W9-CTW-226

Twentieth-Century Literary Criticism

Excerpts from Criticism
of the Works of
Novelists, Poets, Playwrights,
Short Story Writers, and
Other Creative Writers,
1900-1960

Dedria Bryfonski
Phyllis Carmel Mendelson
Editors

Gale Research Company
Book Tower
Detroit, Michigan 48226

STAFF

Dedria Bryfonski, Phyllis Carmel Mendelson, *Editors*

Sharon K. Hall, *Associate Editor*
Susan Johnson, *Assistant Editor*

Sharon R. Cillette, *Production Editor*

Linda M. Pugliese, *Manuscript Coordinator*
L. Elizabeth Hardin, Jeanne A. Gough, *Permissions Coordinators*
Judith Fischer Rutkowski, *Research Coordinator*
Cherie Abbey, Laura A. Buch, Thomas Gunton, Carol Sherman, *Editorial Assistants*

Special acknowledgment to Gerard J. Senick, *Editor,* **Children's Literature Review**

Library of Congress Catalog Card Number 76-46132
ISBN 0-8103-0175-X

CONTENTS

Preface vii

List of Authors to Appear in Early Volumes ix

Authors Included in Volume 1

PREFACE

It is impossible to overvalue the importance of literature in the intellectual, emotional, and spiritual evolution of humankind. Literature is that which both lifts us out of our everyday life and helps us to better understand it. Through the fictive life of an Emma Bovary, a Lambert Strether, a Leopold Bloom, our perceptions of the human condition are enlarged, and we are enriched.

Literary criticism is a collective term for several kinds of critical writing: criticism may be normative, descriptive, textual, interpretive, appreciative, generic. It takes many forms: the traditional essay, the aphorism, the book or play review, even the parodic poem. Perhaps the single unifying feature of literary criticism lies in its purpose: to help us to better understand what we read.

The Scope of the Book

The usefulness of Gale's *Contemporary Literary Criticism (CLC),* which excerpts criticism of current creative writing, suggests an equivalent need among literature students and teachers interested in authors of the period 1900 to 1960. The great poets, novelists, short story writers, and playwrights of this period are by far the most popular writers for study in high school and college literature courses. Moreover, since contemporary critics continue to analyze the work of this period—both in its own right and in relation to today's tastes and standards—a vast amount of relevant critical material confronts the student.

Thus, *Twentieth-Century Literary Criticism (TCLC),* an annual publication, will present significant passages from published criticism on authors who died between 1900 and 1960. Because of the difference in time span under consideration (*CLC* considers authors living from 1960 to the present), there will be no duplication between *CLC* and *TCLC.*

Each volume of *TCLC* will be carefully designed to present a list of authors who represent a variety of genres and nationalities. The length of an author's section is intended to be representative of the amount of critical attention he or she has received. Each *TCLC* author section will represent the scope of critical response to that author's work: some early criticism will be presented to indicate initial reactions, later criticism will be selected to represent any rise or fall in an author's popularity, and current retrospective analyses will provide students with a modern view. Since a *TCLC* author section is intended to be a definitive overview, the editors will include between 40 and 50 authors in each 600-page volume (compared to approximately 200 authors in a *CLC* volume of similar size) in order to devote more attention to each author. Unlike *CLC,* no attempt will be made to update author sections in subsequent volumes, unless important new criticism warrants additional excerpts.

The Organization of the Book

An author section consists of the following elements: author heading, identifying paragraph, list of principal works, and excerpts of criticism (each followed by a citation). The *author heading* consists of the name under which an author most commonly wrote, followed by birth and death dates. Thus, in volume 1, William Sidney Porter can be found under the name of O. Henry. Uncertainty as to a birth or death date is indicated by a question mark. The *identifying paragraph* contains biographical and other background information about an author that will elucidate his or her creative output. The *list of principal works* is chronological by date of first publication and genres are identified.

Preface

In those instances where the first publication was other than English language, the title and date of the first English-language edition are given in brackets. *Criticism* is arranged chronologically in each author section to provide a perspective on any changes in critical evaluation over the years. Each piece of criticism is accompanied by a complete *bibliographical citation* designed to facilitate location of the original essay or book by the interested reader.

Acknowledgments

No work of this scope can be accomplished without the cooperation of many people. The editors especially wish to thank the copyright holders of the excerpts included in this volume, the permission managers of many book and magazine publishing companies for assisting us in locating copyright holders, and the staffs of the Detroit Public Library and Wayne State University Library for making their resources available to us.

Suggestions Are Welcome

If readers wish to suggest authors they are particularly anxious to have covered in coming volumes, or if they have other suggestions, they are cordially invited to write the editors.

AUTHORS TO APPEAR
IN EARLY VOLUMES

Authors to Appear in Early Volumes

Mansfield, Katherine 1888-1923
Marriott, Charles 1869-1957
Martin du Gard, Roger 1881-1958
Martínez Sierra, Gregorio 1881-1947
Masters, Edgar Lee 1869-1950
Mencken, H(enry) L(ouis) 1880-1956
Meredith, George 1828-1909
Meynell, Alice 1847-1922
Millay, Edna St. Vincent 1892-1950
Milne, A(lan) A(lexander) 1882-1956
Míro, Gabriel 1879-1936
Mistral, Frédéric 1830-1914
Mistral, (Lucila Godoy Alcayaga) Gabriela 1889-1957
Mitchell, Margaret 1900-1949
Monro, Harold 1879-1932
Moore, George 1852-1933
Moore, Thomas Sturge 1870-1944
Morgan, Charles 1894-1958
Morley, Christopher 1890-1957
Muir, Edwin 1887-1959
Murray, (George) Gilbert 1866-1957
Natsume, Sōseki (Kinnosuke Natsume) 1867-1916
Norris, Frank 1870-1902
Noyes, Alfred 1880-1958
Olbracht, Ivan (Kemil Zeman) 1882-1952
Orczy, Baroness (Emmuska) 1865-1947
Orwell, George (Eric Hugh Blair) 1903-1950

Owen, Wilfred 1893-1918
Pasternak, Boris 1890-1960
Pavese, Cesare 1908-1950
Pinero, Arthur Wing 1855-1934
Pirandello, Luigi 1867-1936
Pontoppidan, Henrik 1857-1943
Porter, Eleanor H(odgman) 1868-1920
Porter, Gene(va) Stratton 1886-1924
Powys, T(heodore) F(rancis) 1875-1953
Proust, Marcel 1871-1922
Quiller-Couch, Arthur 1863-1944
Rawlings, Marjorie Kinnan 1896-1953
Reid, Forrest 1876-1947
Reymont, Ladislas (Wladyslaw Stanislaw Reymont) 1867-1925
Richardson, Dorothy 1873?-1957
Richardson, Henry Handel (Ethel Florence Richardson) 1870-1946
Riley, James Whitcomb 1849-1916
Rinehart, Mary Roberts 1876-1958
Roberts, Elizabeth Madox 1886-1941
Robinson, Edward Arlington 1869-1935
Rölvaag, O(le) E(dvart) 1876-1931
Rolland, Romain 1866-1944
Rostand, Edmond 1868-1918
Runyon, (Alfred) Damon 1884-1946
Sabatini, Rafael 1875-1950
Saint-Exupéry, Antoine de 1900-1944

Saki (Hector Hugh Munro) 1870-1916
Santayana, George 1863-1952
Sayers, Dorothy L(eigh) 1893-1957
Schnitzler, Arthur 1862-1931
Seeger, Alan 1888-1916
Service, Robert 1874-1958
Seton, Ernest Thompson 1860-1946
Shaw, George Bernard 1856-1950
Sherwood, Robert E(mmet) 1896-1955
Sienkiewitz, Henryk 1846-1916
Sinclair, May 1865-1946
Slater, Francis Carey 1875-1958
Squire, J(ohn) C(ollings) 1884-1958
Stephens, James 1882-1951
Stevens, Wallace 1879-1955
Stockton, Frank R. 1834-1902
Supervielle, Jules 1884-1960
Sutro, Alfred 1863-1933
Svevo, Italo 1861-1928
Swinburne, Algernon Charles 1837-1909
Symons, Arthur 1865-1945
Synge, John Millington 1871-1909
Tabb, John Bannister 1845-1909
Tagore, Sir Rabindranath 1861-1941
Tarkington, Booth 1869-1946
Teasdale, Sara 1884-1933
Tey, Josephine (Elizabeth Mackintosh) 1897-1952
Thompson, Francis 1859-1907
Tolstoy, Count Leo (Nikolayevich) 1828-1910

Turner, W(alter) J(ames) R(edfern) 1889-1946
Twain, Mark (Samuel Langhorne Clemens) 1835-1910
Tynan, Katharine 1861-1931
Unamuno, Miguel de 1864-1936
Undset, Sigrid 1882-1949
Vachell, Horace Annesley 1861-1955
Valéry, Paul 1871-1945
Vallejo, César 1892-1938
Van Dine, S.S. (Willard H. Wright) 1888-1939
Van Doren, Carl 1885-1950
Van Druten, John 1901-1957
Vazov, Ivan 1850-1921
Verga, Giovanni 1840-1922
Verne, Jules 1828-1905
Wallace, Edgar 1875-1932
Wallace, Lewis 1827-1905
Walpole, Hugh 1884-1941
Wassermann, Jakob 1873-1934
Webb, Mary 1881-1927
Webster, Jean 1876-1916
Welch, Denton 1917-1948
Wells, Carolyn 1869-1942
Wells, H(erbert) G(eorge) 1866-1946
Werfel, Franz 1890-1945
Wharton, Edith 1862-1937
Wister, Owen 1860-1938
Wolfe, Thomas 1900-1938
Wren, P(ercival) C(hristopher) 1885-1941
Wylie, Elinor 1885-1928
Young, Francis Brett 1844-1954
Zangwill, Israel 1864-1926

Readers are cordially invited to suggest additional authors to the editors.

James Agee

1909-1955

American journalist, novelist, film critic, screenwriter, and poet. Agee's film criticism established the highest standards for that genre, and as a novelist he was considered to have great potential which, however, went largely undeveloped because of his consuming interest in journalism (he wrote for *Time, Fortune,* and *Nation*) and his compulsion to experiment with many literary forms. Agee's fictive concern is with the dignity of the anonymous individual; a concern which he skillfully develops through his precise observation of daily events. "To him," according to Walker Evans, "human beings were at least possibly immortal and literally sacred souls." He died at forty-five with only a small body of work completed. It was his Pulitzer Prize-winning novel, *A Death in the Family,* that achieved for him posthumous fame.

PRINCIPAL WORKS

Permit Me Voyage (poetry) 1934
Let Us Now Praise Famous Men (essay, with
  photographs by Walker Evans) 1941
The Morning Watch (novel) 1951
A Death in the Family (novel) 1957
Agee on Film: Reviews and Comments (film criticism)
  1958
Agee on Film: Five Film Scripts (screenplays) 1960
The Letters of James Agee to Father Flye (letters) 1962

In *The Morning Watch,* . . . James Agee has come close to a small triumph; he has pierced the protective shell of a boy's personality and exposed the religious exaltation of the boy without once falling into bathos. During the [Good Friday] watch in the chapel, [twelve-year-old] Richard's deepest thoughts and feelings are disturbed by weak flesh and childish imaginings: he is kneeling, and his knees and back hurt, disturbing the purity of his devotions; he remembers his silly effort at self-mortification through eating worms; he imagines himself upon the cross and hearing the school's best athlete whisper, "Jesus, that kid's got guts." And dismayed because every other thought seems tinctured with pride, he fervently prays: "O God forgive me! forgive me if you can stand to!"

After the watch, Richard and two others play hooky and head for a swim. The shift from the atmosphere of the chapel to the outdoor freshness of a spring morning is achieved in descriptive language of unusual beauty. . . . The swim itself and the boyish killing of a snake afterwards are described in flashing language. But it is just here that . . . Agee falters, clothing the action with symbols for which he furnishes no clear keys. As Richard and the others march back to school to face their punishment for playing hooky, Agee's final meaning lags somewhere behind, among the Freudian trees.

Yet throughout *The Morning Watch,* . . . Agee has achieved many things with a fine economy of language: an adolescent's mysticism, sliced through with normal childishness; a shy boy's painful awareness of his own inadequacy among blustering, sometimes grossly obscene classmates; the confused images of the Lord's death and the death of Richard's own father.

All of this is handled with great sympathy and written as few living U.S. writers can write. (pp. 119-20)

> "Richard's Ordeal," in Time (reprinted by permission from Time, The Weekly News-magazine; copyright Time Inc. 1951), April 23, 1951, pp. 119-20.

A Death in the Family is not a completed novel, but a collection of brilliant narrative and lyric fragments given *editorially* the semblance of a novel. In its present state (fixed by the premature death of the author), it hesitates between two ambitions, one of which would have made it a tight, highly unified novella, covering only some three or four days; the other of which would have expanded it in the direction of a thick, family saga, spanning in its main action five to ten years—and including by indirect reference many more. Only the novella-germ seems to have been worked out in anything like final form; while the saga survives as a handful of trial studies, not integrated into the main fiction by the author but somewhat arbitrarily placed in the present book by the editors.

The single unifying factor of a novella and saga—aside from their common raw material of family history—is the mind of a small boy, the death of whose father and the coming to moral maturity of whose mother is the center of the three-day narrative. Yet here, too, there is confusion; for Agee had apparently not yet solved the problem of point of view; and the book, as it has been patched together, shifts disconcertingly from a post of observation just behind the head of the small boy to one which moves nervously. The incomplete work hovers between the subjective and objective, between the lyrical and the novelistic.

The book turns, it seems to me, about four major themes: the threat and temptations of drunkeness, the clash of utterly different families joined in a marriage resented by both, the terrible illumination implicit in the fact of death, the conflict of Protestantism and Catholicism. The last two are sufficiently rendered, in a discreet and subtle poetry, within the limits of the novella. The first two are only suggested in the fragments of the saga which survive. The family of the dead husband, for instance, comes to life briefly in the opening, is further illuminated by a visit to his great-grandmother in the deep country (the opposition between the families involves that between urban and rural, instinctive and intellectual), but is lost at the book's close—where that family simply drops out of sight in a lapse unforgiveable in a finished work. (p. 25)

I think, that Agee's talent is peculiarly *visual,* that the world comes to him in sharp, fragmented sights—all detailed foreground. He paints his scenes sometimes like a miniaturist, and this hovering, scrupulous attention to detail obscures both the kind of infinitely receding background and the sense of forward motion necessary to the novel.

Yet it would be ungrateful and unforgiveable not to say what *pleasure* there is in his visual revelations. The sights (and though primarily these, beyond them, the smells, tastes, textures, sounds) of Knoxville, Tennessee, some forty years ago, are rendered with an astonishing tact and precision, with a kind of freshness that belongs, for most of us, only to the memories of childhood. It is in the lyrical, free, sensual evocation of a boy's world as seen for the first time, the world of experience upon which our others depend and from which they hopelessly decline that Agee excels.

The tone of the book (at its novella-heart) is nostalgic: a longing to recapture the seen-for-the-first-time, to relive the child's sense of warm, safe involvement in love, to believe again that such security is immune from death and change, to be what we were before we felt the need to identify ourselves. Yet the nostalgia is seldom sentimental; for it is essentially religious. It does not, that is to say, deny the reality of death or pain or suffering, the necessity of the fall from the child's peace or the exclusion from the child's Great Good Place; it only affirms that that peace and that place are real, too; and somehow they survive the disappearance of the people and the houses, the sights and sounds which sustained them.

To attempt to translate the book's meaning out of its expression is to realize that, whatever its failure to achieve novel form, it is, in the full sense, poetry: an unanalysable fusion of theme and image, significance and language. It is the language of the book, at once luminiscent and discreet, the language of Agee, *Agee,* that remain in the mind in this time of meagre, undistinguished prose, the prose of authors pledged to pretend that they are not really there. (pp. 25-6)

> *Leslie A. Fiedler, "Encounter With Death,"*
> in The New Republic *(reprinted by permission of* The New Republic; © 1957 by The New Republic, Inc.), December 9, 1957, pp. 25-6.*

To the dozen or so good reasons that have been suggested for our having no new major novelists in America I should like to add one more. America now maintains so many areas in which a creative talent can find room for exercise that a writer whose gifts at one time would have assured us a long series of good fictions is now invited to divert his energies in a dozen different directions. And for an example of what happens to solicit some talents I would offer the case of James Agee, who had a great gift and would, one suspects, have written some fine novels. (p. 212)

When *Permit Me Voyage* was published. . . in the "Yale Series of Younger Poets," Agee was shortly out of college and earning his living as a writer on *Fortune;* and the two main lines that his life as a writer would take were already evident. The book revealed a kind of agonized (self-searcher who would go on for the rest of his life trying to put his feelings about himself and the world into some acceptable order. His work on *Fortune* revealed a craftsman who could lose himself, with complete detachment, in any ephemeral piece of writing which happened to challenge his skill. (It was clear that he could, at least temporarily, lose his troubles in it also.) The self-searching would go on in his poems, in his study of sharecroppers, and toward the last of his life in what little fiction he had time left to write. The craftsman wrote articles for *Fortune, Time,* and *Life,* movie reviews for the *Nation,* and the movie scripts he published as well as those which were filmed in Hollywood. What may be harder to believe is that both lines of activity were so important to him. (pp. 212-13)

Agee had no illusions as to what was expected of him as a writer for *Fortune:* he was supposed to take an assignment and turn the material he and his researcher could gather into a sufficiently slick and smooth-running story. There was no doubting his sincerity when he said that he was working "in a whorehouse," but there was also no doubt that he took great satisfaction in concocting, out of the most recalcitrant technical materials, what have to be called masterpieces of that kind of journalism.

His ability to plunge so deeply into a *Fortune* assignment was the first manifestation of what it was in Agee that has since made people say he did not keep his "promise." Conventionally, if one writes a book of poems which "show promise" then one must go on and write another book of poems or the promise is not "kept." But Agee lacked, even more than other writers of our time, the traditional respect for genres. He went one step beyond Baudelaire's notion that any work of art contains an obstacle which the artist creates as part of the act of conceiving what he is going to do, and then conquers in the execution. For Agee, if not in theory at least in his practice of writing, the presence of an obstacle, in any kind of writing job whatever, was enough to give the job the status of a work of art. It would be false, of course, to say that he set as high a value on a *Fortune* article as on a poem or a piece of fiction, but it is gospel true that he could lose himself as completely in writing of one kind as in writing of the others. What counted was the job, the problem that was presented to the craftsman. (p. 216)

[By] 1934 his poetry had become a rather desultory pursuit. Agee had always been superbly indifferent about what happened to finished manuscripts. (Still further evidence that for him the important part of any writing job was the doing.) He kept no records. A piano bench in his apartment was overflowing with manuscript, but he told one New York publisher that he did not have the material for a second book of poems. (p. 217)

Fortunately, an assignment to an article on the life of typical sharecroppers sent Agee back to the South in 1936 and opened the way to a new round of self-examination. Walker Evans, a photographer known for the puritanical severity of his work, was assigned to the sharecropper topic along with Agee. The two overstayed their time in rural Alabama and brought back to New York a pile of text and photographs which belonged legally to *Fortune* but which *Fortune,* for reasons which the editors were not obliged to make public, decided not to use. It took Agee and Evans a year to get a release of their material, work it over into a book, and take the book to a publisher.

By the time Houghton Mifflin brought out the volume, it was 1941. For bad timing, a book on sharecropping in 1941 probably sets some kind of record. Writers like Erskine Caldwell had been working that side of the street for years. The poor white, like the Okies and Arkies of Steinbeck, had already hardened into a fixed image in the popular mind. Events like the 1939 Hitler-Stalin pact had thrown our attitudes toward local social problems into a nameless confusion. And we were only months away from war. *Let Us Now Praise Famous Men* was probably a poor title anyhow, one hardly calculated to attract readers. According to one report, the book sold fewer than six hundred copies before it was remaindered.

Yet Lionel Trilling called this book "the most realistic and the most important moral effort of our American generation," and he was right. Agee had come upon one of those facts which create, when the individual confronts them, profound emotional disturbance. He had always known about the wretchedness of the tenant farmers of the Central South and had taken the appropriate liberal attitudes toward their predicament, but now he had been thrust up against the human reality of sharecropping and felt called, impelled, obsessively driven to tell about it. . . . That there had been other books about sharecroppers made no difference, because his real, deep subject was not the sharecroppers themselves; it was the emotional experience of meeting the fact of sharecroppers. For this subject, everything he had learned on *Fortune* and elsewhere about making prose do what he wanted, and everything he had learned about words from writing poetry, would barely be adequate.

Like most of his generation Agee had always had an immense scorn of the phony. More than most he distrusted himself, suspecting the phony in his own nature. . . . The problem, in other words, was one of telling the truth about what had been seen and felt by a man whom Agee distrusted—himself. To let the reader see the truth, he had to tell him enough about the man Agee so that the reader could at least guess how much the truth was being distorted in passing through the refracting apparatus of a temperament. This was a preoccupation, of course, with what Henry James called "point of view," and would have concerned Agee equally if he had been writing a novel instead of *Let Us Now Praise Famous Men.* But in this case the problem was more agonizing because the people Agee was writing about existed independently of him, and his obligation was deeper than, and different in kind from, a novelist's obligation to his characters. The truth about a char-

acter is what the novelist asserts to be the truth. The truth about the sharecroppers was what it was; the writer could only distort it at best. Thus this book—which is catalogued in my local library under Economics—became a covert autobiography. (pp. 217-19)

He had conceived *Let Us Now Praise Famous Men* as the opening book of a much longer job, probably in three volumes, to be called "Three Tenant Families." So far as I know, the rest of it was never finished. One suspects why: the longer work would have had to be a more thoroughly "objective" piece of reporting, and this was not what Agee was interested in. His essential work was done when he had finished with his own emotions. (p. 220)

[During] the years before *Let Us Now Praise Famous Men* was published, he had discovered the possibilities of the movie script. From childhood he had been an abandoned movie-goer, capable of watching the same film with unremitting attention a dozen times. . . . Gradually he had come to see the script itself as a kind of literary form, and one which will permit a writer to do what he cannot do in other forms. The ordinary movie script is dialogue plus some directions—not much more. Agee's notion of a script, on the other hand, was that it should be a work of imagination unhampered by the material limitations under which even the best directors have to work. (p. 221)

When finally he went to Hollywood to write scripts for John Huston, he went not as a hack looking for a job but as a practitioner of a special art; the relationship was like that of a writer looking for a publisher. (p. 222)

He also took over the movie column of the *Nation* at that last fine moment in the *Nation's* history when Diana Trilling was writing about fiction, Joseph Wood Krutch covering the plays, and Randall Jarrell reviewing current poetry. The editors put no restrictions on him except that he turn in his copy on time. His reviews were not really reports on current entertainment. His eye was on what a movie had done, even accidentally, that had not been done —or done so well—before, and widely open to spot missed opportunities for greatness. As always, his prose was turned into an instrument for a special purpose. (p. 223)

The whole point of tracing out his career is that at the end of it Agee wrote a short novel, two short stories, and part of a longer novel, all of such quality as to bring home to the reader a realization of what this man could have left behind if his great gift had not been channeled off in other directions. If he had "kept his promise" by writing what was expected of him instead of what he most wanted to write, he would have had his paragraph in the histories of fiction. (p. 224)

He could be intricate when he wanted, as anyone who has followed his early writing and particularly his verse can testify. But in *A Death in the Family* the intricacy shows up not in the arrangement of perspective but in the handling of minute detail, usually visual. (pp. 227-28)

There is no way, of course, to illustrate the function of this kind of vision in the novel as a whole; quotation would show how it works, but not how steadily, and its steadiness is what makes it so valuable. But anyone who reads the book at all alertly will, I believe, recognize its peculiar quality. The selecting, narrating vision moves through scene after scene, like the lens of a camera directed by someone who knows what the directors of the old silent films had to know if they were to survive: how to narrate visually. The consistent vision creates a tone common to all the scenes, obviates most of the need for transitions between them, holds the novel together. If a novelist must have a method, then this way of seeing was what constituted Agee's. (pp. 228-29)

A novel which leans as heavily upon autobiography as this one does would not have been sufficient to establish Agee as a novelist of first rank. . . . We do not know that if he had lived to finish this novel he would have attempted fiction again. What *A Death in the Family* does demonstrate, very thoroughly, is that Agee had the equipment of a very considerable novelist, and of a very original one from the angle of technique. The question is whether he would ever have made much further use of the equipment. Given the special motive which led to his writing what little fiction he did in his maturity, the answer might very well have been negative.

Whenever Agee had to state his occupation, he simply put down "writer"—not journalist or novelist or poet. He was fully aware of how many different kinds of writing could give him satisfaction, and of how little he wanted to give himself to one, excluding the others. If he had wanted to pour his prose—and his almost embarrassing, indiscreet honesty—into, first, a novel about Harvard, then a novel about working for the Luce magazines, perhaps after that a novel about sharecroppers, and finally a novel about his family, he might have died at forty-five a well-known man and a "loss to American letters." But the truth is that with all the different possibilities open, he did not want to choose one and put the rest aside. (pp. 229-30)

> W. M. Frohock, "James Agee–The Question of Wasted Talent," in his The Novel of Violence in America, *revised edition, Southern Methodist University Press, 1957, pp. 212-230.*

Agee was a writer who actually did better in popular and journalistic media—where certain objective technical requirements gave him a chance to create something out of his immense tenderness and his high sense of comedy—than when he let himself go in purely speculative lyricism. He was a natural literary craftsman, not a literary intellectual, and it was only *avant-garde* associations that ever misled him. His most beautiful poems—like the title poem of his first book, *Permit Me Voyage*—are those which are most traditional in form.

Like so many Southern writers . . . he had such an immense capacity for feeling and such easy access to the rhetoric of English poetry that when not taken in hand by his medium, he could oppress the reader with merely beautiful words. His almost ecstatic feeling for music itself led him to seek unexpected dimensions in prose, and extraordinarily like Thoreau in this, he tried, in *Let Us Now Praise Famous Men*, to convey his feeling for the American land in highly charged rhythms that would stick close to the facts. Still, it is easy to overrate *Let Us Now Praise Famous Men,* for so many other books of the 1930s now seem unbelievable. Agee wrote of the sharecroppers with such love and rage that it is impossible to read the book without sharing his suffering. But despite its overpowering beauty of language and its immense personal nobility, the book is a

turbulent preparation for a work of art that was not achieved.

Agee published in 1951 a short novel, *The Morning Watch,* and at his death he left a virtually complete manuscript which has now been published under Agee's own title, *A Death in the Family.* To anyone who knows how introspective and self-accusing Agee's less successful work could be, both these books show a disciplined control of his narrative material which, if anything, went too far. In both, Agee worked from his earliest memories in order to show the impact on a child of what was plainly a major factor in Agee's own life—the death of his father in the early Twenties. . . .

[What] makes the book so significant is actually not the dramatic qualities of a novel, but a universe of feeling, of infinitely aching feeling, which is built up so thoroughly, with meticulous truth to the agony of bereavement, that we finally have the sense of a wholly tangible sorrow, a materialization of human grief. The book is remarkable as a literary performance because, although obviously written from within—almost as if in obedience to a hallucination—it tries entirely to describe it as an objective situation. (pp. 186-87)

The trouble with the book as a novel, however, is that although Agee wrote with an almost unbearable effort at objectivity, one feels from the writing that this effort was made to externalize a private grief, not because he thought of the characters in the book as outside himself. The personality of the dead father actually comes through better than any of the living, for he is the single fact outside them to which they all respond as one.

To speak of faults in a book by James Agee is to point up the absurdity of literary comparisons. Agee's book cannot be judged as another novel-of-the-week; it is an utterly individual and original book, and it is the work of a writer whose power with English words can make you gasp. A brother-in-law, looking at the dead man, feels that he is looking down "upon a horned, bruised anvil; and laid his hand flat against the cold, wheemed iron; and it was as if its forehead gave his hand the stunning shadow of every blow it had ever received." The sense of the father in this book, of both the place he filled in life and of the emptiness created by his death, is one of the most deeply worked out expressions of human feeling that I have ever read. And to think of Jim Agee, with his bad heart, writing with such fierce truth so soon before his own death is to marvel, all over again, how literally it is himself that a writer will give to his task. (p. 187)

> Alfred Kazin, "Good-by to James Agee" (1957), in his Contemporaries (copyright © 1924, 1946, 1952, 1955, 1956, 1957, 1958, 1959, 1960, 1961, 1962 by Alfred Kazin; reprinted by permission of Little, Brown and Co. in association with the Atlantic Monthly Press), Atlantic-Little, Brown, 1962, pp. 185-87.

Though a poet in his resonance and quality, Agee found, in the looser prose evocation, an ideal form for his sensibility. In his homage to images of pastoral simplicity, he invoked a rhetoric heavy with baroque sinuosity, courtly in its posture and eloquence. It is a language with a moral as well as an esthetic intention; against an archetypal modern consciousness, fragmentary, complacent, desiccated with rationality, Agee's language sets fiercely a passionate unity.

In the *Partisan Review* symposium on Religion and the Intellectuals, Agee wrote with grief of the suspect status in which feeling and intuition are held; of the isolation of sensation, and the respect which is reserved alone for the thinking faculty: himself, he rejected the division, choosing "interplay, mutual discipline and fertilization." Finally, and it is the paradox which places him firmly in the American grain, Agee's sacramental attention to life was rooted in the ecstasy of his wonder at death. . . .

Agee's world—the world of [the] two lyrical prose evocations [*The Morning Watch* and *A Death in the Family*], and of the earlier *Let Us Now Praise Famous Men*—is everywhere a ceremony, and to be known only by its hieratic gestures, its rich stuffs and incantations: a world supremely of being. It is not possible to read *A Death in the Family* with a fictional stringency. To the narrative sense, Agee concedes little; to the dramatically lyrical, all. There is no articulation of pattern, no velocity but that of grief, a fragmentary imposition of character as action, and above all, no movement through that stream which is the medium of the great novels: the stream of time. *A Death in the Family* does not pass, as fiction, beyond its single major event: the sudden extinction of a young husband and father in a capricious automobile accident. What it takes for substance after that is a dramatized ritual of those moments—hours and days, weeks perhaps, even longer—in which we do not live but merely endure: passages when time is annulled, and the current of life is brought up against a disabling check: death, radical shock, any obsession, the intensities of passion or love discovered. (p. 591)

Agee's tender fidelity to the actual—to the precise sounds of a cranking automobile engine on a summer night; to the precise way a man will settle his shirttails—is a function of his love, issuing from his conviction of each human destiny as unique but profoundly anonymous, solitary as a thumbprint yet drowned in time as those generations of men which fall in Homer, like leaves. This vision—void of anything like personal egotism or insistence, so infinitely, gently attentive to the specific—has not many American masters, one only, I would think: Whitman, the chanter. It is a dangerous mode, vulnerable to an easy lyricism and disembodied rhetoric, to catalogues. There is, indeed, a point at which "detail" may become an evasion, and *A Death in the Family* does not always transcend it.

Yet what we should imagine at work in Agee's labor of precision is the poet's old assumption of the task of epiphany, of creating a new lexicon of the world by naming each object and restoring to it a virginal freshness. He was interested, Agee, supremely in the child—not, be it noted, in the adolescent, that ambiguous figure who rams his horny way through our literature, and not, certainly, in the child as moral magnifying glass, or victim of adult guile—but in the child as a faculty of wonder: a gift Agee kept himself to a degree rare in mature experience. Which is to say, he would explore not so much the self as that old imponderable, Life and things in their pristine glamour, uniqueness and fatality.

The poet works in metaphor, by apprehending the relationships between objects and discovering, in the endless variety of these, a secret unity. And it is uncommon how, in

Agee's work, we are dominated by the polar tension of his metaphors—of age and youth, of violence and peace, virility and tenderness, death and life—each being known always only in relation to its antinomy. The images of his world have thus an undistracted force—a quality of extremity—proper not so much to the novel as to poetry. Indeed, these intensities of *The Morning Watch* and *A Death in the Family* are the distillation not so much of poetic rhythms as of poetic concepts, for in this search and thirst after an absolute wonder, only the ideal demands to be made real. Agee had a signal power, at once majestic and intimate, to project into language what is most deeply and dumbly felt in man's experience, and so sadly, often, soiled in the agonized or joyous telling. (pp. 591-92)

With the maturity of *The Morning Watch* and *A Death in the Family,* he arrived at something like a rhetoric of splendor, weaving all that is courtly, choice and honorable in human expression into an elaborate artifact of verbal images, a ceremonial invocation through which man's experience in the world is not only known but constantly reborn. (p. 592)

> *Richard Hayes, "Rhetoric of Splendor," in* Commonweal *(copyright © 1958 Commonweal Publishing Co., Inc.; reprinted by permission of Commonweal Publishing Co., Inc.), September 12, 1958, pp. 591-92.*

[Agee] had forsaken [film criticism] some years before his death for screen-writing, some of which he did superbly; but the change of occupation could not have brought him much nearer the perfection for which he stubbornly ached.

Following the posthumous success of his novel *A Death in the Family,* [*Agee on Film*] appears, containing every film review he wrote for *The Nation* (1942-1948), a selection of his anonymous reviews for *Time* in the same period, and various film articles he wrote for *Life, Partisan Review*, and *Sight and Sound.* . . .

The specialist reaches for a book like this automatically, but the general reader wants to know why he should bother to read reviews of movies long gone, no matter how well written. Well, few general readers will be interested in every word here, but many will be moved by the central figure that this book creates: that of a man of sensibility and mind putting every nerve and brain-cell, every memory and hope, completely at the disposal of a major contemporary art and passing on to us, as through a literary cardiograph, the effect on him of that art. Thus he provides us with a picture of the horrors and aspirations of an age, and of the torment and vision of an explorer who dares to leave the cozy nest of acceptances.

That is a large statement but not hyperbolic. See, for substantiation, his three-part review of *Monsieur Verdoux*, his essay on the Hollywood Ten, his review of *Man's Hope*. (p. 18)

What was Agee's stature as a critic? The best critic is one who illuminates whole provinces of an art that you could not see before, who helps to refine the general public's taste (which is never good enough—they haven't time, they're busy studying something else or doing their jobs) and who serves as a sounding board for serious artists. (This last word is a drastic need; for instance, many serious writers work for years in this country without one valuable piece of criticism, even though they get many reviews.) But fundamentally you take a critic's hand and let him lead you further, perhaps higher, only if you are initially convinced of a substantial area of mutual sympathy and interest.

For me, then, despite his rare virtues, Agee is a deficient critic. We have a large basic disagreement. At bottom he has, I believe, little regard for or understanding of the art of acting; indeed, throughout this collection there are numerous references to his preference for well-directed non-professionals as against actors. This, to me, is a blindness, a literalness puzzling in a man of his imagination. (pp. 18-19)

The sternest criticism that can be made of these collected articles is that, from them, emerges not so much a critical intelligence or a Promethean appreciator of an art as a lovable and admirable man. Sometimes his lines soar; sometimes they merely gush. Sometimes his rhapsodic stabs penetrate to the heart; sometimes they flounder. He is given to meaningless distinctions. ("*Verdoux* is not the best of Chaplin's films, but it is the most endlessly interesting." The better ones were less interesting?) But he had what is missing from most criticism today—of films and all arts: fierce intensity. The bitter image he leaves is not of a facile, corrosive cynic but of a blazing pessimist. (p. 19)

> *Stanley Kauffman, "A Life in Reviews," in* The New Republic *(reprinted by permission of* The New Republic; © *1958 by The New Republic, Inc.), December 1, 1958, pp. 18-19.*

James Agee was the most intriguing star-gazer in the middle-brow era of Hollywood films, a virtuoso who capped a strange company of stars on people's lips and set up a hailstorm of ideas for other critics to use. . . .

The writers who flowered in 1939-47 movie columns of liberal middle-class journals had the same kind of reader-employer freedom that encouraged good sportswriters in the 1920's—i.e., they served an undemanding audience that welcomed style and knew hardly anything about the inside of movies. Agee wrote reasonable exaggerations, beautifully articulated, about dull plodding treacle that stretched from Jean Simmons to Ingrid Bergman. (p. 84)

Even where he modified and showboated until the reader had the Jim-jams, Agee's style was exciting in its pea-soup density. As in his beloved films (*Treasure of the Sierra Madre,* Olivier's work), his criticism had an excessive richness that came from a fine writing ear as well as cautious hesitancy, ganglia, guilt. The sentences are swamps that are filled with a suspicious number of right-sounding insights. . . .

As he shellacked the reader with culture, Agee had one infallibly charming tool in his kit: an aristocratic gashouse humor that made use of several art centuries, a fantastic recall of stray coupons—like old song lyrics and the favorite thing people were saying in February, 1917—and a way of playing leapfrog with clichés, making them sparkle like pennies lost in a Bendix. (p. 85)

At least half of the growing Agee legend—that he had a great camera eye, writing equipment, and love for moviemakers—is fantasy. Agee's visual recall, so apparent in *tour de force* pieces on Sennett's gang that hit like a cold shower of visual needles, is always wedded to a blindness

to chic artiness. His humanity has a curious way of leveling performers with flattery, and over-competing with directors by flooding their works with a consuming sensibility. (p. 86)

If Agee had struggled more with the actual material of the popular nonartist, it is inconceivable that he could have missed the vapidity of so much "good" film art. (p. 87)

Agee is perhaps as bewitching as his bandwagon believes, if his whole complexity of traits is admitted in the record. Seldom has more personality walked through American criticism with such slyly cloaked overpossessive manners. The present Hollywood film, in which a mishmash knowledge of faintly old modern art is presented in show-biz language, owes part of its inauthentic soul to a fine critic, who even felt obliged to place pictures he disliked in a company with "all the good writing of this century, the films of Pudovkin and Pabst, and some of the music of Brahms." (p. 88)

> *Manny Farber, "Star-Gazing for the Middlebrows," in* The New Leader (© *1958 by the American Labor Conference on International Affairs, Inc.), December 8, 1958 (and reprinted as "Nearer My Agee to Thee" in his* Negative Space: Manny Farber on the Movies, *Praeger Publishers, 1971, pp. 84-8).*

Had James Agee been more productive of the poetic fiction he seemed destined to write, [*Letters of James Agee to Father Flye*] . . . presumably would not have been published. . . .

A fever of self-importance is upon American writing. Popular expectations of what literature should provide have risen so high that failure is the only possible success, and pained incapacity the only acceptable proof of sincerity. When ever in prose has slovenliness been so esteemed, ineptitude so cherished? In the present apocalyptic atmosphere, the loudest sinner is most likely to be saved; Fitzgerald's crack-up is his ticket to Heaven, Salinger's silence his claim on our devotion. The study of literature threatens to become a kind of paleontology of failure, and criticism a supercilious psychoanalysis of authors. I resist Agee's canonization by these unearthly standards. [Updike notes that both the flap copy and the introduction to *Letters of James Agee to Father Flye* "invite us to lament over Agee's aborted and tormented career."] Authors *should* be honored only for their works. If Agee is to be remembered, it should be for his few, uneven, hard-won successes. The author of the best pages of *Let Us Now Praise Famous Men* and *A Death in the Family* owes no apology to posterity. As to "the quarter of a million unsigned words," surely a culture is enhanced, rather than disgraced, when men of talent and passion undertake anonymous and secondary tasks. Excellence in the great things is built upon excellence in the small; Agee's undoing was not his professionalism but his blind, despairing belief in an ideal amateurism.

The truth is that we would not think of Agee as a failure if he did not insist on it himself [in *Letters of James Agee to Father Flye*]. "Meanwhile I am thirty and have missed irretrievably all the trains I should have caught." "Or briefly, though the impulse is OK, / I haven't, really, a damned thing to say." "I am depressed because whether I am to live a very short time or relatively longer time depends . . . on whether or not I can learn to be the kind of person I am not and have always detested; and because, knowing my own character pretty well, I know pretty well what my chances are, even though I will try." These letters brim with self-accusations. (p. 23)

Of course, in writing to Father Flye, Agee is addressing not only a priest but the embodiment of his boyhood aspirations. Agee was religious in preferring self-disgust and even self-destruction to any downward adjustment of these aspirations. "I would certainly prefer death to reconciling myself." Among the things he refused to be reconciled to was his own nature as a writer.

Alcohol—which appears in the first Harvard letters . . . and figures in almost every letter thereafter—was Agee's faithful ally in his "enormously strong drive, on a universally broad front, toward self-destruction." But I think his real vice, as a writer, was talk. "I seem, and regret it and hate myself for it, to be able to say many more things I want to in talking than in writing." . . . And what are these letters but a flow of talk that nothing but total fatigue could staunch? "The trouble is, of course, that I'd like to write you a pretty indefinitely long letter, and talk about everything under the sun we *would* talk about, if we could see each other. And we'd probably talk five or six hundred pages. . . ."

He simply preferred conversation to composition. The private game of translating life into language, or fitting words to things, did not sufficiently fascinate him. (pp. 23-4)

In the last of these letters, mostly written from the hospital bed where his overstrained heart had taken him, there are hints of reconciliation. His work with the movies—the coöperative art *par excellence*—affects him rather cheerfully. His prose takes on crispness. The tortuous, grinding note of self-reproach diminishes. Looking back on his career, he is pleasantly "surprised I have gotten done even the little that I have." He coherently and masterfully sketches several script ideas—a scene from *Candide,* a moral (*and* satiric) film fantasy about elephants. His versatility, his ardent interest in "that, that and the other thing," were beginning to find channels; perhaps there *was* some use in talking. But his body was ruined, and abruptly his magnanimous spirit and eager intelligence vanished from the world of American letters, to whose Manichaean stresses he had been so sensitive, and whose opportunities he had been so ingeniously reluctant to seize. (p. 24) [See also R. W. Flint's reply to Updike, below.]

John Updike, *"No Use Talking,"* in The New Republic *(reprinted by permission of* The New Republic; © *1962 by The New Republic, Inc.), August 13, 1962, pp. 23-4.*

I do not for a minute believe in John Updike's "very sick literary situation" ("No Use Talking," August 13) and I do not see how he can live down in Ipswich and believe in it. Are "popular expectations of what literature should provide" afflicting him down there? For years Ipswich has run an arts festival all summer on the old Crane estate—all very elegant and luxurious—but never that I can remember has any poet or other literary man been asked to perform. Are "slovenliness" and "ineptitude" really esteemed and cherished as much as all that? Isn't it more likely that a few slovenly writers like Kerouac have a journalistic interest that some armchair craftsmen often lack? . . . But who *esteems* the slovenliness? What circles does Updike frequent? Are Bellow or Roth or Malamud slovenly?

No, I think the publication of Agee's letters is mainly an act of piety, by a publisher with a long memory, towards a writer who, *mutatis mutandis,* was the Stanley Kauffmann of his age. I used to read his film reviews on my carrier in the Pacific and they gave me a sense of a new way of thinking about movies to put in practice when I got back. He lived in the Model-T age of American film criticism, and took the same impressionistic attitude towards films that Rosenfeld took a generation earlier towards art. *Let Us Now Praise Famous Men* was a document of highbrow populism that saved a whole generation of bright, leftist Harvards and Yales the bother of going down South and agonizing, sometimes eloquently, over the sharecroppers. *A Death in the Family* seemed to me a terribly overstrained and uncomfortable book, but it had a purity of intention that lingered in one's mind when everything else about it was forgotten. (pp. 30-1)

R. W. Flint, "How Sick Is the Literary Situation?" in The New Republic *(reprinted by permission of* The New Republic; © *1962 by The New Republic, Inc.), September 3, 1962.*

The late James Agee's *A Death in the Family* . . . is an odd book to be written by a serious writer in this country and century, for it is about death (not violence) and love (not sex). Death is conceived of in a most un-American way, not so much a catastrophe for the victim as a mystery, and at the same time an illumination, for the survivors. As for love, it is not sexual, not even romantic; it is domestic—between husband, wife, children, aunts, uncles, grandparents. This love is described tenderly, not in the tough, now-it-can-be-told style dominant in our fiction since Dreiser. The negative aspects are not passed over—Agee is, after all, a serious writer—but what he dwells on, what he "celebrates," is the positive affection that Tolstoy presented in "Family Happiness" but that now is usually dealt with in the women's magazines. Very odd.

There are other original features. We are used to novels that describe the professional and regional background more fully than the human beings, but here there is no "local color," and we are not even told what the father's occupation is. We are used to novels about "plain people" that are garnished with humanitarian rhetoric and a condescending little-man-what-now? pathos, as in *The Grapes of Wrath* and such exercises in liberal right-mindedness. But Agee felt himself so deeply and simply part of the world of his characters—the fact that they were his own family by no means explains this empathy—that he wrote about them as naturally as Mark Twain wrote about the people of Hannibal. . . . We are used, finally, to novels of action, novels of analysis, and novels that combine the two, but not to a work that is static, sometimes lyrical and sometimes meditative but always drawn from sensibility rather than from intellection. It reminds me most of Sherwood Anderson, another sport in twentieth-century American letters—brooding, tender-minded, and a craftsman of words. (pp. 143-44)

I had always thought of Agee as the most broadly gifted writer of my generation, the one who, if anyone, might someday do major work. He didn't do it, or not much of it, but I am not the only one who expected he would. He really shouldn't have died, I kept thinking, and now this posthumous book makes me think it all the harder.

The book jacket is, for once, accurate when it describes Agee as "essentially a poet." For this is really not a novel but a long poem on themes from childhood and family life. The focal point is the death, in an automobile accident, of Jay Follet, a young husband and father. . . . [There] is no plot, no suspense, no development, and thus no novel. The point of view is mostly that of Jay's six-year-old son, Rufus, who is in fact James Agee, who is writing about his actual childhood and about the actual death of his father. Even those parts that are not told directly in terms of Rufus-Agee's experience are affected by this viewpoint. The father and mother, although they are major figures, are barely individualized, since to a small child his parents are too close to be distinctly seen. The more distant and lesser figures, like Aunt Hannah, are more definite. Parents are big, vague archetypes to a child (Strength, Love, or—alas— Coldness, Failure), but aunts are people. In this child-centered structure, at least, *A Death in the Family* is in the American grain. (Why are our writers so much more at home with children than with adults?) Many of the best things are connected with Rufus: his delight over his new cap, his comic and appalling relations with his little sister, his nightmares ("and darkness, smiling, leaned ever more intimately inward upon him, laid open the huge, ragged mouth"), his innocent trust in the older boys, who tease and humiliate him with subtle cruelty. These parts of it can be recommended as an antidote to *Penrod.*

Agee was a very good writer. He had the poet's eye for detail. "Ahead, Asylum Avenue lay bleak beneath its lamps. . . . In a closed drug store stood Venus de Milo, her golden body laced in elastic straps. The stained glass of the L & N depot smoldered like an exhausted butterfly . . . an outcrop of limestone like a great bundle of dirty laundry. . . . Deep in the valley, an engine coughed and browsed." (pp. 144-45)

Although *A Death in the Family* is not a major work, Agee, I think, had the technical, the intellectual, and the moral equipment to do major writing. By "moral," which has a terribly old-fashioned ring, I mean that Agee believed in and—what is rarer—was interested in good and evil. Lots of writers are fascinated by evil and write copiously about it, but they are bored by virtue; this not only limits their scope but prevents a satisfactory account of evil, which can no more be comprehended apart from good than light can be comprehended apart from darkness. Jay Follet is a good husband and father, Mary is a good wife and mother, and their goodness is expressed in concrete action, as is the evil in the boys who humiliate their son or the lack of "character" Jay's brother, Ralph, shows in a family crisis. (Character is another old-fashioned quality that interested Agee.) The theme is the confrontation of love, which I take to be life carried to its highest possible reach, and death, as the negation of life and yet a necessary part of it.

Admittedly, the book has its *longueurs,* and very long *longueurs* they are sometimes, but for the most part it is wonderfully alive. For besides his technical skill, his originality and integrity of vision, Agee had a humorous eye for human behavior. The nuances of the husband-and-wife relationship come out in a series of everyday actions. . . . The bondage and the binding of marriage are both there. This is realism, but of a higher order than we have become accustomed to, since it includes those positive aspects of human relations which are so difficult to describe today without

appearing sentimental. The uneasiness the Victorians felt in the presence of the base we feel in the presence of the noble. It is to Agee's credit that he didn't feel uneasy. (pp. 147-48)

A Death in the Family should be read slowly. It is easy to become impatient, for the movement is circular, ruminative, unhurried. He dwells on things, runs on and on and on. Perhaps one *should* be impatient. What Agee needed was a sympathetically severe editor who would prune him as Maxwell Perkins pruned Thomas Wolfe, whom Agee resembled in temperament, though I think he was superior artistically. A better comparison is with Whitman, who also runs on and on, hypnotizing himself with his material, losing all sense of proportion, losing all sense of anyone else reading him, and simply chanting, in bardic simplicity, to himself. Like Whitman and unlike Wolfe, Agee was able at last to come down hard on The Point and roll it up into a magically intense formulation; the weariest river of Ageean prose winds somewhere safe to sea. After pages of excessive, obsessive chewing-over of a funeral, including a morbid detailing of the corpse's appearance and several prayers in full, Agee comes down, hard and accurate, to earth and to art: "[Rufus] looked towards his father's face and, seeing the blue-dented chin thrust upward, and the way the flesh was sunken behind the bones of the jaw, first recognized in its specific weight the word, *dead.* He looked quickly away, and solemn wonder tolled in him like the shuddering of a prodigious bell." Should one be impatient? I suspect one should. Granted the preceding *longueurs* were necessary for the writer if he were to work up enough steam for this climax, it doesn't follow that they are necessary for the reader. Would not a more conscious, self-disciplined writer have written them and then, when he had reached the final effect, have gone back and removed the scaffolding? It would have been interesting to see if Agee would have done this had he lived to give final form to *A Death in the Family.* (pp. 149-50)

In some literary circles, James Agee now excites the kind of emotion James Dean does in some non-literary circles. There is already an Agee cult. This is partly because of the power of his writing and his lack of recognition—everyone likes to think he is on to a good thing the general public has not caught up with—but mainly because it is felt that Agee's life and personality, like Dean's, were at once a symbolic expression of our time and a tragic protest against it. It is felt that not their weakness but their vitality betrayed them. In their maimed careers and their wasteful deaths, the writer and the actor appeal to a resentment that intellectuals and teen-agers alike feel about life in America, so smoothly prosperous, so deeply frustrating. (p. 150)

Although he achieved much, it was a wasted, and wasteful, life. Even for a modern writer, he was extraordinarily self-destructive. He was always ready to sit up all night with anyone who happened to be around, or to go out at midnight looking for someone: talking passionately, brilliantly, but too much, drinking too much, smoking too much, reading aloud too much, making love too much, and in general cultivating the worst set of work habits in Greenwich Village. This is a large statement, but Agee's was a large personality. "I wish I knew how to work," he said to a friend. He wrote copiously, spending himself recklessly there, too, but there was too much else going on. He seemed to have almost no sense of self-preservation, allowing his versatility and creative energy to be exploited in a way that shrewder, cooler men of talent don't permit. His getting stuck for so long in the Luce organization is an instance; like Jacob, he drudged fourteen years in another man's fields, but there was no Rachel in view. (p. 152)

The waste one senses in Agee's career had other roots as well. He was spectacularly born in the wrong time and place. He was too versatile, for one thing. In art as in industry, this is an age of specialization. There is a definite if restricted "place" for poetry; there is even a Pulitzer Prize for it, and poets of far less capacity than Agee have made neat, firm little reputations. But his best poetry is written in prose and is buried in his three books. Nor was he solely dedicated to literature. Music was also important to him, and the cinema, so closely related to music, was his first love, and his last. I think he never gave up the dream of becoming a director, of expressing himself directly with images and rhythm instead of making do at one remove with words. His best writing has a cinematic flow and immediacy; his worst has a desperate, clotted quality, as though he felt that nobody would "get" him and was trying to break through, irritatedly, by brute exaggeration and repetition. But he was typed as a writer, and the nearest he could come to making movies was to write scripts—scripts that go far beyond what is usual in the way of precise indications as to sequence of shots, camera angles, visual details (the raindrops on a leaf are described in one), and other matters normally decided by the director. They are the scripts of a frustrated director.

The times might have done better by Agee. They could exploit one or two of his gifts, but they couldn't use him *in toto*—there was too much there to fit into any one compartment. In another sense, American culture was not structured *enough* for Agee's special needs; it was overspecialized as to function but amorphous as to values. He needed definition, limitation, discipline, but he found no firm tradition, no community of artists and intellectuals that would canalize his energies. . . .

If his native land offered Agee no tradition to corset his sprawling talents, no cultural community to moderate his eccentricities, it did provide "movements," political and aesthetic. Unfortunately, he couldn't sympathize with any of them. He was always unfashionable, not at all the thing for the post-Eliot thirties. His verse was rather conventional and romantic. In the foreword to *Permit Me Voyage*, Archibald MacLeish, an expert on literary fashions himself, accurately predicted, "It will not excite the new-generationers, left wing or right. . . . Agee does not assume . . . a Position." Ideologically, it was even worse. In an age that was enthusiastic about social issues, Agee's whole style of being was individualistic and anti-scientific. He was quite aware of this; oddly, considering the constellation of his traits, he had a strong bent toward ideas. (pp. 153-54)

The incompatibility of Agee and his times came to a head in the sensational failure of *Let Us Now Praise Famous Men*. It is a miscellaneous book, as hard to classify as that earlier failure *Moby Dick,* which it resembles, being written in a "big" style and drawing poetry from journalistic description, and making the largest statements about the human condition. It is mostly a documentary account of three Southern tenant-farming families, illustrated with thirty-one magisterial photographs by Walker Evans, Agee's close friend. . . . But it is many other things—philosophy, narra-

tive, satire, cultural history, and autobiography. It is a young man's book—exuberant, angry, tender, willful to the point of perversity (for example, the clumsy and undescriptive title), with the most amazing variations in quality; most of it is extremely good, some of it is as great prose as we have had since Hawthorne, and some of it is turgid, mawkish, overwritten. But the author gives himself wholly to his theme and brings to bear all his powers; he will go to any lengths to get it just right. From this emerges a truth that includes and goes beyond the truth about poverty and ignorance in sociological studies (and "realistic" novels), the truth that such squalid lives, imaginatively observed, are also touched with the poetry, the comedy, the drama of what is unexpected and unpredictable because it is living. (pp. 156-57)

The critics disliked it—Selden Rodman, Lionel Trilling, and George Marion O'Donnell were honorable exceptions—and it sold less than six hundred copies the first year. (p. 158)

The mischance that dogged Agee's career is evident in the timing of his death. Those who knew him best say that in the last few years of his life Agee changed greatly, became more mature, more aware of himself and of others, shrewder about his particular talents and problems. In the very last year, he had even begun to pay some attention to doctors' orders. He was by then getting such good fees for scripts that he was looking forward to doing only one a year and spending the rest of the time on his own writing. He might even have found out who he was. *A Death in the Family* contrasts significantly with *Let Us Now Praise Famous Men:* [the later book] is written in a more controlled and uniform style; it has more humor and none of the self-consciousness that often embarrasses one in the earlier work; its structure is classical, without Gothic excrescences; and, most significant of all, human beings are seen objectively, with the novelist's rather than the poet's eye. There is also the remarkable short story, "A Mother's Tale," he wrote three years before his death: a Kafka-like allegory, perfectly ordered and harmonious all through, of the human situation in this age of total war. I think only a thoroughly developed writer could have done it. Like Keats, Agee died just when he was beginning to mature as an artist. That Keats was twenty-five and Agee forty-five doesn't alter the point. Agee was an American, of a race that matures slowly, if ever. (pp. 158-59)

> *Dwight Macdonald, "James Agee" (originally published in a slightly different version with a different title in* The New Yorker, *November 16, 1957), in his* Against the American Grain *(copyright 1952, 1953, 1954, © 1956, 1957, 1958, 1959, 1960, 1961, 1962 by Dwight Macdonald), Random House, 1962, pp. 143-59.*

[Agee] had an extraordinary generosity of feeling for any effort that wasn't phony and an instant perception of anything that was. . . .

One of Agee's enthusiasms was for the cinema, and when he moved into the job of cinema reviewer for *Time,* he found himself as a journalist. He was certainly the best film critic *Time* has ever had, and I think some of his writing that went into those pages was first-rate. Later, because he felt cramped within the limits of *Time,* it was agreed that he could also review movies for the *Nation*. His *Nation* reviews were printed exactly as he wrote them. Perhaps I was biased, but I thought his *Time* reviews were better. (p. 22)

It was thought (and I was one who thought it) that Agee stayed too long on *Time;* that he should have left before he did and written "his own stuff." He did finally get out—and went straight from that frying pan into the fire of Hollywood. He might have written more and better than he did. Everyone who knew him wishes he had lived longer; but no one was surprised when he didn't. (p. 23)

> *T. S. Matthews, "James Agee—'Strange and Wonderful'," in* Saturday Review *(copyright © 1966 by Saturday Review, Inc.; reprinted with permission), April 16, 1966, pp. 22-3.*

The reasons for the reversal of the critical awareness of Agee [after his death] are complex. Only a few of them will be suggested here. First of all, Agee's death at forty-five immediately evoked the image of the young genius cruelly brought to an end before his prime. . . . Secondly, Agee's career seemed a spectacular waste of talent, and as such it seemed to denounce in certain ways the American way of life. Instead of writing the great American novel, Agee spent sixteen years writing impeccable prose for the Luce empire, first on *Fortune* and later on *Time,* and this, in itself, is an arresting image of the predicament for the creative imagination in contemporary America. Thirdly, Agee's ability to survive, and preserve his integrity, in the world of journalism and, later, in Hollywood, became a testimony to the possibility of being a nonconformist in a conformist age and society; and in the late fifties and sixties this has been a dominant concern of a good many intellectuals.

In an age when *avant-garde* artists can move from obscurity to financially and culturally rewarding fame in a matter of weeks, Agee has become an enviable image of the artist's integrity in a hostile society, recent enough to be relevant to the contemporary situation, yet distant enough to be worthy of veneration without imposing too seriously demanding obligations. No wonder, then, that Agee has become almost a culture hero, whose life has more significance than his work. (pp. 2-3)

Although this sudden reversal of one man's literary reputation is interesting as a demonstration of the fickleness of the public literary mind, there is more than this to be learned from Agee's literary career. For Agee's work may serve to illuminate, by contrast, a good many of the preoccupations of twentieth-century American literature. In 1934, for instance, Agee published a collection of poems, *Permit Me Voyage.* The title was taken from a poem by Hart Crane, and the collection as a whole showed the considerable influence of Whitman, neither one of whom was accepted as a literary model after the thirties. Furthermore, the poetry was basically romantic and conventional in form at a time when everybody was experimenting with the breaking down of poetic form.

At a time when science was asserting itself most strongly, even in the field of psychology, Agee displayed a distinctly anti-scientific attitude, suggesting that scientific truth was only a partial truth and true only so far as it existed in the realm of "Truth" which he had the courage to assert as an absolute. And, finally, at the time when Eliot's Anglo-Ca-

tholicism was becoming fashionable, Agee's religiosity was at once more skeptical and more deeply felt and asserted itself more seriously as a matter of life and death rather than, as in Eliot's case, a matter of intellectual and poetic necessity. (p. 4)

When *Let Us Now Praise Famous Men* was published in 1941, five years after it was begun, the sharecropping problem was no longer in fashion. . . . [Furthermore, the] book attacked not only certain inhuman social conditions but also a good many of those intellectuals who might have been expected to sympathize with the ambition of Agee's exposé. . . . In an age which provided an abundance of political as well as aesthetic "movements" and saw the placing of allegiance as meritorious conduct, Agee's religiously observed individualism must have appeared oddly removed from all the contemporary trends. (pp. 5-6)

Finally, the posthumous publication of *A Death in the Family* brought Agee's mistimed career to its climax. For although it received the Pulitzer Prize and its prose was praised in glowing terms, many critics found it impossible to judge adequately a work which was never finished by its author and, furthermore, wondered whether it really was a novel at all. It seems only appropriate that this book, which derives ultimately from Whitman and the romantics in its method and sensibility, should have been published at a time when critical opinion found it difficult to accept Whitman as a model and demanded in literature order, unity of themes, imagery, character and action, and structure. This literary climate was hardly conducive to the appreciative reception of a work which is in itself a fragment and which shirks structure in favor of "texture."

The question raised by James Agee's literary career is not why he failed to conform to the trends of twentieth-century American literature and culture, but why all those movements which have embraced so many off-beat phenomena failed to see Agee's talent for what it was. (p. 7)

Everybody seems to agree about Agee's poetic talents: the blurb writers assert that "Agee was essentially a poet"; . . . yet nobody seems to be willing to claim that Agee is even a minor poet of the twentieth century. While mentioning his poetry, most critics seem to prefer to go on to talk about the great lyrical qualities of Agee's novels, his screenplays, and his remarkable book about Southern sharecroppers. (pp. 12-13)

On the whole, it can be said that Agee's poetry, especially in *Permit Me Voyage,* exists in a field between two poles: one of them is the example of the sixteenth- and seventeenth-century Elizabethans, Donne, Shakespeare, and others; the other is provided by such American poets as Whitman and Hart Crane. Agee was of course familiar with the metaphysical poets; in his letters he writes: "I've been reading a good deal of John Donne and Herbert, Vaughan, and Emily Dickinson, whose work bears a remarkable resemblance to Donne." (p. 22)

The sonnet cycle . . . reminds one of the Elizabethans in its meditational nature: all twenty-five sonnets deal with the human condition conceived in Anglo-Catholic (or, for that matter, Catholic) terms. (pp. 23-4)

Agee is constantly concerned with the quality of human failure (and, . . . in *Let Us Now Praise Famous Men,* the artistic problem becomes one of taking failure into account during the creation of a work of art, to make the very failure itself into art). Instead of turning this awareness of failure into a gloomy righteousness over human depravity, Agee sees it as what must be affirmed if one wants to be human. . . . (p. 27)

[The] sonnets at least attempt what Agee meant when he said, "I want to *write symphonies*. That is, characters introduced·quietly (as are themes in a symphony, say) will recur in new lights, with new verbal orchestration, will work into counterpoint and get a sort of monstrous grinding beauty. . . ." For while the theme of the whole cycle is the condition of man as defined by religious doctrine, it occurs with many subtle variations in new settings to throw new light on a different situation. This is perhaps the most noteworthy achievement of the cycle as a whole and it points up to what Agee was later to attempt. Considered separately, as poems, the individual sonnets are not always successful; in general, they suffer from their close approximation of seventeenth-century poetics and a slightly archaic style, but when they do succeed, as do sonnets XX, XXII, and XXIV, to cite only three, they have a clear precision of language, a delicate concreteness of imagery, and a subtle sense of rhythm.

[In *Defense of Reason*] Yvor Winters . . . called "A Chorale" a "remarkable poem" (without explaining why), but perhaps the most remarkable thing about the poem is simply the effort to write "a chorale." The choice of genre is itself symptomatic of Agee's strong commitment to his religious background, and the poem struggles to find adequate expressions for this commitment in a world which has turned its back on it. Thus, the poem grows out of the poet's sense of religion as providing a standard for judgment, and it is the radical nature of the poet's choice which is perhaps more amazing than anything else. For it would seem that the poem remains too strongly bound by its own sense of archaism to be quite effective: instead of the awareness of tradition in a new dress (such as we can find it in, say, Eliot or Auden), the poem gives us an elegantly contrived pastiche. (pp. 30-1)

Despite this failure, however, it is the tone of the poem which attracts attention. The poet's attitude to his material reveals an uncompromising attempt to judge the deterioration of the modern world from certain basic values of the Christian tradition. The poem also shows clearly that the poet has realized the need for a rhetoric of some sort to lift the matter out of its everyday connections and make it "poetically" true. In other words, we find here Agee's realization that the conflict between the Christian tradition and the decay of the modern world cannot be resolved in realistic terms if it is not to turn into a trivial quarrel; the high rhetoric is needed to lift the poem to a level on which the conflict can be meaningfully resolved in the minds of the poet and his reader. Unfortunately, Agee's rhetoric borrows so much from the Elizabethans that the poem becomes little more than a pastiche; but the attempt is in itself worthy of notice for it foreshadows the kind of attack on a literary problem which appears in *Let Us Now Praise Famous Men*. Above all, there is evident in the poem passion as well as compassion, high seriousness, and humility. . . . (pp. 32-3)

It is impossible to know if Agee would ever have become a major poet had he concentrated more of his talents on verse. . . . [He] was acutely aware of the medium he was working in, he felt dissatisfied with traditional form and expressed a desire to write "musically" and to evolve a new kind of poetic diction. In this, he hardly succeeded, not because he lacked the talent, but because his ambition was so out of the ordinary and, also, because, as it turned out, prose proved to be a better medium for it than poetry. The early poetry simply shows a talented young man working with language, developing his skill in handling words, rhythms, images, and metaphors, and, above all, emotions. And all that is best in the poetry, the clear and precise language, the high rhetoric, the human involvement, the moral effort, the search for a huge symphonic structure accommodating the details of human experience, simple and complex, all looks forward to what he was to attempt more decisively in *Let Us Now Praise Famous Men*. The poetry, try as it may, does not entirely succeed in fusing that improbable combination of an Anglo-Catholic tradition and a Whitmaniacal "feeling of love for everything." . . . [In] "Dedication," where the Anglo-Catholicism is used as a perspective or a point of view rather than as a theme, Agee does succeed in building a "musical" structure with a powerful, reiterative impact in the manner of Whitman. (pp. 46-7)

Let Us Now Praise Famous Men is, of course, an uncomfortably original work, and it is easier to say what it is not than what it is. It is not a novel, or a documentary, or a journal, or a philosophical treatise, or a sociological study. A work which so refuses to fall into any of the comfortable classifications must, by necessity, disturb the equilibrium of most critics. Nevertheless, it is surprising that so far nobody has attempted to define exactly what *Let Us Now Praise Famous Men* is through correlating Agee's explicit statements about the book (in the book) with the book as a whole. . . . In the preface . . . [for example,] Agee states clearly the basic intention of the work:

> Actually, the effort is to recognize the stature of a portion of unimagined existence, and to contrive techniques proper to its recording, communication, analysis, and defense. More essentially, this is an independent inquiry into certain normal predicaments of human divinity.

These two sentences accurately predict all of the preoccupations of Agee later in the book. (p. 55)

Despite almost forbidding originality, it is well to remember that *Let Us Now Praise Famous Men* grew out of the Depression and the thirties in general. (That it was not published until 1941 only adds, in a superficial sense, to its originality.) . . . Communism in the thirties was not just a political party one might choose depending on individual political philosophy; it was part of a much larger call for action that went up in many areas in the wake of the Depression. This emphasis on action even infiltrated the world of art: as Harold Rosenberg [wrote in "Insurrections," *The New Yorker*, March 14, 1964], "the mixing of art with action philosophies had from the twenties forward become a major innovating factor in literature (Social Realism, Existentialism), as in painting (Action Painting) and on the stage (the Theatre of the Absurd)." In writing *Let Us Now Praise Famous Men*, Agee certainly conceived of it as a call to action, but he was also intelligent enough to see that it would have to be something more than the descriptive propaganda afforded by Social Realism in general which could be comfortably read in the living room and reduced to literary clichés, judgments on style, and comments on the "shocking" subject matter. What he aimed for, instead, was a "human effort which must require human co-opera-tion".... This means that the *only* way to see Agee's work is not as a book about "sharecropping" but as a book about the writing of a book about "sharecropping," and this, in turn, means that what the reader is experiencing is not the ordinary fictionalized (or pseudo-fictionalized) ac-count of reality but the writer's performance of an action or gesture in words as a response to an *actual* human situa-tion.

This action or gesture cannot easily be defined in ordinary terms: its complete definition is, of course, the book itself. But casting around for suitable metaphors, one is perhaps most arrested by the idea that the book as a whole is a prayer.... In the book, the momentum of Agee's under-taking takes him from the simple fury of recording the abuse of the universe on the lives of certain people to the complex acceptance of this reality.... Thus, the modified joy and happiness of the final section of the book is the re-sult not of a placid acceptance of a social abuse but of the realization that even human misery and failure must be af-firmed as part of life itself before these miseries can even be perceived clearly. In that sense, the whole book is simply a hymn to praise the glory of God. (pp. 105-07)

One can compare *A Death in the Family* with *Let Us Now Praise Famous Men,* in the oblique nature of the technique employed. The earlier book asked the question: How is it possible to comprehend the existence of another human life? And, coming to the conclusion that this is finally im-possible, it succeeded, obliquely, in creating the presence of the writer. The novel asks the opposite question: How can one actually comprehend death? And while concluding that it is, finally, impossible, it asserts simply that the world exists. In the process of showing nothingness and death invading the world, that world has been created and cele-brated. This world may be only fictional, but, in a deeper sense, this is insignificant, for the writer's response to his "material" is just as valid a human emotion even were that world real. What matters is not whether the world exists in a book or not; what matters is the response to it, and in that sense the world in *A Death in the Family* is the real world. (p. 212)

It is impossible to know exactly what revisions Agee would have made had he lived to complete *A Death in the Family.* Still, it is worth noting that no matter how he might have changed the arrangement of the chapters outside the central story, the basic nature of the book itself would have re-mained unchanged. It is not in the chronological arrange-ment that the meaning of the work is to be found; rather, it is in the shifting point of view, in the sense of detail, rele-vant or irrelevant, and in the implicit recognition of lan-guage as reality, that the work declares its intention. Like Whitman, adding to *Leaves of Grass,* like Pound, writing new *Cantos,* Agee could have added on to *A Death in the Family* without losing the essential nature of the experi-ence. That he did not live to do so may be tragic, as it de-prives us of literature that would have been rich and mean-ingful, but at least his novel remains, for all its fragmentary appearance, as one of the most remarkably original and carefully executed works of the twentieth century. (pp. 213-14)

Let Us Now Praise Famous Men is autobiographical in the same sense that "Dedication" is: Agee exists in the book, not as that abstract entity, "the author," but as James Agee, poet, journalist, and human being. In his effort to present the lives of certain people as inescapable human reality, Agee breaks down the distinction between art and life by not only presenting certain material but also talking about the aesthetics of his undertaking and the fallacy of supposing that human lives can ever be "material" for any kind of writing. Thus, the book as a whole becomes an ex-tension of Baudelaire's notion that, as W. M. Frohock ex-plains it, "any work of art contains an obstacle which the artist creates as part of the act of conceiving what he is going to do, and then conquers in the execution." *Let Us Now Praise Famous Men* is only nominally a book about three tenant families in Alabama; essentially, it is the record of a struggle between life and art, between the desire to immortalize a segment of human reality and the fact that this cannot be done by any art. It is this struggle which ex-ists as "an effort in human actuality"; and the struggle is won only with the realization that the endeavor is finally hopeless and also meaningless. In the end, although the ar-tistic ambition meets with failure, the recognition of this failure becomes the most moral (and human) thing to do, and since the book constantly declares exactly those values to be infinitely superior to those of art, the work is brought to a successful close.

This deeply original work has always been accused by critics of being formless and chaotic; but if Agee ever was formless, he had a purpose for it. In effect, *Let Us Now Praise Famous Men* has a carefully designed structure which constantly stresses the urgency and reality of the struggle with human experience. One reason why this structure has been so largely overlooked, apart from the radical innovation of the method in general, may be that it tries, in the simplest ways possible, to approach the kind of symmetry (and asymmetry) which Agee saw in the tenant farmer's simple pine-board shack. The complexity of Agee's struggle with the nominal subject matter *seems* to obscure the classical dramatic structure of the work. (pp. 222-23)

There is something unmistakably American about Agee's life and works. Part of this is accounted for by the influence of Whitman's expansive sense of himself as a symbolistic writer or by a comparison with Melville, who started out as a successful promise, produced an unrecognized master-piece, and retired into obscurity, not even bothering to pub-lish his last work. But, more than this, it is the sense one has of Agee as a man using literature for private rather than public ends and often, in fact, insisting so strongly on his personal integrity as to defy all public expectations. This is the opposite of what has been called literature as institu-tion; it is literature as a means of private discovery, and that notion certainly underlies the greatest of American writers: Whitman, Melville, Hawthorne, and Thoreau. (pp. 225-26)

Peter H. Ohlin, in his Agee *(copyright 1966 by Peter Ohlin; reprinted by permission of Astor-Honor, Inc.), Ivan Obolensky, 1966.*

A writer of awesome versatility, Agee still seems spectacu-larly out of place, for he failed to supply critics with a neat little bundle of poems or novels that could be unraveled by modern critical expertise. He wrote too little and, at the same time, too much. His mind played freely over wide areas, and categories fail to enclose him. He was always a poet, but he wrote relatively little poetry. He had a natural bent for fiction, but he produced only one full-length novel. He was a sensitive critic, but he spent his energies flailing away at grade B movies. Consequently, and for lack of anything else to say about him, some commentators discard him in that vast graveyard of American authors whose promise was never fulfilled, and James Agee shares a common grave with such spectres as Harold Frederic, Thomas Wolfe, and Vachel Lindsay.

Like that of composer Gustav Mahler, however, Agee's time seems about to come. (p. ix)

Agee, standing in thunderstorms, was struck by lightning five or six times, but each time by a bolt from a different Muse—a fact which confuses all definitions of "good" and "great" and points out Agee's uniqueness. In his short lifetime he produced a volume of poetry, a novel, a book on southern tenant farming, countless film reviews, several film scripts and short works of fiction, and numerous letters. Agee's greatness, therefore, is not conventional, for the quality of his work is spread throughout half a dozen different genres. A great writer, James Agee confounds our traditional notions of greatness. (p. 1)

The most important event of Agee's childhood occurred when he was six years old: his father, Hugh James Agee, died. For the remainder of his life, there was something of Telemachus in James Agee—as there is, perhaps, in all men. But any attempt at psychological analysis proves futile, for it took Agee thirty years to discover his complex reactions to his father's death. Our major concern should be that his discoveries resulted in *A Death in the Family.* (pp. 3-4)

To see James Agee merely as a writer of "unkept promise," as a creative artist lured to destruction, like the Lady of Shalott, by commercial tinsel and glitter, is to belittle his distinguished achievements. Rather than a victim of society, Agee was a product of his society. In an age that was evolving new media of expression such as television and elevating others such as reportage and motion pictures to unprecedented levels of national importance, Agee was truly an avant-garde artist. He viewed the motion picture, for example, with a scholar's seriousness before it was fashionable to do so, and he wrote experimental drama for television in the days when literate tv drama was still a possibility. He wrote a book which was, and still is, an unclassifiable oddity, and he brought the poetic potentiality of English prose to a level unsurpassed by any of his contemporaries. In an age of specialization and fragmentation, James Agee was a total writer, a professional who earned his living solely by his pen. In short, Agee fulfilled his promise, but in his own way, after a long search and after abandoning many modes of expression, and he fulfilled it in a manner peculiar to an American writer of the post-thirties. That he was denied the final accolade of his time is merely further indication that James Agee, like all great writers, was both of his time and ahead of it. (pp. 15-16)

He was a natural poet: all of his writings reveal an instinct for exact words, striking images, detailed observations, and rhythmical lines. His poetry is intensely lyrical, and at its core is a vein of melancholy and a universal concern with the mutability of love, human relationships, and existence.

In addition, it is a specifically American poetry; although no Frost or Sandburg, Agee harbored an almost mystical love for America's history, tradition, and people. . . .

Agee's poetry, strangely conservative in style, blatantly romantic in subject matter, and peculiarly religious in tone, often seems a prelude to something that never came. The fusion of fresh idiom and complex meaning that Agee so earnestly pursued generally fails to come through in his poetry; the powerful surge of great verse, sweeping beyond the barriers of mere technique, is too seldom evident in *Permit Me Voyage.* (pp. 17-18)

Another reason for dissatisfaction with Agee's poetry is that he chose to work almost slavishly within the limits of form, meter, and rhyme. Agee required the discipline of form to restrain his natural verbosity. . . .

Nonetheless, Agee's poetry is a solid achievement, the work of a writer who has a genuine feeling for the sound and shape of words. His best poems are lyrical, intense, and kinetic. . . . (p. 19)

[Like] that of the Elizabethans, the structure of Agee's poetry is often argumentative and the tone is frequently paradoxical. Yoking passion and intellect, Agee's verse seems closer to the Elizabethans than does that of other modern poets whose metaphysical borrowings have gained considerable commentary.

In addition, Hart Crane and Walt Whitman are the two most important and obvious American influences on Agee's verse. Agee borrowed much from Crane, including the title *Permit Me Voyage* from Crane's "Voyages III." A vivid clustering of image associations, syntactical complexity, and the persistent theme of the ecstasy and omnipotence of love, dominant qualities in Crane's work, dominate Agee's poetry. (p. 23)

Although it is difficult to detect any clear structural pattern to *Permit Me Voyage,* the opening poems, concerned with mutability and earthly frustrations, and the final devotional poems provide a clue. One can see the pattern of a spiritual quest for meaning in a world of fleeting values. The poems, in both tone and subject matter, move from earthly despair to spiritual acceptance. To insist on the presence of such structure, however, may be making too much of too little. It is more likely that the poems, broken up as they are into distinctive groups, stand separately.

The opening poems of *Permit Me Voyage* are entitled merely "Lyrics," suggesting that they have a singing quality and are words set to imaginary music. Always meaningful in Agee's life, music proves influential in his verse. (p. 24)

[The] first ten poems form a kind of overture, an introduction of major themes, to the remainder of the work. We find here the mutability of human life, deceit of lovers, frustrated ideals, and the glory of the creation—some of the themes that Agee returns to in later poems. *Permit Me Voyage,* in short, seems unified musically as well as substantively. (p. 25)

[Agee] abandoned poetry not because of his inability, but because of poetry's inability to do what he wanted it to do. Confined by the limitations of the poetic line and its accoutrements of meter, rhyme, and form, Agee turned from poetry to modes of expression more suited to his vision.

His entire career, in fact, seems a search for a manner of expression that would best enable him to see his artistic creation as a living reality in the present moment. Abandoning both poetry and prose, he eventually found an ideal form, one that enables an artist to create a world that exists solely in the present, that captures—or, at least, can potentially capture—each movement, detail, and nuance of physical reality: the motion picture. But Agee's early talent was reportorial and descriptive, and it was natural that after poetry he would turn for adequate expression to reporting, as he did in *Let Us Now Praise Famous Men.* (pp. 38-9)

Let Us Now Praise Famous Men is another Agee paradox. History, sociology, economics, philosophy, and, in part, fiction, the book rejects all attempts at easy classification and simple analysis. It is appallingly overwritten, yet it is seldom boring. It has a most unliterary subject, tenant farming in the South, yet it contains some of the finest poetic prose in American writing, poetry which Agee was unable to achieve in *Permit Me Voyage.* Agee's attitude toward his subject is idealized, sometimes almost mawkish, yet his writing is always sincere and accurate. The student of literature must resign himself to the fact that *Let Us Now Praise Famous Men,* like *Moby Dick,* achieves greatness through excess, paradox, and sheer linguistic power.

It is with Melville's masterpiece that Agee's book most clearly compares. Both works are written on an epic scale in a rhetoric that is often ecstatic, sometimes ponderous, and always awesome. . . . Like Melville, too, Agee had an awareness of the darker gods, a fascination for the abominations that dog man's footsteps to the grave. Agee's spectres were poverty and oppression, less overwhelming than Melville's whale but no less important, and his hatred of them gave the problem of tenant farming a universal quality and appeal. (p. 42)

The structure of the book, much maligned by critics and readers, is a problem, but not an insurmountable one. It is not that the book is devoid of structure. On the contrary, it has several structures. One consists of four planes. . . . These four planes might also be described as flashback, chronological narrative, imaginative reconstruction, and central consciousness. The device of flashback allowed Agee to contemplate and recall the events that led up to the present moment, while chronological narrative presented events in their logical time sequence. Imaginative reconstruction differed from flashback in that the former was free to invent, to fictionally recreate in order to gain complete perspective. Finally, central consciousness was the detailed account of the perceiving mind of the artist. Agee used each of these methods, and each provided him with a vantage point from which to record.

A second structure might best be seen in terms of music. The book has a pattern, much like the sonata form, consisting of two major themes. . . . The initial theme—poverty—dominates this symphonic structure, while the second, injustice, appears as a subdominant theme. Better still, the entire work is a set of variations or a *grosse fugue* on the theme of poverty and human suffering.

Still a third structure can be found in the dramatic form of the book. . . . [The] book divides into three parts, which correspond to the three acts of a play. Agee even provides, in the opening pages, a cast of characters. (pp. 47-9)

Lying behind the beauty and poetry of this book, however,

is a bitter social criticism, a barely restrained anger at all those whose complacency and cruelty "in so immane and outrageous, wild, irresponsible, dangerous-idiot a world" extinguishes the godhead in the heart, nerves, and center of other human lives. (p. 52)

Let Us Now Praise Famous Men . . . is flawed in two important ways. The first flaw is a moral one, the second is artistic. [Lionel] Trilling, in his 1941 review [see excerpts above], pointed out that Agee's was "a failure of moral realism" that lay in his "inability to see these people as anything but good." . . . Essentially correct, Trilling misses part of the point. Agee, attempting to record experience through his own consciousness, is recording *his* attitudes, not inherent qualities of the tenant farmers. There is no malice or meanness in these people because Agee came to see them as noble human beings, almost folk-heroes, as "famous men." Surely Agee is not saying that there is no malice or darkness in these human souls; he is, however, saying that through suffering comes nobility and that everything that is, even the dirty, barefoot child of a tenant family, is holy. . . . I think it is more accurate, then, to see Agee's vision in *Let Us Now Praise Famous Men* as a consciously restricted point of view rather than a failure.

Agee's second error was an artistic one. Although, as I pointed out, there are several structures in *Let Us Now Praise Famous Men,* the book still lacks unity and discipline. The structures are general, and what one misses is the shaping hand of the skillful artist. The book, like an oversized suit, hangs loose in several places. . . . Agee's insistence that the things of this world have an absolute beauty of their own and need no assistance from art betrays him into a shameless lack of responsibility in his use of language.

Agee's "failure" might better be termed a failure of reality, the failure of the real to be as interesting, inevitable, and perfect as fiction. (pp. 53-6)

If Agee's book fails, it fails—like so many other books in American literature—in the grand manner. *Let Us Now Praise Famous Men,* despite its flaws, failures, and excesses, is an outstanding document in American writing. . . . (p. 57)

It was precisely because of his attempt to reproduce in words a cinematic vision of experience that James Agee turned to fiction. Poetry, with its necessities of conciseness, rhythm, and control, was too limited a medium to reproduce this vision, to represent the interplay of human personalities in a faithfully realistic setting. Reportage was restricted to the details of reality; it left no room for the creative imagination. Only in fiction could Agee paradoxically find the necessary discipline and freedom that his artistry required. Only in fiction could Agee find all of those qualities which give a work of fiction the semblance of actuality and, at the same time, make it into something more, that which we distinguish as "art." And fiction, too, made fewer disciplinary demands upon an author like Agee, whose prose often slipped its confines and galloped off uncontrollably. (p. 61)

No mere summary of plot can fully convey the complexity and interrelationships of characters and themes in *A Death in the Family.* The novel has an almost symphonic arrangement, and anyone who has listened to Samuel Barber's *Knoxville: Summer of 1915* knows how readily Agee's prose can be set to music. In musical terms, the novel is a set of variations on the themes of love and death, Agee's *Tod und Verklärung*.

What is equally difficult to convey is Agee's cinematic technique in the novel. One must remember that while writing *A Death in the Family* he was also at work on screenplays, and this influence upon his writing is profound. The novel abounds in long sections of dialogue, vivid cinematic descriptions, and techniques usually associated with drama and motion pictures. The structure of *A Death in the Family,* not only symphonic, is also the pyramid structure of the drama, a rising and falling action. (pp. 78-9)

It is impossible to read *A Death in the Family* without feeling the author's immense compassion and concern for his fictional characters. Some readers, however, believe that this is precisely what mars the novel. Agee, they say, was too closely identified with his characters and was unable to achieve the proper detachment necessary to all great works of art. Such criticism, I feel, is wrong. It is because of Agee's involvement, his overwhelming concern for his fictional creations, that the reader is able to envision the Follets and Lynches as living human beings instead of allegorical figures. A labor of love, *A Death in the Family* moves us because it moved its author. (p. 81)

Although *A Death in the Family* is Agee's finest achievement, it is an odd book to have appeared in the 1950's and in America. It touches upon no contemporary social problems or minor psychological ones, and it ignores the modern concern with bedroom, boredom, and brutality. It is, moreover, a conservative book stylistically, with no technical innovations or mythopoetic complexity. The author tells his tale simply and lyrically in a straightforward narrative. And finally the theme of the novel is commonplace in modern literature: it is primarily the story of a young man's maturation, and as such stands with Lawrence's *Sons and Lovers,* Joyce's *Portrait of the Artist as a Young Man,* Wolfe's *Look Homeward, Angel,* and Salinger's *Catcher in the Rye.*

What then, we must ask, makes *A Death in the Family* the excellent novel that it is? . . . Agee's novel is a successful work of literary art largely because of its craftsmanship, the rich pattern of significance that emerges from the structure and the language of the novel. *A Death in the Family* is a tightly constructed work (despite the italicized portions Agee never wove into the whole), with the dramatic structure and tension of a play and the lyrical intensity of a poem. The plot of the novel is simple, but its simplicity is the deceptive kind of much great literature. . . . (pp. 90-1)

Secondly, the book's value lies in what Henry James called the amount of "felt life" in the novel—in this case, American life. *A Death in the Family* is a specifically American novel, so much a part of our unique tradition and language that it would seem impossible for a European to share its private vision. (pp. 91-2)

The novel is valuable, too, for the insights into human nature that it gives us. Fiction, involving more than plot, character, and structure, does not exist in a vacuum. It touches in clearly discernible ways the life of man, holding the mirror up to his human personality and, at times, radically changing it. *A Death in the Family* achieves a high level of human insight because it focuses on portions of human experience that we all recognize: death, childhood, and parental love. One of the major themes of the novel is death and resurrection. Jay's soul is spiritually reborn in the form of a butterfly at the end of the novel, but it is also physically reborn in Rufus. (p. 93)

Discussions of Agee center around his wasteful life, his excesses, and his "sensibility" (discussions of his sensibility have become almost a cabala). He is criticized for having failed to objectify his experiences in writing, for being too "autobiographical." Most of all, he is dismissed as a promising writer who was corrupted by commercial pursuits and by Hollywood. (p. 129)

If there is any pattern to the entire body of Agee's work, it lies in his cinematic vision of experience. Each genre that Agee worked in—poetry, reportage, social doctrine, and fiction—was a stage toward the achievement of a more complex vision of reality which he unsuccessfully sought to express in the motion picture. It is difficult to trace this development biographically, for at no time does Agee express such a conscious pursuit. . . .

A close examination of Agee's writings reveals two basic reasons why his work moved increasingly closer to a kind of cinematic reality. The first reason is an aesthetic one, the belief that words "cannot embody; they can only describe." Agee's preoccupation with bringing words as near as possible to "an illusion of embodiment" served only to undermine his faith in words and to enhance the possibilities of the motion picture camera. (p. 131)

Agee's entire career, therefore, was a search for form, for the one medium that would have the impulse of life itself. In spite of his abandoning one form after another, all of his work was of high quality. Agee's writings reveal that he kept his "promise," that he fulfilled whatever expectation others held for him as a writer, but he fulfilled it in his own way and in a manner specifically modern and American. (p. 134)

To speculate on the poetry or fiction that he might have written is to envision James Agee as someone other than the man he was: a versatile and accomplished artist whose mind played freely over all possible media of expression and whose ability with the English language was exceeded by none of his contemporaries. Truly an avant-garde artist, Agee was a writer whose career implies a new direction that American writers may be taking. (p. 141)

> *Kenneth Seib, in his* James Agee: Promise and Fulfillment *(reprinted by permission of the University of Pittsburgh Press;* © *1968 by the University of Pittsburgh Press), University of Pittsburgh Press, 1968.*

The Collected Poems consists of *Permit Me Voyage* . . . , the only collection published in the poet's lifetime, printed here with revisions; of later verse published in periodicals or located in manuscript; and of *John Carter,* a long poem begun when Mr. Agee was in college, but never completed. (p. 409)

Mr. Agee has enough good lines to keep a lesser talent in business for years. His problem is in getting from one to the next without doing violence to his own idiom.

Nor screaking bat, whose wings hook through the gloom,
Nor mournful owl, whose lost and dreary yell
The monstrous deities of the dark invokes

The bat is excellent, the owl cliché, the syntax, at the end,
awkward. . . .

The editor praises the poet's rhythms, but they seem to us
a series of song meters extended metrically and otherwise
beyond what they can bear. The poems are full of love,
death, nature, and all that, but what, actually, are they
about? The theology of the early work is rudimentary, as is
the sociology of the later. One remembers, maliciously,
that when Mr. Agee was young Edna Millay was a very
famous poet, and Appalachia was going through one of its
periodic cycles of chic. (p. 410)

The talent was great; it came to nothing. However, as Hans
Sachs says, *in holder Jugendzeit* we are all of us poets, and
Mr. Agee's poem on Brahms defines exactly the measure
of his own shortcoming.

> Fulfilled, the long, the well-wrought life,
> Accomplished, the undeviant years.   (p. 411)

> *Turner Cassity, in* Poetry (© *1969 by The
> Modern Poetry Association; reprinted by
> permission of the Editor of* Poetry), *September,
> 1969.*

Of the thirteen selections in [*The Collected Short Prose of
James Agee*] edited by Robert Fitzgerald only the famous
A Mother's Tale reads as an entirely successful and mature
work. Not that the other dozen are entirely unsuccessful,
immature, or without value. Ranging from stories first published in *The Harvard Advocate,* through a brilliant list of
proposed projects Agee submitted to a Guggenheim committee, to a portrait of Brooklyn with its stirring coda-like
description of animals at twilight in the zoo, here is the intense young writer, here, too often, the sophomore.

Agee was the young writer, however, to have been voted
most likely to succeed had only these prose pieces existed,
as full as they are of the improbable and the controlled
flight, forced and real humor, bathos and pathos. Reading
them today, aware of his triumphant *Death In The Family*
and *Let Us Now Praise Famous Men,* we are in for some
shocks, pleasant, not so pleasant. "Why, 1930!" one
thinks, reading *Death In The Desert,* a story of extraordinary compassion and perception, "he was only twenty-
one!" Equally impressed, perhaps only a little disconcerted
by the appearance more than once of such phrases as
"rhomboid of light" and "the deliberate edge of evening",
we read *They That Sow in Sorrow Shall Reap.* But then as
the irony weighs deadeningly and humor is boyishly overworked in a satire called *Dedication Day,* we are a little
surprised to discover it was written sixteen years later. It is
disarming, touching to be told, "I know that I am making
the choice most dangerous to an artist, in valuing life above
art . . ." when we have often felt in his writing the ardent
opposite.

Nevertheless, there is great contagion in the prose of James
Agee. There is an infectious joy in Agee's search for and
discovery of the word, the phrase. Three detailed notes for
motion pictures betray that his particular power, a tension
of focus on an object, face, landscape, was one he took
from the camera. What the camera could do was the art he
admired. . . . (pp. 411-12)

In his Memoir [included in this collection], Robert Fitzgerald quotes a good deal from Agee's letters, and these are
full of energetic observation and feeling. I hope the day will
come when there is a complete edition of the letters of
James Agee. . . .

This small book, framed by the opening Memoir, closing on
the sombre myth *A Mother's Tale,* is a fine portrait of the
artist as the eternal young man. (p. 412)

> *David Jackson, in* Poetry (© *1969 by The
> Modern Poetry Association; reprinted by
> permission of the Editor of* Poetry), *Septem-
> ber, 1969.*

An intense desire to know himself marked Agee's work in
the three great pieces of sustained prose that lie at the heart
of his achievement. In *Let Us Now Praise Famous Men*
Agee describes the process by which he came to a new and
deep understanding of himself and his world. In *The
Morning Watch* he looked back at himself as at the age of
twelve he had come to an earlier appreciation of his own
identity and importance. In *A Death in the Family* he looks
even farther back and exposes the roots from which that
twelve-year-old character had grown. And of the three
works perhaps the frankest and most revealing is *A Death
in the Family.* (pp. 36-7)

Whether this novel is considered the capstone of the career
or a description of the first steps in a long-continuing search
for certainty, it is one of the most important things that
Agee wrote. It has been compared on the one hand to the
work of the young James Joyce and on the other it has been
pointed to as proof that Agee should have devoted himself
exclusively to what he always called "his own work"
rather than skittering about and fooling with things like the
movies and criticism. But, whatever our opinion on this
matter might be, it seems clear that Agee did during his life
what he wanted to do. (p. 44)

> *Erling Larsen, in his* James Agee (*American
> Writers Pamphlet No. 95;* © *1971, Univer-
> sity of Minnesota*), *University of Minnesota
> Press, Minneapolis, 1971.*

The writings of James Agee are diverse, but his poetic sensibility is fundamental to all he accomplished. Throughout
his writing, from poetry to informal criticism, a consistency
is revealed in his reverence for actuality. He was so concerned at times that actuality be honored that he argued for
a blurring of distinctions between art and life. Agee saw
and loved the world in its immediacy, and he was angered
when others (with words, or improper use of camera) failed
to see it. Correspondingly, his writing manifests an increasingly precise observation of the ordinary.

Agee's literary work constitutes the act of perception. (p. 9)

No point is gained in lamenting what he did not accomplish.
His literary work possesses integrity. At times he relied
upon satire or sarcasm, but even that posture reveals the
truth as he experienced it. His unfinished manuscript for *A
Death in the Family* is, above all, an affirmation of life.
Those fictionalized memories demonstrate that Agee
achieved the "inner vitality, and harmony, and integrity,"
which is the proper "business of the artist."

This study documents Agee's conviction that poetry resides in the commonplace and depends upon remembrance.

His film criticism, many projected ideas for analysis, and his prose also reveal this conviction. Just as the wide visions of Walt Whitman and William Carlos Williams allowed a broad poetic awareness, Agee's inclusiveness permitted him to see diverse materials and their relatedness. (pp. 9-10)

James Agee, while alive, was considered a genius with words, and his diverse writings validate this appellation; but, when commentators who knew him attempt to characterize his writing, the result often is homage to a man whose personality was luminous. . . . He loved people and interchange with them; inevitably, this characteristic is reflected in remembrances of him. Thus, while the writing stands alone, the strength of Agee as a person remains fundamentally important; he did honor to living. Ultimately to ignore Agee the man is impossible if one is to appreciate the writing. His best prose grew directly from personal experience. A problem that some critics would hasten to add is that Agee did not husband his talents; he sought too much and too many kinds of accomplishment which resulted in an overextension of talent and energy. . . . Agee arrested many moments within a world which, for him, was always best perceived in the full and continuous weight of its reality. Samuel Taylor Coleridge, whom he admired, wrote that, if a poet properly apprehends any particular, it has the potential of suddenly taking on universality; and Agee, as writer, was continually concerned with rendering particularity through language so as to suggest universality. (pp. 17-18)

In whatever Agee wrote he sought an appropriate mode of transfiguring the texture of commonplace experience. He was fascinated with the daily events of living which were intertwined with death; and, although he respected life above art, he accepted the challenge given any poet. . . . The poet is able to distill the ordinary in an extraordinary way and to present his knowledge through language; he is able to reorder reality. Often, as one reads Agee's works, he is reminded of Agee's fascination with the beauty of minute intersections of time, space, and consciousness. (pp. 26-7)

Agee's uses of language are often compared to the camera. . . . True, Agee realized a camera could capture an instant of time, and a photograph properly seen reveals immense amounts of knowledge; but he also knew that, to give the texture of feeling within a particular period of time, words possessed potentialities absent in photography precisely because a person is not a strip of film. Sometimes his preciseness of language suggests that he is attempting to write as a camera might reproduce reality, but his vision remains intensely humane, and his involvement contributes a lyrical quality. (p. 28)

Agee was, as Walker Evans has remarked, "a born sovereign prince of the English Language." But Agee was also a special kind of person. Open and interested, quickwitted and aware of the complexity of all things in a complex universe, he was always beginning again, always looking again to see if there might be a different, or better, way of seeing and writing. (p. 29)

[One] can separate the early prose into two groups; stories that seem to rely heavily upon imagination; and those which grew out of personal experience, or at least are limited to emotional experiences that someone as young as

Agee could have experienced and adequately presented. "Boys Will Be Brutes" is successful because its apparent basis is in an actual, or a believably portrayed, experience. (p. 39)

In contrast, stories written at about the same time which are more limited in scope are careful accomplishments. One of the best examples is "Death in the Desert," a story which limits itself in large part to the stream-of-consciousness revelation of the mind of the narrator. (p. 40)

As Agee encountered the complexity of the world, he began to realize that he could not intellectualize without losing the immediacy of experience. When one looks at the whole of his literary career, minute areas of experience, such as the encounter described in "Death in the Desert," became of greatest value for him as subjects about which to write. Interestingly, much of this writing resulted in poetry of which some of the lyrical passages in *Famous Men* ("On the Porch," "A Country Letter") are illustrative. Although one might describe this development in method as a dislike of abstraction, Agee sought ways to write which would falsify as little as possible. His respect for the quotidian brought about a change in emphasis.

Agee came to realize that the "actual" was a series of moments which flowed together to provide a texture unique in itself. The analogy between apprehension and the film is obvious. (pp. 40-1)

At no point in his career was Agee ever classifiable within a movement or by an ideology. (p. 44)

"Plans for Work: October 1937," which accompanied his second application for a Guggenheim Fellowship, included an outline for forty-seven separate proposed projects. . . . These elaborate proposals contain outlines for various kinds of analysis, poetry, and collection of data; in fact, enough is suggested to keep scores of writers busy for many years. Most of the plans are only ideas, but they reflect Agee as he overflowed with hopes to examine how men see or fail to see their world. These plans best illustrate his turning away from conventional writing. . . . His hope for a new kind of film, akin to the lyric poem, is only now beginning to be explored some thirty years after its suggestion.

A predominant idea found in many of the proposals emphasizes a need for methods to analyze everyday realities. . . . He argued that a record of a street or a room "in its own terms" has a distinct value different from its use as atmosphere in a work of fiction. He was fascinated with the possibilities which the ordinary world offered for analysis and as a challenge to communication. (pp. 61-2)

Of the several types of fugitive writing by Agee that appear during [the middle 1930s], some is clever parody and criticism of society; other poetry is experimental; but the best of this transitional writing is of a personal nature. His "Lyric" which begins "From now on kill America out of your mind," published in *Common Sense* in 1937, seems almost a set of instructions for his better work during these years. Its speaker says that little is to be gained from thinking about abstractions associated with the nation. To think of individuals and "the land / Mutually shapen as a child of love" is far better.

The lyric "Vertigral," which begins "Demure morning morning margin . . .," and establishes a very quiet mood, is an experiment with word music. This Agee poem is the only one clearly derived from the poetry of Gerard Manley Hopkins. But intricate interplay of sound is pursued in many other works of this period, and there is no doubt that Agee had absorbed much of the method of inscape from his reading of Hopkins in Robert Hillyer's versification class at Harvard. (p. 65)

Agee's text [to *Let Us Now Praise Famous Men*] both is and is not a "literary" work. His approaches to reporting the *un*imagined had been in a process of gestation for years preceding the trip to Alabama. A total experience, from biography to the manner in which the book was set into type, ultimately became important to this text's composition. Agee's attempt to wrestle with myriads of inaccuracies and distortions is the core of the work. However, a fundamental assumption which undergirds the text—ironically a work of "Art," despite Agee's belabored distinctions that it is not—is that any attempt to provide an accurate record of what he observed was doomed from the start. For this reason, Agee insists on making his reader aware of the complexity of his goals. (p. 76)

A basic notion which had to be communicated was that distinct persons were apprehended within a unique texture. Each was "a human being, not like any other human being so much as he is like himself".... Because each was respected as distinct and "holy," the dignity of the human person is Agee's basic motif; his language and the obvious external use of religious forms support this fact. But, while trying to adhere to particularities, Agee knew that he had been affected by what was experienced. And he believed that his reactions were finally just as important as what had caused the reactions. *Famous Men*'s aesthetic, therefore, focuses attention on details as remembered, but often as modified by reflection. The writer's presence provides knowledge of the limitations of consciousness; but, since such knowledge is part of any accurately recorded experience, Agee's reactions are included. (p. 77)

Famous Men functions like poetry even though Agee insists that a work of art was not intended. . . . Agee wants his reader to feel as close as possible to the living situation. For this reason, the aural or musical quality of the text is fundamental. In the preamble Agee suggests that the text might be read aloud (he read the book aloud to friends as he wrote it); and he indicates that he is striving for a new literary form which would be analogous to music. Ultimately, the form he developed relies upon several techniques which flow into one another. Particular kinds of experiences are emphasized within different units; and, because of the complexity of the variegated experience, several techniques were necessary. (p. 78)

[As a film critic, Agee] refused to remove himself from his commentary, and he sought to avoid a simplistic view. . . . His reactions, as an "amateur," are a combination of his sense of beauty and of the morally correct. . . . When his movie criticism was later collected, some reviewers complained of an apparent inconsistent aesthetic. But Agee's veneration of reality and honor for the individual unifies his enthusiasm, just as in all of his characteristic work. (pp. 98-9)

Agee's scripts are conceived like novels. The reliance upon the first-person plural in directions is a novelist's point of view. In many instances Agee provides so much detail and

suggestion that little is left for the imagination of the director. . . . Agee felt compelled to go beyond retelling the story, and his scripts can be described, because of their elaborate suggestions for gesture, sound, and camera use, as the production of a frustrated director.

The similarity of theme in each adaptation indicates that Agee must have exercised discretion in choosing projects; for in each case, he chose a literary work in which the regenerate or unregenerate Adamic motif is basic. He was fascinated with the idea of the confrontation of innocence with evil—a situation which is immediately obvious in both of the Stephen Crane stories for which he did scripts, "The Blue Hotel" and "The Bride Comes to Yellow Sky." (p. 120)

Agee knew that religious emotion, for any person, was a combination of many different elements conjoined; but, as one matures, religious feeling is difficult to reconcile with other ways of feeling and thinking. . . . Sometimes he felt a return to formal religion might be necessary for him, while at other times he was sure he would never return. But, along with these vacillations, he could say "at all times I feel sure that my own shapeless personal religious sense . . . is deepening and increasing." Whether or not he might ever again have been a formal believer [after the late 1940s, that is], his interest in religion remained important; for one of his letters of that period says simply "I certainly feel no doubt to which side I am drawn 'as between Christ and those against him.'" (pp. 140-41)

[*A Death in the Family*], while simple on the surface, confronts death as the negation of life, but as a necessary part of it. The book provides an image of life which contrasts with the change brought about by sudden death, and commentators have described the book as the fulfillment of a vision where innocence and compassion meet. . . . But, while *A Death in The Family* remains a private book, it is also about all who have undergone similar experiences; for Agee was aware that what he fictionalized possessed archetypal meaning. (p. 145)

His fictional method is an extension of his continuing interest in documentation: everything remembered became potentially useful. A great respect for the commonplace is at the base of what is accomplished; and remembrances take on significance simply because they contributed to a previous atmosphere. The word "poetic" often occurs in descriptions of the novel; and many perceptive insights about its form derive from the realization that *A Death in The Family* is more like a poem than a novel. Its open form provides a tension between the chaos of reality and the poet's way of writing about it. Through careful attention to ordinary aspects of human experience, Agee reveals larger meaning. (p. 146)

In all of Agee's writing, there is an elegiac tone, for his are songs to moments which are passing. This nostalgia for the past and respect for the moment are his best achievements. His books are valuable because they are precise records of moments which are in process of passing away from memory. *Let Us Now Praise Famous Men, The Morning Watch,* and *A Death in the Family* each reflect particular moments Agee honored; his success is that he catches moments for others to appreciate.

Characteristic of Agee's vision is that, while realizing the transitoriness of all man's endeavors, he could pour all of his energy into a particular project at hand. (p. 158)

Famous Men is the keystone in Agee's career and there he made his most sustained contribution to American letters. His way of documenting what others had not even taken time to see is his most significant contribution to modern literature. His respect for the unsung beauty of common lives in rural Alabama is prophetic of a new kind of journalism, perhaps now best practiced by writers like Norman Mailer. Agee's importance in modern literature rests on his ability to write poetry and prose which go beyond traditional modes. (p. 159)

The quality of [his] moral vision is a final reason why Agee's works have enduring value. He was a writer for whom there was little separation between moral and aesthetic judgments. There was never a question of anything being right if it did not honor the human spirit. He suspected any kind of construct which removed man from the immediacy of life ("kind, obscene philosophy" he some-times said). But he knew that such frameworks were necessary if man were to be reminded of the immediacy of living and the continuity of life. The ultimate value of his poetry and prose is a celebration of immediacy bounded by death. In Agee's writing a continual celebration is of the ordinary facts of existence. A child's wonder, the pleasure to be gained from a chance encounter, the emotion of true religious faith—these are the kinds of things about which he wrote best. Always these are things which quickly pass, but through language they are arrested so that others can behold them. (p. 160)

Victor A. Kramer, in his James Agee *(copyright 1975 by G. K. Hall & Co.; reprinted with the permission of Twayne Publishers, A Division of G. K. Hall & Co., Boston), Twayne, 1975.*

Sholom Aleichem

1859-1916

(Also Sholem or Shalom; also Aleikhem; pseudonym of Sholem Rabinovich; also translated as Solomon Rabinowitz) Yiddish novelist, dramatist, and short story writer. Considered one of the founders of modern Yiddish literature, Aleichem remains the most widely read Yiddish author of all time. For his ability to capture the flavor of popular speech and to write with warmth and humor about the everyday lives of the Yiddish-speaking Jews of Eastern Europe, Aleichem came to be known as "the Jewish Mark Twain." He is best known for his tales of Tevye the dairyman, which were adapted into the enormously popular Broadway musical *Fiddler on the Roof*. A man of the people all his life, Aleichem remained so in death, requesting in his will that "I want to be placed not among aristocrats or among the powerful, but among the plain Jewish laborers, among the very people itself, so that the gravestone that is to be placed upon my grave should illumine the simple graves about me; and these simple graves should adorn my gravestone, even as the plain, good people during my lifetime illumined their *Folkesschreiber*."

PRINCIPAL WORKS*

The Old Country (short stories) 1946
Inside Kasrilevke (short stories) 1948
Tevye's Daughters (short stories) 1949
Adventures of Mottel, The Cantor's Son (short stories) 1953
The Great Fair: Scenes from My Childhood (autobiographical short stories) 1955
Selected Stories of Sholom Aleichem (short stories) 1956
Stories and Satires by Sholom Aleichem (short stories) 1959
The Tevye Stories, and Others (short stories) 1965
Old Country Tales (short stories) 1966
Some Laughter, Some Tears (short stories) 1968
The Adventures of Menahem-Mendl (epistolary novel) 1969

*titles and dates are for first English-language publication

Although Shalom Aleichem's tales do not rank with those of the great professionals, as tiny monuments to the customs and emotions of a race they are excellent. In their rich orthodoxy and their somewhat patriarchal good-humour they contrast strongly with the typical Bowery literature of America. The stories, however, are weakened by a too facile lyrism, as the author cannot narrate for two consecutive pages without breaking into song. (p. 432)

> The Dial (*copyright, 1922, by The Dial Publishing Company, Inc.; reprinted by permission of J. S. Watson, Jr. and Scofield Thayer), April, 1922 (and reprinted by Kraus Reprint Corporation, 1966).*

The strength of Samson lay in his hair. There are writers whose greatness is similarly concentrated. Sholom Aleichem is one of these: his strength lies in his humor. (p. 41)

Forgiveness is both the bitterest root and the sweetest fruit of humor.

The most valuable, most human trait of Tevye [sometimes spelled Tevieh, Tuvia, Tevyeh, or Tevya] the Dairyman, one of Sholom Aleichem's most wonderful characters, is precisely the ability of this common man to understand and forgive everything. To understand and forgive is a virtue of philosophers. And in every authentic humorist there is also something of the philosopher. Tevye the Dairyman is a philosopher, though of the heart, not the head, which is even better.

Though his head is the head of an ignorant and not overly sophisticated village Jew, he has the splendid philosophical ability to turn everything inside out, so as to discover the standpoint from which everything may be justified. (pp. 41-2)

In this delicate but penetrating irony of Tevye's, when the philosopher in him suddenly speaks out, we recognize not the pious but the knowing Jew, not the man of faith but the cheerful pessimist who knows that you can find an answer for everything if you want to, or no answer to anything if you want not to, so that it is better to pose no questions and admit no complaints against the Lord. (p. 42)

The exceptional delicacy and complexity of feeling in Tevye—who is, after all, a simple, ordinary Jew—derive from his hidden store of humor, thanks to which he can transcend the pressure of immediate influences and surrender to life on terms that are not forced or slavish, but liberating. His liberating attitude of "taking it as it comes" creates a cloak of peace, tolerance, and submissiveness in which Tevye envelops his behavior, and which extends to his relations with other people. (p. 43)

It is a mistake to think that the diaspora-Jew speaks through Tevye's mouth, or the *nebbish*, the humble man, the character whose formula is "this-too-is-for-the-best." Not at all. Tevye's healthy human instincts have been neither dulled nor weakened. He knows what is good in this world, and feels very keenly the misery of life. But since he cannot control it from the outside, he uses humor to sweeten it from the inside. Only in this delicate humorously sarcastic sense does he put up with the "world as it is." Only after conquering it from within does he submit to it outwardly. (p. 44)

Tevye has been seen by many as a representative of the old-fashioned, small-town Jewish masses; only the Jew in him was recognized. It seems to me, however, that precisely in the depiction of this simple villager Sholom Aleichem has also transcended that which is specifically Jewish. Tevye does have certain typical Jewish traits and mannerisms, including the characteristic Jewish ability to laugh out of one side of his mouth. Yet he also embodies something appreciably richer and fresher than the cold, angry, embittered Jewish irony, and he stands ten heads taller than the average ordinary small-town Jew.

If you see in this an idealization of Tevye, you must bear in mind that Sholom Aleichem himself idealized Tevye. He treats him quite differently from the other Kasrilevkites. Most of the men and women who people his stories are comic characters, objects of laughter, but Tevye is humorous. Sholom Aleichem stoops to the other characters in describing them, but Tevye he raises to his own level. He endows him with his own most beautiful talent—the ability to laugh. . . .

I have called Tevye Sholom Aleichem's beloved hero. I might have said his *most beloved hero*. Sholom Aleichem was not unfond of the other heroes of his novels, like Stempenyu, Yosele Solovey, Rafalesco of *Wandering Stars*. But whereas his love for them is of the "heroic" kind, his love for Tevye could be called simply "human." The above-mentioned and other romanticized heroes of Sholom Aleichem's works overshadow those around them because they are novelistic heroes—heroes by profession. God has blessed them with exceptional virtues and talents: one is a magnificent violinist, another a famous singer, the third an inspired actor. But Tevye is an everyday Jew, a common woodcarter, a simple villager. Thanks only to Sholom Aleichem's pen did Tevye become Tevye. When the heroes of the romances set out on their great adventures, when they soar to great heights and "speak poetry," it is no wonder; but Tevye had to be instructed by the author in what to say and what to think when he is alone with nature, or alone with himself. To Tevye the Dairyman the author entrusted his own role, the role of humorous story-teller, psychologist, portraitist, jokester, master of language—in short, the role of the writer. Consequently *Tevye the Dairyman* is not only the most moving and most likeable, but also the most intimate of Sholom Aleichem's books. (p. 45)

The humorist and the child have one great virtue in common: their innermost carefreeness. The child *does not know* about life's cares, the humorist chooses to ignore them. That is why they understand each other so well, and why all humorists are writers for children.

It is interesting that with the exception of Tevye, Sholom Aleichem endowed only one of his other major characters

with a humorous approach to life—Motl [sometimes spelled Mottel or Motel], Peysi the Cantor's Son.

In the book by that name, subtitled, "Writings of an Orphan," most of the characters are comic or tragi-comic. Only Motl is humorous; only he looks down upon the others with a gentle smile that suggests either simple childish innocence or a deep but rarified pain; he alone is set apart, at a slight distance from the others. We feel pity for the Kasrilevkites whose pain and suffering is described in these writings, but we feel nothing more than pity. Though Motl endures as much, if not more, than the others, we do not pity him at all. We love him. We love him because he doesn't need our help. In fact, with his bright and comforting smile, he may be able to help us in *our* need. His superb, calm humor enables him to tell us of many indescribable migrations, anxieties, and hardships, all in the tone of an idyll.

When Motl grows up he will become a Tevye. There is already something of Tevye in his nature, but for the time being he is still a boy, so his natural humor is not as overcast as that of Tevye, who is the father of children, with all the problems of raising them. Motl's humor is as yet much more innocent, pure, and bright than that of his close relative, Tevye. (pp. 48-9)

Were we to ask ourselves whether Sholom Aleichem himself stood closer to Tevye or to Motl, we would say, to the latter. Like Motl, Sholom Aleichem cannot be satisfied with the tragic. Like Motl, he loves to laugh, simply and effortlessly. "Laughter is healthy; doctors prescribe laughter" is the motto of his writing.

The God of Laughter who reveals himself in H. D. Nomberg's Yiddish legend had two faces: one that laughed, and the other that grieved. There is of course a grieving face in Sholom Aleichem too, but it is hidden. Only the face that laughs and inspires laughter is revealed. Other writers have been able to tell happy tales; but no one else would take sad, often tiresome stories, and tell them for our pleasure, so that in our delight we might forget what is really going on, and like a child, ask no questions. Though his stories about Jewish life are almost always sad, they evoke not a sigh but a smile, and often a hearty laugh. He is always able to add something to the narrative that will ease our pain or dull it, or something to hide it from us so that we can forget. We thank Sholom Aleichem not because he awakens new ideas but to the contrary, because he is able for a moment to banish the thoughts that disturb our peace. We thank him for making the child his reader, but also for teaching his reader again to be a child. (pp. 49-50)

> *Shmuel Niger, "The Humor of Sholom Aleichem" (1926), translated by Ruth Wisse, in* Voices from the Yiddish: Essays, Memoirs, Diaries, *edited by Irving Howe and Eliezer Greenberg (copyright © by The University of Michigan 1972), University of Michigan Press, 1972, pp. 41-50.*

The world of Sholom Aleichem is mostly—not wholly—the internal world of Russian Jewry forty, fifty, sixty, and seventy years ago. It is—again mostly—the world of the Jewish Pale of Settlement, with special emphasis on a section south and west and east of Kiev. Hereabouts Jews had lived their separate life from very ancient times. There were synagogues in the Crimea long before there were

churches, and Jewish pedlars long before there were pogroms. . . . But the world of Sholom Aleichem had no
connection except by collateral descent with the original
communities of southeastern Russia. Khazar kings and
Hebrew merchants were absorbed by masses of Jewish
immigrants who came eastward under the pressure of the
Crusades, bringing with them the language which developed into Yiddish, and a way of life which retained its identity for a score of generations. (pp. 3-4)

[Sholom Aleichem] was a part of Russian Jewry; he was
Russian Jewry itself. It is hard to think of him as a
"writer." He was the common people in utterance. He was
in a way the "anonymous" of Jewish self-expression,
achieving the stature of a legendary figure even in his own
lifetime.

Many other writers have left us records of Russian-Jewish
life, and some of them compare well with the best-known in
the Western world. None of them had this natural gift for
complete self-identification with a people which makes
Sholom Aleichem unique. He wrote no great panoramic
novels in the manner of a Balzac or a Tolstoy. He did not
set out with the conscious and self-conscious purpose of
"putting it down for posterity." He wrote because of a
simple communicative impulse, as men chat in a tavern or
in a waiting crowd with their like. He never tried his hand
at solemn passages and mighty themes, any more than
people do in a casual, friendly conversation. But his language had an incomparable authenticity, and his humour—
he is the greatest of Jewish humorists, and in the world's
front rank—was that of a folk, not of an individual. (p. 6)

We could write a *Middletown* of the Russian-Jewish Pale
basing ourselves solely on the novels and stories and
sketches of Sholom Aleichem, and it would be as reliable a
scientific document as any "factual" study; more so, indeed, for we should get, in addition to the material of a
straightforward social inquiry, the intangible spirit which
informs the material and gives it its living significance. (pp.
6-7)

> *Maurice Samuel, in his* The World of
> Sholom Aleichem *(copyright 1943 by
> Maurice Samuel; reprinted by permission of
> Alfred A. Knopf, Inc.), Knopf, 1943.*

"The Old Country," a collection of Sholom Aleichem's
tales, is more than a book. It is the epitaph of a vanished
world and an almost vanished people. The salty and hilarious folk of whom it tells—the Jews of Europe—are dead.
All the Tevyas whose souls and sayings, whose bizarre and
tender antics Sholom Aleichem immortalized in the richest
Yiddish prose ever written—were massacred, six million
strong, by the Germans. And all the quaint and heart-
warming villages in which the Jews of Europe lived are no
longer on the map.

In Sholom Aleichem's book you can see all the ghosts. And
what a sturdy set of ghosts they are! You can read in "The
Old Country" capering tales full of rueful laughter, and
these tales are not merely the report of a people. They are
their historical farewell to a civilization that wiped them
out. . . .

"The Old Country" is the best of the Sholom Aleichem in
translation I have read. Maurice Samuels' excellent book,
"The World of Sholom Aleichem," is not shamed in any

fashion by the appearance of his hero in English clothes.
Almost, the fresh, desperate wit of the great Yiddish writer
animates these English tales. Almost the immortal hilarity
of Sholom Aleichem lives in their American pages. That
they lack the earthy impact of the original masterpieces is
no fault of the translators, Julius and Frances Butwin. The
Butwins have done an inspired job. The lack is one which
must befall anyone who touches the genius of Sholom Aleichem and tries to carry it into another tongue.

For Sholom Aleichem's was the genius of idiom. He and
his characters all spoke as if literature had never been invented. They spoke out of a naturalness that must pale in
translation as a folk pales in migration. Their idiom was no
mere argot, no marriage of slang and humor. It was a verbal
rag bag of a dozen languages in which the entire culture,
tragedy and wit of a people were hidden. The words in this
rag bag had more than meanings. They had overtones beyond their syntax, flavors beyond their content. There were
derisions and contradictions in the flattest of statements.

I can best explain it by saying that the people of Sholom
Aleichem do not speak words. They act them. And their
Yiddish words are themselves actors, not language. The
words are as full of hidden chuckles, grimaces and meanings as if they were part of a plot—a plot called "Jews"—
rather than of a vocabulary.

The tales in "The Old Country" are, however, sufficiently
exciting in themselves not to spend more time bemoaning
that they are now merely literature and not "performance."
In English they take their place beside the best of Mark
Twain, Dickens, Ring Lardner and the translations of
Gogol and Gorki. This is a fine enough place without
wishing for any finer. It is only that, were I writing of the
Yiddish Sholom Aleichem, I would write that he stands
alone. (p. 5)

[The Jews of the old country] were poor and toiled mightily
to keep fed and clothed. Misfortune was their brother—and
they examined it with a leer, a grin and a preposterous misunderstanding. They wangled meanings out of misfortune
that almost disarmed it. They suffered, grubbed, collapsed
and died—but when you look into their eyes during these
performances you see a twinkle deeper than their tears.
And you hear out of them sagacities so rueful and cock-
eyed as almost to convince you that you are in the presence
of a tribe of clowns—almost, but not quite.

Sholom Aleichem's people loved life more than misfortune.
And when there was nothing else to sustain them they
managed to live a little madly on their own wit.

In "The Old Country" there are scores of picaresque and
ribald characters, there are events and dénouements of
every stripe—but there is only one plot. The stories picked
from the pile of Sholom Aleichem volumes fit together as if
they had been written as a single book with a single pattern.
They all tell the tale of a Cinderella who does not go to the
ball. (pp. 5, 22)

To say that the pages of "The Old Country" squeeze the
heart even as they stir chuckles and guffaws, is to report
tritely but honestly. The hurly-burly of rabbis, students,
beggars, teachers, housewives, rogues, gamins, wits and
vagabonds, saints and knuckleheads that fill these pages are
more real than any troupe I know of in fiction. To meet
them is to meet more than people. It is to meet the life of a

people, the thousand and one smells and sounds of a Jewish world now gone. (p. 22)

> *Ben Hecht, "Tales of Capering, Rueful Laughter," in* The New York Times Book Review *(© 1946 by The New York Times Company; reprinted by permission), July 7, 1946, pp. 5, 22.*

Toward the end of his life, the great Yiddish writer Sholom Aleichem began to work on a children's book [*Adventures of Mottel*]. It was never completed, death intervened; but the manuscript that remained, forming a kind of children's picaresque of loosely connected episodes, quickly became one of his most admired works. Mottel is a little scamp who rejoices in the accumulation of trouble ("Hurrah! I'm an orphan!") and after some lively adventures in trying to scrape together a living with his big brother in the old country, wanders across Europe and finally settles in New York. Together with Menachem Mendel the *luftmensch* who personifies the quixotic, speculative principle in Jewish life and Tevye the Dairyman who speaks with the authentic folk voice, Mottel was one of Sholom Aleichem's three major characters.... Mottel symbolized the tragically abbreviated childhood of the ghetto, where life did not flow evenly from one phase of experience to another but childhood, adolescence and manhood were all compressed into one....

The whole book is not so impressive as a selection of six or seven pieces might be: Sholom Aleichem was an uneven writer who could not always evaluate his work....

Translating from the Yiddish is, of course, immensely difficult, particularly in the case of Sholom Aleichem, whose prose is simply a mesh of idiom. The Mottel stories are rich with Yiddish diminutives, which creature a kind of miniature world in language, while in English, alas, there are no diminutives. More important, it seems generally true that the closer a writer is to his native audience, the more difficult it is to present him in an alien language; a writer like Sholom Aleichem, who is a genuine "culture hero" in Jewish life, does not need to explicate, he can wink, shrug, imply in ways his readers immediately grasp. (p. 21)

From Sholom Aleichem's children's stories there stems a whole tradition of Yiddish literature. The completely care-free story about the adventurous boy that is so favored in English, is virtually absent from Yiddish, if only because that kind of boy was virtually absent from ghetto life. In the Yiddish story, the child almost always carries a social burden heavier than we in America are accustomed to believe appropriate for children.... It is this note of deprivation—a deprivation that has its roots in both religious fanaticism and the pervasive poverty of ghetto life— that dominates Yiddish children's stories....

Perhaps all that I have been trying to say is that in the world of Sholom Aleichem there is still some remnant of community. And because of this, he is able to approach his material through an astonishing variety of tones. Yiddish fiction is not nearly so well-made as American, nor so deeply inquisitive into character, nor so tautly dramatic. But a writer like Sholom Aleichem can shift from one key to another in the boldest manner, simply because he knows his world so intimately and thoroughly. (p. 22)

> *Irving Howe, "The World of Childhood," in*

The New Republic *(reprinted by permission of* The New Republic; *© 1953 by The New Republic, Inc.), April 6, 1953, pp. 21-2.*

Sholom Aleichem wrote for the family circle and his attitude was that of an entertainer. Hebrew was the language of serious literature among the Jews of the Pale; Yiddish the secular language and the language of comedy. A popular writer, a caricaturist and sentimentalist, Sholom Aleichem had much more in common with Dickens than he had with Mark Twain, to whom he has often been compared. He was a great ironist—the Yiddish language has an ironic genius—and he was a writer in whom the profoundly sad, bitter spirit of the ghetto laughed at itself and thereby transcended itself....

As a novel, "Mottel the Cantor's Son" [Sholom Aleichem's last novel] is not entirely successful; it is loosely constructed and undramatic, but it contains more remarkable characters than any five ordinary novels and it has its pages of incomparable comedy.

> *Saul Bellow, "Laughter in the Ghetto," in* Saturday Review *(copyright © 1953 by Saturday Review, Inc.; reprinted with permission), May 30, 1953, p. 15.*

Sholom Aleichem's *The Adventures of Mottel the Cantor's Son* is the comic Odyssey of a Jewish family traveling from Kassrilovka to New York in the early years of the 20th century. It is not, I believe, considered one of Sholom Aleichem's major works; but if it doesn't rank with the Tevyeh stories, Sholom Aleichem's characteristic genius is still there....

The American sketches were written immediately before Sholom Aleichem's death in New York in 1916, and they are certainly inferior to the marvellous chapters on Kassrilovka begun nine years earlier. The humor of the last section is a little too cosy; for once the exuberance seems a bit forced. Despite this, *Mottel* remains a great work of comic literature, and Mrs. Kahana's fine translation ought to dispel any lingering doubts about whether Sholom Aleichem is "universal" enough to carry over into English. We can see now that there is nothing parochial about his humor, and his sense of life, though peculiarly Jewish in some respects, is not the less intelligible on that account.

Sholom Aleichem lived through the breakup of the Yiddish-speaking world. As a result of persecution from without— especially the May Laws of 1881—as well as the pressure of criticism from within, the walls of the ghetto had begun to crack. There were mass emigrations to America, and amorphous Zionist sentiment was collecting into a powerful political movement. Life in the ghetto or the Pale of Settlement had been hard, but it was also secure, clannish, and changeless. If such a life has no other advantage, it at least permits its creatures a clear knowledge of who and what they are. But with the disintegration of this dirty though cosy world, doubts and confusions about their own identity spread among the Jews at large. And the fact that there had been dozens of attempts during the 19th century to re-define the content of Jewishness by Zionists, Hebraists, emancipationists, assimilationists, and a host of others, did not simplify matters for the *shtetl* innocents going abroad for the first time.

The various schools of thought on what constituted "Jewishness" disagreed in many details, but they were unanimous on one point—that a real Jewish identity could be maintained outside the ghetto, that, in fact, the Jewishness of the ghetto was not actually Jewishness at all, but a withered, stunted version of it. . . . Consequently, all the movements for . . . rehabilitation [of the Jews] invariably began with attacks on the *manners* of the "ghetto Jew": the clothes he wore, the beard he grew, the food he ate, even the language he spoke—all were stigmatized, sometimes naively, as the cause of anti-Semitic outbreaks, more often as barriers to the building of a new and better world. (pp. 261-62)

What were the Jews—a civilization, a religion, a political entity? What was their proper language—Yiddish, Hebrew, English? How were they supposed to behave and dress? Sholom Aleichem answered these questions by refusing to believe in their validity; it is one aspect of his greatness. To him, Jewishness was not a matter of "values" or "essential characteristics" of race or nationality or both; it was nothing abstract, neither a civilization nor yet a peculiar kind of religion. Jewishness was simply the way Jews behaved; it was, in short, the very manners and habits despised by the *avant-garde,* and it was the rich diversity of attitudes implied by the things they did and the way they did them.

And what a marvellous conception of their own threatened identity he conveyed to a people deserted by external reality and harassed by the suspicion that perhaps they didn't really exist at all. He portrayed them not as they were told they ought to be, or as they might turn out to be, but truly as they were. Jewishness was sister-in-law Brocha with the big feet, father-in-law Jonah the biscuit-man, Pinney with the nose, Eli with the temper, Fat Pessie the neighbor, and the eternally weeping Mama. They are types still to be met in any Jewish neighborhood in New York or London or Paris; so right was Sholom Aleichem about the weird persistence of manners. . . . But above all, Jewishness was Mottel, the image of the adaptability, resilience, energy, resourcefulness, and—most important—the *durability* of the Jew.

The Jews of Eastern Europe considered childhood a phase to be got over as quickly as possible, a sort of malignant disease the curing of which justified the use of any means, no matter how drastic. Consequently, Mottel's relation to the world—like that of the Jews to the peoples around them —is one of conflict, the battle between an irrepressible child and adults who can neither understand nor tolerate him, a world to which his very existence is an offense. (p. 262)

The adult world, then, is a great tissue of absurdities to the child. The absurdity comes out in many ways. For example, in Mottel's eyes the whole of reality is a Garden of Eden like Mrs. Doctor's garden in Kassrilovka. . . .

There it all is, offering itself to him, yet Mottel is kept out of the garden by a high fence with horrible spikes and a dog that must really, he thinks, be a wolf. Now why on earth shouldn't he be allowed to pluck a fruit or two from the trees? Fruit was obviously made to be eaten before it gets too ripe, when it's still sour enough to make your lips pucker. But this fruit will never be eaten, not by Mottel or anyone else; it winds up as mouldy jam in Mrs. Doctor's cellar. . . .

This conception of reality as insanely irrational is common to the comic literature of oppressed peoples. . . . What is unusual about Sholom Aleichem is that he makes the absurd malevolence of the world all part of the fun and richness of living. This is a way of accepting life even when life is most niggardly in its gifts. And it is an attitude that strikes me as quintessentially Jewish, the perfect comic expression of a culture in which theology—i.e., the attempt to understand the problem of evil in rational terms—never flourished. Like Mottel's—and like Job's—the privations and sufferings of the Jews bore no relation whatever to anything they did; they suffered only because of what they *were*. And despite the attempts from time to time by pseudo-theologians to make sense of a classically senseless situation, the Jewish answer was still the answer of the Book of Job—that there is no answer. And if there is no answer, one can either rage like a Dostoevsky, or laugh. Sholom Aleichem laughed. His laughter has something to teach modern apologists for Original Sin who believe that optimism and a love of life must necessarily reflect superficiality of spirit. (p. 263) [See also Ivan B. Abrams' reply to Podhoretz, below.]

> *Norman Podhoretz, "Sholom Aleichem: Jewishness Is Jews" (reprinted from* Commentary *by permission; copyright © 1953 by the American Jewish Committee), in* Commentary, *September, 1953, pp. 261-63.*

Although the main body of Norman Podhoretz's article "Sholom Aleichem: Jewishness Is Jews" (September 1953 [see excerpt above]) is excellent, the philosophy inherent in his concluding paragraph is ultimately as corrosively destructive of Sholom Aleichem as it is of Judaism. If Stanley Edgar Hyman could call books that appear to be novels, and are not, "pseudo-fictions," then surely one is justified in calling Mr. Podhoretz's concept of Jewishness pseudo-Jewish. It is a nice gay glib concept: "to make sense of a classically senseless situation, the Jewish answer was still the answer of the book of Job—that there is no answer." And previously Podhoretz has compared Mottel to Job (!), saying that "the privations and sufferings of the Jews bore no relation whatsoever to anything they did; they suffered only because of what they *were*."

It is indeed possible to carry casuistry a long way, and it is terribly possible to misinterpret the Book of Job. And if Job —and the Jews—have any meaning at all, it is that they "were"—and are—precisely because of what they *did*. . . . [One] must not treat the Book of Job as if Genesis did not precede it.

We get one clear and distinct interpretation from Genesis, not "no answer" as Podhoretz blithely says. Though it is true that "one can either rage like a Dostoevsky, or laugh," this is only permissible if one's rage or one's laughter is directed toward clarification, not simply senseless smashing of the skull against a brick wall or braying like a jackass at cosmic inanity. Both Dostoevsky and Sholom Aleichem sought earnestly . . . and with all their beings to clarify. (pp. 591-92)

Neither Job, Dostoevsky, nor Sholom Aleichem would for a moment agree that the lesson of the Jews is to recognize man's involvement in a "classically senseless situation." They would all agree "that optimism and a love of life must necessarily reflect superficiality of spirit." *That is*—if and when, as Mr. Podhoretz assumes they do, these two concepts form a logical dichotomy. As they don't, never have, and never will, they would say man's situation, far from being senseless, is clear for those who *will* understand, and if you *will* understand you can do no less than be optimistic and love life! (p. 592)

*Ivan B. Abrams, "The Need to Clarify"
(reprinted from* Commentary *by permission;
copyright © 1953 by the American Jewish
Committee), in* Commentary, *December,
1953, pp. 591-92.*

The way to read Sholom Aleichem is to remember from the outset that he is writing about a people, a folk: the Yiddish-speaking Jews of Eastern Europe. There are a great many Jews and non-Jews who resent the idea that the Jews are a people, for they think this requires all Jews to speak the same language and to live in the same territory. But Sholom Aleichem's characters already are a people. They are a people not merely because they speak the same language, Yiddish, or because they live in the Pale of settlement that the Czarist government kept Jews in. They are a people because they think of themselves as a people. And what is most important, they are a people because they enjoy thinking of themselves as a people.

This is the great thing about the Jews described by Sholom Aleichem. They enjoy being Jews, they enjoy the idea of belonging to the people who are called Jews—and "their" Sholom Aleichem, perhaps more than any other Jewish writer who has ever lived, writes about Jewishness as if it were a gift, a marvel, an unending theme of wonder and delight. He is one of those writers whose subject is an actual national character, a specific type—the Jew as embodied in the poor Jew of Eastern Europe. In a way he does remind us of Mark Twain, [As Kazin observes in a footnote: "Sholom Aleichem was so often called 'the Jewish Mark Twain' that Mark Twain on meeting him, referred to himself as 'the American Sholom Aleichem'."] who was so entranced with a new character, the Western American, that he was always trying to weigh him, to describe him, as if he, Mark Twain, had discovered a new chemical element. (pp. 271-72)

It is this European, seasoned, familiar pleasure in the national circle of one's own people, that lies behind Sholom Aleichem's stories. But what kind of enjoyment can these people derive from being Jews, since they are incessantly harassed by the Russian government and surrounded by peasants who are usually anti-Semitic and can easily be goaded, with the help of the usual encouragement from the government itself and a lot of vodka, into making pogroms? What is it, in short, that makes for *enjoyment* in these local terms? The answer is that one enjoys being a member of a people because one shares in the feast of their common experience. You share in something that is *given* to you instead of having to make every institution and every habit for yourself, out of nothing, in loneliness and with exertion. The secret of this enjoyment consists not so much in physical solidarity and "togetherness," in the absence of loneliness, as in the fact that a deep part of your life is lived below the usual level of strain, of the struggle for values, of the pressing and harrowing need—so often felt in America—to define your values all over again in each situation, where you may even have to insist on values themselves in the teeth of a brutish materialism. (pp. 272-73)

This is the fabled strength of "the old country," which deprived the Jews of Eastern Europe of every decency that we take for granted, but allowed them to feast unendingly on their own tradition—and even to enjoy, as an unconscious work of art, their projection of their fiercely cherished identity. The very pen name "Sholom Aleichem" is an instance of this. . . . *Sholom aleichem* is the Hebrew greeting, "Peace be unto you," that is technically exchanged between Jews. It is said with more lightness and playfulness than you would guess from the literal translation. Its chief characteristic, as a greeting, is the evidence it gives of relatedness. Now Solomon Rabinowitz, who actually belonged to the prosperous and more "emancipated" middle class of Russian Jewry (he even married into its landed gentry), took this pen name precisely because he found in the phrase an image of the sweet familiarity, the informality, the utter lack of side, that is associated with the Yiddish-speaking masses of Eastern Europe. A Yiddish writer who calls himself *Mister* Sholom Aleichem tells us by this that he has chosen cannily to picture himself as one of the people and, modestly, to be a register or listening post for his people. Sholom Aleichem! The name's as light as a feather, as "common" as daylight, as porous to life as good Yiddish talk: it is the very antithesis of the literary, the mannered, the ornate. If you didn't know anything else about Mister Sholom Aleichem (several of his characters address him so when they bring their stories to him) you should be able to guess from the name the role that he has chosen to play in his own work. He is the passer-by, the informal correspondent, the post office into which Jews drop their communications to the world. All he does, you understand, is to write down stories people bring him. He invents nothing. And need one say—with that name, with that indescribably dear, puckish, wrinkled face of his—that you will never learn from him *what* he has invented, that he has all Yiddish stories in his head, that any one story people bring him will always be capped with another?

In the world of Sholom Aleichem, nothing has to be made up, for the life of the Jews, to say nothing of the Jewish character, is an unending drama. Nor can it be said of anything that it's never been seen or heard of before. The Jews have lived with each other for a very long time, and they know each other through and through—and this, often enough, is what they enjoy. Their history, alas, has too often been the same, and everything that you see in Kasrilevka (the little Jewish town which is all little Jewish towns) or Yehupetz (Kiev, the big city) can be matched from something in Mazeppa's time, which is late seventeenth century, or that of Haman, who tried to kill all the Jews in Persia in the fifth century B.C. Nor, indeed, is anything ever said just *once*. Everything is real, everything is typical, and everything is repeated.

You must understand, first, that Sholom Aleichem's characters possess almost nothing except the word—the holy word, which is Hebrew, and the word of everyday life, which is Yiddish. They are "little" people, not in the sense that they are poor little victims, but in the sense that they are unarmed, defenseless, exiled, not in the world, not in *their* kind of world. All they have is the word. They talk as poor people always talk—because poor people live near each other, and so have a lot of opportunity to talk. They talk the way the European poor always talk—Cockneys or Neapolitans or Provençals: they talk from the belly; they roar, they bellow, they grunt, they scream. They imitate the actual sounds that life makes, and they are rough and blunt. But most of all, they are poor Jews talking, i.e., they find an irony in language itself. Their words strive after the reality, but can never adequately express the human situation. (pp. 273-75)

Yiddish is the poor Jew's everyday clothes rather than his Sabbath garment, Hebrew. But in the Jewish consciousness it is precisely the life of everyday that is contrasted with the divine gift of the Sabbath, and it is this awareness of what life is actually like (seen always against the everlasting history of this people and the eternal promise) that makes the very use of Yiddish an endless commentary on the world as found.

And it is a commentary on the spirit of language itself. One of the things you get from Sholom Aleichem is this mockery of language, a mockery which—need I say it?—carries a boundless pleasure in language and a sense of the positive strength that goes with mighty talk. (p. 275)

> *Alfred Kazin, in his introduction to* Selected Stories of Sholom Aleichem *(copyright © 1956 by Alfred Kazin; reprinted by permission of Random House, Inc.), Modern Library, 1956 (and reprinted as "Sholom Aleichem: The Old Country" in his* Contemporaries, *Atlantic-Little, Brown & Company, 1962, pp. 271-78).*

"My muse is a poor but cheerful one," Sholom Aleichem once wrote. The remark, and even more the nom de plume he chose for himself—the Jewish greeting which means "Peace be with you"—is a central clue to his literary identity. For this most revered of Yiddish writers was indeed a peacemaker, mediating in his lifetime between the Jewish community of the *shtetl,* or Central European village, and its experience of self, and continuing to mediate today between a dwindling number of transplanted Jews and their memories or the memories that are preserved in their families.

This is not to say that Sholom Aleichem is available only within a Jewish context; he has been compared to Mark Twain and to Dickens, and if the comparison is not a particularly accurate one it does testify to certain universal qualities he shares with those most internationally read of authors. The nineteen stories and sketches in [*Stories and Satires*] . . . are not tribal documents or private jokes. There is, however, something to be understood about Sholom Aleichem's special relationship to his audience, and about Yiddish literature in general, if some central values are not to be lost. (p. 505)

To give birth to itself, as Yiddish literature was compelled to do by the absence of any usable tradition, to be its own source, vision and critique, meant that an extraordinary purity and directness were possible, but also that the price would be circumscription, a narrowed area of imaginative encirclement and intellectual thrust, springing from isolation and from a naked concern with basic problems of form.

More than most Yiddish writers, . . . Sholom Aleichem managed partly to transcend the conditions of his literary situation. His battle with craft and the recalcitrance of a language rich and expressive but unused to formal strategies issued in a conversational, story-teller's style that was flexible and lyrical enough to move beyond recapitulation

into discovery, and intellectually robust enough to produce something with a tautness and complexity that folklore can never display.

Revolving around a profound but domesticated ("we are neither tragedians nor dispensers of melancholy") insight into the root irony of Jewish existence—its simultaneous awareness of itself as Chosen People and most put upon of creatures—Sholom Aleichem's work gave *shtetl* life shape, coherence and inviolability, arming it with self-appraisal, fusing its contrarieties at all but their most extreme points, and presenting it with an image, affectionate and mordant at the same time, of its previously uncelebrated reality.

For a later generation he offered, and continues to offer, a sustaining myth that is no less true for being selective: that life in the Old Country was human—and all too human—after all; that the misery and degradation were offset and transfigured by an immense dignity arising from self-possession, from tenacity and half-mocking faith ("I am, with God's help, a poor man," a character says), and from a pervasive generosity that shared suffering as well as joy with an unfathomably sophisticated recognition that the two experiences are inseparable. (pp. 506-07)

The stories in this volume constitute a gallery of the Jewish personality in most of the recognizable manifestations, with blank spaces at either end, since, typically, we encounter no true hero and no real villain.

But apart from this it is a fairly diversified congregation: the saintly fool, the shlimazel (he of infinitely bad fortune), the shrewish yet loyal wife, the Torah-meditating husband, the schnorrer (the man who always drops in at dinnertime), the ambitious mother with a marriageable daughter, the frenetic intellectual, the romantic youth, the beleaguered and enduring housewife.

If there is a weakness in the collection it lies in its disproportionate number of satirical sketches and tales. Many of them are marvelously funny, but they do an injustice to the full range of Sholom Aleichem's work. His richer creations are somewhat scanted, those in which a loving ironic light plays upon scenes of domestic crisis, personal or communal misfortune.

Sholom Aleichem in profile then. But if anyone who read this volume is led by his satisfaction with it to investigate further . . . he will come upon the full face of an authentic master, minor but nearly perfect. (p. 507)

> *Richard Gilman, "Minor Master," in* Commonweal *(copyright © 1960 Commonweal Publishing Co., Inc.; reprinted by permission of Commonweal Publishing Co., Inc.), January 29, 1960, pp. 505-07.*

Fifty or sixty years ago the Jewish intelligentsia, its head buzzing with Zionist, Socialist and Yiddishist ideas, tended to look down upon Sholom Aleichem. His genius was acknowledged, but his importance skimped. To the intellectual Jewish youth in both Warsaw and New York he seemed old-fashioned, lacking in complexity and rebelliousness—it is even said that he showed no appreciation of existentialism. (p. 207)

The conventional estimate—that Sholom Aleichem was a folksy humorist, a sort of jolly gleeman of the *shtetl*—is radically false. He needs to be rescued from his reputation, from the quavering sentimentality which keeps him at a safe distance.

When we say that Sholom Aleichem speaks for a whole culture, we can mean that in his work he represents all the significant levels of behavior and class in the *shtetl* world, thereby encompassing the style of life of the east European Jews in the nineteenth century. In that sense, however, it may be doubted that he does speak for the whole *shtetl* culture. For he does not command the range of a Balzac or even a Faulkner, and he does not present himself as the kind of writer who is primarily concerned with social representation. The ambition, or disease, of literary "scope" leaves him untouched. (p. 208)

Sholom Aleichem speaks for the culture of the east European Jews because he embodies—not represents—its essential values in the very accents and rhythm of his speech, in the inflections of his voice and the gestures of his hands, in the pauses and suggestions between the words even more than the words themselves. To say that a writer represents a culture is to imply that a certain distance exists between the two. But that is not at all the relationship between Sholom Aleichem and the culture of the east European Jews: it is something much more intimate and elusive, something for which, having so little experience of it, we can barely find a name. In Sholom Aleichem everything that is deepest in the ethos of the east European Jews is brought to fulfillment and climax. He is, I think, the only modern writer who may truly be said to be a culture-hero, a writer whose work releases those assumptions of his people, those tacit gestures of bias, which undercut opinion and go deeper into communal life than values.

In his humorous yet often profoundly sad stories, Sholom Aleichem gave to the Jews what they instinctively felt was the right and true judgment of their experience: a judgment of love through the medium of irony. Sholom Aleichem is the great poet of Jewish humanism and Jewish transcendence over the pomp of the world. For the Jews of Eastern Europe he was protector and advocate; he celebrated their communal tradition; he defended their style of life and constantly underlined their passionate urge to dignity. But he was their judge as well: he ridiculed their pretensions, he mocked their vanity, and he constantly reiterated the central dilemma, that simultaneous tragedy and joke, of their existence—the irony of their claim to being a Chosen People, indeed, the irony of their existence at all.

Sholom Aleichem's Yiddish is one of the most extraordinary verbal achievements of modern literature, as important in its way as T. S. Eliot's revolution in the language of English verse or Berthold Brecht's infusion of street language into the German lyric. Sholom Aleichem uses a sparse and highly controlled vocabulary; his medium is so drenched with irony that the material which comes through it is often twisted and elevated into direct tragic statement —irony multiples upon itself to become a deep winding sadness. Many of his stories are monologues, still close to the oral folk tradition, full of verbal by-play, slow in pace, winding in direction, but always immediate and warm in tone. His imagery is based on an absolute mastery of the emotional rhythm of Jewish life; describing the sadness of a wheezing old clock, he writes that it was "a sadness like that in the song of an old, worn-out cantor toward the end of Yom Kippur"—and how sad that is only someone who has heard such a cantor and therefore knows the exquisite rightness of the image can really say.

The world of Sholom Aleichem is bounded by three major characters, each of whom has risen to the level of Jewish archetype: Tevye the Dairyman; Menachem Mendel the *luftmensch;* and Mottel the cantor's son, who represents the loving, spontaneous possibilities of Jewish childhood. Tevye remains rooted in his little town, delights in displaying his uncertain Biblical learning, and stays close to the sources of Jewish survival. Solid, slightly sardonic, fundamentally innocent, Tevye is the folk voice quarreling with itself, criticizing God from an abundance of love, and realizing in its own low-keyed way all that we mean, or should mean, by humaneness.

Tevye represents the generation of Jews that could no longer find complete deliverance in the traditional God yet could not conceive of abandoning Him. No choice remained, therefore, but to celebrate the earthly condition: poverty and hope. (pp. 208-10)

Menachem Mendel, Tevye's opposite, personifies the element of restlessness and soaring, of speculation and fancy-free idealization, in Jewish character. He has a great many occupations: broker, insurance agent, matchmaker, coal dealer, and finally—it is inevitable—writer; but his fundamental principle in life is to keep moving. The love and longing he directs toward his unfound millions are the love and longing that later Jews direct toward programs and ideologies. He is the utopian principle of Jewish life; he is driven by the modern demon. Through Tevye and Menachem Mendel, flanked by little Mottel, Sholom Aleichem creates his vision of the Yiddish world. . . .

Sholom Aleichem came at a major turning point in the history of the east European Jews: between the unquestioned dominance of religious belief and the appearance of modern ideologies, between the past of traditional Judaism and the future of Jewish politics, between a totally integrated culture and a culture that by a leap of history would soon plunge into the midst of modern division and chaos. Yet it was the mark of Sholom Aleichem's greatness that, coming as he did at this point of transition, he betrayed no moral imbalance or uncertainty of tone. (p. 211)

The world he presented was constantly precarious and fearful, yet the vision from which it was seen remained a vision of absolute assurance. It was a vision controlled by that sense of Jewish humaneness which held the best of—even as it transcended—both the concern with the other world that had marked the past and the eagerness to transform this world that would mark the future. His work abounds in troubles, but only rarely does it betray anxiety. (p. 212)

Sholom Aleichem believed in Jews as they embodied the virtues of powerlessness and the healing resources of poverty, as they stood firm against the outrage of history, indeed, against the very idea of history itself. Whoever is unable to conceive of such an outlook as at least an extreme possibility, whoever cannot imagine the power of a messianism turned away from the apocalyptic future and inward toward a living people, cannot understand Sholom Aleichem or the moment in Jewish experience from which he stems. . . .

The stories Sholom Aleichem told his readers were often stories they already knew, but then, as the Hasidic saying goes, they cared not for the words but the melody. What Sholom Aleichem did was to give back to them the very essence of their life and hope, in a language of exaltation: the exaltation of the ordinary. (p. 214)

Sholom Aleichem did not hesitate to thrust his barbs at his readers, and they were generous at reciprocating. Having love, they had no need for politeness. But the love of which I speak here is sharply different from that mindless ooze, that collapse of will, which the word suggests to Americans. It could be argumentative, fierce, bitter, violent; it could be ill-tempered and even vulgar; only one thing it could not be: lukewarm. . . .

[The] power to see the world as it is, to love it and yet not succumb to it . . ., that is the power one finds in Sholom Aleichem. (p. 215)

> *Irving Howe, "Sholom Aleichem: Voice of Our Past," in his* A World More Attractive: A View of Modern Literature and Politics *(© 1963; reprinted by permission of the publisher, Horizon Press, New York), Horizon, 1963, pp. 207-15.*

Successful as he was in creation of character, Sholom Aleichem was too much the humorist to write first-rate fiction. At the outset of his career, eager to wean the naive Jewish reader from the lurid Shomer romances, he wrote *Sender Blank, Stempenu,* and *Yosele Solovey,* authentic stories of Jewish life. To make them palatable he infused the action with elements of human interest. Yet the love displayed by his characters was the reticent and repressed emotion of the traditional Jew. In *Stempenu,* for instance, Rachel, though unhappy in her marriage, buries her love for the musician deep within her and resists strong temptation. (p. 80)

Authentic and wholesome as was the life he depicted, it nevertheless lacked the depth and sustained insight of great fiction. This was equally true of his later novels—*The Deluge, Wandering Stars,* and *The Bloody Jest,* written as newspaper serials under trying circumstances. *The Wandering Star,* for example, describes the conditions obtaining at the birth of the Yiddish theater in Eastern Europe and in America. The atmosphere is presented realistically and humorously, but the injection of sentimental romance deprives the protagonists of artistic vitality. It was as if something of Shomer had infiltrated the action. His several plays likewise have the stamp of his warm humor, yet fail to measure up to his major works.

Although Sholom Aleichem's humor stresses the peculiarities and incongruities of a people undergoing radical transformation and oppressed by a hostile government and inimical social forces, he has achieved his best work in the creation of character. He has given Yiddish literature a number of fictional beings more real to his readers than the people around them; creations that grow, mature, and rise to imaginative heights. The following four major individuals embody his supreme artistic achievement.

When a well-known Jew became endeared to his townsmen, his name underwent expansion. Reb Yosef, the old rabbi of Kaserilevke, early came to be called Reb Yosefel. Not a soul in the town but adores the venerable man when he enters the pages of Sholom Aleichem's writings. He is indeed an idealized sage. The hero of numerous stories, he is portrayed as a revered octogenarian, blessed with good sense and actuated by the deepest altruism. Afflicted with loneliness, indigence, and illness, he retains his implicit faith in the goodness and rectitude of Jehovah. Considering himself but a speck in the ever-to-be-praised world of God, he is always modest and humble. With the phrase, "Vanity

of vanities, all is vanity," he has succeeded in allaying his misery. . . .

Reb Yosefel was delineated as a noble leader of a medievally oriented Jewry—the rabbi who was disappearing together with the static culture he fostered. He was still the old patriarch, concerned for his flock not merely because they were his parishioners but also because they were human beings. Honest and sincere in all things, loving all living creatures, keeping soul and body in their respective places with rigorous piety, he succeeded in inspiring his fellow Jews with the reverence, awe, and poetry which went far to nullify the unsavory effects of their superstitious and blighting beliefs. Endowed by his Creator with the composite Jewish virtues, he was dedicated to the service of his people. And he found much to do! He went about Kaserilevke soothing the sore at heart, advising the perplexed, chastising the selfish, and collecting alms for the needy. In the process he talked, moved, and thought with unforgettable reality. (pp. 81-2)

Chief of Sholom Aleichem's boy creations, [Motel, the cantor's son] is molded pretty much in the image of his own childhood. Motel represents the transitional generation in its youthful state: inheritor of Kaserilevke culture and destined exemplar of the urbanized Jew. . . .

Every word, every act, appears comical to him if it does not coincide with his preconceived idea of it. When his father becomes very ill and his mother is forced to sell the furniture piece by piece to pay the doctor and buy medicines, he thinks it amusing that she should conceal the truth from his father. It appears to him a violation of ethics for a mother to lie and a father to be fooled. But if concealing the truth is to him a laughable matter, the manner in which it is done is even more so. (p. 84)

Motel grows and develops with every related incident. If he seems too knowledgeable for his age, it is because, as a product of Kaserilevke, he too soon becomes a little adult. He reveals his inmost thoughts in a manner that stamps them indelibly upon the reader's mind. His impressions are charged with sensitiveness and humor. He describes everything and everybody as his senses perceive and his imagination interprets. Each narrative adds to the wholesomeness, simplicity, and fineness of the boy's spirit. Impressionable and pliant, he adjusts himself to every situation without a jolt or jar. His heart throbs with warm sympathy; his love of living things is quick and strong; his intuitive mind in time perceives the more delicate nuances of life. He is in truth a child philosopher, always eager to probe into the why of everything, and underlying his entire being is a rich vein of humor, gentle and refined. (p. 86)

Menachem Mendel . . . is a citified Yoshe Heshel become the supreme *luftmensch,* a grotesque product of the 2000-year struggle of the Jews to survive under adverse and at times almost impossible conditions. Business, speculation, get-rich-quick schemes have become to him not merely a means of earning a livelihood but a passionate and irresistible end. He is fascinated not by wealth itself but by the idea of acquiring it suddenly and fortuitously. His repeated failures do not for a moment keep him from plunging into the first quixotic scheme that comes his way. In his excitement he often borders on paranoia; Dr. Eliashev, the first important Yiddish critic, interpreted him as "the Jewish insanity streak in the person of an insignificant Jewish businessman." (p. 87)

Menachem Mendel is essentially a comic character. A dreamer, mentally agile, earnestly eager, he is at the same time childishly naive and helpless in a world of hard and shrewd traders. He is at the mercy of an overexcited fantasy which leads him into absurd behavior. For Reb Yosefel and Tevieh religious faith was the mainspring of their existence; Menachem Mendel has no such solid anchor and is buffeted by the whims of chance. Consequently his every impulsive act and move, stimulated primarily by desperate hope of fortuitous gain, appears exaggerated and ludicrous, since inevitably each one fails. In describing his gullible enthusiasm over matters doomed to disappoint him, Sholom Aleichem makes clear that this behavior is not so much the result of a diseased imagination as of an inimical environment. Trained, as so many of his kind, in neither a trade nor a profession, without worldly sophistication, with his opportunities for earning a living greatly restricted by a hostile government, yet with a mind steeped in Hebrew lore and medieval ways, Menachem Mendel is depicted as more a victim of unfavorable circumstances than of his own inadequacy. No man is in full control of his intellect when in the grip of chronic starvation. Menachem Mendel's effort to free himself from penury, stimulated by his *luftmensch* upbringing, forces him to trust in luck and in his naive ingenuity until he becomes addicted to speculation. His implicit faith in his unrealistic and ridiculous schemes merely emphasizes the pathos of his misfortune. Because his conceit combined with gullibility make his behavior extreme and ludicrous, he appears an object of laughter; but the laugh takes not the form of ridicule but of compassion. One feels that he has not really deserved his repeated failure and despair.

Every major writer secretes his inmost self into at least one of his works. Sholom Aleichem was no exception. Although he has stamped his personality and art upon most of his writings, the stories of *Tevieh the Dairyman* best display his greatness. In this rustic, traditionally religious Jew he has embodied his highest humor, his truest philosophy of life; during the score of years in which he concerned himself with the character, he concentrated his utmost affection, warmest sympathy, and deepest spiritual probings upon this unfortunate milkman.

Tevieh differs conspicuously from Menachem Mendel in both attitude and behavior. Indeed, these two characters represent the polarization of nearly all of Sholom Aleichem's creations: one verging on the pathological and the other being spiritually centripetal. Tevieh is a typical, if artistically heightened, product of orthodox Jewry: he adheres unquestionably to his faith in Jehovah, accepts the buffeting of fate as God's will, procures his bread with the proverbial sweat of his brow, and considers the idea of wealth a satanic temptation. Menachem Mendel is a Kaserilevkite in the process of urbanization, tossed about on the stormy waves of economic precariousness, with his fantasy rising rocket-like on imaginary gain and sinking to despair at the impact with hard reality. (pp. 89-91)

Sholom Aleichem's generation of Jews was fertile with elements of humor. It was in the inevitable process of transition; harsh circumstances were relegating its medieval form of life to the irrevocable past, forcing each one to adapt himself to modern ways as best he could. Naive, quite gullible, wholly unprepared, these Jews were bewildered by the maze of urban modernity, confounded by their inability to tell the real from the apparent; necessity gave them no reprieve, compelling them to seek the means of subsistence hastily and haphazardly. (pp. 95-6)

[Sholom Aleichem] perceived the oblique direction of their transitional behavior and exposed the pathos of their altered status with compensating humor. . . .

His self was blended so successfully with the spirit of his people that in one sense his writings do not bear so much the stamp of individual authorship as that of genuine folklore, poetically interpreted. (p. 96)

As he was ever with and of the Jews of his time, he unwittingly became their literary chronicler, recording their deeds and aspirations, their misfortunes and tribulations, with the accuracy and sympathy of the intuitive writer. (p. 97)

For all the folkloric effect of his writings, he was ever the conscious and painstaking artist. Poverty and the conditions of newspaper serialization—the chief medium of publication in Yiddish—forced him to write regardless of his health or state of mind. Yet he never considered a work finished until he had revised and improved it to his heart's content. To a friend he wrote:

> A kind of Mephistopheles sits within me, and he laughs, mocks, pokes fun at my writings. Every time I write something and read it with enthusiasm, as is usual with an author, he only whistles through his lips and his eyes smile. If I could catch him I would choke him! It sometimes happens that he listens to me quite seriously and nods his head. This makes me think that he approves, and I send it to the printer—when he explodes with laughter—this Mephistopheles, may he burn! . . .

[To] the very end of his life he continued to choose his words and phrases as if he were matching pearls. (p. 98)

> *Charles A. Madison, "Sholom Aleichem,"*
> *in his* Yiddish Literature: Its Scope and
> Major Writers *(copyright © 1968 by Frederick Ungar Publishing Co., Inc.), Ungar, 1968, pp. 61-98.*

As we enter the world of Shalom Aleikhem we become conscious of a tremendous bustle of activity, greater than was necessary for that ironic humor with which the author loved to entertain and amuse his fellow Jews amid the depressing conditions of Eastern Europe. . . . Shalom Aleikhem's humor is rooted not in any light-hearted banter about a nonsensical world, but in the most grievous problems of Jewish life—social and economic, communal and individual, cultural and religious. Even his short stories, which give the impression of having been written as merely casual pieces, allude to these problems, while the longer stories are overtly set against the background of the contemporary Jewish scene—a fundamentally tragic background illumined by the luster of the author's Jewish compassion and reflected in the mirror of his humor.

Shalom Aleikhem devoted all his literary powers to creating the characters of his stories, the highly individualized figures of *Tuvia the Milkman, Menahem Mendel the Dreamer, Mottel ben Peisi the Cantor,* and *Children of Israel.* It is as though the contemporary Jewish scene flowed into his characters, became part of them, and found its ultimate expression through them. Shalom Aleikhem's stories, as we have noted, reflect the Jewish world of his day with remarkable clarity: the collapse of family life in the wake of the new winds blowing into the Jewish village from the outside world, the disintegration of class distinction within the towns, the split in religious leadership, the mass emigration to America, and the spiritual confusion created by "the breakdown of boundaries".... All the realism, however, is woven into the personal tragedy of the individual, and it is this personal note which gives his stories their profundity. The finest instance is, of course, Tuvia himself. Tuvia gazes at the world around him through his own little world, seeing the suffering which the Almighty pours down upon His Chosen People and learning from that what is relevant to himself and his household—Golda his wife, and his six grown-up daughters—and to his own toil and suffering; in fact, to his "all in all." This very perception constitutes Shalom Aleikhem's artistic success. The more Tuvia gazes into himself and his tragic lot, the more vividly does he come to life. Tuvia knows that his own suffering forms part of the suffering of the Jewish community as a whole, yet he still regards his lot as a personal one, a hidden mirror according to which he acts and which gives his life an individual significance. Whatever happens to him is symbolic of the entire community, whether it is his hard struggle for a livelihood, or the fact that his daughters have grown up and that each in her own way is destroying the foundations on which Jewish family life rests; whether it is the loss of his money, which he has invested in the worthless writings of Menahem Mendel the Dreamer, or the expulsion of his family from the village, stripped of all they possessed. And yet he wonderingly treats everything that impinges on him from the outside world as if it reflects some inner meaningful purpose in the very depths of his soul. (pp. 16-17)

Shalom Aleikhem is the first author of modern Jewish fiction, either in Hebrew or Yiddish, who gave his "little people," drawn from the real, contemporary world, those tragic dimensions that the novel of the non-Jewish world had provided since the early 1820's. It is this achievement that places Shalom Aleikhem among the great figures of the modern Hebrew novel. True, he used the technique of the monologue, which perhaps disqualifies him as a novelist in the technical sense, but it was that very monologue, with its humorous irony, that, in contrast to the modernistic struggles of I. L. Peretz, presaged a great psychological change in the Hebrew literary revival. (p. 19)

It was Shalom Aleikhem's urge to create a new type of Jewish character, without any literary precedent, that drove him to employ the monologue.... In *Tuvia the Milkman, Manahem Mendel the Dreamer, Mottel ben Peisi the Cantor* and *Children of Israel*, the monologue functions as a sensitive psychological mechanism that rectifies all that the satire of the Enlightenment had spoiled. Tuvia is not a scholar, nor is he wealthy; he is not a president of a synagogue, nor even well connected; yet the author gives him a certain inner refinement inherent in his psychological make-up so that Shalom Aleikhem is able to "trust" him to speak in his own name and relate the story. The flow of talk that the author allows his character is not the sole "plot" of the tale, for he offers Tuvia new vantage points from which he can gaze at his own spiritual troubles and find words to express his own personality. The monologue was thus an

artistic necessity for Shalom Aleikhem, the source of his irony and humor, allowing him to create the characters of his "little people" and turn them into heroes.

Tuvia keeps chancing upon Shalom Aleikhem, and at once begins to tell him all about himself and his home and about some catastrophe that has happened to one of his daughters. As he thinks aloud he seems to lay the world bare, as if he were saying: "This world is full of blemishes; this is the way the Lord of the Universe treats His mortals, and then He calls it a just universe!" At this level Tuvia's soliloquy serves as an ironic protest liable at any moment to turn into something more than a momentary sense of bitterness. Yet at that very instant there is a marvelous counterbalance; the irony, in the very flow of words, turns into humor. The bitterness of the protest vanishes before Tuvia's response to the heavenly comforts hidden behind bereavement and failure. This is the motive force that gives light and shade to his speech, the technique that so endears Shalom Aleikhem to his readers and that makes him a wonderful Jewish author. The humorous smile, breaking through the irony directed at the real, everyday world, gives Tuvia his peculiar depth of character. (pp. 19-21)

[In] the revival of modern Hebrew and Yiddish literature, [Aleikhem's] use of the monologue is no less important than this mingling of humor and irony. It is only by means of monologue that Tuvia and Mottel ben Peisi the Cantor can achieve knowledge—knowledge of their place in the real world of society and family, and knowledge of their own world, which gives true meaning to their existence. It is in this monologue that the hero is truly himself. He speaks for himself and we come to know him directly, not through the indirect descriptive form of narration usually employed by authors who only rarely let the characters speak. The first-person narrator, however, prevents the other characters from coming to life and speaking for themselves, so that they tend to become mere satellites revolving around the central figure and existing only through him. This is the main drawback of the monologue in general and of Shalom Aleikhem's use of it in particular . For this reason, Tuvia's daughters can never move beyond the orbit of their father's monologue, can never be seen as individual people except through the eyes of Tuvia himself. Their tragic fate forms a central theme of the entire book, but it never becomes dramatized as their personal tragedy. Each phase of the tragedy is in the final analysis related directly to the speaker himself, in terms of his own private world of grief, suffering, complaint, and acceptance. Nevertheless, for all its drawbacks, Shalom Aleikhem's use of the monologue marked an important contribution to the need of post-Enlightenment literature to create individualized characters. (pp. 22-3)

> *Isaiah Rabinovich, in his* Major Trends in Modern Hebrew Fiction, *translated by M. Roston (© 1968 by The University of Chicago; reprinted by permission of Mrs. Sarah Rabinovich), University of Chicago Press, 1968.*

Tradition has it that Sholom Aleichem gave Mendele Mocher Seforim (Mendele the Bookseller) the title "Grandfather of Yiddish Literature." (p. 23)

The publication of Mendele's *Dos Kleine Mentshele* (in English translation, *The Parasite*) in 1864 is generally regarded as the beginning of modern Yiddish literature. . . . Prior to 1864, what passed as "literature" was largely confined to tehinnot (a sentimentalized liturgy written exclusively for women), translations of the Pentateuch or Yiddishized versions of, say, the Arthurian legends. (pp. 23-4)

With the advent of the Hassidic movement during the latter part of the eighteenth century, Yiddish suddenly emerged as an important vehicle for religious expression. What had once been the province of women and only the most uneducated of the male population, was now the medium of religious story literature, parable, and even prayer. (p. 24)

To be sure, even the growing influence of Hassidism could not make Yiddish a respectable language overnight. (pp. 25-6)

Isaac Meir Dick (1813-93) became the first author of the Haskalah [Jewish "Enlightenment"] movement to exploit the possibilities of publishing Yiddish fiction and, from 1847 on, his novels formed the foundations on which Mendele and, later, Sholom Aleichem, were to build their own fictive worlds. (pp. 27-8)

Most of Mendele's early work—including such satiric novels as *Dos Kleine Menshele, Die Takse (The Meat Tax* [1869]) and *Die Klatshe (The Dobbin,* 1873)—were sensationalist exposes of the *Kahal* (ghetto officials, politicians, etc.) whom Mendele blamed for the impoverished condition of Russian Jewry. In these novels, Mendele attacked the corruption of institutions and put forth solutions which were implemented some forty years later. (pp. 29-30)

However, conventional satire and social reform were destined to play a minor role when writers like Sholom Aleichem and Peretz burst onto the scene some twenty years later. By this time, Mendele was an established Yiddish writer, but the renaissance of folk literature made his earlier satires seem too dated, too obsolete—even too "literary." . . . What the folkmentsh needed were not so much novels that would tell them how corrupt things were, but rather stories which might suggest how they could survive in the midst of it. (p. 30)

Sholom Aleichem had hardly learned his *aleph-beys* (the first letters of the Hebrew alphabet) when Mendele published *Dos Kleine Menshele* in 1864. In fact, Sholom Rabinowitz—the man who was to become Yiddish literature's greatest folk writer—was born in 1859, a scant five years before. His earliest training was in Hebrew literature and his first creative effort was a Hebrew version of *Robinson Crusoe*. (p. 39)

By now, the story of his meeting with American humorist Mark Twain has become a part of the entrenched apocrypha handed down from teacher to student. Presumably Twain came to see Sholom Aleichem when he first arrived in America because, he said, people kept calling him "the American Sholom Aleichem." . . . However, it is in his differences from an author like Mark Twain that Sholom Aleichem's achievements can best be measured. For all his apparent popularity, I suspect Twain was really misunderstood by his staunchest admirers. Novels of Twain's later period—say, *The Mysterious Stranger*—were considered atypical Twain (the product of a disillusioned and aging mind) and all too many of his readers preferred to see the earlier novels—say, *Huck Finn*—as nostalgic portraits of an unfettered boyhood. To be sure, Twain's vision was more complicated, but my point is simply that Sholom Aleichem had less problems where rapport was concerned. Although his family was comparatively wealthy and his education far surpassed normal ghetto fare, his allegiance to the poor was undivided. I suspect that Twain's fundamentally low view of man made a genuine sympathy with the "folk" a difficult matter. (pp. 39-40)

Although Sholom Aleichem did not devote full time to "writing" until some sixteen years prior to his death, his literary productivity is nothing short of phenomenal—some forty volumes of stories, plays, and novels. He is best known, of course, as the author of the *Tevye* stories. . . . (p. 41)

For Sholom Aleichem, Tevye was a great tragic figure, a man symbolic of his generation and caught in a rapidly changing world over which he had little, if any, control. If he tends to sentimentalize the poverty of the shtetl, to reject Mendele's satiric solutions for an even heavier dose of characteristically Yiddish humor, it is because the values of Yiddishkeit itself were crumbling and the shtetl was being threatened by forces both within and outside its boundaries. As Yiddish literature moved into the twentieth century, it was a Tevye who best exemplified that sense of innocent suffering and self-awareness which had always been at the heart of Yiddish literature. To be sure, Tevye thinks of himself as a schlimmazel—a man more sinned against than sinning, and to the extent that the folkmentsh could identify with his sufferings and his adjustments, they would have agreed. For a Tevye, life is a matter of suffering, but that notion did not foreclose the matter of a life-affirming stance or a humor of self-mockery. On the contrary, Tevye—and, presumably, Sholom Aleichem's readers—could see a connection between a fidelity to a moral identity (with all its subsequent poverty and suffering) and a notion of tragic grandeur. Far from the sort of schlemiel who was the rightful recipient of the shtetl's condescending laughter, a figure like Tevye was as much the "hero" to his society as, say, Achilles had been to the Greeks. (p. 42)

[It] is in the values of the heart—rather than, say, the "head" or, certainly, the pocketbook—where Tevye scores his biggest gains. In him, the shtetl found an etiquette book full of the proper postures to use when your son began to read Spinoza or your daughter threatened to date a Gentile. More than any other figure, the life of Tevye seemed to suggest that the shtetl really wasn't so bad after all—at least it had solidarity, warmth, a sense of humor, and most of all, an undisputable value structure.

Although Sholom Aleichem created a wealth of individual character types, they all shared in a poverty which was the basis of his humor: Mottel, the cantor's son, became the archetype of the Jewish child-in-literature. Full of bounce and an unfailing good cheer, Mottel meets every tragedy in his life—even orphanhood—with an unquenchable optimism. . . . Menachem-Mendel, a relative of Tevye, is the archetypal luftmentsh. He is the very essence of accommodation and the will to survive. With his eye continually twinkling, due to yet another get-rich-quick plan or perhaps a new "occupation," Menachem-Mendel wanders from place to place as the luckless schlimmazzel. (p. 43)

In "Modern Children," Tevye stands with one foot rooted firmly in the past while the other searches uneasily for a solid foundation in the present. (p. 47)

With the world of the shtetl all but disintegrated, and "modern children" threatening to abandon the Tradition entirely, Tevye not only still continues to pattern his life on the Old Ways, but has a perfect faith that they will, somehow, prevail. On the other hand, however, Tevye has the wisdom necessary to see that the world around him is changing and that his daughters both demand and, more important, require a different sort of "love" than had existed between himself and Golde. As Julius and Francis Butwin said of Tevye: he is the "perfect *schlimazel* (i.e., the man for whom all things go wrong) and also the perfect *kasril,* the man whom nothing in life can down." And now, more than fifty years after Sholom Aleichem's death, Broadway audiences and an increasing American readership have come to see Tevye's "wisdom" as less parochial than they had imagined. (pp. 48-9)

> *Sanford Pinsker, in his* The Schlemiel as Metaphor: Studies in the Yiddish and American Jewish Novel *(copyright © 1971, Southern Illinois University Press; reprinted by permission of Southern Illinois University Press), Southern Illinois University Press, 1971.*

Sholom Aleichem . . . established a genealogy of modern Yiddish letters when he designated Mendele Mocher Sforim as the *zeyde,* the grandfather. The title with its implied kinship was accepted by Mendele and ratified by public consent although the two men were barely a generation apart. Even as it acknowledges the resemblances between the two writers, the appellation emphasizes the relative distance between them. In developing the concept of the schlemiel, as in his writing generally, Sholom Aleichem is directly indebted to Mendele but plays astonishing variations on the master's theme. (p. 41)

The humor of Sholom Aleichem, usually described as optimistic, is the result of a profoundly gloomy appraisal of Jewish life in Eastern Europe and a conscious decision to ease its sufferings. Almost all those who represent new directions in his work—the modern set in the story "Cnards," who mock the superstitions of their backwoods shtetl; Pertchik the revolutionary of "Hodel"; the mother who feels compelled to get her son into the state high school in the story "Gymnasium"—all are reproached for their attempt by the internal verdict of the fiction in which they figure. Emancipation to his characters means escape from the confinement of stultifying Jewish practice and belief. But to Sholom Aleichem, its precondition, the abandonment of the civilizing Jewish structure, was a ridiculous price to pay, especially since the real prospect of "emancipation" was chimerical. The only ones who may successfully challenge the tradition are the children, whose alternative is not another society, but the escape to nature or to art. (p. 43)

Sholom Aleichem conceived of his writing as a solace for people whose situation was so ineluctably unpleasant that they might as well laugh. The Jews of his works are a kind of schlemiel people, powerless and unlucky, but psychologically, or, as one used to say, spiritually, the victors in defeat. (p. 44)

Sholom Aleichem's most exhaustive study of the schlemiel is Menahem Mendl, a luftmensch, or a schlemiel in his economic dimension.

Menahem Mendl, an epistolary novel written between 1892 and 1913, consists of an exchange of letters between Menahem Mendl, the errant husband, and Sheyne Sheyndl of Kasrilevke, the steady wife. The two voices of the ironic proverbs are here expanded into two full-blown characters, one voicing trust and optimism, the other convinced that "Kreplach in a dream are not kreplach, but a dream." (p. 49)

In spite of an unbroken record of failures, the hero succeeds in his determined hope; Menahem Mendl wrests victory from defeat not by any tangible achievement of his purposes, but simply through his continuing capacity to dream. . . .

The characteristic features of the schlemiel are exemplified in the figure of Menahem Mendl: his masculinity is never considered; it is thoroughly extinct. The traditional male virtues such as strength, courage, pride, fortitude, are prominent only in their absence. Wife treats husband like an overgrown, overly fanciful child. Behind the wife stands the more formidable mother-in-law, and together they could undermine the virility of an Ajax. (p. 51)

[But] Sholom Aleichem's schlemiel, for all his simplicity, or naïveté, or weakness, or dreaminess, or predisposition for misfortune, or whatever tendency it is that makes him a schlemiel, retains a very firm sense of his distinct self. His sense of personal identity and worth is not seriously disrupted by the bombardment of environmental harrassments. The schlemiel represents the triumph of identity despite the failure of circumstance.

The full power of that identity is communicated to the reader by having the schlemiel tell the story in his own voice. Sholom Aleichem generally employs the technique of monologue, of which the epistolary form is but a variation, to convey the rhythms and nuances of character, and to underscore the extent to which language itself is the schlemiel's manipulative tool. Through language the schlemiel reinterprets events to conform to his own vision, and thereby controls them, much as the child learns to control the environment by naming it. (pp. 53-4)

Moreover, the richness of the language in some way compensates for the poverty it describes. There is in the style an overabundance of nouns, sayings, explanations, in apposition. Even the names are multiple: Menahem Mendl; Sheyne Sheyndl, or Meir-Motl-Moshe-Meir's. (p. 54)

Yet on the deepest level, Sholom Aleichem is making poverty the metaphor for spiritual wealth, and using the superabundance of language, particularly the rich veins of wit and humor, to suggest the cultural affluence that may be nourished by physical deprivation. The schlemiel is the bearer of this ironic meaning. (p. 55)

Menahem Mendl might be called the purest of Sholom Aleichem's schlemiel studies because of his entirely limited self-awareness and his total insensitivity to the incongruities of his situation. . . . Menahem Mendl is humorous because he is so consistently blind to these contradictions. At the same time Sholom Aleichem wants us to recognize that this very blindness rules out metaphysical doubt or despair. The "rigidity" that makes Menahem Mendl comical also keeps him throbbingly alive.

Menahem Mendl is a naked attempt to go beyond satire and to draw from an example of the most pitiable, laughable creature of society a model for psychic survival. (pp. 56-7)

Ruth R. Wisse, "Ironic Balance for Psychic Survival," in her The Schlemiel as Modern Hero (© 1971 by The University of Chicago), University of Chicago Press, 1971, pp. 41-57.

Sherwood Anderson

1876-1941

American novelist and short story writer. Anderson was a laborer, advertising copywriter, and soldier in the Spanish-American War before becoming a paint manufacturer in Elyria, Ohio. According to a famous story, Anderson walked out of his plant one day, never to return, in order to express his growing conviction that industrialization was corrupting rural/small-town America and to devote himself to serious fiction. Greatly affected by the work of Gertrude Stein, Theodore Dreiser, and D. H. Lawrence, Anderson was among the first to explore the psychology of sexuality and the unconscious in his fiction. His influence on Hemingway, Faulkner, Fitzgerald, and Wolfe is widely recognized, and his work in the short story was significant in the development of that genre away from the neatly plotted tales of O. Henry and his imitators. *Winesburg, Ohio* is considered his most important work.

PRINCIPAL WORKS

Windy McPherson's Son   (novel)   1916
Winesburg, Ohio   (short stories)   1919
Poor White   (novel)   1920
The Triumph of the Egg   (short stories)   1921
Horses and Men   (short stories)   1923
Many Marriages   (novel)   1923
A Story Teller's Story   (autobiography)   1924
Dark Laughter   (novel)   1925
Tar, A Midwest Boyhood   (autobiography)   1926
Beyond Desire   (novel)   1932
Death in the Woods   (short stories)   1933
Kit Brandon   (novel)   1936

In American novels, the words remained the dreariest, most degraded of poor individuals. But out of these fallen creatures, Sherwood Anderson has made the pure poetry of his tales. He has taken the words surely, has set them firmly end to end, and underneath his hand there has come to be a surface as clean and fragrant as that of joyously made things in a fresh young country. The vocabulary of the simplest folk; words of a primer, a copy-book quotidianness, form a surface as hard as that of pungent fresh-planed boards of pine and oak. Into the ordered prose of Anderson the delicacy and sweetness of the growing corn, the grittiness and firmness of black earth sifted by the fingers, the broad-breasted power of great labouring horses, has wavered again. The writing pleases the eye. It pleases the nostrils. It is moist and adhesive to the touch, like milk.

No rare and precious and technical incrustations have stiffened it. The slang of the city proletariat has not whipped it into garish and raging colour. Even in his pictures of life on the farms and in the towns of Ohio, Anderson is not colloquial. Very rarely some turn of language lifted from the speech of the Ohio country folk, gives a curious twist to the ordinary English. The language remains homely sober and spare. The simplest constructions abound. Few adjectives arrest the course of the sentence. At intervals, the succession of simple periods is broken by a compound sprawling its loose length. Qualifying clauses are unusual. Very occasionally, some of the plain massive silver and gold of the King James version shines when biblical poetry is echoed in the balancing of phrases, in the full unhurried repetition of words in slightly varied order. But the words themselves are no longer those that daily sweep by us in dun and opaque stream. They no longer go bent and grimy in a fog. Contours are distinct as those of objects bathed in cool morning light. The words comport themselves with dignity. They are placed so quietly, so plumbly, so solidly, in order; they are arrayed so nakedly, so four-squarely; stand so completely for what they are; ring so fully, that one perceives them bearing themselves as erectly and proudly as simple healthy folk can bear themselves. Aprons and overalls they still wear, for they are working-words. But their garments became starched and fragrant again, when Anderson squared and edged his tools. They leave us freshened as gingham-clad country girls driving past in a buggy do. If they are a little old and a little weary, they hold themselves like certain old folk who wear threadbare shawls and shiny black trousers, and still make their self-regard felt by their port.

It is the voice of Anderson's mind that utters itself through the medium of words. It is the voice of his lean, sinewy mid-American mind that marshalls the phrases, compels them into patterns. In this dumb American shoot of the Ohio countryside, a miracle has begun to declare itself. The man is brother to all the inarticulate folk produced by a couple of centuries of pioneering in the raw new world. (pp. 29-31)

The hysterical American mouth with its fictitious tumult and assurance, its rhetorical trumpeting, is set aside in him, disdained. There is no evasion of the truth in him. There is no pink fog over the truth of the relationship of men and women in this country. There is no evasion of self-consciousness by means of an interest centred entirely in the children; no blinding dream that entrance into a house full of spick furniture and nickled faucets will suddenly make life flow sweet-coloured and deep; no thankfulness to God that He has made a universe in which every one, or every one's offspring may climb to the top of the heap and become rich or a leader of the bar, that murderer of nascent sympathy. Nor does he speak Main Street in denigrating Main Street. (p. 31)

The most ordinary objects glimpsed from an office-window high in the loop . . . give Anderson the clue of a thin grey string, and set him winding through his drab and his wild days to find the truth of some cardinal experience and fill himself. The premature decay of buildings in America, the doleful agedness of things that have never served well and have grown old without becoming beautiful, the brutality of the Chicago skyline, open to him through a furtive chink some truth of his own starved powerful life, his own buried Mississippi Valley, his own unused empire. (p. 32)

Out of the unconscious the style arises, the words charged with the blood and essence of the man. For quite as Anderson hears his own inner flux through the persons of other men, through materials and constructions, so, too, he hears it in the language itself. Words, like corn, like horses themselves, and men, give Anderson pricking sensations. Strange and unusual words do not have to be summoned. He hears the thin vocabulary of his inarticulate fellows not only as concepts of concrete objects, but as independent shapes and colours. (pp. 35-6)

All Anderson's artistry consists in the faithfulness with which he has laboured to make these overtones sound in his prose, to relate the simple words so that while remaining symbolic of the outer men, they give also their inner state. At first, in the two early novels, *Windy McPherson's Son* and *Marching Men,* the word quality was fairly thin. . . . In the next book, *Winesburg, Ohio,* however, form obtains fully. The deep within Anderson utters itself through the prose. (pp. 36-7)

And, in his latest work, in the best of the stories in *The Triumph of the Egg,* and in the pieces of *A New Testament,* it works with always simpler means, begins to manifest itself through a literature that approaches the condition of poetry, that is more and more a play of word-timbres, a design of overtones, of verbal shapes and colours, a sort of absolute prose.

There has been no fiction in America like this. . . . The short-stories show him the fine workman most. The novels, the *nouvelles, Out of Nowhere Into Nothing,* wander at times, are broken in sweep by evasions and holes. A many-sided contact with life is not revealed. The man is not an intellectual critic of society. His range is a fairly limited one. There is a gentle weariness through him. And still, his stories are the truest, the warmest, the most mature, that have sprung out of the Western soil. (p. 37)

> *Paul Rosenfeld, "Sherwood Anderson," in*
> The Dial *(copyright, 1922, by The Dial Publishing Company, Inc.; reprinted by permission of J. S. Watson, Jr. and Scofield Thayer), January, 1922 (and reprinted by Kraus Reprint Corporation, 1966), pp. 31-42.*

Mr Anderson has not completely subdued his material to form, has not thoroughly penetrated it with interpretation. It remains recalcitrant and opaque. But as his work has progressed he has shown constantly a firmer grasp on his problem, a more complete conception of the difficulties of approach, and the resources and limitations of his art. . . .

It is natural to speak of Sherwood Anderson's work in metaphors of physical achievement, for his struggle is first of all an athletic one with the crude stuff of life in a material world. (p. 79)

He has made it his first object to see American life as it is, without illusion. It is a grim spectacle, and he confesses his inability to see it beautifully. . . .

We are a crude people, but not dull. In some strange way the human forms which this life assumes have a grotesque quality which makes them as fascinating as gargoyles. Over and over again Mr Anderson has drawn them for us. . . .

It is true that Mr Anderson has been influenced by the technical experiments of his predecessors, but in so far as he has yielded to them he has failed. His first novel, *Windy McPherson's Son,* begins with a transcript from middle-Western life so faithful that it seems autobiographic; but having established a complete groundwork of reality the author in an endeavour to maintain interest or to disengage significance has recourse to the romantic formula. The point is clearly perceptible at which his fact passes over into fiction. In *Marching Men* the substance of the book is indubitably experience, but the material is subordinated to a thesis which is more than a part of the psychology of the hero. *Poor White* is the best of the three novels. Here the realism in which Mr Anderson works so confidently is raised to significance by a symbolism which is so immediate in its process that it seems unpremeditated and unconscious. But the large sweep and scope of the story somehow carry it beyond the author's control. Somewhere he loses his grasp on the meaning of events, the clue to their interpretation, and presents them with an emphasis which is misplaced, and with a conclusion which is mechanical and arbitrary. *Winesburg, Ohio* revealed Mr Anderson's true vehicle in the short story. . . . The stories reveal by flashes the life, the activity, the character of the little mid-Western town as completely as the persistent glare of Mr Sinclair Lewis's searchlight upon Gopher Prairie. *The Triumph of the Egg* has, through greater diversity of material and wider variety of method and style, the same compelling unity, a unity not geographical, but cosmic. (p. 81)

> *Robert Morss Lovett, "The Promise of Sherwood Anderson," in* The Dial *(copyright, 1922, by The Dial Publishing Company, Inc.; reprinted by permission of J. S. Watson, Jr. and Scofield Thayer), January, 1922 (and reprinted by Kraus Reprint Corporation, 1966), pp. 79-83.*

Mr Anderson's habit of stripping his characters of their incidentals—their clothes, their furniture, and their social relations—which in his best stories produces a sort of classic simplicity, in *Many Marriages* leaves them strangely pale, as if they had been stripped of their personalities, too. (p. 399)

Yet, for all the feebleness, even flabbiness, of the texture of *Many Marriages,* it is not wholly devoid of the strange impressiveness which one feels in all Mr Anderson's work. Here, as elsewhere, we are at once disturbed and soothed by the feeling of hands thrust down among the deepest bowels of life—hands delicate and clean but still pitiless in their explorations. My only quarrel with Mr Anderson is that he has not gone down so far as usual. . . . Yet even here we feel that Mr Anderson has the advantage that his banality is not derived from the banality of other people. It is something he has arrived at by himself. At his best, he functions with a strange ease and beauty in a world at the roots of life—as if in a diving-bell of the human soul—which makes the world of the ordinary novelist seem a painted literary convention; and at his worst, in *Many Marriages,* one feels as one can do in the case of almost none of his contemporaries, that he is at least making his own mistakes in the pursuit of his own authentic ideal and not merely failing from an imperfect attempt to imitate someone else's. (p. 400)

> Edmund Wilson, "Many Marriages," in The Dial *(copyright, 1923, by The Dial Publishing Company, Inc.; reprinted by permission of J. S. Watson, Jr. and Scofield Thayer), April, 1923 (and reprinted by Kraus Reprint Corporation, 1966), pp. 399-400.*

Up to the present time Mr Sherwood Anderson has published four novels, two books of short stories, and a collection of poems. He has been termed by respective critics "the Dostoevsky of America," a great and original figure in American literature, a "phallic Chekhov," and the link that at last connects the old world with that of the new. . . . With the final *Dial* award, Mr Anderson issued completely from those dim recesses hitherto penetrated only by enthusiastic critics and a small reading public, into the safely entrenched ranks of the so-called "best sellers."

Anxiously and hospitably one feels one's way through the pages of his novels in search for those especial qualities which have impelled his admirers to shower so unstintedly upon him their approval. Yet it is at the command of a voice that one finds oneself proceeding—a voice exhorting, suppliant, prophetic, simulating stridency, sentimentalizing, and dwindling at recurring moments to a bewildered whisper of inquiry. Never, no never, touching for more than a fleeting second that subtle art of restraint and aesthetic arrangement which we have come to associate with the most distinguished writing. Never, in spite of his continual use of the word "clean," which serves apparently all purposes, and plays over his pages like an agitated pawn vainly seeking equilibrium on a tilted chess board, giving one a sense of a technique sharp, pure, unmuddied by the stirred sediment of somewhat impuissant emotions. We move among wraiths of "purposeful" or "wistful" men, "straight," "fine" women or women misunderstood, or dulled beyond reprieve. Penetrating, imaginative passages there are, to be sure, an arresting use of a word here and there, a sense of the beauty of old weathered things, of the pitiless craft and hypocrisy of man in his most predatory moments. "How cunning they were, the men who had been successful in life. Behind the flesh that had grown so thick upon their bones what cunning eyes." And when he notes

the rapid growth of Chicago as illustrated by the marks of a lumberman's ax on logs which, once part of an adjacent grove, now remain buried under the debris of a slum district crowded with warehouses, he presents with an economy of means a convincing picture which the tediousness of his later descriptions comes near to obliterating altogether. (pp. 243-44)

With the possible exception of *Poor White* one feels that in his novels Mr Anderson is subject to an ever recurring species of shell shock which projects him *volte face* towards the prickly actualities of life, and in his efforts to regain his spiritual poise he drags one about with him in a cloud of splintering conventions and mysterious clogged desires through passages too cluttered to permit of escape into the clear light of day. (p. 244)

It is only in turning to his short stories that we experience a grateful though guarded relief. In his *Winesburg, Ohio,* and *The Triumph of the Egg* he has recorded in varying situations the obscure emotional states of people, wistful, restless, or maladjusted to the crass routines of life, people who do sudden strange things seeking release for thwarted desires, people who have clung lingeringly to old "pure" ideals as they passed over the curve of puberty into a world too raw for their troubled timidities. Why does one feel, however, that these stories in spite of their eloquent reply to *Main Street,* in spite of their occasional charm and originality, their gentleness and pity, never fully achieve art? One has but to compare even so moving and poetically conceived a story as *The New Englander* to de Maupassant's *Miss Harriet,* of similar theme, or *Senility,* so like Chekhov in conception, to one of that author's delicate masterpieces, to perceive the difference between writing weakened by a groping intellect and writing that arrives radiant and ineluctable from the pens of great imaginative artists. Even Mr Theodore Dreiser, with whose name that of Mr Anderson's has been so often associated, achieves in his brooding candour a freedom from the dragging weight of self-consciousness. "I am a confused child in a confused world" writes Mr Anderson in his *Mid-American Chants,* but it is not from confused children, however engaging they may be, that one looks for art. And with what banalities he is content to fill his pages—"she is fine and purposeful"—"hungry to the roots of her"—"He had lived clean body and mind"—"filled with the white wonder of it."

Then why, one asks oneself, in spite of so many lapses, so much obvious awkwardness in the handling of his material, so little understanding of how the minds of certain women work under circumstances of repression, so much rhetorical self-indulgence and lack of aesthetic arrangement has Mr Anderson created for himself so large and unmistakable a following? It is, we believe, because of a certain perturbed integrity, a thwarted infantile idealism which seeks to construct a new salvation for the human race and cries out for new definitions, new sex emancipation. Where Mr Dreiser like a giant mole with strong flat hands tore up the soil and prepared the ground for a more liberal treatment of sex in American literature, Mr Anderson, nervous and mystical, follows along like the anxious white rabbit in *Alice in Wonderland* clasping instead of a watch the latest edition of Sigmund Freud. . . . He succeeds, however, in depicting with historical perspective the disorder and meaninglessness of the American scene, the loss of our richer heritages, even while permitting such explanations to obtrude upon the development of his characters. . . . (pp. 245-46)

But unfortunately for American letters it must be conceded that when all has been said Sherwood Anderson taps on occasions deeper veins than almost any other of our contemporary novelists. Whether he will achieve a greater perfection in the short story, that realm of literature in which he is most at home, depends largely upon his ability to extricate himself from the debilitating influences of other writers and to think out his problems alone. At present, we feel, he somewhat resembles a man, who, having planted a fine bed of radishes, tends them rather carelessly and sells them before their time, so that when one comes at last to buy them in the open market they turn out, unfortunately, rather softer than any good radish has a right to be. To have attained their legitimate freshness and pungency they should, one strongly suspects, have been left to reach maturity in the promising and well-manured soil of Winesburg, Ohio. (p. 246)

> *Alyse Gregory, "Sherwood Anderson," in* The Dial *(copyright, 1923, by The Dial Publishing Company, Inc.; reprinted by permission of J. S. Watson, Jr. and Scofield Thayer), September, 1923 (and reprinted by Kraus Reprint Corporation, 1966), pp. 243-46.*

Sherwood Anderson, dreamer, philosopher, corn-fed mystic, [was] a man who gathered into himself all the torment of life, who suffered, to some extent voluntarily, all its pangs and ecstasies. (p. 111)

Writing in America, [Anderson] feels, deals entirely with exteriors—"the doctor's office, the city street, the vacant lot beside the factory, are described with an amazing finality and fulsomeness of detail. Into these places people are cast, wearing the ordinary clothes such as one is accustomed to see wrapped about the bodies of his friends and neighbors. Having tricked your reader by these purely mechanical details into having faith in the people they are writing about, you simply make these people do and say things no human being has ever really been known to do or say." (p. 115)

He [tried] to apply his philosophy that life is not a mean thing to be tamed and held to hard and fast canons, but a beautiful, wild thing of ecstasies and dreams, something that must be lived deeply to be understood. (p. 116)

The author [of "Winesburg, Ohio"] presents the impression that he is discovering for the first time the situations that he reveals to the reader, consequently he leads up to them as haltingly, as slowly, as a child opening a door and entering an old, unused room. In the end the effect is cumulative and powerful. It is "Winesburg, Ohio" that permits us to link Sherwood Anderson's name with that of Tchekov. (pp. 147-48)

The troubles [the people of Winesburg] brood over seem to be the troubles many persons have, so that our words "realistic" and "romantic" need to be defined anew. On the critical horizon the appearance of these stories created a sensation. H. L. Mencken recognized their power and truth at once and spoke of "Winesburg, Ohio," as "a brilliant procession of little tragedies, a vivid and moving picture, Dreiserian in its fidelity and almost Conradian in its irony of the insoluble riddle at the heart of human existence. He gets into the minds and souls of his remote and unregarded yokels and what he finds there is not the mere sordid farce

that one glimpses from the train windows but the eternal tragedy of man." (pp. 149-50)

Let us say this for Sherwood Anderson: he is one of the few native novelists in America whose field is the human mind; where writers of thirty years ago concerned themselves wholly with the external happenings in the life of a character, Sherwood Anderson is concerned almost wholly with their mental life. His appearance is not on the highroad of American literature, but marks a deflection from the main currents, a variation. That he will become the founder of a school is doubtful; that he will have followers is certain; that he will profoundly affect American writing along the lines he first preached about—simplicity and honesty—is assured. His influence exerts itself in two ways —in theme, and in treatment; in subject-matter and in technique. (pp. 176-77)

Sherwood Anderson is a naive product of our soil who owes little to our deeply-rooted Anglo-Saxon culture, nor derives from "immigrant sources," or more recognized continental influences. In spite of that he more nearly approaches the homely Saxon speech than many carefully trained writers, and often invests it with a deep spiritual significance that gives new power to the plain, belabored words. He is a mystic and a dreamer, a groper after truth, deluded at times by his childlike faith in his own dreams and imaginings, and yet, like a child, a little nearer truth by reason of his dreams. (pp. 178-79)

> *Harry Hansen, "Sherwood Anderson: Corn-Fed Mystic, Historian of the Middle Age of Man," in his* Midwest Portraits: A Book of Memories and Friendships *(© 1923 by Harcourt, Brace and Company, Inc.; 1951 by Harry Hansen; reprinted by permission of Harcourt Brace Jovanovich, Inc.), Harcourt, 1923, pp. 111-79.*

[Of surrendering] to the current of reality, . . . letting nature have its way, Sherwood Anderson in his short stories has given the most distinct and outstanding examples in American fiction. This fact makes his case perennially and recurrently interesting, in spite of the unevenness of his work in detail, and the ambitious failures of his novels. The latter illustrate the difficulty of construction of a long work without the guidance of a predetermined theme, and, to some extent, Mr Anderson's own surrender to a method not his own. But in them, as in his short stories, it is clear that his chief effort is a quest for meaning through that objective reality of which his senses and his human contacts bring him so vivid an account. With the lavishness of material which his method permits and encourages he can afford failures. And after each novel he clears his intention and his art by a return to his true medium, the short story. (p. 275)

> *Robert Morss Lovett, "Horses and Men," in* The Dial *(copyright, 1924, by The Dial Publishing Company, Inc.; reprinted by permission of J. S. Watson, Jr. and Scofield Thayer), March, 1924 (and reprinted by Kraus Reprint Corporation, 1966), pp. 274-76.*

As for the parables [of *A New Testament*], or poems, or gnomic prose, in which we are to find Mr. Anderson's "doctrine" (*qui d'ailleurs n'existe pas*), the best one can say for it is that it is, unmistakably, imaginative. But beyond that one cannot go. For Mr. Anderson's symbolisms and parables are too wholesale to be effective, too amorphous to be clear, too structureless and humorless to be anything more than readable. Once or twice, when he condescends to be simple and forthright, as in "Young Man in a Room" or "In a Workingman's Rooming House," he gives us a vigorous and moving bit of poetic prose, succinct and real. But for the most part one feels that he is trying too hard, that he is a little overweening. His reach exceeds his grasp. The profuseness with which he empties his unconsciousness, the indiscriminateness with which he allows image to lead to image and one autistic chain of thought to bud another, defeats his own end, and in the upshot one has a mere welter of pictures, some bad and some good, but in the main meaningless.

One feels of Mr. Anderson that he has simply lost himself hopelessly in his own little poetic chaos, in the illusion that he has there discovered the ultimate truth. (p. 132)

> *Conrad Aiken, "Anderson, Sherwood" (originally published under a different title in* New York Post, *July 9, 1927), in his* Collected Criticism *(copyright © 1935, 1939, 1940, 1942, 1951, 1958 by Conrad Aiken; reprinted by permission of Oxford University Press, Inc.), Oxford University Press, 1968, pp. 130-32.*

In his *Story Teller's Story,* and in *Tar,* Sherwood Anderson tells very satisfyingly about the things one really wants to know of a story-teller—about how his feeling for life grew into something articulate, and about how the story-telling inclination was born in him and persisted in him now as a dreamer and now as liar, an ornate and disinterested liar, and now as a discontent who did not know that he ought to be doing something particularly different from the thing that did not satisfy him, now as an "ad" writer whose trade value was greater since he was rumored to have sold some fiction but not enough to keep him alive, and finally as a manufacturer who one day discovered that, instead of selling his goods not very fast, he was actually selling his soul. He is quite detached in the telling of it, neither vain nor proud. He gives more space to his father than to anyone else, because he understands the histrionic self-glorification of the man as something that led to story-telling, though to exactly the kind of stories that the son has always abjured. For he shows that the tales he tells are one with the life he has lived. (pp. 157-58)

What he deliberately chose to do, and what he is doing with almost all his energy, was to become the fine craftsman, working honestly with the rough material of middle western village life and chiseling it into form with the words which are his tools. He wanted to carve out the figures inherent in the stones that lay on every side. He wanted to work in full respect for the fine craftsmanship of the carvers who had wrought before him; not to adopt the mere tricks of a trade but to do the essential thing that they had done. It was life that he was after and not plot. It was the appropriate language that he wanted to use and not literary English. He must never lose his real interest in the people about him; and when he became aware of a story pleading to be told he must lend himself to the simple people who lived it, or might have lived it, and believe in those people until he and they were one. This is the desire of the creative artist and

he has striven to fulfil himself in this fashion. But there was still a way out for him when the desire to be bold and bad intrigued him. In the very reality of his people there was an element that the story-tellers just before him had avoided recognizing. The Victorians, on both sides [of] the Atlantic, had been reluctant to acknowledge the persistence of sex feeling. He could maintain his artistic integrity by dwelling on this with ruthless persistence, and he could be a little shocking in the name of art. (p. 166)

Mr. Anderson is in fact a sensitive artist and sensitive to most hostile comment. The criticism that any of his characters are not worth putting into fiction hurts him; but the criticism that he is a wicked man with a wicked mind carries no such sting. It may be that he is not fully aware of this himself; just as other men and women are not conscious of the subliminal sex feeling on which he harps; but to the friendly and unshocked observer he does seem to be somewhat Whitmanic in his keeping his hat on indoors or out and sounding his barbaric yawp over the roofs of the world, or raising the roof if he happens to be in the bedroom beneath the eaves. It is too conscious, like the removable front of O'Neill's house under the elms.

I do not mean to be either patting Mr. Anderson on the back, or disposing of this aspect of him with a quip. They are both much too substantial for that. I say merely that the truth lies somewhere between the prevailing implications in many of his pages and the loudest outcries of his most hostile assailants—that the problem does not loom so large as he suggests and that he is not so morbid as they insist. It is a case of overemphasis on both sides. The sex impulse is only one of several dominant desires. Any one of them becomes the more interesting as it pushes its way out of proportion. Perfect balance may serve as subject matter for statuary but literature yearns for ruling passions. For a century and more fiction in English has turned to all the other abnormals but sex abnormals. Now it is paying the penalty for repression which errs as far on one side as current expression does on the other. Among the contemporaries Mr. Anderson is doing his share to restore the balance of the age by indulging in some degree of unbalance in his own work. And he is doing it in a manner that is seldom circumstantial and never sickly. (pp. 167-68)

Behind and beyond his interest in the relations of men and women, and in the passion which is only a part of love, Anderson is dealing with the whole experience of men and of women, of which love is only a part. (p. 169)

The difference between *Marching Men* and *Dark Laughter* is parallel to the difference between Anderson the manufacturer and Anderson the author. When he had passed from thinking of men as slaves to the industrialism from which he had escaped, and had come to thinking of men and women as living in a world of primary experiences so vital that their inciting causes faded into unimportance, the factory lost interest as a factory and the slum as a slum, though they still might be used as backgrounds. The one matter that counted was to catch the rare moments when people were really living and to find the words that could record these moments.

And these rare moments were the moments when individuals were able to surmount or penetrate or break down the walls by which they were cut off from their fellows. The metaphor, once noted, recurs insistently throughout the stories. The wall, the wall, the wall. Only now and again do humans come into each other's spiritual presences. Partners, plotters, husbands, and wives are all held apart by impalpable barriers. (pp. 171-72)

[Mr. Anderson's prose] is a medium for that sort of American life to which he was born and to which he is devoting himself. This is far from all of America, and it is part of America whose fineness is crudely articulated and largely devoid of nice nuances of manner. (pp. 176-77)

> *Percy H. Boynton, "Sherwood Anderson,"*
> *in his* More Contemporary Americans (© *1927 by the University of Chicago), University of Chicago Press, 1927, pp. 157-77.*

It is beyond any question that *Winesburg, Ohio,* and *The Triumph of the Egg* are two of the most interesting books of short stories ever written. The story that gives its name to the second volume is a beautiful grotesque which, like a great deal of Chinese art, like the more whimsical Greek bronzes, like much Maya sculpture, like the Buddha himself, achieves through its grotesquerie a serene effect that art directed and censored by idealist considerations can rarely attain. . . .

[Simultaneous excitement and serenity, perhaps the most agreeable sensation permitted to man, is what] Mr. Anderson gave to his readers in *The Triumph of the Egg* by the ambivalence of his feeling for the father, his affection for him, his dislike for him, his contempt for him, his respect for him, his patience with him, his capacity for being endlessly entertained by him. Just as he gave it in *A Story Teller's Story,* that beautiful book, by his co-equal love and hate of himself, of his father, of America.

But I refuse to accompany Mr. Sherwood Anderson on all his adventures. *Dark Laughter* made me feel that negroes must be a lot more easily amused than I am. . . . [In *Many Marriages* his] characters were unable to become Scandals. They never seemed to attain the dignity of complete nudity; their complexes clung to them like dark woollen socks. And *Poor White,* for all its magnificent beginning, was spoiled for me by subsequent passages describing how the hero, unable to face the duty of consummating his marriage, although he liked his bride, wandered about the arable land in the neighbourhood all night until her father and brothers came and fetched him, all looking positively deformed with taciturnity. . . . (pp. 309-11)

Mr. Anderson's latest book, *Tar, a Mid-West Childhood,* . . . has . . . that curious falsification of character in the direction of flatness which belongs to books about children written by most adults. If one casts one's mind back to one's childhood and does not flinch, one has to admit that one then possessed all the emotional characteristics that are called adult in a far more marked degree than one ever had them later. . . . But we cannot bear to admit this, since it means that we who are mature and no more than mature, nevertheless, have already begun to suffer a decline. . . . So we frequently ascribe to childhood an insipidity of nature, a temperance of heart, which is actually an attribute of old age. Thus comes into being the mawkish common run of children's books, which, being lies, die quickly. Those which survive do not repudiate this intensity of youth. (pp. 313-14)

There is in *Tar* just a trifle of this depreciation of the essen-

tial quality of childhood, and the lack of interest in children, which is its root. Mr. Anderson inquires surprisingly whether there can be such a thing as a vulgar child, and pronounces it inconceivable. Yet there could surely be nothing more evident than that there are innumerable children who come out of the everywhere into here wearing a made-up tie. . . . [The] small boy Tar is painted in pale sepia tints to square with the common ideal of the mediocrity of the young; and the representation is still further weakened by indulgences of Mr. Anderson's curious tendency to drag the *tempo* of life, by breaking up movements that in normal humanity are easy and sweeping into delayed, puttering motions, by inserting inarticulateness like a plum in the mouths of his characters. This is an irritating trick of his, because it does not belong to his artistic vision of life. (pp. 314-15)

Certainly Mr. Sherwood Anderson is an unequal writer and *Tar* is disfigured with flatness and sham *naïveté,* but that does not, of course, affect my conviction that he has genius. Unequal writing is less of a condemnation of an author than it ever was before, for the conditions in which modern writers choose their mediums ensure that they shall constantly be setting themselves difficulties which they cannot always surmount. The people who wanted to write about a man's private adventures, those that go on within his own breast, used always to write verse. But now they are impatient of using metre and rhyme. They like to sport among the subtler rhythms of prose. (pp. 318-19)

That Mr. Anderson is wrong to listen to such inquiries has been proved by the fact that his art has always shown itself at its worst in his novels, at its best in short stories and the go-as-you-please rhapsodic form of *A Story Teller's Story.* When he follows his bent he may seem to be violating the traditions of fiction, but he is being loyal to the tradition of poetry, which after all is older and of greater importance: just as Mr. Sherwood Anderson, fussy and humourless and hell-bent on disharmony, as he often is, is nevertheless more important than half a dozen of the glibber novelists of the day, because of his vein of authentic inspiration. (p. 320)

> *Rebecca West, "Sherwood Anderson, Poet," in her* The Strange Necessity (*copyright 1928,* © *1955 by Rebecca West; reprinted by permission of The Viking Press), Doubleday, Doran, 1928, pp. 309-20.*

[To] one interested in the relation of current literature to modern life, [Anderson] is the most instructive of our contemporaries. (p. 115)

Anderson affords a key to the understanding of this country in his sentence, "The living force within could not find expression." The people are baffled because their lives offer no channel through which their vitality can discharge itself. That is why they are all, as he himself has more than once pointed out, grotesque, misshapen, deformed by their own bottled-up energy. They are uncomprehending because their world offers them nothing to comprehend; their existence is an interminable reiteration of meaningless detail, and the innate incapacity of man to be a vegetable makes the tragedy. This is the land, not of repressed, but of unfulfilled, desires. Nor, although sex plays an enormous rôle in this country, is it true that these desires are exclusively sexual. The drama is not chiefly the struggle of sex with convention, nor even the struggle of desire in general with convention or with inhibition of any sort. It is something vastly wider: it is the rebellion of all desire against the inanity of life. (pp. 117-18)

Because, in this country, everything important happens below the surface, Anderson does not often develop the setting to any great extent. His writing is not conspicuous for the sensuous imagination it evinces. . . . And so it is likewise with his characters: there are no complete, rounded-out portraits; they do not possess an independent, tri-dimensional existence of their own—compare them in this respect, for example, with the grotesques of Dickens. There is no one in Anderson's stories who is remembered as an individual like Quilp or Micawber. For Anderson's great faculty is not the imagination that bodies forth the form of things unseen, but rather the insight which probes and penetrates. Yet the process by which he works is not analytical dissection; he is not in the usual sense a "psychological" writer. . . . He truly "enters in," as if the experience had been his own. And he enables the reader to do the same—not to watch an experiment in vivisection, but to explore the depths of living personality by himself getting inside the skins of other men and women. (pp. 118-19)

His people are dismantled energies. . . . (p. 119)

His pity is the prime motor of his work; the pressure of his compassion gives his world its potency and concentration. . . . At his best, Anderson conveys precisely that sense of constriction about the heart and that difficulty of breathing which one gets from the finest lyrics. . . .

His writing has the quality of a well scrubbed plank floor— its clean freshness, its frank homeliness, and its slight roughness and unevenness. He uses no subterfuges and no tricks. In part, his art consists in a remarkable freedom from artifice. He is the opposite of an "artful dodger"; he knows no smartness. Such utter straightforwardness as his is a triumph. (p. 120)

His best stories seem to have no technique at all: each deals with an episode, a crisis in one or two lives, and Anderson first gives what information is needed concerning the participants, and then proceeds with his anecdote. As a writer, his outstanding trait is his integrity; to maintain such integrity against all the lures and pressures of twentieth-century America is a notable feat which speaks highly for his instinct as a workman. To possess not only the story-telling knack but also the critical sense and the severity of taste necessary for strict self-discipline—for certainly he received no outside aid of consequence—that is singular good fortune. Anderson must have been endowed with the rigorous conscience of the true craftsman. (p. 121)

The comparative poverty of his imaginative world is due to the fact that the environment has been ill adapted to meet the needs of his particular mental bias. It has been rich in those qualities with which he is little concerned: in the beauty of nature, in the obvious commotion of city streets, in the achievements of a mechanic civilization, in all that spectacular pageantry with its violent contrasts of which Dreiser is enamoured, in all those external or non-human aspects which fascinate Sandburg. But it has been poor in the things for which Anderson cares, for his interest is in the human soul, in dramatic or poetic human values, and in the relations and interactions of men and women with one another. (p. 130)

Among our present writers, he is one of the few real mystics. At first glance, he may look like much the same sort of naturalist as the others. The world as shown in his portrayal is naturalistic, like the world of Henry Adams, Sandburg, and Dreiser—chaotic, unintelligible, purposeless, with man the sport and victim of forces he cannot understand or control. It is a futile and a tragic world; yet Anderson, unlike certain others, does not make the assumption that it has always been and must always continue to be futile and disordered. He does not first reduce American behavior to a theory of life and then erect it into a scheme of the universe. His standard is never quantitative, and he is never an uncritical worshiper of mere force. The law of the jungle is not for him eternal and immutable. He obscurely apprehends that there may be a solution and a remedy, and this solution he finds in a mystical relation between the human unit and the universe. His quest has always been for the source of a more abundant life, and such a source he discovers in a union or identification of the individual with something outside himself, a merging of the single personality in something larger. Hence his preoccupation with the breaking down of the walls and barriers that hem in and isolate each man and separate him from the world about him and from the others of his kind. (pp. 132-33)

Since, as he says, he has no God, Anderson's is a nature-mysticism much like Whitman's. He advocates a return to a simpler and more primitive way of life, to the condition of savages and even of beasts and plants. (p. 134)

In his theory and thought . . ., as well as in his practice, Anderson is a thorough-going champion of the poetic temper and of the life of realization against all their enemies. His work, for all its high merit within its severe limitations, has quite as much social as literary importance. No other poet, novelist, or dramatist is so fully conscious of the American situation or drives it home so forcibly as does Anderson, both in his imaginative creation and in his critical comment. His picture of human starvation and frustration, his historical explanation of the condition he presents, his suggestions concerning the way to a better and fuller life —all combine to lend him a unique significance in present American letters. (pp. 136-37)

> *T. K. Whipple, "Sherwood Anderson," in his* Spokesmen: Modern Writers and American Life *(copyright © 1928 by Prentice-Hall, Inc.; reprinted by permission of Prentice-Hall, Inc., Englewood Cliffs, New Jersey), D. Appleton & Co., 1928, pp. 115-38.*

[Anderson] is not yet a spent force, but his influence has been absorbed. He has given no evidence that he can produce anything upon a massive scale, but no American writer of the second rank has been so stimulating. His effect has been greater than his achievement. (p. 339)

[He] was the first American writer to cultivate the device of under-statement. It is a manner that lends itself to parody and to unskillful imitation. (pp. 342-43)

Mr. Sherwood Anderson is a comparatively mild rebel for whom dissatisfaction with things as they are is mainly, if not merely, an incentive to self-expression. In *Marching Men* he made his only contribution to the social revolutionary idea. By inclination he is an individualist who thinks that every man must work out his own salvation. He realized, and rightly we think, that his own lot was to be a teller of tales rather than a maker of garments, or whatever his factory produced. He therefore turned the lock in the door, and confronted the world as a manufacturer of words. To the end of his career he has been creating people of crude strength, adversaries of circumstance who win no battles but never acknowledge defeat. He has constituted himself the poet of a shirt-sleeve civilization with none of the amenities of life to compensate its rigors, and whose inarticulate heroes have none of the satisfactions which even the distressed artist enjoys. He excels in the short sketch; the larger canvas confuses him, for he has never envisaged life as a coherent whole. His best long work is in the books where the trembling mirage of the past supplies the theme. *Tar* is reminiscential, poetic, and therefore successful. *Dark Laughter* is far from being a great novel, but in its light way it is as interesting a technical experiment as America has produced. All the usual props of fiction are discarded. Narrative is restricted to the irreducible minimum, and dialogue, whose main virtue is normally to produce the impact of the present moment, is almost all "recovered." There are many fragments of remembered conversation that drift through the minds of the characters, but dialogue contemporaneous with the action of the story is extremely rare and most exiguous when found. (pp. 346-47)

Despite the elimination of all the usual expository material of the novelist the book is crystal clear, and substantially not so thin as many novels fashioned in the conventional mold. (p. 347)

> *Pelham Edgar, in his* The Art of the Novel: From 1700 to the Present Time, *The Macmillan Company, 1933 (and reprinted by Russell & Russell, 1966).*

A revaluation of Sherwood Anderson must necessarily take account of the extraordinary impact that he made upon American literature almost at his appearance. In spite of the crudity of his first novels the impression was general that an original and distinguished talent was to be reckoned with. . . . This verdict may be accounted for by Anderson's possession, in truer balance than any other of his contemporaries, of three qualities marked by Maeterlinck as requisites for great literature: a sure touch upon the world of our senses; a profound intimation of the mystery that surrounds this island of our consciousness; and the literary technique comprehended in the term style. (pp. 88-9)

"Winesburg, Ohio" represents the solution of the problem that Anderson consciously set himself. His own experience, unusually rich and varied, gave him his grip on the actual world in which he was to live so abundantly. He has borne testimony to this in his numerous autobiographical writings, but as an artist his aim was constantly to emerge from the chrysalis stage of realism into the winged career of imagination. (p. 91)

It is in thus seizing on scraps of reality and projecting them beyond the small range controlled by the senses that Sherwood Anderson's imagination brings fiction to the enhancement of life, and enlarges his art beyond the limits of naturalism into expressionism. Not the fact, but the emotion with which the artist accepts it, is the essence of living.

"Winesburg, Ohio" is not only an instance of the evolution

of a literary theory; it marks also Anderson's achievement of a craftsmanship which is an essential part of that theory. (pp. 92-3)

For the communication of the immediate scene Sherwood Anderson has mastered his instrument. But, as he repeatedly asserts, mere realism is bad art. His peculiar quality resides in his intuition of something behind the scene. . . . It is in states of consciousness which eventuate in moments when the unconscious wells up and overwhelms personality with a sense of completion in the larger unity of life that his creative power resides, and it is with such moments that his characteristic stories deal. A recurring theme in them is the effort of the character to break down the wall which confines the individual in isolation from this general life which he shares with his fellows. (pp. 93-4)

Naturally in this pursuit of unity, in this breaking down of separateness, Anderson is much concerned with human relations and especially with sex. Through sex is maintained the great flow of the race of which each individual is but a drop. Sexual intercourse seems the most hopeful point of assault upon the wall which keeps each individual a prisoner. (pp. 94-5)

Anderson's later novels bear an increasingly definite relation to the social scene. For him, the Middle West reveals on a large scale the restless striving, the frustration of unfulfilled purpose, which is so often the theme of individual life treated in his short stories. (p. 95)

The best of Anderson's novels is undoubtedly "Dark Laughter." It is not only a good novel in structure and movement, but more subtly than "Poor White" or "Many Marriages" it is of that thoughtful quality which entitles it to rank among the novels of ideas. The two themes which are woven together are leading ones with Anderson— freedom through craftsmanship, and through love. (p. 97)

Anderson put forth a brief statement in *Story Magazine* which emphasizes what is true of his writing at its best— that in its fact, and its imaginative penetration beyond fact, it is a phase of his experience. . . . (p. 98)

> *Robert Morss Lovett, "Sherwood Anderson," in* After the Genteel Tradition: American Writers Since 1910, *edited by Malcolm Cowley, first edition, 1937 (copyright © 1936, 1937, 1948, 1964 by Malcolm Cowley; reprinted by permission of Southern Illinois University Press), Southern Illinois University Press, 1964, pp. 74-81.*

It would be worth pointing out that the great difference between Miss [Gertrude] Stein and Mr. Anderson is the difference between head and heart, if that were not to deny Miss Stein sentiment and Mr. Anderson intelligence. . . . There is a sense in which Sherwood Anderson may be said to have *felt* his characters and to have realized them in this way. After his talk with Gertrude Stein, Anderson felt (he was always to *feel*) that it was important for him *to think*. The results are seen in what he wrote after 1921.

Anderson's only thoroughly conscious primitivistic novel, *Dark Laughter*, . . . is an ineffectual book. Yet in conception it was excellent. Anderson meant to contrast the easy love of the negroes with the thwarted and abortive loves of intellectual people. . . . [One] cannot help thinking that Anderson's idea should have germinated a play rather than a novel. Yet had Anderson attempted it, the play would have been a more complete failure than the novel, for he cannot produce the talk of cultured people. (pp. 328-29)

Despite the bafflement of the heroine, despite brief excursions into pathology, *Kit Brandon* is one of the most readable of Anderson's books: living beings move through swift rounds of action, spiral to significance, or are hurled off centrifugally into the predestined void. Without offering a tenable conclusion as to a course of action, Anderson accomplished his purpose of revealing the social and psychological illness of America. And he did this literally without injury to his status of amateur—the one thing he seemed to hug as most precious. Yet perhaps he was right—amateurism is usually so briefly preserved in America that, if one can maintain his, he should make every effort to do so. That Anderson died, still a "gifted amateur" at sixty-four—at least in his public's notion of him—is not the least of his triumphs. (p. 331)

[To] employ intelligently the new Freudian psychology meant to depart from [his] preconceived simplicity and to affect a new subtlety and erudition. Gertrude Stein saw this, and despite the fact that her early grounding was in psychology, she refused for this reason to incorporate the "discoveries" of the Freudian school in her work. It is impossible to convince anyone who has really studied Sherwood Anderson sufficiently to appreciate the intelligence which has gone into the making of his short stories, say such masterpieces as "Hands," "I'm a Fool," and "I Want to Know Why," that Sherwood Anderson did not see this, too. He had, however, a far greater predilection for sexual themes than Miss Stein (whose writing is almost ascetic), and the new psychology appealed to him profoundly. How could he resolve the dilemma? There was one easy way, and being yet a creature of impulse, he took it. That way was to pretend to less intelligence than he had, to grope his way, apparently blindly, to Freudian themes. If he could persuade the reviewers that he was a humble earthworm in the purlieus of sex, they might ignore the rather startling incongruity of an earthworm on plush. So for a time Sherwood Anderson became progressively less intelligent. This plan worked admirably so far as the reviewers were concerned (they at once adopted the adjective "groping" for Anderson and have rung the changes on it ever since), but one has misgivings as to how the critics in time to come will view his affected witlessness. (pp. 676-77)

The Triumph of the Egg . . ., a collection of short stories and verse, is a key-book to the later Anderson. It opens with a poem which cannot be regarded as anything other than a deliberate advertisement of the author's alleged stupidity. "The Dumb Man," it is called, and it tells of three men waiting in a room while a woman on the floor above them keeps an assignation. Of these entirely unrelated meetings he can only say, "I have a wonderful story to tell but no way to tell it." Then, after the wholly admirable Primitivistic story, "I Want to Know Why," appears a narrative called "Seeds," in which the author himself is the chief character. . . . The story "Seeds" makes it clear that Anderson qualified his acceptance of Freud—he didn't believe in the Freudian cure of neuroses. . . . Freud was a pessimistic determinist because he believed that the *libido* controls our destinies; Anderson was no less a determinist and a far greater pessimist in that he believed that the libidinous intellectuals cannot deflect a diverted or frustrated

love stream into the proper channel it should run in. Put "Seeds" and "The Dumb Man" together and Anderson appears to the reader as he wanted to appear: the stupid ruminator on problems to which he knows there is no solution, the groper, the bovine Eye. (pp. 678-80)

"The Other Woman" is an attack upon the idea that an affair is necessarily detrimental to ultimate happiness, but in accomplishing this dissociation, Anderson forgets his attitude towards the Freudian cure. This kind of stupidity, we may be sure, is not deliberate. To offset, however, the not wholly satisfactory treatment of frustration in *The Triumph of the Egg* are three completely satisfactory Primitivistic studies: "I Want to Know Why," "The Egg," and "Motherhood." The impressionistic study called "Senility," repulsive though it is, is one of the best things Anderson did. (p. 681)

Oscar Cargill, in his Intellectual America: Ideas on the March *(reprinted with permission of Macmillan Publishing Co., Inc.; copyright © 1941 by Macmillan Publishing Co., Inc.; 1969 by Oscar Cargill), Macmillan, 1941.*

To the young intellectuals of the years after the First World War, Anderson seemed an authentic master. Though few of them shared his cult of the past, most of them understood that it expressed nothing but his despair of the future—and this, they shared fully. Like Anderson, they were adrift, and knew with certainty only what they did not want. They, too, were in revolt against materialism, mechanics, business, bigness and prudery. They agreed with him that it is only at rare moments that we live, and they were no more clear than was he about the nature of such moments. But, most of all, they responded to his resentment against all social dogmas or, as he called them, man-made truths. For they felt, as he did, that the moment one of the people took one of the truths to himself, called it his truth, and tried to live his life by it the truth he embraced became a falsehood. . . .

Though his radicalism of feeling made him seem contemporary, his point of view was actually that of an older generation. He spoke for those Americans who, dubious about the social effects of industrialization, still wished to think their life worth living when, to look at what it contained, it might not have seemed so. His books were significant chiefly because they recorded an average American's bewildered effort to find some meaning in his life. The meaning eluded Anderson, yet he never doubted that one existed. But this problem seldom occurred to his juniors. Most of them started from the premise that life has no meaning whatever. (p. 148)

Lloyd Morris, in his Postscript to Yesterday: America: The Last Fifty Years *(copyright 1947 by Lloyd Morris; reprinted by permission of Random House, Inc.), Random House, 1947.*

It has sometimes been said that Anderson's fiction marks a step in the naturalistic presentation of American life. This is hardly true in any vital sense of the term. For naturalism, although it presents the facts of life in detail, supposes no order nor outcome of them. Anderson was fundamentally an exuberant optimist. The superficial crudity of American life existed as a fact which must be taken into consideration in the presentation of life. In a brief essay called "An Apology for Crudity," which he published in *The Dial* in 1917, he made this clear, but with such stress that academic criticism, keen on the classification of literature, seized the phrase and forgot the intent.

Anderson called his characters "grotesques," but they were "grotesques" because of their involvement with the disorder of society. His apology for crudity was not a plea for it. Anderson's plea was actually for a resolution of the grotesqueness into a conformity with a world which was truly ordered. (p. 55)

At times Anderson would laugh at the didactic moralism of the New England gods whom he would so willingly discard, "trying to find honest, mid-western American gods." But he himself was the most moral of men and the most concerned with the lesson he could teach his time. He was not unique in this respect of course. The writers of his time, like the writers before them, were moralists. Dreiser, Masters, Mencken, Cabell, Stein, and the others, all shook fingers and pointed ways. But what marked Anderson and gave him his particular appeal to men younger than himself was his capacity for love and his sense of optimism. He restored the possibility of beginning again. He maintained the irrepressibility and vitality of youth. Brushed by the inadequacies of society, he was a reformer rather than a revolutionary, a revitalizer rather than a cynic. He could find again and again the joy of re-discovery and of crashing down the old barriers encrusting belief and the power of feeling. In the front ranks of the assault on Puritanism, Anderson was a leader among the New Puritans. (pp. 57-8)

Art was a means of devotion, and the poem or tale was a form of prayer. Words and rhetoric, formalized into clichés, were a barrier to communication, as liturgy had been. Anderson sensed this as others did, and as Emerson had done in his own efforts towards a renaissance. (p. 59)

The poets of our time, following in the same anti-intellectual path of intuitive affirmation, have been great, but great as lyric poets. Pound, Eliot, and Hart Crane, as examples, have even in their most ambitious works never achieved more than a string of linked lyrics. Anderson's strong emotional feeling could be sustained and formalized within the short story as though it too were a lyric. His novels were often linked tales.

The public did not always see the prose of Sherwood Anderson as an optimistic affirmation of the possibilities of American life. They saw the grotesques who figured the pages of his books, and saw them only as grotesques. But the writers and artists of his own time, and those younger than himself, learned to see as he saw, and learned partly by his example. (pp. 61-2)

> *Norman Holmes Pearson, "Anderson and the New Puritanism," in* The Newberry Library Bulletin: Sherwood Anderson Memorial Number *(copyright, 1948, by The Newberry Library), December, 1948, pp. 52-63.*

If read as social fiction *Winesburg* is somewhat absurd, for no such town could possibly exist. If read as a venture into abnormal psychology the book seems almost lurid, for within its total structure the behavior of its hysterics and paranoids is quite purposeless and, in the absence of any

norms to which their deviations might be compared, even incomprehensible. In fact, if read according to the usual expectations of 20th-century naturalistic or conventionally realistic fiction, *Winesburg* seems incoherent and the charge of emotion it can still raise inexplicable. . . . (p. 97)

In rather shy lyrical outbursts the book conveys a vision of American life as a depressed landscape cluttered with dead stumps, twisted oddities, grotesque and pitiful wrecks; a landscape in which ghosts fumble erratically and romance is reduced to mere fugitive brushings at night; a landscape eerie with the cracked echoes of village queers rambling in their lonely eccentricity. Again and again *Winesburg* suggests that beneath the exteriors of our life the deformed exert dominion, that the seeming health of our state derives from a deep malignancy. And *Winesburg* echoes with American loneliness, that loneliness which could once evoke Nigger Jim's chant of praise to the Mississippi pastoral but which has here become fearful and sour. (p. 98)

The two dozen central figures in *Winesburg* are hardly characters in the usual novelistic sense. They are not shown in depth or breadth, complexity or ambiguity; they are allowed no variations of action or opinion; they do not, with the exception of George Willard, the book's "hero," grow or decline. For Anderson is not trying to represent through sensuous images the immediate surface of human experience; he is rather drawing the abstract and deliberately distorted paradigm of an extreme situation, and for that purpose fully rounded characterizations could only be a complicating blemish.

The figures of *Winesburg* usually personify to fantastic excess a condition of psychic deformity which is the consequence of some crucial failure in their lives, some aborted effort to extend their personalities or proffer their love. (pp. 98-9)

Winesburg may . . . be read as a fable of American estrangement, its theme the loss of love. The book's major characters are alienated from the basic sources of emotional sustenance. . . . (p. 101)

In the book's best stretches there is a tension between its underlying loose oral cadences and the stiffened superimposed beat of a prose almost Biblical in its regularity. Anderson's prose is neither "natural" nor primitive; it is rather a hushed bardic chant, low-toned and elegiacally awkward, deeply related to native speech rhythms yet very much the result of literary cultivation.

But the final effectiveness of this prose is in its prevalent tone of tender inclusiveness. Between writer and materials there is an admirable equity of relationship. None of the characters is violated, none of the stories, even the failures, leaves the reader with the bitter sense of having been tricked by cleverness or cheapness or toughness. The ultimate unity of the book is a unity of feeling, a sureness of warmth, and a readiness to accept Winesburg's lost grotesques with the embrace of humility. Many American writers have taken as their theme the loss of love in the modern world, but few, if any at all, have so thoroughly realized it in the accents of love. (pp. 108-09)

For Anderson and for others like him, writing was at least as much a means by which to forge a personal identity as it was an objective discipline of the imagination. No wonder so many of the writers who came after Anderson, both

Thomas Wolfe the individual and the innumerable facsimile Thomas Wolfes, recognized in their lives one or another variant of his legend. Anderson seemed the archetype of all those writers who were trying to raise themselves to art by sheer emotion and sheer will, who suspected intellect as a cosmopolitan snare that would destroy their gift for divining America's mystic essence, and who abominated the society which had formed them but knew no counterpoise of value by which to escape its moral dominion.

It is in terms of his legend, and the needs which impelled him to advance it, that we can best understand Anderson's literary stances and stratagems. Consider, for one, his persistent assumption of innocence or what, in another context, has been called the credo of defenselessness: that literary approach to complex situations and ideas which insists on discounting their complexity in the name of creative passion. After a time, no doubt, Anderson did exploit his innocence, perhaps because he sensed that there are situations in which defenselessness frankly acknowledged is the only possible defense. (pp. 246-47)

In one strand of his work, the lesser strand, legend and deprivation can be seen reinforcing each other. This is the Anderson of the political mindlessness of *Marching Men,* the emasculated sexuality of *Many Marriages,* the folk clichés of *Dark Laughter;* the Anderson who took to cultural fashion the way other novelists take to drink; who staked everything on enthusiasm and sentiment and in their absence tried awkwardly to simulate them; who saw the artist's life as an unambiguous struggle of defiant rectitude against commercial contamination; who was forever concerned with a search for freedom but lacked the spiritual rigor to define that freedom in terms of the scope and tension it had had for the great writers of the past. (pp. 247-48)

Read for moral explication, as a guide to life, his work must seem unsatisfactory; it simply does not tell us enough. But there is another, more fruitful way of reading his work: as the expression of a sensitive witness to the national experience and as the achievement of a story teller who created a small body of fiction unique in American writing for the lyrical purity of its feeling. So regarded, his best work becomes a durable part of the American literary structure.

Unquestionably durable is Anderson's testimony on the most dramatic social development in American life, the transition from an agrarian to an industrial society. No novelist, no historian has portrayed this segment of American experience with an intimacy and poignancy superior to Anderson's in *Poor White* and in his stories; no other American writer has so thoroughly communicated the sense of that historical moment when the native sweetness had not yet been lost to our life, when the nation fumbled on the verge of outwardness and began to stir from provinciality but had not yet toughened into imperial assurance. In the shabby crevices of this world Anderson discovered the lonely and deformed souls who would never be noticed by official society. In the craftsmen of the towns, whom history had passed by and left stricken and helpless, he found concealed reserves of feeling, of muted torment and love. More than most of his contemporaries among American writers, Anderson insisted that frustration and deprivation were at the base of American life, but he did so in order to credit the unused emotional resources, the unmeasured potentials that were also there. (pp. 249-50)

Almost always we categorize him as a writer who moved us greatly in adolescence but now lacks the power to affect us in maturity—as if it were quite safe to assume that our adolescent responses were so patently invalid and unworthy of selective preservation, or as if we could safely compartmentalize our lives, simply discarding in adulthood what we were in our youth. When we use the tag of adolescence to dismiss Anderson's work we forget that even in our first reading his stories appealed to our sense of "oldness" rather than immaturity, that often enough it was in those stories that we were first touched by forebodings of decay and loss. By falsely reducing adolescence to the merely callow and sentimental, we evade the real problem posed by Anderson's work, which is to discriminate between feeling realized and feeling forced or simulated. And when we say—this is the favorite gambit of hostile critics—that Anderson's work deals not with reality but with adolescent gropings, we ignore the reality of those very gropings; we ignore, as well, the fact that from these gropings none of us is or should be exempt. (p. 251)

Anderson's work becomes objectionable only when he ceases to grope, ceases to extend his curiosity and affection; only when he begins to imitate and unwittingly caricature the eagerness and openness of his best writing. The critic's job then becomes one of discriminating between that part of Anderson's work in which callowness and sentimentality frequently corrupt his achievement and that more durable part in which adolescence comes through in a radiant comeliness, a sweet surge of affectivity. Once such a distinction is made there can be no question about the value of *Winesburg* and *Poor White,* of "Death in the Woods" and "The Man Who Became a Woman."

It now becomes possible to consider the question that must suggest itself to every student of Anderson's career: what should he have done after his brief burst of fertility, after *Winesburg* and *The Triumph of the Egg*? The critical point of his career came at about 1923, the year when both *Horses and Men* and *Many Marriages* were published. *Horses and Men* was the last sustained expression of his most successful native manner, and *Many Marriages* the beginning of his disastrous venture into Lawrencian precincts. Among Anderson's friends and critics there have been two opinions about the crisis he then faced. For his Chicago friends and a few of his critics Anderson was essentially a folk or sectional writer who did his best work in the Midwest and was bewildered and contaminated by the cosmopolitan East. For his New York friends and most of his critics Anderson was a writer of undisciplined talent who, after a few creative years, desperately needed a sustaining vision of life and an organized knowledge of craft.

Abstractly, either of these estimates of Anderson, if they led to a consistent course of action, might have helped him avoid his debacles. Had he deliberately restricted himself to the short forms in which his talent was most at home, to those subjects he knew surpassingly well, and to a program of selective and sparse publication, he might have continued producing first-rate stories in the *Winesburg* manner. Had he made a herculean effort to educate himself to the complexities of modern life and thought, to use his mind at its full potential, and to relate himself actively to the great tradition of the novel, he might just possibly have become an interesting social novelist. But in actuality neither of these choices was available to him.

Anderson's Chicago friends ignore the fact that he was "contaminated" by cosmopolitanism before he left the Midwest; the whole bent of his literary life was toward the big city, toward the aggressively modern. (pp. 252-53)

Still less practical was the other proposed course. By 1923 Anderson was a man in his late forties who had gone through the most painful struggles merely to become a writer and had at last won praise to an extent he could hardly have anticipated. The kind of transformation which might have made him a highly conscious artist would have been possible only under the urging and guidance of an authoritative body of literary opinion. But it was precisely this opinion which was missing from American life: the culture of the 1920's was itself beset by the weaknesses that would soon cripple Anderson. (Scott Fitzgerald, for example, wrote that *Many Marriages* was Anderson's best book!) To have urged, in these circumstances, that Anderson attempt a total self-transformation would merely have been an oblique way of suggesting that he stop writing. It was his tragedy that after the early 1920's he was trapped between two worlds: he could find sustenance neither in the deep kinships of the folk bard nor in the demanding traditions of the sophisticated artist. (p. 254)

There is a sense in which it may be said that Anderson has not had an appreciable influence on American writing. To be sure, there are Steinbeck and Saroyan who have brought to extremity the inferior aspects of his work. And there is Hemingway who repudiated Anderson in the name of craft but still owes him many debts. But while Steinbeck and Saroyan could enlarge on his occasional sentimentalism and Hemingway could tighten and rigidify his style, no American writer has yet been able to realize that strain of lyrical and nostalgic feeling which in Anderson's best work reminds one of another and greater poet of tenderness, Turgenev. At his best Anderson creates a world of authentic sentiment, and while part of the meaning of his career is that sentiment is not enough for a writer, the careers of those who follow him—those who swerve to Steinbeck's sentimentality or Hemingway's toughness—illustrate how rare genuine sentiment still is in our literature. (p. 255)

But surely there is, there should be a place in our culture, even if only a minor one, for Sherwood Anderson. His faults, his failures and defeats can hardly be ignored: he was almost always limited in moral sensibility and social perspective. Yet there were a few moments when he spoke, as almost no one else among American writers, with the voice of love. (p. 256)

> *Irving Howe, "The Book of the Grotesque"*
> *(originally published in the* Partisan Review,
> *Winter, 1951; copyright © 1951 by Partisan*
> *Review, Inc.) and "An American as Artist,"*
> *in his* Sherwood Anderson *(copyright, 1951,*
> *by William Sloane Associates, Inc.; re-*
> *printed by permission of William Morrow &*
> *Co., Inc.), William Sloane, 1951, pp. 91-109,*
> *243-56.*

[Anderson] expected people to make fun of, ridicule him. He expected people nowhere near his equal in stature or accomplishment or wit or anything else, to be capable of making him appear ridiculous.

That was why he worked so laboriously and tediously and indefatigably at everything he wrote. It was as if he said to himself: "This anyway will, shall, must be invulnerable." It was as though he wrote not even out of the consuming unsleeping appeaseless thirst for glory for which any normal artist would destroy his aged mother, but for what to him was more important and urgent: not even for mere truth, but for purity, the exactitude of purity. His was not the power and rush of Melville, who was his grandfather, nor the lusty humor for living of Twain, who was his father; he had nothing of the heavy-handed disregard for nuances of his older brother, Dreiser. His was that fumbling for exactitude, the exact word and phrase within the limited scope of a vocabulary controlled and even repressed by what was in him almost a fetish of simplicity, to milk them both dry, to seek always to penetrate to thought's uttermost end. He worked so hard at this that it finally became just style: an end instead of a means: so that he presently came to believe that, provided he kept the style pure and intact and unchanged and inviolate, what the style contained would have to be first rate: it couldn't help but be first rate, and therefore himself too. (p. 5)

[He] was sometimes a sentimentalist in his writing (so was Shakespeare sometimes) but he was never impure in it. He never scanted it, cheapened it, took the easy way; never failed to approach writing except with humility and an almost religious, almost abject faith and patience and willingness to surrender, relinquish himself to and into it. He hated glibness; if it were quick, he believed it was false too. (pp. 6-7)

> *William Faulkner, "A Note on Sherwood*
> *Anderson" (originally published under a dif-*
> *ferent title in* Atlantic, *June, 1953), in* Es-
> *says, Speeches & Public Letters, edited by*
> *James B. Meriwether (copyright © 1965 by*
> *Random House, Inc.; reprinted by permis-*
> *sion of Random House, Inc.), Random*
> *House, 1965, pp. 3-10.*

Sherwood Anderson influenced and inspired me perhaps more profoundly than any other American writer. The critics and reviewers may not like this statement, and a few of them may cast a brickbat or two at me because many of them have committed themselves in print to the assertion that Theodore Dreiser was the biggest influence in my literary career and that I have been and am a disciple of Dreiser. In denying this I am guilty of no disservice to Dreiser. I have written extensively on his work, and I have never denied a debt to it and to him. But in 1927, when I was an aspiring and unpublished young writer, it was Anderson who touched me most deeply. (p. 164)

[Anderson's] work was closer to my own areas of experience. As a boy I had jeeringly been called "Four Eyes." Because of this and other experiences I had sometimes felt that I was a goof. Anderson's sympathy for the grotesque, the queer, the socially abnormal, evinced with feeling, sensibility, and simple humanity in *Winesburg, Ohio*, struck immediate chords of response within me. I was more like Anderson's characters than I was like Dreiser's.

The book of Anderson's which influenced me most was *Tar, a Midwest Childhood*. This is a re-created story of Anderson's own boyhood. It is not an accurate autobiography. Rather, it exhibits that fixed tendency in Anderson to fantasize himself and his past. But in *Tar* he re-created, with meaning and significance, the inner life, the dreams and aspirations of a country boy.

I read *Tar* in a gasoline filling station at Thirty-fifty Street and Morgan Avenue early in 1927. I burned and thrilled with excitement. The drab industrial scene about me, the bare ugly factory walls, the noisy dusty corner all fled from my mind. I lived in this book and in an Ohio countryside. And I found in this experience with *Tar* a means of reaffirmation of self. I can formulate now the logic of what I then intuitively felt. If the inner life of a boy in an Ohio country town of the nineteenth century was meaningful enough to be the material for a book like *Tar,* then perhaps my own feelings and emotions and the feelings and emotions of those with whom I had grown up were important. My self-confidence grew in one leap. My ambition to write was solidified and strengthened. I thought of writing a novel about my own boyhood, about the neighborhood in which I had grown up. Here was one of the seeds that led to *Studs Lonigan.*

Sherwood Anderson was one of the most sensitive, significant, and influential American writers in this century. His stories such as "I Want to Know Why," "I'm a Fool," "Death in the Woods," "The Triumph of an Egg," and those of *Winesburg, Ohio* are among the finest ever written by any American. His use of idiom has a rare flavor and his simple prose rises to a level of poetry. In a few short pages, the hearts and inner lives of his men and women and boys open up for us. He endows his characters with something of his own great creativity. He found a strain of poetry in the experiences of boyhood, and in the spirit of sad, neglected, and queer people. (pp. 165-66)

By and large, much of American humor had been directed against the physically or the socially abnormal, the freak, the odd person, the foreigner, the person who in one way or another deviates from the stereotype of the middle-class regular fellow. But Sherwood Anderson showed most sympathy for those who deviated from the standard stereotypes in one way or another. In fact, he characterized *Winesburg, Ohio* as a book of grotesqueries. In these seemingly grotesque people he saw something very human and very common—a spark of creativity. Grotesqueness, freakishness, aggressiveness are treated and interpreted as a substitute, a negative expression for a frustration of the creativity and of the need for love in human beings. The singular humanness of his characters is bound up with insights of this order. The need for creativity and expression, which he himself felt, aided and guided him in perceiving the same need in others, in people who were simple, uneducated, and, sometimes, psychologically or socially peculiar. (pp. 166-67)

It is probable that Anderson never read such a book as Thorstein Veblen's *The Instinct of Workmanship.* Nonetheless, there is some parallel between him and Veblen. . . . In the last years of the nineteenth century and the early ones of this, Veblen observed many of the psychological effects of industrialism on the nature of man. Positing an instinct of workmanship, a conception which bears resemblance with what Anderson saw in the need of human beings to be creative and to express themselves, Veblen analyzed how the development of industrialism was thwarting this so-called instinct. And what Veblen analyzed is similar to what Sherwood Anderson revealed directly and concretely with the insight and feelings of an artist.

Similarly, it is fairly certain that Anderson never read any of the philosophical articles of the late George Herbert Mead. But again there is a parallel. Mead saw, much as did the writer, the basis for communication and the development of the self. In Anderson, there is a continuous groping to gain a sense of another. One way of enlarging our understanding of Anderson's work is to see it in terms of the question or problem of identity. Searching and questing for a clearer realization of his own identity, Anderson sought it in others, and he sought for a sense of others in himself. (pp. 167-68)

> *James T. Farrell, "A Note on Sherwood Anderson," in* Perspective *(copyright 1954 by* Perspective), *June, 1954 (and reprinted in his* Reflections at Fifty and Other Essays, *Vanguard Press, 1954, pp. 164-68).*

Because Anderson wrote again and again of flights, because his style and structure were deliberately fugitive and elusive in character, because of his many marriages, because in a genuine sense his life for the nearly thirty years after 1912 hinged around repeated flights, it is easy to see in his work nothing but flight—that, of course, being one from reality. Such a judgment is not wholly false, but it is partial. . . . Anderson . . . was more seeker than fugitive. What he found was without doubt nebulous, but his search was none the less genuine. In his writing there was little to suggest that he ever came upon a body of finally satisfying ideas or experiences, but, if one look at his work rather than through it, the achievement of Anderson's search can be defined. It was nothing less than a sense of self, to be achieved in the craft of writing, which the world of business and middle class propriety had destroyed. He, in a radical sense, had rejected that world, but having done so he turned to the creation of another world which could be put in its place. His effort, no doubt, was quixotic, but in one way it accomplished its end. Anderson did in a genuine sense, define himself in his best work. Stories of the quality of "Death in the Woods," "The Man Who Became a Woman," or "The Egg," gave to him what he sought, and they conveyed an act of fulfillment to the reader. They were realizations of what, potentially, Anderson could be—the imaginatively honest and acute narrator of his own bewildering quest. His achievement was lyrical, but, within that limit, one of occasional high success. (pp. 48-9)

[This], for Anderson, [was] a crucial change, that from writing vitalistic propaganda to himself, or of plotting his course in his writing, to imaginative creation for its own sake. This was the essential difference between the two early novels and the great stories of *Winesburg, The Triumph of the Egg,* and *Horses and Men,* and it remained throughout his career the difference between all his work of the first rate and that below first rate. Literature was a creating of persons, a respecting of them, and a realizing by the writer's imagination of their truth. Anderson as craftsman, his key word in this regard, was to be two things simultaneously. He was the artist of language and the artist of life. (pp. 53-4)

The early Anderson had been, as much as he could, a pessimistic rebel crying to himself the news of doom. After *Mid-American Chants* with their broad acceptance, he could pick up the pieces of what he still regarded as a spoiled and broken life for detailed and genuinely loving treatment. *Winesburg* and the *Triumph* stories were not acts of judgment but of commiseration and understanding. . . . Anderson's new approach to the Midwest drew its strength from humility and love. There was also the unabashed lyricism which, though it was to be transmuted in the later work by sympathy, here cut loose from the clogs of realistic convention. But particularly, the *Chants* revealed a concentrated effort to make poetry out of Anderson's own language. This was simple and limited, frequently not sufficient to the demands he put upon it. In the *Chants,* for the first time, he came down upon his language, not to prune and order, but to let come from it whatever was, in nature, there. This was a part of his acceptance. He had felt in Gertrude Stein the achievement of poetry in the aggressively simple. And that, in a literary way, was where his own work must begin and end. (pp. 55-6)

> *Bernard Duffey, in his* The Chicago Renaissance in American Letters: A Critical History *(copyright © 1954 by The Michigan State University Press), Michigan State University Press, 1954 (and reprinted in* The Achievement of Sherwood Anderson: Essays in Criticism, *edited by Ray Lewis White, University of North Carolina Press, 1966, pp. 46-61).*

Sherwood Anderson, as no one needs to be told who has ever read a page of his, was a very lonely man. He was throughout his actually brief literary career also a very uncertain man, who could never be quite sure that he had made good in that unpredictable literary world for which he had abandoned a business career. . . . And he was at the same time a man who just had to keep writing—writing was a profession, a way of life, a condition of his survival. He needed to write all the time, and what he wrote most of, we know now, were letters. He often wrote dozens of letters before settling down to his daily task; he sometimes spent a whole day writing letters, though he did not always mail them—they gave him contact with others, they released and stimulated him to write stories and novels, and above all they kept him in motion, at the very act of writing.

So there are a lot of letters by Sherwood Anderson—five thousand in the Newberry Library in Chicago. Out of these Howard Mumford Jones and Walter B. Rideout have selected four hundred, which cover exactly the twenty-five years of Anderson's literary career, from 1916 to his death in 1941, and have been chosen, the editors tell us, to represent Anderson's attitudes toward writing and his relations with other writers. (p. 223)

The fact is—it will hardly astonish anyone who knows his mind—that Anderson on the subject of writing is moving rather than interesting. There are wonderful moments in this correspondence, for Sherwood Anderson was an extraordinarily open, charming and generous person. But he did write too many of these letters just to keep himself writing; he wrote even when he had little to say—or, what is the same thing for anyone writing letters—he often wrote to people as if he were writing novels at them rather than because he had something to say *to* them that could be said only in a letter. What one misses in this correspondence is the poise, the close directness, even the gossipiness, of the great letter writers—whose letters are great because they are in the world, and are not trying to remake it, and themselves, out of their loneliness. Anderson's letters are almost too serious to be good, and they are so full of his being a

writer that it is sometimes hard to tell whether we are reading a page from his novels or an apologia for them. . . . For Anderson, writing was not just a means of personal expression, but a search for salvation; it was the way he saved his own life, every day he wrote, in the hope that he was also helping to save his country.

But this is a very American fault: writing for itself alone, writing as something really gratuitous, inwardly free and wise, is the rarest thing in our literature. Reading these letters, with their heartbreaking recital of all those projects begun but laid aside, of books he finished but were not good enough to publish—and all the while writing had to give him a living, satisfy his conscience, and release him from himself—one wonders if the tragedy of Anderson was really, as is so often said, that he began so late. (pp. 224-25)

[We] must take him as he was, with all his high hopes, his suffering, his naive artfulness, his fidelity to the vision. And here the letters have their own story to tell; here is where they become genuine, as a portrait of the artist in America. The early letters to Waldo Frank, Paul Rosenfeld, Van Wyck Brooks show him humbly deferential to his mentors and "betters". . . . These early letters, with their authentic Whitmanesque cry of "Brother," their eagerness and high hopes for a whole generation fighting its way out of the nineteenth century, are a moving reminder of the fraternalism among writers that died with our entry into the First World War.

It is when we get into the 'twenties, when *Winesburg* so quickly became a classic and Anderson enjoyed the one unqualified success he ever really knew, that we begin to catch those first notes of entreaty, of panic, of needing to attach himself to some cause or doctrine, that was the symbol of Anderson's trouble. For successful as he was and generally admired, he was simply not growing as an artist must. How many cities he tried to escape to! The very names on the letters are a silent record of Anderson's desperate flights around the country, of his search for the "primitive" in New Orleans or Mexico or wherever, of his broken marriages, of his hopes to find in some out-of-the-way hotel either comradeship with "simple" people or just peace enough to get on with his novels. These letters already prepare one for that visible breakdown of his talent in the 'thirties which led him to attach himself to tenant farmers in the South and to labor struggles as he had once attached himself to "the man and woman thing." "Anyway," he writes in one terrible and revealing sentence, "I am going to try that now." . . . By the late 'thirties he seems to have been often desperate, glad to get commissions from magazines he formerly despised, and—though the most generous of friends—inevitably saddened by the extent to which his erstwhile protégés, Faulkner and Hemingway, had outdistanced him.

Yet even in this last, painful period we catch, amid the yearning and repetitiousness, more than one reminder of the essential, the unforgettable, the beautiful Anderson. How like him to say, still: "Always the imagined world is more important than what we call reality". . . . [How] well he understood that "Man's real life is lived out there in the imaginative world, and that is where we sell him out"; how real he was, in what he really was. He never let go of that trembling vision of love which is all we ever offer to the great mystery around us. (pp. 226-28)

Alfred Kazin, "The Letters of Sherwood Anderson," in his The Inmost Leaf: A Selection of Essays *(© 1953 by Alfred Kazin; reprinted by permission of Harcourt Brace Jovanovich, Inc.), Harcourt, 1955, pp. 223-28.*

Anderson renders qualities of personality and dimensions of experience beyond anything in the work of Crane, Norris, London, or Dreiser. He is far freer from taboos than they; he works on smaller areas; he does not condescend to his characters nor does he feel obliged to defend them. As a result he has laid bare an American heart which had not been known until it was caught and felt in his stories. Whereas by the severest standards Dreiser is ponderous, Norris turgid, Crane staccato and tense, and London often close to ridiculous, Anderson is mellow, lyrical, controlled, and glowing with sonorous warmth. (pp. 157-58)

Anderson, in almost everything he writes, searches out the emotional values involved in an experience. . . .

Anderson explores two major themes. One is discovery, the other inhibition. These themes correspond with the demands of the two branches of the divided stream of transcendentalism. (p. 159)

The theme of inhibition [which appears in almost every story of Anderson's] obviously reflects the materialistic branch of the transcendental stream when it identifies spiritual and material privation. If Anderson ever suggested that all we need in America is a tradition of manners and devout observances to control the wildness of the yokel, he would be returning to orthodoxy and dualism. This he never does.

Rather he evolves the concept of the *grotesque* to indicate what small-town life has done to its people. The grotesque is the person who has become obsessed by a mannerism, an idea, or an interest to the point where he ceases to be Man in the ideal sense. [This condition is] the state wherein the defect has become the man, while his potentialities have remained undeveloped. (p. 160)

Again and again the stories of Anderson are marked by a union of surprise and insight. What was apt to be merely shocking or horrendous or sensational in the work of Zola and Norris acts in Anderson's stories as a key to a fuller grasp of the extraordinary range of "normal" reality. He has got into the heart of bizarre, even fantastic experiences which are nevertheless also universal. (p. 161)

These ideas are all in the naturalistic tradition in that they are motivated by the feeling of need for their expression of the "inner man." Anderson assumes that this inner man exists and is good and "should" be permitted to fulfill itself through love and experience. The need is alive and eager; it is the social order that prevents its satisfaction. (p. 162)

Anderson does not master the structure of the novel. His poignant sketches, which contain some of the best and most memorable writing in our literature, do not "connect" naturally into the sustained expression of the longer form. Perhaps the scale is too narrow or the feeling too intense and special. Perhaps Anderson could not achieve the necessary objectivity. Certainly the patterns of protest and socialism do not provide the sort of frame upon which he could weave. . . .

As a device of presentation he tells his stories through the minds of ignorant—or certainly unstudied—narrators who have no sense of selection and arrangement and so give a story that has the tone and flavor of free association. Here in the mixture of impressionist rendering of experience and the device of the story told by a disorderly narrator we find the heart of Anderson's form. He makes a virtue of beginning a story at the end and ending it at the middle. He gives away information which would create suspense of the conventional sort and yet contrives to produce a surprise and a satisfaction at the end of his story by a psychological revelation or a sharing of experience that suddenly becomes coherent out of the chaos of the narrator's apparently objectless rambling. Often what begins as incoherence emerges as the disorder caused by emotion which the story discloses and which indeed turns out to be the cause of its telling. (p. 165)

Charles Child Walcutt, "Sherwood Anderson: Impressionism and the Buried Life," in his American Literary Naturalism: A Divided Stream *(© 1956, Charles Child Walcutt), University of Minnesota Press, Minneapolis, 1956 (and reprinted in* The Achievement of Sherwood Anderson: Essays in Criticism, *edited by Ray Lewis White, University of North Carolina Press, 1966, pp. 156-73).*

[The] temptation to ascribe an actual influence [of Freud on Anderson] is easily indulged. The reasons for this easy ascription are not obscure. Most important, of course, was the recognition that Freud had contributed to American criticism the term *repression,* which acquired new significance, almost immediately, for the fields of sociology, history, biography, and literary criticism. Anderson was hailed as the leader in the American fight against conventional repression; his novels appeared coincidentally with the beginning of the interest in the new psychology. He dealt with frustration, in many cases with the frustration of normal sex expression. . . . Anderson hesitated himself to acknowledge any influence; that is, he never committed himself fully, in answer to his critics. Though in many other cases, such as the influence of Gertrude Stein, George Borrow, and James Joyce, he was ready enough to admit influences, and in some cases to embrace his "mentors" enthusiastically, he was oddly silent about Freud and psychoanalysis. (pp. 182-83)

Anderson's themes are primarily bound by his search for the causes of man's frustration. What makes men more decent and moral, than healthy and sensual beings? The figures of *Winesburg, Ohio,* and of *Poor White* are victims of both external restrictions and of their own timidity—a sort of perverted gentleness. The source of much impotence lies in basic repressions of society—the business world, industrialism, middle-class decorum. Anderson is anxious to point out that primitive life in unimpeded by such barriers to happiness. He offers a variety of suggestions to imprisoned man: the totalitarian, rhythmic discipline preached by Beaut McGregor in *Marching Men;* simple repudiation, as practised by John Webster in *Many Marriages* and by Aline Grey in *Dark Laughter;* the communism of *Beyond Desire.* Fundamentally, Anderson offers no real solution to the problems he raises.

Anderson himself admits the power of dreams and visions

in the creative life. It is as though he deliberately constructed a world whose particulars and relationships would be valid only in the imagination. He is rarely content with simple realism; he abhors the world of fact—the world of the Puritan, he calls it. His frame of reference is almost always the psychic center of personal experience. (pp. 190-91)

The author's critical judgment which ordinarily manifests itself in selection of judgments stated or implied, is replaced in Anderson by *sympathy*—that is, in the etymological sense of that word, a "suffering with." This is especially true, since there is an autobiographical fragment in almost every one of his creations—they are creatures both of his imagination and of his temperament. This preoccupation with the soul of himself, as one critic has put it, demands recognition of Anderson as a writer whose explorations of the psyche are peculiar to him. (p. 191)

Anderson proceeded originally from a recognition that "something was wrong"; the *bête noire* was not clearly known. It is referred to variously as industrialism, the business mind, the sophistication of the civilized man, the white fear of wholesome impulses.

Were the critics altogether wrong in calling Anderson the "American Freudian"? There is no evidence that he wrote with Freud's works, or a psychoanalytic dictionary, at his elbow. The critics labeled Anderson as they did for this reason: almost any one of his characters could, at a certain stage of his career, have walked into an analyst's office and been justified in asking for treatment. . . . In all cases the clinical report and Anderson's narrative report would have had a different conclusion. There is some justification in noting the parallel courses of psychoanalysis and Anderson's fiction, but there seems little evidence to prove that those two courses intersected at any vital points. It is as though Anderson [in *Dark Laughter*] were thrusting upon Freud the burden of clarifying the artist's analysis: "Men who have passed the age of thirty and who have intelligence understand such things. A German scientist can explain perfectly. If there is anything you do not understand in human life consult the works of Dr. Freud." . . . If you have been unable to follow with me into the lives of these characters, Anderson seems to be saying; if they still seem queer to you—if their acts are merely violent and inexplicably so—Dr. Freud has studied these matters calmly and scientifically, and he will aid you. But if you do go to him, you will have failed to understand much of what I wish to say to you. (pp. 191-92)

> *Frederick J. Hoffman, in his* Freudianism and the Literary Mind *(copyright © 1957 by The Louisiana State University Press), second edition, Louisiana State University Press, 1957 (and reprinted in* The Achievement of Sherwood Anderson: Essays in Criticism, *edited by Ray Lewis White, University of North Carolina Press, 1966, pp. 174-93).*

[Sherwood Anderson] is one of the purest, most intense poets of loneliness—the loneliness of being an individual and of being buffeted in the current, the loneliness of isolation and that of being swallowed. One type represents the traditional retreat into the self for self-possession; the other, and its adversary at times, arises out of the angry resentment of a sensible man in an assemblyline civilization. Anderson's work is a manual of the ways in which loneliness can be used. It was his nourishment and sometimes his poison. (pp. 56-7)

The romantic sentimentalist held up his mirror to look at his world, peered deeply, saw himself instead, of course; wrote painfully about what he saw; and it turned out that he was writing about the world after all, squeezing it by this palpitating mid-western honesty out of his grandiose sorrows and longings. Sometimes, anyway. He was not a pure man; he had a kind of farmer cunning, plus his groaning artiness and pretense, with which he hoped to convince the "word-fellows" and the pretty girls that he was a Poet although not a young one. What he really wanted was to be alone in that succession of gray furnished rooms he talked about so eloquently, making immortal the quiet noise and gentle terror of his childhood. (p. 58)

All his work, the abysmal failures and the successes which have helped to construct the vision Americans have of themselves, represents an innocent, factitious, improvised, schemed reflection and elaboration of the elements of his own life. He turns the private into the public and then back into the private again. (p. 59)

The line between the subjects of Anderson's stories and Sherwood Anderson himself is barely drawn. His relation as artist to his material, as shaper of his material, is as intense and personal as that of any modern writer. Unlike most writing dealing with unhappy and frustrated people, Anderson's work is absolutely authentic in the double sense—not merely in communicating the feeling of these people as people, but also in giving us the conviction that the author shares both their bitter frustration and their evanescent occasional triumphs. By comparison with Sherwood Anderson, Dostoevsky is a monument of cool detachment. . . . He has a primitive idealism, a spoiled romanticism like that of Rousseau: we could be all innocent and pure in our crafts if the machines of America and the fates that bring machines did not cripple us. (p. 61)

In many writers dealing with the grim facts of our lives, the personal sense of triumph at encompassing the material adds a note of confidence which is at variance with the story itself. Hemingway is a good example; his heroes go down to defeat, but Papa Hemingway the chronicler springs eternal. In Anderson this external note of confidence and pride in craft is lacking. . . . The stories of Winesburg are unselfconsciously committed to him as he is sworn true to them; the identification—a variety of loyalty —is torturingly complete; he is related to his material with a love that lacks esthetic detachment and often lacks the control which comes with that detachment. They are practically unique in this among modern storytelling, and it is partially this that gives them their sometimes embarrassing, often tormenting and unforgettable folk quality. (p. 63)

Except for the poetic schoolteacher and a very few others, women are not women in Anderson's stories. There are the girls who suffer under the kind of sensitivity, passion, and lonely burning which was Anderson's own lot; and then there are the Women. For Anderson women have a strange holy power; they are earth-mothers, ectoplasmic spirits, sometimes succubi, rarely individual living creatures. In "Hands" they are not girls but "maidens," where the word gives a quaint archaic charm to the creature who taunts poor, damned, lonely Wing Biddlebaum. The berry-picking "maidens" gambol while the boys are "boisterous," and the hero flutters in his tormented realm between the sexes. (pp. 64-5)

He carried his childhood like a hurt warm bird held to his middle-aged breast as he walked out of his factory into the life of art. The primitive emotions of childhood are the raw material of all poetry. Sometimes the indulgence of them to the exclusion of the mature perspectives of adult life prevents Anderson from equalling his aspiration and own best work. (p. 67)

> Herbert Gold, "The Fair Apple of Progress" (originally published under a different title in The Hudson Review, Vol. X, No. 4, Winter, 1957-58), in his The Age of Happy Problems (copyright © 1958 by Herbert Gold; used by permission of The Dial Press), Dial, 1962, pp. 56-67.

[Anderson's] ideal of literature seemed partly to have been derived from his training as a composer of advertising copy: he liked to make simple statements and to emphasize them by repetition—often to the ennui of his readers; and partly from the *Dial* and the Stieglitz group and other writers whom he had met when he came to New York and who had encouraged him to take himself seriously. All these persons were city-bred, and they had had no such experience of the common life as that from which Sherwood Anderson had gleaned his Mississippi stories. For most of them, the practice of literature was a formal affair for which one dressed, or even a kind of sacrament for which one put on priestly robes. It is true that he came to the defense of Mark Twain when Van Wyck Brooks was taking him to task for falling short of the writer's high rôle, and that he felt, as he wrote to Brooks, that his own story *I'm a Fool* was in the vein of *Huckleberry Finn*. But this story and its companion piece *I Want to Know Why* are exceptional in Anderson's work. He preferred to develop in a void those dreamlike and humorless fables in which people almost never talk like the kind of provincial Americans among whom the author had spent most of his life; and it rarely occurred to Anderson to exploit for the purposes of his fiction the immense amount of material—anecdotes, adventures, queer characters—which, for purposes of conversation, he had always so entertainingly on tap. (pp. 127-28)

> Edmund Wilson, in his The American Earthquake: A Documentary of the Twenties and Thirties (reprinted with the permission of Farrar, Straus & Giroux, Inc.; copyright © 1958 by Edmund Wilson), Octagon, 1971.

[For] the conservatives of 1919, *Winesburg* may have appeared to be tunneling under all the established values of American life. And for some of the radicals of the day, *Winesburg was* exposing the sewers, and opening for public inspection the inadequate drainage system of the luxurious American psyche. (p. 234)

Yet, preoccupied as Anderson may seem to be with sexual maladjustment, very early in the book you realize that his concern is not with human copulation, as it were, but with human isolation: and sex, which is a prelude to love as well as an ending, is the method used by Anderson, like D. H. Lawrence, to convey this isolation. (p. 235)

The point of *Winesburg* is precisely that, while human understanding is so often disfigured and disjointed here—it is still possible. These people *are* lovers, and if their object of love hasn't been found, it *can* be found. 'People live and die alone even in Winesburg,' Anderson says, and the 'even,' which invites a comparison, embodies the theme. This is surely the central meaning of the volume: the psychological factor that holds these apparently scattered and 'plotless' sketches together and gives them an inner unity, just as the village scene gives them an outward unity. (p. 236)

No, *Winesburg* is not a radical but a nostalgic document. This opening gun for a decade of revolt is not an indictment but an evocation of a society. As you follow Anderson's course to this point—the increasing fear of a standardized American social arrangement and the distaste for contemporary life which pervades his early novels as against the return, in *Mid-American Chants,* to the belief of his fathers in village streets and to those rich mid-western cornfields through which you approach his group of Ohio tales—you see, certainly, that *Winesburg* answers his early conflicts. Like the stranger of his story, Anderson has found his 'thing to love,' the thing for which he has been searching, and without which, so he believes, his own destruction would be inevitable. (pp. 237-38)

Yet the central issue remains: when Anderson turns from this rural scene, what is there in his own age that he can equally give himself to and belong with in order to avoid the threat of spiritual destruction? (p. 239)

If Sherwood Anderson is one of the first social rebels of the early twenties to attack the illusions of civilization in the United States, and in this sense helps to set the tone of the decade, he is also—and this is the main sense of his work as a whole—one of the last to believe in the possibility of civilization in the United States. (p. 250)

[Blocked] on all sides by the apparently unbeatable America of the machine age, the writer turns in upon himself.

During the years from 1924 to 1929 will ensue that stream, that flood of reminiscences, memoirs, accounts, autobiographies, and barely disguised novels of childhood, adolescence, and maturity—those voluminous introspective studies of Anderson's which have to a large degree obscured his early and late concern with the life around him, and given him the connotation of an egoism which he least of all deserves. (p. 251)

A Story Teller's Story . . . occupies a transitional place in the shift from social scrutiny to personal introspection. . . . In fact, most sharply of all his books to this point, *A Story Teller's Story* indicates the quality of Anderson's cultural insight: his feeling for, knowledge of, preoccupation with, that entire American social scheme which just then the more fashionable intellects of the middle twenties were consigning to the categories of farce and fantasy. (pp. 252-53)

If *A Story Teller's Story* has summarized the struggle of an American writer to exist in an environment that is hostile to the best sort of human life . . ., so the autobiography introduces us to another pattern of inner conflict: a personal birth struggle, as it were, which will now preoccupy his thoughts and form the core of his work during the middle twenties. (pp. 253-54)

[When] this older exile looks back upon the exile of infancy, it is difficult not to feel the acute crisis of 'place' in Anderson's history. The cultural tension of Anderson's maturity is doubled by the earlier psychological tension: the writer now without a home in a modern society that is itself 'too big, too fast,' seeks in vain the home of his youth. (p. 259)

Within this entire framework of values we can realize the intensity of Anderson's search for a more genuine meaning to life in America: for 'the right place and the right people.' The boy who had never owned a foot of the vast American earth, and who had then rejected the concept of a purely material possession, must nevertheless own it all in his spirit—belong to it, become part of it. (pp. 260-61)

Late in his maturity, Anderson records his decision to return to the American town life he has loved: to see to what degree the white radiance of eternity *is* stained by life's dome of many-colored glass—to act out now, in person, and day by day, that provincial life he has been retracing in his thoughts over these many years. (p. 263)

Anderson was not a novelist. The novel form may have increased his difficulties—his essential gift was that of intuition and a brief and brilliant illumination—and perhaps we should accept the simplest explanation—one, however, that is apt to be a little simple-minded, too. The fact is that *Dark Laughter*—as well as being praised as 'one of the most profound novels of our time' by the urban intellectuals whom our provincial groper must surely have respected—was also one of the most popular of Anderson's books. It was perhaps the most widely read of them for precisely those literary elements which make it one of the least effective of his works; even today it is considered a 'typical' Anderson. Well, if he had wanted to, Anderson could have written a series of novels in the same vein, and it was seven years before his next one. All the same, *is* the next novel, which is *Beyond Desire*—is it, in effect, another of Anderson's bids for that general acclaim and worldly prestige which have haunted and tormented his existence: a temptation resting in the depths of his temperament from his earliest childhood days, repressed time and again, and everywhere else but here—but a temptation to which he must finally yield, if only once in every 'long year' of his life? (p. 270)

It is [the] view [that there is] a certain inevitability in human destiny, and . . . an equal human necessity to make its condition a little less inevitable; it is that final Andersonian 'surrender' to life . . . which is now no less quick and alive and gay—that sets off the *Memoirs* of 1942. (pp. 281-82)

But, if Sherwood Anderson is talking about himself again in the *Memoirs,* you can listen to him endlessly now. Because he is also talking about provincial ascetics and pagans in the Ohio of the nineteen-hundreds; about that Chicago epoch which produced the Little Renaissance and the Children of the Arts in the late teens; about Sandburg, Masters, Dreiser, O'Neill, and Theda Bara; about New York aesthetes in the nineteen-twenties and about New York revolutionaries in the nineteen-thirties; about automobiles; and apple pie and Herbert Hoover; about a certain large radical delegation which was scheduled to arrive in Washington, out of which there appeared only a Negro, a Jew, and, naturally, Sherwood; and about his own southern countryside and people. Anderson is also talking about American morals, habits, types, trends, and movements over the last half-century—about the American *character*—about, in short, everything but himself—and if you can, you ought to listen to him. For the *Memoirs* are a triumph of tone, of a native tone; of a 'grand style' arising from its natural sources and couched in its natural idiom—and of a maturity difficult to achieve in life, and particularly, perhaps, in American life. Never knowing the answers, Anderson knows enough by now. . . . What a long way indeed he has come: this groping provincial, so full of anguish in an age full of uncertainty, who saw the modern Medusa and turned all the more into flesh. Among all the untaught Americans who make up the bulk of our literary annals, which ones, say, have taught themselves more? (pp. 282-83)

Maxwell Geismar, "Sherwood Anderson: Last of the Townsmen," in his The Last of the Provincials: The American Novel, 1915-1925 *(copyright © 1943, 1947, 1949, 1975 by Maxwell Geismar; reprinted by permission of Houghton Mifflin Company), Houghton, 1947 (and reprinted by Hill & Wang, 1959), pp. 223-84.*

Sherwood Anderson was the only story teller of his generation—he was born in 1876—who left his mark on the style and vision of the generation that followed. Hemingway, Faulkner, Wolfe, Steinbeck, Caldwell, Saroyan, Henry Miller . . . each of these owes him an unmistakable debt, and their names might stand for dozens of others. . . .

Rereading Anderson's work after many years, one is happy to find that its moments of vision are as fresh and moving as ever. They are what James Joyce called "epiphanies"; that is, they are moments at which a character, a landscape, or a personal relation stands forth in its essential nature or "what-ness," with its past and future revealed as if by a flash of lightning. For Anderson each of the moments was a story in itself. The problem he almost never solved was how to link one moment with another in a pattern of causality, or how to indicate the passage of time. (p. 16)

These moments at the center of Anderson's often marvelous stories were moments, in general, without a sequel; they existed separately and timelessly. That explains why none of his seven published novels was a unified work and why, with a single exception, he never even wrote a *book* in the strict sense of the word. A book should have a structure and a development, whereas for Anderson there was chiefly the flash of lightning that revealed a life without changing it.

The single exception, of course, is *Winesburg, Ohio,* and that became a true book for several reasons: because it was conceived as a whole, because Anderson had found a subject that released his buried emotions, and because most of it was written in what was almost the same burst of inspiration, so that it gathered force as it went along. (p. 17)

Malcolm Cowley, "Anderson's Lost Days of Innocence," in The New Republic *(reprinted by permission of* The New Republic; *© 1960 by The New Republic, Inc.), February 15, 1960, pp. 16-18.*

[In *Winesburg, Ohio*] Anderson is . . . clear (novelistically speaking) that the artist's essential quality must be defined as a capacity for the growth which he refuses to attribute to any of the grotesques. It is indeed the very description of their grotesqueness that each of them is forever frozen somewhere below the level of a full and proper development. Sometimes this incompletion is "their fault," sometimes not (unless it be more true to say that such a question of ultimate responsibility is meaningless); but there can be no doubt about Anderson's clear perception of the *fact*.

It is not enough, however, to see these figures as incomplete and to sense the pathos of their plight. It is not enough even to see that it is the glimmering awareness of their inadequacy that drives them to their futile efforts at revelation and communion. Ultimately it is only a sentimental reading of *Winesburg, Ohio* that fails to recognize that the grotesques' anxiety to escape their isolation is in itself excessive and truly symptomatic of their grotesquerie. It is of the utmost importance that their counterweight, George Willard, is almost alone among the inhabitants of *Winesburg* in being able to accept the fact of human isolation and to live with it. His willingness to do so is at once the sign of his maturity and the pledge of his incipient artistic ability. . . .

Anderson obviously sees the relation of art and life as from one point of view illuminated by an opposition between the freedom and flexibility which are necessary to the creative role and, on the other hand, the extremes of static and rigid over-commitment instanced by the grotesques. (p. 109)

To remember that the "grotesques" are . . . distorted and misshapen by their insistent involvement with life itself is to share Anderson's realistic perception of "normal" or "ordinary" people (as distinguished from the artist, who is "normal" in a different way); it is to participate imaginatively in Anderson's remarkable vision of humanity, a vision tender without sentimentality, tough without rancor. . . . Actually it is almost useless to attempt to retain any usual conception of "normality"—except in the sense of more or less "developed"—when dealing with Anderson . . ., for at the heart of his feeling is his uncommon ability to like people for what they are instead of for what they might be . . . while in the very act of seeing them as they are. (p. 110)

And so easy is it to allow one's attention to be monopolized by the grotesques! Their problem is presented first and their bizarre revelations continually keep it at the forefront of our perception. Meanwhile, . . . the current of the book is setting away from them toward the final story, "Departure," and, before that, the climactic tale, "Sophistication," wherein George Willard's maturity is to be realized and the final opposition between artist and society drawn. (p. 111)

The artist, [Anderson concludes], is not necessarily different from other people, after all. Primarily, he is defined in terms of maturity and in terms of the practical mastery of his craft (throughout *Winesburg,* George Willard has been busy as a reporter, learning to fit words to life felt and observed). The craft is his special secret, and it is not required that "normal" or "ordinary" people have it. They will have other skills, other secrets. But what they might all share, ideally, is that mixture of participation and detachment, love and respect, passion and criticism, which is, Anderson tells us, the best privilege offered by the modern world to those who wish to grow up, and toward the attainment of which the writer's case—at first glance special, but

ultimately very general—may serve as an eminently practicable pattern of virtue. (p. 113)

> *Edwin Fussell, "'Winesburg, Ohio': Art and Isolation," in* Modern Fiction Studies *(copyright © 1960, by Purdue Research Foundation, West Lafayette, Indiana, U.S.A.), Summer, 1960 (and reprinted in* The Achievement of Sherwood Anderson: Essays in Criticism, *edited by Ray Lewis White, University of North Carolina Press, 1966, pp. 104-15).*

One will not find in Anderson any echoes from the Social Darwinists, nor any techniques learned from Zola but his connections with literary naturalism are none the less clear. One sees this in his sympathy for his "grotesques" who have not been equal to the struggle for life and have become stunted, "regressed," or, as he calls them, "queer." One sees it too in his remarkable studies of the hungers and uncertainties of his adolescents for whom emergence into maturity, particularly sexual maturity, is difficult and painful. (p. 168)

He differs markedly from most of the older literary naturalists in that he permits his characters, even the most bewildered of them, at least a momentary flash of self-illumination, a glimpse of the wonder of life. This epiphanal moment is usually the climax of the Anderson story and he concentrates in it all the symbolic meaning which he can command. (pp. 169-70)

> *Willard Thorp, in his* American Writing in the Twentieth Century *(copyright © 1960 by the President and Fellows of Harvard College; excerpted by permission of the publishers), Cambridge, Mass.: Harvard University Press, 1960.*

[Each of the] best of [Anderson's] essays . . . [is] an attempt to come closer to an understanding of an individual, a group, or a set of circumstances [and] . . . is dominated by careful attention to craftsmanship as well as by penetrating intuitive understanding of the essence of the material, and in them Anderson focuses attention on the significance of the small, the seemingly unimportant, and the easily ignored in human life. (p. 248)

[The] concept that dominated both his life and works from 1929 to his death [is that] man is his brother's keeper . . ., whether he would acknowledge the fact or not. It was the realization of this truth that made human life meaningful, and its rejection, brought about by a preoccupation with things, that led to the inevitable dehumanization of American society. . . . [Only] the individual himself could prevent the material from completely nullifying his potential in his own life.

Anderson's works as a whole record his discovery of this truth, one that a more sophisticated man possessed of more education would have accepted as obvious and then promptly forgotten. (p. 251)

In style more than anywhere else Anderson has come closer to reproducing and interpreting a vital part of the American experience.

The spirit of Anderson's work is the spirit of life, and this, too, will endure. The wonder of human life, a compassionate regard for it, and a compelling sense of discovering significance in the commonplace permeate his works, giving rise to a lyric beauty even in despair. . . . Life is not only the great adventure for Anderson; in the final analysis it is the universal value. (pp. 255-56)

> *David D. Anderson, "Sherwood Anderson after 20 Years," in* The Midwest Quarterly *(copyright, 1962, by* The Midwest Quarterly*), Winter, 1962 (and reprinted in* The Achievement of Sherwood Anderson: Essays in Criticism, *edited by Ray Lewis White, University of North Carolina Press, 1966, pp. 246-56).*

Without attempting either to defend his work or to label or classify it, I should like to consider the several roles of Anderson's "voices" in the American literary scene. He was, first of all, an advisor of his contemporaries, generous and often wise, and much abused by them. He was a "theorist of the imagination," who took down innumerable notes on the creative process and its several kinds of psychological *angst*. He was pre-eminently a literary analyst of the several variants of human loneliness, its causes and its relations to larger social dilemmas. Finally, he was an important "historian" of the period of transition and change (roughly from 1870 to 1915) to American industrialized society. In each of these roles Anderson performed seriously and often wisely, but with only occasional and often indifferent success. Indeed, it is one of the curious paradoxes of modern literature that a man of whom one can say so many things in praise turns out after all to be the author of so little that is first-rate or enduring. (pp. 6-7)

The role of adviser to his celebrated contemporaries left him extremely vulnerable. [Hoffman is referring to the well known caricatures of Anderson's style by Faulkner and Hemingway.] He could help them; they could do little for him. (pp. 7-8)

The American *isolé* is peculiarly a product of Anderson's imagination, as the European *isolé* is of Conrad's. Anderson's figure comes out of the nineteenth century and into the twentieth: a composite of Lincoln, Huckleberry Finn, and (in at least some versions of it) Henry Ford. Most of all, it is the adolescent's predicament of coming for the first time into adult experience: a vague sense of uneasy curiosity and disappointment, the surprise that there should be more than one world and more than one way of seeing them. Faulkner's more vigorous imagination made it possible for him to embellish the experience, but the pull of innocence and the terror of knowing are also there, as they are in Hemingway's Nick Adams and Frederic Henry, as indeed they are in Thomas Wolfe's Eugene Gant. Over all of these creations, Anderson cast an anxious and admonitory eye; they were successes of which Anderson was envious and to the realization of which he had himself made important contributions. His role was the pathetic one of encouraging artists to do better than he seemed able himself to do, and for the most part receiving something less than little thanks for doing so. (p. 9)

Anderson speaks of the world of the imagination as the "other world," to which one withdraws in order to gather strength for the creative act. It is also the world of dreams, in which the artist is relieved of the world of necessity. It is a world of "lies," of the kind that enlarge the real and gro-

tesquely disfigure the truth. Anderson's reputation in this one of his "voices" comes not from any precision he was able to give the theory of the creative process, but from the peculiar values he was able to give the human situation of loneliness. To this aspect of human life he was able to bring insights of extraordinary power and tenderness. (p. 10)

The figure of the "grotesque" is a common enough creature in American literature. There is much to be said for the notion that we have grown old before we have matured, or that the transition from childhood to adulthood has been sudden, abrupt, and painful. Anderson's voice speaks in *Winesburg, Ohio* and in the short stories of the disasters that have resulted in the human personality. It is a fascinating and an arresting image. It involves us in the nostalgia for a "pastoral stillness," an Edenic world that we have always thought we had but never actually achieved. It also suggests a kind of aberration of the American personality, who wishes to be loved and respected but is put off from knowing how to assert himself without shock or outrage.

Anderson's great contribution is to define the misery of these eccentricities, which come directly from the extension of American self-consciousness into a world of industrial and commercial crudeness. The major assertion of Anderson's heroes is to "walk out," to protest, and to engage in a journey of self-discovery. But the truth he offers is more profound, as it is more precise, than that. Again in this matter Anderson is a typical psychologist of American manners. The voyage in space does not suffice. The only satisfactory journey is the journey inward, of self-discovery. But circumstances inhibit, and tragedy (or more frequently, melodrama) results.

Winesburg succeeds in ways in which the other books fail. Too often (in *Dark Laughter, Windy McPherson's Son, Many Marriages*) Anderson does not himself know what to do with the truth he has discovered; and he can only write what often amounts to a parody of what he has intended to write. . . . [The characters of *Winesburg*] lack the means to move gracefully from adolescence to maturity. This is a primary American fable. It is one of Anderson's most authentic voices, and its importance cannot be over-estimated. (pp. 11-12)

Winesburg is like no other work of modern American literature. It does not yield to any effort to classify it, but is instead a semi-poetic study of loneliness, of the grotesqueries of lonely spirits seen in a half light. These are symptoms of a desperate sense of loss and of an equally desperate and forceful desire to regain human love and contact.

The remaining voice is the "historical"; or, it is Anderson's attempt to put the *Winesburg* situation within an historical perspective. He is "historical" only in this sense, that having established contact with the figure of the *isolé*, he wants to give cause and reason for his condition. The critical time in Anderson's survey is the period between the Civil War and World War I. Since he was born in 1876, these are also the years when he grew to maturity. They are times of agony, of quick unthinking progress, and of the loss of a sense of leadership.

Anderson's image of American greatness often comprehended two figures: that of Lincoln, lost forever to the American scene in 1865; that of the Mississippi River, as Mark Twain and Huckleberry Finn saw it. (pp. 12-13)

Anderson tried to recover a lost purity in his fiction, but succeeded only in describing variations of abnormal failure. He was the "man of liberal good will," whose virtues came from an earlier and simpler time, and who did not possess intellectual strength enough to give force to his diagnosis. His heroes and heroines are always victims, with varying degrees of pathos, of an ugly civilization they cannot understand.

Anderson's weakness was in a lack of intellectual force. But it may be said ironically to have been an advantage of a sort. He so felt his own inadequacies as to invest his characters with a strength of sympathy and a rapport that were the result of his sharing them with him. An abundant good will combines with a feeling of distress over its not quite being enough to preserve the world from its own trickery. (p. 13)

The most important fact of Anderson's work is its native simplicity. Not that he did not try for sophistication; his worst writing came as a result of his attempts to imitate the sophistications of others. But, in *Poor White* and in *Winesburg,* there is a sense of "simple profundity," which comes from his having attended to his creatures on his level and on theirs. There are more significant things to say about them than Anderson got around to saying. D. H. Lawrence said many of them, as did Freud, in quite another context. Anderson's virtues are most clearly manifest when he tries to be the spokesman of his times. The delicacy of sentiment with which he invests his adolescent narrators in such stories as "I Want to Know Why" cannot be improved on by a superior taste, cultivation, or intellect. The miraculous moments of revelation in "The Egg" and "Death in the Woods" are *sui generis;* Lawrence sometimes comes very close to them in his short stories, but Anderson owes nothing to Lawrence—or to anyone else—for them.

I should say that at his best Anderson succeeds because he is closer to his world than most writers are to theirs. His elaborate attempts to explain the "life of the fantasy" and the "life of dreams" (in *A Story Teller's Story* and other works of autobiography or semi-criticism) are not valuable in themselves; as theory they are vague and meandering discourses. As an explanation of his own "vision," however, they have a considerable merit. (pp. 16-17)

Anderson is not a prophet (or at any rate, he is not a good prophet). He possesses instead a great delicacy of sentiment and sympathy, a power of attracting to him (because it is within him) a human substance of the most varied kind. (p. 17)

I should regard it as the worst of misunderstandings, however, if I have given the impression that Anderson was "a valuable writer" simply because he was "a valuable human being." The point I wish to make is far more important than that. He spoke in a genuine "voice" because he *was* that voice, because it had a style that at times closely approached the desperate gaucheries of his clumsy, frenzied creatures, frantic to be heard and understood and loved. Again and again, he avoided sentimentality by making his speech like the hard, twisted, bitter apples of *Winesburg.* He was a master of the speech of the anxious, troubled, naive adolescent, and of the equally troubled and naive old man or woman. At either end of the scale, a precious innocence is preserved at the menacing and hostile center of its enemies. There is something hauntingly pitiful about these "lost souls" who want somehow, anyhow, to prove themselves, and end by proving that they are "queer" or violent or apparently purposelessly mad. (p. 18)

Anderson's value for us comes down to these facts: that he knew the virtues and the limitations of innocence; that he could plot the history of its decline; and that he could speak of that decline in genuine accents and with genuine feeling. (pp. 18-19)

> *Frederick J. Hoffman, "The Voices of Sherwood Anderson," in* Shenandoah *(copyright by* Shenandoah; *reprinted from* Shenandoah: The Washington and Lee University Review *with the permission of the Editor), Spring, 1962, pp. 5-19.*

[One] is indeed struck on first reading [*Winesburg, Ohio*] by its apparent simplicity of language and form. On second or subsequent readings, however, he sees that the hard, plain, concrete diction is much mixed with the abstract, that the sentence cadences come from George Moore and the King James Bible as well as from ordinary speech rhythms, that the seemingly artless, even careless, digressions are rarely artless, careless, or digressive. What had once seemed to have the clarity of water held in the hand begins to take on instead its elusiveness. If this is simplicity, it is simplicity—paradox or not—of a complicated kind. (p. 20)

Realism is for Anderson a means rather than an end, and the highly abstract kind of reality found in Winesburg has its valuable uses. The first of these is best understood in relation to George Willard's occupation on the *Winesburg Eagle.* (Clyde's weekly newspaper was, and still is the *Clyde Enterprise,* but Sherwood Anderson was never its reporter.) It has been suggested that the author may have made his central figure a newspaper reporter in order that he could thus be put most readily in touch with the widest number of people in town and most logically become the recipient of many confidences; yet Anderson's point is that exactly insofar as George remains a newspaper reporter, he is committed to the surface of life, not to its depths. (p. 22)

As reporter, George is concerned with externals, with appearances, with the presumably solid, simple, everyday surface of life. For Anderson the surface is there, of course, as his recurring use of place and personal names indicates; yet conventional "reality" is for him relatively insignificant and is best presented in the form of sketch or abstraction. What is important is "to see beneath the surface of lives," to perceive the intricate mesh of impulses, desires, drives growing down in the dark, unrevealed parts of the personality like the complex mass of roots that, below the surface of the ground, feeds the common grass above in the light.

But if one function of Anderson's peculiar adaptation of realism is, as it were, to depreciate the value of surfaces, a corollary function is constantly to affirm that any surface has its depth. (pp. 22-3)

Yet a third function of Anderson's abstract, or shorthand, kind of realism is to help him set the tone of various tales, often a tone of elegiac quietness. . . . [The] Winesburg tales he conceived of as for the most part occurring in a preindustrial setting, recalling nostalgically a town already lost before he had left it, giving this vanished era the permanence of pastoral. Here, as always, he avoids the realism of extensive detail and makes only suggestive references. . . . (pp. 23-4)

If Anderson's treatment of locale in his tales turns out to be more complex than it seems at first, the same can be said of his methods of giving sufficient unity to his book so that, while maintaining the "looseness" of life as he actually sensed it, the tales would still form a coherent whole. Some of these methods, those that I shall be concerned with, have a point in common: they all involve the use of repeated elements. One such device is that of setting the crisis scenes of all but five of the tales in the evening . . . [and] many of the tales end with the characters in total darkness. Such a device not only links the tales but in itself implies meaning. *Winesburg* is primarily a book about the "night world" of human personality. The dim light equates with, as well as literally illuminates, the limited glimpse into an individual soul that each crisis scene affords, and the briefness of the insight is emphasized by the shutting down of the dark.

Another kind of repeated element throughout the book is the recurrent word. Considering the sense of personal isolation one gets from the atomized lives of the "grotesques," one would expect a frequent use of some such word as "wall," standing for whatever it is that divides each person from all others. Surprisingly that particular word appears only a few times. The one that does occur frequently is "hand," either in the singular or the plural; and very often, as indeed would be expected, it suggests, even symbolizes, the potential or actual communication of one personality with another. . . . [The] possibility of physical touch between two human beings always implies, even if by negative counterpart, at least the possibility of a profounder moment of understanding between them. (pp. 24-5)

> *Walter B. Rideout, "The Simplicity of 'Winesburg, Ohio'," in* Shenandoah *(copyright by* Shenandoah; *reprinted from* Shenandoah: *The Washington and Lee University Review with the permission of the Editor), Spring, 1962, pp. 20-31.*

By the time he set to work on *Kit Brandon*, Anderson was prepared to bring to a quantitatively imposing tradition of fiction about the mountaineers his own genius as a proletarian writer. He was not an innovator in this challenging new field. . . .

It is unfortunate that critics and writers on American fiction have apparently not been prepared to perceive the significance of Anderson's fusion of techniques in his handling of what were for him new materials in *Kit Brandon*, which, when studied from the vantage point of one acquainted with the history and the usually shoddy and superficial interpretation in literature of eight million Southern mountaineers, turns out to be not only one of the few genuinely significant interpretations in fiction of the Southern mountaineers and in general a carefully written and well plotted novel, but also Anderson's final triumph in the proletarian novel. In *Kit Brandon* he subordinates the sure touch of the primitivist to the techniques of the naturalist which he had not quite mastered even in *Poor White,* but more dramatic materials lay immediately around him than he had found at hand in writing *Poor White*. Most significantly, Kit's narrative is not obscured by propaganda. (p. 58)

Like most novelists who have worked in mountain fiction, Anderson chose to create his story around the mountain woman, the symbol of continuity. Kit, enlightened by experience and reading, sees her cultural heritage in a clear perspective, and in her the mountaineers have come up from the eighteenth century to the threshold of the basement door in an industrial age. (p. 59)

The novel apparently has failed to appeal to critics and the academic historians of American fiction because it does not fit easily into any *mythos* created recently to encompass large samplings of American fiction. Mountain girls, hillbillies, and moonshiners, after all, are of concern only in a small eddy of the main stream, but the fact remains that Sherwood Anderson handled them faithfully and with integrity in a fresh and original way in a novel bringing together the skills that had shaped *Poor White* on the one hand and *Winesburg, Ohio* and *Dark Laughter* on the other. (p. 61)

> *Cratis D. Williams, "'Kit Brandon': A Reappraisal," in* Shenandoah *(copyright by* Shenandoah; *reprinted from* Shenandoah: *The Washington and Lee University Review with the permission of the Editor), Spring, 1962, pp. 55-61.*

Like Dreiser, Anderson presents [in *Windy McPherson's Son* and *Marching Men*] a Naturalistic picture of people caught up in social "forces"—specifically, by a repressive, individualistic economic system and by an outworn Puritan morality which have defeated the weak and made egoistic monsters of the strong. But, unlike Dreiser, Anderson judges society against an ambivalent nature in which man may choose between harmony and discord, between a moral order based upon concord and a chaotic social system grounded in egoistic competitiveness. . . . Anderson departs further from the traditional Zolaesque and Dreiserian reductive Naturalism in providing his heroes with a choice between a nature of strife on the one hand and a nature of harmony on the other—between an egoistic, competitive life and one of sympathetic communion with others. (pp. 33-4)

The Adamic journey became the characteristic narrative metaphor in all of Anderson's subsequent novels, assuming social and psychological as well as moral and mythical dimensions. Like McPherson and McGregor, Hugh McVey of *Poor White* . . . , John Webster of *Many Marriages* . . . , Bruce Dudley of *Dark Laughter* . . . , Red Oliver of *Beyond Desire* . . . , and Kit Brandon of *Kit Brandon* . . . embrace variously the ethics of success; the doctrine of progress; standardized, hypocritically sexual notions of love and courtship and marriage; or the bloodless piety of Puritan morality. And like McGregor and McPherson, they all rebel against the spiritual confinements of society and try to find and live by a principle of order in the face of the social disorder they have observed everywhere and the inner disorder they have felt in themselves and seen in others. All have a strong instinctive need for order—for example, McPherson's efforts to make an "art" of business and McGregor's obsession to "bring an end to disorder" in society—which reflects the chief cause of Anderson's own psychic crisis in 1912. And all escape from the disorder of their lives and begin a new life that develops into a moral quest, a groping effort to construct a new moral world.

Such a narrative metaphor lends itself to penetrating literary examinations of a cross-section of American life. The assumptions implicit in the moral journey Anderson's heroes take are not hard to identify, for they comprise the strange amalgamation of Jeffersonian agrarian primitivism and secular Calvinism that made up the "folklore of Populism" which was—and to some extent still is—a powerful ideological force in Anderson's Midwest. (p. 37)

The intellectual problems implicit in confronting a corrupt and complicated modern society with an Adamic hero equipped with little more than a strong but recently gained moral conscience were to plague Anderson to the end of his career. But traces of the kind of work he was to do in *Winesburg, Ohio* are evident in these books, particularly in *Windy*; and suggestions of a more useful character type than the Adamic hero—distinguished by a perverse obsession with an innocence that violates conventional modes of behavior—appear in the early sections of both books. (p. 41)

It was in the tale, concerned primarily with the inner life of the individual rather than with the social relations of the group, that Anderson was to excel in writing. If he was unable to solve the problems of the individual in American society through the moral journey of his Adamic heroes in the romances, he did successfully portray in the tales that make up *Winesburg, Ohio* both the broken inner lives that characterized that society and the growth to maturity and consciousness of a Midwestern youth. (p. 43)

> *Rex Burbank, "The Populist Temper," in his* Sherwood Anderson *(copyright 1964 by Twayne Publishers, Inc.; reprinted with the permission of Twayne Publishers, A Division of G. K. Hall & Co., Boston), Twayne, 1964 (and reprinted in* The Achievement of Sherwood Anderson: Essays in Criticism *edited by Ray Lewis White, University of North Carolina Press, 1966, pp. 32-45).*

Anderson did not have the speculative intellect of a Plato, but he had the natural integrity of a fine elm, or a fertile sow, or a potato; he had a burly, carnal mind which was always very close to his urgent, lustful hands and nose, and his books he begat, rather than wrote. Stieglitz made a marvelous photograph of the midland genius, with his bangs of hair (almost like those of Gertrude Stein, whom he admired and imitated) and his mouth, which was voluptuous like a woman's.

Along with Dreiser, Anderson had a great distrust of the mind. . . . Books were necessary for Melville, but had Anderson been a greater reader he would have overeaten.

Anderson had a manual intelligence: he had large, animal hands, like a peasant's, and all his wisdom was in his fingers. That is why he hated the machine, which can make the hands stupid and morose. A workman turning a wheel all day long in a factory will lose patience with ordinary life; indeed, much of human kindness comes from being casual and slow. Anderson was no hurried man; he had time to shake hands, make friendships, or engage in a mettlesome argument. (pp. 17-18)

He was very unsure of himself; that is why he was never in a hurry with anybody, for it takes a long time to understand —or to misunderstand—people. He never had the American "busy" malady. Nor had Dreiser; if you wanted to see him, he always asked you to come over right away. (p. 18)

The way to understand a man like Anderson is not to read about him but to read him. Reading him, you find that all those workinghand words of his are redolent of hay and grass and midwest stables. Get *Winesburg, Ohio,* or *Poor White,* or *Tar,* or the *Notebook,* or his still unrecognized verse, *A New Testament* and *Mid-American Chants.* Anderson's books have the heady pollen of good orchards. . . . Remembering old-style American habits, the lumbering wagon hello, and the easy country-morning how-do-you-do, is enough to make one understand Sherwood Anderson's genius, which is a compact of goodness and of love and of a patient willingness to sit and talk with people. (p. 19)

> *Edward Dahlberg, "Midwestern Fable," in his* Alms for Oblivion *(© 1964, University of Minnesota), University of Minnesota Press, Minneapolis, 1964, pp. 16-19.*

The major theme of Anderson's writing is the tragedy of death in life: modern man, lacking personal identity and with his senses anesthetized, has become a spiritless husk unfitted for love of man and community. This perennial theme is common enough in our time, though it was relatively dormant in the late 1910's when Anderson first enunciated it. It became his leitmotiv when, in 1912, at the age of thirty-six, he suffered a nervous breakdown and rejected his past. Thereafter he viewed this event as a symbolic rebirth which had purified him of false values and freed him from the confines of deadening institutions.

The pattern is classic in Western culture. It has recurred often in American life since Puritan times, with special frequency in the nineteenth century after the rise of transcendentalism. But in the 1920's it was somewhat anachronistic for a man to present himself dramatically, not only as artist but also as human being, in the messianic role of someone who had achieved a second birth and now had come forth to utter prophetic truths. Nor did Anderson's lower-class origins in Ohio, his vaunted and obvious lack of education, his emphasis upon the American and the common, his bohemian dress and manners, his concern with lust and love, and his charismatic religious overtones make him more palatable either to the intellectual or to the average man. (p. 6)

Anderson's reverent attitude toward language was a wholesome sign of his promise as a writer. In the 1900's, it was useful to him because of his limited vocabulary and his unfamiliarity with the range of rhetorical devices to be found in literature. But his emphasis upon "words" as self-sufficient entities, and his lack of concern with their meaning, foreshadowed his later obsessive preoccupation with them. As he struggled unsuccessfully with the expression of ideas and emotional nuances in his first two novels, he came to believe that his failure resulted from the faulty character of his words rather than from the absence of that profound imaginative experience which willy-nilly finds vivid expression even in a limited language. "There is a story.—I cannot tell it.—I have no words," he would write in 1921. . . .

On the one hand, then, Anderson's love and fear of the word stimulated stylistic purity; on the other hand, this ambivalence also led on occasion to a "basic mistrust of the language itself" and to the artistically destructive belief that "reality remains ultimately inexpressible". . . . (p. 12)

The invigorating effect of Gertrude Stein's experimentation with language in *Tender Buttons* is evident in *Marching Men.* . . .

For Anderson, Miss Stein always remained a "writer's writer," a literary pioneer, not a writer for the general reader. He recognized that her abandonment of conventional syntax, punctuation, and spelling was therapeutic for the American writer because it made him conscious of the deadness of conventional language and rhythm, of a literature based on literary custom rather than on objects, associations, functions, and speech freshly articulated. In 1914 such a revivification of style was needed. Gertrude Stein was a pioneer in the undertaking, soon to be joined by Anderson, Pound, Eliot, Joyce, the Dadaists, Cummings, Hemingway, and Faulkner. The poetic repetition and variation of words and phrases, the uncluttered images of objects, the varying musical beat and swing of sentences and paragraphs, noticeable in . . . passages . . . from *Marching Men,* were stylistic techniques Anderson learned from her and passed along to Hemingway and Faulkner. (p. 21)

Winesburg, Ohio had delineated the arid context of Anderson's first life. Having given it aesthetic form, he believed it imperative to create—again in art—the context of his new life. (p. 26)

Mid-American Chants . . ., a collection of free-verse poems in the Whitmanian manner which Anderson began writing early in 1917, illustrates one phase of his attempt to fill his void. The poems are generally inept. Only a few manage coherently to unite their fragmentary rhapsodic ejaculations with the kind of sustained emotional energy, intellectual content, and symbolic structure present in Whitman's best poems. (p. 28)

Poor White was the high point of Anderson's novelistic career. However, it represented a mere refinement of the structure and materials of *Windy McPherson's Son* and *Marching Men* rather than a significant advance. All three novels are essentially accounts of the distortion of a man in youth, his subsequent involvement in a maturity of social fraud and emotional impoverishment, his attempt to attain self-fulfillment in escape and love with an unsatisfactory woman who symbolizes reason and convention rather than emotion and revolt, and the uncertainty of the man's future at the conclusion. (p. 32)

Anderson's next novel, *Many Marriages* . . ., exemplifies the impasse to which such writing could lead. . . . Abandoning the chronological time sequence of the early novels, *Many Marriages* focused upon an extended moment of escape. This was given a past by means of flashbacks that vividly re-create the inhibition of feminine passion. (pp. 32-3)

Anderson published three more novels: *Dark Laughter* . . ., *Beyond Desire* . . ., and *Kit Brandon* . . .. All of them, like his preceding novels, have extraordinary scenes and passages whose high quality has been overlooked. These last novels also show that he endeavored to cope with the problems of extended narrative fiction in different ways; his solutions, however, were generally unsatisfactory, whether it was the attempt to portray the stream of consciousness in *Dark Laughter* or the device of having a central character relate her life story in an extended monologue in *Kit Brandon.*

Anderson's letters and writings from the mid-1910's until shortly before his death reveal that the objective novel, particularly the social novel, had interested him deeply only before the composition of the Winesburg tales. During the

late 1910's, before the publication of *Poor White,* he began and abandoned several novels. After 1925, the pattern was repeated. His impulse was for expression in short forms: the poem, prose poem, and lyrical short story. But he was compelled, particularly since he had begun his career as a novelist, to continue writing novels. (p. 33)

It was not merely the pressure of publishers, as well as readers and critics, which pushed Anderson toward the novel against his natural inclination to work in shorter forms. Anderson shared the erroneous cultural belief that a novel is qualitatively as well as quantitatively more valuable than a short work. Had he been a younger man in the late 1910's and early 1920's, it is possible that he might have been able to develop the lyrical novel, a delicate form that would have best utilized his talents as it did those of Virginia Woolf, his admirer. But he had insufficient time in which to work slowly and perfect his art in every form. (p. 34)

Nevertheless, the bulk of Anderson's important creation is far greater than most critics and readers appear to have realized. His significant contribution to American literature begins with *Winesburg, Ohio* and includes many pieces of prose and poetry published in books and magazines from 1916 to 1941. (pp. 34-5)

One reason Anderson's writing has not received full recognition, apart from the disappointment aroused by his novels, is the uneven character of his books. (p. 35)

Another reason for the relative neglect of Anderson's total accomplishment is the special nature of his talent. He wrote in an age which believed it could master the disorder of existence with patterns of order derived from myths and ideologies of the past or else with descriptions of objects and behavior that possessed the irreducible precision of scientific writing. Because Anderson did not adopt either one of these solutions, his reputation was severely damaged during the 1920's. A reassessment is now in order, for his alleged weaknesses ironically have become strengths which link him with some of the most vigorous currents in contemporary literature. Anderson's vision and method reappear triumphantly in recent American literature in the writing of Carson McCullers, Bernard Malamud, Flannery O'Connor, Tennessee Williams, Edward Albee, Saul Bellow, and John Hawkes. Anderson's pioneering conglomeration of the picaresque, the antiheroic, the grotesque, the passionate, and the rebellious is no longer puzzling nor is it a sign of irresponsible "mindlessness."

One of the most interesting discoveries to be made is that sentimentality is not one of the chief characteristics of Anderson's writing. When dealing with characters whose suffering and confusion he delineated at excessive length, failing to complicate and particularize their uniqueness or to impart visible moral and intellectual significance to their predicaments, he did become pathetic and sentimental. . . . But Anderson's critical temper conflicted strongly with his tendency toward acceptance and complacency. (pp. 35-6)

Essentially Anderson was a lyric writer. Having accepted middle-class thought uncritically at first, then having rebelled against it, he feared that any other system of thought would be equally delusive, would limit and frustrate him, especially since reason tended to become abstract and to ignore the heart. (p. 37)

The uncertain, groping narrator of an Anderson story employs an art of suggestion to articulate his search for pattern and meaning in human existence. His experiences are fragmentary, incoherent, inexplicable. The chronological sequence of time may be interrupted and reversed by memories, inadvertent thoughts, gusts of emotion, and frustrated attempts at comprehension. Objects and people are haphazardly perceived, grotesquely distorted. Absurdly helpless, the narrator may succumb to impotence, give vent to explosive stirrings in his subconscious, flee the envelope of his body in mystical anguish or ecstasy, obsessely focus upon trivialities such as a bent finger, find momentary relief in the muscular health and grace of animals.

Since the story is an articulation of the narrator's experience, its movement is repetitive and circular; it is not rounded off with a meaningful conclusion, for that would violate the narrator's integrity, his stance of wonder and search. Anderson's rejection of conventional plot and climax was aesthetically appropriate. So was his frequent representation of physical detail as incomplete image and generalized noun, his emphasis upon the musical sound of language before it becomes sense in order that he might portray the transformation of undifferentiated sensation and emotion into intelligible form. (p. 39)

The welter of sensuous and emotional perceptions is integrated—despite the powerful centrifugal impulse—by various unifying elements. The narrator maintains a consistent tone of voice. Whether youth or adult, light or serious, comic or satiric, critical or suppliant, he is also visibly interested and compassionate, anxious to discern the reality behind appearance. Moments in the story—episodes, sensations, repetitions—suddenly blaze up to give intense thematic illuminations. Objects, gestures, and events are encrusted with symbolic meaning. These symbols recur and invest the narrator's perceptions with deepened or new significance. Often these symbols are transformed into archetypal patterns of elemental human experience, such as sacrifice, initiation, and rebirth; Anderson's corn seed, for example, is a fertility symbol, its planting a ceremonial drama of death and resurrection. (p. 40)

The vivacity and insight of Anderson's memoirs are remarkable in view of the severe decline of his reputation in the mid-1920's and the lengthy emotional depression that affected him thereafter. To those critics who did not read his works attentively or at all after 1925, when *Dark Laughter* appeared, and to those who know Anderson's writing only on the basis of *Winesburg, Ohio* and two over-anthologized stories—"I'm a Fool" and "I Want to Know Why"—the vibrancy of the memoirs will be truly inexplicable. . . .

Since Anderson was an avant-garde writer, however, a "little magazine" phenomenon, he was at first more enthusiastically received by young writers and critics interested in an American literature that was original, complex, unsentimental, and bold in dealing with taboo subjects such as sex. (p. 42)

But before long even the recognition of the avant-garde was qualified or withdrawn. It generally began to misjudge and overlook Anderson's method and to conclude mistakenly that he was an elderly, provincial American realist because he wrote about the Midwest and praised Dreiser for his human sympathy and his frankness in the treatment of sex.

Anderson's persistent criticisms of Dreiser's style as clumsy and of Sinclair Lewis' style as superficial were ignored. (p. 43)

The ultimate test of a writer's permanence is the power of his words to rekindle generations other than his own. Not until all of the fine writing which Anderson produced during the sixteen-year period after 1925 has been assembled and read will it be possible to undertake the "proper evaluation" for which Faulkner called. Meanwhile, an important place in American literary history seems assured. With characteristic humility Anderson himself had said in 1921 "that after all the only thing the present generation of men in America could expect to do is to make with their bodies and spirits a kind of fertilizing element in our soil." The issue of final grandeur and fame was a matter he left to others. (p. 45)

> *Brom Weber, in his* Sherwood Anderson *(American Writers Pamphlet No. 43;* © *1964, University of Minnesota), University of Minnesota Press, Minneapolis, 1964.*

Traditionally, the decline in quality and appeal of Sherwood Anderson's work has been accounted for by blaming his failures on the influence of the literary movements in which he took part. Thus it would seem that Anderson's association in the Chicago Renaissance led to his best work—*Winesburg, Ohio* and the early short stories. Then the writer was adopted and advised by the "intellectuals," who taught him about Freud, Lawrence, and Marx. Supposedly, the examples and theories of these men corrupted some natural genius in Anderson, who had been heralded as the untutored spokesman for small-town America. Trying to please his educated friends, Anderson wrote as they advised but not so well as they expected, causing them to desert him for the more appealing figures of Hemingway, Faulkner, and Wolfe.

There is some basis for this view of Anderson's career. Feeling uneducated and slightly pitied by those intellectuals who liked his work and who offered their praise and advice, Sherwood Anderson expanded his role-playing, a constant factor in his personality, to include the roles of prophetic midwestern bard, Freudian and Lawrencian philosopher, and socialist tractarian. However, such an explanation ignores the rather obvious impossibility of an author's remaining forever at an early stage of his career, no matter how successful that period may be. As great as *Winesburg, Ohio* is, one cannot imagine Anderson's writing ten volumes of Winesburg stories. A writer must respond more to his genius than to his critics, and Sherwood Anderson's creative spirit demanded that he write novels, poetry, and plays, as well as short stories. There is almost no evidence that Anderson seriously listened to sound literary advice, although his tremendous ego was cut by every word of harsh criticism directed toward him. (pp. 16-17)

Few American writers have lived as colorfully and as spontaneously as Sherwood Anderson, and few authors have committed as much of themselves to the public gaze, consciously playing various roles to establish a "legend." The complexity of Anderson's character, the unusual circumstances of his becoming a writer, and the movement of his career can never be reduced to any simple analysis. Similarly, Sherwood Anderson's writings defy any definitive study; as much as students of Anderson may wish for the "final word" on his accomplishment, it is doubtful that such a study could be written or, if written, that it would long remain the standard comment on the writer who accepted for himself the term "minor." (p. 17)

> *Ray Lewis White, in his introduction to* The Achievement of Sherwood Anderson: Essays in Criticism, *edited by Ray Lewis White (copyright © 1966 by The University of North Carolina Press), University of North Carolina Press, 1966, pp. 3-19.*

Almost a half century has now gone by since the publication of Sherwood Anderson's *Winesburg, Ohio*. During that time it has made its way into a small group of indubitable classics of American literature. The attempts, particularly during the twenties and thirties, to reduce the source of its power to a manageable pigeon-hole now seem dated and largely irrelevant. It is a rich and complex book, perennially fresh and vital, that defies any easy critical or historical formula. It is, to be sure, a book about small town tyranny, the agony and waste of sexual repression, and the dislocations and dehumanization of a growing industrialism. But Anderson weaves these themes into a splendid yet sad vision of the human condition that gives the book a universal vitality.

If we are to understand that vision, I believe we must modify what is becoming a standard interpretation of the book. In this interpretation George Willard is seen as the central character who stands in a contrastive relation to the grotesques; the tension and meaning of the book are located in the grotesques' attraction to George, who represents everything they yearn desperately but futilely for. . . .

Carried a step further, *Winesburg* becomes in this interpretation a kind of parable of the artist in the modern world. . . . (p. 95)

In an obvious sense George is of course the central character of the book. He is the only character who appears repeatedly in the stories, a youth whose innocence and promise draw out the grotesques from the dim shades of their isolation and despair. Furthermore, George's role as a newspaperman and his similarities with Anderson himself clearly justify our seeing him as the artist. To have made these observations, however, is to suggest, it seems to me, a point of departure for critical study rather than a conclusion. . . .

There can be no quarrel with Irving Howe's description of the "typical action" of *Winesburg* as a series of attempts by the grotesques to establish human contact with George, a momentary and abortive attempt to break out of their isolation. (p. 96)

There is another "typical action" (perhaps pattern would be a better word) which lies closer to the center of that vision, binding virtually every story together in lyric and aching sadness. That is the pattern of blighted hope, of frustrated and wasted human worth and, most profound and universal, of lost innocence. A significant and I believe central group of stories embody this pattern by means of an identical narrative structure.

In each of these stories we are introduced to the central character in his present state of half-articulate and final grotesqueness, and then, through a flashback, we learn of the crucial episode, often a catastrophic or traumatic betrayal, which has left him irremediably scarred. These disastrous experiences have occurred at the very moment when each of them stood before the world in youthful hope and innocent expectation that their capacity for goodness and love would somehow be welcomed and requited. It was the very purity of their goodness and love, of their simple but profound dignity and worth, which made the betrayal so catastrophic. Through all of them, there radiates the dim and quiet afterglow of what was once a blaze of joy in being alive, in facing a world commensurate with their capacity for goodness and love.

This is the pattern governing the structure of "Hands," "Paper Pills," "Mother," "The Philosopher," Part III of "Godliness," "Respectability," "The Strength of God," "Loneliness," "The Untold Lie," "Drink," and "Death." It is not, however, a pattern which Anderson employs mechanically and monotonously, but rather the recurrent and underlying pattern which binds together and gives cumulative power to the diverse and unique biographies of the grotesques. (pp. 96-7)

In other stories the catastrophe is not the result of a single act but the cumulative consequence of a long series of acts, of days and months and years. But the same pattern of wasted potential, of goodness and love turned into silent bitterness or despair, is enacted. (pp. 97-8)

In these stories Anderson's lyric, parabolic style creates a kind of rare perfection. It enables him to convey at once the feeling of days and years of quiet desperation which turn hope to despair, love to hate, potential to waste, and yet to render this slow process with a sharp focus and poetic intensity. Unlike Wing Biddlebaum and the other grotesques whose betrayal occurs with a single, transfixing act, Dr. Parcival, Elizabeth Willard, Alice Hindman, the Reverend Hartman, and Ray Pearson grow into bitterness and the sense of betrayal almost imperceptibly over a long period of time. Yet Anderson's use of the technique of the flashback (we are introduced to the characters in their present state of grotesqueness) and the nonrealistic, lyric style turns those long years into a single, timeless moment which is the central fact in these characters' lives.

But this is only part of the impressive skill of these stories. In each of them, the dramatic climax occurs in the present (in contrast to the first group, where it occurs in the past), a burst of illumination, a frantic resolution to act so that the long wasted years may be retrieved, even if vicariously. At this moment of illumination, the grotesque feels those long years of slow waste and unfulfilled hope as a single and timeless instant, like a dying man whose life passes before him instantaneously. (p. 98)

If the unique biographies of the grotesques are given a thematic unity by the recurring pattern which I have been describing they are linked at a yet more abstract and universal level. All of them are victims of a social order or ethos which inexorably and ineluctably breaks them because they ask of life what the modern world cannot give them: love, tenderness, and communion. Like Hemingway's heroes, they face a world indifferent to or incapable of giving them what they want. The world therefore breaks them.

It is the mark of both their pathos and their beauty that they cannot mend at the broken places. (p. 99)

Yet out of the gloom and sad waste which is the powerful

cumulative ambience of the individual lives of the grotesques, within the recurring pattern of youthful betrayal which convulses each of the grotesques into permanent grotesqueness and the fatality that the ethos of modern industrialism represents, there is a muted undertone of hope which rises to the surface and dominates only one story, the beautiful "Sophistication."

In contrast to every other story, "Sophistication" presents a relationship between two human beings which is complete and satisfactory.... That "thing" [for which the grotesques desperately search], Anderson makes clear, is the innocence and spontaneity of youth irretrievably lost and so poignantly remembered by the grotesques.... George and Helen's youthful innocence is a state of grace making their communion possible.

The way in which Anderson describes this communion makes clear, however, that the thing they have taken hold of transcends their individual lives. (p. 102)

More specifically, "Sophistication" resolves the theme of sexual love which figures prominently in so many of the stories. The pathos of so many of the grotesques is that finally and naturally they hope to achieve communion through physical contact, often in its most intimate form of sexual surrender. But the world they are trapped in brutally insists in interpreting it in purely carnal terms....

The sexual content of George and Helen's communion contrasts illuminatingly with that of the others. Their encounter includes but transcends the merely physical....

The key terms Anderson uses to describe the communion are "respect," "reverence," and "dignity"—qualities which in the world of *Winesburg* cannot be attached to physical love....

"Sophistication," the only story to move from frustration and tension to completed communion, is the final story. "Departure," which closes the book, ... is hardly a story at all, but a kind of epilogue.... What George will make of [his] past lies, of course, beyond the final page of the book. The epilogue becomes the prologue to a life we cannot know. (p. 103)

But if we cannot know that life we can know that in "Departure" Anderson carefully and delicately balances the dominant tone of quiet joy felt by George as he faces away from Winesburg with a countertone of sadness and the possibility of failure, an undercurrent that flows backward into the central darkness and despair of the lives of the grotesques. (p. 104)

Without denying George's special role in *Winesburg, Ohio,* then, we must recognize the possibility that his departure is merely the first step in yet another reenactment of the pattern underlying the biographies of all the grotesques: the pattern of hope blighted, potential wasted, and innocence lost. (p. 105)

> *Richard Abcarian, "Innocence and Experience in 'Winesburg, Ohio',"* in The University Review *(copyright 1968 The Curators of the University of Missouri), December, 1968, pp. 95-105.*

[From] 1913 on, Anderson was working toward ... his masterpiece, *Winesburg, Ohio*.... (p. 309)

He was not happy with the more or less conventional novel form that he had already twice attempted. He was no more happy with the prevailing fashions in the short story, either in the formal sense (the contrived melodrama of Poe, for example, or the slick machinery of O. Henry) or in the conventional interpretation of village life (the sentimental romanticism of Booth Tarkington and other writers of the Hoosier School). He had himself observed the pathos, the suffocation of hope and dream in small-town characters, the flight into eccentricity and neurosis, the cruelty no less than the comedy. And in form he wanted something loose and impressionistic and without the contrivance of "plot" that would permit him to get under the surface of manners and character, into the secret life, and into what he felt was the soft, warm flow that, taken together, all the secret lives made into life itself. (p. 310)

He had heard talk of Sigmund Freud and psychoanalysis in bohemian Chicago, and this helped him. He was reading or was about to read the fiction of D. H. Lawrence, and this would help him, too. But above all he had the example of Gertrude Stein's *Three Lives.* It may very well have been this example that urged on him the notion of the plotless, flowing story that would put nothing between the reader and the directly presented contours of the buried life itself. And it was she, of course, who helped him most precisely to discover the language that he now knew he wanted to use—the colloquial language of Mark Twain, of everyday America, of country roads and village streets; but more than that, the naïveté of manner engendered by the simplest words, the simplest, least sophisticated of syntactical forms, the constant repetition.

Finally, it was *Three Lives* that encouraged a habit of plainness, a certain bareness even in content itself—a kind of concentration on essentials and the elimination of all else, so that his characters are divested of "their incidentals," as Edmund Wilson called them—"their furniture, their houses, their clothes, their ordinary social relations." (pp. 310-11)

Yet she could not, in spite of all this, help him in the larger problem of unity and form. This problem was not solved until 1915, when he read Edgar Lee Masters's long poem, *The Spoon River Anthology,* that collection of voices of about two hundred and fifty dead people, all buried in the cemetery of a single Midwest town, each speaking out the essential truth of his secret life, and many of these characters reappearing in the reflections of many of the others. As Masters had done it in free verse, so Anderson would do it in prose, and with two important additional elements of unification.

Like Masters, he would give a certain unity to the separate stories of his twenty-two characters through the common background of the town, Winesburg, As the stories progressed, characters would keep reappearing; someone who had been a minor figure in one story would presently emerge as the major figure in another, and so on, until a whole sense of the community would emerge. Then he would employ a single narrator, George Willard, who would himself appear in many of the stories and would finally climax the whole. While the other characters would come to George in the dumb expectation that he could somehow understand and perhaps tell their stories, their stories would also be like gifts to him, gifts that would help him grow until, at the end, he was mature and made the characteristic gesture of flight into freedom. And Anderson would have one further means of unification—a theory embodied in the opening section, a prelude called "The Book of the Grotesque."

A grotesque is formed, Anderson tells us, when an individual seizes on some single truth from the whole body of truths and tries to live by that alone. A single truth, a single wish, a single memory, a single obsessive ambition that distorts the self even as it compels it—these are the motivations of Sherwood Anderson's grotesques. But what is probably a further consequence of these motivations is perhaps more important than the grotesques themselves: in their single pursuits, the characters isolate themselves from one another, and in their isolation, they are at once lonely and mute. Everyone in this world seems to grope helplessly toward everyone else, but no one can communicate with anyone else—or only with the artist-reporter, George Willard. And that, as Anderson came to understand it, is the function of the artist: to absorb the lives of others into himself, and himself to become those others and their lives. (pp. 311-12)

[It is in the later stories—those following the Winesburg sketches—] that we can best see why Sherwood Anderson was a revolutionary force in the American short story, why he in turn became a model for younger writers, and why the short story was the form most suited to the full expression of his talent. These later stories, like the Winesburg pieces, seemed to contemporary readers to be a new victory for realism, and in a sense they were. It was in that light, certainly, that Theodore Dreiser and H. L. Mencken, for example, read and praised them. These stories seemed to close their eyes to nothing, to gloss over nothing, neither the brutalities of men nor the beauty of animals. Their relatively candid concern with the sexual relationship and with sexual motivations and repressions, their implied criticism of a society that frustrates individuality and of an individualism that creates a society of hermits, their accurate report of such physical detail as they employ and of a certain range in the speaking voice—all this and more made Anderson seem to be the champion of realism both in subject matter and in method. Yet when we put stories like "The Egg" or "I Want to Know Why" beside the work of such a realist as Stephen Crane or such a naturalist as Theodore Dreiser, we see readily enough that, with their impressionistic method, the first story is more nearly a fable and the second more nearly a poetic lamentation than either is a conventionally realistic or naturalistic report. Anderson's important observations are at once under the surface of manners and transcendent of the surface of society.

The short story was perfectly calculated to articulate those glimpses—and glimpses rather than sustained vision they were; James Joyce's word, "epiphany," is not inappropriate to Anderson's gift—those glimpses into the secret, inarticulate life that was his special province. Yet over and over he would attempt the longer form of the novel where, over and over, he would lose his imaginative grip on his materials.

Even before *Winesburg, Ohio* was published, Anderson began his next novel, *Poor White* . . . [It] is probably his best attempt in the form, but still much less satisfactory than the best of the stories. Bringing to it what he had learned about style in *Winesburg, Ohio* and hoping again to accommodate a certain "looseness" of structure by making

the community itself the unifying center (the explicit theme now is the transformation of an agrarian to an industrial way of life), the narrative focus shifts so frequently and so drastically that the total is not "a new looseness" but a thematic confusion. (pp. 313-14)

> *Mark Schorer, in his* The World We Imagine: Selected Essays *(reprinted with the permission of Farrar, Straus & Giroux, Inc.; copyright © 1948, 1949, 1953, 1956, 1957, 1959, 1962, 1963, 1968 by Mark Schorer), Farrar, Straus, 1968.*

For Anderson . . . America evoked both intense devotion and recurrent despair—perhaps an inevitable dualism in one whose deepest cultural convictions were grounded in an ante-bellum version of the American dream as articulated by his five greatest Americans [Jefferson, Lincoln, Emerson, Whitman, Henry Adams]. Jeffersonian as he essentially was, he inclined to trace the confusion and vulgarity of his age to the displacement of the agrarian base of American society. This older America he could envision in *Windy McPherson's Son* as a kind of pastoral paradise. . . . It was this agrarian faith, he wrote in *Mid-American Chants*, that had lured the immigrant races westward and had developed a deep affinity with the earth spirit, with the fields as "sacred places" in whose fertility the impulses to human aggression had vanished. And as small organic centers in this agrarian richness, he felt, there had developed the Midwestern villages, which, in turn, had nurtured a vital individualism whereby both men and women lived with courage and hope and with a pride in craftsmanship and independence such as that joyously possessed by Sponge Martin in *Dark Laughter*. (pp. 6-7)

The snake which had crept into this agrarian Eden and its village culture was, in Anderson's reiterated view, a new reliance on the external benefits supposedly conferred by technological progress rather than on the inner resources conferred by Nature and the Soul on the Emersonian and Thoreauvian and Whitmanian self. On this contest of the humane self and the nonhuman machine most of Anderson's major works revolve—especially *Windy McPherson's Son, Winesburg, Poor White, Dark Laughter,* and *Beyond Desire.* . . . [In] villages like Winesburg, as Anderson declared in his *Memoirs*, the blind faith in machines had not brought beauty but had left a residue of fragmented grotesques—villagers who, as he explains in introducing the stories of *Winesburg,* in the disintegration of the agrarian community had been driven to seize upon some narrow or partial truth and, in a desperate attempt to sustain their lives, to make it an obsessive and destructive absolute. (pp. 7-8)

Anderson's mythic focus, however, lay below the national or politico-economic level. America and the West were at last but symbolic media or indices for him, as they had been for the Transcendentalists—transient entities to be valued only to the degree that they proved instrumental in releasing the deific forces or primal satisfactions of man's being. (pp. 8-9)

Convinced as he was that the greatest obstacle to the return to the "oldness" and the "great tradition" lay in the fidelity to fact espoused by the realistic school, Anderson insisted that American writers look primarily within themselves, for "there is this common thing we all have . . . so essentially alike, deep down the same dreams, aspirations, hungers." In effect Anderson was urging a mythopoeic approach to the same native scenes that Howells and Twain had often depicted. (p. 9)

Though by the mid-1920's Anderson felt obliged to abandon many of the mythic assumptions of his Midwestern years, he could not renounce entirely the demands of his mythopoeic imagination. During the last fifteen years of his life, therefore, he sought new centers and media for a viable myth which would bring unity and beauty to his life. This he found in the mill towns of the new industrial South and in the girls who worked therein. Formerly the South had been for Anderson New Orleans and the southern Mississippi, where the dark, ironic laughter of the Negroes had seemed to express for him an elemental spontaneity and a vital sense of life—a "touch with things" such as stones, trees, houses, fields, and tools, as Bruce Dudley enviously concedes in *Dark Laughter*—which made the members of a subject race humanly superior to the sterile life about them. In the later Southern novels the Negroes have all but disappeared, and though the mill girls, who as a vital center supplant them, are too much at the mercy of their factory world to embody any mythic assurance, they do point to a redemptive feminine principle which Anderson, like Henry Adams, found in his later years the surest counteragent to the disintegrating power of the machine. (pp. 14-15)

[His] treatment of the machine in his late works often discloses a new ambiguity. As his recourse to woman for salvation reflects Adams's adoration of the Virgin, so his discovery of the poetry as well as the power of the machine follows the example of another of his five "greatest Americans," Whitman, who abandoned the pastoral milieu of "the splendid silent sun" to discover the poetry of ferries and locomotives and crowded streets. Yet Anderson, with his earlier sustained distrust of the machine, could not free himself from an ambivalence in his later years; he felt both awe and impotence, he confessed, in the presence of the vast order and power and beauty of machinery, and his tribute to Lindbergh as an emergent culture hero, the new type of machine man, as well as his sympathetic portrayal of the speed-obsessed Kit Brandon, the heroine of a late novel, betrays an uneasiness not present, say, in his characterizations of Sponge Martin and the Negroes in *Dark Laughter*. Yet watching the superb technology of the whirling machines, his hero Red Oliver, in *Beyond Desire*, no doubt reflected much of Anderson's later attitude by confessing that he felt "exultant" and that here was "American genius" at work—America at "its finest." . . . Modern American industry, he concluded ambivalently in *Perhaps Women* . . . , was indeed a "dance," a "flow of refined power," to which men lifted up their eyes in worshipful adoration. Surely in such statements the failure of Anderson to approach the machine as if it were mountains and rivers is manifest. The earlier mythopoeic imagination has become bifurcated into myth and poetry; the validity of the myth is not felt, and the poetry is an act of will rather than of imagination. In this bifurcation and desiccation one may no doubt find much of the explanation for Anderson's decline in his later years.

To his inclination and commitment to a mythopoeic approach to American experience both Anderson's literary achievements and his shortcomings may ultimately be traced. From the time of the First World War until his

death at the beginning of the Second, he consistently aligned his writing with a focal purpose summarily stated in *A Story Teller's Story:* "It is my aim to be true to the essence of things." In probing for the "essence" he ran the romantic risk of neglecting the existential substance of American experience, and hence one may feel, as Lionel Trilling has asserted, a deficiency of the sensory and concrete in his work. If one adds to this mythic concern for patterns and forces behind the phenomenal world Anderson's addiction to the psychic and intuitive as the arbiters of reality, one approaches what to Anderson seemed the "poetic" factor in the mythopoeic imagination. (pp. 15-16)

Anderson's style, like his larger fictional perspective, is an organic product of his mythopoeic approach. Rooted in the naive, in wonder, in the mystic and the intuitive, his expression shapes itself subjectively from emotions or associations . . . at the expense of tight syntax, controlled structure, and purified or precise diction. And yet Anderson's vagaries are, for the most part, those which he inherited (and somewhat intensified) through a major native tradition initiated by the Transcendentalists and involving in its course Whitman, Twain, Stein, and Salinger. If from Anderson's pen this style becomes one in which each sentence affords only a fragmentary glimpse, . . . perhaps the limitation is in part explained by Anderson's conclusion that in an immense land where all men are strangers to one another, the writer can "only snatch at fragments" and be true to his "own inner impulses." . . . Early in his career Anderson in "An Apology for Crudity" asserted that if American writing were to have force and authenticity, it would have to forgo objectivity for the "subjective impulse," and that an honest crudity would have to precede the "gift of beauty and subtlety in prose." However consciously stylized and contrived his own apparent artlessness may be, his "subjective impulse" extended outward like Whitman's in an effort to catch "the essence of things," and his reputation will be most secure among those who can accept the mythopoeic assumptions which nurtured and shaped his imagination. (pp. 17-18)

Benjamin T. Spencer, "Sherwood Anderson: American Mythopoeist," in American Literature *(reprinted by permission of the Publisher; copyright 1969 by Duke University Press, Durham, North Carolina), March, 1969, pp. 1-18.*

Writers of fiction may for convenience be grouped according to their retrospective or prospective qualities, with the war always present as a sign of the historical process. The retrospective writers are those whose techniques and mental sets were determined by the past; they were not necessarily traditional in Eliot's sense, but they were dominated, consciously or not, by tradition. This generalization holds true for Europe, too, although the European outline may differ from the American. Retrospection was first and most obviously a matter of generation, second and more significantly a matter of sensibility. The prospective might be seen as rebellion and a disposition to experiment in technique, but only secondly as a matter of generation. Sherwood Anderson . . . , according to this description, is retrospective by generation and accomplishment despite his ardent will to rebellion and experimentation. . . . (p. 16)

Sherwood Anderson's high reputation in the twenties was made possible by the war, even though he took no direct part in it, and if we are to credit the evidence of his work, letters, memoirs, or biographers, the war made no impact upon him whatsoever. His references to it are few and bombastic. Although Anderson wrote only one work that may endure, *Winesburg, Ohio* ..., and the slightest handful of memorable sketches thereafter, both his contemporaries and later critics were remarkably kind to him. Reasons for that kindness lie deeply embedded in the American mind and spirit at the end of the war, as well as in the rather panhandling personality of Anderson, who begged for and in a sense enforced generosity to himself. With characteristic shrewdness, Anderson contrived to appear to Van Wyck Brooks and Paul Rosenfeld at the end of the war as a middle-aged Lochinvar come out of the West, a genuine American to reinforce their hope for a distinctively American future. (pp. 16-17)

Brooks and his companions knew Anderson through Waldo Frank, with whom Anderson had begun to correspond in 1916. Frank had asked Anderson to contribute to *The Seven Arts* [a pacifist review], and when he received the story "The Untold Lie," Frank wrote an article entitled "Emerging Greatness" for the first issue, thus originating a view of Anderson that has been maintained ever since. Frank, Rosenfeld, and to a lesser degree Brooks himself, saw Anderson as the embodiment of their call for native American genius, for a voice having not the slightest European accent to it, an answer, in brief, to a loud, long American appeal from the eastern seaboard to the midwestern prairie. The difference between what Waldo Frank and his friends saw in Anderson and what Anderson really was is a fair guide to the ambiguity in Anderson's posthumous reputation. A devious man always, Anderson posed as a midwestern original and was so received. In fact, he was the opposite; his strength as a writer lay in his representativeness not his originality. Until very recently, every midwestern factory of any size and every small town has had an Anderson in it: the local self-proclaimed intellectual who drank and whored with the boys, yet who dabbled in the arts and read books on the side. (pp. 18-19)

While posing as a shy countryman to his new-found friends, he was in truth a successful advertising salesman and copywriter who announced what a "smooth son of a bitch" he was as a salesman. In his raw pleas to Brooks and Rosenfeld for mental sustenance, he was not so much envying them their culture and education as setting himself up as the untutored genius. (p. 19)

Readers have been teased by the problem of whether *Winesburg, Ohio* is a novel, a collection of short stories, sketches, or whatever. That problem is interesting, for it places in relief Anderson's salient strengths and crippling weaknesses. Most of the matter in the collection was written as independent short stories, tales, vignettes, or sketches. Anderson then found an apparent solution in his title and his device of creating a linking personage, George Willard. Willard is the prototype of the Andersonian hero: questioning, unhappy, wounded, uncomprehending, but through it all burning for escape from small town life and longing for "freedom." He enters briefly into or bounces off the narratives of the other characters, and his own narrative and theme of freedom introduce and conclude the book. The other device, as mentioned, is the title. By implication, the work concerns not individuals, but the community of Winesburg.... Anderson said that he had found a

new, "looser form" for the novel and justified that form in his belief that "Life is a loose flowing thing." (p. 23)

Winesburg, Ohio is not a novel, but rather what Anderson called it before his publisher changed the title, *The Book of the Grotesque,* or what we might call a book of grotesques. On the evidence of his work, Anderson was apparently incapable of writing a novel, in spite of several works approximating the genre. His talent was not for sustained narrative but for fictionalized meditation and for the creation of highly charged, momentary states of emotion. The characters of *Winesburg, Ohio* qualify as "grotesques" because their emotional time is not solar, but lunar or sidereal; each contains Anderson's notion of a "truth," usually of a sexual nature, about humanity as he conceives it: that some men are homosexual; that some men prefer to sleep with women but do not; that some women prefer to sleep with men but do not; that mores in Winesburg are stupefying, and the like. In his free use of symbolism, Anderson extended the confining bounds of naturalism, but his curious declarative quality frequently made his symbolism easy, then forced, so weakening its power. (p. 25)

In many respects, Anderson is the American Lawrence. Years before reading Lawrence, he had established the brooding, essayistic, declarative tone, together with the impulse toward transcendental freedom to be achieved through fidelity to the senses and emotions, a fidelity possible only by the rejection of industrialism and the affirmation of something very like Lawrence's fatuous doctrine of "blood." Anderson did discover authority in Lawrence for certain of his insights about sex, but to consider him only as a disciple is to do him injustice.... If Lawrence lacked Anderson's attractive freshness and directness, his prose often possessed a nobility that we cannot find in Anderson. Lawrence's was the finer and subtler mind, yet his characters are closely akin to Anderson's. They, too, are "grotesques." (p. 26)

Like many other American writers before and since, Anderson was forced back upon himself exclusively, and his work displays the occasional strengths and frequent weaknesses of that self. His deviousness is witness to a lack of integrity, not in any social or moral sense, but integrity to word and fiction. He brooded not about art but about "being an artist," and he wasted energy trying to encompass themes that were foreign to his talent. His limitations kept him provincial and retrospective, never more so than when he tried to be "modern." Needing ideas, he was born to a time and a society in which the ideas served up to him could not serve him.... When Paul Rosenberg and Van Wyck Brooks greeted him as the savior, as the authentic American of the new era, they did him a disservice. He was at first delighted, then uneasy, then despairing at the impossibility of maintaining the role thrust upon him. A sentimental, retrospective interpretation of the American past could only distort a view of the American post-war present. (pp. 27-8)

John McCormick, in his The Middle Distance: A Comparative History of American Literature: 1919-1932 *(reprinted with permission of Macmillan Publishing Co., Inc.; copyright © 1971 by The Free Press, a Division of The Macmillan Company), The Free Press, 1971.*

Only rarely was [Anderson] able to engage that kind of truly educated speculation over human motivation and action which resides as a latent force in all first-class writers of fiction. "It was his ignorance of 'reality' and 'real people,'" as Alfred Kazin once remarked, "that crippled his books." (p. 569)

If "Winesburg" attains a unity beyond those of time and place, one must seek it elsewhere than in the theory of the grotesque. Waldo Frank thought that Anderson's dominant idea was to trace "a line of decay, a domain of deprivation" within an outmoded "agrarian culture." . . . This is perhaps why so many of the tales take place in a crepuscular atmosphere, partly in light but more often in shadow or darkness visible, as if the town and its environs were meant as an image for the interior of a mind, as no doubt they might have seemed to Anderson's imagination.

Deprivation, search, and *release* are key terms for the recurrent patterns in "Winesburg." So also is *repression.* (p. 575)

Although there is no extant evidence that Anderson had read either Joyce or Lawrence before writing "Winesburg," he afterwards numbered them among his few literary heroes. It may not be merely adventitious, it may actually have been a sign of the times that the Irishman, the Englishman, and the American should all three have chosen, more or less simultaneously, to underscore the necessity of freedom from those forms of mental and moral paralysis that bind their fictional people to drab lives, suffocating jobs, dreary marriages, and all the multifarious distortions that loneliness and lovelessness can produce. (pp. 576-77)

> Carlos Baker, "Sherwood Anderson's Winesburg: A Reprise," in Virginia Quarterly Review (copyright, 1972, by the Virginia Quarterly Review, The University of Virginia), Vol. 48, No. 4 (Autumn, 1972), pp. 568-79.

If the unity of *Winesburg* is to be appreciated, it behooves us to set straight the relevance of the prologue ["The Book of the Grotesque"] especially since the novel's unity, partly by intent and partly because of its lapses, is loose to begin with. Granted, the prologue is invested with typical Andersonian nebulousness, and by itself it oversimplifies: it does not account for the external forces that contribute to his characters' grotesqueness or for the complications of their inward struggles. But this is not to say that it contradicts the stories or has little or no bearing on Anderson's attitude toward his characters. Moreover, however deficient as an autonomous whole, the prologue is a piece of narrative art (a fact sometimes overlooked), a story with a central character; and, considered as such in retrospect, braced and amplified by subsequent stories, it helps us to understand the resolution of the novel's theme and how the book is rounded out. No, *Winesburg* is sufficiently of a whole, unified by Anderson's philosophical vision if not by a sometimes errant formal instinct. (p. 994)

Because their dreams emanate from the depths of their being and express their humanity, the first paradox of Anderson's concept is that grotesqueness is a sign of worth elevating his characters above the rabble. . . . As their dreams are beautiful, so most of the grotesques are beautiful. They are fanatics, but their guilt is qualified by inno-

cence and their social defeat by personal or spiritual triumph. This coincides with one meaning . . . of the novel's key metaphor, "the sweetness of the twisted apples," . . . the savoring of which saves the unnamed girl in "Paper Pills." Like the apples, the grotesques are the twisted crop of the human harvest, their essence having gathered to a gnarl, and hence they too are rejected. But for the very same reason, they are also the "sweetest"—as there are few perfect apples and untouched people, so there are few twisted apples and deformed people; the majority are undistinguished variations in between the two extremes. Or again, considered as a story about the vocational calling of a budding writer, the novel moves toward the realization in George of his capacity to dream, by which he finally escapes the debilitating provincialism of Winesburg and is thrust into the life of the imagination. . . .

[The] grotesques have picked up fanaticism as a shield against hostile forces external to them. That these forces— brutality, lust, and ignorance, the lack of parental love and excessive parental love—are the sole, or even the crucial, cause of their broken lives, however, is difficult to accept. The grotesques are victimized and indeed warrant our sympathy, but in most of the stories our response is mitigated by irony of one kind or another. . . . Moreover, for most of the grotesques the traumas around which their stories and lives revolve occurred in the past, and, with the possible exception of Wing Biddlebaum, there is no reason to believe that their original defeat was so devastating that it is now impossible for them to emerge from their isolation or, most pertinent of all, that they are haunted thereafter by oppressive forces *other than life itself.* (p. 996)

As a symbol of their condition, the "room" can be misleading if we fail to recognize that it is insular and a refuge as well as confining. It is important to see that more relevant to their distended minds than either the traumas they have experienced or the dreams they pursue is the grotesques' fanatical desire to cling to those dreams despite the dehumanizing effects this desire begets. (pp. 996-97)

In a word, the philosophical substance of the novel consists of the conflict between ideal and the real, between spirit and flesh, between subconscious longing and conscious dread; and the inherent flaw of the grotesques is their unwillingness to accept this conflict and what it denotes—that their dreams can never be fulfilled in this world.

Considered as a model of subsequent stories, "Hands" can be summed up in the following way. Society's repression of Wing exemplifies the outcome of the grotesques' crises with forces external to them, these forces, by and large, having similarly engendered sexual fears which prohibit them from growing beyond adolescence. But they have had such an impact because they awakened in the grotesques a conscious awareness of their flesh and hence of their existential guilt, at which point their fanaticism and their victimization are formally fused. In other words, their social crises are simply the external and metaphorical counterparts of their struggle against the internal limits of their being, of their innate finitude, of contingencies which circumscribe their dreams from within and which the grotesques attempt to transcend: they are bent upon immortality. If they seem to be fanatics without will, as it were, this is because they have allowed the unswerving thrust of their emotions to govern their will, and their will in turn has paralyzed their intellect; having met with the opposition of experiential fact but seeking in their hearts the apotheosis of their emotions, they discredit the objective reality of the first and make absolute the subjective reality of the second. And, when this fails, they tend to regard their finitude as absolute: they make of objective reality the totality of all there is. (p. 998)

[The] most important corollary to Anderson's use of myth is that grotesqueness, to him, was nothing more than a metaphor of the natural condition of man, of his being at cross-purposes with himself, of his compulsive hearkening to the infinite call of transcendence which his finitude makes impossible from the start. . . . What distinguishes the grotesques from most of us is that they conduct their lives as if the Fall had never occurred, or as if the "truth" each has seized will deliver them unto their mythic and authentic selves, and hence their regressive groping in the dark. And hence, too, Anderson's compassion for them. He shared their transcendental yearnings, without which, he believed, life is meaningless and false, restricted to the biological and the mechanical. All the same, only a sentimental reading of the stories would maintain that he sanctions without qualification what, in their case, the grotesques' yearnings have produced: narrowness of vision, a refusal to grow, the wilful denial of experience—in short, their fanaticism. Their suffering, after all, clogs and takes them nowhere; it is neither fulfilling nor cathartic. (p. 1001)

He goes on to affirm the rationality and beauty of grotesqueness—"the sweetness of the twisted apples"—and thereby transcends grotesqueness, sanctifying his characters' dreams and yearnings with the promise that they will be returned to the original garden through Death. Anderson dramatizes all this in the two stories that involve Doctor Reefy: the airy "Paper Pills," in which Anderson's key metaphor appears; and "Death," in which George Willard's destiny as an artist has its true inception. Moreover, these stories define the bounds of grotesqueness and, developmentally, bring us back to the prologue. (pp. 1001-02)

Within the context of grotesqueness and its various modes, all the self-immolated characters in the novel who cling to their dreams are suspended metaphysically between Elizabeth and Reefy's young bride, who are polarized. Elizabeth's grotesqueness is ugly and negative because she has capitulated, has surrendered her dream to the empirical world, finding release only in death. The grotesqueness of Reefy's young bride, on the other hand, after she has discovered the "sweetness of the twisted apples," is beautiful and positive.

Of more interest than either of his lovers is Reefy himself, whom Anderson obviously treats as someone special. For one thing, excepting his bride, he alone of all the grotesques undergoes an essential change in character. . . . He has not only learned to live in solitude, this is to say; he has expanded and altered his vision, transmuted the anguish of grotesqueness into something positive. Most noteworthy in this respect is his singular power of communication, the fidelity of his rhetoric to his vision. . . . (pp. 1002-03)

[Owing] specifically to the life and death of Elizabeth, the catalyst of his transformation, Reefy alone among the char-acters understands grotesqueness in the abstract and has gained ascendancy over it. (p. 1003)

[Reefy] knows that the human need and desire for communion and fulfillment is a kind of terminal illness from which there is no immunity and for which there is no lasting cure except death, an enigma his paper pills contain and his bride thrives on. . . . And yet, all the same, man need not despair. If he cannot attain the perfect fruit in this life, he can attain at least the "sweetness of the twisted apples," a temporary palliative to the human condition: man can transcend his existential crisis through the knowledge that all humanity shares in this crisis, a purgative awareness which unites him with others in reverence and in the communion of the human spirit, an awareness of the subsuming beauty and order of all things, including grotesqueness.

Such is the essential content of Reefy's and, we can assume, Anderson's vision. At any rate, we know that the same vision sustains the old writer in the prologue, whom Reefy in his old age resembles. (pp. 1003-04)

By analogy, then, Reefy is more than just a spiritual healer or a village guru; like the old writer, he is also a priest of words, the only man in Winesburg who truly communicates —he is "almost a poet." (p. 1004)

Reefy's change of character and the vision born of this change bear vitally on George's identity and spiritual role as a writer. As the perfect artist and the arbiter of dreams, Reefy is at once the embodiment of all George aspires to and the hope of all the grotesques, who look upon George as their potential savior: through the artistic imagination their lives will be redeemed: though they will not be made whole and beautiful, the peculiar value of their twisted state will be recognized. And since Reefy in this capacity is identified with the old writer in the prologue, and insofar as George fulfills his destiny, this is also to say that George *is* the old writer, symbolically if not actually. Or, to reverse our perspective, the old writer is George in his old age, years after his departure from Winesburg.

This resolution is crystallized in "Death," in which Reefy's and George's metamorphoses simultaneously begin. (pp. 1004-05)

George's destiny is contingent upon the lives of the grotesques, whose suffering will become the substance of his art, and whose fulfillment is contingent upon the dreams they have inspired in him, dreams which will become the infusing and uplifting spirit of his art. In short, for the same reasons that we return to Anderson's novel, George must come back to Winesburg. And this he does, not in fact but from the transcendental perspective of the artistic imagination. (p. 1006)

Ralph Ciancio, "'The Sweetness of the Twisted Apples': Unity of Vision in 'Winesburg, Ohio'," in PMLA, 87 *(copyright © 1972 by the Modern Language Association of America; reprinted by permission of the Modern Language Association of America), October, 1972, pp. 994-1006.*

(Sir Henry) Max(imilian) Beerbohm

1872-1956

English satirical essayist, caricaturist, short story writer, critic, and novelist. Beerbohm was celebrated for the witty satire that he directed primarily at social and aesthetic targets. A contributor to the *Yellow Book,* he joined in his early twenties the literary circle that surrounded Oscar Wilde. In 1898 he succeeded Bernard Shaw (by whom he was dubbed "the incomparable Max") as drama critic of *Saturday Review* and served in that post with the grace of a perfect stylist and the affect of a perfect dandy. He resigned in 1910, marrying in the same year the American actress Florence Kahn, and immediately retired to Rapallo, Italy, where he continued to draw the marvelous caricatures for which he is best known. Beerbohm was knighted in 1939.

PRINCIPAL WORKS

Caricatures of Twenty-Five Gentlemen (drawings) 1896
The Works of Max Beerbohm with a Bibliography
  (essays) 1896
The Happy Hypocrite (short story) 1897
More (essays) 1899
The Second Childhood of John Bull (drawings) 1901
A Book of Caricatures (drawings) 1907
Yet Again (essays) 1909
Zuleika Dobson; or, an Oxford Love Story (novel) 1911
A Christmas Garland (parodies) 1912
Fifty Caricatures (drawings) 1913
Seven Men (short stories) 1919
And Even Now (essays) 1921
Rosetti and His Circle (drawings) 1922
Things New and Old (drawings) 1923
Around Theatres (essays and criticism) 1924
The Dreadful Dragon of Hay Hill (short story) 1928
A Variety of Things (short stories) 1928
Mainly on the Air (broadcasts and essays) 1946
Max's Nineties: Drawings 1892-1899 (drawings) 1958

If Mr Beerbohm intends to contribute anything substantial to our civilization ("or whatever it is") he had better begin at once. I notice an unusual exasperation in the reception of his latest works, and it is clear that the world which has been indulgent to his frivolity for such a long time is at last demanding that he put his gifts to their proper use. (p. 522)

Resentment against a neatness too long drawn out is . . . natural and silly enough. The other element in the decline of Mr Beerbohm's prestige is a trifle more complicated. An emphasis has been put upon the one thing in his career as an artist which is entirely unimportant. It was always the aristocrat, and not the artist, that was marked; the patrician, not the individual. His delicacy and his detachment, his irony, his wilfulness, were not put forth as the elements of his nature, but as the insignia of his rank. The very circumstance that *he* put forth nothing and that Max as an aristocrat in letters was created by his admirers was also noted as part of his superiority. (p. 523)

In Mr Beerbohm's case it was even suggested that the patrician could do no wrong, that he had never published a dull paragraph or a stupid caricature; it was never suggested that what makes him interesting is his imperturbable habit of being himself. I mean by this that he has been dull because he has been dull, and not because some one else, who became famous for it, had been dull before him; if his manner was laboured, it was because he found no other way to say what he wanted to say. (pp. 523-24)

He learned how to write by observing the habits of others; but he never used anything until it had become his own, and never unless it corresponded to something in himself. His work is traditional and affected; but he mastered the tradition and his affectations are his own. (p. 524)

It is because Mr Beerbohm has been with remarkable consistency himself that one does not mind his lapses. I would be willing to omit from the canon all but a few pages of *More,* all but a few paragraphs of *Yet Again.* There are a few pages almost dreary in *The Works* and a few not entirely satisfactory in *And Even Now;* just as there are in each volume of caricatures some which please in no way at all. But there is not, as far as my judgement goes, anything written or drawn with that peculiar kind of badness which betrays imitative and sloppy and dishonest work. (pp. 524-25)

Gilbert Seldes, in The Dial *(copyright, 1922, by The Dial Publishing Company, Inc.; reprinted by permission of J. S. Watson, Jr. and Scofield Thayer), May, 1922 (and reprinted by Kraus Reprint Corporation, 1966).*

Sir Max is as literary as a quotation from Horace. It is never life itself, only the cultivated, the artistic, the aristocratic life, that he savors or satirizes; and when he savors it is not to make converts, any more than when he satirizes it is really to protest. His work exists simply to give pleasure of the most delicate kind—simply to distill all that we mean by temperament into something characterized by all that we mean by style.

His sheer spoofing aside, most of Sir Max's work may be summed up as the manipulation of a personality. He began manipulating it when it was not yet formed, and when his style, whatever its merits, was still a little absurd. He began impudently; not with the callow impudence of youth, but as a precocious and sort of parthenogenic man of the world. The art that reveals art came before its most celebrated opposite, if indeed the opposite ever quite came at all; the fun in Max lies not in wondering about his dexterity but in watching it. He is acrobat, not conjurer. At the start, however, he was not entirely deft: in *The Works* and *More* the cleverness is fatiguing, the personality obtrusive, the matter quite often thin. (pp. 227-28)

What is cardinal to the manipulation of a personality is a completely expressive style; and that, despite an instinctive finesse, came late. Max's style, being mannered, never needed perfect naturalness; but it did need perfect ease. And as late as *Yet Again* and *Zuleika Dobson* there is too often a slight strain in the writing, as there is a slight stretching in the contents. It was the many years that separate *Yet Again* from *And Even Now* that brought perfection. Finally everything came right: the proportions, the tone, the touch that is both intimate and reserved, the *unex-hibitionistic* wit, and the Tory point of view that is worn, not as in too young a man, outrageously; nor defiantly, as in too insecure a one. Above all, the personality has found a prose that exactly suits it. It is a personality raised out of life into art, and one that while seeming to confide continues to elude one. (p. 228)

Perhaps in the factual sense we have never been given the true Max Beerbohm. Artistically it makes no difference—though it is my own guess that Max has usually been altogether candid, exploiting the worldling's knowledge that the truth is the last thing people ever believe.

But beyond the question of fact or fabrication lies the *effect* of personality through style; the juggling, so to speak, of the first person singular. It is probably the most ticklish problem that can confront a writer. . . . There is [also] the peril, the besetting peril for the familiar essayist, of coyness. And though Max escapes all the other pitfalls, at times even he becomes rather coy. Yet the redeeming thing is that he does not become so oftener, particularly as his style can be very irritating. Even his mature style trades too freely in inversions, in Latinisms and archaisms, in double negatives, in "do but" and "averse from" and "belike" and "how great soever"—becoming precious, conspicuous, waxen; and I suppose one is riled the more from knowing that Max indulges in all these mannerisms with a quiet smile. . . . (pp. 228-29)

It is personality that animates Max's work, but form and finish that will go far toward preserving it. The essays are not simply serpentine excursions in personality; they are real essays, often perfect essays, that explore a subject without seeming to exhaust it, that move suavely and wit-

tily from point to point, till they reach a sound resting-place and stop. They breathe culture, but never down your neck; they are as light, but certainly not as colorless, as air; they are as beckoning and satisfying as his own Golden Drugget. One sometimes wonders just why Sir Max's best essays so completely transcend everyone else's in our time, and one seems to find the answer in their tone. Somehow the most noticeably precious of our writers is also the most genially conversational; he chats with us as Chesterton never did, as Shaw—for all his greatness—never could. He shows the reader every courtesy, but his greatest concern is for the essay form itself—which shall remain an essay and never become a dissertation, an impromptu, or even an out-and-out memoir. (pp. 229-30)

It took Max a long time to master his tune; for all his finest essays are to be found in *And Even Now*. . . . Here is "No. 2 the Pines," that glowing memoir of Swinburne which is saved by its impish touches and sly sidelights from being too reverent. Here is that perfect trifle "A Clergyman." Here, again, is "Hosts and Guests," the model and despair of anyone who would write an essay that is exactly, supremely, an essay. Here, indeed, with very few exceptions, is one good thing after another. Yet, before turning away from Max's essays, one ought to note how in all periods they exhibit—though in late periods most keenly—his wit. (p. 231)

Sir Max's only novel [*Zuleika Dobson*] is not a great favorite of mine. . . . [For] me *Zuleika* is unsteadily poised between fantasy and satire, when indeed it is anything more than a classicist's picnic or an Oxford family joke. As to form, perhaps it might better have been a long novelette: stretched into a novel, it has to be elaborate to avoid seeming thin, and it doesn't avoid seeming thin. As to content, the story it tells does not altogether come off. Possibly I lack the delicate imagination that is needed to enter with a whole heart into Sir Max's conspiracy. But possibly the author himself lacked the robust imagination that is needed to make something of this kind really succeed. In satiric fantasy the author must somehow, with a bold maneuver, steal (rather than woo) the reader's credulity; and however great Sir Max's finesse, it is not finesse—and certainly not archness—that a story like *Zuleika* most needs; it is high spirits, lively turns, audacity. And that is just what it frequently lacks. (pp. 231-32)

Sir Max is by all odds the greatest parodist, as he is the greatest essayist, of our time; and the best things in *A Christmas Garland* are almost beyond praise. (p. 233)

All Max's finest parodies are at the expense of writers he loves or appreciates. . . . The parodies of Wells, say, or Kipling, are extremely clever; but they fall short of the piece on Gosse or James because they are conceived in antipathy. Max bludgeons Wells, but somehow Wells escapes only bruised; but he kills James, in the sense that each man kills the thing he loves.

If Max partly failed with his one novel, he brilliantly succeeded with that other work of fiction, *Seven Men*. These stories make up a book almost as original as it is captivating. In "Enoch Soames" and "Maltby and Braxton" Max has spoofed the literary temperament of the nineties, and of more than the nineties—its affectations and insane vanities, its snobbery and emulousness—with superb skill. In these tales Max found his perfect material, reviving with precision and nostalgia a real world of real people, and then, through fantasy, standing it squarely on its head. (pp. 233-34)

Sir Max's theater criticism doubtless suffers from the fact that its author was never deeply drawn to the theater, or powerfully held by it. No one could have been less stage-struck than that reviewer, who confessed he was bored by the play he saw on his tenth birthday. But his critical approach has, besides a certain personal charm, a certain solid usefulness. By not surrendering easily to the theater's "glamour," Max was saved from swallowing a lot of its silliness. He saw the stage for what it was and largely still is: the least impressive, the least adult of contemporary arts. He never, like Shaw, attacked it frontally; he just slowly undermined its pretensions by quietly underlining its stupidities. I suspect that, in the perspective of half a century, we get a sounder estimate of the English theater of his time from Max than we do from his more knowledgeable and responsive colleagues Walkley and Archer. To be sure, Max's temperament led him into errors and inadequacies. He underrated Gorki, for example, and overrated Maeterlinck. There is again no gusto in his criticism; but there is much unprofessional shrewdness, there is fairly much professional observation, there is mild wit and—mixed blessing —an essayist's emphasis on form. Max was not an outstandingly good critic; nor, like Shaw, so superb a journalist and electrical a personality that he himself still holds up where his subject-matter doesn't; but he wrote the sort of antiseptic criticism that, by not succumbing to the moment's emotionalism, has more than the moment's value.

As to Sir Max's general "place" in literature, one can more easily dispute how high it is than how permanent. Of all the writers of their time, it is men like Max and A. E. Housman—men who in their minor way frequently achieved perfection—that we can feel surest will be read with pleasure for many generations to come. They cared more for art than for life, for art, moreover, that has shapeliness rather than size; and the preference greatly limits them in stature. But it should also preserve them in time, in the sense that enamel outwears flesh. In terms of posterity, perfection is much less of a gamble than greatness. How big Max's audience will be a generation, or a century, hence is indeed something else again. Max was always caviar; probably he always will be. But a dozen of his essays and two or three of his stories should survive as long as there is a civilized point of view. (pp. 234-35)

> *Louis Kronenberger, "Max Beerbohm" (1947), in his* The Republic of Letters: Essays on Various Writers *(copyright © 1947 by Louis Kronenberger; reprinted by permission of Alfred A. Knopf, Inc.), Knopf, 1955, pp. 224-35.*

Max is quite complex, and that complexity and the intelligence it generates are what—given his double talent, a complexity in itself—have made him interesting beyond what one might expect from work that seems at first sight so playful. (p. 432)

There had always been perceptible in his work an alien point of view not amenable to English standards.

This alien side of Max Beerbohm declares itself most fully and frankly in the album of drawings called *Rossetti and His Circle,* published in 1922, when Max had lived more than a decade in the country of Rossetti's origins. (p. 433)

For the alien element in Max is at least as exotic as Rossetti. He says somewhere in his theatrical criticism that the rococo is his favorite style; but this element, when he gives it its head, does not stop with being rococo. In its gemminess, its artificiality, its excrescences of grotesque fancy, it sometimes becomes positively Byzantine. The Englishman in Max, on the other hand, is moderate and unassertive, dominated by common sense—and not merely correct and prosaic, but even occasionally a bit of a Philistine. It was the Byzantine that made him love the nineties and led him to find Beardsley enchanting; it was the Englishman that kept him steady, so that, almost alone of his group, he survived the *fin de siècle* without tragedy, breakdown or scandal—and he walked out of the pages of the *Yellow Book* and into those of the *Saturday Review* as politely and unperturbedly as he might have gone to dine at Simpson's after absinthe at the Café Royal. It was the Byzantine that pricked him to cultivate his early preciosity of style; the Englishman that taught him the trick, which it has amused him to practise so often, of letting this preciosity down, with deprecating and comic effect, by a descent into the flatly colloquial.

This mixture of contrasting tendencies appears in all Max Beerbohm's work, sometimes with confusing results. In the title of *Zuleika Dobson* there is a simple juxtaposition of the exotic and the British; but in the novel itself the two are entangled in a curious way.... The trouble, I believe, is due to the fact that in this case the two sets of colors, instead of being blended in a fabric, have got into a kind of snarl. What is the pattern or the point of *Zuleika*? Is it satire or parody or nonsense or what? It is full of amusing things and patches of clever writing, but it has also tiresome stretches of the thought and conversations of characters who do not even have the two-dimensional kind of life— like that of the people of Congreve or Firbank—that is possible within a comic convention. (pp. 434-35)

Neither *Zuleika* nor *The Happy Hypocrite* is a favorite of mine among his works; and *The Dreadful Dragon of Hay Hill* is perhaps the only really bad thing that he has allowed to get into a book. These stories force unworkable conceits; they get queerly out of range of Max's taste. He is much better when—in *Enoch Soames* or *Not That I Would Boast* —he sticks closer to a real background. Yet this is not enough, with Max, to produce one of his first-rate stories: the feeblest of the *Seven Men* are the ones that are least fantastic. Max's talent for impersonation, extraordinary in its way, is almost exclusively literary—that is, he can give you a poem, a play, a letter, a speech in Parliament, but he is unable to give you people—the heroine of *Zuleika,* for example—whose style can have no basis in reading. When Zuleika begins to talk like a book, she has to explain that she has picked up the habit from a certain Mr. Beerbohm, "who once sat next to me at dinner." The two short stories mentioned above are the virtuoso pieces of a parodist, as is the best thing in *Mainly on the Air,* a portrait of a sententious old fraud called *T. Fenning Dodsworth;* and *Zuleika,* it seems to me, succeeds best when the comedy is verbal, when it arrives at its own kind of parody by exploiting a preciosity that is half burlesque. (pp. 436-37)

[In] the series of political cartoons, done during the Boer War and called *The Second Childhood of John Bull,* as well as many of his other drawings between then and the first World War, ... Max gave ... the impression of being something of a middle-class liberal. In any case, there was sometimes in his caricatures, less often in his writings, an unmistakable accent of anger. His impudence was by no means so childlike as his caricatures of himself, wide-eyed and wispy-limbed, seemed calculated to make one expect; but his animus was never derived from political or moral principle: it was simply an intense dislike of certain vulgarities, stupidities, impostures. (p. 438)

It is really the whole modern world that Max Beerbohm despises and dreads; but he has never worked out a consistent line for dealing with contemporary problems. His point of view is instinctively that of the cultivated merchant class. He may admire the feudal nobility, but he is not necessarily sympathetic with them. He prizes the security and freedom of the old-fashioned middle-class gentleman, but he hates all the horrors and rigors, on the masters' side as well as the workers', which have eventually resulted from the system upon which these advantages were based. The difficulties of his position are disarmingly exposed in his essay on servants in *And Even Now*—it appears that he does not like to be waited on and would be glad to see domestic service abolished—in which he calls himself a Tory anarchist.

This is deplorable from the point of view of the man who thinks that "art is a weapon" on one side or other of the class war; but it has not prevented Max Beerbohm from being one of the great critics of his time. Max the critic has a personality somewhat different, though never quite distinct, from Max the storyteller and personal essayist. The writer that emerges, for example, in the two volumes of theatrical notices contributed to the *Saturday Review* has stripped himself, after the pieces of the first few months, of . . . coyness. . . . In the course of his twelve years of service, he had reduced the arabesques of his earlier style to the sobriety of his later prose; and one meets here, as in no other department of his work, the mind that gives a base to the whole: very flexible, very free from prejudice (he has dropped his undergraduate poses), but completely sure of itself (though he has sometimes to revise his first verdicts), very definite and firm in its judgments, and very direct and courageous in registering unpopular opinions. In its different way, this body of writing is as remarkable as the dramatic criticism of Max's predecessor Shaw—who suggested him to fill his own place on the basis of the young man's attacks on Shaw's *Plays Pleasant and Unpleasant*. Max's caricatures of contemporaries, which are a criticism of public life, also give us the tougher Beerbohm (though, for some reason, the forewords to the albums are sometimes pitched in his coyest lisp). But the field in which his critical faculty is happiest and most at home is that of literature, and here the parodies of *A Christmas Garland*—the most searching, except Proust's, of our time—have their place in a body of comment which has undoubtedly left a deeper imprint than the lightness of its tone ever promised. (pp. 439-40)

Edmund Wilson, "An Analysis of Max Beerbohm" (1948), in his Classics and Commercials: A Literary Chronicle of the Forties *(reprinted with the permission of Farrar, Straus & Giroux, Inc.; copyright 1950 by Edmund Wilson), Farrar, Straus, 1950, pp. 431-41.*

If your youth or even part of it was misspent in the twenties in this country it is very likely that some of your more profitable hours were passed reading certain things of Max Beerbohm's: essays, observations, and "Zuleika Dobson." There he ever so presently was, a celebrated member of the older literary generation, a man who knew the world in the most desirably worldly way. He was a wit and his sayings went the rounds. He did famously funny caricatures of other celebrated persons and he wrote, oh, what charming good-tempered pieces about anything that struck his interest.

He must have got pretty tired in those days of reading reviews about his "mellow" style. It may have been this recurring word, or maybe his self-caricature, or a stray photograph, but one did have in mind the image of a round, well-nourished, middling old gentleman—he was in fact a perfect Methuselah, at least forty-five or fifty years old—carefully garbed and groomed, chubby cheeked, hair thinning on top, who no doubt did his writing seated, bland and kind as a pitcher of milk, at a desk in his very exclusive London club.

It may well be asked what attraction such a specimen could have for the brash young in a time when, in certain literary circles at least, even a trace of good manners was looked upon as a moral weakness, if not proof of positive reactionary political tendencies. It was possible that one saw through his disguise, his toughness of mind and intransigent though restrained character.

He managed to get some very sharp things said through the mesh of that excellent, disciplined way of writing. After thirty years these things [collected in *And Even Now*] seem as sharp and even more timely. (pp. 75-6)

Katherine Anne Porter, "Max Beerbohm" (originally published in The New York Times Book Review, *October 22, 1950), in her* The Collected Essays and Occasional Writings of Katherine Anne Porter *(copyright © 1970 by Katherine Anne Porter; reprinted by permission of Delacorte Press/ Seymour Lawrence), Delacorte Press, 1970, pp. 75-6.*

Like most of his caricatures, Beerbohm's imaginary portraits are faces seen through the 'illuminative fog of memory'. From this it follows that they are not faithful copies of reality, but that, owing to the distorting quality of the medium, they have undergone a change. In both spheres of Beerbohm's art the natural product of this distorting process is a caricature, that is to say, a representation of reality in which the irrelevant details are left out while the essential features are exaggerated. His imaginary portraits are, therefore, not reproductions of reality, but—though in a lesser degree than his fairy-stories—fantasies founded on fact. The result of this procedure is that, as in his caricatures, the satire is implicit, because the author, instead of obtruding his own personality—as he does in his essays— lets his characters speak for themselves. This does not mean that the author is entirely absent from these pages; on the contrary, in most of these sketches he is present as one of the *dramatis personae*. . . . 'All fantasy must be rooted in reality' . . ., Max once wrote. The happy result of this technique is a series of portraits which, with all their caricatural exaggeration and inherent satire, strike one as uniquely representative of their period or milieu. (p. 115)

Beerbohm's greatest achievement as a fantasist is his 'novel' *Zuleika* (pronounced *Zu-leek-a*) *Dobson: or, An Oxford Love Story.* (p. 116)

Zuleika Dobson—which, unlike *The Happy Hypocrite,* is a story without a moral—is the record of the devastating effect on the youth of Oxford of a popular, but unscrupulous adventuress and amateur juggler, for whose love the whole body of undergraduates commits a ceremonious suicide by jumping into the Isis on Eights Day. After having taken full toll Zuleika calmly orders a special train for Cambridge, and goes to bed. (p. 117)

The Duke is undoubtedly the principal character . . . [and the] attitudes satirized in the Duke are far more characteristic of the author's *Id* than any of those ridiculed in the beautiful adventuress. . . . [The] Duke is nothing but the satirical embodiment of the idea of *noblesse oblige,* i.e. of 'deportment' everywhere, and under all circumstances. As the means by which this satirical effect is achieved are largely caricatural, the device most frequently employed is exaggeration. (pp. 117-18)

[With respect to Beerbohm's parodies, it] is in the narrow margin between *his* colour range and that of his original that the secret of his incomparable mockery lies. The special nature of this art presupposes an existing literature and an initiated public. It can only flourish in a cultivated and literary-minded milieu, because comparison with its original is the *sine qua non* of its enjoyment. But it also carries its risks. We have seen that in at least one of his essays—that on Cosmetics—the author identified himself so well with the object of his mockery that, by the unenlightened, he was equated with it. In *The Happy Hypocrite,* finally, he seems to transcend the limits of parody. The mimicry in this story is so completely integrated into the harmless-looking fairy-tale frame that, on the face of it, the piece seems to have lost its critical character, so that even the discriminating were deceived. Its subsequent history resembles that of *Gulliver* which, like Beerbohm's parody, will always live on its merits as a story. The reason for this curious shift of accent is to be sought in the special texture of Beerbohm's parody. Its strength lies in the almost imperceptible exaggeration of his mimetic pose, and its operation is so subtle that it largely depends on the response of the reader whether it assumes the character of mockery, or not.

It is this tendency to 'play the sedulous ape' which enables us to connect the art of Beerbohm, the parodist, with that of 'Max', the caricaturist. Though in some of his caricatures the unity of both arts is already symbolized by the letterpress which accompanies and complements them, it is really the similarity of intention and technique which proves that, in Beerbohm's case at least, there is a close affinity between parodist and caricaturist, between writer and artist. In his parodies as well as in his caricatures Beerbohm assimilates and, at the same time, exaggerates the essential features of his original. The degree of exaggeration, however, varies according to the medium used. In his caricatures there is more of it than in his parodies, because the pictorial medium, by its very nature, is less capable of expressing a living thought than the verbal. But in either medium his art springs from the same source—his satirical temper—and tends to the same end—criticism. The way in which he achieves this object both in his writings and in his caricatures is always typically individual, that is, typically 'Max', and therefore, in the full sense of the word, 'incom-

parable'. It was undoubtedly this aspect of Beerbohm's art that Shaw, more than fifty years ago, had in mind when he applied his famous epithet. But it should be remembered that, with regard to much of his work, especially his parodies, it can only be interpreted paradoxically. (pp. 145-46)

[Beerbohm] was a sound, though not a very original critic, with a finely-developed ear for prose. The fact that many of his criticisms of contemporary writers still impress one as remarkably fresh testifies to his sure taste. Perhaps his most valuable contribution to the history of prose criticism is his insistence on style as the essayist's chief means of self-expression. His proviso that the application of this criterion should be restricted to the essayist's art proves that, as a critic, he had nothing in common with the old, Wildean school but his own infatuation with prose. His ideal was not the aesthete's Art for Art's sake. It was Art for Life's sake. (p. 180)

In its more general qualities as well as in its special features his style faithfully reflects the characteristic traits of his personality. It is . . . subtle, impertinent, aristocratic, and urbane; archaic and dainty; dandyish and sophisticated; but above all, mocking, ironical, witty, and humorous. His subject-matter, too, is equally characteristic. . . . [The] great issues of the day left him comparatively untouched. For him the graces of the Regency period were far more real than the problems of the Twentieth Century, while top hats, music-halls, and the oddities of life and literature engrossed him more than the two World Wars which he outlived and which, indeed, he hardly ever refers to in his works. Instead of taking the gross realities of contemporary life for his subject-matter, he always, in his own words, danced 'on the trimmest, narrowest and most devious terraces of literature'. . . . This means that he selected his themes in accordance with his fastidious taste, and only after a meticulous polishing process deemed them worthy of being clothed in equally choice and polished words. (p. 181)

One of the most striking general qualities of Beerbohm's style is its power to mock. . . . It will at once be seen that, with Beerbohm, the medium through which the mockery manifests itself is fourfold. It may be parody . . ., irony, wit, or humour, but hardly ever satire in the strict sense. His purpose, evidently, is not to amend hateful morals and manners by holding them up to malicious public ridicule. He is neither a reformer nor a hater. Consequently his mockery (which, on account of its subtlety, will never appeal to the generality of readers) is not destined to offend, because, in its happiest flights, its ultimate ratio is invariably a feeling of sympathy, reverence, or love—both in his writings and in his caricatures. (p. 182)

Beerbohm's use of wit, too, as a medium for mockery, is of the kind 'that pierces without leaving a wound'. (p. 183)

In order to achieve a desired effect Beerbohm, more than any other writer, makes use of a number of extraordinary devices—to be compared with the conjuring tricks of which he, and his heroine Zuleika, were so fond. It is these devices in particular that lend his style its strange air of irresponsibility and whimsicality. Foremost among them ranks the skilful mixture of fancy and fact, of fiction and reality, which he manages in some of his essays, in his imaginary portraits, and in his 'novel'. Thus Enoch Soames is a fictitious character wandering among a crowd of well-known artists, and, on the face of it, made of the same stuff as they are. But almost imperceptibly the story takes off; the world of reality sinks under our feet and soon dwindles into nothingness; and before we have time to realize our position we find ourselves in mid-air, fully engrossed in the wonders of this topsyturvy world, with the author himself as the slender, and none too solid link with reality. (pp. 189-90)

Another of Beerbohm's favourite juggling-tricks, akin to the one discussed above, is his habit of building up an elaborate structure of make-believe. The artistic function of this device is to weaken the unwary reader's resistance against the shock with which, at a time thought fit by the smiling conjurer, he is undeceived by a solution which is often as witty as it is unexpected. (p. 191)

In view of the limited range of the feelings and thoughts expressed in Beerbohm's writings, any attempt to claim absolute greatness, or even classic status . . . for him must be frivolous. Max himself was aware of his limitations when he wrote: 'My gifts are small. I've used them very well and discreetly, never straining them'. . . . Sir Max Beerbohm's greatness is not in the comprehensiveness of his expression. It is in the absolute perfection of it. (p. 212)

> *J. G. Riewald, in his* Sir Max Beerbohm: Man and Writer *(copyright 1953 by Martinus Nijhoff, The Hague, Netherlands), Martinus Nijhoff, 1953.*

From the first [Beerbohm] stood alone, contemplating his small chosen world, moving the long lashes of his grey, hooded eyes in a continuous and innocent surprise at its folly and charming *bêtise*. But he was unlike the puritanical satirist; it seemed to be precisely this folly and *bêtise* which gave the admirable rest its eminence for him. With Lytton Strachey he was typically a child of the new century in his wish to show that the great are human. . . . (p. 270)

His indifference to Russian literature, like his later indifference to Proust and the novels of D. H. Lawrence, was certainly genuine, and thus his satire has never bothered with it, except for that one reference to the works in Gibrisch of the great Luntic Kolnyatsch. No, it has always been to those things with which he has most sympathy that he has turned his satire.

It was a paradox which mystified the Edwardians, and at first they thought of 'Max' as an exquisite misfit in their age. They could not quite understand his odd combination of frivolity, irreverence and what they took to be malice. . . . Few noticed the paradox of his work, that when his subject was most unsympathetic to him he was at his mildest, that his wickedest and most delighted satire was reserved for those whom, in some secret chamber of his mind, he could reverence.

In spite of all this one cannot think of Sir Max as anything but a perfect and eminent Edwardian. . . . However equivocally 'Max' was an Edwardian, he retired from the London scene as soon as the decade was over. He had mapped it and defined it in his fashion, and could well live on his memories and impressions of it for the rest of his days. (pp. 271-72)

> *Michael Swan, "Sir Max Beerbohm at Eighty," in his* A Small Part of Time: Essays on Literature, Art and Travel, *Jonathan Cape Ltd., 1957 (and reprinted by Dufour Editions, Inc., 1961), pp. 269-75.*

Wilde had said truly that the youthful Max was strangely mature. But the reverse was to prove equally true. The mature Max proved strangely childlike. Children—unlike grown-up people—are able to occupy themselves by "playing." "Go away and play," says the grownup to the child; and the child, if he has any imagination, can thus occupy himself indefinitely. For most people the capacity to do this goes as early as the age of nine; Max kept it till he died at eighty-four. He did not need regular work or varied companionship to be happy; he did not need to feel he was fulfilling a duty or making an impression. He wanted someone to look after the practical things of life for him and, since he was affectionate, he wanted that person to be someone he could love. His wife filled the role required. With her to act as nurse and mother he was free to retire, childlike, to an imaginary world in which he could play indefinitely.

It was a comic world: his games there were humorous games. Max was primarily a humorist, one of those rare human beings to whom the comedy of life is its most significant feature. His favorite and most natural activity was making jokes. (p. 35)

His most memorable stories, too, are largely satirical. In *Zuleika Dobson* he satirizes Oxford; in *Enoch Soames* he satirizes the poets of the nineties; in *Maltby and Braxton,* fashionable life in the Edwardian era.

These stories are not only satiric. Even more are they expressions of a fantastical humor that seizes on some preposterous hypothesis and then works it out in exact and whimsical detail. The results are highly imaginative—as it were, the poetry of laughter. (p. 38)

Max is at his best when he is making fun of something he likes. He says somewhere: "Reverence is a good thing, and part of its value is that the more we revere a man the more we are struck by anything in him (and there is always much) that is incongruous with his greatness." Further, as I have said, his humor is an expression of his wish to play. A man plays most successfully when he is in a good temper. . . .

Max seems to have been himself one of the few writers who could set a just value on himself, neither too much nor too little. Surprisingly, this faculty was bound up with his playfulness. Since he took neither himself nor others very seriously, he was able to judge both with calm impartiality. (p. 40)

> *David Cecil, "The Man Who Never Stopped Playing," in* Horizon *(© 1961 by American Heritage Publishing Co., Inc.), May, 1961, pp. 33-40.*

One might suppose that a collection so curious, a portentously served potpourri of private jokes and *déjà vu,* would add up to a worthless book. But *Max in Verse* is precious in both senses; it is both overrefined and valuable. Its value, which is felt in terms of delight, can perhaps be understood through some consideration of light verse. (p. 258)

Language is finite and formal; reality is infinite and formless. Order is comic; chaos is tragic. By rhyming, language calls attention to its own mechanical nature and relieves the represented reality of seriousness. In this sense, rhyme and allied regularities like alliteration and assonance assert a magical control over things and constitute a spell. . . . The bulk of great English poetry, from Shakespeare to Milton, from Wordsworth to Wallace Stevens, is unrhymed. And those poets of the first rank, like Pope, who habitually rhyme do so unobtrusively. . . . The last considerable poets who preferred to rhyme are Emily Dickinson, Yeats, and Housman. . . . In this situation, light verse, an isolated acolyte, tends the thin flame of formal magic and tempers the inhuman darkness of reality with the comedy of human artifice. Light verse precisely lightens; it lessens the gravity of its subject. (pp. 259-60)

Max in Verse is an enchanted island of a book, and its Ariel is a hovering, invisible, luminous insistence on the comedy (above and beyond the wit of the precious little that is being said) *of versification itself.* (p. 262)

> John Updike, "Rhyming Max" (originally
> published in The New Yorker, March 7,
> 1964), in his Assorted Prose (copyright ©
> 1961 by John Updike; reprinted by permis-
> sion of Alfred A. Knopf, Inc.), Knopf, 1965,
> pp. 256-63.

As a literary critic, Max was wise to confine himself for the most part to literary parodies of the few writers he knew well. Of poetry, as of music, he had no understanding—Henley's "Invictus" was one of his favorite pieces—and both his taste and his reading in fiction were too limited to make him a critic of note. His table-talk criticism is sound enough as far as it goes: he is never mean—though he should have spotted the difference between Virginia Woolf's handling of "the stream of consciousness" and Joyce's—and even in writers whom he finds antipathetic he is always ready to admit their virtues. If his admiration for "Eminent Victorians" now seems excessive, one can understand it: he recognized that Strachey's literary ideal was akin to his own. (p. 380)

As a parodist, he is probably the finest in English. . . . Unfortunately, literary parodies can never appeal to more than a limited and highly sophisticated public, for they can be appreciated only by a reader who is intimately acquainted with the authors parodied. Caricature, or visual parody, is much more accessible, since to "get" a caricature it is not necessary to have seen the subject oneself. Thus, while Max's caricatures should delight almost everybody, the only writings of his which are likely to reach a wide public are the stories—*Zuleika Dobson, Seven Men, A Variety of Things.* (pp. 380-81)

> W. H. Auden, "One of the Family" (origi-
> nally published in The New Yorker, Oc-
> tober 23, 1965), in his Forewords and After-
> words, edited by Edward Mendelson
> (copyright © 1973 by W. H. Auden; re-
> printed by permission of Random House,
> Inc.), Random House, 1973, pp. 367-83.

A Christmas Garland is surely the *liber aureus* of prose parody. What makes Max, as a parodist, incomparable—more than the calm mounting from felicity to felicity and the perfectly scaled enlargement of every surface quirk of the subject style—is the way he seizes and embraces, with something like love, the total personality of the parodee. He seems to enclose in a transparent omniscience the genius of each star as, in *A Christmas Garland*, he methodically moves across the firmament of Edwardian letters. Anyone who has forgotten the difference between Ches-

terton and Belloc could have no better refresher than Beerbohm's parodies of them. Chesterton's preposterously nimble good cheer and Belloc's robust and defiant *angoisse* are each crystallized in absurdity, but the amber is so clear we can glimpse even the sombre spots. "Pray for my soul," the puppet-Belloc abruptly concludes, and the reader is touched by a real shadow. Whereas most parodies are distinctly written from beneath their subjects, Beerbohm for the occasion rises to an equality with his great victims; a vintage parody by him is, as the Greek etymology would have it, a "parallel song." . . . One puts down *A Christmas Garland* wondering why the man who wrote it did not, in his own voice, write great things. Parody this fine is rare perhaps because it requires gifts that usually drive a man to try something more important. When all due homage has been granted to the uniform refinement of Beerbohm's total production—and special tribute paid to those famous radio broadcasts whose impeccably enunciated nostalgia borrows gallantly from the context of blitzed London—there remains something abortive and not entirely pleasing about Beerbohm as a literary figure.

Pure parody is purely parasitic. There is no disgrace in this. We all begin life as parasites within the mother, and writers begin their existence imitatively, within the body of letters. (pp. 244-45)

But "decent" is exactly what his style remained. His criticism, so acute and daintily just, is rendered pale by our impression that he himself was never burned. His own efforts at fiction are bounded by a landscape of books. His most extended invention, *Zuleika Dobson*, miscarries, it seems to me, in its climactic holocaust; he treats his paper creations too heartlessly. His essays do show flashes of terrestrial daylight, of felt experience. The most memorable of them, "The Golden Drugget," tells of a strip of light projected across the road through the open doorway of an inn near Rapallo. This sign of human company comforts him as he walks the dark road; he is tempted to enter but, to preserve his illusions, never does. "Don Quixote would have paused here and done something. Not so do I." Art imitates Nature in this: not to dare is to dwindle. . . . Beerbohm's persistent gloating upon his own "littleness" became somewhat grating, and in the end his delicate belittling of the lack of littleness in others seemed virtually nasty. Magnanimity was reduced in his conversation to a species of conceit, zeal to a form of presumption. Everything withered under the gentle touch of Beerbohm's equanimous depreciation, and his creative energy, which he could never refine quite out of existence, was solipsistically focussed on the ornamentation of his private library with private jokes. As, in his amniotic cave in Rapallo, he continued to play the young man's game of parody, it turned into a childish fiddling with scissors and paste, footnotes and mustaches; in his own drawings of himself, the wispy, ethereal, top-hatted Puck of the London days evolved backward into an elderly fetus with a huge square head, bulging eyes, and a tiny hunched body—an emblem, as ominous as wonderful, of the totally non-quixotic man. (pp. 245-46)

> John Updike, "Beerbohm and Others"
> (originally published in a slightly different
> version in The New Yorker, September 16,
> 1961), in his Assorted Prose (copyright ©
> 1961 by John Updike; reprinted by permis-

sion of Alfred A. Knopf, Inc.), Knopf, 1965, pp. 241-55.

It was evident that [Max] personally disliked Bernard Shaw, as it was plain that he loved Henry James. . . . One felt . . . that Max could not stand the idea that Bernard Shaw had become a great man. He himself had perhaps a little always felt on the margin of things, and he was likely to betray irritation in dealing with great men who took themselves seriously and became public institutions: see his attitude toward Goethe in *Quia Imperfectum*. He had, in any case, by a cunning use of ink, turned the photographs of such people as William Morris and Granville Barker into horrible prognathous gorillas. One felt that he really wanted to degrade Bernard Shaw and everyone connected with him. (pp. 47, 49)

Though Max makes all his subjects absurd, though no one is ever idealized except in a comic way, there is a hierarchy of values here: men he despises and men he admires, men that he rejoices in and men that he likes to make ugly. His work as a caricaturist is in general on a higher imaginative level than his stories, his essays and his parodies. (p. 57)

Yet I read and reread Max Beerbohm as I do not do any other British prose writer of the period in which I grew up, with the exception of Bernard Shaw. It seems to me queer when I find Max Beerbohm speaking, as he does in some essay, of G. K. Chesterton as "a genius" whose brilliance quite put Max in the shade. The paradoxical epigrams of Chesterton, which became so mechanical and monotonous, are mostly unreadable today. But Max Beerbohm's prose has endured. (pp. 57-8)

One feels, when one has seen [the original drawings] as he made them, larger in scale and stronger in color, a quite formidable vitality and power. They have the Bloomsbury "significant form" as well as something like creative passion in their rendering of personalities. He has sometimes been carried away by the form-producing imagination as he never is in his prose. The figures, in being distorted, become, not grotesque monsters, but wonderful inspired shapes. (p. 58)

> *Edmund Wilson, "A Miscellany of Max Beerbohm," in his* The Bit Between My Teeth: A Literary Chronicle of 1950-1965 *(reprinted with the permission of Farrar, Straus & Giroux, Inc.; copyright © 1939, 1940, 1947, 1950, 1951, 1952, 1953, 1956, 1957, 1958, 1959, 1960, 1961, 1962, 1963, 1965 by Edmund Wilson), Farrar, Straus, 1965, pp. 41-62.*

[*The Works of Max Beerbohm with a Bibliography*, his mock-scholarly first book,] is Oscar Wilde estheticism, eighteenth-century sentiment, and uncloyed reminiscence, all made compatible by Beerbohm's wit. Like a good journalist, he does not pretend to tell "all," but only that which will interest. Unlike many journalists, he relies on taste and discrimination rather than on shock. Detachment, not involvement, sets the tone. (p. 47)

[As drama critic for *The Saturday Review*, Max Beerbohm] considered himself a poor substitute for the brilliant Shaw. He took, he said, "neither emotional nor intellectual pleasure" in drama. He had no critical theory nor any knowledge of such traditional critics as Hazlitt, Lamb, and George Henry Lewes. He could, it was true, "recite backwards" most of the successful plays of the past ten years; and he had (through his half-brother Herbert Beerbohm Tree) an acquaintance with many actors. He could only console himself, he concluded, by reflecting that his lot as critic was less uncomfortable than that of a porter in the underground railway.

Witty exaggeration aside, it is really true that Beerbohm approached dramatic criticism with no formal theory and, apparently, no intention of forming one. He trusted his own taste, though he was willing to examine it, to revise it, and even to admit errors. He stated his response to a play and tried to explain the reasons for it. If, from time to time, he seemed to commit himself to large abstract principles, he felt free to limit their application in later essays. His writing about the theater thus retained the quality of good talk: omission of the obvious, exaggeration for effect, and willingness to say part of the truth well. (p. 60)

Beerbohm recognized certain limitations of the theater. It existed for the upper class, and always had, even in Athens and in Elizabethan England. In modern England he thought the public virtually incapable of esthetic pleasure of any kind, and the very hours of performance tended to reduce the theater to mere recreation. He accepted Realism as the major vital impulse of his time, but his conception of it he carefully distinguished from reality itself. Dialogue, for instance, must be edited and compressed. . . . (pp. 60-1)

Realism should not rule out fantasy, since good fantasy has its roots in reality. Melodrama was repeatedly characterized as a dead form because of its stereotyped avoidance of reality, and its failure to project credible characters. A good dramatic idea, Beerbohm thought, was one that enabled the dramatist to show fresh observation of a human situation. (p. 61)

[Beerbohm's novel] *Zuleika Dobson* [eventually] became one of those special books, not central in a syllabus of the English novel, but highly esteemed by readers who discover it. No synopsis of this famous story ever makes it sound very appealing or impressive. The plot is deliberately preposterous. (p. 101)

How did Beerbohm sustain interest in [such] a story, and why? Both questions can be answered if the novel is regarded as a caricature in fantasy. Just as a caricature bears recognizable relation to reality, no matter how great the exaggeration, so the story of Zuleika reflects real life in the very act of distorting it. (pp. 102-03)

Instead of trying to represent the political battles by which rank and hereditary rights were undermined in the quarter century before World War I, Beerbohm puts before us a more insidious and dangerous challenge: the New Woman. Aggressive, rational rather than traditional, Zuleika is not impressed by the Duke's titles and estates. In 1885, Henry James (Beerbohm's favorite novelist) had treated seriously the same theme: Isabel Archer, in *The Portrait of a Lady*. . . . (p. 103)

Not only does [Beerbohm's] story caricature the New Woman; it caricatures the theme of romantic love, which had its most extreme statement in the Pre-Raphaelite paintings and poems and in the Wildean esthetic movement which preoccupied the 1890's. (p. 104)

The elements of which *Zuleika Dobson* is composed—the

New Woman, the life of privilege, Oxford tradition, Zuleika's association with London music halls, the echoes of classic legend—are brought together with extraordinary structural skill. Without an even more skillful style, however, the book could not succeed. The style is a blend of wit and beauty so subtle that shifts in tone occur before they can be distinguished. Description is filled with evocative echoes, and dialogue moves easily from the colloquial to the grandiloquent. If it is asked why Beerbohm never wrote another novel, there is only this reply: he had done the satiric fantasy as well as it could be done; and he never found another kind of story that he wished to develop into a novel. (p. 108)

Next to *Zuleika Dobson,* Beerbohm's most sustained creation is the collection of five narrative sketches entitled *Seven Men.* Beerbohm is involved in all of them, and one sketch concerns two men; hence the title. Though the five narratives were separately published over a period of five years and were collected only as an afterthought, a kind of unity is achieved through playful improbability and an indulgently reminiscent tone. The juxtaposition of actual people with fictional characters reduces the implausibility of events. (pp. 112-13)

Seven Men is a work of extraordinary skill, and those who take an interest in Beerbohm and his period will always delight in its verbal felicities and in its shrewd sense of character. Yet, like all parody, it is derivative and will win few readers by itself. *Zuleika Dobson* and the sketches in *Seven Men* suggest that Beerbohm had capacities for fiction that for reasons obscure even to himself he never fully developed. (p. 115)

As dramatist, Beerbohm joined the long list of drama critics who, knowing a great deal about the stage and having great skill with words, have yet been unable to write great or even good plays. His first attempt, the one-act dramatization of *The Happy Hypocrite* in 1900, was his most successful. (pp. 115-16)

No discussion of Beerbohm as a writer can ignore his caricatures. Many of his most memorable drawings are of literary men such as Wilde, Kipling, and Shaw. The writer who skeptically analyzed Shaw's plays and the artist who drew Shaw standing on his head were the same man. Moreover, the artist pointed up the effect of his drawing by putting himself in it and adding these words: "Mild surprise of one who, revisiting England after long absence, finds that the dear fellow has not moved." Beerbohm condemned the illustration of literary texts, and his early drawings make their point without captions. By 1900, however, the typical Beerbohm caricature combines visual and verbal effect. (p. 125)

No one has ever considered Max Beerbohm a "major" literary figure, whatever that nebulous term may mean. Surely he never saw himself as a Milton, thundering from some secluded mountain top of meditation. Dr. Johnson, a somewhat Miltonic figure on occasion, once advised Boswell to clear his mind of cant; and young Beerbohm, born in 1872, when there was a good deal of cant around, set out to clear his mind of it. In the long run, and it was a very long run for him, he succeeded. This statement is the best answer to the questions: was he conservative, was he anti-democratic? In his youth, he mocked aristocracy and royalty; in later years, he mocked Labour, socialism, and the worship of the Common Man.

Like his older friend Henry James, Beerbohm was shocked that the seemingly civilized world in which he had grown up could lead to the brutalities of the 1914-18 war. Yet the word "gentleman" continued to be for him an honorable term, and he himself exemplified some of its best connotations. Leisure was natural and enjoyable to him, but he could work hard and well. (p. 149)

At present, a romantic haze invests the period of Beerbohm's youth, just as a strong fascination drew him to the 1850's. Beerbohm would be the first to insist that Aubrey Beardsley was a far greater artist than he, yet the drawings of Beerbohm have a range of interest far greater, and less dated, than Beardsley's. In Beerbohm's drawings the great literary and political figures of his day appear to us with a humorous interpretation seldom found in textbooks. No one can be said to "know" the turn of the century who has not looked repeatedly at such a selection as *Max's Nineties* affords. As an essayist, Beerbohm will be fair game for anthologists as long as essays are valued, and selections from him are bright pages in any volume. . . . *The Incomparable Max* [S. C. Roberts' selection,] is an achievement as distinctive and as durable as Lamb's *Essays of Elia* or as Thackeray's *Roundabout Papers*.

Of *Zuleika Dobson,* it is hard to make a prediction. As Oxford itself loses more and more of its nineteenth-century character, Beerbohm's story becomes more and more dated, as do drawings that show the university as it was in 1800. Even so, the theme of the story, its stucture, and, above all, its style, invite the appreciation of the knowing. (pp. 149-50)

The twelve-year stint as dramatic critic for *The Saturday Review* Beerbohm accepted with reluctance and gave up with relief. And it is true that his weekly essays, good as they are, seldom if ever reach the level of his best freelance writing. On the whole, however, the post of dramatic critic was fortunate. It required regular writing, and it kept constantly before Beerbohm the problems of theme, character, structure, and style. Within limits, his position required and nourished independence. In no clearly definable sense is there development in Beerbohm's criticism. A late article on Shaw or Shakespeare would be difficult to distinguish from an early one. Yet Beerbohm was a different man in 1910 from what he had been in 1898, and his experience on *The Saturday Review* is part of the difference. (pp. 150-51)

Beerbohm served his own generation extremely well. He succeeded as essayist, staff critic of drama, novelist, parodist, and caricaturist. His achievements in these different capacities are held together by acute common sense, unsentimental whimsy, and a sense of beauty fresh and individual. Above all, he was a stylist who made himself heard without shouting. (p. 151)

In an early uncollected article, Beerbohm shows that he carefully considered the problem of style. Without a style, he thought, writing is nothing. Writing is essentially talking without the aid of gesture, facial expression, and "the infinitely variable pauses of the human voice." (p. 152)

Talking—and listening—Beerbohm learned the possibilities of language. He did not record the "good things" he got off in conversation and save them for his essays, nor did he indulge in the annoying habit of quoting his own writings. The give and take, the spontaneous shift of strategy, the note of parody, the mingling of the intellectual and the colloquial that characterizes good talk he adapted to the printed page. This was the secret of his style. In the early essays, and in *Zuleika Dobson,* there is sometimes an exaggerated straining for effect. In later writings, as in the paragraph from "Laughter," the effects are better because they appear more natural. (pp. 154-55)

As this [study] indicates, Beerbohm was no thinker. He himself would heartily agree. It was not for systematic ideas that he was valued in his own day, and his fame will endure for other reasons. So long as the late nineteenth century continues to be of interest, Beerbohm's drawings, his writings, and his early career will be indispensable comments on the age. So long as drama entertains and enlightens us, Beerbohm's dramatic criticism will speak for the discriminating and articulate playgoer. For knowing readers, his style will preserve his prejudices as well as his wisdom, and sorting the prejudices from the wisdom will be part of the fun. American readers, in particular, will find Beerbohm as independent as Thoreau and as sophisticated as *The New Yorker*—a journal which is almost inconceivable without the English precedent of the incomparable Max.

Mention of *The New Yorker* suggests that Max Beerbohm's future role will chiefly be to stimulate writers who address themselves to intelligent, lighthearted readers. Such writers will always be able to learn from Beerbohm's skill, even when he expresses prejudices no longer viable. Some readers, too, will discover Beerbohm as one of those minor writers whose work perpetuates its charm as greater figures go in and out of fashion. (p. 159)

Bruce R. McElderry, Jr., in his Max Beerbohm *(copyright 1972 by Twayne Publishers, Inc.; reprinted with the permission of Twayne Publishers, A Division of G. K. Hall & Co., Boston), Twayne, 1972.*

Robert Benchley

1889-1945

American humorist, essayist, drama critic, actor, and screen-writer. Benchley began his career in his student days as president of the *Harvard Lampoon*. Benchley's humor derives from the situation of the hapless Little Man whose tranquility is threatened on all sides by the complexity of everyday life in the twentieth century. With Dorothy Parker, James Thurber, Robert Sherwood, George Kaufman, and Franklin P. Adams, Benchley was a member of the Algonquin Round Table, the group, according to Margaret Case Harriman, whose "influence on American literature, drama, and humor was acute, untiring and permanent."

PRINCIPAL WORKS

Of All Things (humorous essays) 1921
Love Conquers All (humorous essays) 1922
Pluck and Luck (humorous essays) 1925
The Early Worm (humorous essays) 1927
20,000 Leagues under the Sea; or, David Copperfield
     (humorous essays) 1928
The Treasurer's Report (humorous essays) 1930
No Poems; or, Around the World Backwards and Sideways
     (humorous essays) 1932
From Bed to Worse (humorous essays) 1934
Why Does Nobody Collect Me (humorous essay) 1935
My Ten Years in a Quandry, and How They Grew
     (humorous essays) 1936
After 1903-What? (humorous essays) 1938
Inside Benchley (humorous essays) 1942
Benchley Beside Himself (humorous essays) 1943
Chips off the Old Benchley (humorous essays) 1949

It is in the treatment of . . . rudimentary types that Mr. Benchley is seen at his best—extracting always the rich earthiness and humor which underlies the middle western peasantry. . . . It is only in his focus and his values—so much better handled by Flaubert—that we find lapses almost unaccountable in the work of so scrupulous an artist. —If Mr. Benchley were only a little better we might describe them as "lapses lazuli". (p. 636)

[*Love Conquers All* is] a fiction of the first rank, a clout for the dunderheads and slumgullions—a soft soughing of adjectives and adverbs, of pronouns and prepositions. A book to read and to reread. A book to care strongly for. A book to take to bed every night—a devastating book. It will put Mr. Benchley at once in the forefront of American writers. There has been nothing since "A Child's Garden of Verses" which has the delicacy of these little poems. I don't know when a mere written thing has moved me so. It is a superb bit of work. I say that Benchley is a genius and head and shoulders above the mass of his contemporaries. He is, with Mr. Nock and Mr. Rascoe, the chief hope of American letters and upon Mr. Benchley's ample shoulders the chief hope of American letters rests. Like good wine, he needs no bush. (p. 637)

> *Edmund Wilson, Jr., "The Scarsdale Aristotle," in* The Bookman (*copyright, 1923, by George H. Doran Company), January, 1923, pp. 636-37.*

"Ars celare artem" is nowhere truer than in the most subtle and difficult of all literary enterprises, viz., that of tickling the risibilities, einsteining the force of gravity, and purveying spasms to the multitude. . . . So fastidiously captious are we on this point that even though we fain would be amused, yet we cannot (or will not allow ourselves to) be amused to the full, if we but feel that our amuser deliberately intends to be amusing; the bloom, the bouquet, vanishes under the blight of premeditation. Worse than the sun in March, or an offer of free tuition in college athletics, the taint of professionalism in jokesmithing doth nourish agues. "A jest's prosperity lies in the ear of him that hears it," doubtless; but economists tell us that nine-tenths of prosperity is credit, and the jester's sole negotiable credit is the illusion of spontaneity. A forced joke is like a pressed drive in golf: labor and sorrow, soon cut off; frantic ambition which o'erstrains itself, and falls flat on the other; in short, no good at all. We must enter laughter's paradise by the gateway of surprise.

These observations are perhaps strictly applicable only to the characteristically American type of funmaking, which features the broadly comic or frankly ludicrous effects resulting chiefly from exaggeration, paradox, *reductio ad absurdum,* and appalling audacity. It is not generally known that Mark Twain, in the heyday of his eminence as supreme commander of American humorists, selected for his vice-president and successor the late John Kendrick Bangs, and that Mr. Bangs recently passed on his crown to

Professor William Lyon Phelps. This is the authentic line of descent in the distinctively American tradition, and to this school (if not in the direct line of the apostolic succession) Mr. Benchley, willy-nilly, belongs.... Mr. Benchley, at his best, would shake the very midriff of despair with laughter (albeit ["Love Conquers All"] is less continuously hilarious than was his first venture).... [The volume is] marred by too many essays of the routine, stereotyped, machine-made order; but Mr. Benchley largely succeeds in offsetting the stigma of professionalism by his cheerful effrontery, riotous high spirits, and monstrous fertility in preposterous invention (p. 363). ...

> *Lawrence Mason, in* Literary Review, *January 6, 1923.*

Robert C. Benchley is the great philosopher in short pants. He represents the thought of America inversely ratioed. He is the Santayana of the Algonquin, the Plato of Broadway. "Pluck and Luck" ... is a masterpiece of unreason. It is funny, wise, absurd—a delicious collection of thises and thats and then-agains. If we have a humorist in America who performs his feats more skilfully or more consistently, I should like to see him. Whether he writes of the digestive tract or of family life, he does it with perfect control of the pen and of the windpipe. There is much to be said for Mr. Benchley's books' being adopted by the schools. The schools should institute each day a half hour for the cultivation of laughter. There should be organized propaganda for Mr. Benchley in a cutaway, of course, and with a silk hat and a cane, as Gluyas Williams so aptly portrays him. The cane is an adjunct. Mr. Benchley is an adjunct, too—as an adjunct he is even more effective as a philosopher. *But,* it is primarily as a philosopher that I recommend him to you. (pp. 713-14)

> *John Farrar, "The Latest Laugh," in* The Bookman *(copyright, 1926, by George H. Doran Company), February, 1926, pp. 713-14.*

Mr. Robert Benchley is one of the most popular men in the business of being funny today. He has syndicated his skits, at various times, to a large number of newspapers; his books have sold well above 120,000 copies; he has done well on the stage, on the screen, and on the radio. (p. 280)

The pages of the books he wrote ... often remind one of the humor of his forerunners. Many times he shapes his paragraphs and sentences as they did: instinctively, probably, he hits on tried and true ways of making people laugh. But there is a difference between his writings and the older ones which ... seems significant.

This difference is suggested by a look at the kind of a character who woefully makes his way through the strange happenings set down in Mr. Benchley's writings. Any of the books shows the chief thing about this poor devil—that his whole life is a series of humiliations and frustrations. He is constantly bedeviled by all sorts of petty little things which a masterful man would easily be able to take in his stride. As a critic of this writer, Mr. Bryant [that is, J. Bryant III, in an article published in *Saturday Evening Post,* September 23-October 7, 1939], says,

> ... he sees himself ... not the master of
> high comedy, but the victim of low tragedy.

King Lear loses a throne; Benchley loses a filling. Romeo breaks his heart; Benchley breaks his shoelace. They are annihilated; he is humiliated. And to his humiliations there is no end. His whole life has been spent as the dupe of "the total depravity of inanimate things." Today a knicknack leaps from his hand and shatters to the floor. Tonight his slippers will crawl away and wheel around backward. ...

Happier men could laugh little troubles like these off—but they happen so often to the fellow who appears in the Benchley pieces that he develops a persecution complex about them.

A book of his, aptly called *My Ten Years in a Quandary,* shows this character sloshing around in a sea of troubles. Furious, eager to take arms—as Shakespeare puts it—against the waves, he finds himself unable to do anything. All the time he is bothered by frustrations—in general and in particular. He cannot leave a party at a decent time, cure hiccoughs, wear a white suit, smoke a cigarette, or read while eating—though he wants passionately to do all these things. Pathetically, this victim of suppressions looks forward to a total eclipse, when darkness will give him "a chance," as he says, "to do a lot of things I have planned to do, but have been held back from." And what are these daring deeds to be? Simply these—he will put on a white suit, pick some flowers, waltz, exercise on a rowing machine, read some books, and make some faces. All these innocent little diversions he has been afraid to enjoy in the bright light of day.

Plainly, the difference between this victim of fate and healthier men is that the healthier men would not want to do such things or—if they did—would do them. But the man in a Benchley sketch, paralyzed by these tremendous frustrations, worries and worries about them. A chronic worrier, he is tormented by other things besides those which have been mentioned—fur-bearing trout, a bird which breaks down his morale, a ghost which worries him into spending a whole night in the Grand Central Station, meteorites, a Scottie (to which he feels inferior), the Younger Generation (which he fears is hatching a sinister plot), and dancing prairie chickens.

Read on in the book and you will find that even more serious troubles pester him. When this poor creature lies down to sleep, his throat closes up and he stops breathing. He has dementia praecox and a phobia for barber chairs, and he goes crazy in a lonely shack on the seashore. All these psychopathic woes are made known in one volume. Read the rest of his volumes, and it will be clear that the man—if his books are to be believed—is just a mess of frustrations and phobias. As Mr. Bryant has said, "Madness so dominates the landscape of his humor that a second reading is necessary to recognize its other features." (pp. 281-83)

When Mr. Bryant tries to get at the basis of Mr. Benchley's humor, [he concludes that] "Benchley ... is misfortune's fool.... A Benchley short is simply the refinement of Benchley humiliation. It is commotion recollected in tranquillity. Yesterday's tragic ineffectuality has become today's comic effect." Not only is this the definition of all humor; in addition it makes plain that "I" is the same person as his creator. More, it makes clear that the humor does not depend upon a contrast between an utterly stupid man in the foreground and a sufficiently wise man in the background.

In the writings of [Benchley and Thurber], satire has been expanded so far that it has lost a great deal of its sting. Old-timers made fun of only a small group of men—the ones who did not use their gumption to arrive at sound opinions. These modern humorists make fun of all mankind, and of all its opinions except one—the opinion that no ideas are very sound. Mankind is made up, they hint, of Benchleys and Thurbers who lack their skill to record its follies in tranquillity.

To such negative philosophers, horse sense becomes folly. When, under the title "Chips from an Old Philosopher," Mr. Benchley writes his closest parallel to the stuff Josh Billings turned out, he dishes up a series of aphorisms which either contradict one another or are sheer nonsense. . . . Naturally a man who gets no closer to insight by using his head than Mr. Benchley does would be a little squeamish when he sat alone with his thoughts. (pp. 292-93)

Such futilitarians as these two humorists, in short, take little stock in Josh Billings' old-fashioned claim that "you hav got to be wize before you can be witty." Their point seems to be that nobody is wise, and nobody can be. (p. 294)

> *Walter Blair, in his* Horse Sense in American Humor from Benjamin Franklin to Ogden Nash *(copyright 1942, 1970 by Walter Blair), University of Chicago Press, 1942 (and reprinted by Russell & Russell, 1962).*

Though a great many earnest students have tried, the nature of humor has never been very satisfactorily defined—there are too many tastes and nothing is terribly funny to everybody—and it is a reckless thing to try to put any writer into a neat and permanent compartment. It is especially hard for me with Benchley, because the extra fact of known personality inevitably gets into it, too. Rereading his pieces, that is, my judgment is influenced by a clear picture of how he would have looked telling the same story, punctuating it with the abandoned laughter that used to be so famous at opening nights, and assisting himself with gestures of quiet desperation.

It is also conditioned by another absurdity not apparent in the text. For the most part, he wrote about his own polite New England bafflement in the face of strange but negligible crises; the actual fact was that he led one of the most insanely complicated private lives of our day and did it, on the whole, with extraordinary composure. It is possible that this secondary information makes his stories seem funnier to me than they really are, so that my estimate of his talent may be a little high. I can't honestly say that he made me laugh more than any other humorist writing in his time—some of Thurber's maniacal experiences in Columbus, Ohio, still seem to me incomparable as examples of comic genius operating on what must have been an extremely favorable environment—but I think he was, by far, the most brilliant and consistent of the school, originating with [Stephen] Leacock, who performed such dizzy miracles, with parody, non sequitur, garbled reference, and all the other materials of off-center wit.

He avoided with a very acute instinct the monotony that can come from a reiterated comic device and the disaster that comes from crossing the strict line which divides high comedy from awful foolishness. He was sure, wonderfully resourceful, and his style, really based on a lifelong respect for good writing, would have been admirable applied to anything. It was no secret, I guess, that his later appearances in the movies and on the radio bored and depressed him, though he was enormously successful at it, for he was dedicated to writing, and he suffered bitterly when, mistakenly or not, he decided that he couldn't do it any more, and never did.

> *Wolcott Gibbs, "Robert Benchley: In Memoriam," in* The New York Times Book Review *(© 1945 by The New York Times Company; reprinted by permission), December 16, 1945, p. 3.*

My "favorite" Benchley was the man himself—but that was a privilege reserved to a few, the most fortunate few in the world. . . .

Benchley *was* humor. His writings were only one of the outward and visible evidences of the inner grace, the divine essence. But one must not make the mistake of considering humor as a sort of electric heater which one plugs in when one needs the illusion of warmth and happiness in the best of all possible worlds. Benchley *did* give out a radiant glow; his friends and his millions of readers *did* warm themselves and feel better because of his presence. But he was not one to be operated by a switch; he was a flame, capable of leaping out of the fireplace and bitterly scorching the hypocrite, the pretentious, the inhumane.

> *Donald Ogden Stewart, "Mr. Humor," in* The Nation *(copyright 1954 by The Nation Associates, Inc.), October 16, 1954, p. 343.*

One special thing that Robert Benchley had, in addition to the obvious attributes of charm and humor and sympathy and the capacity for indignation and—cheapened word but rare quality—integrity, was his relationship with the famous. At a tableful or in a roomful of the household-word names, Benchley's presence made people out of them. I am tempted to say that he relaxed them, but that isn't quite it. To a certain extent he did not relax them one bit. Without being tough about it, he brought them down to size. Indeed, far from being tough about it, he was often gentle about it, although he could be tough.

In the twenties and thirties he flourished, first, because of the quality of his writing about the theater and, to the somewhat larger public, because he was the funniest man in print. He was not a jokesmith, but he practically invented what is now known as situation comedy. It turned out that he was just as funny acting it as writing it. But what made his company uniquely his own was a matter of attitude, of point of view. He was a person and a personality, and so enormously each that he was never compelled to make an effort to project either. (p. 6)

> *John O'Hara, in* Collier's *(copyright, © 1955, by The Crowell-Collier Publishing Co., Springfield, Ohio; reprinted by permission of Random House, Inc.), January 6, 1956.*

Humorist Frank Sullivan once wrote of humorist Robert Benchley, "His lance pierced more shams than all the preachments of the indignation boys and do-gooders."

To borrow a phrase from some anonymous high-school boy, Mr. Sullivan is full of prune whip all the way up to the eyebrows. Benchley had no lance, and a good solid preachment from just one indignation boy could pierce more shams than Benchley pierced in his whole bumbling, laughing lifetime.

Benchley did pierce the sham of using "V" instead of "U" in carving words in stone ("ѕᴠᴍᴍᴇʀ ʙᴠɪʟᴅɪɴɢ") and he did strike a blow for freedom from the mercilessness of hostesses intent upon their guests having a good time, but that's about the extent of it. . . .

Robert Benchley was no detached professional humorist, efficiently grinding out gags and jokes about the inefficiencies of life. . . . He seems to have achieved that rare Kierkegaardian reduplication: His life and his work were one.

And it was his life he wrote about, sort of. That was his contact with the reality any good humorist has to have lurking somewhere in his background. His trivia had none of the serious overtones of, say, Thurber, but he did write more or less about a real person—himself. He seems really to have had trouble saying "Guess I'll toddle along" at parties, and he really did flee "like a wild, hunted thing" at the first sign of dancing, and he did have difficulty knowing when to call his floor on an elevator, his voice ranging from rich baritone to rasping tenor. He was his own Walter Mitty.

A standard word about Benchley and, as he would say, his ilk, is that they were mild, sensitive men who couldn't work the gadgets of a gadget-minded civilization. . . . Benchley was a major victim of that tendency of things to be against us—the unfoldability of newspapers, the rolling away of pencils, the self-hiding of needed objects.

But it wasn't just the resistance of things and gadgets to which Benchley was responding; it was that still more awesome phenomenon, the earnestness of human beings. It was not the machine he kidded, but organized and purposeful society. Or, rather, he joshed his own inability to fit into that society, the world of charts, diagrams, Treasurers' Reports, and Getting Things Done. Against the American idea of rational, efficient, productive, well-organized man, his paragraphs presented the bemusing image of Robert Benchley.

In our determined world of career, progress, and tangible success, Benchley represented that still, small voice which whispers softly, "Why?" or "Don't," or possibly just "The hell with it." That's why we like him best when we are sophomores, when the juices of irresponsibility are flowing freely. . . .

His "pieces" consequently deprecated himself and his writing. Springing to Einstein's defense, he would say he did it because they were more or less in the same line of work (writing). His style was a continual joking about the writing as he went along: "With the advent of water-power and the subsequent water pistol, Luke (Luke was the fellow I was speaking of a few yards back) didn't know what to do. Unless I am greatly mistaken, this paragraph belongs in another article."

Maybe this humor has the result of suddenly, candidly showing up the limits of our deadly serious purposes. Maybe it gives perspective and a sense of something larger than all the solemn projects in which we become embroiled. But don't ever accuse it of taking up lances and directly intending to do that.

> *William Lee Miller, "There Really Was a Benchley," in* The Reporter *(© 1956 by The Reporter Magazine Co.), January 12, 1956, p. 39.*

Benchley, Thurber, and Perelman depict different characters but similarly rebel against ancient standards. Speaking of this group, "The literary comedians . . . presented themselves as Perfect Fools," says Bernard De Voto, "whereas our comedians present themselves as Perfect Neurotics." "There is no other difference," De Voto claims. This may be true; but the difference is revolutionary. He points out an important element of kinship which he supports by noticing that older humorists and modern ones make much use of "erratic association" and citing Max Adeler's "My First Political Speech" as an earlier version of Robert Benchley's famous "The Treasurer's Report.". . .

Each of Benchley's books shows that he constantly assumes the role of "a Perfect Neurotic.". . . A reader is not surprised to find this assumed character ticking off one after another the symptoms of dementia praecox and finding that he has all of them. (p. 171)

"Some of this," writes his son [Nathaniel] in a biography, [*Robert Benchley, A Biography*] "was exaggerated, but not as much as might be supposed. Benchley was a highly subjective writer, and most of what he wrote was conditioned by his feelings about himself." This modern humorist, then, exaggerates—as did the oldtime humorists who told tall tales. But whereas the oldsters exaggerated the difficulties which they had to overcome and their ability to cope with them, Benchley exaggerates the smallness of the difficulties he has to overcome and his inability to cope with them. And the author's own troubles are like those of his comic character. J. Bryant III subtitles his profile of the humorist "A Study in Professional Frustration," and indicates Benchley's conception of himself is of a man constantly humiliated and defeated by trifles. . . . Benchley's humor constantly makes use of such humiliations and the failure of the assumed character to handle trifling problems. Not surprisingly he has spoken of working in "the dementia praecox field" and has voiced a preference for humor that has "a mad quality." (p. 172)

Now mild or temporary or even violent and permanent aberrations were far from unusual in the older humor. Artemus Ward, it will be recalled, was described as one yielding "a literal obedience to every absurd suggestion of thought and language"; many literary comedians—including Mark Twain—made people laugh, as Stephen Leacock notices, at their "amiable idiocy." But the difference between the assumed character and the character of his creator was an important incongruity. Charles Farrar Browne played up the differences between himself, sane, logical, sound in his attitudes, and Artemus Ward, mildly mad, illogical, unsound in his attitudes. The contrast made for irony, and the irony often made for satire. Just as Clemens stood apart from Pap Finn while Pap lauded racial discrimination and by standing apart attacked an attitude which Clemens abhorred, or as Locke stood apart from the copperhead Nasby with whom he violently disagreed and thereby attacked copperheadism, many literary comedians made the "I" in their writings obviously, comically, and satirically different from his creator.

The new emphasis was not on differences but on resemblances. Benchley, as his son says, exaggerates; but he exaggerates what he believes are his own qualities. And the expectation is that instead of feeling superior to the comic character whose qualities are enlarged versions of Benchley's own characteristics, the reader will identify with that character, will sympathize with him. "The fellow," he will say, "suffers from much the same frustrations, the same fears, the same incompetency I suffer from." And he will join the assumed character in being irritated by all the self-confident people he encounters—clerks, advertising men, efficiency experts, go-getters, clubwomen, scholars, scientists—all those well-adjusted (and quite probably self-deceived) clods. (pp. 172-73)

But native American humor has always dealt comically with worries and tribulations—the struggles of a democratic nation to get going, frontier hardships, wartime tragedies, the upheavals accompanying the shift from an agrarian, rural society to an industrial, urban society. In that sense, Day, Benchley, Thurber, and Perelman write in an old and honorable tradition. Also their assumptions and beliefs are in tune with attitudes of their era. But the different nature of their assumptions and the great change in their beliefs have led them to write humor strikingly different indeed from that of the past. (p. 180)

> *Walter Blair, in his* Native American Humor *(copyright © 1960 by Chandler Publishing Company, Inc.; reprinted by permission of Thomas Y. Crowell Company, Inc.), Chandler, 1960.*

Benchley got off to a fast start ahead of all of us on *The New Yorker,* and our problem was the avoidance of imitation. He had written about practically everything, and his comic devices were easy to fall into. [E. B.] White once showed me something he'd written and asked anxiously, "Did Benchley say that?" In a 1933 preface I said that we were all afraid that whatever we were engaged in had probably been done better by Robert Benchley in 1924. (p. 149) It got harder and harder for Benchley to write, and he gave it up before he was fifty, but he had done five hundred pieces. Of one of the last he said, "It was written in blood, I can tell you that." He left behind a rich legacy of humor, comedy, satire, parody, and criticism—all rolled into one in those thirty-five magnificent movie shorts—but he didn't think he was very good at anything.

"Being simply a person who writes little articles sporadically, and with no distinction," he once wrote, "I am always forced to have something in mind about which to write." We all heard him say this, in paraphrase, a dozen times.

The heavier critics have underrated Benchley because of his "short flight," missing his distinguished contribution to the fine art of comic brevity. He would thank me not to call him an artist, but I think he was an artist who wouldn't give up to it, like a busy housewife fighting the onset of a migraine headache.

It was an artist, to cite outstanding proof, who wrote that brilliant and flawless parody of Galsworthy called "The Blue Sleeve Garter." He had all the equipment for the "major flight," but he laid it aside to lead one of the most crowded private lives of our century. Even so, he somehow found time to work on an ambitious enterprise, a book about the satirists of the Queen Anne period, which he later turned into a history in play form. For all its seriousness, it seems to have been a kind of monumental hobby, and a man is never done with a hobby. Benchley didn't finish his.

In all Benchley, a fresh wind stirs in every page. In all his books, you find him ducking swiftly, looking closely, writing sharply. (p. 150)

Benchley has been placed in the Leacock "school," but this is too facile a classification. For just one thing, Benchley did more funny things in, and to, banks than Stephen ever dreamed of. Leacock was an "I" writer and Benchley, even in the first person, a "You" writer. Leacock is Leacock, but Benchley's Mr. Ferderber is practically every man.

Comparison is easy. A facet of the Benchley fancy resembles the comic approach of the late Max Adeler, but I never heard him mention the Comparable Max—or Leacock, either. To most of us, he stands alone, in a great, good place all his own. (p. 151)

> *James Thurber, "The Incomparable Mr. Benchley" (originally published in* The New York Times), *in his* Credos and Curios *(copyright © 1962 Helen Thurber), Harper, 1962, pp. 146-52.*

Generally speaking, the most important feature of Benchley's humor was a character-type which may be labeled the "Little Man." In the nineteenth century, John Phoenix, Charles Heber Clark, and others had sometimes depicted gentle, bewildered fumblers trying unsuccessfully to cope with an environment too big and too complex for them. . . . Stephen Leacock, whose influence Benchley generously acknowledged, evolved a meek middle-class character who was so scared by the atmosphere of a bank that he asked for his fifty-six dollars "in fifties" and the remainder in sixes." Leacock's little man in *Literary Lapses* (1910) was much like Benchley's ten years later: he spoke college-level English, had a white-collar job and a modest income, and lived in a respectable flat, or, more often, in the suburbs. Most important, he was mentally disturbed but never quite lost his moral sense.

Between 1910 and 1919, while Benchley was painfully developing a style that included the mask of the Little Man, Irvin S. Cobb was impersonating a comic fat man at the mercy of doctors and other agents of civilization, and A. A. Milne in Britain was writing about a mild-mannered suburbanite who was baffled by the simplest mechanical devices, such as a geological hammer, the nib of his pen, and his squeaky collar. In developing his own Milquetoast-Bumstead figure, Benchley was joining and augmenting a trend.

Doubtless, Benchley had no intention of making it easy for scholars to categorize him as a humorist of the Little Man; his type-figure was an expression of his own character, only slightly exaggerated. After three years of manual training in high school, Benchley still couldn't drive a nail without bending it; and later, on a movie set, his bumbling drew from a carpenter the remark, "My God, he's a born one—he does it without thinking!" The trend toward this sort of humor, however, helped Benchley's variety of it to "take" with [Harvard] Yard audiences and later with readers of *Vanity Fair, Life, The New Yorker,* and other periodicals for the literate. (pp. 24-5)

Significant also in Robert's humor was a moral zeal, derived perhaps from his New England background and from his crusading family. . . . This urge to do good, outstanding in Benchley even during the era of Woodrow Wilson and of the Progressive party, caused him to worry continually about whether his writing was helping the cause of progress, and led him to do settlement work with a New York City boys' club. It also cost him two jobs. . . . Nathaniel Benchley has stated that his father was, in a non-denominational way, a deeply religious man—a trait not easy to infer from Robert's humor—but Heaven did not protect these working journalists, nor did Benchley expect it to. Whatever his feelings about the next world, he knew from experience that this world was an absurd mess, not the least of its absurdities being the tendency of some people, himself among them, to obey a conscience that did not make cowards of them. (pp. 35-6)

Much of Robert's humor had an anti-organization slant that was only a slight exaggeration of his personal relations with governmental machinery and business bureaucracies. Benchley, [Robert] Sherwood, and Dorothy Parker made their stay at *Vanity Fair* brisk and brief with gay rebellion against office routine and managerial arrogance. (p. 51)

Although he collected material for a full-length historical play about the Queen Anne period, he published no single masterpieces of scope and depth enough to warrant sustained analysis. Rather, his impact is in the total effect of a large number [more than six hundred] of short pieces, whether read in Benchley's first ten books or in the four anthologies of material reprinted from them. (p. 58)

[A] brief look . . . [at] some of Benchley's books may help give an overview of his writing career. *Of All Things!* . . . is made up largely of material which Benchley wrote for *Vanity Fair* and *Life,* although he drew on *Collier's* and *Motor Print* for several selections and on the old Sunday *Magazine* of the New York *Tribune* for "Call for Mr. Kenworthy!" The most effective touches of what Dorothy Parker recalled as the "old madness"—not so old then—of Benchley are his irrelevant dedication of the book to Henry Bessemer for having invented the steel converter and his acknowledgment of various magazines for permission to reprint this material: "As a matter of fact, permission was never asked, but they probably won't mind anyway." Three parodies of well-known magazines are placed together as "Tabloid Editions," and in *Love Conquers All* . . ., his second volume, twenty-eight selections from his book column in the New York *World* are grouped under "Literary Department"; otherwise no scheme for arrangement of the pieces in these first two volumes is discernible. In fact, many of the selections in the second book were written before some of those in the first.

Three years passed after the publication of *Love Conquers All* before *The Early Worm,* his third collection, appeared; but this volume and subsequent collections do not differ greatly from the first two in content or in quality. By the time Benchley's second book was assembled, he had fully developed his style and had hit a plateau of quality. "The Social Life of the Newt," one of his most hilarious pieces, leads off his first collection; and "The Treasurer's Report" winds up his sixth (although composed several years earlier). One of his best parodies, "Family Life in America," is in his second book, and another, "Love Among the Thinkers," strengthens *From Bed to Worse,* his eighth compilation. The pieces in his last two original collections, *My Ten Years in a Quandary* and *After 1903—What?,* tend to be shorter than those in the previous books, possibly because many of them were culled from the column of chit-chat he was grinding out three times a week for King Features Syndicate during 1933-1936. By the time he dropped the King column, writing had become a chore; but some of his best quips and paragraphs pepper these two volumes. (pp. 58-9)

By 1930 Benchley was beginning to tire of writing humor. He pounded out pieces for another ten years, including some of his best; but he wrote less social commentary than he had in the 1920's. However, the meekness and frustration of the Little Man as fixed in print mainly by Benchley made this figure readily adaptable by other writers as an agent for airing the economic and social problems that baffled Americans during the "angry decade." In contrast to the decline in effectiveness of Mencken's cocksure iconoclast, the Little Man grew during the 1930's partly because he was not tied too closely to any one writer's presuppositions and partly because the sources of his bedevilment—gadgets, political bunkum, the mass media, suburban life, sex, the family, and the brutal complexity of modern living—transcended the differences between prosperity and slump. Thurber, [E. B.] White, [S. J.] Perelman, Frank Sullivan, Wolcott Gibbs, and Russell Maloney were among the younger writers who followed Benchley in making the Little Man deal with social and economic realities as well as with more personal ones. (p. 74)

Benchley was typical of the revitalizers of high-level humor in wearing the self-satirical mask of a Little Man who interpreted only such elements in great problems as affected his own experience. The humor occasioned by this Little Man's bafflement is not that of insanity but of reason and common-sense in a world so absurd and overpowering as to make the sane man seem the opposite. Benchley often depicts his unheroic hero through dramatic monologue and through dialogue, partly because he was fascinated by the stage and platform and partly because these forms are convenient vehicles of parody. Monologue, dialogue, and the indirect opening were three of the ways in which Benchley helped to rejuvenate the familiar essay. (p. 101)

Thurber said that "In all Benchley, a fresh wind stirs in every page." A main source of these zany zephyrs is Benchley's handling of the English language—his quips, his diction, his plays on words, his syntactical acrobatics, and his free association, which ranges from simple digression through non-sequitur to nonsense of a caliber and frequency previously achieved in America only by Gelett Burgess. Striking imagery and sudden irony also whip up whitecaps in the reader's mind, though they seldom send him into gales of laughter. (p. 102)

Long before his death Benchley had become (the label would have amused him) at least a major-minor American humorist. Beginning as a casual exploiter of collegiate topics for the amusement of fellow-students and alumni, he developed his talent until he had enriched the familiar essay with learning, wit, suavity, whimsy, and irony—all of a sort that demanded but well rewarded a relatively high level of reader understanding. Other writers were doing all this, but Benchley went farthest in building his pieces around a self-caricature of the author as a bumbler upset but unconquered by technology, mass media, and mass-man.

Benchley had his weaknesses and his obvious limitations. Despite his devotion to "freshness," there are stale sentences in his prose, usually because of a willingness to let three, five, or seven words participate where two, three, or four could have done the work. Like most humorists, he wrote too much on the same few themes and rewrote himself more and more frequently. More seriously, his range of subject matter and of feeling was narrow; he showed indignation at social abuses, but his work yields little pathos or suspense. Moreover, Benchley's bumbler is too incompetent and too well adjusted to his incompetence; his anxieties are petty even when stimulated by major problems. Fear, awe, crushing defeat, sex, joy, a sense of fate, or a vital awareness of the God in whom the author believed could not be conveyed through such a figure—at least were not so conveyed by Robert Benchley.

Some of these defects, however, have had a way of turning into virtues. Even without the pictorial drolleries of Gluyas Williams, the pompous figure of Benchley's Little Man would have worn deep grooves in the American consciousness—he is so utterly incompetent, and that incompetence is shown so completely and with such persistent, though sympathetic, irony in piece after piece. The effect of Benchley has inevitably merged with that of his contemporaries and followers, but it is no guess to say that the humorous monologue and the archetypal Little Man would have been very different, and poorer, without him. (pp. 136-37)

Norris W. Yates, in his Robert Benchley *(copyright 1968 by Twayne Publishers, Inc.; reprinted with the permission of Twayne Publishers, A Division of G. K. Hall & Co., Boston), Twayne, 1968.*

Ambrose Bierce

1872-1914?

American journalist, poet, essayist, and short story writer. Bierce served with distinction in the Civil War and later drew on that experience—the "golden time" of his life—for many of his stories. He became a journalist in San Francisco following the Civil War, and, for his misanthropic humor and scathing observations on the personalities and events of the day, became known as "the wickedest man in San Francisco." A careful craftsman who peopled his fiction with grotesques, his influence can be discerned in the works of Conrad Aiken, Ernest Hemingway, Nathanael West, and William Faulkner. Bierce is best remembered for his macabre and grim short stories which are often compared to those of Poe. In 1913 he went to Mexico to be close to that country's civil war; he was never heard from again.

PRINCIPAL WORKS

Nuggets and Dust Panned Out in California [as Dod Grile] (sketches) 1872
The Fiend's Delight [as Dod Grile] (sketches) 1873
Cobwebs from an Empty Skull [as Dod Grile] (sketches) 1874
The Dance of Death [with Thomas A. Harcourt under the joint pseudonym of William Herman] (satire) 1877
Tales of Soldiers and Civilians (short stories) 1891 [reissued in 1892 as *In the Midst of Life*]
Black Beetles in Amber (poetry) 1892
The Monk and the Hangman's Daughter [with Gustav Adolph Danziger] (translators and adaptors) 1892
Can Such Things Be? (short stories) 1893
Fantastic Fables (homilies) 1899
Shapes of Clay (poetry) 1903
The Cynic's Word Book (aphorisms) 1906 [retitled *The Devil's Dictionary* in 1911]
The Shadow on the Dial, and Other Essays (essays) 1909
Write It Right (essay) 1909

Bierce was apparently a most attractive personality, who could make friends incapable of forgetting or not loving that unfathomable, deep-lined face, that great head, sensitive but invulnerable, lined and deepened into a native nobility like some king of the peasants. He could write to these friends, and to strangers as well, diffident, considerate, and charming letters, in which was combined gentleness of feeling with a square-cut simplicity of language, but whatever else he wrote, no matter how powerful, how striking, how carved from deep and simple quarries of speech, was somehow profoundly unattractive. It was tainted, subtly poisoned by the ever-present idea of death, a phenomenon which repelled him and drew him to itself with fascinated horror. He never accepted death as a mere terminal; death was not only an end, but an end in itself, a thing never solved, never absent, a mouthful of life from which no amount of chewing could ever expel its sweet and bitter taste.

There seems to have been no gayety in Bierce. He had wit, a savage macabre humor which made him feared and famous in the early newspaper days on the coast. In the columns of little California sheets he flayed weekly, in heavily venomous and brilliant verses, the local criminals and politicians. His favorite method was to imagine his victim in hell, and turn him over and over upon red-hot couplets. . . . The roasting was often wickedly neat and malicious, but how the black and red threads, fire and death, persisted, until one turned away from this sadism in horror. (pp. 184-85)

Bierce's claim to fame rests chiefly upon his stories of war. . . . Horror and death start from these pages and stifle us as if from the note-book of an eyewitness whose purpose in taking down the last details of the scenes about him was eventually to horrify a reader. Realism? No, curiously enough; these stories of war, though they seize attention as in a trap, are utterly unreal when we think of Tolstoy's Sebastopol. Much of Bierce's detail is poignantly lifelike, but he rolled and twisted these details up into a creature of his own death-ridden, fate-tortured imagination. The cruelty and irony of the war seem to have warped his sense of the real; nothing happens casually, spontaneously, irrelevantly; all is subordinate to that final twist or trick. . . . Under his unrelaxed grip the story moves tensely, unnaturally to an end predetermined with irony, bitterness and clenched teeth. This craftsman's inexorable chisel cuts dead true to pattern, so that no living tree seems to have been the father of this rigid piece of wood. Once in a while the tight grip loosens a little, and we have that noble, solid, almost poetic last ride on the white horse into the enemy's lines.

Bierce's stories belong to a species which, thanks to the influence of Chekhov, Katherine Mansfield and many others, who adapt life rather than twist it to their creative ends, is far less popular than it was. It is the kind of story which, from the very beginning, is built up and hammered together for the sake of the final twist, the dramatic or melodramatic dénouement which in Bierce's case was often as violent as the kick of a mule in the reader's face. Once or twice, as in the story of Peyton Farquhar's hanging, this final trick is handled with superb skill and suspense, but in story after story such decapitation of the reader's attention on the last page becomes tiresome. This is very discouraging in view of Bierce's accurate eye and skillful hand in the piling up of natural detail toward his unnatural and artificial end. After many pages in which we hear real bits of life and catch glimpses of real people, the closet door opens with a crash and out upon the floor falls a rattling skeleton. We are jarred, but we somehow suspected this would happen, for though the skeleton is concealed until the end, Bierce had it so much in mind, and was saving it up so eagerly that he could not keep it from rattling faintly from the beginning of the story. It was his obsession, this constant sense of death, it was his honey and his poison, and it was one of the sardonic, self-destructive twists in the mind of a man who was extraordinarily gifted, and who might, one feels, have been great. (pp. 186-88)

> *Robert Littell, "Bitter Bierce" (originally published in* The New Republic, *1926), in his* Read America First *(© 1926 by Harcourt, Brace and Company, Inc.; reprinted by permission of Harcourt Brace Jovanovich, Inc.), Harcourt, 1926, pp. 183-88.*

If Bierce were writing at present there would be a market for his products in the up-and-coming magazines. If his collected works had appeared ten years later they might have met with a welcome. But for any popular hearing Bierce emerged on the American scene betwixt too early and too late; though posthumously he seems to be coming into a modest repute. (pp. 76-7)

In both his journalism and his artistry Bierce was more nearly in tune with the nineteen twenties than with the eighteen nineties which chose to ignore him in his prime. (p. 78)

In his best-known volume, *In the Midst of Life,* Bierce painted a series of pictures that are marvels of sheer vividness. Once read they are cut deep into the memory both by the vigor of the etching and the momentous significance they contribute to the stories that contain them. "An Occurrence at Owl Creek Bridge," although not above the level of Bierce's most effective writing, is most often cited because of its ingenious construction and its surprise ending. . . . (p. 84)

Bierce often turned naturally to war episodes, because, although actual, they were farthest from the even tenor of normal life. Even in these it was the rarest occurrence for him to reveal any sense of humankind in general. The mass, the herd, the crowd, was a dim background for one man living at the highest pitch and more often than not dying of the tension. And the individual himself was less a character than a piece of susceptibility played on by overwhelming emotions. (p. 85)

Quite at the apex of Bierce's literary achievement is his longest piece of prose, "The Monk and the Hangman's Daughter," in which he most effectively combines his sense of beauty with his gift for subjective analysis. In a circumstantial Foreword he attributes the original to a German—who pretends to derive it from an old manuscript—and the first English version to a faithful but uninspired translator. His own version, he says, is a free rendition of this. . . . The source of the plot is a matter of small moment. In its present form the tale is an evidence of what Bierce could achieve when he released his powers in pure artistry.

His gifts as an artist lay in altogether different and conflicting powers. On the intellectual side he was a sardonic wit and a humorist. The special endowment of the wit is based on a capacity for acute and often acrid wording of nice discriminations. He sees a discrepancy or an incongruity and brands it with a phrase or a sentence. (pp. 86-7)

In the fashion of Thackeray and Holmes and Bret Harte, Bierce tried his hand at parody, and he succeeded perhaps as well as they, which was only moderately well. For he was a satirist rather than a parodist; he quite lacked the flexibility of the latter. . . . Always, whether as wit or humorist Bierce was taking the offensive against sentimentalism. On this ground he was more than a little suspicious of faith, hope, and charity. Feelings of any sort except distrust, scorn, and wrath seemed rather dangerous to him. The intellect must be a strong fortress against them all.

And yet sense was in the balance with sensibility, for Bierce was in the very nature of the case a man of feeling. So on the aesthetic side he added the delicate perceptions of the portrait painter to the caustic judgments of the cartoonist. The attitude and the utterance of the two are in complete contrast. The intellectual Bierce was always on the offensive; always ready to express himself in brilliant brevities. But the Bierce who wrote of the mysteries and the thrills of individual experience was receptive, deliberate, and deliberative, ready to surrender to a mood in a wise passiveness; willing to court in the shadows the shy thoughts that would not come out into the sunlight.

His shorter narratives inevitably suggest Poe, and can be comfortably laid on the Procrustes' bed erected by Poe in "The Philosophy of Composition." In scale, determination of effect, adoption of tone, establishment of background, and the rest of it, they submit to the same tests as "A Cask of Amontillado" and "The Fall of the House of Usher." But Bierce very properly resented the common report that he was a disciple of Poe. The tonal resemblance of their stories is clear, and it is clearly the result of their own resemblances in mind and temper; but in the most insistent feature of Bierce's workmanship, the elaboration of a single point of time for its subjective values, his stories are more imperatively suggestive of Victor Hugo's before him or of Stephen Crane's that were to come. (pp. 88-90)

The time when Bierce should have gained a hearing was between 1890 and 1910. His thinking, though not markedly original, was independent and aggressive and today seems somewhat provocative. He saw fairly straight when he looked at actual conditions, and he said very plainly what he saw. His printed resentment met with no general response. Much of what he had to say was implicit in Bellamy's *Looking Backward* which fascinated the multitude with an explicit picture of a communized Boston before communism had become a pariah in the public mind. It was rather more than suggested in Howells' *A Traveler from Altruria* with its strictures on the ways of the fortunate and its flavor of sugar-coated socialism. But Bierce's methods were more direct and his opinions less hopeful. He did not believe in Arcadias or Utopias or Altrurias or Platonic republics. He rejected communism and socialism, and he was as devastating in his comminatory passages as the plain-spoken objectors in the Platonic *Dialogues* who are set up for the not always convincing rebuttals of Socrates. (pp. 90-1)

If Bierce were writing today he would have his audience. His social theses would not attract much attention—they are no longer startling—but they would be either condemned or approved. And the best of his narratives, equal in bulk to the best of Poe's, would be read, let us say, by the readers of Aldous Huxley and Arthur Machen, Sherwood Anderson, and Joseph Hergesheimer. For those who like good writing, whether it was done yesterday or last week, it is not yet too late to turn to the narratives of Ambrose Bierce. (p. 93)

> *Percy H. Boynton, "Ambrose Bierce," in his* More Contemporary Americans (© *1927 by the University of Chicago), University of Chicago Press, 1927, pp. 75-93.*

Bierce, I believe, was the first writer of fiction ever to treat war realistically. He antedated even Zola. It is common to say that he came out of the Civil War with a deep and abiding loathing of slaughter—that he wrote his war stories in disillusion, and as a sort of pacifist. But this is certainly not believed by anyone who knew him, as I did in his last years. What he got out of his services in the field was not a sentimental horror of it, but a cynical delight in it. It appeared to him as a sort of magnificent *reductio ad absurdum* of all romance. The world viewed war as something heroic, glorious, idealistic. Very well, he would show how sordid and filthy it was—how stupid, savage and degrading. But to say this is not to say that he disapproved it. On the contrary, he vastly enjoyed the chance its discussion gave him to set forth dramatically what he was always talking about and gloating over: the infinite imbecility of man. There was nothing of the milk of human kindness in old Ambrose; he did not get the nickname of Bitter Bierce for nothing. What delighted him most in this life was the spectacle of human cowardice and folly. He put man, intellectually, somewhere between the sheep and the horned cattle, and as a hero somewhere below the rats. His war stories, even when they deal with the heroic, do not depict soldiers as heroes; they depict them as bewildered fools, doing things without sense, submitting to torture and outrage without resistance, dying at last like hogs in Chicago, the former literary capital of the United States. So far in this life, indeed, I have encountered no more thorough-going cynic than Bierce was. His disbelief in man went even further than Mark Twain's; he was quite unable to imagine the heroic, in any ordinary sense. Nor, for that matter, the wise. Man to him, was the most stupid and ignoble of animals. But at the same time the most amusing. Out of the spectacle of life about him he got an unflagging and Gargantuan joy. The obscene farce of politics delighted him. He was an almost amorous connoisseur of theology and theologians. He howled with mirth whenever he thought of a professor, a doctor or a husband. His favorites among his contemporaries were such zanies as Bryan, Roosevelt and Hearst.

Another character that marked him, perhaps flowing out of this same cynicism, was his curious taste for the macabre. All of his stories show it. He delighted in hangings, autopsies, dissecting-rooms. Death to him was not something repulsive, but a sort of low comedy—the last act of a squalid and rib-rocking buffoonery. (pp. 260-62)

He liked mystification, and there are whole stretches of his long life that are unaccounted for. His end had mystery in it too. It is assumed that he was killed in Mexico, but no eye-witness has ever come forward, and so the fact, if it is a fact, remains hanging in the air. (pp. 263-64)

Unluckily, his stories seem destined to go the way of Poe's. Their influence upon the modern American short story, at least upon its higher levels, is almost nil. When they are imitated at all, it is by the lowly hacks who manufacture thrillers for the cheap magazines. Even his chief disciples, Sterling and Scheffauer, did not follow him.... Meanwhile, it remains astonishing that his wit is so little remembered. In "The Devil's Dictionary" are some of the most devastating epigrams ever written. "Ah, that we could fall into women's arms without falling into their hands": it is hard to find a match for that in Oscar himself. (p. 264)

His life was a long sequence of bitter ironies. I believe that he enjoyed it. (p. 265)

> *H. L. Mencken, "Ambrose Bierce," in his* Prejudices: Sixth Series *(copyright © 1927 by Alfred A. Knopf, Inc.; 1955 by H. L. Mencken; reprinted by permission of Alfred A. Knopf, Inc.), Knopf, 1927, pp. 259-65.*

[It] was one of [Bierce's] fundamental beliefs that the emotions were to be distrusted. He demanded that they be severely restrained, disciplined, and reduced to the positions of servants of the intellect. Since he was of a highly emotional nature it was very difficult for him to follow this programme in his life. In his writings he succeeded somewhat better, for he could exercise a more severe censorship over the written word than over his acts. (p. 88)

A good many people have attributed his actual and reputed bitterness to the fact that he felt defeated by life.... [But] most of his bitterness was due to emotional instability. In his calmer moments he was not a bitter man. As I see it, the defeat he sustained worked out in quite another way than personal bitterness. It took the form of hampering his utterance. He left his work half done; his thoughts half expressed; his capacity for fiction only partly carried to fruition. (p. 90)

Another thing that made it impossible for Bierce to reach his full stature was the fact that he was at odds with his environment all the time. He was a perfectionist at a time when public morals were very low and private morals were nine tenths hypocrisy. He set up a high code of morality and judged all men by their deviation from it. He was an aristocrat when democracy was an unquestioned dogma.... In literature he was opposed to all the dominant trends and to all who supported them. It is, in fact, almost impossible to find a single topic upon which Bierce agreed with the general run of intellectuals of his day.... He could not even imagine a public for his ideas and consequently felt small urge to bring them to full expression. In this sense he was defeated by his time. (pp. 92-3)

There is probably not another writer in American literature

who had so high an ideal of literature as Bierce. It is probable, too, that few writers ever found the practice of their day so low and despicable. In presenting Bierce's ideas on this or any other topic it is necessary to give an exposition of his view of actuality as well as of his view of the ideal. The two are always diametrically opposed.

Bierce found himself a complete outsider in the literary world of his day. He did not accept the novel, realism, local colour, or slang. He resisted the environmental pressure that was making American literature deficient in heartiness. On his side in this particular combat he found Goethe, Shakespeare, Cervantes, Molière, and Rabelais and was satisfied. He despised magazine fiction and poetry through their whole range. He was at odds with every critic who supported the contemporary situation. He once lapsed into Johnsonese and called the critics "microcephalus bibliopomps." As a coat of arms for American letters he proposed an illiterate hoodlum rampant on a field of dead authors: motto, "To Hell with Literature."

His inability to find much of anything hopeful in contemporary literature produced a terrific reaction and resulted in his amazing portrait of literature as he conceived it to be practised. Starting from the tools of authorship and working up, he damned everything. (pp. 100-02)

Bierce was first and foremost a disciplinarian. He placed great emphasis on the technique of fiction and verse. He was constantly eager to be correct, and to see that others were correct even in the details of punctuation. . . . Yet however much he emphasized the technique of writing he was not an aesthetician. He scoffed at the idea that in writing a story an author solved any "aesthetic problem." (p. 118)

Bierce's rejection of realism and acceptance of romance was based upon his fundamental distaste for the reality he found himself immersed in and his abhorrence of human character as it exhibited itself to him. . . . In his own work in romance Bierce dealt principally with three topics—war, the supernatural, and religion. With the exception of the last each was handled in the short-story form. His philosophy of the short story was similar to that of Poe. He sought, like Poe, to make a single vivid impression upon the reader. To that end he eliminated all extraneous references. Furthermore, each story is a complete world in itself, controlled by the writer's logic, not by the illogicality of life. Since Bierce saw no point in reproducing the flat tones of ordinary life, he found an interesting topic only in the impingement of the extraordinary or the unreal on the normal course of events. . . . Nevertheless, it was Bierce's peculiar power to make these unusual happenings seem as vivid and real as the most "true-to-life" stories recorded by professed realists. (pp. 121-22)

Bierce's war stories, contained in *In the Midst of Life* and *Can Such Things Be?* number but nineteen. With these nineteen stories he has made a reputation greater than that of any other American writer about war with the exception of Stephen Crane. Yet even within that narrow range Bierce was unable to keep from repeating himself. . . . [We] are struck by the fact that the plots are lacking in any extraordinary brilliance. It seems, therefore, quite just to say that Bierce was lacking in inventiveness. It is highly improbable that he put all he had to say about the war into nineteen brief stories. He did not go on, in all probability,

simply because he could not find more extraordinary incidents to treat. This seems to me to reveal a fundamental weakness in his theory of art. It placed too much emphasis on mere inventiveness. It did not place enough emphasis on what seems to me the factor that makes fiction moving, the reflection of life through a contemplative consciousness. In the hands of a man whose inventiveness outran his capacity for observation and reflection the literary value of the products would quickly become negligible. (pp. 143-44)

Bierce never demanded that the reader approach his stories [of the supernatural] with a "will to believe." He saw to it that within the story itself were incorporated all the facts and sidelights necessary to lead into a state of mind that would minimize skepticism. The effects he achieved, then, are the product of a careful mixture of the facts of ordinary life with the supernatural. Neither one is allowed to dominate. It is difficult to tell where one leaves off and the other begins. That Bierce himself did not know seems to me logical to suppose.

It has been suggested to me that there must have been some obscure psychological reason for Bierce's interest in the horrible. I do not think so. It may well be that there was a twist in Bierce's mind that led him to deal with such matters with particular pleasure, but my point is that I do not think we need be worried if we cannot isolate it. (pp. 181-82)

Bierce himself, apropos his war stories, remarked: "If it scares you to read that one imaginary character killed another imaginary character, why not take up knitting instead of reading?" It may, however, be noted that it is extremely unfortunate that Bierce did not treat other than "nerve-racking" subjects. He certainly had all the literary skill necessary for widening his range of topics. If he had, his books would have been more balanced and the possibility that his effects would become tedious by repetition would have been avoided. (pp. 182-83)

[A] good deal of his satire is dull and almost unreadable today. It has lost its relevancy because it was directed against temporary situations. Bierce's satire as a rule was not directed against permanent foibles of the human race. In the same way a good deal of his wit was aimed to annihilate persons of such slight importance that they cannot be identified now by the moderately well-informed reader. Nevertheless, it is possible to make out a better case for his wit than for his satire. The latter had better be left to moulder undisturbed. (pp. 184-85)

Unfortunately, he had one fault that takes the edge off some of his wit. He was not satisfied to startle by paradox, to be wise and bleak; he thought it necessary to score a knock-out every time he took up his pen. His wit is of the knockdown variety. (pp. 186-87)

As a poet, Bierce was a failure. His hostility to emotional utterance was an impenetrable barrier to his success in poetry. He had some sense of rhetoric, but it was conventional rhetoric. Indeed, I am unable to find any redeeming qualities of importance even in [that]. . . . (p. 190)

It is almost beyond question that Bierce's mind was keener [than Mark Twain's], more disciplined, more penetrating, and in every way of a higher quality. If their cynicisms run parallel it is because they were both underfed intellectually and both betray a lack of culture. But the quality of their minds was quite different, and the potentialities of Bierce impress me much more than those of Mark Twain.

Yet in the bulk of work actually done, the fact remains that Mark Twain is far ahead of Bierce. In the final reckoning Mark Twain is an infinitely more important writer than Bierce. This may, perhaps, be attributed to the fact that Mark Twain was gifted with a greater creative capacity than Bierce, and creation has little to do with incisiveness of intellect. (pp. 265-66)

I do not think that Bierce was essentially a man of letters. . . . He was essentially a man of action who chose to function in letters. He needed something to fight against to arouse his best powers. The mere act of composition gave him small satisfaction. . . . He regarded his skill in expression in the same way that a swordsman regards his skill with the rapier. It was a convenient weapon with which to dispose of the fools and rogues he disliked.

In spite of all these reservations it is still possible to regard Bierce as one of the most important writers of his day and a significant figure in American literature. He stands out from every other writer of his generation for his independence, for the fact that he spoke out in meeting in no uncertain terms, and for the originality of his thinking. . . . [His] limitations sink into insignificance before the fact that he saw that the greatest limitation on authorship in America was the lack of a demand for independence on the part of the writers themselves. (pp. 269-71)

> *C. Hartley Grattan, in his* Bitter Bierce: A Mystery of American Letters *(copyright © 1929 by Doubleday, Doran & Company, Inc.; reprinted by permission of Doubleday & Co., Inc.), Doubleday, 1929 (and reprinted by Cooper Square Publishers, Inc., 1966).*

Whenever I meet a man with a pretense to critical sagacity in the matter of American *belles lettres,* I have an annoying habit of asking him his opinion of the late lost, strayed or stolen Mr. Ambrose Bierce. If, upon the question, he imparts to me a crisp wink, I put him down in my mental files as a fellow worth cultivating. If, on the other hand, he goes into an encomiastic clog, I dismiss him as one whose critical faculties have still not outgrown their adolescence. For I believe that an admiration of Bierce, among men of my generation, is invariably an unconscious hangover from the enthusiasm of their youth, when an epigram—provided only it were sufficiently cynical—was the last word in worldly wisdom and when any story of the occult in which the tall grass was mysteriously agitated by something (spelled with a capital S) was a dark-shudderful masterpiece.

Bierce's persistent reputation as an eminento of letters is undoubtedly due to these long-pants laudators with an unrevoked short-pants rapture. (p. 74)

In every smaller city, there is and always has been some writer or newspaper man who is singled out for matinée-idolizing by his cronies and certain of the town folk. . . . Bierce was the selection in the San Francisco of his time. (p. 78)

> *George Jean Nathan, in his* Passing Judgments *(copyright © 1935 by George Jean Nathan; reprinted by permission of Julie Haydon Nathan), Knopf, 1935.*

The dominating tendency of American literature and social thought, from Benjamin Franklin to Sinclair Lewis, has been optimistic. It has believed in man, it has believed in American man. It has at times been satirical and even bitter —but not negative. It gave the world the positive statements of the Declaration, the Constitution, the Gettysburg Address, Emerson, Whitman, William James, Henry George, John Dewey. This has been the stronger current. But along with it there has coursed a narrower current, the shadowed stream of pessimism. Perhaps its obscure source lies in the southern philosophers of slavery or in the bleak hell-fire morality of early puritan divines. . . . It flows hesitantly in Hawthorne, with fury in *Moby Dick* and *Pierre,* with many a subtle meander in the dark symbolisms of Poe. It may appear in part of a writer (the Mark Twain of "The Mysterious Stranger" and "The Man That Corrupted Hadleyburg") and not in the whole of him. It runs through Stephen Crane. You may trace it in an out-of-the-main-stream philosopher such as Thorstein Veblen. You will find it in the thought of H. L. Mencken and the stories of Ring Lardner. And you will see it plain, naked, naive, and powerful, in the strange fables of Ambrose Bierce.

Bierce's nihilism is as brutal and simple as a blow, and by the same token not decisive. It has no base in philosophy and, being quite bare of shading or qualification, becomes, if taken in overdoses, tedious. Except for the skeleton grin that creeps over his face when he has devised in his fiction some peculiarly grotesque death, Bierce never deviates into cheerfulness. His rage is unselective. The great skeptics view human nature without admiration but also without ire. Bierce's misanthropy is too systematic. He is a pessimism-machine. He is a Swift minus intellectual power, Rochefoucauld with a bludgeon, Voltaire with stomach-ulcers.

Nevertheless he may appeal to a generation which all over the world is being carefully conditioned to believe in nothing but Force. His cynicism, phrased with really extraordinary concentration, appalled his contemporaries; but it may attract rather than appall us. His *Fantastic Fables* may strike us as neither fantastic nor fabulous. He seems quite a man of our time.

I do not wish to overstate the point, for much of Bierce is old-fashioned. His prose at its worst is flawed with the bad taste of his period; his weakness for melodrama occasionally makes us squirm; he frequently overdoes his effects. Yet it is difficult to forget, for instance, the best of the stories in *In the Midst of Life:* "An Occurrence at Owl Creek Bridge," less interesting as a trick than as a heart-freezing symbolical presentation of the depth of the passion for survival; "Chickamauga," which, by a device of brilliant originality, rams home the pure insanity of war; "One of the Missing," which, like so many of his tales, shows a completely modern interest in and understanding of abnormal states of consciousness. Bierce, despite his almost Spanish admiration for "honor," was one of the earliest American writers to dismiss the flapdoodle of war and hold up to our gaze something like its true countenance. It is not so much that he hated war; indeed these stories are marked by a sort of agony of joy over war's horrors. Perhaps Bierce took a cold pleasure in war as the perfect justification of his view of mankind. He may even have liked war—no true lover of war has ever been so weak-kneed or weak-stomached as to attempt to disguise its brutality. But, however complicated Bierce's attitude toward war may have been, what he writes has the bitter-aloes taste of truth. He helped blaze the trail for later and doubtless better realists.

It is pertinent that Bierce, who disliked human beings and scoffed at social relationships, should have written so much and on the whole so well about ghosts, apparitions, revenants, were-dogs, animated machines, extrasensory perception, and action at a distance. It is as though the man's inability to stomach the real world forced him to try to establish citizenship in the country of the occult. He was so obsessed by the horror of real life that he had to call in the aid of another dimension in order to express it. . . . Bierce's morbidity is too controlled to have about it any touch of the insane; it merely expresses his fury at our placid healthiness. . . . It is this emotional drive behind his most calculated horrors that makes him much more than an American Monk Lewis. His Gothicism is no hothouse flower but a monstrous orchid.

Bierce's morbidity was exceptionally fertile—he made it produce humor as well as chills. I should say that in this extremely narrow field of the sardonic, of the ludicrous ghost story and the comical murder, he is unrivaled. He begins by somehow making you accept his basic premise: death is a joke. The rest is dead-pan elaboration, with the dead pan occasionally relieved by the rictus of a ghoul trying to laugh. Perhaps the two best examples are "My Favorite Murder" and "Oil of Dog." "My Favorite Murder" really creates a new shudder, a shudder in which laughter is grotesquely mingled. It is outrageous, it is frightening—it is funny. One finishes it in thorough agreement with the narrator that "in point of artistic atrocity" the murder of Uncle William has seldom been excelled. The humor of the unbelievable "Oil of Dog" depends on a careful, indeed beautiful use of ironical understatement, and the exhaustiveness of the technique whereby the macabre is pushed to such an extreme that it falls somehow into the gulf of laughter. (pp. 148-52)

The nuclear Bierce is to be found in the *Fantastic Fables*. One should not read more than a dozen of them at a time, just as one should not read more than a dozen jokes at a time. Their quality lies in their ferocious concentration of extra-double-distilled essential oil of misanthropy. They are so condensed they take your breath away.

The theme is always the same: mankind is a scoundrel. But the changes rung upon the theme demonstrate an almost abnormal inventiveness. They have no humor—they do not resemble at all, for instance, the fables of George Ade. They have wit but little fancy, they are undecorated, and they sting painfully. The brutal Bierce allows no exceptions. He aims to make mincemeat of all civilized humanity. . . . (p. 152)

Bierce is not, of course, a great writer. He has painful faults of vulgarity and cheapness of imagination. But at his best he is like no one else. He had, for example, a mastery of pared phrasing equaled in our time perhaps only by Wilde and Shaw. (pp. 152-53)

His style, for one thing, will preserve him, though for how long no one would care to say; and the purity of his misanthropy, too, will help to keep him alive. It is good that literature should be so catholic and wide-wayed that it affords scope to every emotion and attitude, even the unloveliest. It is fitting that someone should be born and live and die, dedicated to the expression of bitterness. For bitterness is a

mood that comes to all intelligent men, though, as they are intelligent, only intermittently. It is proper that there should be at least one man able to give penetrating expression to that mood. Bierce is such a man—limited, wrong-headed, unbalanced, but, in his own constricted way, an artist. (p. 153)

> *Clifton Fadiman, "Portrait of a Misan-*
> *thrope," an introduction to* The Collected
> Writings of Ambrose Bierce *(copyright,*
> *1946, The Citadel Press), The Citadel Press,*
> *1946 (and reprinted in* Party of One, *World*
> *Publishing Co., 1955, pp. 145-53).*

[Bierce's] claim to a position in American literature rests wholly on . . . two books [*Tales of Soldiers and Civilians* and *Can Such Things Be?*], a slender enough chain upon which to hang a reputation; but, as it happens, a strong one from the standpoint of the apocalyptic tradition. Bierce wrote fiction exclusively and solely in this vein; he modeled his form and his subject matter directly upon Poe, and while he never achieved the artistry or the psychological overtones of his master, he exhibited some aspects of the imagination never seen before. Irked as he was by contemporary jibes at his Poe-idolatry, it is nevertheless perfectly apparent that Poe was his inspiration and exemplar, and hardly any other influence can be detected in his work.

If it be objected that Poe's characters seldom seem lifelike, what must be our objection to Bierce's? They have absolutely no relevant characteristics that strike us as human, save their outward description; it is never for the character's sake but always for the plot's sake that a Bierce story exists. Bierce was interested, even more than Brown, Poe or Melville, in the *idea* of the story—seldom in the human significance of it. In fact, some of the stories exist essentially for the whiplash ending, which in Bierce's handling antedated O. Henry. But the Bierce story can be reread with some profit, for there is real evidence of a technician's hand. The element of atmosphere contributes a good deal to the effectiveness of these stories, which in all cases deal with the bleak, gloomy or horrible aspects of life. Madness induced by fright, terror of the supernatural, death in battle, these are the Biercean themes. There is no humor in any line of Bierce's creative work; in fact, Bierce never wrote a humorous sentence in his life, though there is plenty of death's-head grinning throughout the *Collected Works*. It is doubtful if any of the apocalyptic writers from Brown to Faulkner have perceived what humor is, or been able to write it; they have excluded it from the categories of human behavior; their definition of life rules out the possibility of real levity. In its place we find a savage and bitter gibing at human frailty, the more savage because the more heartbreaking to the shattered idealist who has found humanity is frail. The best these writers can do is show us a caricature of comedy, and from Poe to Faulkner we find them offering as "humorous" what is merely grotesque.

However, of Bierce we can say that he never tried to be funny in his fiction; he did try most desperately for shocking effects, and he succeeded greatly. . . . The soldier in "A Horseman in the Sky" reveals in the penultimate sentence that he has shot his father; and we feel the shock. We can go through the story backwards, pick up the threads that led us to this denouement, and find that Bierce had made a nice puzzle for us and untangled it skillfully. We react to the story as we might to a cleverly demonstrated mathematical problem; but we do not feel the human sympathy or identity which serious fiction ought to arouse.... We read through [his] stories of war, and toward carnage an attitude emerges which is entirely realistic and quite modern. Bierce wrote from the viewpoint of the individual sufferer in war; he never attempted to glorify any aspect of killing; and on the reportorial level, the *Tales* are the best minor pictures of modern warfare up to their time. No doubt Crane's *Red Badge of Courage* owed much to Bierce. (pp. 80-2)

[In the supernatural tales] the actors are pawns but what they do is calculated to induce that thrill of fear which is one of the lesser functions of fictional art but surely still a function. Diabolism seldom reached such heights as in this collection; and if read properly, accepting the limitations Bierce imposed upon himself, these tales are worth considering; they compare favorably with many of Poe's similar stories. (p. 82)

> *George Snell, in his* The Shapers of American Fiction: 1798-1947 *(copyright 1947 by George Snell; reprinted by permission of the publishers, E. P. Dutton), Dutton, 1947.*

[Bierce] wrote with a certain elegance of which he was highly conscious and extremely proud,—he liked to correct the grammar of his rivals in the press, as he censored their factual mistakes and their errors in logic. (p. 203)

It was through his association with authors and artists in London, moreover, that the semi-literate Bierce learned really to write. He had had little education, his early work was rough and coarse and his tardy discovery of good English rather went to his head, as one could see by the manner in which, as an unofficial teacher, he later gave his little Senate laws. For he was the master of a group of disciples in writing. (p. 204)

Bierce was quite without Poe's magic, but he had qualities that were wholly his own, qualities that owed virtually nothing to a predecessor, and, even when he most resembled Poe, the situations of his tales were new, whether invented or fruits of observation. (p. 209)

Never obliged to match his wits with first-rate minds, he rode his hobbies freely and indulged his whims, dogmatizing at his ease with a too facile cynicism that over-expressed his somewhat acrid spirit. More than occasionally really witty, with a singular force of imagination that gave permanent value to a dozen or a score of his tales, he poured out a mass of uncensored writings, epigrams, essays and stories, that filled twelve tasteless volumes at the end of his life. Quite out of touch with the mind of his time, he never read a new book save, as he remarked, by way of penance,—he had stopped growing, in fact, before 1890; and yet there was something to justify Jack London's letter to George Sterling the poet saying that Bierce had "crystallized" before they were born. "It is too magnificent a crystallization to quarrel with," Jack London observed, and for all his intolerance Bierce was a "splendid old man." (p. 211)

> *Van Wyck Brooks, "San Francisco: Ambrose Bierce," in his* The Confident Years: 1885-1915 *(copyright, 1952, by Van Wyck Brooks; reprinted by permission of the publishers, E. P. Dutton), Dutton, 1952, pp. 201-16.*

It may very well be true [as some biographers claim] that the special ferocity and gusto with which Bierce played the Devil's advocate, as well as his readiness to castigate others as "wantons," liars and thieves—that is, blastingly, out of hand, from the point of view of old-fashioned morality—and the curious Puritanism that underlay his San Francisco rakishness, were due to a Calvinist background.

In any case, it is certainly true, not only that, as has been said by Clifton Fadiman, Death itself is Bierce's favorite character, but that, except in *The Monk and the Hangman's Daughter,* a rewriting of a story by someone else, Death may perhaps be said to be Ambrose Bierce's only real character. In all Bierce's fiction, there are no men or women who are interesting as men or women—that is, by reason of their passions, their aspirations or their personalities. They figure only as the helpless butts of sadistic practical jokes, and their higher faculties are so little involved that they might almost as well be trapped animals. But Bierce does succeed in making Death play an almost personal role. His accounts of battles he took part in are among the most attractive of his writings, because here he is able to combine a ceaseless looking Death in the face with a delight in the wonder of the world, as the young man from Elkhart, Indiana, finds himself in a land where "unfamiliar constellations burned in the southern midnights, and the mocking-bird poured out his heart in the moon-gilded magnolia." . . . [The] enchantment that Bierce's war memories had for him was partly created by the charms of the South, so different from anything he had previously known. But eventually, in his horror stories, the obsession with death becomes tiresome. If we try to read these stories in bulk, they get to seem not merely disgusting but dull. The horror stories of Poe, with which they have been compared, have always a psychological interest in the sense that the images they summon are metaphors for hidden emotions. The horror stories of Bierce have only in a very few cases such psychological interest as may come from exploiting dramatically some abnormal phenomenon of consciousness. There is, otherwise, merely the Grand Guignol trick repeated again and again. The executioner Death comes to us from outside our human world and, capriciously, gratuitously, cruelly, slices away our lives. It is an unpleasant limitation of Bierce's treatment of violent death that it should seem to him never a tragedy, but merely a bitter jest. He seems rarely to have felt any pity for his dead comrades of the Civil War, and it is characteristic of him that he should write [of them] as if in derision. . . . (pp. 622-23)

Bierce's short stories are often distinguished from the hackwork of the shudder magazines only by the fact that the shudder is an emotion that for the author is genuine, and by the sharp-edged and flexible style, like the ribbon of a wound-up steel tape-measure. He has also a certain real knack for catching, in his stories about the West, the loneliness of solitary cabins, with their roofs partly fallen in and with a grave or two among the trees; of worked-out diggings in Nevada hills with a skeleton at the bottom of the shaft; of empty buildings in San Francisco of which nobody knows the owners but into which some unknown person creeps at night—all places where the visit of Death seems peculiarly blighting and final, where, in pinching out a tiny human spirit, it renders the great waste complete.

In most other departments of Bierce's work—his poetry,

his commentary on public events, his satirical and humorous sketches—the reign of Death is only less absolute. He seems interested in denouncing political corruption mainly from the point of view of its giving him an opportunity to imagine macabre scenes in which the miscreants are received in Hell or left to survive alone in a universe divested of life. In his poetry, God and the angels and even the figure of Christ, as well as the Devil and his agents, are sometimes brought on to the scene, but these powers, celestial and infernal alike, act only to reject and to damn. (p. 624)

As for Bierce's opinions and principles, they were, as someone said of Voltaire, "a chaos of clear ideas." The dismay and the doubt which for such men as Bierce, in the era of big profits and abundant graft, came to cloud the success of the Union cause is given vehement expression in certain of his poems. And he detested the melodrama that the Northerners had made of the Civil War.... [At one time he wrote]: "They found a Confederate soldier the other day with his rifle alongside. I'm going over to beg his pardon."

There are moments when, like Justice Holmes, he is inclined to think that war itself is a purgative and bracing institution.... (pp. 625-26)

Ambrose Bierce, in the department of religion, was not a militant atheist as he might have been expected to be. Though he baited and made fun of the clergy, he had several clerical friends, and, according to the memoir of Walter Neale, he especially esteemed Jewish rabbis, for their "broad scholarship," their "devotion to the traditions of their religious order" and their "tolerance of other religions." He was respectful toward all the faiths, but conceived them to be all the creations of men.... [He] was haunted by visions of judgment, and he talks about God in a way which, even when he is being facetious, makes one feel that the conception is still real to him, that—remote above the power of Death—it still presides in Bierce's mind.

As for Bierce's political and social views, the disruption of the Republic by the Civil War, in shattering the integrity of the republican ideal, had shaken Bierce's faith in its purpose; yet, like Holmes, he was too much an old-fashioned American to feel himself really at home with the new ideals of social justice—with the socialists or with Henry George. The result was that, in commenting on current affairs in his San Francisco newspaper column, he was often quite inconsistent.... The degradation of public life that followed the Civil War and the activities of omnivorous Business which had worried Walt Whitman and others, were now causing younger men to conclude that if this was what democracy meant, there must be something wrong with democracy. The insistence of Ambrose Bierce on discipline, law and order, and on the need for the control of the disorderly mob by an enlightened and well-washed minority has today a familiar fascistic ring. Though Bierce sometimes jeered at the English, he was really—having lived for three years in England (1872-75)—quite distinctly an Anglophile, and he was sympathetic with British imperialism. He seems to have believed that monarchy was the most satisfactory form of government. (pp. 626-28)

[There is a] disconcerting contrast between the somewhat unpleasant impression that we are likely to get of Bierce when we read him or read about him at length, and the attraction which he evidently exercised on those with whom he came in contact.... And it is reported by several persons that Bierce seemed to exert a magnetic power over the animals he kept as pets, and that, by giving a "soft call" in the woods, "half a whisper and half a cry," he could bring the birds to perch on his shoulders and hop about on his uplifted hands; yet there is no love of life in his writings, and barely a flush of responsive warmth toward any other human being. Of the sunlight and flowers and fruit, of the gaiety and good wine and good eating, of the love affairs and friendships that Bierce enjoyed in and about San Francisco for something like thirty years, there is hardly a trace in his work.

Even the best of his fiction is monotonous and almost monomaniacal in its compulsive concentration on death, and the general run of his journalism would seem to have been equally sterile and even more disagreeable in its monotony of personal abuse.... [His] biographers cite many instances of his kindness and consideration. Yet the impression one gets from his journalism is that of a powerful impulse to denigrate for the lust of destroying. (pp. 628-30)

He abominated dialect literature and wanted to outlaw American colloquialisms. As Mencken says, "It never seems to have occurred to him that language, like literature, is a living thing, not a mere set of rules." It is the hand of death again. The best qualities of Bierce's prose are military—concision, severe order and unequivocal clearness. His diction is the result of training and seems sometimes rather artificial. The soldier commands one's respect, but the queer unsatisfactoriness of Bierce's writing is partly due to the fact that this marble correctitude is made to serve as a mask for a certain vulgarity of mind and feeling.... Bierce was aware of his crudeness, and it is plain from ... books about him that he resolutely struggled against it. But there was something besides the crudeness that hobbled his exceptional talents—an impasse, a numbness, a void, as if some psychological short circuit had blown out an emotional fuse. The obsession with death is the image of this: it is the blank that blocks every vista; and the asthma from which Bierce suffered was evidently its physical aspect.... His writing—with its purged vocabulary, the brevity of the units in which it works and its cramped emotional range—is an art that can hardly breathe.

Ambrose Bierce lacks the tragic dimension; he was unable to surmount his frustration, his contempt for himself and mankind.... (pp. 631-32)

> *Edmund Wilson, "Ambrose Bierce on the Owl Creek Bridge," in his* Patriotic Gore: Studies in the Literature of the American Civil War *(copyright © 1962 by Edmund Wilson; reprinted by permission of Farrar, Straus & Giroux, Inc.), Oxford University Press, 1962, pp. 617-34.*

[Bierce's] reputation after his death seemed about to be submerged by the rising tide of naturalism in fiction. Literary developments since then have taken such a turn, however, that Bierce now seems a prophetic writer. Many of the techniques developed by Bierce anticipate those employed by such writers as Conrad Aiken, Ernest Hemingway, Nathanael West, and William Faulkner, to name only the major ones.... We must assign him a minor role in literary history, but that role grows larger as the tradition of the grotesque develops in the twentieth century. It is now possible to see Bierce as a writer who has had some influence upon the course of American literature. (pp. 5-6)

Bierce's targets for satire, sarcasm, and invective ranged over the personality and habits of journalists, officials, ministers, and all figures in public life. His subjects most often were religion, politics, and public immorality. This mixture was a popular one, and, although he might tread upon various toes, his column ["Town Crier"] was avidly read, even by those whom he abused. (p. 13)

He coveted the polish of literary respectability. With aristocratic tastes he scorned appeal to a mass audience and insisted upon his own standards as opposed to local color, dialect, and realism. He regarded himself as a satirist in the classical tradition. Nonetheless, at the behest of his London editors he tried his hand at the breezy humor popularly associated with the Far West. (p. 14)

The curious student who tries to find some significant change between early and later work will be disappointed. Apart from technical skill there is little to distinguish Bierce's fiction of 1871, when he first contributed "The Haunted Valley" to the *Overland,* and that of 1908, when he sent his last stories to *Cosmopolitan.* The only valid generalization concerning such a change is perhaps that he modified the humor. Some early stories, like "Curried Cow," show a kinship with the boisterous tall tale; but uniformly the late work is pessimistic, its humor sardonic and cynical. (p. 24)

Many of Bierce's narratives deal with death by violent means, and in this respect he invites comparison with certain other writers of his day. Violent death seems to have been common on the American frontier. Bret Harte saw in it a picturesque part of the "local color"; Mark Twain saw it as a subject for humor. Ambrose Bierce saw it for what it was. Curiously, the literary historians have classed Harte and Twain as realists and have accepted Bierce's own classification of himself as a romantic.

It is not easy to pin a label on his fiction. His contemporaries compared him most often to Poe. Bierce resented the comparison, not because he disliked Poe but because he was irritated by the narrow critical view that gave Poe a priority right to the supernatural. (p. 30)

Bierce's stories, though many are bloodcurdling and deal with the supernatural, often have a rational explanation and display psychological insight. He is a master of the outré. What interests him is not the ordinary, but the unusual, and this is part of his conscious opposition to the school of realism, headed by William Dean Howells, that objected to any breach of probability.... The outré, the unusual, is not enough to define Bierce's subject in fiction. The story must have a cynical ironic twist. The old man turned away from the Home for the Aged must be the philanthropist who, in his palmier days, founded the place. (pp. 30-1)

In 1909 a volume of his essays, *The Shadow on the Dial,* was published in San Francisco. The reviews were uniformly critical of his inconsistencies, lack of information, and journalistic haste. The book was a grab bag collection of assaults on government, socialism, women's rights, and labor unions. They betrayed their hastily written origins; as one reviewer said, "These wrathful passages seem to have

no natural glow—only the steam heat of journalism." (p. 40)

The autobiographical essays, however, show Bierce at his stylistic best when deeply engaged by his subject; they are based upon personal experience, chiefly in the Civil War. The prose is clear, simple, straightforward, and effective. The narrative portions make absorbing reading and compare favorably with Mark Twain's prose in *Life on the Mississippi,* without the colloquial character, but with the same stylistic ease and grace of the born raconteur. One is moved to speculate upon what Bierce might have accomplished had he not fenced himself in with his literary prejudices. But then he would not have been Bierce, for these eccentricities go far toward defining his personality and character. (p. 41)

Bierce set himself obstinately against the tide of realism associated with Howells and his followers—a tide which was dominant well into the third decade of the twentieth century and is still the moving force of most best sellers. But serious fiction in the forties and fifties has exhibited certain changes that make Bierce seem less remote. For one thing, the realistic works that survive strike us now as fundamentally symbolic. For another, the literature of the grotesque and absurd appears increasingly significant. Both characteristics bring Bierce closer to a tradition of importance in our literature. (pp. 44-5)

Precise definition is difficult because like any vital tradition this one changes as it develops. Certain characteristics, however, are associated in varying degrees with the fiction identified with it. There is a marked concern for abnormal or heightened psychological states. Characters frequently deviate widely in the direction of grotesque, twisted, or alienated personalities. Often physical appearance will symbolize the inner state. The events depicted are disposed toward the unusual rather than the ordinary, particularly the perverse, the violent, and the shocking. Similarly there is a disposition toward fear, terror, horror, insecurity, and the failure of love. There is a tendency to see problems within the individual soul, psyche, or unconscious rather than in terms of outward circumstances—society and institutions, for example.

Ambrose Bierce is squarely within this tradition. In his best work he has given us a number of powerful symbolic studies firmly grounded upon psychological insights into bizarre incidents and characters. The theme of war in its grotesque and horrible aspects, so intimately associated with Bierce, seems not so much his private property as it once did. (p. 46)

The chief flaws in his work seem to proceed from a limited range of emotional experience. Bierce never matured emotionally. Much of his iconoclasm has the fervor of adolescence; he could not see the many-sidedness of human behavior. Much of the violence in his work seems as much an extension of his personal and journalistic aggression as it does a result of direct observation of life. His personal aloofness, even in his closest relationships, is reflected upon his work. There is not sufficient sympathy in his stories to allow any all-out attachment; the characters, especially the women, are two-dimensional. The great compression and economy so characteristic of his stories keep the reader from becoming involved; we are left detached and remote. Though this situation sometimes reinforces the ironic treatment, more often it prevents a full realization of the story's possibilities. Bierce's satire, despite the allure of its surface wit and force, suffers from the same cause. Much of it is trivial, and even the best seems to lack a substratum of human sympathy; he never earned by his compassion the privilege of harshly indicting his fellow man.

Despite his faults—perhaps partly because of them—Bierce makes us aware of a distinctive voice; if not one of the best in our literary chorus, it is nonetheless an interesting one important to an understanding of a significant part of our literature. (p. 47)

> *Robert A. Wiggins, in his* Ambrose Bierce *(American Writers Pamphlet No. 37;* © *1964, University of Minnesota), University of Minnesota Press, Minneapolis, 1964.*

If Bierce has proved a protean figure, his fiction, at least, has a curiously homogeneous quality which originates in his obsessive vision. Specifically, Bierce's fiction takes its form from a series of violent oscillations between art and life, idealism and cynicism, and a richly romantic imagination and a rational awareness of life as a diminished thing. It was the pressure of the warring impulses Bierce could never manage in his own life that determined the controlling conception of his short stories. The conception itself severely restricted the range of his ideas and finally destroyed him as a serious writer. But in a handful of his war tales, it also enabled him to do what time may judge to be his finest writing. (pp. 2-3)

As certain of his essays, and particularly his letters, make evident, behind all the raillery and bitter satire lay a romantic temperament and a frustrated idealism that left Bierce stranded when he could find no way to justify them through his experience. By his own admission and the testimony of friends, Bierce had once approached life filled with extravagant expectations and youthful dreams of achievement. Specifically, this time of promise was the period covered by Bierce's war service, which Bierce always regarded as the most exciting and significant experience of his life and looked back on with an almost incredible nostalgia. It became the focal point of his existence, against which he opposed the dreary civilian aftermath, a means of defining the gulf between former youthful hopes and dreams and a present experience that mocked all sanguine assumptions about life. Bierce talked about the war, thought about it, wrote about it, all his life, and paid repeated visits to the Civil War battlefields where he had fought. Emotionally, he never left the army at all, and as his disillusionment and frustration increased, his war days became increasingly a cherished memory. . . . It is difficult to understand Bierce as a writer without reference to his divided sensibility and to his contradictory responses to experience. Although the conflicts in Bierce are apparent to anyone reading his journalism and correspondence, . . . their relevance to his short stories has never been explored. . . . Bierce's inability to reconcile extremes in his temperament determines the very form and texture of his imaginative world. Too many critics have regarded his fiction either as mechanically contrived or as a fictional version of his cynicism and misanthropy. While this is true of his least successful stories, it misses the significance and symbolic complexity of his war fiction, which is highly idiosyncratic. . . .

In his imaginative literature Bierce instinctively turned away from the prosaic constricting world dissected in his journalism. He did so either by returning to the scenes of his war experience, with all their ambiguous associations or, less successfully, by working within the tradition of terror and the supernatural. This impulse to seek out the remote or unusual, part of his romantic theory of art and the imagination, explains why Bierce never dealt in his fiction with the world of everyday experience and why his stories fall within sharply defined limits. They are circumscribed by the fact that the impulse to withdraw into a world of imagination was invariably blocked by Bierce's pervasive sense of the futility and emptiness of life itself. A recurrent pattern in Bierce's fiction is one in which the imagination is denied or frustrated by rational knowledge and empirical experience. (pp. 12-14)

In his journalism and satiric verse, and especially in *The Devil's Dictionary,* Bierce is primarily concerned with castigating a flawed humanity. . . . In his short stories, on the other hand, Bierce's characteristic theme is the inscrutable universe itself, whose mechanisms checkmate man's every attempt to assert his will or live his dreams. If the universe is not actively hostile or malevolent, as in many of his tales of the supernatural, it is at best always indifferent to human need. . . . This dismal concept of the human situation is Bierce's central imaginative impulse in his short stories, the idea that gives shape to his fictional world. (p. 19)

As a scientific determinist, Bierce believed in evolution through natural selection, but to him it implied no march toward human perfection. Instead, he saw man caught in an eternal round of progress and disintegration. As a part of nature's principles of force and strife, man, innately selfish, engaged in an endless series of wars which destroyed the capable and strong while preserving the feeble and incompetent. Man's attempts at humanitarian and social reform, such as the rehabilitation of criminals, salvaged the very misfits and "incapables whom Nature is trying to 'weed out.'" (p. 21)

With the paradoxical irony some modern existentialists are so fond of, Bierce regarded self-destruction as a kind of creative act, a weird moral achievement in a universe virtually drained of moral purpose and meaning. It was as if the individual could only assert his will by relinquishing it altogether in a final destructive act. Suicide became a last salute to all those dark forces conspiring against man, a Pyrrhic victory that ushered in the "good, good darkness." (p. 31)

The fate that overtakes such characters as Jerome Searing, William Grayrock, and George Thurston, originates in what Bierce conceived of as the "pitiless perfection of the divine, eternal plan." Whether this fate manifests itself as some arbitrary pattern of external circumstance or as an inner "constitutional tendency" makes no difference. The result is the same: the annihilation of the protagonist or of his private dream. Sometimes death is preceded by a stupefying sense of disillusionment or horror; sometimes it comes so swiftly there is no time for reflection. In many of the war stories, Bierce creates a bitter contrast between the main character's hopes or youthful dreams and the harsh reality that reduces him to a meaningless cipher. . . . To Bierce, the ultimate horror of the "eternal plan" was that man could learn nothing from his ordeal except the lesson of his own futility and purposelessness. (pp. 37-8)

[The] sense of man's helplessness, of the terrible inevitability of his fate, is the most persistent theme running through Bierce's stories, especially those dealing with war. For Bierce, war was the ideal metaphor to define the human predicament, not simply because he had known war intimately, but because it was the clearest demonstration of how the instinctive and the accidental combined to thwart human endeavor. But war's most important function was to represent what Bierce regarded as the central fact of existence: one's physical annihilation. Believing that the "mind or spirit or soul of man was the product of his physical being, the result of chemical combinations," Bierce looked upon death as the "awful mystery," awful because of its irreducible finality, its negation of all of man's hopes and creative impulses.... Bierce's war stories are fables of life's essential movement toward disillusion, defeat, and death. They concentrate and accelerate the inexorable process of disintegration. (pp. 44-5)

In Bierce's most convincing stories we see little of that intemperate and sometimes hysterical assault on human folly that characterizes his expository writing; that is, his main characters are seldom the object of the narrator's scorn or abuse. Bierce is conscious of unmerited suffering and his despair is consequently centered not so much on man as on the destructive nature of his experience. This focus enabled him to manage tone more successfully in his war tales than in his other writings, and while it did not prevent his showing the human condition to be meaningless, it kept it from becoming merely absurd. (p. 46)

Because it was the reality of their suffering and frustration that Bierce responded to, his war figures make a serious claim upon our attention. Only in the war stories does Bierce achieve the sense of genuine concern for human frailty endlessly cheated and baffled by life. His characters are credible even when their dilemmas are not, because he believed in the agony of their ordeal, even if he believed in little else. (p. 53)

The essays are particularly useful as evidence of a strain of emotional fervor and romantic idealism which Bierce found increasingly untenable in the face of certain indigestible facts of his experience. (p. 57)

Bierce seems to have been bent on convincing himself that ideals had no real meaning, that there were no principles except those of expediency and, therefore, that they had no power to hurt or disappoint. They were the products of an idle fancy and emotional wishful thinking. As his writing clearly shows, he came to feel that all painful emotions could be laughed and mocked out of existence. That such a strategy convinced some people is shown by the frequent charge of "inhumanity" leveled at Bierce's work. But Bierce was hardly inhuman, and his intellect never subverted his heart, although he prided himself on some sort of Olympian tragic vision, of looking down from "the dominating peaks austere and desolate" and "holding a prophecy of doom." (p. 78)

In going back to war's actions and images for the best fiction he ever wrote, Bierce was not simply drawing upon his own experiences. By the time Bierce began writing his tales, the war itself had crystallized into a symbol combining his youthful expectations of life and his postwar disillusionment. His perspective was one conscious of the distance between what once had *seemed* and what now *was*,

between a sensuous involvement in experience and a detached contemplation of its limiting conditions. It is this perspective, in turn, which determines the symbolic action of Bierce's plots. The inward sense of impoverishment and frustration is externalized as some form of death or defeat which comes upon the protagonist through no fault of his own. He is carried along relentlessly by a whimsical destiny which propels him from illusions and false assumptions about life to a situation that points up the disparity between the knowledge and the dream. The success of the war tales generally lies in Bierce's ability to get outside himself sufficiently to objectify his own dilemma while at the same time his characters and their destructive experiences are close enough to be taken seriously and regarded with a measure of compassion. (p. 89)

Because Bierce saw nothing in life to look forward to, he spent much of it looking backward. His truest art is the result of his nostalgia, which he objectifies as some false assumption experience ruthlessly denies. Perhaps just because it had proved so insubstantial and unreliable in his own case, Bierce sometimes wrote about the imagination as if it were itself a "dream" he could never hold on to. Only in sleep and dreams did it have a valid existence, and so "the dreamer is your only true poet." ... (p. 94)

In view of his emphasis upon the primacy of imagination, it is hardly surprising that next to poetry, Bierce regarded the romance as the noblest literary form. It was, in fact, the only type of fiction that Bierce would allow, the only kind that could be dignified with the name of "art." (pp. 94-5)

Unable to mediate between his head and his heart, between his rational self and his imaginative idealistic self, Bierce ended by exploiting the differences with a ruthless cynicism that reflected his frustration. As a writer he first distrusted, then tried to deny, his most creative impulses. He was always being pulled in opposite directions by his realistic satirical journalism and his romantic views on literature, by his antifactual imagination and his distrust of all that was not fact. (p. 103)

The polarity which Bierce was most conscious of, and which best summarizes all the others, was that between the true and permanent art he hungered for and the largely ephemeral journalism which took up his time and energy for almost forty years. It is not a question of Bierce's newspaper work leaving little opportunity for fiction—many writers with equal or greater demands upon their time have produced more imaginative literature than he did. The real significance of his journalism is that it defines, just as it intensified, the split between Bierce's imaginative and his empirical responses to life, between his desire to create an imaginary world of beauty, order, and permanence and an even stronger impulse to destroy a painfully real civilian world of windy oratory and business chicanery, of cheap patriotism and crass materialism. Both his short stories and his expository writing sprang from the common source of his postwar disillusionment which gave force and substance to his newspaper work while at the same time it undermined his attempts at serious fiction. (p. 104)

[A] good deal of Bierce's disillusionment stemmed from a gnawing sense of his own artistic limitations, as well as from his revulsion at a culturally starved and morally sick America. This is why Bierce always stressed an irreconcilable distinction between journalism and literature and why he actually despised the career which in his own day brought him considerable recognition. . . . What journalism lacked for Bierce was the quality of imaginative vision he prized so highly. It dealt only with prosaic facts and was, therefore, like the new realism he ridiculed, "mere reporting." (p. 106)

He never seems to have considered that true art also comes from close observation and experience of things as they are; he saw it instead as a mysterious realm far removed from real life. And that is why he idealized it, just as he idealized his war memories and the past in general. At the same time that he looked back nostalgically at the period of youthful ideals and enthusiasms, he distrusted his imagination for playing him false, so that his attitude wavers between sentimentality and bitter derision of all sentiment and untested assumptions. (p. 109)

Convinced of an impossible gulf between satirical personal journalism and imaginative literature, Bierce decided to make the most of his destined career. (p. 110)

Bierce's tales of terror and the supernatural derive from his love of the romance and from his belief that literature must treat themes and situations far removed from everyday life. Because he looked upon it as a distant dream and the most memorable period of his life, the Civil War provided the desired diversion from a dreary world. When he had exhausted its possibilities in a few tales, he naturally looked for inspiration in what he calls in one of his stories "the realm of the unreal." . . . His interest in the supernatural is only another manifestation of a romantic temperament, as well as of a mind that habitually looked upon the dark side of life. (p. 124)

Although Bierce has frequently been praised for fertility of imagination, his imagination was actually restricted to a few conceptions which he repeats in story after story. . . . He could never seem to break out of the charmed circle circumscribed by his vision of futility and inevitable defeat. Bierce may have read Darwin and Spencer along with other pessimists of the age, but he knew determinism at first hand, in his own warring impulses and inadequacies and in an environment which, to say the least, violated "his keen sense of the beautiful." The knowledge served only to feed his frustration and his resentment. (p. 143)

> *Stuart C. Woodruff, in his* The Short Stories of Ambrose Bierce: A Study in Polarity *(reprinted by permission of the University of Pittsburgh Press; © 1964 by the University of Pittsburgh Press), University of Pittsburgh Press, 1964.*

Ambrose Bierce . . . has maintained a curious kind of underground reputation, less as a maker of books than as a personal legend, a minority saint for the cynical and disenchanted. (A passion for taut, precise, desentimentalizing English is a special part of this legend.) Growing up into the holocaust of the Civil War, in which he served with honor and was badly wounded, he became a writer whose voice and outlook are more impressive than the literary uses he managed to put them to. He survives as a figure of bitter dissent and disaffiliation—from the bluster and prodigality of the Gilded Age, from its daydreams of comfort and success, from all its gross connivance in hypocrisy and untruth. It was as such, a scarifier of his times and an honest measure of their moral shabbiness, that the critic Percival

Pollard celebrated Bierce in *Their Day in Court* (1909) as "the one commanding figure in our time."

The very peremptoriness of his naysaying, however, limited Bierce's authority as a satirist and moral critic. Nonetheless his *Fantastic Fables* . . ., sardonically reviewing the rules and conditions for success in contemporary society, do pungently underscore the more formidable critique of the sociology of the leisure classes that Thorstein Veblen published in the same year; Bierce's indictment is less substantial but rather more absolute. His point of view is even more starkly expressed in *The Cynic's Word Book* (. . . reissued as *The Devil's Dictionary*), a book worth keeping in print and commending to the young and their teachers, although by reason of its piecemeal form this collection of "old saws fitted with new teeth" loses bite when read straight through. Bierce's major achievement is rather in his two volumes of stories, *In the Midst of Life* (. . . also issued as *Tales of Soldiers and Civilians*) and *Can Such Things Be?*. . . . Even these stories are perhaps most impressive as emotional gestures. The second title suggests their essential form: a shocked outcry against the horrors and violations of life in what is called peace as well as in war. There is not much invention or variation in these stories. Eventually the ironies they turn upon appear mechanical. . . . We begin, in fact, to see that the fidelity of these savage anecdotes is not to the way "things are" in the world but to the shocked and haunted consciousness of the writer himself. Yet the feelings he writes from—outrage, despair, desolation, grim resignation—do him credit. (pp. 77-8)

Always tightly made, Bierce's stories renew a standard of form set by his master, Poe. Like Poe's they are distinguished by descriptive intensity and a strict economy of means; they are as compact and bare as mathematical equations—which is partly why they are not greatly interesting as stories. Where they are most effective is in indicating the weariness and the barbarism of men in the front lines of war; and, as we sense that for Bierce these front-line conditions are somehow only an intensification of the norm of human life, we must grant that we cannot easily argue him wrong. Perhaps the real terror of his work is in suggesting how naturally men can be brought to give to the anguished question, "Can such things be?" the numbed answer, "Yes, of course."

The vision of life in Bierce's work, though intensely personal, is also very much of its time. It is close to that of the school of "naturalism," which was entering American literature around 1900 with the generation of Norris, Stephen Crane, and Dreiser. Under the assault of the mindless, amoral forces of nature—or of a society equally savage—men are seen as victims and casualties of agencies beyond their control. If they survive, it is by some crippling process of dehumanization. (p. 79)

> *Warner Berthoff, in his* The Ferment of Realism: American Literature, 1884-1919 *(reprinted with permission of Macmillan Publishing Co., Inc.; copyright © 1965 by The Free Press, a Division of The Macmillan Company), The Free Press, 1965.*

[Bierce] had a fairly free hand as to what he would put into his columns [in the *San Francisco Examiner*]. The American scene appeared to him to have all the senselessness of battle without the glory and the rules, and he attacked with vigor both the wielders of privilege and their victims. Without benefit of Nietzsche, he had arrived at a philosophy that looked with contempt both on the viciousness with which the plunderers plundered and the foolishness with which the plundered allowed themselves to be plundered. (p. 167)

Bierce held to the dictum that life was the writer's material. . . . It meant that he, Bierce, had little to learn from other writers, and it also meant that his wartime experiences could be held in suspension within him and made to stand for all the books and all the other experiences life could afford. Accident Bierce defined as "an inevitable occurrence due to the action of immutable natural laws," and in this he was not merely twitting the complacent. He was rationalizing his arrested outlook, so that war, which abounded in violent reversals, became the pattern of life, and everything that occurred outside his window could be accounted for, as were events in war, as the chance happenings of a universe in which moral causation bore no relation to events.

Realism, then, which presented the commonplace in terms of some immediately recognizable causal pattern was contemptible, and Howells became a constant target for Bierce's abuse. He preferred Poe's romances because they relied on the imagination to throw up pictures of the horrors of life, "and the first three essentials of the literary art are imagination, imagination and imagination." (p. 168)

To preserve his sense of himself as a man of letters temporarily engaged in a base trade, Bierce developed a style which, though with echoes of Bret Harte, also anticipates the school of Mencken. In his reporting, as also in his stories, he employed an extremely formal, literary language—latinate words, periodic sentences, foreign borrowings—and used it to surround the sordid events with which he dealt so as to demonstrate two things central to his outlook. First, he revealed his contempt for what he was treating by exploiting the incongruity of its vocabulary with his syntax and diction. The object of satire was not just attacked, it was, as it were, dangled contemptuously from a cultured hand. Second, he showed his reader that he had a style which was adequate to more than he was at the moment undertaking and that if he but thought it worthwhile he could excel in the literary craft. (p. 169)

An entire twentieth-century style of wise-guy journalism may be found summed up in a typical Bierce sentence. Inversion, lofty diction, and foreign borrowings consciously clash with slang. . . . (p. 170)

While Bierce was read and admired by many another writer, it is difficult to see his work as a direct influence on the journalistic style of later practitioners, few of whom possessed his skill. The same factors which formed his techniques—the cynicism which allowed him to live with conditions he felt himself powerless to affect; his fascination with words and their syntactic combinations as opposed to straight reporting styles—could have led others to imitate him unconsciously. But the imitations, conscious or unconscious, lacked Bierce's distinguishing mark, the tone of arrow-like contempt, because they were assumed as an artificial way of dismissing the troubles of the world. Bierce's tone was a natural outgrowth of a personality so shocked by war that it held itself together only by the com-

pulsive demonstration that meaningless slaughter contained all the meaning there was.

The Civil War stories which Bierce published in the nineties reflected this attitude. . . . Grotesque coincidences abound, in contempt of the natural laws of probabilty, and, to enforce the unnaturalness of war, Bierce turns time and again to the slaughter of kin either in the unconscious fury of war or in the fulfillment of a military duty higher than the normal requirements. The men who respect orders, who are heroic, who are honorable, are glorified, although they always die. Through following the arbitrary military code they respond cleanly to the violence of life, whereas those who view life as essentially tranquil and give in to feelings which they regard as natural are only deluded. In story after story family and feelings lead only to destruction—not the clean death of the hero who accepts the code, but the horrible death of the betrayed man who has misapprehended the conditions of his existence. The only connoisseur of heroism is he who pursues it to death, just as the only gourmet is he who eats the meat; but he must be conscious of what he is about. The most famous of Bierce's stories, "An Occurrence at Owl Creek Bridge," holds up for display a man who pathetically yields to instinct and in imagination flees for home rather than accepting the death that the rules of war require of him. He should have known better, says the snap of the strangling noose.

In peacetime, Bierce felt, the same values apply. Commerce is based on cheating, and cheats and counter-cheats are a peacetime war far more degrading than the real thing. "That is all nonsense about the 'horrors of war,'" he wrote, "in so far as the detestable phrase implies that they are worse than those of peace; they are more striking and impressive that is all." In war what is expedient is what is moral, and, Bierce believed, in life the same is true. (pp. 170-71)

Life, like war, was impersonal, and the recurrent theme of his art was the way personality went smash in its failure to comprehend this. Better to grasp this fact and run headlong into the inevitable consequences.

But Ambrose Bierce himself hung back from the plunge and, unable to write long fiction because of disbelief in the rational continuity of experience, he interspersed his slashing journalism in the nineties with brief tales and poems of bitter attack on men who would not see what he saw. Still, he knew what all this meant for himself—that a life as cruel as the one he saw rendered art meaningless and that he was better off dead. (p. 172)

Ambrose Bierce's bitterness stood at one pole in the range of experience available to the writer coming of age in the nineties. His scorn for collective action, his dismissal of the realistic novel, his admiration for Poe and the role of the imagination in literature, and his immersion of the vernacular in a sea of latinate diction timed to the rhythms of formal syntax, all found followers, or, at the least, unconscious echoers. . . . [He] became a tempting guide for some writers in the twentieth century. Whenever life was seen as chaos by a writer who was committed to capturing some shred of that chaos as he condemned it, there Bierce stood as a model. His nearly brutal wrath might maim; but his imitators, lacking that wrath, were in danger of posing. (p. 173)

Larzer Ziff, in his The American 1890s: Life

and Times of a Lost Generation *(copyright © 1966 by Larzer Ziff; reprinted by permission of The Viking Press, Inc.), Viking, 1966.*

The Devil's Dictionary, a lexicon of Bierce's scorn for mankind and all its institutions, . . . stands today not only as the distillation of Bierce's thought but as epigrammatic misanthropy bordering on genius. . . .The novelist or essayist is a careful householder, hoarding his resources; the aphorist tosses his shiny gold coins on the floor, seeking neither to save nor to order them. That is why the art of aphorism has rarely been considered major. Yet it is through his misanthropic aphorisms that Bierce should enter literature for keeps. The confident, eupeptic American spirit also has its dark side. And of those writers who chose to dwell on its shadows, few perceived or portrayed them with greater clarity than Bierce. His agonized view of human perfidy, which he found everywhere, raps imperatively on contemporary consciences.

> *"The Misanthrope," in* Time *(reprinted by permission from* Time, The Weekly Newsmagazine; *copyright Time Inc. 1967), May 5, 1967, p. 102.*

The only factor that alleviates what has been called [Bierce's] Puritanism of hate is the luxury of sophisticated verbal play. (p. 162)

Bierce is the naked model of antitheticism in American humor, the bare thing itself in all the social antagonism and painstaking comic fury he embodies. Only Charles Addams, in later American humor, is an adequate rival. Bierce misses few opportunities of fierce antipatriotism, a kind of compounded blasphemy when it takes the familiar semi-hymnal form. . . . His antidemocracy, like Poe's, is a means of aristocratic self-identification and therefore pervades his work, an adjunct to his misanthropy. His essay on *Disintroductions,* begins: "The devil is a citizen of every country but only in our own are we in constant peril of an introduction to him." The final pronoun is generic, accounting for every companionable, social, affable democratic type one is in danger of meeting in our streets. (pp. 163-64)

Tawdry violence and wanton cruelty in all the pieces of Bierce's "The Parenticide Club" constitute something more than the ruling influence of Poe on Bierce's mind. . . . The question of literary influence, after all, is always answered by susceptibilities. One is never tyrannized by an influence, but subjects himself to it, for his own reasons. . . . The black or sick humor is a measure of Bierce's recoil from a whole cultural system of sentimentality and falsification, and the key word is "treachery." His mistake is not in unmasking society, for that is a prime function of comedy, particularly in America. His error is to fall in love with the death's head revealed. But that act shows his fundamental passion . . . to love, practically at any cost.

The proper humorist is less compulsive. He is basically more disengaged, more dispassionate, in order precisely to bestow a more discriminate love where it is deserved. He is paradoxically more strict and credulous. And he has trained himself to look things in the face with less revulsion when, stripped, they do not conform to subjective ideal. Which is to say that black or sick humorists, like Bierce, are infallibly romantic and that in a realistic age they are necessarily more and more prone to the dark expression . . . of themselves, primarily. They are, in the end, lyricists; the beauty or perversity of what they say depends on the material and tenor of the age. Their need is to express rather than to report or truly dramatize.

In all his haughty severities, Bierce thus reveals himself. He had no middle stage like Twain; he was a lifelong versifier and prose poet of black humor who could never really objectify his themes in another character outside of himself. . . . And we never hear the slightest change of voice throughout his entire work. A strident subjectivist, he provides the essential clue to black humor in any day: his relentless abuses are reverse rhapsodies. Black subjectivist humorists are disenchanted poets. This point distinguishes them from authentic comedians, who have not been particularly enchanted to begin with or register, at least, a prolonged period of objective disengagement sometime in their career. (pp. 170-72)

He was . . . firmly opposed to realistic, colloquial speech, and therefore avoided the humor of slang. . . . He thought the practice unliterary, commercial, and cheap, and would have nothing to do with it. The principle is related to his antidemocratic beliefs as a whole and to his scorn of local color, which focused on low, ignorant characters. Still, he descended to popular practice in a number of other ways, including understatements so extreme that they fit squarely into the native mode of all-out extravagance. (pp. 177-78)

Added to his unvarying subjectivism and tone are [his] penchant for farce and the whole strategy of explicitness in his humor, a crucial disadvantage because it makes the comedy too readily exhaustible. Bierce preferred to think of himself as a wit and farcicist rather than mere humorist, vastly appreciating his own directness and devaluating the techniques of indirectness and objectification. But, in addition to the excesses of his own point of view, his technique becomes far too predictable and heavy.

Up to now, in fact, enough of Bierce went a long way with most readers, due as much to the technical load as anything else. . . . In a time of almost epidemical sick humor, Bierce is recognized as a source or old spore, the more virulent the better. (p. 178)

> *Jesse Bier, in his* The Rise and Fall of American Humor *(copyright © 1968 by Jesse Bier;. reprinted by permission of Holt, Rinehart and Winston, Publishers), Holt, 1968.*

Bertolt Brecht

1898-1956

German dramatist, poet, and theatrical producer, Eugen Berthold Friedrich Brecht's major contribution to drama was his invention of "epic theater" in which dance, soliloquy, song, and choral reading, among other forms, are used to achieve dramatic effect. Departing from Sophoclean theory, he promoted distance between cast and audience, thereby denying the legitimacy of the catharsis derived by the audience from emotional participation in the play. His intent was to motivate his audiences to action by disturbing them intellectually, wishing them "to think rather than feel." Essentially a poet, Brecht combined in his plays lyrical beauty and political propaganda. Following the advent of Hitler in 1933, Brecht went into self-imposed exile in Scandinavia and the United States, where he wrote many vigorous plays, radio scripts, and poems decrying Hitlerism. A man of genius who feared for his freedom, he took Austrian citizenship before accepting the East German invitation to settle in East Berlin. There he founded his famous company, The Berliner Ensemble.

PRINCIPAL WORKS

Baal (drama) 1922
 [*Baal*, 1964]
Trommeln in der Nacht (drama) 1922
 [*Drums in the Night*, 1966]
Das Leben Eduards des Zweiten von England (drama)
 1924
 [*Edward II: A Chronicle Play*, 1966]
Die Hauspostille (poetry) 1927
 [*Manual of Piety*, 1966]
*Im Dickicht der Städte; der Kampf Zweir Männer in der
 Riesenstadt Chicago* (drama) 1927
 [*In the Jungle of Cities*, 1957]
Mann ist Mann (drama) 1927
 [*A Man's a Man*, 1957]
Aufstieg und Fall der Stadt Mahogonny (drama) 1929
 [*The Rise and Fall of the Town of Mahogonny*, 1960]
Die Dreigroschenoper (drama) 1929
 [*The Threepenny Opera*, 1949]
Der Jasager und der Neinsager (drama) 1930
 [*He Who Said Yes/He Who Said No*, 1946]
Die Massnahme (drama) 1931
 [*The Measures Taken*, 1956]
Die Heilige Johanna der Schlachthöfe (drama) 1932
 [*St. Joan of the Stockyards*, 1956]
Dreigroschenroman (novel) 1933

[*A Penny for the Poor*, 1937; *Threepenny Novel*, 1956]
Die Mutter (drama) 1933
 [*The Mother*, 1965]
Fünf Schwierigkeiten beim Schreiben der Wahrheit
 (essays) 1934
 [*Writing the Truth: Five Difficulties*, 1948]
Die Ausnahme und die Regel (drama) 1937
 [*The Exception and the Rule*, 1954]
Furcht und Elend des Dritten Reiches (drama) 1941
 [*Fear and Misery of the Third Reich*, 1942]
Das Verhör des Lukullus (drama) 1940
 [*The Trial of Lucullus*, 1943]
Der Kaukasiche Kreidekreis (drama) 1949
 [*The Caucasian Chalk Circle*, 1948]
Kleines Organon für das Theatre (essays) 1949
 [*Little Organ for the Theatre*, 1951]
*Mutter Courage und Ihre Kinder; eine Chronik aus dem
 Dreissigjährigen Krieg* (drama) 1949
 [*Mother Courage and Her Children*, 1949]
Herr Puntila und sein Knecht Matt (drama) 1950
 [*Puntila*, 1954]
Der Gute Mensch von Sezuan (drama) 1953
 [*The Good Women of Setzuan*, 1941]
Die Gesichte der Simone Marchard (drama) 1956
 [*Visions of Simone Marchard*, 1965]
Leben des Galilei-II (drama) 1957
 [*Galileo*, 1952]

By grafting his poetry upon conventions that lay outside the usual orbit of "book" literature, Brecht has gained for it an edge and a kind of contemporaneity rare in elevated modern writing—or rare until lately. I cannot help thinking that Auden may have learned something from Brecht about how to convert slang, modish phrases, the flat axioms of Marxism, the clichés of intellectual journalism, into serious verse. Auden, too, parodies nursery rhymes and prayers, ballads and popular song. What he does with these is quite different—and politer—than what Brecht does, but he seems to move in a similar direction.

There emerges from the anonymity and parody in the *Hauspostille* poems a highly personal and consistent style. Its characteristics are dryness and simplicity; a deliberate, therefore aggressive affectation of restraint and understatement; sudden shifts of tone and transpositions of key, discords, dissonances. Matter-of-factness unfurls into Biblical grandiloquence; the sententious passage collapses into a banal expression or a trivial image; the rhyme, or the main stress, will fall on an auxiliary verb or an enclitic; the horrible or the squalid alternates with the idyllic, the brutal with the sentimental, the cynical with the naive, the honestly cynical with the falsely naive. There is a process of inflation and deflation; anticlimaxes succeed one another until the universe of affect is flattened out and everything becomes equivalent. All possible catastrophes and all imaginable banalities are assimilated. . . . (pp. 256-57)

Neither in the *Hauspostille* poems nor in the plays he wrote during the same period, does he attack the specific kind of society he happens to be living in. He is against established society in general, and while his pariahs and gutter people complain, they do not criticize. Only one value survives Brecht's early nihilism: that of comradeship pure and simple, which is found at its purest and simplest on the fringes of society, among outcasts; in army platoons, in ship's crews, in the bohemias of tramps and criminals and misfits, where human solidarity is less tinged with self-interest. (p. 259)

The tradition of the poet who starts out as a reckless rebel and ends up as a pillar of society tends to be more frequently confirmed in Germany than elsewhere, and Brecht has followed this tradition in his own way. His conversion to Bolshevism, which was like a change of personality, meant a return to responsibility. Abandoning his previous insouciance, he adopted an attitude so earnest as almost to be suspect. He began to see, beyond the ends of poetry as art, the obligation to show the poor and the ignorant how to change the world. (p. 261)

His style and manner began to change in a "Bolshevik" direction . . . in the choruses and recitatives with which his *Lehrstücken* of the late twenties and early thirties are interspersed. There, he first began to use unrhymed free verse, supposedly because it accorded better with the rhythms of plain talk and dispensed with such embellishments as might dissemble the austerity of Bolshevik method. In the directions accompanying the texts of these "didactic pieces," Brecht emphasizes the necessity of a "dry" delivery. Poetry was to become stripped and bare—prosaic. The principles of its organization were to be no longer metrical or musical, but forensic and rhetorical, in the service of a message that was designed to change the lives of those who heard it. (p. 262)

Yet, for all his sobriety, and for all the strenuous earnestness and literalness of his new manner, Brecht continued to be a complete poet in the old-fashioned sense which he pretended to repudiate. When he put Lenin's dicta into verse they became parables, and their context became mythological. Whatever doubt this may have thrown on the revolutionary efficacy of the result, it was certainly in harmony with the style of devotion that Stalinism instilled in its faithful. Indeed, Brecht can be said to be the only writer to have wrested from genuine Stalinism anything that is or resembles genuine high art. (pp. 263-4)

Brecht is far better known as a playwright than as a poet, and the plays with which he made his reputation were in prose. Poetry seems to have been a side issue at first. Yet it was largely due, I feel, to the fact that he was a poet, and

wrote verse with conscience, that he developed as boldly and uniquely as he did. We have become too accustomed to taking it for granted that drama can dispense entirely with poetry. In Brecht's case, it is poetry that fires both prose and verse; his instincts and habits as a poet enforce the shape, measure, and incisiveness which belong to almost everything he writes. His gift is, above all, the gift of language, and that gift provides the right kind of vehicle for what seems to me the most original literary temperament to have appeared anywhere in the last twenty years. (p. 265)

> *Clement Greenberg, "Bertolt Brecht's Poetry" (1941), in his* Art and Culture: Critical Essays *(copyright © 1961 by Clement Greenberg; reprinted by permission of Beacon Press), Beacon Press, 1961, pp. 252-65.*

The root idea of Brecht's Epic Drama is expressed in the name. Of the three types of literature—epic, dramatic, and lyric—the first two are to be fused, and Brecht has no objection to admitting the lyrical element too. This is against all the laws of the elders. . . . There have long been two types of dramatic structure too: the open, diffuse play which starts early in the narrative and proceeds through it in many scenes and, on the other hand, the closed, concentrated play which has a late point of attack and lets us look back on the story from its climax—which is the play. . . . Brecht's Epic procedure is this open structure. (pp. 253-54)

Brecht is not a Naturalist; but he is a naturalist. He wishes to be as faithful as possible to objective facts. . . . Zola's Naturalistic theater, dedicated to actuality, was a theater of illusion, phantasmagoria, and—it might even be maintained —escape. It differed from its ostensible opposite Neo-Romanticism in that one escaped to an ugly not to a beautiful island. . . .

If Expressionism and Neo-Romanticism were a rebound from the earlier Naturalism, Epic Drama was a rebound from the New Romanticism and Expressionism. If the earlier Naturalism came in with the discovery of the "true meaning of life" in Darwinist science, the later Epic Drama came in with the discovery of the "true meaning of life" in Marxist science. (p. 258)

The dramatic art of Brecht has so far gone through four phases. In the first, his apprenticeship, he took up the problems of the theater where Strindberg and Wedekind left them, that is to say, he had to think through the whole question of form almost from scratch. To help himself in this task he studied, and made adaptations from, Chinese, Elizabethan, and Spanish plays; and before the end of the twenties he had written four outstanding original works. Two were plays in a style of highly personal naturalism, two were operettas equally idiosyncratic. Only the last of all these to be written—his version of the *Beggar's Opera* —is fully developed Epic Theater. Hence it is the culmination of Brecht's first period.

If the first phase is cynical and brilliant and very much of the twenties, the second is stark and solemn and very much of the thirties. If the works of the twenties permitted hostile critics to dismiss Brecht as a cabaret wit, the works of the thirties permitted them to dismiss him an "artist in uniform," a "minstrel of the GPU." Though Brecht's bleakest, barrenest works belong to this period, so also does his *Saint Joan of the Stockyards,* a rich satire, and a kind of prelude to the third phase, the first years of exile from Germany, during which Brecht wrote two full-scale dramatic fantasies about the Nazi movement. But probably the major works of the middle thirties are *Mother Courage and Her Sons* and *Fear and Misery of the Third Reich*. In the first Brecht withdrew from the current struggle to compose another Epic play in verse and prose, in song and monosyllabic conversation, a sardonic and circumstantial record, based on the seventeenth-century writer Grimmelshausen, of the process of war. In *Fear and Misery* Brecht and the Third Reich are for the first time face to face. The title is a parody of Balzac's *Glory and Misery of the Courtesans*, and the work itself—a portrait of one cell after another in the social organism—is a twentieth-century *comédie humaine* in miniature. In a series of over twenty scenes, unconnected by characters or plot, connected only by theme, the people of Hitler's Germany are revealed. Between the scenes a choric voice is heard, and (in the shorter stage version) a group of Nazi soldiers sings Brecht's words to the tune of their party hymn at the beginning and end of each act. (pp. 261-62)

There is a Brecht below the political level, a Brecht whose traits gradually become clear to those who absorb his works. . . . The political Brecht is a socialist. Beneath the socialist is what we might call the Confucian—by which I mean that Brecht's economic interpretation of human life, his materialism, is at the service of a finely humane, ironic, salty appreciation of normal experience. When he defends the normal, the ordinary, and the common, he is not therefore championing vulgarity and mediocrity; he is championing human nature. It is this that makes the average socialist writing appear bourgeois by comparison, for the average socialist writing is socialist only, so to speak, in terms of party policy. It is this that makes Brecht a poet of democracy in a sense deeper than that applied to the zealous supporters of particular causes. Today his is an uncommon sort of belief in the common man. (p. 268)

Both Brecht and Sartre are attempting a synthesis of the individual and the social. They differ in coming at it from opposite directions. Brecht reaches the individual via the collectivity, Sartre reaches the collectivity via the individual.

They are rival revolutionaries. Brecht's revolution is Marx's. It is "from without," for man is not independent of "externals." Sartre's revolution is—shall we say Nietzsche's? the Existentialists'? Christ's? It is "from within," for man is not simply a piece of the landscape. Yet Sartre's "inner" revolution leads to the liberation of Argos, and Brecht's "outer" revolution would bring "inner" peace to Shen Te. Sartre's hell is personal, yet a vote of censure against a society is inferred. Brecht's hell—Sezuan—is social, yet it is its meaning in individual lives that is measured. Perhaps Sartre's argument starts from a metaphysic, but its significance spreads out over the natural life of man. Perhaps Brecht's argument is simply socialism, but its significance is seen much more concretely, dramatically, poetically than in so-called "proletarian literature". . . . (p. 271)

When, to secure a more faithful version of the external world, Brecht gave up more and more of the methods of stage realism in favor of Chinese and other conventions he was using non-naturalistic techniques for naturalistic ends. He was mixing the two primary elements of art—nature and

convention—in a new way. When his plays took the form of operettas and fantasies, parables and abstract moralities, he was approaching a synthesis of what the naturalists and their antagonists had intended. (pp. 271-72)

Whatever the future for tragedy and comedy, for naturalism and non-naturalism, the work of Sartre and Brecht—in ways that are often different and sometimes the same—is a fairly adequate apologia for the playwright as thinker. (p. 272)

> *Eric Bentley, in his* The Playwright as Thinker: A Study of Drama in Modern Times *(copyright 1946, 1974 by Eric Bentley), Reynal & Hitchcock, 1946.*

Brecht's type of theater he himself has called Epic on the grounds that it is a narrative form as opposed to the degenerate "dramatic" theater of our era in which narrative or plot has lost its priority. . . . I would maintain that when Brecht's method differs from conventional theater, it differs consistently along the lines of a mature common-sense theory of the stage. . . . [A] good term for this method . . . [is] Epic Realism. One could simplify the matter still further and say: Narrative Realism.

As a method of staging, Narrative Realism stands midway between the two extreme methods of the modern theater, which we may call naturalism and symbolism. A naturalistic stage setting of a room is a literal reproduction of the room—or what looks like such a reproduction—except that the fourth wall is missing. A symbolistic setting presents a number of objects and forms which form a substitute for the room: a door, for instance, is represented by two vertical posts. (p. 147)

The Narrative Realist neither reassembles the whole room nor tries to substitute symbols for actualities. He tries to avoid the remoteness from actuality of symbolism by using real objects, and the laborious explicitness of naturalism by making a more fastidious selection from among the all too many objects that make up the real scene. In representing a room, he will use only things that actually make up a room, but he won't attempt to show the whole room: one part of it will suffice—a piece of wall, or a door, some pieces of furniture. (p. 148)

Being inevitably involved in polemical disputes, Brecht has had to overstress the negative aspects of this sort of staging, the fact that it destroys the illusion of reality. (p. 149)

Because Brecht does not believe in an inner reality, a higher reality, or a deeper reality, but simply in reality, he presents on the stage the solid things of this world in all their solidity and with all the appreciation of their corporeality that we find in certain painters. (Brueghel is the painter from whom Brecht has learned most.) This means that he is more interested in the beauty and vitality of things than are the naturalists. . . . Here we must remember that Narrative Realism is not a dogma, is not exclusive. Where, for instance, a symbolistic idea seems the most practical solution, the Narrative Realist can use it. Symbolism can be used whenever naturalism is impossible. Thus a disk can represent the sun. Yet if we use such a symbol, we must not fool ourselves into believing that it is not a symbol but the reality. (pp. 149-50)

[Being] fundamentally didactic in intention, Brecht remains a poet in method. To the general "alienation" of life which is effected by form, he adds many particular "alienating" devices, more or less deliberate. One that must surely be very deliberate occurs in *The Caucasian Chalk Circle.* This is the scene in which Grusha feels the temptation of goodness, the temptation to pick up and save the abandoned baby. Grusha acts the whole scene out in pantomime while the Singer in the third person and the past tense relates what she is doing. In this the Singer is doing for Grusha exactly what Brecht, in his essay "A New Technique of Acting," suggests should be done to help an actor emancipate himself from the Stanislavsky procedure. If an actor hears his role talked about in the third person and his deeds talked about in the past tense, he stands apart from the role and the deeds and renders them, not as self-expression, but as history. When he uses the device in *Chalk Circle,* Brecht of course is radically "alienating" Grusha's actions so that we do not lose ourselves in our compassion. He uses the third person, the past tense, the art of pantomime, and a refined language as massed alienation effects. (pp. 154-55)

Brecht is primarily a poet, and words are the backbone of his plays, but he has also worked out, in theory and practice, a kind of theater in which the non-verbal arts play an essential and considered part.... [The] methods of Brecht's theater—its use of interruption and "alienation," for example—do constitute a kind of irritation. Yet if this is all we say, the conclusion drawn by many will be that, in order to annoy everyone, Brecht destroys his plays by deliberate incongruities and impertinent interpolations. In a play like *Mother Courage, Puntila,* or *Chalk Circle* the idea is not to annoy but to awaken, and this, not by flying in the face of dramatic art, but by the re-creation, the enrichment, of dramatic art. (pp. 155-56)

[Nine] students out of ten today, when asked to name a dramatic painting, would name something like Géricault's *Raft of the Medusa,* and not something like Brueghel's *Battle of the Carnival and Lent.* Géricault's painting is dramatic in the popular sense: it presents a standard "exciting situation." It is also dramatic in the academic sense: it is simple rather than compound in construction, it has a single focus. Brueghel's painting is dramatic in neither of these senses. It offers no solace to the eye that seeks swift, strong sensation. It invites the eye to linger on this detail and that. The eye that accepts the invitation discovers one "drama" after another in the picture and even a total drama of the whole, discovers a thoroughly dramatic way of looking at life.

The eye that can relax over a Brueghel painting and yet find it highly dramatic can relax over a Brecht play and yet find it dramatic. During a Brecht performance one can relax and look with pleasure at the various parts of the stage—the wardrobe of Peachum, or the kitchen utensils of Mother Courage. The eye is not glued to one spot. Because suspense has been reduced to a minimum, one is not always asking what will happen next. One is not interested in the next scene, one is interested in *this* scene. . . . Thus, in the Notes to his *Threepenny Opera,* Brecht ridicules the accepted notion that a playwright must "embody" everything in the characters and the action. Why should not comment from the outside also be possible? The words of the songs are superadded comment, the music is a comment on these words. In *The Threepenny Opera,* ironical titles are projected on screens; so are drawings by Georg Grosz, drawings of nothing specifically mentioned in the play. In *The*

Good Woman of Setzuan, characters throw out comments in the shape of short asides in verse. And so on. (pp. 156-57)

To my mind, Brecht's theory of theater *is* a theory of comedy. Something very like the dramaturgy described by Brecht was practiced by Aristophanes. Something very like the kind of acting described by Brecht was practiced (one is inclined to think) by the *commedia dell' arte* players. (p. 158)

Brecht would give us a very modern Shakespeare, doubtless; the hope would be that the modern style would contain more of the original Elizabethan spirit than the romantic style did. The theater of Narrative Realism (this reiteration may stand as a conclusion) has more in common with the great theater of the remoter past than with the theater of today and yesterday. (p. 160)

> *Eric Bentley, "The Stagecraft of Brecht" (1949), in his* In Search of Theater *(copyright © 1948, 1949, 1950, 1951, 1953 by Eric Bentley; reprinted by permission of Atheneum Publishers, New York), Atheneum, 1953, pp. 144-60.*

Brecht has viewed the past and present with a twentieth-century mind. His political outlook has always been far left of center, although his left-wing orthodoxy has been questionable even when he has spoken dogmatically. He is essentially an extreme individualist, if not indeed a bohemian artist-intellectual, weaving his way through mazes of collectivist ideals and policies as a poet rather than as a politician. Like others of his time, he has ridden the two horses of idealism and materialism, or of romanticism and Marxism, without any particular sense of discomfort or incongruity. He has also been a moralist of contemporary caliber for better or worse, pondering ethical problems in relation to political realities and expedients until ethics and strategy become indistinguishable in his thought—a dangerous way of thinking mitigated in his case by an essential humanism apparent in his passion for justice and his sympathy for the underdog. For Brecht does not quite succeed in suppressing the human sympathy that he would theoretically banish from the stage, if his theories are construed rigorously. He has endeavored to make drama out of themes and material usually excluded from a theatre dedicated to private emotion. In ways that recall the efforts of Koestler, Malraux, and other contemporary novelists, Brecht has certainly tried to make political reality the center of his art and the springboard of his inquiry into private and public conduct. Even when his main characters themselves have only a hazy awareness of politics, they exemplify the political nature of human existence, and the "human condition" with which Brecht has concerned himself has always been intrinsically a political condition. How Brecht's outlook has determined his form is, however, the paramount question; for his uniqueness as an artist lies not in his content or politics, common enough these days, but in the manner in which he has translated a bias into drama, production style, and dramatic theory. (pp. 83-4)

Galileo . . . is not merely a biographical drama such as we are accustomed to, but a cool analysis of the problems and state of mind of a man who stands between two worlds and compromises between intellectual integrity and personal safety. . . . It was written with the intention of exposing a situation rather than emotionally involving the spectators; we are not made to sympathize with Galileo but to understand his problem . . . [and] a historical situation which may repeat itself and therefore must be comprehended. . . . Brecht's intentionally cold dramaturgy, whether we like it or not, has a special place in modern theatrical art, if due attention is given to the expansion of radio, television, and motion picture documentary or semi-documentary drama. His objective method does seem the most appropriate one for treating historical events. Sidney Howard's *Yellowjack,* which employed the documentary style, would actually be more effective in my opinion if the dramaturgy and style were "colder"; the audience would be less disappointed then because the play isn't "warmer," in the sense of being closer to conventional affective drama. At the same time, Howard's play would have been more lyrical, too, if Brecht had been the author. It is an error to make lyricism invariably synonymous with "feeling"; Brecht, like Aristophanes, John Gay, and W. S. Gilbert, has the talent to achieve "non-emotional" and ironical lyricism. (p. 87)

The Caucasian Circle of Chalk, . . . [though somewhat] unwieldy, . . . is, nevertheless, a good example of the manner in which Brecht deliberately turns even an intrinsically emotional situation into an exposition of attitudes and values. He is the anti-sentimentalist *par excellence* even when his subject is sentiment. The other parable, *The Good Woman of Setzuan,* is, in my opinion, a masterpiece, although it is difficult to produce with sufficient verisimilitude, considering the prevailing taste of our theatre, because the same actress must play both a woman and a man —that is, the heroine's cousin. Brecht, however, has little use for verisimilitude, and would be pleased rather than disturbed if the production violated illusion. He is opposed to illusion-mongering and actually wants his audience to know that it is witnessing theatre rather than life; just as the public watching a demonstration knows that reality is not being photographed but being arranged for the purposes of an analysis. Actions in his type of drama are not intended to represent reality but to explain it and to challenge the critical intelligence of the observer.

Here, as in other plays, Brecht avails himself freely of Chinese theatrical style in which verisimilitude is of no consequence. Although he wrote *The Good Woman of Setzuan* with great charm and resorted to fantasy in bringing several little Chinese deities down to earth parable-wise in order to see how the human race is behaving, his object was to demonstrate a far-reaching point rather than to create illusion. . . . There is a sort of sophrosyne in this demonstration of how goodness must be practical and strong but not so "practical" as to take advantage of human helplessness and play the dictator. The sophrosyne at the core of this presentation of the problem of good and evil in social action determines the style and tone of the work. Here, too, Brecht effects a "cooling off" of the drama by means of a quizzical tone, lyric interruptions of the plot, and an "angle of vision" that tilts the picture of life with sardonic emphasis. Brecht, who can be a master of eloquence, knows that "coolness," too, can be a sort of rhetoric—if not an Aristotelian rhetoric of *persuasion,* then a rhetoric of inquiry or analysis. The method is Socratic or, more accurately, Silenic. . . .

Brecht is in all respects a rebel against Aristotelian and post-Aristotelian esthetics. Although Aristotle was the son

of a physician and himself a biologist, he relied on illusion and emotion when he considered dramatic art. Brecht, who was a medical student, is consistently the surgeon; and this not only in his plays but in his ballads, that often vary eloquence with a sudden flatness, with a lapse into caustic colloquialism, and with an eighteenth-century rationalistic sharpness. He is given to pouring cold water on his work whenever it threatens to become overheated. His "epic" theory of drama and stagecraft is a protest against the priority of feeling and the principle of identification in drama. He does not allow feeling to preempt the field of observation, nor does he want us to get into other people's skin, lest we fail to observe them, assess them, and draw objective conclusions.

Brecht is the most anti-tragic of modern artists, not excluding Bernard Shaw; and for the same reason that Shaw was anti-tragic except in *Saint Joan*—that is, because Brecht has unlimited faith in the perfectability of man, the effectiveness of rational inquiry, and the power of men to improve the "human condition" by concerted action. It may be interesting to observe, in fact, that the great ages of high tragedy are not notable for any strong conviction that mankind is committed to progress and capable of it, that improvement is a social rather than individual problem, and that it can be effected by materialistic rather than spiritual means. Tragic art is neither "liberal" nor "radical," in the Western sense of either term since the Renaissance or, at least, since the ultra-optimistic eighteenth-century Enlightenment that promulgated the belief in unlimited progress of mankind on earth. The tragic sense includes a hard truth, harder than anything the tough-fibered Brecht accepts— namely, a sense of "life's impossibilities."

Brecht also abides by the principle of naturalistic objectivity in spite of his rejection of naturalistic technique. One might describe him as a lyric Henry Becque, if we waive the fact that Brecht has favored epic expansion of the drama whereas Becque sought dramatic compression. Brecht, one should add, exercises great economy in building scenes and writing dialogue and lyrics; the expansiveness he requires is of the Elizabethan variety—that is, free-flowing, multifarious, and multi-scened action.

Brecht favors a type of dramatic composition that projects the various facets of man's life in society without accepting an obligation to abide by any strict unity of time, place, action, mood, and style. . . . [Episodes] combined with narrative and lyrical passages, and augmented with pantomime, dance, projected slogans, signs or placards, slides, and even motion-picture sequences, if necessary, all following one another in rapid succession, may form one big tumultuous play somewhat in the manner of the "multiplicity novels" of John Dos Passos.

The result of this horizontal dramaturgy is "epic drama," according to Brecht. Since he also takes an analytical view of reality and institutes an inquiry or demonstrates his argument with every conceivable device, his epic style serves the purpose of social realism, and the most accurate term for his type of drama is "epic realism." Foregoing the esthetic advantages of a complete synthesis by tone or mood (the ideal since the nineteenth century of both the conventional realists and the art-for-art's-sake symbolists), Brecht concentrates on the diversity of a problem or situation, because the interrelationship of many facts and forces comprises its social reality. (pp. 88-90)

No one . . . has gone as far as Brecht in banishing Aristotelian pity, terror, catharsis, unity, and illusion as paramount dramatic values. He prides himself upon reflecting the scientific and analytical spirit of modern society, as well as the specially materialistic dialectic of Marxism. . . .

Nothing, indeed, is more remarkable in Brecht's career than that he should have been able to satisfy two contemporary needs at the same time—to extend realism and invigorate it, on the one hand, and to promote a theatre of imagination and poetry on the other hand. Imaginative drama and realistic drama are supposed to be the opposite poles of theatrical art. Brecht has resolved the major dichotomy of the modern stage in his own work and has proved that it need not exist. (p. 92)

> *John Gassner, "Drama and Detachment: A View of Brecht's Style of Theatre," in his* The Theatre in Our Times: A Survey of the Men, Materials and Movements in the Modern Theatre *(copyright © 1954 by John Gassner; used by permission of Crown Publishers, Inc.), Crown, 1954, pp. 82-96.*

For twenty-four centuries, in Europe, the theater has been Aristotelian: even today, in 1955, each time we go to the theater, whether to see Shakespeare or Montherlant, Racine or Roussin, Maria Casarès or Pierre Fresnay, whatever our tastes and whatever our politics, we determine pleasure and boredom, good and bad, as a function of an age-old morality whose credo is this: the more the public is moved, the more it identifies with the hero; the more the stage imitates action, the more the actor incarnates his role, then the more magical the theater and the better the spectacle.

Now comes a man whose work and thought radically contest this art so ancestral that we had the best reasons in the world for believing it to be "natural"; who tells us, despite all tradition, that the public must be only half-committed to the spectacle so as to "know" what is shown, instead of submitting to it; that the actor must create this consciousness by exposing not by incarnating his role; that the spectator must never identify completely with the hero but remain free to judge the causes and then the remedies of his suffering; that the action must not be imitated but narrated; that the theater must cease to be magical in order to become critical, which will still be its best way of being passionate.

And precisely to the degree that Brecht's theatrical revolution challenges our habits, our tastes, our reflexes, the very "laws" of the theater in which we live, we must renounce our silence or our irony and face up to Brecht. . . .

Whatever our final evaluation of Brecht, we must at least indicate the coincidence of his thought with the great progressive themes of our time: that the evils men suffer are in their own hands—in other words, that the world can be changed; that art can and must intervene in history; that it must contribute to the same goal as the sciences, with which it is united; that we must have an art of explanation and no longer merely an art of expression; that the theater must participate in history by revealing its movement; that the techniques of the stage are themselves "committed"; that, finally, there is no such thing as an "essence" of eternal art, but that each society must invent the art which will be responsible for its own deliverance. (p. 38)

> *Roland Barthes, "The Brechtian Revolution" (1955; originally published in French in his* Essais Critiques, Editions du Seuil, 1964), in his Critical Essays, *translated by Richard Howard (copyright © 1972 by Northwestern University Press, Evanston, Ill.), Northwestern University Press, 1972, pp. 37-9.*

In Brecht's theatre, it is what people do, not what they feel, that counts. Action takes precedence over emotion, fact over fantasy. "*Die Wahrheit ist konkret*" ("Truth is concrete") was Brecht's favorite maxim; for him there could be no such thing as abstract truth. Somebody once asked him what the purpose of a good play ought to be. He answered by describing a photograph he had seen in a magazine, a double-page spread of Tokyo after the earthquake. Amid the devastation, one building remained upright. The caption consisted of two words: "Steel Stood." That, said Brecht, was the purpose of drama—to teach us how to survive. (p. 104)

Brecht's opposition to naturalistic acting was really, as he often insisted, a return to the older forms of popular theatre, including (the list is Mr. [Martin] Esslin's) "the Elizabethan, the Chinese, Japanese, and Indian theatre, the use of the chorus in Greek tragedy, the techniques of clowns and fairground entertainers, the Austrian and Bavarian folk play, and many others." His refusal to permit actors to "identify" with their roles, and thus to create strongly individualized characters, sprang from his conviction that human identity is not fixed but infinitely mutable, dependent on particular social and economic circumstances; this is the Left Wing equivalent of Pirandello's theories, at once frivolous and despondent, about the many-faceted impermanence of the human ego. What Pirandello fatalistically accepted, Brecht sought to explain. His loathing of stage emotionalism is more easily accounted for. It was a violent reaction against the bombast of the conventional German theatre. Life in a Brecht production is laid out before you as comprehensively as in a Brueghel painting, and with many of the same colors—browns, grays, and off-whites. It does not seize you by the lapel and yell secrets into your ear; humanity itself, not the romantic individualist, is what it is seeking to explore. (p. 109)

> *Kenneth Tynan, in* The New Yorker *(© 1959 by The New Yorker Magazine, Inc.), September 12, 1959.*

Brecht was a poet, first and foremost. However much interest his writings may have aroused as expressions of the problems and anxieties of the age, as political pamphlets, manifestoes of stage reform, or social documents, their chief distinction lies in their being "memorable speech." This is their primary significance. It underlies, and from it derives, any other significance they may possess. (p. 171)

Brecht's poetry does not translate well. Its power, to a large extent, lies in its directness and simplicity, in the bold use of hackneyed words in unhackneyed contexts. Inevitably in translation simplicity often turns into mere simplemindedness or banality and the common word subtly used into the merely commonplace.

It is clearly futile to try to *describe* the beauties of a poet's style at second hand. Yet an attempt must be made here to convey, without deeper analysis of Brecht's use of words, syntax, and imagery, some of the features that account for its impact, and to trace the varied sources and influences that lie behind it.

Literary German, and above all stage German, is essentially an artificial dead language. While standard English, standard French, and standard American are spoken, if not by the whole population at least by important sections of it, standard German exists only on paper and on the stage. In ordinary life even the most educated Germans have a clearly defined regional accent and vocabulary. (pp. 171-72)

Brecht, however, achieved the rare feat of creating in his poetry and plays a language all his own, which suggested the rhythms and gave the feeling of real speech without being tied to any particular regional dialect. It is still not a language spoken by anyone in reality—with the exception perhaps of Brecht himself. But while it is a synthesis, it is such a vital and original synthesis, so deeply rooted in a number of different traditions, that it creates the illusion of real speech. (p. 172)

This intensely personal idiom, chaotic and uncontrolled in his early years, disciplined into severe and monumental simplicity later on, is the product of the fusion of many diverse and disparate elements. . . .

These elements, which are already clearly present in Brecht's earliest published writings, are the basis of his personal idiom; the regional Bavarian accent is always to be detected, but never lapses into mere local color. It is stylized and fused with archaic elements from an earlier, baroque layer of the German language. (p. 173)

Brecht's language also has a firm basis in the chief source of modern standard German. Once, when asked by a magazine to name the strongest literary influence in his life, Brecht replied in a single sentence: "You will laugh: the Bible!" . . . He made masterly use of Biblical constructions: the juxtaposition of contrasted half-sentences, parallelism, repetition, and inversion.

Equally marked throughout Brecht's life was the influence of the street ballad, the *Moritat* (morality), as it was sung by balladmongers at country fairs—lurid accounts of murders and executions couched in the strident language of lachrymose sentiment and naïve horror. Brecht turned to this "vulgar" style in protest against the gentility and respectability of the bourgeois society he abhorred. Disgusted by the insipid classical poetry taught at school, he reveled in the powerful emotions and garish colors of the entertainments of the common people, the songs of kitchen maids, and the pleasures offered by the sideshows of fair grounds and beer gardens. (pp. 173-74)

Goethe and Schiller had been the crowning glory of the literary movement of the eighteenth century, whose aim it had been to base the greatness of the united German nation they sought to create upon the sure foundation of a German national literature as respectable and regular, as elegant and polite as the literatures of France and England. To achieve this aim the exuberance of the baroque, the earthiness of the folk tradition had to be banished from polite society. The victory of the reformers seemed complete. Yet among the comics of the beer gardens, in the peepshows and fairground "panoramas" the old German baroque drama, the earlier traditions of Hans Sachs, the Austrian and Bavarian forms of the Italian *commedia dell' arte,* and even some

relics of the mystery plays of the Middle Ages were still alive when Brecht was young. (p. 174)

Brecht's theater with its use of fairy tale elements, musical numbers, and broadly comical characters is a continuation of this old and once despised tradition and has re-established it as a vehicle for the expression of ideas. His language drew much of its vigor and force from the earthy speech of clowns who never failed to call a spade a spade. (p. 175)

Surprising as it may seem at first sight, Brecht was at least as strongly influenced by a poet of an entirely different stamp: Rudyard Kipling. The same impulse that drove him from the drab respectability of provincial society to the vagabonds among the poets, street entertainers, and fair ground comics also made Brecht dream of the wide, wide world he found in the *Barrack-Room Ballads.* There, too, he met a vigorous plebian language—spiced with deliciously exotic names of places and things that breathed an air of boundless freedom and adventure.

Kipling was the main source of the exotic, mythical Anglo-Saxon world which forms the background to a great deal of Brecht's earlier writing. Other elements in it come from Swift and Gay, Upton Sinclair, Jack London, the Chicago stories of the Danish novelist J. V. Jensen (*The Wheel*), Dickens, innumerable crime stories, and gangster films. (pp. 175-76)

Such was the curious mixture of influences that shaped Brecht's early poetry and the tense, extravagant prose of his first plays. While the Expressionist fashion of the period also left some superficial traces in his style, his basic attitude remained fundamentally different from that of the Expressionists. They were entirely preoccupied with their own ego and projected their own personal emotions onto a cosmic plane, while Brecht's poetry, even in its wildest effusions of riotous imagery, remains strangely impersonal. Like the ballads of the street singers, whose strident tones he tried to reproduce, most of his poems are reports on the accidents and crimes of other people, or dramatic monologues whose first person singular or plural is clearly that of historical or imagined characters. The only really personal poems in Brecht's first published volume of poetry, *Domestic Breviary,* are relegated to an appendix, headed "Of poor B.B." (an echo of *"pauvre François Villon"*), and even here the lyrical self-portrait of the author is put forward in the exhibitionist tone of a music hall performer presenting a character sketch, masking the private emotion by the posturing of a public performance.

The publication of the *Domestic Breviary* marks the transition to an even more impersonal approach than that represented by many of the early poems collected in that book. By the time Brecht published these poems . . . his attitude had become austere and didactic. He had made himself one of the main exponents of *Gebrauchslyrik,* the view that poetry should not be an outlet of private emotions but should be judged solely by its social usefulness. (pp. 177-78)

As the frenzy of the Expressionist era died down and the fooleries of Dadaism lost their novelty, many of the younger poets and artists in Germany tried to get away from the fruitless preoccupation with their own selves to the real problems of the age. The plush curtains and ornamental bric-a-brac of the previous, now discredited generation had been torn down and cast aside. The new beauty of the machine, its economy of outline resulting from perfect adaptation to the function for which it had been created, now became the ideal before the artist. This was the creed of a movement labeled *Neue Sachlichkeit.* If social usefulness, however, was to be the new criterion of beauty, literature and the stage also would have to be didactic and to serve the community by teaching it how to live.

And so Brecht's language cast off all ornament and became functional and austere. The *Lehrstücke* and "school operas" are meant to be "teaching aids" rather than art, and their language is severely factual. (p. 178)

It is a measure of Brecht's stature as a poet that he did succeed in achieving the effect of functional elegance he aimed at and that some of the later *Lehrstücke* have a monolithic, stark beauty of their own. The sudden rejection of the anarchic exuberance of his early style reflects Brecht's yearning for discipline and order, which led him to Marxism, and it is significant that one of the models for his new didactic style was provided by a civilization that followed a pattern of equally strict military discipline: the Japan of the samurai. The school operas *He Who Says Yes* and *He Who Says No* are based on a Japanese no play, *Taniko,* in Arthur Waley's translation, and Brecht's most important didactic play, *The Measures Taken,* also derives from this Japanese model.

Arthur Waley's translations of Chinese poetry made a deep impression on Brecht in his next, more mellowed and relaxed stage of development. The Confucian urbanity and courtesy, the quietly ironical tone and free rhythm of these translations became a decisive influence in his progress toward mature simplicity. The gentle politeness of the Chinese, the undogmatic authority of their classical teachers, represented for him the ultimate socialist ideal of friendliness as the basis of human relations. Brecht made German versions of a number of Waley's Chinese poems, and some of his most successful later verse is clearly modeled on them. (p. 179)

[It] is in the great plays he wrote between 1937 and 1947 that the overflowing richness of his early language and the didactic severity of the phase that followed are blended in a masterly idiom unequaled by any other German dramatist of this century. The Biblical allusions, the Bavarian local accent, the exotic names, the archaisms, and the garish rhythms of the street ballad are still there, but controlled and put into their place by the conciseness and economy acquired in the austere atmosphere of the didactic plays and mellowed and relaxed by the influence of the Chinese example. Each play has its own individual tone: *Mother Courage* the earthy flavor of seventeenth century German and the picaresque novels of Grimmelshausen, *Puntila* a racy folk language, *Galileo* the richness of baroque scientific and religious disputation, *The Good Woman of Setzuan* a Confucian urbanity, *The Caucasian Chalk Circle* a different blend of Oriental colors, and *Schweik in the Second World War* a brilliant pastiche of the language of Hašek's novel.

The various and openly acknowledged influences which shaped Brecht's work throughout his life have inevitably led to his being accused of plagiarism and lack of originality. In fact, his originality consisted of his uncanny ability to absorb and assimilate the most diverse and seemingly incompatible elements. (pp. 180-81)

Brecht loved to adapt and to modify the work of others. He needed the challenge of another mind to get the best from his own talent. He based many of his plays on existing originals—Marlowe's *Edward II,* Gay's *Beggar's Opera,* Hašek's *Schweik,* old Japanese or Chinese legends. Again and again he drew on motifs from Shakespeare. His satire against racialism, *The Roundheads and the Peakheads,* contains elements from the plot of *Measure for Measure;* in *Arturo Ui,* in which the rise of Hitler is parodied through that of a Chicago gangster, the character of the villainous hero is modeled on Richard III, so that the murder of Roehm echoes the downfall of Buckingham and the Hitler character woos the widow of one of his victims. But while the Shakespearean models are used with reverence and admiration, the German classics are always ruthlessly parodied. Brecht even went so far as to parody the Bible: Macheath, for example, is betrayed by a kiss on a Thursday evening.

Besides reverent adaptation or cruel parody, Brecht had a third way of assimilating the work of others: the counterplay, written as a reply to, or refutation of, an existing work. His first play, *Baal,* was written to show how Johst's *Der Einsame* could be bettered. *The Days of the Commune* was a reply to Nordahl Grieg, and at the time of his death Brecht planned a counterplay to Beckett's *Waiting for Godot.*

Brecht shares his predilection for literary allusion with writers like T. S. Eliot, Ezra Pound, and James Joyce. It marks him as an intellectual, in spite of his sincere attempts and avowed intention to write for the common people. The use of parody, moreover, particularly the iconoclastic mockery of the German classics, the Bible, and religious hymns and anthems, reveals Brecht's ambivalent attitude toward these models. Parody gave Brecht an opportunity to fulfill an unconscious desire to emulate and follow these examples. Under the cover of ridicule he could indulge the "high-minded," even religious impulses which his rational, cynical self would not allow him to acknowledge. In his later phase, when he had found a positive framework of belief and had attained recognition as a classic of his own time, the tendency to parody great literary examples disappeared, while his love for open adaptation and imitation continued unabated.

Brecht's readiness to sink his own personality in the work of his predecessors and contemporaries, to use the whole storehouse of past literature as so much material for his own handiwork, was in accordance with his views about the nature of poetry itself and the poet's function in society. Here, too, he rejected the mystical, romantic view of the poet as the vessel of divinely inspired intuitions, called upon to fulfill and express his unique personality. To him the poet was a craftsman serving the community and relying on his reason and acquired skill, a man among men, not a being set apart by virtue of some special quality or power. That is why Brecht was ready to accept the advice of numerous collaborators, whom he conscientiously named when his works were published. As he did not consider the work of art divinely inspired, he never hesitated to alter, and often debase, his own work, according to the circumstances of the moment. (pp. 181-82)

> *Martin Esslin, "Brecht's Language and Its Sources," in his* Brecht: The Man and His Work *(copyright © 1959, 1960 by Martin*

Esslin; reprinted in the U.S. by permission of Doubleday & Co., Inc.; and in Canada by permission of Eyre & Spottiswoode Ltd.), Eyre & Spottiswoode, 1959, Doubleday, 1960 (and reprinted in Brecht: A Collection of Critical Essays, *edited by Peter Demetz, Prentice-Hall, Inc., 1962, pp. 171-83).*

The Good Woman of Setzuan is a brilliant matching of Brecht's essential moral complexity with a dramatic method which can genuinely embody it. The moral framework is explicit, as it was in Strindberg's *Dreamplay,* in the traditional device of the gods visiting earth to find a good person. But the action which this initiates is clearer in Brecht than in Strindberg, because the central perception is more precise. In his early plays Brecht had been attracted to morally ambiguous characters, whom he could use to point a cynical paradox about conventional morality. In *The Good Woman of Setzuan* these feelings have developed and clarified. He can now invite us to look at what happens to a good person in a bad society, not through argument, but through a dramatic demonstration. . . . Brecht is always impressive, in his mature plays, in the discovery of ways of enacting genuine alternatives: not so much, as in traditional drama, through the embodiment of alternatives in opposing characters, but by their embodiment in one person, who lives through this way and then that and invites us to draw our conclusions. This is "complex seeing" integrated in depth with the dramatic form, and it is carried right through in that there is no imposed resolution—the tension is there to the end, and we are formally invited to consider it. The ordinary reactions with which we cover this tension are carefully put into the mouths of other characters, so that we can discover their inadequacy while the tension is still there to see. The methods of expressionist drama, normally used to manifest this breaking tension within a single consciousness, are used by Brecht with power and skill, but have acquired a new clarity, a genuine absence of the hysteria characteristic of ordinary expressionism, by the use of controlling and distancing elements which spring from the desire to examine rather than to expose. Brecht is as far as possible, in this play, from the method of special pleading which insists on the spectator or reader seeing the world through the action and tensions of a single mind. This ordinary expressionist emphasis has been transformed by deliberate generalisation, and by the appeal to impersonal judgment. *The Good Woman of Setzuan,* if not Brecht's greatest play, is a profoundly original development of dramatic form in its most important sense. (pp. 156-57)

He is often very like Shaw in this: that he becomes more exciting—more consciously vital and brilliant—as he becomes more confused. About experimental drama, people are often afraid to say this, restricting themselves, because of uneasiness, to comment on the techniques as such. But we shall always fall short of true judgement if we suppose that these isolable qualities are the whole terms of value; we have to look at what the wit is for, what the engaging roughness is for, and in the case of *The Caucasian Chalk Circle* I think we shall discover that in effect they distract both audience and author from a central confusion of experience. . . .

What is important about [*Mother Courage*] is that the drama simultaneously occurs and is seen; it is not an action assumed and then argued. Such an achievement ought not to be rare—it is what all the textbooks prescribe—but it is in fact only rarely (Synge's *Playboy of the Western World* is another good example) that it is unmistakeably there. (p. 158)

[The] point is not what we feel about [Mother Courage's] hard, lively opportunism; it is what we see, in the action, of where this leads. . . . All Brecht's dramatic skill is deployed to lead us to this critical realism; it is not an abstract morality, with force and pressure temporarily set aside, but an active process which is simultaneously moral and dramatic. . . . The contradictions in the characters—that they are sometimes hard, sometimes generous, and so on—are real, but they exist not only at the level of personal qualities; they exist also at the level of the play as a whole. Much of the speech is the play speaking, drawing strength from its characters but also moving beyond them. . . . (pp. 158-59)

[*Galileo*] is a play of the crisis of consciousness, as opposed to the dramatisation of conflicting instincts, conflicting illusions and momentary perceptions, in *Mother Courage*—a play that had rightly to reach crisis with the frantic drumming of one who cannot speak.

It is not that as an individual [Galileo] is a hypocrite; it is that under . . . real pressures he embodies both a true consciousness and a false consciousness—the fact of their coexistence is what Brecht invites us to see. The movement of the play is from the ironic, apparently safe acceptance of false consciousness (what you say to get by, in an imperfect world) to the point where false consciousness becomes false action and is not irony but tragedy and waste. In the end Brecht is showing us not an individual and his history but a structure of feeling and its consequences: this is the central strength of his mature drama.

In the history of drama, Brecht's achievement will perhaps be seen as this: that he took the powerful analytic techniques of expressionism and succeeded in reintegrating them with the main body of humanist drama. Naturalism and expressionism had in common the fact that they were ordinarily static: the unfolding of a character or group of characters: the exposition of a state of mind. Brecht took from expressionism the techniques of exposition, but broke out from its ordinary deadlock by a sense of human history and movement which had been absent from drama for many generations. . . . Continually limited by his own weaknesses—both his constant opportunism, which too often comes through as dramatic cheating, and his vestigial jeering and coarseness, the real dregs of his time and ours— he struggled towards a transformation and in part achieved it. Instead of trying to convert his work to the complacencies of our fashionable despair, or more easily to the grossness of our defensive cynicism, which at times he readily nourishes, we should try to see what it means to drama when in recovering a sense of history and of the future a writer recovers the means of an action both complex and dynamic. In most modern drama, the best conclusion is that that is how it was. Only an occasional major play goes further, with the specific excitement of recognition that this is how it is. Brecht, at his best, reaches out to and touches the necessary next stage: that this is how it is, for this reason, but the action is continually being replayed, and it could be otherwise. And this happens, not in separate stages of seeing and reflection, but in the complex seeing of a single dramatic experience. (pp. 161-62)

Raymond Williams, "The Achievement of Brecht," in Critical Quarterly, *Summer, 1961 (and reprinted by Kraus Reprint Corporation, 1967), pp. 153-62.*

It is true that the final statement of Brecht must be that of his plays. However, after *The Threepenny Opera . . .,* Brecht became mindful of the extent to which the theorist had been betrayed in the reading and performance by others of his drama. As there is thus at least the possibility that two Brechts existed, it would seem only fair to examine first the one which he himself proposed. Because he wrote nothing of any particular significance after the "Organon," ["A Little Organon for the Theatre" . . ., Vol. 12 of his *Versuche*] that pronunciamento can be considered sufficiently terminal to be used as a point of departure.

Brecht starts by removing God from the theater: it is the pastime of men amongst themselves, the construction of living images, of events—historical or imaginary—that occurred among men, and, says Brecht, this is done for recreation. (p. 6)

The stage must be a world that is real to the point of recognition—but no more. (p. 8)

[Music] is a mode of expression meant to remain as distinct from the action as the actor and for the same purpose. . . . The songs scattered through the plays of Brecht are conceived as separate units that mark a break in the action and invite further commentary upon it. In the same way, choreography is supposed to intensify the stage reality even as it objectifies it: stylization of that which is natural must not abolish that naturalness—it must enhance it. And the list continues (stage design, make-up, costume, and so on) in this theater whose every part is laid under contribution in a single effort to achieve an essential realism and an objective spectator.

The substance of Brechtian drama is the story that is told rather than the Aristotelian persona. The characters themselves resist absorption by the drama; their first objective comment about themselves may occur in their self-introduction, a convention drawn from the Japanese noh and interpreted by Brecht as an exercise in spectator detachment. (p. 10)

The "story," which Brecht considers the gist of his drama, coincides with the Marxist's concept of the historical determinant. The characters move according to the dynamics of a given moment in history which their acts exemplify. That which was once considered inherent to all mankind and all times—the essential motivation of the classical protagonist—is considered to be merely the result of a particular set of circumstances. Psychological and metaphysical absolutes are no longer prestated. Instead, Brecht believes that the historical process is shaped by man, or, more properly, by the collective body of men, and that individual psychological states—responses to this process—are thus also subject to change and to correction. The Aristotelian figure that filled the classical theater is therefore replaced with the modest performers of a social "gesture" whose cogency and whose significance are determined by the unfolding tapestry which they compose. . . .

This is not the theater of a single figure. First, there is the independent audience—the autonomous "spectators" who will not become participants in the stage reality. Next, the

stage thus erected *before* the spectator functions as the elaborate, architectonic basis for a demonstration—display and proof: this is the so-called epic theater. (p. 12)

But for Brecht, the term does not refer to an esthetic category. Instead, it keeps as its fundamental definition an appeal to reason rather than the senses and refers to the experimental (scientific) techniques warranted to this end. Epic theater it is because, in the manner of the classical epic, it invites reflection rather than participation. . . .

Whereas the dynamics of the Aristotelian stage work in the direction of absorption (though Brecht sees this absorption effected by the stage rather than by the spectator), the epic form is derived from such principles as will confirm the spectator in his objective detachment from the stage by "awaking" rather than "consuming" his activity. (p. 13)

The spectator is rejected from participation in an action that moves no longer in linear fashion to an attention-centering climax. Instead, he is placed before circular developments of the drama, a series of self-contained units that compel the sustained analysis of a constant movement. The stability of a world based on an assumption of human constants is now viewed for evidence of change whereby to plot the shape of a world to come. (pp. 13-14)

As conceived by Brecht, the didactic play draws upon his anti-Aristotelian wisdom (later outlined in the "Organon") in order to create a play of great apparent simplicity. It is in fact a narrative rather than the performance of an action; the actor is a mediator and an obstacle between the role which he performs and the spectator who represents yet another figure in the debate. . . . (p. 16)

The spectator is excluded from this stage world since he is not a participant in the action which is henceforth referred to as accepted reality by the people on stage. In order to effect a repossession of the world, the spectator must credit—through identification this time—the world in which the actors perform as people, and that world includes the stage judges. No longer on an equal footing with the spectator, these judges now derive their reality from his own. The objective criteria for judgment are destroyed by the subjective criteria of the spectator re-creating in his image the reality of these people; the objective demonstration is lost in subjective "absorption." (p. 18)

Although the theoretical writing of Brecht consistently condemns the negative nature of this "absorption," there is evidence that he accepts its mechanism in his drama. Nearly every play of his, from the earliest, uses this entrapment of the spectator to effect a dramatic—and didactic—dissociation. (pp. 18-19)

[Brecht was] aware that any dramatic statement of illusion and reality through the human presence on stage defies rational analysis and jeopardizes the principles of a theater meant to resist—through analysis—absorption into . . . the hazy land of generalities "incorporeal and abstract." It is presumably for this reason that his people generally evidence little feeling for their own nonideological problems. Whatever they may have to say about themselves or their relationship to others is less the expression of formless and intimate feelings than the crisp outline of a sociopolitical commentary, the value of which—in terms of historical cogency—reflects the degree of their maturity on this sociopolitical stage. The fundamental detachment on Brecht's stage is that of the human actor *impersonating* a character that consciously evinces the symptoms of a human being.

When the human lure is removed from the mechanical creature on stage, its bloodlessness contrasts with a lusty drama loosing upon these stages colorful masses that portray the turmoil of camp life and soldiery (*A Man's a Man; Mother Courage, . . .*), revolution and upheaval (*The Caucasian Chalk Circle; Mahagonny*), the exuberance of carnival crowds (*Galileo*), the gusto and violence of the underworld (*The Threepenny Opera,* whose development follows closely Gay's *Beggar's Opera*), and so on. In the midst of this life and excitement walk surprisingly thick-skinned or indifferent protagonists—generally sexless women or weak men, passive commentators of an action that affects only their commentary. . . . It is only in the late *Puntila* that something like a sensual climate develops thanks to the drunken hero, but that sensuality is frustrated by the moral lesson that denounces the falseness of such drunken humanism. (pp. 23-4)

The reduction of stage people to mechanical objects makes them comical, and Brecht has consciously allowed this to happen to figures which he deemed to be socially unsatisfactory (such as MacHeath and Ackermann). . . . But when the comic context is not justified by the critical position of the author, the mechanical individual voids certain dramatic effects of their intended meaning: blows that signify the oppression of an unenlightened social order rain unconvincingly on such obviously tough hides (as is the case in the bloody beating given to Azdak, the drunken judge who devises the Caucasian chalk circle test). The discursive detachment of the victims reduces the statement of social evils to mere words, and the picture of misery is dissipated in argument—the more so in that Brecht seldom departs from an ironic tone that further lessens the impact of what he is saying, thus calling attention to the detachment of the author. Communist critics themselves have been disturbed by these forsaken characters that are unable to initiate a gesture of revolt or do more than comment on vicissitudes which they endure.

This refusal to acknowledge more than a mental existence is the best guarantee which the character can offer against throbbing with the spectator's pulse; and although it does not always insure the sort of drama which Brecht desired, it resists metabolic stimulation and places the spectator in a position to comment and thus to benefit from that which Brecht considers the theater's greatest good—its power to enlighten and teach. (pp. 25-6)

Whatever the intensity of his speculative thought, Brecht remained fascinated by the fact of the stage. With other postnaturalists, he understood that the first assertion of the stage is an assertion of self and is noncontingent. A stage may show the tread and passage of humanity; but it cannot be a street. (It cannot even show a concern with streets; at the very most, it might express in its own way that which a street is.) All through Brecht's lifetime, he heard Communists insisting that the stage become a mere platform for documentary evidence; and all the while, Brecht insisted that the only evidence of the stage is its own statement at the intersection of fact and figment. And its mystery held him fast. (p. 31)

Several plays of Brecht ask the question: "Does man help man?" It is asked by the chorus in the *Baden Didactic Play*

on Acquiescence . . . that sits in judgment upon a fallen flyer. His admission that he flew for nothing and for no one will require his ultimate banishment from among the living. . . . In 1939, Brecht returned to the question formally—an indication of the central position that it occupies in his ethical system. It is formulated this time by the infernal judges in *The Trial of Lucullus* who must determine whether the Roman general was useful to men. (pp. 34-5)

[The] abiding interest of Brecht in the question of man's social responsibility causes him to pursue it into even more intimate recesses. In *The Caucasian Chalk Circle,* written six years after the first of the *Lucullus* plays, the singer who comments on Grusha's perilous devotion to the child she has saved is moved to exclaim (in the original), "with a ringing voice": "It is a terrible thing / The temptation to goodness!" The problem is no longer debated formally. It is now assimilated within the character of Grusha whose calvary can be linked to the formal lesson only retrospectively and at an intellectual level that is remote from the scene of her suffering. . . . Instead of an intellectual formulation, a living person is laid bare before the spectator, and the rational statement becomes dependent on the vicissitudes of the person that replaces it. (pp. 35-6)

The interest of Brecht in the ethical postulate may derive in part from the dramatic problem which it raises. As a moralist, he refuses goodness when it leads to human misery. . . . But Brecht is unable to resolve the quandary. In *Puntila,* ten years later, the last arguer to state an opinion on the practical value of goodness says: "It depends." (p. 36)

After his first three, Brecht built every play around a moral postulate and in each he hoped for a political lesson, but as often as not, he entrusted that lesson to the dramatic necessities of the play. In so doing, he became a successor to Pirandello and Cocteau: his plays are often interesting commentaries upon, and analyses of, the dramatic process itself. There is an echo to his plays, a depth which is that of the stage. When that dimension is lost, he is as successful as he wished to be—and as no one else wished: the play becomes intellectual, that is to say, merely parodic; a story is told, or commented upon, or imitated—but the depth of the stage is missing.

Speaking of his craft and beliefs, Brecht said, "One cannot conceive an epic theater lacking in artistry, fantasy, without humor, or the gift of sympathy." Sympathy: the ability to suffer with. How many pages of theory and dogma are subverted by those words? And how far was Brecht, ultimately, from Aristotle, who acknowledged, within a special and very lofty sense, the power of tragedy to teach—anagnorisis? (pp. 44-5)

> *David I. Grossvogel, "Bertolt Brecht: The Difficulty of Witnessing," in his* Four Playwrights and a Postscript *(copyright © 1962 by Cornell University; used by permission of Cornell University Press), Cornell University Press, 1962, pp. 3-45.*

Nobody more effectively than Brecht destroyed the well-made play throughout Europe. But there is a considerable debit side to his achievement. For one thing, his plays are necessarily unenjoyable. Since their function is to alert our critical sense they have no universal place for our sense of pleasure. Since, again, they are antibourgeois and antirespectable, they are designed as a threat to the playgoing public rather than a stimulus. It has never been recorded that they had the least influence on the political thinking of either Right or Left—and influence towards the establishment of a Marxist Europe was their primary aim. So that Brecht's undoubted triumphs were unwilling ones. In *Galileo*, in *The Caucasian Chalk Circle*, in *The Threepenny Opera*, he may indeed give pleasure, but that is as far from his intention as the aping of a cleverly sentimental Terence Rattigan technique in "The Jewish Wife," an episode in *Terror and Misery of the Third Reich*. There is a dustiness, a deliberate shabbiness, which, if appropriate to Brecht's larger political ends as a critic of the middle classes, is deeply depressing when it is coupled with so careful a refusal of anything like a heroic gesture. Brecht's characters, like himself, tend to be evasive and self-protecting in moments of crisis. And although it is now fashionable to say that he made a theatrical merit of inconsistency, there is something unattractive, to say the least, in the spectacle of a great writer to whom the art of lifemanship was so supremely important.

I suspect that he will only take his true place in the history of the theatre a generation from now, and that it will turn out to be a less important place than at present seems likely. A considerable part of his reputation today comes from causes unconnected with theatre. . . . But if he is granted four or five masterpieces, I suspect that the perfunctoriness—if deliberate—of much of his playwriting will tell against him in the end. Who can be permanently involved, even detachedly, in the imaginary Chicago of *In the Jungle of Cities,* or tax his receptive powers with what Brecht calls "an inexplicable boxing match between two men"—a theme, incidentally, better treated by Harold Pinter in *The Birthday Party*? All Brecht's plays are permeated by what John Willett calls "an active burrowing doubt." He has based his whole system of thought on unassuageable scepticism. But is this really any wiser than its opposite? Granted that Brecht is a far more copious, a far more versatile playwright than T. S. Eliot, they have it in common that both are above all poets, and both are searching for fresh techniques for the conveyance of an idea. At the moment, Brecht gets all the suffrage because he is clearly the nonsquare of the two. Yet may it not in the end appear that both, despite their incidental felicities, fail for the same reason, by sacrificing their art to a program, and an illiberal program at that? Both are concerned, at bottom, with the same dilemma: how to adjust the individual to his circumstances, and both introduce an overriding power to rectify the ultimate balance. Brecht's power center is Marx plus a box of theatrical tricks, a dead end, surely, unlikely to carry more theatrical traffic than Eliot's classical musings on the Power and the Glory. (p. 24)

Alan Pryce-Jones, in Theatre Arts *(© 1963 by Theatre Publications, Inc.), June, 1963.*

There is a certain ambivalence in most of Brecht's writing which is inimical to strict moralizing. There is always a small "No" or "Maybe" in Brecht's larger "Yes!" No one triumphs easily or irrevocably in his plays.

Brecht is a little contemptuous of Mother Courage for not learning more from her experience: She has not been "converted." Galileo is as much a slob as a saint. . . .

The point of "Mother Courage" is that war destroys even those who would profit from it, but its appeal lies in the

pathetic and indomitable nature of its central figure. The theme of "Galileo" is the moral responsibility of the scientist, but its fascination lies in the portrayal of the tension that pulls its all-too-human hero between his duty and his personal convenience. . . .

Brecht's plays are never pills of redemption for the world's ills; they transcend the naked statement of any political panacea.

Whether or not Brecht wrote what are all too glibly called "great" plays (how many such plays are there in a generation, anyway?) it is my conviction that his plays are the most important to have been written anywhere in the past 35 years. . . .

In the original German, Brecht's writing is a curiously attractive composite of simplicity and sophistication, slang and elegance, pungency and charm, creating a texture the beauty of which is often hard to appreciate in translation. (p. 33)

For Brecht, what creates "psychology" in the person is as much a matter of external circumstances as of individual temperament. To understand why a character behaves in a certain way, we must situate him within the larger framework of his social environment.

In Brecht's plays, moreover, events are narrated, rather than shown as action in the immediate present. The audience thus tends to become an observer rather than a "participant." In short, Brecht strives to induce a certain detachment in the spectator, as if he were a god sitting in judgment on what he beholds and preparing himself to come to some decision.

This method serves to diminish ordinary dramatic suspense. Sometimes Brecht tells us what we are going to see before the event itself. He will deliberately interrupt the flow of scenes so that when they seem about to reach a climax, a song—of sly comment or moral exhortation—is introduced as a choral aside.

We are also prevented from effecting any immediate identification with the place of action by its removal from any readily recognizable locale. . . . The purpose of this removal (in Brechtian terminology, "alienation") is to foster an objective attitude toward the spectacle of the play. All this contradicts our customary habit of mind in the theater.

You might suppose from the foregoing that Brecht's plays and productions lack feeling. Anyone who has seen a Berliner Ensemble production knows that this isn't so. But the emotion aroused by a Brecht play (as he himself produced it) is more akin to that of the classic theater than to that of the run-of-the-mill contemporary show. When Brecht says at the end of one of his plays, "Learn to see, instead of watching stupidly," he means that he does not wish his audience to leave the theater in a frenzy of unthinking excitement. (p. 36)

Though Brecht's material frequently deals with violence and subjects for indignation, he is at bottom forbearing. His final message is affirmative, his ultimate posture a humane assent to life. Even his most brutally pessimistic play—the first one, "Baal"—ends with the line, "It was beautiful . . . Everything." (p. 38)

Harold Clurman, "Brecht Is Global, Except Here," in The New York Times Magazine

(© *1963 by The New York Times Company; reprinted by permission), November 3, 1963, pp. 30, 33, 36, 38.*

It requires great artistry for a modern writer to achieve pristine effectiveness and epic scope with apparently primitive means. That is what Brecht has done. There is something almost medieval, peasantlike and penetratingly poignant in the simplicity of *Mother Courage*. Brecht possesses folk canniness and mother wit, a shrewdness of vision based on intimate experience of life's basic realities. He is both skeptical and direct; his language combines the accents and vocabulary of street and stable with the purity and majestic rhythm of Martin Luther's Old Testament German. The play seems massively sculpted in wood.

Mother Courage is not "propaganda"; not an antiwar tract. It is a comic narrative that mounts to tragedy. Its central figure is a woman without a "soul," an earthbound creature astray in the miserable current of history. . . . She has allegiance to no cause but survival and the care of her brood. She is a pack horse and a "profiteer" of war. She has not the dimmest idea of what all the shooting is about. Nor does she ever grow wiser, learn a lesson. But the war deprives her of everything—her goods, her children, her indomitable vitality. The only heroic and enduringly innocent person in the play is Mother Courage's daughter, who is a mute. Brecht's use of her in the play is a masterstroke. (pp. 130-31)

Much of the play is funny with harsh humor and wry wisdom. There are no villains, barely any sentiment, little pathos. No one preaches, no slogans are enunciated, and even the interpolated songs, which serve as choral comment, might be taken simply as "entertainment." All is impersonal; yet in the end we are moved and feel close to life. (p. 131)

> *Harold Clurman, "Mother Courage" (1963), in his* The Divine Pastime: Theatre Essays *(reprinted with permission of Macmillan Publishing Co., Inc.; copyright © 1946, 1948, 1949, 1950, 1951, 1952, 1953, 1954, 1955, 1956, 1957, 1958, 1959, 1960, 1961, 1962, 1963, 1964, 1965, 1967, 1969, 1970, 1971, 1974 by Harold Clurman), Macmillan, 1974, pp. 130-33.*

Is there any value that Brecht denied consistently, perseveringly, profoundly? Is there any value that Brecht affirmed unyieldingly with all his force and with all his cunning, again and again? Was there a real Nay in him? An authentic Yea?

If Brecht were merely a nay sayer our inquiry would be quickly ended. What Brecht denied in his early poems and in his first play, *Baal*—written when he was twenty-one—Brecht continued to deny with more or less vehemence and subtlety throughout all of his work, in one play after another.

Baal is raucous, exuberant, and at times exquisite; in it, Brecht announces once and for all the object of his enduring hatred, contempt, and disbelief: the individual, that is to say, moral experience. (p. 88)

This is why he was from the start opposed to tragedy—an impossible form if one did not take moral sufferings seriously—and also opposed to realism, the theatrical form inherited from Ibsen in which the individual plays so large a role. In *A Man's a Man* Brecht expressed his hatred for the individual analytically, dramatizing the process by which a so-called individual is rid of his original identity and a brand new one, more serviceable to others, is installed in him. In *Three Penny Opera* Brecht had musicalized his basic negation; in this farcial and boisterous extravaganza, moral experience is ridiculed and all positive values are buried to the wonderful jazz music Brecht had inspired Kurt Weill to write. (p. 89)

[A] year before the production of *Three Penny Opera,* he elected to support the German Communist Party, but in so doing he in no way took back his original negation. Communism for Brecht was still another way of denying the individual, and the value of moral experience as such.

Shortly after *Three Penny Opera,* Brecht wrote a little play, *The Measures Taken,* which was performed in Berlin in 1930. This play is certainly a masterpiece; and in its great virtues and characteristic defects reveals what Brecht would have liked dogmatic Communism to mean to him; Communism would not have that meaning to him for long.

The Measures Taken is a kind of abstract and speculative exercise in the experience of total commitment. . . . What is denied in this play is what Brecht had always denied: the individual, moral experience as such. What is affirmed in the play is something new for Brecht: the absolute authority of the Party bureaucracy.

From the response of the Communists to *The Measures Taken,* Brecht was to learn something about the Party bureaucracy he had not taken into account when he wrote his play: the Party, while it wanted to be treated as an absolute, did not want its pretensions to absoluteness exposed—or even justified. (pp. 90-1)

Brecht never again attempted to present the Party as an absolute value in a dramatic work. Is it so strange or paradoxical then that while remaining a Communist he would in the future protect himself, his rights, freedom, money, and literary works from Communist Party control? Why should he have treated as absolute in fact what he could not celebrate imaginatively as absolute? (p. 92)

[It] is the human body which is the hero of every important play Brecht wrote from then on. The human body in its desire to feed, sustain, and expend itself is the real hero of *Mother Courage, Puntilla, The Caucasian Chalk Circle,* and of *Galileo.* I think it was Brecht's adoration of the body which made it possible for him to view optimistically the decline and death of the individual and even to celebrate it poetically. The ambiguities seen by critics in the main characters of the plays mentioned disappear when it is recognized that Brecht was interested neither in condemning his characters nor in justifying them, though at times it must be admitted he implied he was. When we read the plays carefully we note what the critics have already noted, that the main characters are morally incoherent. But their moral incoherence simply means, I suggest, that Brecht was not interested in them as individuals, but as striking images of the human body in its assertiveness, natural ecstasy, and desire to endure. (pp. 94-5)

The protagonist of *Mother Courage,* the canteen woman who makes a living out of the Thirty Years' War has also raised similar difficulties for critics, apparently even for Brecht himself. (p. 95)

How are we to take Courage then? Certainly, we are not to approve her morally. But the affecting thing about her is not her moral consciousness but her vitality, her physical endurance, her ability to go on from horror to horror, her unabatable animality. All the confusions about her character arise from the error of considering her as an individual, with a moral consciousness of a sort we must condemn or approve. She is not that at all. Her consciousness is as incoherent as Puntilla's desire to be sober and drunk at the same time, and enjoy the advantages of both. Yet Courage is not a negative figure; her positive attributes are those of the body, not of the soul. (pp. 96-7)

But most extraordinary of all Brecht's poetical celebrations of the body is his play *Galileo,* which treats one of the great representatives of Western science. Brecht's play, quietly told in scenes wherein the dramatic conflicts are always understated and never pushed too far, describes the physicist in relation to his own ideas, to rival theorists, to his daughter, to his disciple, and to the Church. In the main the play concentrates on the motives that led Galileo to deny his own theory about the movement of the earth and his recantation of his recantation to his disciple afterward. The play is never really exciting nor does it rise to any great emotional height. One never feels that any tremendous issue is at stake. But it has a wonderful movement, an intellectual beauty, and the figure of the great Galileo charms utterly. This is one of Brecht's best plays, perhaps his greatest.

It has been said that Brecht himself regarded his protagonist, Galileo, as a criminal for yielding to the pressure of the Church, and that Brecht wanted audiences to condemn him for his cowardice. Apparently he thought that science had suffered from Galileo's recantation, and hence that Galileo was a criminal for not enduring martyrdom. (pp. 98-9)

Here again we have a case of what seems to be an insurmountable ambiguity in one of Brecht's main characters, an ambiguity so deep that Brecht himself was never able to explain it satisfactorily or justify it. What are we to think of Galileo? (p. 99)

Very revealing of Brecht's intention is the interest he showed in the physical presentation of his play. For instance, Brecht approved Charles Laughton's way of expounding the Ptolemaic and Copernican systems while taking his morning wash, stripped to the waist. According to Ronald Gray, this was because "Galileo's pleasure here was not merely intellectual, but physical also, in fact his appetite for knowledge has to be shown as part of his appetite for all things." . . . Galileo is shown as a man interested in eating, drinking, and thinking. Someone says of him, "He has thinking bouts." Thought is reduced to a physical activity. And Galileo says: "I don't understand a man who doesn't use his mind to fill his belly." The mind according to Galileo ought to serve the body, in the instance cited— the belly. So consistently in fact has Brecht physicalized Galileo's intelligence that one begins to wonder after a while whether even the word *mind,* with its hint of spirituality, is proper when applied to the great scientist.

The paradoxes and ambiguities of Galileo's character disappear, I suggest, when we think of the great figure in the play *not* as a representative of human spirit at all or of mind either, except in terms of its physical seat, the brain. The remarkable daring of this play, still I think not fully appreciated by critics, is that in it Brecht took one of the greatest scientists of the West and made of him . . . a representative of the human body—in Galileo's case, a representative of the body in its most intellectual posture, but still at a very far remove from what we can very properly call spirit or even mind. (p. 100)

Brecht . . . denied the individual more radically than anyone else and maintained this negation throughout his life. This does not mean, however, that we should judge him a moral cynic.

But if Brecht denied moral experience, can he be called a moralist? This is a more complicated matter; but one point has to be made strongly. Brecht was not, except for a short period in his career, the moralist of commitment to Communist Party authority. . . . Brecht never claimed to be a humanist. He had never affirmed the individual; I think he never believed the individual in this society could be quite real or that moral experience could be anything but an imposture. (p. 101)

What Brecht affirmed was the body, the human body in its warmth, its weakness, its susceptibility, its appetites, the human body in its longing and in its thought. Why did he remain a Communist? He may have thought that even distorted modern Communism, because of its philosophical basis in materialism, was the politics of the human body and hence preferable to Western liberalism based on what he considered a false affirmation of the individual soul.

It may be that his interest in the body extended itself to an interest in the physical details of his own productions, in the material and circumstantial values his plays could have, in their bodies, so to speak, as against their written dialogue, which we may not incorrectly think of as a play's soul. The attention other playwrights have given to the literary form of their plays Brecht devoted indefatigably to the details of his productions. Writers have been honored for their conscientious search for the right word. Brecht was utterly conscientious in his search for the right stage business to bring out the strongest meanings of his plays. (p. 102)

The best of [Brecht's] characters are mainly passive, morally inconsequential, or inconsistent. They live by lies, by fraud, and if, on occasion by feats of thought, the thought generally ministers to their bodies. I think Brecht loved the body, in the abstract, of course, with a feeling similar to what each person feels for his own. (pp. 102-03)

In analyzing Brecht's values, I showed that from the very start of his career as a playwright he rejected the individual and moral experience, so important in the realistic European drama as it was shaped by Ibsen, and in Germany continued by Hauptmann and Sudermann. . . . He could not write realistic plays about individuals, treating their moral conflicts seriously, since he thought the individual a phantom, and hence the dramatization of moral sufferings would have to be comical rather than serious. Certainly the Ibsen type of drama was an impossibility for him, and he knew this from the start. (pp. 103-04)

I have defined metatheatre as resting on two basic postulates: (1) the world is a stage and (2) life is a dream. Now I am not going to assert that Brecht entertained either of these postulates as truths to be demonstrated by his works.

What I do claim is that Brecht, by having rejected the significance of the individual and of moral experience, had to rely on these concepts to give his plays form.

Let us look first at the proposition "the world is a stage." If one does not believe that individuals are real or their sufferings of any great moment, then do not all human actions, reactions, and expressions of feeling immediately seem theatrical? Now what was Brecht's most characteristic theatrical device? It was his deliberate insistence that feelings be played by his actors as if they were acted and not directly felt. One of his favorite devices was to ask his actors to act out a feeling as if they were telling of how some other person felt. Surely this is the furthest possible extreme from the kind of psychological realism we get regularly on the American stage, based very often on the notion that the most infantile and absurd expressions of feeling of so-called individuals are of the very greatest importance. Whether, then, Brecht believed the world to be a stage or not, his plays, his concepts of acting and stage design, were all calculated to produce that effect. The reality in his plays is that of theatre and not that of life, except as the latter happens to become theatrical. (p. 105)

The other proposition of metatheatre is more difficult to ascribe to Brecht than the first. Could this hardheaded, practical-minded man have believed that life is a dream? Again I do not think he would have consciously asserted any such thing. . . . Cool, dispassionate thinking of the sort Brecht always advocated, and claimed he wanted to induce in his spectators, is precisely the kind of thinking that can never assert the reality of any person not oneself. Life, in a way, had to be a dream for Brecht, given his extreme devaluation of individual feelings.

Now the type of play Brecht wrote . . . implies the notion that life is a dream, and that the spectator will either form this notion or feel its suggestiveness as a result of the play's effect. Perhaps Brecht did not want this to happen, and I think it correct to say he did not want this to happen because of his political views. Hence his idea of interfering with, interrupting, restraining the response of the spectator. . . . Certainly Brecht's idea of recalling the spectator back from involvement would be a contradictory one had Brecht been trying to write tragedy or realism; it is not contradictory, considering that what he actually wrote was metatheatre. (pp. 105-06)

> Lionel Abel, *"Brecht: His Nay and His Yea" and "Brecht and Metatheatre,"* in his Metatheatre: A New View of Dramatic Form *(reprinted with the permission of Hill & Wang, a division of Farrar, Straus & Giroux, Inc.; copyright © 1963 by Lionel Abel), Hill & Wang, 1963, pp. 86-107.*

Of all the great modern dramatists, Bertolt Brecht is the most enigmatic—at once both direct and hidden, at once both simple and complex. The great bulk of his work is designed to be an impersonal and schematic contribution to Marxist myth-making. . . . This reminds us of another Marxist dramatist, Bernard Shaw, and, superficially, Shaw would seem to be Brecht's closest companion in the theatre of revolt. Both support a "non-Aristotelian" theatre, characterized not by cathartic emotional effects but by preachment, protest, and persuasion. Both are absorbed with the materialistic motives behind human ideals. Outwardly, both

are social rebels, attempting the salvation of mankind through a change in the external environment. And both involuntarily overcome the narrow utilitarian limitations they impose on their art. Still, for all their surface similarities, Brecht is even further removed from Shaw, temperamentally, than Strindberg is from Ibsen. Whereas Shaw's revolt is modified by the geniality of his character and the meliorism of his social philosophy, Brecht's is intensified by his savage indignation and his harrowing vision of life. Shaw is a suppressed poet who rarely breaks the skin of the unconscious; and though he calls himself a Puritan, he cannot bring himself to contemplate evil in the soul of man. But Brecht is a lyrical, dramatic, and satiric poet of fierce intensity; and few Puritan theologians have been more fascinated than he with the brutal, the Satanic, and the irrational aspects of human nature. (pp. 231-32)

Brecht's Communism is a discipline imposed, by a mighty effort of will, on a self which is essentially morbid, sensual, and anarchical. Beginning his career as an existential rebel, abnormally preoccupied with crime, blind instinctualism, and decay, Brecht becomes a social revolutionary only after he has investigated all the blind alleys of his early nihilism. The Communist ideology helps him to objectify his feelings and rationalize his art; and it encourages him to attribute an external cause to the cruelty, greed, and lust that he finds in life; but it is never fully adequate to Brecht's metaphysical *Angst*. Brecht may try to convince us that man's aggressive instincts are an outgrowth of the capitalist system, but he never seems wholly convinced himself, especially when his own aggressive instincts are so difficult to control. Even at his most scientifically objective, Brecht continues to introduce a subjective note; even at his most social and political, he remains an essentially moral and religious poet. . . . Brecht's revolt, therefore, is double-layered. On the surface, it is directed against the hypocrisy, avarice, and injustice of bourgeois society; in the depths, against the disorder of the universe and the chaos in the human soul. Brecht's social revolt is objective, active, remedial, realistic; his existential revolt is subjective, passive, irremediable, and Romantic. The conflict between these two modes of rebellion issues in the dialectic of Brecht's plays; and the conflict is not fully resolved until the very end of his career. Part monk, part sensualist; part moralist, part diabolist; part fanatical idealist, part cynical compromiser, Brecht is a compound of many different simples; but he combines the discords and uncertainties of our time into a product which, being dramatic poetry, is always more than the sum of its parts. (pp. 232-33)

Despite the studied indifference with which Brecht affects to examine life in this period, however, he cannot disguise his sense of horror at it. (p. 234)

German Neo-Romanticism culminates in the early work of Brecht, where it takes the form of extreme antipathy to the social and natural world. . . . [He] deals obsessively with such Neo-Romantic themes as the meaninglessness of individualism, the inescapable isolation of the natural man, and the vileness of the natural functions, besides displaying a typically Germanic interest in decay and death. Putrefying corpses, drowned girls, dead soldiers, and murdered infants populate the balladic structures of these verses. (pp. 237-38)

This obsession with man and nature in a state of putrefaction is also central to Brecht's early drama, where he deals with lower forms of humanity, deteriorating in a terrible environment. (p. 238)

Like Strindberg, whom he so much resembles in this period, Brecht tries to deal with his own desperation by turning it into art: Baal, Kragler, Garga, Shlink, Bloody Five, Galy Gay, almost all his early characters are aspects of himself, projected into semiautobiographical form. These characters can be roughly divided into two main types: the active and the passive, those who create violence and those who seek to avoid it—but whether victimizers or victims, almost all of Brecht's characters find themselves repelled by their own instincts, and seek to achieve a state of calm beyond the turmoil of the appetitive life. Brecht, who is remembered as an incorrigible womanizer, almost invariably associates some dire penalty with the indulgence of the appetites; for him, physical satisfaction leads directly to catastrophe—which may explain why Bloody Five in *A Man's a Man,* and, later Lauffer in *The Tutor,* resort to such desperate expedients as self-castration in order to control themselves. Not only sex but passions of any uncontrolled kind seem to be a source of anxiety to Brecht: anger, outrage, panic, revenge, violence, all are vital elements of his work, and all stand condemned.

Brecht is probably trying to master these emotions in himself, for his work exposes his desire for absolute submission, a state of being in which he can conquer his unbridled feelings, and, instead of engaging himself with the external world, merge with it. Brecht's favorite symbol for this passionless state is the condition of the child in its mother's womb. . . . To lie still in this water is to give oneself up to existence; to flail about in it is to involve oneself—sexually, socially, actively—with the external world. What Brecht really desires is the Buddhist Nirvana—but his own physical needs and his rebellious spirit continually press him back into material life. Brecht's unremitting attempts to control his rebellious instincts by surrendering to a discipline outside himself are to issue, later, in his submission to the Communist orthodoxy, and, still later, in his aspiration towards Oriental impassivity, where one becomes a vessel of the universe—acquiescent, will-less, and obedient. But whatever form it finds, Brecht's desire for impersonality and control reflects his need to escape from the pulls of the flesh, to subjugate the instincts which force him into unwilling participation in life. (pp. 239-40)

Yet, for all his scorn of Romanticism in its more positive forms, his own Romantic temperament can still be glimpsed in his subjective poetic attack, in his ferocious bitterness and disillusionment, and, especially, in his unremitting rebellion against the straitened conditions of modern existence. (p. 241)

In the Jungle of Cities powerfully suggests the madness Brecht perceives in nature and the chaos he senses in the universe. . . . His attraction to Communism, therefore, can also be ascribed to the fact that it offers a system of regimentation, a form of rational control over his frightening individualism and terrifying subjectivity. Brecht's desire for passivity, in short, stems from his fear of activity. And his rage for order is really an extension of his desire to drift with the tide, for Communism represents a tide with a meaningful direction. (pp. 249-50)

What I am suggesting is that Brecht responded as eagerly to the Communist discipline as to the Communist dogma; there is something almost religious about his attachment to his new creed. Like most new converts, his fanaticism begins to exceed that of the orthodox; using "science" and

"reason" as ritualistic passwords, he turns to ideology as if it were theology, and enters politics as if he were joining a monastic order. Brecht's monkishness is expressed not only in the new simplicity of his poetry, which grows more functional and clipped, but in almost every aspect of his behavior. He begins to wear a simple worker's uniform as if it were a monk's habit; he crops his hair short; his surroundings become more stark and austere; and his private life more ascetic. Most important, he begins to urge the complete extinction of the personality, accompanied by total obedience to a higher order. (p. 250)

Brecht's characters, however, are also victimized now by a cruel society. As we might expect, his Marxist orientation puts social-economic concerns at the center of his art. The rebel against the chaos of nature has turned into a rebel against the social system. (p. 252)

Brecht himself seems to be more responsive to the critical than to the Utopian side of Marx—at least, in his plays. Interpreting life as dominated by the search for food and the lust for money (he wanted money and food to replace sex and power as the central subjects of the drama), he also conceives of man as an aggressive beast of prey who grows fat by battening on the flesh of his victims. (p. 253)

On the social-objective level of his plays, Brecht is drawing a clear-cut moral: Man's instincts are healthy, compassionate, kindly, and courteous, but in a competitive society, he must suppress these natural feelings, exercising selfish reason in order to survive. (p. 255)

Brecht's ambivalence accounts for the dialectical power and texture of his work. Through the clash of opposites, his *Widersprüchsgeist* (contradictory spirit), as he liked to call it, is able to find its complicated expression. Unable to resolve his contradictions, Brecht fails to create unambiguous political ideology. . . . Yet, his failure to be a Utopian ideologist is his triumph as a dramatic poet; like all the great rebel dramatists, he draws his power from the clash of thesis and antithesis, always skirting a fake harmonious synthesis. Whether Brecht is examining the conflict of reason and instinct, vice and virtue, cowardice and heroism, adaptation and revolt, science and religion, Marxism and Neo-Romanticism, he almost invariably concentrates on the opposition rather than the resolution of his terms; and he even suggests, as in these concluding verses from *Saint Joan of the Stockyards,* that life is good *because* it is unresolved:

> Humanity! Two souls abide
> Within thy breast!
> Do not set either one aside:
> To live with both is best!
> Be torn apart with constant care!
> Be two in one! Be here, be there!
> Hold the low one, hold the high one—
> Hold the straight one, hold the sly one—
> Hold the pair!   (p. 257)

How Brecht manages to maintain his scepticism, detachment, and irony while declaring his unquestioning allegiance to the Communist cause is one of the most skillful accomplishments of dramatic literature. But it is the achievement of a man who is split in half. Committed and alienated, active and passive, hopeful and cynical. . . . (pp. 258-59)

Much the same doubleness of vision and unity of tone can be found in *Mother Courage and her Children (Mutter Courage und Ihre Kinder)*, Brecht's masterpiece and, without doubt, one of the finest works of the modern theatre. Completed in 1939, when World War II was just beginning and Brecht was in exile in Scandinavia, *Mother Courage* ostensibly deals with the Thirty Years War, that seventeenth-century feast of death, fire, and pestilence. But its real subject is all wars, as seen from the perspective of one who loathes military heroism. . . . In the background of *Mother Courage* pass the victories, defeats, reversals, sieges, assaults, retreats, and advances which form the substance of history. In the foreground, the private lives of the noncombatants provide a non-heroic contrast. The external course of the conflict is narrated, like newspaper headlines, in the legends preceding each scene, but it interests Brecht only insofar as it influences local commerce: "General Tilley's victory at Leipzig," the title informs us, "costs Mother Courage four shirts." (pp. 267-68)

Mother Courage is the culminating work of Brecht's career, but it is hardly the end of it. During the war and after, in exile and back in East Berlin, Brecht continues to create a profusion of plays—including at least one masterpiece, *The Caucasion Chalk Circle*. But after *Mother Courage*, Brecht's savage indignation begins to leave him, his rebellion progressively cools. Even as his plays become more openly Communistic in subject matter, his approach grows more sweet and even-tempered. Virtuous, maternal women like Kattrin—Shen Te, Simone Machard, Grusha—move in to the center of the action, while his secondary characters develop deeper dimensions, and more complex motivations than simple greed and lust. Instead of castigating humanity, Brecht is beginning to celebrate it; instead of illustrating his themes through ironic comparisons, he is beginning to employ moral allegories and parables. Brecht's later approach to character and his use of less exaggerated comparisons suggest how he is losing his need to rebel against reality; as further proof, Nature has returned to his work—no longer hostile and ugly, but calm, serene, and even beautiful. Less sardonic, more relaxed, Brecht grows more lyrical and carefree: in fact, if Brecht's first period is Büchnerian, and his second Jonsonian, then his third is clearly Shakespearean—some of his plays have an atmosphere akin to Shakespeare's Romantic comedies. Even Brecht's theory is loosening up from the rigid didacticism of his early days. (p. 276)

Brecht's interest in the Oriental drama is accompanied, during this last period, by an interest in the Eastern religious thinkers—Confucius, Buddha, Lao-Tse, the philosophers of obedience through the annihilation of the physical self. It is probable that, with the advance of age, Brecht had finally subdued his troublesome passions. No longer harried by appetite, he gives himself up to that drifting and merging which he desired all his life. Like Strindberg, in short, Brecht works his way through, after a career of fierce rebellion, to a position of resignation; at last, he achieves that security and serenity he associates with the mother's womb. (pp. 277-78)

Brecht's desire for revolt is still satisfied by his identification with Communism; but his desire for peace is now expressed through images of Oriental calm. Brecht, therefore, comes to terms with life only by continuing to reject it—by drifting with a political tide, he overcomes his spiritual

horror and nausea. And this is the only synthesis of Brecht's double revolt. Only by merging with evil did he feel he could still function for good; only by embracing the destroyers could he still join the ranks of the creators. The chicanery and compromises Brecht accepted for the sake of the survival of himself and his art are not always very attractive. And no modern playwright better exemplifies the dwindling possibilities of revolt in an age of totalitarianism, war, and the mass state. But if Brecht sometimes sacrificed his personal integrity to a collective falsehood, then this was in order that his individualism could still be secretly expressed. His drama remains the final measurement of this achievement—acts of bitterness which did not quench his cigar but rather kept it aglow. (p. 278)

> *Robert Brustein, "Bertolt Brecht" (originally published in a slightly different version in* Partisan Review, *1963), in his* The Theatre of Revolt: An Approach to the Modern Drama (© *1962, 1963, 1964 by Robert Brustein; reprinted by permission of Little, Brown and Co. in association with the Atlantic Monthly Press), Atlantic-Little, Brown, 1964, pp. 231-78.*

No dogmatic summary of a political or social belief does *Mother Courage, Saint Joan of the Stockyards,* or *The Good Woman of Setzuan* even the roughest justice. The intellectual tensions in the plays, which give them their greatest creative power even as dogmatic propaganda, come indeed from those moments . . . when the spectator is tempted to the brink of a dogmatic summary, which is immediately denied by an ironic glancing away of character or plot in another oblique direction. (p. 60)

This impulse, however, toward dogmatic simplification, whether in critical comment on his own plays or in his adaptations of others', underlines Brecht's more characteristic mode, that of ironic casuist. It is probable that Brecht's most valuable contribution toward any exploration of contemporary thinking, whether Christian or non-Christian, springs from the moral and dramatic dilemmas inherent in this ironic counterposing of involvement and detachment, the give-and-take of a dramatic technique that is never wholly given to moral judgment. This is best expressed in two moments in his plays when intellectual resolution seems on the brink of crystallization: at the end of *The Caucasian Chalk Circle* Azdak the judge, venal, grotesque, and a caricature of the judicial office, is summarized in the closing choric verses of the Singer:

> But the people of Grusinia did not forget him and
>   often remembered
> His time of Judgment as a brief
> Golden Age that was almost just.

The tone of the final phrase, "almost just," comprehends and goes beyond dramatic irony. It is a comment . . . on the fallibility of all human authority and the proper limitation of all our expectations. The second example occurs at a relatively highly charged moment in *Galileo*. Andrea, Galileo's pupil, has listened to a long examination of the necessary moral role of scientific investigation; Galileo concludes with the flat judgment, "I have betrayed my profession," and, to Andrea's farewell greeting, responds, "Can you bring yourself to take a hand such as mine?" At this point the audience might expect once more a crystallization of judgment, a resolution of the dilemma which Galileo's conduct has posed. Instead, Andrea makes the much more telling, because temperate and equivocal, judgment: "I cannot believe that your murderous analysis [of yourself] will be the last word." The sophisticated urbanity with which Brecht withholds any final, clear-cut dogmatic statement confounds any attempt to reduce his dramatic arguments to a formula.

Irony is a somewhat overworked category in our contemporary criticism, but it is difficult to ignore its pervasive presence in Brecht . . . in particular his ironic manipulation of historical subjects and the more delicate irony of the relation between social justice and law. (pp. 62-4)

In a cultural climate which explores the validity and limitations of all dogmatic statement, all creedal assumptions, the gravity of the Brechtian irony merits full and just assessment. The exploratory theologian, in testing the marginal confines of his own creed, could scarcely write more soberly and responsibly of his craft than did Brecht when he asserted the dignity of the theatre, of the dramatist and the actor as instruments of social experiment: "The little knife must rest lightly in the surgeon's hand when his responsibility is so great." No small part of the "little knife's" keenness is the quality of restless, qualifying irony . . . , a powerful instrument which could be of value to many outside the orbit of Marxist writing. (p. 75)

> W. Moelwyn Merchant, "The Irony of Bertolt Brecht," in Man in the Modern Theatre, edited by Nathan A. Scott, Jr. (© 1965 by M. E. Bratcher; used by permission of John Knox Press), John Knox, 1965, pp. 58-75.

The worst that can happen to a poet is that he should cease to be a poet, and that is what happened to Brecht in the last years of his life. . . . There are a number of very touching lines in love poems and nursery rhymes. And, most important, there are praises of purposelessness. . . . (p. 213)

That Brecht could write such verses at all indicates an unexpected and decisive shift in the poet's mood; only his early poetry, in the "Manual of Piety," shows the same freedom from worldly purposes and cares, and in the place of the earlier tone of jubilation or defiance there is now the peculiar stillness of wonder and gratitude. (p. 214)

Everything indicated that the poet had found a new voice—perhaps "the dying swan's song that is held to be the most beautiful"—but when the moment came for the voice to be heard, it seemed to have lost its power. This is the only objective and therefore unquestionable sign we have that he had transgressed the rather wide limits set for poets, that he had crossed the line marking what was permitted to him. . . . [The] only meaningful punishment that a poet can suffer, short of death, is, of course, the sudden loss of what throughout human history has appeared a divine gift. To Brecht the loss clearly came rather late, and hence it can teach us a lesson about the great permissiveness enjoyed by those who live under the laws of Apollo. . . . It came, finally, after he had settled down in East Berlin, where he could see, day after day, what it meant to the people to live under a Communist regime. (pp. 214-16)

The element of playfulness, so important in his work, could not possibly survive in proximity with the very horrors he used in his plays. It is, after all, one thing to tell your friends and acquaintances when they disagree with you, "We'll shoot you, too, when we seize power," and quite another thing to live where things worse than shooting happen to those who disagree with those who have indeed seized power. (pp. 216-17)

Hence, side by side with the great poet and playwright there is also the case of Bertolt Brecht. And this case is of concern to all citizens who wish to share their world with poets. It cannot be left to the literature departments but is the business of political scientists as well. The chronic misbehavior of poets and artists has been a political, and sometimes a moral, problem since antiquity. (p. 218)

If one wished to classify him, one might say that he was an anarchist by disposition and inclination, but it would be altogether wrong to see in him another member of that school of decay and of morbid fascination with death which in his generation was perhaps best represented in Germany by Gottfried Benn and in France by Louis-Ferdinand Céline. Brecht's characters—even his drowning girls who slowly swim down the rivers until they are taken back into nature's great wilderness of all-encompassing peace; even Mazeppa, bound to his own horse and dragged to his death—are in love with life and with what earth and sky have to offer, to the point where they willingly accept death and destruction. The last two stanzas of the "Ballad of Mazeppa" are among the truly immortal lines of German poetry. . . . I certainly cannot translate them properly. They speak of the end of the three days' ride into death: into silence, the gift of the earth; into rest, the gift of the sky. . . . There is a glorious, triumphant vitality in this death song, and it is the same vitality—the feeling that it is fun to be alive and that it is a sign of being alive to make fun of everything—that makes us delight in the lyrical cynicism and sarcasm of the songs in "The Threepenny Opera." It was not for nothing that Brecht helped himself so generously to a Villon translation into German—something that German law, unhappily, called plagiarism. He is celebrating the same love of the world, the same gratitude for earth and sky, for the mere fact of being born and alive, and Villon, I am sure, would not have minded. (pp. 229-30)

[There is an] element of hellish pride dear to all of Brecht's adventurers and outcasts, the pride of absolutely carefree men, who will yield only to the catastrophic forces of nature, and never to the daily worries of a respectable life, let alone to the higher worries of a respectable soul. Whatever philosophy Brecht may have been born with—as opposed to the doctrines he later borrowed from Marx and Lenin—is spelled out in the "Manual of Piety," being clearly articulated in two perfect poems, the "Grand Hymn of Thanksgiving" and in "Against Temptation," which was later incorporated into "The Rise and Fall of the City Mahagonny." The "Grand Hymn" is an exact imitation of Joachim Neander's great baroque church hymn "Lobe den Herren," which every German child knows by heart. (p. 232)

Nowhere else in modern literature, it seems to me, is there such a clear understanding that what Nietzsche called "the death of God" does not necessarily lead into despair but, on the contrary, since it eliminates the fear of Hell, can end in sheer jubilation, in a new "yes" to life. (p. 233)

Yet there are nihilistic elements in Brecht's early poetry, and no one, probably, has ever been more aware of them than he was himself.... "The Rise and Fall of the City Mahagonny," which is Brecht's only strictly nihilistic play, deals with the last error, his own, the error that what life has to give—the great pleasures of eating, drinking, fornicating, and boxing—could be enough. (p. 234)

Compassion was doubtless the fiercest and most fundamental of Brecht's passions, hence the one he was most anxious to hide and also was least successful in hiding; it shines through almost every play he wrote.... The leitmotiv was the fierce temptation to be good in a world and under circumstances that make goodness impossible and self-defeating. The dramatic conflict in Brecht's plays is almost always the same: Those who, compelled by compassion, set out to change the world cannot afford to be good. (pp. 235-36)

[It] was out of a feeling of solidarity with the downtrodden and oppressed that Brecht wrote so much of his poetry in ballad form. (Like other masters of the century—W. H. Auden, for instance—he had the latecomer's facility in the poetic genres of the past, and hence was free to choose.) For the ballad, grown out of folk and street songs, and, not unlike Negro spirituals, out of endless stanzas in which servant girls in the kitchen lamented unfaithful lovers and innocent infanticides, . . . had always been the vein of unrecorded poetry, the art form, if such it was, in which people condemned to obscurity and oblivion attempted to record their own stories and create their own poetic immortality. Needless to say, the folk song had inspired great poetry in the German language before Brecht.... Also, the ballad in which the poet becomes a storyteller had great predecessors, including Schiller and poets before and after him, and, thanks to them, had lost, together with its original crudeness, much of its popularity. But no poet before Brecht had stuck with such consistency to these popular forms and succeeded so thoroughly in gaining for them the rank of great poetry. (pp. 238-39)

[My] purpose . . . is to present my thesis that a poet's real sins are avenged by the gods of poetry. . . . (p. 242)

[When] he went back to East Germany, essentially for artistic reasons, because its government would give him a theatre—that is, for that "art for art's sake" he had vehemently denounced for nearly thirty years—his punishment caught up with him. Now reality overwhelmed him to the point where he could no longer be its voice; he had succeeded in being in the thick of it—and had proved that this is no good place for a poet to be.

This is what the case of Bertolt Brecht is likely to teach us, and what we ought to take into consideration when we judge him today, as we must, and pay him our respect for all that we owe him. The poets' relation to reality is indeed what Goethe said it was: They cannot bear the same burden of responsibility as ordinary mortals; they need a measure of remoteness, and yet would not be worth their salt if they were not forever tempted to exchange this remoteness for being just like everybody else. On this attempt Brecht staked his life and his art as few poets had ever done; it led him into triumph and disaster. (p. 247)

I have proposed that we grant poets a certain latitude, such as we would hardly be willing to grant each other in the ordinary course of events. I do not deny that this may offend many people's sense of justice; in fact, if Brecht were still among us he would certainly be the first to protest violently against any such exception. (pp. 247-48)

But, for our consolation, this inequality works both ways. One of the signs that a poet is entitled to such privileges as I here claim for him is that there are certain things he cannot do and still remain who he was. It is the poet's task to coin the words we live by, and surely no one is going to live by the words that Brecht wrote in praise of Stalin. . . . [It] is true that mere intellectuals or literati are not punished for their sins by loss of talent. No god leaned over their cradle; no god will take his revenge. . . . [The] example of "poor B.B.," who never wasted a shred of pity on himself, may teach us how difficult it is to be a poet in this century or at any other time. (p. 249)

> *Hannah Arendt, "Bertolt Brecht: 1898-1956" (originally published under a different title in* The New Yorker, *November 5, 1966), in her* Men in Dark Times *(© 1955, 1965, 1966, 1967, 1968 by Hannah Arendt; reprinted by permission of Harcourt Brace Jovanovich, Inc.), Harcourt, 1968, pp. 207-49.*

Brecht's plays lend themselves to controversy of all sorts—literary, theatrical, political. (p. 51)

It was inevitable that Brecht should become the subject of every type of exegesis. For his is the only manifestation of a total theatre style (text and presentation in organic relationship) since the emergence of the Moscow Art Theatre with its climactic peak in the plays of Chekhov and the corresponding development of the so-called Stanislavsky system or Method.

The modern theatre has known such influences as those of symbolism, expressionism, constructivism—impulses and tendencies which characterize certain writers, scene designers, directors, but hardly any of which shaped themselves into a complete body of work with any permanent organ to institutionalize them on every level of stagecraft. . . .

Brecht's plays are picaresque, poetic narrations for the stage. They are based on brief episodes of concentrated action—most of them almost complete in themselves—each of which makes a simple sharp point essential to the understanding of the play's idea as a whole. The intellectual approach is tersely factual, the tone ironic, crisp and detached. Songs in a similar vein embody the ideological point as in an epigram. The aim is frankly didactic. One play tells us that war debases everything and everyone, even those who seem to be outside its antagonisms. Another play tells us that it is virtually impossible to "do good" in a corrupt society. These are morality plays as certainly as anything ever written in the Middle Ages in behalf of the Church. (p. 52)

[These] plays with their somewhat ribald humor—part folk canniness and part twentieth-century sophistication—their starkly naïve "stories," their rude simplicity, their dry, yet poignant songs—witty homilies or grave and austere preachments—inspire a sense of nobility, a kind of humane asceticism which is cleansing and elevating. The spareness of the plays is sinewy; their slightly astringent timbre which might easily be mistaken for cynicism is invigorating; their pathos—and they have a pathos at times bordering on sentimentality—is classically serene. (p. 53)

Brecht's theatre is theatrical theatre *and* is very real. He endeavors to avoid ecstatic, stentorian, sweating, tremulous emotionalism, *and* at the same time his work communicates an emotion as lofty as any we know in the theatre today. (p. 54)

The first thing we recognize in the Brecht productions is their *reality:* an utterly engrossing reality. We feel we are looking directly at the core and substance of what the plays are about. We do not sense any element of staginess, arty ornament or eye-deceiving illusion. At the same time, we are not only at ease—the ordinary naturalistic production always seems a little strenuous by comparison—but thoroughly absorbed. We are at once in the theatre—with all its sense of festival and fun—and soberly in the midst of life. (p. 204)

When one reads a play by Brecht—before or even after having seen it—one is astonished to find that for all the purity, simplicity and, with the plainness, the subtle elevation of its style, one thinks of it not so much as a complete play, but rather as a libretto for the opera of which it is a part, or as a film script in respect to the picture which is to be made of it. That is one reason why Brecht's plays may prove disappointing in productions not created by the Brecht company under the conditions which the Berliner Ensemble has been enabled to foster for itself.

The secret of the total power these plays impart in the productions which the playwright or his colleagues have directed is that everything in them emanates from a sense of life, a conviction, a will, a seed-sentiment transmitted in every moment, movement, color, gesture and thought, shared by everyone concerned in the performance. Not only one consciousness, but a single breath, seems to have given it life. The productions are not so much a collective triumph as they are the body of one spirit. Brecht's word has become flesh; his ideas have taken on visible form. The productions are literally a revelation; that is why—antinaturalistic, anti-"emotional" and (save the mark!) anti-"Method"—they are so unmistakably forceful, so wholly real, so inescapably immediate, so compelling and—for all the infinite care and craftsmanship involved in their making —so unaffected. (pp. 204-05)

Brecht is a poet of classic character. He wished his work to have the authority of an objective statement which needs no stress beyond a simple grace of speech, no "art" beyond the most engaging directness, no "passion" greater than that which the truth will elicit. His technique is a reasonableness which arises when a smiling skepticism sets out in quest of a small area of certainty. This, he hopes, will prove charmingly self-evident. Not wholly in vain did Brecht claim the Chinese and Japanese among his artistic ancestors.

What does Brecht ultimately say? Trust what your senses experience, what your mind has weighed and what your most fundamental human instincts dictate. Act with your fellowmen in the name of what you have all tested and found to be needful to your life in common. Seek always, do not allow yourself to grow rigid at any point and let your goal be the peaceful enjoyment of the goods of life.

From all the contradictions of Brecht's nature, his irony and his radicalism, his homely earthiness and his "peasant" cunning, his culture and folksy common sense, there emerges something that may very well be that ineffable quality: manly virtue. (pp. 208-09)

Harold Clurman, "Bertolt Brecht: His Achievement" and "Brecht in Paris, 1960," in his The Naked Image: Observations on the Modern Theatre *(reprinted with permission of Macmillan Publishing Co., Inc.; copyright © 1958, 1959, 1960, 1961, 1962, 1963, 1964, 1965, 1966 by Harold Clurman),* Macmillan, 1966, pp. 51-5, 203-09.*

Bertolt Brecht is classical in his insistence upon the didactic function of theater. His *Lehrstücke* are usually translated as "learning plays," but the literal "teaching plays" would be more precise. . . . Brecht insisted . . . upon the theatricality of theater. Not a world that is like a stage, but a stage that is like a stage. Theater is theater, and Brecht thought that it should teach by symbolic example, as do parables. To increase the teachability of his audience, Brecht was willing to entertain them, but reluctant to involve them emotionally in the dramatic action. Hence, the celebrated *Verfremdungseffekt,* to prevent the audience from entering too deeply into the illusion of the drama. Brecht delineated specific techniques to estrange the audience from the actors— projections, narrators, harsh lighting, scanty staging, songs of social significance, and direct address by actor to audience. Through such techniques, the audience was to be sufficiently detached from the action to pronounce moral judgment upon it. (pp. 28-9)

Brecht designated a judicatory role for his audience, and he was also partial to judgment scenes in his drama. . . . Occasionally, Brecht leads his audience towards a different verdict from the one pronounced on stage. . . .

Many of Brecht's plays pose the problem of traditional virtue in an untraditional world, and in *The Good Woman of Setzuan,* that problem is underlined through a final court scene, where the would-be good woman appeals to the judge-gods, as Everyman appeals to the Christian judging God. (p. 29)

The Caucasian Chalk Circle dramatizes Brecht's most winning appeal for agreement with an on-stage verdict. . . . [Although] Brecht spurns world-stage imagery, the parable quality of a play like *The Caucasian Chalk Circle* implies a world-stage, which the audience watches in order to arrive at a moral judgment, even as God did in traditional use of the topos. And just as God inevitably damned the sinner, so Brecht expects his audience to damn a non-socialist system.

Brecht and Beckett are often viewed as polar opposites— Brecht the propagandist of social change and Beckett the poet of individual anguish. Not surprisingly, then, Brecht casts his audience in a role of social significance, whereas Beckett demands only their witness. (p. 30)

Ruby Cohn, "'Theatrum Mundi' and Contemporary Theater," in Comparative Drama *(copyright 1967, by* Comparative Drama*), Spring, 1967, pp. 28-35.*

What so obviously fascinated the playwright in Brecht was the drama of Hegel's philosophy. Hegel, like Brecht, delighted in the cunning tricks of reason, in ambivalence and contradiction, in the heady proposition that the opposite of a truth may not be a falsehood, but another truth. Hegel extolled the power of negative thinking. Brecht put it more simply: "Doubt moves mountains."

Perhaps this is why many critics in the West have been baffled or bamboozled by Brecht, and put off by his brazen raising of the red flag, even in a play about Saint Joan. Blasphemous, yes; illogical, no. . . . There is more than a touch in him of the American village atheist secretly reading the Bible in an outhouse.

Like the blue young men in the painting of his friend Picasso, Brecht taught himself to look at the world with two left eyes. This discipline heightened his vision in some directions, but blinded him in many others. His Marxism took him on silly sorties into sophomore economics—"What is the difference, really, between founding a bank and robbing one?" This nonsense mars several of the didactic plays that he wrote while holding a wooden hammer in his left hand.

But when the Hegelian mood takes over, Brecht's poetic insights have the cutting quality of a diamond. Here lies the exciting contradiction of his whole career. His eclecticism gets him a hearing in the West, whereas the Communist East long viewed, and still views, Brecht and his works with glowering suspicion. (p. 111)

Out of [his] constant struggle with himself he made great poetry and ennobled the German language. Today his reputation as poet, as dramatist, as theater man has gone into world orbit. And yet too often in the West, even in West Germany, one of Brecht's fears seems coming true. He is being "theatered down," played as a conventional classic like Schiller, reduced to what he himself derided as "culinary theater." (p. 112)

Brecht [brought] back to the modern stage what the Greek choruses knew, what the Elizabethans practiced, and indeed what the circus does. He turned his actors back toward the audience and thus abolished the "fourth wall" of Stanislavsky and the slice-of-life Method madmen. From faraway Stratford, one hears the applauding murmur of the master. (pp. 112-13)

Brecht taught his actors, sometimes against mulish resistance, to "distance" themselves from their roles, to comment on the character by voice, asides, and gesture, to "act in quotation marks." Although whole volumes have been written about it (including seven by B. B. himself), this is all the famous "V-Effect" really means. And all that Berlin epic theater is. Epic in the sense of narrative, episodic, non-climactic, always taking place in the past. Brecht wanted the audience to see familiar things in this "new light." And it was the audience Brecht was really after.

Did he succeed? Yes and no. . . . The real argument begins with Brecht's anti-empathy and anti-hero leanings. He set out to kill Aristotelian "empathy" in order to make people think in the theater—"I don't write for slobs who want me to warm the cockles of their hearts." Brecht wanted to make people think in the theater—here he is close to Shaw —because he then wanted them to go out and help "change the world." In a good Brecht play, the propagandist is often wrestling with the poet. The delightful, Hegelian paradox is that the poet, who controls the undertones and dramatic asides, invariably wins. Brecht's nonheroes— Mother Courage, Grusche in the *Chalk Circle,* Shen Te in *The Good Woman of Setzuan*—most surely do evoke empathy in the audience. But if Brecht failed . . . , what fine failure. (p. 113)

J. P. O'Donnell, "The Ghost of Brecht," in The Atlantic Monthly *(copyright © 1969 by The Atlantic Monthly Company, Boston, Mass.; reprinted with permission), January, 1969, pp. 110-13.*

It may indeed sound heretical today, but may well be true nevertheless, that posterity might attribute greater importance to Brecht's poems and some of his short stories than to his work as a dramatist; or that of his twenty-one full-length and sixteen shorter plays, and six major adaptations, perhaps no more than half a dozen might stand the test of time. As to his theoretical writings, they have played an important part in creating Brecht's world-wide fame, for they have stimulated discussion about his plays among actors, directors, and critics and have made the study of his work particularly attractive in academic circles. They might, however, also prove the most vulnerable element in Brecht's posthumous reputation, resting, as they do, on the fairly shaky foundations of Brecht's own peculiar view of Marxism, a very questionable conception of the psychological basis of the audience's experience in the theatre, and on many passing fashions of the political and aesthetic climate of his times. (pp. 3-4)

Brecht's career . . . shows a clear pattern of development and its own dialectic: anarchic exuberance (1918-*ca*. 1927) abruptly turning to the opposite extreme, austere self-discipline (*ca*. 1927-1934); a brief interlude of openly propagandist, almost journalistic, work, undertaken to help the good cause of anti-Fascism (1934-38); then, as a synthesis of emotional exuberance, severe Marxist rationalism, and some elements of political special pleading, the great works of the mature phase (1938-47); and, finally, to crown the whole, the period from Brecht's return to Europe to his death (1947-56) when in the theatre he fulfilled his theories by his practice as a great director, while, as a lyrical poet, he reached sublime heights of detached self-knowledge and melancholic self-irony. It is a pattern which bears the marks of the great career of a great man. (p. 8)

The recognition that rebellion to accomplish freedom can only succeed if the rebel's own freedom is ruthlessly suppressed in the discipline of party forms the ironical, yet tragic, *leitmotiv* of Brecht's *oeuvre*. This ambivalence— which must also be seen as a highly characteristic German quality—explains the fascination which the Hegelian dialectic held for Brecht; it is also the basis of his genius as a dramatist. (p. 9)

In their famous essay *On Epic and Dramatic Poetry* (1797) Goethe and Schiller asserted that the "great, essential difference" between the two kinds of literature "lies in the fact that the epic poet presents the event as totally past, while the dramatic poet presents it as totally present." (pp. 11-12)

There can be little doubt that Brecht's entire theory of a truly Marxist theatre springs from his angry reaction against [this] very essay by Goethe and Schiller. . . . In Brecht's theatre the action must *not* take place in a total present, but in a strictly defined historical past—hence the streamers with precise dates for each scene in plays like *Mother Courage;* in Brecht's theatre the spectators must *not* be allowed to identify with the actors on stage to the extent of forgetting their own personalities—hence Brecht's striving for a multitude of *Verfremdungseffekte,* i.e., devices which would prevent identification to the point of annihilating the suspension of disbelief (e.g., the actors stepping out of their parts, or grotesque masks that clearly reveal them to be puppets, etc.). And, finally, the spectator in Brecht's theatre *must be made* to rise to thoughtful contemplation, must be led to detached critical reflection on the play and its meaning. For only a detached spectator could appreciate the *distance* between the historical characters, determined by the social relations of their time on the one hand and contemporary man on the other. . . .

Brecht's theory of "epic—i.e., nondramatic—drama" can thus be seen both as an earnest endeavor to find a Marxist aesthetic of the theatre and as an angry rejection of the official, classical aesthetic codified by those twin deities of the German cultural establishment, Goethe and Schiller. (pp. 13-14)

[Brecht] not only rejected the "classics" and their reactionary aesthetics, he ridiculed them by making them the target of a stream of overt and covert *parody*. And he went for inspiration and example to the alternative sources of a German dramatic tradition: to Baroque dramatists like Gryphius; the Austro-Bavarian folk theatre, whose last living exponent, the great beer-hall comedian Karl Valentin, became Brecht's mentor and friend; and above all to Büchner, a dramatist whose genius is today generally acknowledged to have been at least equal, if not superior, to that of Goethe or Schiller. (p. 15)

Brecht's very first completed play [*Baal*] already contains that characteristic tension that will dominate his entire *oeuvre*: the tension between a desire to drift in the glorious, passive stream of life, on the one hand, and, on the other, a yearning for rationality which rejects that oceanic feeling with its passivity and amoral yielding to sensual impulse. (p. 16)

In the first, anarchic phase of Brecht's career, it is the sensuous, emotional, uncontrolled, passive attitude, the yielding to impulse, which dominates, while the rational, disciplined, activist attitude merely appears in the undertone of satire, mockery, ridicule with which the impulsive demeanor of the main character is portrayed. . . .

Emotion/Reason—Selfishness/Discipline—Chaos/Order, these three polarities sum up the dialectic of Brecht's life and work. (p. 17)

The change from the anarchic to the didactic phase of Brecht's development is clearly marked in the evolution of his language. The Büchneresque exuberance of daring metaphors strung together in chains of image-laden main clauses yields to laconic severity and sparseness of expression. . . . (p. 18)

In the great plays of his years of exile Brecht's style has lost the austerity of his didactic phase; and his characters, who had been reduced to the bare essentials (reminiscent of the highly stylized characters of French classical tragedy, who also lack all individual little human touches), again acquired a rich texture of personal idiosyncrasies. Nevertheless, these plays remain *didactic* in the sense that they are conceived as *parables*, models of human situations, cited, like the parables in the New Testament, not for their own intrinsic interest, but because of their general applicability to *other* human situations and problems. Galilei stands for all scientists who have submitted to the dictates of political au-

thority (and for the atomic scientists of our time in particular); Mother Courage for all little people who do not realize that, deriving their small profit from war or the preparation of war, they are themselves guilty of causing the death of their children and the destruction of their country (as the little people of Hitler's Germany did); Puntila—evil when sober, human when drunk—is an emblem and exemplar of the irreconcilability between capitalistic attitudes and genuine humanity; while Shen Te, the good woman of Setzuan, demonstrates the impossibility of goodness in a world where survival depends on commercial success. The greatest of these plays, *The Caucasian Chalk Circle*, quite openly uses the parable form; it illustrates the solution of a problem which is posed in the prologue: who has the better right to a tract of land in a socialist country—a fairly mythically drawn Soviet Union—the legal owners or those who cultivate the land to the best purpose? . . .

Brecht's use of the parable form expresses another aspect of his revolt against the state of German culture and the German theatre in his youth: as much as he rejected the grandiloquent classicism of the followers of Goethe and Schiller (and, to a lesser extent, of the masters themselves), he also detested the naturalistic theatre which had become dominant in Germany at the turn of the century. All of Brecht's dramatic work can be seen as a refutation of naturalism, the use of the stage to reproduce photographically accurate slices of life. (pp. 19-20)

The quotability of gestures is a key concept in Brecht's aesthetics: for Brecht the essence of art, of poetry, is, indeed, the fact that through its perfection of form, through its concentration of thought, poetry enables truth to become transmittable, accessible to the mass of people. But a merely *verbal* quotation merely transmits an abstract version of the truth. The importance of drama lies, precisely, in its concreteness, in its ability to embody actual models of *human behavior*. Instead of merely hearing people quote the noble words from some play by Shakespeare or Schiller, Brecht wanted them to repeat wholesome, rational, and noble *actions* they might have seen on the stage. Hence his desire to create *quotable gestures*, in his narrative prose as well as in his plays. (p. 23)

Much of German poetry—and therefore also of the poetic language of drama—revels in grand philosophical abstractions and flowery, nebulous concepts. Brecht not only rejected these bombastic abstractions, he also set himself against the subjectivity, the sentimental self-involvement, of the lyrical tradition. (p. 26)

Brecht's *Hauspostille* is typical of his first exuberant, anarchic phase. The ballads it contains celebrate a kind of wild acceptance of nature and its processes of growth and decay. . . . There is no introspection in these poems; even the few which deal with Brecht's personal life treat of him objectively, in the third person almost; there are no elaborate similes: the images are put before the reader directly, starkly, and stand by and for themselves. Formally there is still a good deal of artifice and elaboration: ballad metres, even sonnets, abound. (p. 27)

Brecht's later poetry is more cerebral, severe, and economical. . . . [His] best late poems are short, almost epigrammatic: they speak of the tribulations of exile, the sorrows of the poet's return to his ravaged homeland, aging, and death. They are among the finest poems in the German language. They reveal the real Brecht behind the façade of cheerful support for the East German regime; a wistful, disillusioned man, dreaming of the landscape of his childhood in Augsburg, praising the humble pleasures of homely food, cheese, bread, and cool beer. There even creeps into this private, late poetry a note of wry rejection of the hollow claims of the totalitarian state to which he had committed his fortunes. (p. 28)

Poetry thus holds a central position in any consideration of Brecht as a dramatist as well as a prose-writer. (p. 29)

Brecht's endeavors to create a truly Marxist aesthetic of theatre are brilliant and stimulating and have given rise to endless misunderstandings. Above all, it must be kept in mind that these writings do not present a unitary, finished theory but are, themselves, the documentation of a constant process of changing and developing thought. (p. 33)

[It] is Brecht's unique achievement that he has reconciled two traditions in German literature which had been kept in different compartments before him, a state of affairs which had had most unfortunate effects on the cultural life of Germany. In Brecht the rough, plebeian, popular tradition and the sophisticated, academic, refined, respectable tradition have come together. Thanks to Brecht's achievement the work of the Austro-Bavarian folk comedians and the plays of the *poètes maudits* of the eighteenth and early nineteenth centuries appear in a new light and have assumed a new importance. And what is more: by introducing his new rough, popular, almost dialect tone, Brecht succeeded in forging a new German stage idiom, which is neither the highly refined, but unnatural *Bühnendeutsch* (stage German) of the one nor the broad vernacular regional speech of the other tradition. This is an achievement which has greatly eased the difficulties of the generation of young postwar dramatists and poets in Germany. (p. 45)

> *Martin Esslin, in his* Bertolt Brecht *(Columbia Essays on Modern Writers Pamphlet No. 42; copyright © 1969 Columbia University Press; reprinted by permission of the publisher), Columbia University Press, 1969.*

Brecht was writing against the heritage of the Naturalist theatre, with its concept of the overwhelming natural and social determinants of the fate of man and the virtual futility of any resistance. He started to write as the carnage of World War I sank into the general mind, a sufficient proof as many thought (including a good number of writers like Dos Passos) that human freedom was indeed nonsense. . . .

Brecht's earliest plays . . . reflect the Naturalist spirit. Their "scientific" aloofness to the aims of human actions, their "dispassionate" refusal to believe that any value but consciousness itself has any true value, are but a special and highly talented version of the "moment" which constituted the crisis in theatre, in social life and in thought.

Yet Brecht's thought and vitality already edged beyond the Naturalist limits. To adopt a clinical stance was a means of breaking away from the fruitless grappling that *In the Jungle of Cities* depicted. And if Brecht's characters were not yet as lucid as they were to become, nonetheless they abounded with appetites that burst the narrow limits of action appropriate to the Naturalist state of mind. Then too, Brecht was already for having signs put up where his plays

were acted, urging spectators: "Stop that romantic gaping." Already, he realized that consistency of thought meant that the relationship with the audience, too, had to change.

Here I believe is the source of Brecht's stature which makes him matter to us so much despite all obstacles. He was supremely intelligent among the modern playwrights; he was at the forefront of *concretely* solving the intellectual riddles of our time, as perhaps only playwrights have the ultimate artistic opportunity to be. Of course, like his earliest dramatic hero Baal he, too, could be fantastically charming. But he realized that the ultimate charm of all is—freedom. If Brecht didn't give us many "positive" heroes, he nonetheless infused his creations in myriad big and little ways with the consciousness that meant Naturalism had been superseded.

We needn't be victims. That conviction is at the core of Brecht's allure. (p. 501)

> *Lee Baxandall, "Brecht Returns as a Classic," in* The Nation *(copyright 1971 by the Nation Associates, Inc.), April 19, 1971, pp. 501-03.*

A Man's a Man marks the beginning of a course of development which Brecht [followed] for the remainder of his career as a playwright. Although one will still find, like an almost invisible watermark, the haunting despair of spiritual isolation, Brecht's dominant concern [in and after this play was] to create a theatrical form capable of expressing the conflicts of social personalities as they live within a collective society. His ultimate achievement [was] *Mother Courage*. For Mother Courage is the perfect embodiment of the social personality; she is a woman whose very stature is the result of her being able to sacrifice her individual humanity to the collective system of which she is a part and which she affirms to the end. *Mother Courage* is articulate testimony that to destroy the humanist concept of the individual does not necessarily mean a loss of stature in the theatre, nor the disappearance of dramatic conflict. Rather there is a new kind of character and new kinds of conflict, and Brecht's theatre [provides] the forms and language to express them.

The subject of Brecht's Marxism always seems to create problems. I can think of very few critics who agree. . . . I do not believe that Brecht's temperament was political in any activist way, nor do I believe that he was spiritually attuned to the methods and practices of the Communist party. On the other hand, I am convinced that Marxism did fulfill Brecht's "over-powering impulse to construct a system which will enable him to feel that he does not stand alone but is intimately associated with some force or group infinitely more powerful and significant than himself." I see Brecht's embrace of Marxism as a strategy of despair and while the strategy may have worked successfully, it was nonetheless an act of will imposed by the intellect upon the sadness, the loneliness, the sense of emptiness which were the ground of Brecht's being. (pp. 216-17)

Now while Marx certainly played a major role in the nineteenth-century "re-evaluation of values" which brought about the modernist revolution in the theatre, the modernist view of the irrational is completely incompatible with Marxist thought. (p. 217)

For Brecht, the idea that there are in nature (including human nature) hidden and uncontrollable forces which can dominate the mind has no objective reality whatsoever. Indeed, such forces have no real existence. For him . . . "apparent chaos exists only because our head is not a perfect one and therefore that which remains outside it we call the irrational." Since we cannot know it rationally, it *seems* chaotic; but this "remainder is irrational only in respect to the capacity of our mind for knowing." Thus, while Brecht does not believe in the perfectibility of man (Marx believed that only the powers of reason can master the natural world), he does believe that the mind's range can be stretched. This distinction is crucial because all Brecht's theatrical theories are based upon it.

For example, it is the basis of his anti-empathic theories of production and explains his controversial Alienation-effect. Here Brecht, although he was passionately antipsychological, got his clue from Freud. Just as psychiatric therapy —and I think it is very significant that psychiatrists were first known as "alienists"—seeks to detach us from ourselves so we can begin to see ourselves in a more objective way (almost as an object), so Brecht believed that if the theatre was "to stretch the mind's range" it must not encourage the spectator to identify with the action but must show it so the audience can come to know itself better. . . . So throughout his plays, Brecht is trying to isolate the inconspicuous moral drama, to estrange it, to set it in a sharp light, so that it is not taken for granted before it falls, dragged down by the weight of society. (pp. 218-19)

Seen in this light, *Mother Courage* is not a pacifist tract, nor is Brecht the playwright a polemicist. His most daring achievement in this play is his use of war as an all-encompassing metaphor for the modern world, and his presentation of Mother Courage, who lives off the war and continues to exist because of it, as the symbol of the ordinary human condition. However, the play is not an attack on war, but an attempt to show all aspects of that war which is the central fact of the contemporary human condition. From the ironical speech of the Top Sergeant on the "horrors" of peace in the first scene, it is very clear that Brecht is very much aware of the negative and destructive aspects of our warring condition, but other parts of the play make it equally clear that war does make money, which we hold dear; war does create courage, which we admire; war does support the established institutions of society, which we want to maintain; and war does promote a sense of love and brotherhood, which we find valuable. As the play ends, Mother Courage is seen trudging after another regiment. In her (our) circumstances she cannot do otherwise. The tragedy of the situation, indeed, if it is a tragedy, is that her perception of what is wrong cannot alter her situation as it traditionally does in tragedy. In *Mother Courage* the situation completely dominates the individual. Brecht was in all likelihood not very happy about this, but he has been one of the few playwrights in our time who was capable of facing up to the realities of life in an industrialized collective society without having to abdicate his responsibility as an artist. (pp. 219-20)

Brecht sees that man is changed by the forces of the world outside him. And it follows that he must reject the characteristics of the traditional inner-directed drama in the Aristotelian mode. (p. 220)

Brecht's epic form . . . is his way of expressing the complexity, multiplicity, variety, and even the contradictions of a collective world while still maintaining that unity of form which is essential for art. He uses its episodic structure as a kind of counterpoint of estrangement for the purpose of stretching the limits of the audience's mind. Finally, it is a form that seeks to achieve the capacity of the novel (the literary mode which emerged out of the industrial revolution and is probably best suited to express our times) in dealing with the central issues of the modern world, without sacrificing the immediacy and force of the actor on a stage. (p. 223)

When viewed in the context of an industrialized collective society, Brecht believed the actions of . . . "old-fashioned" heroes tend to be little more than the empty posturings of the foolish, the headstrong, or the selfish. Genuine goodness, such as Kattrin's in *Mother Courage,* is equally irrelevant. While her behavior in the play seems to have a mute nobility about it, Brecht makes it very clear that her dramatic function in the play is to reveal the futility of the instinct to goodness and the impossibility of its surviving in a world in which the evergrowing cult of the celebrity, with its tendency to value charm without character, showmanship without real ability, bodies without minds, and information without wisdom, celebrates the triumph of ordinariness. . . . Thus, beginning with *A Man's a Man,* the idea that the assertion of individuality in the name of virtue is the chief cause of human failure in a collective society is a recurring and dominant theme in almost all of Brecht's plays. However, it should be pointed out that the Marxist playwright Brecht never completely represses the lonely poet Brecht. . . . For while it is true that he sees [some] characters as . . . failures because they give in to their human feelings and good instincts, paradoxically, he also believes that to be overwhelmed by the gratuitous impulse to do a good act is the beginning of freedom. (pp. 224-25)

As a poet he put his trust in words. He believed in the power of verse to deal with the contradictions of reality. He knew that by virtue of elision, concentration, and obliqueness, poetry can create an image of life which is far denser and more complex than that of prose. And, finally, he was aware that his new vision of reality as dialectical had to be expressed in poetry, for only poetry can advance discordant persuasions simultaneously and still retain that gestural quality which is essential to the theatre. Thus it may very well turn out that Brecht's greatest contribution as a poet in the theatre was to create a poetry of the collective. (pp. 228-29)

His life and his work were always in a state of dialectical tension. He rejected nature and emotional feelings overtly expressed and yet the most moving and powerful scenes in his plays are pervaded by the sense of them. He once told Max Frisch that he liked the large picture window in his home which looked out onto the Alps only because it gave lots of light; nonetheless, he chose to live in a house that had a magnificent view. Brecht in his last years was the high priest of collectivist drama, but he never genuflected to communism and as long as he lived he never allowed his theatre to become a shrine. His spiritual makeup always had enough heresy in it to permit the poet in him to work against the grain of orthodoxy. There is no doubt that he embraced the realities of a collective society and sought to find the language, forms, and characters that would best express such a world; but everything he wrote reveals a profound kind of rebellion against such acceptance. (p. 229)

Robert W. Corrigan, "Bertolt Brecht: Poet of the Collective," in his The Theatre in Search of a Fix *(copyright © 1973 by Robert W. Corrigan; reprinted by permission of Delacorte Press), Delacorte Press, 1973, pp. 210-29.*

Brecht was never interested in the "soul," even as a concept, or in the self apart from its situation among others. Or, more accurately, his earliest plays lying somewhat aside, his interest in the self centered on its apprehensible, one could almost say "reportable," qualities, not its mysteries, and particularly on its behavior in social and objective contexts. Above all, he cared about the self's capacity to endure (and the cost of such endurance) and to be "happy," which, as we shall see, he considered its natural condition, thwarted by the political and economic structures of the world. Thus, as Walter Sokel has observed, Brecht "does not begin with the individual but with the problem." His dramatic characters operate in an arena designed for the exhibition and struggle of public issues, transformed by his art into metaphors for the difficulties of personal, though never idiosyncratic, existence itself. (p. 195)

What made Brecht suspect to the end in the eyes of official Communism was precisely his subordination of dogma to perspective, his imaginative use of Marxism as a method of inquiry rather than a storehouse of conviction. In a sense he was far truer to Marx's spirit than were the commissars, since, unlike them, he never used dialectical materialism as a means of confirming assumptions about the world or for the validation of power.

For Brecht, Marxian dialectics was at one and the same time a double mode of perception and a way of seeing the doubleness of the world. It was his means, wielded more explicitly at first and then assimilated into the very fabric of his imaginative method, of becoming able to deal with the perennial gap between men and their social organizations, between values and power, between, in its most profound formulation, human desire and ontological fact. (p. 214)

Brecht's consciousness . . . moved beyond tragedy, or eliminated it entirely as a mode of dramatic vision. Suffused now in politics and economic theory, his notion of aesthetic reality having become increasingly functional, he wishes now not simply to understand the world or even, in Ibsen's manner, to perceive it without illusion, but, like Marx, to alter it. (p. 215)

Because of his pragmatic approach to theory as well as practice, there is no single work in which Brecht's ideas about the theater can be definitively studied and no period in which they can be said to have become fixed into doctrine. (pp. 215-16)

Still, the broad elements of Brecht's theatrical ideas persist without radical change throughout his writings, so that it is a sort of intellectual mug's game to try, as a number of commentators continue to do, to catch him in contradictions or make him appear, through chronological investigations that focus on details, to have been eclectic, inconsistent, or capricious. The fundamentally unchanging constituents of his thought, the basis of his unparalleled influence on the contemporary theater, are these: that the stage ought to instigate consciousness and not lull or confirm it; that drama ought not to be a surrogate for experience but an experience in itself; that acting ought to be the physical or "gestural" expression of consciousness and not a species of emotional enticement.

Out of these convictions—or, really, these intuitions fortified into convictions—Brecht elaborated the particularities of his theatrical theory and practice. They were implacable yet supple too. They remained always subject to the test of experience, and Brecht remained ready to learn from his own temporary dogmas. The central Brechtian terms— "epic theater," "alienation effect," "gestus," etc.— entered his vocabulary, for example, as "attempts" (his own word for them) and not as completed pieces of wisdom, and he was ready to change or scrap them as the need showed itself. What he never abandoned was his vision of the theater as a scene of active consciousness, a needle against slumber. (p. 216)

Richard Gilman, "Brecht," in his The Making of Modern Drama: A Study of Büchner, Ibsen, Strindberg, Chekhov, Pirandello, Brecht, Beckett, Handke *(reprinted with the permission of Farrar, Straus & Giroux, Inc.; copyright © 1972, 1973, 1974 by Richard Gilman), Farrar, Straus, 1974, pp. 190-233.*

Brecht once called [*The Measures Taken*] "a limbering-up exercise for those athletes of the spirit that good dialecticians must be.". . .

For every interpreter . . . who claims the moral of the play is that the end justifies the means, there is another who claims that the moral is to prove the opposite. For every interpreter who believes the moral is that ultimate justice for all takes precedence over attention to every individual injustice, there is another who believes the moral is that communism is ultimately unjust to everybody. For every interpreter who sees the play (written in 1930) as a "forewarning of Stalin's purge trials," there is another who claims that "the only moral of this play is that Trotsky must be eliminated." (p. 699)

[It is] the basic contradictions of the play . . . that explain its intellectual appeal and make it what Brecht called "a learning play." (p. 700)

Rose Mary Mechem, in The Nation *(copyright 1975 by the Nation Associates, Inc.), June 7, 1975.*

Brecht on the run from the Nazis, with his combative and barbed poems, is . . . a stirring figure. Brecht *in situ* as a Communist, with his combative and barbed poems, becomes, as the years go by and Nazism recedes while Communism doesn't, if not a sinister, at any rate a suspect figure. . . .

Brecht's poetry is less likely than the plays to arouse . . . suspicions. Aside from the simple-minded propagandist pieces . . . and some outbreaks of silly bad temper, it has other weaknesses: notably repetitiousness, the vain, over-insistent effort to make minority art look like *vox populi*, and what we might call an excessive fluency in laconicism. What mostly kept Brecht out of danger, and what is most important for and in him, is that—whether or not you share his attitudes—he talked about his times, he was plugged firmly into reality. This kept him, mostly, on the right, decent path. It also saved him from the mere vapid egotism of poets who pride themselves on their concern with the so-called 'eternal verities', while, in effect, concerning themselves narcissistically with themselves. (No objection or offence is intended to the said verities, who, like Brecht's gods, tend to evince themselves in disguise.) But perhaps this is to say no more than Brecht's favourite slogan says: 'The truth is concrete.' And not one's own features 'interestingly' reflected in a pool of still water. (p. 576)

D. J. Enright, "Echt Brecht," in The Listener *(© British Broadcasting Corp., 1976; reprinted by permission of D. J. Enright), May 6, 1976, pp. 576-77.*

If Bertolt Brecht's artistic personality—guarded, self-questioning, tensed against effusiveness—did not inhibit easy affirmations, one could simply assert that [the] English edition of more than 500 of his poems [*Poems 1913-1956*] is a literary landmark. . . .

[Brecht] enters as the Augsburg Rimbaud, the Villon of Bavaria singing raucous cabaret ballads about the harlot Evelyn Roe, the parricide Jacob Apfelbock, thumbing his nose at God but treating nature with the respect due to an antagonist who will outlast man. Already the strands of his mature poetry are evident: the vigorous, even kitschy language of ballads about pirates and shipwrecks and boozing which will be refined into the songs of *The Threepenny Opera* and *Mahogonny*, the ferocious depiction of impassive natural forces and the sobriety of Lutheran-style chorales and pseudo-devotional verses which will later acquire a political content. There is another surprising voice, apocalyptic and sometimes almost Beckettian, in the 'Psalms' in which he speaks of love and the power of natural appetite. (p. 614)

[His] first real advance towards a new poetic idiom occurs in the city poems of the Twenties. After the hedonism and luxuriance of Augsburg, Berlin's brutal massiveness shook him into an entirely different kind of utterance: spindly, spare, austere poems constructed like pincers. 'This Babylonian confusion of words / Results from their being the language / Of men who are going down,' he says. . . .

Brecht began to study Marxism in 1927 and his poetry of the Thirties manifests a different kind of impersonality. Agitational choruses for workers' choirs, Homeric accounts of episodes in the Soviet Union, satirical anti-Hitler hymns, militant lullabies—his poetry pared itself to become immediately utilitarian. But the sense of a resistant self determined to preserve quality and idiosyncracy against the great levelling persists, and grows stronger as Brecht approaches the next endurance test, exile.

From 1934 to 1937, from Scandinavia to California, Brecht was in exile, and wrote his greatest poetry. The sense of tension and tightly-coiled contradiction between mask and face, the pressure in the voice of the man 'who wanted to prepare the ground for friendliness and could not himself be friendly' is screwed up to its highest pitch. And yet the precision of his craft, harnessing the harshest insights into

crystalline patterns based on 'gestus' (a scrupulous attention to the underlying attitude behind any utterance and its precise rhythmic and syntactical form—perhaps Brecht's greatest legacy to poets now), produced works of stoic equanimity. . . .

There is unbearable pathos and fierce denunciation; yet both are constantly tempered by a refusal to overvalue the importance of his suffering or his ability to effect change through his writing.

This modesty—the fruit of his Marxist self-abnegation, of the hard-won artlessness of his forms, and of that persona of the wise Chinese sage distanced from the swirl of events which colours so many of his best poems—is Brecht's distinctive voice in any pantheon of socialist poets. Its realism will always set him apart from the bullying loud-hailers, the hysterical prophets, the agonised lyricists foreseeing heroic martyrdom for the cause. (p. 615)

Michael Kustow, "Exile's Return," in New Statesman *(© 1976 The Statesman & Nation Publishing Co. Ltd.), May 7, 1976, pp. 614-15.*

Threepenny Opera is surely one of the masterworks of the 20th-century theatre. It is peculiarly ravishing: it enchants with sweet sickness. Its impudent snarl delights—most strangely. It is defiant and yet very nearly funereal. The mournful alternates with the heroic. Heartbroken, it manages to laugh. The wretchedness of Germany after World War I, its baleful future, its hope and failure are all here. Beneath the mockery and challenge, it presages the approaching defeat. There is a sense of doom in it, yet it inspires elation by a consciousness of the living moment. It is a play of befouled time struggling to express its malady and to overcome it. . . .

As certain artists in the past sought refuge from dark days of social and personal disease by turning to the Church, Brecht found salvation in a humanistic Marxism. But in 1928, when *The Threepenny Opera* was produced, he was not yet there; he was intellectually convinced of his dawning belief but not yet possessed by it. Much of his skepticism (never altogether dispelled) and a masochistic anguish which the war's aftermath had instilled in him still remained. This ambivalence is what makes the play an enduring work. It is not "propaganda," though the political Right as well as the Left saw it as such and made its first production an occasion for scandal and riot.

If without preconception one leaves oneself open to the full effect of *The Threepenny Opera*, one senses that Brecht was himself infected with the romantic glow of decay, even as he reviled it and aspired to liberate himself from it. Hence the pervasive irony of the work. . . . (p. 636)

Harold Clurman, in The Nation *(copyright 1976 by the Nation Associates, Inc.), May 22, 1976.*

Robert Bridges

1844-1930

English poet, dramatist, and critic. Bridges was trained as a physician but retired from practice in 1882 to devote himself to literature. A Victorian who by choice remained apart from the aesthetic movements of his day, Bridges was a classicist. His experimentation with eighteenth-century classical forms culminated in *The Testament of Beauty*, generally acknowledged as his masterpiece. He succeeded Alfred Austin as Poet Laureate in 1913 and was active in the Society of Pure English, which was founded largely through his efforts. He had an important friendship and correspondence with Gerard Manley Hopkins; his edition of Hopkins's poems is considered a major contribution to English literature.

PRINCIPAL WORKS

Poems (poetry) 1873
The Growth of Love (poetry) 1876
Poems by the Author of 'The Growth of Love' (poetry) 1879
Prometheus the Firegiver (drama) 1883
Poems (poetry) 1884
Eros & Psyche (poetry) 1885
Shorter Poems (poetry) 1890-94
The Humours of the Court (poetry) 1893
John Keats, A Critical Essay (essay) 1895
Poems of Gerard Manley Hopkins (editor) 1918
October and Other Poems, with Occasional Verses on the War (poetry) 1920
New Verse (poetry) 1925
The Testament of Beauty (poetry) 1929
Three Friends (memoirs) 1932

Some day the few among us who care for poetry more than any temporal thing, and who believe that its delights cannot be perfect when we read it alone in our rooms and long for one to share its delights, but that they might be perfect in the theatre, when we share them friend with friend, lover with beloved, will persuade a few idealists to seek out the lost art of speaking, and seek out ourselves the lost art, that is perhaps nearest of all arts to eternity, the subtle art of listening. When that day comes we will talk much of Mr. Bridges; for did he not write scrupulous, passionate poetry to be sung and to be spoken, when there were few to sing and as yet none to speak? There is one play especially, *The*

Return of Ulysses, which we will praise for perfect after its kind, the kind of our new drama of wisdom, for it moulds into dramatic shape, and with as much as possible of literal translation, those closing books of the *Odyssey* which are perhaps the most perfect poetry of the world, and compels that great tide of song to flow through delicate dramatic verse, with little abatement of its own leaping and clamorous speed. (p. 199)

The poet who writes best in the Shakespearian manner is a poet with a circumstantial and instinctive mind, who delights to speak with strange voices and to see his mind in the mirror of nature; while Mr. Bridges, like most of us today, has a lyrical and meditative mind, and delights to speak with his own voice and to see nature in the mirror of his mind. In reading his plays in a Shakespearian manner, I find that he is constantly arranging his story in such-and-such a way because he has read that the persons he is writing of did such-and-such things, and not because his soul has passed into the soul of their world and understood its unchangeable destinies. His *Return of Ulysses* is admirable in beauty, because its classical gravity of speech, which does not, like Shakespeare's verse, desire the vivacity of common life, purifies and subdues all passion into lyrical and meditative ecstasies, and because the unity of place and time in the late acts compels a logical rather than instinctive procession of incidents; and if the Shakespearian *Nero: Second Part* approaches it in beauty and in dramatic power, it is because it eddies about Nero and Seneca, who had both, to a great extent, lyrical and meditative minds. Had Mr. Bridges been a true Shakespearian, the pomp and glory of the world would have drowned that subtle voice that speaks amid our heterogeneous lives of a life lived in obedience to a lonely and distinguished ideal. (pp. 200-01)

There is poetry that is like the white light of noon, and poetry that has the heaviness of woods, and poetry that has the golden light of dawn or of sunset; and I find in the poetry of Mr. Bridges in the plays, but still more in the lyrics, the pale colours, the delicate silence, the low murmurs of cloudy country days, when the plough is in the earth, and the clouds darkening towards sunset; and had I the great gift of praising, I would praise it as I would praise these things. (p. 202)

W. B. Yeats, "The Return of Ulysses" (1896), in his Essays and Introductions *(re-*

*printed with permission of Macmillan Pub-
lishing Co., Inc.; © 1961 by Mrs. W. B.
Yeats; and in Canada reprinted by permission of Miss Anne Yeats, M. B. Yeats and
the Macmillan Co. of London and Basing-
stoke), Macmillan, 1961, pp. 198-202.*

[No] English poet now living carries on the great tradition
of English song, as previously upheld by Wordsworth and
Tennyson, with a finer sense of the poet's mission in a blatant age than does this modest man of science and accomplished classical scholar.

We call him "Dr. Bridges" because it is only courteous to
give a man the title to which professional distinction entitles
him. . . . We notice, however, that certain recent comment
has used the title of Dr. Bridges for purposes of malicious
emphasis, and as indicative of a sort of veiled resentment of
the choice of a poet so little known to the average reader,
and so serenely unconcerned with the issues upon which a
poet, to secure popularity, must now make his appeal to the
general public. For the new laureate is neither spectacular
nor freakish; he does not beat the big drum of the jingo, nor
does he seek to make capital out of whatever form of sentimentalism happens to be current. He is not a poet of imperialism or of democracy; he is neither a society poet nor a
slum poet; he is simply an artist whose guiding spirit is aestheticism and whose work is conceived *sub specie aeternitatis.* He writes of the enduring themes in the enduring
manner, which of course invites the attack of horny-eyed
philistines everywhere, and earns him the titles of old fogy
and conservative and exploiter of old-world themes in outworn forms of expression. (pp. 69-70)

The . . . modern idea of the [laureateship] was that of
Queen Victoria, who regarded it "as the official recognition
of a distinguished poet, sufficiently susceptible to the form
and pressure of the time to be proclaimed without absurdity
as its poetical interpreter." We quote from "The Saturday
Review," which goes on to say: "It is not now a Laureate's business to celebrate his time. All we require for the
office is a poet conspicuously distinguished among his fellows upon whom an official decoration will not indeco-
rously sit." Dr. Bridges answers almost perfectly to this
requirement. In his selection the choice lay between the
abiding elements of beauty in the poetic art and those
ephemeral characteristics which the fashion of the day or
the caprices of popular taste may emphasize, and the
choice has fallen upon a poet of the right type, even if not
upon a poet of the rank of his immediate predecessors. (p.
70)

"Robert Bridges, Poet Laureate," in The
Dial *(copyright, 1913, by The Dial Publishing Company, Inc.; reprinted by permission of J. S. Watson, Jr. and Scofield
Thayer), August, 1913 (and reprinted by
Kraus Reprint Corporation, 1966), pp. 69-
71.*

The poetry of Robert Bridges seems often the most natural
in the world, and sometimes the most cunning in artifice.
And that is because, using words loosely, we hardly stay to
remember that poetry is an artifice, and that no one naturally uses the forms of verse for common speech. But at
least one may say that poetry has never come more near to
common speech and yet remained indubitably poetry, than
in some of Mr. Bridges's blank verse. (p. 319)

His work is of an unusual simplicity, and of a very high
rhythmical quality. It is free from inversion (that tempting
trick of much verse even of to-day), and depends for its
impression upon the sense of life conveyed by the naturalness of its movement, by its responsiveness to the thought.
Verse becomes, here if anywhere, a natural form of speech.
But to say natural is not to say commonplace. . . . (p. 324)

True that the appearance of naturalness in verse is not always easily contrived. Mr. Bridges is a profound student of
questions of prosody, and has for many years been credited
with a knowledge of music unusual, for its intimacy, among
English poets. Such knowledge, such expertry, forms a
great advantage. He brings to the writing of verse a rare
skill in the judgment of sounds and words, and an ear for
delicate cadences. . . . To say that Mr. Bridges is a greater
poet than Tennyson would be gratuitous folly, but he assuredly has a finer sense of rhythm. The rhythm of his
verse is like that of willows caressing and caressed by the
wind, or like the waves' unmonotonous unceasing tossing.
Keeping as Mr. Bridges does mainly to the fair and temperate zone of passion, and shrinking from excess as from
blasphemy (which indeed for thoughtful artists it is), he
nevertheless proves his medium capable of dark and serious
things, as in *Palicio,* or lofty, as in *Prometheus the Firegiver,* or tender, as in the beautiful *Return of Ulysses,* or
familiar, as in *The Humours of the Court.* But whether passionate or lofty, tender or familiar, Mr. Bridges's blank
verse always appears a *natural* form of speech, even though
you know that such fine, felicitous work is never achieved
but by the vigilant cunning of a fine mind. (pp. 326-27)

Of the matter of Mr. Bridges's dramatic writings I do not
propose to speak in detail. He has written two plays upon
Nero, others upon historical events, as *The Christian Captives* and *Palicio;* others again where his scholarship has
served him finely, namely, *Achilles in Scyros, Prometheus
the Firegiver* and *The Return of Ulysses;* and two comedies
standing apart from all the rest and from each other—*The
Humours of the Court* and *The Feast of Bacchus.* The last
named is partly translated from Terence, and is the most
excellently pleasant of all these plays. To suit the easy
comic spirit the author has used a line of six stresses full of
those nice adjustments which Mr. Bridges so happily contrives. The result is a play as truly comic as Molière's
plays, in a medium of familiar verse which preserves faithfully the exquisite commonplace and sly humour of the various characters. (p. 329)

These plays by Mr. Bridges . . . are full of human feeling,
full of wise speech upon near and dear things; and that
speech has the natural free rhythm of unmistakable, spontaneous poetry. (p. 331)

[The] sonnet-sequence, *The Growth of Love,* . . . may be
taken as an introduction to the lyrical poems. The sonnets
are among the earliest of their author's work. . . . Taken
strictly as sonnets they are sometimes irregular in form, but
throughout their beauty is singular. There is a pure morning
air over them. They have not been made, but sung while
swallows flew and shrilled. In so many sonnets there is
stiffness, perhaps wilful, or conscious dignity. Mr.
Bridges's are lyrical cries in sonnet form. . . . There is, it
must be said, little evidence of the "growth" of love in the
sonnets grouped under this title. Love appears full-grown
with nothing tristful, nothing passionate; love as the natural
fulfilment of human life is their note. . . . (pp. 331-33)

It would not be incorrect to say . . . that there is nothing remarkable in Mr. Bridges's lyrics, and to add smartly that they are remarkable in that. They have distinction by virtue of their manner, but not only by virtue of that. And as for the sum of their meaning, to ascertain that you must try to gauge the measure of their intention, the depth of their suggestion. I do not mean that there are any well-hidden treasures of wisdom in the remote chambers of these poems: I do not think there are. There is a way that some writers have of giving their readers flash-light revelations, sudden surprises, lights the more vivid from the surrounding darkness. Mr. Bridges does not do this. His meaning is plain, his emotions not curiously refined, his ideas not very often subtilized. But nevertheless there *is* more than the separate meanings, or than the sum-total of those separate meanings: there is the spirit in which he confronts the form of time and the spectre of eternity. Let the metrical diversity be as wonderful as you please, the separate "notes" as charming, the intentions as wise: yet these can make but faint claim on our serious thoughts if there is nothing more.

Well, one thing that is to be remarked is the essential joyousness of life as viewed in the lyrics. Joy pours in with sun and frost, clouds and dews, sleep and dreams. Usually it is a "passionless passion" that glows in these beautifully fashioned braziers, sometimes a "solemn joy"; but it yet burns undiminishing. (pp. 333-35)

[He] has an earnest and bright love of England, and of her land as being hers and a part of nature. A pure and steady lamp of devotion shines in his reserved unemphatic verse. His feeling for the earth and waters of England is, in truth, filial in its affectionateness; and his renderings of English landscape—making for me the most complete of all the delight of his verse—are as pure and direct and as truly impassioned as those of Gray and Arnold, and only less moving than Wordsworth's. (p. 338)

> *John Freeman, "Robert Bridges," in his* The Moderns: Essays in Literary Criticism, *R. Scott, 1916 (and reprinted by Books for Libraries Press, Inc., 1967), pp. 319-41.*

Throughout the war, and since the war was won, Mr. Bridges has performed a service to which this history [of laureateship] affords no parallel. The war poems of former laureates have sometimes fostered, have usually been content to echo, popular feeling. Jubilation over England's successes, reprobation of her enemies, have been the sufficient theme. But during the years since 1914, the fluctuating impulses that have found vent in a plethora of ephemeral war poetry have passed the laureate by. Neither the initial glamours of the stay-at-home poets nor the subsequent disillusionments of the soldier poets colour his pages. Mr. Bridges is not a 'popular' poet, and he is totally indifferent to the popular notion that the laureate of the moment should be the versifier of what the public is thinking—at the moment. He has not rushed into print, as, for example, Austin did on the occasion of the Jameson Raid; but an examination of *October and Other Poems* amply disproves the accusation of 'unworthy inactivity'. Between the stirring words of 'Wake up, England' (August, 1914) and the heart-searching 'Britannia Victrix' of November, 1918, are thirteen war-poems of memorable quality and substantial length, besides several slighter pieces. If the point were worth arguing, it might be observed that this is a larger number of poems immediately inspired by national events than Tennyson produced during the first seven years of his laureateship—a period which included the Crimean war and the Indian Mutiny; but the public to whom mere facility in rhyming and versing must be the right describing note to know a poet by is, fortunately, not the public that matters. It is not the ephemeral impulses of the war which find expression in Mr. Bridges' pages, but rather the greater emotions—the emotions which will still emerge as the perspective lengthens, and will sum up all the rest. (pp. 214-15)

> *Edmund Kemper Broadus, in his* The Laureateship: A Study of the Office of Poet Laureate in England with Some Account of the Poets *(reprinted by permission of Oxford University Press, Inc.), Oxford University Press, 1921.*

Words and music are with [Bridges] always inseparable: he is at the opposite pole from the man, often not unintelligent in other ways, who forces his material into a strait-jacket of jingle. In this respect his taste is as flawless, his subtlety as unfailing, as any in the records of literature. . . . (p. 126)

It may seem a large assertion, but no Englishman has written so large a body of good landscape poetry. There are two obvious things to be said about it.

The first is that his landscape is the landscape of the South of England, more particularly of the Thames Valley and the downs by the sea. . . . And the second obvious thing is that, being a true landscape poet and not a romantic who exploits nature to find backgrounds for his passions, it is of ordinary landscapes that he writes. Tennyson, too, was an observer, but many of his best-known landscapes are of the selected kind. It is one thing to write of the sort of natural scene traditionally approved as remarkable: sunset on a marsh, sunrise on the Alps, stupendous cliffs, high cataracts, and breakers in the moon. It is another to describe, giving the breath of life to your description, what any man, going out on any day in any season, will see when he looks over a five-barred gate or takes a footpath through the woods. Mr. Bridges writes of nature like a countryman. (pp. 126-28)

And Mr. Bridges, even when at his best, is not only a landscape poet, but a poet cunning in the experiences of the heart. Very many of his poems are love poems and many of them are beautiful: if the fact has not been widely observed it must be because they are happy love poems, or at least because they are not excessive in expression. The proclivity that makes him, in another sphere, write not about storms but about calms after storms, is seen always: he has no violence, no vehement abandonment. . . . He never declaims, never raves, despairs, or burns in print: but he knows the ways of lovers' hearts, and his quiet stanzas, whether their subject be the pain of doubt, or separation, or the joy of union, or calm affection by the warm domestic hearth, have a truth and strength which outwear the ardours of many poets. (p. 133)

> *J. C. Squire, "Mr. Robert Bridges's Lyrical Poems," in his* Essays on Poetry, *Hodder and Stoughton, 1923, pp. 122-39.*

In our own time, at least, very few English poets have inclined to look at life without a wry face. . . . Mr. Bridges is the exception *par excellence*. The peculiar originality of his work is its dominating mood of eager delight, a mood that sparkles with implications of genuine spiritual fulfilment, the outcome of a faith repeatedly expressed, that

> in spite of woe and death,
> Gay is life and sweet is breath.

The basis of his mood is contentment. . . . (p. 88)

One rejoicing lyric after another etches the character of a happy life, until, in his old age, the poet epitomizes his philosophy in the quiet valedictory lyric "Fortunatus Nimium". . . . The greater part of his lyric poetry . . . is the exquisitely simple expression of a positive joy: that is, it stands in complete opposition to that negative "poetry of escape" of which Mr. de la Mare's lovely work (especially its later phases) is the best modern example. (pp. 89-91)

Pictorial verse, like that in which Mr. Bridges has reflected the English landscape, rises into poetry by virtue of the author's colouring mood or not at all. Minute observation and skilful word painting, however finely wrought, are not in themselves enough to raise it. The absence of any direct emotional statement must somehow be counterbalanced, and this can only be done by means of implication, musical or metaphorical. It is not enough merely to record appearances . . . [as have] John Clare, and, in our own time, Mr. Edmund Blunden. But Mr. Bridges, even when he is most the painter, never [commits this error]. His descriptive verse is rife with implications. These are never "metaphorical" (like the implications made, for instance, by such poems as Mr. Robert Frost's "Mending Wall," or Mr. de la Mare's "The Moth," to name no more); they are always musical. For Mr. Bridges writes verse in as many different keys as Schubert used in song. (pp. 100-01)

There is nothing very novel, of course, in the poet's attitude, which has already been described by another critic as "the philosophy of the average man." The originality lies rather in the way that philosophy is reflected in his verse. Mr. Bridges has given us what every poet must try to give, something "common in experience, but uncommon in expression," to borrow the phrase in which Mr. Robert Frost improves on Pope's famous "What oft was thought but ne'er so well expressed." He has never looked far afield for the material of his poetry. It lay ready around him. . . . (pp. 104-05)

Mr. Bridges has certainly deserved his reputation as a "poets' poet." Surrounded as we are by so much that is slipshod in literature, we may count not least among his virtues the delight the Poet Laureate takes in his art. Even his consistent eccentricities have their value. His archaic verb and pronoun forms probably appear musty to people with fixed ideas concerning "poetic diction." More subtle ears will not fail to recognize the value of the old mode, because it not only subserves the delicacy of his verbal music, but also ministers to that urbane tone which is the most noticeable characteristic of his poetic style. (p. 107)

[Bridges' style] has some of the rarest attributes, clarity almost approaching perfection, great simplicity even when it is expressing very delicate shades of meaning, a continual glow from the core, and, everywhere, exceptional economy. . . . The resulting poetry . . . is of the kind easiest to read but from a purely technical point of view hardest to write. It is a poetry that re-informs the old familiar themes with new feeling and original significance, that triumphs over the prosaic, trembling responsively to the mere chiaroscuro of human emotion as well as to its great flushes of color and light; a poetry that, whether delighted or dejected, is still quiet and self-sufficient, always beginning with a deep plunge into music and a straight, clean swim to the banks of silence. (p. 109)

> *Edward Davison, "The Poet Laureate," in his* Some Modern Poets and Other Critical Essays *(copyright © 1928 by Harper & Row, Publishers, Inc.; reprinted by permission of Harper & Row, Publishers, Inc.), Harper, 1928, pp. 77-110.*

We may doubt whether the original poetic instinct in [Robert Bridges] was very strong: in his early dramas there seems to be no inner compulsion; there is nothing in them of humanity or appealing beauty to urge us to overcome the obstacle of their idiom, which is the defunct idiom of another age, the terribly distant age of our grandfathers. But if there was no inner compulsion there was always one passion which is a great compensation—the passion a good workman has in the use of his tools. Dr. Bridges has been sustained over a great number of years by his technical ability, and it is greatly to his credit that when he had wearied of perfection in the old modes, he was not too proud to turn a quizzical eye on new modes. But by then his muscles had set. . . .

The object which the Poet Laureate aims at in his loose alexandrines is identical with that for which the advocates of Free Verse have struggled over a number of years. . . .

Dr. Bridges, by his experiments, acknowledges the need for a change. He achieves a change in his loose alexandrines, but is it a change for the better? It is doubtful. His muse must still lie in the procrustean bed of twelve syllables and (presumably) six accents. Now if the aim in such a situation is to adopt or adapt the natural rhythms of speech, you have, to say the least of it, your work cut out. Rhythmical speech rarely has so many as six accents to twelve syllables. This syllabic dragooning of speech rhythm in Dr. Bridges's loose alexandrines results in *clotted* speech. We lose the expectancy of regular metres, and gain, not the ease of natural speech-rhythms, but these speech rhythms clipped and pruned like a cordon fruit-tree. . . .

Dr. Bridges tends to defeat the possibility of rhythmical beauty. [He] sacrifices the expectancy of a regular measure without gaining the inevitability of direct emotional stress. . . .

The general impression given is one of remoteness from actuality. It is true that much contemporary material is dealt with—the problems of marriage and sex, for example. It is true also that abstract ideas are independent of time and occasion. But there is something dry and disdainful, ascetic and Calvinistic throughout—a lack of warmth and humanity. There is no consciousness of that horror of modern civilization, with which the younger generation is afflicted. Dr. Bridges, in his complacency, can even defend modern warfare. . . . (p. 287)

The fault here is a lack of experience. It is true that the Poet Laureate goes on to speak of "sorrows which no glory of heroism can atone, horrors which to forget were cowardice and wrong," but war is seen as a "scourge of God," a just retribution for "mankind's crowded uncleanness of soul." A point of view more in accordance with reality would see only "man's inhumanity to man," and instead of self-discipline and other reclusive virtues, would cry out for fearless freedom of thought and extreme action. For "mid the smoke and gas of war's new armoury" there was simply no question of heroism, self-sacrifice, and discipline. There was only a predetermined death, a waste of life without accompanying nobility, life given without strife or effort, nothing but machines and despair. There is still little else, and this testament of beauty, high and rare though it be, is too remote to comfort us. (p. 288)

> *Herbert Read, "Poet or Pedant?" in* The Nation and The Athenaeum *(copyright 1929 by the Nation Associates, Inc.), November 23, 1929, pp. 287-88.*

The poetry of Robert Bridges has never been particularly popular. It is probably less read than that of any other poet whose official standing is so high. Even now, when *The Testament of Beauty* has surprisingly taken the English public by storm, it is safe to predict that few people will trouble to read his four volumes or more of classic, or pseudo-classic, masques and plays; and if they do, it is almost as safe to predict that they will come away from that undertaking pretty empty-handed. The real reasons for the unpopularity of Bridges are clearest in these unfortunate experiments: they are cold, dull, precious, actionless, full of affectations and archaisms, primly formal, nigglingly florid. The characters are lifeless, the colors are dim; one feels no warmth in them, no rootedness in that rich life of consciousness which (for example and contrast) everywhere makes the Elizabethan drama so hotly vascular. An occasional song or ode of great beauty and delicacy does little to redeem them from the cardinal sin of deadness.

Even in the shorter poems—the "books" of lyrics—one encounters the same faults. These are the poems on which Bridges' reputation has hitherto chiefly rested, and among them are many lyrics which combine a kind of chilly loveliness with a high degree of technical and prosodic ingenuity. . . . At their best, they tend to the elegiac. They are uniformly gentle, pensive, limpid; a deliberate pastoral note informs almost all of them; the language is prim, and touched here and there with archaisms of word and idiom; in short, they belong to a strain of English poetry which is very "consciously" English. One does not go to such poetry for the terrors or profundities of human experience: one goes to it rather for a mild and healing gospel of beauty, a gospel everywhere charming, but perhaps also a little bit epicene. And also one goes to it for a study of its curious and excellent technique.

The Testament of Beauty is in this respect—perhaps in every respect, but most interestingly in this—Bridges' finest achievement. The development of a quantitative hexameter for use in a long narrative or philosophic poem (with the aim of avoiding monotony) had already begun to concern Bridges even in his earliest work. (pp. 141-42)

[For] the most part [*The Testament of Beauty*] moves closer to the "prose" end of the spectrum than any other quasi-successful poem (of similar length) which one can recall. And on the whole, this queer loose prosaic rhythm, with its oddities of inversion and its eccentricities of spelling, suits surprisingly well Bridges' semi-didactic, semi-al-

legorical purpose. The poem is difficult reading—the familiar faults are here again; here again are the archaisms, the frigidities, the primly florid uncouthnesses and heavy pseudo-classical asides; but they fit the method and the theme, and moreover there are many incidental passages of extraordinary beauty. In short, the poem achieves a queer kind of uniqueness—something analogous, perhaps, to "Mansoul," or "The Dawn in Britain," of Doughty, in which there is the same effort toward the formulation of a pure convention.

Of the content of the poem it is sufficient here to speak very briefly. It is a mildly philosophical essay, a good deal influenced by Santayana's "Sense of Beauty" and "Life of Reason"; very loosely assembled, not always very cogent in reasoning, suffused everywhere with an odd and almost medieval simplicity and old-fashionedness. It reminds one even a little of *The Anatomy of Melancholy;* it has the same air of amateurish charm, the same earnest sincerity. It is a gentle testament, and ingenuous—the gentle praise of a gentle ideal. There is no wrestling here with the dynamics of the soul, no probing of horrors or sounding of wonder; chaos has removed itself from the shores of Albion; everything is peaceful and detached and comfortable; and everything is as consciously and purely English as it can possibly be. (pp. 142-43)

> *Conrad Aiken, "Prose and Music," in* The New Republic *(reprinted by permission of The New Republic; © 1930 by The New Republic, Inc.), March 26, 1930 (and reprinted in his* Collected Criticism, *Oxford University Press, 1968, pp. 141-43).*

The death of Robert Bridges at the ripe age of eighty-six gives us pause, on this side of the ocean, chiefly as a reminder of differences between Britain's poetry of this period and our own. For Bridges was rightfully the Laureate, in that he was typically British, and British of the upper class accustomed to titles and honors; a poet of the more decorous and gentlemanly English tradition, deriving not from Chaucer and Shakespeare, not from the ballad-vendors of King Henry or the swashbuckling player-playwrights of Queen Elizabeth, but from that *preux chevalier* Sir Philip Sidney, from the mannerly Robert Herrick, with Wordsworth and Tennyson, two other laureates, for more immediate ancestors.

Hardy, almost his exact contemporary, was also English, but he was something more; rooted in Wessex, he yet looked beyond the traditions and aristocratic prejudices of his little island, and took the world for his province, with all its heavy load of common people. But Bridges remained in a walled garden discreetly planted among classic colonnades. He had followed the regulation courses at Eton and Oxford; indeed, the frock-coated classicism of Oxford suited him so well that he passed his whole long life in the quiet countryside shadowed by its towers. (p. 146)

For more spacious life he looks to the Greeks and writes poetic dramas from the safe enclosure of a library; and he founds his art on scholarship rather than direct experience of life. In fact, scholarship *is* his life, and his art is a derivation—delicate and precise, and in a sense varied—from his scholarship. (p. 149)

It is this indoorness—or, so far as it gets out-of-doors, this rural quality—which seems to me typical of English twentieth-century poetry. Bridges began in the eighteen-seventies, but if not a true Georgian by date of first appearance, he was the ancestor of the Georgians, and, consciously or unconsciously, they may have learned from him certain quiet virtues of a well-bred art. And it is just here that one must feel the contrast with the American poetry of our time. Ours is certainly more free of boundaries and restrictions, more eager to roam, more conscious of great spaces. The magnificent variety to be found here, scenic, regional, racial, traditional, occupational, is getting into our poetry; is being reflected there in an uncontrollable variety of feeling and thinking, of method and manner. Our poetry may not be well-bred, but there is something of primitive wildness in it, something of spaciousness and assertive power. (p. 150)

> *Harriet Monroe, "Bridges as a Lyricist," in*
> Poetry (© *1930 by The Modern Poetry Association; reprinted by permission of the Editor of* Poetry), *June, 1930, pp. 146-50.*

[Bridges] begins . . . with Nature, and he interprets her by natural, simple means and measures. His study of metre and prosody helped him to enlarge the resources of his art, but he did so by variation rather than by revolt. There was nothing spectacular or arresting in his effects, nothing, for instance, of the anapaestic revelry of Swinburne, or the hard, clean-cut severity of the later empiricists in free verse. He began by experimenting in quantity; he went on to emphasize the importance of stress; his lyrical measures are almost all restrained and modulated in tone. But they are always full of music—for Bridges loved music almost as much as he loved nature—and their harmonies are as much a matter of stress as of sound, of vision as of ear. The perfect picture of an English scene is called up again and again in his poetry through the employment of sounds and echoes as inalienably English as the image they create. (p. 837)

Robert Bridges accepted the laureateship in the year before the outbreak of the Great War; and, in those first months of confused voices, of challenge, fury, and vituperation, there were not wanting fiery counsellors who would have liked to see the country's official poet fulminating from the crest of Boar's Head, and urging on the nations to mutual destruction. . . . [No] poetry at all of that sort was to be won from the poet whom the more irresponsible type of journalist was not ashamed to call "Our Silent Laureate". In its stead, there emerged from the sheltered study above the Oxford spires a book of the finest spiritual quality, a collection of the noblest thoughts and visions with which great Englishmen through the ages had consoled themselves in the hour of tribulation,—that beautiful, stirring, reconciling anthology, *The Spirit of Man.* Looking back to-day, when the weapons of war have perished, and bitter thoughts are hushed in honour to the dead, it is easy enough to recognise that no wiser, or more needed message could possibly have been offered to that fevered hour than the message to be found in those golden pages of courage, peace, and love. And the spirit which animated that book was all the while at work in the poet's mind, preparing his last, and most characteristic legacy to his generation, the wonderful *Testament of Beauty,* in which, on his eighty-fifth birthday, the poet bore witness to the perennial youthfulness of his heart, and to his unfailing faith in the final destiny of man.

There is certainly no denying that this noble "Testament" presents itself in a difficult guise, and demands patient submission of the reader; but it is actually much less difficult than it appears at first sight. The obstacles to facile acceptance are mainly three. In the first place, the poem is written in what the poet describes as "loose alexandrines," a metre which has never proved very congenial to the English language. In the second place, the poet, in order to make the stress and fall of his metre more acceptable to the English ear, has adopted a modified form of phonetic spelling, which lends to the page, at a superficial glance, an air of archaism which is entirely alien from its atmosphere and intention. And finally, the argument is illustrated by a procession of similes, crowded with detail as full as those of Matthew Arnold, in whose poetry the simile sometimes stretches itself out so far that the original picture drops from the mind, as it concentrates upon the opulence of the analogy. This, however, is a comparatively small question of workmanship, which yields its secret to a closer examination; and the other difficulties are not much harder to overcome. The reader will find that, if he reads the verse straight on, as though it were prose, not allowing himself to mark its quantity or, as it were, to chant its melody, he will soon feel the measure shaping itself around its beautiful imagery, and lending clarity to its occasionally intricate argument. In this he will be greatly helped by the emphasis of the spelling, when once it has become familiar; for the doubled consonants and dropped vowels are contrived expressly as aids both to sound and sense, and soon play their part in elucidating the intention. And, as the entire intention of the poem shapes itself in the imagination, its nobility and power are more and more vividly revealed. (pp. 841-42)

With illustrations from history, from metaphysics, and from ethics, he traces the necessity of man's response to Nature and its claims, under the guidance of beauty, and follows up his quest for Nature's meaning, its will, and purpose. . . . From contemplation of Self the poet proceeds to the study of Breed, which "is to the race as selfhood to the individual"; he surveys the mystery of sex, "the allure of bodily beauty"; and the call of instinct, merging in the harmony of union. And so, finally, he comes out upon the shining tableland of *Ethick,* which reveals to man the obligation of Duty; invests him with the knowledge of good and evil; and demonstrates that the choice of good is natural to man, planted in him by the conscience which is personality, and leading him instinctively to the divine practice of prayer and praise. (pp. 842-43)

The Testament of Beauty is such a gift as only a great poet could leave to his generation, the last utterance of a fine and philosophic mind, which from the Pisgah-height of experience saw the vision of eternal beauty face to face, and had no fear to die, having learnt so fully how to live. (p. 843)

> *Arthur Waugh, "Robert Bridges," in* The
> Fortnightly Review, *June, 1930, pp. 832-43.*

Bridges, with all his variety of lyric and essay in existence, had nevertheless a late opportunity to crown his labour with an invention of ampler sway and profounder speculation. He took that opportunity. Normally those who awake to find themselves famous are young in years. Bridges changed all that. . . . 'The Testament of Beauty' was 'the turning-point in his career', as they say. . . . (p. 217)

[In 'The Testament of Beauty'] Bridges displayed the dignity of poetry. Servility or opportunism, that have not one of the many mansions in that palace, found no approach to him. He continued to be the same sensitive melodist and interpreter of scene and thought as before. He was not unwilling to write on a national theme—but then, it would be also his own by nature, as, the tercentenary of Shakespeare. Then, since poetry is only one of the instruments by which the character of a nation is to be cultivated, enlightened, and directed, Bridges continually brought into action his other auxiliary gifts and studies. Those were numerous. He was intent upon (to catalogue these ideals crudely) the speech of England, how he should pronounce it, and how write it down; upon the music of England, and the improvement of voice and verse in religious services; upon the general realization of poetry, in its total influence and its minor construction; upon typography, which plays for better or worse on our daily life; upon the illumining of poetical achievements not generally known; and upon the worth, cheerfulness, aspiration, and endurance of the English people. . . .

But these words are not in the nature of a panegyric; for Bridges remains still with the reader as he personally regards him, a private man, to whose music each is invited without strain or demand. (p. 219)

> Edmund Blunden, "The Ideal Laureate"
> (1930), in his The Mind's Eye, (reprinted by
> permission of A. D. Peters & Co.), Jona-
> than Cape, 1934, pp. 216-20.

It is on his lyrics, along with *Eros and Psyche* and *The Testament of Beauty*, that Bridges's fame rests secure. Other lyrists may have reached greater imaginative heights, or struck a more ardent note of passion: none has produced a large body of verse more varied in music and design and yet so faultless in taste and workmanship. There is nothing freakish or mannered about his language; in poetry as in music Bridges 'loved the purer style', and his diction has the limpidity and ease of the best classical writing. In their form, too, and their melody they are in the line of that great tradition, to which, as he thought, his contemporaries had shown too scant respect. (p. 217)

Bridges's one attempt at the idyll of humble life is as feeble as any of Tennyson's, his few incursions into the weird or the romantic are hardly more successful. He had little of that dramatic sympathy which enables a man to project himself into moods and conditions of life other than his own. Still less is he one of those world-poets who descend into the arena of blood and tears and snatch a victory for their mistress Beauty out of the agony of human conflict, or draw inspiration even from the chaffering of the market place. (p. 227)

His poems of love are eminently characteristic of his art. By reason alike of depth and sincerity of feeling and of flawless execution he is among the finest of our love poets; but here again his range is strictly confined. There is nothing in him of the cross currents of love, of impossible longings, of tragic despair, of the pangs of mad desire, 'enjoyed no sooner but despised straight'. The physical basis of all love is not slighted, but the love he pictures is not Eros, the merely physical. . . . The poems of Bridges have been criticized as lacking passion, and if by passion is meant uncontrolled excitement, the charge is just enough. . . . Clear vision seemed to him to call for calm. There is nothing revolutionary about him; the noisy and the

blustering repel him: beauty to him lies in order and discipline. In life, as in his art, he is the true aristocrat. He knew that moral sanity, though it may not inspire poetry, is yet an indispensable element in it. . . . Bridges is not blind to the darker elements in life, and in his poem *Nightingales* has re-echoed, in music as immortal as Shelley's, the cry that 'our sweetest songs are those that tell of saddest thought'; yet, he holds that the very act of turning sorrow into song is itself an act of joy, and hence that the true artist must perforce know happiness.

Bridges is the aristocrat also in his lofty gift of selection. He is the victim of no optimistic delusions. He has studied nature and human life too closely not to admit their 'mean ugly brutish obscene clumsy irrelevances'; but man, the highest product of nature, is endowed with consciousness and judgement, and of what good is judgement if it does not choose the best? Nowadays, it seems, to revel in the ugly is accounted to a man for strength and realism. But beauty is as real as ugliness, and to Bridges more noteworthy. And so, where he 'holds up the mirror to Nature, She, seeing her face therein, shall not be ashamed'. And of his own moods those which he chiefly delights to celebrate are the most worthy, i.e. the happiest. . . . He is essentially the poet of joy, rather than of sorrow, of attainment rather than of unsatisfied longing. He has himself, indeed, felt the growing-pains of melancholy, but he declines to make easy poetic capital out of them. (pp. 228, 230-31)

He is in a special sense Oxford's poet, both in what he owed her and what, so richly, he repaid. None better than he has expressed the quiet charm of her countryside, none has distilled into a finer fragrance her essential spirit. And like a true son, the praise he most coveted was that which might fall from the lips of those who acknowledge the same loving allegiance. (p. 232)

Taken as a whole *The Testament of Beauty* [Bridges's masterwork, in the opinion of this critic,] is imaginative rather than didactic. And the field of experience over which it ranges is astonishingly wide. It is the 'intimate echo' of the life of one whose home has always been in the land of the Muses, yet who has been a tireless adventurer in many countries, and from them all has brought back with him treasures with which to adorn the shrine of his divine mistress. In reaching his conclusions he has tested against his own experience the findings of many philosophers. Different facets of his thought sparkle in analogies drawn from physics or chemistry or medicine; others are expressed in vivid episodes from ancient or medieval history, or the achievements of the sister arts of painting and music, or the conditions of modern life. The dawn of wisdom in Hellas, the birth of modern poetry at the court of Raymond of Toulouse, the lives of St. Francis and St. Thomas and Henry VIII, the Crusades and the Albigensian war, Raphael's Madonnas and Titian's *L'Amor sacro e profano*, the feasts of city aldermen, and the latest discovery of prehistoric tombs in Mesopotamia—these are but a few of the scenes in which the thought of the poem takes life. The logical argument, indeed, sits lightly upon it; pedants might complain that it sits too lightly, and that some of the incidents are developed out of all proportion to their weight in the argument. But this charge could be met as another poet met it, with the plea that 'his course is often stay'd, yet never is astray'. For in whatever by-paths he wanders, Bridges finds beauty on the road. Beauty is all his argument; and even where poetic inspiration flags there is always the beauty of accomplished art.

Of versification Bridges is a master. If we have had greater poets than he, we have had few artists as impeccable. A classical scholar, who has made a life-long study of the technique of English verse and has probed, as far as they can be probed, the secrets of Milton's incomparable music, he has been also a bold experimenter; and if some of his classical adventures have not proved happy to an English ear, they have doubtless contributed to his own final facility. The new metre which he has evolved, in which our poem is written, loose Alexandrines, or neo-Miltonic syllabics, as he calls them, was suggested by the choruses of *Samson Agonistes,* with as generous a licence in the positions of stress, and the use of elision, substitution and extra-metrical syllables as is compatible with the rhythmical integrity of the line. This metre is a triumph of art. It is capable of infinite variety, as is proved by the ease with which quotations from poets writing in different languages and different metres can be fitted into its mould; and according as it is loosely or strictly handled it is adaptable to any mood and any subject. It can move with the sweet regularity of a softly gliding stream, or dance with the sparkling gaiety of a mountain torrent: it is equally successful in light familiar discourse or pithy reflection; it can assume a dignity consonant with high prophetic utterance. If it cannot rise to the majesty of blank verse, it is much happier than that measure upon the lower poetic levels. In range it can, perhaps, only be equalled by the metre of Byron's *Don Juan,* and in Bridges's hands it is capable of a delicate and subtle music quite out of Byron's reach. By its invention Bridges has definitely extended the musical capacities of our language; whether future poets will be able to develop it still further, or to handle it with his skill, I am not rash enough to prophesy. (pp. 249-50)

> *E. De Selincourt, "Robert Bridges" and "'The Testament of Beauty',"* in his Oxford Lectures on Poetry *(reprinted by permission of The Clarendon Press, Oxford),* Oxford University Press, 1934, pp. 207-56.

Bridges is a poet for students, not for those who read poetry alone for its music and its evocations; he is a poet for students, not for those who read poetry for its rapture or its metaphysical refinements.

As far as rapture is concerned, Bridges would have none of it. The word "joy" was much upon his pen; but as the name of an abstraction. It was his word, perhaps, for some temporary escape of his genius from tutelage; one feels, at least, no joy as one reads, no light-hearted and light-headed nonsensical delight in playfulness. An ethical joy, perhaps. (pp. 258-59)

Bridges was extremely well-read in the poets, and he could imitate old models with remarkable fidelity. He was also, given much leisure, engrossed in the study of the craft of poetry. Here lies his chief influence upon the newer generation of poets, who owe him a great deal (I forget whether they admit the debt). The old models did not satisfy him, and he sought for new. He wanted to experiment in prosody, and to this end he not only practised incessantly, but conned the practice of others and wrote down in book and pamphlet the results of his observations. Invaluable work, devoted and often illuminating, possible only to one who was both poet and scholar. (p. 259)

His original work is always distinguished, and often full of fervour expressed with great dignity and beauty; when it deals with very simple things it is usually exquisite. But it is never unrestrained; it is always, in my wicked view, middle class, the product of genius overlaid by breeding, or rather by those conventions by which the exclusive separate themselves from the world. (p. 260)

> *Frank Swinnerton, in his* The Georgian Scene: A Literary Panorama *(reprinted with the permission of Farrar, Straus & Giroux, Inc.; copyright 1934 © 1962 by Frank Swinnerton; reprinted by permission of Holt, Rinehart and Winston, Publishers), Farrar & Rinehart, 1934.*

Bridges' narrative *Eros and Psyche* and the four mythological dramas are perhaps generally regarded, like Tennyson's *Idylls,* as the sometimes beautiful mistakes of a born lyrist, and the multitude who bought but did not read *The Testament of Beauty* are not likely to discover the long poems written a generation and more ago. Yet these everywhere reveal the poet's special quality, and their defects as well as their virtues illustrate his attitude toward art and life. The scholarly traditionalist, the technical experimenter and contriver of subtle rhythms, the singer of love and joy and beauty, they are all here. (p. 433)

All four of the mythological dramas have a prologue and chorus, but only *Prometheus the Firegiver* . . . approaches at all closely the Greek manner, and it, as "a mask," has very little dramatic realism or conflict or suspense. (p. 437)

Of the choruses some are dramatic and decorative, some less dramatic and more philosophical. The first two ceremonial odes in honor of Zeus and Hera are admirably cool and lucid mythological lyrics. The ode on the spirit of wonder which concludes the first part of the drama is a beautiful and entirely modern utterance. (pp. 438-39)

While Bridges avoided direct competition with his great predecessors, he reminds us at times of both Goethe and Shelley, and the theme of idealistic striving bears some resemblance to Calderon's *La Estatua de Prometeo.* Bridges could not, presumably, have equaled them, but he could have made a finer drama than he did if he had been sufficiently possessed by his subject to follow them in completely reinterpreting it. As it is, he vacillates uncertainly between philosophic modernization and studious reproduction of the antique, and the symbolic parable appears intermittently among bits of flawless writing which are not alive. Except Prometheus—and he is not always an exception—the characters remain too merely mythological; even the fire stolen from heaven is a little too much in the nature of chemical combustion. Further, the action, though chiefly mental, is too simple for the implications of the theme. Still, with all its shortcomings, *Prometheus* is, as an extended and massive lyric, a beautiful performance. Bridges' idealism is not spurious or extravagant, and his exalted purity of tone does more than anything else to show that his faith in beauty and in good is a living faith. (pp. 439-40)

The poet's intellect, temperament, and happy circumstances, if they did not disqualify him for grappling with the problems of good and evil, at any rate over-simplified those problems. . . . Bridges' Reason is a name for the serene idealism and optimistic monism of a sequestered, untroubled student and lover of nature which satisfied him more completely than it may satisfy the less fortunate.

On the other hand we have a way of confusing the real defects of such a poet as Bridges with our own hasty or fashionable prejudices. He has suffered unduly from critics who, accustomed to "gross and violent stimulants," worship only demonic genius, regard a work of art as cold unless it boils over, and find the proof of inspiration in disorder. (Henry James, the Bridges of modern fiction, has suffered in the same way.) Bridges is academic and traditional in the good as well as the bad sense. When an artist does not deal with raw experience it may be that he has weakly recoiled from it; but it may be also that he has gone beyond it. (p. 443)

> *Douglas Bush, in his* Mythology and the Romantic Tradition in English Poetry *(copyright © 1937, 1969 by the President and Fellows of Harvard College; 1965 by Douglas Bush; excerpted by permission of the author and publishers), Cambridge, Mass.: Harvard University Press, 1937 (and reprinted by Harvard University Press, 1969).*

Dr. Bridges' meters have been so often and so fruitlessly discussed that I shall omit entirely to analyze them, though his importance as a subtle and learned renovator of English meters is sufficiently great. It is my belief that he has been long enough patronized as a sugar-coated pill for those who wish to brush up on their metrics, as a minor manipulator of outworn graces, and that he should be recognized once and for all as the sole English rival of Hardy in nineteenth-century poetry, as, in all likelihood, considering his formal versatility, the range of his feeling, and the purity of his diction, a diction so free from any trace of personal idiosyncrasy that a successful imitator of it could never be detected as an imitator but would appear only as that most unlikely of phenomena, a rival, that he should, I say, in all likelihood be recognized as the most valuable model of poetic style to appear since Dryden. (p. 128)

Dr. Bridges possessed much more curiosity about the possibilities of various forms than has been shown by most of our modern experimenters. Mr. Pound, Dr. Williams, and Miss Moore, for example, have all worked in a straight line, as if impelled by some more or less fanatical dogma, toward a certain form or tempo, and, having once perfected it, have become slaves to it. . . . Dr. Bridges seems to have been fully aware that a change of tempo involves a complete or nearly complete change in the range of feeling perceived, that it opens up, in other words, a fresh field of subject matter; if one follows his career step by step one finds him taking up one tempo after another, exhausting its possibilities (for himself) and dropping each, once he has thoroughly mastered it and before it has mastered him. (p. 129)

In his longer and more meditative lyrics, Dr. Bridges achieved a poetry, the norm of which is scarcely more intense than the norm of distinguished prose, but which, thanks to the quality of its diction, syntax and cadence, never falls short of extreme distinction, and which rises at need and without shock from distinction to extraordinary beauty. Poetry of this sort is not inferior to poetry of the shorter and more lyrical sort, though it may be harder to appreciate and is certainly less popular at the present time. It can handle material impossible in the more specialized lyric: what it loses in concentration, it can regain in subtlety of detail, completeness of description, range of material, and structural elaboration. (p. 131)

Dr. Bridges has been so often and so angrily compared to his friend Gerard Hopkins that I may perhaps be pardoned for a word on this subject. Hopkins seems to me to have been a truly great poet, though I cannot carry my enthusiasm as far as do his most violent admirers. The qualities that have won Hopkins almost immediate recognition during the past few years are, I fear, the very reasons for his limitations and his definite inferiority to Bridges. The mere fact that a man is a radical technical innovator does not render him a greater poet than the man who is less an innovator; extreme originality of method almost always involves extreme departure from the norm of experience, involves specialization and limitation of feeling. . . . Hopkins . . . can express with his violent rhythms an extremely special kind of excitement arising from religious experience, but he can express little else, and even the religious experience is incomplete, for if he does not deal wholly with the resultant excitement, he certainly throws his emphasis very heavily upon it. We are told, for instance, in superbly impassioned verses that the mind has mountains, but the nature of those mountains is never wholly clear. In Bridges the nature of the mountains is absolutely clear—that is, the experience is rendered whole—and the terror of the mountains is not isolated from all other experience but is seen in firm proportion. There is in the metrical experimentation in [*The Shorter Poems of Robert Bridges*] quite as much originality of thought as in the experiments of Hopkins, coupled with a much more thorough knowledge of English meters and the complexities of feeling involved in their history. Bridges' technique, if the less obviously original of the two, is the more sensitive and the more widely applicable instrument of perception. In saying this, I do not wish it to be thought, let me repeat, that I am blind to the sensitivity or the power of Hopkins, a poet, who moves me very deeply. (pp. 133-34)

[The] diction of Dr. Bridges is as fresh and living as that of Dr. Williams; his meters allow him greater freedom, or rather greater range; he is in general a more civilized man. It is to be hoped for the sake of twentieth-century poetry, that he will receive the study which his own poetry merits. (p. 135)

> *Yvor Winters, "Traditional Mastery," in his* Yvor Winters: Uncollected Essays and Reviews, *edited by Francis Murphy (© 1973 by Janet Lewis Winters; reprinted with permission of The Swallow Press, Inc.), Swallow, 1973, pp. 127-35.*

[One] very English poet of [the Georgian] time may be said to have had a most distinctive persona: this was Robert Bridges. To contrast his persona with that of Ezra Pound is to contrast two extreme English and American attitudes towards poetry: each of which verges on self-caricature. The comparison is useful in that Robert Bridges was a radical in his conservatism as Pound was in his modernism, as stubbornly English as Pound was brashly American. Like Pound, he was greatly concerned with words and languages and problems of prosody, though the two often arrived at opposite conclusions. (p. 163)

Bridges remained nevertheless exceptional among his English contemporaries in having an extremely critical mind which roved over a very wide area of classical and English poetry. In his lyrics he used a great variety of conventional historic forms based mostly on the Elizabethans, Herrick and, particularly, Campion. He also experimented in classical meters and, late in life, in *New Poems* (a collection which contains *Poor Poll* and some of his most beautiful late lyrics) and in *The Testament of Beauty,* he invented what he called his "loose alcaics," a meter in which he was certainly able to express freely his philosophy of life and his reminiscences, such as those of his friendship with Gerard Manley Hopkins. Like Pound and Joyce, he was inspired by the Greek, writing works called *Prometheus the Firegiver, Ulysses* and *Eros and Psyche.* He was interested, like Bernard Shaw, in simplified spelling, and like E. E. Cummings, in the typographical look of his poems on the printed page. Unlike other English poets whom Eliot by implication criticized for adhering to the idea that poetry should express the poet's feelings and personality, Bridges' poetry, though often about love, has a marked impersonality, burning with what I can only call a flame of ice. In his love poetry Bridges gives the impression of some great millionaire whose wealth no one can doubt, but who never on any account refers to the actual money in the bank or does anything so vulgar as to carry loose change around.

Like Pound and Eliot, Bridges believed that poetry should objectify emotion and not express the personality of the poet: in fact he carried the idea of objectivization to the point of petrifaction. He was in favor of disciplines of strict form, and opposed to free verse, which he called Harum-Scarum, a description which Pound and Eliot might, in the long run, have agreed with (though from Bridges' point of view—as also from Frost's—what Pound wrote was free verse). (pp. 164-65)

The idea that the modern world of science and machinery has produced changes in sensibility which can only be met by poets having to reflect them in language and form—learn the language of this changed sensibility and change poetry to meet it—was utterly alien to Bridges. (p. 167)

Bridges' remarks exclude not only a world of modern things

—and after all he was under no obligation to force himself to write about them—but, what is far more important, the realization that the language itself, in its vocabulary and rhythms, had become altered by those things; so that even to oppose their values, the poet had to work through them.

Bridges' "persona" was opposite to that of Ezra Pound, the extrovert, hectoring, dogmatic and generous modernist. His arrogance, unlike that of Pound, was the starting place not of preaching, writing manifestos and forming movements, but of aloofness and spiritual pride. . . . Beautiful as his poems sometimes are, and impressive as his transformed style became in *The Testament of Beauty,* one never escapes the impression that his ideas were formed in Oxford when he studied Greats as a very young man, and that he never developed beyond them, and that he had a lizard skin which was impenetrable to experience. His technique is always admirable, his observation occasionally stunning, his ideas never interesting. Superiority was, of course, his "thing" and he was in every way superior to his English fellow poets; yet the qualities which he had transmogrified into his aloofness had the same defects of a somnambulistic traditionalism. As the young poet Robert Graves, visiting the poet laureate in his Oxford garden after the First World War, wrote:

> His time and truth he has not bridged to ours,
> But shrivelled by long heliotropic idling
> He croaks at us his out-of-date humours.

What gave the American poets their strength is that it was not Bridges but they who were the bridge builders between past and present. (pp. 168-70)

> *Stephen Spender, "The Persona of Bridges," in his* Love-Hate Relations: English and American Sensibilities *(copyright © 1974 by Stephen Spender; reprinted by permission of Random House, Inc.), Random House, 1974, pp. 163-70.*

Samuel Butler

1835-1902

English novelist, essayist, and satirist. The son of a rector and grandson of a bishop, Butler was also trained for the clergy but abandoned orthodox beliefs after graduation from Cambridge and emigrated to New Zealand. He returned to England five years later a wealthy man from his stint as a sheep farmer. An amateur biologist, Butler was immediately attracted to Darwin's theory of evolution but later contended that Darwin had omitted "mind" from his theory of natural selection. He wrote several treatises on evolution advocating that the true spring of organic evolution was "need" or "want," later expressed by psychologists as "will-to-live" or "libido." *The Way of All Flesh*, a novel engendered by his own conflicts with his father, satirizes hypocrisy in Victorian church and family life. Published posthumously, it is now considered his finest work. In addition to his work as a writer and scientist, Butler was a translator of Homer (to whom he referred in a famous theory as "the authoress of the *Odyssey*"), an artist, musician, and composer.

PRINCIPAL WORKS

A First Year in Canterbury Settlement   (letters and essays)
   1863
Erewhon; or Over the Range   (satire)   1872
*The Fair Haven: A Work in Defence of the Miraculous
   Element in Our Lord's Ministry upon Earth, Both as
   against Rationalistic Impugners and Certain Orthodox
   Defenders*   (satire)   1873
*Life and Habit: An Essay after a Completer View of
   Evolution*   (essay)   1878
*Evolution Old and New; or The Theories of Buffon, Dr.
   Erasmus Darwin, and Lamarck, as Compared with
   That of Mr. C. Darwin*   (essay)   1879
Unconscious Memory   (essay)   1880
Alps and Sanctuaries of Piedmont and the Canton Ticino
   (travel essays)   1882
*Luck, or Cunning, as the Main Means of Organic
   Modification?*   (essay)   1887
*The Authoress of 'The Odyssey', Where and When She
   Wrote, Who She Was, the Use She Made of 'The
   Iliad', and How the Poem Grew under Her Hands*
   (essay)   1897
*Shakespeare's Sonnets: Reconsidered, and in Part
   Rearranged with Introductory Chapters, Notes, and a*

Brief Reprint of the Original 1609 Edition   (essay)
   1899
*Erewhon Revisited, Twenty Years Later, Both by the
   Original Discoverer of the Country and by His Son*
   (satire)   1901
The Way of All Flesh   (novel)   1903

[Butler] set himself, with every argument at his disposal, to urge his countrymen to take a more honest view of life and its responsibilities, and to wash their eyes clean of hypocrisy and pretence. (p. 233)

Certainly the age, against whose standards he raised his protest, was steeped in a poisonous complacency. The utilitarianism of Bentham and Mill had merged into a slack policy of laissez-faire. Society was exceedingly well pleased with itself, and made its own idols of those whom it had itself crowned with material success. (p. 234)

Butler was indeed the exact antithesis to his age. Instead of being self-satisfied, he was perpetually obsessed by shortcomings; in place of self-concentration he bestowed his whole thought upon the environment which hemmed him in. "Erewhon" is a comprehensive satire of Victorian England, drawing out the absurdities of the time to their logical conclusion. . . . Satire was Butler's perfect weapon, but it was a creative satire, not a destructive. It was designed to help the age to rehabilitate itself by getting into honest relations with its own motives and purposes. It was, above all things, the satire of a man who has ideals, and who desires to instil those ideals into his fellow-men; but who, at the same time, having a natural aversion from the preaching business, finds it more congenial to drive his meaning home through an undercurrent of humorous exaggeration. And speaking to the public, he spoke in plain language. He cherished an instinctive distrust for scientific jargon, and went straight for good, clear words to express good, clear thoughts. His suspicion of all religious organisations made him dislike every form of introspection and self-consciousness; the mainspring of his ethical system was a belief in unconscious action, inspired by a naturally attuned nature. The properly harmonised character would, he believed, act morally by its own impulse; but this impulse could only be fostered by heredity. The heredity of Butler, however, was very different from that of Darwin. . . . (pp. 234-36)

Butler separated from Darwin, in short, on the border-line of Darwin's materialism. Heredity with Butler was a spiritual force, working through a sort of unconscious memory. (p. 236)

Butler had no party to serve, and no recognisable programme to carry through. He refused to be solemn, even when he was serious: and the pedants declined to believe that any man, who had seriously conceived the apparently mad notion that the Odyssey was written by a woman, would be content to exploit it in language which always appeared to be laughing in its sleeve. But Butler's way was always the way of quiet laughter, and along that path he sought persistently for truth, and sought it clear-eyed and eager-hearted. He smiled as he went, but he was in deadly earnest all the time. He yearned to get down to essentials, and had little patience with fripperies and decorations. To him Character was the essence of life: Success a mere accident of fortune. (p. 237)

[In his] pages we can read the record of the faults which we are called upon to amend, and read of them (to all the better profit) in that stimulating world of fancy, where Wit and Wisdom go blithely hand in hand. (p. 238)

> Arthur Waugh, "Samuel Butler," in his Tradition and Change: Studies in Contemporary Literature, *Chapman and Hall, Ltd., 1919, pp. 232-38.*

Historically, Butler's books on the great evolution controversy are very important, as he was almost the only writer to attack Darwinism from any other than the Book of Genesis standpoint; he was a neo-Lamarckian, and held that Darwin, with whom he had personally quarreled, was not only absurdly wrong in ascribing so much importance to natural selection as a factor of development, but mischievously deceitful in the exposition of his scientific observations. *Luck or Cunning?, Life and Habit,* and *Evolution, Old and New,* though somewhat put out of date by the newer developments of Mendelism, are not to any extent denied in their scientific principle: and for the clearness of their English and the sweet malice of their polemics are to be read with the same enjoyment as Whistler's *Gentle Art of Making Enemies.*

Whistler and Butler, though their views on art were not sympathetic, had much in common, particularly in their bantering style. Butler, we may notice, cared nothing for style as such ... and only valued writing which was straightforward and studied the convenience of its reader.

Besides his philosophic-scientific writings, among the most important of which is his little-read *God the Known and God the Unknown,* Butler could claim to have contributed notably to Shakespearean, Homeric, and Biblical criticism. His edition of the Sonnets comes nearer than any I know to making them read intelligibly as a story. The strange *Authoress of the Odyssey* theory, which is the one that most infuriated Butler's own generation when they discovered he was not joking, rests on arguments which have never been controverted, and that not because they were unworthy of controversion. *Fair Haven,* an essay on the events of the Crucifixion, is a reasonable, reverent, and most unusual treatment of familiar history, well illustrating Butler's remark about picking up sovereigns in public places. (p. 182)

Butler's actual achievements often do seem to me less im-

portant than the manner in which they were achieved. His age needed not a Juvenal to lash its vices, for it was a progressive age singularly free from the more glaring and violent vices; it needed an *enfant terrible* to shy a few stones at its club windows and ask a few awkward questions in its drawing-rooms.

Butler was the child for the task; his stones smashed many panes and his example smashed many more. His questions vexed many a drawing-room, and he was duly slippered by the critics and sent out through the door. He continued at the keyhole, and his fate was not so horrible that other children did not press his questions and shout them in the street; the beginnings of most contemporary movements toward freedom of opinion on religion, aesthetics, or philosophy can be traced to Butler. To give a single instance, I do not remember seeing it noted that Butler in *Erewhon Revisited* as good as prophesied the psychoanalyst; he looked forward to the time when crime and illness should be interchangeable terms; and the 'straightener' was to be a man to whom patients confessed their delinquencies and who undertook to cure them. This must have read grotesquely in 1872; but to-day there is a rush to the psychoanalyst for confessing the most horrible morbid tendencies, and instead of holding up his hands in horror the straightener undertakes quite calmly, and usually, I may add, quite ineffectually, to cure these. (p. 183)

> Robert Graves, "The Galileo of Mares' Nests," in The Living Age, *January 26, 1924, pp. 180-83.*

Those who have read *Erewhon* and *The Way of All Flesh* will have been struck by the frequency of the biological references they contain. Nor are these references accidental. Samuel Butler was not a novelist, but a biologist who wrote occasional satire to amuse himself and to satisfy his spleen, a fact which the wide popularity of his fictional works has caused to be overlooked. His biological theories, ignored by contemporary scientists and for a dozen years after his death referred to in terms of contemptuous ridicule by the few biologists who condescended to notice him, have recently been vindicated by a number of experiments, the revolutionary bearing of which upon our conception of the universe only continues to escape general notice because of the average scientist's constitutional inability to use his imagination to grasp the implication of his facts. (p. 311)

> C. E. M. Joad, "The Vindication of Samuel Butler," in The Spectator (© 1926 by The Spectator; *reprinted by permission of* The Spectator), *February 20, 1926, pp. 311-12.*

The genius of Samuel Butler was a livid intense flash. It showed blackest darkness about it, then itself grew dim.

The child of a provincial English rectory, he grew up in the narrowest, the most snobbish, the most bigoted and the most ungracious atmosphere which the Protestant nineteenth century produced. He rebelled against it and broke away from it, and he damned it forever in his masterpiece, "The Way of All Flesh," which is likely to survive as one of the classical accounts of how hateful life could become when the successful English middle class mixed avarice with religion. . . .

[Whereas] in "Erewhon" and "The Way of All Flesh" his revolt against his father had inspired him to his most brilliant work, his controversies with substitute fathers became less and less interesting as he grew older, and he himself became a kind of crank.

The shadows of the rectory were closing on him. His wit had attracted attention when "Erewhon" had first come out, but he was never really to become a part of the general culture of the time till "The Way of All Flesh" was published after his death and Bernard Shaw, the great popularizer, began to popularize him. Shaw points out that, despite Butler's rebellion against the intolerance of his parents, in spite of his lifelong yearning toward a world of playful opinions and easy manners, he had become as intolerant about Darwin as his father could ever have become about Samuel. . . .

"Erewhon," however, which was written in Butler's late twenties and early thirties, has the freshness and the bravado of Butler's first defiance of the rectory and of his escape from his father and from England; and it is consequently his most attractive, although not his greatest, book. . . . But he has here in his "Erewhon" period something of true intellectual liberation. (And "The Way of All Flesh" and "Life and Habit" followed closely on "Erewhon.") He touches here more intimately than ever afterwards that race of healthy and natural beings, gay, good-mannered and with easy consciences, which he had imagined as the antithesis of the rectory and who were to haunt him and make him wistful all his life. (It will still be the legend of such a race which will delight him so much in Homer; the "authoress of the Odyssey" is probably a fantasy of such a mate as he might have found among them.) And even the eternal antagonism with his father loses here some of its bitterness and strain. (p. 35)

"Erewhon," therefore, is not a production which one can compare to "Candide" or "Gulliver's Travels": it is not the definite expression of a satiric point of view based on mature experience, it is simply the brilliant first book of a young man. It does not pretend either to the logic of Swift or the singleness of intention of Voltaire: it is rather merely a device for uniting an assortment of satirical ideas—in some cases, reductions to absurdity of English ideas and institutions; in others, whimsically suggested improvements on them; in others, flights of fantastic reasoning of uncertain application. . . .

Butler was a moral philosopher, to use the old-fashioned term: he never became a modern scientist. He stuck halfway in an anomalous position between science and traditional theology. It was again the shell of the rectory which he was never able to shed—and perhaps he felt some envy of Darwin, who had been a pupil of his grandfather's at Shrewsbury School. . . .

How did Butler, five years after "Das Kapital," eighteen years after Dickens's "Hard Times," fail to satirize the profit-motive which was turning the machine into a tyrant? He was far from approving the kind of civilization which the middle class had brought with it in its rise. (p. 36)

Yet Butler, though he could be most amusing about people's mercenary motives, was too much a middle-class man himself to analyze the social system in which, for all his financial difficulties, he occupied a privileged position. (p. 37)

Edmund Wilson, "The Satire of Samuel

Butler," in The New Republic *(reprinted by permission of* The New Republic; © *1933* The New Republic, Inc.*), May 24, 1933, pp. 35-7.*

[Butler] was not an artist. He remarks in one of the notes, 'I never knew a writer yet who took the smallest pains with his style and was at the same time readable.' To have thought twice about the words he used, to have tried to refine his language in order to express his meaning with greater exactitude, this would have been, in his view, to blaspheme against the essential Samuel ('You must take me just as you find me'). Better far to stick down everything as it came to mind. . . . (p. 341)

The perpetual need to generalize from a peculiar personal experience maimed his imagination. Even Christianity he could not consider dispassionately because it was the history of a Father and Son. In *The Way of All Flesh* he avenged a little of his childhood's suffering, but he was not freed from the dead hand. His most serious criticism has the pettiness of personal hate, and how will posterity be able to take with respect attacks on Authority (whether it be the authority of God, Trinity College, or Darwin) when the mask it wears is always the cruel, smug, unimportant features of Theobald Pontifex? (p. 342)

Graham Greene, "Samuel Butler" (1934), in his Collected Essays *(copyright © 1951, 1966, 1968, 1969 by Graham Greene; reprinted by permission of The Viking Press, Inc., and in Canada, The Bodley Head, Ltd.), Viking, 1969, pp. 340-42.*

There are various ways of looking at Butler—and Butler meant them, with all the duplicity of which he was capable, to be more various than they are; but in no aspect did he approach perfection except in that for which he cared for perfection least—that of the humorous essayist or lecturer. (p. 227)

Butler was not a scientist—he was not a master of any of the subjects to which he addressed himself; and that fact may explain the strength and beauty of his invective, the bravura of his wit: these qualities were his real obligation. He was, however, profoundly interested in evolution, and he was by nature large enough to find, and maintain at any expense, views of his own sufficiently definite to make the controversy worth carrying on without regard to its personal inspiration. (p. 229)

"We have the same respect," wrote T. S. Eliot, "for Blake's philosophy (and perhaps for that of Samuel Butler) that we have for an ingenious piece of home-made furniture: we admire the man who has put it together out of the odds and ends about the house." The difference, in this respect, between Blake and Butler is that Blake had nothing to begin with but his collected odds and ends, while Butler had resolutely to labour half his life at getting rid of advantages which had been thrust upon him at Shrewsbury and Cambridge. Butler rejected his education as far as he could, and in the process wrote the three satires, *Erewhon, The Way of All Flesh*, and *Erewhon Revisited*, to which our minds are likely to turn when we think of him. . . . The more thoroughly he seemed to have destroyed a thing the more tenaciously he clung to it, because in destroying he found his need for it, and had never either the courage, or the idea, of putting his soul in peril to do without. (p. 231)

> *R. P. Blackmur, "Samuel Butler" (originally published in* Hound & Horn*), in his* The Double Agent: Essays in Craft and Elucidation *(copyright, 1935, by Richard P. Blackmur), Arrow Editions, 1935, pp. 226-33.*

The Way of All Flesh is one of the time-bombs of literature. One thinks of it lying in Butler's desk at Clifford's Inn for thirty years, waiting to blow up the Victorian family and with it the whole great pillared and balustraded edifice of the Victorian novel. (p. 109)

As Irish life runs to secret societies, so English life seems to run naturally to parricide movements. We are a nation of father-haters. *The Way of All Flesh* assuaged a thirst which, one supposes, began with the law of primogeniture and the disinheritance of younger sons. (p. 110)

But what Butler really opposed to Victorianism was not the sort of responsibility we would oppose to it; Butler opposed a system and its myth not with another system but with the claims of human personality. Against Victorianism he placed himself; himself with both feet on the ground, telescope to blind eye and in perverse self-possession, against people whose dreary will to power—and whose hold on spiritual and material property as well—had dried the sap of sense and life.

We cannot think of Butler without the Butleriana. We always come back to Butler as a man. We come back to the undigested slice of rebel egotism. Full of theories himself, he is constantly leaving the ranks of the specialists and joining the amateur ranks of the human beings. (p. 111)

The worldliness, the curiosity, the plainness, the tolerance, the irony, the comeliness of the eighteenth century are qualities which *The Way of All Flesh* revives. . . . Butler would be at home in the cudgeling matches of Johnson or in Swift's dry and incinerating indignations. *Erewhon* is a straight descendant of *Gulliver*—a poorer book because it lacks savagery and the sublime, plain figure of Gulliver himself—it is no fellow to a mild book like *News from Nowhere*. (p. 112)

One's criticism is that the priggishness of Butler, rather than the roundness, gets into the characters of *The Way of All Flesh*. We must except Butler's working-class characters, those collector's pieces, like Mrs. Jupp, the landladies, charladies and servants. A novelist picks those up as he goes along. It is the great weakness of *The Way of All Flesh* that the characters are dwarfed and burned dry by Butler's argument. They are often very tedious. He chose them for their mediocrity and then cursed them for it. They can't stand up to his tweakings. . . .

[One] ends with the feeling that Ernest Pontifex does not amount to much. Why should he come into his fortune? Merely that the unrighteous should have their reward? One does not feel that Ernest has very deeply developed because of suffering or fortune. He has escaped only. And he seems rather lost without his enemy. The weakness is that Butler is doing all the talking. There is no contradictory principle. Ultimately the defense of orthodoxy, even an orthodoxy as dim as Theobald's, is the knowledge of human passions. The strange thing is that Ernest does not give us the impression of a man who enjoys himself; he sounds like a man whose hedonism is a prig's hygiene. (p. 113)

Butler believed that living, like money, should be in the foreground of human life and not an anxiety in its background. He hated the efficient mechanic doctrine, the mechanistic science and (as one sees in *Erewhon*) the machine with its stereotyped response. He pitied the conscious Ernest who toes the line and tried to inflame in Ernest the healthy sabotage of the unconscious. What, strangely enough, Butler failed to find, in this early introduction of the unconscious into English fiction, was the passion. It was odd going to the unconscious and finding there—what? That chronic perversity: common sense. (pp. 114-15)

> *V. S. Pritchett, "A Victorian Son," in his* The Living Novel *(copyright, 1947, 1975 by V. S. Pritchett; reprinted by permission of Harold Matson Co., Inc.), Reynal & Hitchcock, 1947, pp. 109-15.*

[Butler] had never had any literary ambition, though he was a born writer. . . .

When Butler at last gave up the hope that he could ever be anything more in pictorial art than a mediocre painter aiming at correctness of representation instead of self-expression, he took to composing music in the style of Handel, collaborating with his friend and biographer Festing Jones, a musical barrister of genuine talent, who told me that Butler never could manage any tempo more elaborate than two or three crotchets in a bar and that Beethoven was quite beyond him. So this also was a failure, and Butler, though his simple imitations of Handel might also pass as uninspired originals, had to become Festing's librettist and supply him with some screamingly funny oratorio texts. . . . Canon Butler [his father] was a genial old gaffer out of doors but at home was tyrant, judge, jury, and executioner all in one. A hydrogen bomb could not have blasted his reputation more devastatingly after his death than his dutiful son did with his novel called "The Way of All Flesh." (p. 9)

Butler should be considered in the roll of fame neither as novelist nor biologist but as metabiologist, just as we class Hegel not as physician but as metaphysician. This is perhaps because I call myself a metabiologist and was the first, so far as I know, to bring that necessary term into the vocabulary. (p. 10)

> *George Bernard Shaw, "Butler When I Was a Nobody," in* Saturday Review *(copyright © 1950 by Saturday Review, Inc.; reprinted with permission), April 29, 1950, pp. 9-10.*

Samuel Butler's *Erewhon* [is] a work of genius, but with Dante, Gibbon and Tolstoy setting our standards not to be called great. It has been better described as "a serious book not written too seriously."

Published as far back as 1872, it is difficult to classify—partly a yarn, partly an account of Utopia, partly a satire on Victorian civilization. (pp. 219-20)

Although a rebel, [Butler] was not a reformer. He believed in the conventions, provided they are observed humanely. Grace and graciousness, good temper, good looks, good health and good sense; tolerance, intelligence, and willingness to abandon any moral standard at a pinch. That is what he admired. (p. 221)

Why did this book influence me? For one thing, I have the sort of mind which likes to be taken unawares. The frontal full-dress presentation of an opinion often repels me, but if it be insidiously slipped in sidewise I may receive it, and Butler is a master of the oblique. . . .

Erewhon also influenced me in its technique. I like that idea of fantasy, of muddling up the actual and the impossible until the reader isn't sure which is which, and I have sometimes tried to do it when writing myself. (p. 222)

> *E. M. Forster, "A Book That Influenced Me," in his* Two Cheers for Democracy *(© 1938, 1939, 1947, 1949, 1951 by E. M. Forster; reprinted by permission of Harcourt Brace Jovanovich, Inc.), Harcourt, 1951, pp. 219-22.*

[Butler's *Notebooks*] have the crankiness of nature, the stubbornness of personality. They store up Butler as a character, a minor of the Johnsonian school. They are the sketches of a mind and its habits, year in year out; and, taken together, they make an intimate portrait of a peculiarly English type of Worthy: the man who sets out to make recalcitrance respectable—even demure.

Behind those who make a cult of Common Sense we are usually, though not always, entitled to suspect the wounded heart. . . . Butler, we know, was a hurt man. The love he must have proffered at one time to his father and which, on some stern conception of principle or duty, was rejected, rebounded and became the comic anger of satire. Feeling was cut short, pruned back in Butler and its full expression is rare; one remembers only the lines supposedly written about his love for Pauli and his remorse after the death of Miss Savage. But the latter was expressed with a defensive touch of brutality and our lasting impression of the emotional Butler is a wistful and misanthropic one. The ridiculous and ironical make their protective gestures. He is dryly aware of a dull, edgy, armed neutrality in human relationships and he has the stubborn air of a man too sensitive to private pain. And so sensibility is shut off, the spirit of perversity wakes up, the comic eye aggressively winks, and if imagination is there—but there was more dialectic than imagination in him—it is soon nipped by the sobering eye for fact. (pp. 50-1)

The amusement we get out of Butler comes from his stand for Common Sense, Equanimity, Worldliness and the Plain, and from comparing its downrightness with its underlying timidity. . . . (p. 51)

Like Shaw, Butler is without humbug. Possibly it was a form of humbug on Butler's part to pretend to be unrespectable and rebellious, when he was in fact a conservative and rather prim and tetchy character. He was a true Victorian. . . . One thinks of him as a Victorian because he sallied into the great wars of religion in the 19th centruy but he turned them into private wars, fought with home-made weapons of his own invention. He attacked church religion with autobiography. He attacked it with his personality. Like a minor Johnson, he is pithy, downright and scathing. But where Johnson is orthodox, tragic and frontal in his declarations, Butler drops into the ill-wearing habit of paradox. (pp. 51-2)

In Butler one sees the exasperations of the intelligence; in Johnson the baited bear, the growls that can become the

roar of unanswerable moral rage or emotional agony. Then, one feels, Butler was unlucky in his time. He had, as it were, been forced into the Victorian age against his will; he seems to have been born to parcel out the Moral in the fashion of the 18th century, and not to gnash at its unsightly conversion into the conventional morality of the Victorians. And, in fact, their profession and their inherited wealth preserved the whole Butler family from any notion of what the Industrial Revolution did to England. He really wanted, one suspects, what the earlier century had had: a respectable cut and dried and formal God who, except for holidays with the Wesleyans, left the world alone. (p. 52)

Butler's failure in his own lifetime does not seriously affect his spirits; it makes him more phlegmatic and a little touchy, that is all. The *Notebooks* suggest a packed life, the sword never back in the scabbard. Life in whatever *cul de sac* he gets himself into is so dense in its interest, so transformed by his personal curiosity and by his disagreement with it all, that he is more sorry for the bewilderment of the reader than perturbed by it. (p. 53)

Butler's notes have a dry, almost scientific and specimen-like quality. Compressed, worked upon, shaped, made economical though not elegant, they are uttered without comment. It is the vanity of the aphorist. The good-and-evil, vice-and-virtue themes seem now the poorest, and to a contemporary taste the jokes about religion no longer shock and even require—what damns an epigram—an explanation. (p. 54)

In [the *Notebooks*] he hit upon the form most congenial to him: a system of recording guesses about life. The great damage done to Butler in his childhood gave this able, virile and tender man of immensely original curiosity, a craving for the "normal", and the normal could be surmised only by posing extreme statements and from their collision extracting the mean. His wisdom is a kind of practical guesswork and it has a power to move or convince when we feel the hourly puffing and blowing of his experience behind it. (p. 55)

> *V. S. Pritchett, "Butler's Notebooks," in his* Books in General *(© 1953 by V. S. Pritchett; reprinted in the U.S. by permission of Harold Matson Co., Inc., and in Canada by permission of A. D. Peters & Co.), Chatto and Windus, 1953, pp. 50-5.*

Butler's fight against his parents was logically more than just parricide: it was a denial of the family as a unit at all. The family for Butler was the essence of the Victorian prison house. Capitulation to family life was the end of Butlerian freedom; only perhaps a marriage like Shaw's, which brought one solid dividends, would really win Butler's approval.

Even for the artist this distrustful view of freedom might prove ambiguous: it was exactly the wandering dilettante, bachelor bohemianism of Butler himself and of Norman Douglas that made them in the end clever amateurs of literature rather than great writers. More importantly, however, it was an odd foundation for a brave new world, for the sensible, future-looking citizenship which Butler puts forward in *Erewhon Revisited*. It is one of the contradictions which . . . lay beneath the culture of the progressive middle-class families who were the eventual heirs of Butler's teaching. Good comradeliness and straight speaking may be the most satisfactory basis for an old bachelor's emotional friendships; they do not suffice for the subtle and intricate blood ties of family relationship. (p. 196)

One of the Victorians' deepest sentimentalities which Butler exploded was the concept that poverty and disease were in themselves virtuous—an idea that vitiates even the best of Dickens's work. In *Erewhon* and in *The Way of All Flesh* there is no compromise with this hypocrisy, and Butler's personal taste for health and strength in the male fortified this view. The sick and the poor are unlikely to be masters of their own fates—to be "unlucky" in life was one of the sins against the life force in Butler's code. His attacks on Darwin's Natural Selection—put forward in three large volumes, disregarded by the scientific world because of their amateurish foundation—were actuated partly because Darwin was the great Victorian father figure, partly because Butler rightly saw the tyranny that science was assuming over the popular mind, but, mainly because the whole idea of an evolution, controlled not by man's will but by chance, was repulsive to his obsessive need to believe that the rejection of his past was in his own hands. To Butler it must have seemed that he had demolished the blackness and morbidity of the Christian concept of Sin and Atonement only to see a worse black pessimism return with Darwin's evolutionary materialism. . . .

The gravest defect . . . of Anti-Victorianism was its surface appearance of simplicity. Life, it said, could be healthy, clean, sensible, if men only took it into their own hands; mysteries, subtleties, contradictions—all these were simply part of the Victorian refusal to face facts, of puritan morality and hypocrisy, of pomposity and vested interest. No nonsense and plenty of healthy humor were all that was needed to blow the fog away.

Much of this was due to Butler's own character and circumstances. He was a weak man obsessed with the need for absolute personal freedom; he was also a man whom parental Victorianism had made abnormally suspicious of any rhetoric or embroidery in thought. Imagery, poetry, extravagance of language, all these seemed to him the evasions, the casuistry of Victorian preaching.

We have only to read the grotesques of Dickens—Pecksniff, Chadband, Micawber—to see how the Victorians could inebriate themselves with words. Butler was determined to avoid this word-drunkenness. Clarity and simplicity of style was his aim and he achieved it. He is one of the masters of English prose. . . .; but, alas! clarity of style is often achieved by over-simplification of thought, by the avoidance of the obscurities of life. Butlerian Anti-Victorianism was too straightforward to be adequate to the needs of man's complex nature. (p. 198)

> *Angus Wilson, "The Revolt of Samuel Butler," in* The Atlantic Monthly *(copyright © 1957 by The Atlantic Monthly Company, Boston, Mass.; reprinted with permission), November, 1957, pp. 190, 192, 194, 196, 198.*

If the house caught on fire, the Victorian novel I would rescue from the flames would be not "Vanity Fair" or "Bleak House" but Samuel Butler's "The Way of All Flesh." It is read, I believe, mostly by the young, bent on making out a case against their elders, but Butler was fifty when he stopped working on it, and no reader much under that age is likely to appreciate the full beauty of its horrors,

which are the horrors not of the Gothic novel but of family life. Every contemporary novelist with a developed sense of irony is probably in some measure, directly or indirectly, through Shaw and Arnold Bennett and E. M. Forster and D. H. Lawrence, indebted to Butler, who had the misfortune to be a twentieth-century man born in the year 1835. (p. 225)

> *William Maxwell, "Your Affectionate Son," in* The New Yorker *(© 1962 by The New Yorker Magazine, Inc.), October 13, 1962, pp. 225-31.*

Out of his family quarrels [Butler] built an opposition to established conventions. He attacked vigorously but often with something of the child seeking for attention and basically wanting the security of orthodoxy. He is often perverse, sometimes absurd, in the prejudices which he opposes to the prejudices of society—and he often shows that he knew it. (p. 316)

In *Erewhon* Butler worked out some of his venom against the things which he hated because his parents revered them. The Church is parodied in the 'Musical Banks' where people can build up accounts which are payable only in the next world but whose servants insist on being paid in real, immediately usable currency. He mocks at religion for its social respectability and the insurance-policy calculations of certain types of Evangelical piety. It continued to haunt him all his life, and he kept sniping at it without ever shooting it down. More unusual for the time is his recognition of the connection between crime and poverty and his attack on the injustice of punishing actions for which an unequal society was responsible. In Erewhon people are imprisoned for being ill but sent to hospital and visited with sympathy when they break the law. Higgs sees the trial of a poor man for 'labouring under pulmonary consumption', and the irony came too near to truth for the comfort of his readers. He returned to the style and theme many years later with *Erewhon Revisited* . . ., a slighter work out of a weary mind. The new parody of Christianity is dreary: Higgs has been deified by the people because of his previous disappearance into the sky.

[Comparison] with Swift is not to Butler's advantage. There is nothing in *Erewhon* so savagely ironical as Swift's *Modest Proposal* that the surplus Irish children should be killed and eaten. Nor does the framework of the story contain such a convincingly organic whole as the even more fantastic realms of *Gulliver's Travels*. At his best, Butler can be as stimulating as Swift, but the irony is seldom sustained to be carried to its logical conclusion and beyond. The fact is perhaps that Butler, like many late Victorians who railed against their age, was a man with a zest for life in all its vigour and shared the prevailing optimisim that a better society was attainable and indeed probable. The lack of depth in much that he wrote is often hidden under the easy style which invites the reader's confidence and glossed by the quality of his best descriptive passages. (pp. 316-17)

Once again, Butler's skill should not lead us into excessive admiration [for *The Way of All Flesh*]. He said much that needed saying, but he said it mainly out of his own experience. He was one of those whose technical brilliance can make the particular seem universal. There was more to the Victorian family than hypocrisy and repression; the very conventionality which he attacked might build greater security in the child than the permissiveness without moral certainty of some later homes. . . .

Not objective enough to be pure fiction, too fictional to be documentary, *The Way of All Flesh* still has a great deal to say about Victorian society. Butler attacks his age where it felt most confident—or perhaps was most stoutly defending its anxiety. He strikes at the middle-class values, the axioms of respectability. At a period when satire was a rare literary form, though self-criticism was increasing, he combines the two and batters away at the walls which are bastions for the majority but prisons for him. (p. 318)

As a comic novel, *The Way of All Flesh* has higher quality. . . . Few writers caught so well the weakness of aspects of Evangelicalism and the comedy of the parsonical manner. The detached, satirical tone is maintained by Butler's dual role in the story, as the immature Ernest and as the sceptical narrator Overton. . . .

Butler read *The Origin of Species* and embarked on a number of books on evolution which challenged the mechanistic determinism of Darwin's theory. He carried on a running fight with Darwin as well as with the Church, appealing back to Lamarck and the idea of mind and will working on the evolutionary pattern. It is not those fitted by the chance of body who survive, but those who best use their skill and cunning. (p. 319)

This is a more cheerful doctrine than Darwin's, putting the stakes not on physical chance but on individual virtue and the will to succeed. Butler was a good Victorian after all, not least in his fear of a new tyranny in place of the old. (p. 320)

Raymond Chapman, in his The Victorian Debate: English Literature and Society, 1832-1901 *(© 1968 by Raymond Chapman), Basic Books, Inc., Publishers, 1968.*

(Arthur) Joyce Cary

1888-1957

Anglo-Irish novelist, critic, poet, and political scientist. Cary lived in Africa for several years, serving in both political and military positions, and his early novels reflect this experience. His later novels are distinguished by a wealth of characters, empathically drawn; a Dickensian sense of humor; optimism; and vitality. Cary planned three trilogies around the principal concerns of art, politics, and religion. He completed the first two, abandoning the third when his health failed. His trilogies are distinguished by technical virtuosity, especially in the areas of point-of-view and timeshifts. Cary is now considered an important contributor to the trilogy as a literary form.

PRINCIPAL WORKS

Aissa Saved (novel) 1932
An American Visitor (novel) 1933
The African Witch (novel) 1936
Castle Corner (novel) 1938
Mister Johnson (novel) 1939
Charley Is My Darling (novel) 1940
Herself Surprised (novel) 1941
A House of Children (novel) 1941
To Be a Pilgrim (novel) 1942
The Horse's Mouth (novel) 1944
Marching Soldier (poetry) 1945
The Moonlight (novel) 1946
The Drunken Sailor (poetry) 1947
A Fearful Joy (novel) 1949
Prisoner of Grace (novel) 1952
Except the Lord (novel) 1953
Not Honour More (novel) 1955
The Captive and the Free (novel) 1959
Spring Song, and Other Stories (short stories) 1960

It is [an] eighteenth-century acceptance of life in Mr. Cary which makes his work so unusual today, setting him apart as it does, from the world which shrank and shriveled under the touch of the Romantics and their successors, from the Victorians to today's avant-garde.

Mr. Cary has redone Robinson Crusoe (in "The Horse's Mouth") as Gulley Jimson, adrift and isolated among non-artists, and he has redone Moll Flanders as Sara of "Her-self Surprised." Now [in "Prisoner of Grace"] he gives us man as political animal, as seen by the woman he married. Yet this book—one of his major creations—is much more than a "political novel." It is a fascinating exposition of the political attitude that is involved in the very act of living, particularly in this most remarkable marriage of a most remarkable man.

Nowhere is Mr. Cary's gift of not merely thinking like but of being someone else more brilliantly and provocatively displayed than in the portrait which Nina Woodville draws of herself as she sets down her memoir of her husband, Chester Nimmo. "I am writing this book," she begins, "because I understand that 'revelations' are soon to appear about that great man who was once my husband, attacking his character, and my own." Here at once is Mr. Cary's characteristic note, which is something more full-bodied than irony, more sympathetic than satire. (p. 5)

The brilliant portrait of Nimmo, the political animal, is matched by Nina herself, who is simply woman—the woman of all the jokes men tell each other, who never knows her own mind and always gets her own way, whose sex is undifferentiated weapon and pleasure, who lies by nature, says no and means yes (and always to the wrong man), who cannot be trusted for an instant and, when one naturally locks her in, regards such action as justification for any betrayal. She is also the woman whom two men cannot live without and pursue all their lives in lust and fury; and who says calmly of someone quite different, the brother of one of these passionate fools, "I think perhaps *he* was meant to be my man." (pp. 5, 28)

Mr. Cary's extraordinary sense of life, his almost wicked delight in its cross-currents and contradictions and fertility of paradox; his tremendous ability to unify and shape these forces within the bounds of the novel without cramping or distortion, enable one not only to see more than is expected in a novel but farther around it. The deceptive simplicity with which his material seems merely to present itself while every sentence is yet formed and informed with the personality and the obsession of the dominant character sets him off from his contemporaries and makes him not only a master but unique in the way in which he is a master of prose. (p. 28)

Elizabeth Janeway, "'A Great Man Who Was My Husband'," in The New York

Times Book Review (© 1952 by The New York Times Company; reprinted by permission), October 12, 1952, pp. 5, 28.

There are few walks of life, few classes of society, few occupations, about which [Cary] cannot write with complete authority. His insight into the inmost depths of human beings is profound. His understanding of the social changes which have transformed the world in the last half century is impressive. A novelist who never fails to tell a rousing story, he writes with a gusto and sense of the excitement and drama of life which are rare indeed in this age of mincing talents and literary pretensions. Mr. Cary's inexhaustible imagination and comic zest stem from the great tradition of Dickens and Fielding. To touch one of his books is to touch something alive. (pp. 191-92)

Orville Prescott, in his In My Opinion: An Inquiry into the Contemporary Novel *(copyright, 1942, 1943, 1944, 1945, 1946, 1947, 1948, 1949, 1950, 1951, by* The New York Times; *copyright, 1952, by Orville Prescott),* Bobbs-Merrill, *1952.*

Joyce Cary has played a comparatively lone game among contemporary novelists. Although he has experimented in a number of forms he has on the whole rejected the cults both of 'sensibility' (in the Virginia Woolf sense) and of pessimistic decadence (expressed generally through an obsessive introspection or through a rejection of humane values and potentialities). He is a vigorous and extravert writer, not without the kind of sensitivity most admired by sophisticated readers . . . , but capable of developing that sensitivity outward. (pp. 177-78)

Joyce Cary is a writer whose novels, though far from the 'tough guy' school of inverted sentimentality, have a kind of inner toughness most welcome and refreshing. Sometimes, as in *The Horse's Mouth* (in some respects his most important novel) the vitality seems to become a little forced, but the general effect is of a great and individual vigour. The attempt, in some of his books, to return to a picaresque approach—*Herself Surprised* is almost a twentieth-century *Moll Flanders*—is interesting. Here is a writer striving continuously to escape the polite tradition. (p. 178)

Arnold Kettle, in his An Introduction to the English Novel, *Vol. II, edited by Basil Willey, Hutchinson's University Library, 1953.*

[Cary] is not a "difficult" writer; his prose is lucid; his plots complex, perhaps, but always intriguing; his characters are recognizable as human beings, though the behavior of many of them might, in the hands of any other writer, shock a few of the Mrs. Grundys left in the world. A modest man, he has received all of the literary prizes and honors his country has to offer. . . .

The paradox of Joyce Cary, stated simply, is that the unstinted enthusiasm of critics for Mr. Cary's novels in England and the United States over twenty or more years has not persuaded the American public to buy more than a comparatively few thousand copies of any of his novels, with the exception of "The Horse's Mouth." . . . (p. 12)

What Joyce Cary has accomplished is to confront and attack the almost universal conviction, which the shock of the First World War and the long years of the Depression had created, that life was not worth living; to prove the unreality of that twisted fictional world of the last thirty years, inhabited by psychotics, perverts, and gloomy existentialists who flourish on the craving for imaginary thrills of people who have lost their faith in the future. (pp. 12-13)

Harrison Smith, "Artist of Affirmation," in Saturday Review *(copyright © 1955 by Saturday Review, Inc.; reprinted with permission), May 28, 1955, pp. 12-13.*

Joyce Cary's last novel [*The Captive and the Free*] lacks the clarity of structure he worked hard, sometimes too hard, to impose upon his work. But it is one of his finest books, written with a strength and severity one can readily associate with the circumstances of its composition. For one thing, Cary wrote it in the third person; there is none of the distraction of virtuosity that arises in the trilogies, and there is an interesting new tone, of asperity and impatience. (p. 456)

The free souls of this novel are in some sense captives of unexamined drives, paranoid zeal, and frightening illusions. Their freedom lies in their constantly renewed search for the power of conviction and their willingness to unmake their lives in order to realize their vision. . . . Cary, like the romantics, is less interested in the content of conviction than in its form; like Shaw on the Salvation Army or Blake on the "grey monk" or Wordsworth on the Grande Chartreuse, he is less concerned with doctrine than with the power which is conferred by imaginative vision.

The Captive and the Free has an intensity such as Cary rarely achieved in his earlier novels. This is a matter partly of tone and partly of range. There is a curious mixture of astringency and assertiveness in this study of kinds and degrees of commitment. The book extends to an image of a society and, in the manner of D. H. Lawrence's *Women in Love*, it dramatizes the stresses of that society in the relationships of its central characters. Hooper and Joanna can at least remind us of Lawrence's Gerald and Gudrun; and if Cary had little of Lawrence's poetic intensity, he had, like Lawrence, a mind that worked with more delicacy and originality in the symbols of his fiction than in the direct assertion of his ideas. (p. 458)

Martin Price, in The Yale Review *(© 1959 by Yale University; reprinted by permission of the editors), Spring, 1959.*

Those critics are not necessarily captious who point out that Joyce Cary, though a writer with merits mortised in more than the quarter of a century in which he flourished, has a limitation or two. If his panoramic Nigerians and children and Anglo-Irish be excepted, then the characters he has treated at full length, his Johnson, Sara, Wilcher, Jimson, Tabitha, Bonser, Gollan, Rose, Nimmo, Latter, and Nina, for all their diversified aliveness, turn out to be rather narrow in range. The men are either fact-bound creatures or free-leaping empyreans . . .; the women, even more circumscribed, are various composites of such archetypes as Defoe's Moll, Milton's Eve, and, properly enough, Wordsworth's Woman Nobly Planned.

More narrowly as craftsman, Cary also has something to answer for. Writing with omnivorous zest—something short or long of character in situation always in process, as he has told us—he was bound to allow things without distinction to be published. Though novels like *Castle Corner* are also involved, Cary's facility of expression shows its questionable side more readily, of course, in his short stories. A number of these, like some of Graham Greene's and for similar reasons, are no more than field sketches or otherwise undeveloped efforts. True, they make up an interesting group, but to rate them as more than oddments is to overrate them.

It is no harping on the matter, surely, to add that working in terms of the picaresque or the mosaic as Cary did, he often seems to have come to feel that rendition of experience was its own excuse for being. Nothing else so readily explains what some have called his over-evenness of tone but which can more critically be seen as a creative euphoria in which either gusty detail jostles gusty detail in a blaze of story, or, circumstances altering, the dramatic is joined indistinguishably to the non-dramatic in some accretion of a steady narrative. (pp. 596-97)

Reality: here we come to the heart of Cary. . . . Reality for Cary, there is reason enough to believe, refers not so much to the morality of objective presentation nor to the interplay between will and authority nor to the advancement of the creative spirit nor to the posing of good and evil in people nor yet to the observation of characters condemned to dread freedom, nor, taking a leaf from something he himself has said, to the justifying of life to the feelings; it is, rather, to that which subsumes all of these suggestions, namely, to his application of good sense to the perennial urgencies of man.

For in any cross section of Cary's dealings with the stuff of existence, what does one find? Good sense and ever more good sense at work. (p. 597)

Cary is a much-needed contrast to Byronic posturers and egocentric whiners. His work too is corrective, helping to right, as it does, the balance pulled down for some time now on the side of the immature and the off-beat. Judging its future in the light of the slow but growing appreciation it has had, one should not hesitate to say that it will endure. (p. 598)

> *Max Cosman, "The Protean Joyce Cary,"* in Commonweal *(copyright © 1959 Commonweal Publishing Co., Inc.; reprinted by permission of Commonweal Publishing Co., Inc.), March 6, 1959, pp. 596-98.*

[The] late Joyce Cary was much concerned with the various ways in which man could be 'possessed'; it is an appropriate irony that his last novel, *The Captive and the Free,* courageously finished against time and odds, should be about the most extreme of all forms of possession—possession by God. . . .

Cary, in his time, recorded with love a diversity of human conditions; but many of these were freak conditions, and the proposition he really cherished was that all inspired men are crazed and probably crooked, that those by Power possessed are of their natures semi-lunatic. Thus, though we know Cary was the last man to denigrate religion, such is his obsession with the sheer battiness of the God-driven that we end by thinking more of their quirks than of their Godliness. Cary himself says nothing, in his own voice, to redress the balance, and the impression given is that all religions of the fighting kind take as their prophets gin-stinking

ringmasters who own brothels on the side. . . . Now, much as I detest fighting religions myself, I cannot accept the impression Cary gives as being in any way fair or valid except on a declared level of farce. Cary was not writing at such a level. And therefore the controlled intensity, the cool and unhurried conviction with which he spreads his crazy world before us, are to me the measure at once of his power as a creator here and of his failure—by reference to the highest standards—as a novelist. (p. 334)

> *Simon Raven, in* The Spectator *(© 1959 by The Spectator; reprinted by permission of The Spectator), March 6, 1959.*

Joyce Cary did not finish *The Captive and the Free,* but the novel, edited by Mrs Winifred Davin, is reasonably coherent. . . .

Cary's later novels suffered from . . . preoccupation with ideas. They are prodigious efforts of the imagination; they are full of invention; their technique is dazzling. But they are laborious and academic. They may be statements about a single reality, but they are curiously removed from reality. Some quickening element is missing. It seems that Cary, in his ascetic pursuit of ideas, had denied himself the full use of his novelist's gifts. . . .

The Captive and the Free repeats the pattern of the later Cary novel. It is intellectual and cold; characters are subservient to ideas. . . . We are in the airless world of allegory. The action is not always immediately comprehensible; it has to be worked out and even so is sometimes difficult to follow. But the grandeur of Cary's vision cannot be denied. And in this book, written in such heroic circumstances, his grasp of technique is still astonishing. (p. 376)

> *V. S. Naipaul, in* New Statesman *(© 1959 The Statesman & Nation Publishing Co. Ltd.), March 14, 1959.*

Because Cary was not only a very unimaginative but also a very conventional man, his work has a positive, if non-literary, value as a mirror of the prejudices of his class and his generation. His self-confidence allows him to write with all the dash and vigor of someone breaking new ground, but he never hits his reader with an unexpected or difficult thought, or with any of those discoveries about the development of character that are the novelist's business. (p. 174)

["*Charley Is My Darling*"] has the great defect of all Cary's novels: it isn't about the matters with which it claims to deal. It takes one directly into Cary's opinions and prejudices, and its contact with the world of common experience is so tenuous that its essential characteristic is irrelevance. There is nothing wrong with a writer who handles experience from an idiosyncratic point of view, but what Cary has is not a point of view but an enclosure with a high wall of certainty round it. There is less in his writing—much less—than meets the eye. (p. 176)

> *Anthony West, in* The New Yorker *(© 1960 by The New Yorker Magazine, Inc.), April 30, 1960.*

Joyce Cary is Britain's best contemporary popular novelist. Not that he merely sells well—even *Ulysses* sells fairly well—but he writes what readers are prepared to accept. He does not create much pressure toward self-recognition. He is for freedom, imagination, mother, vitality—and who is not? Most first-rate novels confront an intensely felt wish with a resistance that at least recalls the resistance we ourselves meet in the real world. Cary specializes in the intensely felt wish, and in that sense he is popular. Yet he develops this part of experience with a convincingness uncommon in any period. (p. 82)

Cary's unique comfortableness proceeds from his sense that, though events may be unpredictable, character is not. The restless will rises to meet challenge and begins anew to shape things to its obsession. . . . The reader can remain confident through all the characters' troubles because Cary establishes confidence in them. They will meet difficulties in orthodox or unorthodox ways, but they will not stagnate. For all their eccentricities, they stand squarely for the middle-class virtues of drive and applied intelligence. Unlike Hartley, Cary does not defeat his characters in advance; his people do not become senile. . . . They are restless, rebellious, reckless. But Cary gives them two crucial shifts of emphasis. Though they may use fashions for their own purposes, they are individualists who do not stylize their rebellions. And, even more important, Cary wants above all else to reunite impulsiveness with *moral* purpose. Impulse is not its own excuse. The moral purpose may be revolutionizing literature, developing the airplane, mothering homeless men, or reaching a creative ecstasy in painting. The achievement itself may be almost an accident, but Cary wants desperately to show that the restless temperament need not turn to games or self-conscious myths, but by its very existence changes the world. His comic novels could all begin with the same superscription: directed restlessness is the hope of the age. (pp. 83-4)

The First Trilogy, Cary's most important work, consists of two comic novels separated by one in which comedy is incidental. The division follows directly from the main characters' attitudes toward change. Tom Wilcher, the old man who narrates *To Be a Pilgrim,* has spent his life opposing it and seeing it happen. He records with melancholy admiration his brothers' and sisters' attempts to meet life head-on. By contrast, the heroine of *Herself Surprised* and the hero of *The Horse's Mouth* are geniuses of resiliency. In Cary's work only such people make the comic mode and conciliation possible. Tom Wilcher must be treated sadly. (pp. 85-6)

[The] third novel in the trilogy, *The Horse's Mouth,* is Cary's best, and in it Cary faces some of the real obstacles to being in league with the future. Gulley has extraordinary talent for invective against the world, but he also has an inner problem with possibilities. (p. 87)

The Horse's Mouth . . . presents the hero's strong fantasy of himself and the obstacles to making it prevail in a world with purposes of its own. The apparently rambling story does progress—from self-defeating anger through some release in mockery to artistic celebration, "practically a matter of life and death." Yet imaginative detail so submerges this framework that few admirers of Cary will find it enough to account for the impact of the novel. There is something else.

One something-else is giving the reader all the joys of a scattergun rebellion against family, church, and state without making him leave home. Cary mutes the isolation and loneliness of anarchic individualism, and plays up its fun and warmth. (p. 89)

In general, Cary has had a good press. The disposition to believe what he believes is strong. Critics have attributed to him many virtues and a few weaknesses, largely forgivable. (Narrowness is the most common.) He has so much goodheartedness and merry dissatisfaction that it is hard to subject him to questions; yet in the absence of firmer judgment he is likely to lapse from our attention as a good man not quite relevant to present conflicts. For Cary has one weakness that is hard to forgive completely. He is often dull.

The dullness is not an accident; its causes lie at the heart of his work. *The Horse's Mouth* is harder to reread than most comic novels. The excitement and perceptions are there; they are not illusions. But Cary often mixes in Gulley's ramblings without bringing these into any meaningful relation to the novel as a whole. The lively periods are intermittent, and between them Cary doodles. Yet when he tries, as in the last half of *A Fearful Joy,* to speed up the pace, he loses his spontaneous perception and becomes too demonstrative. He can never wholly integrate his simplified framework with sustained play of mind. . . .

Cary becomes dull frequently because he can find no comic interest in the life of necessity. Conditions that must be lived with or fought against unsuccessfully do not engage his comic imagination, and he only recognizes that they exist. (p. 97)

For the time being, at least, he is the last comic novelist of his kind in England. . . . [That] he sometimes writes dully does not diminish him seriously; it may make possible a more accurate understanding of his achievement. (p. 98)

> *James Hall, "Directed Restlessness," in his* The Tragic Comedians: Seven Modern British Novelists *(copyright © 1963 by Indiana University Press), Indiana University Press, 1963, pp. 82-98.*

[All] of [Cary's] novels are about the world of freedom, a world of perpetual change. "Change itself is my country," Cary wrote in [a] letter, and it is the idea of change as freedom that is the underlying theme of his novels. Thus the free soul stands before all possibilities, creating his own special world in art, religion, and politics. The comedy of freedom is the joy of creation itself, but the very act of freedom brings with it responsibility for its consequences whether for good or evil. Paradoxically, the tragedy of freedom—injustice in the world—is an inevitable corollary of the comedy of freedom, for the free act may create evil as well as good. (p. 1)

Joyce Cary wrote in the multiple novel form throughout his literary career and contributed significantly to its development as a literary genre and to its theory as a literary form. (p. 2)

Cary's early approach to the multiple novel form seems to recapitulate the development of this literary genre. . . . These early attempts in the multiple novel constitute Cary's continuing search for a multiple view of reality. This search culminated in the development of the trilogy in which Cary realized a multiple view of reality through the interaction of narrator and form. (pp. 3-4)

Cary's first trilogy is artistically successful, and it is also a new development in the multiple novel: the three separate narrators, each with his own view of reality and his relationship with the other two narrators, represent a unique approach to the problem of form in the multiple novel. Arnold Bennett in his *Clayhanger* trilogy devoted the pattern of each novel to the development of one of the main characters, but the use of the omniscient third-person point of view results in a totally different perspective: instead of a multiple view of reality, we receive a single, over-all viewpoint. (pp. 4-5)

Cary wanted to write a trilogy on each of what he felt to be the major creative activities of man—art, politics, and religion—and even before the completion of the second trilogy, he had a third one in mind. However, when in 1955 his fatal illness was diagnosed as muscular atrophy, he had to give up any plan to write the third trilogy. He used the remaining time of his life to work on the single novel *The Captive and the Free,* which was published posthumously. . . . Though Cary was unable to fulfill his ambition to complete three trilogies, he did write on all three of man's creative activities, for *The Captive and the Free* treats of the artist of the soul, the religious spellbinder.

The form of the multiple novel used by Cary in the two trilogies is at the opposite extreme of narrative technique from the traditional omniscient point of view. It is important to realize that Cary (like Durrell) was not attempting to achieve a total view of reality simply by multiplying the points of view so that these different views would constitute the whole of reality. On the contrary, though each life touches on the others in interlocking relationships, what is ultimately suggested is that the human mind must be content with partial views of reality. (p. 6)

Mister Johnson should be viewed as the final novel in a series of novels on Africa which dramatize the various facets of the African revolution. *Aissa Saved* explores the conflicting religions and beliefs in the war of incompatible ideals, particularly as they affect the mind and emotions of Aissa, herself both product and victim of the revolution. *An American Visitor* examines the effect of conflicting cultures and ideas, particularly within the white community, but everything the whites do and say also deeply affects what the blacks do and say. In *The African Witch* the battle is openly joined between the two races, and this battle is dramatically focused on the conflict within Aladai's mind between his white man's education and his African origins. And finally, in *Mister Johnson* Cary portrays the tragic effect of the revolution on the susceptible and romantic mind of Johnson who, motivated by the illusory vision of heroic destiny, in reality weaves his own doom while believing he is a free man in a white man's world. (p. 42)

The revolution in politics and art that is portrayed in *Castle Corner* emphasizes both the continuity of this novel with the African novels and the shift that has taken place in Cary's development as a novelist. In theme *Castle Corner* continues the exploration of the war of ideas, but the background of this conflict of beliefs is enlarged in scope to include the whole panorama of Anglo-Irish history—the Irish Land Acts, Home Rule, Parnell, imperialism, the Boer War, Radical politics, pacifism, and even the aesthetic movement, all of which have a direct impact on the lives of characters. In characterization the colonial types and the African characters are only a few of the many characters portrayed as each new generation seeks its own destiny in revolt against the old generation, creating the revolution that makes or destroys its happiness and the happiness of its elders. In form Cary attempts to achieve the complexity

of the African novel series by using the family chronicle, contrasting individuals, families, and generations to explore the tremendous changes taking place in politics, economics, religion, art, science, and social customs. (p. 45)

Though *Castle Corner* contains some very fine scenes, it is artistically the most diffuse and least satisfactory of all his published novels. . . . Cary intended its full meaning and impact to be closely dependent on the interrelationship of this novel with the others in the series. To some extent this is true of all multiple novels or novels in sequence: the interrelationship is an organic one in which each succeeding novel throws new light on the characters or the themes. But to be successful each novel of a series must stand alone. After the reader has completed all the novels of the series, he will perceive the larger pattern of the whole, but each novel must itself have organic unity. This is true of the African novels and of the novels in the two trilogies; it is not true of *Castle Corner*. (pp. 46-7)

Though *Castle Corner* is an artistic failure, it is of great significance to the development of Cary as a novelist. A novel of transition, it separates his African novels from his later books and represents a crisis of failure after which he matured as a novelist. (p. 52)

Without his attempt to write the *Castle Corner* series Cary would have been less prepared to write the two trilogies, but by abandoning the series Cary freed himself to experiment with different styles (the present tense of *Mister Johnson* and *Charley Is My Darling*), with different points of view (the autobiographical first person of *A House of Children* and the objectification of the first-person narration in the first trilogy), and with a different approach to the multiple novel. (p. 53)

In *Charley Is My Darling* Cary concentrates on a single character and a single theme. The simplicity of construction in both novels, after the complexity of *Castle Corner,* was an exploration of technique by which Cary sought to achieve greater control over his material before again attempting the complexity of the trilogy form. In *A House of Children* Cary experimented with one more technique—the first person. (pp. 59-60)

Each novel of the trilogy is a full portrait of a character, narrated in the first person from the point of view of the protagonist; each portrait is different because of Cary's ability to enter into the character portrayed. This negative capability, one of Cary's most important talents as a novelist, was his ability to *be* Sara Monday (*Herself Surprised*), an earthy woman who lives by a code of natural morals but who also has a natural capacity for love and forgiveness; to be Tom Wilcher (*To Be a Pilgrim*), the man whom history and change left behind but whose basic wisdom and moral experience enable him to survive and be a pilgrim in a modern world that is drifting aimlessly; and to be Gulley Jimson (*The Horse's Mouth*), a reprobate artist who speaks from the horse's mouth about art and the artist in conflict with society. Though it does not depend upon these approaches, Cary's ability to submerge his own ego into the personality he creates is best illustrated in the trilogy form and the first person point of view. The form of the trilogy enabled Cary to develop the narrating personalities fully, each according to his or her point of view, yet at the same time he could achieve complexity because the themes and the characters of each novel of the trilogy are further developed in the other two novels. (pp. 67-8)

Each of the three narrators in the trilogy is a prisoner. Gulley Jimson (just out of prison) is a prisoner of his art. Tom Wilcher (who is threatened with "imprisonment" in an asylum) is a prisoner of the past. Sara Monday (who is being sentenced to a prison term) is a prisoner of grace. (p. 71)

To Be a Pilgrim as the middle novel of the trilogy gives coherence to the whole; its theme adds a moral and historical dimension to the lives of Sara and Gulley through the voice of Tom Wilcher. Sara is too unreflective and inarticulate to be an interpretative observer. Gulley Jimson is too much the egoistic artist to be the historian of the past. It is Tom Wilcher, introspective and religious, who interprets the past as a pilgrim's progress and thus gives meaning to the present lives of the other characters and his own. (p. 78)

Tom Wilcher is a pilgrim; his moral conscience is the continuity of England's Protestant heritage and his sense of the past is the continuity of England's democratic tradition unbroken by changes in appearance. Underneath the changing exterior of moral codes, political revolutions, economic and social upheavals, he is the steady undercurrent of tradition and order that asks where are we going, to what purpose, why. He is the heritage of Protestant liberalism that can be shocked by his brother Edward's duplicity and cynicism as a practicing politician (the prototype of Chester Nimmo, the protagonist of the second trilogy). He is the heritage of eighteenth-century rationalism that can be repelled by his sister Lucy's religious fanaticism. He is the heritage of Anglican morality that can still be shocked, not by the fact of Ann's extramarital relations with Robert, but by her cold, clinical attitude. He is the heritage of the past that resists change and yet must bow to it inevitably, not because he is stuffy and old-fashioned as the younger generation would like to see him, but because he questions the sense of destroying all of the past—the good with the bad—merely for the sake of being different. (pp. 78-9)

If Sara is the unchanging Eve creating "a society, a relationship, a spiritual world" for herself and her man, and Gulley is the unchanging Adam, doubting, developing, evolving, destroying that which he has created in order to envision a larger creation, then Tom Wilcher is the unchanging pilgrim in the land of unfulfilled promise. (p. 79)

The first-person narrative method of *The Horse's Mouth* not only reveals the mind of the artist, but also illuminates the tragedy of the creative mind: the comic mask which Gulley wears intensifies the catastrophe at the end. Were it not for this method we would see mainly the comedy of action, the impudence and irreverence of the character. Instead we also see the artist at work. *The Horse's Mouth* is, as Cary says, "A study of the creative imagination working in symbols."

The comedy is Gulley's struggle with society; the tragedy is Gulley's struggle with himself and his art. To Gulley "society" is law, authority, popular taste, the Boorjays, and thus to be defied because the artist must be free. Even art itself becomes hardened into a style and is to be rebelled against. To society Gulley is the bohemian exile, the *avant garde* artist, the immoral and irresponsible man (Gulley does steal, cheat, and lie, but basically it is to get money so that he can go on painting, and he is honest with himself when it comes to matters of art). What then becomes clear is the tragic implications of the artist's struggle to release

the creative vision from the prison within himself and translate it into the discipline of form and technique.

This struggle is parodied on the comic level by Gulley's quarrel with society. But even the comic reveals the tragedy of the artist in the modern world: the artist is not valued by society; it fears him as a creator, hates him as a rebel, envies him as a free man. (pp. 88-9)

[Gulley's] three major paintings—"The Fall," "The Raising of Lazarus," and "The Creation"—are the structural foci of the novel. . . . (p. 89)

"The Raising of Lazarus," Gulley's second painting, recapitulates and completes the theme of *To Be a Pilgrim* as "The Fall" rounds out the meaning of *Herself Surprised.* (p. 93)

The subject of "The Creation" is the final development of the theme of freedom as creation and the celebration of Gulley Jimson the creator. The Adam and Eve theme of the fall into freedom with its regeneration through love and the resurrection theme of rebirth through faith are the symbolic elements of creation. (p. 95)

Gulley never completes his painting, but creation is never complete. Life and art, Cary is saying, both stand before all possibilities. Creation is infinite; beauty unlimited in its variety. Gulley's life is completed, but art and life go on. (p. 97)

As the final novel of the trilogy Cary used *The Horse's Mouth* to extend the meaning of the first two novels and complete the portrait of Gulley Jimson, an artist's self-portrait. Both Wilcher and Jimson complete the portrait of Sara; they see her from different points of view, but together they fill in the missing pieces. Wilcher reveals the human side of Sara, against which Gulley constantly wars; Gulley reveals the aesthetic side of Sara through his art, which Wilcher does not know. Wilcher interprets the past since both Sara and Gulley live entirely for the present. Gulley interprets the present through his art because his art creates the present. Sara sees herself, for neither Wilcher nor Gulley can reveal the whole Sara. Wilcher speaks for himself because neither Sara, who is unreflective, nor Gulley, who is his enemy, can speak for him. Gulley speaks for himself because neither Sara nor Wilcher can speak for the artist. (pp. 97-8)

Cary is clearly on the side of the free against the captives in all his novels. The comedy of freedom is the love, joy, beauty, and happiness of life itself. Paradoxically, the tragedy of freedom is the injustice that exists in life as a necessary condition of freedom. The greatest freedom is achieved in creative activity, whether in politics, religion, or art, but with creativity comes responsibility for evil as well as good. The free are captives of their captivity which makes them free, but as Cary notes, "The Free *perceive* their captivity which is the conditions [sic] of their creative life." To understand one's captivity is to be free. (p. 169)

> *Charles G. Hoffman, in his* Joyce Cary: The Comedy of Freedom *(reprinted by permission of the University of Pittsburgh Press; © 1964 by the University of Pittsburgh Press), University of Pittsburgh Press, 1964.*

Cary seems somewhere between the new and the old. The

"modern" novelist tends to ask questions, not to give answers. The older novelists tended to give the answers: Society is like this; the legal system is wrong for this or that reason; and serving girls who are not circumspect can expect this! The modernist seems to say: Is this the way it is? Cary seems to say, Look, haven't you seen how certain types behave? Listen closely, and you'll hear that tone of voice that is heard all over the Empire. Or, that Mister Johnson, isn't he like impulsive, hard-driving, creative men everywhere? The generalizations are there, but they are tentative, not insisted upon.

The novelist's problem is the discovery of a satisfactory form. Cary was, in a sense, obsessed with that need. In *Art and Reality,* written for Cambridge lectures he was too ill to give, he spoke of two sorts of mind: the analytical-conceptual, and the intuitive-imaginative. Strong on theorizing, Cary would write an essay or give a radio talk at the drop of a hat. He was a great explainer. He was also an artist. . . . His problem was to keep Cary the analyst and Cary the theorizer in check, and to give Cary the intuitive-imaginative man as much freedom as he could take without fouling the reins. (pp. 4-5)

Cary's characters are not so grotesque as Dickens's characters, nor does he create such a variety of them. On the other hand, although he creates them larger than life, he does not rely on caricature. There may be a limitation in Cary's characterizations in that he prefers his characters to have creative imagination. It is, he felt, one of the great treasures. This may be a limitation, but it gave Cary an affirming vision of life that thus far has been very rare in the fiction of the twentieth century. (pp. 6-7)

Joyce Cary looked upon himself as a political writer whose subject was freedom. Nineteenth-century liberals defined liberty as freedom from restraint. Cary defined it as freedom to create. (p. 13)

Cary has been criticized for writing a patronizing book about an ignorant and naive black man, Mister Johnson. But the novel, *Mister Johnson,* is no such thing. Cary does Johnson the honor of treating him as a wildly creative man, the sort of human being that delighted Cary.

Mister Johnson is Cary at his simplest, with a minimum of political and sociological theorizing. Mister Johnson, a joyful creator—of happiness and his own destruction—is a pure Cary type, indifferent to consequences, driven, and imaginative. (p. 21)

Cary was given to trying to force more material into the sequence of a story than character, theme, pace, or plot could comfortably accommodate. The wild, vital life, or the innocuous lassitude, of a given character struggles—and sometimes doesn't struggle—to join the forward motion of a story. In *Castle Corner* inchoate scenes—in this case in Northern Ireland, England, and Africa—touch one another. Beginnings come to little, and things appear not to mean much. (p. 30)

A not inappropriate term to be used if one wishes to be negative about Cary is naturalism. For all of his *joie de vivre,* furious vitality, and Blakean joy, he is a kind of naturalist. His characters do not wrestle with the angel all night, carefully pick or choose, or scrupulously weigh alternatives. Life is force. Lust, parenthood, money, success, fighting, warmth, hope, despair—these and fifty more

forces are the currents, the eddies, the streams in which lives flow.

Nineteenth-century naturalists, outside of their fiction, tended to preach a meliorist doctrine, were socialists, and believers in science. In their fiction, they present forces—atavisms, diseases, the country, the city, the beast in man—and a background glowering darkly, with reddish flames threatening destruction. Man lived at the edge of despair. Cary's naturalism is of a different sort. His Bonsers and Tabithas live their lives fully, joyously. Defeats, despair, humiliations, and anger are leavened by joy. Wars come and go. So too the Liberals and the Conservatives. Art movements flourish and fade. Newspapers wage campaigns against child labor, against the Hun, for Irish home rule, or for understanding of the black masses. The lives of Bonser and Tabitha are affected, or not affected. They go on living, suffering and enjoying. (pp. 34-5)

For Cary life flowed turbulently, abundantly. Probably this is why his short stories, collected as *Spring Song . . .,* seem only outlines for novels. They are too terse to achieve either the comedy or vitality of the best novels. He needed a broad canvas, and perhaps this is why the two trilogies may prove to be his best work. (p. 43)

> *William Van O'Connor, in his* Joyce Cary *(Columbia Essays on Modern Writers Pamphlet No. 16; copyright © 1966 Columbia University Press; reprinted by permission of the publisher), Columbia University Press, 1966.*

Cary, like Joyce in the twenties and thirties, either has received outrageous praise or been subjected to excessive attack, all less for his work itself than for what he stands for and what he is: a link to the past, a novelist interested in morality, a traditionalist who finds workable things of greater importance than the new and the strange, a conservative who cannot conceive of the darkly irrational superseding the rational (even the tumultuous Gulley Jimson in *The Horse's Mouth,* for example, lives according to his own explicable principles). In a way, Cary is a "didactician" writing novels, and his supporters have lined up accordingly. (p. 130)

Anxious to catch an individual at the moment his actions are questioned by another, Cary works out his character relationships without trying to appear a moralist. Yet, despite this effort to be emancipated from dogma and despite the ultra-modern devices that he intermittently uses, there is a curious old-fashioned quality to his work; somehow, his ideas have failed to come to grips with a modern world. The terms of Cary's world, even when he is discussing an anarchic artist like Gulley Jimson, are as ordered as any in the nineteenth century. . . . Jimson is not self-destructive, irrational, or in contact with underground devils; rather, like his nineteenth-century predecessors, he perpetuates himself through the only means he knows: the expression of his individual will through art. For in Cary's world, the individual still thinks his will can conquer and prevail. (pp. 132-33)

It is precisely this reasonable "rounded" property of Cary's characters which gives the old-fashioned quality to his work, making him seem closer to the major nineteenth-century novelists than to those of the twentieth century. Moreover, Cary's castigation of "modern" looseness and aimlessness seems like an echo from a moralistic past, in which directions and goals were more significant than individual deviations. His characters' anarchy is superficial, their lack of control only external, their loss of purpose only partial. Even if they destroy in order to re-create, they destroy with a definite end in view. Their actions are motivated by things they understand: self-interest, ambition, the need to create, the urge to fix a particular design on life.

The only area in which Cary tries to break this pattern is in his creation of female characters, who become, as it were, buffers between the various males and the rest of society. Only his women seem really chaotic, but even they come to operate according to certain principles of behavior imposed from without. (pp. 133-34)

Cary's women . . . exist to make slaves of the men who originally attract them. They turn sexual charm into a moral asset, and although they seem as caught up emotionally as the man they seduce, actually their use of sex is for a predetermined purpose. Still, they are attractive and often seem more sinned against than sinning. In a way, however, they are personally to blame for their downfall, for they operate behind a disguise. Theirs is a vision of the world in which man will be securely tied to the woman of his choice, and his horizons will not extend beyond the family hearth.

Characters of this type, whether male or female, overwhelmed as they are by Cary's moral views and comic sense, cannot go too deep or too far. (pp. 134-35)

Cary rarely stops long enough to create people at their moment of decision; for him, they are fixed by what they are, and they are unable to change or grow. Therefore, despite his interest in character, Cary never comes to grips with people in whom real choice is involved. And although his main themes are concerned with the demands of conscience, ambition, and duty, Cary, unlike C. P. Snow, only infrequently surprises us with the conflicts implicit in a character's awareness of these qualities.

A kindred fault of Cary's novels . . . is the easy acquiescence of his characters to whatever befalls them. (p. 135)

Most of these strictures against Cary tend to destroy his answers to the questions his novels raise. That is to say, important questions are suggested in the narrative: Is genius an excuse for personal expediency? Can freedom and authority be reconciled? How can human liberty and social necessity complement and not conflict with each other? But these questions are rarely answered in terms of the characters, who lack the depth to confront such issues. The answers seem presented, instead, in terms of drifting and sliding characters or hit-and-run comments by the author. The questions, in a way, are in excess of what the answers can possibly be.

This conscious avoidance of thinking characters considerably reduces and thins out Cary's themes; and yet he is evidently more than a simple humorist. (pp. 137-38)

It is, we have seen, his characters' failure to feel conflict that causes the softness and dormancy in a Cary novel. People usually seem the products of their surroundings or of influences upon them, and even his well-rounded successes "arrive" more because of circumstances than inner will. As a philosophical view of the world, this is, of course, perfectly acceptable. One may claim, as several major novelists have, that inner will is less important than

the confusion that characterizes life, and success itself therefore is fortuitous and dependent not upon principle but upon expedience. However, such a view must be dramatized so that the author seems to control his characters. What Cary's characters impose upon the scene is usually less than what is willy-nilly imposed upon them. Unlike Virginia Woolf, for instance, Cary presents distinctly neither the will of his characters nor the muddle of life, and the result is a blurred outline of rapidly moving events.

Cary, we remember, praised Dostoyevsky's ability to let his characters follow their own paths without interference even though they pass beyond the author's own sense of proportion. Nevertheless, in precisely this area, Cary failed. . . . Cary often substitutes successive short and choppy episodes for the kind of analysis that would give meaning to the individual scene, as if his inventive skill were running ahead of his interpretive powers. In the political trilogy, for instance there is a headlong rush of episodes, one following fast upon the other, one scene breathing, so to speak, down the neck of the one ahead, so that the reader is rarely permitted to focus on the immediate situation. The characters themselves seem to be dashing toward the end of a requisite number of episodes, several of which, taken individually, are humorous and effective, but with their overall sense of dramatic inevitability lost along the frenzied way.

To compare Cary once again with C. P. Snow, a writer clearly lacking the former's verbal facility and sense of wit, we can see that Snow has an essential quality that Cary fails to demonstrate: the ability to convey intellectual content in characters who are supposed to have minds. (pp. 141-42)

[Cary's] strength, throughout, rested on his exuberance, his vitality, the vibrancy of his prose, the variety of his characters. All these virtues are real. But while one should not castigate Cary for having failed to expand the novel form any further, one can admonish him for not having availed himself of what existed. Although he reworked many techniques with which Joyce and Virginia Woolf had experimented (*The Horse's Mouth,* for example, is full of interior monologues and attempts at stream of consciousness), nevertheless his novels are full of old-fashioned ideas and characters. . . . The result, for Cary, is to be categorized as a minor novelist with the gifts of a major one, a minor humorist lacking the sweeping vision of a major satirist or ironist, a minor artist simply because he remained, for one reason or another, a minor thinker. (pp. 145-47)

> *Frederick R. Karl, "Joyce Cary: The Moralist as Novelist," in his* The Contemporary English Novel *(reprinted with the permission of Farrar, Straus & Giroux, Inc.; copyright © 1962 by Frederick Karl), Noonday, 1970, pp. 131-47.*

In his preface to *Prisoner of Grace,* Joyce Cary defends Chester Nimmo against the accusation that he is a crook. The defense is interesting, less for the reasons Cary gives to explain why Nimmo was not intended as a crook, than for the fact that he should feel compelled at all to explain how one of his characters should be understood. . . . All the novels before the last trilogy manage to establish values without any equivocation whatever. Fundamental disagreement as to the worth of a character has no precedent in

Cary, and the interesting question of the trilogy is not so much *What* is Chester? but rather *Why* Chester?

Cary's own conception of Nimmo is clear: he is one of his artist-heroes, a man of immense imagination moving creatively through a world which is perpetually renewing itself around him. Nimmo's creative response to his own freedom and isolation—those two basic conditions of living in Cary's universe—is repeatedly emphasized by Cary in his working notes for the novel: "Chester's quickness of *idea,* of *imagination,* a daring mind".... "Plot. *Central Point.* Principle and imagination. Chester always *running into dogma* and then being revived *by imagination.*"

Nimmo, then, clearly fits into the tradition of Mister Johnson, Charley, Sara, and Gulley, the exuberant artist-heroes of the earlier fiction. Although only Gulley creates lasting works of art, for Cary all are artists in their ability to create their own lives out of the freedom and chaos around them.... But to establish Chester's artistic lineage is at once to underline how enormously he deviates from it. For while Cary is forced to dispel the confusion over Chester's moral being, Johnson, Charley, Sara, and Gulley romp gaily outside the law with total immunity, their criminal proclivities never for a moment endangering our sense of their absolute goodness.... Although Chester has obviously inherited their creative genes, he differs fundamentally from his artist ancestors in two respects: he does not do anything nearly as bad as they do, and he is not nearly as good as they are.

The movement from the transparent goodness of the earlier comic heroes to Chester's opaqueness can best be understood as a function of Cary's changed apprehension of the world. Afflicted from the beginning of his career with a profound sense of the suffering and injustice of life, it is clear that by the time he came to the last trilogy Cary could no longer sustain that vision of a sublimely gay innocence which vitalizes *Mister Johnson, Charley Is My Darling, Herself Surprised,* and *The Horse's Mouth....* ["Realness"] is what distinguishes Nimmo and his universe from that of the innocent artist-heroes.... Although Gulley and the others are finally destroyed—as all men must inevitably be in Cary's novels—they manage momentarily to achieve a transcendent serenity not permitted Nimmo (or anybody else) in the second trilogy. Cary's real world does not allow unalloyed goodness or delight to exist.

The darkening of Cary's vision—his loss of faith in the transcendent powers of innocence—is implicit in the political focus of the second trilogy.... The endless manipulation of people and "facts," the unhesitating and callous use of power, the conniving, distorting, and concealing which Cary knows to be an inescapable part of political reality now become for the first time the conditions of personal relationships as well. The background of *Prisoner of Grace* (and accordingly of the whole trilogy), Cary indicates, is "the universal political position—the necessary management of human nature and human beings."

This necessity for management is new in Cary's fiction; in the comic novels, relationships flourish without it. (pp. 332-35)

Nimmo does not share the simple contours of the earlier artists. While they impress us as being larger than life, Nimmo very obviously *is* life with all its attendant complexities and uncertainties. This difference in dimension is important, for life-sized characters do not receive the same immunity from moral censure we gladly grant the others. (p. 336)

[If, in *Not Honour More,*] Jim's political idiocy appears initially refreshing, Cary does not allow us to enjoy it for very long.... Jim's inflexible responses prove inadequate to the demands of a world without solid objects, a complex and difficult world in which the facts are always different from the truth. Insisting on purity in a tarnished world, searching for the absolute when there is only the relative, Jim ends by stripping himself of all credibility as a moral witness....

For Cary, it is precisely the burden of the politician to reject simple formulations. Having accepted the responsibility of managing imperfect people in an imperfect world—a responsibility, Cary feels, involving moral heroism of the highest sort—the politician cannot afford the luxury of easy appeals to truth and honor such as Jim makes. (p. 337)

Chester remains an unanalyzable compound of cynical opportunism and genuine political commitment. Cary is scrupulously careful not to permit us the comfort of isolating the dominant motives in his behavior. The very point on which the whole trilogy insists—the fluid nature of reality which cannot be fixed or defined—is forced upon us in the person of Chester. Unable to categorize him satisfactorily, we must finally accept him in all his elusiveness. However human the desire for certainty, it is something we pursue, as Jim's example is intended to show, at our own peril....

Looked at simply as a sustained creative effort, Chester's life is a miracle of energy and ingenuity.

But if in itself the effort has much about it that is admirable, the final result of that effort, both for himself and for others, has very little.... The sterile wasteland produced by Chester's talents is altogether different from the landscape created by the previous artist-heroes. The debris of his world is not found in theirs: while he leaves behind swamps of poisoned water, Gulley, Sara, Charley, and Johnson leave only enclaves of light and order and affection. The suffering that Chester's "successes" inflict on others is not paralleled in the comic novels.... Surrounded by walls and lies and broken bodies, Chester is the first of Cary's artists whose creativity does not embrace and enrich the world around him.

Nimmo, then, remains ambiguous—as Cary intended him to be. His motives, his methods, and even his achievements cannot be neatly evaluated. In his elusiveness he serves as the appropriate center for the "real" world of Cary's political trilogy, which does not permit the simple moral clarity of the earlier novels. The vision of innocence responsible for the comic novels is finally overwhelmed, in Cary, by the bitter facts of experience, and if Gulley is the proper hero of innocence, so Chester is of experience. Perhaps the best way to understand Chester is suggested by a comment in one of Cary's notebooks—"Nimmo as a *symbol* both of good and evil"—which tells us much about Cary's sense not only of Chester but also of the political world in which he lives. (pp. 338-40)

Michael Rosenthal, "Joyce Cary's Ambiguous Chester Nimmo," in South Atlantic Quarterly *(reprinted by permission of the Publisher; copyright 1971 by Duke University Press, Durham, North Carolina), Summer, 1971, pp. 332-40.*

Throughout *The Horse's Mouth,* Gulley Jimson struggles to liberate himself from the shortsighted concerns of a society that cannot afford to accommodate him. While he remains focused on an eternal, innocent world where truth and beauty are one, most of the people around him are committed to a corrupt, practical existence where truth is harsh, brutal, ugly—and where beauty is seldom noticed, much less penetrated to reveal a fresh vision of hope and wisdom. As his society stumbles along the shallow, shadowy surfaces of life, Gulley concerns himself solely with the substance—the pure energetic beauty at the heart of all life. His pursuit of the divine in a decayed, secular atmosphere is reminiscent of Aschenbach's quest for moral and aesthetic perfection in plague-ridden Venice. [Seltzer's reference is to Thomas Mann's *Death in Venice*.] But whereas Mann's hero watches in horror as his ideal becomes infected by the reality it had struggled vainly to transcend, Gulley truly believes his ideals to be immune from the contaminated touch of the concrete world. A true Platonist, Gulley is neither deceived nor depressed by the world of appearances, because the surface of reality becomes increasingly dispensable as all things open up to reveal their divine essence; everything sings the wonder, ecstasy, glory of God's creation. This is the only music Gulley cares to hear, and so he concentrates more and more on the eternal form rather than its earthly cover or equivalent. (pp. 491-92)

Here is the greatest irony of all: Gulley is to use Hitler's eyes to reflect the full glory of God's creation; the symbol of political malevolence becomes the artist's means for rendering his vision of divine benevolence. Dismissing the single attribute of the man we consider the most important —i.e., his moral character—Gulley selects only those features useful to him, as though Hitler were no more than an object. Just as Gulley need know nothing about a model's values in order to paint his feet, Hitler's political identity could not be less relevant to the artist who is, after all, on his own mission. (p. 500)

Cary needn't have mentioned Hitler in his story of Gulley's struggle and oppression—and he certainly could have introduced Sara's death at a different point. But by delaying the reader's knowledge of Sara's death until [the] tavern scene discussion of Hitler, Cary has made it impossible for us to ignore the social implications of Gulley's commitment to his art. We are forced now to see that Gulley is ultimately not all that different from Hitler in his willingness to sacrifice anyone or anything to his cause. The Jews got in Hitler's way very much as Sara got in Gulley's way. For Gulley too, then, ends have been made to justify means with horrifying results. As a murderer, Gulley, who proclaims freedom, becomes his own contradiction of the vision he wants to express. We can no longer say that art and politics do not mix, for we are now made to realize that they really can and in fact *do* mix, sometimes quite atrociously. The inevitable outcome for the committed artist is to fail somewhere in his commitment as a man to other men and to the best in himself. (p. 501)

Alvin J. Seltzer, "Speaking Out of Both Sides of 'The Horse's Mouth': Joyce Cary vs. Gulley Jimson," in Contemporary Literature *(© 1974 by the Board of Regents of the University of Wisconsin), Vol. 15, No. 4, Autumn, 1974, pp. 488-501.*

Willa (Sibert) Cather

1873-1947

American novelist, short story writer, poet, and journalist. Willa Cather was born in Virginia, lived in Nebraska from the age of eight until after graduation from college, moved to Pittsburgh to work as an editor, journalist, and educator, toured Europe several times, then moved to New York. A strong literary influence in her work was Sara Orne Jewett's advice that she write from her own background; the Nebraska novels of pioneer and immigrant life that followed are among America's most impressive fiction. The spare purity of her prose and her serious treatment of aesthetic and moral concerns take her far above the ranks of merely regional writers. Cather won the Pulitzer Prize in 1922 for *One of Ours;* however, *My Ántonia* and *Death Comes for the Archbishop* are now considered her most distinguished works.

PRINCIPAL WORKS

April Twilight: Poems (poetry) 1903
The Troll Garden (short stories) 1905
Alexander's Bridge (novel) 1912
O Pioneers! (novel) 1913
The Song of the Lark (novel) 1915
My Ántonia (novel) 1918
Youth and the Bright Medusa (short stories) 1920
One of Ours (novel) 1922
April Twilights, and Other Poems (poetry) 1923
A Lost Lady (novel) 1923
The Professor's House (novel) 1925
My Mortal Enemy (novel) 1926
Death Comes for the Archbishop (novel) 1927
Shadows on the Rock (novel) 1931
Obscure Destinies (short stories) 1932
Lucy Gayheart (novel) 1935
Not under Forty (essays) 1936
Sapphira and the Slave Girl (novel) 1940
The Old Beauty, and Others (short stories) 1948
On Writing (essays) 1949

Something more than Miss Cather's own experience first upon the frontier and then among artists and musicians has held her almost entirely to those two worlds as the favored realms of her imagination. In them, rather than in bourgeois conditions, she finds the theme most congenial to her interest and to her powers. That theme is the struggle of some elect individual to outgrow the restrictions laid upon him—or more frequently her—by numbing circumstances. . . . Pioneers and artists, in Miss Cather's understanding of their natures, are practically equals in single-mindedness; at least they work much by themselves, contending with definite though ruthless obstacles and looking forward, if they win, to a freedom which cannot be achieved in the routine of crowded communities. . . .

Miss Cather would not belong to her generation if she did not resent the trespasses which the world regularly commits upon pioneers and artists. For all the superb vitality of her frontier, it faces—and she knows it faces—the degradation of its wild freedom and beauty by clumsy towns, obese vulgarity, the uniform of a monotonous standardization. Her heroic days endure but a brief period before extinction comes. Then her high-hearted pioneers survive half as curiosities in a new order; and their spirits, transmitted to the artists who are their legitimate successors, take up the old struggle in a new guise. (p. 92)

Fiction habitually strives to reproduce passion and heroism, and in all but chosen instances falls below the realities because it has not truly comprehended them or because it tries to copy them in cheap materials. It is not Miss Cather's lucid intelligence alone, though that too is indispensable, which has kept her from these ordinary blunders of the novelist: she herself has the energy which enables her to feel passion and the honesty which enables her to reproduce it. Something of the large tolerance which she must have felt in Whitman before she borrowed from him the title of "O Pioneers!" breathes in all her work. . . .

Taste and intelligence hold her passion in hand. It is her distinction that she combines the merits of those oddly matched progenitors, Miss Jewett and Walt Whitman; she has the delicate tact to paint what she sees with clean, quiet strokes; and she has the strength to look past casual surfaces to the passionate center of her characters.

The passion of the artist, the heroism of the pioneer—these are the human qualities Miss Cather knows best. (p. 93)

> *Carl Van Doren, in* The Nation *(copyright 1921 by the Nation Associates, Inc.), July 27, 1921 (and reprinted in his* Contemporary American Novelists: 1900-1920, *Macmillan, 1922).*

Miss Cather ranks with Mrs. [Edith] Wharton, Mr. [Booth] Tarkington, Mr. [Joseph] Hergesheimer, and a few others as one of the American talents which are not merely agreeable but worth the most exact study. . . .

Yet her name is, even after such novels as *My Ántonia* and *O Pioneers!,* scarce known to the general public. . . . Her style is so deftly a part of her theme that to the uncomprehending, to the seeker after verbal glass jewels, she is not perceivable as a "stylist" at all. But to the more discerning Miss Cather is a phenomenon to be examined excitedly, both as a pure artist and as an interpreter. (pp. 171-72)

In the world of the artist it is the little, immediate, comprehensible things—jackknives or kisses, bath sponges or children's wails—which illuminate and fix the human spectacle; and for the would-be painter of our Western world a Sears-Roebuck catalogue is (to one who knows how to choose and who has his imagination from living life) a more valuable reference book than a library of economics, poetry, and the lives of the saints. This axiom Miss Cather knows; she has lived by it not only in her prairie novels but in the sketches of that golden book *Youth and the Bright Medusa,* in which the artist's gas stove and the cabman's hat are paths to everlasting beauty. In *One of Ours* that truth does guide the first part of the book, but she disastrously loses it in a romance of violinists gallantly turned soldier, of self-sacrificing sergeants, sallies at midnight, and all the commonplaces of ordinary war novels. . . . (p. 173)

> *Sinclair Lewis, "A Hamlet of the Plains," in* New York Post *(reprinted by permission of the* New York Post*; © 1922, New York Post Corporation), September 22, 1922 (and reprinted in* The Man From Main Street: Selected Essays and Other Writings, 1904-1950, *edited by Harry E. Maule and Melville H. Cane, Random House, 1953, pp. 170-74).*

[Miss Cather's] merit lies in her exceptional honesty; she has not, in the novels of Nebraska, written a meretricious line. It lies in her having an intelligence above that of most practitioners of her art. It lies in a certain dignity.

Honesty, intelligence, and dignity are no mean equipment when they are joined to a special faculty which is the power to communicate. (p. 438)

Let modern aesthetics persuade us that the two things coincide, that the impression conditions the expression (or communication); the reader of Miss Cather's novels cannot help feeling a small abyss between them; he cannot help feeling that the impression must have been a little more intense than it seems; that the lines of communication have somewhere broken down. . . .

Despairing, possibly, of the novel afflicted with too protrusive a point of view, she has managed to write one [*One of Ours*] with none at all; she has recorded without creating; she has described without evocation. (p. 439)

[That] this book fails to come to life is not to be set down to a lack of genius, for a fair talent can make a book live. It is due, I think, to the calculated pursuit of a purpose alien to fiction, the purpose to record, rather than to create.

When this purpose is forgotten Miss Cather's deliberate care in statement, her occasional utterance neither shrill nor weak of passion, lead her to veritable creation. . . . The

small successes are fine indeed and from them one gathers certainty that Miss Cather can do pretty nearly whatever she wants to do; one feels from them that the fields of ripe corn and the tides of human joy and suffering have with intensity been present in her mind's eye, that she has checked the buoyant power, the humour, the vitality which tried to get into her book. Possibly she found no place for them in a record of small and dispirited things and people. It is an error in conception, and the error in design (common in her work: the book breaks in half) illuminates. For the trouble is not that the war cuts off the solution of Claude's problem in marriage; it is that the second half of the book is *about* the war, and cuts off the solution of the aesthetic problem as well. (p. 440)

> *Claude Bovary, in* The Dial *(copyright, 1922, by The Dial Publishing Company, Inc.; reprinted by permission of J. S. Watson, Jr. and Scofield Thayer), October, 1922 (and reprinted by Kraus Reprint Corporation, 1966).*

[Although it is possible that] Miss Cather's avoidance of big scenes, her preference for significant detail, is a sign of literary tact in her, [one] comes to doubt whether her ability to write is equal to the strain of the big scene. Signs are not lacking that her art is extraordinarily conscious, chiefly conscious exclusion. . . . The completed work is not the crystallization of the conception; if it were, she would not be tempted to digress or to strike false notes. Her unity is attained, if at all, not under compulsion of an inner force, but by careful pruning off of excrescences. Her earlier novels especially seem not to have grown from a germ but to have been put together, built up—even to owe much to a notebook.

This flaw (if my analysis is not in error) is all the stranger because Miss Cather obviously has passion. Intensity of feeling, especially a keen sympathy, is manifest in all her work. The trouble is that it is seldom communicated to the reader; we perceive its presence, but we do not ourselves fully experience it, at least not more than two or three times in a novel. Her emotion should fire her imagination, and so, in turn, her writing; but there is a break somewhere in the chain. . . .

Nothing is more striking about the Cather country than the vein of hardness, as of iron or flint, that runs all through it. Sometimes it is harsh, even brutal. No other quality of Miss Cather's is more impressive than her sense of fact, then her clearness of eyesight and honesty of mind. If she may properly be called refined and fastidious, these traits come not from squeamishness, not from the shrinking, timorous *noli me tangere* which vitiates so much American writing. . . . She is at once fine and strong, and this uncommon union more than anything else distinguishes her from her contemporaries. She has poise and balance.

A similar distinction from other writers of the day lies in the fact that her world is tragic (otherwise she would not be a modern) but not futile. Whether her protagonists succeed or fail, the tragic aspect is there; if, like Alexandra and Thea, they succeed, it is at great cost in suffering and in a sort of hardening of the spiritual arteries. If they fail, the waste is still more obvious—for the essence of her tragedy, as perhaps of all tragedy, is the waste of human possibilities. Yet, with all its waste, life in her rendering is not futile. In her favorite theme, the struggle of a superior individual with an unworthy society, there is compensation in the very fineness which separates her protagonists from their neighbors. Passion is its own reward; to have cared intensely about anything, even if one has not gained it, is not to have lived in vain. . . .

Perhaps the shrewdest criticism yet made of Miss Cather is that she represents the "triumph of mind over Nebraska." The victory was not bloodless; it has left its scars. Among her many difficulties, much the most serious has been that in her youth her imagination was undernourished. A desiccated and sterilized life affords little sustenance to poet, dramatist, or novelist. The marvel is that she has been able to achieve so much, to discover so much humanity in that flat and vacant land, with its rich soil and human poverty. If her books suffer in comparison with those of writers who have grown in a more fertile society, they are yet opulence itself compared, say, with those of Sinclair Lewis. If the world of her creation does not abound in variety and intrinsic interest, it is because the material on which her imagination fed was lacking in those elements. She has extracted from it all the meagre juices it afforded.

Yet Miss Cather has triumphed. She has not sought refuge in Europe or in romantic fancies. She has had the strength to give herself to her natural environment, and in "A Lost Lady" she has actually succeeded in transforming her material into the universal forms of art—no easy conquest. (p. 332)

> T. K. Whipple, "Willa Cather," in the Literary Review, *December 8, 1923, pp. 331-32.*

[Like] many of her literary contemporaries, [Miss Cather] is unable to discover in American life at the moment either the grounds for a national faith or the prospect of a national destiny. Another writer might have summoned us, as pioneers, to a new task; that of subduing the material organization of our life to human uses and the service of the race, as our predecessors once subdued the continent. But she has been content occasionally to point out that, as our life now stands, it is the race that is subdued to the exigencies of material organization. (p. 643)

The new frontier, Miss Cather suggests, occurs within the imagination. In the arts there are always unbroken lands open for settlement, and her pioneers of yesterday become the artists of today, turning from the conquest of the land to a fresh contest with an equally obdurate spiritual environment. In default, perhaps, of any ideal sufficiently comprehensive to claim an undivided loyalty, the undisciplined and unemployed spiritual energy of the race is pushing forward its discoveries in the creative life of the arts. (p. 645)

It is perhaps not without significance that Miss Cather, who is among the most thoughtful of our contemporary novelists, has failed to isolate in our national life any ideal faith or noble purpose deserving the allegiance that awaits its discovery. So remote is she from that discovery that she intimates the futility of the quest. (p. 646)

It is only in *A Lost Lady* . . . that Miss Cather seems to have achieved a balanced control over both content and structure. That book stands, from the point of view of art, as her most notable performance up to the present. It is all but faultless in structure; it possesses evident beauty of de-

sign and proportion, and the form of the story seems only an inevitable expression of its content. Miss Cather's use of the indirect method of presentation, perhaps the last vestige of the influence once exercised upon her by Henry James, has sometimes been challenged. It has been asserted that she suffers from a disability akin to that of James, a limitation of imaginative scope which prevents her from recording action and emotion except at second hand. But her use of the indirect method is amply justified by *A Lost Lady,* in which the channel of presentation is inextricably implicated in the action presented. (pp. 650-51)

At her best she has created characters of distinction and significance and represented experience in some of its permanent aspects. At her best, therefore, she has achieved art by interpreting comprehensively what her somewhat narrow world has offered for her contemplation. (p. 652)

> *Lloyd Morris, "Willa Cather," in* The North American Review *(reprinted by permission from* The North American Review; *copyright © 1924 by the University of Northern Iowa), Spring, 1924, pp. 641-52.*

One of Ours . . . seems to me a pretty flat failure. . . . I feel, in the case of this book as I did with her collection of short stories, *Youth and the Bright Medusa,* that it has cost Miss Cather too much effort to summon her people from the void and that, even when she has got them before us, they appear less like human beings, or even the phantoms of human beings, than like pale unfeatured silhouettes, pasted on cardboard backs and, skillfully but a little mechanically, put through the paces of puppets. (pp. 39-40)

Admirers of Willa Cather will declare that this kind of criticism is based on a misunderstanding; that her method is not to get inside her characters—as Dostoevsky does, for example—and depict their emotions directly, but rather, in the manner of Turgenev, to tell you how people behave and to let the inner blaze of their glory or grief shine through the simple recital. But the reader, in either case, must demand that the characters come to life. In this novel, they never do. (p. 40)

Let it be counted to her for righteousness, however, that, like Flaubert, she has devoted her life to her art; that—even though her colors are faint and the characters she animates shadowy—she understands how fine work should be done. She knows that in a decent novel every word should be in its place and every figure in its right perspective, that every incident should be presented with its appropriate economy of detail. (pp. 40-1)

A Lost Lady . . . does something to atone for *One of Ours.* Miss Cather seems to suffer from a disability like that of Henry James: it is almost impossible for her to describe an emotion or an action except at secondhand. (p. 41)

In *A Lost Lady* . . . Miss Cather falls back on the indirect method of James—who was a great artist, . . . and she achieves something of James's success. Here her problem is to present the vicissitudes of a young and attractive woman, with a vigorous capacity for life, in the course of her marriage, during the pioneering period after the Civil War, with an elderly contractor of the "railroad aristocracy," who has brought her from California to live somewhere between Omaha and Denver. For this purpose, she invents another of those limpid and sensitive young men to whom she has always been rather addicted and makes him the Jamesian glass through which we are to look at her heroine. (p. 42)

In any case, *A Lost Lady* is a charming sketch performed with exceptional skill. Willa Cather is, in fact, one of the only writers who has been able to bring any real distinction to the life of the Middle West. Other writers have more enthusiasm or animation or color or humor, but Miss Cather is perhaps unique in her art of imposing a patina on that meager and sprawling scene. . . .

There run through Miss Cather's work two currents of profound feeling—one for the beauty of those lives lived out between the sky and the prairie; the other—most touchingly in *A Wagner Concert,* my favorite among her short stories, and . . . in certain scenes of *A Lost Lady*—for the pathos of the human spirit making the effort to send down its roots and to flower in that barren soil. (p. 43)

> Edmund Wilson, "Two Novels of Willa Cather" (1924), in his The Shores of Light: A Literary Chronicle of the Twenties and Thirties (reprinted with the permission of Farrar, Straus & Giroux, Inc.; copyright 1952 by Edmund Wilson), Farrar, Straus and Young, 1952, pp. 39-43.

The most sensuous of writers, Willa Cather builds her imagined world almost as solidly as our five senses build the universe around us. . . . She has within herself a sensitivity that constantly presents her with a body of material which would overwhelm most of us, so that we would give up all idea of transmitting it and would sink into a state of passivity; and she has also a quality of mountain-pony sturdiness that makes her push on unfatigued under her load and give an accurate account of every part of it. (p. 233)

Her work has not that air of claiming to cover all the ground which gives the later novels of Henry James the feeling of pretentiousness and futility which amazingly co-exists with the extremes of subtlety and beauty and which is perhaps due to his attempt to account for all the actions and thoughts of his characters by motives established well in the forefront of consciousness. . . . Hers is to move on the sunlit face of the earth, with the gracious amplitude of Ceres, bidding the soil yield richly, that the other kind of artist, who is like Persephone and must spend half of his days in the world under the world, may be refreshed on emergence. (pp. 247-48)

> Rebecca West, "The Classic Artist," in her The Strange Necessity (copyright 1928, © 1955 by Rebecca West; reprinted by permission of The Viking Press), Doubleday, Doran, 1928, pp. 233-48.

Willa Cather's is one of the most complex, if not difficult and contradictory, minds in our letters. If we must admire the conscience, it won't always be easy to follow the logic of this artist. . . . Among the whole group of our feminine novelists, Willa Cather is in some ways the most interesting of them all: less restricted than Edith Wharton, more intense than Ellen Glasgow. (pp. 155-56)

There is no doubt that Cather's pioneer portraits are fore-shortened in perspective to a certain degree, a little reduced in size, and also, after one has escaped from the spell of the craft itself, curiously static in their final effect, almost like a tableau of Grant Wood's. Both *O Pioneers!* and *My Ántonia* are georgics of the frontier, or idylls of western fortitude. . . . It is against [the] whole emerging pattern of both rural and urban life in America that Cather has actually set her earlier western individualists, her pioneer makers and ancestors, as an example of a better, a freer, a more heroic and worthy time.

In some part this accounts for both the eloquence of Cather's frontier tales and the final effect they produce of being isolated and almost static episodes, as I say—of being separated *out* of a larger and more complex historical situation. If this is a return to the childhood world of the artist, it is also a sort of childlike return. Moreover, as the chronicle of the pioneers is carried forward through the early western towns of *My Ántonia* to the metropolitan centers of *The Song of the Lark,* there is the same note of isolation and hostility in the later defense of the artist in a purely materialistic society. . . . And yet there are other elements and more curious undertones here. Does the central emotional pattern of Cather's work—that particularly Catheresque sense of an intense splendor in life and of its inevitable loss, of a brief ecstasy and of a long and bitter resignation to suffering—stem back to her first novel, which contains, in fact, not only the fullest statement of this theme, but the most complete human relationship of the first period of her writing? After *Alexander's Bridge* the lyrical note is increasingly subordinated to the stoical, while the line of her superior matriarchs is established, and Thea Kronborg again expresses their central conviction of 'standing up under things,' of 'meeting catastrophe without any fussiness,' of 'dealing with fate bare-handed.' (pp. 170-71)

[But] is it also the fate of Cather's dominant and increasingly inaccessible women to be 'always surrounded by little men,' . . . to be worshiped from afar . . . and to sacrifice marriage, love, and, finally, friendship in the interests of an artist's career, as in the case of Thea Kronberg? Isn't it something of a catastrophe to avoid all deeper human involvements, as her women seem to be doing . . . , though it may be in the interests of the most admirable or illustrious cause? . . . (p. 171)

As a matter of fact, one *could* view Willa Cather's representation of her pioneer and artistic heroines as a turning-away, not only from a distasteful contemporary society, but also from a sensitive and crucial area of emotional experience: that is, from all the more or less involved consequences of what we call ordinary human relationships. In any case, the work of her second period will record the stress of an increasingly acute spiritual conflict, if not that of an actual psychic wound. For there, indeed, her figures will learn to live without delight, as she says, and will fall out of 'all domestic and social relations.' (p. 172)

The Professor's House is a symbolical novel, and in the framework of allegory which we gradually catch on to, even the apparent flaws in the story—the exaggerated finesse of the St. Peter household, the curious sense of remoteness from the world—take on a certain validity. . . . [Here,] in terms of the central human relationships of the novel—husband and wife, parent and child, brother and sister—are some of Cather's most sensitive and acute observations on the human family in general: and here the persistent undertones of suffering in these human relationships, of thwarted desire, of broken delight, of jealousy, malice, and actual anguish, become more marked. That familiar wound of

Cather's, 'healed and hardened and hopeless,' begins to throb. In a remarkable series of minor episodes, an underlying pattern of emotional despair becomes dominant, as, step by step, *The Professor's House* records the process of St. Peter's withdrawal from his scholarly work, his academic position and associates, his own home—from the whole nexus of those close family relationships which have always, in the past, sustained him through their warmth and friendliness. (p. 184)

Thus, while *The Professor's House* is an allegory of human imperfection in terms of its outward scene ("My fortunes have corrupted honest men"), it is even more clearly a chronicle of inner defeat and spiritual withdrawal. In this context the curious episode in the novel which is called 'Tom Outland's Story' . . . contains the crux of the novel's meaning. . . .

For the Parable of the Mesa is at once the climax of Willa Cather's search for a sort of transcendent splendor in life and the most extreme point of her own withdrawal from all domestic and social relations—and I mean, of course, that whole industrial and engineering society from which, as we saw, the first period of her work already represented a sort of escape into a more heroic or idyllic past. In terms of the pioneer novels themselves, we noticed her hostility to the increasingly respectable age of rural wealth and machines which, in *One of Ours,* she is not only scornful of but hardly tries to understand. And if *A Lost Lady* depicts the 'sunset of the pioneer,' not indeed in terms of fact, but in Cather's own view of the facts, isn't it clear that the glow, the intensity, the actual 'magic' of her last frontier tale, come out of a more intense need for mystery and enchantment in the face of her growing disenchantment about contemporary life? A disenchantment that is marked precisely by the increasing sense of weariness and frustration, and by that final acceptance of spiritual defeat and withdrawal which is recorded in *The Professor's House.* (pp. 185-86)

Yet there are some curious elements in the crucial episode at the middle of Cather's career. Is it, in fact, a conversion or a trauma? For the transfiguration on the mesa also seems to answer that more obscure sense of guilt and retribution which is evident in her work from her earliest short stories and which parallels her search for a special splendor and enchantment in life—a desire *for* an irremediable disaster. And the final realization of the search, the glorious feeling of a world above the world, the marvelous air, the consuming light of the mesa—are they, after all, too much for a single individual to bear? . . .

And this singular spiritual ambivalence, this equivocal dialogue between the forms of life and the forms of death—and by now it is difficult to say which is which—is carried on into the period of Cather's better-known and more strictly religious novels. (p. 187)

My Mortal Enemy is a sort of farewell to Cather's earlier American scene of wealth and cultivation. This is her last story to deal with it for almost a decade, and her return to it, in the *Lucy Gayheart* of 1935, will be under quite different circumstances. It is worth noticing, too, that the central theological image of *Death Comes for the Archbishop,* in 1927, should be that of the Virgin Mother ('Only a Woman, Divine, could know all that woman can suffer'), while the central psychological image should again be that of the Rock. In these pages, whatever doubts we may have

had as to the significance of the Mesa in Cather's work are clarified by her reflections on the Cliff Cities of the Acomas. . . . (p. 191)

Here the Mesa has become identified with the Rock: stark, grim, enduring. Isn't it curious, though, that Cather's Sanctuary should be so clearly now a leap *away* from the earth, a barren mesa, indeed, on which there is "not a tree or a blade of green . . . not a handful of soil," except, perhaps, the graveyard? Here, too, her hero has lost that first mystical exaltation, the sense of a final and absolute freedom, of a communion with space and solitude in a world above the world. (p. 192)

Shadows on the Rock may be viewed almost entirely as a children's story. In any case it is *as* a fairy tale of the Church and the New World—as a glowing account of Christian heroes, saints, and martyrs, and of ecclesiastical legends and miracles—that her last religious novel most clearly shows the direction of her middle period and the true nature of her goal. Just as the central spiritual vision of *Shadows on the Rock* is that altogether safe, soothing, and ornamental universe of Cather's Ursuline Sisters, the actual psychological scene is centered around the proper and tidy home life of the apothecary Auclair and the apothecary's daughter, the gentle, sweet, and pious Cécile herself; this innocent and untouched heroine of Cather's, who, without passion or the capacity for passion, grows up in a well-ordered sphere of loving-kindliness and cleanliness. (pp. 197-98)

Both *Death Comes for the Archbishop* and *Shadows on the Rock* are tracts of divine love and of golden goodness which exclude just that uncertainty and anguish of human love, or that deeper sense of good and evil, which have been the distinguishing mark of her best work. By now the emphasis on religious ceremony has almost taken the place of the original emphasis on religion, while the artist's stress on the rich surface of things only serves to remind us of a lost richness of feeling. That 'mortal enemy' of Myra Henshawe's—that vain, selfish, worldly woman—was also in a sense her truest friend, for wasn't it out of this sort of emotional matrix that Cather had formed her true art? (p. 200)

[The] 'goal' of *Obscure Destinies* has pretty nearly fixed the course of its path. We realize that the volume is intended to indicate the whole range of her new values and beliefs and to present her mature view of the contemporary American scene. And this somewhat overpowering emphasis on the nobility of her literary spokesmen marks an odd return to that human family whose corruption and malice the Willa Cather of *The Professor's House,* just seven years before, had condemned, and all of whose social relationships she had apparently renounced. (pp. 200-01)

If the whole course of Cather's development over these seven years can be summarized by that leap from the earth to the rock, and from the rock to the dais, the final step of this whole curious circular literary pilgrimage is nevertheless a descent again: from the dais to the kitchen. (p. 201)

Lucy Gayheart . . . does mark a return in both theme and tone to the pattern of her earlier writing. But it is very far from the 'lavender and old lace' which has been generally used to describe it. (p. 209)

[Just] as *Lucy Gayheart* contains the most complete love

relationship in the range of Cather's work, with the possible exception of *Alexander's Bridge*, it is also among her most convincing works. The sense of immediacy that we have in regard to both the scene and the emotions of the central story is a remarkable achievement for an artist who is approaching her sixties. (p. 212)

[On] the plane of critical speculation, you might say that the true inner pattern of Cather's early work is that of a kind of traumatic wound; that the whole burden of her middle period is the attempt to reach a spiritual equilibrium through a formal mode of religious conversion—and that it was only *after* this conversion, and within the framework of its security, that the original emotions of the writer could approach something like a full aesthetic expression.... You may notice that in the later sections of *Lucy Gayheart* Cather does at last reach down into the mystery and drama, or even the mingled splendor and terror, of that *ordinary* human life, that common everyday existence of humanity which, lying directly between her need for worldly glamour and her sense of religious guilt, has constantly eluded her grasp. (p. 213)

In its central framework *Sapphira and the Slave Girl* is probably Cather's most ambitious book, the first of her novels to attempt to come to grips with a difficult and complex social environment. It is interesting to notice how close she comes to the psychological implications of this environment; that is, to the underlying sexual corruption which was attendant upon the institution of slavery; the debasement of the deepest human drives which was implicit in the buying and selling of human flesh, as well as of human souls, and which in a way did less fundamental harm to those who were the 'material' of the merchandising than to the merchants themselves. (pp. 214-15)

For the whole range of Cather's values, standards, tastes, and prejudices, her tone, is that of an inherent aristocrat in an equalitarian order, of an agrarian writer in an industrial order, of a defender of the spiritual graces in the midst of an increasingly materialistic culture. Miss Cather is quite aware of her predicament.... And Cather's narrow and almost deliberately naïve view of the past, of history, and therefore of human nature itself, has also affected the whole texture of her work. (pp. 217-18)

> *Maxwell Geismar, "Willa Cather: Lady in the Wilderness," in his* The Last of the Provincials: The American Novel, 1915-1925 *(copyright © 1943, 1947, 1949, 1975 by Maxwell Geismar; reprinted by permission of Houghton Mifflin Company), Houghton, 1947 (and reprinted by Hill & Wang, 1959), pp. 153-220.*

[All Willa Cather's] novels and stories . . . were animated by a single great theme as they were graced by a single felicitous style. The theme was that of the supremacy of moral and spiritual over material values, the ever recurrent but inexhaustible theme of gaining the whole world and losing one's soul.

Willa Cather was a traditionalist and a conformer; the tradition that she so triumphantly maintained was peculiarly American, the standards to which she so instinctively conformed those that had sufficed her mentors, Sarah Orne Jewett and Henry James and, in an earlier day, Hawthorne. Her roots were deep in the American and the Christian past.... (p. 150)

Miss Cather rejected the "overfurnished" novel as she rejected the overfurnished countryside—rejected alike the furniture of sociology, of psychology, and of physiology, for "a novel crowded with physical sensations is no less a catalogue than one crowded with furniture." She thought the traditional themes of love and despair, truth and beauty, the struggle with the soil and the struggle for artistic honesty, far from exhausted.... (pp. 150-51)

From *Alexander's Bridge* to *The Old Beauty* she wrote life itself, wrote it so passionately that the characters she created seem to us more authentic than the characters of history.

The best of Miss Cather's novels all deal with the frontier, in one sense or another, but the frontier is never the object but rather the setting, and her stories are never, as with Bret Harte or Hamlin Garland, frontier stories. For just as Turner, when he placed himself on the vantage point of the frontier, was able to see the significance of the whole of American history, so Willa Cather, when she looked out upon life from the prairie or mesa or from one of those Rocks which figure so largely in her books, was able to see, from those vantage points, the real meaning of life in America. It was because the frontier simplified, clarified, and dramatized universal moral problems that she returned to it again and again for inspiration, and rarely in vain.

What was it about the pioneer West that inspired Miss Cather's elegiac mood, commanded her affection and respect, and, by contrast, made the busy world of the East seem so brash and pushing? It was, first of all, the land itself, and Miss Cather indulged in that pathetic fallacy which ascribed to the land not only spaciousness and beauty but endurance and serenity and strength. (p. 151)

Nature, however, was usually something that seemed to belong to the past; modern man had ignored it or exploited it, and therein lay its weakness. But those pioneers who had first gone out to the high plains, Miss Cather asserted, had been concerned with more than material conquest or exploitation: it was a romantic assertion, to be sure, and not wholly supported by the facts, but it was a mark of Miss Cather's triumph that she made nature and history conform to her art. (p. 152)

The passing of this pioneer generation meant, to Miss Cather, the passing of all the old virtues, and she was incapable of believing that there could be different virtues in a civilization whose standards were those of the counting-house, whose habits were predatory, and whose rewards were social and ostentatious rather than spiritual and private. (p. 154)

It was entirely natural that her search for the permanent should have led her, as it led Henry Adams, to the Catholic church, with "its safe, lovingly arranged and ordered universe, not too vast, though nobly spacious."

"It takes a great deal of history to produce a little literature," Henry James had written, and the sense of history was strong in Willa Cather, stronger by far than in most of those "historical" novelists whose recreation of the past was so calculated and so artificial. Better than any of her literary contemporaries, she represented the force of tradition in twentieth-century America—the tradition of the artist, the tradition of the pioneer, the tradition, eventually, of the universal church. (p. 155)

Henry Steele Commager, in his The American Mind: An Interpretation of American Thought and Character Since the 1880's *(copyright, 1950, by Yale University Press), Yale University Press, 1950.*

Miss Cather is admired, one gathers from a large body of comment, for her profound sense of the larger motives, for her serene artistry, her purity of language, her moral poise, her ardent but controlled desire for perfection of art, of mind and of spirit. Her principal characters, chiefly artists, pioneers and saints, are valiant spirits who live and die for ideals. Their immense, epic vitality, conveyed by mood rather than through action, derives from intrinsic virtues of mind and heart. But their vitality, far from being abstract, operates in a special region and a special moment of history, so that we are as often aware of the landscape, and the movement of time across it, as we are of the symbolic figures which dominate it. (pp. 69-70)

Occasionally, as in *One of Ours* or in *Sapphira and the Slave Girl,* she tended to describe states of mind rather than persons, and once or twice, due to her imperfect assimilation of the Jamesian technique, she seems to have assaulted rather than to have wooed her subject. But these [are] infrequent lapses. . . . (p. 70)

Speaking by precept, in *Not Under Forty* and in *On Writing,* as well as by example, she opposed the raw and capering naturalism which colored the literary generation of which she was perhaps an involuntary member. Essentially a biographer of the spirit of man, she could not respond to the literature of sociology, of journalism, of mere documentation. Having striven, from her earliest stories, to cultivate a silver style capable of conveying the quiet, melancholy underground tones of memory and mood, she was not unexpectedly oppressed by the violence and crudity, the insufficiently humanized passions of contemporary fiction. . . . She rejected with deliberate anger the contemporary surrender to disorder and anxiety, and turned to those moments of the past when tradition, decency, a classic sense of life could permit her imagination to soar without strain, to hover without danger of collapse. . . .

That her rejection of her own generation should be taken for escapism or, as Maxwell Geismar characterizes it, as infantile malice (the most recent contemporary phrase is "failure of nerve") may readily be understood. . . . Her characters had been remembered, rather than created, her plots had the force as well as the assymetrical form of a memoir, and her writing or composing had come to count for less than the reality they pointed out. . . . (p. 71)

To turn from [the] rich vein [of real memory, which produced *O Pioneers!, The Song of the Lark,* and *My Ántonia*] to the elegiac middle-aged disillusion of *The Professor's House,* and then to the Spanish southwest in the nostalgic *Death Comes for the Archbishop,* and immediately afterward to the French northeast in her reticent and frosty *Shadows on the Rock* certainly could appear to be "evasion of social environment, broken creative framework, dissipation of true energies." (p. 72)

Literary form was her constant preoccupation and yet she allowed her books to carve out their channels, to follow a will of their own, to shift in time and point-of-view, to run up-hill at times, as in *The Professor's House,* where one

digression continues for a quarter of the novel. She had the robust mentality of a man, but remained ineluctably feminine in her spontaneous and detached insights. Preeminently a chronicler of affairs of the spirit, her eyes wandered after the lustier life of her Lena Lingards. She was so devoted to the individual "existential" person that, excepting *Alexander's Bridge,* she refused to plot a course which might interfere with their independence. Nevertheless she is an "essential" novelist, for the central idea—the theme—is nowhere more controlling than in Willa Cather.

These themes, moreover, are often curiously ambivalent, and thus frequently defy her professedly single intention. They concern both the frontier *and* the drawing room, self-realization *and* frustration, constant change *and* eternal truths, Martha *and* Mary. The symbols which she selects to convey these controlling ideas, while less equivocal, are not less rich in contrast. Professor St. Peter, an artistic temperament sprung from pioneer French and Yankee stock, has two houses; one enshrines a silver memory of a golden past, the other the prosperous, brassy and pressurized present. . . .

There are tensions in Willa Cather, but they are rarely revealed in the same character, never wholly revealed in the same book; and, more often than not, they rarely rise above the tight smooth surface of story. Neither are they resolved explicitly; even when, in an attempt to do so, Miss Cather breaks almost all the conventions of prose fiction.

For the direction of Willa Cather's art, as it may be determined from her crucial books—beginning with *My Antonia* and ending with *Shadows on the Rock*—moved steadily away from dramatic form and "solidity of specification" towards the literature of statement, of legend, of mood, towards the fusion of fiction and reality. The normal preoccupations of novelists with contemporary manners and morals, with the cycle of stimulus and sensation, thought and motive, motive and act, act and memory, memory and stimulus, with the dialectic of subject and style, the concern with the growth of a character through successive incidents to a full personality—in short, their attempt to give a complete sense of life—these are not Miss Cather's chief preoccupations. There is memory of growth and change in her novels, but it rarely takes place before our eyes. There is report of stress, even of horror, but the event is quickly succeeded by the shadows which it casts. For the truth is that, for all the realistic tone and texture of her stories, Willa Cather is at heart a symbolic writer. She is far more concerned with the foreshortened essential meaning than the lengthy existent fact, and at one stage of her career more concerned with residual moral value than with elaborate intellectual meaning.

Indeed the crucial books . . ., particularly *My Antonia, The Professor's House* and *Death Comes for the Archbishop,* record progress from one level of meaning and value to another; from the level of nature to the level of mind, and from the level of mind to the level of spirit. In harmony with this progress, one may detect a gradually shifting point of view, in which the ultimate values of life are seen successively in the memory of youth, of middle age and old age. (pp. 73-4)

The symbols in *The Professor's House*—the shabby old place which is a home of the spirit as opposed to the new house which is a mere convenience, the unclouded joy of

Tom Outland's blue mesa as opposed to the contaminated pleasures of life in the university town of Hamilton, Augusta's rough-textured trustworthiness as opposed to the humid sensibilities of his own family—contain the seeds of Willa Cather's future growth. (p. 82)

Death Comes for the Archbishop is not merely a slightly fictitious history of a region. It is that, and many things more, but it is primarily a tribute to the transforming power of the disciplined intelligence of a Latour illuminated by his faith, assisted by the driving energy of that friend of his soul, Joseph Vaillant. The Archbishop and Vaillant are in effect one complete personality, since each exists completely in the other by virtue of their common inspiration and culture. Their temperamental differences serve to render credible the co-existence in that one complete personality of the healthy coarse grain of the pioneer and the tender sensibility of the artist. . . . Taken together, Latour and Vaillant stand for that fusion of action and contemplation, of doing and being, of enterprise and art which was latent in *My Antonia* and emergent in *The Professor's House.*

To say this is to suggest that in *Death Comes for the Archbishop* Willa Cather reached the end of her search for self-expression. But the pattern of her progress towards the spiritual poise of *Death Comes for the Archbishop,* from the lower levels of *My Antonia* and of *The Professor's House,* together with the analogous rhythmical pattern of youth, middle age and old age, is not wholly satisfactory. And it is not satisfactory because the pattern of progress does come to an end. Her next book, *Shadows on the Rock* . . . , for all its splendid episodic action, reveals a fundamentally closed world, too great a sense of contemplation, with an ending which does not contain a new beginning. (pp. 84-5)

[It is possible] that Miss Cather had never properly understood the Christian spirituality which is the informing principle of *Death Comes for the Archbishop* and *Shadows on the Rock.* Her "idea" of Christianity was perhaps too esthetic, too historical, too French, an admiration of Christian art and manners, its order and decency, its culture and its codes. She tried to remember what she had not experienced and perhaps found that her response, that of the culturally starved Protestant, to the greatness of the past, her noble desire to participate in an aristocracy of spirit, did not suffice to capture the reality she aimed at. She had fused art and life. When her vision of reality failed, her art failed with it. She was too honest to feign what she could not represent. (pp. 85-6)

[Willa Cather had] an imperfect sense of what the struggle for spiritual perfection actually meant. For this reason she made no progress beyond the position developed in *Shadows on the Rock,* or for that matter in *Death Comes for the Archbishop.* She failed to keep pace with the movement of her own vision, and losing the pace, she lost momentum, too. She had gone as far as she could go.

To say this is simply to say that her immense and imperishable contribution to American literature is not the most perfect one can imagine. Had she been able to understand that *Death Comes for the Archbishop* and *Shadows on the Rock,* while far superior in their vision of reality to their predecessors, were themselves incomplete, that there were still higher levels of spiritual values and greater depths of spiritual suffering; had she been less content with her ideas of things and with the esthetic gratification of those ideas; had she, in other words, felt fire as well as seen it, she might have been the greatest novelist of her time. (p. 87)

> *Francis X. Connolly, "Willa Cather: Memory as Muse," in* Fifty Years of the American Novel: A Christian Appraisal, *edited by Harold C. Gardiner (reprinted by permission of Charles Scribner's Sons; © 1951 by Charles Scribner's Sons), Scribner's, 1951, pp. 69-88.*

Alexander's Bridge, Willa Cather's first novel, is in a sense a mere literary exercise. Deftly constructed, written with a sensitive precision (learned from Henry James), full of warmly imagined interiors, and containing some fine set descriptions, it nevertheless fails in that the central emotional situations are never fully realized. (p. 9)

Is this merely the study of a man at the "dangerous age" of forty when he is liable to break out into some new kind of emotional life? Miss Cather was clearly interested in this phenomenon, for in later novels she has other male characters similarly break loose at the same age. But the book is not organized in order to illuminate this kind of situation. It is organized, one might say, for the sake of organization, and the neat disposal of the problem by Alexander's opportune death just before he commits himself is no real resolution of the plot but rather the solution by fictional artifice of what has not been solved by the life generated in the novel itself. (p. 10)

O Pioneers! is handling, in its own way, a theme that is to be found in *Alexander's Bridge,* as it is to be found in Henry James—the relation between the Old World and the New. (p. 16)

O Pioneers! is the first of a group of novels in which the impact of a young country on the sad sensitivity of uprooted Europeans is presented with a sympathy and an insight rare in American writers, even the most sophisticated of whom tend to regard the European immigrant as only too happy to leave the bad old world behind and settle down in the land of the free. In *O Pioneers!* as in *The Song of the Lark* and *My Ántonia* we find this impact carefully observed, yet in none of these novels is it Miss Cather's main concern. She knows that for the old people, living on their memories of the past, there is no real hope in America, and she symbolizes this in such characters as John Bergson in *O Pioneers!,* Herr Wunsch in *The Song of the Lark,* and Mr. Shimerda in *My Ántonia:* she leaves these characters almost abruptly, consigning them without too much compunction to decay and death, and turns to their children to study the much more complex phenomenon of their merging of cultures and backgrounds. On the one hand there is the European heritage, and on the other the open spaces of the American west, with its challenge and excitement and its possibilities of new life for those young and adaptable enough to take them. All these three novels move between these two poles. The most interesting characters—Alexandra Bergson, Thea Kronborg, Ántonia—owe much of what they are to their European heritage. . . . (pp. 17-18)

The strong character is the character who knows what to retain of the past and at the same time how to adapt to the present and the future. That, Miss Cather seems to be saying, is the true pattern of American achievement. . . .

Those characters who never discover in America a challenge to achieve themselves but hanker continually after the old country, remain valuable critical agents, reminders, and warnings against complacent provincialism on either side, and when they are allowed to live . . . , they serve as irritants and gadflies, implicit criticisms, even, of "the American way of life."

It may not be too far-fetched to see in Willa Cather's handling of the European-in-America theme a transmutation of one of James's major themes and thus to recognize James's legacy transplanted and put to new uses. (pp. 18-19)

[For] all the tensions between the Old World and the New to be found in [*My Ántonia*] as in so many of the others, the central theme is neither the struggle of the pioneer nor the conflict between generations, but the development and self-discovery of the heroine. (p. 43)

[Ántonia's] growth, development, and final adjustment is a vast symbolic progress interesting less for what it is than for what it can be made to mean. (p. 44)

Throughout the book the narrator's sensibility takes control; and this raises problems which Willa Cather is never quite able to solve. The narrator's development goes on side by side with Ántonia's: indeed, we sometimes lose sight of Ántonia for long stretches at a time, while we can never lose sight of the narrator. Miss Cather tries to solve this problem by emphasizing that the book's title is *My Ántonia*: this is not just the story of Ántonia, but of Ántonia as she impinged on a number of other significant characters. She goes out of the way to use the adjective "my" in talking of Ántonia with reference not only to the narrator but also to other characters—to her father, who first uses the phrase, and to Mrs. Steavens, for example. And yet we cannot say that this is a story of what Ántonia meant to a selected number of other characters of the book: though there are elements in the story which suggest this, the organization as a whole tends to present Ántonia as a symbolic figure in her own right rather than as a character with special meaning for particular individuals. (p. 45)

It seems that the autobiographical impulse that redeemed Willa Cather from what she later considered the barren artfulness of *Alexander's Bridge* had its own dangers and was responsible for the abundance of interesting but not wholly dominated material which is to be found in *My Ántonia* as in *O Pioneers!*. These two novels are in many respects more alike than any other two of her books: . . . both show a remarkable ability to project characters and incidents as symbols; but in both the variety of material is not fully integrated with the main theme, and autobiography or regional curiosity sometimes leads the story astray. (pp. 60-1)

The expansiveness of such novels as *O Pioneers!* and *My Ántonia* gradually gives way, in Miss Cather's work, to more concentrated novels of more limited scope. *A Lost Lady*, though it still has something of the western background, is focused throughout on a single character. In *The Professor's House* . . . the scope is similarly restricted. . . . In both Tom Outland and the professor Miss Cather is exploring certain phases of sensibility, aspects of character which in some degree and at some time are bound to come in conflict with the demands of the conventional world.

We can trace the growth of this interest in the earlier novels. To some extent, it is present in *Alexander's Bridge*,

but it gives way in the pioneering novels to sturdier themes, emerging there only in incidental characters, until we see it again more fully revealed in Claude of *One of Ours*. *The Professor's House* is Miss Cather's first full-length treatment of a theme which has become so important in the twentieth-century novel, the first of her novels which links her, however tenuously, to what might be called the modern novel of sensibility so successfully practiced in England by Virginia Woolf and still very much alive. Not that there is any real resemblance between Miss Cather and Mrs. Woolf in attitude or technique—their art had very different foundations; but the exploration of individual sensitivity, so central in Virginia Woolf's fiction, does come to be one of Willa Cather's main interests at this stage in her career. (pp. 87-8)

As the ideals represented by her midwestern novels disappear in modern life, she moves toward history, indirectly in *The Professor's House*, directly in *Death Comes for the Archbishop*. (pp. 104-05)

Death Comes for the Archbishop is the best known and most popular of Miss Cather's novels, perhaps because its qualities, though considerable, are rather obvious. An episodic and sentimental novel which exploits a cultured religious heroism in a context of picturesque landscape and romantic historical figures, a novel both sophisticated and elemental, both meditative and full of action, an epic success story with a brightly colored surface—such a novel could hardly fail to be acclaimed as her most effective work to date. Yet one wonders whether this lively creation of a golden world in which all ideals are realized is not fundamentally a "softer" piece of writing than, say, *My Ántonia* with its frustrations counterbalancing successes, or than *The Professor's House*, whose main note is of heroic failure. There is, it is true, a splendid sympathy in the treatment of the characters and a most genuine feeling for the period and the natural setting in which the action is laid. But there is no indication here of an artist wrestling successfully with intractable material. The material is all too tractable, and the success, though it is real enough, seems too easy. (p. 105)

Willa Cather's last two novels, *Lucy Gayheart* . . . and *Sapphira and the Slave Girl* . . . , are hardly what one would have expected as the final work of an author who had moved from a self-conscious Jamesian craftsmanship through an exploration of the impact of the Old World on the New in the American Middle West, in which she drew on her autobiography, to a symbolization in historical novels of satisfying cultural patterns which she could not find in contemporary American civilization. (p. 129)

Throughout the whole of the latter part of her career as a novelist Willa Cather kept protesting against the demands of naturalism in fiction; the selection of a few, properly symbolic objects, is what is needed, she claimed, rather than the minute and exact cataloging of as much as possible. (p. 137)

This desire for unfurnishing the novel, combined with her repudiation of any obvious social function in fiction, might have led Miss Cather to a kind of subtle symbolic writing which woman novelists in England have in our time practiced so successfully. But, while in *The Professor's House* she comes as close as she ever did to this kind of writing, she did not take the path chosen by, say, Virginia Woolf.

The influence of James is clear in *Alexander's Bridge,* but it never reappears in any obvious way. The influence of Proust is nowhere discernible. Yet James and Proust have been the novelists most influential on other twentieth-century writers who, like Willa Cather, have endeavored to "interpret imaginatively [rather than naturally] the material and social investiture of their characters; to present their scene by suggestion rather than by enumeration." James and Proust are paramount, for example, in the heredity of Elizabeth Bowen's art. Willa Cather, however, was not interested in any kind of radical experimentation with the technique of the novel, and some interest of that kind was necessary to achieve the delicate texture of such a novel as *To the Lighthouse* or *The Death of the Heart.* Miss Cather's technique remained for the most part sturdily traditional. (pp. 138-39)

She wrote appreciatively of Katharine Mansfield, but what impressed her most about Miss Mansfield's work was her desire to recapture in her stories the quality of her childhood life in New Zealand. Her one critical remark about D. H. Lawrence is contemptuous. She defends her praise of Thomas Mann's Joseph series by insisting that, while the contemporary critics were "concerned only with his forwardness," Mann "also goes back a long way, and his backwardness is more gratifying to the backward"—and among the backward she includes herself.

It is odd that her early Populist sympathies, which led her to be ever more suspicious of modern industrial America, should have ended by making her a nostalgic idealizer of the past. (pp. 184-85)

It might not be going too far to say that in the end this increasing tendency to look backward impaired, if it did not destroy, her art. (p. 185)

There are few writers of her distinction whose achievement is so difficult to sum up. She belongs to no school.... [She] cannot be helpfully classified with respect to either theme or technique. The heroic nostalgia that pursued her until the end first changed her from a minor imitator of James to a novelist of fierce originality and individuality, and from the moment she discovered herself with *O Pioneers!* she went her own way with remarkably little notice of her contemporaries. She developed a style both strong and supple, combining forthrightness with sensitivity: she was one of the least showy novelists of her time. (p. 186)

Her central concern as a novelist came to be more and more that of Sir Walter Scott. Scott, too, was concerned with the fate of heroic ideals in an age of commercial progress and in his best novels presented his essentially tragic perception that progress was incompatible with the survival of the ideal of heroic action. The perception was tragic for Scott, for he wanted both; Willa Cather, as she grew older, wanted less and less of anything the modern world could offer and so withdrew into history with fewer regrets (odd though it may seem) than the celebrated historical novelist.

Other American novelists have written about the pioneers and have gloried in their heroic qualities. But for Miss Cather heroism was not enough, and her accounts of pioneers do not simply glorify their courage and strength of purpose. She was interested in the quality of their imagination, in the passion and brilliance of their ideal, in their discriminating acceptance of a vision, as well as in their will power and endurance. (pp. 187-88)

Her position among American novelists is unique; no other has brought to bear quite her kind of perception on the American scene. Yet the subject she handles most successfully and most characteristically—the subtilizing of courage by vision and discrimination and the search for a culture that combines all three qualities—is more than an American theme. It transcends national problems to illuminate one of the great questions about civilization. (p. 189)

> *David Daiches, in his* Willa Cather: A Critical Introduction *(copyright © 1951 by Cornell University; used by permission of Cornell University Press), Cornell University Press, 1951.*

Miss Cather's prairie (and the principle to which it contributed) was like neither James's London nor Miss Jewett's New England. It made demands on her that the experience of her two principal mentors had not encountered. From James Miss Cather seemed to get her interest in structure, in the use of a point-of-view character, such as Jim Burden, in *My Ántonia,* and in the perfection of sophisticated dialogue. From Miss Jewett, she took chiefly the encouragement she found in her regional successes—the "beautiful writing" which she saw as a consequence of Miss Jewett's steady concentration upon a thoroughly understood scene.... (pp. 54-5)

The great novels of the prairie states are *O Pioneers!* and *My Ántonia....* In these novels, with one emphasis or another, Miss Cather had worked out what she thought were the principal themes that literature might discover in that setting. The first of these was the hardness of the land, which offered its pioneering settlers disappointment and disaster more often than success. It was under these conditions that the challenge to character was most severe, and only the strongest succeeded. (p. 56)

In these novels, the masculine and feminine principles are reversed.... The triumph over the land is due to the endurance of the heroine; but it is through the male's self-defeating sensibility that other values, alien to the land, are preserved. (p. 57)

Throughout these novels there is a second theme—the suggestion that the creative artist is in closest sympathy with what Miss Cather regards as the complete life. As she had pointed out the failure of the pioneer community to understand (or to need) the artist, so later she was to suggest that the life of the small towns rejected both the feminine strength and the masculine sensitivity of the pioneer life. Miss Cather's "defeated souls" were from the beginning artists—singers, violinists, sculptors—who, in one way or another, had to get away from the prairies before their art could be nourished and who were appreciated even then by only a few isolated rebels against the dead-level convention of the towns they had left. In one sense, her strongest and most bitter criticism of the prairie culture was that it could not understand or abide the artistic soul. (pp. 58-9)

Miss Cather's art is nowhere so self-contained [as in *Death Comes for the Archbishop* and *Shadows on the Rock*]. But one has inevitably the feeling that she has given up too much for what she now feels she must have. The purchase price is great indeed. The loss is chiefly in dramatic intensity and in subtlety of representation. The world of these two novels seems a child's world. There are no problems here that cannot be solved by recourse to a simple, abiding faith in a father image. The historical theme which her other novels had tried to give has here been abandoned. However crudely stated, the study of a growing complexity and of a deepening evil in the change from pioneer life to a complex modern life had been vitally given in her earlier novels. (p. 62)

She was right when she took Sarah Orne Jewett's advice to write about what she knew best. But we can only say that her effort to bring to that subject the point of view of the sophisticated Easterner did somehow fail. It was not that the techniques recommended to her in her early apprenticeship were not suited to the Midwestern subject; they are suited to any subject at all. Rather, she had acquired a taste and a cultivation as well; and this taste first led her into an imperfect integration of sensibility with subject, then finally forced her into a distorted view of the subject altogether. . . . [She] was left with the role of chronicler of a simpler society—a society which antedated her distress with the modern world and thus enabled her to avoid that world.

Miss Cather was a traditionalist who, having acquired cultivation, used it to reject the subject that lay at hand. . . . So the manner did her no more than incidental good, and her insistence upon that setting, upon the narrow view of "taste" that dominates so much of her attitude even unto the posthumous *Old Beauty and Other Tales* . . . , damaged immeasurably the opportunity her experience had given her. (pp. 64-5)

> *Frederick J. Hoffman, in his* The Modern Novel in America, 1900-1950 *(copyright © 1951 by Gateway Editions, Ltd.), Regnery, 1951.*

Willa Cather's two collections of short stories . . . live still with morning freshness in my memory, their clearness, warmth of feeling, calmness of intelligence, an ample human view of things; in short the sense of an artist at work in whom one could have complete confidence: not even the prose attracted my attention from what the writer was saying—really saying, and not just in the words. . . .

[At one time I thought] that Miss Cather's reserve amounted to a deliberate withholding of some vital part of herself as artist; not as if she had hidden herself at the center of her mystery but was still there to be disclosed at last; no, she had absented herself willfully.

I was quite wrong of course. She is exactly at the center of her own mystery, where she belongs. My immoderate reading of our two or three invaluably afflicted giants of contemporary literature, and their abject army of camp followers and imitators, had blurred temporarily my perception of that thin line separating self-revealment from self-exhibition. Miss Cather had never any intention of using fiction or any other form of writing as a device for showing herself off. (p. 35)

Freud had happened: but Miss Cather continued to cite the old Hebrew prophets, the Greek dramatists, Goethe, Shakespeare, Dante, Tolstoy, Flaubert, and such for the deeper truths of human nature, both good and evil. (p. 37)

Joyce had happened: or perhaps we should say, *Ulysses,* for the work has now fairly absorbed the man we knew. . . . That subterranean upheaval of language caused not even the barest tremor in Miss Cather's firm, lucid sentences. There is good internal evidence that she read a great deal of

contemporary literature, contemporary over a stretch of fifty years, and think what contemporaries they were . . .; it was as rich and fruitfully disturbing a period as literature has to show for several centuries. And it did make an enormous change. Miss Cather held firmly to what she had found for herself, did her own work in her own way as all the others were doing each in his unique way, and did help greatly to save and reassert and illustrate the validity of certain great and dangerously threatened principles of art. Without too much fuss, too—and is quietly disappearing into her work altogether, as we might expect.

Mr. Maxwell Geismar wrote a book about her and some others, called *The Last of the Provincials* [see excerpt above]. Not having read it I do not know his argument; but he has a case: she is a provincial; and I hope not the last. She was a good artist, and all true art is provincial in the most realistic sense: of the very time and place of its making, out of human beings who are so particularly limited by their situation, whose faces and names are real and whose lives begin each one at an individual unique center. Indeed, Willa Cather was as provincial as Hawthorne or Flaubert or Turgenev, as little concerned with aesthetics and as much with morals as Tolstoy, as obstinately reserved as Melville. In fact she always reminds me of very good literary company, of the particularly admirable masters who formed her youthful tastes, her thinking and feeling.

She is a curiously immovable shape, monumental, virtue itself in her art and a symbol of virtue—like certain churches, in fact, or exemplary women, revered and neglected. Yet like these again, she has her faithful friends and true believers, even so to speak her lovers, and they last a lifetime, and after: the only kind of bond she would recognize or require or respect. (pp. 38-9)

> *Katherine Anne Porter, "Reflections on Willa Cather" (1952), in her* The Collected Essays and Occasional Writings of Katherine Anne Porter *(copyright © 1970 by Katherine Anne Porter; reprinted by permission of Delacorte Press/Seymour Lawrence), Delacorte Press, 1970, pp. 29-39.*

The only present that appealed to [Willa Cather] was the foreground of the world of art, especially the musical world of New York and Chicago, and at the same time she was drawn to French Quebec and to Santa Fé, the remains of venerable civilizations that had strayed across the ocean. (p. 533)

Along with her sensuous imagination, her feeling for colours, tastes, odours and sounds, for the flavour of fresh lettuce and good wine, for the tone of bells, [a] note of composure characterized Willa Cather, all but uniquely at a time when the brilliantly rapid report was the mark of so many novelists, especially of the West. (p. 534)

Willa Cather's conception of her art was all of a piece with her vision of life, her delight in gaiety and grace, ideality and beauty. . . . She was too full of the exhilaration, the excitement of youth and discovery to dwell on the cracks in the mirrors and the gauntness of the houses, while she was constantly on the alert, in her studies of the Western scene, for every trace of distinction, vitality, talent. (pp. 535-36)

Until Willa Cather wrote her stories, no one had ever conveyed a sense of the teeming aesthetic resources of the multi-racial West, the dawning talents of the new immigrant strains that were beginning to find expression and that contributed so largely to the Renascence of the moment. . . . But, with her gift of evocation and what Vachel Lindsay called her "instinct for the horizon," her "passion for the skyline," the air of the great grass plains was most her own, that light dry air "on the bright edges of the world" that had something soft and wild and free about it. Sometimes her note was elegiac, sometimes idyllic, while her style, so luminous, buoyant and fresh, recalled the fragrance of sagebrush and clover, the wind and the snowy peaks flashing against the sky. (pp. 537-38)

> *Van Wyck Brooks, in his* The Confident Years: 1885-1915 *(copyright, 1952, by Van Wyck Brooks; reprinted by permission of the publishers, E. P. Dutton), Dutton, 1952.*

To understand her refusal to move with her era—and her refusal was adamant—we must recognize that Willa Cather was not a child of the 20th century. She had been a child of the frontier; and long after the frontiers were gone she yearned—with an ache that had all the poetry of youth and adolescence in it—for the old, the cherished things she had known. This she expressed in one form and another in 12 novels; it is the best aspect of her talent and the one that gives her a claim upon us on this occasion. It also reflects the limitations of her talent. (p. 2)

[In the short stories, the] fascination for art, and the art world, on the part of Miss Cather's heroes and heroines, was a fascination essentially with success; the energy represented is not aesthetic, it is that of conquest; of overcoming nature and competition and standing firm and free among the Philistines and resisting their inevitable demands that talent become as mediocre as themselves.

Miss Cather's central theme is that of people who pull themselves up by their bootstraps. What is interesting for us in a novel such as *The Song of the Lark* is that once the would-be opera star, Thea, arrives at her goal, the story has nowhere to go. . . . [Characters] discover, perhaps, what Henry James meant when he remarked that success was like having a good dinner. All that you can say is that you have had it.

The inner voice of the early novels of Willa Cather suggests this fascination with, and need to describe, various forms of success—but also certain forms of failure. The drive to power in these books is overriding, with the result that the novels contain no complicated plots, no complexity of human relationships, no love affairs that we can take seriously. (pp. 7-8)

When a writer turns to things as they were, and conveys them with an ache as powerful and poignant as Willa Cather's, we can wonder whether this may not express a profound uneasiness with things as they are. . . . Miss Cather's novels, those she wrote in her second phase [during the early 1920s] leave no doubt that for her the here and the now was deeply depressing. (p. 8)

[For Miss Cather, the] process of growing older, the calm of quieter years, the dropping away of early intensities for later insights, could offer little satisfaction. The only thing that had possessed fundamental meaning for Willa Cather were her striving years. And this [is what I consider] the "paradox of success" in the work and in the life of Willa

Cather. . . . She became involved in one of those anomalies of human existence in which, when the struggle ceases, there seems to go with it all reason for pursuing anything new. (pp. 9-10)

[The] inner story of *Death Comes for the Archbishop* is something quite other than the overt material shows: it illustrates the marvelous way in which the creative consciousness operates in an artist as determined as Willa Cather, as tenacious in keeping her personal world intact and allowing neither time nor world upheaval to alter it. Indeed we might observe that Miss Cather instinctively found a solution, a triumphant solution, in terms of her personal as well as her artistic needs. . . . If the Western frontiers of her own time had disappeared, Miss Cather's inner voice seemed to say to her, there were still older frontiers available—those which existed before her time and which she could relive in the history books, in anecdote, in memories other than her own, and then retell them. Stated in other terms, Miss Cather's greatest fictional success, her chronicle of two missionaries in the Southwest carrying out their great religious and civilizing tasks, was a discovery that she could still—and indeed better than ever—do what she had always done. But see how insistent inner claims can be! The word Death is the first word in the title, even though the novel is once again a novel of conquest, conquest alike of a new land and of the souls of men. Indeed, for all the insistence of the title, the book is in reality not about death; it is about Archbishop Latour's courage and steadfastness, his gentleness and his worldly wisdom. His death at the end is simply the death that comes to all men—but in giving it significance, Miss Cather may have betrayed her deepest awareness that she was herself engaged in this novel in an act of exhuming the dead past. (p. 14)

Miss Cather's life and work constitute a success story of the most characteristic kind. Her books, her best books, are, in their simple and direct appeal, success stories, uncomplicated by subtleties of analysis or complexities of plot. She is a writer of people in action; and their action is characteristically American. She was one of those whose energies in a pioneering world were boundless; Tennyson's words, wafted over the seas during the Victorian century, to strive, to seek, to find—and he added also *but not to yield*—meant much to the pioneers who were striving and seeking and finding and seldom yielding. And Willa Cather had experienced her early life with such extraordinary intensity that she refused ever to let it go. (p. 16)

> *Leon Edel, in his* Willa Cather: The Paradox of Success *(copyright © 1960 by Leon Edel; reprinted by permission of William Morris Agency, Inc.), Library of Congress, 1960.*

Miss Cather had from the beginning tried for a strict definition of manners; it was partly a non-Jamesian expression of a Jamesian taste, partly a morally useful metaphor of the land. In her most famous novels of the prairie states she developed her own kind of international theme: it was the Old World that advanced into the New, settled it, fought its recalcitrance, tutored it, and eventually reduced it to neatly classical squares, triangles, and rectangles of fertile soil. The history was not without its tragedies: the too sensitive European might be overcome in the struggle. . . . (p. 182)

Some human pattern (some classical form of order) must rise from this union of Old World manner and New World necessity. It was a problem of "scale"—how to order a vast, uninhibited geography in human terms; how to make the European virtue responsive to the mid-American challenge. Miss Cather, in *O Pioneers!* . . . and *My Ántonia,* offers a land myth and a land goddess to rule it: a noble creature, strong, patient, robust, sensitive, and enduring, who undergoes a symbolic courtship with the land. The land at first coerces the heroine, but at last she is able to dominate it. It then becomes metaphorically "polite," civilized, classically ordered, and religiously fertile. It acquires a "manner," and the result is a noble, creative, and productive unity of man and nature. Like most carefully wrought designs, this pattern of decorum and fertility is threatened from without. The ugly, venal, amoral cities offer another way of life, a deceptively easy and distracting one. But the cities are not communities; they are huge congested areas in which man lives and dies in isolation—dies frequently *of* isolation. The exploiter—the man who sells what other men make, the man who is interested only in calculating risks and profits—is the villain. . . . (pp. 182-83)

From her reflections upon the moral and religious significance of the pioneer scene, Miss Cather suggests her ideal pattern of morality and decorum. Her hero or heroine has a strong sense of what is proper: great sensitivity (which by itself, however, often leads to disaster), great strength and courage, an almost superhuman talent for heroic struggle and fortitude, most of all, a *faith,* which is realized in the fertility rites of the seasons on the land, the sowing and the harvest, and in ceremonials (both secular customs and religious rituals), which are accepted without question or skepticism. (p. 183)

Miss Cather also withdrew into the past of her imagining; she created an image of history, made of simple and primary qualities, isolated in the past, free from the complications of modern life, with standards so purified as almost to make each human act a ritual exemplar. In so doing—and in stressing the values of traditional religion—she succeeded in vanquishing, to her own satisfaction at least, the unholy modern trinity of science, invention, and war. (p. 189)

Like other forms of traditionalism in the decade, Miss Cather's was motivated by a firm conviction concerning the world as she saw it then, and it was shaped as she acted upon her conviction. . . . Of all the forms of traditionalism, hers was the most apparently, and illusorily, precise and the most unfamiliar to those who naïvely and excitedly answered the challenge of immediacy. (p. 190)

> *Frederick J. Hoffman, "The Text: Willa Cather's Two Worlds," in his* The Twenties: American Writing in the Postwar Decade *(reprinted with permission of Macmillan Publishing Co., Inc.; copyright 1949, 1953, 1954, 1955, 1962 by Frederick J. Hoffman), revised edition, The Free Press, 1962, pp. 181-90.*

Miss Cather's whole body of work is the attempt to accommodate and assimilate her perception of the pioneer's failure. Reared on a Nebraska farm, she saw the personal and cultural defeat at first hand. Her forebears had marched westward to the new horizons; her own work is a march back toward the spiritual East—toward all that is the antithesis of the pioneer's individualism and innovation,

toward authority and permanence, toward Rome itself. (p. 49)

A Lost Lady, Miss Cather's most explicit treatment of the passing of the old order, is the central work of her career. Far from being the delicate minor book it is often called, it is probably her most muscular story, for it derives power from the grandeur of its theme. Miss Cather shares the American belief in the tonic moral quality of the pioneer's life; with the passing of the frontier she conceives that a great source of fortitude has been lost. . . .

But though the best of the pioneer ideal is defeated by alien forces, the ideal itself, Miss Cather sees, is really an insufficient one. (p. 50)

The disappearance of the old frontier left Miss Cather with a heritage of the virtues in which she had been bred, but with the necessity of finding a new object for them. Looking for the new frontier, she found it in the mind.

[Art] is not the only, or a sufficient, salvation from the débâcle of pioneer culture. For some vestige of the old striving after new worlds which cannot be gratified seems to spread a poison through the American soul, making it thin and unsubstantial, unable to find peace and solidity. (p. 51)

Indeed, "making the most of things" becomes even more important to Miss Cather than the eternal striving of art. For, she implies, in our civilization even the best ideals are bound to corruption. (p. 52)

Not the pioneering philosophy alone, but the whole poetic romanticism of the nineteenth century had been suffused with the belief that the struggle rather than the prize was admirable, that a man's reach should exceed his grasp, or what's a heaven for? Having seen the insufficiency of this philosophy Miss Cather must find another in which the goal shall be more than the search. She finds it, expectably enough, in religion. The Catholicism to which she turns is a Catholicism of culture, not of doctrine. The ideal of unremitting search, it may be said, is essentially a Protestant notion; Catholic thought tends to repudiate the ineffable and to seek the sharply defined. The quest for Moby Dick, that dangerous beast, is Protestant; the Catholic tradition selects what it can make immediate and tangible in symbol, and Miss Cather turns to the way of life that "makes the most of things," to the old settled cultures. She attaches a mystical significance to the ritual of the ordered life, to the niceties of cookery, to the supernal virtues of *things* themselves—sherry, or lettuce, or "these coppers, big and little, these brooms and clouts and brushes," which are the tools for making life itself. And with a religious ideal one may safely be a pioneer. The two priests of *Death Comes for the Archbishop* are pioneers; they happen to be successful in their enterprise, but they could not have been frustrated, Miss Cather implies, because the worth of their goal is indisputable. (pp. 52-3)

Church seems to offer the possibility of satisfying that appealing definition of human happiness which Miss Cather had made as far back as *My Ántonia*—"to be dissolved in something complete and great . . . to become a part of something entire, whether it is sun and air, goodness and knowledge."

It is toward that dissolvement that Miss Cather is always striving. She achieves it with the "sun and air"—and perhaps few modern writers have been so successful with landscape. She can find it in goodness and in society—but only if they have the feudal constriction of the old Quebec of *Shadows on the Rock*. Nothing in modern life, no possibility, no hope, offers it to her. (p. 53)

[What] is so irksome in Miss Cather's conception of ordered living . . . is her implied praise of devitalization. She can recognize the energy of assiduous duty but not the energy of mind and emotion. Her order is not the channeling of insurgent human forces but their absence. (p. 54)

But Miss Cather's turn to the ideals of a vanished time is the weary response to weariness, to that devitalization of spirit which she so brilliantly describes in the story of Professor St. Peter. It is a weariness which comes not merely from defeat but from an exacerbated sense of personal isolation and from the narrowing of all life to the individual's sensitivities, with the resulting loss of the objectivity that can draw strength from seeking the causes of things. . . .

Miss Cather's later books are pervaded by the air of a brooding ancient wisdom, but if we examine her mystical concern with pots and pans, it does not seem much more than an oblique defense of gentility or very far from the gaudy domesticity of bourgeois accumulation glorified in the *Woman's Home Companion*. (p. 55)

It has always been a personal failure of her talent that prevented her from involving her people in truly dramatic relations with each other. (Her women, for example, always stand in the mother or daughter relation to men; they are never truly lovers.) But at least once upon a time her people were involved in a dramatic relation with themselves or with their environments, whereas . . . *Lucy Gayheart* has not even this involvement. Environment does not exist, fate springs from nothing save chance; the characters are unattached to anything save their dreams. The novel has been *démeublé* indeed; but life without its furniture is strangely bare. (p. 56)

> Lionel Trilling, "Willa Cather," in After the Genteel Tradition: American Writers, 1910-1930, *edited by Malcolm Cowley (copyright © 1964 by Malcolm Cowley; reprinted by permission of Southern Illinois University Press), revised edition, Southern Illinois University Press, 1964, pp. 48-56.*

The country has shrunk, and our sense of the weight and relevance of Willa Cather's observation of Nebraska has shrunk with it. Nebraska is no doubt still there, but as a distinct imaginative possibility it has for the moment simply disappeared. As in so many other cases we are left confronting the artist who has been abandoned by his ostensible subject. The artist we now see is one whose energies are largely lavished on defensive maneuver, on masquerade. The power she now exercises is a measure of the degree to which the masquerade is itself something American. It is a small power when compared with Whitman's, but it is, despite the shellwork of fictional convention, a power of the same kind which engages us in "Song of Myself": a delighted absorption in the capacity of the self to embrace the world. In Whitman this play is overt; in Willa Cather it is masked. (p. 28)

The critics of the shrunken country spend more time discussing Willa Cather's characteristic emotional gestures than in trying to recall Nebraska. . . . Now that she has lost her cultural office, her relation to an older strain in American writing has become apparent: we may now see that she has all along a cultural office of a different kind. To discuss (I take the chief example) Whitman's America is to discuss him, and the play of all the selves he projected: the two are coterminus. Is there not, in Willa Cather and most of the writers who have tried to put us in imaginative possession of the continent, a child at play with his great mother? Taking possession of the continent is a function we have largely left to those who have themselves preserved a strong sense of their "preadolescent integration."

O Pioneers! . . . , *The Song of the Lark* . . . , and *My Ántonia* . . . are novels which turn on the moment of consciousness in which the child—often the child at the instant of waking—seizes on his world entire, undivided by sex, by possessions, by caste. The world is a fostering scene which sanctions his impulse to conquer, to be a large somebody. The overall effect is not nostalgic; it is the consequence of judging all the phases of human life from the standpoint of a state in which the world seems wholly vulnerable to the powers of the self. Yet, when dressing for school, the commanding self must acknowledge the family, adult expectations, the narrow village view. These constraints become the business of the shrewdly managing public self, which like Huck Finn, caters to adult desire. Within, the "second self" plots its freedom, which is found in the primal activities of growing and preparing food, of raising children, or in the work of the artist who momentarily unites the hidden selves of his public. (pp. 29-30)

The self-limiting character of the fables about artists and earth mothers is obvious. But this is only the first phase of Willa Cather's work; act one of her masquerade. The second is comprised of *A Lost Lady* and *The Professor's House*, in which the two selves are actually seen to be at war in the central figure. . . . In these two novels the cost of the assumption of specific sexual roles is the subject.

The third phase resumes the first with an enormous simplification: since the leading characters are Catholics their subordination to a great mother is externally justified. The Virgin succeeds Antonia and Alexandra. The churchmen of *Death Comes for the Archbishop* have put off their male roles, and together with the little girl of *Shadows on the Rock*, may take possession of the world in Mary's name. The great charm of *Death Comes for the Archbishop* is its exquisitely sustained resolution of the contradiction between its stony, wide-stretching, violently colored scene and an Auvergnat domesticity. Father Vaillant and Bishop Latour happily devote their public selves to the Virgin's secret ends; they are her housekeepers.

It would be foolish to scold the elegist of the undivided self for her failure to represent transitive human roles, dramatic encounters, the felt passage of time, and its changes of perspective, or the meaning of death for grown-ups. Nobody can die out of more lives than he has had, and Miss Cather's confusion of death with merging is, like Whitman's, wholly consistent with her way of seeing things. The emotional makeup which made Whitman our national poet is founded on a similarly infantile choice of object, his love of his own body, and the whole cast of selves that lived in it, and of the world as extension of himself, the world which fostered him and which he joyfully fostered in return. (pp. 30-1)

Whitman's acceptance of his role was not open to a woman; instead Willa Cather carried on a masquerade which made it appear that she was accepting the conditions of adulthood while actually rejecting them. It was a shrewd woman of 40 who published *O Pioneers!*, and discovered the terms of her disguise. Her literary career is a kind of inversion of Melville's story of the confidence man. He is making a bitter assault on the very thing Willa Cather cherished, the notion of a people who in their virgin wholeness might be conceived of as she conceived of the inhabitants of Mesa Verde—as worthy children of the continental mother. Melville's fable announces that no such wholeness is possible; the mingling of fraud and innocence is literally inextricable. But Willa Cather's basic antithesis is one that lies within the emotional territory she herself occupies: it is between wholeness and greed. Her last novel of any consequence, *Shadows on the Rock*, brings its characters into the beautifully ordered Auclair kitchen to be judged. In that kitchen a little girl prepares and serves food with ritual care, taking the place of the worshipped mother, her own, the Virgin, the great continent itself. In her last phase Willa Cather's America is a ravished kitchen, a primal order despoiled by greed. (p. 31)

> *Quentin Anderson, "Willa Cather: Her Masquerade," in* The New Republic *(reprinted by permission of* The New Republic; © *1965 by The New Republic, Inc.), November 27, 1965, pp. 28, 30-1.*

[In] 1912, when she was on the brink of forty, . . . [Willa Cather] resigned from *McClure's* and took a long holiday trip to the American Southwest. The landscape of Arizona and New Mexico, the Indians and Mexicans, the survivals of Aztec beauty were a shock and a great delight to her. She had discovered for the first time an American past that had significance to her, and she was to make great use of it. (pp. 96-7)

[For] all its approach to sentimentality *O Pioneers!* is the work of a major novelist who has at last discovered her form and her subject. One would never suspect that it was written by the author of *Alexander's Bridge*. At its best it is almost as good as Willa Cather was ever to write. Its theme is the conquest of virgin soil by pioneers. (p. 99)

Elizabeth Sergeant records that Willa Cather agreed with her criticism that *O Pioneers!* lacked a sharp skeleton, but argued that the Nebraskan prairies (which presumably dictated her structure) had no sculptured lines or features. . . .

Willa Cather said of her next and longest novel, *The Song of the Lark* . . . , that it should have ended with Thea Kronborg's first surmountal of her difficulties, that having escaped to Chicago from the stultification of Moonstone, where a concert or operatic career was inconceivable, and having discovered at last that her instrument was not the piano but the voice, she should have been left, one foot firmly set on the first rung of her long ladder. Perhaps. (p. 100)

Yet . . . [the] trouble with the second part of the novel, which tells of [Thea's] triumph as an opera star, is not, as Miss Cather thought, that a great singer becomes less interesting as she loses herself in her art, but that *she* loses Thea Kronborg. . . . *The Song of the Lark* . . . ceases to be a book about an opera singer and becomes a book about opera. And opera lovers, even Miss Cather, have a tendency to be fulsome in writing of their love. There are bits of *The Song of the Lark* that sound like intermission notes on a Saturday afternoon broadcast of the Metropolitan Opera.

Even the plot in the second half becomes hurried and blurred. The romance with the rich, handsome Fred Ottenburg—a *Jane Eyre* tale of planned bigamy—is slid over, for Thea seems little affected either by his love or by his fraud. Its real function seems to be to introduce the scenic grandeur of the Southwest—which Willa Cather always used to great effect—when Thea and Fred take their trip to Arizona. . . . The trouble is that one does not see Thea as an opera star at all. She is too noble, too dedicated, too pure. She has no men, no temperament, no ego. She cares more about being Sieglinde than being applauded as Sieglinde. She is too much an artist, too little a woman; too much a musical instrument, too little a diva.

Willa Cather made no secret of having modeled her, at least in part, on Olive Fremstad, the beautiful Swedish opera star (raised in Minnesota) who retired from the Metropolitan at the peak of her powers at the age of forty-two. . . . But one may doubt the likeness. One suspects that the young Thea has more of Willa Cather in her than anyone else and that Thea, the great star, is Willa Cather's fantasy of herself, with Fremstad's looks and Fremstad's voice, singing Sieglinde. (pp. 101-02)

Miss Cather was never much interested in what was or what was not a "novel." Fact, fancy, reminiscence, invention, what difference did it make? The mood, the unity, the finished product was all. (p. 104)

Willa Cather once said that in 1922 the world had broken in two and that she belonged to the earlier half, but this statement was simply the culmination of a habit of thinking that had begun before the war. . . . This preoccupation with the cheapness and tawdriness of the twentieth century was to eat even more deeply into Willa Cather's heart than it ate into Edith Wharton's or Ellen Glasgow's. Luckily, however, for the artist in her, she had something with which to balance it. She had her vision of the past. (p. 109)

As there were no historical links between the Pueblo Indians and twentieth-century Americans, any bridge had to be a mystical one, and her attempt to create it was to give a unique quality to her later work and to save her from degenerating into a shrill and ineffective female version of H. L. Mencken.

In 1922 . . . she was confirmed into the Episcopalian Church. The split between the woman and the artist was from now on to be increasingly distinct, one hostile to the disarray of the times, more and more conservative, even reactionary, the other immersed in the very special task of working a rich spiritual pattern out of the bits and pieces of the past. (pp. 109-10)

Willa Cather had now discovered that in using the past she did not have to limit herself to the past of her own or even of her parents' recollection. Indeed, the further back she went, the closer she seemed to approach the essence of that pioneer spirit from which she felt that the twentieth century was a tragic falling away. It is certainly healthier for a novelist to admire the past than to deplore the present. Edith Wharton was on the same right track when she wrote *The Age of Innocence,* as was Ellen Glasgow in the early chapters of *Vein of Iron,* but the right track, alas, was the exception and not, as with Willa Cather, the rule, in their later work. Miss Cather allowed the woman but never the writer to become a crank. (p. 114)

The paradox in Willa Cather's theory of fiction, the novel démeublé, or stripped of all unnecessary descriptions and stratagems, the novel that must almost flow by some process of artistic free association from a mind that has fully assimilated the characters and scenes to be portrayed, is that she herself did not abide by it. Although her completed novels may be somewhat shapeless, they are filled with little gems of short stories, insets, that might have been conceived and plotted by Guy de Maupassant himself. Critics have leaned over backwards to relate these to the novels in which they appear, and critics who are not themselves novelists are apt to make wide allowances for seeming irrelevancies in this respect. (pp. 115-16)

The historical novel not only served to eliminate Willa Cather's grudges against modern life; it provided the skeleton on which the most disparate and unconnected matters could be hung. *Death Comes for the Archbishop* is like a gallery of brilliantly lit dioramas in a historical museum illustrating life in the American Southwest a century ago. Everything falls into place because the reader accepts the era and the locale as in themselves creating a frame and hence a form. It is the same in *Shadows on the Rock.* . . . (p. 116)

If Willa Cather started with the impact of America on poor immigrants and went on to explore the impact of European culture on America, she ended, most significantly, with the impact of America on educated European pioneers. It is her vision of Father Latour's vision of the Southwest and of Pierre Chardon's vision of Canada that is her highest achievement. Neither Latour nor Pierre ever want to go back; they have seen a beauty as fine as anything that elicited the gasps of the young Henry James. In *Death Comes for the Archbishop* there is quite as deep a sense of the past as in *The Ambassadors.* The mesas are as old as anything in Paris, and eternity broods over the desert. Henry Adams was one of the few American writers of his time to find as much in America and in the Pacific to stimulate his imagination as in Europe. It is a pity that he did not survive to comment on Miss Cather's historical novels. (pp. 118-19)

> *Louis Auchincloss, "Willa Cather," in his* Pioneers & Caretakers: A Study of 9 American Women Novelists *(© 1965, University of Minnesota), University of Minnesota Press, Minneapolis, 1965, pp. 92-122.*

[Willa Cather] matured late and hardened early, in the American fashion. . . . Not surprisingly the explicit message of much of her own later writing has to do with maturity of spirit or the want of it. For Willa Cather such maturity is invariably a condition to be attained by way of surrendering the self to some heroic and transcendent service. Self-indulgence, of sense or desire, even of natural human hopefulness, is the abyss to be avoided; from the pathetic early story, "Paul's Case," through the clumsy parable of *Alexander's Bridge* . . . , her first novel, to the vindictive cartoon harassment which at fifty she chose to inflict upon her "lost lady," this abyss yawns before her characters as the very earnest of degradation and spiritual disaster. Opposed to it—radiant and redemptive for all this

author's studied coolness in defining alternatives (and clearly the opposition projects a division in her own nature which she could not resolve except wishfully)—is the moral discipline Willa Cather particularly admired, the idealized self-discipline of, interchangeably, the artist and the saint. It is for her a total dedication of being, a conscientious withdrawal from worldly pleasures and benefits into the heaven-haven of a liberating spirituality. (pp. 256-57)

It is of course a noble thought—but in Willa Cather's later work we gradually discover that it operates to hold life at arm's length, and at no small cost to our belief in its relevance to the life around us. By the time she had formulated this thought in so many words, it served her not as an instrument of imaginative exploration and measurement but as a protective screen against the unnerving disorder of common experience. . . . The ideal of an uncontaminated and immunized art led her steadily away from the kind of recollective realism she had settled upon in the brief prime of her career. Yet it is this work of her prime which really illustrates her moral-aesthetic principle of self-surrender. For it was only when, just at mid-life, she turned back to the Nebraska of her childhood—turned back, that is, to that one life to which she had already surrendered her unguarded private consciousness beyond recall—that she did in fact free her imagination to accomplish something wholly "worth while" and (as a novelist) recreate a substantial and convincing fictional world.

Willa Cather's secure work is recollective and memorial. Except as a register of incontrovertible past impressions her moral intelligence is uninteresting; her direct moral precepting invariably surrounds itself, in her work, with a kind of vacuum of demonstration. . . . As a craftsman Willa Cather has surely been overpraised or praised for the wrong things. Her architectural sense is limited and easily overtaxed; indeed her rather narrow and uncertain talent for story-telling seems to flourish in the degree that she departs from the requirements of coherent dramatic representation and orderly plotting. *O Pioneers!* and *The Song of the Lark* are episodic and discontinuous, and her best book, *My Ántonia,* is not a novel at all but a loose chronicle of community remembrance. But in this way, one feels, all three are so much the more open to the free flow of uncoerced observation through which, in the writing, Willa Cather's intensely personal confrontation of life could be creatively reabsorbed into the collective history of a world she had had no choice not to participate in and without reserve. (pp. 257-59)

In American writing of this period *My Ántonia* possesses a rare steadiness of formal apprehension, an achievement back of which we may recognize the liberating conjunction of two decisive factors: unstinted personal emotion and a remarkably firm and objective knowledge of an actual pattern of regional, and national, history. (p. 263)

> *Warner Berthoff, in his* The Ferment of Realism: American Literature, 1884-1919 *(reprinted with permission of Macmillan Publishing Co., Inc.; copyright © 1965 by The Free Press, a Division of The Macmillan Company), The Free Press, 1965.*

In Willa Cather's fiction the land exists as more than mere backdrop or place of action; the land fundamentally conditions the action and characterization in her novels and short stories. . . . I shall use the coined term "land-philosophy" to suggest the whole range of symbolic meanings of the land and the rock in the fiction of Miss Cather.

In her fiction the land demands attention in its own right, but it also serves as a controlling image that gives philosophical meaning to the facts of ordinary life. Within her comprehensive land image she employs the land-rock polarity to express an over-arching vision that extends from pioneering existence close to the wild land through man's life at the level of highest cultural achievement. It is a vision which finds in the land the roots of honesty and strength, imagination and desire—a vision that provides for active acceptance of reality and its eventual transformation into art and culture, and, finally, the transcendence of all through love.

At the same time, however, that one admits the consistent reality of Willa Cather's "land-philosophy," especially as revealed in her major and minor land images, one must hasten to assert that she does not consciously operate from a formulated world-view. Rather a view emerges from a whole configuration of particulars. (p. 58)

It will be helpful here to differentiate briefly between the two elements in the imagery—the land and the rock—and to point out their complementary function in Willa Cather's fiction.

Persisting as it does, yet being subject in its fruits to birth, death, and rebirth, the land for Miss Cather involves immersion in a reality that is limited yet which points perpetually to something beyond itself that is lasting. The rock, on the other hand, signifies an achieved transcendence, in the sense of an other-worldly satisfaction of human longings—sometimes in the human sense of the discovery of an elevated but now extinct civilization and at other times in the divine sense of final union with God.

Obviously the two large images—the land and the rock—complement one another in Willa Cather's fiction. A truly human life in the here-and-now cannot be complete with only one of the basic elements that the land-rock imagery represents. The complete human person must actively accept or love the land—the underlying reality that repeatedly gives nourishment to life and love and art—and he must simultaneously transcend that essentially limited yet nonetheless inspiring force to realize a life and a love that constitute the ultimate order and beauty and meaning of his existence. (p. 59)

The first cardinal point in Willa Cather's "land-philosophy" is her use of the land as an expanding symbol for essences. The fact that words and phrases referring to such essentials as "strength," "genuineness," "vitality," "freedom," "generosity," "active acceptance," "discipline," "almost boundless satisfaction," and "power to love" are expressed or implied as intrinsic to the land throughout her fiction is one verification of this judgment. (pp. 59-60)

At the root of her feeling for the land and her evaluation of it and its effects on other persons stands the second cardinal point of her "land-philosophy": The land is good in itself by nature; but sometimes in its effects or in a person's response to it, it appears evil in its operations. . . .

A third cardinal notion in Willa Cather's "land-philosophy" consists in the "pull" of the earth, what I shall call an almost "gravitational" attachment to reality—the necessary

foundational contact with the underlying forces from which life and art, however defined, receive their impetus and their enrichment. In Miss Cather's view, one does not achieve these "roots" in the land automatically, either by birth on the land or by direct involvement with it. Rather one must actively accept what the land is; one must be open to it; in fact, one must consciously love it. And since the land means for Willa Cather that which is whole, real, and living, a satisfactory relation to the land constitutes a precondition for the creativity of art. Thus creativity follows living, and living follows upon positively willed acceptance.

Leading up to the final point of Willa Cather's "land-philosophy" is a fourth main point, that is, the idea of the plains as bespeaking openness and breadth of vision, purposeful freedom and a yearning for greatness. On the open plains Miss Cather's sympathetic characters find that their spirit has a wide range that enables a person to eschew triviality and to reach out, with determination, toward challenging—if perhaps unformulated—goals.

The fifth and final cardinal point, the land's fostering of transcendence, pervades Willa Cather's land-fiction, appearing alone as well as in relation to other major notions of her "land-philosophy." According to her thinking, the wild land holds the promise of ultimate possibilities, and the rock "cities" offer a cultured civilization that gives the human spirit a taste—a whetted appetite—for realized fulfillment, limited though that fulfillment be. But both wildness and civilization merely give impetus and direction to the one questing for the transcendent. It is important to assert, however, that the place of transcendence in the total scheme of things does not, for Miss Cather, mean a rejection of those natural goods and human achievements that have, of themselves, proved inadequate to the complete fulfillment of desire. In her vision the need for transcendence does not emerge from a vacuum but rather from a long continuum of human effort exercised upon a very real and complex world. (pp. 60-1)

Looked at chronologically, Willa Cather's fiction reveals a vigorous continuum of application of her "land-philosophy," despite a certain evolution of "land" meaning. The early stories show that from the very beginning of her career as a fiction writer, Miss Cather saw the land as symbolizing a sense of reality and a yearning for the unknown, the ultimate, the transcendent. Nevertheless, at this point she exhibits more of a sociological approach to the people of the land than an interest in characters as persons in their own right. No convincingly dramatized, fully satisfactory relationships of persons with the land obtain in her early short stories.

Yet the fact remains that rapport with the land constitutes for Miss Cather the *sine qua non* condition for portrayal of a sympathetic character. (pp. 62-3)

Through her "land-philosophy," finally, Willa Cather suggests a personal as well as an impersonal good; through it she tells not only of transcendence and power, but of involvement and love as well. (p. 63)

Sister Lucy Schneider, "Artistry and Intuition: Willa Cather's 'Land-Philosophy'," in South Dakota Review, *Winter, 1968-69, pp. 53-64.*

If, as is often said, every novelist is born to write one thing, then the one thing that Willa Cather was born to write was first fully realized in *My Ántonia* (1918). (p. 237)

One technical device which is fundamental to the greater concentration and suggestiveness of *My Ántonia* is the point of view from which it is told. Both of the earlier "Nebraska novels" had been reported over the protagonist's shoulder, with omniscient intrusions by the author. Here the whole story is told by a narrator, Jim Burden, a boyhood friend of Ántonia, later a lawyer representing the railroads. The use of the narrative mask permits Miss Cather to exercise her sensibility without obvious self-indulgence: Burden becomes an instrument of the selectivity that she worked for. He also permits the easy condensation and syncopation of time—an indispensable technical tool in a novel that covers more than 30 years and deals in a complex way with a theme of development. Finally, Jim Burden is used constantly as a suggestive parallel to Ántonia: he is himself an orphan and has been himself transplanted and is himself groping for an identity and an affiliation. In the process of understanding and commemorating Ántonia, he locates himself; we see the essential theme from two points, and the space between those points serves as a base line for triangulation. (pp. 240-41)

[The] name Willa Cather chose for [Jim Burden] was not picked by accident. For Jim not only, as narrator, carries the "burden" or tune of the novel; he carries also the cultural burden that Willa Cather herself carried, the quintessentially American burden of remaking in the terms of a new place everything that makes life graceful and civilized. To become a European or an easterner is only to reverse and double the exile. The education that lured Jim Burden away from Nebraska had divided him against himself, as Willa Cather was divided. Like people, the education that comes from elsewhere must be modified to fit a new environment. In becoming a man of the world, Jim Burden discovers that he has almost forgotten to be a man from Nebraska. It is Ántonia, who now achieves some of that quality of earth goddess that Alexandra Bergson had had in *O Pioneers!*, who reminds him that no matter where his mind has been, his heart has always been here. (p. 247)

Jim Burden is more than a narrative device: his is an essential part of the theme, a demonstration of how such an American may reconcile the two halves of himself. And Ántonia is more than a woman and a character. Jim describes her toward the end as "a rich mine of life, like the founders of early races."

Miss Cather, who did not believe in laboring a point any more than she believed in over-furnishing a novel, clearly wanted us to take away that image of Ántonia. A mine of life, the mother of races, a new thing forming itself in hardship and hope, but clinging to fragments of the well-loved old. Hence *My Ántonia*—any American's Ántonia, Willa Cather's Ántonia. No writer ever posed that essential aspect of the American experience more warmly, with more nostalgic lyricism, or with a surer understanding of what it means. (pp. 248-49)

> *Wallace Stegner, "The West Authentic: Willa Cather," in his* The Sound of Mountain Water *(copyright © 1969 by Wallace Stegner; reprinted by permission of Doubleday & Co., Inc.), Doubleday, 1969, pp. 237-49.*

My Ántonia is, I believe, a commentary on the American experience, the American dream, and the American reality. (p. 112)

The novel is, in some sense, about a national experience—the frontier or pioneer experience—and its rapid diminishment and disappearance from the national memory. But more than an experience is involved and at stake. Obscurely related to the experience and its consequences is the American dream. Was it a trivial or mistaken impulse all along, magnified in the imagination beyond its possibilities? Was it a reality that was in some blundering way betrayed by us all? Or was it, perhaps, an illusion, created out of nothing, and, finally, disappearing into nothing, and well forgotten. (p. 114)

In short, Jim has all the appearances of one who has lived the American dream and achieved fulfillment. But the material fulfillment has not brought the happiness promised. (p. 117)

In some dark sense, Jim's experience is the American experience, his melancholy sense of loss also his country's, his longing for something missed in the past a national longing. (p. 123)

> *James E. Miller, Jr., "'My Ántonia' and the American Dream," in* Prairie Schooner *(© 1974 by University of Nebraska Press; reprinted by permission from* Prairie Schooner*), Summer, 1974, pp. 112-23.*

Raymond Chandler

1888-1959

American mystery and screen writer. Chandler, raised and educated in England, returned to America to become first an oil executive and then a full-time writer. With his own mentor, Dashiell Hammett, Chandler is considered one of the founders of the detective-story-as-literature, hard-boiled crime fiction characterized by a high degree of literary craftsmanship. Philip Marlowe, working in Los Angeles's "neon wilderness," is his private detective.

PRINCIPAL WORKS

The Big Sleep (novel) 1939
Farewell, My Lovely (novel) 1940
The High Window (novel) 1942
The Lady in the Lake (novel) 1943
Red Wind (short stories) 1946
The Simple Art of Murder (short stories) 1950
The Long Goodbye (novel) 1954

Chandler writes not out of habit and not with synthetic materials, as do so many mystery writers, but with an artistry of craftsmanship and a realism that can rank him with many a famous novelist. In his hands, words do become beautiful and wonderful things, operating with economy and precision. What a delight it is to come upon a writer who tosses off a good image on almost every page. . . .

Chandler is prodigal in his imagery. If they seem more wisecracks than high-flown literary similes, I will point out that Chandler writes the characteristic American speech and uses characteristic American humor. In doing this he comes closer to literature than other writers who disdain the native brand of thought and language. . . .

There are descriptive passages that a poet might envy; and phrases . . . [that] have a beauty which shows that Chandler cannot be pigeonholed merely as an expert in tough language.

There is more of the tough language in Chandler's works than of the other kind, but this is because he writes of a world and order of society in which there is little beauty or serenity. (p. 123)

He believes, and rightly I think, that most murder stories no longer have any relation to real life—that they have become a literary form and convention remote from realism. If we were to judge from most murder stories, murders are most prevalent among the middle and upper classes and as often as not are solved, not by the police, but by private individuals possessed of bulging brains and a vast assortment of strange knowledges. It is manifestly ridiculous. Chandler in his works has returned to that world where murder is a commonplace: the world of racketeers in drugs and liquor, in gambling and prostitution; a world in which police and racketeers and politicians are often mixed up in sub-surface alliances. It is not a bad thing that we should be told about the murky depths of our civilization, that this realism should be Chandler's subject, for, as we well know, this is indeed the area of American society in which murder is most frequent.

It is strange to meet a murder-novel writer who attacks his work with the earnest attention and serious social thought which are supposed to be the prerogative of eminent novelists. This is what Chandler does; and, so doing, he has removed his work from the realm of merely conventional entertainment to the point where it becomes a serious study of a certain kind of American society. This quality, and a grim sense of humor allied with an even grimmer sense of realism—for example, his description of the seedy Fulwider Building in *The Big Sleep,*—plus a superb writing ability, have produced five novels which are worth the attention of more readers than just those alone who are interested in the literature of murder. . . .

Mr. Chandler has done his vigorous best to explode the empty convention behind ordinary murder stories, but he ought not to set up a convention for himself. We who read three or four shockers a week can't stand monotony in murder. (p. 124)

D. C. Russell, "The Chandler Books," in The Atlantic Monthly *(copyright © 1945, 1973, by The Atlantic Monthly Company, Boston, Mass.; reprinted with permission), March, 1945, pp. 123-24.*

To be caught with a Raymond Chandler whodunit in hand is a fate no highbrow reader need dread. When *The Big Sleep*, his first, was published . . . , it not only wowed the choosiest mystery reviewers; it also won him a large audience in which even the most determined intellectual could feel at home. . . . Chandler proved in his next three books that the cheers were justified. They had everything a good detective story needs: ingenuity, suspense, pace, credibility. But they had a lot more. Their private-eye hero, Philip Marlowe, was just tough enough, just sentimental enough to move like a born natural through the neon-nylon wilderness of a Los Angeles world that the movies never made until Chandler showed them how. Chandler's tense situations mushroomed naturally with almost no trace of fabrication. Best of all, he wrote fresh, crackling prose and it was peppered with newly minted similes. . . . (pp. 82-3)

Chandler is at his best in conveying the special flavor of depressing police-station offices, the even more depressing outlook of cynical policemen and cheap-hotel dicks. He makes Marlowe good, but not too good to make mistakes, human enough to feel resentment and despair. Yet . . . , [moving] over & over again in the same groove, even genuine talent can get to be a cliché. Shamus Marlowe is in real danger of becoming an old retainer, Chandler of becoming a gifted hack. (p. 83)

> *"Murder at the Old Stand," in* Time *(reprinted by permission from* Time, The Weekly Newsmagazine; *copyright Time Inc. 1949), October 3, 1949, pp. 82-3.*

Mr. Chandler has emphasized his own dislike for plot-construction. The realistic method, he says, has freed him from "an exhausting concatenation of insignificant clues," . . . and he can now let the characters work out the story for themselves.

Here we see the main weakness in Mr. Chandler's novels. From the first page he goes whooping along at high speed, magnificently if somewhat confusedly, until he reaches the last chapter. There he takes one sweet spill into a net. He thrashes wildly, but he can't get out; he can't explain why his characters acted as they did, and he can't even talk intelligibly. This, presumably, is realism.

Mr. Chandler is a serious-minded man, and it would be unjust not to take him seriously. . . . He can write a scene with an almost suffocating vividness and sense of danger— if he does not add three words too many and make it funny. His virtues are all there. If, to some restraint, he could add the fatigue of construction and clues (the writer he most admires, Mr. Hammett, has never disdained clues and has always given them fairly)—then one day he may write a good novel.

I say nothing of new ideas or plot-twists, because Mr. Chandler does not have them. He will never disturb the laurels of Mr. Queen or Mr. Gardner or Mr. Stout. Perhaps it is best to let him alone, and offer no suggestions. . . .

When he forgets he cannot write a true detective story, when he forgets to torture words, the muddle resolves and the action whips along like a numbered racing-car. . . .

Mr. Chandler will do even better when he discovers that you cannot create an American language merely by butchering the English language.

> *John Dickson Carr, "With Colt and Luger," in* The New York Times Book Review *(© 1950 by The New York Times Company; reprinted by permission), September 24, 1950, p. 36.*

Raymond Chandler . . . left behind five . . . solid thrillers [which] will probably be read by ordinary readers for . . . [as] long . . . as the taste for violent thrillers endures and [as] long as Southern California has a place in people's imagination.

Whether Chandler will ever be elected into literary history is another question. The odd thing is that he is known and enjoyed by those who have the power to vote him in—critics, writers, scholars, literary historians—and even so it begins to look as though his nomination for membership may not be seconded. To be sure, any comprehensive literary chronicle of the age will certainly list him along with Dashiell Hammett and Mickey Spillane as one of the chief practitioners of the "tough-guy mystery"; but this is indiscriminate and flattering. . . . (pp. 354-55)

I would bet a good deal that right now (1) most of the literary folk of the country have read some of Chandler's best work with pleasure and profit but, ashamed of their pleasure, would deny it any literary value; and (2) these same people have read of Wallace Stevens' poems few more than the often-anthologized pieces, and those without anything like full comprehension or pleasure, and yet would grant high value to the body of his poetry. Well, I do not mean to suggest that I think Stevens is less than excellent or that Chandler is more than pretty good. But I do suggest that it is time we publicly honor Chandler (and Hammett his master). . . .

There is no use pretending that the detective story has much to recommend it as a form. In fact, I should imagine that no novel written within its conventions could be first-rate, just as no opera written within the conventions of the Broadway musical could be first-rate. . . . The detective story damagingly interferes in what is of the very essence of a novel; it manipulates the motives and relationships of its characters for an artificial and trivial end. Even in those rare detective stories where the motives are credible enough and the relationships are reasonably subtle and valid, the reader is kept from apprehending them in a way that is really serious. Knowledge of motive and relationship is parceled out to him for reasons of plot excitement—a matter of some, but low, value—and this very excitement works against a profound or thoughtful or complexly moving appreciation of the characters' essential natures. (p. 355)

Chandler's novels are a good deal more successful as thrillers than as detective stories, and a thriller, as demonstrated by the example of Graham Greene (he's respectable), need not distort motive or relationship very much. It forbids that contemplation which is essential to reading great fiction, the movement of which is most of the time quite slow. But a thriller can do a good many things of literary value, and some of these things Chandler does admirably.

The obvious accomplishment of his thrillers is to generate a sort of nervous tension which is the literary analogue to the tension generated just by being an American citizen. Tension alone is not so much: one can induce it by chain-smoking a couple of packs of cigarettes and slugging down a fair amount of liquor, driving eighty miles an hour to a juke box joint where one drinks black coffee and plays a slot machine, then driving home again chortling every so often, "We sure had a good time, didn't we?" In fact this sort of tension-making is an unexceptional way to spend the evening in Southern California, and if Philip Marlowe did not do things like it we would not believe in him. (pp. 355-56)

But, as I think, these tension-making actions are only externalizings of deep and chronic and ill-conceived trouble within the actor-reader. (There is something drastically wrong with the world and with me as part of it; I don't know what it is, it isn't what they tell me it is, I don't think I could figure it out if I tried; anyhow I am afraid to look too closely.) One temporary relief from this malaise, and I think many suffer from it much of the time, is to read a story which produces in the reader a safe version of the same thing and which purges this induced tension by showing a Marlowe who figures out what's wrong with at least part of the world and then remedies it.

Good enough. This is a considerable endeavor for a novelist to undertake. To accomplish it adequately, he must have, and make us share, a clarifying and steady vision of the evil which infects the world he shows, and he must persuade us that the hero's action is more than a simple wish-fulfillment, is a possible and dignified deed however bitterly limited it may be.

Hammett's vision was of a society so corrupt that it corrupts all individual relationships; it is not surprising that he turned to left-wing politics. Spillane's murked vision was of a human nature so corrupt that no clean action is possible; it is fitting that he turned for solace to the wet-mud notions and dry-mud practices of the Jehovah's Witnesses. Chandler's vision was of a world which is no less violent, ugly, unjust, or loveless than theirs; yet it is not exactly corrupt. Moral corruption implies a prior innocent nature, whether Christian or Rousseauistic, to be corrupted. Chandler's attitude is to look at what's there in the expectation that good and evil are all mixed together; consequently he does not suffer such rage as do the other two. It is a stoic vision. In his novels Chandler did not quite sustain it, being much too romantic and not quite courageous enough to bear the full bitterness of that vision: Marlowe's solutions are morally too easy; they promise, dreamily, to remedy more than they ever could, as he recognizes, despairingly, at the end of each novel. (p. 356)

Chandler has a good many of the lesser virtues and vices of a romancer. Two of the locations for these are his style and the way he treats blondes.

Some of the style is of the genre—Marlowe's hyper-aggressive truth-telling, for instance. . . . Surely no American since Mark Twain has invented so many wisecracks as this British-educated classicist. . . . The dialogue, when it is not hobbled by plot work, is fast, glittering and tough. . . . The famous language of his style is a fabrication based only in part on the argots of police and criminals. For this is the world of romance and the style is a romantic style. (pp. 356, 358)

If you say that all this provides somewhat meager fare for romance, I must agree. But if you say that this distorts life beyond recognition, I must object that you do not know that meager region, Southern California, as well as Chandler did.

His chief accomplishment, it seems to me, is to create for the place a fictional image which corresponds to the ac-

tuality more vividly and more accurately than anything written by anyone else. . . .

If you want the feel and aspect of Los Angeles and vicinity during the thirties, forties and early fifties, you could hardly do better than to read his fictions. There is a considerable change in this fictional world between *The Big Sleep* and *The Long Goodbye;* part of this change was a deepening in Chandler as a writer and part of it was, no doubt, a result of his greater acquaintance with the region; but part of it too took place in Southern California itself. As it has grown in population, wealth and importance, its appearance has become less macabre and its vileness has turned inward, hidden behind solider false fronts. (p. 358)

Chandler saw his region not just as it saw itself but in his own way too. And his version of it was so congenial and so strong that it affected his readers' versions. Chandler's fictions are one of the reasons Southern California now is seen as it is seen.

If you object that in the long view this is not so much for a writer to do, I cannot disagree. What I would maintain, though, is that he did as much as the J. F. Coopers of our literature ever did and that his novels are, for the time being, a lot more fun to read. (p. 360)

> *George P. Elliot, "Country Full of Blondes," in* The Nation *(copyright 1960 by the Nation Associates, Inc.), April 23, 1960, pp. 354-56, 358-60.*

In reading *Raymond Chandler Speaking*, a collection of the late mystery writer's letters and literary fragments, one gets a sense of the peculiar loneliness of the writer of integrity who works in a popular genre that attracts few writers like himself and that the American literary culture tends to dismiss with easy, contemptuous generalizations. Chandler was a talented and devoted craftsman, one who spent his life either in spurts of hard work on his novels or in long periods of lying fallow and brooding about the lack of serious understanding and appreciation with which his work was received. (p. 158)

At the same time, this feeling of being left out, of working at a vocation in which one's best and most conscientious efforts were underrated and misunderstood, can also be seen to have informed Chandler's fiction.

His great theme was not crime and punishment, though his letters reveal him to have had a sound technical knowledge of criminal history, psychology, and technique. His theme was, rather, an exploration of the belief that the moral man, who refuses to play the game of life in a conventionally immoral or amoral way, is doomed to the kind of loneliness Chandler himself suffered.

This understanding of Chandler and his theme provides, in turn, for speculation about the decline of a once promising figure in popular mythology, the private eye. As created by Dashiell Hammett and developed by Chandler, [the private eye] offered a unique perspective on loneliness as a central condition of modern urban existence. Philip Marlowe, Chandler's detective, masked his feeling of emptiness behind a protective set of tough-guy mannerisms, and it is because Chandler's legion of imitators borrowed them, but not Marlowe's inner spirit, that the hard school is no longer very interesting. The books are sometimes amusing as puzzles, but nothing about them catches in the mind. Marlowe did. (pp. 158-59)

Marlowe, like his creator, was a plodder, the intensity of his dangerous moments heightened by the contrast with the lonely boredom of his normal life. This gave Chandler the opportunity to write about boredom, that great modern subject, without ultimately becoming boring himself. A quick turn of the plot always saved him and the reader from ennui. . . .

Chandler was a master of this milieu. Of today's serious writers, only Graham Greene has given us a comparable rendering of the habits and habitats of the individual at loose ends in a great city. Greene came, in time, to see the squalor of the bed-sitting room as a symbol of man's alienation from God. Chandler never went quite that far. A striving for faith becomes the moral imperative in Greene's later work. A gruff, typically American sentimentality is Chandler's equivalent to it. It is pragmatic and limited; it says no more than that everybody has the right to be left alone. So, with Chandler, mood becomes dominant, and response to it is everything in the appreciation of his work.

The atmosphere of cheap furnished apartments, of second-rate bars where one can always find a conversation and sometimes a woman, the very feel of an empty city street to the man who has just killed the evening alone in a second-run movie house, are done with wonderful rightness. So are the psychic defenses of the lonely man. Marlowe plays endless games of chess with himself, carefully setting up the classic problems, then spending the evening trying to solve them, sipping at a bourbon highball. He is persnickety, in an old-maidish way, about small things like coffee. The careful construction of an ideal cup of it occupies a lovingly written paragraph in almost every Marlowe novel. In fact, popular misapprehension to the contrary, Marlowe is more interested in good coffee than he is in booze, good or otherwise. Nor is Marlowe much of a boudoir athlete. He is rather offhand about women, perhaps a little defensive. Physically, of course, he needs them, but emotionally he knows they pose a threat to his independence. Consequently, he is wary, though gallant, in his treatment of them.

But why, since Marlowe is reasonably attractive, reasonably intelligent, does he do nothing to change his lot? Chandler answers this question in one of his letters, stating explicitly what is implicit in the novels.

> If being in revolt against a corrupt society constitutes being immature, then Philip Marlowe is extremely immature. If seeing dirt where there is dirt constitutes an inadequate social adjustment, then Philip Marlowe has inadequate social adjustment. Of course Marlowe is a failure and usually he knows it. He is a failure because he hasn't any money. A man who without physical handicaps cannot make a decent living is always a failure and usually a moral failure. But a lot of very good men have been failures because their particular talents did not suit their time and place. (p. 159)

The two great private detectives of the hard school, Marlowe and Hammett's Sam Spade, were both code heroes, like those of Hemingway (whose style also had its influence on that school). . . . Consciously or unconsciously, the classic private eye represents an attempt to transfer the man with a code from the lost Eden of the 19th-century American West to the modern Jungle of the Cities. Hammett was the first to make the attempt in the pulp magazines of the 20's. His original private eye, the Continental Op, discovered that his code of personal conduct, which consisted mostly of "doing the job," was inadequate to cope with the magnitude of the evil opposed to him. . . . In 1939 Chandler published his first novel, *The Big Sleep,* and introduced Marlowe to the world. His tales would not be as bloody or as smoothly fast-moving as Hammett's, but Marlowe would prove to be a character of more depth than any Hammett ever created.

Marlowe rarely tangled with the kind of organized crime that the Continental Op encountered in *Red Harvest.* He was called upon only to pit his private morality against private immorality. Even so, the literary left tried to claim Marlowe for its own, tried to invest his struggle against evil with political significance. Chandler resented this deeply. As far as he was concerned, politics was merely an extension of criminality by legal, but certainly not moral, means; he never fell victim to the kind of inner conflict that silenced Hammett.

Still, like it or not, Marlowe was a class figure. He was most believable when there were distinct differences between the styles of the rich, or at least upper middle class, and lower middle class. He began to seem a little out of place in the prosperous 50's, when even college professors were being cut in on the wealthiest society in human history. His stubborn refusal to join up with the rest of society seemed more eccentric than heroic, more adolescent than mature. . . . Marlowe had begun to suffer from cultural lag. (pp. 160-61)

Chandler, in his concern with the real psychological issues of his time, and in his ability to focus these issues by his excellent anti-hero, was at least the equal of a middle rank "serious" novelist—perhaps the equal, on occasion, of a first-rate one. (p. 161)

> *Richard Schickel, "Raymond Chandler, Private Eye" (reprinted from* Commentary *by permission; copyright © 1963 by the American Jewish Committee), in* Commentary, *February, 1963, pp. 158-61.*

Chandler's achievements are impressive: he mastered the American style—a combination (as he defined it) of idiom, slang, wise-crack, hyperbole and tough talk that in the hands of a man of genius can be made to do anything; he had a view of the world more serious and more valid than a good many craftsmen working in a more respected genre; he invented a hero, Philip Marlowe, who has been called a "great creation"; he expressed his vision with wit and vigor, though occasionally with sentimentality; he is indisputably the best writer about urban California, and he wrote the best novel about Hollywood. But all these achievements seem somehow not enough to overcome the fact that he realized them while working in the mystery genre. This fact has kept him out of any serious literary discussion, a silence which even some honorable exceptions (Richard Schickel, George P. Elliott, Auden, Maugham) have not broken. (pp. 171-72)

Philip Marlowe (detective, sleuth, gum-shoe, private eye, private investigator, PI—take your pick) grew out of the pulps, especially *Black Mask,* in which the hard-boiled detective story was being perfected. Chandler has called Marlowe a fantasy, "an exaggeration, but at least an exaggeration of the possible." He's a "great creation," according to Richard Schickel. H. B. Parkes has traced his descent from other figures of popular American and literary culture, heroes who fled into the wilderness to escape the corrupting influences of civilization, figures like the trapper and the cowboy, and heroes such as Leatherstocking, Ishmael, Huck Finn, Nick Adams, who could still associate innocence and Nature. But Marlowe, like Hammett's recurrent hero, the Continental Op, is among the first urban heroes in that tradition. For both, the frontier is closed, the identification of nature and innocence is no longer possible; but while Hammett's Continental Op worked within an organization, and cooperated with the police, Marlowe, a decade later, finds no one to trust; the police are both reflections and victims of a corrupt society, and of the powers within it or without—the man of wealth, or the gangster—who manipulate it. (p. 176)

Chandler's hero does not think, he has character, and he responds to character in others. He knows and understands character; he makes distinctions between people; he responds to their moral qualities and is himself moral; he believes in truth, and justice, and honesty and fidelity, and he will go to any length to protect those in whom he sees these qualities, usually the aged (with some important exceptions). Just so, he responds to the qualities of the city; and just so, Chandler gives a richness and fullness to his style. There are all gradations of class and milieu and speech and diction in Chandler's novels. For these reasons, Chandler, through Marlowe, succeeds as no one else has succeeded in portraying Los Angeles, including Hollywood, and it seems at times that it is neither the violence nor the solution of the mystery Chandler is interested in as it is the city and the people, through the whole range of which, in the solution of the crime, Marlowe moves.

Yet Marlowe, though heroic, tough, and wise, is a sad character. For all the personal life he has and the people he can trust, he might as well be in the wilderness. He is a lonely figure, a man without personal life. (pp. 177-78)

In *The Long Goodbye* Chandler came closest to writing the mystery novel that isn't a mystery novel, the realistic novel with a couple of murders in which character is more important than anything, except style. (p. 180)

Marlowe's major motive is again sentimentality allied to loyalty in one part of the double plot-structure, but there is an improvement in that sentimental loyalty; the motive in the primary and enveloping plot is causally related to the novel's second group of episodes, in which Marlowe is called on to protect a lush who is a writer from homicidal and suicidal impulses. This part of the novel becomes a fairly realistic study of an upper-class L.A. group living in a restricted community called Idle Valley.

This further extension of the form affects the style. The realistic novel does not lend itself to hyperbole, wit, and wise-crack, to the humorous exaggeration of the usual; the style is tame in the more realistic series of episodes. (The problem does not exist in his incomplete novel of manners; on the contrary, as in the Restoration plays from which it derives, the novel of manners has always thrived on exaggeration, on contrast of speech, and style, and attitude.) On the other hand, Chandler is as vivid as usual. . . . (p. 181)

This is the farthest that Chandler had gotten with the character of Marlowe, as opposed to his catalytic function, until, in the unfinished *The Poodle Springs Story* he was to treat him as character in domestic conflict with wealth and in public conflict with unlawful power, with some suggestion that this conversion of convention into character would undermine the legitimacy of the convention. Marlowe as character would destroy Marlowe as function. With Marlowe's function destroyed, the mystery novel could indeed not go beyond Chandler. . . .

But if in his last novel, Chandler had finally begun to question the very idea of his hero, whose validity he had hitherto assumed, in an earlier novel, Chandler had already indicated the limits of the mystery as mystery, by opposing to the ritual of the mystery novel—murder, suspicion, complication, solution—a much older ritual. (p. 182)

Thus Chandler's continual experimentation with his genre had led him to study the possibility of the convention of his catalyst and of the strength of his plot. Turning his hero into a character had shown him the improbability of his hero, and counterpointing his ritual to a far older one had shown him the weaknesses of his plot. Beyond this, in his historical view of California—from a kind of paradise to the land of the chiseler, the shyster, the angle-boy—Chandler had also accurately studied . . . the last frontier of continental America. He set an end to the fictional coverage of America, and provided America incidentally with a most devastating concluding image. (p. 185)

> *Herbert Ruhm, "Raymond Chandler: From Bloomsbury to the Jungle—and Beyond," in* Tough Guy Writers of the Thirties, *edited by David Madden (copyright © 1968, Southern Illinois University Press; reprinted by permission of Southern Illinois University Press), Southern Illinois University Press, 1968, pp. 171-85.*

In those four miraculous novels, *The Big Sleep, Farewell, My Lovely, The High Window,* and *The Lady in the Lake,* Chandler stopped the Los Angeles kaleidoscope; he arrested its spinning, so confusing to most writers who have tried to see the city clearly; and then he fixed in prose of poetic intensity the brilliant bits and pieces, until we find in his "Big Four" a glittering mosaic of greater Los Angeles from San Bernardino to the sea. (p. 372)

What distinguishes his treatment of Los Angeles from that of most other novelists is his wealth of precise observation and power of description. His vision was clear, with prose to match it. Through his transparent language we see landscape and life in exact register without blur.

As I said, he stopped the kaleidoscope. His pages glitter with brilliant descriptions. They are like the view of the city from aloft, either in the sharp light of late afternoon or after dark, when a day of Santa Ana has swept the coastal plain of smog and the Queen of the Angels is her former naked self. Time and place are of the essence in a Chandler novel. (p. 376)

By literature, Chandler meant any sort of writing that reaches a sufficient intensity of performance to glow with its own heat. "There must be magic in the writing," he said, "but I take no credit for it. It just happens, like red hair." His pages have this magical glow and give off heat that comes from the incandescence of his own style. He took the American vernacular as it is concocted in the melting pot of Los Angeles and made it an expressive instrument. . . .

Chandler's stories are melodramas, which is to say they are exaggerations of violence and fear in which emotion is overcharged and time and event are compressed beyond probability. And yet they are relevant to the milieu they transform. (p. 377)

Not only does Chandler describe environment with poetical realism, his people are vividly alive, even the most minor. . . . (p. 378)

In a little more than four years of concentrated creativity, Chandler said it all and at such a level that never again could he regain that height. *The Little Sister, The Long Goodbye,* and *Playback* are what was left after the cream had been taken off. They are the tail of the rocket, the tricks without the magic. And yet every Chandler addict will read them and long for more. (pp. 378-79)

> *Lawrence Clark Powell, "'Farewell, My Lovely': Raymond Chandler," in his* California Classics: The Creative Literature of the Golden State (*copyright © 1971 by Lawrence Clark Powell*), Ward Ritchie, 1971, pp. 371-81.

Long before Raymond Chandler died in 1959, his private investigator, Philip Marlowe, was an American folk hero. Chandler became famous in the forties during and immediately after World War II, and Marlowe was a perfect escapist hero for the period, one who took readers away from the war. . . . The violence is entirely local, the product of individual weakness and greed, and shabby, incorruptible Marlowe is there to see the crooked record set straight. . . .

Well, throughout his writing life Chandler demanded to be taken seriously. He came to crime fiction late in his career, and was shocked to discover that the people who wrote it were a lesser breed living below the salt, who were expected to bark gratefully for any scraps of notice they received. (p. 13)

[The] fact that Chandler was an introverted romantic is important, especially in relation to his detective, Philip Marlowe.

You get the romanticism most obviously in that famous phrase about a man going down the mean streets where crime takes place, "who is not himself mean, who is neither tarnished nor afraid." . . . It is no wonder that Chandler originally meant to call Marlowe Mallory, for the link with some of the characters in Sir Thomas Malory's "Morte d'Arthur" is strong.

Chandler said various things about his detective at different times. Marlowe was nobody, but just grew out of the pulps. Marlowe had a personal conscience, not a social one, and like his creator didn't give a damn who was President because he was bound to be a politician. He was just over six feet tall, weighed about 190 pounds, drank almost anything alcoholic provided it was not sweet, and would be best represented among film actors by . . . Cary Grant. (p. 22)

If we compare Marlowe with Dashiell Hammett's Sam Spade, he looks a romantic fiction. If we put him side by side with Ross Macdonald's Lew Archer, Marlowe is less believable than Archer, but he is more vivid because Archer is deliberately made a figure who in many stories is merely a catalyst for violent action. . . . Marlowe as a folk hero fitted the time. Conceived a few years earlier, he would have been harder and more nearly corrupt, like Hammett's Ned Beaumont. But Marlowe, like his creator, was, beneath the surface flippancy and nose-thumbing, a virtuous and even sentimental man. . . .

"The Big Sleep" was an astonishing piece of work. Chandler's skill in conveying atmosphere, especially of a claustrophobic kind, is evident in the very first scene, when Marlowe takes on an assignment from old General Sternwood in an overheated orchid-filled conservatory, where the plants smell "as overpowering as boiling alcohol under a blanket." And the dialogue fairly fizzes with excitement and blackish humor. . . .

The book didn't exactly make Chandler famous, but the three that followed in the next four years did. They all had the same qualities: crackling dialogue, shaky plotting ("I do my plotting in my head as I go along, and usually I do it wrong and have to do it all over again"), tremendous pace and excitement—and of course Marlowe, the slightly shabby man of integrity moving through the corrupt California scene. . . .

Success makes many authors uncritical about their own work, but with Chandler things went the other way. His last two long novels, "The Little Sister" and "The Long Goodbye," cost him many more pains than the earlier books, and they are the better for it. The plot of "The Long Goodbye" is as beautifully smooth in its intricacies as the lock of a good safe. . . .

And he took more and more care with the texture of his writing, working phrases and passages of dialogue over with immense care, regarding the first draft of a book simply as raw material, distilling what he needed from it and discarding the rest. . . .

He simply found, once he had emancipated himself from the bang-and-bash routine of pulp magazines, that he was a naturally gifted writer, sharply observant of the way people look, and with a marvelous capacity to bring his chosen California settings to life. In the early books there is a good deal of routine violence—in those days it was slightly shocking for a woman even to have her face slapped. In the later ones Chandler managed with much less. (p. 25)

In the private-eye or tough-guy genre (both dated phrases, but what else can you use?), America has produced three considerable writers, Hammett, Chandler and Ross Macdonald. . . . In America, the crime story is still playing Cinderella for critics, but it seems to me that Hammett's "The Glass Key" (which André Malraux also greatly admired) can stand with any American novel of its decade, the thirties.

Neither Chandler nor Macdonald is quite on this level. I'd be inclined to put them together, although their intentions are very different. . . . All of Macdonald's recent novels dig into the past, looking for a family secret, a distant traumatic event which influences the present. By contrast, Chandler offers a series of sparkling surfaces, below which he doesn't care to look. And he doesn't want us to look below the surface either. . . .

[Within] the limits of what he tried to do, he became a very good writer indeed. Into the adventures of Philip Marlowe he put all the witty remarks he never made, the violent adventures he would probably have shrunk from, the lovely girls he didn't know. He always wanted to be judged by the standards of art, and knew how often he fell short of them. (p. 27)

Julian Symons, "The Case of Raymond Chandler," in The New York Times Magazine (© *1973 by The New York Times Company; reprinted by permission), December 23, 1973, pp. 13, 22, 25, 27.*

In addition to the revelation of guilt, the projection of the subconscious onto the narrated events, the *tough* or *black* detective novel also deals with violence as a pattern of social relations inherent to the City and to Urban Man. Certainly, Chandler narrates from a North American perspective, and this perspective, these fictional events, are marked by the Depression, the Second World War, the Cold War, McCarthyism, and the dawn of today's consumer society. In present-day Latin America and Spain, where Chandler is consumed and consulted (like an oracle?), the historical situation is slightly different. But the violence is the same—an unspeakable fact, of multiple echoes, which conditions urban life and marks it with a permanent scar.

Every detective novel, even the roughest and most pessimistic . . ., supplies adventure, the mystery inherent to the genre. Chandler's work constitutes the proof, rather than the exception, to this rule, together with a solid realism and an internal system of signs that protect its central verisimilitude.

Even the detective Philip Marlowe emerges as a moralist straight out of romanticism. Ross MacDonald, unquestionably the best detective novelist of our time, used to point out that Marlowe always solves his cases, and this "solution" implies, at least temporarily, the restoration of order. In other words, the individual, by public, ethical action, can put things back in place. . . .

But, like all good books, Chandler's novels give rise to many readings which, while they free him from identification with any one genre—or, in any case, enrich the possibilities of that genre—at the same time serve as the basis or justification for pointing to Chandler as one of the best writers of his time in the United States. (pp. 48-9)

Among the constants of Chandler's fiction, one stands out —the dialectical opposition implied by the confrontation of power + money with marginality + poverty. Chandler dissects this opposition—it is also one of the constants of capitalist society itself, part of the definition of that society—until he has reduced it to a sort of Gothic code in which the deepest motives, that is, the most essential ones, turn out to be decadence and death.

As a rule, Marlowe, or the detectives who precede him, is hired to solve a crime committed in "high places." Generally, the crime (or better, the wrongdoing) comes to involve men and women from the slums, anxious to escape their poverty and to climb up Vance Packard's pyramid. Such oppositions expose the primary structure which generates the confrontation: the competitiveness of a stratified society. Corruption and human beings who can be bought and sold serve as rungs for ascending or descending the social ladder, for acquiring a new status. (p. 50)

The "hard-boiled novel" is, to put it precisely, a realistic novel dealing with violence. It found its greatest cultivators in Dashiell Hammett and Raymond Chandler. Other great writers in the genre have been Horace McCoy, Charles Williams, and Frederic Brown (also Nathanael West, although his novels are not, strictly speaking, detective stories).

Chandler struck the highest, the deepest, and the most desolate note. In *The Long Goodbye,* he pushes the genre to such an extreme that only the recent writings of Ross MacDonald, twenty years later, can be said to present a new angle, a fresh turn of the screw. Everything else looks like a rhetorical variation.

The "hard-boiled novel" is also the Elizabethan tragedy of the common man. Marlowe, like the characters he encounters, is a pathetic figure. Pushed around by events, by the corrupt and the corrupters, he makes no attempt to understand the superstructure of the system, nor will he risk his safety to keep it functioning (he distrusts the police on principle, because the police are essentially repressive, and Marlowe is at heart a libertarian); he merely seeks to restore a certain bygone coherence capable of explaining humanity and the strange acts of its members. (p. 51)

Whatever the reason [for the widespread reading of Chandler's work in Latin America], his realism functions as a hazy but photographic picture of our own realities. The picture stirs many resonances. Marlowe lives as badly as we do, and his big-shots are as powerful as the ones who control our countries. And, however much we may lament it, we too understand the language of revolvers and machine guns—another Chandler constant.

In any case, these themes are part of the surface, the tip of the iceberg. For there is another Chandler, richer and more difficult to classify, that emerges from Marlowe's existential world view. Loneliness, the impossibility of communication, and the need to survive force Marlowe to confront his life in philosophical terms. He does not make a philosophy out of action; instead, action leads him to reflection, a reflection colored by anguish.

Marlowe is an exile, an outcast, in the eyes of society. And the social system exists to serve the Other. The world of other men becomes another form of alienation, something hopelessly external and incomprehensible.

His struggle carries with it the seeds of its own defeat. Something deep and bitter waits beneath the events of the plot, like a secret foundation, unshakeable. The final impression is inexorable—a grey, Kafkian metaphor slightly rationalized by the sour smell of fish. The rancid smell of decay.

But Marlowe is the axis that allows this world to be turned upside-down. Or at least to have doubt cast on its values. Marlowe is a man alienated, defeated, and cast out by *this* world, in *this* context, among *these* social alternatives.

If anything sums up Marlowe's character, it is that his very existence is a challenge.

His actions throw the defenses of the world around him into disorder. What is behind Marlowe? Nothing; almost nothing, or, at most, very little. But no sooner do we dig deeper, seeking the roots of his *method,* of his popularity, then we find that this "nothing—almost nothing—very little" begins to grow and take on complexity. Because the "nothings" are relative to an opulent and decadent capitalist society. And any question aimed at widening the field of discussion must refer to the Other.

The Other is Marlowe's original point of reference: the unmentioned, underlying, but possible alternatives beyond Marlowe's world: another social order.

Marlowe is a libertarian, because his ideology places him in a rebelious attitude toward the State and, as he questions, criticizes, and violates its rules, in the end leads him to attempt its overthrow.

His ideology is confused. On the surface, he operates like a mercenary. He sells his services for $25 a day, plus expenses. But in reality he isn't interested in this recompense, nor are we. He has his own set of values, which is unshaken. These values clash openly with the ones established by society. Marlowe's value system is meant for marginal men in a marginal society. It defines certain goals and defends certain principles. None of the moral codes of a puritanical United States coincides with the Marlowe code.

Marlowe hires himself out because plot and realism demand it. His profession allows him to right wrongs like a new Quixote. He will never violate the limits of his individualist code. But in this case, individualism does not mean selfishness. Marlowe's code is based on human relationships, on solidarity. It is in conflict with the other code, the one that orders and defines the larger society, because the latter is competitive, mercenary, and depraved. . . .

[His] acts provoke, they call into question. The detective always seem to be saying, "that's not true," "that sounds suspicious," "that's got to be looked into."

Marlowe "rubs people the wrong way." He's disagreeable, shabbily dressed, and far from accommodating. He antagonizes because he's different, and the contrast shows up the faults of others. . . .

In a time of crisis, Marlowe secretes disturbances. He asks too much. In the midst of everyday violence, of the endless struggle to keep things as they are, a man appears who is incorruptible and demoralizing, who calls attention to the truth across the street. And who unearths ugly crimes, unspeakable thefts, kidnappings, and tricks that sound like swindles.

Marlowe is, then, an irritant who manages to intimidate because he doesn't fit in. What do you want? What does he want, after all?—these are the questions that he is asked, that the characters ask each other.

He wants to live in a democracy, but not the relative, almost non-existent democracy of the Establishment. He wants the other kind, the one that is synonymous with Justice and Liberty, for which men have fought since the beginning of time, for which a man can fight and die.

He asks too much.

And so Marlowe must become an outcast.

And the "outcast" readers, loudmouthed, disreputable, and controversial, are the ones who consume him. It is safe to say that at least the majority of them come from the middle strata of Latin American society, economically dependent but far from agreeing with the policies of those in power.

It is here that Chandler-Marlowe makes his last appeal, turning, with political connotations, to the realities of Latin America, so contemporary and so difficult to overcome.

All this helps to define Chandler, but it does not exhaust him. It is a *the last* . . . that can serve as a subtle prelude to a definitive reading. (pp. 52-3)

> *Carlos Alberto Moran, "A Latin American Reading of Raymond Chandler," translated by Paula Speck (originally published in* Imagen, *No. 103/104, 1975), in* Review 76 *(copyright © 1976 by the Center for Inter-American Relations, Inc.), Spring, 1976, pp. 47-53.*

It is remarkable how much [Chandler] seems, in his life and in his art, consistently inconsistent, doomed never to be simply himself. (p. 1)

Chandler's fiction—like much in popular culture—is interesting insofar as its best effects are determined by a style, difficult to master, that is restricted to elemental crudeness in feeling and mind. . . .

Chandler felt that, within the limits of the mystery story form, he achieved so much that he could be considered a serious novelist, but he also felt—in a wretchedly defensive way—no writer ever achieved more than he. . . .

What [is] evident . . . is not only Chandler's radical ambivalence, but also that it is extremely difficult for some writers—perhaps most writers—to produce entertaining, financially successful, democratically popular, high quality junk. And, from their point of view, this achievement is not absolutely distinguishable from what intellectuals consider serious literature in the modern age. (p. 26)

> *Leonard Michaels, in* The New York Times Book Review *(© 1976 by The New York Times Company; reprinted by permission), May 16, 1976.*

Chandler . . . is the most considerable American literary artist ever to write [what might be called] formula fiction. He was a better and more conscientious writer than a number of others—Sinclair Lewis, James T. Farrell, John O'Hara come to mind immediately—whose reputations are far more secure. Yet only now is he beginning to receive the kind of recognition and attention he deserved and so desperately wanted in his lifetime. . . .

Working with much greater care and precision than was usual in the field, he put himself to school writing for the pulps—three stories one year, three stories the next, and so on—until at last he was ready to try a novel. This he managed by a process he called "cannibalizing"—that is, taking stories he had already written, stitching them together into novel-length continuity, and rewriting them. In this way he produced *The Big Sleep* . . . , *Farewell, My Lovely* . . . , and *The Lady in the Lake* . . . , three of his best, which raised the hard-boiled detective story to the level, if you will, of the mimetic novel. He showed it could be done. It was only with his valedictory, *The Long Goodbye* . . . , that he again managed to achieve the standard he set with those three.

With Chandler, rewriting made all the difference. He worked painstakingly, through draft after draft, to achieve the seemingly casual flow of his idiomatic first-person narrative. Philip Marlowe, his detective, is a creation of pure style—an attitude, a set of values implicit in a distinctive diction. Chandler had little talent for the sort of intricate plotting associated with the classic detective story—hence his stitched-together novels. He knew his weakness, and he didn't mind in the least: "the mind which can produce a coolly thought-out puzzle can't, as a rule, develop the fire and dash necessary for vivid writing."

Raymond Chandler was the purest sort of literary artist, and MacShane's claims for him [in his *The Life of Raymond Chandler*]—that he was "one of the most important writers of his time as well as one of the most delightful"— seem not all exaggerated. Chandler was totally absorbed in writing itself—not in getting across a message, and certainly not in merely revealing whodunit. (p. 26)

> *Bruce Cook, in* The New Republic *(reprinted by permission of* The New Republic; © *1976 by* The New Republic, Inc.*), June 12, 1976.*

[Raymond Chandler's] loneliness at the end of his life was [painful] to see and revives equally distressing memories of that of Auden at the end of his life. Although Auden was a far closer and more long-standing friend, and we had beliefs in common, sitting over luncheon at Carlton Hill was quite like sitting over tea in our kitchen in Loudoun Road with Auden, discussing 'LIFE'. Though their achievements were of a totally different order, in history they were not unlike; both devoted to memories of 'saintly' mothers and both always searching to be mothered, both concerned with the discipline aspect of writing and justly proud of their craftsmanship, both in old age nervy and demanding, both childless, both drinking, and both craving only companionship and a gentle round of domestic chores—nothing more. But where Raymond in work and life was sentimental, a fantasist and self-deluding (his drinking had a long life history), even self-pitying, Auden was absolutely non-fantasist, controlled and stoic, his daily litany being a counting of his blessings. In Raymond it is possible that childlessness explained his skirmishes against both Christianity and psy-

choanalysis, for both creeds recognise the primacy, vulnerability and sacredness of childhood. Auden's Christianity originated in his relationship to a loving mother; his compassion was easily accommodated in both creeds, Raymond on occasions found it hard to keep in touch with his. Raymond was proud to think of himself as a 'passionate moralist', which sounds comparatively merciless towards himself and others; Auden believed benevolently in redemption and forgiveness, and was a 'compassionate moralist'. (p. 25)

> *Natasha Spender, "Raymond Chandler's Own Long Goodbye," in* The New Review *(© The New Review Ltd., 11 Greek Street, London W1V 5LE), June 27, 1976, pp. 15-28.*

Chandler knew that *Farewell, My Lovely, The Lady in the Lake, The Long Goodbye,* and other detective fictions *were* his serious literary work, and this awareness led him into a kind of bifocalism about his reputation. He hated to be considered with—or reviewed by—most other crime novelists, yet was honored in his last year to be elected president of the Mystery Writers of America. He was pleased when W. H. Auden said his books were "serious studies of a criminal milieu" and should be judged "not as escape literature but as works of art," yet he later complained, "Now I look at everything I put down and say to myself, Remember, old boy, this has to be a serious study of a criminal milieu." (p. 16)

Although he prided himself on his sense of character, his novels are inhabited less by people than by powerful physical presences. He got these wrongos exactly right but they remained merely types. Since he was more interested in the dramatic consequences of a crime than in its causes, motivation was taken for granted and was not at all problematic. (p. 17)

> *Ruth Mathewson, "The Mystery-Writer as Novelist," in* The New Leader *(© 1976 by the American Labor Conference on International Affairs, Inc.), July 19, 1976, pp. 16-17.*

G(ilbert) K(eith) Chesterton

1874-1936

English novelist, poet, critic, essayist, journalist, biographer, and historian. He is remembered for his witty essays, his poem "Lepanto," his fantastic novel *The Man Who Was Thursday*, and, best of all, for the Father Brown stories, in which that lovable and absent-minded Catholic priest performed his detective work with Holmesian wizardry. Critics generally agree that the very diversity of Chesterton's literary subjects and his self-proclaimed role as a mere journalist are together responsible for his reputation as a "master who left no masterpiece."

PRINCIPAL WORKS

Robert Browning (criticism) 1903
The Napoleon of Notting Hill (novel) 1904
Heretics (essays) 1905
Charles Dickens (criticism) 1906
The Man Who Was Thursday: A Nightmare (novel) 1908
Orthodoxy (essays) 1908
George Bernard Shaw (criticism) 1909
What's Wrong with the World (essays) 1910
The Ballad of the White Horse (poetry) 1911
The Innocence of Father Brown (short stories) 1911
Manalive (novel) 1912
The Victorian Age in Literature (criticism) 1913
The Flying Inn (poetry) 1914
The Wisdom of Father Brown (short stories) 1914
Wine, Water and Song (poetry) 1915
The Man Who Knew Too Much (short stories) 1922
St. Francis of Assisi (biography) 1923
The Everlasting Man (essays) 1925
The Incredulity of Father Brown (short stories) 1926
The Secret of Father Brown (short stories) 1927
Four Faultless Felons (short stories) 1930
St. Thomas Aquinas (biography) 1933
Autobiography (autobiography) 1936
The Paradoxes of Mr. Pond (short stories) 1936

I have tried to like [Shaw and Chesterton]. I have tried to tolerate them. I have tried to believe that they are serviceable to mankind from some point of view which is not yet revealed to me. I do believe this; but I believe it with the head and not with the heart. The following reflections are, after all, a mere groping toward the light, and the tapping of the staff of a blind man. (p. 149)

Shaw and Chesterton . . . seem to have become partners in a sort of game of buffoonery—for the world will have its jesters. They are tumblers on a raft, floating down stream, surrounded by a whole Henley regatta, an armada of applauding multitudes, on barges, wherries, tugs, and ferryboats and river-craft innumerable, whose holiday passengers shout their admiration to the performers on the raft, and egg on the favorites to superhuman effort. (p. 151)

The loss which Shaw and Chesterton share in common is a loss of delicacy. They are crude: they are all edge. They are, indeed, a little vulgar. But this is not the serious objection to them. The serious objection to Shaw and Chesterton is that they have no intellectual independence. They are moving with the show. It will pass, and they with it. (p. 152)

> *John Jay Chapman, "Jesters," in his* Learning and Other Essays *(copyright, 1910 by John Jay Chapman), Moffat, Yard and Company, 1910, pp. 149-52.*

Those who read [Chesterton] do so for his Chestertonisms, for his fun, for his chunks of common sense, and they try to forgive him for his belief that if you say a good thing once, it becomes twice as good if you say it twice. But they do not read him for his message. What is his message? Does any reader get anything from his book on Divorce, except that in the recesses of his alert hide-and-seek brain he has beautiful mystical thoughts about marriage? Really I do not think it matters much what Mr. Chesterton's subject is. Stardust, Lobsters, Bric-à-brac, Ireland—the subject is merely a peg to hang Chestertonian daydreams on. His method is simple. He might begin an essay thus: "You may think that in the jungle a tiger acts like a tiger. It does not: it acts like a geranium. The reasons are obvious. . . ."

He is a figure in the literary world in a wider sense than usual. Usually and rightly an author's personal appearance is regarded as something separate and apart from his writings, as sacred as his home life. But Mr. Chesterton's great bulk, massive face, and wild crop of untidy hair are as well known and popular as were Dr. Johnson's appearance and idiosyncrasies. Each is a legend. Chesterton himself is by no means shy on the subject. It is on record that, at a public dinner, a speaker said that Chesterton's chivalry is so splendid that he had been known to rise in a tramcar and offer his seat to three ladies. Mr. A. G. Gardiner, who tells this story, adds that Mr. Chesterton's laughter sounded high above all the rest. "You may laugh with him, and at him, and about him," adds Mr. Gardiner, "but there is one thing, and one only, about which he is serious, and that is his own seriousness." (pp. 56-7)

He has a typical Protestant mind, yet he loves ritual, superstition, legends, saints, fairies, and he still believes, so he has told us, that the moon is made of green cheese; he is always for the underdog, the voiceless, and the lost cause; he is a Little Englander, an Englishman who resents Belfast and reacts rhythmically to Dublin. (p. 58)

Mr. Chesterton is the outstanding type of the literary journalist. It is as an essayist that he earns his living and wins his fame. I fancy that he would, if he could, be a maker of romances and draw as near to the success of Stevenson as the public would allow. He does not succeed. I can enjoy passages of "Manalive," "The Flying Inn," "The Napoleon of Notting Hill," and "The Man Who Was Thursday," but reading them through is an effort. They are shaped like romance; they ought to be riotously romantic and funny, but they are not. As for the Father Brown detective stories, if I want to read such things I go to Sherlock Holmes.

If I were asked to select three of Chesterton's books for a public library, which could not afford the whole of his Brobdingnagian output, my choice would fall upon his "Browning," his "Dickens" and "Irish Impressions."

He has also published poems, sometimes humorous. . . . [And] as a poet he can be very serious and very fine. It is quite likely that "The Wild Knight" and "The Ballad of the White Horse" (a ballad that took the bit between its teeth and raced into a book), and his "Lepanto," a poem that has already drifted into the Anthologies, will be read when "Heretics" and "Tremendous Trifles" are forgotten. Somebody should always be standing by his side when he is writing essays, saying, "Gilbert be dull for a bit. Paradox should be a soufflé, not a joint." (pp. 58-60)

> *Charles Lewis Hind, "G. K. Chesterton,"*
> *in his* Authors and I, *John Lane Company,*
> *1921 (and reprinted by Books for Libraries*
> *Press, 1968), pp. 56-60.*

Mr. Chesterton was sent into the world by an All-Just God for the exclusive purpose of saying the opposite to Mr. Shaw. With the most complimentary intention I say that Mr. Chesterton's job in the world is, when Mr. Shaw speaks, to reply, "On the contrary! . . ." He has to restore the balance which Mr. Shaw very vigorously disturbs. (pp. 92-3)

Roughly, one may say that Mr. Chesterton stands for the common man against the very clever man. He believes more in the People than he believes in Particular Persons. . . . He believes in tradition, even in legend, which is the wisdom accumulated by Man, not out of his mind so much as out of his experience. . . . He does not believe in Progress as Mr. Wells, for example, believes in it, and he will tell you very emphatically that the common man was

happier in the Middle Ages than he is to-day. There are times when it seems to me that Mr. Chesterton's "common man" is as mythical as the "average man" of the newspapers and the "economic man" of the economists; and I am very dubious about the happiness of the poor people of the Middle Ages. It would be foolish to carry one's doctrine too far, but if there is anything in this theory of Man deriving wisdom from experience, surely it is reasonable to suppose that human beings, having discovered a means of living which ensures some comfort and security to them, will not easily be deprived of it. (pp. 95-6)

Mr. Chesterton believes, too, in what he calls "the ancient and universal things" as against what he calls "the modern and specialist things." He has invented a theory which establishes man as the great specialist and woman as the great amateur, and he would keep woman out of the polling-booth, not because the vote is too good for her, but because it is not good enough. He demands that the woman shall stay in the home, not for the Teutonic reason that she is inferior to man and must work in a narrow area, but for the Chestertonic reason that she is capable of more varied work than man and can only find adequate range for her variety in the broad dominions of the home. (p. 97)

Mr. Chesterton's style and his thought [are] a mixture of soundness and unsoundness, in which the two things merge so imperceptibly that there is difficulty in distinguishing the one from the other. . . . [Furthermore,] I suspect that the home is not quite the broadening influence Mr. Chesterton declares it to be. . . . (pp. 98-9)

But he helps us to keep a balance. His service to us is that when we are inclined to run frantically after the superman, he reminds us of the existence of the common man. . . . There are times indeed, when his faith in the common man undergoes a sea-change, and he utters sentiments that might be spoken by Mr. H. L. Mencken, who cannot abide the common mind. (pp. 109-10)

His anger is almost completely impersonal. His pardon is on the heels of his condemnation. The sins of jealousy and hatred are unknown to him. . . . We are all children of the one God, in his belief, even if some of us are Jews, and in some mystical manner he contrives, in his anger, to discriminate between the human being and the thing which the human being does. If ever he is moved to slay a sweater or an international financier or a Prohibitionist, he will do so entirely without prejudice to that person's right to be called a child of God. . . . He is Don Quixote in the body of Sancho Panza. (pp. 111-12)

> *St. John G. Ervine, "G. K. Chesterton"*
> *(originally published in a slightly different*
> *version in* North American Review, *October, 1921), in his* Some Impressions of My
> Elders *(reprinted by permission of The Society of Authors as the literary representative of the Estate of St. John Ervine; © 1922*
> *by St. John G. Ervine), Macmillan, 1922,*
> *pp. 90-112.*

[My] chief claim to know and interpret Chesterton is, of course, a permanent and active personal friendship, through which we were very close companions for more than 30 years and during nearly the whole of his literary activity. (pp. 6-7)

The group to which he and I belonged recognised that the main social event of our generation was the destruction of freedom through the universal growth of Capitalist monopoly, and the ruin of economic independence in the mass of private citizens. (p. 10)

It is essential to a comprehension of Gilbert Chesterton's life, even in the field of literature (which stands half apart today from politics), to understand that this *political* aim to which he and I and all our group were vowed, the Restoration of Property, the struggle against Communism and the Capitalism whence Communism springs, was our (and his) chief temporal aim. (p. 11)

But such a temporal object must, like all external worldly objects, depend upon an underlying internal spirit. Only a philosophy can produce political action and a philosophy is only vital when it is the soul of a religion.

Now here we come to the thing of chief value and of chief effect in Gilbert Chesterton's life and work: his religion. (pp. 11-12)

The main points of what I have to say . . . upon the conditions of survival in Gilbert Chesterton's writings, may be tabulated as follows:

I. The leading characteristic of Chesterton as a writer and as a man (the two were much closer identified in him than in most writers) was that he was *national*. . . .

II. The next characteristic was an extreme precision of thought, such as used to be characteristic of Englishmen, though in modern times it has broken down and people have forgotten how native it was to the English mind in the past.

III. The third characteristic I note about his writing and thought is a unique capacity for *parallelism*. He continually illumined and explained realities by comparisons. This was really the weapon peculiar to Chesterton's genius. It was the one thing which he in particular had, and which no one else in his time came near to, and few in the past have approached. It is the strongest element in his writing and thinking, after the far less exceptional element of sincerity.

IV. The structure upon which his work, like that of all modern men, had been founded, was historical: but it was only in general historical; it was far more deeply and widely *literary*. (I believe I notice this the more because with me it has always been the other way about; I have a very great deal of reading and experience upon history, far less upon literature.)

V. Charity. He approached controversy, his delight, hardly ever as a conflict, nearly always as an appreciation, including that of his opponent.

VI. Lastly there is that chief matter of his life and therefore of his literary activity, his acceptation of the Faith. (pp. 14-16)

The nationalism of Chesterton was providential, not only for his own fame but for its effect upon his readers. It formed a bridge or link between the English mind as it has been formed by the Reformation (and particularly the later part of the Reformation, during the 17th century), and the general culture of Europe which was created by, and can only be preserved through, the Catholic Church. (pp. 22-3)

One example of this national character and style is the way in which the word suggests the word in his writing: a thing not unconnected with the effect of the Jacobean Bible on the English mind since the 17th century, particularly the Epistles of St. Paul. . . . It is in this connection that the frequent use of puns, or, when they are not puns, plays upon words in Chesterton's writings, should be noted.

Lastly, there is the national character of high individualisation, which some have also called "localisation"; the preference of concrete connotation to abstraction. Chesterton is in the full tradition of those creative English writers from Chaucer to Dickens, who dwell not upon ideas but upon men and women, and especially is he national in his vast survey of English letters. (pp. 26-7)

Chesterton's passion for precision of thought was an overwhelming advantage for him over all his modern opponents in controversy, especially for his modern opponents of English speech, or rather of Protestant English culture. (p. 29)

Chesterton is perpetually pulling up the reader with a shock of surprise, and his pages are crammed with epigram. . . . The heart of his style is lucidity, produced by a complete rejection of ambiguity: complete exactitude of definition.

While there is in this . . . a peril to his contemporary effect and to its permanence in one way, because he wrote in the English tongue and for a public melted into the last dilution of English Protestantism—a public therefore which was almost physically incapable of appreciating precision in the major matters of life—there is, on the other hand, a strong chance of permanence in another way. For your precise thinker stands unchanged: unaffected by the fluctuations of fashion in expression.

Here, as in many other connections, the permanent effect of Gilbert Chesterton's writing must largely depend upon our return or non-return to the high culture we have lost. This means in practice the return or non-return of England to the Catholic Church. The English-speaking public, apart from the Irish race, is now Protestant. It has been strongly and increasingly Anti-Catholic for now 250 years. Through the effect of time it is to-day more soaked in Protestantism than ever it was before.

Here, as in every other matter, the permanence of Chesterton's fame will depend upon that very doubtful contingency —the conversion of England. (pp. 33-6)

His unique, his capital, genius for illustration by parallel, by example, is his peculiar mark. . . . Now parallelism is a gift or method of vast effect in the conveyance of truth.

Parallelism consists in the illustration of some unperceived truth by its exact consonance with the reflection of a truth already known and perceived. (pp. 36-7)

He introduces [a parallelism] in more than one form; with the phrase . . . "It is as though," or more violently, the phrase "Why not say while you are about it," followed by an example of the absurdity rebuked. (pp. 38-9)

My next point is Chesterton's *historical* basis.

Gilbert Chesterton, having for his supreme interest the business and fate of his own country and of Christendom, occupied himself with history and literature, as supports and nourishment to the philosophy which it was his main business to expound. (pp. 45-6)

[Some] of his finest verse was historical and the history

therein was just, with a particular appreciation of the defence of Christendom against the barbarian and the Mahommedan. No one else but Gilbert Chesterton could have written such a poem as *Lepanto* in English, and no one has attempted it; while the *Ballad of the White Horse* is an extension of the same theme. (pp. 48-9)

But his triumph (if I may so call it), in the historical field was his appreciation of Ireland. No other English writer has come near to Chesterton in understanding both the nature of Ireland and the overwhelming importance of the Irish in the English story. (p. 49)

Everything he wrote upon any one of the great English literary names was of the first quality. He summed up any one pen (that of Jane Austen, for instance) in exact sentences; sometimes in a single sentence, after a fashion which no one else has approached. He stood quite by himself in this department. He understood the very minds (to take the two most famous names) of Thackeray and of Dickens. He understood and presented Meredith. He understood the supremacy in Milton. He understood Pope. He understood the great Dryden. He was not swamped as nearly all his contemporaries were by Shakespeare, wherein they drown as in a vast sea—for that is what Shakespeare is. Gilbert Chesterton continued to understand the youngest and latest comers as he understood the forefathers in our great corpus of English verse and prose. (pp. 53-4)

[His] influence in explaining English letters to Englishmen was great, though perpetually frustrated. He was here a teacher who should have led but who was not permitted to lead. However, he was a teacher who was more listened to than if he had expended the same energy on, and had acquired the same voluminous acquaintance with, history. (p. 55)

Chesterton's connection with the Faith is much the most important aspect of his literary life. . . . (p. 56)

That one of Chesterton's innumerable pieces of work wherein the effect of the Faith is most evident is also his best piece of work. Of all his books ["The Thing"] is by far the most profound and the most clear. . . . If ["The Thing"] is forgotten, that will mean that thought is failing. . . . (pp. 66-7)

All men one may say, or very nearly all men, have one leading moral defect. Few have one leading Christian virtue. That of Gilbert Chesterton was unmistakably the virtue of Christian charity: a virtue especially rare in writing men, and rarest of all in such of them as have a pursuing appetite for controversy—that is, for bolting out the truth.

He loved his fellow-men. Through this affection, which was all embracing, he understood the common man; and that virtue, which was so conspicuous in all his private life and broad river of daily speech, was both a strength and a weakness to his fame.

It was a strength because it gave him access to every mind; men will always listen to a friend; and so much was he a friend of all those for whom he wrote that all were prepared to listen, however much they were puzzled. (pp. 79-80)

The drawback, however, of this virtue of charity as regards its action upon his fame was that it prevented the presence in what he wrote of that acerbity or "bite" which gives an edge or rather a spearhead to every effort at persuasion. (p. 80)

He wounded none, but thus also he failed to provide weapons wherewith one may wound and kill folly. Now without wounding and killing, there is no battle; and thus, in this life, no victory; but also no peril to the soul through hatred. (p. 81)

Christendom would seem to be now entering an ultimate phase in the struggle between good and evil, which is, for us, the battle between the Catholic Church and its opponents. In that struggle, those will stand out in the future most vividly who most provoked hostility. To his lasting advantage in the essential things of the spirit, of his own individual soul, he did not provoke it. (p. 82)

> *Hilaire Belloc, in his* On the Place of Gilbert Chesterton in English Letters *(reprinted by permission of A. D. Peters & Co. Ltd.),* Sheed & Ward, 1940.

Chesterton's occasional essays are usually more interesting than his attempts at wholly imaginative writing, whether in fiction or verse. His novels are perhaps even more neglected than they deserve, for one of them at least—*The Man who was Thursday,* which is not a novel at all but a symbolic romance—deals with a potentially major theme: the whole problem of personal identity, so intriguing to our own age. But we need only compare it with, say, Kafka's symbolic fables on comparable themes, to see that Chesterton's story never rises above the level of a charade, or at least a prolonged and ingenious joke. (p. 126)

It is in the essays that we most often find the characteristic Chestertonian vehicle and weapon, the paradox, which has been variously described as 'truth standing on her head to attract attention' and 'truth cutting her throat to attract attention'. . . . [It] is certainly true that Chesterton's use of paradox frequently degenerates into a mannerism, but it is equally true that he used it as earlier nineteenth-century thinkers had used other stylistic devices— . . . as a means of mediating a total view of life. It is well known that Chesterton 'invented' Christian orthodoxy for himself before discovering that it really existed, and he similarly arrived at a *Weltanschauung* that was basically Thomist before he had even heard of Aquinas. . . . Every event in man's life, and everything in the universe, had for Chesterton an ultimate ontological purpose. Secure within an all-embracing and rationalistic world-picture, he could make adroit semantic analyses of his opponents' statements and wittily point out the errors and false assumptions contained in them. And this is the essence of the 'paradoxical' method. Engaged by the wit and precision of the observation, and the urbanity of the tone, one is forced to concede that some kind of point *is* being made, even if one does not agree with it: to that extent one has had, momentarily, to accept the Chestertonian *Weltanschauung* and abandon one's own. In this way Chesterton's paradoxes have a rhetorical function, comparable to the stylistic tricks of Arnold. But they worked a good deal better in that pre-1914 Age of Reason, the period of the great debate between Chesterton and Belloc and Shaw and Wells, when men believed in the power of reason and were prepared to use it vigorously and combatively to prove that they were right and their opponents wrong, than they do now, when we are suspicious of *any* discussion of pure ideas, and a logic which deals in such clear-cut categories as 'right' or 'wrong' seems pretty crude. Whether this is a good thing or not is not at the moment my concern, but it explains why Chesterton—and the rest of his generation, Catholic or otherwise—seem such strange and remote figures nowadays. We are more concerned with a subtle and discriminating attention to particular facts than with fitting events into a total world-picture (of course, we will still have one, though it will possess the dubious advantages of being unconscious and unexamined). And here, admittedly, Chesterton is often deficient. His overriding concentration on a two-valued dialectic sometimes led him into some very unsatisfactory literary valuations. (pp. 126-28)

> *Bernard Bergonzi, "Chesterton and/or Belloc" (1959), in his* The Turn of a Century: Essays on Victorian and Modern English Literature *(© Bernard Bergonzi 1973; reprinted in the U.S. by permission of Harper & Row, Publishers, Inc., Barnes & Noble Import Division; and in Canada by permission of A. D. Peters & Co.), Barnes & Noble, 1973, pp. 124-33.*

Each story in the Father Brown Saga presents a mystery, proposes explanations of a demoniacal or magical sort, and then replaces them at the end with solutions of this world. Skill is not the only virtue of those brief bits of fiction; I believe I can perceive in them an abbreviation of Chesterton's life, a symbol or reflection of Chesterton. The repetition of his formula through the years and through the books (*The Man Who Knew Too Much, The Poet and the Lunatics, The Paradoxes of Mr. Pond*) seems to confirm that this is an essential form, not a rhetorical artifice. (p. 82)

Chesterton was a Catholic, he believed in the Middle Ages of the Pre-Raphaelites ("Of London, small and white, and clean"). Like Whitman, Chesterton thought that the mere fact of existing is so prodigious that no misfortune should exempt us from a kind of cosmic gratitude. That may be a just belief, but it arouses only limited interest; to suppose that it is all Chesterton offers is to forget that a creed is the underlying factor in a series of mental and emotional processes and that a man is the whole series. In Argentina, Catholics exalt Chesterton, freethinkers reject him. Like every writer who professes a creed, Chesterton is judged by it, is condemned or acclaimed because of it. His case is not unlike that of Kipling, who is always judged with reference to the English Empire.

Poe and Baudelaire proposed the creation of a world of terror, as did Blake's tormented Urizen; it is natural for their work to teem with the forms of horror. In my opinion, Chesterton would not have tolerated the imputation of being a contriver of nightmares, a *monstrorum artifex* . . . , but he tends inevitably to revert to atrocious observations. (p. 83)

Chesterton restrained himself from being Edgar Allan Poe or Franz Kafka, but something in the makeup of his personality leaned toward the nightmarish, something secret, and blind, and central. Not in vain did he dedicate his first works to the justification of two great gothic craftsmen, Browning and Dickens; not in vain did he repeat that the best book to come out of Germany was *Grimm's Fairy Tales*. He reviled Ibsen and defended Rostand (perhaps

indefensibly), but the Trolls and the creator of *Peer Gynt* were the stuff his dreams were made of. That discord, that precarious subjection of a demoniacal will, defines Chesterton's nature. For me, the emblems of that struggle are the adventures of Father Brown, each of which undertakes to explain an inexplicable event by reason alone. ["Most writers of detective stories usually undertake to explain the obscure rather than the inexplicable."] That is why I said, in the first paragraph of this essay, that those stories were the key to Chesterton, the symbols and reflections of Chesterton. That is all, except that the "reason" to which Chesterton subjected his imaginings was not precisely reason but the Catholic faith or rather a collection of Hebrew imaginings that had been subjected to Plato and Aristotle.

I remember two opposing parables. The first one is from the first volume of Kafka's works. It is the story of the man who asks to be admitted to the law. The guardian of the first door says that there are many other doors within, and that every room is under the watchful eye of a guardian, each of whom is stronger than the one before. The man sits down to wait. Days and years go by, and the man dies. In his agony he asks, "Is it possible that during the years I have been waiting, no one has wanted to enter but me?" The guardian answers, "No one has wanted to enter this door because it was destined for you alone. Now I shall close it.". . . The other parable is in Bunyan's *Pilgrim's Progress*. People gaze enviously at a castle guarded by many warriors; a guardian at the door holds a book in which he will write the name of the one who is worthy of entering. An intrepid man approaches the guardian and says, "Write my name, sir." Then he takes out his sword and lunges at the warriors; there is an exchange of bloody blows; he forces his way through the tumult and enters the castle.

Chesterton devoted his life to the writing of the second parable, but something within him always tended to write the first. (pp. 84-5)

> *Jorge Luis Borges, "On Chesterton," in his* Other Inquisitions: 1937-1952 *(copyright © 1964 by the University of Texas Press; reprinted by permission of Emecé Editores, Buenos Aires, República Argentina), University of Texas Press, 1964, pp. 82-5.*

G. K. Chesterton . . . and Hilaire Belloc . . . have suffered a steep decline in popularity over the last three decades. Chesterton is read more and more selectively by fewer and fewer people; and Belloc is in almost total eclipse. The world-famous partnership that George Bernard Shaw dubbed 'the Chesterbelloc' has had a great fall, and few seem interested in putting it together again.

There are many reasons for this. The Modern Movement in literature, which Chesterton and Belloc either opposed or ignored, has become classical for our culture, and their own work looks thin and faded in comparison. The form to which they devoted so much of their time and energy—the whimsical, ruminative essay—is dead and unmourned. Their intellectual amateurism is unfashionable. And the ideas for which they stood have largely lost their relevance.

Those ideas were always controversial, but they once commanded considerable respect, and the support of a large Christian, specifically Catholic, reading public. The

Chesterbelloc's brand of Catholicism however—triumphalist, proselytizing, theologically conservative, Europe-orientated—is hardly congenial to the mood of the Church since Pope John XXIII and the Second Vatican Council. Chesterton and Belloc were the propagandists and cheerleaders of the Catholic ghetto, dedicated to proving that it was really the City of God. (p. 145)

There is a certain irony in associating Chesterton and Belloc with the Catholic 'ghetto', because one of the major factors in the decline of their popularity is that they have the reputation of being anti-semitic. For liberal, non-Catholics this was always an objection to their work. (pp. 145-46)

The alleged anti-semitism of these two writers is not perhaps a purely literary question; but they were not purely literary writers. The charge has undoubtedly affected the reception of their work, yet it has never, as far as I know, been properly documented by their accusers, or honestly investigated by their defenders. It seems worthwhile, therefore, to try and establish exactly what the Chesterbelloc's attitude to the Jews was, how it fitted into the total structure of the two men's ideas, and how it related to attitudes and events in society at large. (p. 146)

The Christianity of both men was of a romantically conservative character, yearning back to a somewhat idealized medieval Christendom—the period when the demonology of anti-semitism was fully developed. Chesterton, particularly, was emotionally and imaginatively attracted to the aggressive Christianity of the Crusades, and in a late poem, 'The Modern Magic', he contrasts the chivalrous conflict of Christian and Saracen with the cynical mercenary realities of the Jewish National Home in Palestine. . . . There is [, in fact,] quite as much political and economic animus behind this verse as religious. . . . (p. 149)

Both Chesterton and Belloc were intensely critical of industrial capitalism. So, perhaps, were most enlightened men of their time; but whereas the latter tended to espouse some form of socialism as the solution, Chesterton and Belloc saw this as only promising a different kind of political and economic slavery. (p. 149)

To Chesterton and Belloc, nineteenth-century capitalism was essentially usury, and the fact that Jews (most notably the Rothschild family) were prominent in the field of high finance was evidence that capitalism was essentially alien to Christian culture. Much (though not all) of their 'anti-semitism' consisted of identifying Jewry with the evils of modern capitalism. (pp. 149-50)

Belloc was always the more violently anti-Jewish half of the Chesterbelloc, partly because he was more of a natural hater, a hard and aggressive man compared to the genial and much-loved Chesterton. . . .

Before he met Belloc, Chesterton wrote a poem, 'To A Certain Nation', deploring the persecution of Dreyfus. When he reprinted it in 1905 he noted that he had changed his mind about the subject. This instance, noted by Maisie Ward, is only one of many indications that Belloc was a strong influence on Chesterton's attitude to the Jews. (p. 152)

Basically, theirs was a failure of imagination. Celebrated for wit, humour, irony and paradox, they never seem to have turned these liberating modes of perception upon their own assumptions and prejudices. (p. 156)

David Lodge, "The Chesterbelloc and the Jews," (originally published in The Critic, *1970), in his* The Novelist at the Crossroads and Other Essays on Fiction and Criticism *(copyright © 1971 by David Lodge; reprinted by permission of the author),* Cornell University Press, 1971, pp. 145-58.

Every good name dropper has a vested interest in how his names are doing, their current exchange value, and the likely quotation when memoir time comes around. My own best coins, Chesterton and Belloc, have, alas, devalued steadily. Strictly speaking, I didn't see that much of either of them in the flesh—Chesterton just once at my christening when I disappeared into his lap (sorry to sound like an English lady diarist, but that's the way I heard it)—but they filled my childhood like Mardi gras balloons. (p. 259)

My meetings with Chesterton were . . . spectral. My mother was working on his biography from roughly my seventh to my thirteenth year, a strange way to encounter someone. I knew his letters and unpublished drawings before I exactly knew who he was: a bit like knowing a man's galoshes and the smell of his pipe tobacco, but never quite seeing his face. Chesterton, I understood, was simply what the word "genius" meant: a spirit so huge and fertile that it could grow poetry, novels, detective stories, turnips and mimosa all at once. I'll swear I grew up thinking that physical fatness had something to do with it.

At fifteen or so, I waded through his books on my own and found to my surprise that the estimate held up pretty well. It seemed to me that any writer combining imagination and good sense at that level of intensity could accomplish anything he wanted. So, when Lionel Trilling placed Chesterton's social criticism on a line between Cobbett and Orwell, I agreed; when Jacques Maritain, the Thomist, called G. K. a better natural metaphysician than himself, I only wondered at the understatement. I even thought that a short essay of his on dreams knocked Jung out of the ball park.

Larger than life, I suppose. No one is that good. Taking the lowest possible consensus, Chesterton was a brilliant philosophical journalist, who wasted too much time cutting up other journalists and journalistic ideas, and an inspired dabbler in other forms; Hilaire Belloc was a grand master of language, so willfully cranky in its use that he seemed to *demand* a minor place in letters. Still, they towered over the hedge at our place; and to write about them now, with all the fake judiciousness that follows, seems dizzily unreal, as well as something of a betrayal.

Chesterbelloc was, I believe, a word coined by Bernard Shaw, in order to have a bigger and clumsier target to his right. If so, the old stage manager was being his usual shrewd self, because the two reputations have long since sunk of their combined dead weight, where either might have survived on its own. (pp. 259-60)

The toughest chain binding the dead men is undoubtedly their combined reputation for anti-Semitism, and this might be a good place to start separating them. Auden himself was put off by it, but finally blames the whole thing on Belloc and on Chesterton's brother Cecil. There is some historic verification for this. (p. 262)

Yet an explanation that blames it all on someone else

bothers in its own way. Chesterton was in other respects a thinker of visibly painful independence, an arguing machine, who dearly wanted to agree with everyone he wrote about, but just couldn't. (p. 263)

[He] fastened on certain Bellocian positions out of simple loyalty, and with less of his early skepticism (he had always feared that his hairshirt itch to question everything might lead to madness; Belloc's affirmations were an antidote). It could be that anti-Semitism was a small part of the package: although small to vanishing as his mind regained its strength.

Yet even this is misleading. Chesterton probably trusted Belloc as much out of laziness as anything else (he was always happy to have someone else go to the library); but he would have picked Belloc's general philosophy to pieces in five minutes if it hadn't paralleled some thought-out position of his own. Although his anti-Semitism (which he preferred to call Zionism—i.e., get them out of here) differed from Belloc's in quality and stress, both were based on a doctrine of place: in Chesterton's case a real place, the London of his childhood; in Belloc's, a memory and a yearning. . . .

Chesterton's quarrel with the Jews was of [a] fuzzy kind, . . . a distrust of their alleged universalism as Belloc gave him to understand it: that is, with a people who maintained their own identity at heavy cost, but seemed bent on persuading other people to blend theirs. (p. 264)

The Jewish problem was that the Jews lacked their own land; they must be given a real nation and, if necessary, cantons in other nations. They must become farmers as well as lawyers. No word comes off a Chesterton page with a heavier sneer on it than the word "cosmopolitan." (p. 265)

For both [Chesterton and Belloc], the Jew was primarily an agent of change: both, I'm convinced, would have been horrified to find these agents of change being liquidated in Prussian gas chambers; both, in fact, hated Germany, and only distrusted Jews. (p. 269)

Humor was actually the strongest link between [Belloc] and Chesterton, not any kind of prejudice, and an account that leaves that out reminds one, for earnest foolishness, of the new revisionism on the Algonquin wits.

Oddly enough, no one ever talks about the influence of Chesterton on Belloc. It could be that the latter simply would not submit to influence; but there may have been some anyway, of a subtle, personal kind—G. K. raising his friend's heavy spirits, sharpening his comic gifts, maintaining a schoolboy atmosphere in which a middle-aged man could still enjoy writing light verse. The influence the other way is superficially obvious. Chesterton's political instinct dozed, and this great quintessential Cockney even wound up joining an unassimilated international organization, the Catholic Church. (pp. 273-74)

Yet Chesterton's own philosophical trajectory remained true enough. As a journalist, he had to keep all his horns blaring at once, and he was probably tempted to leave some of it to Hilaire. His main line of interest in the last years was the religious experience of mankind, and the paradoxical nature of Being itself, and on this his thinking proceeded vigorously on its own way, even when one feels he was too written-out to get it down right or scrape off the fat. (p. 274)

The range of Chesterton's talent was almost alarming, like a glandular growth, and the area he shared with Belloc was comparatively small. And I think he shared it because he wanted company. His wife had removed him from London (one always blames somebody else for Chesterton—perhaps his one great flaw) to get him away from his drinking friends; so he had to assert his solidarity in print. Also, he must have been one of the rare geniuses with absolutely no taste for the part, no wish to be unique. Artistic perfectionism was too pushy for him, wisdom too pretentious. The spillover of his thinking leaves us (if anyone can find it) a body of aphorisms universal enough to belong to literature—Shaw looks like an old newspaper in comparison—yet he did not set up as a sage. His Cockney soul wanted, even intellectually, to be one of the boys, a comrade in battle line and pub. And as if to prove it, he accepted equal billing, and a few ideas, from a man of lesser intelligence and dramatically lesser wisdom, Hilaire Belloc. . . . (pp. 274-75)

Wilfrid Sheed, "Chesterbelloc" (1971), in his The Morning After: Selected Essays and Reviews *(reprinted with the permission of Farrar, Straus & Giroux, Inc.; copyright © 1963, 1965, 1966, 1967, 1968, 1969, 1970, 1971 by Wilfrid Sheed), Farrar, Straus, 1971, pp. 259-75.*

Thirty years ago, when Belloc wrote his essay 'On the Place of Chesterton in English Letters' [see excerpt above], he concluded that his friend's reputation would ultimately depend upon 'that doubtful contingency—the conversion of England'. This absurd proposition assumes, as every other Catholic writing about Chesterton has assumed, that he was a 'Catholic Author', and that posterity would read him, if at all, for the same reason that it would read the *Spiritual Exercises*. Belloc neglected, as Chesterton's Catholic admirers have tended to neglect, those great merits in his work that do not appeal to doctrinal minds and are not to be explained in doctrinal terms. (He also neglected the fact that Chesterton was a Roman Catholic for only the last fourteen years of his life.) This parochial regard has given Chesterton's reputation a kind of parish-newspaper security, but it has not helped him with the larger literary audience. It is time that Chesterton was removed from the loving disservices of his co-religionists; above all, he needs secular attention.

Even so, the elevation of Chesterton will be uphill work. For one thing, he didn't work seriously in the right forms. He called himself a journalist and a man-of-letters (terms which could still be understood, in Edwardian times, as sometimes synonymous), and he practised his profession on whatever subject came to hand. He was a political pamphleteer, a religious polemicist, an informal essayist, a sociologist, a novelist, a poet—and all without ceasing to be a journalist. (pp. 80-1)

Certainly he has no present place, even an insecure one, in the history of English literature. He made no important contribution to any major literary form, and he has had no success in the academies; his novels are not taught in university courses in modern fiction, his poems are not anthologized, and scarcely anyone even remembers that he wrote plays. If there were such an academic subject as The History of Controversy, or if the casual weekly newspaper essay were susceptible to heavy scholarship, then Chesterton might figure importantly; but as it is, he is cast among Miscellaneous Authors, the writers-on-everything. (p. 81)

Chesterton had a genius for the shape of wickedness; that is to say, he had an allegorical imagination. All of *The Man Who Was Thursday* is a dark conceit, and so is *Manalive* and *The Ball and the Cross* and *The Napoleon of Notting Hill*. Even the Father Brown stories have something in them of allegory or parable: each offers an inscrutable, irrational, often obscurely unnatural event, and then explains it, through Father Brown's understanding, as an aspect of the intelligible order of existence. At the end of each story the sanity of the world has been defended against the stark anarchies, and we are reassured.

It is in his uses of his allegorical imagination that Chesterton seems most 'modern', for nightmare is the allegorical form for our time, an allegory of the unconscious by which our deepest anxieties and fears are revealed. . . . [It] is not surprising that a parabolical writer like Jorge Luis Borges should admire Chesterton, or that he should have written the best short appreciation of Chesterton's imagination [see excerpt above].

The sense of the world as a moral battlefield is at the centre of Chesterton's thought: it underlies his allegorical fiction, and it informs his criticism. It made it possible for him to live in a world of anarchies and negations and yet preserve that moral energy that he called optimism. 'This world can be made beautiful again', he wrote in his *Charles Dickens,* 'by beholding it as a battlefield. When we have defined and isolated the evil thing, the colours come back into everything else. When evil things have become evil, good things, in a blazing apocalypse, become good.'

It is in part because he saw the world in this way that he was so excellent a critic of the Victorian period; for he understood the importance of religious struggle for the age, and emphasized it even at the peril, as he put it, of making the spiritual landscape too large for the figures. He was born into that landscape, and he sympathized with the Victorians in their High Seriousness. But he was also an Edwardian, removed enough from the past age so that he could see it whole, and thus become the first Victorianist. His *Victorian Age in Literature* is still the best single work on the subject. . . . (pp. 84-5)

Perhaps because Chesterton was so good a Victorian, and so great an Edwardian, he made a poor Modern. Unlike Bennett (who was his elder by seven years) he did not change with the times. . . . The difference is simply that Bennett was entirely a literary man, who could admire a man for writing well, while Chesterton, a man with a philosophy and a religion, founded his judgments on his beliefs. He believed in a way of ordering the world, and as he grew older he saw that way lost; and he judged the writers of those later days as symptoms of the universal decline. (pp. 85-6)

He was a skilful versifier, a good maker of ballads and ballades and sonnets, and a master of rhymed narrative, but his poems scarcely seem to belong to the century in which they were written. . . . No doubt there are still Chestertonians here and there who continue to read the satirical verses, and who recognize that Chesterton was the cleverest of modern satirists, but most of those witty attacks have faded with the fading of their subjects, and no amount

of wit will make the follies of F. E. Smith and Walter Long compelling reading. Which is a pity, for the skill and the wit are remarkable, and there has been no popular poet to match him since his day. (p. 86)

[He] is one of the greatest of modern stylists, because he believed in something else. If he was witty and epigrammatic, it was in order that deep beliefs might be well and pungently expressed; and if he was illogical and paradoxical, it was because the world did not strike him as logical, but as a great Impossibility, a miracle. Because he believed, he was a controversialist; he could think of no better use of his marvellous style than the defence of his faith. Consequently his best writing is not concentrated in the most literary works, but is scattered carelessly over everything, even his most casual letters to editors. He wrote no perfect book, nor even any book on which he seems to have spent quite enough time; he was always hasty and prodigal, like a man for whom a merely literary immortality was unimportant. One is less likely to admire a whole work by him than to cherish portions—marvellous episodes, skilful arguments by paradoxical example, turns of phrase that no one else could have written. Surely Chesterton would approve of this, for he was, as he always maintained, a journalist and not an artist, and he would rather be savoured than revered. (pp. 86-7)

> *Samuel Hynes, in his* Edwardian Occasions: Essays on English Writing in the Early Twentieth Century *(copyright © 1972 by Samuel Hynes; reprinted by permission of the author, Oxford University Press, Inc., and Routledge & Kegan Paul Ltd.), Oxford University Press and, in England and Canada, Routledge & Kegan Paul, 1972.*

I have always enjoyed Chesterton's poetry and fiction, but I must admit that, until I started work on a selection for a publisher, it was many years since I had read any of his non-fictional prose.

The reasons for my neglect were, I think, two. Firstly, his reputation as an anti-Semite. Though he denied the charge and did, certainly, denounce Hitler's persecution, he cannot, I fear, be completely exonerated. . . . [It] remains a regrettable blemish upon the writings of a man who was, according to the universal testimony of all who met him, an extraordinarily "decent" human being, astonishingly generous of mind and warm of heart.

My second reason for neglecting Chesterton was that I imagined him to be what he himself claimed, just a "Jolly Journalist," a writer of weekly essays on "amusing" themes, such as *What I found in my Pockets, On Lying in Bed, The Advantage of having one Leg, A Piece of Chalk, The Glory of Grey, Cheese* and so forth.

In his generation, the Essay as a form of *belles-lettres* was still popular. . . . Today tastes have changed. We can appreciate a review or a critical essay devoted to a particular book or author, we can enjoy a discussion of a specific philosophical problem or political event, but we can no longer derive any pleasure from the kind of essay which is a fantasia upon whatever chance thoughts may come into the essayist's head.

My objection to the prose fantasia is the same as my objection to "free" verse (to which Chesterton also objected), namely, that, while excellent examples of both exist, they are the exception not the rule. All too often the result of the absence of any rules and restrictions, of a meter to which the poet must conform, of a definite subject to which the essayist must stick, is a repetitious and self-indulgent "show-off" of the writer's personality and stylistic mannerisms.

Chesterton's insistence upon the treadmill of weekly journalism after it ceased to be financially necessary seems to have puzzled his friends as much as it puzzles me. . . . Whatever Chesterton's reasons and motives for his choice, I am quite certain it was a mistake. . . . His best thinking and best writing are to be found, not in his short weekly essays, but in his full-length books where he could take as much time and space as he pleased. . . . Oddly enough, since he so detested them, Chesterton inherited from the aesthetes of the eighties and nineties the conviction that a writer should be continuously "bright" and epigrammatic. When he is really enthralled by a subject he is brilliant, without any doubt one of the finest aphorists in English literature, but, when his imagination is not fully held he can write an exasperating parody of himself, and this is most likely to happen when he has a dead-line to meet.

It is always difficult for a man as he grows older to "keep up" with the times, to understand what the younger generation is thinking and writing well enough to criticize it intelligently; for an overworked journalist like Chesterton it is quite impossible, since he simply does not have the time to read any new book carefully enough. (pp. 395-97)

Critical Judgment and Personal Taste are different kinds of evaluation which always overlap but seldom coincide exactly. On the whole and in the long run, Critical Judgment is a public matter; we agree as to what we consider artistic virtues and artistic defects. Our personal tastes, however, differ. For each of us, there are writers whom we enjoy reading, despite their defects, and others who, for all their virtues, give us little pleasure. In order for us to find a writer "sympathetic," there must be some kinship between his imaginative preferences and our own. As Chesterton wrote:

> There is at the back of every artist's mind something like a pattern or a type of architecture. The original quality in any man of imagination is imagery. It is a thing like the landscape of his dreams; the sort of world he would wish to make or in which he would wish to wander; the strange flora and fauna of his own secret planet; the sort of thing he likes to think about.

This is equally true of every reader's mind. Our personal patterns, too, unlike our scale of critical values, which we need much time and experience to arrive at, are formed quite early in life, probably before the age of ten. In "The Ethics of Elfland" Chesterton tells us how his own pattern was derived from fairy-stories. If I can always enjoy reading him, even at his silliest, I am sure the reason is that many elements in my own pattern are derived from the same source. (There is one gulf between us: Chesterton had no feeling for or understanding of music.) There are, I know, because I have met them, persons to whom Grimm and Andersen mean little or nothing: Chesterton will not be for them. (pp. 402-03)

W. H. Auden, "G. K. Chesterton's Non-Fiction," in his Forewords and Afterwords, *edited by Edward Mendelson (copyright © 1954 by W. H. Auden; reprinted by permission of Random House, Inc.), Random House, 1973, pp. 395-403.*

[Chesterton the] Polemicist, thickly or thinly disguised, turns up virtually everywhere in Chesterton's fiction, and it must be said of him at once that he is rarely less than entertaining and often lends argument an elegance and an epigrammatic sting worthy of the best of the author's avowed polemical writing. (p. 29)

[Chesterton] the Melodramatist . . . does much of his work in dialogue, though he also operates through the heroic gesture, the stroke of symbolism, through *coup de théâtre* and *peripeteia* and transformation scene. (p. 30)

No one doubts that Chesterton was deeply interested in people and their relations with one another, but at least in his fiction—parts of his literary criticism may be a different matter—he does not go in much for 'characterization' as it is normally thought of, for differentiating, developing, showing response to circumstance. (p. 31)

Chesterton never developed a character who is and remains a child, but his tales are full of insights into childhood, celebrations of it and of the disregarded truth that the adult who has missed or rejected any part of what it is to be a child is a sad, stunted creature. In [one] novel he speaks of 'that concrete and material poetry which a child feels when he takes a gun upon a journey or a bun with him to bed'. (I can still remember the gentle shock of reading that sentence for the first time, the flash of realization, not that you fully understand the author, but, far rarer and more memorable, that the author knows all about you.) (pp. 31-2)

Chesterton the Painter . . . does the service of reminding us that the author started his career not as an author, but as a painter in the proper sense, or at any rate as an art student at the Slade. I wonder very much whether the pictures he produced at that time, if any, show the fascination with the effects of light . . . which constantly reappears throughout his novels and stories. Every such reappearance seems fresh, different from all the others; we see not only London (though we see London most and perhaps best), not only the town or the village or the castle or the inn, but countryside from the lush to the stark, salt-flat, seashore, estuary, river (light on water, as might be expected, particularly attracted him), at all times of day but with a preference for dusk and dawn, in fog, in rain, in lightning, under snow. Chesterton the Impressionist? (pp. 32-3)

In the later novels, the Melodramatist bows himself out and, *pari passu,* the Impressionist is reduced to the status of a scene-painter: any old time of day and most places will do as background to conversation. It is the Polemicist who comes increasingly to the fore. Part of him is propagandist, the champion of Roman Catholicism against its various foes, but it is a much smaller part than people with a sketchy knowledge or recollection of the real Chesterton would have us believe. (p. 36)

With no more than three or four exceptions, the best of Chesterton's work in the shorter form is to be found in the Brown saga. This consists of what are much closer to being detective stories than most of his other fiction is close to any accepted category. Before turning to it, I might just remark on the pertinacity, or desperation, with which he clung to the detective form in nearly all his short pieces. For a writer with little interest in, or aptitude for, narration as such, a crime or mystery plus investigation plus dénouement is a convenient clothes-horse over which all manner of diverse material can be draped. . . .

The Impressionist . . . is in top form throughout the Brown stories, even those written after, say, 1918, when he had all but disappeared from the novels. In 'The Sins of Prince Saradine' and 'The Perishing of the Pendragons' and elsewhere he achieves some of the finest, and least regarded, descriptive writing of this century. And it is not just description; it is atmosphere, it anticipates and underlines mood and feeling, usually of the more nervous sort, in terms of sky and water and shadow, the eye that sees and the hand that records acting as one. (p. 38)

In these stories, the Polemicist and the Melodramatist are often hard to distinguish from the Impressionist and from each other. Between them, the three produce wonderfully organized puzzles that tell an overlooked truth, parables that touch the emotions, syllogisms that thrill the senses. (pp. 38-9)

Of Chesterton's seventeen volumes of fiction, seven or eight, with another half-book or so of odds and ends, are worth keeping and re-reading; not a bad score. Very well, he remains a minor master in the genre, but there he remains, in spite of the glaring fact that so much of what interested him was irrelevant or even directly inimical to fiction as we usually think of it. His reader can promise himself . . . a very entertaining evening. (p. 39)

> *Kingsley Amis, "Four Fluent Fellows: An Essay on Chesterton's Fiction," in* G. K. Chesterton: A Centenary Appraisal, *edited by John Sullivan (copyright © 1974 by Kingsley Amis; reprinted by permission of A. D. Peters & Co. Ltd.), Paul Elek, 1974, pp. 28-39.*

All lovers of poetry, I imagine, would rather quote from poems they admire than talk about them. Once read or listened to, their merits should be immediately apparent. One feels this all the more strongly in the case of a poet whom, like Chesterton, one suspects to be out of fashion and little read. (p. 73)

Consciously or unconsciously, every poet takes one or more of his predecessors as models. Usually, his instinct leads him to make the right choice among these, but not always. In Chesterton's case, for example, I think that Swinburne was a disastrous influence. That he should ever have allowed himself to be influenced by Swinburne seems to me very odd, when one thinks how utterly different their respective views about Life, Religion and Art were, but he was and always to his harm. It is due to Swinburne that, all too often in his verses, alliteration becomes an obsessive tic. In Anglo-Saxon and Icelandic poetry where the metrical structure is based upon alliteration, its essential function is obvious. In modern·verse, based upon regular feet and rhyme, alliteration can be used for onomatopoeic effects, but only sparingly: in excess it becomes maddeningly irritating. The other vice Chesterton acquired from Swinburne was prolixity. Too often one feels that a poem would have been better if it had been half the length. 'Lepanto', it seems to me, exhibits both faults. (pp. 73-4)

In the case of his longest and, perhaps, greatest 'serious' poem, *The Ballad of the White Horse*, I do not, however, I am happy to say, find the length excessive. When, for example, Elf the Minstrel, Earl Ogier and Guthrum express in turns their conceptions of the Human Condition, what they sing could not be further condensed without loss. (p. 74)

Chesterton never disregards the actual visible appearance of things. Then, unlike Wordsworth, his imagination is stirred to wonder, not only by natural objects, but by human artifacts as well.

> Men grow too old to woo, my love,
> Men grow too old to wed:
> But I shall not grow too old to see
> Hung crazily overhead
> Incredible rafters when I wake
> And find I am not dead.

Probably most young children possess this imaginative gift, but most of us lose it when we grow up as a consequence, Chesterton would say, of the Fall.

[When the] Swinburnian influence [is not in evidence, one can detect behind the verses] the whole tradition of English Comic Verse, of Samuel Butler, Prior, Praed, Edward Lear, Lewis Carroll and, above all, W. S. Gilbert. It was from such writers, I believe, that Chesterton, both in his verse and his prose, learned the art of making terse aphoristic statements which, once read or heard, remain unforgettably in one's mind. (pp. 76-7)

I cannot think of a single comic poem by Chesterton that is not a triumphant success. It is tempting to quote several, but I must restrain myself. Instead, I recommend any reader unacquainted with them to open *The Collected Poems* . . . and sample 'The Shakespeare Memorial' . . . , 'Ballade d'une Grande Dame' . . . and 'A Ballade of Suicide'. . . . His parodies of other poets are equally good, especially those of Browning and Kipling. (p. 78)

By natural gift, Chesterton was, I think, essentially a comic poet. Very few of his 'serious' poems are as good as these. (p. 79)

> *W. H. Auden, "The Gift of Wonder," in* G. K. Chesterton: A Centenary Appraisal, *edited by John Sullivan (copyright © 1974 by W. H. Auden; reprinted by permission of Harper & Row Publishers, Inc., Barnes & Noble Import Division), Paul Elek, 1974, pp. 73-80.*

It would be fair, I think, to call G. K. Chesterton the archetypical Edwardian writer. 'Edwardian' is not an established term quite like 'Romantic' or 'Augustan', yet for me at least it has a fairly precise meaning. It suggests a writer formed by, and attuned to, the Harmsworth era. Shaw and Kipling were Edwardian writers in this sense, though not chronologically; and in saying this one is saying something about the nature of their imagination. What I mean is, that the imagination of the 'Edwardian' writer is nurtured not so much by the sap of nature as by printer's ink. It is an *ad hoc* imagination, a product of the will and of opinion. Everything, even in Kipling, is there to make a case and can be converted back into a case.

If one accepts this definition, then what one notices about 'Edwardian' writers, as compared with the modernist artists like Yeats and Joyce who were coming to maturity at the same period, is that the Edwardians were much more natural men. To cultivate the true, unconscripted imagination in art, as Yeats and Joyce did, consumes all the artist's natural humanity and leaves him a stiff and unnatural monster in real life. Shaw, Wells and Chesterton, by contrast, splashed about in the intellectual life in a thoroughly carefree way; perhaps no other group of writers has ever done so to the same degree. And why I have called Chesterton the archetypical Edwardian is because, while possessing as much verve and invention as any of his contemporaries, he was franker in admitting to himself that it was all paper and printer's ink. There is a moral good taste in Chesterton which prevents him, as it does not always prevent Shaw—think of *St Joan*—from asking you to accept his impromptus as true imagination. In his fantastic novels you never for a moment leave the weekly column or the debating-hall; it is simply that the whole universe becomes a debating-hall, and the argument happens to be continued on the dome of St Paul's or the pantomime battlefield of Notting Hill.

How Chesterton became the kind of writer he was makes, biographically speaking, a curious story. As we learn from Maisie Ward [the author of two Chesterton biographies], he did not reach puberty until he was eighteen or nineteen—evidently he suffered from some mild glandular disorder, as one might have guessed from his later fatness. The fact was clearly important. For to come to puberty so belatedly, when in most other respects you are in the midst of adult life, must be a very strange, and perhaps shattering, experience; and so it proved with Chesterton. He became a victim of phantasmagoric sexual obsessions, which convinced him of the close and immediate presence of the devil. And, more to the point, it gave to the intellectual movements of the day, in which he had already taken a cheerful debating-society interest, a sulphurous flavour of diabolism for him. His reaction was to combat them with the weapons of his childhood—with a toy-theatre medievalism, pasteboard swords and debating-society high jinks. It was a reaction of genius, restoring his moral balance and leaving his intellect untrammelled and free. None the less it left him with some extremely odd, and rather comic, misconceptions. It prevented him from having much real notion of what Ibsenism, or Zolaism, or Symbolism or Schopenhauerian pessimism were about. It even left him feeling that there was something sinister, and metaphysically subversive, in Impressionist painting—at least, he thought that his own 'black night of the soul' might partly be laid at its door. (pp. 16-17)

There is another slight oddity in Chesterton's formation as a writer. He was a refugee from the *fin-de-siècle,* and yet he borrowed almost all his equipment as a writer from it. He was evidently fascinated by Wilde, as all his contemporaries were, and took over the paradox from Wilde, in order to turn it against him. In Wilde the paradox was expressive of a quarrel with nature. It was the emblem of those who lived 'A rebours'—against the grain, at odds with nature, using the wrong organs of the body in sex, and so on. Chesterton took it over as a weapon against just this attitude, as a device for bouncing oneself into a fresh vision of the ordinary and the natural. And he wielded it much in Wilde's style. In that alliance of the fanatic and the joker cemented at the end of *The Napoleon of Notting Hill,* the joker, Auberon Quin, is, in essentials, Wilde. His epigram, 'The

reversal of the obvious is as near as we can come to ritual with our imperfect apparatus' echoes Wilde's philosophy and tone with great fidelity. (p. 18)

Likewise Chesterton's idea of the poet, flaming-haired and gorgeous-tongued, is Wildean; it is Swinburne as transmitted by Wilde. And so, again, is his intellectual bravado, his love of impromptu, and—what goes with them—the cheerful ignorance. . . . Chesterton, of course, did not conceal his ignorance, he announced it blithely. And perhaps one should not call it ignorance, for he read enormously; but whatever it was—say, a beaming disregard for dates and details—it became part of his costume and role. Nevertheless there was a kinship to Wilde here. Wilde loved to allude, in a grand gesture or generalization, to vast tracts of (in his case largely non-existent) knowledge. And with more to support it, this was Chesterton's habit too. It was the Fleet Street method, the method of a thinker living his intellectual life in public. (pp. 19-20)

Here, I need hardly say, we are at the heart of Edwardianism. Never did ideas so run rampant. . . . It was an inspiriting time, and one feels a nostalgia for it. Though, on the other hand, it was this period which, understandably, produced in modernist writers their distrust of all 'ideas' as the enemy of art. Chesterton, said Eliot, had a mind as full of ideas as a rabbit-warren; 'but I have yet to see evidence that he thinks'. It was a most unfair, and rather Chestertonian, remark; and it has always remained a somewhat dark mystery what Eliot meant by 'thinking', a word with which he sandbagged many opponents. Yet there was some truth in the jibe. The faith in 'ideas' of Chesterton and his fellow-prophets was part of the optimism of that brief post-Victorian moment and perhaps wasn't fitted to survive it. All the same, we should not write off Edwardian polemics as mere mock-battles, or as some kind of indoor game. So much free intelligence playing round fundamental issues could not fail to leave a deposit of truth and to have effect on events. (p. 20)

So much for Chesterton's formation and role as an 'Edwardian' writer. Now a word about his central belief, which he evolved—and which, he said, preserved him—when in 'the darkest depths of the contemporary pessimism'. I mean the belief that 'Even mere existence, reduced to its most primary limits, was extraordinary enough to be exciting'. That 'At the back of our brains . . . there was a forgotten blaze or burst of astonishment at our own existence' and 'the object of the artistic and spiritual life was to dig for this submerged sunrise of wonder'. As we know, the belief did sustain him throughout his career and was the basis for some of his most engaging fantasies—such as that of *Manalive,* in which the hero, to revive his excitement at his own existence, burgles his own house and elopes with his own wife. (pp. 21-2)

Of [Chesterton's] novels, I would think *The Man Who Was Thursday* the best fitted to survive. It is the profoundest and most aerated, the one springing from the deepest paradox and most completely pervaded and penetrated by its paradox. It is not surprising that a doctor once told Chesterton that the novel had been a great help in treating mental patients. As a parable of outfacing paranoiac imaginings—that classic one, especially, of the whole world being in a conspiracy against you—the book has great force and originality. It is a true comedy of psychosis, exploring that absurd and tireless logic with which the insane create their own dilemmas and make evil out of what is innocent. And absurdest and most logical of all, funniest and most like some theorem of the reversibility of all propositions, is the duel-scene. (p. 25)

Whether in fact this, or any of the novels, will live I am not sure. What I am surer of is that Chesterton will live as a moralist. If he was weak in aesthetic taste, he was, on the other hand, extraordinarily strong in moral taste. It is this which . . . makes him worth listening to as a literary critic. (p. 26)

> *P. N. Furbank, "Chesterton the Edwardian," in* G. K. Chesterton: A Centenary Appraisal, *edited by John Sullivan (copyright © 1974 by P. N. Furbank; reprinted by permission of Harper & Row Publishers, Inc., Barnes & Noble Import Division),* Paul Elek, *1974, pp. 16-27.*

Chesterton himself did not attach great importance to the Father Brown stories. Ordered in batches by magazine editors and publishers, they were written hurriedly for the primary purpose of helping to finance his Distributist paper, *G. K.'s Weekly*. And though they have proved to be the most popular of Chesterton's writings, critical attention to them has been casual. This is partly because they are detective stories; and the detective story is commonly dismissed, without argument, as a very low form of art. That it is also a very difficult and demanding form, in which many clever writers have failed, is not regarded as relevant. Nor is there much respect for the innovators in this genre, or much comment on their remarkable rarity. If there were, Chesterton's reputation would stand very high; for his detective stories, while they may not be the best ever written, are without doubt the most ingenious. But to show ingenuity and originality in the detective story is for the superior critic merely to have a knack for a particular sort of commercial fiction. It is not the sort of thing he takes seriously. And Chesterton himself, it seems, would have agreed with him. (p. 58)

What is Chesterton saying in the Father Brown stories? Their meaning must be understood in terms of their genre. . . . Chesterton, like all detective story writers, derives from Poe. Indeed, it might be said that he derives from a single story of Poe: many of the Father Brown stories can be regarded as ingenious variations on the theme of 'The Purloined Letter'. . . . There are no chemical analyses or careful checking of alibis in these stories. Nor is there the dry intellectuality of Dupin. . . . [Between] Poe and Chesterton comes Conan Doyle. (pp. 59-60)

Every imaginative writer must choose his genre, and every genre has limitations. Those of the detective tale are obvious, and the most serious is this: no character can have depth, no character can be done from the inside, because any must be a potential suspect. It is Chesterton's triumph that he turned this limitation of the genre into an illumination of the universal human potentiality of guilt and sin. No character in the stories matters except Father Brown. But this is not a fault, because Father Brown, being a man, epitomizes all their potentialities within himself. 'Are you a devil?' the exposed criminal wildly asks. 'I am a man,' replies Father Brown, 'and therefore have all devils in my heart.'

This ability to identify himself with the murderer is the 'secret' of Father Brown's method. Some readers have misunderstood Chesterton's intention here. They suppose that Father Brown is credited with special spiritual powers, pertaining to his rôle as a priest. They see him as a thaumaturgic Sherlock Holmes. . . . But it is made quite clear that Father Brown owes his success not to supernatural insight but to the usual five senses. He is simply more observant, less clouded by conventional anticipations and prejudices, than the average man. (pp. 61-2)

Father Brown is, then, not a thaumaturge. But it must be granted that, apart from his powers of observation, he has exceptional moral insight. It is well known that Chesterton conceived the idea for this character after meeting a priest whose 'unworldliness' proved to be compatible with an inside knowledge of crime and wickedness. His 'innocence' was of a kind that would have shocked the would-be sophisticated young men whom Chesterton soon afterwards heard patronizing the clergy for their ignorance of the world. Chesterton makes a good deal of play with the contrast between Father Brown's appearance, moonfaced, blinking, dropping his umbrella, and the reality of his insights into men's minds and hearts. But Chesterton's aim is not really a psychological study of such a man. Almost at once Father Brown becomes largely a mouthpiece for Chesterton's own wit and wisdom. (p. 63)

The artistic reason for Father Brown's powers of repartee, and his wittiness in general, is that we look straight at him as we do not look at Sherlock Holmes, who is reflected in the—sometimes exasperated—admiration of Dr Watson. Chesterton has dispensed with a Dr Watson; and so Father Brown has to seem brilliant to *us*. And the only way this can be done is by making him brilliant. . . . Father Brown by himself has no solidity. He is not a credible priest; he seems to be away from his parish as often as Dr Watson was away from his practice. He comes and goes from nowhere. The temptation to make him a semi-symbolic figure must have been great. Agatha Christie succumbed to a similar temptation in her stories about *The Mysterious Mr Quin*. But this is false to the genre. Chesterton's stories, though often fantastic, are not fantasies. Again and again it is emphasized that Father Brown in himself is an ordinary man: an extraordinarily ordinary man.

But Father Brown's ordinariness is ordinariness *à la* Chesterton. He shares his creator's aesthetic sense. Indeed, his detective powers are closely connected with his aesthetic sense. . . . It is an aesthetic sense that sometimes provides Father Brown with an essential clue; as in 'The Worst Crime in the World,' where his perception of the balanced arrangement of a hall enables him to spot that one suit of armour, out of what must have been a pair, is missing. (pp. 64-5)

Finally, Father Brown's detective skill owes much to that linguistic sensitivity which he shares with his creator. (p. 65)

Father Brown, then, is represented as at the same time an ordinary man, of simple tastes, who enjoys simple pleasures, and a clever, shrewd person, with observation and sensitiveness beyond the ordinary. But he is not a mystic. He remains true both to traditional theology, and to the genre of the detective story, in never decrying reason. It is when Flambeau, disguised as a priest, does this that Father

Brown is certain he is a fraud. Of course, Father Brown is represented as a religious man. It is not by accident, and not merely to find a new twist to the Sherlock Holmes formula, that Chesterton makes him a priest. (p. 67)

The abundance of quacks, mystagogues, sorcerers in [these stories] is not only due to the desire to point a contrast with Father Brown. It is to illustrate, in terms proper to the genre in which Chesterton is writing, his belief that what Christianity has shown is that the age-old effort of man to grasp the Divine is bankrupt. Man cannot come to God. Christianity says that God came to man. This was what Chesterton was saying over and over again, in different tones and with varying degrees of humour or earnestness. Orwell claimed that writers like Chesterton seem to have only one subject: that they are Catholics. One might as well retort that Orwell's only subject seems to be that he was not one. Either the Catholic faith is relevant to the whole of life, or it is relevant to none of it. That, at any rate, was Chesterton's position. (pp. 67-8)

But the most memorable of the stories are not witty parables . . . , but imaginative fairy tales. What some readers remember most in the Father Brown stories is Chesterton's powers of description. His liking for a twilight setting—dawn or dusk—has been noted; and so has the constant sense we have that the action is taking place in a toy theatre, where the weird and wonderful backcloth dominates everything, and the tiny puppets that gesticulate in fight or dance in front of it seem faceless and featureless. And these backcloths have a décor which links Chesterton to Swinburne and the Decadents. His moral and religious outlook could not be more different from theirs; but his imagination has been formed on their work. (p. 69)

[The] child-like quality in Chesterton [that is, the intensely visual quality of Chesterton's imagination] attracts some readers and repels others. Those whom it repels dislike the association he makes between childish fantasies about winged daggers and flying vampires, and serious themes of good and evil. They feel that the former degrade the latter. (p. 71)

We might say, then, that Father Brown is imagined by Chesterton as a child whose vision is undistorted. The psychological critic will no doubt see in the contrasting distortions of perspective, the 'wrong shapes', the murderous yet strangely unheated fantasies of the stories, some relationship to the child's bizarre notions of the behaviour of adults. For reasons of temperament, period, and literary mode, Chesterton avoids overtly sexual themes in the Father Brown stories. Yet it was presumably the real Father Brown's knowledge of sexual depravities that shocked Chesterton. And in 'The Secret of Father Brown' the priest confides to his interlocutor that he 'acted out' in his imagination all the crimes that he had investigated. What renders Father Brown invulnerable is precisely this anterior playacting.

The main critical problem posed by these stories, as by Chesterton's work as a whole, is how to distinguish between the child-like and the childish. (pp. 71-2)

> *W. W. Robson, "Father Brown and Others," in* G. K. Chesterton: A Centenary Appraisal, *edited by John Sullivan (copyright © 1974 by W. W. Robson; reprinted by permission of Harper & Row Publishers, Inc., Barnes & Noble Import Division), Paul Elek, 1974, pp. 58-72.*

(Sidonie-Gabrielle) Colette

1873-1954

French novelist and journalist. Colette's widely read "Claudine" novels were published by her first husband, Henry Gauthier-Villars, an unsuccessful author, under his own name, "Willy." She was divorced in 1906 and for nearly ten years thereafter lived a Bohemian life in Paris as a music-hall dancer and mime. During her second marriage she created Mitsou and Cheri, the fictional characters that made her famous; during her third she was elected to both the Academie Royale Belge and the Academie Goncourt. All of her later work derives from her need for independence and the severing of relationships is often a central theme. Colette's magnificent fluid prose, much admired by Proust, places her among the greatest French writers.

PRINCIPAL WORKS

Claudine à l'école   (novel)   1900
   [*Claudine at School*, 1930]
Claudine à Paris   (novel)   1901
   [*Claudine in Paris*, 1958]
Claudine en ménage   (novel)   1902
   [*The Indulgent Husband*, 1935; *Claudine Married*, 1960]
Claudine s'en va   (novel)   1903
   [*The Innocent Wife*, 1934; *Claudine and Annie*, 1962]
L'Ingénue libertine   (novel)   1909
   [*The Gentle Libertine*, 1931; *The Innocent Libertine*, 1961]
La Vagabonde, roman   (novel)   1910
   [*The Vagabond*, 1954]
L'Entrave, roman   (novel)   1913
   [*Recaptured*, 1931; *The Shackle*, 1964]
Mitsou; ou, Comment l'esprit vient aux filles   (novel) 1919
   [*Mitsou; or, How Girls Grow Wise*, 1930]
Chéri, roman   (novel)   1920
   [*Chéri*, 1929]
La Maison de Claudine   (novel)   1922
   [*My Mother's House*, 1953]
La fin de Chéri, roman   (novel)   1926
   [*The Last of Chéri*, 1932]
La Seconde   (novel)   1929
   [*The Other One*, 1931]
Sido   (novel)   1929
   [*Sido*, 1953]
La Chatte, roman   (novel)   1933
   [*The Cat*, 1936]

Duo   (novel)   1934
   [*Duo*, 1935; *The Married Lover*, 1935]
Gigi   (novel)   1944
   [*Gigi*, 1952]

Colette's excellence, long recognized by a European public that includes her fellow artists, is not easy to define by English-speaking standards. That she is a born writer and an exceptionally sensitive woman is evident. Her full-bodied gusto, her fresh senses and compassion unspoiled as a child's, are immediately clear to the running eye. She is not erudite. Her pages are singularly free from allusion and echoes of literature. She can be compared to little but herself because she has written her discoveries down just as she herself made them. She has lived her life—as a provincial girl, the wife of a Parisian man-about-town, a dancer in music hall, a woman of letters—and written of it concurrently. (pp. 75-6)

The novelist . . . works in a dangerously malleable form. . . . Animus, stupidity, inaccuracy, and condescension, if disguised by a neat and fashionable manner and a long wind, can easily pass unnoticed. The good novelist is distinguished from the bad one chiefly by a gift of choice. Choice, itself a talent, as taste is a talent, is not however, enough. Only extreme sanity and balance of selection can give to prose fiction the dignity and excitement inherent in more rigid forms of writing: drama, poetry, and the exposition of ideas.

Colette makes perfect choices. She writes with the naive freedom of the amateur who has only himself for audience, and with the artist's unwavering adherence to form. . . . The stories of Katherine Mansfield, so obviously influenced by Colette, illustrate the Frenchwoman's method of attack without giving a hint of her quality. For Katherine Mansfield's talent leaves off where Colette's begins. (p. 76)

In *Chéri*, Colette chooses for her subject one of the most difficult situations in the rather limited gamut of relationships possible between men and women: the love of an aging woman for a young man; the dependence of a young man upon the passion and tenderness of an older woman. She makes her problem perfectly clear and does not slight its implications. . . .

Mitsou is so lightly blocked in, so delicately developed, that it barely merits the heavy title of novel. (p. 77)

Turning the light formality of French fiction to her own uses, Colette has colored French prose, for a long time rather grayed by reflections from Parisian streets, with the varied green of provincial gardens. Honest, sensuous, and witty, she has produced a solid body of work that owes little to masculine attitudes. (p. 78)

> *Louise Bogan, "Colette" (1930), in* A Poet's Alphabet, *edited by Robert Phelps and Ruth Limmer (copyright © 1970 by Ruth Limmer as Trustee), McGraw-Hill, 1971, pp. 75-8.*

In thirty years [Colette] has been putting into infallible artistic form her gross, wise, limited, eternal views about life, at times leaving *The Well of Loneliness* beaten at the post, at times producing little candid pearls of innocence, since these too are aspects of the universe. It is one of the peculiar virtues of the French race that it can take the kind of sturdy long-lived strength which in other countries remains dedicated to the body and yoke it to the service of the mind. (p. 181)

> *Rebecca West, "Formidable," in her* Ending in Earnest: A Literary Log *(copyright 1931, © 1957 by Rebecca West; reprinted by permission of The Viking Press), Doubleday, Doran, 1931, pp. 180-81.*

One of the most interesting aspects of [the Claudine] books, whose heroine Claudine has created a durable type, is the contrast between the circumstances of the author and the spirit they exhale. Colette was then very young, very serious, very unhappy, very unwell; Claudine had the sensuous gayety, veined with melancholy, of a piece by Mozart. Yet none of the four books is entirely non-autobiographical. (pp. 93-4)

In 1920 Colette published *Chéri* . . ., and in 1922 the entrancing *Maison de Claudine*. Since this book is admittedly autobiographical, its title acknowledges Claudine to have contained a part of Colette; but in its pages the figure of the *enfant terrible* with her little-boy's curls melts, like a figure in a film, into the more seriously delectable figure of the young Colette in whom passion and irony were mixed in so rare a manner, who was as remarkable for intellectual probity as for simply expressed sensuality. And it was into this book's unforcedly pastoral scenes that she first introduced her mother, to whom she was eight years later to devote one of her most superb books, *Sido*. . . .

Colette's technique is exquisite; her vocabulary immense . . . , and everything she writes gives the effect of effortlessness. (p. 94)

Colette's first specifically original contribution to literature was her treatment of the human senses; this, and the fact that she treated them without the fanfare that might have been expected from a writer of her period, but with accuracy, good taste, and warmth. The magnitude of this contribution has been kept from English-speaking readers—those dependent upon translation—by the circumstance that these translations, being less good than one could wish, have deforming proprieties. Imprisoned in them, like Ariel in the hollow tree, Colette's books have acquired a pornographic label. This is extremely inappropriate.

It is true that Colette has devoted much of her talent to expositions of love—the love of a child for its mother, the passion of a young girl for her lover, the devotion of a woman to her husband, the adoration of an elderly woman for a boy, among other forms—but auscultation is only part of her equipment. And human reactions to food, climate, scent and sound, to animals, forests, and rivers have an even more remarkable place in the sensual inventory to whose compilation she has devoted a formidable intellect. (pp. 94-5)

> *Monica Stirling, "Colette," in* The Atlantic Monthly *(copyright © 1946, 1974, by The Atlantic Monthly Company, Boston, Mass.; reprinted with permission), July, 1946, pp. 92-5.*

In France [Colette] has been known and loved and read from the beginning, and though one always heard of her as "a light writer," that was no term of disrespect—quite the contrary. The French above all know how much strength and discipline and even sheer genius it takes to write lightly of serious things; they never called her frivolous, far from it.

Yet there was always that tone of particular indulgence, reserved for gifted women who make no pretentions and know how to keep their place in the arts: a modest second-best, no matter how good, to the next ranking male. . . .

[That] she is the greatest living French writer of fiction; and that she was while Gide and Proust still lived; that these two preposterously afflicted self-adoring, frankly career-geniuses certainly got in Colette's light; they certainly diminished her standing, though not her own kind of genius. She lived in the same world, more or less in the same time —without their money or their leisure. Where they could choose their occasions, she lived on a treadmill of sheer labor. Compared to their easy road of acknowledged great literary figures, her life path was a granite cliff sown with cactus and barbed wire.

But she had the immense daylight sense of reality they both lacked and, beyond that, something that Gide tried all his life to have, or to appear to have, and which he lacked to the end: a genuine moral sense founded on a genuine capacity for human feeling. She never attempts to haul God into criminal collusion with the spiritual deformities of her characters. Being a generous woman born to be exploited by men, she has for some of them the abject tenderness and indulgence which is so terribly womanly. Yet she knows this; she does not deceive herself. And her women, if possible less attractive even than the men, are still women, which Proust's never were. (p. 5)

Stupidity is the inability to learn in spite of experience. Innocence can lead the innocent into evil; stupidity is itself an evil. Colette is the wisest kind of artist; the light of her quick intelligence plays over this Limbo, in her warmth of emotion she cannot reject or condemn them, and here is the strangest thing—the stories are full of light, and air, and greenery and freshness, the gayest sparkle of laughter, all in a way misleading, if you like; for there is a satire of the sharpest kind in this contrast between the sordidness, the obstinate dreariness, of human conduct and motive, and the disregarded, the ignored, the unused possibilities for human happiness.

Colette conceals her aim, her end, in her method. Without

setting her up in rivalry with her great jealous, dubious male colleagues and contemporaries, let us just be glad of such a good, sound, honest artist, a hard-working one; we could really do nicely with more "light writers" like her. The really light-weight ones weigh a ton beside her. (p. 52)

Katherine Anne Porter, "A Most Lively Genius," in The New York Times Book Review *(© 1951 by The New York Times Company; reprinted by permission), November 18, 1951, pp. 5, 52.*

As much as Paris belongs to Colette so does Colette belong to Paris. Each has the same kind of capriciousness and lightness of heart; the alert sensibility; the mercurial intellect, tender, curious and analytical; the restless melancholy; and the basic knowledge of the relative cost of pleasure and pain. The city made the woman famous and the woman's work makes the city more memorable; for in Colette's forty or more books is the wonder and delight of Paris, like a harlequin's ghost beckoning the fair ones and the dispossessed.

It is of these fair ones and these dispossessed that Colette writes. They are fair not because of their deeds nor dispossessed because of their politics: each finds his particular heaven and hell in the simplicity and complicity of love. . . .

Structurally Colette is a conscious stylist; a determined excavator of the adroit word, of the consummate image; an instinctive perfectionist ever alert to the influence of atmosphere and undertone. Fundamentally Colette is an artist, able to reveal with a sharp impressionable truth the many facets of direct and indirect experience. (p. 210)

There she is in her books, distributing her varied selves in the precocious experimentalism of *Claudine;* in the watchful narrator of *La Retraite Sentimentale,* in Renée of *La Vagabonde* and *L'Entrave,* and in *Chéri* too, she is there. Impossible to locate precisely, Colette is narrator, heroine, hero, incidental character and unintentional spectator. (p. 211)

And what is [the] love on which Colette squanders [her] artistry? It is an exposed nerve. A strident insistent theme of sensual desire which has no relation to the simplicity of wedlock and the passivity of family continuity. (p. 214)

To illustrate and describe this love Colette, the artist, brings her sensibility and her experienced appreciation of all that life so closely and intimately links with love. Participator and watcher, Colette knows that love possesses a sensuality beyond the actual physical desire, a sensuality of loss, of departure, of death, of time, of place. (p. 215)

Kay Dick, "Colette," in The Saturday Book, *edited by John Hadfield (copyright © 1952 by Hutchinson), Hutchinson, 1952, pp. 209-15.*

If Colette has recently been the subject of a flourishing revival in France that can only be in part because she seems so remote from contemporary preoccupations, because her complete absorption in a private world refreshes a generation almost obsessed with global affairs and esoteric philosophies, because even what was once thought the naughtiness of her occasional frank sensuality seems centuries away from a generation to whom "love" means neither sentiment nor normal sensuality but violence, hatred, and, often, some form of perversity.

Few writers have ever been less engaged. This does not mean merely that she has no political or social ideas and no ethical convictions beyond those which an unthinking generosity and kindliness suggest. It means also an introversion so complete that she is a prisoner of herself and unaware of things outside herself except in so far as she can make them part of that self. As blind as a child to everything not part of her own experience she is also childishly alert to and absorbed in everything which is. . . .

By [her] confession . . . there is no literary art as that term is now usually defined. By the evidence of the writing itself here is presented a world where there are no politics, no philosophy, no religion, and no morality—though cruelty and kindness, indifference and compassion, ugliness and beauty, are vivid realities. The sum total makes something more vivid, more intense, and more solidly founded than one would have expected.

Joseph Wood Krutch, "Fox without Guile," in The Nation *(copyright 1955 by the Nation Associates, Inc.), March 26, 1955, p. 268.*

For the French, one of the qualities that made Colette classifiable as unique was the fact that as a writer she was—in the purist's sense of the word—amoral. Her catlike—her tiger-like—gold-flecked eyes were so feral that she seemed to be literally looking at the world with the eyes of a fine animal, or at any rate observing it without the refraction of moral judgment. She was also esteemed because she never wrote in generalities. (p. 138)

She knew the vegetation she wrote about; she knew the animals in her stories, and how they lived, fed, and died. In her nostalgic references to the country, she always identified any tree she wrote of by name, to determine its architecture and silhouette, and to supply it with its own spring smell of sap, or its summer color. (p. 141)

Janet Flanner, "The Story of Colette," in The New Yorker *(© 1955 by The New Yorker Magazine, Inc.), April 2, 1955, pp. 137-38, 141.*

There is . . . no one book where readers ought to begin and by which Colette must be judged. There is only the creation of a single character, Claudine-Renée Néré-Colette. Perhaps all three persons are co-equally autobiographical ('I have been able', [*The Blue Lantern*] says, 'to tell only of what I know'). More probably, they are all equally fictitious.

The Blue Lantern takes its title *(Le Fanal Bleu)* from the reading lamp for which Colette rigged up a shade out of the blue paper she wrote on. By its light the character Colette rigged up for herself (likewise, one might say, out of the paper she wrote on) is still vigorously at all its old devices and vices. Here is the usual talk about animals—for which all honour to her, especially in so anti-animal a society as France: but there is also the usual talk *by* animals. Colette is still name-dropping: Cocteau, of course, and if Cocteau, then naturally Jean Marais. (p. 265)

[As] a writer, Colette is against the French grain. She, rather, *has* a grain: whereas the *génie français* has, since Racine, flowed classically without one. Where the whole tendency of French literature is, magnificently or banally, to substitute an abstract for a concrete and an intellectual antithesis for a tangible gesture, Colette's prose is forever bringing you up against whorls and knots—not merely substantives, but particular, even peculiar, substantives. . . .

The personality this implies may be fake all through. I could believe she never set foot in the countryside, that she hired someone to coach her in her Burgundian accent, got her botany out of books, could not tell tulip from turnip, dog from cat or man from woman, and ate the revolting water-caltrops solely to provoke her friends' incredulity. . . .

What is authentic is the literary power which evokes these things in more than *trompe-l'oeil*—in *trompe-la-langue* and *trompe-le-nez*—actuality. Impatiently, one might ask by virtue of what, except Colette's opportunist eye for publicity, one instantly recognises 'Pauline' as Colette's housekeeper, or what on earth it can matter whether Colette was or wasn't lesbian. The answer is that it matters for the same reason as it does about Albertine: that one knows Pauline in the sense one knows Françoise.

Colette's perseverance in the truly Proustian creation she carried out in life as well as on blue paper measures her narcissism. Almost auto-erotically she played with her own name (she even got as far as 'Willette Collie' [her husband's pseudonym was Willy and for a time she used the name Colette Willy]); and by the same symptom she revealed that her sexual ambiguity went back to an indecision about whether to identify herself with her mother or her father. She inclined first towards the father. To call herself simply by her (and his) surname, Colette, shorn of female first names, was as blatant a claim to masculinity as the shorn hair which she adopted soon after. (Claudine herself is named for her father—his Christian name is Claude.) Maturity and fame made Colette into 'Madame Colette'—which was, of course, what her mother was. Colette's reconciliation and identification with her mother shewed itself not only in the open mother-worship she put (safely after her mother's death) into *Sido* but also in her ability to incarnate herself in the disreputable mother-figures of the novels. . . . (pp. 266-67)

The appreciating eye, the pampered body: both are Colette's. If she never actually went to bed with a woman, it was probably because she could not bear another woman to be the object of sexual admiration. (Her best novel is the one where Claudine actually does; but it may be good through its truth to Colette's fantasy life rather than to her life.). . . In the over-circumstantially furnished nineteenth-century-baroque brothel which was Colette's imagination, Colette was the tart (seventy-five-year-old heart not of but set on gold), the madame and even the establishment cat. Indeed, she was even the client. (pp. 267-68)

> *Brigid Brophy, "Call Me Madame Colette" (originally published in* New Statesman, *August, 1963), in her* Don't Never Forget *(copyright © 1966 by Brigid Brophy; reprinted by permission of Jonathan Cape Ltd.), Holt, 1967, pp. 264-68.*

[Colette's] work is divorced from . . . French concerns with the theory of fiction or with embodiments of philosophy in fiction. She had no taste for theory, feeling that "feathered hats, general ideas, and earrings" did not become her. She spoke of her own thoughts as though they were cows wintering in a barn: "They have grown used to waiting, half asleep, for their feed of fresh words." Her commitment to

the concrete was so absolute that words and even single letters, the two abstractions she could not escape, became things for her: she saw the capital *S* "standing on end like a protecting serpent."

It is this attachment to the visible that prompts the conception of Colette as naturalist and, by extension, as pantheist. . . . Colette had, certainly, a tendency toward excess, toward an emotive extravagance, the aspect of her work which an unpleasant friend labeled "rustic poetics." But it seems more difficult to be a Wordsworth in France, especially in Paris, and the checks which Colette imposed upon her sensuous excursions are not romantic. (p. 720)

Colette undeniably possessed, and enjoyed, an animal-like sharpness of the senses. Few could say of a rose that it smelled like "crushed ants," and it is as doggy as it is witty to say that another rose smelled "like a gymnasium frequented exclusively by young redheaded women.". . . But within her books, these rapacious senses are supervised by ironic severity. . . . The current questions of fiction, how to weather ennui, how to initiate action, are alien to Colette. It is not the prolongation of torpor which frightens her but her possible capitulation to excitement. (pp. 720-21)

More often, as romanticism is close to solemnity, Colette determines upon what she calls frivolity. She excuses a snake as though he were a nephew: "He's young, after all, and intelligent." Her memory fastens on the defect which a friend found in that most blatant image of natural beauty, the peacock: "He is beautiful . . . but it's mistaken of him to wear long, snuff-colored knitted underpants." She can turn the same frivolity on human beauty, "the bottomless, radiant imbecility of Mlle. d'Estouteville," on feminine histrionics, "It's four o'clock . . . at five I have my abyss." . . .

That quality in Colette which Gide considered vulgarity but which in Sido is called a "scandalous sincerity," results in the acumen of the least lyrical observations: "nasty little curtains fit for wrapping up abortions."

There is, after all, something here that we have appropriated as modern, a working against the grain. . . .

What one continues to read of Colette is apt to be [the] books out of which *Earthly Paradise* is formed, the books in which Colette chooses a high perversity, working distrust against impulse. (p. 721)

> *Mary Ellmann, "Colette: A Scandalous Sincerity," in* The Nation *(copyright 1966 by the Nation Associates, Inc.), June 13, 1966, pp. 720-21.*

Colette has always seemed to me the most authentic feminist heroine of all women writers. Like Aphra Behn and George Sand, she made her living by her pen. She was professional in that fundamental sense. Unlike so many others, she did not take her own life, but did the far braver thing of living to a ripe old age (writing all the while). She chronicled every stage of a woman's life from girlhood to old age. And almost alone of women writers, she presents a pattern for living and working which seems attractive. Not easy, not painless—but somehow rich, various, and *alive*. Her life contained many lives: writing, performing, running a cosmetics business; three marriages, many lovers of both sexes, the birth of a daughter, a close and enduring relationship with her mother. Colette did not find any secret, magical way to combine love and work; she struggled with the problem all her life. But she never gave up, and her life is moving precisely because it is the life of a survivor. (p. 31)

Colette is one of our authentic literary geniuses. She is an important innovator because she dared write out of a female consciousness and because she "dared to be natural" (as Francis Jammes, one of her earliest critics, recognized). It is a sad paradox that when male authors impersonate women (Tolstoy as Anna Karenina, Flaubert as Bovary, Richardson as Clarissa, Lawrence as Constance Chatterley, John Berryman as Mistress Bradstreet), they are said to be dealing with "cosmic, major concerns"—but when we impersonate *ourselves* we are said to be writing "women's fiction" or "women's poetry." Unfortunately, Colette has been the victim of that sort of prejudice in America—and to some extent in her native country. The male literary establishment has created the impression that she is slightly precious, supersensitive, effusive, and gushy. She is none of these. In fact there are many reasons why Colette's work has particular relevance to us now. First, because it tells the story of a soul's quest for liberation—not political liberation but spiritual liberation (which, of course, is the better part of the same thing). Second, because it is extremely modern in its aims and techniques: it is pseudoautobiography, pseudoconfession, subjective writing which *seems* artless and utterly natural but is really full of invisible artistry. Third, because it asks all the questions about marriage, love, jealousy, bisexuality, maleness and femaleness—which our generation sometimes flatters itself it has invented. Fourth, because it is great writing, full of sights, smells, colors, birds, beasts, love, hate, and the beautiful rhythms of words. And fifth, because Colette is an inspiration, a survivor, a hardy plant.

If you are tired of reading women's novels (or biographies) which end in madhouses, gas ovens, car crashes, leaps from open windows—then read Colette. She will not present a retouched picture of the world or pretend that life is painless. But she will show you the pure and the impure, the earthly paradise which flourishes in an imperfect world, the pleasures to be snatched from the jaws of mortality. She will show you cats and gardens, cups of chocolate and green grapes, sexual passion and friendship, rivalry and amity, imprisonment and freedom. She might have said with Wallace Stevens, "The imperfect is our paradise."

What a pleasure it is to know she's there—more than 50 volumes of her! (p. 33)

Erica Jong, "Retrieving Colette," in Ms. (© 1974 Ms. Magazine Corp.), April, 1974, pp. 31-3.

"Is it autobiographical?" they always ask you after you have written a novel. And the honest author can only reply: "I don't know." . . .

Colette's wonderful short novel *The Vagabond* raises this question in the most fascinating way. . . . Colette is an artist whose first and best creation is herself. If she sticks close to reality in small details, it is only so as to have greater freedom where it counts: in her literary artistry. . . .

During the years when Colette wrote *The Vagabond,* she was living in close (possibly lesbian) relationship with an older woman who mothered her and protected her. Not a trace of this relationship appears in *The Vagabond.* Yet the novel is always said to be "autobiographical" and "confessional," and is often treated as if it were straight reportage about Colette's life. Why? Presumably because the heroine looks like Colette, went on the stage like Colette, wrote like Colette, had the same ex-husband, and so on. But the whole thrust of Renée Néré's search is different from her creator's. Colette was, in fact, very dependent and in need of shelter at this time in her life. Yet she wrote about a woman who gives up shelter, renounces dependency and insists on solitude as the price of her soul. Is it autobiographical? Well, in a psychological way, it *is*. Perhaps because Colette felt deeply her own dependency, she was impelled to write a novel about a woman who chooses independence. But *The Vagabond* is certainly not autobiographical in a literal way—despite Colette's deliberate carelessness about putting "disguises" on all the characters. For the writer, a novel is often like a dream (or waking fantasy) in which one is far braver than one ever could be in life. It is a tribute to Colette's authenticity of tone that nearly everyone takes her books as straight autobiography. Perhaps the brash question, "Is it autobiographical?" is really a compliment. It means: "Sounds *true* to me!" And it *is* true; but true to fantasy, not fact. (p. 108)

Erica Jong, in Mademoiselle (copyright © 1974 by Erica Mann Jong; reprinted by permission), May, 1974.

Joseph Conrad

1857-1924

(Pseudonym of Teodor Jozef Konrad Korzeniowski) Polish-born English novelist. Son of a poet and revolutionary, Conrad was orphaned before he was twelve. He went to sea at seventeen, worked first with the French marine service and then, after four unsettled years involving gun-running, a passionate love affair, and attempted suicide, joined a British freighter. In 1886 he became a naturalized British subject and earned his Master Mariner's Certificate. As ship's captain he voyaged to the Far East, the South Pacific, and the Upper Congo. In 1896 he married and retired permanently from seafaring to devote the rest of his life to writing. Although Conrad did not learn English until he was twenty, he became one of England's greatest novelists and finest prose stylists. Conflict and convergence of emotional and physical landscapes, morality, fidelity, solidarity, betrayal, and self-deception are organizing concepts in Conrad's fiction. One of his most important stylistic methods—now commonplace but remarkable in 1900—was his use of time shifts accomplished through the introduction of a narrator, who also provided a contrasting perspective on the other characters. In 1924, the year of his death, Conrad declined a knighthood.

PRINCIPAL WORKS

Almayer's Folly, a Story of an Eastern River (novel) 1895
An Outcast of the Islands (novel) 1896
The Nigger of the "Narcissus" (novel) 1897
Tales of Unrest (short stories) 1898
Lord Jim: A Romance (novel) 1900
The Inheritors: An Extravagant Story [with Ford Madox Ford] (novel) 1901
Typhoon (short story) 1902
Youth: A Narrative, and Two Other Stories (short stories) 1902
Romance: A Novel [with Ford Madox Ford] (novel) 1903
Nostromo: A Tale of the Seaboard (novel) 1904
The Mirror of the Sea (autobiography) 1906
The Secret Agent: A Simple Tale (novel) 1907
A Set of Six (short stories) 1908
Under Western Eyes (novel) 1911
Some Reminiscences (autobiography) 1912
'Twixt Land and Sea (short stories) 1912
Chance (novel) 1914
Victory (novel) 1915
Within the Tides (short stories) 1915

The Shadow Line (novel) 1917
The Arrow of Gold (novel) 1919
The Rescue (novel) 1920
Notes on Life and Letters (essays) 1921
Notes on My Books (essays) 1921
The Rover (novel) 1923
The Nature of a Crime [with Ford Madox Ford] (novel) 1924
Tales of Hearsay (short stories) 1925
The Sisters (short stories) 1928

I hope that "One Day More" . . . is not the only alms that Mr. Conrad will bestow on our needy drama. Mr. Conrad is just the sort of person who ought to be coaxed into writing plays. . . . When [a master] does actually condescend to write a play, we ought all to dance around him and pat him enthusiastically on the back, crying "Continue!" I hasten to dance thus around Mr. Conrad. But my gyrations recall painfully to me those of the famous bee who tried to "swarm alone". (p. 495)

Mr. Conrad has not worked on that scale which offers serious difficulties in technical construction. He has not written a full-sized play. He has but turned one of his short stories into a little one-act play. And the short story chosen by him for this purpose happens to be one which any child could dramatise effectively. Indeed, I am not sure that it was not originally conceived in dramatic form.

[As] it stands, ["One Day More"] is a quite straightforward and well-knit play. The characters come on and go off quite naturally. There is no technical blemish whatever. But, even if this play were evidently the work of an amateur, and scored all over with technical blemishes, how lamentable a lack of critical insight were revealed by a criticism insistent on these blemishes, and impercipient of the originality and the fine humanity and strength underlying them! (pp. 496-97)

In other words, it is a powerful tragedy. And, therefore, I delight in it. What I want from art is some kind of emotion. It matters not at all to me whether the emotion be in itself one of pleasure or one of pain. In whatever way I be quickened, I am grateful. I pity the critics who can find no aesthetic pleasure in "One Day More". They ought to give up criticism. (p. 498)

The reason why the play is inferior to the story is simply that the dramatic form is, generally and essentially, inferior to the literary form. In the one. . . . Hush! Am I not a dramatic critic? And is not my immediate aim to coax Mr. Conrad, for our drama's sake, to further dramaturgy? (p. 499)

> *Max Beerbohm, "Mr. Conrad's Play" (1905), in his* Around Theatres, *Vol. II (copyright © 1930 by Max Beerbohm; reprinted by permission of Simon & Schuster, Inc.), Knopf, 1930, pp. 495-99.*

"A Set of Six" will not count among Mr. Conrad's major works. But in the mere use of English it shows an advance upon all his previous books. In some of his finest chapters there is scarcely a page without a phrase that no Englishman would have written, and in nearly every one of his books slight positive errors in the use of English are fairly common. In "A Set of Six" I have detected no error and extremely few questionable terms. The influence of his deep acquaintance with French is shown in the position of the adverb in "I saw again somebody in the porch." It cannot be called bad English, but it is queer. (p. 39)

Mr. Conrad still maintains his preference for indirect narrative through the mouths of persons who witnessed the events to be described. I daresay that he would justify the device with great skill and convincingness. But it undoubtedly gives an effect of clumsiness. . . . The best pages in the book are those devoted to the ironical contemplation of a young lady anarchist. They are tremendous. (p. 40)

> *Arnold Bennett, "Joseph Conrad and the 'Athenaeum'" (1908), in his* Books and Persons: Being Comments on a Past Epoch 1908-1911 *(copyright, 1917, by George H. Doran Company; reprinted by permission of Doubleday and Co., Inc.), Doran, 1917, pp. 36-40.*

Honour, loyalty, faith, crown his conceptions, and [Conrad] involves in them whatever beauty and strength is discernible in man's desire and achievement. I am not sure that this simple and tremendous moral impression is not of all Mr. Conrad's effects the most weighty and lasting. I am quite sure that it is the most characteristic. He sees life as a conflict: in *Victory,* the latest novel, the conflict of one disdaining strife with spirits of absolute evil; in *Chance,* the conflict of girl's tragic bewilderment with a man's magnanimity; in *Nostromo,* the conflict of pride with the spell of treasure; in *Under Western Eyes,* the conflict of a passion for independence and order with a base fear. Chiefly, as in *Lord Jim,* it is the inward clash of human aspiration with secret falseness that fascinates his imagination. . . . *Noblesse oblige,* might be inscribed in all his books as in those of Henry James; for they form, in a very real and direct sense, a Song of Honour. (pp. 250-51)

Mr. Conrad is a poet in all but the shaping spirit of verse. He has been oddly compared with Browning, for the moral rather than the purely poetic character; and the comparison on either ground is astonishing. He is an Odysseus among poets, passing lonely, half-glimpsed and unrecognized through the people of his own creation. . . . Not invention nor description but imagination marks his quality, making him a poet among prose writers. He has something of the careless reproductive power of natural life, something of its intensity, something of its variety, something of its mystery. His interest is as keenly fixed on characters of pure evil as on Lord Jim or Heyst; he is not concerned to judge or condemn or excuse, for there is always something that he cannot explore, a darkness he cannot pierce. (pp. 258-59)

In *Chance* his method is perhaps most conspicuously indirect, but really simple. Of all his books it is the richest in intuition, the clearest in its reading of the unusual and remote. . . . The value of Mr. Conrad's method is that his story has not one life but many lives. He tries to apprehend character in action. So you have the briefest description of Lord Jim, but his actions and his influence (his character *in being*) are detailed with immense patience. . . . Mr. Conrad seeks to involve his reader in his narrative, to bring you to the table where men talk still of these things; to appeal to your recollection, your apprehension, your sympathy; for it is his passion that you should possess the whole story, not simply as a procession of events or as an unfolding of character, but as a web of events and characters acting and reacting as living things. Not everything can be told; sometimes you may but guess, and in one extraordinary scene in *Chance* Marlow himself can only guess dimly what happened, what *must* have happened. . . . (pp. 259-61)

> *John Freeman, "Joseph Conrad," in his* The Moderns: Essays in Literary Criticism, *R. Scott, 1916 (and reprinted by Books for Libraries Press, Inc., 1967), pp. 243-64.*

[The essays composing Conrad's *Notes on Life and Letters*] suggest that he is misty in the middle as well as at the edges, that the secret casket of his genius contains a vapour rather than a jewel; and that we need not try to write him down philosophically, because there is, in this particular direction, nothing to write. No creed, in fact. Only opinions, and the right to throw them overboard when facts make them look absurd. Opinions held under the semblance of eternity, . . . and therefore easily mistaken for a creed.

As the simple sailorman, concerned only with his job, and resenting interference, he is not difficult to understand, and it is this side of him that has given what is most solid, though not what is most splendid, to his books. . . .

He has no respect for adventure, unless it comes incidentally. If pursued for its own sake it leads to "red noses and watery eyes," and "lays a man under no obligation of faithfulness to an idea." Work filled the life of the men whom he admired and imitated and whom, more articulate than they, he would express. (p. 138)

He does not respect all humanity. Indeed, were he less self-conscious, he would probably be a misanthrope. He has to pull himself up with a reminder that misanthropy wouldn't be quite fair—on himself. . . . It becomes a point of honour not to be misanthropic, so that even when he hits out there is a fierce restraint that wounds more deeply than the blows. He will not despise men, yet cannot respect them, and consequently our careers seem to him important and unimportant at the same time, and our fates, like those of the characters of Alphonse Daudet, "poignant, intensely interesting, and not of the slightest consequence."

Now, together with these loyalties and prejudices and personal scruples, he holds another ideal, a universal, the love of Truth. But Truth is a flower in whose neighbourhood others must wither, and Mr. Conrad has no intention that the blossoms he has culled with such pains and in so many lands should suffer and be thrown aside. So there are constant discrepancies between his nearer and his further vision, and here would seem to be the cause of his central obscurity. If he lived only in his experiences, never lifting his eyes to what lies beyond them: or if, having seen what lies beyond, he would subordinate his experiences to it—then in either case he would be easier to read. But he is in neither case. He is too much of a seer to restrain his spirit; he is too much Joseph Conrad, too jealous of personal honour, to give any but the fullest value to deeds and dangers he has known. (pp. 139-40)

Neither explicitly nor implicitly does Mr. Conrad demand friendship: he desires no good wishes from his readers: the anonymous intimacy, so dear to most, is only an annoyance and a hindrance to him. (p. 141)

> *E. M. Forster, "Joseph Conrad: A Note" (1920), in his* Abinger Harvest (© *1936, 1964 by E. M. Forster; reprinted by permission of Harcourt Brace Jovanovich, Inc.), Harcourt, 1936, pp. 136-41.*

In the midst of a futile meliorism which deceives the more, the more it soothes, [Conrad] stands out like some sinister skeleton at the feast, regarding the festivities with a flickering and impenetrable grin. . . . It was not an artistic choice that made him write English instead of French; it was a choice with its roots in considerations far afield. But once made, it concerned him no further. In his first book he was plainly a stranger, and all himself; in his last he is a stranger still—strange in his manner of speech, strange in his view of life, strange, above all, in his glowing and gorgeous artistry. . . . (pp. 28-9)

[Conrad] is no more a moralist than an atheist is a theologian. His attitude toward all moral systems and axioms is that of a skeptic who rejects them unanimously, even including, and perhaps especially including, those to which, in moments of aesthetic detachment, he seems to give a formal and resigned sort of assent. . . . His show fascinates, but his philosophy, in the last analysis, is unbearable. And in particular it is unbearable to women. One rarely meets a woman who, stripped of affection, shows any genuine enthusiasm for a Conrad book, or, indeed, any genuine comprehension of it. (pp. 31-2)

As for Conrad, he retaliates by approaching the sex somewhat gingerly. His women, in the main, are no more than soiled and tattered cards in a game played by the gods. The effort to erect them into the customary "sympathetic" heroines of fiction always breaks down under the drum fire of the plain facts. He sees quite accurately, it seems to me, how vastly the rôle of women has been exaggerated, how little they amount to in the authentic struggle of man. His heroes are moved by avarice, by ambition, by rebellion, by fear, by that "obscure inner necessity" which passes for nobility or the sense of duty—never by that puerile passion which is the mainspring of all masculine acts and aspirations in popular novels and on the stage. If they yield to amour at all, it is only at the urging of some more powerful and characteristic impulse, *e.g.*, a fantastic notion of chivalry, as in the case of Heyst, or the thirst for dominion, as in the case of Kurtz. (pp. 33-4)

I used to wonder why Conrad never tackled a straight-out story of adultery under Christianity, the standard matter of all our more pretentious fiction and drama. I was curious to see what his ethical agnosticism would make of it. The conclusion I came to at first was that his failure marked the limitations of his courage—in brief, that he hesitated to go against the orthodox axioms and assumptions in the department where they were most powerfully maintained. But it seems to me now that his abstinence has not been the fruit of timidity, but of disdain. He has shied at the hypothesis, not at its implications. His whole work, in truth, is a destructive criticism of the prevailing notion that such a story is momentous and worth telling. The current gyneolatry is as far outside his scheme of things as the current program of rewards and punishments, sins and virtues, causes and effects. He not only sees clearly that the destiny and soul of man are not moulded by petty jousts of sex, as the prophets of romantic love would have us believe; he is so impatient of the fallacy that he puts it as far behind him as possible, and sets his conflicts amid scenes that it cannot penetrate, save as a palpable absurdity. Love, in his stories, is either a feeble phosphorescence or a gigantic grotesquerie. (pp. 34-5)

[Conrad's] concern, one may say, is with the gross anatomy of passion, not with its histology. He seeks to depict emotion, not in its ultimate attenuation, but in its fundamental innocence and fury. Inevitably, his materials are those of what we call melodrama; he is at one, in the bare substance of his tales, with the manufacturers of the baldest shockers. But with a difference!—a difference, to wit, of approach and comprehension, a difference abysmal and revolutionary. He lifts melodrama to the dignity of an important business, and makes it a means to an end that the mere shock-monger never dreams of. In itself, remember, all this up-roar and blood-letting is not incredible, nor even improbable. The world, for all the pressure of order, is still full of savage and stupendous conflicts, of murders and debaucheries, of crimes indescribable and adventures almost unimaginable. One cannot reasonably ask a novelist to deny them or to gloss over them. . . . (pp. 42-3)

Here, in brief, you have the point of essential distinction between the stories of Conrad, a supreme artist in fiction, and the trashy confections of the literary artisans—*e.g.*, Sienkiewicz, Dumas, Lew Wallace, and their kind. Conrad's materials, at bottom, are almost identical with those of the artisans. He, too, has his chariot races, his castaways, his carnivals of blood in the arena. . . . But always he illuminates the nude and amazing event with shafts of light which reveal not only the last detail of its workings, but also the complex of origins and inducements behind it. Always, he throws about it a probability which, in the end, becomes almost inevitability. (p. 45)

But always it is the process of mind rather than the actual act that interests him. Always he is trying to penetrate the actor's mask and interpret the actor's frenzy. It is this concern with the profounder aspects of human nature, this bold grappling with the deeper and more recondite problems of his art, that gives him consideration as a first-rate artist. (p. 47)

This superiority is only the more vividly revealed by the

shop-worn shoddiness of most of his materials. He takes whatever is nearest to hand, out of his own rich experience or out of the common store of romance. He seems to disdain the petty advantages which go with the invention of novel plots, extravagant characters and unprecedented snarls of circumstance. (p. 48)

To this day there are marks of his origins in his style. His periods, more than once, have an inept and foreign smack. In fishing for the right phrase one sometimes feels that he finds a French phrase, or even a Polish phrase, and that it loses something by being done into English. (pp. 51-2)

There is a notion that judgments of living artists are impossible. They are bound to be corrupted, we are told, by prejudice, false perspective, mob emotion, error. The question whether this or that man is great or small is one which only posterity can answer. . . . We are not dead yet; we are here, and it is now. Therefore, let us at least venture, guess, opine.

My own conviction, sweeping all those reaches of living fiction that I know, is that Conrad's figure stands out from the field like the Alps from the Piedmont plain. He not only has no masters in the novel; he has scarcely a colourable peer. (pp. 61-2)

H. L. Mencken, "Joseph Conrad," in his A Book of Prefaces *(copyright 1917 by Alfred A. Knopf, Inc.; 1945 by H. L. Mencken; reprinted by permission of Alfred A. Knopf, Inc.), 3rd edition, Knopf, 1920 (and reprinted by Knopf, 1922), pp. 11-66.*

The quality of Mr. Conrad's art is seen in his faculty of making us perceive men's lives in their natural relation to the seen universe around them; his men are a part of the great world of nature, and the sea, land and sky around them are not drawn as a mere background, or as something inferior and secondary to the human will, as we have in most artists' work. [It is this] faculty of seeing man's life in relation to the seen and unseen forces of nature . . . that gives Mr. Conrad's art its extreme delicacy and its great breadth of vision. It is pre-eminently the poet's gift, and is very rarely conjoined with insight into human nature and power of conceiving character. . . . To reproduce life naturally, in its close fidelity to breathing nature, yet to interpret its significance, and to make us see the great universe around—art cannot go beyond this, except to introduce the illusion of inevitability. (pp. 87-8)

The critic, pressed for an explanation of Mr. Conrad's special power by which he accomplishes particular feats beyond his rivals', may boldly declare that he has a special poetic sense for *the psychology of scene,* by which the human drama before us is seen in its just relation to the whole enveloping drama of Nature around, forming both the immediate environment and the distant background. In Mr. Conrad's vision we may imagine Nature as a ceaselessly flowing river of life, out of which the tiny atom of each man's individual life emerges into sight, stands out in the surrounding atmosphere, and is lost again in the infinite succession of the fresh waves of life into which it dissolves. The author's pre-eminence does not lie specifically in his psychological analysis of character, but in the delicate relation of his characters to the whole environment—to the whole mirage of life in which their figures are seen to move. (pp. 93-4)

His method of poetic realism is, indeed, intimately akin to that of the great Russian novelists, but Mr. Conrad, often inferior in the psychology of character, has outstripped them in his magical power of creating the whole mirage of Nature. (p. 97)

Edward Garnett, "Mr. Joseph Conrad" (1921), in his Friday Nights: Literary Criticisms and Appreciations *(copyright 1922, 1950 by David Garnett; reprinted by permission of Alfred A. Knopf, Inc.), Knopf, 1922, pp. 83-101.*

There is nothing colloquial in Conrad; nothing intimate; and no humour, at least of the English kind. And those are great drawbacks for a novelist, you will admit. Then, of course, it goes without saying that he is a romantic. No one objects to that. But it entails a terrible penalty—death at the age of forty—death or disillusionment. If your romantic persists in living, he must face his disillusionment. He must make his music out of contrasts. But Conrad has never faced his disillusionment. He goes on singing the same songs about sea captains and the sea, beautiful, noble, and monotonous; but now I think with a crack in the flawless strain of his youth. It is a mind of one fact; and such a mind can never be among the classics. (pp. 77-8)

My theory is made of cobwebs, no doubt, . . . [but] of this I am certain. Conrad is not one and simple; no, he is many and complex. . . . And Mr. Conrad's selves are particularly opposite. He is composed of two people who have nothing whatever in common. He is your sea captain, simple, faithful, obscure; and he is Marlow, subtle, psychological, loquacious. In the early books the Captain dominates; in the later it is Marlow at least who does all the talking. The union of these two very different men makes for all sorts of queer effects. You must have noticed the sudden silences, the awkward collisions, the immense lethargy which threatens at every moment to descend. All this, I think, must be the result of that internal conflict. . . . In Conrad's novels personal relations are never final. Men are tested by their attitude to august abstractions. Are they faithful, are they honourable, are they courageous? The men he loves are reserved for death in the bosom of the sea. (pp. 78-9)

He sees once and he sees for ever. His books are full of moments of vision. They light up a whole character in a flash. . . . The beauty of surface has always a fibre of morality within. I seem to see each of the sentences . . . advancing with resolute bearing and a calm which they have won in strenuous conflict, against the forces of falsehood, sentimentality, and slovenliness. He could not write badly, one feels, to save his life. (p. 80)

[The ships] are more feminine than his women, who are either mountains of marble or the dreams of a charming boy over the photograph of an actress. But surely a great novel can be made out of a man and a ship, a man and a storm, a man and death and dishonour? (pp. 80-1)

Virginia Woolf, "Mr. Conrad: A Conversation" (1923), in her The Captain's Death Bed and Other Essays *(© 1950 by Harcourt, Brace and Company; reprinted by permission of Harcourt Brace Jovanovich, Inc.), Harcourt, 1950, pp. 76-81.*

There are three qualities which stand out in Mr. Conrad's

novels: the love of beauty, the insight into the mind, the sense of character. . . . The passions he has portrayed, it is true, but he has portrayed them preëminently in their effect upon the mind and upon character. In short, he has studied them under glass, and as a psychologist and a moralist. The soul he has not tried to know at all. The conflict in his novels is not the spiritual, but the moral, conflict. . . . Neither Mr. Conrad nor his characters mentions the name of God, and we feel it is because they would consider it insincere, even theatrical, to do so. (p. 48)

Mr. Conrad, then, is preëminently artist, psychologist and moralist; in other words, he is interested essentially in beauty, the mind, and character. And he is interested perhaps in beauty primarily. He writes by instinctive choice of beautiful things; of the sea, of ships, of tropical skies, and of men whose lives have still the atmosphere of romance around them—of seamen, of barbarians, of South American bandits whose minds have something of the naïve morality of the Renaissance. And he never writes, as Stevenson constantly wrote, with the design of being "romantic." His beauty is not stuck on. On the contrary, when he describes a scene it strikes us first by its astonishing truth and then by its astonishing beauty. (p. 49)

But when Mr. Conrad turns aside from his description of the beautiful, in which there is so much noble passion, he becomes at once the detached student of humanity. In his vision of nature a poet, he is in his investigation of the mind and the passions almost a scientist. To study passion, he might tell us, it is necessary above all to eschew passion. Certainly the passions he shows are sterilized passions—sterilized by his unique attitude to life. He is interested in life, but he does not love it; and in detaching himself as an artist entirely from life, his interest in it has actually become greater, has become interest and nothing else. (p. 51)

It is because [his characters] are not men and women (it is both a censure and a compliment to Mr. Conrad's art to say so); they are something much more definite than that: they are specimens of humanity, collected and docketed with incredible finesse. . . . Mr. Conrad's characters exist insulated by the resolve of the author to study them; they exist in a laboratory of psychology. (pp. 52-3)

The rationalist who peeps out of Mr. Conrad the psychologist, reveals himself completely in Mr. Conrad the moralist. In his ethics it is reason that is moral, and the irrational that is immoral. The moral conflict is therefore the conflict between man in so far as he is a rational creature, and nature as a thing, amoral and unknown. Nature against the conscious, the discovered, the ordered—that is to Mr. Conrad the real antinomy of existence. He gives the highest value, therefore, to the known, to the little in the ocean of the irrational which man has been able to wrest away and precariously to maintain. This alone is certainly good. The symbol of the immoral is always nature in one of her moods —sometimes the sea, sometimes the impulses in man's breast. . . .

Mr. Conrad's heroes are at once fortifying and discouraging; they fight, but they fight with their back to the wall. They have not the right to despair, however; for if they can not win, they may not be defeated! Their endeavor, of course, is not to advance and to conquer—that would appear to Mr. Conrad the most extreme romanticism—but to maintain one or two things without which they would

perish. And these are a few truisms. Man voyages over the devouring waste of existence on nothing more stable than a few concepts, a few platitudes.

This conception, so simple in appearance, is, in fact, extremely subtle. Only a profound mind could have given such fundamental meaning to platitude. It is the conception of a skeptic who is sure of one or two things; who accepts the minimum, who accepts platitude, indisputable platitude, because he is sure of nothing else. He has found two or three planks to put between him and the incommensurable, and that suffices him. And thus while he denies himself hope, as austerely he denies himself despair. (pp. 54-6)

> *Edwin Muir, "A Note on Mr. Conrad," in his* Latitudes *(copyright, 1924, by B. W. Huebsch., Inc.), Huebsch, 1924, pp. 47-56.*

[Conrad's] shortcomings [as a dramatist] were due, partly, to the almost insuperable difficulties of adaptation [his three plays, *One Day More, Laughing Anne,* and *The Secret Agent,* are all adaptations from stories] and, partly, to inadequate mastery of trick work which has to be learned. In other words, he had not given enough time to the dramatic form. He did not quite know how to balance his effects, how to economise his words, or how to keep his line of action clear and inevitable. (p. 181)

[One] is glad he didn't give time enough to play-writing. Those of us who remember that amazing cab drive in the novel—the gem passage in *The Secret Agent*—unrenderable on the stage, realise very well that his time was better concentrated on an unfettered fidelity to his moods in his unflinching scrutiny of men and things, on his power of painting in words, and on a psychological insight unsurpassed for depth and subtlety. (pp. 182-83)

> *John Galsworthy, "Preface to Conrad's Plays," in his* Castle in Spain and Other Screeds *(reprinted by permission of Charles Scribner's Sons; © 1927 by Charles Scribner's Sons), Scribner's, 1927, pp. 175-84.*

Conrad was the great experimentalist of his day. He was as ill content with ready-made ways of putting a story together as with ready-made ways of interpreting character. And he did more than any one else to limber up the stiff machine of fiction. (p. 332)

It is obvious that, while Conrad never formulated any rules, he was forever trying out new methods, hitting upon this or that new procedure, it may be, by instinct rather than by deliberation; but it was the instinct of a man profoundly concerned with method, forever on the lookout for some new way of cheating oblivion and saving his chosen art from the dry-rot of monotony and academicism. Given his temperament he could never be content with the neat little formula of the well-made novel, with its crystalline simplicity of logic and its steady rigor of method. Life must have seemed to him much too complex, much too vast and elusive a creature to be caught in any such net—and still more that illusion of life, which, rather than the thing itself, is what such writers are most concerned to capture and display. (pp. 337-38)

[His] subject-matter, interesting as it was on its own account, must have created difficulties not encountered by friends like Galsworthy and Bennett. . . . [It] was no mean task throwing the illusion of truth over subjects so strange and fantastic.

It is not merely that he used the subject-matter of romance, that he occupied and immensely enlarged the realm of Cooper, Stevenson, and Kipling. He was not content to work the traditional motives of chivalry, fealty, bravado, and revenge. Life was not so simple as that, nor so monotonous. His grotesque imagination fills his pages with monsters and vermin. . . . He loves to trace the slimy involutions of morbid psychology. And when it comes to his heroes, he loves to envelop them in a cloud of Slavic mysticism. (p. 339)

Of course Conrad hated the Russians on patriotic, on political grounds, and he was a decidedly political-minded man. He wanted to be identified, himself, with "Europe," and insisted that the true classification of Poland was with Europe and not with Slavic and Asiatic Russia. Again, he may have disliked in Dostoevski the specifically religious cast of his "mysticism." . . . [But he] certainly shared with Dostoevski a profound feeling of the mysteriousness, the almost transcendental character of human motives. This psychological cast is something as exotic as his subject-matter, and is another reason why he found so arduous the novelist's task of making his reader *see*.

Now, the most obvious means of making the reader see is simply the use of adequate words. And that Conrad most earnestly cultivated this means we have, what we hardly need, the testimony of Mr. Ford Madox Ford (then Hueffer), who collaborated with him in the writing of three novels, and that at a most critical time in Conrad's career. . . . Their notions of style were not identical, Conrad being inclined, Ford thought, to make his writing *trop chargé*. This was one thing Wells admired in Conrad, and he begged Ford not to collaborate with him for fear he should spoil his magnificent "Oriental style."

Conrad's Oriental style is one of the features for which he is most admired. But over and over again, especially in his earlier novels, before Ford came on the scene, one must feel that he would have profited by the critical spirit of the Englishman. Conrad had often the tendency to use too many words. It is as if in his search for the *mot juste* he tried out three or four or a dozen words, and then, instead of keeping the one which just suited his need, he kept them all. (pp. 340-41)

Conrad's emotion is too warm and turbulent to be confined within the dry dikes of the *mot juste*. Over and over again, when he broods upon man's destiny, his great heart, and the futile stir he makes upon the vast impassive face of Nature, he reaches heights of imaginative splendor which would be impossible to a more critical artist. (pp. 341-42)

[Conrad's] conception of human nature was one which made much of its mystery, its protean elusiveness. No one angle of vision would suffice to catch it in its completeness. . . . [His] problem was to secure the advantage of the many points of view without losing that of coherence. It was to make a real composite of these many pictures taken from so many diverse angles, to make a *synthesis* of material so disparate. And he solved that problem most successfully through the help of Captain Marlow.

This person he had created in the short story "Youth," and also used in "Heart of Darkness". . . . (p. 353)

The Oriental style, in [the] word-of-mouth narrative [that is *Lord Jim*], gives place largely to a natural, anecdotal man-

ner, the manner of one speaking with authority of things of which he knows, and yet—in such a strange story—striving for plausibility, striving to convert his audience to sympathy with his point of view, arguing with them over the character of his hero, producing evidence for his knowledge of this or that episode. All this gives to the narrative an amazing air of authenticity. . . . (p. 354)

[There is another] feature of Conrad's technique that is particularly favored by the use of Marlow as narrator. This is his apparently freakish and eccentric chronology. (p. 359)

[Conrad] had always shown a disposition to get his character in first with a strong impression and then work backward over his past before going on with the dramatic present which brought the story to its climax. (pp. 361-62)

The method . . . is the actual strategy of many an excellent raconteur. It is for this reason a system which gives naturalness to Marlow's narrative.

But the esthetic rationale goes much deeper. It is Conrad's sense of the elusiveness of human nature which leads him not merely to view his subject from so many angles and strain it through so many media, but also to keep moving his camera backward and forward in time so as constantly to get the subject into some new illuminating perspective. It is as if human nature were a rare and skittish bird which he must approach with every circumstance of precaution and which must by all means be taken by surprise. The method of James is to lay regular siege to Life; the method of Conrad is to lie in ambush for it.

Conrad's material in "Nostromo" . . .—character, incident, setting—is perhaps richer than that of any of his other books. In fact, it is much too rich even for a book of this size, the longest of his novels. . . . The chronological looping method is used throughout, with evident good intentions but with very dubious results. (pp. 363-64)

The book is of course a most striking example of what I have called the *deformalization* of the novel. And it was not labor altogether wasted. The "impressionistic" method outlined by Ford does go far to give life and naturalness to the story. But it must be acknowledged that Conrad here indulged in excesses of such impressionism. In "Victory" . . . he managed without Marlow, partly because he did have a center of interest. But the great triumphs of his technique are "Lord Jim" and "Chance," in which his impressionism was chastened and controlled by the use of the word-of-mouth narrator Marlow. (p. 365)

Joseph Warren Beach, in his The Twentieth Century Novel: Studies in Technique *(copyright, 1932, Prentice-Hall, Inc.; copyright, 1960 by Mrs. Dagmar Doneghy Beach; reprinted by permission of Prentice-Hall, Inc., Englewood Cliffs, New Jersey), Appleton-Century-Crofts, 1932.*

Conrad's revolutionaries are hardly lovable types; the psychology of his social rebels is strongly pessimistic in kind; and his scepticism of social utopias is revealed in the description of one insurgent of "an immense and nice hospital with a garden of flowers, in which the strong are to devote themselves to the nursing of the weak," whereas another, a miserable little terrorist and professor of dynamiting, dreams of quite another kind, a world like a slaughterhouse, whither the "weak" are carried to be extinguished.

But all this sarcasm is hardly bourgeois in intention. (pp. 241-42)

Disregard for art, for what constitutes the things of the mind, combined with boundless credulity and reverence for utilitarian science—that Conrad feels to be bourgeois. (p. 243)

In his judgment of the sexes he is objective: speaks of the sensitivity that can exist in the masculine nature alongside exasperating brutality; and finds that women are naturally more artful than men and much more ruthlessly avid for detail. So also he is aloof and critical in his attitude toward classes and masses, to all the apparent and temporary contradictions in the world. The sarcasm he directs against "hygienic idleness" as a form of existence is quite good socialism. . . . (p. 246)

Conrad's objectivity may seem cool; but is a passion—a passion for freedom. It is the expression of the very same love and passion that drove the young Pole to sea; and that —as once in the case of Ivan Tourgeniev—was doubtless the profoundest motive of his cultural relations with the West. This love of freedom cannot be confused with bourgeois liberalism, for he is an artist; and it is far too robust to be classed as aestheticism. The extent of Conrad's artistic success in Germany will be measured by his talent. His intellectual message will be for those among us who believe— in opposition to the views of the large majority—that the idea of freedom has a rôle to play in Europe that is not yet played out. (p. 247)

> *Thomas Mann, "Joseph Conrad's 'The Secret Agent'," in his* Past Masters and Other Papers, *translated by H. T. Lowe-Porter, Martin Secker, 1933 (and reprinted by Books For Libraries Press, 1968), pp. 231-47.*

The contribution of Conrad to the technique of the novel was his invention of narrating a story by means of two or three people who had had an opportunity of knowing the facts. This method became tiresome even in the hands of Conrad himself; in the hands of his imitators it became exasperating. Nor was there any real gain for actuality. The strain of a writer's apparent omniscience upon his reader's credulity is certainly great when readers begin to question his Olympian status; but the method which offered the reader an explanation of how the writer came to know certain facts about people in his tale imposed an equal strain, for the reader could not help asking how any listener could have had the physical endurance to remain silent while such a figure as Marlow prosed on for hours, that unending and remorseless old man of the sea, as Henry James called him once to myself. The reason why Conrad adopted this device was probably less out of any desire to improve the technique of the novel than out of an anxiety to conceal his own inability to write English dialogue. Conrad was for ever proclaiming his hatred of dialogue in a novel, and in conversation he was himself always dependent on French, which should have made his disciples suspect the disinterestedness of his criticism of English dialogue. (pp. 170-71)

Not a little of Conrad's merit as a novelist is due to the means he took to surmount the handicap of writing in an acquired language. Paradoxically, the difficulty of finding the right word secured him a vocabulary larger than that of most contemporary English novelists, and this wide vocabulary gave his prose a richness which made it seem better prose than it really was. (p. 172)

It is perhaps not a fair charge to level against Conrad that his tales of the sea can only be read by landsmen; but it does suggest ground for criticism, and that this should be so does suggest a doubt of the permanence of his reputation. In asserting that his tales cannot be read by his fellow-seamen I should except *The Nigger of the Narcissus,* and it is significant that *The Nigger of the Narcissus* was one of his earliest books, written before he had settled down to become something of a "literary gent." It may not be equally significant, because it is the expression of a merely personal opinion, when I say that of all Conrad's books, that which in retrospect comes back to me most vividly is *The Secret Agent,* for that is one of the few books in which the sea plays no part. *Lord Jim,* to which I suppose most people would give the palm, has always seemed to me a great short story ruined by protracted spasms of wearisome psychology.

My prejudice may be due to a surfeit of critical eulogy which was not inspired by a genuine appreciation of Conrad, but prompted by a belief that to praise Conrad reflected the critic's own good taste. Conrad always appealed to that English delight in the art which does not conceal itself. . . . Possibly, too, I am prejudiced by the enthusiasm which Conrad roused in the United States. . . . Probably the Germans are the most readily deceived by the *faux bon* in literature; but after the Germans the Americans are the most gullible. (pp. 173-74)

> *Compton Mackenzie, "Joseph Conrad," in his* Literature in My Time, *Rich & Cowan Ltd., 1934 (and reprinted by Books for Libraries Press, Inc., 1967), pp. 168-74.*

Nostromo was the first book of Conrad's to be built or manufactured. For the first time he departed from the imaginative reconstruction of lives and episodes drawn from the fibre of his own experience. He invented a whole milieu. From a single paragraph in a book of reminiscence he derived the hint for a tale involving many lives, and he planned this with the most profound seriousness and wrote it with scrupulous care. Unquestionably the result was a disappointment to him, for *Nostromo,* however highly praised, was a failure with the public and always remained a comparative failure. I think I can understand why. The book is very elaborate; it is as rich as can be in comprehensions and in diverse characters; but its movement is extremely slow, the detail of its intrigue is not always intelligible; and it does not quite escape dullness. In vain does one dwell upon its qualities; the truth is that in place of that concentrated intensity of imagining which gives Conrad's finest work its thrilling dramatic force there is a generalized interest which the reader admires only at the bidding of his sense of literary duty. He knows that he should admire whatever is very difficult or very elaborate, whatever has cost the writer great pains or great ingenuity, and he admires most manfully, the more so as he is consicous that if the book were not so good he would yawn his head off. But since "Nostromo has never been intended for the hero of the tale of the Seaboard" and "Silver is the pivot of the moral and material events, affecting the lives of everybody in the tale," it is perhaps allowable to say that for once Conrad forgot that motto of his, to the effect that "Something human is dearer to me than the wealth of all the world," and paid accordingly for his forgetfulness. (pp. 149-50)

Conrad objected to the general belief that he was a writer of sea stories. He said: "It seems to me that people imagine I sit here and brood over sea stuff. That is quite a mistake. I brood certainly, but. . . ." He regarded himself as a psychologist. "I insist not on the events but on their effect upon the persons in the tale." . . . As he grew older he sought for greater subtlety and for finer shades, but his true gift was for the reproduction of scene and atmosphere, not for analysis. (p. 154)

> *Frank Swinnerton, in his* The Georgian Scene: A Literary Panorama *(copyright 1934 © 1962 by Frank Swinnerton; reprinted by permission of Holt, Rinehart and Winston, Publishers), Farrar & Rinehart, 1934.*

It is, singularly enough, *The Secret Agent* that most affects me when, ten years after the death of Joseph Conrad, I sit in New York and read his works. . . . Should this come to be the final verdict on the work of that great and romantic poet, it would singularly appease his poor ghost. For he never tired of protesting that he was not a writer about the sea; he detested the sea as a man detests a cast-off mistress, and with the hatred of a small man who has had, on freezing nights of gales, to wrestle with immense yards and dripping cordage; his passion became to live out of sight of the sea and all its memories. . . . (p. 57)

It was a curious and wanton nemesis. For many years of his life almost all the English whom Conrad met were men connected with the sea. And, with his highly developed sense of nationalities, Conrad was almost superaware of the immense part that the sea has played in the history of the English race—of the Anglo-Saxon congeries of nations. (p. 58)

[Ironically, though,] while he was still under the spell of sea-following and the hypnotism of mariners, he did his best and, as it were, cleanest work. For I think it is to *Youth, Heart of Darkness,* and the matchless *Nigger of the Narcissus* that those epithets must be ascribed, leaving *Almayer* and *The Outpost of Progress* to be considered as his prentice work. (p. 61)

The sea has two disadvantages as pabulum for the writer. Seen from the shore it cuts your horizon in half. If you write about human voyages upon it, your work will inevitably be set down as boys' books. (p. 64)

Conrad . . . left women, for a great part of his writing career, altogether out of his books and supplied their place with the epicene great waters, attributing to them all the passions and pretty ways of he-male rages and feminine coquetries.

But, as he left the hated sea further and further behind him, women and non-seafarers came more and more into his books—and political intrigues and the careers of republics entered more and more largely. *Nostromo,* an immense book, the first that he evolved after he had definitely left the sea far behind, is the first of his political romances—and the one he loved best. It retained, still, some of his early quality of gusto. To give it a frame, he must needs invent a whole human cosmogony—a whole republic, with a governing machine, a constitution, intrigues, commerce, industry, graft . . . and a gallery of women from Mrs. Gould downward.

And, as he went onward, women became of more and more importance in his political romances—and it was more and more the political romance that occupied his mind. *The Secret Agent* is the romance of international communism, with Mrs. Verloc as its *dea ex machina*; *The Arrow of Gold* is the romance of royalist machinations, with the Rita of his first love dominating its every sentence; *Under Western Eyes* is the romance of Russian-Swiss nihilism, over which floats continuously, as mists float above a city, the serene and beautiful spirit of Miss Haldin. (pp. 64-5)

Conrad was, at heart, an aristo-royalist apologist; the whole Left in politics was forever temperamentally suspect for him, and, at the bottom of his heart, all his writing wistfully tended towards the restoration of the Kingdom of Poland, with its irresponsible hierachy of reckless and hypersophistically civilized nobility. He saw in nothing else the salvation of mankind. . . . But he was a poet even before he was a Polack *pan*. . . . In any case he was a great poet and a great novelist. I imagine that few men have had much more power to see vividly the opposing sides of human characters. (pp. 65-6)

> *Ford Madox Ford, "Conrad and the Sea," in his* Portraits from Life *(copyright © 1936 and 1937 by Ford Madox Ford; 1965 by Janice Alaine; reprinted by permission of Houghton Mifflin Company), Houghton, 1937 (and reprinted by Greenwood Press, 1974), pp. 58-77.*

The crisis in almost every one of Conrad's novels—many of which form a prolonged and exhaustive analysis or sublimation of crisis—arrives when, by a stroke of accident, or by an act of decision or error rising from the secret necessities of temperament, a man finds himself abruptly committed to his destiny. It is a commitment to which all men of morally significant quality are bound. It is the test and opportunity of fundamental selfhood, and there is no escape from it. (p. 68)

It is this drama of alienation and spiritual recognition which appears in the characteristic novels of Mann, Gide, and Kafka, in Robinson's poems, in Joyce and Hemingway. . . . One of its latest appearances is in the novels of the French existentialists. . . . But it is doubtful if any of these writers has achieved a more successful *dramatic* version of the problem than Conrad did—a more complete coincidence of the processes of psychic recognition and recovery with the dramatic necessities of the plot; and this for a reason which distinguishes Conrad's contribution to modern fictional method: his imposition of the processes of psychological experience, notably the experience of recognition, on the structure of the plot.

The conditions that mark the plight of a Conrad character who is caught in the grip of circumstances that enforce self-discovery and its cognate, the discovery of reality or truth, are remarkably consistent in his books. The condition of moral solitude is the first of them. (pp. 75-6)

But if isolation is the first condition of these lives, it is never an isolation that brings independence or liberty. Freed by choice from normal human ties and obligations, Conrad's men find themselves in the inescapable presence of conscience. (p. 76)

It is here that Conrad's work enters a dimension which is

ostensibly psychological and which, for purposes of drama and characterization, must appear validly so. But it goes farther. It encounters the problem of appearance and reality, of bringing into single focus the processes of subjective intuition and the conditions of social and moral necessity—the values of egotism and those of ethical fact. It may treat these in terms of the relativity of appearances and sentiments as Proust defined it, but it will also insist on relating the psychic and moral ambiguity of human nature to the ambivalence of reality as art embodies and struggles with it, and finally to the metaphysical condition of value itself. When Conrad enters that dimension fully he leaves his sentimental limitations and prejudices behind him and takes his place as one of the authentic creative imaginations of our time—one who certainly outdistances the other English novelists of his generation.

The order of art to which Conrad addressed himself, less apparently by conscious intention than by instinct and personal necessity, is one that has become paramount in the literature of the Twentieth Century. The ambiguity of truth, the conflict of appearance and reality, the rival claims of the secret and the social self—these are now integral to modern fiction in its major manifestations, whether in Proust or Mann, James or Kafka, Gide or Sartre. They arrive at something like the condition of paradigm in Pirandello's *Six Characters in Search of an Author*. (pp. 77-8)

It is not only art that is at odds with life; it is human comprehension itself. But the question insists: can life ever do justice to its own reality? Are suffering, agony, tragedy comprehensible in their own condition? Is it possible for them to achieve comprehension until consciousness, moral sympathy, or art intervene to interpret and define them? Can man, or life, be said to exist in terms of significance until these modes of definition and justice succeed in embodying them? The dilemma, driven to the extreme lengths of suspense and contradiction, ends finally in enigma and fiasco. The question remains unresolved. It collapses under the test of resolution. Conrad's problem in *Lord Jim* was this same problem. There too, in spite of driving Jim's fate to the logic of catastrophe, the question of the reality of his moral identity ends in enigma. But the problem of resolving it had become an obsession with Conrad. It taxed him continuously to the end of his life. At times he resorted to desperate measures of heroism, suicide, or moral compromise to resolve it; sometimes he fell back on the arbitrary formulas of ethical duplicity of stoicism. But it remained to the end the essential theme and animus of his drama. (pp. 78-9)

"The Secret Sharer," as Miss M. C. Bradbrook has pointed out, is the microcosm of the basic concept in Conrad's fiction.... From this germinal presentation of the case Conrad's drama of the self widens until, in his most ambitious books, it comes to include the larger workings of that law in society and politics, even in the destiny of nations and of races. The growth in his thought from an idealistic conception of life to a critical one, from his temperamental romanticism to his later realism of values, is the drama of his genius in its difficult emergence, its strenuous self-discipline, and its eventual successes. That growth appears most typically in the three novels that show his dramatic method most explicitly—*Lord Jim, Under Western Eyes,* and *Chance,* but it is extended to more sheerly creative feats of dramatization in three other books —*Nostromo,* his most complex historical and political

drama, a comprehensive matrix of his moral and ethical sensibility, resonant of a profoundly riddled debate of moralities and creeds of conduct; *The Secret Agent,* his highest achievement in tragic irony; and *Victory,* his most concentrated symbolic narrative. (pp. 81-2)

> *Morton Dauwen Zabel, "Chance and Recognition" (1945), in his* Craft and Character in Modern Fiction *(copyright © 1957 by Morton Dauwen Zabel; reprinted by permission of The Viking Press, Inc.), Viking, 1957 (and reprinted in* Modern British Fiction, *edited by Mark Schorer, Oxford University Press, 1961, pp. 65-83).*

I have been reading some of the Malayan novels again, after a lapse of twenty years—books like *Almayer's Folly, The Outcast of the Island, The Rescue, Lord Jim* and shorter pieces like *Youth, The Secret Sharer* and *Freya of the Seven Isles.* What struck me was how vague and even falsified these books were in my memory. The atmosphere one remembered, of course. But even stories like *Almayer's Folly* were muddled in my mind like the memory of a dream. They *are* dreams, these books. Their color, their unreal major characters, their insectile minor ones, their tortuous action, live in the compelled twilight of a hypnotic dream, a dream that slows down to the intense heat of nightmare. Here and there the temperature becomes colder and, as in the yacht episode of *The Rescue,* you touch that *Tatler*-like actuality of the Maugham subject, but it is only for a moment. The half-light comes down, the shadow and the sun-shot fog of Conrad's ruminations cloud the obvious issue, and the dream thickens in the head. Afterwards it will be difficult to say once more what *was* the issue Conrad had in his tentative, evasive, suspicious and rather exasperated imagination. (pp. 143-44)

[Though] Destiny is a laconic conception, it is one which encourages wordiness in novelists; and the reader of Conrad feels a baffled irritation, as if he were a commercial traveler getting heavy admonitions every day from an importunate head office. One ought not to feel like this, and I am convinced that one would not do so in Conrad if one felt that Conrad's Destiny was endowed with the sublime and indispensable gift of inevitability. Conrad's Destiny seems to be an idea poisoned by exile, dwarfed by a bad temper and embittered by a failure to meet great men worth destroying. To [his characters], Destiny can only be nasty, as the police are nasty to tramps.

The valuable side of Conrad's conception of Destiny is that it is a sense of history—a sense of history which the Slavonic imagination has made theatrical. (p. 145)

It has been said that Conrad does not draw the Malay as he really is, and that his Malays are idealizations. They are really transplantations from Polish history. They are an exile's interpretation of the bloody history of the islands, and of the historical situation at the time he was writing. And knowing the situation, he knows the intrigue—how it is something which goes far deeper than human idiosyncrasy and private jealousy or ambition, but is the ferment of a defeated society itself.... [When his gift for handling intrigue in his novels] turned from society to psychology, that is to say, to a man's intrigue with himself, as in *Lord Jim,* then Conrad is less successful. (pp. 145-46)

As Conrad exhausted his early material, his imagination

naturally turned to improvization. He who had been . . . an historical novelist, now became a prophetic one. What is a prophetic novelist? He is hard to define, but I should say he is one to whom human beings are timeless; they are souls and not persons, and good and evil and fate fight for the possession of their future. This element had always been in Conrad's work and gave his realism the distorting stamp of a spiritual vision. But, on the whole, in England we reject the prophets; it is so obvious that they are disappointed men. . . . [His] problems are esoteric. *Lord Jim* was not a good man gone wrong, but, like the outcast, a compulsive neurotic. The charge of morbidity originally brought against Conrad must be sustained; his morbidity was in fact the irritant which created the Conrad fog.

The excellencies of Conrad do not lie, in my opinion, in that dubious Romantic over-world, but in his real observation, in his feeling for real life. (pp. 146-47)

The genius of Conrad was directed to intensifying the life of a man or a woman and to contrasting that intensity with the slacker, ragged commentary of their real circumstances. His characters live on the edge of a great anxiety, an unbearable exasperation, a threatened loss. They are faced by the sardonic refusal of life to play up. (p. 148)

> *V. S. Pritchett, "A Pole in the Far East," in his* The Living Novel *(copyright, 1947, 1975 by V. S. Pritchett; reprinted by permission of Harold Matson Co., Inc.), Reynal & Hitchcock, 1947, pp. 143-48.*

The great English novelists are Jane Austen, George Eliot, Henry James and Joseph Conrad . . . [later in his introduction to the "great tradition" Leavis adds D. H. Lawrence to complete his list of five great English novelists], major novelists who count in the same way as the major poets, in the sense that they not only change the possibilities of the art for practitioners and readers, but that they are significant in terms of the human awareness they promote; awareness of the possibilities of life. (pp. 1-2)

There is a habit nowadays of suggesting that there is a tradition of 'the English Novel,' and that all that can be said of the tradition (that being its peculiarity) is that 'the English Novel' can be anything you like. To distinguish the major novelists in the spirit proposed is to form a more useful idea of tradition. . . . It is in terms of the major novelists, those significant in the way suggested, that tradition, in any serious sense, has its significance. (p. 3)

When we come to Conrad we can't, by way of insisting that he is indeed significantly 'in' the tradition—in and of it, neatly and conclusively relate him to any one English novelist. Rather, we have to stress his foreignness—that he was a Pole, whose first other language was French. . . . Conrad's themes and interests demanded the concreteness and action—the dramatic energy—of English. (p. 17)

Conrad's great novels, if they deal with the sea at all, deal with it only incidentally. But the Merchant Service is for him both a spiritual fact and a spiritual symbol, and the interests that made it so for him control and animate his art everywhere. Here, then, we have a master of the English language, who chose it for its distinctive qualities and because of the moral tradition associated with it, and whose concern for art—he being like Jane Austen and George Eliot and Henry James an innovator in 'form' and method

—is the servant of a profoundly serious interest in life. . . . Like James, he brought a great deal from outside, but it was of the utmost importance to him that he found a serious art of fiction there in English, and that there *were,* in English, great novelists to study. (p. 18)

As being technically sophisticated he may be supposed to have found fortifying stimulus in James. . . . But actually, the one influence at all obvious is that of a writer at the other end of the scale from sophistication, Dickens. . . . Conrad is in certain respects so like Dickens that it is difficult to say for just how much influence Dickens counts. . . . This co-presence of obvious influence with assimilation [of what he needed from English literature] suggests that Dickens may have counted for more in Conrad's mature art . . . than seems at first probable: it suggests that Dickens may have encouraged the development in Conrad's art of that extraordinary energy of vision and registration in which they are akin. . . . We may reasonably, too, in the same way see some Dickensian influence, closely related and of the same order, in Conrad's use of melodrama, or what would have been melodrama in Dickens; for in Conrad the end is a total significance of a profoundly serious kind. (pp. 18-19)

[The] major quality [of Conrad is that] he is one of those creative geniuses whose distinction is manifested in their being peculiarly alive in their time—peculiarly alive *to* it; not 'in the vanguard' in the manner of Shaw and Wells and Aldous Huxley, but sensitive to the stresses of the changing spiritual climate as they begin to be registered by the most conscious. His interest in the tradition of the Merchant Service as a constructive triumph of the human spirit is correlative with his intense consciousness of the dependence, not only of the distinctive humanities at all levels, but of sanity itself and our sense of a normal outer world, on an analogous creative collaboration. His Robinson Crusoe cannot bear a few days alone on his island, and blows out his brains. (pp. 21-2)

> *F. R. Leavis, in his* The Great Tradition *(reprinted by permission of Chatto and Windus, Ltd.), George W. Stewart, 1948.*

There is no reason to suppose that [Conrad] found the English braver or more honourable than his own countrymen; but he will have found them gentler in the expression of their virility and more inclined to make light of the grimmer sides of personal experience. . . .

The nineteenth-century English gentleman is a mysterious figure; and here Conrad was admirably placed, by the nature of his temperament and imagination, to grasp the outline and significance of a type which reaches back, beyond Corneille, to the ideals of fifteenth-century Spain. Love, Duty: in the widest acceptance of these two words are contained the conflict and resolution within a view of life which needs nothing else for its fulfilment. Such a system is only by accident associated with Christian belief; essentially it is Stoic. . . . It is a conception in which Silence plays an important role, analogous to the gigantic rests in Beethoven's musical style: silence which is not mere void but a form of transition. . . . In his masterly variations on this ghostly passacaglia Joseph Conrad shows himself the last of the great nineteenth-century novelists. . . . For all [his] elaborate articulateness, [he places] the highest value—the most brilliant accent—on the peak of silence. In a sense [his] plots are so constructed as to lead up to it. . . .

On a spiritually lower level, but of correspondingly higher dramatic tension, is the silence of suspense of which Conrad is so fond. (pp. 72-3)

An acute sense of the human mystery, which has landed many novelists of to-day in despair and contempt of life, led Conrad to a high opinion of men and women. His disgust when they betrayed the standard he expected of them was incompatible with resignation to human frailty. As a novelist he was no less intransigent; when the creatures of his imagination fail to rise to his occasions, then the nervous exasperation, which was so striking a feature of his own personality, shows itself in bursts of violent disdain. This cavalier treatment is responsible for much that is bad in his high-toned novels.... The sense of romance (the feature of his work which seems to 'date' most strongly just now) gave Conrad his preference for melodramatic plots, unaccompanied by any love of telling a story for its own sake. He has left it on record that in his opinion the point of the universe is probably spectacular. Such a view is perfectly consistent with a strong sense of man's responsibility to develop his powers to the utmost....

That Conrad was an efficient sea captain there is no reason to doubt; hidden in the depths of his reserve were the anguish and the self-distrust which visit all men who are responsible for the lives of others, and supremely, perhaps, in that great symbol of life, the sailing ship. (pp. 74-5)

The weaknesses that great men successfully overcome tell us more about them than the façade they present to the world. To dramatise these frailties becomes their most cherished ambition. In Conrad's case the moment of silence could have been filled only in this manner. (p. 76)

> *Edward Sackville-West, "The Moment of Silence," in his* Inclinations, *Secker & Warburg, 1949, pp. 72-7.*

Nostromo is central for Conrad's work. When *Nostromo* appeared in 1904, . . . the world of Conrad's imagination already had exhibited its characteristic persons and issues.... The characteristic themes and situations and persons had emerged, but had emerged piecemeal, though in *Lord Jim* and "Heart of Darkness" Conrad had begun to move toward the massive synthesis and complex interfusion which was to engage him in *Nostromo*. As the earlier fiction seems to move toward *Nostromo,* so the later fiction seems to represent, by and large, specializations and elaborations of elements that had been in suspension in that work.

To take some examples, Dr. Monygham is an older and more twisted Lord Jim, the man who had failed the test, not like Jim by abandoning his post and breaking the code of the sea, but by betraying friends under the torture of a South American dictator. His personal story, like the story of Jim, is the attempt to restore himself to the human community and to himself, though he, unlike Jim, survives the attempt. (pp. 34-5)

Gould himself is a kind of cousin of Kurtz of "Heart of Darkness," though Gould is doomed to his isolation, not like Kurtz by avarice, vanity, and violence, by refusing his mission as a light-bringer, by repudiating the idea, but accepting his mission as light-bringer and bearer of the idea.... Kurtz betrays his Intended to the Heart of Darkness, so Gould betrays his wife to what he takes to be the Heart of Light. (pp. 35-6)

Without too much wrenching we may take Nostromo's significance as a parallel to that of Captain Brierly in *Lord Jim*. (p. 37)

But we cannot speak of the characters as such, for Conrad, in one sense, had little concern for character independently considered. He is no Dickens or Shakespeare, with relish for the mere variety and richness of personality. Rather, for him a character lives in terms of its typical involvement with situation and theme: the fable, the fable as symbol for exfoliating theme, is his central fact. (p. 39)

Fidelity and the job sense make for the human community, the solidarity in which Conrad finds his final values, "the solidarity of all mankind in simple ideas and sincere emotions." It is through the realization of this community that man cures himself of that "feeling of life-emptiness".... (p. 40)

The characteristic story for Conrad becomes, then, the relation of man to the human communion. The story may be one of three types: the story of the MacWhirr or the Don Pépé or the Captain Mitchell, the man who lacks imagination and cannot see the "true horror behind the appalling face of things," and who can cling to fidelity and the job; the story of the Kurtz or Decoud, the sinner against human solidarity and the human mission; the story of the redemption, of Lord Jim, Heyst, Dr. Monygham, Flora de Barral, Captain Anthony, Razumov.

The first type of story scarcely engages Conrad.... We may almost say that [the] significance [of the simple men] is in their being, not in their doing, that they have, properly speaking, no "story"; they are the static image of the condition which men who are real and who have real "stories" may achieve by accepting the logic of experience, but which, when earned, has a dynamic value the innocent never know. The man who has been saved may reach the moment of fulfillment when he can spontaneously meet the demands of fidelity, but his spontaneity must have been earned, and only by the fact of its having been earned is it, at last, significant. Therefore, it is the last type of story that engages Conrad most fully, the effort of the alienated, whatever the cause of his alienation, crime or weakness or accident or the "mystic wound," to enter again the human communion. And the crisis of this story comes when the hero recognizes the terms on which he may be saved, the moment, to take Morton Zabel's phrase, of the "terror of the awakening." (pp. 40-1)

Conrad's skepticism is ultimately but a "reasonable" recognition of the fact that man is a natural creature who can rest on no revealed values and can look forward to neither individual immortality nor racial survival. But reason, in this sense, is the denial of life and energy, for against all reason man insists, as man, on creating and trying to live by certain values. These values are, to use Conrad's word, "illusions," but the last wisdom is for man to realize that though his values are illusions, the illusion is necessary, is infinitely precious, is the mark of his human achievement, and is, in the end, his only truth.

From this notion springs the motif of the "true lie," as we may term it, which appears several times in Conrad's fiction. (p. 45)

[His] work itself is at center dramatic: it is about the cost of awareness and the difficulty of virtue, and his characteristic story is the story of struggle and, sometimes, of redemption. (p.48)

In [*Nostromo*] Conrad endeavored to create a great, massive, multiphase symbol that would render his total vision of the world, his sense of individual destiny, his sense of man's place in nature, his sense of history and society.

First, *Nostromo* is a complex of personal stories, intimately interfused, a chromatic scale of attitudes, a study in the definition and necessity of "illusion" as Conrad freighted that word. Each character lives by his necessary idealization, up the scale from the "natural" man Nostromo, whose only idealization is that primitive one of his vanity, to Emilia Gould, who, more than any other, has purged the self and entered the human community.

The personal stories are related not only in the contact of person and person in plot and as carriers of variations of the theme of illusion, but also in reference to the social and historical theme. That is, each character is also a carrier of an attitude toward, a point of view about, society; and each is an actor in a crucial historical moment. This historical moment is presumably intended to embody the main issues of Conrad's time: capitalism, imperialism, revolution, social justice. (pp. 48-9)

If in *A Personal Record* Conrad declares himself an "imperfect Esthete," in the same sentence he admits that he is "no better philosopher." Leavis goes so far as to affirm that Conrad cannot be said to have a philosophy: "He is not one of those writers who clear up their fundamental attitudes for themselves in such a way that we may reasonably, in talking of them, use that portentous term." . . . [In] my judgment Leavis takes Conrad's work as too much a casual matter of temperament. For I think that even if Conrad is as "imperfect" philosopher as esthete, he is still, in the fullest sense of the term, a philosophical novelist. (pp. 57-8)

> *Robert Penn Warren, "'The Great Mirage': Conrad and 'Nostromo'" (1951), in his* Selected Essays *(copyright © 1958; by Robert Penn Warren; reprinted by permission of Random House, Inc.), Random House, 1958, pp. 31-58.*

[Conrad] was no Art-for-Arter, this artist who, incredibly, wrote his books in a foreign language which he learned as an adult, and wrestled with his novels in a way reminiscent of Flaubert, the novelist whom he most admired. And by "moral discovery" he did not mean merely the illustration of some preconceived moral truth. It was in the creation of the work of art that the discovery was made. This seems to me very important. The very act of artistic creation, that moulding into significant form of some thing or part of life, is in itself a discovery about the nature of life and ultimately its value will lie in the value of that discovery. . . . The explanation undoubtedly lies in this word "discovery." It was in his artistic grappling with life, not in his logical thinking about it, that Conrad delved deepest and with best result. (p. 68)

[He had] no creed, but an unflinching respect for facts, the facts of the world he lived in. The moral discoveries are always based on facts.

The most important fact of all to Conrad is the social nature of man. It is a fact (or, if you will, an opinion based on fact)

which permeates his books and informs, not least, that hard and "jewelled" style, generally so concrete in its imagery, so controlled in its movement. (p. 69)

As he grew older the moral discoveries he drew from his art became rather more fully rationalized. His hatred of financial speculation (what he calls "material interests") may be an opinion rather than a creed, but it is an opinion which permeates several of the later novels. . . . I wish merely to emphasize that Conrad's concern with imperialism is no chance interest but is central to his whole work which is the presentation through his art of man as a social being. (p. 70)

Nostromo is, from the technical point of view, an amazing *tour de force*. The method Conrad uses is of particular interest because his problems are the characteristic problems of the modern novelist—to present a wide canvas in which essentials are not lost in too great detail; to convey political and social movement on various levels (conscious, unconscious, semi-conscious); to suggest the almost infinite interrelatedness of character and character, character and background; to give each character a real individuality and yet see each as part of a concrete whole: in short, to show men in society. Conrad's method is to over-simplify somewhat individual character in the sense of giving each individual very sharply-defined personal characteristics, frequently reiterated, so that each stands out clearly, not only in contrast to the others, but against the clear, concrete, surface-objective background of the whole. (p. 71)

Conrad succeeds moreover in the immensely difficult task of conveying the inter-relation between the individual and society, the one and the many. The people in *Nostromo* are what they are because they are part and parcel of a social situation; and at the same time they change and modify the situation. You cannot abstract them from the situation or the situation from them. (p.75)

The difference between the treatment of the dispossessed in *Nostromo* and in the contemporary novels and plays of pessimistic neurosis is that Conrad sees their problem not as a symbol of life itself but only as a part of life. That he shares to a degree their despair is true and he expresses that despair most powerfully. . . . But though the theme is so poignantly done it retains the status of a theme, overtopped by the prevailing vitality, the sense of life developing.

Conrad succeeds in fact in the enormously difficult task (which has defeated more 'politically-conscious' writers since) of revealing imaginatively that "every man is a piece of the continent, a part of the main," and his triumph is the more remarkable because in his personal outlook he would seem to have been far from clarity. (p. 77)

Conrad . . . has no conscious, intellectualized solution for the problems of the society which in *Nostromo* he depicts with so much truth and insight. And indeed it is foolish to talk glibly of the 'solution' offered by a work of art; the experience of the work of art is in itself a kind of solution, a synthesis, a discovery of the nature of the problem. (pp. 80-1)

> *Arnold Kettle, in his* An Introduction to the English Novel, *Vol. II edited by Basil Willey, Hutchinson's University Library, 1953.*

Isolation and conscience are the dominant motifs in the novels of Joseph Conrad and, two of them especially, *The*

Secret Agent and *Under Western Eyes*, become more and more suggestive to the contemporary reader. They attract because they are free from that sudden fogginess, that enlarged bad temper which Conrad called Destiny, and from the melodrama or rhetoric, which play tricks with the lighting and climate of many of his ambitious works. They have the compactness, the efficiency of that peculiarly modern form of writing, the thriller with a bitter moral flavour. (p. 216)

Conrad is a reactionary; for him the old despotism and the new Utopianism are complementary forms of moral anarchy. Their end is cynicism, more despotism, more destruction and to that opinion some have now reluctantly come. But Conrad was a fixed reactionary; he had never tried to tack across the revolutionary tide; he hated the Russian revolution as a Pole who was already a generation away from the hatred of his time; his hatred was glued into the past. The positive contribution of his political views is that they double the precision of our dilemmas of conscience by presenting them in reverse. (p. 217)

Conrad himself found a strong if not lasting interest in the order and discipline of life at sea, and his scorn is softened in *Under Western Eyes* by the attempt of one kind of Slav to understand another. In *The Secret Agent* there is no such emotional entanglement; his scorn, unrestrained, now becomes almost overpoweringly rich and pungent and his irony leaves nothing standing. (p. 219)

Conrad's genius was for picturesque discussion rather than for narrative—he was tortured, one is told, by the difficulties of invention—and what always impresses is his rummaging about, back and forth, in the lives of his characters. (p. 220)

Conrad, the exile, the isolated man, was the master of any atmosphere. That gift comes at once to the sensibility of the emigré. Like the French novelists, like Meredith and Henry James, he moves in narrative from idea to idea, to the change in moral climate rather than from event to event. . . . Conrad's novels are marked by . . . crucial sentences, which change a whole view of life, and his dramas are the dramas of the change of view. (p. 221)

> *V. S. Pritchett, "An Emigré," in his* Books in General *(© 1953 by V. S. Pritchett; reprinted in the U.S. by permission of Harold Matson Co., Inc., and in Canada by permission of A. D. Peters & Co.), Chatto and Windus, 1953, pp. 216-22.*

[Conrad] was, as anyone may see from his books, a very rigid moralist and politically far from sympathetic with revolutionaries. (p. 86)

Of all that he had written I admired most the terrible story called *The Heart of Darkness*, in which a rather weak idealist is driven mad by horror of the tropical forest and loneliness among savages. This story expresses, I think, most completely his philosophy of life. I felt, though I do not know whether he would have accepted such an image, that he thought of civilized and morally tolerable human life as a dangerous walk on a thin crust of barely cooled lava which at any moment might break and let the unwary sink into fiery depths. He was very conscious of the various forms of passionate madness to which men are prone, and it was this that gave him such a profound belief in the importance of discipline. (p. 87)

The two things that seem most to occupy Conrad's imagination are loneliness and fear of what is strange. (p. 88)

Conrad's point of view was far from modern. In the modern world there are two philosophies: the one, which stems from Rousseau, and sweeps aside discipline as unnecessary; the other, which finds its fullest expression in totalitarianism, which thinks of discipline as essentially imposed from without. Conrad adhered to the older tradition, that discipline should come from within. He despised indiscipline, and hated discipline that was merely external. (p. 89)

> *Bertrand Russell, "Joseph Conrad," in his* Portraits from Memory and Other Essays *(copyright © 1951, 1952, 1953, 1956 by Bertrand Russell; reprinted by permission of Simon & Schuster, Inc.), Simon & Schuster, 1956, pp. 86-91.*

Conrad is an English writer and the Poles have never tried to assimilate him into their literature. (p. 41)

[But certain] themes, and even the rhythms of certain passages in his novels, are reminiscent of [Polish] verse lines. . . . What happened in Conrad was a perfect fusing of two literatures and two civilizations. (pp. 41-2)

[But as] we go more deeply into the biographical materials we come to the conclusion that a carefully hidden complex of treason is discernible in some of his writings—a feeling that he had betrayed the cause so fanatically embraced by his compatriots and, above all, by his father.

Literature in Poland and Russia—and this is one of the rare features of similarity between these two dissimilar countries —has traditionally been viewed in a way differing from that of Western Europe. There it is conceived of as an arm in the struggle for the community good. Conrad did not believe in the future of his country and this provided him with a self-justification. But no amount of self-justification [could] insulate [him] from doubts about the rightness of [his] choice. (p. 42)

If we restore its proper meaning to the term "cosmopolitanism" . . . and recognize that it covers bad as well as good qualities, then we may say that Conrad, though he traveled to distant parts of the world and wrote about different peoples speaking many different languages, was not really a cosmopolitan. It was impossible for him to be one because of his need for roots. But he knew how to maintain a certain equilibrium between the demands of his double fidelity. (p. 43)

The "Heart of Darkness," which appeared at the very beginning of our century, was a Cassandra cry announcing the end of Victorian Europe, on the verge of transforming itself into the Europe of violence. The First World War, which ushered in the new epoch, destroyed many illusions. In this respect Conrad's fear of anarchy found its somber confirmation. (pp. 43-4)

> *Czeslaw Milosz, "Joseph Conrad in Polish Eyes" in* The Atlantic Monthly *(copyright © 1957, by The Atlantic Monthly Company, Boston, Mass.; reprinted with permission), Anniversary Issue, 1957 (and reprinted in* The Art of Joseph Conrad: A Critical Symposium, *edited by R. W. Stallman, Mich-*

igan State University Press, 1960, pp. 35-45).

It is Conrad the moralist, with his simple idea of fidelity, who chooses the central situation of the early stories: the test. Conrad wishes to explore that most important moment in an individual's life, the moment which reveals whether or not he is faithful to the community. Here Conrad is the traditional moralist; each of his stories is a kind of pilgrim's progress (but without God!). Thus his natural story, the voyage, is perfectly congenial to his moral view. (pp. 14-15)

Conrad sees experience as a test, and his characters' responses to the test determine their place in his moral hierarchy. It is here that the simple Conradian ideas become more involved. In the best works of the early period, we find three major types of character and one minor type, all of them defined through response to a moral crisis, to a question of right or wrong, to the issue of fidelity or betrayal. The first of these types is *the simple hero:* the unreflective, courageous, loyal seaman. He meets his crisis, often some disaster at sea, with unthinking devotion. His guide is the code we have just been considering. This code unites him with a large group of similarly loyal people, so that he is seldom oppressed by any sense of isolation. He is unimaginative and tends not to sympathize with more complex persons. The second type is the man with the "plague spot"; the man who, confronted in isolation with a crisis, necessarily fails. He is Conrad's most difficult, most complicated character, and he is also the central figure in most of the full-length novels of the early period. He has caused many to misread the novels because he often seems to be a conventional hero. Let us call him (since he *does* fail), *the vulnerable hero.* . . . The third and last major type of character in the early period partakes of aspects of the other two. He understands, appreciates, and subscribes to the ethical code of the simple, unimaginative man. But he shares the terror and the weakness of the man with the plague spot. Unlike the simple seaman, he is complex and introspective. Unlike the vulnerable hero, he meets his crisis successfully. The measure of his success is not, however, the fact of meeting the crisis; his success lies in his achievement of self-knowledge. Let us call him, for convenience, *the perceptive hero.* Finally, there is one minor type. Like the vulnerable hero, he fails his crisis, but unlike him, he would never be mistaken for a true hero. He has no moral sense and, hence, no shame. Moral crises do not interest him. We shall call him the villain. (pp. 15-16)

Conrad persuades the reader to admire his simple, faithful, hard-working seamen by suggesting that their heroism is of mythical proportions and by magnifying achievement through understatement. . . . At the same time that Conrad suggests that his seamen have quasi-supernatural qualities . . . , he emphasizes certain unattractive physical details. . . . These details act as effective understatement. By diminishing his heroes physically, Conrad makes their spirit seem even more intrepid. These men, moreover, are supposed to be ordinary, very much of the human community. (pp. 17-18)

Perhaps, too, Conrad the psychologist does not quite believe in his moral heroes; his tendency to assign to them more-than-human virtue suggests that they do not exist, are a myth, an ideal. . . .

If fidelity is the highest virtue of Conrad's moral code, its opposite—betrayal—is the central theme of the early period. The second type of character, the man who fails, interests Conrad more deeply than the man who succeeds in the ranks. (p. 19)

The theme of self-knowledge in *Lord Jim* and Marlow's role as perceptive hero demonstrate how subtle the early Conrad's thinking is, how much more complex the book than the simple "sin and redemption" interpretation it first received. Jim fails on two counts: first, his leap from the *Patna* clearly violates the seaman's code; second, in his inconclusive interviews with Marlow during the Inquiry he avoids the self-knowledge that is Marlow's chief interest. (p. 24)

If the early Conrad is conservative and hates revolt, he also scorns complacency. We find, therefore, in the background of the early novels a vaguely defined group of people who appear to be secure only because they have never been tested. . . . Conrad's attitude toward Jim's people gives us an interesting key to his early complexity. On the one hand, he idealizes them as the solid folk of England. On the other hand, by contrasting their safe existence to Jim's disreputable failure, he raises serious doubts as to their superiority to Jim. . . . The imperceptive, untested character is really as reprehensible to the early Conrad as his corrupt and comic villains. (pp. 27-8)

[The] early Conrad devotes his energies chiefly to creating vulnerable heroes who fail to support the human community. . . . Certainly this is what interests Conrad: not the superficial how of his characters' actions but the fundamental why, and particularly the why of moral failure. (p. 29)

Isolation in Conrad is . . . more than a striking image. It is the condition of the test which each of his major characters must undergo; it is a chief cause of their failure; and it tempts them to seek unlawful successes. (p. 30)

If loneliness is the condition of most of Conrad's characters, it is a condition largely self-imposed. Whether simple or complex, his vulnerable heroes are all egoists. Their deepest impulses and longings are directed not toward a dutiful place in the ranks but toward self-aggrandizement. They are alone chiefly because they have thoughts for no one but themselves. This is one of the central convictions of Conrad the psychologist, that egoism is the motive force of most men's actions. (p. 31)

Finally, in his anatomy of moral failure, Conrad dramatizes the idea that man, with his egoistic longing to escape reality, desires—more profoundly than power and glory—irresponsibility, peace, even death itself. (p. 34)

Though Conrad of course sees self-destructiveness as a fault in his vulnerable heroes, he nevertheless has to admire the vigor with which they go about it. After all, it is Jim's "intensity" that makes Marlow admit that Jim is "none the less true." Most readers respond in the same way. Surely the glamor, the energy, the intensity of the hero of *The Great Gatsby* owes something to the self-destructive Jim. (p. 35)

Clearly the early Conrad's use of language is but one more aspect of his complexity. Through irony, symbolic imagery, and even sentence structure, he is able constantly to suggest that there are other sides to the question, that things are not quite what they seem. Though his morality is apparently simple enough, his characters' responses to their moral tests, his analysis of their responses, and the organization and the expression of his art—all these are very complicated.

Few novelists using the English language can match Conrad in any single aspect of his art. None, it may be asserted, has ever been able to combine so successfully such moral and psychological awareness with so complicated and rich a technique. (p. 49)

More unusual than his pessimism is the inhibiting effect of sexual subject matter on Conrad's creative processes. The failure of imagination in the love stories can be seen in the woodenness of the actors and their lack of perception. Let us take Conrad's villains as an example. Insofar as they participate in love stories, they fail as caricatures. (p. 127)

Conrad differs radically from other great modern novelists in his lack of understanding, in his almost belligerent lack of genuine, dramatic interest in sexual problems. Although the Conradian villains could be labeled neurotic, exhibitionist, and unconsciously homosexual, they are really just cardboard figures plucked from nowhere and thrown up as obstacles to sexual consummation. Yet such characters would inspire a Dostoevski to his most intense efforts. Ford Madox Ford claims that Conrad was fascinated by the subject of incestuous love, and we have seen some suggestions of incest. But once again, incestuous love exists in Conrad's novels only as a barrier to sexual consummation, not as a deeply felt human emotion. (p. 128)

While Conrad does sympathize with the homeless female waif, his sympathy is not as complete as Hardy's or Dreiser's. He will not believe with Hardy that man deserves better than he gets or with Dreiser that man is the pawn of heredity and environment. Conrad's temperament is not that of the naturalist. His characters' crises are moral crises; his characters must *act,* and their actions must be judged. Although Conrad relaxes his moral judgment in the later period, the later novels still move in the same pattern as the early ones. Now, however, Conrad asserts (but cannot show) that his characters are morally triumphant.

Conrad's moral sense, demanding that his characters act upon their own volition, conflicts with his misogyny. Woman in action, woman as the competitor of man, is insufferable. Thus, Conrad's sympathy for the homeless waif vanishes as soon as she makes a gesture of self-assertion. (pp. 159-60)

[The] later Conrad's denial of individual guilt and his espousal of repose result in the almost total destruction of the early, profound hierarchy of characters. In the place of faithful seaman and vulnerable hero, we find the untried boy and the impeccable hero. The perceptive hero disappears; the popular-magazine heroine and the unremittingly black villain dominate the scene. The only bright spot in the later characterizations, the handling of Flora [in *Chance*] and Lena [in *Victory*] in certain scenes, seems rather the reflection of the early Conrad's sympathy for lonely figures than of any new perception into his characters. (p. 163)

Style as well as structure suffers from the later Conrad's view of the world. (p. 172)

[The] later Conrad either did not wish to or could not recover his early symbolic imagery and emotionally evocative prose. Most critics, however, tend to assert that in the last novels Conrad returned to his early style, a style they do not applaud. Actually, it is doubtful whether the Conrad of 1919 could write with the suggestive power of even some of the poorer specimens of early Conradese. Throughout the later period there are clear examples of the later Conrad's ineffectual imitation of early Conradese. This is true of *Chance,* which belongs to the time when, according to some readers, Conrad has "purged" himself of the early style. (pp. 177-78)

His rejection of a concrete and suggestive style is of a piece with his altered view of the world and man's place in it. In his early work, he sternly judges those of his characters who try to evade responsibility and seek peace. Moreover, these characters go about their self-destruction with vigor of purpose and intensity of emotion. But in the later work, Conrad evades the question of moral responsibility and passively acknowledges peace as man's greatest good. If this is affirmation, it rises not out of serene old age but out of a desperate weariness. (p. 178)

[The] productions of Conrad's last years are virtually without a redeeming feature. They reveal that Conrad has exhausted his creative energy. He has no longer anything to write about and must rework old materials, cling to someone's memoirs, or, in the case of *The Rover,* spin nearly three hundred pages out of almost nothing. Even more seriously, the last novels show that Conrad has finally lost control of the basic tools of his craft. He can no longer focus on his subject: the novels contain many beginnings but virtually no endings. The characters lack substance, and Conrad can only assert their emotions and ideas—he cannot dramatize them. The prose of the last works is very faulty. When Conrad tries his hardest to make a scene important, the prose drifts into thin, vague pretentiousness. Although Conrad writes awkwardly at times in all of his novels (least so perhaps in *Lord Jim* and the shorter sea pieces), the prose of the last novels stumbles on every page. Sometimes he cannot even execute a sentence. Besides the specific faults in technique, the last novels give a general feeling of weariness. All the characters, young and old, seem very tired, eager to sit or lie down. Moreover, the difficulty with which their creator manipulates them indicates clearly the source of their fatigue. (p. 180)

> *Thomas Moser, in his* Joseph Conrad: Achievement and Decline *(copyright © 1957 by the President and Fellows of Harvard College; excerpted by permission of the author and publishers), Cambridge, Mass.: Harvard University Press, 1957.*

The very virtue of *Nostromo* is that it combines the austere soul-searchings of the absorbent tragic hero (or rather heroes) with a great deal of 'land entanglement'; that, after the manner of the *Iliad,* it pictures not only man's private struggles with his destiny but also a whole phase of man's political and social life. However closely tied together the parts of *Nostromo* may be, it is immensely suggestive of issues wider than that of the hero's predicament. That Conrad can suggest so much through so incredibly concatenated a plot is precisely his triumph. (p. 127)

Conrad is at home equally with idealist and scoundrel, with audacity and cowardice, with simple and complex people. . . . Conrad's greatest triumph . . . is that he creates the illusion of life being lived all at once by a great number of very different people. He does this partly by his technique of passing backward and forward in time, thereby removing from the reader all temptation to thin out events by stringing them on a long chain. But he does it also by his miraculous power of keeping everything and all people present simultaneously in his head. And he reveals that power through the sheer wealth of unexpected small touches, touches we are absolutely certain were not contrived casually on the spur of the moment but are minute and highly significant revelations of all the more permanent wealth that lies beneath them. It is the same power that Homer commands in the *Iliad* when he suddenly mentions the insignificant military class of store-keepers or tells us that Patroclus's captive maid-servants, when they lamented his death, were in reality lamenting their own unhappy lot. Conrad is in complete command of the total life of his Sulaco, not to speak of life outside it. (pp. 135-36)

It is the special distinction of the English novel during the nineteenth century and the first quarter of the twentieth to invest places, existent or imagined, with an air of compelling reality.... [For] the sustained compulsion to see and believe in an imagined town and its surroundings no English novel can challenge *Nostromo,* not even when its imaginings are founded on an actual place. (p. 138)

It is usual to centre the action of *Nostromo* on the San Tomé mine and the corruption it works in the minds of Charles Gould and of Nostromo. And that habit is correct except for not including enough. Conrad himself seems to support it by his ceaseless insistence on the silver, even to the extent of giving the Garibaldino silver-rimmed spectacles and risking an irrelevance by introducing the word into the last sentence of the book. Nevertheless, the silver of the mine not only expresses the temptation of avarice, and the pressure on the modern industrialised world of 'material interests', but represents *any* ideal to which a man gives himself and for which he works. (p. 141)

Conrad's concern with the abstracted ideal is given both beauty and weight through being centred symbolically in the single, dominant snow-peak. And that singleness and domination give point to the many varieties in the inevitable failure of human beings to live up to the ideals on which they attempt to found their conduct....

Nostromo contains superb pictures of men short-sighted in evil. And at the same time it is the short sight of the well-intentioned that causes the corruption of their ideals. (p. 145)

The terrible truth, then, that every ideal is corrupted as soon as it is translated into action is not without its mitigations. Though it allows of no exceptions, the extent of its working varies enormously, and the power of the human imagination may prevent its taking an extreme form. Conrad also allows that the humbler the ideal and the simpler the person pursuing it, the milder is the corruption involved. (p. 147)

Conrad believed that every man has his Achilles heel and that the Stoics were wrong in holding that the self-reliant man of virtue, the man in Horace's phrase *justus et tenax propositi,* could survive all ordeals, including the collapse of the world itself. But he also believed that some men (like Captain MacWhirr) were lucky and were subjected only to those ordeals to which they were equal. (p. 149)

Critics have usually seen in Conrad's admission of the Achilles heel a profound pessimism; they attribute to him a terrible belief in the darkness at the centre of every human mind, in an area of uncertainty capable at any time of confounding every noble or decent feeling or thought that exists in its other areas. And when, in his later novels, Conrad seems less obsessed with the heart of darkness, they suspect him of escapism and comparative dishonesty. But they forget that in *Nostromo* Conrad combines his theme of the heart of darkness with the other theme that in actual fact some men are not subject to its tyranny. (pp. 149-50)

If . . . you are convinced that Christianity is in essence pessimistic, you will find Conrad to be so too. Otherwise you will find that his pessimism is not incompatible with the Christian scheme. Christianity has always opposed the Stoic's notion of self-sufficiency and has always held that the mind of fallen, unaided man is prone, some limited natural motions towards good apart, to fall into a state of chaos. It is Christian thought that is behind Conrad's conception of human destiny. The very prayer not to be led into temptation may be taken to imply that for every mortal some temptations are indeed too strong. And when Conrad both admits this and records that in actual fact some men seem to survive their ordeals, he is not straying from the religion in which he was brought up. And if thereafter he does nothing more definite than recognise and present a mystery, can more be expected of him as an artist or can it be said that Shakespeare did otherwise? On the contrary, in its richness and its mystery Conrad's presentation of the human predicament reminds me of Shakespeare's most of all. (p. 150)

One of Conrad's tiresome habits is to overdo the theme or the symbol iterated for the sake of the construction. He overdoes the darkness theme in the *Heart of Darkness* and the youth theme in *Youth.* And in *Nostromo* he does the same with silver and 'material interests'. (p. 151)

Speaking of Conrad and Yeats, [M. C.] Bradbrook observed that "both deserve the epithet *majestic;* their power to write of the great simple heroic themes almost frightens the modern reader". And this sentiment confirms my experience of constantly thinking of Homer when reading *Nostromo.* . . . Conrad's treatment of the great themes of action and reflection, of material interests and moral idealism, recalls the Homeric theme in the *Iliad* of the irreconcilable virtues of heroic valour and the ordered domestic life. Conrad's union of colour and romance and fairy-lore with irony and the most accurate eye for the living detail recalls Homer's union of the fabulous with the actual in the *Odyssey.* And they are alike in the span of life they cover and in the sense of teeming life within that span. This spontaneous comparison of *Nostromo* with Homer suggests that in this one book Conrad achieved an epic in the medium of prose fiction: a suggestion confirmed by the control Conrad maintained over his multifarious material and the force of later opinion of which he has become the mouthpiece. (pp. 166-67)

> *E.M.W. Tillyard, "Conrad: 'Nostromo',"
> in his* The Epic Strain in the English Novel
> *(copyright © E.M.W. Tillyard 1958), Chatto
> and Windus, 1958, pp. 126-67.*

Victory is . . . a novel intimately concerned with questions of truth and reality, as it is with lies and illusion. Those big considerations force themselves on the imagination of the characters, and hence upon that of the reader; for it is that kind of novel, the kind Conrad normally attempted to write. (p. 148)

Revisiting *Victory* today, one cannot help being struck by its "existentialist" qualities—by how much it shares the intellectual preoccupations and postures notable in continental literature during recent decades. Here, for instance, is an elaborated image of human isolation: the isolation not only of man from man, but even more of man from his metaphysical environment.... Here is the articulated obsession with the feeling of existence and of non-existence, as clues both to character and action.... Here are modes of nihilism yielding to modes of self-annihilation, in the oddly similar catastrophes of both hero and villain. Here, in short, is a tale of violence that oscillates richly between the fundamental mysteries of being and nothing. Conrad, we are inclined to say, is the still insufficiently acknowledged grandfather of the most recent literary generation.

To say so is not necessarily to praise Conrad; and it is more likely, indeed, to impose upon him a false identity. *Victory* is not—and it cannot be discussed as—a novel of ideas.... (p. 149)

Conrad did of course display attitudes, and he had a stiff little set of convictions. But E. M. Forster has rightly, if unsympathetically, made the point that Conrad had no "creed"—no coherent order of intellectual principles [see excerpt above]; and no more than other novelists writing on English soil did Conrad possess that occasional French and German talent for making the war of thought itself exciting....

He wanted to exploit the power of words, as he said, in order "to make you hear, to make you feel—before all to make you *see*"; and the end of each of his best novels was simply its own composition.... *Victory* dramatizes basic aspects of truth and being; but as regards the human condition, its main aim is only to observe it in the way of art—with that idle but no less intense and sustained attention for which Conrad accurately thought he had a natural ability....

The novel's final word—"Nothing!"—is, accordingly, less a cry of appalled metaphysical recognition than the quiet acknowledgment that the adventure is over and the art that described it has peacefully exhausted itself. (p. 150)

And yet. If there is no metaphysical vision or purpose at work in the novel, there can nevertheless be felt running through it something like a metaphysical tide. Or better, perhaps, one senses the active presence, the dangerous undertow, of a metaphysical current giving the story its energy and its direction. In the same way, if the tale is not plainly intended as an allegory, one feels in it nevertheless something like an allegorical swelling, as though everything were about to become bigger than itself. That very impression affects the nerves of the persons in the book. "I have a peculiar feeling about this," says Mr. Jones. "It's a different thing. It's a sort of test." In the long list of Conrad's writings, *Victory* also comes to us as a different thing and a sort of test. It is Conrad's test of the nature of fiction: in general, of the ability of drama to move toward allegory while retaining intact its dramatic form and essence; and in particular, of the ability of fiction to move toward drama

while retaining its identity as fictional narrative. It is a test of the way truth and reality can become the subject matter of a novel which hangs on to its novelistic nature. And the result, in my judgment, is indicated by the last word Conrad actually did write in this book, as he tells us: the single word of the title. (p. 151)

Nostromo and *Victory* . . . stand in a relation similar to the relation between *King Lear* and *Othello* (or perhaps like that between *The Possessed* and *Crime and Punishment*). Both *Nostromo* and *King Lear* comprehend more of the world and of human experience than the mind can comfortably contemplate; both are made up of a variety of parallel plots and involve several different groups of persons; in each we discover what Francis Fergusson calls "action by analogy," and the action so richly exposed in its multiplicity of modes reveals something not only about the individuals concerned but about the hidden drift of history, the secret and tragic movement of the universe. Both works engage the artist's most disturbing power—the prophetic power—which is of course not the ability to read the particular and immediate future, but the ability to read the future implicit in every grave and serious time, the future man is perennially prone to. In *Victory*, on the other hand, as in *Othello*, the action emerges directly from the peculiar temperaments of a few eccentric individuals. What happens, both artistically and psychologically, happens as a result of the impact of one unique personality upon another. This is not to deny any largeness to *Victory*; it is only to identify the source of the special largeness it does reveal. It is to say that the novel shows an allegorical swelling rather than an allegory, and that the creative force is less a pre-existent design the characters are re-enacting (for example, the myth of Eden, of the man and the woman in the garden and the invasion by the serpent) than the jarring effect of the human encounters. (pp. 152-53)

Victory is, in a sense, . . . an admonition about the tendency of both fiction and criticism to intellectualize the art—to lose the drama in the allegory—or to deform the art—to lose the novel in the drama. The form of *Victory* grows dramatic, and it gives forth intimations of allegory. But it remains faithful to its own nature, for it never makes the mistake of Mr. Jones—it never fails to take account of the variable and highly unpredictable character of individual human beings. (pp. 168-69)

> *R.W.B. Lewis, "The Current of Conrad's 'Victory'" (1959), in his* Trials of the Word: Essays in American Literature and the Humanistic Tradition *(copyright, 1965, by R.W.B. Lewis), Yale University Press, 1965, pp. 148-69.*

Joseph Conrad is the first important modern novelist in English [in the sense that] his finest novels and stories are all concerned, directly or obliquely, with situations to which public codes—*any* public codes—are inapplicable, situations which yield a dark and disturbing insight which cannot be related to any of the beliefs or rules which make human societies possible. (pp. 26-7)

Conrad makes it quite clear that the heart of darkness is a symbolic experience of what lies at the heart of much human profession and activity. Commerce, progress, imperialism, politics, society—in the last analysis they are based on what does not bear looking into. And in the last analysis they are not *real*, but conscious or unconscious covers for something else—perhaps merely for a great nothingness. . . . [We] have the suggestion that outside individual experience there is perhaps no reality, that society can never be wholly real. (p. 41)

David Daiches, "Joseph Conrad," in his The Novel and the Modern World *(© 1960 by The University of Chicago), University of Chicago Press, 1960, pp. 25-62.*

[Everything] about Conrad's characters is interesting to him except what they say, and so they say very little, and when they say it they are interrupted constantly by the narrator's lush sensory monologue. . . . Conrad never seemed to realize that the technique to which he was committed made meaningful dialogue practically impossible. He kept trying to write plays. One wonders where he thought the actors' speeches were going to come from, and after reading his unrecognizable dramatic version of *The Secret Agent* one still wonders. A true Conrad play would be a kind of pantomime with everyone looking deep, gesturing madly, and brushing aside mosquitoes and palm fronds, to perfectly tremendous background music.

This is not to say that the pantomime would be devoid of hard facts. It is only to say that the actors involved would not be expected to vocalize about them; indeed they would be speaking out of character if they did so, for their awareness of hard facts was conceived by Conrad to be an emotional rather than conceptual awareness; their response to the hard facts had, accordingly, to be somehow more or less than verbal, a response that they themselves could not be expected to describe any more than Benjy could have been expected to write the first chapter of *The Sound and the Fury*. And so, dramatically, such characters were the weakest of reeds; they needed their author to be on stage constantly, mouthing for them, telling the audience what their thoughts and feelings were. This is one reason why Conrad *was* on stage all the time, why his novels took the form they did, and why they were completely unsuited to the theater. (pp. 152-53)

When a character speaks to us directly he may be judged directly for what he has said; but when a character is not permitted to speak he may be known to his audience only at secondhand; the audience's opinion of him is thereby diverted by its interest in the intermediary, the author who created him. Thus we arrive at a kind of paradox that the artist like Conrad, who is concerned with the immediacies of Life, with the here and now in the most obvious and defensible meaning of the here and now, the here and now of an individual's sensations and feelings—we come to the paradox that this kind of artist is apt to be . . . a contriver, . . . One has to get over the hump of the method before the hard facts, if there are any, emerge.

Obviously Conrad's admirers have gotten over that hump. His rather conspicuous artistry, his verbal mystification, his concern with transitions and point of view, all the matters that [H. G.] Wells professed to be scornful of, have not prevented them from discovering the realist in him. (p. 153)

Reed Whittemore, "The Fascination of the Abomination—Wells, Shaw, Ford, Conrad," the introduction to Browning *(copyright © 1960 by Richard Wilbur; reprinted by permission of Dell Publishing Company, Inc.), Dell, 1960 (and reprinted in his* The Fascination of the Abomination, The Macmillan Company, 1963, pp. 129-66).*

Conrad brought a new vision into English fiction, and if, as many people think, the sense of human isolation and the search for individual identity is the most characteristic feature of the serious twentieth-century novel, the fact that *Lord Jim* was published in 1900 makes it a symbol of the new trend. (p. 156)

Just as Conrad's vision of life, his grave, lonely and ironic perception of the human condition, reveals a new atmosphere in fiction, so do his experiments in technique. Revolutionary writers are always forced into new technical experiments, because what they have to say will not fit into the old molds: a new way of seeing life demands a new way of writing about it. "Life does not narrate," says Conrad, "it makes impressions on our brains." Hence he had to find a new way of telling his story. . . . The author may pretend he is writing an autobiography, or he may be outside his material and present it with differing degrees of objectivity; but wherever he takes his stand, the plot development, the growth of the characters and the over-all theme emerge in a linear pattern of cause-and-effect progress.

Conrad changed all that. *Lord Jim* is one of Marlow's memories, and though Conrad never read any Freud, nor of course any Proust, he was well aware that association and not chronology is the basic principle of the memory process. The opening chapters of straight narrative are technically clumsy, in spite of some wonderful writing, because there is really no way by which Conrad, who is supposed to know the story only through Marlow, could be familiar with the inner and outer aspects of Jim's earlier life. But from the entrance of Marlow in Chapter 4, the sequence becomes that of the associations and digressions in Marlow's mind. They play all over time and place, picking up new illuminating perspectives at every turn.

All chronological sequence is abandoned. (pp. 165-66)

Through all these personalities we see Jim and his conduct from many points of view, and in essence, see the human condition in the same way. What each of these people sees is to him the reality of the matter. The facts are added to, or distorted, or ignored as they are refracted through different eyes. No wonder that Marlow declares that reality and illusion cannot be separated: "there is so little difference and the difference means so little." No wonder too that Marlow feels fated "never to see him clearly," and that we leave him "at the heart of a vast enigma."

That mistiness, with its confusing outlines, through whose rents the "moments of vision" form themselves into clear-cut external events, is sustained as a symbol throughout. Conrad is again a forerunner of the twentieth-century novelists in his careful creation of symbolic significance. In certain passages he elaborates his imagery so as to give a new dimension to descriptive writing. The external details are vivid in themselves but they do not remain merely scenic. Each has a symbolic value which deepens and enriches the emotional and moral elements involved in the picture. . . .

The whole thing can be left at the level of description; but a study of the language reveals that Conrad is playing "the game of art" in every detail. The universe, the ship, and

Jim all *seem* part of a changeless placid pattern: a pattern of simple lines, curves and circles; of simple effects of light and dark on a flat surface: the rays of the stars, the curve of the moon, the sea extending "its perfect level to the perfect circle of a dark horizon''; and this "circular stillness of water and sky with the black speck of the moving hull remaining everlastingly in its centre." Conrad then suggests that this apparent static peace is not really all-inclusive. The black smoke from the funnel, the discordant grinding of the wheel chains, the fragmentary light from the binnacle are all disharmonies; and the intermittent glimpses of the black fingers of the steersman, "alternately letting go and catching hold of the revolving spokes" remind us of the wheel of fortune. . . . (pp. 168-69)

It is easy to find fault with certain aspects of Conrad's writing. F. R. Leavis says that he is sometimes too intent "on making a virtue out of not knowing what he means," and that he insists too often that "the vague and unrealizable are profoundly and immensely significant." Yet this impossibility of comprehension is exactly what Conrad is trying to convey. He does perhaps overwork words like *inscrutable, unspeakable, inconceivable,* and in places his prose is overdecorated and overcadenced in his enjoyment of "purple patches." Yet when these things are said, he remains a great and original artist, whose work lives up magnificently to what he himself put forward as his aim. In his Preface to *The Nigger of the Narcissus* Conrad describes his conception of what the novelist's art should be. It should evoke both the sense of isolation of the human soul and its sense of solidarity with its fellows; it should appeal primarily to the spontaneous, intuitive emotions rather than to the intellectual side of man's nature; and its moral truths should be implicit in the actions, the characters, the scenes, without the direct intrusion of interpretation by the author. (p. 171)

> *Elizabeth Drew, "Joseph Conrad: 'Lord Jim'," in her* The Novel: A Modern Guide to Fifteen English Masterpieces *(copyright © 1963 by Elizabeth Drew; reprinted by permission of Dell Publishing Company, Inc.),* Dell, 1963, pp. 156-72.

One must conclude that though Conrad was an emotionally complex man, he was intellectually simple. His aesthetic principles, like his philosophical principles, were few and plain: a half-page of note paper would contain all the ideas that he had. . . . This near-solipsism is a philosophical stance that Conrad shared with many of his contemporaries, and certainly it defines a line of English fiction from James to Virginia Woolf. If there is only the consciousness of ourselves, then the only possible matter of fiction is consciousness, and the sensations that consciousness records. And that is precisely Conrad's understanding of his art. . . . To hear, to feel, to see—if that is everything, it is so only in a world limited to the apprehension of sense data. The world that Conrad's novels propose is such a world—a world of isolated consciousnesses, each open to the rich, mysterious data of experience, but closed to one another. Conrad did not believe in the illuminated heart, and though he recorded the 'vain and floating appearance' of the world with scrupulous exactitude, he left the motives and awarenesses of his characters shrouded in obscurity and cloudy rhetoric—not because he could not invent clear motives, but because he could not imagine a human relationship in

which motives would be mutually comprehensible. . . . (pp. 49-50)

It is through this truth-to-sensations that Conrad introduces the idea of *craft.* The true rendering of one's perceptions requires an austere and rigorous technique, and the elimination of elements that are not fundamentally sensational; the authorial voice, for example, must go, not because it is inartistic, but because it implies assumptions about the nature of truth that are invalid; similarly, a chronological ordering of events is wrong because it is untrue to the realities of perception, in which human histories do not come to us in straight lines.

The forms of Conrad's novels are therefore difficult and obscure by intention. . . . This is the central point about Conrad as a thinker-about-fiction: that his forms emerged from his vision of things, and not from theories. . . .

[To] Conrad, art was subject to the same pressures and uncertainties as life, and was to be lived in the same way. Consequently his thoughts about fiction are thoughts about life—interesting for what they reveal about Conrad's mind at work, but not generally illuminating of the novel as a genre. (p. 51)

> *Samuel Hynes, "Conrad and Ford: Two Rye Revolutionists" (originally published in* Sewanee Review, January/March, 1965), in his *Edwardian Occasions: Essays on English Writing in the Early Twentieth Century (copyright © 1972 by Samuel Hynes; reprinted by permission of the author, Oxford University Press, Inc., and Routledge & Kegan Paul Ltd.),* Oxford University Press *and, in England and Canada, Routledge & Kegan Paul, 1972, pp. 48-53.*

In Conrad's view civilization is the metamorphosis of darkness into light. It is a process of transforming everything unknown, irrational, or indistinct into clear forms, named and ordered, given a meaning and use by man. Civilization has two sides, curiously in contradiction. To be safe, civilized man must have a blind devotion to immediate practical tasks, a devotion which recalls the Victorian cult of work. For Conrad as for Carlyle work is protection against unwholesome doubt or neurotic paralysis of will. "A man is a worker," says Conrad. "If he is not that he is nothing. . . ." (p. 14)

Civilization is at once a social ideal and an ideal of personal life. The ideal society is imaged in the relation among men on board a well-ordered ship: a hierarchical structure, with those at the bottom owing obedience to those above, and the whole forming a perfect organism. As a personal ideal, submission to civilization may mean being one of the stolid, unimaginative people, like Captain MacWhirr in *Typhoon.* It may also mean setting up for oneself an ideal of glory, the winning of power and fame for the accomplishment of some difficult project. A man who does this accepts as the meaning of his life the value he has in the eyes of other people. (p. 16)

The human world is a lie. All human ideals, even the ideal of fidelity, are lies. They are lies in the sense that they are human fabrications. They derive from man himself and are supported by nothing outside him. There is a gap between man and the world, and what remains isolated within the human realm is illusory and insubstantial. Nostromo's goal in life is an egotistic sham, as is Lord Jim's, Lingard's, or Razumov's. (p. 17)

Conrad's pessimism has a double source. It is a recognition that ethical terms have no meaning because they do not refer to some thing outside man which tells him what he ought to do. . . . On the other hand, the tragedy of man's existence lies in the fact that he is cut off irrevocably from the truth of the universe. As long as he remains human he will remain exiled in a nightmarish realm of illusion. (p. 18)

The aim of all Conrad's fiction is to destroy in the reader his bondage to illusion, and to give him a glimpse of the truth, however dark and disquieting that truth may be. His work might be called an effort of demystification. It attempts to rescue man from his alienation. His problem in reaching this goal is double: to lift the veil of illusion, and to make the truth appear. The second aim is especially difficult, for Conrad's truth is the exact opposite of precise images and events. (pp. 18-19)

The first step in his method of demystification consists, strangely enough, in accentuating the lucidity of vision typical of civilized man. The characteristic stance of Conrad's narrators is one of cold, clearheaded, ironic objectivity. . . . His habit of multiplying narrators and points of view, so that sometimes an event is told filtered through several consciousnesses, his reconstruction of the chronological sequence to make a pattern of progressive revelation, his use of a framing story—all these techniques increase the distance between the reader and the events as they were lived by the characters. (p. 19)

The interpretations ordinarily connecting man to things are broken, and the world is put in parentheses, seen as pure phenomenon. . . .

The most extraordinary aspect of this experience is the deceptive ease with which it occurs. No great catastrophe is necessary. A momentary absence of mind, a new way of looking at a familiar object, a slight change of routine may be enough to shatter the structure of a life. (p. 20)

To see the world without interpretations is to see it reduced to pure quality. Instead of namable things, only patches of dark on light are seen. . . . This recognition of the qualitative aspect of sense experience is an ultimate point reached through the vision of the world as dreamlike. . . . What the thing is can no longer be said because the attention is absorbed and fascinated by how it is.

Conrad habitually calls attention to the conflict between the qualitative aspect of things and the interpretation of what is seen into recognizable objects. The world is often perceived simultaneously as colors or incomprehensible sounds and as things which can be identified. The reader is balanced precariously between two ways of being related to the world. . . . (p. 24)

The culmination of the vision of the world as pure quality is the recognition that behind "the overwhelming realities of this strange world of plants, and water, and silence" . . . is something else, something more than human and more than natural, an "implacable force brooding over an inscrutable intention" [*Heart of Darkness*]. This is the darkness. The impressions things make on the senses are no more ultimate reality than their interpretation into meanings and objects. Qualities are a thin layer of scintillating light spread over the formless stuff of things, like the moonlight's silvery glitter on the jungle river or on the primeval mud. . . . The attempt to render the exact appearances of things is not an end in itself. Its aim is to make the truth of life, something different from any impression or quality, momentarily visible. (pp. 26-7)

The universe exists for Conrad, as for Dylan Thomas, as a process of the birth of things out of a genetic darkness and their return to that darkness. . . .

It would be an error to identify Conrad's darkness with Sartrean nothingness, just as it would be an error to identify it with the Freudian unconscious, or with evil, if that implies the existence of some opposing principle of good. The darkness is not nothingness, and it is not limited to the depths of human nature. It is the basic stuff of the universe, the uninterrupted. It is what remains, horrifyingly, when every thing or color has disappeared. . . .

The crucial experience for Conrad's characters is the moment when they escape from their enclosures in the sane bounds of everyday life and encounter the heart of darkness which beats at the center of the earth and in the breast of every human being on earth. (p. 29)

The deepest experience of truth is a moment which is neither past, present, nor future, but out of time altogether, like death itself. Many of Conrad's characters reach this state, but not necessarily by dying. The crucial experience for many of them is a moment which hovers on the threshold of the invisible. *The Rescue* offers important examples of this. (pp. 31-2)

Existence corresponds to the all-embracing night, to a world of flashes of light, impalpable shapes in the fog. Life corresponds to the vision of things as significant objects projected in broad daylight. . . .

Life is the voluntary commitment of one's energies to the fulfillment of a noble idea, in Lingard's case his promise to get Hassim and Immada back on their thrones. But life is only an unreal scene performed before a black curtain, and the curtain negates the play acted before it. Black is the color which absorbs all colors, the place where contradictions meet, the force that turns all forms and judgments into nothing, but there is a way of being which is not separate from it: existence. (p. 33)

People in Conrad's world are in an intolerable situation. The Apollonian realm of reason and intention is a lie. The heart of darkness is the truth, but it is a truth which makes ordinary human life impossible. . . . A man who reaches the truth is swallowed up by a force which invades his reason and destroys his awareness of his individuality. To know the darkness is to know the falsity of life, and to understand the leap into emptiness man made when he separated himself from the wild clamor of primitive life.

Throughout his career Conrad recognized that there is no way to relate existence and life, no way to evade the tragic contradictions of the human situation. (pp. 33-4)

J. Hillis Miller, "Joseph Conrad," in his Poets of Reality: Six Twentieth-Century Writers *(copyright © 1965 by the President and Fellows of Harvard College; excerpted by permission of the author and publishers), Cambridge, Mass.: Harvard University Press, 1965, pp. 13-40.*

Conrad's first book is a slight affair; yet in a study of the transition from closed to open form at about the turn of the century, *Almayer's Folly* has a significance beyond itself. For Conrad did not simply conceive his earliest book in the open form; he did so in a detailed way which not only turned to the newer pattern but explicitly rejected the older one. (p. 77)

Conrad in this slender, beginning work is by no means content merely to give us a narrative experience which is finally not closed. Like Hardy, he is preoccupied with the *necessity* of closing off the expanding moral agony of his central character; and like Hardy he is preoccupied with the necessity of making clear to the reader that no such closing off is *possible*. Almayer tries (as hard as any central character ever has) to reverse the disaster of the climax, he wrestles to achieve a moral reorganization which will contain the damage, and he fails. It is all very explicit. The closing of his stream of conscience is not simply ignored or discarded or unachieved; it is undermined by the author's intention. . . . [The] specific tension between the necessity for a narrowing experience in fiction and the realities of a widening one becomes the recurrent tension through which the book is organized and which gives it form. (p. 78)

These are the conditions of Almayer's innocence, and the central movement from innocence to experience in the book is his, not his daughter's or Dain's. The simple sequence of frustration built upon these conditions, which gives the story its fundamental structure, is exceedingly direct. (p. 79)

The central self of the moral experience envisions an "opening"—a necessary but shaming conclusion in which, at the moment of crucial moral choice, he gives up the attitudes, ideals, dignity, and effort of a lifetime. . . . The book's method of conclusion then—the struggle to forget—is a rigid decision, personal, social, and moral. And all the final events—from Almayer's erasure of his daughter's footprints to his last resort, opium—represent his attempts to close off, morally and emotionally, the intense disaster of the book's climax; to close off, in fact, the previous movement of twenty-five years of frustration culminating in the departure of his daughter and the utter loss of hope.

So, deliberately, the book's last pages are there for the conventional reason: to suggest finality by suggesting a containment of the climactic movement, a closing down and a tapering off of moral experience. (pp. 81-2)

But the careful, the over-careful, the single point of Conrad's mockery is that Almayer's programmatic attempt cannot and does not work, not at all, not in the slightest. Despite the formal "sequence of events, a detailed programme of things to do . . . and then forgetfulness would come easy" . . . , no moral or emotional containment of the overwhelming climax will ever be possible for his protagonist. . . . We are now close to the central moral organization not only of this small volume, but of much of Conrad's work: the very blatant irony of this story is that Almayer's folly, frustration, and degradation continue to expand after the climax despite his program for their containment. In thus mocking (too easily, too grossly in this tale) his central character's final effort to bring his life into accord with his own ideas and ideals, Conrad is both asserting and denying the familiar narrative and ethical myth. (pp. 82-3)

Nostromo's experience becomes emblematic—a pattern for the corrupted experience of others, and a pattern for the corrupted experience of the country. (p. 88)

"Nostromo" is "our man" (*nostr'uomo,* "our man" in Italian); and Ourman is the hero of this secular morality in the same sense that Everyman is the hero of the more famous morality. Ourman's centrality, of course, is not so easily achieved. The tying together of multifarious careers in *Nostromo,* and in particular the tying-in of the hero's corrosion with the corrosion of the world, is a kaleidoscopic affair. (pp. 89-90)

The tying together, the weaving of Nostromo's life into the bigger, thicker, more important texture of the novel—he is "indispensable," he "saves" every major character in one fashion or another, and then he "saves" the nation as a whole—thus becomes a method for the formal expansion of his experience. (p. 90)

[Surely] it is Conrad's point that the process which the novel depicts from its very beginnings in the nation and in Ourman—the corruption of the spirit by "material interest" —is not only still going on, but still expanding. . . .

[The] form of *Nostromo* is that of a malignancy. Once the cancerous growth begins, it consumes Nostromo's life and the novel in a single forward-moving development. (p. 96)

The central experience in a Conrad story—the sequence of inward and outward responses—traces almost invariably the hero's dogged refusal to embrace whatever moral and emotional expansion events still more doggedly force upon him; and formally, that pattern of experience operates as a brake against any mere mounting of "effects" into sensationalism. Conrad's novels are continually *about* to open outward. One is aware of an imminent explosion as the "progression" intensifies; but the inward refusal holds the cumulative force in check under increasing pressure; and the story "opens" only at the end. There is a sudden crumbling of resistance, an eruption at maximum moral intensity. The point I wish to make is that these last throes of emotional response only *seem* to be crucial containments of disturbing moral experience. They seem that way because Conrad is divided against himself, and consciously so. (pp. 98-9)

Conrad does *not* imagine always, as he does in *Nostromo,* an expanding current of conscience which is finally not reduced, controlled, or contained by his ending. Nevertheless, the recurrence of the conflict of intentions in Conrad deserves observation. It is the struggle between his effort to "close" his form morally and his refusal to do so; and I refer to a conflict both in his critical mind and in his imaginative work. The two impulses can be discerned in both clearly. They are not only opposed but contradictory; as a result, the imagined "ends" to which they give rise are morally ambiguous conclusions; and that specific tension in Conrad helps to indicate the slow turn of the novel, the progressive emergence of a finally open experience as normative for fiction. (p. 99)

He is attempting to make real the pattern of fiction by making it resemble the pattern of "life" (rather, *his* vision of *his* life). The struggle to produce something "incomplete" is a positive need. . . . He is struggling toward the vision of fiction in which "events crowd and push and nothing happens." (p. 100)

Alan Friedman, "Joseph Conrad 'The End,

Such As It Is'," in his The Turn of the Novel *(copyright © 1966 by Alan Friedman; reprinted by permission of Oxford University Press, Inc.), Oxford University Press, 1966, pp. 130-78.*

The final Conradian gesture, whether of courage or duty or tragic pessimism or human solidarity, gets more . . . attention [from critics] while the mental turmoil that precipitated it gets lip service. What is engaging about Conrad for me and I daresay for others is the part of his imagination that is prior to this withdrawal into gesture—the part that Marvin Mudrick refers to darkly, without explanation, as Conrad's "suppressed . . . nightmares". (p. 43)

Conrad's most significant level of discourse is the unconscious level, where inadmissible wishes are entertained, blocked, and allowed a choked and guarded expression.

The atmosphere of Conrad's fiction is only partly one of physical challenge; there is always an opposite pull toward easeful death. The source of this urge is obviously his own depressive tendency, which he fought, disguised, and tried to negate in his art as in his life. And yet he is a consistently autobiographical writer; the effort to shout down his deepest impulses entails an incessant recasting of his psychic history. . . . [The] concern with the posthumous grip of the parents [on Conrad's heroes] amounts to an oblique assigning of blame for the inhibition which characterizes Conrad's protagonists and is never adequately explained on "realistic" grounds. Conrad tells us in effect that his characters cannot involve themselves emotionally because they suffer from fixation; they are too busy fending off resentments and longings toward the departed elders to permit themselves anything more than the most furtive encounters with their contemporaries. (pp. 45-7)

Like Hemingway, Conrad wavered between a maudlin *Weltschmerz* and a defensive assertiveness about the importance of manly style; the two attitudes are psychologically consistent in that one is an antidote to the other. The value of action for such a writer is measured by the inertia that must be overcome to achieve it. Manhood is always in doubt, and its reconfirmation can only be made believable in an exclusively masculine ambience hedged with rules and physical difficulties. Hence the otherwise inexplicable feeling in Conrad that nautical duty and discipline and trial constitute a welcome respite from something more fearsome. In a word, that something is sexuality. Conrad can permit himself to imagine a love relationship only if it is a matching of racial opposites—that is, if it contains an alibi to the accusation of being latently incestuous. . . . His heroes, for all their exotic adventures, amount to virtual eunuchs, while his heroines tend to be awesome, androgynous, self-sufficient monoliths who can be fought over but not fertilized. His heroes' mortality rate rises sharply as they approach these Brobdingnagian ladies, who evidently pose a menace more forbidding than any hazard of the male world. Death is at once a symbol of castration and the surest escape from it, a flight from incest and a return to it —and, of course, by killing off his heroes Conrad spares himself the awkwardness of trying to depict love scenes when his mind is possessed by fantasies of this sort. (pp. 47-8)

Conrad's uniqueness does not consist in the virtues for which he is most often praised—vivid detail, evocative

scenery, suspense, moral concern, a sense of the heroic— but in the fact that he carries these traits along in a nose dive toward self-destruction. He is simultaneously terrified at existence and a connoisseur of its heightened moments, at once a nihilist and a raconteur. This tension is sustained by the "adjectival" rhetoric which looks so foolishly obfuscating when it is extracted for analysis. Even the memorable sentences, the ones that strike us as profoundly true, serve to mediate among Conrad's contrary impulses. Take, for instance, his haunting remark in *Nostromo* that "in our activity alone do we find the sustaining illusion of an independent existence as against the whole scheme of things of which we form a helpless part." That is classic Conrad, not only because it contains a flash of tragic insight but also because it blurs responsibility: to think of oneself as helpless within a metaphysical void is to assign an external cause for one's prevailing depression. I suggest that this quasi-confessional mode is Conrad's forte and that we are more affected by it than we may care to admit. Conrad indulges our fears of isolation, neglect, and victimization by malign higher powers—the fears of an anxious infant— without locating their source. There is something luxurious about the Conradian *Angst;* it comforts us because it is shared, indeed it is built into the order of things, and we combat it with the fellowship of our orphanage. (pp. 48-9)

The real agon in Conrad is the struggle against inhibition. It is no small point in his favor that he always tried to resist the impulse—indulged, for example, by Henry James—to pretend that his taste for sexless irresolution was a superior achievement of some sort. Every Jamesian plot puts a thick moral varnish on the necessities of the Jamesian temperament, but Conrad did what he could to oppose the passivity which usually has the final say in his works. Common human experience was sacred for Conrad, as it distinctly wasn't for James, because he grasped at it for rescue from the real destructive element, his instinct for failure. (pp. 49-50)

[Conrad's] engagement in his plots would seem to have more to do with self-exculpation than with dispassionate analysis. The semblance of irony is thrown up by his need to review his misgivings about himself, but when the misgivings become too insistent they must be replaced by muddle. Conrad typically diverts our interest from the hero's gloomy mind to his lush surroundings, which are stocked with misplaced energies; we expect confessions and instead we get tropical storms. The very fact that the plots are so crammed with adventure is comprehensible in this light. The hero is kept too busy staving off real "savages" and villains to spare time for self-inquiry, and in most cases we are finally meant to think of him as a victim of hard luck. Thus Conrad avails himself of projection—into the landscape, into "the whole scheme of things of which we form a helpless part"—in order to blunt an insight which would amount to self-analysis. . . .

For the comfort of disavowal Conrad pays a price in stereotyped characterization, melodramatic incidents, and the overworking of exotic props. (The three traits are really one, the negation of what is complicated, personal, and paralyzing by what is simple, alien, and active.) Not surprisingly, the works that have stood up best—nearly all of which were written in the so-called "Hueffer decade" of 1899-1909, when Conrad felt himself to have an ally against despair—are those which come nearest to self-confrontation. (p. 50)

Significantly, the most conspicuous change [in the late novels, such as *Chance* and *Victory*,] occurs in Conrad's treatment of women. Though he never at any period recognized that misogyny is more an affair of male psychology than of female sin, in his later phase he felt compelled both to idolize womankind and to denigrate it with slanderous generalities, both to try his hand at idyllic love scenes and to wilt them with . . . abhorrent language. . . .

[*Victory*] is built upon an anomaly which Conrad seems unable to control: as the hero gets (verbally) more committed to involvement in the world, his remarkable passivity is not overcome but intensified. (p. 51)

The novel's aesthetic incompleteness is a consequence of its censored self-debate: the details that stand out as blemishes are coherent only as replies to charges that Conrad has suppressed in the interest of his dubious tranquillity. (p. 53)

The trouble with *Victory* is that Conrad wants no part whatsoever of the forces that are tyrannizing over his plot; the result of his divided purpose is a sulky and confusing reticence. In all his finest novels and tales he is moving toward, not away from, a recognition that character is destiny. In these works [*Chance, Victory, Suspense*] the charged language, the undercurrent of double entendre which was bound to be present anyway, works with the momentum of the plot, and we are carried through an experience that feels single and whole. (pp. 53-4)

Conrad was on the whole a good Victorian, which is to say that he was earnestly overwrought about maintaining order and decency in his mind, and was apt to mistake the effects of repression for the structure of the universe. Even in his own time he was not a "modern." He lived long enough to call Lawrence's writings "Filth. Nothing but obscenities"; and he used his resonant prose to shore up semblances of the piety which all the great modern writers began by smashing. There was no real choice involved in his continuing to work his customary vein, telling fireside tales of adventure after Joyce and Lawrence and Yeats and Eliot had turned their backs on the philistine public of their day. Conrad and the *hypocrite lecteur* needed each other's company; in order to have access to his creativity he had to believe he was engaged in validating common mankind's good opinion of itself. (p. 54)

[The] Conradian experience, while intense and cathartic, is built around taboos that have lost much of their sacredness. Given the Victorian rules of the game, Conrad's grandiose but barely sustained duplicity with himself can be understood as the enabling condition of his narrative energy. (pp. 54-5)

"Heart of Darkness" . . . is surely Conrad at his best. This is not to say that its intellectual content is especially profound or even clear; on the contrary, the one definite point that emerges from the cacaphony of explication is that the appeal of this story cannot rest on its ideas. I suppose it was by working in an irresolute state that Conrad managed to keep the source of his inspiration so extrordinarily open. What matters, in any case, is that nearly everyone can respond to the symbolic experience at the base of his plot and feel the consonance between overt and latent emphasis. (p. 55)

If [the] plot were recounted to a psychoanalyst as a dream

—and that is just what Marlow calls it—the interpretation would be beyond doubt. The exposed sinner at the heart of darkness would be an image of the father, accused of sexual "rites" with the mother. The dreamer is preoccupied with the primal scene, which he symbolically interrupts. The journey into the maternal body is both voyeuristic and incestuous, and the rescue of the father is more defiant and supplantive than tender and restitutive. The closing episode with the "phantom" woman in a sarcophagal setting would be the dreamer-son's squaring of accounts with his dead mother. He "knows" that parental sexuality is entirely the father's fault, and he has preserved the maternal image untarnished by imagining that the father's partner was not she but a savage woman, a personification of the distant country's "colossal body of the fecund and mysterious life". . . . But given the anxiety generated by his fantasy of usurpation, he prefers to suppress the father's misdeeds. Such a tactic reduces the threat of punishment while reestablishing the "pure" mother-son dyad. Only one complaint against the sainted mother is allowed to reach expression: the son tells her with devious truthfulness that the dying sinner's last word ("horror!") was "your name". . . . (pp. 56-7)

"Heart of Darkness" is in the most agitated sense an autobiographical work. Far from criticizing Marlow, Conrad was using him to recapitulate and try to master the Congo experience he himself had sought out and undergone in 1890—an experience that led not to philosophical conclusions but to a physical and nervous collapse. Conrad's Congo interlude presents exactly the interpretive problem for his biographers that "Heart of Darkness" does for his critics; in both cases he went out of his way to make a real journey coincide with an unconscious investigation of his morbidity. . . . Conrad as well as Marlow is rattled by the idea of Kurtz, who is melodramatically overdrawn and yet scarcely permitted to appear.

In a broader sense we can see that Conrad's involvement in the unconscious allegory of "Heart of Darkness" explains its combination of hallucinatory vividness and garbled ideas. The whole account of European imperialism in the Congo is brilliantly convincing, not because of any developed ideology on Conrad's part, but because in his struggle with Oedipal "savagery" he feels within himself the pathology of men who want both to improve the brutes and to exterminate them. . . . No one is better at investing real observations of folly and sadism with the fever of a mind that has already imagined the worst criminality and severest punishment. What he cannot do, however, is relinquish this charmed mood or think clearly about its basis. Since everything that is necessary to Marlow's sanity is necessary to Conrad's, he cannot crawl out of Marlow's mind even for a moment. Hence the difficulty he has in conceiving of the Congolese except as objects of persecution or diabolical headhunters . . .; he still aspires to put down the heathen in himself. In short, Conrad finds no point of repose from which to assess the ordeal he puts us through. All he can muster as a substitute are dabs of moral philosophy—treasured like scripture by his critics—to plaster over his confusion about the causes of his melancholy.

To a certain degree, then, "Heart of Darkness" *is* a clinical document, a record of persisting misery. This is not to deny its power as art but on the contrary to suggest where its power must lie. Despite some details which owe their significance to memories that have not been made available in the text, the anxiety of the whole story comes across unmistakably.... [Conrad's] curse and opportunity was his need to deal at close range with the gaping monster of his fantasies. Whoever begrudges him his distracting maneuvers has not sufficiently understood the precariousness of the civilized equilibrium he sought to maintain. In retrospect Conrad's lurking skepticism about the strength of conscious decency looks so warranted by public events that we may feel tempted to credit him with a clairvoyant modernity, a vision of general collapse, but precisely because he writhed under the nightmare of history he could not be its interpreter. He did not formulate contradictions, he lived intensely with them and transcribed them into the terms of art. (pp. 58-60, 62)

> Frederick Crews, "Conrad's Uneasiness—And Ours" (originally published under a different title in Partisan Review, 1967), in his Out of My System (copyright © 1975 by Frederick Crews; reprinted by permission of Oxford University Press, Inc.), Oxford University Press, 1975, pp. 41-62.

One may ... raise the question of the possible influence of the scenic method of Henry James, whom Conrad called his dear master. Although he stood in awe of the older writer, near whom he lived for several years, there is little indication that he had read much if any of James before he revealed his own interest in drama. Moreover, there are certain differences in focus between the two. James seems the more centripetal, interested primarily in states of consciousness and awareness. Conrad is the more centrifugal, concerned with the relationship, at times the conflict, between the interior and the exterior. Conrad's technique of dramatic embodiment is substantially different from James's scenic method.

Ford Madox Ford must also be taken into account; not only did he and Conrad collaborate on two novels, they theorized extensively around the turn of the century on the art of fiction.... Aware that in real life our understanding of character and events proceeds, not in serial order, but by indirection, they thought fiction should reflect this indirection. They called the method literary impressionism. Yet Ford's influence, which he and others have thought to be considerable, should not be overestimated. Although Conrad embraced the theory of indirection, his best fiction involves the reader in a considerably more active role than that of receiving impressions. His reader becomes directly involved, is drawn into the game, either by the exercise of his own filtering consciousness, as is the case in *Nostromo,* or by the presence of a dramatic narrator such as Marlow, who is himself a central character.

Marlow, a virtuoso of indirection, is at once a literary device and far more than that, as he tells and retells his stories and inextricably intertwines himself and us with them. Suitably, he is an ambiguous figure, a loner, surrounded not only by the inscrutable universe but by a welter of scholarly pronouncements as well. Some consider him English, to others he is a Pole. He may have been based on a friend of Conrad's, but the prevalent view is that he came into being in response to the internal demands of Conrad's art, which posed the necessity of finding the proper vehicle for dealing with the increasing complexity he found himself confronted with as he came of age artistically. (pp. 6-7)

The real separation between Marlow and Conrad is nowhere more in evidence that in Marlow's incomplete perceptivity. His partial perceptions serve as foil for our own; from the resulting dialectic, additional meaning radiates. And it is of course Conrad who arranges the synthesis. (p. 7)

> Robert S. Ryf, in his Joseph Conrad (Columbia Essays on Modern Writers Pamphlet No. 49; copyright © 1970 Columbia University Press; reprinted by permission of the publisher), Columbia University Press, 1970.

Conrad's experiences down the Congo in 1890, which led to the writing of *Heart of Darkness,* ruined his health. He was profoundly shocked by the exploitation of the natives, and the dark, primitive jungle chaos haunted his imagination. When eventually he settled in England he may have felt that he had deserted Poland. Many writers on Conrad have ascribed the obsession with guilt and atonement in his fiction (*Lord Jim* and *Under Western Eyes,* for example) to his own sense that he had betrayed his country. All these reasons for his depressive state fed his philosophical pessimism, his belief that the new scientific discoveries of the nineteenth century made the universe seem absurd.

The breakdown in 1910 proved a turning point in his life. After this terrifying illness, Conrad increasingly repressed the sensitive, imaginative side of his nature, and forced his mind into safer, more normal channels of thought. There were still moods of anxiety and disturbance, of course, but he increasingly assumed the role of the Polish gentleman cased in British tar. Who can blame him? Like so many of us, he kept his sanity by suppressing the sense of horror and alienation which had dominated his waking dreams during the period from 1898 to 1910, the time of his greatest imaginative achievements.

The result was a growing superficiality in his later writings. It is now generally agreed that *The Arrow of Gold ...,* *The Rescue ...* and *The Rover ...* incline too much to sentimentality, and that they lack the disturbing complexities of novels such as *Nostromo ...* and *The Secret Agent....*

In his later years Conrad wrote a series of author's notes for his novels which mis-represent his true achievement. He put himself forward as a simple man with a conventional faith in duty, fidelity and the seaman's code of discipline. After he died, many commentators took this picture as self-evidently true....

It was not until 1957 that it was discovered that Conrad's autobiographical writings owed as much to fantasy as to fact.... There is no doubt that Conrad lied to his wife about [his] attempted suicide, and that he created fantasies to cover up the turbulent neuroses of his early days.... (p. 22)

On the one hand [Conrad] committed himself to work, to the concept of duty exemplified by the old seaman, Singleton, in *The Nigger of the 'Narcissus'*. In contrast, he had moments, like Decoud, when all activity seemed an illusion, and evasion of the futility of our lives....

Conrad has more to tell those of us who claim to be normal. His life and work were a desperate struggle to avoid the claims of suicide, to find meaningful forms of conduct amidst all the apparent absurdity of the universe. (p. 23)

C. B. Cox, "The Two Conrads," in Books and Bookmen (© *copyright C. B. Cox 1974; reprinted with permission), August, 1974, pp. 22-3.*

We have been told that Conrad was of a 'conservative nature' so often that we've come to accept it as an indisputable fact. . . . The fact that he wrote almost exclusively about life outside the social milieu in which he lived, and that when he did write about that milieu he was invariably scathing in his comments, suggests he was anything but 'conservative' by nature. . . . (p. 32)

In 'The Secret Sharer', . . . Conrad makes it abundantly clear that he does not share the 'conservative' view that justice and the Law are the same thing. When it comes to *The Secret Agent* he is more explicit. . . . In this grim novel, which deals with terrorism and violent deaths, there is a desperate irony similar to that of Jacobean drama, at times even a sense of black comedy. Law and order, as a concept, is equated with anarchy. And Conrad refers us back implicitly to 'Heart of Darkness'. There, Marlow insists on the security of the city, of civilised life being a world apart from the jungle: 'You can't understand. How could you?—with solid pavement under your feet. . . .' Here, Conrad finds London, the centre of civilisation and progress, an 'enormity of cold, black, wet, muddy inhospitable . . . bricks, slates and stones, things in themselves unlovely and unfriendly to man'. When the Assistant Commissioner goes out 'his descent into the street was like the descent into a slimy aquarium from which the water had been run out'. So much for civilisation, for law and order. . . .

Nostromo is perhaps Conrad's most political, most anticapitalist work. (p. 33)

It was Conrad's tragedy that while he could see that capitalism is an evil and destructive, as so-called civilisation is an illusion, he could find no other force (for good) in the world to take its place. Certainly he did not find it in the revolutionaries of *The Secret Agent* and *Under Western Eyes*. Certainly he did not look to the Church for it in the way that Eliot, who saw the human dilemma much as Conrad saw it, did, retiring behind the blinkers of authoritarian Christianity so that he should not have to face reality. 'I am not blind to its services,' Conrad once wrote, 'but the absurd oriental fable from which it starts irritates me . . . it has lent itself with amazing facility to cruel distortion and is the only religion which . . . has brought an infinity of anguish to innumerable souls—on his earth.' . . . It was Conrad's triumph as a man that he was able to face the truth to the end of his life, to live with the horrors he had seen in the heart of darkness, and to fight back against malignant fate by creating a moral order and a sense of human dignity in his art. Alienated from life, suffering in an isolation that brought periods of almost lethal depression, he was able to survive only by committing himself to his writing. Perhaps it was because he was obliged to put everything into his novels and stories that he achieved so much more than any subsequent writer of fiction in our language has done. . . . (pp. 33-4)

Frank Granville Barker, "Conrad's Mirror of Despair," in Books and Bookmen (© *copyright Frank Granville Barker 1974; reprinted with permission), October, 1974, pp. 32-4.*

Joseph Conrad uses the novel to excavate the core of reality buried beneath a familiar surface of people and events, but because that core cannot be cracked by any tool at the author's disposal, the result is a novel which contemplates rather than penetrates experience. Pursuing the truth beneath appearances, yet never getting beyond the appearance of truth itself, Conrad remains fixated on the subject that eludes him and finally forces the reader into the same position. Contemplation becomes, then, both subject and method of his novels: resigning himself to the futility of ever knowing enough to interpret facts—yet scorning the facts alone as worthless—Conrad turns life's mystery into his main theme. (p. 80)

If chaos is defined as a situation in which things do not fit together in meaningful patterns for the human mind, then *Lord Jim* is surely a work focused on chaos so consistently that it finally becomes the central subject of the novel. (p. 81)

The whole novel, is, I think, an effort on Conrad's part to wriggle his way out of the net which confines his comprehension of reality—"trying to find a weak spot, a crevice, a place to scale." The novel recounts his failure, and the failure itself is the whole point of the novel. (pp. 82-3)

Language for Conrad is inadequate because it falsifies certain feelings by rendering them explicit. If life's elusiveness is to be his main theme, then words must be used to suggest that idea without expressing it so directly that we feel the security of knowing truth. Articulation invariably distorts, and so even he who has perceived truth in its silent suggestiveness must resign himself to the inevitable failure of his attempts to communicate it in direct terms. Once the author himself has acknowledged the futility of language, however, he is left in a paradoxical position which must be satisfactorily resolved before he can advance very far—and again, Conrad's solution is a method of indirectness. Although feelings themselves cannot be communicated, the situation giving rise to them, if transmitted in its entirety, *can* reproduce similar feelings in the receiver. Words do, after all, have evocative powers, and so long as they are used to evoke rather than express, they can be used to establish some viable, if minimal, kind of communication. Shadowy thoughts cannot be conveyed, perhaps, but the *sense* of shadows can be projected with enough intensity to settle in another's imagination.

Vision, then, embodies thought, and language, in turn, can be used to project vision. But because truth can never be detached from the terrain in which it grows, but is suggested only through successful visualization of the appearances through which it glows so faintly, Conrad's method of communicating his vision will be as indirect as his manner of telling the story. It is not surprising, therefore, that he uses nature metaphorically, and that his descriptions of nature consistently insinuate his sense of moral and philosophical chaos. (pp. 87-8)

Alvin J. Seltzer, "The Rescued Fragment: Elusiveness of Truth in Conrad's 'Lord Jim'," in his Chaos in the Novel: The Novel in Chaos (*copyright © 1974 by Schocken Books, Inc.), Schocken Books, 1974, pp. 80-91.*

Unquestionably, the work of Conrad does not countenance fully relative value schemes. His view of ethics is not blurred, and his major work deals with the precise conflict between the image of the self and the patterns of conduct which fate causes us to enact. This clash usually takes the shape of a betrayal of trust, and the only reconciliation in Conrad ... is to acknowledge both parts of the self: the inviolate image and the equally representative acts, even when they are dark.... The inscrutable, unalterable nature of their act and the rigorously logical network of consequences give rise to a strange monologue in Conrad, wherein the protagonist queries in disbelief how such a damning pattern can, in fact, be his life. The problems of self-knowledge are matched by a corresponding epistemological impasse: how does one learn of others? ... The variety of responses to [Lord] Jim ... asserts both the tentative, arbitrary nature of judgment and Conrad's interest in perception as theme.

Of course, the elaborate Conradian presentation may be viewed as the author's failure to distinguish between matter and manner. Thus we have Wayne Booth's query: "Is 'Heart of Darkness' the story of Kurtz or the story of Marlow's experience of Kurtz?" (pp. 51-2)

In short, the search for the self, instigated from the inside or the outside, constitutes the visible impulse of Conrad's work, but the desired object is at best elusive, at worst nonexistent.

All we really see is the apparatus of observation. The political or ideological or even moral conflicts seem to matter less than the problems of scrutiny, interpretation, surveillance, and surmise. Conrad is drawn to secret agents, double agents, speculating professors, and philosophical men of the sea because the mechanics of inquiry strike him as more real, possibly even more ethical, than the fatal gestures themselves. (pp. 53-4)

What emerges from Conrad is not that our uncontrollable acts expose us, but rather that life erratically and brutally foists roles upon us, and we are stuck with them. For the truth is a void, and, rather than accept that, we live out the procedural drama of fighting against masks. The most authentic note in Conrad is that the masks do not fit. But they are all we have. That is why codes are so precious to Conrad, especially the seaman's code. (pp. 54-5)

Conrad's fiction depends on belief in ... dark, ineffable realms, for they generate the compulsion of his work. Despite the verbosity and the analytical passages, the novels never clarify or lay bare the sources of energy. They cannot. There is a wager in such an aesthetic, almost a plea that the expressed appearances do, in fact, hint at, or stem from, something too fine or too prodigious for language. (p. 56)

Because of its emphasis on vision and its sense of the void, the Conradian novel can emerge only when fact, or the straightforward narration of a story, no longer carries the credibility or the "magic suggestiveness" that its author needs for his faith and defines as the condition of his art. Conrad's codes and forms are more truly generative than prescriptive because the sought-after self can be brought to life only through the complicity of character, narrator, and reader. (p. 57)

Arnold L. Weinstein, in his Vision and Response in Modern Fiction *(copyright © 1974 by Cornell University; used by permission of Cornell University Press),* Cornell University Press, *1974.*

In *Heart of Darkness,* the nature of Marlow's "a kind of light" has piqued critics for decades. Some readers still prefer to focus upon the novel as a tale of adventure or, at a second level, as criticism of "Christian" societies that abhor incest and cannibalism but condone economic aggression against less advanced people. Yet it is clearly descent into inner darkness that most deeply engages Marlow; it is equally clear that Marlow emerges from the descent "a changed and knowing man." ... Conrad—or Marlow—never really clarifies his insight. He has glimpsed something so dark, so alien that it can be expressed only indirectly through an overlapping haze of foreshadowing and revelation as the tale uncoils. Through Marlow, Conrad seems at least to be saying that there is an inner darkness in man untouched by beliefs current at his time; he seems at most to be saying that there is more than one way to get a true vision of man's universe—that a Kurtzlike vision downward to darkness may be as valid as a vision upward to light. This is not a particularly Christian concept, despite the symbolism inchoate in Conrad's snake-like river, or the Inferno of the dying slaves at the Coastal Station. It is, if anything, suggestive of the Manichaean belief in a universe where a demonic creator is equal to god.... Yet Conrad, deliberately or not, never specifically repudiates the Christian conceptions of light and dark, good and evil, God over all. He never specifically advises embracing what the serpent has to offer. (pp. 23-4)

Rose Salberg Kam, in Extrapolation *(copyright 1975 by Thomas D. and Alice S. Clareson), December, 1975.*

Self-possession is ... the primary 'article of creed' in Conrad. Being 'the first condition of good service', it is necessarily anterior to all that is subsumed by that ideal, to the effective deployment of the characteristic Conradian virtues of fidelity, solidarity, duty, discipline, courage, endurance—to compliance, in short, with the code of the Merchant Marine, to which Conrad subscribed in his first life and used as an initial moral marker in his second. If the world rests on a few simple ideas, those ideas or values are dependent for their realization on a prior condition of being.

It is a condition about which Conrad clearly felt very strongly, and in a directly personal way which adds a further dimension to its importance in his life and work. That he should declare he has 'a positive horror' of losing his self-possession 'even for one moving moment', and again admit to 'an instinctive horror' of such a loss, is indicative not only of the supreme value accorded the quality but also, in the unexpected excess of the sense of horror, of a personal insecurity, a radical uncertainty as to the tenure of his hold on the one thing really his. And indeed in ordinary, everyday life, if not under the pressure of stresses encountered at sea or at his desk, Conrad was on occasion revealingly unable to live up to his ideal. (p. 17)

Given the ... moral and psychological ramifications of the issue of self-possession in Conrad's life, it might well be expected that it constitute a steady nuclear complex in his work. I believe this to be the case, and, confining myself to the literary aspects of the question, wish to trace the development of the theme of self-possession in Conrad through a critical analysis of his major fiction. (p. 19)

If self-possession may be seen as Conrad's obsessive preoccupation, it is at once striking that the obsession should manifest itself in repeated depictions of loss of self. The ways in which self may be lost are varied, there being, I believe, four main variations which interest Conrad. There is, first, abandon, the letting go or surrender of self in passion; then there is panic, the losing of one's head in a situation which demands physical self-possession; third, there is nullity or vacancy, the loss of self that is a concomitant of spiritual disintegration; and finally there is suicide, the deliberate destruction of self. These, I suggest, are the four points of Conrad's literary compass.

The question of self-possession figures in Conrad's earliest work in relation to that of passion. Sexual abandon was not a subject which Conrad was psychologically equipped to handle successfully. . . . (p. 20)

In the works I have selected for analysis Conrad strenuously asserts the necessity for self-possession, but is led to a sympathetic and constantly deepening apprehension of panic and nullity and suicide. The works may be divided into two groups. From *The Nigger of the 'Narcissus'* to 'Typhoon' Conrad is primarily concerned with the question of physical self-possession, though in his portrayal of Kurtz in 'Heart of Darkness' he makes his first (largely unsuccessful) attempt to analyse a case of nullity. In the storm scenes in *The Nigger of the 'Narcissus'* and 'Typhoon' and in the journey up the river in 'Heart of Darkness', Conrad succeeds in depicting men who are endowed with a saving self-possession; but his imagination would appear to be most strongly seized by varied manifestations of panic and of abandon, both physical and spiritual. This phase culminates in *Lord Jim*, in which he arrives at a definitive account of the nature of the inner weakness that may make a man fall to pieces; and in 'Typhoon', in which he shows how a potential Jim may acquire inner strength and be braced into indomitability. Conrad would seem to have exhausted the theme of physical self-possession by the time he had completed 'Typhoon'—it is notable that a capacity for such self-possession is simply taken for granted in *Nostromo*—but he unexpectedly recurs to the subject in 'The Secret Sharer', where it undergoes a crucial development.

In the next phase, from *Nostromo* to *Under Western Eyes*, Conrad's interests are generally thought to have turned to the political, and the three major novels in this group are usually linked together as 'the political novels'. It is clear that in this period the setting is affairs of state rather than the whirl of typhoons, but the essential drama, it seems to me, is unchanged. I believe, that is, that Conrad is still fundamentally concerned with the problem of selfhood, though he now explores new ways in which a man may lose the full possession of himself. In this phase he is concerned with manifestations of spiritual nullity and with suicide rather than with physical panic. The nullity, he shows time and again, is the product of abandon, of the surrender of the self to a non-sexual but consuming passion, which is most often represented as a fixed idea or obsession. The state of nullity is conceived as a condition of spiritual vacancy, and it manifests itself outwardly in a pervasive moral nihilism. The phenomenon of obsession, moreover, is shown to have self-destructive implications, and, in the case of Martin Decoud in *Nostromo* and Winnie Verloc in *The Secret Agent*, to lead in the end to suicide.

The two phases are unified by more than a common concern with the loss of self. When a man loses possession of himself in Conrad, he lays himself open—[as in the case of] Willems in *An Outcast of the Islands*—to a counter-possession. Such a man, whether he abandons himself to passion or to panic, to obsession or despair, is conceived in almost legendary terms as a man possessed. This . . . is the case with both Kurtz and Jim in the first group of works, and—cutting across the division between the two phases—it is equally shown to be the case with Gould and Nostromo and Decoud and Dr. Monygham, with Winnie Verloc, and with Razumov. Men possessed, it would seem to follow, may be saved only by dispossession; but, though this would appear to be an obviously logical development, it was not until *Under Western Eyes* that Conrad could comprehensively and centrally portray it. I assume he was inhibited by the corollary that, in order to be dispossessed, a man must be ready to let go—for such a conception, as I have pointed out, was anathema to him. His art, however, soon began to confront him with situations in which it was clearly necessary for a character to let go, and also to pose the need for an authorial acceptance of the fact of unrestraint. Conrad's reluctance to follow the drive of his own art led, first, to the blurring of a crucial aspect of *The Nigger of the 'Narcissus'*, and then to the botching of the end of 'Heart of Darkness'.

Conrad took a significant step forward in this regard, however, in his portrayal of Dr. Monygham in *Nostromo*. Possessed by a sense of his own earlier disgrace but impelled by a love which he knows will remain unrequited, Monygham lets go customary restraints and risks his life for Mrs. Gould. The effacement of self that he demonstrates tacitly emerges at this point as a further necessary preliminary to dispossession. He is the first character in Conrad to move beyond a state of possession, and may in this respect be viewed as a forerunner of the more complex Razumov in *Under Western Eyes*. Razumov's self-effacement at the moment of dispossession is so radical that he envisages it as a surrendering of the self to destruction. Risking himself with abandon, he too is impelled by love, though he knowingly renounces the object of his passion when he lets go. Ultimately it is this kind of renunciation, with its concomitant self-effacement, that is set against the inability of self-centred men like Gould and Nostromo to renounce that which possesses them. To be dispossessed, that is, a man possessed must be ready to give up what is most precious to him. Since such self-effacement is worked by love, however, it would appear (in a manner that is analogous to a sexual loss and finding of self . . .) to lead paradoxically to the re-establishment of self—as proves to be the case with both Dr. Monygham and Razumov. What Conrad's art finally insists on—and the captain-narrator in 'The Secret Sharer' (whose climactic risking of his ship parallels an experience of the young Captain Korzeniowski) is a further striking instance of this—is that true self-possession is based on a capacity for abandon. (pp. 23-5)

In 'The Secret Sharer' Conrad's imagination seems to have seized on the fact that ideal seamanship may depend on the integration of qualities that are potentially subversive of it.

Leggatt would certainly seem to be strikingly endowed with the quality that is the first condition of good service. From the start, it is his self-possession that most strongly characterizes him. (p. 174)

[Leggatt] gives way neither to despair nor panic when put to the test at sea. Aboard the *Sephora* in 'a sea gone mad', it is Captain Archbold who gives up hope when the main topsail blows away and, with 'all his nerve [gone] to pieces altogether' . . . , fails to give the order to set the foresail; it is Leggatt who, realizing what should be done, gives the necessary order, sees that it is carried out, and saves the ship. . . . But it is also on that occasion that he kills an un-ruly member of the crew. . . . The vivid picture we are given . . . of Leggatt at the man's throat, frozen in that posture, as it were, since we are to understand that he 'was holding him by the throat' for 'over ten minutes', provides us with one of the most significant images—and epiphanies—in all Conrad. For what Leggatt's posture symbolizes is a holding on that is simultaneously a letting go. The letting go is implicit in his having maintained such a grip for so long a time; and when he says, in retrospect, that it was clear he 'meant business', he seems to recognize how he in fact abandoned himself to his impulse, even though he may have had no conscious intention of killing the man when he sprang at him.

The young captain-narrator, in his response to Leggatt's story, uses an image which helps us to clarify the implications of a holding on that is also a letting go. He tells Leggatt that he 'quite [understands]':

> It was all very simple. The same strung-up force which had given twenty-four men a chance, at least, for their lives, had, in a sort of recoil, crushed an unworthy mutinous existence.

The way in which the captain envisages Leggatt as having let go is vividly evoked by the image of the 'recoil' of the 'strung-up force'; but that it is 'the same force' which saves life and destroys life suggests that the force is itself a tension of opposites, that the quality of self-possession, which, strung-up to a pitch, saves the ship, contains or controls the quality of abandon, which, released in recoil, kills the man. But then the force may be said to contain the abandon in another sense—to contain it as a constituent; and Conrad, after ten years of sustained grappling with the problem, had thus articulated an intuition that he seemed to be groping after in 'Heart of Darkness', where the self-possession of Kurtz's savage woman . . . [appears] to be founded on a capacity for abandon. The novelist's unexpected return to the question of physical self-possession, therefore, may be seen as an attempt to take the matter further than he had been able to by the end of *Lord Jim* and 'Typhoon'; it may also be explained by a need, at the point he had reached in *Under Western Eyes,* to substantiate a similar intuition that he had been moving towards in the intangible sphere of the spirit in the more palpable terms of the flesh—and of the life at sea that he knew so well.

Such paradoxes of being, however, are not easily accommodated by a conventional morality, whether of the formally strict or practically tolerant variety. Captain Archbold, for instance, at once concludes that Leggatt's action has made him morally unfit to retain his position as an officer aboard the *Sephora*. . . . The captain-narrator, on the other hand, concludes that Leggatt was morally justified in doing what he did because of the danger that threatened the ship; and though this is the more lenient judgement that we are implicitly asked to accept as final, we cannot but be aware that, when he says 'it was all very simple', he is ig-

noring some of the disturbing implications of the thrusts of force he has so vividly discerned. A concern for life, for example, which may be assumed to have impelled Leggatt in his desire to save it, would seem to coexist with a contempt for life—or, at any rate, for certain manifestations of it—that is seen to lurk behind his readiness to destroy it. (pp. 174-76)

The narrator [in *The Secret Sharer*] is about to enter literally on a new phase of existence as a captain, and he appears to believe that the 'long and arduous enterprise' of the coming voyage will measure his fitness not only to command but to live since to command is 'the appointed task' of his existence. He regards the voyage, that is to say, as a test of himself both as a man and a captain, and what he consequently '[feels]' most' before its start is his being 'a stranger to the ship' and 'somewhat of a stranger' to himself. At the outset, therefore, he finds himself in a paradoxical situation: in order to be sure of being able to meet the test he must know both the ship and himself, to a degree that he may take both its adequacy and his own 'for granted'; he can only achieve such knowledge, however, by testing himself and his ship to the utmost. In the event, it is this that he soon proceeds to do. And he may then be assumed to be seeking to live up to 'that ideal conception' of his personality which he has 'set up for himself secretly'.

The fact that the young captain has set up such a shadow figure suggests he has a secret sharer even before Leggatt appears on the scene. When Leggatt comes aboard, the captain not only identifies with him but would seem to regard him as an embodiment of his own ideal conception of self. (pp. 179-80)

If the captain does not at once commit himself to protecting Leggatt, he responds with an immediate humanity and compassion to his need of physical help. His fellow-feeling for Leggatt, which rapidly expands into a sense of identification with him, imposes on him a choice between loyalty to the man, which requires his continued aiding of him, and fidelity to the social and legal code, which necessitates his surrendering him to the captain of the *Sephora* when he arrives. . . . The captain has so strong a sense of the mitigating circumstances of Leggatt's crime that it outweighs the kind of 'pitiless obligation' which the captain of the *Sephora* feels he must adhere to. . . . In protecting Leggatt, therefore, the captain stands by his own moral judgement, accepting the obligation not of the law but of an individual moral responsibility. (p. 181)

The captain's story is illustrative, we begin to realize, of paradoxes of being that are analogous to those dramatized in the case of Leggatt. And just as Leggatt is most notably characterized by the image of him at the sailor's throat, so the quality of the young captain is epitomized for us in the picture we are given of his handling of his ship when he helps Leggatt to escape. He tells Leggatt he has decided to 'edge [the ship] in to half a mile [of the shore], as far as [he] may be able to judge in the dark—' in order to give him a chance to swim for the island of Koh-ring. . . . It is evident it is not out of a sense of obligation to Leggatt that the captain regards it as 'a matter of conscience' to take his ship so dangerously close to the shore, for he knows that Leggatt is a strong swimmer. . . . He would seem to be driven rather by a need to put both himself and his ship to an extreme test as a necessary preliminary to his taking effective possession of it as its captain. It is striking, in this respect, that the test should be depicted (as in the case of Leggatt's killing of the sailor) in terms of a holding on that is simultaneously a letting go: 'under any other circumstances', the captain reflects, he 'would not have held on a minute longer', but he does in fact hold on, letting the ship go closer and closer, giving it its head, as it were, until the 'black southern hill of Koh-ring' seems 'to hang right over the ship like a towering fragment of the everlasting night' and to be 'gliding irresistibly' towards it. (pp. 181-82)

Unlike Leggatt at the sailor's throat, however, the captain never loses his self-control, and at the last moment succeeds in bringing the ship round. . . . Though the captain may start as 'a stranger to the ship', he comes to full knowledge of it as a result of this experience, the 'silent knowledge' that he has of it evoking, in its context of 'mute affection' and 'perfect communion', the sort of knowledge that a man may take of a woman. The captain, that is, sees himself as having fully taken possession of his ship; we see, furthermore, that he has ceased to be 'somewhat of a stranger' to himself, and that, having learnt to know his own resources, he has also taken full possession of himself. During the manoeuvre, the self-possession he demonstrates in snatching the ship from disaster is shown to coexist with a capacity for letting go; just as his fitness for the responsibility of command (which he proves at the same time) is seen to coexist, given the way in which he risks the safety of his ship and the lives of his crew, with a pronounced tendency to irresponsibility. But the sort of knowledge he comes to as a result of the experience suggests the integration of these dark Dionysian qualities in a self that will henceforth be proof against their disruptive influence. . . . (pp. 182-83)

H. M. Daleski, in his Joseph Conrad: The Way of Dispossession *(© 1976 by H. M. Daleski), Holmes & Meier, 1977.*

(Arthur Annesley) Ronald Firbank

1886-1926

English novelist, poet, dramatist, and short story writer. Born in London of wealthy parents, Firbank attended Cambridge, where he adopted the lifestyle of a leisured aesthete. His principal genre was the novel, and his central concern in this genre was the sensitive individual as isolated and lonely victim in an absurd and often depraved world. This potentially dreary theme was developed with a satirical elegance and brittle gaiety. Firbank had a taste for original characters and a disdain for plot (the latter were consequently wispy). His dialogue, however, was brilliant and his prose meticulously patterned. His impressionistic, Dadaistic style was consistently marked with an idiosyncratic wit both artificial and fantastic. Firbank would, for example, quote from imaginary sources, textbooks, and history. Sojourns in Italy, Spain, France, North Africa, and Cuba provided the exotic settings of his novels. His technical innovations were borrowed by Aldous Huxley, Evelyn Waugh, Ivy Compton-Burnett, and Iris Murdoch, among others. Individualistic, almost "high camp" in his personal life, Firbank's hobbies ran to such activities as witnessing wills and attempting for years to grow a palm tree in his London apartment. His health was as fragile as his genius. Firbank hated the idea of being forty, a fact that made his death from pneumonia at the age of thirty-nine a timely one.

PRINCIPAL WORKS

Vainglory (novel) 1915
Inclinations (novel) 1916
Caprice (novel) 1917
Valmouth (novel) 1919
The Princess Zoubaroff (drama) 1920
The Flower beneath the Foot (novel) 1923
Sorrow in Sunlight (novel) 1924
    [published as *Prancing Nigger*, 1925]
Concerning the Eccentricities of Cardinal Pirelli (novel) 1926
The Artificial Princess (novel) 1934

Ronald Firbank is the only authentic master of the light touch I have discovered. His touch is so light, indeed, that after reading one of his books I find even Max Beerbohm a trifle studied, a little composed. (p. 172)

Firbank is, perhaps, the only purely Greek writer that we possess today. There is no sentimentality or irony in his work; hardly even cynicism. There is, indeed, a baffling quality about Firbank's very lucidity, his gay, firm grasp of his trivial peccancies. His ellipses serve the same purpose as the descending curtain at the close of the first act of *Die Walküre*. His form arranges itself for the most part in a diagram of dialogue . . . and such dialogue! No matter how many ancient clouds of glory he trails behind him, and there is Greek, Firbank is more than up-to-date. He is the Pierrot of the minute. Félicien Rops on a merry-go-round. Aubrey Beardsley in a Rolls-Royce. Ronald in Lesbosland. Puck celebrating the Black Mass. Sacher-Masoch in Mayfair. A Rebours à la mode. Aretino in Piccadilly. Jean Cocteau at the Savoy. The Oxford tradition with steam from the Paris bains de vapeur. The cubists are remembered. Firbank plays Picasso's violin. The decorations serve more than their purpose. Flippant, impertinent symbols are the tools of his impudicity. Fruits, flowers, bees, and even mice play eccentric rôles in these concentric comedies. Roses and nightingales impose their furtive intentions. Cathedral towers and organ recitals are to be noted among the minor gems in a by no means despicable collection. At last, apparently, Tinker Bell's life is no longer in danger. Can it be possible that this impudent young man is satirizing D. H. Lawrence, or is this the true picture of English life? (pp. 172-73)

To such affairs of the world as those for which he has no taste he is utterly indifferent. He does not satirize the things he hates. He flits airily about, arranging with skilful fingers the things he loves. Make no mistake: what he wants to do he does, and is a master of the doing of. The delicate tranquillity of his prose, shot through with icy stabs of wit and shimmering gleams of sophistication, is very rare and very original. When you compare him with other authors, logically you can go no further than the binding. His utterly own manner alienates him completely from the possibility of any other form of estimate. He is unique, a glittering dragon-fly skimming over the sunlit literary garden, where almost all the other creatures crawl. (pp. 173-74)

Carl Van Vechten, "Ronald Firbank," in his Excavations: A Book of Advocacies *(copyright 1926 by Carl Van Vechten; reprinted by permission of Alfred A. Knopf, Inc.), Knopf, 1926, pp. 172-74.*

[Ronald Firbank] is *fin de siècle,* as it used to be called; he belongs to the 'nineties and the *Yellow Book;* his mind inherits the furniture and his prose the cadences of Aubrey Beardsley's *Under the Hill.* . . . Is he affected? Yes, always. Is he self-conscious? No; he wants to mop and mow, and put on birettas and stays, and he does it as naturally as healthy Englishmen light their pipes. Is he himself healthy? Perish the thought! Is he passionate, compassionate, dispassionate? Next question! Is he intelligent? Not particularly, if we compare him with another writer whom he occasionally resembles—Max. [Beerbohm, of course.] . . . What charms us in him is his taste, his choice of words, the rhythm both of his narrative and of his conversations, his wit, and—in his later work—an opulence as of gathered fruit and enamelled skies. His very monsignorishness is acceptable. It is *chic,* it is *risqué,* to titter in sacristies and peep through grilles at ecclesiastical Thesmophoriazusae, and if he becomes petulant, and lets a convent or a pipkin crash, it does not signify, for likely enough we have thrown down the book ourselves a page before. Yes, he has genius, for we are certain to take up the book again. . . . (p. 118)

> E. M. Forster, "Ronald Firbank" (1929), in
> his Abinger Harvest (© 1936, 1964 by E. M.
> Forster; reprinted by permission of Har-
> court Brace Jovanovich, Inc.), Harcourt,
> 1936, pp. 115-21.

Firbank's was a world of pure fancy: it was the extreme of escapism, but one should add that though it meant escape from life, it meant equally escape *to* a temperament. It was an artificial, a downright unreal world—a world which with its curiously wrought "sophistication" evoked stagey night-scenes brilliant with electric light. But the truth about Firbank's world does not lie, for all that, with those who regard it as merely silly; one might as well call "Alice in Wonderland" silly. And the escapism of Ronald Firbank lies much closer to the escapism of Lewis Carroll than it does, let us say, to that of Carl Van Vechten or Cabell. For its artificiality is genuine, and—except as art—is complete; its scenes, its sentiments, its values are not, as Van Vechten's or Cabell's are, mixed. With Firbank we are well on our way toward Dada except that Firbank still bravely attempts a kind of continuity and roundedness of pattern, as if he could somehow miraculously expand his one-dimensioned universe into three. But actually his success lies in quite the other direction: he is at his best in disoriented moments of non-sequitur, in unfettered flights of madcap fancy, in amalgams of poetry with nonsense. He is at his best when he archly mingles absurdity with charm.

And Firbank who was genuinely witty and by no means unimaginative, only misses being first-rate entertainment because he is too much given to fuss and feathers. He is never spontaneous and never simple. With an artistry always at the mercy of his temperament, he sought to achieve complicated effects; and by doing so, usually failed of any effect at all. Most of Carroll's nonsense is naked and direct: it does not impede the tempo of his narrative, or blur the outlines of his scene. But Firbank, a follower of the cult of the petit maitre, is always obsessed with painting in the last subtle touch; and it is one touch too many. Thus a man with many stylistic talents was doomed to a labored style. Thus a really witty writer ends by being tiresome. Thus a man who might have become skillful at baroque became, instead, affected. Thus a man with an eye for loveliness never got beyond a mastery of cosmetics. He is only really successful with a snapshot or a phrase.

It need scarcely be added that Firbank had nothing whatever to say. But at least, unlike the other sophisticates of his day, he was unpretentious. He remained true to his temperament, even though its over-refinements betrayed him. As for his decadence, it was not of a willful or immoral sort, but merely the natural possession of a man who shied away from light and air. He lived in a hothouse because he liked a hothouse, and it might have surprised him to learn that he was odd in doing so. Meadows, to him, would have seemed sprawling and unkempt; and he would have been forced to the trouble of reminding you that the dandelion is a weed, and not a flower. (p. 24)

> Louis Kronenberger, "Hothouse Blooms,"
> in The New York Times Book Review (©
> 1935 by The New York Times Company;
> reprinted by permission), November 17,
> 1935, pp. 7, 24.

Firbank has been so obscured by the tiresome adulation of the claque which adores his pre-1914 "wickedness" and by the legend he constructed about himself that almost a quarter of a century after his death it is still difficult to disentangle the serious artist from the effeminate posturer who tried so hard—and with indifferent success—to astonish the bourgeois. Sociologically he belongs to the history of sensitive young men who escape from the materialism which has brought money into the family straight into the materialism of the aesthete and the social snob. . . . Until the last ten years of his life, when, for all his flittings about, he settled himself earnestly to becoming a writer, he was engaged in a seemingly sterile pursuit of the amusing and the beautiful.

The very settings of his novels record this flight from the world of his grandfather into the refinements of another kind of materialism. . . . Firbank is the first novelist to celebrate cafe society.

As an artist he often succeeded in spite of himself. He worked hard at his writing, but he tried to make it sound like the purely casual comment of the most elegant dilettante. Sex, for him, was always a matter for comedy, but just as in life his infantilism betrayed him into preposterous affectation, so in his novels the comedy of sex is frequently marred by an almost obsessional bravado and sniggering; for the exquisite and frivolous dream world of his fiction, with its international élite and rococo palaces, is a Nirvana in which, like Negroes in Paris in the twenties, homosexuals are the ultimate *chic.* Even in his own time he was old-fashioned in his toyings with the ceremonial of Rome, his aesthetic interest in evil, "if for no other purpose, to add color to life," and a dandyism which would have revolted Baudelaire. . . . But—and this is what saved him as an artist —he was never really fooled by [his world]; there is always a tough core of common sense to his dallyings with the trivial; he merely found the substance of his art in the fantastic behavior of the inhabitants of a fantastic milieu. . . . He is one of the few Georgian novelists who scrupulously eschewed the dead-end of realist-cum-naturalist fiction. Today his pictures of a vanished and usually an improbable world stand up far better than novels which in his own time seemed indestructible.

Firbank's writing is reminiscent of the Wilde of "Dorian Grey," of Baron Corvo, most of all perhaps of Ivy

Compton-Burnett with the passion left out, of Max Beer-bohm and of Max Ewing, whose "Going Somewhere" (a piece of anthropological curiosa and the middlebrow's Firbank) ought also to be reprinted. But all this is only approximate. "His work," says a character in "Vainglory," his first novel, describing a writer clearly meant to be Firbank, "calls to mind a frieze with figures of varying heights trotting all the same way. If one should by chance turn about it's usually merely to stare or sneer or to make a grimace. Only occasionally his figures care to beckon. And they rarely touch." This is an effect which might be predicted of a writer who habitually collected on little pieces of paper the remarks which occurred to him or which he overheard, later fitting them together into a careful mosaic. His early novels, indeed, tend to be all talk conducted on the same level. Later—to read him chronologically is to see his art developing—he created magnificent grotesques. They do not "touch," if by that we mean the passion which sometimes breaks so wonderfully through the comic mask in Molière or Congreve, for Firbanks's satire never operated on the passional level. But too much has been made of their artificiality. They stem from the rich tradition of British eccentricity, which was at its height, since eccentricity could then best be afforded, in the world in which Firbank lived. A glance at the sober reporting of Sir Osbert Sit-well's memoirs should dissipate any notion that their goings-on are merely extravagant invention.

Firbank worked almost entirely in terms of what seem to be superficial and frivolous externals. The trappings of circumstance were alike fascinating in themselves and indices to the most complex states. Like Joyce and Virginia Woolf, he relied on the methods of poetry, the drama, and impressionist painting. A phrase does what pages of analysis and description are intended to do in the novels of his contemporaries; the most unlikely opposites are juxtaposed for comic purposes; scenes are described in terms of the remarks which float through them—all this with such deceptive flippancy that the inner complexity and the satire may escape the casual reader. The language is private. . . . He makes his sympathetic reader a member of [his] little group. Fleetingly and joyfully one has the sense of belonging to the inner circle. Read Firbank aloud to grasp the subtlety of his dialogue.

His favorite device, and one which, I think, explains a good deal about Firbank as a human being, is a kind of watered-down romantic irony. He is constantly deflating the objects of his concern. So, although he burlesques themes popular in nineteenth-century English fiction for a satire turned upon the bourgeois milieu from which he had escaped, this satire is also turned upon the never-never-land which was only half his loving contrivance. (pp. 520-21)

There is a consistent satiric intent in these novels, aimed at the usual objects of social satire. And the touch is so light, so deft, the rapier flicking even those ineffably beautiful and world-weary figures the artist most loves. There is also a perverse moral grandeur. For all the scandal of his end, in death Firbank's Cardinal Pirelli is triumphant. . . . And one has only to read a page or so of Firbank at random to note the sense of mortality, of the transience of all the earthly beauty he loved so well, which makes these novels, with their curious materialism, their praises of the rich and the exotic, poignant as well as comic. (p. 521)

Ernest Jones, "The World of Ronald Fir-
bank," in The Nation *(copyright 1949 by the Nation Associates, Inc.), November 26, 1949, pp. 520-21.*

One may have thought, when one first looked at [Firbank's] books in the twenties, that they were foamy improvisations which could be skimmed up in rapid reading. Yet when one tried to run through them, one found oneself pricked by something that queerly impressed; one was aware of artistic seriousness, even if one did not linger to find out what the writer was up to. When one returns to them today, one realizes that Ronald Firbank was one of the writers of his time who took most trouble over their work and who were most singlemindedly devoted to literature. The memoirs of him testify to this. His books are not foolish trifles, scribbled down to get through the boredoms of a languid and luxurious life. They are extremely intellectual, and composed with the closest attention: dense textures of indirection that always disguise point. They have to be read with care, and they can be read again and again, because Firbank has loaded every rift with ore. The effect of his writing is light, but it differs from the flimsier work of the nineties, which, at first sight, it may resemble, in the tension behind it of the effort to find the felicitous or the witty phrase which will render the essence of something. The little dyed twirls of plume and the often fresh sprays of flowers, the half-stifled flutters of laughter and the *fusées* of jewelly fire, have been twisted and tempered in a mind that is capable of concentration. It is a glancing mind but rarely wobbles. . . . [Phrase] by phrase, sentence by sentence, paragraph by paragraph, chapter by chapter, the workmanship is not merely exact but of a quality for which the craftsman must gratuitously tax himself. (pp. 491-92)

[His work is] in an old and strong English tradition: it belongs to the school of comedy that had its first great practitioner in Ben Jonson, that was exploited in its purest form by Congreve and the other Restoration dramatists, and that persists through a variety of modifications in Peacock, Gilbert and Aldous Huxley. The true products of this school are at the opposite pole from the hearty and hilarious English humor (though in some writers the two are combined). It is polished and coldly reasoned and rarely admits any kind of idealism. It is occupied with worldly values and if it ever turns its attention to general ideas, it makes mock of them all indiscriminately. Though it sometimes introduces a moralist who is supposed to act as a touchstone in showing up the faults of the other characters, it usually verges on cynicism, and it is always non-romantic and non-sentimental. There is nothing, so far as I know, quite like this English comic tradition in the literature of any other country. Distinguished, unscrupulous, hard; carved, gilded and decorative; planned logically and executed deliberately; of good quality, designed for long wear; intellectual but never intelligent—no people could have developed it but the English. You may feel, when you first approach Firbank, that his talent is too effeminate to claim ancestry from this masculine line; and it is true that a number of his books are occupied almost exclusively with women, and that his writing is full of trailed dots, coy italics and little cries. Yet these latter, always calculated, are really a part of his subject: the mannerisms that go with the habits of his special group and time. You may think that his effete preciosity has little in common with the brutality and elegance of *Love for Love* and *The Way of the World*. Yet the fact that Ronald Firbank is dealing with a later and less lusty phase of the same society as Congreve should not keep us from appreciating that his formal panels are no less finely painted.

Ronald Firbank wrote one play, *The Princess Zoubaroff*, and it affords a useful opportunity to compare his methods and point of view with those of Restoration comedy. The men and women in Wycherley and Congreve are all engaged in chasing one another: they lack sentiment but have vigorous appetites. The men and women in Firbank, for the most part, have neither sentiment nor keen desires. To them marriage means as little as it does to the characters of Congreve; but the alternative is not a succession of more or less piquant adulteries: it is likely to be an adolescent falling-back on members of their own sexes. (pp. 492-93)

Where the speeches in Congreve are set-pieces, where the scenes have the give-and-take of an energetic well-played game, the dialogue in Firbank is all vague innuendos, gasps and murmurs, light caresses, small digs. Yet as writing it is no less consummate—and much finer than that of Wilde when he is working in the Congreve tradition. Not that Firbank's fluttering absurdities are more skillful than Wilde's ringingly turned epigrams; but there is always in the comedies of Wilde an element of conventional theater—of melodrama or simple farce—though in this he is of course running true to the tone of his late-Victorian time. *Lady Windemere's Fan* has passages that might almost have been written by Pinero; *The Importance of Being Ernest* is still not far from *Charley's Aunt*. Firbank's comedy belongs to a society that is as non-moral as the Restoration and quite detached from the middle-class standards that still make themselves felt in Wilde.

One finds also in Firbank, however, besides this durable old English tradition, a certain influence from modern France—notably, I should say, from *Histoire Contemporaine,* Anatole France's Bergeret series. One seems to find the Anatole France formulas both in Firbank's tricks of style and in his presentation of episodes. In the latter connection, Firbank seems also to have reproduced France's faults—for the weakness of his narratives, like the weakness of France's, is a lack of continuous development. One chapter does not lead to another, but each makes a little vignette which, significant and finished though it is, does not always fall into place as part of a coherent scheme. (pp. 494-95)

The Artificial Princess—*Vainglory, Inclinations* and *Caprice*—are all attempts, most successful in spite of their apparent fanciness, to depict English life and character. Ronald Firbank has caught certain aspects of these as perhaps no one else has done—particularly the English habit of pretending to disregard what is uppermost in people's minds and always talking about something else. In Firbank's next novel, *Valmouth,* he is dealing still with the English scene but has found his own vein of fantasy, and develops in terms of high caricature the theme of the English capacity for carrying on unperturbedly in the presence of the scandalous or the catastrophic. (pp. 496-97)

[Turning] to religion from the life of the world is a theme in all Firbank's later books. If you should read *The Flower Beneath the Foot* without knowing Firbank's work well, you might think this was all a joke, that he was merely being silly and witty, as he was in *The Princess Zoubaroff*, about the fashionable aspects of religion. But that was not the case. (p. 499)

Ronald Firbank was the poet of the *fou rire*. That is the key to the whole of his work. There is anguish behind it all—and the more ridiculous it is, the better he is expressing this anguish. *The Eccentricities of Cardinal Pirelli* is at once his most preposterous book and the one that has most moral meaning; it combines his most perverse story with his purest and most beautiful writing. He has here expressed his ideal conception, quite heretical but not irresponsible, not lacking in serious intention, of what a Catholic priest might be, and this has enabled him, for the first time, through art, fully to accommodate his imperfections, to triumph over his disabilities. It may be that the dead Cardinal's serenity had been won by him, too, for a moment in the few weeks of life that were left him. (p. 501)

> *Edmund Wilson, "A Revival of Ronald Firbank" (December 10, 1949), in his* Classics and Commercials: A Literary Chronicle of the Forties *(reprinted with the permission of Farrar, Straus & Giroux, Inc.; copyright 1950 by Edmund Wilson), Farrar, Straus, 1950, pp. 486-502.*

[In Firbank's novels] was to be found a new if minute world, which existed by its own pulse of time and exhibited its own standards of behavior. Strange, fresh tides of rhythm played and lapped round its breathless shores, on which figures that, however etiolate, were sufficiently substantial for the reader never to be able to forget them, moved to their own measure and were left striking the most unexpected attitudes against the mauve and lime-green horizon. Each book, as it appeared, was a new revelation of style, and of a wit that rippled the surface of every page without ever breaking it. The virtuosity of the author was able to net any situation, however crazy or occasionally even obscene, and let it loose in the realms of a harmless reality. Just as in the autumn the silver cobwebs lightly cover the trees with a thin mist of impalpable beauty, so a similar highly stylized but intangible loveliness hung over every page, while wit ran in, round and underneath each word. But the chief claim that is to be advanced for the author, I think, is his startling technical achievement. His dialogues are quicker and lighter than had hitherto been designed for a novel. He altered the pace of the dialogue for the novel, and already his influence can be detected in writers of more content than himself, and indeed, in the most unlikely quarters. (pp. 79-80)

The first impression of him in conversation must always have been surprise that so frail, vague and extraordinary a creature could ever have arranged—let alone have created—a book. But there it was: he was a born, as opposed to a self-made, writer. (p. 88)

> *Sir Osbert Sitwell, "Ronald Firbank," in his* Noble Essences: A Book of Characters *(copyright © 1950 by Sir Osbert Sitwell; reprinted by permission of Little, Brown and Co. in association with the Atlantic Monthly Press), Atlantic-Little, Brown, 1950, pp. 77-100.*

[Firbank] is one of the pioneers of the moment-by-moment novel. The moment-by-moment fashion has now outlived its usefulness, but it dominated a certain kind of sensibility for thirty years. . . . In reality, it is not so much a technique as an attitude of mind, which suggests that a writer can only learn anything of life *through the immediate present,* i.e., he should confine his art to what he can see and hear. . . . No attitude could be more sterile. It is not in the least how one learns about life in actual fact. In knowing a human being, one does not restrict oneself to the seconds in which one hears him speak and watches his face: one thinks about him, corrects one's thoughts, investigates his past and guesses his future, listens to others' opinions, and gradually forms a kind of composite of feeling and observation which, though it includes moment-by-moment pictures, is utterly different in kind. That is the way in which the great human novelists have always worked: it is, incidentally, the way in which anyone who studies people for a living has to work. . . .

The moment-by-moment vision looked to its pioneers as though it might reveal startling truths, but it has turned out arid. Its characteristic works have sacrificed both mind and emotion—which, in any literary form, is altogether too big a sacrifice. That is why a number of contemporary novelists are making a fresh start.

With all that said, Firbank has several claims on our admiration—a genuine originality (when he began writing there was no one in the least like him), a remarkable eye, a kind of eldritch gaiety. He also possessed another quality which, while it is not strictly a literary virtue, increases his impact, especially on the young. He was totally devoid of moral vanity; he was the least stuffed of men; he exposed the nerve of his perverse sexual temperament, with an abandon that few writers had done before him. Often this quality—irrespective of artistic merit—turns out to have an appeal for the sensitive young, puzzled and sometimes dismayed by facets of their own temperament with which they have not yet come to terms. Several writers, not quite of the first rank, have derived a large slice of their reputation because they have, through their self-exposure, calmed the fears of others. They have, as it were, presented some of their readers with the latch-key. Among these latch-key novelists, Firbank has, and may for some time continue to have, his own peculiar place. (p. 82)

> *C. P. Snow, in* The Spectator (© *1951 by* The Spectator; *reprinted by permission of* The Spectator) *January 19, 1951.*

We *need* all the Firbank we can get. We need the example of his splendid inconsequence—seen backward with special effect through the work of Henry Green—to deliver us from the dull consequence of plot. We can be stimulated by the strategies of his dialogue: the constant flow of talk, at once witty and silly, real and artificial, to which no one listens, and into which everything, action and introspection, is dissolved—even the author's comment becoming just another voice among drawing-room voices. The effect is that of extreme fenestration; his works are all window and no wall, every possible element of structure sacrificed for the sake of light.

We need his practice chiefly, however, as a specific against the thick novel of merciless documentation. I remember recently putting down "The Wall" [Fiedler is probably referring to John Hersey's novel, new when this review was written], opaque, earnest, and unconvincing, *wrong* as fiction, and picking up "Cardinel Pirelli," slight, mannered, and impudent, with the sense of coming home to the authentic literary experience. Time has delivered Firbank

from the misleading connotations of the titillating and the chic, so that we can see him now as a classic instance of the uses of convention. We are all the time somehow forgetting that the truth of fiction is in inverse proportion to its resemblance to any superficial "reality." Even great masters of the convincing grotesque like Faulkner or Dickens or Dostoevsky become so familiar that we come to think of them as "realistic." At that point we must turn to some master of a new convention, or a revived one, to which we are no longer immune, and learn again that the essential skill of the novelist lies in protecting his fictional standards of truth from any adulteration with the standards of actual life. This is the use of Firbank now. (pp. 381-82)

Yet . . . Firbank is himself so much a party to the witty snobbery of his characters that he ends with a second-rate irony, negative and exclusive, rather than the positive, inclusive irony of, say, Moliere's "Misanthrope." There is an ultimate irony of love to which Firbank for all his skill and wit and sincerity cannot attain. (p. 382)

> *Leslie A. Fiedler, "The Relevance of Irrelevance," in* The Nation (*copyright 1951 by the Nation Associates, Inc.), April 21, 1951, pp. 381-82.*

Concerning the Eccentricities of Cardinal Pirelli . . . is in some ways, I believe, the best book of Ronald Firbank's I have read—certainly one of the very best written and one of the freest from the curious "gagging" with which Firbank has had a way of shutting off the vividness and charm of his characters by reducing them to the mere comic names of a sophisticated funny-paper. Ronald Firbank has usually been treated as a less important representative of the fashionable school of ironic romance (Van Vechten, Aldous Huxley, etc.); but, though at first glance he looks the most trivial, he seems to me to have felt the artist's vocation more authentically than many of the others. These others, in general, are graceful writers; but Firbank is not really a graceful writer: he works always in brief discontinuous strokes which appear to have cost him some pains. Whatever else he may not take seriously, he is serious about literature. (p. 264)

But Firbank, in some ways so highly developed, is fatally deficient in others. . . . In their subjects themselves, Firbank's novels seem to reflect some fundamental malformation; it is not merely the reader who finds them unsatisfactory, but the author who expresses dissatisfaction. All the heroes and heroines of Firbank—in those books that I have read, at least—have the most unfortunate fates; possessed by a bizarre variety of passions, they are almost invariably frustrated in their efforts to satisfy them. This final novel, indeed, seems a fable for the author's own case: can we fail to recognize in the Cardinal, with his "very great distinction and sweetness," whose ecclesiastical career is blighted by his worldliness and frivolity, by his inveterate excessive indulgence toward the weaknesses and vagaries of his flock, a symbol of the fate of that English novelist, distinguished by some very rare qualities, who never came to anything in the world of letters. . . . (p. 265)

[An] incongruous bitterness . . . sometimes makes itself felt in Firbank. . . . Firbank [has] a cool and trivial cruelty that we might call cattily feminine if it were not so plainly something else. And in [his] sensitiveness, [his] subtle intelligence, [his] taste for fine and gorgeous things, as well as in

[his] malice, [his] manias and [his] incurable tic of silliness, [he has] much in common with the uncomfortable character of Proust's M. de Charlus. (p. 266)

> *Edmund Wilson, in his* The Shores of Light: A Literary Chronicle of the Twenties and Thirties *(reprinted with the permission of Farrar, Straus & Giroux, Inc., copyright 1952 by Edmund Wilson), Farrar, Straus and Young, 1952.*

[The] wild satires and fairy tales of Ronald Firbank . . . are antics in a void left by life, elegies on burst bubbles. They celebrate the unworldliness of the rich, the childishness of aristocracy, the ubiquity of priests, the vim of the sensual life, the venom and the languor of taste and pleasure. They commemorate the comi-tragedy of the superlatives and fashions in which the heart thrills and dies a hundred times a day. . . . [It] is a simple fact that technically Firbank cleared dead wood out of the English novel, in one or two convulsive laughs; laid down the pattern for contemporary dialogue twenty or thirty years ago and discovered the fact of hysterical private humour—the jokes the mind makes and does not communicate. . . . [If] we can safely let characters speak for themselves and then fail to keep up a conversation, if we can create an emotion by describing something else, it is in part due to Firbank's frantic driving.

Let us grant that Firbank's baroque paradises, his jazzband kingdoms, his over-heated and flower-stuffed conservatories would have been intolerable if he had been a larger writer, and had not the skids and evasions of startling economy by nature. . . . One inhales him and it is important not to take too much at a time. Even so, he is tricky; for as one turns the page for the next hilarious breath, the story is over and one is caught with an empty nose. It is not easy to say what the novels are about, though we shall remember surgical sentences and wounding paragraphs by heart. *Prancing Nigger,* the most felt of his books, and one which was originally intended as a kind of documentary study on the unhappy condition of Haiti, can be defined, perhaps, more closely than the rest. . . . [There] is in this book a rumble of indignation which replaces the stylish horror he lets fall in his satires on fashion and chic. A not very happy moral note is in this tale, and there is a rather gummy sentence or two about the evils of rootlessness, which are heavy on the tongue of a dandy; one cannot go in for both the stylish and the moral. But *Prancing Nigger* is made by its warmth and its lyrical pathos; and although Firbank may have made his Negroes sing hymns like

> Time like an ever-rolling stream
> Bears all its sons away

for the lark of it, the sentiment was close to his own sensibility to the transient in life. Time is his subject. He is a poet of the surface of life and the writers who can feather a surface are rare. The comedy is in the inconsequence; the poetry in the evanescence; the tragedy in the chill of loneliness and desolation which will suddenly strike in a random word. The element common to all these novels is melancholy. . . . His comic genius rises from the fatality of rarely seeing life steadily and never seeing it whole. It is in bits.

His art is to make stained glass out of the unlikely bits. (pp. 229-32)

The Eccentricities of Cardinal Pirelli has a cloying and faded corruption and naughtiness. In general, the brilliant indecencies of Firbank (so wonderfully timed and without the tedium of lascivious lingering) are best when he is not being naughty about the nuns and priests. This kind of joke is wearying, a sort of Catholic convert smut which Firbank (who was a convert) did not escape. . . . For myself, *The Flower Beneath the Foot,* with its wild account of an African visit to a European court, is the most successful of the satires. (p. 233)

It is a surprise that so much of Firbank has survived from the Twenties, but as he is totally unreal and Fashion is eternal, he is dateless, though one can see that his freakishness may be despised and its décor become a bore. There is a force of feeling, scattered in his works, which recalls the ambiguous emotions we meet in John Betjeman's poems, and which gives his absurd world a vitality and determination of its own. . . . It is the strength of detail that counts in writers like this; the taste—if that can outlast a generation —for a certain tone of voice, breathless, snobbish, frightening and full of malice. Unlike Max Beerbohm he is the incumbent of a fundamental literary innocence. In life, a hermit almost speechless, helplessly gesticulating, a bizarre and feather-headed traveller unable to communicate, Firbank would be found sitting among the silliest illustrated papers, "getting ideas" from them, and seeing life—by some alarming but beneficent deprivation—flat and without perspective. Of our contemporary satirists he alone has the traditional quality of total artifice. (pp. 233-34)

> *V. S. Pritchett, "Firbank," in his* Books in General *(© 1953 by V. S. Pritchett; reprinted in the U.S. by permission of Harold Matson Co., Inc., and in Canada by permission of A. D. Peters & Co.), Chatto and Windus, 1953, pp. 229-34.*

Eroticism plays over Firbank's surfaces like sunlight on a Watteau sleeve; and because it is so evanescent, resting for so brief a space on each facet, the effect, as with Watteau, is of tragedy. . . . The Firbank technique is that of mosaic in a glittering material. The more ruthless and masterly he became, the more spaces were left deliberately unfilled by anything except his immense power of suggesting whole characters *in absentia.* The later books are discoveries of fragmentary mosaic pavements, like the discovery of a Sappho fragment in *Vainglory.*

In his interstices lies Firbank's flexibility, which in the end encompassed not only tragedy and his unparalleled wit but farce (four lines in *The Flower Beneath The Foot* state virtually the whole of *Clochemerle*) and wisecracks which, for their combination of no meaning with double meaning, resemble only Groucho Marx's. (p. 246)

Firbank is by no means a 'nineties author left over: he is a pioneer of twentieth-century art. One has only to snatch at this conversational fragment from *Inclinations* (1916)— 'There's the Negress you called a *Gauguin*'—to recognise that by 1924 Firbank had produced, in *Prancing Nigger,* something which, in its tropically enervated vitality, simply *is* a Gauguin. Firbank's emergence from the aesthetic movement is parallel to Gauguin's from the mists of Puvis de Chavannes or Picasso's from the pretty but (like Firbank's) Maeterlinck-verging pathos of his rose and blue periods. It is all part of the characteristically twentieth-century fusion of 'nineties decadence with those primitive motifs from overseas which were among the last booty sent home by the empire builders: a fusion which amazingly, and almost overnight, turned mauve into *fauve.*

Unerring, Firbank adopted for his last book the new rhythm: jazz is also one of the twentieth century's fusions of decadent with primitive. To the Negro patois he had invented for *Prancing Nigger,* Firbank now adds a free fantasia on white American slang. The novel is set in New York, where Firbank had never been. So he gives it to one of his New Yorkers to confess 'Somehow I've no desire much to visit England. I seem to know what it's like', and himself goes boldly on to invent New York, spreading over it 'a sky like the darkest of cinerarias'. (p. 247)

> *Brigid Brophy, "The New Rhythm and Other Pieces" (originally published in* London Magazine, *October, 1962), in her* Don't Never Forget *(copyright © 1966 by Brigid Brophy; reprinted by permission of Jonathan Cape Ltd.),* Holt, 1967, pp. 243-48.

Firbank's evanescent prose and his air of ephemerality place him among the most elusive of writers. Because of these baffling qualities, the diversity of opinion among Firbank's critics (each using a different rack) has been remarkable. Considered variously baroque and rococo, Catholic and pagan, amoral and immoral, decadent and robust, a minor classic and a major mistake, Firbank is some of these things maybe but not all of them. (p. 3)

A central theme in his novels is the dilemma of the individual, often a female, who is isolated from the surrounding world and then destroyed by it. (pp. 4-5)

"A Study in Temperament," though it owes much to the comedies of Wilde, still represents an original attempt at social satire—an attempt, moreover, in which some unique effects are gained through carefully patterned dialogue. The title is, in itself, meaningful, for all of Firbank's novels are studies in temperament. . . . In "A Study in Temperament" Firbank not only discovered his subject matter but cleverly experimented with a dialogue technique which he was later to refine, complicate, and perfect. (p. 7)

Notwithstanding the calculated blasphemies, the high jinks of clerics, and the hocus-pocus of ritual in Firbank's novels, his attitude toward Catholicism remains equivocal and mysterious. . . .

At first one suspects that, like Wilde, Dowson, Beardsley, and Lionel Johnson, Firbank was attracted by the aesthetic dimensions of the Roman Church. Given his love of visual beauty and ordered elegance, it is easy to understand the appeal which Rome would have for him. Nevertheless, evidence suggests that it was the mystic, rather than the aesthetic, element of Catholicism which profoundly moved him. In any case, Firbank, formerly an Anglican, was received into the Roman Church in 1907. . . . (p.11)

Firbank thought of applying for a post at the Vatican, in preparation for which he talked of going into retreat, as much for his looks, he chirped, as for the welfare of his soul. The Church apparently failed to reciprocate Firbank's equivocal devotion, and the Vatican was thereby spared the uncertainty of Firbank's peculiar talents. It was also rumored in 1909 that Firbank failed to gain acceptance by the Society of Jesus. These incidents may account for his later remark to Lord Berners: "The Church of Rome wouldn't

have me and so I laugh at her." This mocking attitude toward Rome colored Firbank's fiction deeply. (pp. 12-13)

Firbank's ironic impulse, the most fundamental element in his nature, forestalled his taking one creed as the only possible form of truth. All enthusiasms seemed valueless in the cold light of his wit, and even the pursuit of beauty without pretension was not proof against it. (p. 19)

With his irresolutions, inconsistencies, and ironic postures, it is extremely difficult to formulate anything so ponderous as Firbank's "philosophy of life." His deepest convictions about life, rarely found unguarded, tended toward a detached, but comprehensive, pessimism. As a rule, Firbank did not err, when he could help it, on the side of righteousness. (p. 20)

Many memoirs written about Firbank, allegedly by friends, present the Firbank myth which Firbank himself perversely inspired and fueled. This myth, in the most tiresome tradition of English eccentricity, preciously exhibits Firbank in his horrid roles as coddled, wealthy *flâneur,* squirming aesthete, giggling snob, darling gossip, and drunken Catholic homosexual. It is heartening to know that Firbank derived cynical satisfaction from his myth, because it has been used, with a telling vengeance, against both him and his novels. (p. 21)

Firbank initially adopted a Pateresque principle of life, a pessimism which led to a fascination with the beauty of the moment and a desire to capture that moment in prose. Although he never entirely rejected the philosophy of aestheticism, he subordinated it to the objectives of self-discovery and social satire. . . . Announcing no doctrines, publishing no manifestoes, converting no disciples, Firbank earnestly experimented with the art of fiction. His painstaking experiments resulted in a series of unique, richly comic novels which, like their author, brook few comparisons.

Unlike many of his contemporaries—Lawrence, Forster, and Huxley, for example—Firbank had few explicit messages. Human beings suffer, life is sad, the comic mask conceals anguish. These are the conditions of life in his luxurious world, with its surface of gossip, fine moods, and cold boredom. No propagandist, Firbank overtly deals with the trivialities of fantastic characters who inhabit fantastic milieus. But, as an artist, he was no more self-deceived by his predilections than he was by the world he chose to create. There is always a cutting edge and a tough core of common sense to his dallyings with the trivial, which provides no more than the substance of his art. He was well aware of the pervasive international and social upheavals that threatened or raged just beyond the self-imposed limits of his own elegant world. Large-scale events, like World War I, could influence his work profoundly, but Firbank would view them only out of the very corner of his eye. This was his life-style, from which his literary indirection seems to derive. (pp. 24-5)

Firbank's vision of the world was, ultimately, a vision of the absurd, with gaiety maybe and some horror. Consonant with this vision, his only consistent theology was irony, which faithfully served him as universal solvent, although the solvent could dissolve, itself, on occasion, into half-articulated phrases. (p. 26)

Like Evelyn Waugh, who learned much from him, Firbank used humor verging upon the insane to define the fragmented society around him. Encompassing the chaos, disbelief, ennui, and frustration of his (and our) time, the world of Firbank's fiction explicitly parallels many of the central literary achievements of this century. By reducing human values and conduct to the absurd and by insisting upon the omnipresence of human folly, Firbank qualifies as a distant relative of Dadaists and the funnier Existentialists. To claim, however, that he was a member of any "school of thought" would be tedious—if not wrongheaded. Like himself, Firbank's vision was comminatory. Affording no consoling philosophical solutions, Firbank's aloof, negative world charitably offers, nevertheless, an abundance of maniacal, introverted laughter. If the laughter fails to provide comfort, Firbank insinuates, one must then be content simply to laugh at the laughter. (pp. 26-7)

Firbank's humor is there to be enjoyed by those who have a taste for it, but it is probably too individual and intangible to become a significant literary influence. Although his characters and situations are often extremely amusing in themselves, Firbank's humor derives, primarily, from the idiosyncrasies of his style. Depending on the very form and cadence of a sentence, this humor tends to be purely verbal: it lies in the inflection and tone of voice. Firbank, who wrote his novels with immense care, shrewdly designed each sentence to produce exactly the right effect. Every word tells, and a phrase fills out a paragraph. Like Pope, Firbank was a master of the glancing image. Myriad possibilities lurk behind a single, darting phrase, and dialogue teems with innuendo. Few other novelists have traveled so light, or convey so much in proportion to weight. (pp. 27-8)

Curious misspellings, shifts in tense, and dangling participles are common enough in Firbank's novels, but he always wrote with a horror of the cliché. To avoid the outworn and the obvious, Firbank paid close attention to the values of words and syntax. His chief effects, which can be overdone, are produced by syntactical inversions and the eccentric placing of words, especially adverbs. He will write, for example, "Is the worst of the storm yet over, Fowler, do you consider?" or "Winsome Brookes would spend whole hours together grooming fitfully his hair." (p. 28)

These inversions, in which syntax is intentionally twisted and strained, give Firbank's prose, as Jocelyn Brooke observes, a kind of "'syncopated' quality," which more than suggests the influence of jazz music, of which Firbank was extraordinarily fond. Occasionally Firbank's wit sounds more like the nonsense poetry of Edward Lear. (p. 29)

Like Joyce, Firbank obviously enjoyed playing with language. He was able to catch the exact tones and modulations of real speech, however inconsequent or preposterous that speech was in content. If, at times, he took a sheer delight in writing nonsense, the nonsense was always spilling over into a kind of poetry. Firbank's seemingly senseless catalogues of funny names, for example, are comparable to Dadaist "poems" or Lewis Carroll's "Jabberwocky." Full of double meanings and symbolism, these absurd names also suggest Restoration drama, Richard Brinsley Sheridan, vaudeville, and comic strips. (pp. 29-30)

Firbank's technical contributions to the novel, all highly idiosyncratic, were threefold: structure, the art of dialogue, and elements of comic organization. First of all, Firbank relied primarily upon dialogue, reducing narration and de-

scription to a minimum. He used dialogue not only to reveal aspects of character but to amuse, shock, suggest, and to further whatever plot he had. Frequently, he used it to do all these things at once. Applying the economy of poetry to the novel, Firbank proceeded by hiatus. He made few concessions to the conventions of realism and ruthlessly deleted discursive explanations from his prose. He thought nothing of filing fifty pages down to make a crisp paragraph, or even a row of dots. But his rows of dots are often more eloquent than some other novelists' chapters. (p. 32)

[The] essential characteristics of Firbank's dialogue [are] incomplete and suggestive fragments; inverted word order; italicized words; constant use of the dash, exclamation point, and question mark; ellipses; sly implications and bawdy innuendo.... Firbank's "conversational" techniques, which give adequate direction, precision, and economy to his flickerings of neurasthenic talk, often generate monotony because the resulting tone of ominous unease seems unvarying. Apart from the mildly offending dialects of his Negroes, it is difficult to distinguish one of his characters from the next. Twittering with the same witty disconnectedness, they are all overfastidious, very bored, and pained by the sexual politics they dabble in. When the talk becomes too coy, it represents little more than the tiresome stream of consciousness of a hypersensitive, effeminate socialite. Indeed, Firbank's characters all seem projections of his own set of jangled nerves.

The verbal *pointillisme* of Firbank's dialogue, on the other hand, is best illustrated by the long passages of overheard fragments which he liked to compose in an "impressionistic" manner. These snatches of conversation at first sound like mad jabberings, but they gradually make sense. The logic of skipping unnecessaries, of using only key words, of conversing by means of ideas brought to mind by a chance word or phrase, is the logic of Firbank's mind. This kind of writing, absolutely dependent on the momentary awareness of the comic, is remarkably well attuned to the tensions which run just below the level of social chatter. (pp. 34-5)

Firbank's second major technical contribution was to the structure of the novel. He was among the first modern writers to solve for himself the aesthetic problem of representation in fiction, to achieve a unique and balanced interrelation of subject and form. Nineteenth-century novelists usually achieved a balance only by complete submission to the idea of the succession of events in an arbitrarily limited period of time. They were fettered by the chain of cause and effect. Most important novels of this century—the work of Proust, Gide, Joyce, and Virginia Woolf comes to mind—were experiments in making an art form out of the raw material of narration. Firbank's significant experiments not only enabled him to make an art form out of this raw material but allowed him to maintain, simultaneously, an objective attitude toward his material. Remaining objective, Firbank emphasized the fact which many of his subjective contemporaries were neglecting, namely, that the novel should be directed toward entertainment.

Firbank achieved his unique, balanced interrelation of subject and form by developing his novels through a series of vignettes or animated tableaux rather than through coherent action. His books, which are almost wholly devoid of any attributions of cause to effect, have the barest minimum of direct description. Intricately and with a balanced alternation of wild extravagance and austere economy, his compositions are built up with conversational *nuances*. There is little exchange of opinion in Firbank's dialogue, but the highly selective talk goes on, chic, delicate, sharply comic, and seemingly without point or plan. Then, quite gradually, one is aware that a casual reference on one page links up with some particular inflection of phrase on another until a skeleton of plot—often shockingly outrageous—emerges. (pp. 36-7)

In time, one becomes used to Firbank's abrupt shifts from character to character or from scene to scene. His carefully plotted hints and inferences, the salient features of his indirection, coalesce and begin to make sense. This oblique method of presentation [resembles] cinematic montage. . . . (p. 37)

Firbank's third technical innovation was the development of a comic technique for setting off a ridiculous chain of events and then burying further reference to it in the midst of other inconsequential material. The device, essentially a variation of "counterpoint," is Firbank's (or Sterne's) method of indirection applied, with adroitness and compression, to a subplot or digression rather than to the main action of a novel. (p. 40)

Firbank's sensibility and the methods he employed for expressing it were ideally suited for rendering the mood of the society in which he flourished. Taking perversion for granted as the basic moral norm, this society was weary, passion-ridden, and depraved. For the sake of evading anguish and maintaining a minimal coherence, it became self-dedicated to the pursuit of fashion and the preservation of flawless surfaces, which Firbank adroitly chronicled. As fascinated as he was by the aristocracy, his own aristocrats have no deeply established roots in land, money, or manners. Although they are feeble and absurd, their chief prerogatives are snobbery and eccentricity; they are dominated by silly women and chic. It is clear, then, that Firbank's peculiar comedy reveals something more than silliness, or supersilliness. In the most striking way, it reveals his whole attitude toward the nature of his time. (p. 43)

> *Edward Martin Potoker, in his* Ronald Firbank *(Columbia Essays on Modern Writers Pamphlet No. 43; copyright © 1969 Columbia University Press; reprinted by permission of the publisher), Columbia University Press, 1969.*

Firbank's essential limitations stem from the narrowness of his interests and the severity of his estheticism. In a letter to his sister, he once remarked that "there is bound to be *ennui,* when things become real," and he described ordinary life as "a nightmare of ugliness." To escape he lived in his imagination and created in his novels an idiosyncratic secondary world in which wit, exoticism and outrageous affectation banish boredom and diminish pain. Loss, cruelty, terror and death are, of course, present in Firbank's fiction, but rarely in ways that seriously disturb the brilliant effect of his decorative design. . . .

Firbank himself rarely made imprecise or exaggerated claims for his talent. When *The Flower Beneath the Foot* was published, he told Carl Van Vechten: "its parfum is what concerns me most & if it is exotic & elusive & bafflingly *embaumé*, the gardener, (poor dear), will be glad." That (and perhaps Edmund Wilson's essay in *Classics and Commercials* [see excerpt above]) is about all one needs to read Firbank. (p. 26)

> *Lawrence Graver, "The Flower Beneath the Footnotes," in* The New Republic *(reprinted by permission of* The New Republic; © *1973 by The New Republic, Inc.), June 30, 1973, pp. 25-6.*

F(rancis) Scott (Key) Fitzgerald

1896-1940

American novelist, short story writer, and scenarist. Both Fitzgerald's life and his work have been seen as a study in the pursuit of an elusive American dream. The son of modestly well-off midwestern parents, Fitzgerald became an outsider among the rich, a breed that both repelled and fascinated him throughout his life. He went East to Princeton and spent most of the rest of his life on the eastern seaboard and in Europe. He used the material of his experiences as an undergraduate in his first novel, *This Side of Paradise,* an immediate critical and popular success. He quickly became spokesman for the "jazz age" and was plunged into the world of rich and careless sophisticates who were to people his fiction. Throughout the glittering world of his fiction run the themes of moral waste and decay and the necessity of personal responsibility. His marriage in 1920 to Zelda Sayre was critical, for her extravagant tastes and their lavish parties forced him to compromise his talents between writing for well-paying popular magazines and his more serious efforts. Ironically, the first of his major works, *The Great Gatsby,* coincided with his decline in popularity, although he enjoyed considerable prestige among his fellow writers. He spent his last years in Hollywood and died of a heart attack in 1940, believing himself to be a failure. At the time of his death, all of his books were out of print and his last novel, *The Last Tycoon,* remained uncompleted. A Fitzgerald revival began in the late 1950s.

PRINCIPAL WORKS

Flappers and Philosophers (short stories) 1920
This Side of Paradise (novel) 1920
The Beautiful and Damned (novel) 1922
Tales of the Jazz Age (short stories) 1922
The Great Gatsby (novel) 1925
All the Sad Young Men (short stories) 1926
Tender Is the Night (novel) 1934
Taps at Reveille (short stories) 1935
The Last Tycoon (novel) 1941
The Pat Hobby Stories (short stories) 1962

It has been said by a celebrated person [Edna St. Vincent Millay] that to meet F. Scott Fitzgerald is to think of a stupid old woman with whom someone has left a diamond; she is extremely proud of the diamond and shows it to everyone who comes by, and everyone is surprised that such an ignorant old woman should possess so valuable a jewel; for in nothing does she appear so inept as in the remarks she makes about the diamond. . . . (p. 27)

Scott Fitzgerald is, in fact, no old woman, but a very good-looking young man, nor is he in the least stupid, but, on the contrary, exhilaratingly clever. Yet there *is* a symbolic truth in the description quoted above: it is true that Fitzgerald has been left with a jewel which he doesn't know quite what to do with. For he has been given imagination without intellectual control of it; he has been given the desire for beauty without an aesthetic ideal; and he has been given a gift for expression without very many ideas to express.

Consider, for example, the novel—*This Side of Paradise*—with which he founded his reputation. It has almost every fault and deficiency that a novel can possibly have. It is not only highly imitative but it imitates an inferior model. Fitzgerald, when he wrote the book, was drunk with Compton Mackenzie, and it sounds like an American attempt to rewrite *Sinister Street.* . . . [One] of the chief weaknesses of *This Side of Paradise* is that it is really not *about* anything: its intellectual and moral content amounts to little more than a gesture—a gesture of indefinite revolt. The story itself, furthermore, is very immaturely imagined: it is always just verging on the ludicrous. And, finally, *This Side of Paradise* is one of the most illiterate books of any merit ever published (a fault which the publisher's proofreader seems to have made no effort to remedy). Not only is it ornamented with bogus ideas and faked literary references, but it is full of literary words tossed about with the most reckless inaccuracy.

I have said that *This Side of Paradise* commits almost every sin that a novel can possibly commit: but it does not commit the unpardonable sin: it does not fail to live. The whole preposterous farrago is animated with life. It is rather a fluttering and mercurial life: its emotions do not move you profoundly; its drama does not make you hold your breath; but its gaiety and color and movement did make it come as something exciting after the realistic heaviness and dinginess of so much serious American fiction. (pp. 27-9)

In regard to the man himself, there are perhaps two things

worth knowing, for the influence they have had on his work. In the first place, he comes from the Middle West—from St. Paul, Minnesota. Fitzgerald is as much of the Middle West of large cities and country clubs as Sinclair Lewis is of the Middle West of the prairies and little towns. What we find in him is much what we find in the more prosperous strata of these cities: sensitivity and eagerness for life without a sound base of culture and taste; a structure of millionaire residences, brilliant expensive hotels and exhilarating social activities built not on the eighteenth century but simply on the flat Western land. And it seems to me rather a pity that he has not written more of the West: it is perhaps the only milieu that he thoroughly understands. When Fitzgerald approaches the East, he brings to it the standards of the wealthy West—the preoccupation with display, the appetite for visible magnificence and audible jamboree, the vigorous social atmosphere of amiable flappers and youths comparatively untainted as yet by the snobbery of the East. In *The Beautiful and Damned,* for example, we feel that he is moving in a vacuum; the characters have no real connection with the background to which they have been assigned; they are not part of the organism of New York as the characters, in, say, the short story *Bernice Bobs Her Hair* are a part of the organism of St. Paul. Surely F. Scott Fitzgerald should some day do for Summit Avenue what Lewis has done for Main Street.

But you are not to suppose from all this that the author of *This Side of Paradise* is merely a typical well-to-do Middle Westerner, with correct clothes and clear skin, who has been sent to the East for college. The second thing one should know about him is that Fitzgerald is partly Irish and that he brings both to life and to fiction certain qualities that are not Anglo-Saxon. For, like the Irish, Fitzgerald is romantic, but also cynical about romance; he is bitter as well as ecstatic; astringent as well as lyrical. He casts himself in the role of playboy, yet at the playboy he incessantly mocks. He is vain, a little malicious, of quick intelligence and wit, and has an Irish gift for turning language into something iridescent and surprising. He often reminds one, in fact, of the description that a great Irishman, Bernard Shaw, has written of the Irish: ''An Irishman's imagination never lets him alone, never convinces him, never satisfies him; but it makes him that he can't face reality nor deal with it nor handle it nor conquer it: he can only sneer at them that do . . . and imagination's such a torture that you can't bear it without whisky. . . . And all the while there goes on a horrible, senseless, mischievous laughter.''

For the rest, F. Scott Fitzgerald is a rather childlike fellow, very much wrapped up in his dream of himself and his projection of it on paper. For a person of his mental agility, he is extraordinarily little occupied with the general affairs of the world: like a woman, he is not much given to abstract or impersonal thought. Conversation about politics or general ideas have a way of snapping back to Fitzgerald. But this seldom becomes annoying; he is never pretentious or boring. He is quite devoid of affectation and takes the curse off his relentless egoism by his readiness to laugh at himself and his boyish uncertainty of his talent. And he exhibits, in his personality as well as in his writings, a quality rare today among even the youngest American writers: he is almost the only one among them who is capable of lighthearted high spirits. . . . His characters—and he—are actors in an elfin harlequinade; they are as nimble, as gay and as lovely—and as hardhearted—as fairies: Columbine

elopes with Harlequin on a rope ladder dropped from the Ritz and both go morris-dancing amuck on a case of bootleg liquor; Pantaloon is pinked with an epigram that withers him up like a leaf; the Policeman is tripped by Harlequin and falls into the Pulitzer Fountain. Just before the curtain falls, Harlequin puts on false whiskers and pretends to be Bernard Shaw; he gives reporters an elaborate interview on politics, religion and history; a hundred thousand readers see it and are more or less impressed; Columbine nearly dies laughing; Harlequin sends out for a case of gin. (pp. 30-2)

Since writing *This Side of Paradise*—on the inspiration of Wells and Mackenzie—Fitzgerald has become acquainted with a different school of fiction: the ironical-pessimistic. In college, he had supposed that the thing to do was to write biographical novels with a burst of ideas toward the close; since his advent in the literary world, he has discovered that another genre has recently come into favor: the kind which makes much of the tragedy and what Mencken has called ''the meaninglessness of life.'' Fitzgerald had imagined, hitherto, that the thing to do in a novel was to bring out a meaning in life; but he now set bravely about it to contrive a shattering tragedy that should be, also, a hundred-percent meaningless. As a result of this determination, the first version of *The Beautiful and Damned* culminated in an orgy of horror for which the reader was imperfectly prepared. Fitzgerald destroyed his characters with a succession of catastrophes so arbitrary that, beside them, the perversities of Hardy seemed the working of natural laws. (p. 33)

To conclude, it would be quite unfair to subject Scott Fitzgerald, who is still in his twenties and has presumably most of his work before him, to a rigorous overhauling. His restless imagination may yet produce something durable. For the present, however, this imagination is certainly not seen to the best advantage: it suffers badly from lack of discipline and poverty of aesthetic ideas. Fitzgerald is a dazzling extemporizer, but his stories have a way of petering out: he seems never to have planned them completely or to have thought out his themes from the beginning. This is true even of some of his most successful fantasies, such as *The Diamond as Big as the Ritz* or his comedy, *The Vegetable.* On the other hand, *The Beautiful and Damned,* imperfect though it is, marks an advance over *This Side of Paradise:* the style is more nearly mature and the subject more solidly unified, and there are scenes that are more convincing than any in his previous fiction.

But, in any case, even the work that Fitzgerald has done up to date has a certain moral importance. In his very expression of the anarchy by which he finds himself bewildered, of his revolt which cannot fix on an object, he is typical of the war generation—the generation so memorably described on the last page of *This Side of Paradise* as ''grown up to find all gods dead, all wars fought, all faiths in men shaken.'' There is a moral in *The Beautiful and Damned* that the author did not perhaps intend to point. The hero and the heroine of this giddy book are creatures without method or purpose: they give themselves up to wild debaucheries and do not, from beginning to end, perform a single serious act; yet somehow you get the impression that, in spite of their fantastic behavior, Anthony and Gloria Patch are the most rational people in the book. Wherever they come in contact with institutions, with the serious life of their time, these are made to appear ridiculous, they are subjects for scorn or mirth. We see the army, finance and business successively and casually exposed as completely without point or dignity. The inference we are led to draw is that, in such a civilization as this, the sanest and most honorable course is to escape from organized society and live for the excitement of the moment. It cannot be merely a special reaction to a personal situation which gives rise to the paradoxes of such a book. It may be that we cannot demand too high a degree of moral balance from young men, however able or brilliant, who write books in the year 1921: we must remember that they have had to grow up in, that they have had to derive their chief stimulus from the wars, the society and the commerce of the Age of Confusion itself. (pp. 33-5)

> *Edmund Wilson, "F. Scott Fitzgerald" (March, 1922), in his* The Shores of Light: A Literary Chronicle of the Twenties and Thirties *(reprinted with the permission of Farrar, Straus & Giroux, Inc.; copyright 1952 by Edmund Wilson), Farrar, Straus and Young, 1952, pp. 27-35.*

Scott Fitzgerald, rather surprisingly, has written a tragedy [*The Beautiful and Damned*], an almost uncompromising tragedy, which is more than their critics have led us to expect from one of the younger generation. He has felt the implications of a rudderless society steering gayly for nowhere and has followed them down the rapids to final catastrophe. Not, of course, in any Puritan fashion nor with an Ibsen view of the sins of the race, but simply because his story led him that way; and defiantly scoffing at lessons, joyously dwelling upon the life that leads his friends to perdition, he follows. I admire him for it; and if *This Side of Paradise* showed in certain passages and in the essential energy of the whole that he had glimpses of a genius for sheer writing, this book proves that he has the artist's conscience and enough intellect to learn how to control the life that fascinates him.

He has not yet learned that lesson, a lesson which even those who believe, as he pretends to believe, that life is meaningless, must learn. He has chosen to wallow in naturalism, to be a romantic unrestrained, and he must pay the price. The scenes of debauchery in this book will be very much censured, by some on moral grounds, by others (more justly, I think) on artistic; his verbose excursions into philosophy and literary criticism will be mentioned without favor. And it will be his own fault. Following what he believes to be popular taste, he has decided to gratify curiosity as to what they do on Broadway after midnight with the fullest detail, and to supply scenes at riotous country-house week-ends regardless of taste and proportion. Following his own desire, he has reported his own reactions to life and its problems in general with a fulness only justifiable in a young man's diary. Like a reporter with a moving-picture camera, he has squirmed into hallways and hid behind café tables until the result is an endless film of racy pictures, relieved by aesthetic vaporings. "Give 'em all the truth," has been his motto, and therefore from one point of view *The Beautiful and Damned* is not so much a novel as an irresponsible social document, veracious, in its way, as photographs are always veracious in their way, but often untruthful, as photographs are often untruthful, and with about the same relation to the scope

and significance of life that is possessed by a society drama in the films. (p. 318)

[When] he is not showing off in pseudo-wit, or trying to shock the bourgeoisie, or discovering profound truths of philosophy which get muddled before he can grasp them, how this novelist can write! . . .

Mr. Fitzgerald is too much in the whirl, too much in love with its abandoned irresponsibility, to understand it, and to be detached while still sympathetic. . . .

He will write better novels, but he will probably never give us better documents of distraught and abandoned but intensely living youth. (p. 319)

> *Henry Seidel Canby, "The Flapper's Tragedy," in* New York Post *(reprinted by permission of the* New York Post; © *1922, New York Post Corporation), March 4, 1922 (and reprinted as "'The Beautiful and Damned': The Flapper's Tragedy," in* F. Scott Fitzgerald in His Own Time: A Miscellany, *edited by Matthew J. Bruccoli and Jackson R. Bryer, Kent State University Press, 1971, pp. 317-19).*

It would not be easy to find a more thoroughly depressing book than this new novel by F. Scott Fitzgerald, "The Beautiful and Damned." Not because there is something of tragedy in it—tragedy may be and often is fine and inspiring —but because its slow-moving narrative is the record of lives utterly worthless and utterly futile. Not one of the book's many characters, important or unimportant, ever rises to the level of ordinary decent humanity. Not one of them shows a spark of loyalty, of honor, of devotion, of generosity, of real friendship or of real affection. Anthony Patch, most important of them all, lacks even physical courage. His one admirable quality is that of "understanding too well to blame," and the reader more than suspects that this refraining from blame is due more to his general laziness, his general inertia, than to anything else. . . .

About [the protagonists, Anthony and Gloria,]—and naturally enough, since people, like water, seek their own level —move a number of other small-souled individuals. The women most closely associated with Gloria are even cheaper than she is, and though the men who are Anthony's "friends" never quite fall into the abyss of physical degradation which engulfs him, it would be difficult to find anything to say in their favor. . . . Patriotism being in Mr. Fitzgerald's view, mere foolishness and hysteria, it is not surprising that he should depict the [soldiers] Anthony meets in camp as another worthless lot. He is not ill-treated; officers and men are not cruel, but merely stupid and contemptible. . . .

So far as its style is concerned, much of the novel is well written, and Anthony's gradual loss of his mental curiosity, his gradual degeneration into "a bleak and sordid wreck" is convincingly depicted, though to the reader he never seems one-third as intelligent as the author apparently thinks him. . . . The general atmosphere of the book is an atmosphere of futility, waste and the avoidance of effort, into which the fumes of whisky penetrate more and more, until at last it fairly reeks with them. The novel is full of that kind of pseudo-realism which results from shutting one's eyes to all that is good in human nature, and looking only upon that which is small and mean—a view quite as false as its extreme opposite, which, reversing the process, results in what we have learned to classify as "glad" books. It is to be hoped that Mr. Fitzgerald, who possesses a genuine, undeniable talent, will some day acquire a less one-sided understanding. (p. 16)

> Louise Maunsell Field, in The New York Times Book Review and Magazine (© 1922 by The New York Times Company; reprinted by permission), March 5, 1922.

If it was haste and insolence which hurt *This Side of Paradise,* what hurts *The Beautiful and Damned* is deliberate seriousness—or rather, a seriousness not deliberated quite enough. Bound to bring some sort of instruction in, Mr. Fitzgerald pushes his characters downhill as if gravitation needed help. He must have lost some of his interest in them as they went down; at least he imparts interest less and less as they advance; his imagination flames only while they are at the summit. Few current writers can represent young love in its incandescence as he can, but his knowledge—so far as this novel goes to show—does not extend with the same accuracy to the seedy side of life which he has felt he must explore. He has, . . . without adding much to the body of his style, sacrificed—or lost—some of the poetry which illuminated the earlier narrative and which illuminates the higher places of this one with a light never present unless there is genius not far off. Why did he have to mix good poetry with indifferent moralism? Moralists are plenty but poets few. (p. 328)

> Carl Van Doren, "The Roving Critic," in The Nation (copyright 1922 by the Nation Associates, Inc.), March 15, 1922 (and reprinted as "'The Beautiful and Damned'," in F. Scott Fitzgerald in His Own Time: A Miscellany, edited by Matthew J. Bruccoli and Jackson R. Bryer, The Kent State University Press, 1971, pp. 327-28).

The impression Mr Fitzgerald's work makes on his elders is so intense that one is grateful for the omission of the name of the Deity from his new title [*The Beautiful and Damned*]. To his contemporaries, "interested only in ourselves and Art," his revelations are of quite secondary importance and he has neither the critical intelligence nor the profound vision which might make him an imposing figure. His elders, naturally, do not require these things of him, since they have other sources of supply, and they are the best judges of his immediate significance. To them he presents a picture of the world which is no longer theirs, and even when they doubt his supreme truthfulness they can safely go behind the book to the author and say that this is what the younger generation would like us to think.

It cannot, of course, continue indefinitely, because even about so bright and cheerful a talent as Mr Fitzgerald's the shadows of the prison house are bound to close. Especially since he has been considered as a revealer and an artist he has had to grow quickly, and he can say (I speak not of his private life with which I am unacquainted, but of his fiction) "my grief lies onward and my joy behind." (p. 419)

Tragedy, and particularly in our own time a rather meaningless tragedy, are quite the natural thing for young people to deal in; it was surprising and creditable to him that Mr Fitzgerald's first book held so steadily to a gay worldliness.

Nor is it Mr Fitzgerald's increasingly detailed naturalism which marks the change in him. The new thing is his overburden of sentiment and his really alarming seriousness. Sentiment, to be sure, has been surreptitiously conveyed, and so made more poignant and, when it doesn't come off, more objectionable, by being presented always with scepticism. (This is, I believe, the real nature of the author's noted irony. . . .) It is whenever he approaches either the mind or the soul of his characters that Mr Fitzgerald becomes romantic. (pp. 419-20)

The pellmell of ideas, or rather of the names of ideas, in [*The Beautiful and Damned*] is startling, and more startling is the incipient philosophy of the author; but the book is important not for these. It is important because it presents a definite American *milieu* and because it has pretentions as a work of art; the degree of success (the degree, that is, of importance) comes out in comparison with the work of another American novelist: Mrs Edith Wharton. (p. 420)

The failure to carry Gloria through, his seeing her as a flapper and not as a woman, marks the precise point at which Mr Fitzgerald now rests—this side of innocence, considerably this side of the mad and innocent truth. He is this side, too, of a full respect for the medium he works in; his irrelevance destroys his design. I have nothing against his sudden descents into the dialogue of the printed play, if that is the most effective way of presenting his scene, although I wish he did not do this whenever he has a crowd to handle and something in itself insignificant to tell. His interludes are usually trivial and never contribute to the one thing they can create, his atmosphere. But I do wish that Mr Fitzgerald would stop incorporating into his novels his wingéd words and his unrelated episodes as they are published from time to time. It indicates a carelessness about structure and effect which one who has so much to gain from the novel ought to find displeasing. (p. 421)

> Vivian Shaw, "This Side of Innocence," in The Dial (copyright, 1922, by The Dial Publishing Company, Inc.; reprinted by permission of J. S. Watson, Jr. and Scofield Thayer), April, 1922 (and reprinted by Kraus Reprint Corporation, 1966), pp. 419-21.

Scott Fitzgerald was born with a knack for writing. What they call "a natural gift." And another gift of the fairies at his christening was a reckless confidence in himself. And he was quite intoxicated with the joy of life and rather engagingly savage toward an elder world. He was out "to get the world by the neck" and put words on paper in the patterns his exuberant fancy suggested. He didn't worry much about what had gone before Fitzgerald in literature. He dreamed gorgeously of what there was in Fitzgerald to "tell the world."

And all these elements contributed to the amazing performance of *This Side of Paradise,* amazing in its excitement and gusto, amazing in phrase and epithet, amazing no less for all sorts of thoroughly bad writing pitched in with the good, for preposterous carelessness, and amazing as well as for the sheer pace of the narrative and the fresh quality of its oddly pervasive poetry. Short stories of flappers and philosophers displayed the same vitality and flourished much the same faults. *Tales of the Jazz Age* inhabited the same glamour. *The Beautiful and Damned,* while still in the mirage, furnished a more valuable document concerning the younger generation of the first quarter of the Twentieth Century. But brilliant, irrefutably brilliant as were certain passages of the novels and tales of which the "boy wonder" of our time was so lavish, arresting as were certain gleams of insight, intensely promising as were certain observed facilities, there remained in general, glamour, glamour everywhere, and, after the glamour faded, little for the mind to hold except an impression of this kinetic glamour. (pp. 352-53)

But . . . *The Great Gatsby* reveals thoroughly matured craftsmanship. It has structure. It has high occasions of felicitous, almost magic, phrase. And most of all, it is out of the mirage. For the first time Fitzgerald surveys the Babylonian captivity of this era unblinded by the bright lights. (p. 353)

> *William Rose Benét, "An Admirable Novel," in* Saturday Review of Literature *(copyright © 1925 by Saturday Review, Inc.; reprinted with permission), May 9, 1925 (and reprinted in* F. Scott Fitzgerald in His Own Time: A Miscellany, *edited by Matthew J. Bruccoli and Jackson R. Bryer, Kent State University Press, 1971, pp. 352-54).*

There has never been any question of the talents of F. Scott Fitzgerald; there has been, justifiably until the publication of *The Great Gatsby,* a grave question as to what he was going to do with his gifts. The question has been answered in one of the finest of contemporary novels. Fitzgerald has more than matured; he has mastered his talents and gone soaring in a beautiful flight, leaving behind him everything dubious and tricky in his earlier work, and leaving even farther behind all the men of his own generation and most of his elders. . . .

Scenes of incredible difficulty are rendered with what seems an effortless precision, crowds and conversation and action and retrospects—everything comes naturally and persuasively. The minor people and events are threads of colour and strength, holding the principal things together. The technical virtuosity is extraordinary. (p. 162)

The Great Gatsby is passionate as [Ford Madox Ford's] *Some Do Not* is passionate, with such an abundance of feeling for the characters (feeling their integral reality, not hating or loving them objectively) that the most trivial of the actors in the drama are endowed with vitality. The concentration of the book is so intense that the principal characters exist almost as essences, as biting acids that find themselves in the same golden cup and have no choice but to act upon each other. And the *milieux* which are brought into such violent contact with each other are as full of character, and as immitigably compelled to struggle and to debase one another.

The book is written as a series of scenes, the method which Fitzgerald derived from Henry James through Mrs Wharton, and these scenes are reported by a narrator who was obviously intended to be much more significant than he is. The author's appetite for life is so violent that he found the personality of the narrator an obstacle, and simply ignored it once his actual people were in motion, but the narrator helps to give the feeling of an intense unit which the various characters around Gatsby form. (pp. 162-63)

Fitzgerald has ceased to content himself with a satiric report on the outside of American life and has with considerable irony attacked the spirit underneath, and so has begun to report on life in its most general terms. His tactile apprehension remains so fine that his people and his settings are specifically of Long Island; but now he meditates upon their fate, and they become universal also. He has now something of extreme importance to say; and it is good fortune for us that he knows how to say it. (p. 163)

The variety of treatment, the intermingling of dialogue and narrative, the use of a snatch of significant detail instead of a big scene, make the whole a superb impressionistic painting, vivid in colour, and sparkling with meaning. And the major composition is as just as the treatment of detail. There is a brief curve before Gatsby himself enters; a longer one in which he begins his movement toward Daisy; then a succession of carefully spaced shorter and longer movements until the climax is reached. The plot works out not like a puzzle with odd bits falling into place, but like a tragedy, with every part functioning in the completed organism. (p. 164)

> *Gilbert Seldes, "Spring Flight," in* The Dial *(copyright, 1925, by The Dial Publishing Company, Inc.; reprinted by permission of J. S. Watson, Jr. and Scofield Thayer), August, 1925 (and reprinted by Kraus Reprint Corporation, 1966), pp. 162-64.*

Mr. Fitzgerald has enjoyed a spectacular career as a writer of short stories for American magazines; and in these, as well as in *This Side of Paradise,* his first novel, he showed (mixed with much magazine shoddy) enough ability to make one fearful lest he should allow himself to be manipulated, by his audience and by his success, as O. Henry was manipulated. In his latest collection of stories, *All The Sad Young Men,* he appears still all too manipulatable; though in one or two of the stories he also makes it evident that his conscience is not yet wholly dead. *Absolution* is an attempt at a close psychological study of hysteria which has good things in it but as a whole is somewhat forced: one feels that Mr. Fitzgerald is not speaking his own language. In this, and in *The Rich Boy,* he fails to detach, and to make clear, his effect—so much so that one suspects him of not seeing it too clearly himself.

In *The Great Gatsby,* however, Mr. Fitzgerald has written a highly colored and brilliant little novel which, by grace of one cardinal virtue, quite escapes the company of most contemporary American fiction—it has excellence of form. It is not great, it is not large, it is not strikingly subtle; but it is well imagined and shaped, it moves swiftly and neatly, its scene is admirably seized and admirably matched with the theme, and its hard bright tone is entirely original. Technically, it appears to owe much to the influence of the cinema; and perhaps also something to Henry James—a peculiar conjunction, but not so peculiar if one reflects on the flash-backs and close-ups and paralleled themes of that "little experiment in the style of Gyp," *The Awkward Age.* Mr. Fitzgerald's publishers call *The Great Gatsby* a satire. This is deceptive. It is only incidentally a satire, it is only in the *setting* that it is satirical, and in the tone provided by the minor characters. The story itself, and the main figure, are tragic, and it is precisely the fantastic vulgarity of the scene which gives to the excellence of Gatsby's soul its finest bouquet, and to his tragic fate its sharpest edge. All of Mr. Fitzgerald's people are real—but Gatsby comes close to being superb. He is betrayed to us slowly and skill-fully, and with a keen tenderness which in the end makes his tragedy a deeply moving one. By so much, therefore, *The Great Gatsby* is better than a mere satire of manners, and better than Mr. Fitzgerald's usual sort of superficial cleverness. If only he can refrain altogether in future from the sham romanticism and sham sophistication which the magazines demand of him, and give another turn of the screw to the care with which he writes, he may well be-come a first-rate novelist. (pp. 209-10)

> *Conrad Aiken, "Fitzgerald, F. Scott" (orig-inally published under a different title in* New Criterion, *October, 1926), in his* Col-lected Criticism *(copyright © 1935, 1939, 1940, 1942, 1951, 1958 by Conrad Aiken; reprinted by permission of Brandt & Brandt),* Oxford University Press, *1968, pp. 207-10.*

Tender Is the Night is a good novel that puzzles you and ends by making you a little angry because it isn't a great novel also. It doesn't give the feeling of being complete in itself.

The theme of it is stated in a conversation among the three principal characters. "What did this to him?" Rosemary asks. (p. 225)

The question remains victoriously buzzing in the reader's ears long after the story has ended. Fitzgerald tries to an-swer it, obliquely. (p. 226)

Here is a magnificent subject for a novel. The trouble is that Fitzgerald has never completely decided what kind of novel he wanted to write—whether it should center round a single hero or deal with a whole group. Both types of ap-proach are present, the individual and the collective, and they interfere with each other. We are conscious of a di-vided purpose that perhaps goes back to a division in the author himself.

Fitzgerald has always been the poet of the American upper bourgeoisie; he has been the only writer able to invest their lives with glamor. Yet he has never been sure that he owed his loyalty to the class about which he was writing. It is as if he had a double personality. Part of him is a guest at the ball given by the people in the big house; part of him has been a little boy peeping in through the window and being thrilled by the music and the beautifully dressed women—a romantic but hard-headed little boy who stops every once in a while to wonder how much it all cost and where the money came from. (Fitzgerald says, "There is a streak of vulgarity in me that I try to cultivate.") In his early books, this divided personality was wholly an advantage; it en-abled him to portray American society from the inside, and yet at the same time to surround it with an atmosphere of magic and romance that exists only in the eyes of people watching at the carriage entrance as the guests arrive in limousines. Since those days, however, the division has been emphasized and has become a liability. The little boy outside the window has grown mature and cold-eyed: from an enraptured spectator he has developed into a social his-torian. At the same time, part of Fitzgerald remains inside, among the dancers. And now that the ball is ending in a tragedy, he doesn't know how to describe it—whether as a guest, a participant, in which case he will be writing a purely psychological novel; or whether from the detached point of view of a social historian. (p. 227)

> *Malcolm Cowley, "Fitzgerald's Goodbye to His Generation," in* The New Republic *(re-printed by permission of* The New Republic; *© 1934 by The New Republic, Inc.), June 6, 1934 (and reprinted in* Think Back on Us . . .: A Contemporary Chronicle of the 1930's, *by Malcolm Cowley, edited by Henry Dan Piper, Southern Illinois Univer-sity Press, 1967, pp. 225-28).*

It is our guess that very young men wrote the obituaries for F. Scott Fitzgerald. Not only were they somewhat unin-formed . . . but they were also inclined to be supercilious. He was the prophet of the Jazz Age, they wrote patroniz-ingly, who never quite fulfilled the promise indicated in *This Side of Paradise.* As an approximate contemporary of Mr. Fitzgerald's and, we suppose, a survivor of the Jazz Age ourself, we find this estimate just a little exasperating. He undoubtedly said and did a great many wild and childish things and he turned out one or two rather foolish books; he also wrote, however, one of the most scrupulously ob-served and beautifully written of American novels. It was called, of course, *The Great Gatsby.* If Jay Gatsby was no more than could be expected of Amory Blaine, Manhattan Island has never quite come up to Peter Stuyvesant's early dreams. (p. 9)

> The New Yorker *(© 1941, 1969 by The New Yorker Magazine, Inc.), January 4, 1941.*

Scott Fitzgerald drew the finest and purest tone from the English language of any writer since Walter Pater, who also, as fate would have it, never had anything to say half worthy of his incomparable ability to express it. (p. 478)

[Fitzgerald] had a queer Keltic tendency to enjoy ill-luck as some people enjoy ill-health. He liked to dramatize to him-self the inevitability of both his latest and his next defeats.

If anything was wrong in his life, and something always seemed to be, even during his Long Island and Riviera days when the world appeared to be his oyster, then everything was all wrong, and he seemed rather to enjoy saying so. He was the same way about a story. In life and letters both he was such a perfectionist that he was always prone to exag-gerate minor excellences and minor defects away out of their proportionate importance to the average perception.

Here at *Esquire* he was the seven-year despair of our proof-room. Very seldom did we manage to get to press with any of his writing without receiving from one to four revised versions after the original had been set in type. . . . More than once we received revised versions of the Hobby sto-ries either on or after the date of their actual appearance on the newsstands. Each time that happened he would act as if his whole career had been torpedoed without warning. (p. 479)

Oddly enough, or perhaps appropriately enough, his most beautiful book, *Tender Is the Night,* was also his most ugly and was the least perfectly realized piece of work of all four of his novels. It was a magnificent failure in many ways, and it contains passages of haunting loveliness, but it suf-fered from the very phenomenon with which it was con-cerned, a split personality. It was really the malformed twin embryo of two books, one of which might have been a mas-terpiece. That book, which ought to have a prominent place on the shelf of the great unwritten books of lost time, was to have been titled simply *Richard Diver*. It might have been an even better book than *The Great Gatsby* but the story got lost and twisted and came out imperfectly and misshapenly as an unassimilated half of *Tender Is the Night*. Well, he's gone and we shall miss him. We shall miss both the writer that he was and the one that he might have been. (pp. 480-81)

> *Arnold Gingrich, "Editorial: Salute and Farewell to F. Scott Fitzgerald," in* Esquire Magazine *(reprinted by permission of Esquire Magazine;* © *1941, 1969 by Esquire, Inc.), March, 1941 (and reprinted in* F. Scott Fitzgerald in His Own Time: A Miscellany, *edited by Matthew J. Bruccoli and Jackson R. Bryer, Kent State University Press, 1971, pp. 477-81.)*

F. Scott Fitzgerald . . . made a major contribution to Primitivism and a minor one to literature, in 1925, with *The Great Gatsby*. (p. 342)

[It] is one of the swiftest moving of modern novels. Its speed and its hard surface polish should have made it more popular with a generation which was fond of quick acceleration, high lacquers, and bright chromium. From the point of view of appeal to the class of readers who like these things, however, the book has two weaknesses: first, Buchanan's affair with Mrs. Wilson is too muddy; and secondly, the most brilliant writer who ever lived could not attack the popular conception of the ex-football hero, as Fitzgerald does, and expect a wide audience. The least read of all his novels (prior to its inclusion in the Modern Library), *The Great Gatsby* has proved, however, to be the one most influential upon other writers. The author aimed to present the rich, selfish athlete and his wife as less ethical than the bootlegger, Gatsby; and so far as Tom and Daisy are concerned the portraiture is hardly to be surpassed, but in sharpening the lines of their sterile and selfish natures, he softened and sentimentalized his drawing of the lawbreaker. It is but a step from *The Great Gatsby* to *Little Caesar* (1929) by Burnett, *To Have and Have Not* (1937) by Hemingway, and other attempts to lionize the gangster and bootlegger. *The Great Gatsby*, then, not only brought new materials to Primitivism, but it also vulgarized Primitivism. Fount of a kind of degeneracy, the novel is still better than many of the books it has influenced. (pp. 345-46)

> *Oscar Cargill, in his* Intellectual America: Ideas on the March *(reprinted with permission of Macmillan Publishing Co., Inc.; copyright 1941 by Macmillan Publishing Co., Inc.; 1969 by Oscar Cargill), Macmillan, 1941.*

A progression might easily be established, I think, from Henry James to Fitzgerald to John O'Hara—a steady materialization and vulgarization of the idea of an aristocracy, and a corresponding increase in the importance of an artificial propriety of dress and behavior in a society which is losing all inner, spiritual propriety. O'Hara seems at times to be aware of this; but Fitzgerald, in his own longing to sit down among the rich, among the right people, in his own admission that his art was somehow not so much a value in itself as a means of procuring for him these other values, seems to have failed to recognize it in himself or in his work. However that may be, he certainly suffers, like his

contemporaries Wolfe, Hemingway, and Faulkner, from the lack of a view of life, a set of standards in which both he and his readers can share. (p. 112)

> *Charles Weir, Jr., "An Invite with Gilded Edges: A Study of F. Scott Fitzgerald," in* Virginia Quarterly Review *(copyright, 1944, by the* Virginia Quarterly Review, *The University of Virginia), Vol. 20, No. 1 (Winter, 1944), pp. 100-13.*

The Great Gatsby is the fable of its period, and I believe it will be read when most of the novels of the Twenties are entirely forgotten. It will stand as one of a small group in which I would place Lewis's *Main Street, Babbitt, Arrowsmith,* and *Dodsworth,* Willa Cather's *A Lost Lady, My Mortal Enemy,* and *Death Comes for the Archbishop,* Ellen Glasgow's *Barren Ground,* Hemingway's *A Farewell to Arms,* and Elizabeth Madox Roberts's *The Time of Man,* as comprising the Twenties' small packet for posterity. (p. 89)

Of *The Last Tycoon* it may confidently be said that . . . there is, in the little more than one hundred pages that he left, the best piece of creative writing that we have had about one phase of American life—Hollywood and the movies. Of all our novelists, he was by reason of his temperament and his gifts the best fitted to re-create that world in fiction. The subject needs a romantic realist, which Fitzgerald had become; it requires a lively sense of the fantastic, which he had; it demands the kind of intuitive perceptions which were his in abundance. . . . The book is a tragic fragment, for it revealed a Fitzgerald approaching a long-delayed maturity. His craftsmanship was already sure, but his grasp upon life was not. (p. 90)

> *J. Donald Adams, in his* The Shape of Books to Come *(copyright* © *1944 by J. Donald Adams; reprinted by permission of The Viking Press, Inc.), Viking, 1944.*

There are novelists who find their material almost entirely outside themselves, and there are others who find it almost entirely within themselves. Scott Fitzgerald's talent lay in an unusual combination of these two modes. The basis of his work was self-scrutiny, but the actual product was an eloquent comment on the world. He was that rare kind of writer, a genuine microcosm with a real gift of objectivity. The combination explains his success. It is the reason that the force of his best work always transcends its subject matter. (p. 187)

"The Crack-up," like almost everything else Fitzgerald wrote, is excellent in the degree by which it transcends mere pathos. This comes in part from his writing itself, which is marked by a colloquial ease that persistently achieves genuine poetic effects. But these effects, in turn, depend on his capacity to hit upon details which invoke an atmosphere much larger than their own. . . .

His evaluations were not always satisfactory. Certain well-known and jejune predilections clung to him throughout life. When he imposed a political observation or a social prejudice on his material, his irony as often as not turned into a kind of snide charlatanism. An instinctive artistic tact kept these elements, in any explicit form, out of his finished work, but, of course, they circumscribed his subject matter, which was narrow. That is why evocation was an absolute necessity, and that is what he had most abundantly. (pp. 187-88)

> *Mark Schorer, "Fitzgerald's Tragic Sense," in* The Yale Review *(© 1945 by Yale University; reprinted by permission of the editors), Fall, 1945, pp. 187-88.*

It is tragic that Scott Fitzgerald did not live to finish *The Last Tycoon*. Even as it stands I have an idea that it will turn out to be one of those literary fragments that from time to time appear in the stream of a culture and profoundly influence the course of future events. His unique achievement, in these beginnings of a great novel, is that here for the first time he has managed to establish that unshakable moral attitude towards the world we live in and towards its temporary standards that is the basic essential of any powerful work of the imagination. A firmly anchored ethical standard is something that American writing has been struggling towards for half a century. (p. 339)

The old standards just don't ring true to the quicker minds of this unstable century. Literature, who for? they ask themselves. It is natural that they should turn to the easy demands of the popular market, and to that fame which if it is admittedly not deathless is at least ladled out publicly and with a trowel.

Scott Fitzgerald was one of the inventors of that kind of fame. As a man he was tragically destroyed by his own invention. As a writer his triumph was that he managed in *The Great Gatsby* and to a greater degree in *The Last Tycoon* to weld together again the two divergent halves, to fuse the conscientious worker that no creative man can ever really kill with the moneyed celebrity who aimed his stories at the twelve-year-olds. In *The Last Tycoon* he was even able to invest with some human dignity the pimp and pander aspects of Hollywood. There he was writing, not for highbrows or for lowbrows, but for whoever had enough elementary knowledge of the English language to read through a page of a novel. (p. 342)

In *The Last Tycoon* he was managing to invent a set of people seen really in the round instead of lit by an envious spotlight from above or below. *The Great Gatsby* remains a perfect example of this sort of treatment at an earlier, more anecdotic, more bas relief stage, but in the fragments of *The Last Tycoon*, you can see the beginning of a real grand style. Even in their unfinished state these fragments, I believe, are of sufficient dimensions to raise the level of American fiction to follow in some such way as Marlowe's blank verse line raised the whole level of Elizabethan verse. (p. 343)

> *John Dos Passos, "A Note on Fitzgerald" (originally published in a slightly different version in* The New Republic, *February 17, 1941), in* The Crack-up *by F. Scott Fitzgerald, edited by Edmund Wilson (© 1945 by New Directions; reprinted by permission of New Directions Publishing Corporation), New Directions, 1945, pp. 338-43.*

We may agree that [Fitzgerald] went in heavily and childishly for fireworks, beautiful in the immediate darkness, a mess of wire and cardboard in the morning. We want something better than lips which are stated to be thrilling and day-dreams drifting over fatuity. But there can be no doubt that in *The Great Gatsby* we have something better. . . . An impression . . . which I wish to encourage is that it is a masterpiece.

The word need not be pretentious nor invoke wild rivalries with Hawthorne or Stendhal. Let us mean by it a work of the literary imagination which is consistent, engaging, and dramatic, in exceptional degrees; which exhibits largely mastered a human subject of the first importance; and which seems in retrospect to illuminate the whole physical and spiritual situation of which it was, by the strange parturition of art, an accidental product. One easy test will be the rapidity with which, in the imagination of a good judge, other works of the period and kind will faint away under any suggested comparison with it. Now a small work may satisfy these demands as readily as a large one, and *The Great Gatsby* satisfies them, I believe, better than any other American work of fiction since *The Golden Bowl*. (pp. 197-98)

[Gatsby] is described at the outset as possessing "an extraordinary gift for hope, a romantic readiness," "some heightened sensitivity to the promises of life," and it is clear that this is the quality that drew Fitzgerald to his creation. (p. 199)

Carraway is not permitted to understand . . . fully [the obsession which dominates Gatsby, the man and the book, and provides the permanent theme of Fitzgerald's serious fiction], but I have no doubt that Fitzgerald himself did and wished his reader to do. In the Introduction he wrote in 1934 for a reprint of *Gatsby* occurs this startling claim: "How anyone could take up the responsibility of being a novelist without a sharp and concise attitude about life is a puzzle to me." It was not intended, probably, as a claim, but a claim it is; and although Fitzgerald looked on himself as a moralist (and plainly is one) this seems to me less a reference to morality than to an attitude or pattern of the most general kind, a "figure in the carpet" as James called it. What is the "figure"?

It is not an idealism, and not Hope, though it is kin to these. It is hardly even an attitude toward experience, although it is a way of taking Life. It is a view of Life in which the creature's supreme admiration is commanded by that which the artist knows to be *wrong*, in which the supreme allegiance is forced to be felt—producing "creative passion"—toward a hopeless error. It insists that the enthusiast be *impersonal* or selfless, and *certain*. It is as if a young artist, a young man, saw every road blocked and sent his characters forward singing. There is helpless irony in the mounting of such a theme, owing to an incongruity between what the hero is made to be obsessed by, his impersonal devotion and confidence, and what the author knows, his own despair. But this irony is not tragic in Fitzgerald; it is as unhappy and tender as a farewell. The superior knowledge has no condescension or rebuke. Carraway knows for instance that Gatsby's chance for Daisy is long past, but there is only love in his witness to Gatsby's fantastic vigil,—or there is envy. This feeling is as idiosyncratic and as literal as some of Wordsworth's feelings, and as difficult to understand for the same reason: most people are familiar with the attitude in some diffused form but cannot imagine that anyone really believes it in a strict form. What Fitzgerald valued was a beauty and intensity of attachment, which his imagination required should be attachment to something inaccessible. For the wholly inaccessible he admitted two modes, the never existent and the already past. He drove his characters sometimes towards the first, as in certain of the stories which are actual fantasies, but regularly toward the second, as in *Gatsby*. And his finest work is saturated with the desperate or ecstatic nostalgia, the firm hope and the firmer despair, of the superb conclusion of this novel. (pp. 199-200)

Tender is the Night . . . [is] diffuse, lush, uncertain, and badly designed. There are admirable things in it, a few scenes, some description, some epigrams; but it is hard to believe that anyone ever found it as a story anything but a failure. Perhaps Nicole is all right. The other characters are not, and one hears a personal insistence in the degeneration of Dick Diver and Abe North which seems external, morbid. It would wreck a firmer book than this. Episodes too, almost uniformly disagreeable, are hurried in and out without reason,—simply, one guesses, because they *happened* once. The style alters senselessly from section to section, as if the book were a series of exercises. Most of the second half can hardly be read as continuous narrative. All the talent of Carraway's summer has gone to bits.

Six years later Fitzgerald left *The Last Tycoon* unfinished when he died. Resisting the inclination to exaggerate the merit of posthumous work, as James's *The Ivory Tower* has been overpraised and Stephen Crane's *The O'Ruddy* would be if it were read, one must testify that Fitzgerald had gone far enough with it to demonstrate a reassembled gift. His film producer, Monroe Stahr, comes from the imagination that made Jay Gatsby. . . . The opening chapters are excellent, the writing compact as well as rich, the symbols working plainly and quietly. . . . There is no doubt that we suffered in losing the novel's completion. To try to measure the loss is futile, although I should note that Fitzgerald was having extraordinary difficulty already with his point of view. . . . (pp. 201-02)

Then there are the magazine stories, of which he collected the least trivial from time to time into volumes. Claims have been made for some of these, without much justification, unless perhaps for "The Rich Boy." The two most ambitious strike me as about equally false: "May Day," banal, fundamentally disordered, and "Absolution" [relying] unduly upon Joyce's profound story called "The Sisters". . . .

It is little to show for fifteen years of the fulness of such a gift. The fulness?—hardly. If the similarity of Gatsby's story and Stahr's suggests to us that the gift was a limited one, we should remember that not only did Fitzgerald not *develop* it beyond 1925 but he hardly exercised it at all thereafter. . . . [He] could not use his gift because he no longer had it. He had sold it for money. . . .

I am not concerned to judge his long apostasy, but merely to look at some of its results, because no other recent history known to me exhibits so sharply the difficulty and danger an artist undergoes who must do his work in a culture essentially confused in the way and to the degree that ours is. (p. 202)

Fitzgerald for instance appears to have lived his whole life in the well-heeled infantile world of American popular writing. . . .

What did it cost him, besides the ability to practice his art? It cost him, first, the criticism that might have saved him:

by shaming him from his bad work, stiffening his conscience, protecting him against his abasements. (p. 203)

It cost Fitzgerald, second, his sense of reality. He could not write, and publish, what he felt, so at intervals for years he abandoned the realm of truth altogether: he wrote fantasies, one his intolerable play *The Vegetable,* the rest stories, of ghosts, diamond mountains, men growing young. Here he could construct his own laws, and his own conscience, for feeling; not even his own reproaches would reach him. It cost him, last, his faith in art. (p. 204)

John Berryman, "F. Scott Fitzgerald" (originally published in The Kenyon Review, Winter, 1946), in his Freedom of the Poet (reprinted with permission of Farrar, Straus & Giroux, Inc.; copyright 1946 by John Berryman; 1973 by Kate Berryman), Farrar, Straus, 1976, pp. 197-204.

Fitzgerald's great accomplishment is to have realized in completely American terms the developed romantic attitude, in the end at least in that most responsible form in which all the romantic's sensuous and emotional responses are disciplined by his awareness of the goodness and evilness of human experience. He had a kind of instinct for the tragic view of life. . . . (p. 333)

From the very beginning he showed facility and that minute awareness of the qualities of times and places and persons which is sharpened to a fine point in the romantic writer by his acute consciousness of the irrevocable passage of everything into the past. . . . A romantic writer of this kind is bound to take as his characteristic subject his own past, building out of the people and places of his time fables of his own inner experience, working his way into his material by identifying himself with others. . . .

At its best the attitude Fitzgerald possessed produces an effect which is compounded of three clearly definable elements. There is in his mature work an almost historical objectivity, produced by his acute sense of the pastness of the past; there is also a Proustian minuteness of recollection of the feelings and attitudes which made up the experience as it was lived; and there is, finally, cast over both the historically apprehended event and the personal recollection embedded in it, a glow of pathos, the pathos of the irretrievableness of a part of oneself. (p. 334)

Until he wrote *The Great Gatsby* Fitzgerald's ability to evoke the nightmare terror of disaster was greater than his ability to motivate the disaster. (p. 335)

[It] is obviously true that the general idea and structure of *This Side of Paradise* were suggested by [Compton Mackenzie's] *Sinister Street* and that Fitzgerald had little realization of the importance for this episodic kind of book of unity of tone. The lack of unity of tone in the book is partly due to its being made up of stories written, over a considerable period of time, before the novel was contemplated. (p. 338)

The quality which [Edmund] Wilson ascribes to the book's being immaturely imagined [see excerpts from this essay by Wilson above] displays itself most in the latter part and especially in the accounts of Amory's love affairs. Fitzgerald's lovers conduct their affairs by making speeches at each other, full of sentiment from Swinburne and of sweeping generalizations about "Life"; as lovers they show all the hypnotized egocentricity and intellectual immaturity of college freshmen. (pp. 338-39)

Yet for all these faults the book is not essentially a bad one. There is in the writing something of the intensity of felt experience which is in the language of Fitzgerald's mature books. This is especially true of the first part, for the experience of Princeton life on which this part of the book was based was far enough behind Fitzgerald to have been to some extent emotionally distanced and evaluated. But even in the latter part of the book, beneath all the author's naïve earnestness about the romantic cynicism and "philosophizing" of Amory and Rosalind and Eleanor, you feel something of the real suffering of unhappiness. Fitzgerald's judgment and technique are inadequate almost everywhere in the book, but the fundamental, almost instinctive attitude toward experience which emerges, even at times through the worst of the book's surface, is serious and moving. (p. 339)

The Beautiful and Damned is an enormous improvement on *This Side of Paradise,* more than anything else because Fitzgerald, though he has not yet found out how to motivate disaster, has a much clearer sense of the precise feel of the disaster he senses in the life he knows. The book is also a great advance on its predecessor technically, much more unified, much less mixed in tone. The tendency to substitute lectures for dialogue is subdued. . . . (p. 340)

[The] sense of tragedy is very real with Fitzgerald and his ability to realize the minutiae of humiliation and suffering seldom fails him. His difficulty is in finding a cause for this suffering sufficient to justify the importance he asks us to give it and characters of sufficient dignity to make their suffering and defeat tragic rather than merely pathetic.

Nor is it quite true that Fitzgerald did not try to give the disaster a motive and meaning. There is a fairly consistent effort to make Anthony the sensitive and intelligent man who, driven into a difficult place by his refusal to compromise with a brutal and stupid world, finds his weaknesses too strong for him. He is tempted to cowardice and drifting by his own imagination and sensitiveness. . . . The trouble is that Anthony is not real as the sensitive and intelligent man; what is real is the Anthony who is weak, drifting, and full of self-pity. The Anthony who drifts into the affair with Dot under the momentary stimulus of his romantic imagination, knowing perfectly well that he does not believe in the thing; the Anthony who is continually drunk because only thus can he sustain "the old illusion that truth and beauty [are] in some way intertwined"; the partly intolerable, partly absurd, partly pathetic Anthony who seeks again and again to sustain his now fantastic vision of his own dignity and honor; this Anthony is marvelously realized. But the thing that would justify this pathos, the conviction that here is a man more sinned against than sinning, is wholly lacking. *The Beautiful and Damned* is full of precisely observed life and Fitzgerald is often able to make us feel the poignancy of his characters' suffering, but he is able to provide neither an adequate cause for their suffering nor an adequate reason within their characters for their surrender. In the end you do not believe they ever were people who wanted the opportunities for fineness that the freedom of wealth provides; you believe them only people who wanted luxury. They are pitiful, and their pathos is often brilliantly realized; but they are not tragic. (pp. 341-42)

The Great Gatsby was another leap forward for Fitzgerald. He had found a situation which would allow him to exploit without loss of probability much more of his feeling about his material, and he had arrived at the point where he understood the advantage of realizing his subject dramatically. (p. 344)

[Though] Fitzgerald would be the last to have reasoned it out in such terms, *The Great Gatsby* becomes a kind of tragic pastoral, with the East the exemplar of urban sophistication and culture and corruption, and the West, "the bored, sprawling, swollen towns beyond the Ohio," the exemplar of simple virtue. (p. 345)

Against Nick's gradual understanding of the incorruptibility at the heart of Gatsby's corruption, Fitzgerald sets his gradual penetration of the charm and grace of Tom and Daisy's world. What he penetrates to is corruption, grossness, and cowardice. . . . To the representation of this double contrast Fitzgerald brings all his now mature powers of observation, of invention, of creating for the scenes and persons the quality and tone the story requires. Because of the formal perfection of *The Great Gatsby,* this eloquence is given a concentration and intensity Fitzgerald never achieved again. The art of the book, in the narrow sense, is nearly perfect. Its limitation is the limitation of Fitzgerald's nearly complete commitment to Gatsby's romanticism. . . . Fitzgerald's book is a *Troilus and Cressida* with an Ajax but no Ulysses. (pp. 346-47)

Tender Is the Night, though the most profoundly moving of all Fitzgerald's novels, is a structurally imperfect book. To this difficulty must be added the fact that its central theme is not an easy one. We believe overwhelmingly in the collapse of Dick Diver's morale because we are made to see and hear, in the most minute and subtly shaded detail, the process of that collapse. It is very like the collapse of Fitzgerald's own morale as he describes it in "The Crack-Up." But it is not easy to say in either case what, in the immediate and practical sense, happens to cause the collapse. As do many romantics with their horror of time and age, Fitzgerald tended to think of spiritual resources—of courage and generosity and kindness—as he thought of physical resources, as a sum in the bank against which a man draws. (p. 348)

At the very beginning Dick Diver has to choose between becoming a great psychologist and a fully human being when Nicole, beautiful and schizophrenic, falls in love with him. . . . [He] accepted the responsibility of being loved by Nicole and, gradually, of being loved by all the others whom his life drew around him. To them he gave lavishly of his strength, of his ability to translate into their terms the necessary human values and so remind them of their best selves. . . . But the people he worked this trick for had no energy of their own, and gradually he exhausted his supply, spun out all his strength for other people until he had none left. (p. 349)

Whether one accepts Fitzgerald's conception of the cause of . . . spiritual death or not, *Tender Is the Night* remains his most brilliant book. All his powers, the microscopic observation of the life he describes, the sense of the significance and relations of every detail of it, the infallible ear, and the gift of expression, all these things are here in greater abundance than ever before. And as never before they are used for the concrete, dramatic presentation of the inner significance of human experience, so that all the people of his book lead lives of "continual allegory" and its world is a microcosm of the great world. Its scope is such as to make *The Great Gatsby* seem small and simple, for all its neatness and perfection, and its dramatic realization so complete that Fitzgerald need not ever say what is happening: we always see. (p. 350)

> *Arthur Mizener, "F. Scott Fitzgerald (1896-1940): The Poet of Borrowed Time," in* The Lives of Eighteen from Princeton, *edited by Willard Thorp (copyright © 1946, 1974 by Princeton University Press; reprinted by permission of Princeton University Press), Princeton University Press, 1946, pp. 333-53.*

Fitzgerald does not allow a single redeeming characteristic to his Jewish gambler [Wolfsheim, in *The Great Gatsby*], not even so much redemption as Shakespeare allows to Shylock in his dominantly villainous portrait. . . .

I shall grant that Fitzgerald is writing a satire, and that some of the non-Jewish characters are even harder hit than the Jew is. *The Great Gatsby* is nothing so simple as a piece of propaganda against the Jews. If it were, that would have been pointed out long ago. *But anti-Semitism is a component part of the novel.* It is not the mad anti-Semitism we find in Ezra Pound. Nor is it the kind of anti-Semitism we find in Dostoevski.

Fitzgerald's is the *fashionable anti-Semitism* of the 1920's, of the sort we find in T. S. Eliot at the same period. (p. 510)

It will not do simply to say that there are Jews such as Mr. Wolfsheim, and that Fitzgerald is being objective in the portrayal of a certain type, without casting any aspersions upon other kinds of Jews. Wolfsheim is a character without any compensations. His moral physiognomy is as distinctive as his physical one, and both stand out with the isolation of a caricature in *Der Stuermer*. If we compare Fitzgerald's satire with Proust's, I think that my meaning will become clearer. There is little difference between Fitzgerald's portrayal of Wolfsheim and Proust's portrayal of Bloch. Yet there is not the faintest trace of suspicion that Proust is anti-Semitic. . . . Proust, in other words, does not leave Bloch hanging in mid-air as Fitzgerald leaves Wolfsheim; he provides a balance and a milieu that make of Bloch not the general representative of his people, but only an individual example. There is no objection to the portrayal of a Jew, however bad he is, provided that the reader cannot read into it the implication that this is a picture of *the* Jew. (pp. 510-11)

When the intellect reaches a certain stage of development, there seems nowhere left for it to go except back into the primitive. It bathes and purges itself in popular emotion, from which it has been excluded so long. Perhaps modern anti-Semitism may be considered most fruitfully as the backwash of the romantic movement, that reaction against a preceding "age of reason" (an age, by the way, from which the liberation of modern Jewry dates). It was romanticism which originally brought into favor the music of Wagner, the philosophy of Schopenhauer, the folk ballad, and various other seemingly anti- or sub-intellectual forms.

In any case, it is a rare member of the avant-garde of the 20's who feels as does Stephen Dedalus in Joyce's *Ulysses*

that "history is a nightmare" from which he is trying "to awaken." Many of them seem to think that it is a nightmare that ought to be encouraged. And they bring forward to it their own little "trifles for a massacre" (the actual title of Céline's first anti-Semitic book, which was so violent that André Gide in his review thought it a satire of genuine anti-Semitism). (p. 513)

Fitzgerald was an artist rather than a philosopher, and he was therefore at his best when creating images, not when thinking about them. It is instructive to compare the richness and meaningfulness of his picture of American decay during the drinking 20's with the poverty of his interpretation of that picture. . . . Almost the last comment Nick makes in the book, a few pages from the end, is most significant, if not illuminating:

"That's my Middle West. . . . I am a part of that. . . . Even when the East excited me the most, . . . even then it had always for me a quality of distortion. . . ."

It would take a long time to disentangle the threads of this attitude and categorize them, but in general the passage represents the basis of his feelings about Meyer Wolfsheim. The West in this passage represents the forces of tradition (a curious change from the days of the frontier when it stood for everything that was crude and uncultured), and the East stands for decay. . . . Gatsby, the romantic baby turned into a clown by the surrounding waves of scepticism and nihilism, is so uprooted from tradition and a healthy connection with the people about him that he is reduced to considering a Wolfsheim his closest friend. Nevertheless, Gatsby remains the hero of the book precisely because to Fitzgerald he is a tragic victim. As a whole, *The Great Gatsby* is a kind of left-handed defense of romanticism and betrays Fitzgerald's ambivalent mixture of contempt, nostalgic admiration, and sympathy for this Don Quixote on Long Island (or, as he thought of naming the book at one time, "Trimalchio of West Egg"). (p. 514)

[The] evidence justifies our applying to Fitzgerald the statement from Goethe's sympathetic obituary on Byron: *"sobald er reflektiert ist er ein Kind."* As soon as he begins to think he becomes a child. His cartoon of *the* Jew is the product of this thoughtlessness, though it surely is far from systematic anti-Semitism.

Fitzgerald's last word on the Jews remained only half spoken. *The Last Tycoon,* interrupted by the author's death, is the merest fragment, but it promised to be an interesting book and of an import somewhat different from that of *The Great Gatsby*.

The available portions of this last book show Fitzgerald playing with a number of ideas. The one that must concern us here is in the sharpest opposition to the Wolfsheim theme. The abstract concept of *the* Jew (perfect or imperfect) is split up by the concrete reality of *Jews*, good, bad, and indifferent. It is as if his Hollywood experience forced Fitzgerald, at least in this problem, to think a little harder and observe a little more closely. . . . [Stahr, the protagonist,] belongs to the only type for which the author had any indulgence. He is a self-made, romantic millionaire, a dreamer. The more one thinks about him, the more he seems to resemble Jay Gatsby. With one important difference—he is a Jew. . . . For Fitzgerald to admit that a Jew might be a romantic was equivalent to his ceasing to be an anti-Semite. This perhaps reinforces the suggestion that his anti-Semitism was a superficial, merely "fashionable" thing from the beginning.

Certainly Fitzgerald's attitude toward Stahr is ambivalent, but so was his attitude toward Gatsby, whom he regarded constantly with an inextricable mixture of love and contempt. . . . [He] can write of Stahr, with a kind of tenderness and humility. . . . Stahr is surely no representative of the tradition of the Middle West, as Gatsby was, but by this time, perhaps, Fitzgerald had lost his sentimental nostalgia for that tradition. . . . [The] complicated interplay of conflicting attitudes in the portrait of Monroe Stahr is thus a sign of greater maturity and responsibility in the writer. (pp. 514-15)

> *Milton Hindus, "F. Scott Fitzgerald and Literary Anti-Semitism: A Footnote on the Mind of the 20's" (reprinted from* Commentary *by permission; copyright © 1947 by the American Jewish Committee), in* Commentary, *June, 1947, pp. 508-16.*

Where *This Side of Paradise* marked the first brilliant flaring of Scott's talent, *The Beautiful and Damned* is in some respects the sputtering-away of the bright flame. The two brief years which have elapsed between the two novels appear to have encompassed two decades of bitter experience: an experience that has no sufficient counterpart in the external facts of the writer's life over this period. (p. 304)

For F. Scott Fitzgerald, . . . the prime Muse of the Jazz Age, James Gatz of North Dakota—granting the inevitable exception of his millions—is almost the equivalent of a proletarian protagonist. Yet, as the Great Gatsby, he is more than a class symbol. He is a sort of cultural hero, and the story of Gatsby's illusion is the story of an age's illusion, too. The bare outlines of his career—the upward struggle from poverty and ignorance; the naïve aspirations toward refinement and the primal, ruthless energy of these aspirations; the fixation of this provincial soul upon a childlike notion of beauty and grace and the reliance upon material power as the single method satisfying his searching and inarticulate spirit—these are surely the elements of a dominant cultural legend in its purest, most sympathetic form. And through a consummate choice of detail Fitzgerald has made the legend live. Gauche, ridiculous, and touching as James Gatz is, he is surely our native adolescent, raised on the western reverberations of Vanderbilt and Gould, entering a new world full of shining secrets 'that only Midas and Morgan and Maecenas knew'—a barefoot boy in the land of steel, and even, in a rather deeper sense, a cousin, say, of Huck Finn, but now drifting in the eddies and backwaters of the Long Island Sound. Whatever there is of permanence in *The Great Gatsby* derives from the fact that here, by one of those fortunate coincidences which form the record of artistic achievement, the deepest inner convictions of the writer have met with and matched those of his time and place. The 'illusive rhythm, the fragment of lost words' that Nick Carraway tries to recall are the rhythm and words of an American myth. (pp. 319-20)

Tender is the Night . . . is a novel of lost causes, or lost cures, as it represents Fitzgerald's most precipitous descent into the abyss, and fulfills the pattern of disaster which has been the core of his work. Yet what actually lies in these depths where now the writer wanders, without light, through Keats's 'tender' night? What discordant impulses

have led Fitzgerald to make this recurrent plunge into darkness? . . . [One] has the curious impression at times that the novel is really about something else altogether—and yet *Tender is the Night* is certainly at the center of Fitzgerald's recurrent aesthetic conflict and brings into focus some of the more obscure elements we have noticed in his previous work. (pp. 332-33)

[We] have the final cleavage of this tragically divided writer: the cleavage of his writing itself. On the one hand, the 'psychological' novels—*The Beautiful and Damned* and *Tender is the Night*—intense, powerful, and unco-ordinated: the force of their discordant impulses reflected in the ragged ending of the first, and the disorderly ending of the second novel. And on the other hand, the 'social' novels—*The Great Gatsby* and *The Last Tycoon*—very skillful, often superb technically, and yet curiously hollow at times, and in a sense quite 'unreal' underneath, since they reflect without carrying through the real emotions of Fitzgerald's writing.

One needn't labor the loss here, or the wider cultural implications. The young Fitzgerald, disowning his own heritage, leaving his criminals just on the edge of 'crime,' attempting with all his tormented heart to pass as a Nordic—this Fitzgerald was in the American grain. The rich, too, are an American novelist's natural prey, just as the nineteen-twenties and nineteen-thirties were among the best decades in the nation's history to observe the rich in the polar extremes of their existence. (p. 350)

Yes, *The Great Gatsby* fades a little with its last 'dying fall'—but it is still the warm and touching chronicle of our deceptive native romance, just as 'The Diamond as Big as the Ritz' is among our best shorter parables of wealth, as 'May Day' has all the faintly bitter fragrance of the age of pleasure, and as *The Last Tycoon* is still the closest that an American novelist has got to the truth about the histrionic home of the Success Story. Although Fitzgerald remains the folklorist of the rich in their more restricted aspects, and, like his own Munro Stahr, who had never learned enough about the feel of America, still retains 'a certain half-naïve conception of the common weal,' there are few others who could have given such a bright and glowing intensity to such a shallow world. (p. 351)

> *Maxwell Geismar, "F. Scott Fitzgerald: Orestes at the Ritz," in his* The Last of the Provincials: The American Novel, 1915-1925 *(copyright © 1943, 1947, 1949, 1975 by Maxwell Geismar; reprinted by permission of Houghton Mifflin Company), Houghton, 1947 (and reprinted by Hill & Wang, 1959, pp. 287-352.*

Horror and compassion were what Fitzgerald quickly came to feel for the segments of American society he chose to explore. These segments were as narrow as those claimed by Henry James and Mrs. Wharton, but they were equally representative. They exhibited the way of life deliberately adopted by those who were absolutely free to choose. And, while they represented the reality of only a very few, they also represented the aspiration of the many. Almost from the first, Fitzgerald had been pretty aware that living wasn't the reckless, careless business these people thought. And, in even his earliest tales, unnoticed by most readers, there was always a touch of disaster—"the lovely young creatures in my novels went to ruin, the diamond mountains of my short stories blew up, my millionaires were as beautiful and damned as Thomas Hardy's peasants."

Damned, certainly. Not only because effort was futile and failure inevitable. Not only because life was meaningless so what the hell. Almost without exception, the hereditary members of Fitzgerald's smart world exhibited a singular callousness of heart. There was in them a streak of brutishness. It seemed to result from the absence of something which enabled the normal human to distinguish between those actions which will nourish life, and those which will destroy it. . . . For him, it did more than characterize the privileged products of American success. It expressed the national frame of mind during a period when the maximum of national prosperity coincided with the extreme of national corruption.

It was the coincidence of these two factors which, in the nineteen-twenties, gave a peculiar tone to American life. In Fitzgerald, it produced what he said was an abiding distrust, an animosity, toward the leisure class—not the conviction of a revolutionist but the smoldering hatred of a peasant. More accurately, his hatred was intellectual and moral. It was the resentment which any intelligent American might have felt after exposure to, and disillusion by, the world he had been bred to revere. Like most middle-class Americans, Fitzgerald had been shaped by an environment in which the acquisition of wealth was the sole test of worth, and the ways of those who possessed it the sole criterion of excellence. (pp. 151-52)

In Fitzgerald's view, there was something inherently evil in a society which elevated as models those who were so demonstrably rotten at the core. Was not the average American being deceived and ruined by what his environment proposed for his emulation? . . . Like the "little people" of his friend Ring Lardner's stories, Fitzgerald's "outsiders" were pathetic victims of a myth. The function of the myth was to keep prosperity going. (p. 152)

What came to be called "defeatism" was implicit in Fitzgerald's mature work. . . . And although in his youthful first novel Fitzgerald had found hope in a vague kind of socialism, in middle age he had no faith in the success of any high intentions toward the future. From his station in an unlovely present, all that he could affirm as spiritually useful was the wise and tragic sense of life. (p. 153)

> *Lloyd Morris, in his* Postscript to Yesterday: America: The Last Fifty Years *(copyright 1947 by Lloyd Morris; reprinted by permission of Random House, Inc.), Random House, 1947.*

Nothing happens, nothing ever pans out; life is infinite boredom, futility, and frustration. [This] is the theme . . . of Scott Fitzgerald, the most gifted of all the novelists of the twenties, the incomparable historian of gilded youth, of the jazz age, of the rich and the near rich, of the great prosperity and the great disillusionment. His characters are, for the most part, extravagantly rich, but they differ from those of Lewis and Lardner chiefly in circumstances, not in aspirations: it is when we contrast Fitzgerald's playboys and demimondaines with their equivalents in Edith Wharton or Henry James that the comparison is qualitative. Nor do West Egg or the Riviera or Hollywood differ greatly from Gopher Prairie or Zenith or the Big Town, except that their inhabitants live what the hapless denizens of the sticks dream and thus reveal the tawdriness of the dream. (p. 265)

First implicitly in *This Side of Paradise,* then more explicitly in *The Beautiful and Damned, The Great Gatsby,* and *Tender Is the Night,* and finally in the wonderful fragment of *The Last Tycoon,* Fitzgerald laid bare the pathology of that generation which Gertrude Stein had called "lost," and it is relevant to remember that pathology derives from pathos. His theme—as surely as that of Dos Passos—was the Big Money, and he showed, not with malice but with compassion, what money did to his generation, how its standards conditioned life, dictated habits, condemned to futility, and led, in the end, to that "crack-up" which he himself experienced. He is the chronicler of the Beautiful but especially of the Damned, of All the Sad Young Men, of the golden bowl of riches that was so fatally flawed.

Of all Fitzgerald's novels, *The Great Gatsby* best mirrors not so much the economy as the economic fantasies of the twenties. . . . *The Great Gatsby* is one of the saddest novels in American literature. It is not that, in the end, Gatsby lies dead in the symbolic swimming pool and the rooms of the fabulous mansion are silent; it is rather that while he lived he realized all his ambitions. (p. 266)

> *Henry Steele Commager, in his* The American Mind: An Interpretation of American Thought and Character Since the 1880's *(copyright, 1950, by Yale University Press), Yale University Press, 1950.*

[If] all of Fitzgerald's most memorable characters are finally broken by society, some of them, especially in the early stories, are destroyed trying to get inside; and some of them, especially in the later stories, are destroyed because they are too much in the center, too much in the sun. In the former case, we have the sad and brilliant series of initiation rites gone wrong—like a college initiation in which the joke gets out of hand and the pledge is injured or killed. In the latter case, we have the brutal and perhaps necessary tribal drama of the scapegoat: the ludicrous Christ, the despised vessel of society's confession and absolution. This was the way traversed by Fitzgerald—from initiate to scapegoat; it is unmistakably the story of the stories, and when it is told in a manner faithful to its legendary form, it will turn out also to be the story of the life. (p. 306)

The stories up to and including *The Great Gatsby,* are, I suggest, attached essentially to the local tradition of the unfallen innocent—the godlike young man exempted from family and race, dreaming a pure dream nourished by the unfolding and undefined west: the hero of the vast inchoate legend of The American Adam. No such figure was conceivable in England or on the continent; but American fiction and poetry threw up image after image of this absurd, attractive and helpless fellow. He ought to have disappeared, along with Turner's frontier, before the turn of the century; but if Fitzgerald commits him once again to his inevitable catastrophe in a story of the twenties, Adam at least has a suitably changed appearance and encounters his incomprehensibly evil enemy in a suitably new guise. The uninitiated innocent is buried beneath a guessed-at corruption and hidden in a gorgeous pink rag of a suit; Whitman's singer of Adamic songs has got himself somehow involved with the man who fixed the World Series of 1919; the old hero is as veiled from the eye as the flock of sheep Nick

Carraway almost imagines seeing on Fifth Avenue one summer afternoon. But he is there all the time, greatly there; and he has failed once again, and now with a kind of finality, to grasp the fact of wickedness, and so to survive, and so to grow up. (p. 307)

[It] is another mark of Fitzgerald's stature that his style is not intended to call attention to itself, but to illuminate the action or character or thought that it is standing for. His words are never in love with themselves. But along with his directness, his strength and his accuracy, there are also qualities of melody and brightness; so that Fitzgerald's prose not only lights up its object, it also makes us conscious of the shadows that lie around it. This is to say that Fitzgerald mastered what must be the supreme problem for the American novelist, in his steadily more successful accommodation of the visible and concrete to the ideal or ethical. The story of the style would be one of a development towards this end, and it could be summarized in three stages: in the first, the fusion is imperfect, and the prose consists of conventional phrasing interrupted by occasional darts of realistic detail; in the second, the convention acts as a counter-poise—it is being used by Fitzgerald to designate possible false habits of perception; and in the third, the convention has been absorbed and reprojected in a fresh and vital form. It can readily be seen that the story of the style is not different from the other stories: the second stage, for example, can be recognized in the long list of tales in which the hero attempts success in conventional terms (money, fame and power), and in which the point of the story is precisely the catastrophic intrusion of an actual rhythm of life into the meretricious fairy-tale formula. (p. 308)

> *R.W.B. Lewis, "Fitzgerald's Way," in* The Hudson Review *(copyright © 1951 by The Hudson Review, Inc.; reprinted by permission), Vol. IV, No. 2, Summer, 1951, pp. 304-09.*

The Fitzgerald legend threatens to become something of a bore. For some time now the vogue of the twenties has been booming in all branches of our popular entertainment, as if all America were sighing with nostalgia for its lost youth.... The legend ... threatens to fasten upon those things in Fitzgerald's life and writings that are most perishable; and before it does, we ought to put ourselves at a little distance from it, and ask why this legend itself should become so urgent for us now, and whether it does not conceal a meaning a little more damaging than we had thought to our own American self-esteem. (p. 433)

Fitzgerald was, to put it quite simply, a genius—the term cannot now be denied him—but he did not become a great writer, if we use this adjective with a sober consciousness of literary history that in his best moments he would have wanted us to invoke....

The last pages of *Gatsby* remind us that Fitzgerald's imagination sought for its furthest meanings in the total image of America itself, a reference that takes us well beyond the "fabulous" twenties or the Success Story that still echoes like a tinny tune of that decade; and if we are to find any meaning to his career, it ought to be one commensurate in scope with this total image of America on which, as his notebooks show, he brooded all his life. I suggest that the real drama of Fitzgerald's life is as part of the general drama of the American's emotional innocence before life. Other writers have treated the theme of American innocence, and Henry James, for one, has given the subject much more explicit and mature treatment in his fiction. But Fitzgerald lived this subject matter, at once wide-awake and violent, with a completeness that leaves us unable to face the stark and unpleasant truth of our innocence from the rather shielded and sometimes even self-indulgent point of view provided by the fictions of James. (p. 435)

Character is fate, and Fitzgerald willed his own destruction; observing this, we are not likely to say Fitzgerald was done in by America, the boom and the bust, his wife, the shifting literary climate of the thirties, or any other such external cause; but, having granted all that, we are not altogether exonerated thereby from the question that would relate his self-destruction to the peculiarly destructive and unstable character of so much of American life: Might not a reckless and gifted individual like this have found in another culture some stable way of life, some support outside himself which he might have hung on to, which could not indeed have prevented him from doing himself harm but might at least have preserved him a little better and a little longer from his own nemesis? ...

The American, in the face of and in spite of everything in life, wishes to persist in believing in his own innocence. When Fitzgerald's innocence could no longer maintain itself against the facts of his own life, there followed the breakdown, the despair, and the howl of disappointment of "The Crack-up." (p. 436)

On the positive side, the emotional innocence of the American is also a condition of discovery, and Fitzgerald's work without his wide-eyed romanticism would not be filled with so many things sharply seen and sharply felt.... (p. 439)

> *William Barrett, "Fitzgerald and America" (originally published in* Partisan Review, *1951), in* The Partisan Review Anthology, *edited by William Phillips and Philip Rahv (copyright © 1962 by Holt, Rinehart and Winston, Inc.; reprinted by permission of Holt, Rinehart and Winston, Publishers), Holt, 1962, pp. 433-39.*

With a sense of the destructive impulses of his time that can only be compared with Hemingway's, [Fitzgerald] yet lacked Hemingway's stabilizing gift—the ability to get rid of the bad times by writing of them. Fitzgerald never got rid of anything; the ghosts of his adolescence, the failures of his youth, the doubts of his maturity plagued him to the end. He was supremely a part of the world he described, so much a part that he made himself its king and then, when he saw it begin to crumble, he crumbled with it and led it to death.

But the thing that destroyed him also gave him his special distinction. His vision of Paradise served him as a medium of artistic understanding. Through it he penetrated to the heart of some of the great illusions of his time, discovering their falsity as if he were discovering his own. If that vision —like Hemingway's correlative of loss which it so much resembles—was limited, it was at least adequate to Fitzgerald's purpose; and it was a means of contact between his art and the experience of his time. (p. 41)

> *John Aldridge, "Fitzgerald: The Horror and*

the Vision of Paradise," in his After the Lost Generation (copyright © 1951 by John W. Aldridge), McGraw-Hill, 1951 (and reprinted in F. Scott Fitzgerald: A Collection of Critical Essays, edited by Arthur Mizener, Prentice-Hall, 1963, pp. 32-42).

This Side of Paradise . . . was as revolutionary a document for its time as Main Street and The Grapes of Wrath were to be for theirs. The book is an individual manifesto, a kind of portrait of the artist as a young Princetonian. Its notes of decadence and protest and its salute to change announce that here is a generation born disenchanted.

Yet for all its reputation as the definitive work on the Jazz Age, This Side of Paradise is a tentative book, one dedicated not to being but to becoming. (p. 138)

Unlike Stephen Dedalus (whose problems "puzzled and depressed" him), Amory will not cloak himself in the arrogance of art. Significantly, he is himself artifact, and here he will put his trust. The book comes to an ambiguous close, for as Mencken observed in his Smart Set review: "What, after such a youth, is to be done with the fellow?"

Gloria [in The Beautiful and Damned], like all of Fitzgerald's heroines, possesses a masculine mind. Anarchic sentiments may vaguely haunt his heroes; his heroines are ruthlessly Nietzchean. The will to power, the will to immolation and to annihilation consume them. Eleanor, the willful descendant of Maryland aristocrats in This Side of Paradise, runs her horse over a cliff in a moment of defiance; Gloria munches gum drops.

The "war between the sexes," a dominant American theme, is fought with increasing bitterness in Fitzgerald's books. (p. 139)

Most of Fitzgerald's short stories are negligible as art, but they achieve significance in terms of the American myth of progress, for which he was, in his moments of acceptance, spokesman. But in spite of their surface approval of American life, these stories reveal a profound disquiet, and the serious and commercial ones have the curious effect of contradicting one another's premises. "All of the stories that came into my head," he wrote in his last years, "had a touch of disaster in them. . . ." In one of the stories Fitzgerald speaks of the millennial book to be written, the book patently of his own ambition. "It will be neither cheerful nor pleasant but will contain numerous passages of striking humor." This is a remarkably apposite characterization of the short stories. (pp. 140-41)

The Great Gatsby . . . , the fable for which Fitzgerald's name will always be known, achieves . . . passages of striking humor and a delicate wit. Its wit arises not so much from new material as a fresh way of looking at the old. The book ties together themes Fitzgerald had used before—most memorably those of the outsider from the West and the penniless young man of promise who meets and loves the girl "safe and proud above the hot struggles of the poor."

There are but two kinds of hero in Fitzgerald: the man who had money and must now live without it; and the man who was born without money and who has, by one species of outlawry or another, come late to the acquiring of it. Jay Gatsby, born James Gatz, is one of the latter. (p. 141)

The story of Jay Gatsby's tragedy escapes triviality and sordidness through its allegorical power. The book is a juxtaposition of scene and symbol from beginning to end; it is "metaphysical" in the modern sense. Everywhere is the sign of contradiction. Brooding over a Long Island out of El Greco are the enormous billboard eyes of Doctor T. J. Eckleburg, eyes which "look out of no face, but, instead from a pair of enormous yellow spectacles which pass over a non-existent nose." These eyes do more than survey the dumping ground which separates the valley of villas from the city. They are, ambiguously, but certainly, Fitzgerald's symbol of value. (pp. 141-42)

Because Fitzgerald was essentially rootless—what use, in the 'twenties, were loyalties to Catholicism, to Francis Scott Key, to the mid-Western virtues?—he was powerfully attracted to contemporary currents, which he mistook for ideas. Often self-conscious and mistrustful of self, yet at times going to his own books for advice, he was painfully aware of the lack of substance in his work. Somewhere, he hoped, in the right books, in making the timely gestures, learning and wisdom could be stumbled upon. When he reached out for ideas, he was not likely to find them; but intuitively, brooding upon his deficiencies, his inchoate protests, and his feelings of betrayal, he happened upon many insights which were later to become truisms. Amory Blaine's harangue on socialism in the closing pages of This Side of Paradise is sophomoric. But it is portentous. Fitzgerald never entertained ideas purely, for their own sake; or pragmatically, for what they could do. Most of all, he wanted people to like his mind. (p. 146)

And for all that we think of him as, so to speak, a naturally mannered stylist, Fitzgerald spent most of his creative life wrestling with the problem of form. His first novel, indeed, is an instance of the triumph of form over the novelist. . . . On the occasions, unfortunately rare in his total work, when Fitzgerald was successful with form, his meaning attained a clarity it did not otherwise have. It is true of Fitzgerald, as it is of all writers not absolutely of the first rank, that he could achieve idea, achieve the thing only through form. He had no other than oblique utterance.

Such is the indirection, the elevation of form into meaning which takes place in The Great Gatsby. Nothing Fitzgerald had done before really prepares one for this book. Some of its themes he had touched on before, and was to treat again. It derives, it is true, from his own life. But it is the only one of his novels to derive as well from his view of life. Tender Is the Night and The Last Tycoon present, as did the two earlier novels, the flat, mirrored surface of the author's experience. Only Gatsby is prismatic. For this effectiveness Fitzgerald is more beholden to literature than to life. Without his acquaintance with Conrad and Henry James, Gatsby would not be the book we know. For one thing, the Conradian device of the involved observer lends dimension. (Up to this time, in his life and books, Fitzgerald had striven for "an almost theatrical innocence by preferring the role of the observed to that of the observer.") Without Nick Carraway, Jay Gatsby would not be in focus. Gatsby started out to be someone he knew, the author tells us, and then became himself, for Fitzgerald could not keep himself out of his fictions. In the first two novels the author's identification with the hero is embarrassingly complete; in the last two the identification is diffused: he assumes one mask after another. Only in The Great

Gatsby is there disjunction between the author and the objects of his compassion.

The verdict of time on Fitzgerald's work will never permit it to be entirely lost to us. Much of it will be forgotten, of course, because Fitzgerald was a profoundly unoriginal writer, and his time had no enduring stamp. He himself felt that "the ennui of changing fashions" would "suppress" him and his books. Few of his writings, it would seem, other than *The Great Gatsby* and a handful of the short stories, will be remembered as anything more than period pieces. Historians will go to them for data on that era in our national life when frivolity was a prime social force. The student of our literary history will, it may be, turn to Fitzgerald to examine the personality of a man who wrote in half a dozen different styles.

For there were at least three Fitzgeralds: the allegorist of *This Side of Paradise* and *The Beautiful and Damned*, both with their morality-play characters and sermonizing; the fabulist of *The Great Gatsby* and "The Diamond as Big as the Ritz"; and lastly the impressionist of *Tender Is the Night* and *The Last Tycoon*. In the first two novels the clash of conventionality in style and form with the shock of new ideas is characteristic of the 'twenties. In the following decade form and matter merged into one another, and Fitzgerald caught the manner of it. In the last two novels, the very syncopation of the nervous 'thirties, the Angry Decade as someone has called it, has gotten into the author's bloodstream. His prose is a remarkable barometer of the sensibilities, of the very pulse, of the successive decades which produced it.

F. Scott Fitzgerald, the unrivaled poet of the thousand dollar bill, was the last of the romantics. Early and late he was perplexed with the dualities of life and the dream. Each was escape from the other. (pp. 147-49)

But *The Great Gatsby* is the dream made palpable, tender and lasting. There the ambiguities are resolved, fashioned into art out of failure and regret. And behind the book, finally unreached and perhaps unanalyzable, is the haunting figure of Scott Fitzgerald, self-dispossessed heir to all the ages. (p. 149)

> *Riley Hughes, "F. Scott Fitzgerald: The Touch of Disaster," in* Fifty Years of the American Novel: A Christian Appraisal, *edited by Harold C. Gardiner (reprinted by permission of Charles Scribner's Sons; © 1951 by Charles Scribner's Sons), Scribner's, 1951, pp. 135-50.*

In Kierkegaard's definition, *despair*, the contrary of *faith*, is the Sickness unto Death arising from an impotence in the self to choose and to become itself. In this precise sense, Fitzgerald was a man in despair. (p. 147)

> *D. S. Savage, "The Significance of F. Scott Fitzgerald" (copyright © 1952 by D. S. Savage), in* Arizona Quarterly *(copyright © 1952 by the* Arizona Quarterly*), Vol. 8, No. 3, Autumn, 1952 (and reprinted in* F. Scott Fitzgerald: A Collection of Critical Essays, *edited by Arthur Mizener, Prentice-Hall, 1963, pp. 146-56).*

The source of Fitzgerald's excellence is an uncanny ability to juxtapose the sensibilities implied by the phrase "romantic wonder" with the most conspicuous, as well as the most deeply significant, phenomena of American civilization, and to derive from that juxtaposition a moral critique of human nature. (p. 43)

Roughly speaking, Fitzgerald's basic plot is the history of the New World (ironic *double entendre* here and throughout); more precisely, of the human imagination in the New World. It shows itself in two predominant patterns, quest and seduction. The quest is the search for romantic wonder (a kind of febrile secular beatitude), in the terms proposed by contemporary America; the seduction represents capitulation to these terms. Obversely, the quest is a flight: from reality, from normality, from time, fate, death, and the conception of *limit*. In the social realm, the pattern of desire may be suggested by such phrases as "the American dream" and "the pursuit of happiness." Fitzgerald begins by exposing the corruption of that dream in industrial America; he ends by discovering that the pursuit is universally seductive and perpetually damned. Driven by inner forces that compel him towards the personal realization of romantic wonder, the Fitzgerald hero is destroyed by the materials which the American experience offers as objects and criteria of passion; or, at best, he is purged of these unholy fires, chastened, and reduced.

In general, this quest has two symptomatic goals. There is, for one, the search for eternal youth and beauty, what might be called the historic myth of Ponce de Leon. ("Historic" because the man was really looking for a fountain; "myth" because no such fountain ever existed). The essence of romantic wonder appears to reside in the illusion of perennial youth and grace and happiness surrounding the leisure class of which Fitzgerald customarily wrote; thus the man of imagination in America, searching for the source of satisfaction of his deepest aesthetic needs, is seduced by the delusion that these qualities are actually to be found in people who, in sober fact, are vacuous and irresponsible. But further, this kind of romantic quest, which implies both escape and destruction, is equated on the level of national ideology with a transcendental and Utopian contempt for time and history, and on the religious level, which Fitzgerald (whose Catholic apostasy was about half genuine and half imagined) persistently but hesitantly approaches, with a blasphemous rejection of the very conditions of human existence.

The second goal is, simply enough, money. The search for wealth is the familiar Anglo-Saxon Protestant ideal of personal material success, most succinctly embodied for our culture in the saga of young Benjamin Franklin. It is the romantic assumption of this aspect of the "American dream" that all the magic of the world can be had for money. Both from a moral, and from a highly personal and idiosyncratic Marxist standpoint, Fitzgerald examines and condemns the plutocratic ambitions of American life and the ruinous price exacted by their lure. But the two dreams are, of course, so intimately related as to be for all practical purposes one: the appearance of eternal youth and beauty centers in a particular social class whose glamor is made possible by social inequality and inequity. Beauty, the presumed object of aesthetic contemplation, is commercialized, love is bought and sold. Money is the means to the violent recovery or specious arrest of an enchanting youth.

In muted contrast, Fitzgerald repeatedly affirms his faith in an older, simpler America, generally identified as pre-Civil

War; the emotion is that of pastoral, the social connotations agrarian and democratic. In such areas he continues to find fragments of basic human value, social, moral, and religious. But these affirmations are for the most part subordinate and indirect; Fitzgerald's attention was chiefly directed upon the merchandise of romantic wonder proffered by his own time and place. . . . His keenest perception, and the one that told most heavily for his fiction, was the universal quality of the patterns he was tracing, his greatest discovery that there was nothing new about the Lost Generation except its particular toys. The quest for romantic wonder and the inevitable failure were only the latest in a long series. (pp. 43-5)

> *Edwin Fussell, "Fitzgerald's Brave New World" (copyright © 1952 by The Johns Hopkins University Press), in* English Literary History, *December, 1952 (and reprinted in* F. Scott Fitzgerald: A Collection of Critical Essays, *edited by Arthur Mizener, Prentice-Hall, 1963, pp. 43-56).*

[We] have reached the point from which the 'twenties, Fitzgerald's 'twenties, can be regarded with the maximum nostalgia; we readopt the hairdos, the songs—and the authors. We see him now as one who refused to whore after strange Marxist gods, our lonely St. Anthony, faithful to literature in the sociological desert. The versions of Fitzgerald that these estimates imply are perhaps not quite true, but they are believed in and will do. And yet the *essential* appeal of Fitzgerald is elsewhere—astonishingly enough, in his *failure*. (p. 71)

Edgar Allan Poe provides the prototype, of course: dope, whisky, the shadow of madness, poverty and early death—and Fitzgerald is the perfect modern avatar. It is the Fall not of a King, but of an Artist, the disaffected son of the middle class, of us all, that we demand to stir our pity and terror. For the great quasi-literate public, Fitzgerald is providing right now the *tragic experience:* creating, in the great amphitheater without walls of articles in *Life,* abridgments in the *Atlantic Monthly,* paragraphs in the papers, and 25-cent reprints, a debased equivalent of what the Athenian found in the *Oedipus Rex.* When any American writer refuses to live into the conventional public myth, the people remake him, as even Poe was retouched by Griswold, who invented in malice the American Writer, and as Stephen Crane was lied and vilified into the image necessary to us all.

But Fitzgerald *willed* his role as a failure, for all his paeans to success. Long before his own actual crack-up, he dreamed it, prophesied it in his stories and novels. . . . (pp. 71-2)

The greatest drunken writer whom Fitzgerald created . . . appeared in none of his books—being, of course, Fitzgerald himself. A part of the apparent waste of Fitzgerald's life stems from his having invested most of his energy in composing himself. . . . (p. 73)

All his life, he moved uncertainly between the demands of his own erratic sensibility and a desire to please a great, undefined audience—to be loved by everybody. Like one of his own epicene coquettes, he postured and flirted with all comers, trying to cling meanwhile to a virginity which became more and more a technicality. To be wanted and admired, he was willing to seem to say less than he meant, to

appear merely chic; so that it is still possible to read even his best books with no understanding and much pleasure. How could he ever find time to learn how to put a novel together with skill! All his life, point-of-view baffled him, and he was forced to make his transitions with such awkward links as: "To resume Rosemary's point of view, it should be said . . ." or "This is Cecilia taking up the story . . .". (p. 75)

But, beyond all this, one feels in his work a great theme, however elusive and imperfectly realized. It is not love, though love is superficially everywhere in his writing; nor is it Europe, though he lived there and set one book and many stories in the expatriate background. Though he was educated in Catholic schools, it is not religion. His books have no religious insights, only religious décor—the obsessive metaphor of the "ruined priest," a theatrical making of the cross to close a book, a belated Aubrey-Beardsley-ish priest. The sensibility of the Catholic in America becomes, like everything else, puritan: the devil, self-consciously introduced in *This Side of Paradise,* shrinks to an evil aura around a tart's head. There is in Fitzgerald no profound sense of evil or sin, only of guilt; and no gods except the Rich.

The Rich—there is the proper subject matter of Fitzgerald, as everyone has perceived: their difference from the rest of us, and the meanings of that difference. . . . Of course, the wealthy in Fitzgerald are not *real,* but that is precisely the point. Whether in declared fantasy like "A Diamond as Big as the Ritz" or in nominally realistic novels, they resemble veritable millionaires as little as Natty Bumppo resembles an actual frontiersman. But they are, at least—like that Cooper character and unlike the nasty rich in proletarian novels—myths rather than platitudes, viable to the imagination. (pp. 75-6)

The world where a penny saved is a penny earned is the world of anti-art. The lower middle class in particular, Fitzgerald felt, were the enemies of style. He wanted a class that knows how to *use* writers, or at least desires a kind of life in which the imagination would have a chance to live. It was a hopeless dream, and in the end Fitzgerald learned two things: first, that the rich, whatever the quality of their living, regard the artist not as an ally but as a somewhat amusing *arriviste;* and, second, that to live the life of high style is to remain a moral child, who destroys whatever does not suit his whim. To be "rich," in the sense he dreamed, is to refuse responsibility, to deny fate, to try (as in the terrible scene toward the close of "The Diamond as Big as the Ritz") to bribe God. There is implicit in such a life a doom as absolute as its splendor, and in this sense alone the career of the very rich is like that of the artist.

It is a vision atrocious and beautiful enough to be true, and it survives in Fitzgerald's work, despite the incoherence and sentimentality, with the force of truth. It is fitting that our chronicler of the rich be our prophet of failure. To those who plead that Fitzgerald could not face up to life and success, it can be said that at least he kept faith with death and defeat. (p. 76)

> *Leslie Fiedler, "Some Notes on F. Scott Fitzgerald," in his* An End to Innocence *(copyright © 1955 by the Beacon Press; 1971 by Leslie Fiedler; reprinted by permission of Stein and Day Publishers), Beacon*

Press, 1955 (and reprinted in F. Scott Fitzgerald: A Collection of Critical Essays, *edited by Arthur Mizener, Prentice-Hall, 1963, pp. 70-6).*

It was in the very nature of Fitzgerald's mind to sculpt the contours of experience in such a way that the light falling on them, from his own ready charm and vivid perception of tragedy, would suggest some content they did not represent. He had learned early in his career—not with *This Side of Paradise,* which was juvenile, but with his first intensive stories of the jazz age and *The Great Gatsby*—that his talent was colorful rather than deep, immensely resourceful in suggestiveness and blending, and that it was futile for him to try for more. Life, or at least the America and tourist France of the 'twenties, appeared as a succession of brightly lit scenes whose significance emerged not from the frank and frontal realization with which he could mold them —the idea-giving power—but from the prompter's quickness with which he underscored the scenes. The emphasis was always on the immediate light irony of some human encounter, the placing of the characters to each other in such a way that they were silhouettes of a mood, quickly inserted into a scene and as quickly releasable from it. The living rhythm of the work was in the movement of the filmy curtain through which he saw it. Everything had to be faintly and deliciously supported on a lightly running river of little golden words. Just as the story of *Tender Is the Night* was heartbreaking without ever being definite, too thickly suffused, for all the delicacy and grace, in the unmistakable glare of the American Mediterranean, so in *The Crack-Up* even the most awesome admission of personal bankruptcy and irretrievable loneliness had to be subtly bent to sound good, to put a subtly diffusing eloquence between the emotion and the fact.

Yet what comes through, so far as one can break through the walls of an experience so coated and painted and glamorized, so heightened and modulated by the strategy of a mind that sought grace at any price, is a very American confession, an unrealized but agonized revolt against certain basic American patterns by which Fitzgerald knew himself to be imprisoned. . . . The good fairy who showers gifts always does so with some final reservation to remind us that life is a coil of many springs and never a straight road. To Scott Fitzgerald she gave talent as a weapon rather than as a gift; it was to be a means to success rather than the content of some ultimate human success in itself. (pp. 119-20)

Since he was Gatsby, and could never really admit the fact into the course of the novel, he made a bargain with himself. He would make Gatsby an object of rich historical pathos, but a kind of anonymous figure, and easy to patronize, to whom the cool amused narrator of the book (Fitzgerald himself, as we were led to think) would not seem related. He could create Gatsby only at the price of never admitting that he *was* Gatsby. . . . (p. 122)

Monroe Stahr, the sad, skilled, burned-out genius of manipulation . . ., was as much the refracted image of himself at forty as Gatsby had been at twenty-five. Stahr is unquestionably the greatest of Fitzgerald's achievements; even in the half-pages of the unfinished *The Last Tycoon* he has a depth, a variety of human color, that was missing from the young dancers of the 'twenties, the nostalgia of Gatsby, or the arbitrary innocence of Dick Diver. Stahr was a man whose true life was all *inside;* who was a success in the worldly sense and yet above success; an artist of gravity and importance and immense responsibility, but one who did his work casually and quietly; he was occupied with a tragedy. It was important to Fitzgerald to create Stahr; it was even more important for us to have him. For no very good American artist had ever taken the movies seriously enough before. Dos Passos in *The Big Money* caricatured and mauled Josef Von Sternberg, and the caricature remains a caricature. Fitzgerald did something deeper and more enduring. Out of the very heart of the American dream, at the topmost pinnacle of American success, he plucked an alien, a "mere" producer, a Jew, and gave him back to us as one who might have been with White-Jacket and Huck Finn, Lambert Strether and Sister Carrie. And if the success did not bring home "the old white light" of the heart; if Monroe Stahr stood among tinsel miracles; what would? What had? Fitzgerald had found *mon semblable, mon frère;* he gave him everything for a while; and suddenly he died. (p. 126)

> *Alfred Kazin, "Fitzgerald: An American Confession," in his* The Inmost Leaf: A Selection of Essays *(© 1946, 1974 by Alfred Kazin; reprinted by permission of Harcourt Brace Jovanovich, Inc.), Harcourt, 1955, pp. 116-26.*

Unable to dominate the society he both idolized and despised, Fitzgerald was also unable, even unwilling, to destroy it. Although he finally scorned the worship of the bitch goddess, Success, he turned against it too late, and his tragedy was neither the tragedy of noble defeat nor of proud failure, but the casualty of irresolute and unresisting compromise. (p. 701)

> *Louis Untermeyer, "F. Scott Fitzgerald," in his* Makers of the Modern World *(copyright © 1955 by Louis Untermeyer; reprinted by permission of Simon and Schuster, Inc.), Simon & Schuster, 1955, pp. 691-701.*

From the start, Fitzgerald's personal dreams of romance contained the seeds of their own destruction. In his earliest works, his optimistic sense of the value of experience is overshadowed by a personal intuition of tragedy; his capacity for naive wonder is chastened by satiric and ironic insights which make surrender to the romantic impulse incomplete. (pp. 54-5)

Inevitably, then, Fitzgerald saw his romantic dream threaded by a double irony. Those who possess the necessary means lack the will, motive, or capacity to pursue a dream. Those with the heightened sensitivity to the promises of life have it because they are the disinherited, forever barred from the white palace where "the king's daughter, the golden girl" awaits "safe and proud above the struggles of the poor." . . . The successful entrepreneurs of Gatsby's age are the panderers to vulgar tastes, the high pressure salesmen, and, of course, the bootleggers. Yet once, Fitzgerald suggests, there had been opportunity commensurate with aspiration, an unexplored and unexploited frontier where great fortunes had been made or at least romantically stolen. And out of the shifting of opportunities from the West to Wall Street, he creates an American fable which redeems as well as explains romantic failure. (p. 56)

> *Robert Ornstein, "Scott Fitzgerald's Fable of East and West," in* College English *(copyright © 1957 by the National Council of Teachers of English), December, 1956 (and reprinted in* Twentieth Century Interpretations of "The Great Gatsby," *edited by Ernest Lockridge, Prentice-Hall, 1968, pp. 54-60).*

Gatsby, as has often been said, represents the irony of American history and the corruption of the American dream. While this certainly is true, yet even here, with this general legend, Fitzgerald has rung in his own characteristic changes, doubling and redoubling ironies. At the center of the legend proper there is the relationship between Europe and America and the ambiguous interaction between the contradictory impulses of Europe that led to the original settling of America and its subsequent development: mercantilism and idealism. At either end of American history, and all the way through, the two impulses have a way of being both radically exclusive and mutually confusing, the one melting into the other: the human faculty of wonder, on the one hand, and the power and beauty of things, on the other.

The Great Gatsby dramatizes this continuing ambiguity directly in the life of Gatsby and retrospectively by a glance at history at the end of the novel. Especially docs it do so in the two passages in the novel of what might be called the ecstatic moment, the moment when the human imagination seems to be on the verge of entering the earthly paradise. The two passages are (1) the real Gatsby looking on the real Daisy, and (2) the imaginary Dutchmen, whom Nick conjures up at the end of the novel, looking on the "green breast" of Long Island. (pp. 99-100)

No one knew better than Gatsby that nothing could finally match the splendors of his own imagination, and the novel would suggest finally that not only had the American dream been corrupted but that it was, in part anyway, necessarily corrupted, for it asked too much. Nothing of this earth, even the most beautiful of earthly objects, could be anything but a perversion of it.

The Great Gatsby, then, begins in a dramatization, as suggested, of the basic thesis of the early Van Wyck Brooks: that America had produced an idealism so impalpable that it had lost touch with reality (Gatsby) and a materialism so heavy that it was inhuman (Tom Buchanan). The novel as a whole is another turn of the screw on this legend, with the impossible idealism trying to realize itself, to its utter destruction, in the gross materiality. (p. 101)

Allegorically considered, Nick is reason, experience, waking, reality, and history, while Gatsby is imagination, innocence, sleeping, dream, and eternity. Nick is like Wordsworth listening to "the still sad music of humanity," while Gatsby is like Blake seeing hosts of angels in the sun. The one can only look at the facts and see them as tragic; the other tries to transform the facts by an act of the imagination.... They are generically two of the best types of humanity: the moralist and the radical.... A lesser writer might have attempted to make Nick a literal sage and Gatsby a literal prophet. But it is certain that such a thought would never have entered Fitzgerald's head, as he was only dramatizing the morals and manners of the life he knew. The genius of the novel consists precisely in the fact that, while using only the stuff, one might better say the froth and flotsam of its own limited time and place, it has managed to suggest ... a sense of eternity. (p. 103)

> *John Henry Raleigh, "F. Scott Fitzgerald's 'The Great Gatsby': Legendary Bases and Allegorical Significances"* (copyright © 1957 by John H. Raleigh), in The University of Kansas City Review, Autumn, 1957 (and reprinted in F. Scott Fitzgerald: A Collection of Critical Essays, edited by Arthur Mizener, Prentice-Hall, 1963, pp. 99-103).

[Fitzgerald] was a romantic, and he had considerable integrity, which survived his success and period of literary prostitution unscathed. In the nineteenth century, he might not have come to a great deal of harm; the penalties and temptations of success were less great then.... Fitzgerald's significance is to point out that the modern Outsider has a new problem that did not exist in previous ages. In the past, the Outsider's chief enemy was the indifference of his time, his failure to communicate, failure to achieve self-expression. Ours is the first age in Western history in which the Outsider has had to face the other danger—horrifying because it is so insidiously attractive—of arousing too much sympathy and interest, of being paid and flattered by the age "for telling people you feel as they do." (pp. 90-1)

Fitzgerald was the dupe of his time; its appearance of riches and prosperity took him in. For all his talent, he was not big enough to be a representative figure of the twentieth century. He did not understand his own age. (p. 91)

> *Colin Wilson, in his* Religion and the Rebel *(copyright © 1957 by Colin Wilson; reprinted by permission of Victor Gollancz, Ltd.), Houghton, 1957.*

Thomas Wolfe's nostalgia, his cry of *"Lost, lost, lost—"* was a cliché he neither transformed nor examined, but Fitzgerald made of it a form of consciousness. Nostalgia, quite simply, is *all* there is. In plumbing this sentiment to its depths, rather than merely using or abusing it, Fitzgerald dropped to the deep, dead-end center of the American mind. He let his line out deeper than Hemingway and Twain, deeper than the Mississippi and the Big-Two Hearted River, down to that sunken island that once mythically flowered for Dutch sailors' eyes.

That was where the dream began, he tells us, that still pandered to men in whispers: that was where man held his breath in the presence of this brave new world. It was Fitzgerald, dreaming of paradise, who was compelled to an aesthetic contemplation that made of nostalgia, that snare and delusion, a work of art. (p. 25)

Fitzgerald *knew*. That was the hell of it. He was the first of his generation to know that life was *absurd*.

It is fitting that Fitzgerald, the aesthete of nostalgia, of the escape clause without question, should be the first American to formulate his own philosophy of the absurd. But nostalgia, carried to its conclusion, leads nowhere else. (p. 26)

He did not know, however, that art can sometimes begin where life stops. He was too profoundly and incurably committed to life itself. (p. 29)

But the quiet streets and lanes of nostalgia soon turn upon

themselves, a labyrinth without an exit, both a public madness and a private ecstasy. The strings of reminiscence tangle on themselves, they spin a choking web around the hero, and he must either surrender himself, without a struggle, or risk cracking up. Fitzgerald ran the risk. He did not, with Wolfe's adolescent bellow, try to empty the house of its ghosts by shouting, nor did he, like Faulkner, generate his escape with an impotent rage. He simply faced it. But he faced it too late. Having dispensed with his resources, he cracked up. The artist in him, as self-aware as Henry James, went on plying its hand, sharpening all the old pencils, but the man within him had died of nostalgia. The sign of *Cave Canem* that hung above his door meant exactly what it said. (p. 31)

> *Wright Morris, "The Function of Nostalgia: F. Scott Fitzgerald," in his* The Territory Ahead *(© 1958 by Wright Morris; reprinted by permission of Harcourt Brace Jovanovich, Inc.), Harcourt, 1958 (and reprinted in* F. Scott Fitzgerald: A Collection of Critical Essays, *edited by Arthur Mizener, Prentice-Hall, 1963, pp. 25-31).*

In one sense Gatsby is the apotheosis of his rootless society. His background is cosmopolitan, his past a mystery, his temperament that of an opportunist entirely oblivious to the claims of people or the world outside. His threadbare self-dramatisation, unremitting selfishness, and attempts to make something out of nothing are the same in kind as those of the waste-land society, and different only in intensity. Yet this intensity springs from a quality which he alone has: and this we might call "faith." He really believes in himself and his illusions: and this quality of faith, however grotesque it must seem with such an object, sets him apart from the cynically armoured midgets whom he epitomizes. It makes him bigger than they are, and more vulnerable. . . .

The tragedy—for [*The Great Gatsby*] is a tragic novel, though of an unorthodox kind—lies in the fact that Gatsby can go only so far and no further. Faith can still remove sizeable molehills, but is absolutely powerless when it comes to mountains. The ultimate romantic affirmation, "I'll always love you alone" cannot be brought to life: certainly not in the waste land; not when people like Daisy, and Gatsby himself, are involved. Gatsby's faith has to break, in the end, against a reality radically incompatible with it. But in so breaking, it makes him a tragic figure: and unites him symbolically with many men more worthy than himself—with, indeed, the general lot of mankind. (p. 44)

[Carraway] cannot make reality more acceptable than it is, or find a way out of the waste land, or suggest a cure for the cynicism which is eating out the heart of society. He can, however, prize the highest human values that he sees, and respond to the misfortunes of others with a pity which has in it a feeling for human suffering as a whole. It is characteristic that in the closing sentences he should find in Gatsby's tragic awakening a symbol of the disenchantment of mankind as a whole—and end on a note which, transcending both Gatsby's personal fate, and the *folie-de-grandeur* of the America which he also represents, achieves a universal tragic vision as haunting as any I can think of in a novel. (p. 48)

> *A. E. Dyson, "'The Great Gatsby': Thirty-*

> *Six Years After," in* Modern Fiction Studies *(copyright © 1961, by Purdue Research Foundation, West Lafayette, Indiana, U.S.A.), Spring, 1961, pp. 37-48.*

[The same] fatalistic determinism [found in the later short stories] marks the only novel Fitzgerald completed after 1929, *Tender is the Night*. If the short stories . . . represent a hyperbolic treatment of some of the circumstances of Fitzgerald's own life, the novel traces the moral decline and fall of practically everyone. The men and women that inhabit the novel are no longer the daring, fun-loving throng of the author's earliest vision of the twenties. They are unsavory couples with dissolving marriages, Americans dying in barroom brawls, and decadent nobles with homosexual sons. The moral themes of the novel are the same as those in the short stories, and the resolution of moral issues is handled the same way. (p. 75)

A great deal has been written about the incest motif that dominates the book. Diver, it has been observed, is sapped of his strength because he is forced to become the father-figure first to Nicole Warren, the woman he marries, then to Rosemary Hoyt, Hollywood star of "Daddy's Girl," and finally to the whole group of immature, inebriated Americans that frequent the Riviera after the First World War. As a device for indicating both the decadence and the infantilism of the twenties this is highly successful. If the novel did nothing more than evoke a mood, critical discussion could stop with revealing the Oedipal relationships within it.

Such is not the case, however. Dr. Diver is perhaps the most appealing personality Fitzgerald ever created, and one cannot view him as merely one more indistinguishable face in the crowd or regard his fate with indifference. One wants to know why Diver meets his doom, why he has succumbed to the kinds of demands that his friends place upon him, and, above all, how this has happened to a man who knows himself as well as a man in Diver's profession must. The answers, of course, lie partly in the nature of the time Diver is living in. His self-knowledge was attained before the war and hence, to Fitzgerald, in another era; it is no longer adequate in the face of new needs. One of those new needs is a way of coping with the prosperity that came with the twenties. The problem as it is defined in *Tender is the Night* and as it is faced by Dick Diver is essentially a moral one. (pp. 75-6)

Diver . . . acts as though he had been created without any will at all. Consequently it is virtually impossible to make any sort of moral evaluation of Diver's actions. He has been destroyed by forces he could neither control nor even fully understand, and the moral judgment he had once possessed was of no use.

The fate of Dick Diver furnishes another insight into Fitzgerald's later moralism and the nature of his contrition for past sins. To him it was believable that a man should lose his zest for work, his desire to make any contribution to society, if the profit motive is removed. And without work a man's character crumbles. This begins to sound remarkably like the Protestant ethic. If profit is, then, to some extent the measure of virtue, the fact that Fitzgerald's writing didn't sell served to aggravate the frustrations of his other personal adversities. It increased his sense of guilt without increasing his understanding. (pp. 76-7)

The fragment of a novel that Fitzgerald left at his death is in some ways anticlimactic. It seems almost as though the author had effectively passed judgment upon his life and work in "The Crack Up," and might have been spared the effort of a literary second coming. A casual glance at *The Last Tycoon* seems to indicate that he had, indeed, broken sharply with his earlier writing and had chosen a new and very different subject.

Yet the difference is more apparent than real. It is obviously the work of the same man, no longer preoccupied with the sparkle and then the tarnish of the twenties, but still grappling with the same kinds of problems. (p. 78)

There is the descent into evil, for which Stahr is not entirely responsible. . . . There is the recognition of evil and the desire to halt its consequences, which is thwarted by circumstances beyond the control of the protagonist. The only moral difference between Stahr and Wales is that the former is not permitted to meditate over the consequences and the implications of what he has done. He is spared this by being handed the fate that Fitzgerald usually reserved for his women characters, escape through death or insanity.

To say all this is not to suggest that Stahr is only a type. Fitzgerald was too good a writer to have created a mannikin. Stahr is differentiated from almost anyone else who appears in his fiction. Most distinctive is the fact that Stahr knows himself more thoroughly than Dick Diver or Charles Wales or Donald Plant or Louis Trimble knew themselves. He is aware of the extent and limitations of his mental, moral, and physical capacities. He is a somber figure who has accepted the burden of the past, and whose actions in the present are not crippled by it.

Yet it remains true that Fitzgerald came to his last work, so different in scenario and outward characterization from most of his other writing, with essentially the same moral concepts, the same ideas of guilt and responsibility that had long marked his writing. More important than the nature of Fitzgerald's moralism, of course, is its quality. The most serious charge that must be leveled against him is that he never made a really searching inquiry into the sources of his moral ideas or of the reasons behind the situations that moved him to render moral judgment. His own specific references to his tendency to moralize were always oblique, as though he felt he should either get rid of this predilection or make light of it. Instead of trying to understand it, he tried to direct his reader's attention to something else. When this was no longer possible, he found himself in the midst of a tangle of sometimes adolescent, sometimes senile ways of coping with the moral issues raised in his fiction and in his life.

The absence of a mature, well-defined position of moral perception in a writer is important only if it damages the effectiveness of his writing. In Fitzgerald's case it is clear that his work was damaged, and seriously so. This deficiency kept him from realizing the brilliant potentialities of some of the characters he created. It meant that even the best of them must be only pathetic creatures lost in a world they never made, a world that was hopelessly bewildering.

Only in *The Last Tycoon* did Fitzgerald approach a more sophisticated treatment, and even there he left much to be desired. The moral outlook of Monroe Stahr was that of a latter-day Stoic . . ., but [one who was] still not entirely the master of himself. For inherent in this brand of Stoicism is the abandonment of the effort to understand—one only accepts.

For Fitzgerald himself the absence of a clear moral vision meant that he continued to be torn by an ambivalence that thrust him back and forth between the two poles of guilt and innocence. (pp. 80-1)

> *Kent and Gretchen Kreuter, "The Moralism of the Later Fitzgerald," in* Modern Fiction Studies *(copyright © 1961, by Purdue Research Foundation, West Lafayette, Indiana, U.S.A.), Spring, 1961, pp. 71-81.*

Fitzgerald now seems to us to have been a kind of exoticist who wrote about a bright, brittle kind of life whose attraction, for his audience, lay in its unfamiliarity. A part of him thus functioned as his reader's surrogate. The significance of this becomes clear if one compares his attitude with Hemingway's and *The Great Gatsby* with *The Sun Also Rises.* Jake Barnes tells his story in a tone which assumes that you know already what the central experience is all about. This kind of complicity between author, character, and reader is exactly what Fitzgerald's stance does not let him achieve. In *The Great Gatsby,* in *Tender Is the Night,* and (one gathers from the notes even more than from the published draft) in *The Last Tycoon,* the characters of Nick, Rosemary, and Cecilia Brady are *on* the scene but not completely *of* it; they stay near the edge to help the reader see in, without being completely in themselves. All of them, so to speak, are in some measure transplants from Minnesota. (p. 37)

Hemingway wrote with . . . admirable unity of tone because he thought of his readers as a homogeneous group. The taste that underlies his prose may displease many, but at least it is a single taste; even when he exaggerates the characteristics of his style until he sounds like a parody of himself, as I think he does in *To Have and Have Not,* the unity of taste is still present. . . . Fitzgerald did not lack the talent it takes to get a similar unity of tone. There are plenty of pages, even in *The Great Gatsby,* so clearly keyed to the internal necessities, so "clean, and hard, and true," that there can be no question of his ability to write prose "of integrity." But at the point in history when the editors of the *New Yorker* were making epochal announcement that their magazine would not be written and edited for "the old lady from Dubuque," and every number of Mencken's *American Mercury* was heaping slurs on the Middle West, Fitzgerald was writing for an audience which may have included the old lady herself and certainly took in her half-emancipated daughters. This need not mean—and I don't mean—that Fitzgerald pandered deliberately to a taste which demanded that paragraphs end with soggy phrases about the infinite variety of life. (pp. 45-6)

There was a taste abroad with which were identified writers like Tarkington, just as there was also a taste, then forming though not fully formed, for writing reflecting the more rigid standards of men like Hemingway. The broad American audience Fitzgerald wrote for shared both in varying proportions, and Fitzgerald shared them, too. It was implicit both in his subject matter and in the stance he assumed toward it that he should do so. (p. 46)

A final estimate of Fitzgerald has to include the fact of his preferring . . . immature characters for the point of view. . . . What each of them is busy trying to pick through is not the surface of an ethically complex situation but the eggshell of his own emotional and social inexperience. The distance which separates such instruments of the moral imagination from one on the order of Lambert Strether is vertiginous.

All this suggests that Fitzgerald falls somewhat short of the eminence as moralist which recent criticism would like to attribute to him. Actually, there is some reason to doubt that Fitzgerald was really devoted to the use of the central moral consciousness as such; i.e., he used it, but not especially for the purposes of the moralist. . . . One has to conclude that if the temporarily central position of these characters was important to Fitzgerald, the reason for the importance has no connection with moral observation. For such a character to be a useful means of indirect moral analysis he would have, obviously, to maintain his privileged position throughout the story, the end of which should be at least as morally significant as the beginning. (pp. 50-1)

I suspect . . . that most of his audience do not take Fitzgerald to be a moralist at all. They take Gatsby's career as being all of a piece with the sensibility which did not object to ending a paragraph with a cliché about life's inexhaustible variety.

For its proper purpose, that sensibility is a perfectly useful one. But the purpose has to do not with morals but with manners. It was because Fitzgerald was dealing essentially with manners that he could work so hard on the "central" characters of two of his novels, only to let them drop back out of their central positions. Their role was to introduce the reader to, and ease him into, a new strange world; once he was acclimated their importance declined. They were there to help him report the "feel" of a certain kind of life, the precise sensation of it. And because, after all, "felt life" is a synonym for "novel," we honor Fitzgerald's achievement. (p. 52)

The Great Gatsby should not be taken as satire. Satire assumes an understanding on the part of the reader which Fitzgerald's novel may not—a reasonable familiarity with the human foibles which it exposes. Satirizing something one's audience does not know runs just as much chance of success as parodying a totally unfamiliar poem. *The Great Gatsby* comes no closer to being satire than would a *Satyricon* written by a recent arrival from Transalpine Gaul. (p. 61)

As a moralist he suffers from an inability to find a solid position of his own. As a novelist of manners he merits complete respect in so far as his report can be credited; but there is a point beyond which crediting it becomes extremely difficult. As a stylist he is often admirable, but there are moments when his difficulties with manners and morals corrupt his style. There is always the "but," the qualification of the praise, and each time we pronounce it we return to the subject of displacement in America, the effect on our writing of the universal problem of cultural adjustment.

On the other hand, none of these considerations diminishes him with respect to the accomplishment for which we should, and possibly do, honor him most. He made the great myths of his time—the myth of going to college, the myth of the unhappy expatriate, the myth of the Jazz Age

itself. He had help, of course, but he was still the principal contributor. The debt we owe him is the one we acknowledge to those writers, rarely more than two or three in each generation, who help us understand ourselves in relation to our time. To merit this it was no obstacle to him to be a transplant, a displaced person writing about other displaced persons. Probably being such was an advantage. Possibly it was even the one indispensable condition. (p. 62)

> W. M. Frohock, "F. Scott Fitzgerald: Manners and Morals," in his Strangers to this Ground: Cultural Diversity in Contemporary American Writing (© 1961 Southern Methodist University Press), Southern Methodist University Press, 1961, pp. 36-62.

[Fitzgerald's] highest achievement was not the nostalgic evocation of an age. It was not even the recreation of an essential American myth: the green light Gatsby believed in at the end of Daisy's dock; not even in the exquisite and affecting prose he found to communicate the dream—at its best, the finest that American fiction can offer. Fitzgerald's genius, an almost tragic genius, as *Tender is the Night* gives witness, was fully to understand the hopelessness, even the appalling viciousness of the romantic ideal he created. In a way not unlike far greater artists, he could both wholly believe in the ideal—in Gatsby, Gatsby's green light, the drunken butterfly world of the twenties, the whole grand American dream—and consciously recognize its ugliness and folly. (p. 168)

> David Littlejohn, "Fitzgerald's Grand Illusion," in Commonweal (copyright © 1962 Commonweal Publishing Co., Inc.; reprinted by permission of Commonweal Publishing Co., Inc.), May 11, 1962, pp. 168-69.

Fitzgerald looks very different when regarded primarily as a short story writer and secondarily as a novelist. He looks better, too. Nothing, I imagine, will unseat *The Great Gatsby,* in critical opinion and popular reception, as the finest thing Fitzgerald wrote. It is also by far the shortest of his novels and, in terms of the span of years covered in the life of its main character, more compressed than many of his stories. The big novels have always met with grumblings of dissatisfaction from Fitzgerald fans. *This Side of Paradise,* as everyone knows, was a true first novel—half literary pastiche, half jazz—covering the facts and fantasies of Fitzgerald's own life from birth through college. His second novel, *The Beautiful and Damned,* carried on the story, with somewhat more seriousness, to Fitzgerald's courtship of his wife and early married life in the United States. *Tender Is the Night,* which everyone would like to be Fitzgerald's major work, but which simply doesn't make the grade, carries on the autobiography through the Fitzgerald's European years and Mrs. Fitzgerald's mental breakdown. Its worst parts are autobiography, its best are the romance of hero-worship at which Fitzgerald excelled. The same judgment holds for *The Last Tycoon,* his unfinished novel.

The Fitzgerald of the short stories, including *The Great Gatsby,* is one of the least egotistical of authors. When he draws himself as the protagonist of a novel, self-disgust, shame, guilt, in short the failure to make himself a hero, cast an embarrassing pall over the whole book. When he puts himself into a short story, he figures as the naive, the weak, the incompetent but utterly attractive and characteristically American innocent. The narrators of *Gatsby*, of "The Rich Boy," of "A Short Trip Home," of "The Last of the Belles," have the short end of the stick, but wave it with extraordinary grace.... [These are] the two great themes in Fitzgerald's work: power as an emanation of personality and, conversely, the pains and pleasures, above all the survival, of the weak. The other theme was Love, which Fitzgerald seemed to believe was something the powerful inspired and the weak felt. (p. 526)

In the parlance of the American literary world it is customary to say we sell a short story but publish a novel. Selling is a literary sin, and it follows that an author's lucrative work must be his worst. Now Fitzgerald liked to eat (and drink) and felt an odd compulsion to pay his bills in full (eventually); what is more, he fell in love with a poor girl. So that, instead of saving his manuscripts for the genteel, unremunerative applause of posterity, he sold them for cash. In fact he sold most of them to the *Saturday Evening Post* and similar journals that paid best. And it can be argued that Fitzgerald's best work, with the one exception of *The Great Gatsby*, appeared in the "slicks." The two dozen or so first-rate stories among those bought by the *Post*, *McCall's*, *Red Book*, *Liberty*, and so on easily contain more first-rate work than he put into any one of his long novels. (p. 527)

It is curious that Fitzgerald has kept for so long the reputation for being in love with the idle rich, when he demonstrated repeatedly his Midwestern, middle-class reverence for "honest" work. "The Rich Boy," the story from which Hemingway quoted derisively the line about the very rich as "different from you and me," sets out to describe the life of a young man born into a solid old New York family with millions, but soon turns into the account of an extraordinarily hard-working Wall Street man, who achieves a partnership and a handsome income through his own exertions—and not in the family firm. Of all Fitzgerald's fiction, "The Rich Boy" demonstrates best how little he knew, or cared to learn about, the established rich of the Eastern seaboard. Fitzgerald was certainly in love with the idea of being rich himself, but he never thought up any way to get there other than hard work. (p. 530)

> *Ellen Moers, "F. Scott Fitzgerald: Reveille at Taps" (reprinted from* Commentary *by permission of Curtis Brown, Ltd. and Com-mentary; copyright © 1962 by the American Jewish Committee), in* Commentary, *December, 1962, pp. 526-30.*

What went into *The Great Gatsby* ... was the result of five years of erratic but earnest search and experiment. In the years following *This Side of Paradise*, [Fitzgerald's] occasional reviews of novels mention again and again the need of "selectivity," of taking a firm grasp upon character and scene, of recording ideas and "plot" through scenes....

It was a question of where the author stood with respect to his subject and his material. It was also a question of *how*: by what means could a set of details and circumstances be presented without losing the reader altogether in them or confusing him about point of view and judgment. It is obvious that Conrad was a major tutor in these years. (p. 6)

The obvious sources of help were Conrad's *Lord Jim* and *The Heart of Darkness*, whose Marlow served the limited but significant role Nick Carraway was to serve in *Gatsby*. But other works also interested him. Joyce's *Ulysses* impressed him as a novel preeminently worked out from what Wilson called a "precise technical plan." Surely *Ulysses* impressed him as a masterful warning of the need of careful attention to technique, though there is no specific indebtedness in *Gatsby*. James was another master of technique to whom Fitzgerald might have turned, but there is not even any indication that he had gone beyond *Daisy Miller* and *The American* by the time he had written *Gatsby*, if indeed he had read that far. But James's uses of point of view, his scenic maneuvers, his care for the refashioning of dialogue (to make it precisely adequate), are not in any way inimical to Fitzgerald's thinking and practice. Perhaps Willa Cather was more nearly contemporary and intelligible. [James E.] Miller points out the similarities of *My Ántonia* and *A Lost Lady* to Fitzgerald's interest, but then quite properly discounts the former and asks that the parallel of the latter with *Gatsby* not be pressed too far. The truth is that Fitzgerald needed to borrow not a subject (which he had uniquely and in abundance), but a method and a technique; and these he worked out from whatever sources were available: Conrad, James, Cather, Ford Madox Ford. In Ford's *Personal Remembrance* of Conrad (first published in 1924 in his *transatlantic review*) the problems of scenic representation and point of view are carefully worked out, in such a manner as could have helped Fitzgerald immensely. (p. 7)

Gatsby is linked to the 1920's world itself, but he is also historically associated with the "American dream," with the progress of American wealth and ambition from the very dawn of New World aspirations. In many ways, *Gatsby* is a marvel of symbolically compressed cultural history: of the original promise, seen in the "fresh, green breast of the new world" ..., of the growth and decline of that promise as the history of American money-getting moved into the twentieth century; of the vulgarization and venality of the privilege conferred by wealth; but above all, of its association with a romantic view of time and the past. This romantic "illusion" is at the core of Gatsby's characterization as a figure of tragedy or pathos. (p. 8)

[The] role of money in *The Great Gatsby* involves one, by implication and indirection, in three major cultural symbols: that of the social role of wealth, which became a moral and aesthetic convention in James and Howells; that of the Manhattan underworld, the source of Gatsby's fortune; and that of the world of appearances, especially of young and privileged love. All three of these are present in Fitzgerald's other works; all of them receive masterful treatment in *The Great Gatsby*. Perhaps for the first time Fitzgerald saw the world of his subject clearly and with a moderate objectivity. The pathos of Gatsby's vulgarity is evident not only in the glare of his parties but also in the obscenity and tragic indifference with which his invitations are used and received. But it is a most complex symbol, involving not only Gatsby and his indifferent guests, but the Buchanans from across the bay, and Carraway himself.... Most of all, the social value of money serves as the means of testing and measuring the vitality and the integrity of human impulses and desires: the network of contrasts and confusions involved in Tom Buchanan's two women and in Gatsby's being mixed up with both, sets up the basic uses of wealth in the novel. These uses are revealed in the four scenes of residence (the three houses on East and West Egg, the apartment on 158th Street), in which the arrangements of space are brilliant clues to taste, moral discretion, human arrogance and humility, and romantic impulse. (pp. 8-9)

Above all, *Gatsby* is successful because it is *presented* and not merely "told." The succession of "party" chapters, 1, 2, and 3, provide as good an opening as there is in modern fiction. The *places* are suggestively given before the full significance is known of those who inhabit them. In each case, the place and the manners of those who move in and about them leave something of a mystery, that needs to be both defined and solved in the action that follows. Fitzgerald maneuvers present and past in a succession of scenic records: Louisville, Long Island, Minnesota, Europe are all seen, whether in memory or in the impact of present action.

This interweaving of present and past is especially important, in the light of Nick Carraway's role as narrator. The real triumph of *The Great Gatsby* lies in its combining two principal strands of emotional and intellectual development: Carraway moves toward an understanding of Gatsby (he must "solve the mystery" of what appears at first to be a "purposeless splendor"); but he also comes to *accept* Gatsby, as the mystery recedes and the "young roughneck" vulgarity is discounted, for the "romantic readiness for hope" that transcends it.

These are the major means of the novel. It is, therefore, a novel with both Gatsby and Carraway as heroes. Only Carraway grows in the novel; but that is because Gatsby had very early in his life decided his destinies and in his case it is circumstance rather than personal inadequacy that affects it. Carraway's virtue is one of limitation; Gatsby's greatness comes from his having impulsively, anxiously, and absolutely committed himself to an illusion that transcended all limit. The two qualities are the polarities of American "promise," as Fitzgerald saw it. Gatsby has gone "all the way" before we have even seen him; Carraway must go much of the way toward him. They meet "on Gatsby's side, and alone" . . ., but Carraway's sense of restraint is sufficient to make him stop short of Gatsby's absurdity, the uncomprehending vulgarity of his means, and to cause him to appreciate the romantic purity of Gatsby's ends without submitting to its almost ludicrous and pathetic moral chaos of means. (pp. 9-10)

> *Frederick J. Hoffman, in his introduction to* "The Great Gatsby": A Study, *edited by Frederick J. Hoffman (reprinted by permission of Charles Scribner's Sons; © 1962 by Frederick J. Hoffman), Scribner's, 1962, pp. 1-18.*

[Fitzgerald frequently] portrayed his heroines in settings and in situations that attracted his readers and gave him quick financial returns; but he was often depressed, and not infrequently outraged, by his knowledge that his heroines were dishonest with themselves and with others. . . . His judgment of Daisy was severe; as the final, particular embodiment of Gatsby's purpose, she was unequal to the task, first of understanding his love, then of realizing the effort he had made to recover the one moment in the past that seemed worth while to him.

From being the younger generation's most brilliant and charming spokesman, Fitzgerald in a few short years became its most perceptive and incisive judge. In order to assume that role, he had (or thought he had) in *The Great*

Gatsby to measure the younger generation against the only person who merited his respect. Gatsby scarcely deserved the position Fitzgerald gave him, and he deserved not at all the romantic adulation Carraway offered his memory in the last paragraphs of the novel. Fitzgerald's effort to point to the "disaster" implicit in the behavior of the very young led him to an excess of admiration for Gatsby in untenable and in almost intolerable terms. For all its grace of style and tightness of structure, *The Great Gatsby* was a sentimental novel, with several fatal lapses of taste and judgment.

Fitzgerald was not quite equal to the task he set for himself. Throughout his career he sought the adequately "correct" modern hero—a man of bright promise, trying to realize himself and defeated inevitably by the indifference, the selfishness, the corruptibility of those about him, as well as by a fatal weakness within himself. But his fiction almost never escaped a sudden shift in his attitude toward his characters. His criticism, even in the best of his work, was blunted or turned aside or maneuvered into unlikely compromises with his subject.

Partly because of this his work is a revealing story of the very young in the decade. He is, in his life and in his tastes, an inseparable part of that story, a victim of the decade's own standards of judging people. He never quite makes the proper intellectual use of the disaster implicit in the behavior of the very young. Gatsby, his most remarkable creation, is judged only in terms of himself; and Gatsby's indiscretions, which are enormous, are first forgiven, then sanctified and romanticized. . . . [There] are crucial failures of control in Fitzgerald's art. The details are presented with brilliantly accurate insight, greater than any other found in modern American fiction, but there are places where the control fails, and as in the case of Gatsby, the opportunity to judge becomes an occasion for attachment and sentimental defense. (pp. 142-43)

> *Frederick J. Hoffman, "The Text: Fitzgerald's 'The Great Gatsby'," in his* The Twenties: American Writing in the Postwar Decade *(reprinted with permission of Macmillan Publishing Co., Inc.; copyright 1949, 1953, 1954, 1955, 1962 by Frederick J. Hoffman), revised edition, The Free Press, 1962, pp. 135-43.*

What is most appalling in an F. Scott Fitzgerald book is that it is *peopleless* fiction: Fitzgerald writes about spectral, muscled suits; dresses, hats, and sleeves which have some sort of vague, libidinous throb. These are plainly the products of sickness. . . . There is nothing left in the urban, peopleless novel but the national smirk, and that is what the billboard eye of the oculist in *The Great Gatsby* really is. It is the closest that Fitzgerald ever came to seeing the human eye. (p. 68)

Everybody in a Fitzgerald book is denatured, without parents or family, for the mortuary home has taken the place of the old frame house with porch, weedy steps, a clothesline in the yard. Tom Buchanan, athlete with polo ponies and a big automobile, is married to Daisy, the perennial vestal spinster. They have a modern utilitarian relationship based on the most subhuman inertia; their marriage reminds us of our conveniences in comfort, fruits, and self-service. Seedless grapes, seedless oranges, seedless wedlock all go together in a cafeteria marriage like Tom Buchanan's, a dreary, enervated husband casually helps himself to his wife, for nobody wants to bother about anything any longer. The more inventions we have, the more apathetic we are toward others.

In the peopleless realism of Fitzgerald the author appears to have no role in the narrative. For the sake of a humbug objectivity the novelist becomes as dingy, as depleted, and as seedless as the objects and the deanimated persons in the book. The Fitzgerald men are effete male ingenues, brutish and shrewd, like Stahr in *The Last Tycoon*. Tom Buchanan breaks his wife's nose because he is an athlete and has to do something with his body. (p. 69)

Fitzgerald's fiction is filled with slovenly writing. . . . Whitman, Norris, Crane, Hamlin Garland, and Dreiser wrote a bluff barbaric vulgate which is sometimes very nimble and very manly. Their words, deriving from the old, manual occupations, are far more masculine and energetic than the lymphatic ones that come from advertising and from inventions that are emasculating the human faculties. . . . I don't care for forceless platitudes (even though they are employed by most of the people) any more than I do for cheating, stealing, lying, or murder. (p. 70)

> *Edward Dahlberg, in his* Alms for Oblivion
> (© 1964, University of Minnesota), Univer-
> sity of Minnesota Press, Minneapolis, 1964.

[As] a basis for exploring Fitzgerald's literary consciousness, it is useful first to relate him to one of the most significant literary events of his time. . . . [Most] historians of contemporary literature have found the event a dramatization, in concrete terms, of the clash of two opposing forces or movements in our literature. The event is the James-Wells controversy, which reached its climax and conclusion in the exchange of personal letters in July, 1915.

Fitzgerald did not participate in this controversy, and, indeed, he may not even have been aware that it was in progress. But when he began his literary career with *This Side of Paradise*, he was under the influence of the literary movement to which Wells was wholeheartedly dedicated; and in the next few years, he gradually became aware of the opposing movement, which was vigorously supported by James. By the time he wrote *The Great Gatsby*, Fitzgerald had completely shifted his allegiance. (pp. 1-2)

[Four] concepts (character as the center of the novel, very little or nothing as irrelevant in the novel, author-intrusion as a virtue in the novel, and the novel as a vehicle for problem discussion) can probably be best implied by Wells's term "discursive." (p. 4)

James believed that that author is best who is heard but not seen, that that method is best which succeeds without obtruding, that that art is best which is not apparent as art. This "law" precludes the author's stepping forward to chat with the reader. Conrad had developed his narrator or narrators as characters within the framework of his story, a technique far different from the author-intrusion so precious to Wells. (p. 8)

Wells continued to see the novel as some kind of literal transcription of life. James's plea for method or selection, which would give the illusion or effect of the complexity of life without in itself being discursive and irrelevant, seems to have eluded Wells's comprehension entirely. (pp. 8-9)

Selection (or foreshortening) was for James a matter of technique rather than of quantity; selection was not mere addition or omission, but a "figuring synthetically" or a *method* of treatment. Wells desired irrelevance in order to imitate life; James desired selection in order to convey the *effect* of life. (p. 9)

To James, the novel was a work of art; to Wells, it was a vehicle—a vehicle for the discussion of social and other problems. (p. 11)

[The] views held by Wells and James were being debated on Fitzgerald's native grounds during his formative years as a novelist. And the trend was away from documentation or saturation toward selection and experimentation in technique. (p. 15)

Fitzgerald began the first version of *This Side of Paradise* during his undergraduate days at Princeton. From the time that he started writing the novel up to the completion and publication of the third and final version in 1920, Fitzgerald was, as his letters show, steeped in the literature of the Wells side of the Wells-James controversy. (p. 16)

The characterization of Amory Blaine, and not a continuous action, is the center of interest, and this emphasis on character allows for the "felt" of irrelevancies which Wells considered necessary to make the novel lifelike. *This Side of Paradise* even has the intrusive author which Wells defended; and the latter part of the book, devoted to debates on capitalism and socialism, is certainly utilized as a vehicle for the discussion of social problems. (pp. 23-4)

Granting *This Side of Paradise* its method of *saturation,* we can still critically examine its technique. Indeed, most critics have agreed that the crucial failure in the book was the failure of Fitzgerald to see his material objectively—that is, a failure in point of view. (p. 26)

The point of view in *This Side of Paradise* is, in one sense, conventional. The author assumes omniscience but visualizes most of the story through the eyes of the protagonist, Amory Blaine. (p. 31)

Fitzgerald's rapid transition . . . from one technique to another [demonstrated in *This Side of Paradise*], as it suits his narrative purpose, shows that he was familiar with and fairly adept in the use of a variety of methods. Some justification can be offered for his use of a specific technique for a specific situation: when Amory is contemplating the poor of the city, some control is needed to give his imaginative conception of their lives coherence and to lead logically into the examination of his own life; when he is sorting through his own problems, the question-answer method serves well to dramatize the uncertainties of his own mind; when he has posed for himself the unanswerable question "Where are you drifting?" (with both physical and spiritual implications), the stream-of-consciousness method, with all of its discursiveness, serves well to dramatize the blending of those "desires, worries, exterior impressions and physical reactions" . . . which inundate him in his crisis.

The techniques Fitzgerald uses in the representation of events are, in one sense, as conventional as those he uses in manipulating point of view. The happenings are related chronologically, not in a tightly knit plot sequence but, in the tradition of the saturation novel, in a series of independent scenes only loosely related. (pp. 38-9)

The representation of events in *This Side of Paradise* varies from the dramatic to the panoramic, a wide range not unusual in itself, but Fitzgerald's technical devices reach the extreme in both directions. (p. 40)

Many of the "episodes" in *This Side of Paradise,* separated from each other by the subtitles in the book, are no more than "snapshots," or brief summaries of significant events in the life or education of the protagonist. Fitzgerald gathers several of these episodes together under the title, "Snapshots of the Young Egotist".... [The] "narration" consumes less than three pages. This documentary method suits Fitzgerald's intention admirably, if his intention is to present to the fullest possible extent the influences which shaped Amory's character. (pp. 41-2)

The letters Fitzgerald uses in *This Side of Paradise* force him by their very nature to panoramic representation. Letters are "reports" of events by one character to another and, as technical devices, have certain advantages. They permit the covering of much ground rapidly; they permit the revelation of certain facts or events without violation of a point of view which has been established; they inform a character (and the reader) of important facts or events which he has no logical way of learning or observing at first hand; and they may reveal a perspective on the action other than that of the fiction's primary point of view. The use of letters for panoramic representation of happenings is demonstrated fully in "Interlude," the brief section compressed between the two books of the novel. (pp. 42-3)

In spite of its faults, perhaps in part because of them, *This Side of Paradise* continues to appeal. In its very immaturity lies its charm; it is an honest and sincere book by youth about youth, containing the emotions, ranging from ecstasy to despair, of the immature which the mature can neither easily recall nor evoke. (p. 44)

A large part of *The Beautiful and Damned* is concerned with Anthony and Gloria's rejection of the kind of life Grandfather Patch symbolizes. Were this rebellion central throughout, the theme would be simply a definite statement of that revolt which was but a "gesture" in *This Side of Paradise.* (p. 62)

[The] two themes in *The Beautiful and Damned,* one concerned with the revolt of youth and the other with the meaninglessness of life, [are] both developed side by side but never quite merging into a unified view. (p. 63)

In *The Beautiful and Damned,* Fitzgerald uses the conventional omniscient point of view, telling the story primarily through the eyes of Anthony and Gloria but not hesitating, when occasion requires, to reveal the thoughts or adopt the perspective of various minor characters. Fitzgerald himself is a less obtrusive author than in *This Side of Paradise,* but he still occasionally addresses himself directly to the reader. (p. 69)

Although Fitzgerald, at the time of writing *The Great Gatsby,* was apparently not under the direct influence of James, he could have felt an immense indirect attraction through any number of writers who themselves had gone to school to the master.

By 1925 Fitzgerald had transferred his former enthusiasm for Wells, Mackenzie, and Mencken to a number of other writers. James Joyce, Willa Cather, and, most important, Joseph Conrad—all figured prominently in the evolution of Fitzgerald's concept of the novel as a work of art. (p. 84)

It seems likely that the degree to which Fitzgerald was indebted to Willa Cather is greater than has been heretofore realized. From either Willa Cather's essay, "The Novel Démeublé," or from her novels, possibly from both, Fitzgerald probably learned a great deal about technique, especially about the manipulation of point of view and about form and unity....

Probably the greatest influence on Fitzgerald during the gestation period of *The Great Gatsby* was Joseph Conrad [in particular, that author's artistic manifesto prefacing *The Nigger of the Narcissus*]. (p. 92)

He was indebted to Conrad also for more specific elements: for the use of style or language to reflect theme; for the use of the modified first person narration; and for the use of deliberate "confusion" by the reordering of the chronology of events. (p. 94)

In *The Great Gatsby,* Fitzgerald abandoned the omniscient point of view he had previously used in his novels and resorted to first-person narration, after the manner of Joseph Conrad. Until Conrad's special use of the first person, the method had been in disrepute among writers who thought of fiction primarily in terms of technique. (p. 106)

Fitzgerald used the modified first-person in *The Great Gatsby* much as Conrad used it in the Marlow stories. Nick Carraway is charged with relating the story as he sees it, reconstructing by some means whatever he himself has been unable to witness. His qualification as a sympathetic listener is carefully established on the first page of the novel: "I'm inclined to reserve all judgments...." Such a characteristic is mandatory for an observer who must rely to a great extent on other people for information about those events which he himself is unable to witness.

There are three methods by which Nick Carraway informs the reader of what is happening or has happened in *The Great Gatsby:* most frequently he presents his own eyewitness account; often he presents the accounts of other people, sometimes in their words, sometimes in his own; occasionally he reconstructs an event from several sources —the newspapers, servants, his own imagination—but presents his version as connected narrative. Nick is initially placed at the edge of the story.... [He] becomes, in spite of his reluctance, involved in Gatsby's pursuit of Daisy.... Nick's position becomes such that he is naturally able to witness and report personally a maximum of the "contemporary" action. Various devices are used to keep him on stage when Fitzgerald wishes to represent an event scenically through him. (pp. 108-09)

When Fitzgerald needs to inform the reader of material about which his narrator can have no firsthand knowledge, he sometimes permits Nick to listen extensively to an individual who has the information. (p. 109)

After *The Great Gatsby,* there were no great shifts as there had been before in Fitzgerald's fictional technique; but he did not in his later work continue to achieve the brilliance of his third novel. As he himself realized there was a relaxation, a looking back, which he came to regret near the end of his brief life.... (p. 128)

In *Tender Is the Night* Fitzgerald's technique, especially his manipulation of point of view, is highly varied and sophisticated. Indeed, it might be said to suffer from an embarrassment of riches. It has all the variety of the technique of *This Side of Paradise,* but without that novel's ring of exuberant experimentation. It is more complex in conception than the technique of *The Great Gatsby*—but *Tender* never gives the impression of absolute certainty of control that *Gatsby* gives. Fitzgerald seems sure of his craft, and the craft seems always on the verge—but never quite—of bringing all the disparate materials of the novel into clear, thematic focus. Most readers finish *Tender* with a vivid impression of its ambitious complexity. (p. 139)

Dick's story [in *Tender is the Night*] is a story of the losing of a self, the disappearance of an identity. The structure of *Tender* may be conceived as a large X, with the one line marking Dick's decline, the other Nicole's rise. There is a kind of spiritual cannibalism or vampirism going on in the novel. As Nicole imbibes Dick's overflowing vitality, she rises from the depths of her soul-sickness to new heights of stability and self-possession—while Dick descends into spiritual exhaustion and emptiness below the level even of despair. It is as though for Dick and Nicole there is only one soul, first in Dick's possession, finally in Nicole's. The tragedy lies in the attempt, by these two people, to share what they cannot by their very nature share. In the attempt, as the marriage hangs precariously in the balance, there are only suspicion and fear, antagonism and bitterness. Possession must be all or none. (p. 140)

In his quest for identity, Dick is confronted at every turn with reflections of the self, and it is here that the novel seems to achieve much of its rich and complex texture. The book may be said to have a mirror or echo structure: a number of the characters who revolve about Dick Diver reflect one or another of his weaknesses in isolation. As he looks about him, he can see not the self he is in process of dissipating, but the several selves warring like vultures to take over the carcass of his soul. In a way, the book with its mirror structure may be read as an allegory, with Everyman (or at least American Everyman) Diver journeying through a multitude of temptations—and succumbing to all of them: Money, Liquor, Anarchy, Self-Betrayal, Sex. These abstractions take carnal embodiment in Baby Warren, Abe North, Tommy Barban, Albert McKisco, and Rosemary Hoyt. But each of these characters is supplemented with additional figures who echo and re-echo the vice set to trap the selfhood of the unwary wayfarer. (pp. 142-43)

Tender Is the Night tends in its thematic complexity to move rhythmically both inward and outward, inward to an exploration in depth of the spiritual malaise of Dick Diver, outward to an examination in breadth of the sickness of a society and a culture. (p. 146)

In its scope . . . *The Last Tycoon* resembles *Tender Is the Night* more than *The Great Gatsby.* (p. 150)

What has all the marks of a melodramatic plot turns out to be remarkably believable, if not commonplace, in Fitzgerald's skillful rendering, at least in the six finished chapters of the projected nine. His notes show him taking great care to work out the method for telling his story. The most notable technical device he has hit upon is to use the young, somewhat sophisticated, partly naive girl, Cecilia Brady, as narrator. . . . (p. 151)

In creating an appropriate narrator, Fitzgerald was no doubt discovering his own attitude toward his material. It would have been easy, in depicting a Hollywood tycoon, to perpetuate a stereotype, either Hollywood's romantic conception of its own, or an anti-Hollywood caricature. Distance, Fitzgerald saw, would be everything if he were to escape both cynicism and sentimentality. Cecilia would provide just the right tone for making Monroe Stahr breathe the breath of life. . . . Cecilia does provide the breathless quality that we have come to identify as that special evocation of Hollywood—but without compromising the serious note that Fitzgerald wanted to sound. Her freshness, not unlike Rosemary Hoyt's in *Tender Is the Night,* revitalizes what might be tired material. Her bright young passion for Stahr endows him with a glamour that does not cheapen or mock. (pp. 151-52)

But, as Fitzgerald indicated in one of his notes, he did not leave the whole task to Cecilia. In letting her "imagine the actions of the characters," he freed himself from the absurdity of inventing excuses for her being present at or learning about everything that had to be represented in the action. (pp. 152-53)

The last note included with *The Last Tycoon* is written in capitals, as a kind of warning, "ACTION IS CHARACTER". . . . Fitzgerald's novel seems to be something of a demonstration of this "rule." We are never told directly what kind of man Monroe Stahr is, but we are shown continuously through his varied activities—and, furthermore, we see him as many others see him, each through his own distorting lens. It is not easy, then, to assess the special quality of his being that arouses such a complex mixture of respect and distaste, irony and awe. But this complexity is not new with Fitzgerald's heroes—Jay Gatsby and Dick Diver both attracted and repelled. Though radically different in their motives and their careers, their lives and their milieus, all these heroes, in spite of their shortcomings, share a kind of moral awareness that ultimately wins our grudging admiration. (p. 154)

If the existing chapters of *The Last Tycoon* reveal that the novel was to be about Stahr and about Hollywood, they suggest also that it was to be in some sense about modern life, about American life. No doubt the theme would have emerged with clarity from the finished novel, but there are enough signs to indicate Fitzgerald's direction. (p. 157)

Like *The Great Gatsby, The Last Tycoon* might well have provided a commentary on the ultimate debasement of the American dream. As it is, we must accept the chapters that we have and the notes that survived with them for what they actually are—interesting evidence of Fitzgerald's involvement not only with plot but with technique as well. The outpourings of *This Side of Paradise*—the novel of saturation—have long since been replaced by a style that is the result of conscious and avowed concern for structure and selection. (p. 158)

> *James E. Miller, Jr., in his* F. Scott Fitzgerald: His Art and His Technique *(reprinted by permission of New York University Press; copyright © 1964 by New York University), New York University Press, 1964.*

[Fitzgerald] used himself so mercilessly in his fiction, there is often such a complete fusion between his life and his stories, that conscientious criticism will always have to remember D. H. Lawrence's warning to biographically-minded critics: don't trust the artist, trust the tale. There is, however, another order of difficulty in appreciating Fitzgerald's best work. His attitude toward money and moneyed people has been much misunderstood.

One way to begin a consideration of Fitzgerald's attraction to the American rich as the prime subject matter of his fiction is to look at the most famous Fitzgerald literary anecdote. As Ernest Hemingway originally wrote it into his story "The Snows of Kilimanjaro," published in *Esquire* in 1936, it went this way. Hemingway's writer-hero is musing on his own life among the American rich. "He remembered poor Scott Fitzgerald and his romantic awe of them and how he had started a story once that began, 'The very rich are different from you and me.' And how someone had said to Scott, Yes they have more money. But that was not humorous to Scott."

Although the exchange never actually took place it has become part of the story of our two most legendary modern novelists. The moral implications of the anecdote, political, personal, and artistic, have usually been chalked up to Hemingway's score. It is significant for understanding the distance that separated the two men at this point in their friendship that Hemingway could make such demeaning use of Fitzgerald as a character in a piece of magazine fiction. The anecdote concludes with this comment, "He thought they were a special glamorous race and when he found they weren't it wrecked him just as much as any other thing that wrecked him." This was the public burial of a has-been writer, and Fitzgerald was deeply offended.

Hemingway's rebuke belongs to the general charge against Fitzgerald made frequently in the thirties that he was captivated by the rich and their expensive manners, and forgot that too much money in America is always supposed to be a sign of vulgarity and wickedness. Applied to Fitzgerald's fiction this moralism is simple-minded. To disprove there is exhibited in the novels and stories all the moral energy that Fitzgerald spent "fixing" the rich. Since we read Fitzgerald's stories of the rich in a more affluent American society, in which the rich have become less shocking because they are now less removed from middle-class mores, we should more easily detect the moral and cultural confusions in Fitzgerald's fiction if they are really there. Americans living through a new postwar society can no longer feel superior to Fitzgerald's interest in the American greed for fine cars, the right clothes, and the pleasures of the best hotels and offbeat entertainment. The American people now seem to be less embarrassed than they once were at the snobbery of large parts of their social system. Contemporary social analysis has shown them how far ahead of his times Fitzgerald was in describing the rigorous systems of status that underlie that rather contradictory American term, the Open Society.

We may in fact be today more responsive readers of Fitzgerald's stories of money and display and expensive charm than many of his contemporaries were. . . . Nowadays we may be more ready to accept as he did the final complexity of our society and to recognize that we create a large part of our moral selves as we become engaged in that society. This is the theme that runs through his fiction—and through his life. We do him an injustice if we assume at the start that in order to understand the dreadful sanctions of social prestige—that is, money—Fitzgerald had to make a fatal submission of himself to the glamorous rich. (pp. 82-4)

One of the safest generalizations that can be made about Fitzgerald is that he is America's most sentient novelist of manners. (p. 87)

It is hard in coming to terms with Fitzgerald to follow Lawrence's advice and learn to trust the tale, not the author. But if we succeed we shall learn that the aspects of himself that he continually made into the characters in his fiction are imaginatively re-created American lives. He often wrote that high order of self-revelation that reveals humanity. (p. 117)

> *Charles E. Shain, "F. Scott Fitzgerald," in* Seven Modern American Novelists: An Introduction, *edited by William Van O'Connor (© 1964, University of Minnesota), University of Minnesota Press, Minneapolis, 1964, pp. 81-117.*

All during Fitzgerald's life, Keats was his favorite poet. "For awhile after you quit Keats all other poetry seems to be only whistling or humming," he wrote to his daughter; and he has several times remarked on the frequency with which he read Keats when he was very young. In the year of his death he wrote that he still could not read "Ode to a Nightingale" "without tears in my eyes." Keats's strong verbal influence in the more poetic passages of Fitzgerald's prose is obvious—perhaps in *The Great Gatsby* most of all. But one guesses that essentially it was Keats's attitude to experience that seized and dominated his imagination, and may have exerted some influence on Fitzgerald's choice of themes and subject matter.

Throughout Keats's poetry there is a sense of transience and loss, at times an almost unbearably poignant sense of passage and dissolution. The origin of this is understandable in terms of Keats's biography; but there is a somewhat similar sense of transience in Fitzgerald's writing. In the latter case it is a little difficult to guess its cause, but it is pervasive. (pp. 156-57)

Fitzgerald never learned to triumph over this theme of loss and defeat in his fiction as Keats does in his poetry. In Fitzgerald's case it moves from the elegiac to the tragic but never to victory, as it does, for example, in the great speech from "Hyperion" in which Oceanus, the vanquished Titan, accepts the infinite loss entailed in a fall from divinity. . . . (p. 158)

Fitzgerald's ultimate subject is the character of the American Dream in which, in their respective ways, his principal heroes are all trapped. If the American Dream seems delusively to carry a suggestion of infinite possibilities, it tolerates no fresh perfections beyond its own material boundaries. If it engenders heroic desires in the hearts of its advocates, it can only offer unheroic fulfillments. For this reason Fitzgerald's novels, and *Gatsby* above all, are tragedies. The heart of the tragedy is that these heroes must die of a love for which there is no worthy object. (pp. 158-59)

> *Marius Bewley, "Scott Fitzgerald: The Apprentice Fiction" (originally published in* The New York Review of Books, *September 16, 1965), in his* Masks & Mirrors: Essays in Criticism *(copyright © 1965, 1970 by Marius Bewley; reprinted by permission of Atheneum Publishers, New York), Atheneum, 1970, pp. 154-59.*

Gatsby is Fitzgerald's most brilliant image of his deepest conviction, the conviction that life untouched by imagination is brutal and intolerable and that the imagined life must be made actual in the world if a man is to become anything more than a self-indulgent daydreamer. It is, I believe, a peculiarly American attitude. Americans are no doubt proud of their wealth and of the enterprise that is at least in part responsible for it. But they are seldom content with a merely material life; that kind of life seems to them, as Gatsby's life seemed to him after he lost faith in Daisy, material without being real. Only when it is animated by an ideal purpose does it seem real to them. This is, in fact, what we mean by "The American Dream," insofar as that dream is something possessed by each of us individually. (p. 190)

T. S. Eliot once called *The Great Gatsby* "the first step in American fiction since Henry James," for in it Fitzgerald realized, for the first time in twentieth-century terms, James's understanding of the dramatic conflict between good and evil that is inherent in American life. (p. 191)

> *Arthur Mizener, "F. Scott Fitzgerald: 'The Great Gatsby'," in* The American Novel: From James Fenimore Cooper to William Faulkner, *edited by Wallace Stegner (©️ 1965 by Basic Books, Inc., Publishers), Basic Books, 1965, pp. 180-91.*

Despite his gift for phrase, and it is a notable one; despite one luminous novel and a small handful of first-rate short stories; despite his high and tender morality and his seldom-failing taste, Fitzgerald is a writer pathetically limited in the artist's ability to control his materials, to advance beyond the limitations of his own—and his wife's or his first love's—personality, and to refuse to bow to the demands of the "buck," however crude that sounds. (p. 278)

[To] read *This Side of Paradise* today is to wonder what all the fuss was about. Granted that it expressed the collegiate mores of the generation immediately after the war; granted too that it had a youthful buoyancy and charm and that it found a market ready for it. . . . But reading *This Side of Paradise* today is far from an illuminating experience; the novel is merely sophomoric. It is a literary curiosity: professionally phony, grossly immature, it happened to come along when the time was right. Contemporary reviews were either encomiastic or sharply critical, and both were right; the former sensed the talent, the latter the carelessness of form and detail.

The Beautiful and Damned is a diary, and it reads as if Fitzgerald had kept a journal of his married life, and rewrote it as a novel. Fitzgerald was honest, even daring, for publishing to the world a *roman* so obviously *à clef*. He somehow believed that the daily record of *his* experience was important to somebody, somewhere. But this is what every young person believes—and very shortly outgrows. *The Beautiful and Damned* deserves small attention: the *deus ex machina* resolution is enough to destroy it, although its continuous concern with money gives it a passing interest to Fitzgerald *aficionados* for whom Daisy and Anson Hunter and Monroe Stahr are definitive accounts of the rich.

Tender Is the Night . . . is a failure, and not a noble failure at that. It is unfocused from beginning to end, for the author had inadequate control over his materials and suffered from a faltering sense of purpose and design. The novel is a failure of art, for it lacks discipline.

The Last Tycoon is also the last Fitzgerald. It holds moments of distinction that the Pat Hobby stories do not. Even though it was unfinished at his death, it has an atmosphere found only in Fitzgerald's very best work. But as a novel, it has only a little more impact than the one good short story of the same place and subject, "Crazy Sunday."

And so we were left, among the novels, with *The Great Gatsby,* a novel viable enough, we may say with reluctant irony, to have been made into two movies, one television drama, and a paperback selection of critical studies. Of all the five, only *The Great Gatsby* bears the marks of what might be called an achieved novel, one in which the author has control of his characters, his theme, and his idea. It is the only one of his novels in which character is clear (Nick, Jordan, Tom, Myrtle, Gatsby) from beginning to end, and in which sense and symbol (the ash heaps of a Canarsie, the green light at the end of Buchanans' dock, and the eyes of Dr. Eckleburg) grow naturally out of the novel itself. (pp. 278-79)

The Great Gatsby, however luminous its scenes, however graceful its phrases, however clearly it establishes Gatsby as a romantic gone almost paranoid in his attempt to regain the past, may not stand up very much longer as a notable novel. For whatever of Fitzgerald's time, talent, and struggle went into its making, *The Great Gatsby* remains a trivial novel, and today's students in the classrooms occasionally use that very adjective. They use it hesitantly, out of fear that they are running counter to the ponderous traditions that their professors proclaim, but they use it—and they are very probably right.

Let us now turn to a consideration of the short stories of F. Scott Fitzgerald. In round figures they number two hundred. As every Fitzgerald buff knows, they were his bread and butter. And as every critic knows, they were also his near-ruination as an artist. (p. 280)

The short stories of Fitzgerald vary greatly in quality. At the best, they are timeless; at the worst, they are just so much fancy fiction read by stenographers riding the rackety subway home—and forgotten as soon as they are read. These stories express the two sides of Fitzgerald's creativity much better than the novels do: the half-dozen tales of enduring merit represent the highest reaches of Fitzgerald's talent as a literary artist; the remainder are the work of the purveyor to the slick magazines. (pp. 280-81)

The best of Fitzgerald's short stories are entitled to rank among the best in American fiction. Curiously enough, they do not belong to any period: they range from his early years to his last in 1940. And the hallmark of his great short stories is that they are free of the contaminating marks of self-conscious writing for a market. They are the work of a writer asking to be heard, not to be sold. (p. 281)

[Two] alone stand as the best of *all* F. Scott Fitzgerald. As the anthologists have already made clear, "Rich Boy" and "Babylon Revisited" are superb stories, the former of the pre-Depression period alcoholic, the latter his post-Depression equivalent. It doesn't matter at all that Anson Hunter and Charlie Wales are forms of F. Scott Fitzgerald. It only matters that these stories came very close to artistic perfection. They evoke the moods of pre- and post-Depression, the gorgeous spree and the morning after, and the High Judge's sentence of loneliness in both cases.

These stories belong to Fitzgerald's thirtieth and thirty-fifth years—years, one may say, of at least the beginning of maturity. But five earlier stories demand consideration. Two of them are the "Catholic" stories: "Benediction" and "Absolution." Both have the hallmarks of Fitzgerald at his best. They are lucid, graceful, and honest. Surprisingly, they aroused controversy. Mencken was characteristically facetious when he said he was amazed at Catholic reaction to "Benediction," which, he wrote in *Smart Set*, "brought down the maledictions of the Jesuits and came near getting the magazine barred from Knights of Columbus camp-libraries." Fitzgerald actually received furious letters from Catholics about "Absolution." But Mencken, in the same review, noted that "Benediction" rings true—and it does.

"The Ice Palace" too openly shows its structure, but it remains in the memory as a contrast of cultures and as a rare Fitzgerald example of symbol emerging from the story, not superimposed, as in "Cut Glass Bowl." (p. 282)

"The Diamond as Big as the Ritz" is probably the best of the Fitzgerald stories in the category of fantasy. One can hardly deny that it is readable; one can easily deny that it is a great story. Once again appears the theme of the attractions of wealth, here carried to the level of science fiction; and once again, to satisfy the demands of a movie-going public, the hero and heroine magically escape. It is written by and for an intelligent child, but it deserves admission among the better of Fitzgerald's short stories, although it lies some distance below "Babylon Revisited" and "Rich Boy." "Winter Dreams" and "Crazy Sunday" . . . belong to the best of Fitzgerald's fiction because both clearly evoke a time, a mood, and a milieu that the lesser stories do not. "Crazy Sunday" dangerously nears a B-picture scenario, especially at the end, but it sharply delineates the Hollywood party—if that is important—as very few other stories do, including Faulkner's and Hecht's movietown narratives.

The Basil Duke Lee and the Josephine stories, clear and readable, and here and there touching, can scarcely be regarded as enduring. Reading them a second time makes one wonder why anyone considers them significant. Not one of them is memorable, not one—through force of writing, of character, or of plot—really stays in the mind. They entertain but they do not haunt; they do not penetrate the memory, to hang there like pictures in a gallery to be enjoyed for years—the touchstone and the hallmark of all enduring literature. (pp. 282-83)

He will be remembered for his gift of phrase and for being the supreme exemplar in our generation of a single theme, the poor boy in love with the rich girl. His world is narrowly circumscribed; it is the world of Fitzgerald, Zelda, and Ginevra. No one, of course, will be disaffected by the fact that Fitzgerald had a single theme. The troublesome question is whether it is a great enough theme. For all the variations he played upon it, Fitzgerald's theme is, in the end, at best a minor one. No one has treated this theme with greater versatility than Fitzgerald, but it remains a minor theme, an immature theme, and failure to grow beyond it sharply marks the limitations of Fitzgerald as a writer. (p. 283)

H. Alan Wycherley, "Fitzgerald Revisited," in Texas Studies in Literature and Language *(copyright © 1966 by the University of Texas Press), Summer, 1966, pp. 277-83.*

There is evidence especially in *The Great Gatsby* that Fitzgerald's admiration [for Conrad] extended as far as imitation, and the similarity between [*Gatsby* and *Heart of Darkness*] enables us to challenge claims for Fitzgerald's intellectual and artistic merit by showing how much better Conrad could think and write.

The most important of the similarities between the two novels is the use of the first-person narrator as a character in his own story. (p. 70)

In some novels the first-person narrator is merely a convenience in achieving selectivity, and in others at the opposite extreme the narrator himself is the object of our study. In *Heart of Darkness* both purposes are served; Marlow is both a technical device and part of the subject-matter. In *The Great Gatsby* the situation of Carraway is the same as that of Marlow, but I believe that Fitzgerald, never a great critical theorist, did not realize the dual nature of his narrator and therefore handled him very clumsily—and very revealingly.

When a narrator is also a character, with all that this implies of personality, individuality, and responsibility, we readers are forced to be more alert. We must question the accuracy of the narrator's account. When he makes judgments, we have to decide whether his special interests betray the truth and whether the meaning of each particular event and of the whole fable differs from the interpretation he offers. In *Heart of Darkness* Conrad is highly conscious of these problems and takes steps to solve them. (p. 71)

It is quite legitimate to ask why Fitzgerald should follow Conrad closely in narrative technique except for those elements which warn us that the narrator may be giving us a truth which is anything but unvarnished. Why remove Conrad's surrogate audience and inset narrative? Why exchange the honest hesitancy of Marlow's manner for Carraway's literary imitation of charming spontaneity? Carraway is a disarmingly frank chap, and, as with most such fellows, his self-revelations are highly contrived. Is his opening characterization of himself as accurate as it is influential? During the narrative he tells us what to think of his actions, but should we judge by what he says or what he does? It is an obvious enough point, but it is exactly here that readers go astray and that Fitzgerald's artistic and ethical inferiority lie. Conrad knew that problems would arise and provided material to alert the reader. Fitzgerald promptly abandoned that material and led readers to follow Carraway's interpretation of events without realizing that there should be a difference, a gap, a huge gulf, between Carraway's and their conceptions of the affair. (p. 72)

Carraway tells us that Gatsby's great redeeming quality is his "heightened sensitivity to the promises of life." Whether we criticize or praise Carraway for being sufficiently young to believe that life makes promises, we should notice at once that it is the promises—not the realities—of life to which Gatsby is sensitive, and that Carraway is in fact praising that very attempt to deny the past and reality whose failure he is recounting. (p. 74)

In fact Gatsby himself is Carraway's romantic dream. The

only difference between the world that Carraway despises and the man he admires is that Gatsby does things more spectacularly. In not seeing this, Carraway reveals that just like Gatsby he is willing to accept only those parts of reality which please him. He wants Gatsby to be different from the rest of the world; therefore Gatsby *is* different from the rest of the world. If we look at Carraway's behavior more closely, we may see that he shares others of Gatsby's failings, and that if Gatsby is no romantic hero, Carraway is even less the pleasant, anonymous, and highly principled character that he seems to be. (pp. 74-5)

It is usually considered that Fitzgerald intended *The Great Gatsby* to warn us against the attempt to deny reality. My interpretation of the novel goes further to suggest that unwittingly, through careless technique and cloudy thinking, Fitzgerald in fact created a novel which says that it is impossible for us to face reality. One would like to think that Fitzgerald knew what he was doing, that in the opening pages he intended Carraway's priggishness and enervation to warn the reader against the narrator. Certainly there is enough evidence in the novel to support such a view, which can no more be completely disproven than can similar readings of *Moll Flanders* and *Gulliver's Travels,* but before we accept it we have to answer two questions: was the young Fitzgerald capable of such ironic perception, which would involve an extraordinarily complex attitude not just to his characters but to his readers and to himself as writer and individual? and if so, why did he choose deliberately not to make the irony clearer to the reader, especially with the example of Conrad in front of him? My own belief is that Fitzgerald achieved something other than he intended. Knowing that he always had difficulty in distinguishing himself from his characters (and admitted to being even Gatsby!), we can legitimately suspect that Carraway's failure is Fitzgerald's failure, and that Fitzgerald himself was chronically unaware of the dangers of romanticism. If Daisy is Gatsby's dream, and Gatsby is Carraway's dream, one suspects that Carraway is Fitzgerald's dream. (p. 80)

We may no longer be able to read [*The Great Gatsby*] as a description of the fate that awaits American innocence, but we can see it as a record of the worse dangers that confront American sentimentality. (p. 81)

> *Gary J. Scrimgeour, "Against the Great Gatsby," in* Criticism *(reprinted by permission of the Wayne State University Press; copyright 1966 by Wayne State University Press), Vol. VIII, No. 1 Winter, 1966, (and reprinted in* Twentieth Century Interpretations of "The Great Gatsby," *edited by Ernest Lockridge, Prentice-Hall, 1968, pp. 54-60).*

There is only one story that Fitzgerald knows how to tell, and no matter how he thrashes about, he must tell it over and over. The penniless knight, poor stupid Hans, caddy or bootlegger or medical student, goes out to seek his fortune and unluckily finds it. His reward is, just as in the fairy tales, the golden girl in the white palace; but quite differently from the fairy tales, that is not a happy ending at all. He finds in his bed not the white bride but the Dark Destroyer; indeed, there is no White Bride, since Dark Lady and Fair, witch and redeemer have fallen together. But it is more complicated even than this. Possessed of the power of wealth, Fitzgerald's women, like their wealthy male com-

peers, who seem their twins rather than their mates, are rapists and aggressors. . . . In a real sense, not Daisy but Jay Gatz, the Great Gatsby, is the true descendant of Daisy Miller: the naïf out of the West destined to shock the upholders of decorum and to die of a love for which there is no worthy object.

In Fitzgerald's world, the distinction between sexes is fluid and shifting, precisely because he has transposed the mythic roles and values of male and female. . . . With no difficulty at all and only a minimum of rewriting, the boy Francis, who was to be a center of vision in *The World's Fair,* becomes the girl Rosemary as that proposed novel turned into *Tender Is the Night.* Thematically, archetypally even such chief male protagonists as Gatsby and Dick Diver are females; at least, they occupy in their stories the position of Henry James's Nice American Girls. It is they who embody innocence and the American dream. . . . (p. 313)

Fitzgerald apparently never managed to accommodate to the fact that he lived at the moment of a great switch-over in roles, though he recorded that revolution in the body of his work. His outrage and self-pity constantly break through the pattern of his fiction, make even an ambitious attempt like *Tender Is the Night* finally too sentimental and whining to endure.

Only in *The Great Gatsby* does Fitzgerald manage to transmute his pattern into an objective form, evade the self-pity which corrodes the significance and the very shape of his other work—and this is perhaps because Gatsby is the most distant of all his protagonists from his real self. . . . Daisy, rich and elegant and clean and sweet-smelling, represents to her status-hungry provincial lover, not the corruption and death she really embodies, but Success—which is to say, America itself. In Fitzgerald, the same fable that informs James is replayed, subtly transformed, for like James he has written an anti-Western, an "Eastern": a drama in which back-trailers reverse their westward drive to seek in the world which their ancestors abandoned the dream of riches and glory that has somehow evaded them. Fitzgerald's young men go east even as far as Europe; though unlike James's young women, they are in quest not of art and experience and the shudder of guilt, but of an even more ultimate innocence, an absolute America: a happy ending complete with new car, big house, money, and the girl. (pp. 314-15)

> *Leslie Fiedler, in his* Love and Death in the American Novel *(copyright © 1960, 1966 by Leslie A. Fiedler; reprinted with permission of Stein and Day/Publishers), revised edition, Stein and Day, 1966.*

The best of Fitzgerald is matchless. "Absolution," which I consider his one completely successful short story, in its beginning and end rises to an intensity of vision almost Blakean. Scene after scene in *The Great Gatsby* shows absolute mastery: Gatsby's stretching out his arms to the green light at the end of Daisy's dock; the reunion of Gatsby and Daisy, with Daisy crying into the heap of his beautiful shirts; Daisy and Tom sitting over cold fried chicken and ale, after Daisy has killed Tom's mistress; Nick's final thoughts. *The Last Tycoon* has such miracles too: Kathleen's first appearance, floating on a head of Siva; the telephone call from the orang-outang; Stahr and Kathleen, after their carnal congress, sitting with the soles of their shoes touching; the Emersonian Negro on the beach.

Most of the stories in *The Fitzgerald Reader* are terrible. . . .

Fitzgerald was a writer with only one story to tell: the story of his life. In his inferior work he told it transparently, with gossamer disguises. . . . In his superior work, on the other hand, Fitzgerald managed to get some aesthetic distance from himself as subject, by feats of splitting, dissociation, and combination. Gatsby was based on a man Fitzgerald knew, combined with the romantic half of Fitzgerald (the realist half became Nick Carraway, the narrator). In just the seven chapters of *Tender Is the Night* included in the *Reader:* Tommy Barban has Fitzgerald's good looks; Abe North is a composite of Ring Lardner's wit and Fitzgerald's pranks and lack of productivity; Rosemary, awed and gushy at Dick Diver, is Fitzgerald awed and gushy at Gerald Murphy; Diver himself combines Murphy's strengths and Fitzgerald's weaknesses.

The splittings and combinations of Fitzgerald in *The Last Tycoon* are even more astonishing. (pp. 192-93)

Lunatic as this process sounds, it was necessary to enable Fitzgerald to write his finest work, and his finest work— "Absolution," *Gatsby*, parts of *Tender* and *Tycoon*—is small in quantity but just as great as they say. Gatsby is Great because he transforms himself into a work of art, and Fitzgerald was great only when he was able to accomplish the same thing. (p. 193)

> Stanley Edgar Hyman, "The Great Fitzgerald," in his Standards: A Chronicle of Books for Our Time (© 1966; reprinted by permission of the publisher, Horizon Press, New York), Horizon, 1966, pp. 189-93.

In *The Great Gatsby,* and in nearly all of his best and most serious short stories, Fitzgerald's artistic achievement was measurably "classical" in kind. But two things are especially remarkable about Fitzgerald's acquiring mastery of the *art* of fiction: first, that in his formally most perfect works his innately "romantic" sensibility was neither overwhelmed nor falsified; and second, that after having so notably achieved conventionally modern novelistic "form" in *Gatsby,* he could go on, in *Tender Is the Night* and *The Last Tycoon,* to allow himself the new freedoms he needed in order to say new things.

Furthermore, because, as an artist, he was so intensely himself as a man, he could tell other lesser artists what they needed to know, especially in a period dominated by the critical imperatives of mere formalism, in order to make their work artistically alive. (pp. 148-49)

[Unlike] Yeats or Eliot or Hemingway, all of whom in their different ways seemed to be chasing after their artistic destinies most of their lives, Fitzgerald's first instinct was to try to run away from his, until some time after *Gatsby* (perhaps not finally until Zelda's collapse) he was caught and devoured by it; and from then on he tended to speak about writing in a quietly consistent voice from the still center of his knowledge. It was always the same knowledge. Writing in 1933 in the pages of *The Saturday Evening Post* as "one of the champion false starters of the writing profession," Fitzgerald discussed the identity of an artist:

Mostly we authors must repeat ourselves— that's the truth. We have two or three great and moving experiences in our lives. . . . Then we learn our trade, well or less well, and we tell our two or three stories—each time in a new guise—maybe ten times, maybe a hundred, as long as people will listen.

Fitzgerald . . . would not, or could not, abandon [*This Side of Paradise* and *The Beautiful and Damned*] because they were part of his identity as a writer, and because he knew that, for all their badness and falseness, they had their true, their living, moments.

It is the simplicity and purity of Fitzgerald's loyalty to the life of his imagination that makes him rare and moving in the role of artist in the twentieth century. He had a cruelly honest eye for his own capacities for the cheap and the facile. And yet he was ultimately proof against the chief distractions of professionalism—critical cant and the blandishments of current literary fashion. With small literary sophistication and large vanity, Fitzgerald nevertheless came to know the last and best lesson that the critical sense can teach: that if a writer's genius is true he must be true to it, and that to be true to it he must not only evade *mere* professionalism but also learn to respect his genius without sentimentality or false reverence. He was a writer whose final sophistication as a true professional was deeply interfused with and qualified by his intuitive self-knowledge as a man. His significance for contemporary critics and writers lies in the extraordinary integrity of his artistic enterprise. (pp. 155-56)

> Richard Foster, "Fitzgerald's Imagination: A Parable for Criticism," in The Minnesota Review (copyright 1967 by the Bolingbroke Society, Inc.), Vol. VII, No. 2, 1967, pp. 144-56.

For the first clarion voice of "a new generation . . . grown up to find all Gods dead, all wars fought, all faiths in man shaken," . . . *This Side of Paradise* . . . revealed a continual concern with matters of religion. In every scene, whether recalled in summary exposition or dramatized through detailed dialogue, the protagonist Amory Blaine self-consciously raises questions of faith, of formal religious affiliation, of the spiritual lurking somehow in the mundane. Even when he claims agnosticism or non-belief, he does so with a kind of bravado, as if he knows only too well that he is a misbehaving child, or with an uncomfortable uncertainty, as if his early conditioning remains stronger than his youthful and fashionable rebellion.

The tone vacillates between satire, an approach at its best when the criticized patterns of behavior have been frozen into established attitudes and honorific gestures, and sentimental seriousness, suggesting after all that the mockery was a kind of collegiate covering up of emotions that persist in spite of the contemporary code. (p. 7)

[Amory] turns over the problems of good and evil as they apply to personal relationships with his classmates, to romantic relationships with girls, and to the large social issues of pacifism and war, the concerns of any questioning and sensitive young man trying to understand himself and his world. He is genuinely concerned that in the midst of his moral and broadly philosophical inquiries his Catholicism is "without priests or sacraments or sacrifice." Priests, sacraments, and sacrifice remained pivotal in the awareness of Fitzgerald throughout his works, central to his content, his imagery, and his structure.

This Side of Paradise evolves as a "quest" book. . . . It is a story of the coming-of-age of Amory Blaine, his ritual journey from childhood, through preparatory school, through his college experience, to the threshold of manhood, Amory's quest to discover his identity and to define his society. (p. 8)

The first of two important lessons is Monsignor Darcy's admonition to Amory to be not merely a "personality," but a "personage," a bar on which a thousand things, "glittering things sometimes, as ours are," are hung and used "with a cold mentality back of them," replaced and replenished when necessary, left behind consecutively for "the next thing." This direction is a call to a vocation, a kind of ordination, asking from Amory a sense of his specialness, an aloofness from the world, a faith in what Fitzgerald would have later called his "bright promise." Ordination is in one sense or another the point to which every youthful journey-of-learning takes a protagonist who is ready for courageous self-discovery, for a fearless sense of identity midway between the sacrament of the literal beginning and the sacrament of the physical end. . . . [Amory] comes to a realization in the final statement of the book, "I know myself, but that is all," that although he has finished with his youth, "his ideas were still in riot." (pp. 9-10)

Darcy's second important lesson . . . is that one cannot be "romantic without religion," that for himself and Amory "the secret of success" is "the mystical element in us." (p. 10)

Amory arrives at a goal of sacrifice, of bearing the burdens of others, of defining one's own identity through what he does for others. . . . Amory has taken the blame in a prohibition episode involving girls and boys drinking in a hotel room, a particularly sexless episode in which Amory has played a peripheral role at best. Clinching his hands "in quick ecstatic excitement" over his self-consciously magnanimous role, post-adolescent at most, Amory feels almost mystically that God is talking to him, that sacrifice must be "arrogant," "impersonal," "eternally supercilious." Here is the height of specialness, presented in the very terms of the supreme ordination, that is, God the Father's designation of Christ the Son as sacrificial hero. But the ordinariness, the lowness, the youthful foolishness of the episode in which Amory plays his grand part inverts the mystery, the glory of sacrifice as a pivotal religious concept. (pp. 11-12)

Edwin M. Moseley, in his F. Scott Fitzgerald: A Critical Essay *(copyright © 1967 by Wm. B. Eerdmans Publishing Co.; "Contemporary Writing in Christian Perspective" Series; used by permission), Eerdmans, 1967.*

Fitzgerald sensed that the myth of the American Adam and the American Eden was bankrupt, had indeed always been morally indefensible, even though he was unable to find another faith to live by. *The Great Gatsby* is truly a document of the Lost Generation. It is self-criticism without constructive purpose. (pp. 152-53)

Nick Carraway, like a Hemingway hero, sees himself as free from the burden of culture, able to live directly with and by the facts of experience, without the illusions and myths which tormented the bourgeoisie; he represents the relationship of the expatriate to the middle-class imagination. Europeans had fled the Old World to escape its corruption and to find innocence, to escape timefulness and to find timelessness. These middle-class people believed that innocence was possible if man turned away from the false theories of medieval civilization to live by the concrete facts of experience. To Fitzgerald, this was only the appearance of a pragmatic or empirical outlook. In reality, it was a platonic philosophy; it assumed the perfect organic expression of the ideal in material form. For the European bourgeois coming to the New World, the ideal expressed itself in two major material forms—the American landscape and money. As Fitzgerald presents the career of Nick Carraway, he is posing an embarrassing question for the Lost Generation: What is the essential difference between the innocence of Nick Carraway, the expatriate, and that of the American middle class? (p. 153)

For Fitzgerald, there was no Europe and no America, there was no East and no West. There were only hypocrites who pretended that innocence was to be found in America and not in Europe, or in the West and not in the East, or in some individuals and not in others. . . . (pp. 154-55)

Nick knew that this dream had not found fulfillment and never could. But like Fitzgerald, he cannot imagine an alternative to this "greatest of all human dreams." Stoically, he accepts the burden of innocence which dooms him to the hypocrisy and sterility of the Lost Generation. He can see no other future but that which "year by year recedes before us. . . . So we beat on boats against the current, borne back ceaselessly into the past." (p. 160)

David W. Noble, in his The Eternal Adam and the New World Garden: The Central Myth in the American Novel Since 1830 *(reprinted by permission of George Braziller, Inc., Publishers; copyright © 1968 by David W. Noble), Braziller, 1968.*

Fitzgerald's fiction always, in one form or another, reveals a strong element of moral judgment against which the heroes can be seen. The Fitzgerald hero is . . . a special person in the sense that the romantic hero is always someone particularly sensitive, intelligent, and vulnerable. But against the romantic hero Fitzgerald places a moral judgment, a stern rebuke, functioning either within the character or from the outside, which inevitably limits the freedom and possibility of the romantic hero. The romantic hero would be God, would dominate through his own individual capacity, but the moral judgment demonstrates that no man, no matter how special in secular terms, can play God. The hero is also, simultaneously, the archetypal contemporary American, the confident and eager representative of his country trying his talents against an older and more universal moral order.

In Fitzgerald's earliest novel, *This Side of Paradise* . . . , the moral framework is not fully developed, and the romantic hero's sin never reaches proportions sufficient to earn inevitable damnation. The next novel, *The Beautiful and Damned* . . . , however, articulates the doom of the special creature, and in *The Great Gatsby* . . . , Fitzgerald echoes the paradox implicit in the doctrine of original sin, the concept of man inevitably trapped by the difference between what he would desperately like to be and what he is. In subsequent novels, *Tender Is the Night* . . . and the unfinished *The Last Tycoon* . . . , the romantic hero is also doomed, but the moral framework, the judgment that makes the usurping hero's damnation inevitable, is more equivocal, more questionable, less confidently a statement about man's destiny. God weakens in Fitzgerald's last two novels, and although the hero, the man who would be God, never achieves his vision of experience, the forces that prevent him are more accidental and capricious, less articulately a moral order. The hero sometimes seems doomed by the lingering residue of firm moral commitment. (pp. 64-5)

Contemporary America, as Fitzgerald depicts it [in *The Beautiful and Damned*], rewards hypocrisy, simplification, the person who restricts his humanity to the salvageable single pose and rules out any humanely contradictory impulses. Anthony and Gloria are "beautiful" because they do not simplify, and they are spoiled because they represent something exceptional to the people around them; but their inability or unwillingness to simplify, to restrict themselves, insures their damnation in contemporary America.

The novel's flaw lies in Fitzgerald's failure to work out convincingly the balance between the couple's inability and unwillingness, or to develop any coherent relationship between their responsibility for their doom and an indictment of the American society that dooms its "beautiful." Responsive, directionless, impulsive, capable at times of love for each other, as no other characters in the novel are capable of love, Anthony and Gloria try to sustain their status as special people. . . . In the novel, however, contemporary America, despite all its opulence, is a land of "ignorance and necessity," a land that requires hard simplification, callous dishonesty, or rigorous moral restriction from those who are determined to survive. The "beautiful," the flexible and evanescent, are "damned." Because of the depiction of America, the relentless environment that promises so much and punishes so fiercely, Anthony and Gloria gain sympathy well beyond that usually accorded to illustrations in a moral parable. Hollow as they finally are, and harshly as Fitzgerald judges them, Anthony and Gloria are still preferable to all the self-seeking simplifications around them. Although Fitzgerald never makes the relevance of the moral judgment clear, never allows the judgment to stand as a final statement about the principal characters, he never modifies the stringency of the judgment itself.

The moral structure of *The Great Gatsby* is far more coherent. The narrator of the novel, Nick Carraway, more honest than anyone else, serves as "a guide, a pathfinder, an original settler," . . . [and] provides the perspective through which the issues of the novel are apparent. (pp. 70-1)

Jay Gatsby . . . is the embodiment of the American Dream: the mystery of its origins, its impossible romanticism, its belief in its capacity to recapture a past that may never have existed (as Gatsby believes he can re-create his past with Daisy), its faith in an unknown future, its ultimate futility. He attempts to create a new Eden, derived from the past, through money, silk shirts, and an Oxford accent. Gatsby is also the Horatio Alger hero in his dedication to "dumbbell exercise," the study of "needed inventions," and the pure vision of the future that involves making a lot of money.

Gatsby's vision might have been a more plausible version of experience in an earlier, simpler America. . . . Yet in another sense, as Nick clearly sees at the end of the novel, the dream Gatsby represents was always flawed, always impossible to achieve, the promise of the glittering new land which could never be fulfilled no matter how dedicated the aspirant. . . . In *The Great Gatsby,* Fitzgerald's tightest novel both artistically and theologically, both sides of man are locked, the romantic hero's aspiration and defeat are equally necessary. Man's destiny, the sin of the attractive romantic hero, is immutable in Fitzgerald's moral and religious perspective. (pp. 72-3)

Fitzgerald's morality in *The Great Gatsby* is not the simple morality of single-minded judgment, of excoriating the unrighteous. Rather, as articulated through the wise and temperate Nick, the morality is the inflexible necessity of the harsh dilemma of human experience, the invariable human defeat involved in the difference between vision and reality. Because he understands and accepts this, Nick is able to survive and look back on the events of the novel through distance and time. (pp. 73-4)

[In *Tender Is the Night,* Dick Diver] fails, like Jay Gatsby, partly because his innocent and moral ideals no longer apply to contemporary experience. Increasingly throughout the novel, Dick's public moralism is inappropriate in a new, more private world that he cannot understand. (p. 74)

In the moral ambiguity of *Tender Is the Night,* much of Fitzgerald's attention shifts from the vertical relationship, the transmission of truth or moral values from parent to child, to the lateral relationship, the equivalent relationship between man and woman, the mutual recognition of humanity. The focus often changes from fathers to women, to the representatives of an amoral principle of accepting what is and holding "things together." For Fitzgerald, the father is more characteristically, although not entirely, connected with America, a continent that is a "nursery." (pp. 77-8)

The structural reliance on only the theme of Dick's decline almost seems a substitute for the failure to control fully the ultimate skepticism about God and the issues of lateral relationship in the novel. Yet, despite this failure and the lack of a universal order as tight as that of *The Great Gatsby,* a sense of richness, density, and disordered humanity emerges from *Tender Is the Night.* (p. 80)

The point of view of *The Last Tycoon* is never developed sufficiently to order all the elements. . . . And, in secular as well as religious terms, no structurally coherent device, at least none apparent in the unfinished novel, manages to articulate all that is there.

In his last two novels, Fitzgerald's compassion grew. His concern for his characters increased, as did his sympathy for their human struggles and relationships, for all the questions they could never answer. Correspondingly, the element of morality or judgment diminished, and God or truth disappeared; the romantic hero, although still doomed, seemed doomed less by a moral order or original sin than by accident. Still unable to control his own destiny as he so powerfully wanted to, the romantic hero turned his attention to the very human relationships that contributed to his doom, sometimes even, as in the instance of Monroe Stahr [in *The Last Tycoon*], ironically learning from them. Yet despite the interest in the strictly secular relationship and the lack of an implicit moral order, Fitzgerald's form was always that of the parable, no less in *Tender Is the Night* than in *The Beautiful and Damned*. In the last two novels, the parable form was less appropriate, less able to summarize and direct the issues of the novel, and Fitzgerald never found a form to express coherently the greater human dimensions and complexity of his later fiction. The form broke, particularly in *Tender Is the Night,* in which the energy and perception of the novel leap out from the inadequate structure and the ultimately superficial point of view. Yet in the very breaking of the form, the very collapse of the parable as an explanation that can support the weight of contemporary experience, the sense of Fitzgerald's achieved compassion inheres. Compassion seldom is tidy or neatly measurable in a formal equation, and Fitzgerald's last two novels explode from the tidiness of judgment and evaluation of the "American experience" into deeper questions, as well as richer and less systematic understandings about the perplexities of man. (pp. 84-5)

> *James Gindin, "Gods and Fathers in F. Scott Fitzgerald's Novels," in* Modern Language Quarterly, *March, 1969, pp. 64-85.*

Gatsby in many ways marks the logical end of the [Horatio] Alger tradition. He is, to put this differently, the end product of the American Dream, the grotesque embodiment of what America can offer its ambitious young. (p. 110)

Gatsby becomes the absurd incarnation of Benjamin Franklin and the Gilded Age tycoon. . . . He came to embody the values that Henry James turned from in terror in *The American Scene*. He came to represent the decline of cultural ideals which Henry Adams warned us about in apocalyptic terms in his autobiography. (p. 111)

What is important is Gatsby's attitude toward Daisy. . . . For the aim is not to have Daisy, but to want her; and when she appears to be Gatsby's or when she is lost forever, the world changes. As long as Daisy was beyond his reach, the green light on her dock was a resplendent symbol of desire. When Gatsby meets Daisy after five years and feels her love for him return, it became once again a mere "green light on a dock. His count of enchanted objects had diminished by one." . . . Fitzgerald clearly makes Gatsby into the Faustian man, the man who must have an object of desire. Once Gatsby loses his sense of expectation—and Nick in great part shares with him this experience—there is nowhere to go, nothing to live for. (p. 112)

When the dream fails them, Fitzgerald's characters look first nostalgically to the past and see it in terms of what might have been. Soon this nostalgia turns to horror as they realize how they have betrayed the promises of youth, how they have wasted their talents. Thus we move from one circle of experience to another in *The Great Gatsby*, the personal experience duplicating and reinforcing the cultural experience, Gatsby's sense of lost promise duplicating the lost promises of America itself. (p. 113)

> *Richard Lehan, "Focus on F. Scott Fitzgerald's 'The Great Gatsby': The Nowhere Hero," in* American Dreams, American Nightmares, *edited by David Madden (copyright © 1970, Southern Illinois University Press; reprinted by permission of Southern Illinois University Press), Southern Illinois University Press, 1970, pp. 106-14.*

[The American Dream] dies a most savage death in the case of Jay Gatsby; and *Tender Is the Night* is a most savage postmortem. The central concern of that work is the tension between the Dream and the harsh reality underlying it; and this theme is developed primarily in terms of the personality of Dick Diver. Indeed, the contradictions inherent in his character are the same as those of the Dream as a whole; the Dream evaporates and Dick dies for much the same reasons and with the same inevitability.

The narrative thread of the novel is interwoven with certain recurrent motifs. The first of these I call the "two-worlds" motif. We sense from the novel's start that all its major characters straddle two continents, with greater or less success. . . . But the two-worlds motif applies in a special sense to Dick and Nicole Diver; the physical fact of their expatriation might in fact be taken as merely a symbol of their far more profound emotional isolation. Their "two worlds" are interior as well as geographic. The surface they present to society is that of the well-adjusted husband and wife; the hard fact of the matter is that they are actually doctor and patient as well, preserving their ultra-sane appearance in the face of a quite real insanity. Let me take this a step further and point out that in one sense they are not expatriates at all, since they really inhabit neither America nor Europe. . . . Rather, they live in an intensely personal world that floats somewhere outside of our own notions of space, a world that Dick has created in hopes of saving Nicole: "in fantasy alone she finds rest." (p. 116)

Fitzgerald, then, has set up a play situation, a personal dream; and the central question then becomes whether or not the dream world Dick has created can survive the realities underlying it. Book 1 ends with the revelation of Nicole's insanity; and it is at this stage in the narrative that the theme takes on more universal dimensions. Book 2 is basically a rather violent denunciation of America in terms of this same dream motif; the dream in this instance is the American Dream, but the facts beneath it are no less brutal. (p. 120)

[At the end, the] real world, changing, fragmented, violent, has reasserted that dreams cannot endure. The revelation is gradual, and so is the consequent decline; but it is natural; it is inevitable. (p. 125)

> *Frank Kinahan, "Focus on F. Scott Fitzgerald's 'Tender Is the Night'," in* American Dreams, American Nightmares, *edited by David Madden (copyright © 1970, Southern Illinois University Press; reprinted by permission of Southern Illinois University Press), Southern Illinois University Press, 1970, pp. 115-28.*

Because it is such a perfect critic's piece—compact, complex, and propertied with symbols—*The Great Gatsby* has been one of the most written about classics of modern fiction in English. It has also been, surely, one of the most peaceably written about. Practically to a man the critics have praised its "form," by which they have chiefly meant the control, distancing, and complication which Fitzgerald gives to the portrait of Gatsby through his subtle use of intelligent, detached, principled, skeptical and ironic, but humanely compassionate Nick Carraway as narrator. A few years back Robert W. Stallman disturbed the peace somewhat by taking the view that Nick is a sentimental hypocrite and moral paralytic whose presence as narrator has the effect of radically heightening, through contrast, the shimmer of Gatsby's heroic radiance. Frederick J. Hoffman, speaking for established critical opinion, peremptorily dismissed Stallman's reading as "an exaggerated and often incorrect interpretation." A more recent critic [Gary J. Scrimgeour, from whose essay excerpts appear above], also unable to ignore the obtrusive evidence of Nick's gravely flawed conscience and spirit, saved himself from a like censure by deciding that, after all, the novel is an intellectual and formal failure and its creator soft-headed.

This last judgment, though attached to a shrewd enough analysis of Nick Carraway, is not very much more difficult to put aside than was Eliot's devaluation of Milton or Ransom's of Shakespeare. But it nevertheless suggests, as does Stallman's reinterpretation, that the praise accorded *Gatsby* by a whole generation of critics may have been based on a mistaken, or at least distorted, perception of its object. If so, Nick Carraway seems to have been the cause of the trouble. For as exemplars of a neoclassical and "formalist" age of criticism, the critics seem to have found it both right and natural to identify their own style of moral intelligence with that of neoclassical Nick. And perhaps, therefore, the style of their regard for the novel—like Nick's of its hero—has cheated it of its warranted full measure of recognition as a deft masterpiece of affirmative romantic imagination. (pp. 94-5)

Because we see Gatsby and the world he inhabits only through Nick's eyes, an objective understanding of Nick is vital to our understanding of Gatsby and the moral meaning of his story. And Nick, as I shall argue, is not quite what he takes himself to be, nor what most commentators on the novel, agreeably seeing him as he sees himself, have taken him to be.

Nick sees the world, twentieth-century America, as a moral and spiritual wasteland. . . . He sees Gatsby as an Apollo or Prometheus, the type of the hero or god reincarnate, who transforms, for a brief term, not only himself but the world around him before he becomes the half-absurd, half-tragic victim of history's inevitably reasserted laws. To Nick, Gatsby is a beautiful if fragile redeemer of modern secularist materialism, creating out of that very substance quite another reality. Beauty and meaning are born where Gatsby casts his glance. (pp. 95-6)

Gatsby has that rare and magically creative endowment of personality first isolated and defined as "radiance" in *This Side of Paradise*. And throughout the novel Nick hungrily drinks in this "radiance" of Gatsby's as if it were rich spiritual nourishment. (p. 96)

[The] hardest lesson yielded up by Nick's questing pilgrimage in the east—that the dream-led hero is doomed to destruction by the reductive laws of the reality that he would transform and transcend—is also the last . . ., and Nick turns back to the prudential stabilities of his Middle West. As the novel's narrative form itself implies, though Nick's perception and understanding have been augmented and changed by his experience, Nick himself has not. Back home again, the style of his life will return to essentially what it had been before his removal to the East. He has seen Gatsby, appraised him, valued him, witnessed his cause and been touched, moved, exalted by the prospect of his tragic destiny. Like Gatsby himself, he has come into

the possession of a new vision. But unlike Gatsby he has not been possessed by it. He does not, as he says Gatsby does, become born anew from some "Platonic conception of himself" derived from his vision of Gatsby. To discern how and why this is so—to adjudicate and interpret the radical opposition of Gatsby and Nick in terms of the polarities of value and motive that form the conflicts of *The Great Gatsby*—is to uncover meanings in the novel which considerably complicate and deepen those more available ones that have already been discussed. (pp. 97-8)

Opposite as they are in certain very obvious ways—mostly in the area of self-knowledge—there is a striking moral similarity between Nick Carraway and Tom Buchanan, especially when one views the two in comparison with Gatsby. The similarity is not easy to name definitively, but it has to do with dreaming and feeling. Tom, the rich boy born to the power of wealth, cannot learn the meaning of aspiration nor know what it is to "dream" as Gatsby does. . . . He is less human, as a consequence, than he should be. He has been brutalized by the luck of his birth. But so, in another way, has Nick. For Nick is also one of the "very rich," though in another sense. As Tom has been born to riches, Nick has been born, as he himself knows and confesses, to moral certainty. Tom is one of the powerful, Nick one of the righteous. And though both can know the frustration of the child who is denied, neither can know what it is to undertake the hazardous remaking of life in the lineaments of some dream. This is why dangerous Tom fears and hates Gatsby, while ironic Nick eyes him with the timorous passion of the fan-club cultist. (pp. 100-01)

Gatsby is *alive,* as Nick and Tom are not. But one distinction between Nick and Tom on this ground is of course that Nick knows it and Tom does not. (p. 101)

Nick the scorner of artifice in others is all artifice himself. When things become too real for this detached epicure of the flights and failures of others, specifically when the currents of actual life threaten to envelop him, Nick draws back. He prefers the role of onlooker, and he even enjoys watching himself play it. (p. 102)

As the materialist, the illusionist, and the moralist, or however else one might appropriately name them and indicate their relationships to each other, Tom, Gatsby, and Nick together add up to a paradigm of the permanent tendencies, drives, and tensions, the universal "laws," of human temperament operative in any time or place. But the strong local and historical feeling of *The Great Gatsby* as a novel—the sense throughout it that the world has got itself into a grim historical *cul de sac*, that values are "dead," and so on—invites an understanding of these characters' roles, and the "laws" of human thought and feeling suggested by them, in the historical perspective as well. Viewed against the background *Angst* characterizing the historically predicated "modern world," Nick seems to take on the special significance of having changed, *as a type,* under the effects of history, while his compeers, as types, have not. His moral essence shows signs of permutations, theirs do not. Gatsby is Hotspur reborn as a modern and he flourishes and falls in this world much as he did in that other where "honor" was a reality. And Tom is an arrogant, as truculent, as "careless," and even though he does not go under, is as pitifully blind and vulnerable, as Shakespeare's Caesar. But Nick, whom we recognize as the contemplative man, the knower and thinker, is no Brutus, certainly no

Hamlet. He could not be either one of them in this world and yet survive to function as the Jacques-Thersites commentator on the bitterly comic tragedy of absurdities that history has concocted for his witness.

Though Fitzgerald admitted to having learned much from the art of Joseph Conrad, the novelist he admired above all others, Nick is no Conradian narrator, above all no Marlow [as Scrimgeour claims]. At their worst Conrad's narrators are simple, never bad, nor even weak. They were born and bred in reverence of the old heroic virtues, and it is this standard of human value that they bring to bear on the stories they tell and interpret to us. Nick is very different, not only because he never lived the life of action that Marlow did, but because he was formed by that "modern" world that had only begun to be born when Marlow disappeared. Furthermore, Nick's return to the West at the end of the novel is quite obviously a very different thing from the moral nobility of Jim's return, in *Lord Jim*, to the "destructive element" of life that he had once fled, or Isabel's return to face the grim music of marriage to Osmond in James' *Portrait of a Lady*. But it is not, after all, so very different from Lambert Strether's ostensibly renunciatory return from Europe and the joys and challenges of "life" to Woollett, Massachusetts and the justice of Mrs. Newsome in *The Ambassadors*. And because it is not, it tends to expose, in its incisive portrayal of the self-camouflaging weaknesses and hypocrisies of the Carraway-Strether type, the basic sentimentality of that celebrated—and, incidentally, hyperironic—work of James. Prufrock is Strether in parody. And Carraway is Prufrock, in turn, taken seriously, given his due as well as his knocks, in that he is shown possessing in spite of his negativeness, a disturbing effectiveness. Nick Carraway is the modern man of integrity; and Fitzgerald's characterization of him as subtly corrupt and potentially corrupting in his relations with the unlucky people he observes constitutes a shrewd and original comment on the new laws of consequence that make the modern world modern. The skill with which Nick masks chronic fear and neurotic curiosity as tenderness of feeling and piercing intelligence is nearly that of a poet. It is a skill largely of words. And in this novel words are the life-medium of the impotent man.

Nick's weavings of words compose and interpret the most part of the moral reality confronting our judgment and understanding as we read *The Great Gatsby*. And sometimes, as in those last magnificent paragraphs about the meaning of America, the end of history, and the deathlessness of man's tragic appetite for wonder, he is a very great and true poet indeed. But he is also suggestively placed as a character in relation to other characters within the action whose narration his sensibility controls, encompasses, and so effectively shades and highlights. He has *his* author, too, that is to say; and he cannot, as Ford's Dowell could not, entirely becloud the fact that he is an object within the purview of yet another intelligence. Tested by the norms of that intelligence, Nick's moral vision is at best of an uncertain purity, and his harsh, poignant, gross, beautiful, and always engaging recreations of it in words, are a kind of siren song whose seductions are quite clearly discerned and definitely to be resisted. Nick Carraway's moralism is insistently negative. There is nothing one can "do" with his counsel except turn from life, retreat, grieve, and perhaps pine away listening to the beautiful music of his statement of his vision, and like Keats, drunk with the music of his

nightingale, die rapturously at last into oblivion. (pp. 105-08)

Putting behind him Nick Carraway's rendering of a blind-end world in *The Great Gatsby,* and taking with him that part of it which has value as usable human truth, Fitzgerald went on, as an artist, to the "next thing" in *Tender Is the Night,* which is the story of a man who, with much fuller knowledge of the inexorable laws of reality than innocent Gatsby had, nevertheless pitted his character, his integrity, his personal vision and energy, flawed and imperfect as they were, against the futility and despair that he knew were the ruling truths of his world. (p. 108)

> *Richard Foster, "The Way to Read 'Gatsby'," in* Sense and Sensibility in Twentieth-Century Writing, *edited by Brom Weber (copyright © 1970, Southern Illinois University Press; reprinted by permission of Southern Illinois University Press),* Southern Illinois University Press, 1970, pp. 94-108.

Fitzgerald has the archaic virtues of being a classic—of being old-fashioned. We read him at a distance, safely, measuring the frivolities and irresponsibilities, the youth, of another era. We admire the chiseled prose of his later period, his fine perceptions, his wit, his developing sense of tragedy; but we know that we are reading of something—a "romantic readiness" to believe in the possibilities of life, of idealism and hope, of simplicity, of the awkward, youthful gesture—that has left our lives and that Fitzgerald knew was leaving the lives of the people in his generation. (p. 222)

[If] his art is indeed retrospective, and if the early loss of idealism causes it to be retrospective, then the nature of that idealism assumes more than ordinary significance. The May day riots in 1919 and the stock market crash in 1929 not only mark Fitzgerald's arbitrary dates for the Jazz age, but they also mark a profound shift in American literature —and a measurement of Fitzgerald's achievement is one way of estimating the nature of that changing perspective.

It would be wrong to assume that Fitzgerald's early work is characterized by an innocence and idealism that are only in sharp contrast to his later work; for the tone of *This Side of Paradise,* as Fitzgerald assured Edmund Wilson before the book was published, is neither "sensational nor trashy," its romantic qualities are controlled by a wit and satire that Fitzgerald would later make less pretentious and more organic to his general intentions; moreover, in spite of the fact that Amory Blaine is so young, Fitzgerald already expresses, through his hero's undeveloped sensibility, his own disillusionment in the possibilities of heroism. . . .

Now, Amory's loss of faith suffers from the most trivial kind of attitudinizing, and is burdened by a sentimentality and false intellectualism that Edmund Wilson, among dozens of later critics, justly condemned [see excerpts from one of Wilson's early essays above]; but Fitzgerald's central idea is already present—the hero sees himself in the midst of his own decline, he witnesses the death of his idealism—and though Fitzgerald has neither the language nor the narrative with which to develop his idea, one can sense, in *This Side of Paradise* and in *The Beautiful and Damned* as well, the validity of his perception: one can understand Gertrude Stein's approval of the young Fitzgerald as the man who "really created for the public the new generation." (p. 223)

Few American writers have been so self-consciously literary as Fitzgerald, and it is the early Fitzgerald who is most self-conscious, most intent upon displaying his intellectual wares. . . . As [the] later heroes grow less intellectually pretentious, Fitzgerald's own style becomes less flaccid and more virile, less dependent upon itself for effects, less intent upon merely dazzling. (p. 224)

Both of Fitzgerald's early novels [*This Side of Paradise* and *The Beautiful and Damned*] grope towards tragedy, they fumble in their attempt to mourn the death of Gods, the loss of faiths—they want so eagerly to be tragedies; but they are really suggestions rather than statements, and they suffer from an uncertain perspective towards the tragedy that Fitzgerald feels but cannot dramatize effectively. The most convincing portions of these novels trace the decline of the central figures—then Fitzgerald seems certain, then he writes with authority for he writes of failure; the early sections that present the characters in their impulsive naiveté are too obviously written for and serve as a prelude to the elegiac commentaries at the end of each novel. And these commentaries seem hollow and artificial because they rest upon ideographs rather than characters, upon the idea of a story rather than the story itself; where there should be story, there is gesture, and, as Edmund Wilson suggests, we are left with striking beginnings and "with a burst of ideas toward the close," but with no narrative center.

Fitzgerald solved this problem of perspective by presenting the tragedies of his major novels retrospectively: the irrevocable fate that awaits Gatsby and Daisy, Dick and Nicole, Stahr and Kathleen, is grounded in experiences that have occurred before the present action; and the suggestive qualities that give a great density to these characters grow out of their past, a past that bears them ceaselessly back to a moment of greater strength which now is irrevocably lost. Furthermore, the point of view, which Fitzgerald first successfully controls in *The Great Gatsby*, colors the past events with a certain morbidity that intensifies the former heroism of the central figure. . . . The morbidity that attaches itself to the past inevitably affects the present and permits Fitzgerald to exaggerate those extraordinary characteristics of his heroes: for if Gatsby is preyed upon by the meanness of his society then we can accept more readily his literally absurd behavior; if Nicole suffers from relapses of her illness then we can understand Dick's inability to pursue his own career, we can believe in his erratic behavior; if Stahr is constantly threatened by death, then his eagerness to live his last moments intensely almost resurrect in him his earlier heroism. By connecting his tragedies to a past that broods over the present action and by informing the present with the unhealthy atmosphere of uncertainty, Fitzgerald is able to describe the decline of the heroic and idealistic posture in his generation. (pp. 225-26)

Gatsby is real only in his innocence (his state of romantic possibility) or his defeat (his state of helpless grandeur). There is no tragic dimension for Gatsby; the girl for whom he has sacrificed his life has always been limited. At the beginning she was a child, at the end she is really still a child, still unable to act—"What'll we do with ourselves this afternoon," she cries, "and the day after that, and the next thirty years?"—and Gatsby seems never to have realized the smallness of her character, the fundamental cruelty

of her character; the dream of self-fulfillment has always been behind him, as Fitzgerald states explicitly in the last paragraphs, although Gatsby seems to have lost any quality of self-perception he once may have possessed.

Gatsby is indeed much closer to a clown than to a tragic hero; in the title itself we feel that we are privy to a circus show in which the Great Gatsby will perform. . . . Fitzgerald has created a tragic conception of America but not a tragic character; his prose, his setting, his point of view, his idea or donné, as James would have put it, all contribute to the sense of tragic loss, but the character is never really noble, except as his gestures are interpreted and refined and given greater symbolic dimension by Nick Carraway. (p. 228)

[Questions about technical imperfections in *Tender Is the Night*] seem superficial when one considers Fitzgerald's achievement: the convincing description of this vast group of expatriates, each suggestive of some inner decay, each drawn with a concision and subtlety that imply the novelist's knowledge of his characters' entire lives; the sense of place, permanently and naturally beautiful in contrast to the ephemeral and artificial beauty, charm, and—in Nicole's case—the human illness of the people themselves; and, finally, the highly polished prose, fixed on the page like words on granite, Keatsian in its heavy, somber, sensuous luxuriance, firmly controlled in contrast to the insecurities of the people it describes. (p. 231)

Tender is the Night seems to be not only a far more ambitious novel than [Hemingway's] *A Farewell to Arms* but one that is artistically more satisfying—more satisfying, indeed, and richer in its total achievement than any other novel in twentieth-century American literature, with the exception of Faulkner's early work—*The Sound and the Fury, Light in August,* and *Absalom, Absalom!*

The great advance in *Tender is the Night* lies in Fitzgerald's conception of Dick Diver. . . . [Unlike Gatsby's], his tragedy is not only symbolic in its significance but personal as well—we always feel the human consequences in *Tender is the Night*. (p. 232)

And as we measure Fitzgerald's achievement we realize that his special significance lies in his dramatic awareness of those elements that "will not come again into our time"; of idealism and hope, of the singular individual fashioning his future as if a future can be fashioned, of the "romantic readiness" that informs his central figures but that inevitably is crushed by the hardness of the very rich, as in *The Great Gatsby*, or by the atrophying will of the idealist himself, as in *Tender is the Night*, or by the forces of history, grown monopolistic and predatory and increasingly centralized, as in *The Last Tycoon*. (p. 238)

> Theodore L. Gross, "F. Scott Fitzgerald: The Hero in Retrospect" (originally published in a slightly different version in South Atlantic Quarterly, Winter, 1968), in his The Heroic Ideal in American Literature (reprinted with permission of Macmillan Publishing Co., Inc.; copyright © 1971 by Theodore L. Gross), The Free Press, 1971, pp. 221-39.

[Fitzgerald's] single, pervading theme [is] the Flaubertian theme of the sentimental education with its allied depiction of the character's failure to grasp the disparity between youthful illusion and the world's mauling of that illusion in maturity. It is a useable theme for the moralist and satirist that Fitzgerald was. Historically considered, it is the great theme that the romantics made available to fiction, and one which many writers found useful after World War I. That Fitzgerald was aware of its full possibilities is clear from the fact that the theme lies at the center of all his fiction; he was able to realize it fully only in *The Great Gatsby* . . . and to approach it again in *Tender Is the Night.* . . . Fitzgerald gave the theme of the sentimental education a particular American coloration, to become "the thesis that Beauty is a concealed form of Money." It is characteristic of Fitzgerald that he apprehended his theme only fitfully and intuitively; it was not the product of disciplined study. His conventionally good education introduced him only to individuals and social groups, not to ideas. He left Princeton unscathed by formal education, but with a mass of dimly perceived literary ideas and the friendship of such men as Edmund Wilson and John Peale Bishop, who were to help him discard the trash with which he had burdened an unpowerful mind. He was not an intellectual, but he was a born writer who possessed an integrity to the word that Anderson never approached. (pp. 28-9)

The elements of pastiche in *This Side of Paradise* mar a sprightly, energetic surface, but they do not form a major weakness; its weakness lies in the fact that the novel is not really written. At this point in his career, Fitzgerald was unable to invent imaginative material, and when he departed from lived experience, he violated his own canon of truth, a canon that we dimly apprehend in a welter of contradictory impressions. Although he could register manners brilliantly, his talent was never for naturalism, nor even for realism, but for moral fantasy made firm by a tone of voice and mind—in brief, by style. When in his first novel he lapsed into conventional realism, he violated his particular gift. Fitzgerald could construct fantasy upon observed experience, but he could not invent and dress his invention in the clothing of reality. (pp. 30-1)

Fitzgerald is like Henry James in being a distinctly indoor writer. Whenever narrative forces him out into the open, fantasy again takes the place of typical American realism or naturalism. Nature is a setting, sweet if not sickly, an occasion for drama reflecting the states of mind of his characters, but never a force to be mastered or a challenge to be overcome. Thousands of stars glimmer in his skies, water sparkles in his lakes, waves break in his oceans, but the apprehension is fantastic, not naturalistic. In this sense, Fitzgerald's imagination was un-American and even refreshing. It set him apart from Anderson, Faulkner, Hemingway, and most of his American contemporaries.

Because he was a moralist, Fitzgerald wrote novels of ideas of a sort. Part of his power as a writer derived from his incapacity for abstract thought. Lacking intellectual tidiness, he was forced to grope his way through narrative, through the fictional comings and goings of his characters, to an essence which he himself grasped imperfectly and fleetingly. (pp. 31-2)

One is at a loss to account for what happened to Fitzgerald between the writing of *The Beautiful and Damned* and *The Great Gatsby;* to account in any real sense, that is, for the difference in so brief a time between the clever amateur and the near-master. In retrospect, it is clear that the earlier novel served to indicate to Fitzgerald what he could not do, and perhaps to guide him to what he could do. He could write neither *L'Education sentimental* in twentieth-century terms nor a counterpart to *A Portrait of the Artist as a Young Man*. Biography does not give us the answer, nor can it ever do so. . . . He seemed not to possess the kind of mind that was open to primary influence, while he himself complained that he needed to learn everything in writing by trial and error. If there was an influence at work upon *The Great Gatsby,* I suspect that it was again the influence of Flaubert, specifically *Madame Bovary*. . . . Both of Fitzgerald's earlier novels had suffered from the vice of contemporaneity, the attempt to catch and record the fashionable moment. Fitzgerald had seized upon the present and had tried to isolate it from the immediate past and from history.

In *The Great Gatsby,* by contrast, Fitzgerald returned, however unwittingly, to that richest of veins for the American novelist, to history itself, to the continuities and disparities between possibility and reality as conceived by the historical imagination. Much of *The Great Gatsby*'s staying power has to do with the fact that in this novel Fitzgerald took his place alongside Hawthorne, Melville, and James as a writer who realized the marvelous possibilities of the historical dimension in fiction. As in certain of the novels of his contemporaries—Hemingway, Dos Passos, and Faulkner—Fitzgerald perceived the past as a resonant and moving force upon the present, a force that liberated him from the curse of contemporaneity while it also made possible a degree of control over his materials that was lacking in his earlier work. History does not intrude disproportionately, however, as it does through rhetoric in Sherwood Anderson's work, or in some of Faulkner's through both rhetoric and obsession. Complex yet brief, *The Great Gatsby* is unique in American fiction for its lovely justness of proportion. Unlike other American writers who strove for proportion, Willa Cather for one, Fitzgerald here was not bloodless or dry. His novel is fully realized, not only in terms of history but also in terms of manners. It is a brilliant rendering of what is and is not possible in the society he set out to depict. (pp. 35-6)

More fictional narrators fail than succeed; although the use of a narrator solves the writer's problems of immediacy and continuity, the device also creates problems of strategy and credibility. Too often the narrator is likely to resemble Proust's, out in the bushes peering through the window at the shenanigans of Mademoiselle Vinteuil and her lesbian playmate. Fitzgerald's narrator, Nick Carraway, succeeds unequivocally for a variety of reasons. The principal reason is that he is not a mere structural device; he is rather a fully imagined character who not only relates the narrative but also interestingly debates the matter while telling it, and through his debates, judges it. . . . If Conrad's Marlowe stays in the mind as a man in need of a pipe cleaner and still another match, Carraway remains in the mind as a man of wit, charm, and intelligence rather than as a mechanical narrator. (p. 37)

Jay Gatsby succeeds as a character (where Dick Diver fails) because he is the projection of an intuition of life rather than a "true" character; he is a "fantastic," but he emphatically is not an Andersonian grotesque. Presented ambiguously as a liar, poseur, gangster, and bootlegger, Gatsby nevertheless emerges not only as sympathetic, but as authentically heroic and authentically tragic. He is a male Bovary whose romantic dream—his *Bovarysme*—is not simply personal and escapist, but representative, historical, and largely American. . . .

[The same] basic situation—the appearance versus the reality of American life—was responsible for most of Sinclair Lewis' work during the same period. What makes Fitzgerald's novel so superior to Lewis' work is the historical dimension, which has been there all along but which Fitzgerald does not insist upon until his beautifully written conclusion. First, we are shown Nick Carraway's Wordsworthian rejection of the wicked, citified east and his return to the "good" midwest: by implication a turning from contemporary moral shoddiness to an earlier, pastoral point in history when men were close to Nature and therefore virtuous. Then Fitzgerald gives us, through Nick's eyes, a remarkable, brief insight into Gatsby's plight, an insight made possible only by history. . . . Gatsby's desire for Daisy . . . transcends mere lust for sexual and material indulgence. He becomes, through his belief in the "orgastic future," however futile, a historical hero in his very denial of history. . . . (p. 39)

Thus Fitzgerald moved on from his earlier theme of youthful illusion and reality, that easy and conventional novel of *Bildung,* to broach a far more interesting theme, one that is at the same time a natural transformation of *Bildung:* the role of will in human destiny. It is one of the great modern themes, and one that permits us to place Fitzgerald within the perspective of a group of fine European novelists, specifically the Unamuno of *Abel Sánchez,* the Pío Baroja of *El Arbol de la ciencia,* of André Gide's best work, and above all, the fiction of André Malraux. At the same time, Fitzgerald's apprehension of history in *The Great Gatsby* allies him to such contemporary poets as Hart Crane in *The Bridge,* T. S. Eliot in *The Waste Land,* and Ezra Pound in the *Cantos.* It is an honorable company. (p. 40)

> *John McCormick, in his* The Middle Distance: A Comparative History of Imaginative Literature: 1919-1932 *(reprinted with permission of Macmillan Publishing Co., Inc.; copyright © 1971 by The Free Press, a Division of The Macmillan Company),* The Free Press, 1971.

The Last Tycoon represents one of the most striking applications of the cinematic imagination to a literary subject that has yet been written. Only the stream-of-consciousness genre and some works in Hemingway's canon possess anything comparable to Fitzgerald's achievement in his last novel. Although the writer had movie construction in mind during the composition of *The Last Tycoon,* he did not commit Dos Passos's mistake in *U. S. A.* of projecting a "movie novel." Fitzgerald's cinematic method remains relatively unobtrusive; the technique is assimilated to the subject, and not the other way around; the emphasis properly remains on character; and without the authority of the writer's presence—that is to say without the tone and style of the narrator—the novel would be nothing. (p. 179)

> *Edward Murray, "F. Scott Fitzgerald, Hollywood, and 'The Last Tycoon'," in his* The Cinematic Imagination: Writers and the Motion Pictures *(copyright © 1972 by Fred-*

erick Unger Publishing Co., Inc.), Ungar, 1972, pp. 179-205.

Fitzgerald never lost a quality that very few writers are able to acquire: a sense of living in history. Manners and morals were changing all through his life and he set himself the task of recording the changes. These were revealed to him, not by statistics or news reports, but in terms of living characters, and the characters were revealed by gestures, each appropriate to a certain year. . . .

He tried to find the visible act that revealed the moral quality inherent in a certain moment of time. He was haunted by time, as if he wrote in a room full of clocks and calendars. (p. 30)

Fitzgerald lived in his great moments, and lived in them again when he reproduced their drama, but he also stood apart from them and coldly reckoned their causes and consequences. That is his doubleness or irony, and it is one of his distinguishing marks as a writer. (p. 31)

The drama he watched and in which he overplayed a leading part was a moral drama leading to rewards and punishments. . . . The morality he wanted to preach was a simple one, in the midst of the prevailing confusion. Its four cardinal virtues were Industry, Discipline, Responsibility (in the sense of meeting one's social and financial obligations), and Maturity (in the sense of learning to expect little from life while continuing to make one's best efforts). Thus, his stories had a way of becoming fables. For virtues they displayed or failed to display, the characters were rewarded or punished in the end.

The handle by which he took hold of the characters was their dreams. These . . . might be commonplace or even cheap, but usually Fitzgerald managed to surround them with an atmosphere of the mysterious and illimitable or of the pitifully doomed. (p. 32)

Fitzgerald himself was a poet who never learned some of the elementary rules for writing prose. His grammar was shaky and his spelling definitely bad. . . . He was not a student, for all the books he read; not a theoretician and perhaps one should flatly say, not a thinker. He counted on his friends to do much of his thinking for him. . . . (p. 33)

Fitzgerald immersed himself in the age and always remained close to the business world which [most serious writers] were trying to evade. That world was the background of his stories, and these performed a business function in themselves, by supplying the narrative that readers followed like a thread through the labyrinth of advertising in the slick-paper magazines. He did not divorce himself from readers by writing experimental prose or refusing to tell a story. His very real originality was a matter of mood and subject and image rather than of structure, and it was more evident in his novels than in his stories, good as the stories often were. Although he despised the trade of writing for magazines—or despised it with part of his mind —he worked at it honestly. It yielded him a large income that he couldn't have earned in any other fashion, and the income was necessary to his self-respect. (pp. 35-6)

He had little interest in the physical objects that money could buy. On the other hand, he had a great interest in earning money, lots of it fast, because that was a gold medal offered with the blue ribbon for competitive achievement.

In his attitude toward money he revealed the new spirit of an age when conspicuous accumulation was giving way to conspicuous earning and spending. (p. 36)

In writing about the romance of money, as he did in most of his earlier novels and stories, he was dealing not only with an intimate truth but also with what seemed to him the central truth of his American age. "Americans," he liked to say, "should be born with fins and perhaps they were—perhaps money was a form of fin." (p. 38)

In Fitzgerald's stories a love affair is like secret negotiations between the diplomats of two countries which are not at peace and not quite at war. For a moment they forget their hostility, find it transformed into mutual inspection, attraction, even passion (though the passion is not physical); but the hostility will survive even in marriage, if marriage is to be their future. I called the lovers diplomats, ambassadors, and that is another way of saying that they are representatives. When they meet it is as if they were leaning toward each other from separate high platforms—the man from a platform built up of his former poverty, his ambition, his competitive triumphs, his ability to earn and spend always more, more; the girl from another platform covered with cloth of gold and feather fans of many colors, but beneath them a sturdy pile of stock certificates testifying to the ownership of mines, forests, factories, villages —all of Candy Town. (pp. 40-1)

His mixture of feelings toward the very rich, which included curiosity and admiration as well as distrust, is revealed in his treatment of a basic situation that reappears in many of his stories. . . .

[*The Great Gatsby,*] Fitzgerald's story of the suitor betrayed by the princess and murdered in his innocence is a fable of the 1920s that has survived as a legend for other times. (p. 47)

> *Malcolm Cowley, "Fitzgerald: The Romance of Money," in his* A Second Flowering: Works and Days of the Lost Generation *(copyright © 1956, 1967, 1968, 1970, 1972, 1973 by Malcolm Cowley; reprinted by permission of The Viking Press, Inc.), Viking, 1973, pp. 19-47.*

It is clear that Scott Fitzgerald, who created Gatsby, understood several things that Horatio Alger, Jr., never felt the need to consider, notably how vast wealth could most plausibly be amassed in a very short time, and how an ambitious youth should best prepare himself for benefactors who may put opportunity of that kind in his way. He had best cultivate Readiness, i.e. poise and how to attain it, and make use of such observations as that people like him when he smiles. He also needs a "Platonic conception of himself," which means the awareness that he deserves to be what he is not, and he needs a fierce determination to become that new self. (p. 26)

He did not so much isolate and reflect upon techniques as observe himself responding to what he read, and sort out what had made for comfortable or uncomfortable reading. . . . That was his chief gift, fidelity to his own responses. Reading in this way, reading everything—*War and Peace,* well-machined junk—he remained quarter-educated . . . , but he learned how to set up situations and manage transitions without fuss.

He also learned how to get a frame around Romance, a necessary accomplishment since his model for Romance, like his model for the docile reader, was himself. Gatsby, he admitted, "started as one man I knew and then changed into myself," and was probably never very different from himself. (pp. 34-5)

The author, who set out to be Nick Carraway, generally forgets to be anybody but Scott Fitzgerald, who could write the lyrical sentence about Gatsby's car, "terraced with a labyrinth of wind-shields that mirrored a dozen suns," and allow Nick Carraway to slip in but two words, "swollen" and "monstrous," among the enchanting forty. Nick is less a narrator than a conscience; though the less he says the better, the knowledge that he is somewhere around, like a saturnine big brother, helps keep Fitzgerald from talking nonsense. (p. 36)

As a narrator, Nick has the deficiencies of the homemade. Henry James, more knowing, would have used him to locate a point of view without trying to pretend he wrote the book, and despite the technicalities of the first person, that is what he turns out to be: a point of view. He is a more useful one than Conrad's Marlow because he relates not merely Gatsby's goings-on but also a revision of his own response to them. That is his real use. As significant an event as the book contains is the shift in Nick's standpoint, reported as the last chapter commences with Gatsby lying dead: "I found myself on Gatsby's side, and alone." Since it is clear by this time that Gatsby lives by bootlegging, by betting rackets, by transactions in stolen bonds, a phlegmatic citizen is needed on his side to save the book from triviality. The glamour was meretricious; now the wealth is criminal. In short, the Poseur Exposed: too slight a plot for a second thought.

So it is important that the Poseur shall not have been Exposed: that a man hard to convince shall have been convinced of his worth, to balance the parasites who desert him, the thugs who prefer not to get involved, and the rigid hypocrite (Tom Buchanan) who would be crying "Ah ha!" much louder did messy terminal circumstances not compromise him. It is important, in short, that Gatsby shall be Great. It is important, because the central myth of the book has to do with Appearance made Real by sheer will: the oldest American theme of all. (pp. 37-8)

Gatsby is a bootlegger and a thief. What matters is the purity of his vision. (p. 39)

Fitzgerald is engaged in [a subtle weaving of] the grotesque so firmly into the real that their textures, however improbable the *Gestalt,* are thread by thread indistinguishable.

Gatsby himself is achieved in a similar manner; it is his very trash that grounds him in the real. . . . [Fitzgerald] even finds it necessary to have Nick say that listening to Gatsby talk "was like skimming hastily through a dozen magazines": and who knew better than F. Scott Fitzgerald what order of reality was contained in magazines? But even when the words are wrong the music is right; the cadence of "painting a little, things for myself only"—cuddling self-deprecation—or of "trying to forget something very sad that had happened to me long ago." That is the authentic music, the cello throb of *Collier's* and the *Post,* purveying with slick effrontery the dreams Horatio Alger could never quite realize to himself. (pp. 41-2)

Hugh Kenner, in his A Homemade World: The American Modernist Writers *(copyright © 1975 by Hugh Kenner; reprinted by permission of Alfred A. Knopf, Inc.), Knopf, 1975.*

If *The Great Gatsby* is not a religious novel—and I am not sure of that—it is at least profoundly concerned with religious issues. Its central issue, indeed, turns out to be a religious one, and the novel defines it in religious terms. . . .

[Gatsby's] religion of course is not Christianity—but it does have a name, implicit in the imagery with which Fitzgerald surrounds Gatsby, and it has an ancient theological history. . . .

Gatsby is associated with magic and witchcraft. Attempting to win a victory over time and mortality, he is the divinity of a world whose distinguishing motif is magical transformation. . . .

In *Gatsby* money creates possibility, another name for freedom, and enables the magical transformations to occur. Money is the solvent, the freer of spirits pure and impure. At the outset Nick Carraway begins his novitiate in this peculiar world of magic. "I bought a dozen volumes on banking and credit and investment securities and they stood on my shelf in red and gold like new money from the mint, promising to unfold the secrets that only Midas and Morgan and Maecenas knew." Most sentences in *Gatsby* are rich in meaning, but that one is especially worth pausing over. J. P. Morgan was an actual person, familiar in the rotogravures, but Midas was a mythical figure and also a magician who performed transformations, while Maecenas, though historical, melts into folklore. The alliteration assimilates Morgan to this magical company. (p. 31)

A powerful counter-current . . . runs through *Gatsby,* asserting itself against the idea of unlimited possibility, and affirming the objective structure of reality. The book handles Jay Gatsby with great tenderness, but it also judges him as heretical in his transactions with reality. All of his avowals come into collision with it: that time is not real, that we do not grow older, that we prevail over experience, that Daisy was never really married and never really loved Tom Buchanan, that crime and idealism can successfully coexist, that he is an Oxford man. Gatsby's whole project of annihilating time, and rolling back the clock to the period before Daisy's marriage to Tom, is really an attempt to deny the reality of man's objective existence *in* time: it is an assault upon the fact of man's mortality. Throughout the book, indeed, time in its objective reality is everpresent, both literally and symbolically. . . .

No, Gatsby cannot annihilate time. Even he, at last, must set the clock back in place with trembling fingers, submit to time. And soon he will be rigid indeed. "Dimly I heard someone murmur 'Blessed are the dead that the rain falls on. . . .'" The touch, light but definitive, is exactly right; the traditional wisdom, the liturgical phrasing, echo with total appropriateness at Gatsby's funeral. Gatsby, as Nick says, paid a high price for living too long with a single dream, and that price was that he literally "lost the world." His mad project separated him from reality. Gatsby's idealism, which throughout the book is implicated in a wider American idealism, represents a kind of treason, a treason to being, and the foul dust that floated in the wake of Gatsby's dreams is the awareness of that treason.

I have noted earlier Gatsby's parodic relationship to Christ —he is a false Christ, Christ as magician or gnostic—but there may also be present in this novel a pattern of imagery suggesting a parodic relationship to the Old Testament as well (I am indebted for some of the following points to James Erwin, a student in a seminar I taught at Dartmouth). The famous valley of ashes can easily suggest the valley of the shadow of death (Psalm 23) where "thou art with me." In the valley of ashes "thou" turns out to be Dr. T. J. Eckelburg. The "fresh green breast of the New World" first seen by the Dutch sailors is a kind of Promised Land. It turns out to be, however, not the land of milk and honey but the land of alcohol and money. Daisy's voice is full of money; Mabel Wilson's breast is violently torn off; and Gatsby dies in his own Canaan, a parodic Moses. The "Jordan" in this book, moreover, is corrupt and deceptive.

Gatsby, then, is a great doomed magician, a heresiarch in his relationship to reality. It is an easy matter to identify him with the gnostic dream identified by Eric Voegelin— the gnostics were heretics who sought salvation within time —a dream replicated in the immanentizing modern consciousness. But Fitzgerald, even as he offers us this profound comment on a powerful thrust within modern and especially American culture, at the same time surrounds it with the laughter of forgiveness and a powerful elegaic tenderness. His comic-elegaic tone amounts to a kind of benediction. . . . (p. 32)

Jeffrey Hart, in The New Republic *(reprinted by permission of* The New Republic; © *1976 by The New Republic, Inc.), April 17, 1976.*

Ford Madox Ford

1873-1939

English novelist, poet, and critic, born Ford Madox Hueffer. Ford is distinguished by his literary associations as well as his contributions to the development of technique in the novel. Coming from a distinguished pre-Raphaelite family of artists and writers, Ford made his debut in print before the age of twenty. His collaboration with Joseph Conrad was an important one, as he was to learn from Conrad the technique of impressionism while in turn helping his coauthor to master English. Ford founded and brilliantly edited *The English Review*, a journal of high literary standing, which was published in 1908-9. A messy marital situation alienated most of Ford's friends but provided him with material which he was later to reflect in his two best works, *The Good Soldier* and *Parade's End* (a tetralogy). In 1924 he founded *the transatlantic review* in Paris and became the center of a group of writers which included Ezra Pound and Gertrude Stein. He was among the first to publish the works of James Joyce and Ernest Hemingway and is considered an important figure in their careers. Ford's achievements are major in the areas of point-of-view and timeshift.

PRINCIPAL WORKS

The Inheritors: An Extravagant Story   [with Joseph Conrad]   (novel) 1901
Romance: A Novel   [with Joseph Conrad]   (novel) 1903
The Fifth Queen: And How She Came to Court   (novel) 1906
Privy Seal: His Last Venture   (novel) 1907
The Fifth Queen Crowned: A Romance   (novel) 1908
Henry James: A Critical Study   (criticism) 1913
The Good Soldier: A Tale of Passion   (novel) 1915
Joseph Conrad: A Personal Remembrance   (memoir) 1924
The Nature of a Crime   [with Joseph Conrad]   (novel) 1924
Some Do Not . . . : A Novel   (novel) 1924
No More Parades: A Novel   (novel) 1925
A Man Could Stand Up–: A Novel   (novel) 1926
The Last Post   (novel) 1928
Henry for Hugh: A Novel   (novel) 1934
Collected Poems   (poetry) 1936
Portraits from Life: Memories and Criticisms   (criticism) 1937

There is no end to the pleasant debts one owes to that Mr. Ford Madox Ford who passes among us breathing heavily because of deep dives, of prolonged natations, in perilous seas of faerylands forlorn, now as novelist, now as poet, now as historian, once—and it was then that many of those debts were contracted—as editor. Most magazines have that look of being predestined to be left which one sees on the faces of the women whose troubles bring them to the Law Courts. . . . Not so was Mr. Ford Madox Ford's *English Review*.

Each number of that was a sturdy member added to the family. Had one left it in the train one would have stopped it, by some of the devices one has seen on the movies, galloping horses, flags; a cultured railroad President would have understood and forgiven. (pp. 249-50)

> *Rebecca West, in her* The Strange Necessity *(copyright 1928, © 1955 by Rebecca West; reprinted by permission of The Viking Press), Doubleday, Doran, 1928.*

It would not, I imagine, please Mr. Ford to be called neglected. He has written more than sixty books . . . [and when] he was in his twenties he was called the most perfect stylist in the English language; Joseph Conrad sought him as a collaborator; and, more recently, his war tetralogy has led to his being compared with Proust. He has not, obviously, been neglected in any ordinary sense. . . . [His] is a . . . puzzling story, the story of a man who has been in the thick of every literary fray and yet is ignored by the literary historians, a man whose individual books have, as they appeared, been greeted as unusual achievements but whose work as a whole has made little impression on the contemporary mind. (p. 364)

[His] book on the literary scene, . . . *Thus to Revisit*, . . . is, of Ford's many books, the most amusing and the most irritating. Ostensibly a treatise on contemporary writers, it concerns itself primarily with one Ford Madox Ford. This Ford, we learn, has "the faculty of absolute indifference to my personal fate or the fate of my work". He is often hailed as the greatest living critic, novelist, and poet. When he is attacked or slandered he merely shrugs his shoulders.

It is, no doubt, Mr. Ford's way of talking about himself that has prejudiced many of his contemporaries against him, and it is quite possible that his tone in such writings is the partial cause of his being neglected: it is difficult to take seriously a man who so recklessly exposes himself to the charge of asininity. (pp. 366-67)

Perhaps it is because there is so much of a career behind Ford—so many books and in such a variety of forms—that critics have hesitated to try to define his position among his contemporaries. The task is not, however, so difficult as it appears; examination of his work soon shows that we may legitimately confine our attention to his novels. Even in his non-fiction Ford is primarily the novelist and should be so judged. His books about France, England, and America have the merits of a novelist's note-books: quickness and accuracy of observation, an interest in the precise rendering of physical and mental qualities, a sense of the dramatic possibilities of situations that are only hastily and fragmentarily seen. His criticism also, though Ford lacks the patience to rear that structure of hypothesis and generalization towards which the judicial critic aims, does show the sensitiveness and discrimination of a thoughtful novelist to whom no phase of his craft can be uninteresting.

One might even, without extravagance, go on to say that Ford's poetry discloses his talents as a master of prose fiction. He has said that the conventional forms of verse are either too easy or too difficult to be worth bothering with, and certainly his own experiments in these forms are little more than the exercises of a bright student. In *vers libre* his performances are more individual, but even here the level of intensity is usually low and the diction often careless. The imagery is fresh, but it is involved and leisurely; usually it could be transferred to a page of prose without the reader's being conscious of any incongruity. Ford probably does not lack the qualities of imagination that are essential to poetry, but he has never made the effort to master poetic expression. The writing of verse seems to be for him a kind of recreation, whereas the writing of fiction is a matter of careful artistry.

Ford has, in short, tried his hand at all sorts of things, and his brilliant resourcefulness has always stood in the way of complete failure; but there is only one literary form that he has taken the trouble to master, and that is the novel. Only the novel has been sufficiently attractive to persuade him to subject his facility to a thorough discipline, and, though his work in other fields is never discreditable, it is his novels alone that entitle him to serious consideration. (p. 367)

The author's interest [in the "Henry VIII" series] is centered in the presentation of states of mind and the rendering of sequences that are largely psychological. Lacking the animation, the pageantry and the simplicity of the true romance, they derive their interest almost altogether from virtues not ordinarily discoverable in works of their kind. Conrad was not far wrong in calling the series the swan song of historical romance; the *genre* cannot flourish long in an atmosphere of sophistication, analysis and artifice. What Ford was clearly working toward was the psychological novel. (p. 368)

To test Ford's success all that is necessary is to read [*The Good Soldier*] a second time. Though you know how the story ends, though you have see,n the characters as they really are, you cannot find a phrase that is misleading nor can you discover any withholding of facts that the narrator could justly be expected to give. On the other hand, you discover in the early chapters references and allusions that

carefully prepare the reader for his final impression. It comes close to being a flawless book, remarkable for its sustained inventiveness and its sound, unfaltering progress. . . .

With all its technical virtuosity, however, *The Good Soldier* is not merely a *tour de force*. There is no disproportion between the technical skill and the solidity of the work. As a revelation of life the book is worthy of the technique, and every formal subtlety adds to the accuracy and force of that revelation. With the utmost tenderness Ford pushes deeper and deeper into the minds of his characters, disclosing realms of passion and agony and meanness. Conrad never attempted to present so complex a situation, and James never ventured to explore emotion so intense and volcanic. When the book reaches its terrifying close, one realizes that only such formal perfection as Ford exhibits could bear the weight of this tragedy. (pp. 368-69)

[Ford] has not departed in any fundamental way from James's aims and methods, and yet he has done certain sorts of things that James could never have done and would not have attempted. Thus he has demonstrated the vitality of the Jamesian novel in our day. . . .

His books have neither the sociological interest of the novels of Wells and his associates nor the experimental interest of the works of James and his followers. However, as the sociological novel continues to decline in favor, and as the experimental novel reveals its limitations, Ford's work may receive more attention. (p. 370)

> *Granville Hicks, "Ford Madox Ford—A Neglected Contemporary," in* The Bookman *(copyright, 1930, by George H. Doran Company), December, 1930, pp. 364-70.*

[*Return to Yesterday*] should not be impatiently put down by the reader because of its inaccuracies and misstatements. It should be considered as an impressionist picture and not as a record. . . . Mr. Ford is a highly accomplished man of letters, and a keen observer whom nearly everything interests. He would tell us that he is a novelist, and it is as a pictorial novel that this volume should be considered. That he has produced a good book in spite of an avowed disdain of accuracy is really a testimony to his powers as a writer. . . .

We are not suggesting that Mr. Ford has consciously distorted anything he has seen or heard. He is an artist; and an artist does not distort. But he is so constituted by nature as to see what he wishes to see, and to believe what he chooses to imagine. What might have occurred is as vivid to him as what actually did; and in an account of what might have occurred he will etch in details which really make the value of his book. And the reason is this: Mr. Ford, as a novelist, knows the supreme importance of details—"atmosphere." His instinct when he enters a room is to seize its atmosphere; and once seized, he will be able at any distance of time to reproduce it in words. That is his gift. As a thinker he is almost negligible. Ingenuity, flexibility, dexterity of phrase are his; but originality and, still more, permanence, are not his. He possesses great humanity, is capable of much devotion to a sufferer, can be generous to stricken cause or individual; but for a word or a look—often subjects of his fancy—he will turn away. For this reason his book makes sad reading. (p. 685)

"Mr. Ford Madox Ford," in The Spectator *(© 1931 by* The Spectator; *reprinted by permission of* The Spectator*), November 21, 1931, pp. 685-86.*

[Ford] has great talent, and much taste, to which he adds considerable coarseness of spirit and a carelessness of statement which constantly spoils a reader's enjoyment of his work. He has written remarkable poetry, some historical romances which just miss being excellent, many novels on modern themes and situations which with much skill and passages beyond the reach of most living authors combine the coldness of the mortuary, criticism which for a paragraph here and there seems very like revealed truth and then drifts off into perversity, and memoirs of his own life and the lives of others which seem all the time to be boasting of his own unpleasantness. (p. 239)

I must not forget to mention that when he wishes to do so he writes with eloquence and beauty. (p. 240)

Frank Swinnerton, in his The Georgian Scene: A Literary Panorama *(reprinted with the permission of Farrar, Straus & Giroux, Inc.; copyright 1934 © 1962 by Frank Swinnerton; reprinted by permission of Holt, Rinehart and Winston, Publishers), Farrar & Rinehart, 1934.*

[Ford Madox Ford] was a man of letters, born and bred. His life work and his vocation happened to be one and the same thing. A lucky man, in spite of what seems, sometimes, to the onlooker, as unlucky a life as was ever lived. (p. 249)

I doubt greatly he ever seriously considered for one moment any other mode of life than the life he lived. I knew him for twelve years, in a great many places and situations, and I can testify that he led an existence of marvelous discomfort, of insecurity, of deep and pressing anxiety as to his daily bread; but no matter where he was, what his sufferings were, he sat down daily and wrote, in his crabbed fine hand, with pen, the book he was working on at the moment; and I never knew him when he was not working on a book. It is not the moment to estimate those books, time may reverse his own severe judgment on some of them, but any of you who have read the Tietjens cycle, or *The Good Soldier,* must have taken a long step forward in your knowledge of craftsmanship, or just what it takes to write a fine novel. His influence is deeper than we are able to measure, for he has influenced writers who never read his books, which is the fate of all masters. (p. 250)

Katherine Anne Porter, "Homage to Ford Madox Ford" (1942), in her The Collected Essays and Occasional Writings of Katherine Anne Porter *(copyright © 1970 by Katherine Anne Porter; reprinted by permission of Delacorte Press/Seymour Lawrence), Delacorte Press, 1970, pp. 249-50.*

As in most great works of comic irony, the mechanical structure of *The Good Soldier* is controlled to a degree nothing less than taut, while the structure of meaning is almost blandly open, capable of limitless refractions. One may go further, perhaps, and say that the novel renews a major lesson of all classic art: from the very delimitation of form arises the exfoliation of theme. This, at any rate, is the fact about *The Good Soldier* that gives point to John Rodker's quip that "it is the finest French novel in the English language," which is to say that it has perfect clarity of surface and nearly mathematical poise, and—as an admirer would wish to extend the remark—a substance at once exact and richly enigmatic. As a novel, *The Good Soldier* is like a hall of mirrors, so constructed that, while one is always looking straight ahead at a perfectly solid surface, one is made to contemplate not the bright surface itself, but the bewildering maze of past circumstances and future consequence that—somewhat falsely—it contains. Or it is like some structure all of glass and brilliantly illuminated, from which one looks out upon a sable jungle and ragged darkness.

The Good Soldier carries the subtitle "A Tale of Passion," and the book's controlling irony lies in the fact that passionate situations are related by a narrator who is himself incapable of passion, sexual and moral alike. His is the true *accidia,* and so, from his opening absurdity: "This is the saddest story I have ever heard," on to the end and at every point, we are forced to ask: "How can we believe *him*? His must be exactly the *wrong* view." The fracture between the character of the event as we feel it to be and the character of the narrator as he reports the event to us is the essential irony, yet it is not in any way a simple one; for the narrator's view, as we soon discover, is not so much the wrong view as merely *a* view, although a special one. No simple inversion of statement can yield up the truth, for the truth is the maze, and, as we learn from what is perhaps the major theme of the book, appearances have their reality.

First of all, this novel is about the difference between convention and fact. The story consists of the narrator's attempt to adjust his reason to the shattering discovery that, in his most intimate relationships, he has, for nine years, mistaken the conventions of social behavior for the actual human fact. That he did not want it otherwise, that the deception was in effect self-induced, that he could not have lived at all with the actuality, is, for the moment, beside our point, although ultimately, for the attitude and the architecture of the novel, it is the whole point. (pp. vi-viii)

Are not the "facts" that the narrator discovers in themselves "conventions" of a sort? We are forced, at every point, to look back at this narrator, to scan his beguiling surprise, to measure the angle of refraction at which that veiled glance penetrates experience. He himself suggests that we are looking at events here as one looks at the image of a mirror in a mirror, at the box within the box within the box, the arch beyond the arch beyond the arch. (p. ix)

The vicious consolations of failure form our narrator. "Men," said D. H. Lawrence, "men can suck the heady juice of exalted self-importance from the bitter weed of failure—failures are usually the most conceited of men." Thus at the end of the novel we have forgotten the named good soldier, and we look instead at the nominated one, the narrator himself. His consolations are small: attendance upon the ill. . . . (p. xii)

And thus we come to the final circles of meaning, and these, like ripples round a stone tossed into a pool, never stop. For, finally, *The Good Soldier* describes a world that is without moral point, a narrator who suffers from the madness of moral inertia. "You ask how it feels to be a deceived husband. Just heavens, I do not know. It feels just nothing at all. It is not hell, certainly it is not necessarily heaven. So I suppose it is the intermediate stage. What do they call it? Limbo." *Accidia!* It is the dull hysteria of sloth that besets him, the sluggish insanity of defective love. . . .

It is in the comedy that Ford displays his great art. Irony, which makes no absolute commitments and can thus enjoy the advantage of many ambiguities of meaning and endless complexities of situation, is at the same time an evaluative mood, and, in a master, a sharp one. Perhaps the most astonishing achievement in this astonishing novel is the manner in which the author, while speaking through his simple, infatuated character, lets us know how to take his simplicity and his infatuation. This is comic genius. It shows, for example, in the characteristic figures, the rather simple-minded and, at the same time, grotesquely comic metaphors. . . . (p. xiii)

Then there are the wonderfully comic events. . . . There are the frequent moments when the author leads his characters to the most absurd anticlimaxes. . . . There is the incessant wit, of style and statement, the wittier for its deceptive clothing of pathos. And, most important in this catalogue of comic devices, there is the covering symbolism of illness: characters who fancy that they suffer from "hearts," who do suffer defective hearts not, as they would have us believe, in the physiological but in the moral sense, and who are told about by a character who has no heart at all, and hence no mind. "I never," he tells us with his habitually comic solemnity, "I never was a patient anywhere." To which we may add: only always, in the madhouse of the world. (pp. xiv-xv)

> *Mark Schorer, "An Interpretation" (originally published in a slightly different version in* The Princeton University Library Chronicle, *April, 1948) in* The Good Soldier: A Tale of Passion, *by Ford Madox Ford (copyright 1955 by Janice Brustlein), Vintage Books, 1955, pp. v-xv.*

Ford had no "philosophy"; that is perhaps the reason for his long neglect. . . . *The Good Soldier* is in more than one way a tour de force. Ford arranges words so as to produce constant surprise, constant small shocks to the attention. He arranges incidents in the same way. Theme words drop into place, key scenes recur in new contexts, an intricate tangle of cross-reference conveys the illusion of living complexity assuming no more and no less order than life assumes. With a technique of far greater virtuosity than Conrad's goes a far greater sense of flexible life. Ford's heroes, like Conrad's, undergo mute ordeals, but without suggesting to the reader a "symbolic" remoteness. . . . Worry is the stuff of his situations. . . . (pp. 167-68)

There is no pretense of detachment; the whole is ordered by a shocked narrator. And the narrator's bewilderment is Ford's most serviceable device; for it prevents him from having to resolve the book. The convention of the book is that the narrator resolves it by writing it: the last turn of Ford the technician's screw. If one seeks for a center, one is driven through ironic mirror-lined corridors of viewpoint reflecting viewpoint, and this is of the book's essence; an optical illusion of infinite recession. Ford, one uneasily supposes, doesn't himself know what his attitude is to the situation he presents. The gap between presentation and "values" is never bridged. Ford's presented values are those of the craftsman; the man Ford, most compassionate of novelists, is himself in an impasse, an impasse of sympathy for all sides. (pp. 168-69)

> *Hugh Kenner, in his* Gnomon: Essays on Contemporary Literature *(copyright © 1958 by Hugh Kenner; reprinted by permission of Astor-Honor, Inc.), McDowell, Obolensky, 1958.*

The problems involved in the interpretation of *The Good Soldier* all stem from one question: What are we to make of the novel's narrator? . . . [What] authority should we allow to the version of events which he narrates? The question is not . . . particular to this novel; it raises a point of critical theory touching every novel which employs a limited mode of narration.

The point is really an epistemological one; for a novel is a version of the ways in which a man can know reality, as well as a version of reality itself. The techniques by which a novelist controls our contact with his fictional world, and particularly his choice of point of view and his treatment of time, combine to create a model of a theory of knowledge. Thus the narrative technique of Fielding, with the author omniscient and all consciousnesses equally open to him, implies eighteenth-century ideas of Reason, Order, and General Nature, while the modern inclination toward a restricted and subjective narrative mode implies a more limited and tentative conception of the way man knows.

When we speak of a limited-point-of-view novel, then, we are talking about a novel which implies a limited theory of knowledge. In this kind of novel, the reality that a man can know is two-fold; the external world exists as discrete, observed phenomena, and the individual consciousness exists. That is, a man is given what his senses tell him, and what he thinks. The "central intelligence" is a narrow room, from which we the readers look out at the disorderly phenomena of experience. We do not *know* . . . that what we see has meaning; if it has, it is an order which the narrator imposes upon phenomena, not one which is inherent there. And we can know only one consciousness—the one we are in. Other human beings are simply other events outside. (pp. 225-26)

In the first-person novel . . . it is at least possible to eliminate authority altogether, and to devise a narrative which raises uncertainty about the nature of truth and reality to the level of a structural principle. (pp. 225-26)

The Good Soldier is "A Tale of Passion," a story of seduction, adultery, and suicide told by a deceived husband. These are melodramatic materials; yet the novel is not a melodrama, because the action of which it is an imitation is not the sequence of passionate gestures which in another novel we would call the plot, but rather the action of the narrator's mind as it gropes for the meaning, the reality of what has occurred. It is an interior action, taking its order from the processes of a puzzled mind rather than from the external forms of chronology and causation. This point is clear enough if one considers the way in which Ford treats the violent events which would, in a true melodrama, be climactic—the deaths of Maisie Maidan, Florence, and Ashburnham. All these climaxes are, dramatically speaking, "thrown away," anticipated in casual remarks so as to deprive them of melodramatic force, and treated, when they do occur, almost as afterthoughts. (pp. 226-27)

The narrative technique of *The Good Soldier* is a formal model of this interior action. We are entirely restricted to what Dowell perceives, and the order in which we receive his perceptions is the order of his thought; we never know more than he knows about his "saddest story," and we must accept his contradictions and uncertainties as stages in our own progress toward knowledge. At first glance, Dowell seems peculiarly ill-equipped to tell this story, because he is ill-equipped to *know* a tale of passion. He is a kind of eunuch, a married virgin, a cuckold. He has apparently never felt passion. . . . He is a stranger to human affairs. . . . And he is an American, a stranger to the society in which his story takes place.

But more than all this Dowell would seem to be disqualified as the narrator of *any* story by the doubt and uncertainty which are the defining characteristics of his mind. One phrase runs through his narrative, from the first pages to the last: "I don't know"; and again and again he raises questions of knowledge, only to leave them unanswered: "What does one know and why is one here?" "Who in this world can know anything of any other heart—or of his own?"

The patent inadequacies of Dowell as a narrator have led critics of the novel to dismiss his version of the meaning of the events, and to look elsewhere for authority. (p. 227)

But the point of technique here is simply that the factors which seem to disqualify Dowell—his ignorance, his inability to act, his profound doubt—are not seen in relation to any norm; there is neither a "primary author" nor a "knower". . . . There is only Dowell, sitting down "to puzzle out what I know." The world of the novel is his world, in which "it is all a darkness"; there is no knowledge offered, or even implied, which is superior to his own.

In a novel which postulates such severe limits to human knowledge—a novel of doubt, that is, in which the narrator's fallibility *is* the norm—the problem of authority cannot be settled directly, because the question which authority answers: "How can we know what is true?" is itself what the novel is about. There are, however, two indirect ways in which a sense of the truth can be introduced into such a novel without violating its formal (which is to say epistemological) limitations: either through ironic tone, which will act to discredit the narrator's version of events and to imply the correctness of some alternative version, or through the development of the narrator toward some partial knowledge, if only of his own fallibility. . . . (p. 228)

It has generally been assumed by Ford's commentators that *The Good Soldier* belongs to the [former class] . . . but in fact it is closer to [the latter]. Ford's novel is, to be sure, . . . ironic . . ., [but] Ford's narrator is conscious of the irony, and consciously turns it upon himself. When he describes his own inactions, or ventures an analysis of his own character . . . he is consciously self-deprecating, and thus blocks, as any conscious ironist does, the possibility of being charged with self-delusion. Schorer [see excerpt above] errs on this crucial point when he says that "the author, while speaking through his simple, infatuated character, lets us know how to take his simplicity and his infatuation." For the author does not speak—the novel has no "primary author"; it is Dowell himself who says, in effect,

"I am simple and infatuated" (though there is irony in this, too; he is not all *that* simple).

The case for reading the novel as Schorer does, as a comedy of humor, is based on the enormity of Dowell's inadequacies. There are two arguments to be raised against this reading. First, Dowell's failures—his failure to act, his failure to understand the people around him, his failure to "connect"—are shared by all the other characters in the novel, and thus would seem to constitute a generalization about the human condition rather than a moral state peculiar to him. Alienation, silence, loneliness, repression—these describe Ashburnham and Leonora and Nancy, and even "poor Florence" as well as they describe Dowell. Each character confronts his destiny alone.

Second, Dowell does have certain positive qualities which perhaps, in the light of recent criticism of the novel, require some rehabilitation. For instance, if his moral doubt prevents positive action, it also restrains him from passing judgment, even on those who have most wronged him. . . . And though he doubts judgment—doubts, that is, the existence of moral absolutes—he is filled with a desire to know, a compelling need for the truth to sustain him in the ruin of his life. In the action of the novel, the doubt and the need to know are equally real, though they deny each other.

Dowell has one other quality, and it is his finest and most saving attribute—his capacity for love; for ironically, it is he, the eunuch, who is the Lover. Florence and Ashburnham and Maisie Maidan suffer from "hearts," but Dowell is sound, and able, after his fashion, to love—to love Ashburnham and Nancy, and even Leonora. It is he who performs the two acts of wholly unselfish love in the book—he crosses the Atlantic in answer to Ashburnham's plea for help, and he travels to Ceylon to bring back the mad Nancy, when Leonora will not. And he can forgive, as no other character can.

This is the character, then, through whom Ford chooses to tell this "saddest story." He is a limited, fallible man, but the novel is not a study of his particular limitations; it is rather a study of the difficulties which man's nature and the world's put in the way of his will to know. Absolute truth and objective judgment are not possible; experience is a darkness, and other hearts are closed to us. If man nevertheless desires to know, and he does, then he will have to do the best he can with the shabby equipment which life offers him, and to be content with small and tentative achievements.

Dowell's account of this affair is told, as all first-person narratives must be, in retrospect, but the technique is in some ways unusual. We know the physical, melodramatic world only at one remove, so that the real events of the novel are Dowell's thoughts about what has happened, and not the happenings themselves. We are never thrown back into the stream of events, as we are, for example, in the narratives of Conrad's Marlowe; dramatic scenes are rare, and tend to be told in scattered fragments, as Dowell reverts to them in his thoughts. We are always with Dowell, after the event.

Yet though we are constantly reminded that all the events are over and done, we are also reminded that time passes during the telling (two years in all). The point of this device is the clear distinction that the novel makes between events and meaning, between what we have witnessed and what we know. All the returns are in, but their meaning can only be discovered (if at all) in time, by re-examination of the data, by reflection, and ultimately by love. And so Dowell tells his story as a puzzled man thinks—not in chronological order, but compulsively, going over the ground in circles, returning to crucial points, like someone looking for a lost object in a dim light. What he is looking for is the meaning of his experience.

Since the action of the novel is Dowell's struggle to understand, the events are ordered in relation to his developing knowledge, and are given importance in relation to what he learns from them. (pp. 229-31)

The effect of this ordering is not that we finally see one version as right and another as wrong, but that we recognize an irresolvable pluralism of truths, in a world that remains essentially dark. . . . There are, as I have said, certain crucial points in the narrative to which Dowell returns, or around which the narrative hovers. These are the points at which the two conflicting principles of the novel—Convention and Passion—intersect. (pp. 231-32)

Ford once described himself as "a sentimental Tory and a Roman Catholic," and it is in these two forms that convention functions in *The Good Soldier* (and in a number of his other novels as well). Society, as Dowell recognizes, depends on the arbitrary and unquestioning acceptance of "the whole collection of rules." Dowell is, at the beginning of his action, entirely conventional in this sense; conventions provide him with a way of existing in the world—they are the alternatives to the true reality which man cannot know, or which he cannot bear to know. From conventions he gets a spurious sense of permanence and stability and human intimacy, and the illusion of knowledge. When they collapse, he is left with nothing. (pp. 232-33)

Passion is the necessary antagonist of Convention, the protest of the individual against the rules. It is anarchic and destructive; it reveals the secrets of the heart which convention exists to conceal and repress; it knows no rules except its own necessity. Passion is, of course, an ambiguous term. To the secular mind it is likely to suggest simply sexual desire. But it also means suffering, and specifically Christ's sacrificial suffering. I don't mean to suggest that Ashburnham is what it has become fashionable to call a "Christ-figure" . . . but simply that the passionate sufferings of Ashburnham (and even of Leonora) are acts of love, and as such have their positive aspects. Convention, as Dowell learns, provides no medium for the expression of such love. (p. 233)

Between the conflicting demands of Convention and Passion, the characters are, as Nancy says, shuttlecocks. . . .

In the action of Dowell's knowing, he learns the reality of Passion, but he also acknowledges that Convention will triumph, because it must. "Society must go on, I suppose, and society can only exist if the normal, if the virtuous, the slightly deceitful flourish, and if the passionate, the headstrong, and the too-truthful are condemned to suicide and to madness." Yet in the end he identifies himself unconditionally with Passion: "I loved Edward Ashburnham," he says, "because he was just myself." This seems a bizarre assertion, that Dowell, the Philadelphia eunuch, should identify himself with Ashburnham, the English county squire and lover ("this is his weirdest absurdity," Schorer remarks of this passage, "the final, total blindness of infat-

uation, and self-infatuation"). But in the action of the novel the identification is understandable enough. The problem that the novel sets is the problem of knowledge, and specifically knowledge of the human heart: "Who in this world knows anything of any other heart—or of his own?" Dowell, in the end, *does* know another human heart—Ashburnham's, and knowing that heart, he knows his own. By entering selflessly into another man's suffering, he has identified himself with him, and identity is knowledge. (p. 234)

Of positive knowledge, he has this: he knows something of another human heart, and something also of the necessary and irreconcilable conflict which exists between Passion and Convention, and which he accepts as in the nature of things. Beyond that, it is all a darkness, as it was. (p. 235)

> *Samuel Hynes, "The Epistemology of 'The Good Soldier'," in* Sewanee Review *(reprinted by permission of the editor, © 1972 by Samuel Hynes), Spring, 1961, pp. 225-35.*

We catch the true Fordian note from the start [of *No More Parades*]. The prose is the quietest and suavest imaginable; to render noise the writer need not become noisy. Ford does not shout at us; rather, he is asking us to *contemplate* noise—battle noise. The tone is composed and the prose is composed; the noise is orchestrated for us. . . . Ford once said that the tone he sought in his prose was that of one English gentleman whispering into the ear of another English gentleman. . . . Here we are given a glimpse of violence in a matrix of quietness, of intimacy being violated by more than sound. *No More Parades* opens brownly upon a world in which gentlemen, alas, will no longer whisper. (p. 466)

When [*Some Do Not, No More Parades, A Man Could Stand Up,* and *The Last Post*] appeared together in 1950 as *Parade's End*, they were widely—and on the whole favorably—reviewed. The reviewers were all united on one point: they seemed preoccupied with the peacetime sections of the book. No one appeared to be much interested in the war. . . . And when Ford had said that his tetralogy was a war book—as he had—he was (Mr. Macauley's words) "hoaxing us." Some of the reviewers discussed the novel's formal qualities and all, of course, its content. But no one seemed much concerned about where the two meet: in the unique angle of vision that danger, and especially war, creates. Or perhaps it would be better to say unique quality of vision, all that takes place under brown light.

Ford himself seems to have been in no doubt about his subject: it was war, and *No More Parades* was the germinal volume. (pp. 467-68)

[The] primary motive of Ford's war novel was scenic—an assertion that may appear improbable to the reader who still thinks of the novelist's trade as "story-telling" or to the other, perhaps more sophisticated, reader who looks at every novel as symbolic action. Nevertheless, Tietjens, Sylvia, Valentine Wannop, General Campion and the rest —their whole complex, funny, and sad imbroglio, and *Parade's End*'s originality of form and style—all exist ultimately in order that Ford may penetrate and encompass that torn scene and recreate the particular kind of countryside that is called a battlefield. Tietjens' long parade begins and ends in a landscape.

Ford, incidentally, was never quite decided whether the

resulting labor was one book or four—and with reason. The separate volumes follow one another more closely than sequels, yet each (with the exception of the last) is formally complete in itself, and, since much of what has happened is recapitulated in each new volume, they are best read with a certain interval of time between one and the next. In any case, to take in the whole tetralogy the critic must stand too far off. A look at a single volume reveals more, since each *in petto* reflects a pattern found in the whole. Of the four, *No More Parades* is probably the best. It also comes nearest to being central.

In structure, *No More Parades* is a strictly scenic novel. There is no general narrative: we are always locked up in a particular scene, but the scene in turn is locked up in a particular mind. It is a worrying mind, both anticipatory and mnemonic, since fragments of a remembered past and a looked-forward-to future are continually being filtered in.... In the opening scene of *No More Parades* there are stressed, almost to the point of claustrophobia, its indoor—even domestic—aspects. About all the doings in that hut there clings a suggestion of a monstrous tea party. The falling, and lethal, insides of shrapnel shells are called "candlesticks." ... The hut is shaped like the house a child draws. Inside, there is a curious air of false domesticity, into which the sounds of the outside come, appropriately, like the falling of a large tea-tray.

This depiction of soldiers under fire is (or ought to have been) the death of a noble cliché: war seen as outdoors living, active, virile. There is much cold, much wet, much mud in Ford's landscape, but there is very little action. Ford knew that war was mostly waiting. He also knew that in war one is always surrounded—if (please God!) not by the enemy, then by one's own side. (pp. 469-71)

[The] technical problem raised by writing of this sort—with its hard cameo outlines—is a matter of continuity: how to get on, how to mediate between one scene and the next. The very sharpness of impression prevents a flow, especially since anything like ordinary chronological continuity is avoided by Ford. Life does not narrate; it impresses itself upon our minds and senses; and that is what Ford sought through his brand of impressionism.

Ford's solution to the problem is hinted at in his curious, and controversial, little book on Joseph Conrad. He warns against the novelist's reporting whole speeches—for example, by a long-winded suburbanite in his garden: "If you gave all those long speeches one after the other you might be aware of a certain dullness when you reread that *compte rendu*. But if you carefully broke up petunias, statuary, and flower-show motives and put them down in little shreds, one contrasting with the other, you would arrive at something much more coloured, animated, lifelike and interesting. ..." The same principle, I believe, holds true for the large garden that is a battlefield: by laying down "in little shreds" such motives as blood, noise, mud, battle neurosis, relations between officers and men, thoughts of home, sexual excitement, interest in nature, etc., Ford creates an effect that might be thought of as fugal. Or—to alter the metaphor—like seeds, these motives will show a strong inclination to grow and force their way from one scene into the next, as they do so often, undergoing curious and interesting metamorphoses. They weave the parts of the book together—and do much more besides. (pp. 472-73)

The war as seen by Ford Madox Ford is not quite the war of Hemingway, or of Tolstoi, or Stephen Crane, or anyone else—though it is tempting to suggest that it might almost have been Henry James's ("a war-novel on the lines of 'What Maisie Knew'"). For other writers the key fact of war and not-war (one hesitates to say peace) is their separation. The soldier is, in action and out, hardly the same man. ... Not so with Ford's soldiers. Each is, as Ford put it, "*homo duplex:* a poor fellow whose body is tied in one place but whose mind and personality brood eternally over another distant locality." It is this persistent doubleness that controls the ranges of horror, of which Ford presents quite a bit. And yet—and this is the point I wish to stress—Ford's presentation of horror is not harrowing. Indeed, on reflection, his depiction of war seems principally comic—though we may have to stretch our conception of comedy and scrap some received ideas about what subjects are intrinsically funny. (p. 476)

[By] far the most important point about Sylvia, and one which might easily be overlooked, is that she is among other things a splendid comic heroine—or comic villainess rather. The embarrassments that she creates are nearly always funny and the humor is not lost on her. She has a keen wit and a sense of the incongruous, even at her own expense.... Sylvia, indeed, comes very close to being Ford's muse, since Ford's continual juxtapositions, the altercations he contrives for his characters, the "perspectives by incongruity," superimposing war on peace and peace on war, create a way of looking at things that can only be described as comic. Comedy permeates Ford's world at even its grimmest. ... (pp. 477-78)

I would like to revert to certain consequences of the curiously closed-in quality of Ford's scene. Out there and a little beyond is unnamed horror: the horror of what lies beyond the front lines, of No Man's Land, of the unknown, from which for the most part we take cover with varying degrees of success. Were the action placed out there, as it is in much of the *Iliad,* it would necessarily be tragic. But Ford's characters remain enclosed, boxed-up, holed-in. We —the readers and the characters—await the inevitable intrusion, and when it comes it is horrid and macabre, but not tragic. It is more than anything absurd, since in this shut-in scene the social norms of a life of reason and common sense (or what passes for them) have, despite all, been preserved, in particular such matters as rank and class. These are simply incommensurate with the intruding horror, and it with them. So, when death enters in the guise of O Nine Morgan, for a brief time the social norms are shattered—for one thing his blood gets on an officer's shoes—but the normal is quickly re-established. It is perhaps this very quickness, indeed, which keeps the rhythm comic.

The phenomenon is of course not merely a wartime one. In peacetime the same is true; death, chaos, and madness being no respecters of our abstractions "war," "peace." This Ford knows as he shows us the same pattern working out quite early in *Some Do Not,* for example at the breakfast with the mad clergyman or, later, a road accident in the fog. Always the scene is an interior (though the walls may be only of vapor) into which there is a violent intrusion, a very brief dispersal, and a quick regrouping. ... As the novel proceeds we are translated, as though by metamorphosis, from one interior to the next, and to the extent that we are aware of this strange transmogrifying process—this sliding-away of panels—we must find the whole process comic. Indeed, these rapidly shifting perspectives are implicit in the minutiae of Ford's writing and, as such, probably make themselves felt from the start. (pp. 478-79)

But at its best the comedy is not obvious at all . . .; and it is not quite like any other writing about war that one can think of, nor like any other twentieth-century prose. It is a high and horrible comedy, with much compassion played off against an unrelenting pressure of the absurd.

The whole movement of Ford's tetralogy comes to a brief rest, as it should, in a fine scene at the end of *No More Parades,* a repetition of the familiar pattern of intrusion—if we can so characterize a general's inspection. The fall of France at this point appears imminent, and the fall of Tietjens with it; yet the ending Ford supplies is comic, light, and gay. (pp. 480-81)

> *Ambrose Gordon, Jr., "A Diamond of Pattern: The War of F. Madox Ford," in* Sewanee Review *(reprinted by permission of the editor, © 1962 by The University of the South), Summer, 1962, pp. 464-83.*

Human nature in [Ford's] books was usually phosphorescent—varying from the daemonic malice of Sylvia Tietjens to the painstaking, rather hopeless will-to-be-good of Captain Ashburnham, 'the good soldier'. The little virtue that existed only attracted evil. But to Mr Ford, a Catholic in theory though not for long in practice, this was neither surprising nor depressing: it was just what one expected. . . .

[The] novels which stand as high as any fiction written since the death of James are *The Good Soldier* with its magnificent claim in the first line, 'This is the saddest story I have ever heard'—the study of an averagely good man of a conventional class driven, divided and destroyed by unconventional passion—and the Tietjens series, that appalling examination of how private malice goes on during public disaster. . . . (pp. 161-62)

I don't suppose failure disturbed him much: he had never really believed in human happiness, his middle life had been made miserable by passion, and he had come through—with his humour intact, his stock of unreliable anecdotes, the kind of enemies a man ought to have, and a half-belief in a posterity which would care for good writing. (p. 162)

[He] brought to his dramatizations of people he had known the same astonishing knack he showed with his historical figures. Most writers dealing with real people find their invention confined, but that was not so with Ford. 'When it has seemed expedient to me I have altered episodes that I have witnessed, but I have been careful never to distort the character of the episode. *The accuracies I deal in are the accuracies of my impressions.* If you want factual accuracies you must go to . . . but no, no, don't go to anyone, stay with me.' (The italics are mine: it is a phrase worth bearing in mind in reading all his works.) (p. 163)

Most historical novelists use real characters only for purposes of local colour—Lord Nelson passes up a Portsmouth street or Doctor Johnson enters ponderously to close a chapter, but in *The Fifth Queen* we have virtually no fictional characters—the King, Thomas Cromwell, Catherine Howard, they are the principals; we are nearer to the historical plays of Shakespeare than to the fictions of [other] historical writers. . . . (pp. 163-64)

If *The Fifth Queen* is a magnificent bravura piece—and you could say that it was a better painting than ever came out of Fitzroy Square with all the mingled talents there of Madox Brown and Morris, Rossetti and Burne-Jones—in *The Good Soldier* Ford triumphantly found his true subject and oddly enough, for a child of the Pre-Raphaelites, his subject was the English 'gentleman', the 'black and merciless things' which lie behind that façade. (pp. 164-65)

Technically [*The Good Soldier*] is undoubtedly Ford's masterpiece. The time-shifts are valuable not merely for purposes of suspense—they lend veracity to the appalling events. This is just how memory works, and we become involved with the narrator's memory as though it were our own. Ford's apprenticeship with Conrad had borne its fruit, but he improved on the Master. (p. 165)

A short enough book it is to contain two suicides, two ruined lives, a death, and a girl driven insane: it may seem odd to find the keynote of the book is restraint, a restraint which is given it by the gentle character of the narrator ('I am only an ageing American with very little knowledge of life') who never loses his love and compassion for the characters concerned. . . . He condemns no one; in extremity he doesn't even condemn human nature, and I find one of the most moving under-statements in literature his summing up of Leonora's attitude to her husband's temporary infatuation for the immature young woman, Maisie Maidan: 'I think she would really have welcomed it if he could have come across the love of his life. It would have given her a rest.'

I don't know how many times in nearly forty years I have come back to this novel of Ford's, every time to discover a new aspect to admire, but I think the impression which will be left strongly on the reader is the sense of Ford's involvement. A novelist is not a vegetable absorbing nourishment mechanically from soil and air: material is not easily or painlessly gained, and one cannot help wondering what agonies of frustration and error lay behind *The Saddest Story.*

It seems likely that, when time has ceased its dreary work of erosion, Ford Madox Ford will be remembered as the author of three great novels, a little scarred, stained here and there and chipped perhaps, but how massive and resistant compared with most of the work of his successors: *The Fifth Queen, The Good Soldier,* and *Parade's End,* the title Ford himself gave to what is often known, after the name of the principal character, as the Tietjens tetralogy—the terrifying story of a good man tortured, pursued, driven into revolt, and ruined as far as the world is concerned by the clever devices of a jealous and lying wife. . . . I think it could be argued that *Last Post* was more than a mistake—it was a disaster, a disaster which has delayed a full critical appreciation of *Parade's End.* The sentimentality which sometimes lurks in the shadow of Christopher Tietjens, the last Tory (Ford sometimes seems to be writing about 'the last English gentleman'), emerged there unashamed. Everything was cleared up—all the valuable ambiguities. . . . [All] are brought into the idyllic sunshine of Christopher's successful escape into the life of a Kentish smallholder. Even Sylvia—surely the most possessed evil character in the modern novel—groped in *Last Post* towards goodness, granted Christopher his divorce, took back—however grudgingly—her lies. It is as though Lady Macbeth dropped her dagger beside the sleeping Duncan.

This is a better book, a thousand times, when it ends in the confusion of Armistice Night 1918—the two lovers united, it is true, but with no absolute certainties about the past. (pp. 167-68)

> Graham Greene, "Ford Madox Ford" (1939 and 1962), in his Collected Essays (copyright © 1951, 1966, 1968 by Graham Greene; reprinted by permission of The Viking Press, Inc., and, in Canada, The Bodley Head, Ltd.), Viking, 1969, pp. 159-71.

As a novelist Ford belonged (as he ceaselessly tells us) to the French tradition of writing, the tradition of which Flaubert, teacher of Maupassant, was the chief master, and whose important Anglo-American descendants have been authors like James, Conrad, Joyce, and Hemingway. It is the school which stresses craftsmanship—the careful, suggestive, economic selection of incident and detail—and which strives to approximate the aesthetic rigor and formal shapeliness associated with poetry and the drama. (p. 5)

Ford's subject matter and his technique are inseparable, each enhancing the other in an extraordinary fashion. "Anguish and Cat's Cradle" as image of Ford the novelist is therefore extremely fitting, for it crystallizes in one phrase the unique effect of his conjoined substance and form.

For "agony" is the emblem of Ford's spiritual universe. . . . One source of this anguish was no doubt personal, springing from Ford's own stricken psyche. (pp. 6-7)

But this sense of pain in Ford's world also derives from a fairly objective vision of the decay, spiritual and material, of England in particular and of the Western world in general. Himself emotionally committed to the values of a life he recognized to be dying—a life feudal, agrarian, local, scaled to human size—he looked with horror on the industrialized, giant, impersonal society which was emerging to take its place, and on the calculating, unrooted type of man he saw it producing. . . . In The Good Soldier, a book which dramatizes the emotional meaning of this change in the life of modern man, Ford's great theme . . . finds its quintessential rendering. (p. 7)

The mark of the Fordian universe, its basic fact, is incompletion. In his world, desire remains unfulfilled, thwarted doubly by the exterior conditions of life—its pointless vicissitudes, a blighting spiritual and social order, the insensitivity and cruelty of humankind—and by the inability of his emotionally crippled figures to act and to take. (p. 8)

The master metaphor of his form, "cat's cradle," was specifically, though subtly, used by Ford himself in a scene of the Fifth Queen trilogy in which the old children's game is played by his chief characters. (pp. 8-9)

Ford's view of his times, we have seen, was fundamentally unaccepting and critical. The whole body of his work makes that plain. Yet, paradoxically, the task which Ford set himself as a novelist (and which he urged on other writers) was the objective registering (constatation) of his age. His business, he said repeatedly, was to reflect, not to reflect on, his times. As Ford once put it, the novelist should be an exact scientist, never appearing, never buttonholing the reader, never moralizing. (p. 12)

The keystone of his intention lies in his statement that "the general effect of a novel must be the general effect that life makes on mankind." The business of the novelist, as he put it, is "to produce an illusion of reality," to "make each of his stories an experience." (p. 19)

Romance is no more pure Conrad than pure Hueffer. Ford has written of the "third artist" who emerged from their work together, and Conrad has spoken of their ideal of "welded" collaboration. . . . Yet the over-all impression of the novel creates is one of disharmony. In vision, tone, and diction, and in narrative style, Romance is a mélange, the struggles between the two temperaments being not so much concealed in the final product as made evident. (p. 29)

Probably the most striking variance is in the handling of the visual. Conrad's world is rendered with extreme physical clarity and vividness—an effect deriving chiefly from his handling of space. Conrad is particularly fond . . . of composing a stage of fixed points upon which his actors perform—dramatically interrelating with each other and, even more, with . . . material objects. . . . It is, in fact, through their motion in juxtaposition with these points of reference, or in static poses which are elaborately detailed, that Conrad's characters take on much of their definition and vital energy. (p. 30)

Ford's physical world, on the other hand, is much more indistinct and subjective. Through his fondness for unusual, slightly startling imagery it takes on an aspect that is more intellectual than visual. (p. 31)

Ford's province as a novelist lies elsewhere. It is the study of society and the psychological interactions of its members —an area for which Romance gave little scope. To understand this, one has only to examine works like The Benefactor, A Call, The Good Soldier, and the Tietjens books, or any of the social satires. Ford's historical novels are mainly psychological in their interest. And it is significant that the Fifth Part of Romance, which is predominantly psychological, is the most effective of Ford's three sections. (pp. 35-6)

What Ford did help Conrad with was his handling of English idiom. . . . That he actually did have a favorable influence on Conrad's writing is clear enough from a comparison of the rhetorical, redundant prose of Lord Jim with the much cleaner, lighter style of Nostromo. (p. 38)

The Good Soldier is . . . one of the literary triumphs of the twentieth century—a creation of the very highest art which must also be ranked among the more powerful novels that have been written. Certainly very few works in English— The Scarlet Letter, Jude the Obscure, Sons and Lovers, The House in Paris perhaps—can match the force of its emotion, while none can equal its duration. And this emotional intensity, which begins on a high pitch in the opening chapter, not only sustains itself throughout but steadily tightens until the final moments. The psychological effect of the novel is that of some relentless spiral cutting deeper and deeper into its human material. It is the extraordinary "turning of the screw," not for 140 pages as in Henry James's famous nouvelle, but for a far more exacting 256, and rendered with a visceral intensity completely unknown to James—one we are more likely to associate with the Greeks. The Good Soldier, in short, is a rare combination of Flaubertian technique and almost Dostoyevskian laceration and power. It is also a book, it is extremely important to add, whose second reading is astonishingly different from its first: in intellectual subtlety, in tone, and, above all, in feeling. (p. 151)

[The] meaning and significance of the book spring not from the story of only one individual but from the interrelationship of all its characters and events, from its total pattern. (p. 152)

The technical importance of Dowell [as narrator] in shaping the responses of the reader is not confined . . . to various poetic, ironic, and stylistic elements. He also enables Ford brilliantly to manage feelings by controlling the tempo and tension of the novel and the degree of its psychological penetration. (p. 169)

Looking back over the earlier novels from the vantage point of the twenties, we can readily see the ways in which the Tietjens books—and *Some Do Not,* in particular—pull together the various strands of his pre-war production. In them are combined the large public canvas of the social satires and the characterization in depth of the novels of "small circles." And from Ford's absorption in his historical novels derives much of their emphasis on the English past as evaluative standard. (p. 190)

The failure of the novels after *Some Do Not* lies . . . in their excessive fluidity. Because they are not composed with scrupulous care or by a fully engaged mind, the imaginative vitality established for the Tietjens world in the first book is mostly lost. In writing these volumes, Ford had ceased to be an artist. (p. 222)

[Also] unhappy is the effect of the interior monologue on the narrative strength of these three books [*No More Parades, A Man Could Stand Up, the Last Post*]. Very little in them is deeply engaging because the method is basically a non-dramatic prison—much of the "action" occurring posthumously, so to speak, in the mind of a character. And since the focus is not on the conflict itself but on the character's thoughts about it, the few dramatic scenes which do take place tend to be muffled and oblique. The method as implemented also makes for an over-all linear impression, in pale contrast to the rich and various world of *Some Do Not.* (p. 224)

The theme of England lies at the roots of nearly all Ford's fictional works, but none of his other novels approaches *Some Do Not* in the range or depth with which the life of his native country is portrayed. Since Ford's intention was to show the impact on the nation of the Great War, its Englishness is hardly accidental: the British milieu required elaboration. It needed to be given the thick, complex feel of actuality—had, in James's phrase, to be "done." Thus the novel is rich with the peculiar motifs, amply developed, of English life: the role and character of the governing classes; the class structure and the demarcation between those "born" and those of undistinguished lineage; political struggles between Conservatives and Liberals; the pervasive dominance of Victorian sexual morality, and the diversity of English types. . . . (pp. 232-33)

Perhaps more than any other single quality, Ford's ability to create the illusion of life actually being lived imparts to *Some Do Not* its authentic literary distinction.

The success of the novel depends, however, on the masterful handling of tools other than point of view and time-shift. Of these, the most important involve the process by which the work moves through time—the relentlessness of its advance and the modulation of its effect. Principles of composition rather than devices, they cut across and in part

draw on the other methods. . . .

Like his other fine novels, *Some Do Not* beautifully illustrates the theory of *progression d'effet.* The novel moves purposefully forward in every word, growing faster and more intense as it proceeds. Every device or effect serves to advance the story and to develop the over-all plan. (p. 246)

[By] temperament . . . Ford [was not] especially well equipped to be a penetrating historian of his times. He was too exclusively literary, and no doubt too uninterested, to saturate himself in the affairs of the world. Although he was sensitive to them, his concern was not—on the accumulated evidence of the bulk of his novels—that of a deeply versed, broadly informed, or particularly incisive student. . . . Quite frequently Ford's insights into his time are fundamental—and, as norms against which to test our ways, they are extremely valuable. But the consequence of his approach and temperament was that the cross-section of life he did cut was too often thin, both intellectually in the grasp of the genuine complexities of the problems of modern life, and aesthetically in the presentation of the texture and "feel" of his milieu. (p. 268)

[The] possibly limited relevance for today of [the] central ideas and vision [of Ford's work might also be mentioned]. . . . There is considerable truth, if not all, in R. P. Blackmur's observation that Ford was a writer in love with the defeat of the past for the sake of that defeat. If Ford was a moralist, he was but infrequently a working one. Too often his vision of the good life was merely traditional, more code than morality. (p. 270)

But, of course, Ford's permanent importance as a novelist will be based, in the end, on his best work—on his two strikingly different masterpieces: *The Good Soldier,* a brilliant small-group novel in the French tradition, mordant and ironic and intensely concentrated in form, subject, and passion; and *Some Do Not,* deriving more from English roots; broad in social scope; populated with a diverse cast of fully drawn, appealing characters; and more relaxed, humorous, and leisurely in spirit. On this pair of works, his reputation will solidly rest. (p. 271)

> *John A. Meixner, in his* Ford Madox Ford's
> Novels: A Critical Study *(© 1962, University of Minnesota), University of Minnesota
> Press, Minneapolis, 1962.*

Most writers focus on individuals at the expense of society or on society at the expense of individuals, or, at best, put their characters on the periphery of either the one or the other. Few have been able to embrace both social reality and personal sensibility, yet one needs the other to give it meaning.

One of the few writers who has, to my mind, been successful in embracing both is Ford Madox Ford. The book: *Parade's End.* Looking at these four volumes as one unit, I think it is possible to discern two interrelated but nevertheless separate patterns, the world of social experience (external reality) and the world of personal sensibility (internal reality), and to show that these patterns culminate in two distinct climaxes. (p. 26)

If *Parade's End* is first an allegory of social decay, the climax must fall on *The Last Post,* and to narrow it down still further, on the felling of the Groby Great Tree. Tietjens' England is freed from the beloved but archaic tradition which has been strangling him. Sylvia, the world of appearances, is now willing to divorce. The book becomes a portrayal of social reality.

But while Ford is a social realist, he is also a profound psychologist and a master of psychological realism. Looking at *Parade's End* from this viewpoint (especially in the first three volumes), it is Tietjens the man, the specific individual man, who engages our attention. (p. 31)

Ford is a writer who would never let a given scene dominate, but subordinated all his scenes to the creation of one "effect." This may be a disturbing technique to those of us who want dramatic explosions to erupt from the page, but it is certainly one way of going about the business. (p. 36)

What is noteworthy about Ford's achievement is that he has been able to represent the individual and society from both within and without. The earlier novelists represented individuals *in* society as a matter of course. By the time Ford began to write *Parade's End,* the individual had become alienated from the old social security to such an extent that Ford was forced to try to bridge a chasm grown so deep and wide that few novelists could even see from one side to the other. . . . He had, that is, to show an individual coming to grips with the new dichotomy of private man and social man, and at the same time to show how the social and private worlds relate. It is a remarkable accomplishment that Ford was able to resolve this complex task. (p. 37)

Sensibility and experience are combined since he embraces social reality as well as the individual consciousness. In both realms he has tried to separate the fraudulent or archaic from the real, and the recognition of these separations makes for two distinct climaxes.

In *Parade's End,* Ford does not focus on individuals at the expense of society nor on society at the expense of individuals. He does not stay on the periphery of contemporary life, nor does he stay on the periphery of the individual consciousness. He penetrates both. In so doing, his perception and his reaction to it are important to us because the questions which he poses are not yet resolved. (p. 38)

> *Marlene Griffith, "A Double Reading of 'Parade's End',"* in Modern Fiction Studies: Ford Madox Ford Number *(copyright © 1963, by Purdue Research Foundation, West Lafayette, Indiana, U.S.A.), Spring, 1963, pp. 25-38.*

The Good Soldier is a novel which explores in a masterful style the interpersonal relationships of four people. It is the magic of the novel that we understand how thoroughly each couple's existence penetrates the other's during the nine years encompassed by the novel. (p. 50)

The narrator does not analyze the events of his life; he dramatizes them. His dramatization, the novel, fails as a heuristic device because he has no insight or understanding. He is convinced that there must be an order to life, and he is frightened when it is not apparent: "And there is nothing to guide us. And if everything is so nebulous about a matter so elementary as the morals of sex, what is there to guide us in the more subtle morality of all other personal contacts, associations, and activities? Or are we meant to act

on impulse alone? It is all a darkness." . . . He constructs a pattern out of events as he remembers them, but his construction, so notoriously coincidental, can never reveal the principles and ordered quality of habitual behavior he assumes to be essential for an ordered world. (p. 59)

There are two reasons why [Dowell] is unable to view Edward objectively: his primarily sexual identification with Edward and his view of Ashburnham as a member of the upper class, a "quite good" person whose behavior need not be censored. Edward, however, does censor his own behavior, and when he finds it intolerable, he kills himself.

Unlike Edward, the narrator does not understand his own character or his place in the events. Since he identifies with Edward, he attempts to explain his own place in the order of things by constructing situations around Ashburnham and fitting himself in. However, his constructions are unreal, and at the end Dowell understands nothing more about himself than he already knew but could not admit. This final irony fills the narrative of the book with a sense of futility and is what Ford might have called, "the Dowell tragedy."

We see, then, that Ford is constructing two tragedies and delineating two characters simultaneously. It is the latter tragedy which concerns Ford, for if we extend our interpretation of Dowell, we see that Ford is writing about the failure to discover meaning during a time which to him must have been one of the gloomiest periods he knew. . . . He is writing about life as he sees it: "a series of such meaningless episodes beneath the shadow of doom. . . ." (p. 60)

> *Patricia McFate and Bruce Golden, "'The Good Soldier': A Tragedy of Self-Deception,"* in Modern Fiction Studies: Ford Madox Ford Number *(copyright © 1963, by Purdue Research Foundation, West Lafayette, Indiana, U.S.A.), Spring, 1963, pp. 50-60.*

The strength of Ford Madox Ford's *The Good Soldier* may be found in Ford's style. The precision of this style is immediately discernible in Ford's metaphor. . . . Besides his great wealth of figurative devices, however, Ford relies on four other stylistic techniques: repetition of thematic elements, which creates a consistent world-view; parallelism, which suggests helpless movement toward a purposeless end and which also embodies the order that underlies apparent chaos; hypothesis, which reveals the reflective and anxious uncertainty of the narrator, John Dowell; and negation, which indicates the narrator's passive response to some of the problems that face man in contemporary society. . . . Ford's style . . . functions on two intersecting levels: on the level of form it reinforces climatic events in the story, connecting these with Ford's dominant themes and patterns; on the level of content it reveals the character of the narrator. (p. 61)

Because it dominates the point-of-view, the narrator's uncertain perspective (which depicts the chaos of human relationships) provides a valid stylistic basis for Ford's obscure labyrinthine structure. (p. 65)

> *Robert J. Ray, "Style in 'The Good Soldier',"* in Modern Fiction Studies: Ford Madox Ford Number *(copyright © 1963, by Purdue Research Foundation, West Lafay-*

ette, Indiana, U.S.A.), Spring, 1963, pp. 61-6.

[Though] reduced to its essential plot *The Good Soldier* is melodrama of a vintage mellowness, complete with the savor of multiple adultery, madness, incestuous desires, two suicides, an escape from a second-story window, the caning of an old Negro retainer, and so on, unfolded as Ford unfolds it the story somehow does not seem much like melodrama but is as queerly insistent as life itself. (p. 69)

One of the assumptions underlying all Ford's writing is the desperate need of communication and the near impossibility of its attainment. Following long periods of silence or conventional chatter the need manifests itself, if sporadically. In *The Good Soldier* each of the main characters makes at some point a confession and, like Prufrock, attempts for once to tell all. Yet, paradoxically, this attempt at communication is successful only to the extent that the person confessing is by nature usually disinclined to make confessions, is reticent, passionate, and proud. (p. 72)

Virtue, in Ford's somewhat old-fashioned view, is silent where points of honor are concerned, even when this silence may contribute to the injury of an innocent victim. . . . (pp. 72-3)

Like Lear or Hamlet, Jean-Paul Sartre, Mr. MacLeish, and Hemingway's old waiter, Dowell is haunted by nothingness. The word "nothing" keeps rising to the surface in his utterances, in part, perhaps, because it is a word with an extraordinarily wide range of contexts, pairing easily with other words to suggest at one extreme triviality ("such nothings") and standing for utter annihilation at the other. . . .

The word turns up frequently in *The Good Soldier* in nearly meaningless, conventional turns of phrase ("nothing less than," "nothing I like better than," "nothing to the point") that perhaps tend to inure us to its ultimate ontological mysteriousness as the opposite of something, the vacuum nature abhors and limbo God permits. (p. 75)

The abyss of *nada* . . . is ultimately no verbal matter, for the abyss denies all words and is, like the Godhead, ineffable, though it can be suggested when speech points to the mystery of silence, a puzzle for all, but especially for the writer who lives by words. (p. 76)

Ford's mutes seem nearer the heart of things than the wordy creatures around them, though whether the heart of things more fully partakes of heaven or of hell is . . . not always easy to say. For that matter, at the center of most of Ford's writing there is silence. . . . (pp. 76-7)

But usually in Ford's universe . . . the silence of the abyss proves to be the deeper and more real. The pleasant lyric quiet usually has something of the illusory, even the fraudulent, about it. So the quietest moments that Dowell has ever known are followed immediately by Edward's jolting all-night confession.

For the purest examples of the deeper silence of the abyss the reader must turn to Ford's writing about war, to scenes in *Parade's End* where the roar of bombardment finally registers on the amazed and outraged eardrum less as noise than as what Ford calls, beautifully, "a rushing silence". . . . (p. 77)

In *The Good Soldier*, however, there is no rushing silence.

Nancy's awful stillness is seen entirely from the outside—and, besides, it is not complete. Ford does not take us into the abyss; we are brought to the edge, invited to look in, and then are permitted to withdraw. This incompleteness is in keeping with the general air of stasis, and is an aspect of the story's sadness. (pp. 77-8)

Ambrose Gordon, Jr., "At the Edge of Silence: 'The Good Soldier' as 'War Novel'," in Modern Fiction Studies: Ford Madox Ford Number *(copyright © 1963, by Purdue Research Foundation, West Lafayette, Indiana, U.S.A.), Spring, 1963, pp. 67-78.*

[There] are more than nineteen . . . passages in *The Good Soldier* that call attention to [the] deification of a loved one by the romantic lover. And the purpose in both *Madame Bovary* and *The Good Soldier* seems clearly the same: to suggest that the principal source of the chaos in the lives of these two suicides is romantic love and the confusion of human passion with divine worship that such love encourages. For while the reward of devotion to God may be heaven, the penalty of a comparable devotion to the merely human is hell. (pp. 81-2)

Although Flaubert, compared to Ford, puts little emphasis on the origin of romantic love in the courtly love tradition of Provence, both labor the point that the immediate source for their lovers is romantic or sentimental literature. (p. 82)

The inescapable similarity between Flaubert's emphasis upon the confusion of "the two forms of love: earthly and mystical" in romantic love, as well as his concern to show its immediate origin in romantic or sentimental literature, and that which Ford gives to these two ideas suggests not only influence but also a need to revise our view of Edward Ashburnham. . . . [Too] many critics . . . have simply failed to consider the character of Edward Ashburnham from a sufficiently objective point of view. He is the direct cause of the deaths of two women, the madness of a third, and the intense unhappiness of his wife. He cuckolds his fellow officers and his best friend. Yet he is without remorse. And he dies the death of the supreme sentimentalist: suicide because of frustrated love.

Is this man simply "passionate, headstrong, and too-truthful"? Impossible! He is Emma Bovary—upperclass, English, male version. And if Flaubert could say of Emma, "*C'est moi*," so too with more truthfulness could the romantic Ford Madox Hueffer say of Edward, "*C'est moi*." (p. 84)

Ford not only employs Flaubert's principal symbols of romance in the sea and the color blue but even gives them the same ironic reversal in significance as a means of pointing to romantic illusion as the chief cause of the tragedy Edward and the other romantics come to. (p. 85)

My own conclusion . . . is that Ford, at forty, set himself the same task that Flaubert did: the exorcism of his own romanticism. And while Flaubert was perhaps too successful, Ford, happily, failed. . . . Ford Madox Hueffer's own commitment to romantic love and to his illusion of himself as an English country gentleman would not allow him to bring off the exposure, manifestly planned, of Edward Ashburnham as a monster, comparable in every way except in station and sex to Emma Bovary. Instead, he deserts his aim and confesses to a wistful devotion to his villain. And it is this desertion . . . that accounts for the extreme divergence of interpretation which has characterized recent criticism of this novel. (p. 92)

> *James Trammell Cox, "The Finest French Novel in the English Language," in* Modern Fiction Studies: Ford Madox Ford Number *(copyright © 1963 by Purdue Research Foundation, West Lafayette, Indiana, U.S.A.), Spring, 1963, pp. 79-93.*

The function of Dowell as narrator [of *The Good Soldier*] is . . . very much an open question. I think one of the difficulties is that critics have not yet seen that Dowell really has two voices. One voice is self-assured and dogmatic. . . . The other voice is hesitant and bewildered: "I don't know. And there is nothing to guide us. . . . It is all darkness." . . . Dowell, in other words, speaks in both a conclusive and an inconclusive way. He at one moment seems to have fitted the pieces together, while at the next the puzzle is still unfinished.

In his book on Henry James, Ford discusses two aspects of the novel form. He maintains that a novel should have a social dimension; he also states that the impressionistic novel is the highest form of narration. In order to understand *The Good Soldier*, I think that it is necessary to see that Dowell is both a dogmatic and an impressionistic narrator. He speaks to the reader out of two intelligences: he knowingly sets his story in a social and political context, and then he enigmatically undercuts the general import of his conclusions, reducing them to conjecture. (p. 220)

Dowell is an essentially honest and reliable commentator, but . . . his final sense of meaninglessness is unjustified. Dowell has given the reader enough information for the story to make sense. Rather than say that Dowell knows more than he tells, I think that it is more correct to say, paradoxically, that Dowell tells more than he knows. While events in *The Good Soldier* seem to happen in a gratuitous and chaotic way, there is really a basis for explanation. Ford's world is not meaningless, but appears so only because Dowell is unable to perceive its essential nature, despite the fact that Dowell has given the reader the key to the tragedy. . . . Reason seems to take Dowell part of the way toward understanding and then to break down, leaving elements that appear inexplicable and inscrutable—absurd, to use a word that is in fashion today. (pp. 220-21)

[In Camus's *L'Etranger*], as in Conrad's *Chance*, the idea of gratuity and the absurd is something that the reader has to accept (it is Camus's and Conrad's donnée, one of the assumptions of the novel to be taken as a metaphysical fact), and it is not a matter of characterization.

Ford does not demand such an act of faith or suspension of belief in *The Good Soldier*. Absurdity is not a metaphysical fact but a state of mind. Characters are not victims of cosmic forces, but victims of human motives—motives not fully understood, leading to acts that bewilder, or at least bewilder and confuse John Dowell. (p. 223)

Dowell . . . sees in double focus and speaks with two voices. One voice is that of Ford himself, and this tells the reader the whole story, as Ford wanted it told, with characters in social perspective. The other voice is that of modern man, and this speaks impressionistically and in terms of dead-ended conclusions because it is on the unknowing side of history. . . . Ford seems to be saying that while the

world may appear to be absurd from Dowell's vantage point, in reality it is not. . . . If Dowell were only to listen to himself, his story would make sense. The facts are there: Dowell, for thematic reasons, just cannot grasp them in any conclusive way. As a result, in *The Good Soldier*, Ford Madox Ford, concerned with one of the major problems for the modern reader, suggests in human terms the origin of absurdity. (pp. 230-31)

> *Richard Lehan, "Ford Madox Ford and the Absurd: 'The Good Soldier'," in* Texas Studies in Literature and Language *(copyright © 1963 by the University of Texas Press), Summer, 1963, pp. 219-31.*

To some of his readers, Ford Madox Ford has seemed one of the more superficial of the late Victorian and Edwardian novelists. He wrote a significant First World War tetralogy, and his 1915 novel, *The Good Soldier,* is considered a masterpiece of novelistic technique. His output was enormous . . . but much of his writing was hack work. And then he was one of those personages—delightful in conversation but dubious in print—who like to spin yarns without regard for fact. This is harmless enough and even beguiling so long as actual persons are not involved. H. G. Wells described this trait in Ford as "a copious carelessness of reminiscence." A heavy, sprawling, walrusy sort of man, generous and easygoing, he had the look of indolence in spite of his industry; for all his splendid definitions of the artist's job, and his legendary collaboration with Joseph Conrad, he did not make an artist's exacting demands of himself. . . .

Ford certainly overwrote. He was a chivalrous man with codes and gallantries and he had wives and mistresses and children to provide for. . . . He would have liked to be a gentleman farmer; and he gardened much in Provence, where he took life as it came, enjoyed the wine and the food, and wrote his thousand words a day. Yet in this continual grind he did produce his four volumes of the Tietjens series. (p. 23)

Ford said that it was "the lonely buffaloes ploughing solitary furrows who produce the great truths of art." He had watched Conrad and he had known Henry James. Though he believed in the truths of art, he had no wish to be a lonely buffalo. . . .

During the Twenties, Ford came often to New York, where he was lionized, his books sold, and he ground out stuff for the magazines. One of the earliest "writers in residence"—at Olivet—he gave himself earnestly to his students, although American education appalled him. He died just before the new war, which he would have hated, for total war had nothing to do with chivalry and gallantry. (p. 24)

> *Leon Edel, "A Good Soldier Himself," in* Saturday Review *(copyright © 1965 by Saturday Review, Inc.; reprinted with permission), September 4, 1965, pp. 23-4.*

[Beside] *Parade's End* a novel like *A Passage to India* seems an attempt to make a major book out of minor material, *Jude the Obscure* seems an interesting muddle, *l'Education sentimentale*—which Ford himself loved so much—becomes a tempest in a teapot, even a fully accepted classic like *Ulysses* seems to have been written in a laboratory. I am not saying these judgments are correct, only that they are not radically out of the question. Of the English fiction of the last hundred years, only Lawrence's three great novels seem clearly superior to Ford's; there a writer is doing all Ford can do in the way of showing how life's ways are history's ways, and something else and something more as well.

But even Lawrence cannot efface Ford. Rereading *Parade's End* is a practically unique reminder of a novelist's resources when he is both superbly intelligent and saturated with the lives he is imagining. Ford's softness, his great willingness to identify with Tietjens and especially with Tietjens' unwillingness to try to save himself, which is the work's one glaring defect, is for one who knows Ford's life an evocation of life's possibilities for art, though it is a real defect nonetheless. But give Ford that, concede him this large single weakness, and he can do anything, almost. Few moments even in Lawrence are more responsive to the relation of landscape to human consciousness than Tietjens' watching the skylarks over the trenches; no one except Tolstoi or Chekhov can make the beastly normal as winning as Ford makes Valentine Wannop, as she lives through and then remembers in scene after different scene how much she wanted Christopher to kiss her that night in the horse trap; if Ford was limited as a writer about war because he knew very little about actual fighting in the trenches, he is unerringly good in his descriptions of the muddle of war and its inevitable toll in psychic dislocation and subsequent torment. Without this book there would be many things we simply would not know. (pp. 517-18)

> *Roger Sale, "The Second Saddest Story," in* The Hudson Review *(copyright © 1971 by The Hudson Review, Inc.; reprinted by permission), Vol. XXIV, No. 3, Autumn, 1971, pp. 511-18.*

The theme [of Ford's Tietjens novels] is recurrent: the defeats of decency, the great sadness that comes of honor. (p. 97)

[Two episodes in "Some Do Not"] are a marvel of tact and craftsmanship. The peregrination in the mist is probably the nearest thing we have in English literature to Turgenev, whom Ford Madox Ford considered the greatest of modern masters. In the empty house, before the rockets go up, Valentine Wannop holds Tietjens' sanity in her grasp, gathering the torn threads one by one, holding off the crazy ghosts. How many readers, today, know either scene? Who but the occasional academic could validate the claim that the influence of Ford Madox Ford on twentieth-century English and American letters was second only to that of Pound?

In good measure the fault lies with Ford himself, and he knew it. (pp. 97-8)

In his two-volume anthology of Ford, issued in 1962, Graham Greene included both "The Good Soldier"—"perhaps one of the finest novels of our century"—and the whole of Ford's historical trilogy, "The Fifth Queen," on Henry VIII, Thomas Cromwell, and Catherine Howard. Greene characterizes it as "a magnificent bravura piece" and asks whether any novel has ever been more cunning in its scenario of light and shadows. One can reread "Ladies Whose Bright Eyes" . . . and "The Marsden Case" . . . with profit and a constant sense of art. "Romance," which Ford wrote in intimate, stormy collaboration with Joseph Conrad, remains a fascinating and oddly underrated novel. Often Ford's theoretical and practical criticism of English

fiction has a shrewder, more technical incisiveness than that of Henry James. (pp. 98-9)

Only "The Good Soldier" and some sections of the Tietjens saga really stand up to time. Beside John Cowper Powys' "Owen Glendower," with its Shakespearean energy of historical re-invention, "The Fifth Queen" seems mannered. Ford's gifts were only sporadically at the level of his intelligence. . . . He was so good a craftsman that books came too easily, that the material did not adequately resist the immediate professional commitment. (p. 99)

[Ford's] aesthetic creed and the ambiguous obsession with gentility could not mesh fully. They had meshed in Turgenev's "A Sportsman's Sketches," which Ford hailed as the supreme instance of the novelist's art. But the Russian condition was different, and Turgenev's aristocracy a natural and scarcely examined attribute. Attempting to yoke together his divided impulses, Ford Madox Ford produced fiction nearly all of which has a covert, uncertain center. It was only when he made this muddle the actual topic of his story, in the affairs of Tietjens and of Captain and Mrs. Ashburnham, in "The Good Soldier," that Ford could turn out coherent, mature novels. Only then was he "in harmony with [his] own soul."

Thus what counts is Ford's role as witness, middleman, and impresario. We owe to him penetrating accounts of James and Conrad at work. He saw D. H. Lawrence and Hemingway at close quarters when they were as yet untried. Ford was an editor of genius. He published Conrad, W. H. Hudson, Thomas Hardy, and a score of younger writers in the prewar *English Review*. After the war, he edited the *transatlantic review* in Paris, and gave vital opportunities to Gertrude Stein, Joyce, E. E. Cummings, and Hemingway. Ford's activities as discoverer and organizer of talent were tireless. He found buyers for indigent artists. He created circles of friends around poets, such as William Carlos Williams, whom he regarded as insufficiently honored or well known. At one end, Ford's life touched the world of Carlyle and Swinburne; at the other, it reached generously into the careers of Henry Miller, Marianne Moore, and Allen Tate. It is difficult to separate his animating presence from the essential tone of modern English and American literature. (pp. 100-01)

> *George Steiner, "Gent," in* The New Yorker *(© 1972 by The New Yorker Magazine, Inc.), February 12, 1972, pp. 97-102.*

"For factual exactitudes I have never had much use," wrote Ford Madox Ford in the epistle prefatory to *Portraits from Life*. . . . That must have been one of the last of his many asseverations to the same effect. . . . [For] Ford subjectivity was truth. . . . He set down what ought to have been, and this then represented the reality. (p. 3)

Is the truth of "reality" no different from that of "imagination"? Granted that all vivid impressions have a truth for the mind which conceives them, is this where we will agree that truth shall be lodged and established—in the mind only? The answer, of course, is that the question is an epistemological one, answered in one way by Realists, who distinguish between subjective and objective truth, and in another way by Idealists, who (more or less) do not. For the mass of mankind, there is, in theory if not in practice, a distinction which leads to calling the violator of it—a liar.

Certainly there are different sorts of liars, something that may redeem Ford from the baser charge. A careless critic once observed that Ford was, after all, only the second biggest (nonpolitical) liar of his time, the biggest being Frank Harris. That was absurd. Harris was an unprincipled liar; Ford the opposite, a liar on principle. Ford's intention was to get at the truth *au fond,* the meaning hidden under appearances. He professed nothing else, though his habit of indulging in "impressionism" even while in the act of explaining a detected "inaccuracy" fortified the stiff-necked suspicions of the enemy. (p. 5)

Ford's whole life was a web of paradoxes. He had to be ironic to be wholly serious. His childhood upbringing had established the necessity of seriousness: the irony was his own addition, or palliative, a mode of defense. Later he was to be attracted to the problem of psychological identity in dealing with the various fictional characters through whose embroilments with fate he inwardly refined his own. But to start with, almost in infancy, he learned to be obsessed with scruple and sin. From this grew his habit of weighing the conscience; of depicting it racked with the temptations of fraud and with the social penalties of virtue (the children of darkness being wiser in their generation than the children of light); and of honoring the lie courteous, the lie merciful, and as well the lie *penetrant* by which the world's hypocrisy is breached. Thus he came to irony. The truth never swimming on the surface of life, he was obliged to fish for it with ironic misrepresentations. These in turn became exaggerative . . ., that is to say comic, by way of drawing attention to the irony and in a sense apologizing for it, or perhaps legitimizing it by recognition.

Had Ford been the only artist of his time who dealt in *duplicities* (if the word may be employed in a laundered sense), it would seem uncannily coincidental that he should have been both Hueffer and Ford—and then, being Ford, be Ford *doubly.* But it was an age of double vision—and double speech. . . . To hunt [Ford's change of name] into symbol country would be ridiculous—and yet . . . he *was* fascinated with doubled characters, *doppelgänger,* the lot. It is a subject which wisdom bids one shun. (p. 8)

Ford, who was a good poet sometimes, was once or twice for a protracted time a great novelist. Yet he has been refused his fame, and it is no accident at all; some of his bad luck was accidental, but his failure to catch on was not. To be blunt, he was the victim of his character, which made him "second-guess" everything; the fact that his artistic motives were superbly decent and his judgments of literature, men, and nations angelically pure was insufficient to gain him pardon from a world whose opinions, and indeed very way of seeing and reflecting, he obstinately flouted. The decency and purity themselves became an outrage. Not that Ford puffed himself morally—but he did so critically. His erotic energy, of course, and his indiscreet exercise of it damaged both his moral and his critical reputation. And then there were the lies. He insisted on making life work like art, on transforming chronicle into parable. But he simulated: he did not dissemble. Ford reminds one of Giordano Bruno in his confidence that truth is found in its antithesis. While only a superior form of irony, such discernment is unsettling to the multitudes. (p. 44)

Grover Smith, in his Ford Madox Ford *(Co-*

lumbia Essays on Modern Writers Pamphlet No. 63; copyright © 1972 Columbia University Press; reprinted by permission of the publisher), Columbia University Press, 1972.

American readers and writers—and not only academics— are keenly interested in technical considerations, whereas the British tend to find these boring and, if pushed too hard, rather an embarrassment. Hence the unending American interest in Joyce—the supreme literary technician of all time—a figure whom many English readers find too strong in gimmicks and too weak in moral seriousness. Ford, too, is an author who offers enormous technical interest to the student of modern fiction. The way the first-person narrative works in *The Good Soldier,* where the true meaning of events has to be construed from the duped and unreliable consciousness of the story-teller John Dowell, is one example of this. Another is Ford's virtuoso use of the timeshift in parts of *Parade's End,* a technique which Ford worked out in collaboration with Conrad but which, if anything, he used more adroitly than Conrad. These are questions which interest American readers more strongly than English ones.

But the American interest in Ford is far from simply academic, and involves more than a sympathetic sharing of his passionate concern with form and method in fiction. During his years in America he aroused a genuine personal devotion in a number of his fellow-writers, including poets like William Carlos Williams and Allen Tate, and this has helped to keep alive the memory of his work there. (pp. 141-42)

The Americans have, [with some exceptions,] regarded their expatriates with tolerance. . . . The British, however, have a habit of withdrawing favour from writers who decide to live elsewhere, and this I think, is one reason why Ford's reputation slumped so disastrously in the twenties and thirties. (p. 143)

In his biography [of Ford, Frank MacShane] provides some plausible clues to the British rejection of Ford. When Ford edited the *English Review* his critical standards were so high that he offended some of the most influential reviewers and moulders of opinion by refusing to print their work. Subsequently, Mr MacShane suggests, they took their revenge on Ford by refusing to countenance him as a serious writer. Knowing the way metropolitan literary life works, it does not seem an extravagant notion. Ford was certainly not helped by his infallible capacity for making a mess of his private life—and often a sadly public mess. . . . (pp. 143-44)

[Ford's] troubles were most marked during the First World War, as his letters show; they were later transmuted into the tribulations of Christopher Tietjens. . . . Ford was a generous man and a dedicated lover of the arts and encourager of the young. But he was also a snob and something of a braggart, or as we might say nowadays, a 'role-player.' . . . There may well have been something about Ford's personality that invited rebuff and irritation; at all events, like Falstaff, he was rejected. This question is not of merely biographical interest: it is desirable to know something about the context in which a writer's work was first read— or not read—if we are to grasp all its aspects. . . . (p. 144)

Tietjens is used by Ford as the focus for a rather romantic portrayal of the crack-up of traditional English aristocratic values, which works by suggestion and implication rather than by direct realism. Americans were accustomed to imagining English society in this heightened and selective way, whereas English readers might find it a distorted picture. (p. 145)

In general, Ford's exotic conception of English life, and his highly conscious artistry, mean that he still hasn't properly 'taken' with English readers. I think that before long his peculiar genius will be more widely recognised, though I doubt if he will ever be really popular in England. . . . It might even be a useful strategy for us to read Ford as if he were, after all, an American novelist of a rather special kind. (p. 146)

> *Bernard Bergonzi, "The Reputation of Ford Madox Ford" (1973), in his* The Turn of a Century: Essays on Victorian and Modern English Literature (© *Bernard Bergonzi 1973; reprinted in the U.S. by permission of Harper & Row, Publishers, Inc., Barnes & Noble Import Division, and in Canada by permission of A. D. Peters & Co.), Barnes & Noble, 1973, pp. 139-46.*

Books written far away and long ago in quite different cultures with different goods and goals in life, about people utterly unlike ourselves, may yet remain utterly convincing—*The Tale of Genji, The Satyricon, Les Liaisons dangereuses, Burnt Njal,* remain true to our understanding of the ways of man to man the more experienced we grow. Of only a few novels in the twentieth century is this true. Ford Madox Ford's *Parade's End* is one of those books.

This is not a rash statement. Most important contemporary critics who have read it agree that it is the most mystifyingly under-appreciated novel of modern times. (p. 124)

Graham Greene once said of *Parade's End* that it was the only adult novel dealing with the sexual life that has been written in English. This is a startling superlative, but it may well be true. Certainly the book has a scope and depth, a power and complexity quite unlike anything in modern fiction, and still more unusual, it is about mature people in grown-up situations, written by a thoroughly adult man.

Like his contemporaries, D. H. Lawrence and H. G. Wells, Ford's best novels are all concerned with the struggle to achieve, and ultimately the tragic failure of what before them had been called the sacrament of marriage. Before *Parade's End* Ford's *The Good Soldier* was probably the best of all the novels on this subject which so tortured the Edwardians, in literature and in life. Besides being a much larger-minded work, *Parade's End* is certainly the best "anti-war" novel provoked by the First World War in any language. The reason is that the two tragedies are presented as one double aspect, microcosm and macrocosm, of a world ill. Ford builds his cast of English people at war like Dante built his tiers of eschatology, and reveals the war as a gigantic, proliferating hell of the love lost—known to itself as Western European Culture. (pp. 126-27)

The complex web of shifting time, the multiple aspects of each person, the interweaving and transmutation of motives, all these appear in the novels Ford wrote with Joseph Conrad, but here, where he is on his own, Ford's talent for once seems to have been fully liberated, to go to its utmost limits.

The result is a little as though *Burnt Njal* had been rewritten by the author of *Les Liaisons dangereuses.* There is the same deadly impetus, the inertia of doom, riding on hate, that drives through the greatest of the sagas. There is the same tireless weaving and re-weaving of the tiniest threads of the consequences of grasping and malevolence, the chittering of the looms of corruption, that sickens the heart in *Les Liaisons dangereuses.* The reader of either novel, or the saga, emerges wrung dry. The difference in Ford's book is compassion. The poetry is in the pity, as Wilfred Owen said of the same war. (p. 127)

> *Kenneth Rexroth, "Ford Madox Ford's 'Parade's End'," in his* The Elastic Retort: Essays in Literature and Ideas *(copyright © 1973 by Kenneth Rexroth; used by permission of The Seabury Press), Seabury, 1973, pp. 124-27.*

Ford's well-known insistence that the right way to start a novel is with a strong opening impression has been subjected to a great deal of criticism. Yet no criticism could be stronger than what is dramatized in *The Good Soldier.* The reader meets a destroyed narrator. Dowell has depended wholly on first impressions, has, as the "good people" do, taken things for granted. The novel measures the enormity of his error. And the technique is decidedly more than impressionistic. It is, rather, a process of vision and revision, impression and query, probing and guessing. . . . The irony, cynicism, and melodrama become credible and moving through our reconstruction. . . . As the book progresses, we must call into question our notion of irony, of melodrama. We are forced to re-evaluate those earlier scenes, reconsider our judgment of Dowell. Our task, in fact, mirrors the education and reversals that Dowell himself has undergone. (pp. 64-6)

We are far from Balzac and Dickens. Education in *Père Goriot* and *Great Expectations* consists basically in insight, penetration of the societal codes in favor of human bonds. Ford too dramatizes insight, but it is a devastating insight, one that erodes and paralyzes more the more one sees. Dowell stated at the outset, in only seemingly exaggerated terms, that "it is not unusual in human beings who have witnessed the sack of a city or the falling to pieces of a people to desire to set down what they have witnessed for the benefit of unknown heirs or of generations infinitely remote." . . . It is for the reader to make more of it than Dowell does. (pp. 67-8)

Perhaps it is hard, from the vantage point of the latter twentieth century, to see *The Good Soldier* as other than ironic; the pieties of Dowell and Edward and Leonora risk seeming so prehistoric as to be preposterous. But Ford may have thought otherwise; although his book is a scathing critique of conventions, it is also a poignant recognition of the fact that conventions are real: Edward *is* his sentimentalism; Dowell *is* his gullibility; Leonora *is* her Catholic upbringing. The pathos of *The Good Soldier* lies in the fact that our blindness and our conventions are part of our flesh. (p. 68)

[However], the vision is controlled. . . . Dowell places the burden of interpretation on the reader, but Ford has arranged the presentation with a sure hand. (p. 69)

Arnold L. Weinstein, in his Vision and Response in Modern Fiction *(copyright © 1974 by Cornell University; used by permission of Cornell University Press), Cornell University Press, 1974.*

The *Fifth Queen* trilogy inaugurates a twentieth-century theme—Shaw's in *Saint Joan,* Eliot's in the Canterbury play and *The Cocktail Party,* Graham Greene's in *The Power and the Glory* and *A Burnt-Out Case*—of the making of a saint. . . . (pp. 80-1)

Ford is at work on a problem [here] he will never let go: whether it is possible to use bad means to a good end. Conrad and he had treated this issue in *The Inheritors* and found every established generation irremediably tied in bad means and every inheriting generation contaminated from the start. Conrad had returned to the issue for himself in *Nostromo* and had concluded . . . that it could not be done —except for a brief and memorable moment, it could not be done. Touch pitch, and you are defiled. Katharine, idealist, refuses to touch pitch. . . . Her strenuous blindness is fatal to her, but is the secret of her call on the reader, who follows her passion and fights for her through every page. This is how the legend of a hero or a saint functions when it takes the form of the historical novel.

Even in the third volume of the trilogy, where we are not brought quite so intimately into contact with Katharine as we were in the earlier books, the same operation prevails. Watching the slow, perhaps slightly stagey, drawing together of the combination against her, following the mad Culpepper as he rushes from Edinburgh to tumble into and spring the trap, we recognize the ignobility of men's behavior and hate and oppose it. Moreover—and this is the special capability of the art that adopts history—we oppose history. The fate of the characters is already familiar. But the author is handling his characters so that our hopes are antithetical to our knowledge of their fate. Like Stephen Dedalus we cry out that history is a nightmare from which we are trying to awake. And we fight against our own ignobility. For we notice our virtue, our idealism, our heroism as readers, and we are bound to contrast the ardour with the painful knowledge that if we had lived in Katharine's time we should have been among those who damaged her or rejoiced in her fall. . . . Ford's Tudor trilogy is written to move us to exert our will against history, against ourselves who are this moment making history. (pp. 82-3)

Herbert Howarth, in Journal of Modern Literature *(© Temple University 1976), February, 1976.*

John Galsworthy

1867-1933

English novelist, dramatist, and short story writer. Born to wealth, Galsworthy prepared to pursue a career in law. However, on a journey by ship to the Far East he met Joseph Conrad, with whom he formed a close friendship and who influenced Galsworthy to become a writer. Galsworthy is noted for his painstakingly thorough depictions of the society of his era. His early novels, not remarkably successful, were written under the pen name of John Sinjohn and show the influence of Turgenev. He then set himself the task of chronicling the spirit of his age and of exposing its evils. This was accomplished most notably in *The Forsyte Saga*, a combination of three trilogies written between 1906 and 1928. Galsworthy was considered a literary giant in the 1920s and was offered a knighthood for his literary achievements, an offer he refused. He did accept the Order of Merit in 1929 and he received the Nobel Prize for Literature in 1932. In his plays Galsworthy dramatized social and ethical problems but was inclined to be an intellectual, rather than a passionate, reformer. Since much of his contemporary acclaim rested on the belief that he was a sociological writer, he was later dismissed as an out-of-date historian. The centenary of his birth brought a television serial re-creation of *The Forsyte Saga*, which gained new popularity for him in Great Britain and the United States.

PRINCIPAL WORKS

From the Four Winds [*as John Sinjohn*] (short stories) 1897
Jocelyn [*as John Sinjohn*] (novel) 1898
Villa Rubein [*as John Sinjohn*] (novel) 1900
A Man of Devon [*as John Sinjohn*] (short stories) 1901
The Island Pharisees (novel) 1904
The Man of Property (novel) 1906
The Silver Box (drama) 1906
The Country House (novel) 1907
A Commentary (essays) 1908
Fraternity (novel) 1909
Strife (drama) 1909
Justice (drama) 1910
A Motley (essays) 1910
The Patrician (novel) 1911
The Inn of Tranquility: Studies and Essays (essays) 1912
The Pigeon (drama) 1912
The Dark Flower (novel) 1913

The Fugitive (drama) 1913
The Freelands (novel) 1915
The Little Man, and Other Satires (essays) 1915
A Sheaf (essays) 1916
Beyond (novel) 1917
Five Tales (short stories) 1918
Another Sheaf (essays) 1919
The Burning Spear (essay) 1919
Saint's Progress (novel) 1919
In Chancery (novel) 1920
The Skin Game (drama) 1920
Tatterdemalion (short stories) 1920
To Let (novel) 1921
The Forsyte Saga (novel) 1922
Loyalties (drama) 1922
Captures (short stories) 1923
Old English (drama) 1924
The White Monkey (novel) 1924
Caravan: The Assembled Tales of John Galsworthy (short stories) 1925
Escape (drama) 1926
The Silver Spoon (novel) 1926
Castles in Spain (essays) 1927
Swan Song (novel) 1928
A Modern Comedy (novel) 1929
On Forsyte 'Change (short stories) 1930
Soames and the Flag (short stories) 1930
Maid in Waiting (novel) 1931
Candelabra, Selected Essays and Addresses (essays) 1932
Flowering Wilderness (novel) 1932
Over the River (novel) 1933
End of the Chapter (novel) 1934

In accordance with my habit of re-reading books which have uncommonly interested me on first perusal, I have recently read again "The Man of Property." Well, it stands the test. It is certainly the most perfect of Mr. Galsworthy's novels up to now [1910]. Except for the confused impression caused by the too rapid presentation of all the numerous members of the Forsyte family at the opening, it has practically no faults. In construction it is unlike any other novel that I know, but that is not to say it has no constructive design—as some critics have said. It is merely to say that it is original. There are no weak parts in the book, no places where the author has stopped to take his breath and wipe his brow. The tension is never relaxed. This is one of the two qualities without which a novel cannot be first-class and great. The other is the quality of sound, harmonious design. Both qualities are exceedingly rare, and I do not know which is the rarer. In the actual material of the book, the finest quality is its extraordinary passionate cruelty towards the oppressors as distinguished from the oppressed. That oppressors should be treated with less sympathy than oppressed is contrary to my own notion of the ethics of creative art, but the result in Mr. Galsworthy's work is something very pleasing. Since "The Man of Property," the idea that the creator of the universe, or the Original Will, or whatever you like to call it or him, made a grotesque fundamental mistake in the conception of our particular planet has apparently gained much ground in Mr. Galsworthy's mind. I hope that this ground may slowly be recovered by the opposite idea. Anyhow, the Forsyte is universal. We are all Forsytes, . . . and this incontrovertible statement implies inevitably that Mr. Galsworthy is a writer of the highest rank. I re-read "The Man of Property" immediately after re-reading Dostoievsky's "Crime and Punishment," and immediately before re-reading Björnson's "Arne." It ranks well with these European masterpieces. (pp. 215-16)

> *Arnold Bennett, "John Galsworthy" (July 14, 1910), in his* Books and Persons: Being Comments on a Past Epoch 1908-1911 *(copyright, 1917, by George H. Doran Company; reprinted by permission of Doubleday and Co., Inc.), Doran, 1917, pp. 214-16.*

[In "In Chancery"], which is a continuation of the Forsyte Saga, Mr. John Galsworthy gives the impression of being in his real right element. There is a peculiar note, a mixture of confidence and hospitality, struck in the first chapter, which seems to come from the happy author warming himself at a familiar hearth. Here, in the very bosom of the Forsyte family, if any man is at home, he is that man. Its ramifications have no terrors for him; on the contrary, the quick, searching, backward glance he takes before setting out upon this book is yet long enough to be a kind of basking which extends to the cousin furthest removed. (pp. 316-17)

"In Chancery" is less solid [than "The Man of Property"] —the shell-pink azaleas escape the control of Soames' conservatory and flower a trifle too freely, as they are also a trifle too shell-pink; the tone is softer. It is not because the author is regarding his subject from another angle, but because all that remains from the deep vein of irony in "The Man of Property" is a faint ironic tinge. In "The Man of Property" what the author made us feel the Forsyte family lacked was imagination; in this new novel we feel it still, but we are not at all certain the author intends us to. . . . It is a very great gift for an author to be able to project himself into the hearts and minds of his characters—but more is needed to make a great creative artist; he must be able, with equal power, to withdraw, to survey what is happening —and from an eminence. But Mr. Galsworthy is so deeply engaged, immersed and engrossed in the Forsyte family that he loses this freedom. . . . Hence we have a brilliant display of analysis and dissection, but without any 'mys-

tery,' any unplumbed depth to feed our imagination upon. The Forsyte men are so completely life-size, so bound within the crowns of their hats and the soles of their shoes, that they are almost something less than men. We do not doubt for a moment that it has been the aim of the author to appeal to the imagination; but so strong is the imposition of his mind that the appeal stops short at the senses. . . . Let us examine for a moment the figure of Soames Forsyte, who is the hero of "In Chancery." . . . He is flesh and blood with a strong dash of clay—long before he is a tormented man; and flesh and blood and clay he remains after the torment is on him. But there never comes that moment when the character is more than himself, so that we feel at the end that what should have happened to him never has happened. He is an appearance only—a lifelike image.

[While] 'In Chancery' is not a great novel, we would assure our readers that it is a fascinating, brilliant book. (pp. 317-19)

> *Katherine Mansfield, "Family Portraits" (1920), in her* Novels and Novelists *(copyright © 1930 by Alfred A. Knopf, Inc.; reprinted by permission of Alfred A. Knopf, Inc.), Knopf, 1930, pp. 316-21.*

Mr. Galsworthy can create people and he can write natural dialogue. "The Silver Box" is a testimony of his power to do so. But in his later plays he has not always allowed his creatures to behave in a creditable fashion, nor has he always written dialogue that exactly fits their tongues. One suspects, too, that he is losing his sense of proportion, that he is not so capable now as he was earlier in his career of distinguishing between things which are important and things which are not. He has developed an interest in trivial questions of sex and has become so absorbed in dilemmas of colliding characters that he has lost sight of the nature of his characters. He has been called a Determinist because he shows his people as the creature of circumstances, but in his later work, particularly in his play "The Fugitive," his Determinism has become wilful: he seems to have made up his mind that his characters shall become the victims of circumstances in defiance of facts and the natures with which he has created them. He deliberately ties their hands behind their backs and then exclaims: "These are the victims of adverse circumstances!" And indeed they are, but the circumstances have been artificially created by Mr. Galsworthy and not by any force that governs the universe. (pp. 128-29)

It is not in ideas that Mr. Galsworthy fails, so far as his later work is concerned—it is in execution. The idea of "The Fugitive" is a notable one. The play, which in its faults is significant of all Mr. Galsworthy's later plays, deals with the tragic failure of a sensitive woman to adjust her life to that of a dull, unimaginative man. . . . The collision is between the finely-perceptive and the totally-imperceptive, and the theme is similar, in one respect, to that of "The Doll's House," and in another to that of "The Shadow of the Glen." But the treatment of it is very inferior to the treatment of it by Ibsen and Synge. Ibsen plainly showed how impossible it was for Nora to continue to live with her husband after she had suffered her disillusionment. He showed with equal clarity how natural it was that she should marry and love her husband, and yet in the end, turn away from him. . . . [Mr. Galsworthy] has taken a longer stretch of Clare's life than Ibsen took of Nora's, but he has contrived to make it smaller than Nora's. One derives an extraordinary sense of completeness and space from "The Doll's House," but does not derive a similar sense from "The Fugitive." Ibsen gives one a sense of familiarity with his people, but Mr. Galsworthy hardly makes one more familiar with Clare Dedmond and her husband than a reader of a newspaper is with the principal parties to a divorce suit. (pp. 129-30)

Synge in his one-act play ["The Shadow of Glen"] has created the atmosphere of starved emotions far more successfully than Mr. Galsworthy has done in his four acts. (p. 131)

Most of the conflict in the Galsworthy novels springs from the reactions of the characters to [the sense of property which he discovers in mankind], and it is laboured to the point of attenuation. The temperamental differences between Soames and Irene Forsyte in "The Man of Property" are obscurely stated, and still more obscurely stated in the dramatized version of their relationship called "The Fugitive," in which Soames and Irene become George and Clare Dedmond, and Bosinney, the architect-lover, becomes Malise, the journalist-lover. . . . Soames and Irene Forsyte may not be able to say why they cannot live together, but Mr. Galsworthy must be able to do so and he must empower his readers to do so, too. . . . He is so busy endowing his people with a sense of property that he occasionally omits to endow them with a sense of humanity. If one compares the Forsyte novels, say, "In Chancery," with Mrs. Edith Wharton's latest book, "The Age of Innocence," one discovers that in each case, the theme is concerned with the institution of the family, with the tribal instinct which makes the majority of minds seek identity rather than dissimilarity. But in Mrs. Wharton's book, this tribal instinct is humanly expressed, whereas in Mr. Galsworthy's it is not. I recognize Mrs. Wharton's people as human beings, but I am sceptical about Mr. Galsworthy's people. . . . I think that Mr. Galsworthy has allowed his theory to get the better of his people, whereas Mrs. Wharton, whatever her theory may be, has kept her eye very steadfastly on human beings. (pp. 146-49)

One entertains oneself with noting how differently an experience of life presents itself to Mr. Galsworthy from the way in which it presents itself to Mr. Bernard Shaw. . . . Mr. Galsworthy sees a gaol as a place where thought is destroyed or embittered: Mr. Shaw sees it as a place where thought is provoked and clarified; and between them, a simple-minded person cannot make up his mind whether to subscribe to the funds of the Howard League for Penal Reform or to advocate penal servitude for every one in the interests of Higher Thought. (pp. 149-50)

I like "The Country House" and "Five Tales" and "To Let" better than anything else that Mr. Galsworthy has written. The human sense is more truly felt in these books than in any others that he has done. There are few figures in modern fiction so tender and beautiful as Mrs. Pendyce in "The Country House" and few figures so immensely impressive and indomitable as the old man in the story called "The Stoic" which is the first of the "Five Tales." The craftsmanship of "To Let" is superb—this novel is, perhaps, the most technically-correct book of our time—but its human value is even greater than its craftsmanship. In a very vivid fashion, Mr. Galsworthy shows the passing of a tradition and an age. He leaves Soames Forsyte in lonely

age, but he does not leave him entirely without sympathy; for this muddleheaded man, unable to win or to keep affection on any but commercial terms, contrives in the end to win the pity and almost the love of the reader who has followed his varying fortunes through their stupid career. The frustrated love of Fleur and Jon is certainly one of the tenderest things in modern fiction. Mr. Galsworthy has a love of beauty which permeates everything that he writes and reconciles his more critical readers to his dubious characterization. (pp. 150-51)

Too many of his people make impotent gestures, and it is remarkable that these important people are nearly always his most idealistic characters. Such an one is Gregory Vigil in "The Country House" who constantly clutches his forehead and tilts his face towards the sky and generally strikes attitudes of despair until one begins to feel that he is the weakest of weaklings. And it is extraordinary to observe what havoc Mr. Galsworthy, ordinarily a very fastidious writer, sometimes makes of the English language. (pp. 153-54)

It is his sincerity and his chivalry and his pity and his sense of beauty, a little too conscious, perhaps, which, much more than his powers of thought, make us read his novels and witness the performance of his plays. These qualities tend to become obsessions in him with the result that his sense of proportion and his verity are disorganized and he is led into sentimentalities, some of which, on first sight, have an impressive appearance which is not maintained after closer scrutiny. (p. 155)

There are few people who can depict the helplessness of dull men so skilfully and movingly as Mr. Galsworthy can. I doubt whether any of his contemporaries could so revealingly describe the state of mind of a man, spiritually imperceptive and puzzled by his inability to understand, as Mr. Galsworthy in his novel "In Chancery" has described Soames Forsyte after he has obtained a divorce from his first wife. The dumb animal bewilderment of this man, . . . is done with the most extraordinary penetration; and it is scenes such as this, which cause his readers all the more to marvel at his obsessions and their attendant failures.

One rises from a consideration of his work in the belief that he pities mankind, but does not love it. He is a spectator of our struggles rather than a comrade in them. (pp. 157-58)

Mr. Galsworthy can tell a story very skilfully. His technique is remarkable, as any one who has read "To Let" or seen a performance of "Loyalties" can testify; but there are too many occasions when he seems to have let go his hold on reality and to be writing out of dim memories which are growing dimmer. His characters resemble people who are hurriedly seen through a window by one who is ignorant of their identity and anxious, chiefly, to be at home. (p. 159)

St. John G. Ervine, "John Galsworthy" (originally published in a slightly different version in North American Review, *March, 1921), in his* Some Impressions of My Elders *(reprinted by permission of The Society of Authors as the literary representative of the Estate of St. John Ervine; © 1922 by St. John G. Ervine), Macmillan, 1922, pp. 113-60.*

Good manners are commonly associated with a safe disposition; a gentleman with well-creased trousers and a nice taste in cravats is not suspected of a bomb under his coat.... The public that neither reads Shaw nor understands him has a vague mental image of a flaming beard, a sardonic smile, a Jaeger shirt, and a Fenian meeting. That is the real thing.... But John Galsworthy? ... The correctness of his demeanor has endeared him to broad and wealthy bosoms. And all the while, in the laboratory of his mind, with instruments of deadly delicacy and serene precision, he has tested the political and moral pretensions of mankind and found them a blunder and a shame. He has seen legal justice to be a cruel farce, romantic love a delusion, rigid marriage an instrument of stupid torture, the crowd's charity an insult, and its windy opinions the weapons of murder and disgrace. But he has neither cried nor striven and rarely condescended to argue. He has used a pair of balances—exquisite, fragile-looking things under a crystal globe—and weighed the issues of life. And the result of his weighing is more devastating than the rioting of an army with scarlet flags.

Yet he has never forgotten that he is an artist. He has never, to use his own words, set down directly "those theories in which he himself believes," but has let "the phenomena of life and character" tell their own story and point their own moral. He has not always been able to adhere perfectly to the logic and to the rhythm of life. In *The Fugitive,* fine and right as the details are, there are also artifice and, at the end, a touch of violence. But by virtue of the inner control and patience of his mind he has been able to follow the rhythm of life oftener than any other English dramatist, and he has been able to reproduce it more richly by virtue of his supreme sensitiveness to the true quality of human speech. The wit and eloquence of Shaw spring from a different impulse and make for a different goal. Galsworthy's dialogue escapes the caging of the printed page at once. No theatre can contort it, no actor vulgarize it with the false graces of his trade. For it is thus that men speak in the eagerness of affairs or under the sting of passion. (pp. 168-70)

The Skin Game has a more timeless touch [than *The Foundations*]. It takes the tragi-comedy of all human conflict, localizes it narrowly, embodies it with the utmost concreteness, and yet exhausts its whole significance. For the staggering truth concerning all human conflict, whether between groups of men or individuals, is that each contestant is both right and wrong; that each has the subjective conviction of being wholly right; that as the conflict grows in length and bitterness each is guilty of deeds that blur his original rightness and bring him closer to the wrongness against which he fights; that hence to be victorious in any conflict is to add your adversary's unrighteousness to your own and to be defeated is to gain the only chance of saving your soul. "Who touches pitch shall be defiled" is the motto of *The Skin Game*. The pitch that defiled the Hillcrists and the Hornblowers was not in either of them but in the conflict that arose between them. Galsworthy has never derived a dramatic action from deeper sources in the nature of man; he has never put forth a more far-reaching idea nor shown it more adequately in terms of flesh and blood.... There are far greater plays in the modern drama—greater in emotional power and imaginative splendor. There is none that illustrates more exactly or searchingly the inner nature,

stripped of the accretions of myth and tradition, of the tragic process itself. (pp. 172-73)

Ludwig Lewisohn, "The Quiet Truth," in his The Drama and the Stage *(© 1922 by Harcourt, Brace and Company; reprinted by permission of Harcourt Brace Jovanovich, Inc.), Harcourt, 1922, pp. 168-73.*

As a playwright Galsworthy is a phenomenon *manqué,* a craftsman endowed with all the arts but one—to breath into the dramatic character a living soul. The root of dramatic craftsmanship is in him; as Bernard Shaw once remarked to me, "Galsworthy can make a coroner's inquest dramatic." But his theatre is essentially experimental; each new play is a Galsworthian demonstration in cause and effect. His characters move about upon the boards with an extraordinary semblance of naturalness; they fall into the most significant groupings; their doings always have a preconceived meaning. That something "rich and strange" which informs warm creatures moving with the rhythm of life is absent; in its place is something thin and familiar, a neat scheme for putting across certain ideas through the instrumentality of essential type figures masquerading as individuals. (p. 471)

[He] speaks as a sculptor, not as a dramatist; he is posing groups of lay figures, not projecting scenes of human life, by possible people in possible situations, through the colored lens of art. (p. 472)

I suspect that *The Pigeon* will eventually rank as Galsworthy's finest achievement in drama. The Frenchman, Ferrand, the wild bird, the untamed gull, is a character so rich in texture, so completely realized that he is permanently added to the galaxy of familiar modern dramatic characters of our acquaintance. Aside from this one character, which gives the play a peculiar eminence, *The Pigeon* falls into the category of the strange Galsworthy technic—plays of social contrast which are inconclusive, and really "get you nowhere." Galsworthy's social philosophy is simple enough in outline: imagination and sympathy, not theory and programme, are the magic symbols of social reform. Here Galsworthy has *not* "lost sight of the individual . . .". (p. 475)

Galsworthy draws the neatest pattern of any contemporary dramatist. His plays are studies in parallelism, not in perpendicularity. They are specimens of social contrast, not of individual conflict. Galsworthy, so far as I know, is the first man in the history of the theatre who refuses to mark the cards, is strictly, almost painfully impartial, and insists on letting the play's meaning rest implicit in the situation and the characters.... Shaw and Galsworthy are poles apart in this respect. Shaw shouts the moral through every convenient mouthpiece, whether appropriately or not; and also writes a lengthy preface to explain the meaning and moral of the play. Galsworthy ruthlessly excises every epigram, witticism, joke which is not in character; and dams back the emotional flood and moralizing impulse of his characters almost at the expense of their humanity. As he himself once wittily observed: "It might be said of Shaw's plays that he creates characters who express feelings which they have not got. It might be said of mine that I create characters who have feelings which they cannot express." It should be added that the inarticulateness of Galsworthy's characters is deliberately imposed on them by their author; Galsworthy insists that by the actions and the circumstances, and not out of the mouths of the characters, shall the story be told and the moral drawn. (pp. 476-77)

[*Loyalties*] is a theatre piece of pure stamp, dramatic to the core; and it will take high rank in Galsworthy's theatre for its "sure-fire" theatric effectiveness. But it is in no sense a great play. One pays Galsworthy due tribute for *Loyalties* by declaring that Pinero could have done no better. (p. 479)

> *Archibald Henderson, "John Galsworthy," in his* European Dramatists *(copyright © 1913, 1926, Prentice-Hall, Inc.; reprinted by permission of Prentice-Hall, Inc., Englewood Cliffs, New Jersey), Appleton, 1926, pp. 467-79.*

The reader is . . . continuously being visited, both in Mr. Galsworthy's fiction and in his drama, by the sense of what ought to be. It might seem his principal reason for writing, the spring-head of the delicate, solicitous, and considered satire, which perhaps more than anything else, his art is. At all events the sense of what ought to be does not fail of presence in any tale of his, from *The Island Pharisees,* in which the feeling of discrepancy between what is and what ought to be forms a burden of something not unlike asperity, to *The Forsyte Saga,* in which the social criticism is somehow splendidly implicit in the creative substance of the novel. Such harmonies of criticism and depiction as obtain in the latter tale are no doubt not easy, and Mr. Galsworthy seems not always to have achieved them, in spite of his apparent conviction that the most effective critical indictment is simply revelation.

At least one must suppose Mr. Galsworthy to hold convictions as to the force of simple revelation, for it is to an art of gently satiric exhibition—exposure, as it were, with malice toward none—that he has seemed to bend his talents. . . . His intellectually artistic resources are very great, and he feels very cleverly—so cleverly that the impression is rather slow in arriving that he feels in considerable share with his mind. But it does arrive, for the occasional thinness of fictive effect in the general range of his work seems inexplicable on any other basis. Such a manner of feeling is, no doubt, well adapted to the aims of his art, for to feel with the mind cannot involve the artist beyond his intended design. . . . Few novelists writing in English show more consistently than he that they know at all moments what they are about. One can be sure, doubtless, that he feels what he writes; but doubtless also, he knows it as much as he feels it. He is not creative, it would seem, out of such an emotionality as, for instance, possesses Thomas Hardy.

To say that the pages of Mr. Galsworthy are beautiful deliberately, beautiful by the contrivances of a well cultivated, complete, and intellectually acute aesthetic sense is not, of course, to say that they are not sincerely felt pages, for sincere they evidently are, to their outmost and inmost. Sincerity and seriousness seem among the indubitable qualities of Mr. Galsworthy's fiction. More than this, there is a gentleness in his satire, a qualified flagellation, even in the sharpest of his damnations of complacency, which might lead us to suppose it not quite satire, were there not ever evident the fact of its singleness about the business of exposing, exposing the blindness that caste and prejudice and self-sufficiency can bring about in character. His singleness to expose has led before now to the suggestion that he does not "see life whole." It has led, too, to the charge of insig-

nificance in the characters that populate his pages. Against these charges he defends himself, in his present prefaces, with great urbanity, moderation, and ability. But the fact still seems to remain that these beautiful situations, beautifully enclosed, and managed with perfect artistic economy, situations which no one knows better than he how to elaborate, are revelatory chiefly of what they are designed to reveal, that is, deficits of character and insight, rather than character in the round. . . . It is only on such splendidly creative occasions as those of his famous old men that Mr. Galsworthy transcends design, and gives us ripe and solid old beings, who walk upon legs, who are both less and more than the designed situation calls for, and upon whom no amount of "exposure" can work a real belittlement. . . . By and large one must feel Mr. Galsworthy's imagination expended more in other directions than that of his characters.

Indeed a reader may very well wonder if Mr. Galsworthy's stated vision of the world is not an example both of the force and the defect of the saying that art is a criticism of life. *His* art certainly is a criticism of life, and a very specific and sweeping one, well-taken, beautifully embodied, grave, sincere, and winning. But its excellence as criticism, together with its occasional failure to satisfy, suggests that we may be looking for something more in art, at least in the art of fiction, than a criticism of life. Perhaps we are looking for an imaginative creation of life itself. Must it not seem that the best of Mr. Galsworthy's work as a novelist, in such books as the Saga, is that in which he overruns the beautiful business of revelation and sets willy-nilly about the creation of life? (pp. 165-67)

> *Charles K. Trueblood, "The Art of Revelation," in* The Dial *(copyright, 1927, by The Dial Publishing Company, Inc.; reprinted by permission of J. S. Watson, Jr. and Scofield Thayer), August, 1927 (and reprinted by Kraus Reprint Corporation, 1966), pp. 165-67.*

We feel such friendliness for Mr Galsworthy as we read these poems [*Verses New and Old*] for his modesty, his fine sense of honour, his love of country scenes, his philosophic temper of mind, that we hesitate, remembering the crude material of which life is made, to express what we really think. But recalling with a courage not to be out-distanced by Mr Galsworthy's own, that higher duty toward art, we force ourselves to admit that this eminent author's poetry lacks everything that the greatest poetry should have except integrity and gravity, and sometimes it lacks the latter. (p. 174)

> The Dial *(copyright, 1927, by The Dial Publishing Company, Inc.; reprinted by permission of J. S. Watson, Jr. and Scofield Thayer), August, 1927 (and reprinted by Kraus Reprint Corporation, 1966).*

What Trollope did for the "country family" in England in the early and middle parts of nineteenth century—taking up the theme about a generation after the point at which Jane Austen dropped it—Mr. Galsworthy has set out to do for the second half of the century, and the early years of the next. The three authors provide us, indeed, with an almost perfect *continuum*. Not only do they deal with the same scene and with the same kinds of people: they also share a common method. It is the "wholeness" of the social picture that interests them, and all three of them go about the presentation of this picture with something of the unexaggerative detachment of the sociologist. Allowing for individual differences—for the shrewder wit of Jane Austen, the generous urbanity of Trollope, the more inquisitive intellectualism of Mr. Galsworthy, and also his keener interest in the purely *dramatic* element in the architecture of fiction—the three authors are very obviously congeners.

[If] Mr. Galsworthy resembles his two predecessors in his comprehensiveness and in his predilection for a level and cumulative realism, he has also his striking differences. He is not as "pure" a literary phenomenon as either of the others: his talent is not, like Jane Austen's or Trollope's, a single and immediately recognizable thing, but rather a kind of synthesis, whether we regard it from the point of view of style or the point of view of method. We can, and should, grant immediately his greater intellectual grasp: he assumes for his purpose a far more complex scene, and this more complex scene he handles with admirable control. Nothing is left out, everything is adequately seen and rendered. If we take the picture as a whole, we can say that it is true and rich, and that in assembling so much material on one canvas he has achieved a remarkable feat of design.

It is when we look at the thing in detail that we begin, perhaps, to be here and there a little disquieted and to feel that for all its energy his talent is not quite so fine or deep, not so individual, as that of either of his literary forbears. (p. 214)

Mr. Galsworthy's prose is an adequate prose, but it is not a distinguished one. It is frequently awkward, frequently monotonous, to the point of becoming actively and obtrusively *not* a good medium for the thing said. . . . Mr. Galsworthy has always been somewhat disposed to purple passages. There are . . . times when he wants something a little better than his "mere medium" for the thing said; he desires to be poetic; an emotional scene or atmosphere is to be conveyed, and accordingly he attempts a prose more charged and ornate. These attempts are almost invariably failures: Mr. Galsworthy's taste fails him. What one usually feels on these occasions is that he is simply unable to express feelings delicately; and that is, perhaps, a definition of sentimentality.

One feels . . . that when one accepts, as one does, Mr. Galsworthy's place in English fiction, one does so with very definite reserves as to the quality of his style. And even the "wholeness" of his picture, which is his major virtue, is not without grave faults. If he gives us admirable scenes, sharp, quick, and living, and admirable portraits . . . he also gives us a good many scenes which we do not believe in for a minute, and more than a handful of portraits which do not belong at all in any such gallery as this, but rather in the category of the Jonsonian or Dickensian "humor." (p. 215)

One has the feeling, occasionally, that he is describing his characters rather than letting them live; that when they face a crisis, he solves it for them *intellectually:* and that again and again he fails to sound the real truth in the situations which he himself has evoked. Soames Forsyte, for example, is a real person, on the whole admirably drawn. But could Soames, granted the sensitiveness with which we see him to be endowed, possibly have lived four years with Irene in so total a blindness as to the real state of things between them? Here was a situation which could have been magnificent. A real "realism" would have luxuriated in the minute-by-minute analysis of this profound disaccord. But Mr. Galsworthy never comes to grips with it.

Something of this failure to get inside his characters shows again in *Swan Song,* the coda to the Forsyte Saga. . . . [We] are given the culmination of the interrupted affair of Fleur and Jon, and the death of Soames. The whole story moves toward, and is focused on, the eventual love-scene between Jon and Fleur: . . . but when it comes, it is quite lamentably inadequate; it is as if the author had gone into a complete psychological funk about it, and had simply not *known* how two such people would have behaved on such an occasion. This scene needed to be the realest and richest and most moving in the book; and given the sufficient actuality of the two people, it could easily have been so. Mr. Galsworthy's failure to give us here anything but a stagey little scene of rhetorical melodrama suggests anew that his gravest fault is his habit of *thinking* his way, by sheer intelligence, into situations which he has not sufficient psychological insight to *feel.* (pp. 216-17)

> *Conrad Aiken, "The Last of the Forsytes,"* in The New Republic *(reprinted by permission of* The New Republic; © *1928 by The New Republic, Inc.), October 10, 1928 (and reprinted as "Galsworthy, John" in his* Collected Criticism, Oxford University Press, *1968, pp. 213-17).*

Galsworthy's contact with many civilizations led him to question the whole range of the English social order as fixed in law and conventions by the Victorians. If a man is to become an author, he has several times said, a narrow selfhood must lose itself in the soul of the world. Galsworthy and Conrad, each in his own way, won their freedom of outlook in lands beyond the seas. Galsworthy was thereby saved from becoming a Soames Forsyte. (p. 528)

Galsworthy's first long novel ["The Island Pharisees"] is an introduction to all he has since written. Having discovered the Pharisee, he immediately proceeded to expose modern Phariseeism in its many phases, obvious and obscure, as peculiar to different social classes, much as Thackeray had once played with the snob idea, detecting the wolf and the ass in sheep's clothing through all ranks and all professions. In the process Galsworthy's art underwent a profound sea-change. Only two years intervene between "The Island Pharisees" and "The Man of Property"; but in tone and manner the two novels are a world apart. Satire approaching cynicism passes into irony. A wandering narrative is subjected to artistic control. And the characterization, hitherto mostly on the surface, now shows psychological insight.

The novelist, one may say, has suddenly reached maturity. But to say that, is not a full explanation. Wide as was his reading, Galsworthy in his first experimental stage followed a confusion of models, no one of which was very good. To Maupassant and Turgenev and to Tolstoi, we have Galsworthy's word for it, he owed his later "inspiration and training." Though the breadth of Tolstoi was beyond him, there never would have been a "Forsyte Saga" had no "War and Peace" gone before, greatly as the two differ in subject, movement, and scope.

As Galsworthy's art was maturing, he became more tolerant in spirit.... Hypocrisy and insincerity were submerged in a more psychological conception of Phariseeism, as lurking somewhere in the unconscious mind. Most of us, Galsworthy concluded, are Pharisees, without knowing it, in our pretense to be other than we are. Phariseeism is a blind spot which no one can see in himself unless he turns "the ironic eye inwards." It is this blind spot in a character that he would expose to view, not so much for condemnation as for enlightenment and humor. (pp. 530-31)

Not known so well as they deserve are Galsworthy's country gentlemen such as the Forsytes and even the Dallisons might have become had they never been drawn into a cosmopolitan atmosphere. His country gentlemen do not care to add to their estates so much as to preserve intact what they have received from their ancestors as a sacred trust to be handed on to their descendants. Land, tenants, and laborers they regard as theirs to do what they please with. (p. 531)

Galsworthy has described his novels, in Matthew Arnold's phrase, as "a criticism of life." One British institution after another passes in review as in a panorama, and a knife is put into each picture. Interspersed in the panorama are plans, schemes, and theories, soberly or humorously set forth, for the regeneration of mankind—pure democracy, socialism, universal brotherhood, a shift in the population from town to country, or emigration to the colonies. These, too, receive the knife as the author proceeds not far from the middle of the road but nearer the side of critics and reformers. Galsworthy is not a revolutionist. His aim is nowhere the complete overthrow of the existing social order; it is rather the elimination of grievous faults in the machine while he would hold fast to what is good in the principles governing the aristocracy and the middle classes.... Taken as a whole, there is little or no direct propaganda in Galsworthy's novels. Such as seems to be is inherent in his naturalistic method which endeavors to transfer to fiction the social scene as it appears to a man who would look beneath the surface. Nor are problems solved in the authoritative manner of H. G. Wells. They are stated and elaborated, and left there for the reader's solution if he has any. Galsworthy's theme is the liberation of the mind. The nearest approach to his ideal of emancipation is the artist, who at least has imagination, while the aristocrat, the priest, and the man of affairs have none. Man is to be saved through art. God, in his freedom to build in his own way, is the supreme artist.

For Galsworthy the artist all roads lead to the world of the Forsytes, which was his early home. In their Saga are most of the ideas lying at the basis of his other novels, here massed and concentered in an abnormal "sense of property" as the central and dominating theme. With a slightly superior air Galsworthy looks back in irony on ways of life he has outgrown. As he fits scene after scene into his patterns, commenting, satirizing, and looking beneath the surface, there are times when he appears to feel that he is thrusting a knife into himself, well knowing that the Forsyte in his subconscious self is still alive, moving and mumbling. (pp. 532-33)

These old Forsytes as they once existed in the flesh are the very people who entered largely into the novels of Dickens and Thackeray. (p. 533)

"The Man of Property" is a dramatic presentation of the clash between two antagonistic groups of social ideas such as Galsworthy invariably has in his mature novels and in the plays he was soon to write. Here the antagonisms, labelled Forsytean and artistic, are brought together in close quarters under one roof, where there is no escape for either except in an explosion. In form and movement the novel is an expanded Greek tragedy, cleverly adapted to modern views and modern conditions.... Emotional undercurrents, as they collide, recede, and collide again, are revealed with little psychological phrasing in an objective art which often becomes very subtle.... Scraps of speech, pauses, echoes, and silences tell the story of a tension fraught with the greatest danger.... Everywhere the texture is tightly woven, giving one the illusion that Galsworthy had already determined what was to be the fate of the characters involved in the dramatic action, and had in mind, too, the ironic train of events which were at last to catch fire. His irony and his silences often remind one of Sophocles. (p. 539)

Reduced to the lowest terms, "The Man of Property" is a study of what will happen in a particular *milieu* when a wife has an aversion for her husband which she cannot overcome. The novel is primarily an emotional study in the physiology of nerves.... The succeeding novels, with the exception of "Indian Summer of a Forsyte," are more objective. (p. 541)

> *Wilbur Cross, "The Forsytes," in* The Yale Review (© *1930 by Yale University; reprinted by permission of the editors), Spring, 1930, pp. 527-50.*

I have to confess that on re-reading [Galsworthy's] *The Man of Property* ... when it was incorporated with other stories in *The Forsyte Saga,* I found a longer experience of life had left me more keenly aware of Galsworthy's faults than of his virtues. The lack of humour and, strange though it may seem to some to say so, the lack of much first-hand experience of human nature, the deliberate manipulation of the natural scene that suggested a theatrical convention, the sentimentalization of flowers and animals, the solemnity of presentation that so often verged upon something akin to pomposity, combined to destroy the edifice, ... took on more and more the air of one of those palaces built to enshrine the spirit of a nation at an exhibition. (p. 155)

The weakness of Galsworthy's method was patent when he attempted in *The White Monkey, The Silver Spoon,* and *Swan Song* to present a picture of England after the war. One began to suspect that his characters were lay figures dressed up with all he could learn from newspapers about the externals of contemporary manners, and in suspecting the authentic life of his later creations one began to ask if his typical late Victorians might not have been the result of a similar resolve to achieve typicality at the expense of individual life. (p. 156)

> *Compton Mackenzie, in his* Literature in My Time, *Rich & Cowan Ltd., 1934 (and reprinted by Books for Libraries Press, Inc., 1967).*

Galsworthy was, I think, the first English novelist to turn for what may be called technical inspiration to Russia. And whereas French realism always directed its attention towards an objective presentation of life, Russian realism was always tinged with philosophy (that is to say, with ethics and metaphysics) and with politics. The same is true of Russian literary criticism. In Galsworthy's case it was never denied that his earliest books were written in direct imitation of the novels of Turgenev; and his whole work was coloured by that humanitarian moralizing to which Conrad—always an acute critic—refers in [a] letter. . . . ["A moralist must present us with a gospel—he must give counsel, not to our reason or sentiment, but to our very soul"]. Galsworthy thought as much of the moral of everything as Alice's Ugly Duchess.

Another point to which I wish to refer is that Galsworthy was the first genteel novelist of the Georgian scene, and only the second genteel novelist in English literature. (p. 192)

All his sympathy with poor people was the sympathy of a sensitive and highly-strung humanitarian who tries to put himself in the place of those whom he does not understand; those between whom and himself there can be no intercommunication. Whether lambs or horses, dogs or guttersnipes, social outsiders or performing seals, all who did not belong to the English affluent middle class—the Forsytes—were in a sense dumb animals. He suffered their pains a thousand times over; but the last plumbing degrees of insight, of identification, were beyond him. As in the case of Gregory, in *The Country House*, it was to his "reforming instinct a constant grief that he had been born refined. A natural delicacy *would* interfere. . . ." That is why, when one has been poor, one never quite accepts Galsworthy's poor people, who are poor before they are human. . . .

In [his early] books he took from Turgenev's method what he needed—measure and delicate precision; and he shared with his master a thrilling sense of beauty, irony, and an extraordinary feeling for tragic young love. Galsworthy often returned to this theme, trying to pitch the note high but always decorously, to catch a pure ray of emotion and at the same time woo reality and escape the namby-pamby. (p. 194)

[A] horror of pain and injustice runs through the whole of Galsworthy's work, and affects its ultimate importance. The artist may rightly see and protest against injustice; but if he does this too narrowly, if he is but a fabulist, he may well miss truth for the sake of his moral. . . . Suffering as he did from that emotional sympathy with the loser in any fight which is the mark of humanitarianism, he unconsciously distorts both sides of a wrangle in order to produce his plea for the unfortunate, the weak, the dumb. He was a pleader. (pp. 195-96)

His strength was in his love of beauty, which was rare. It was greater than his love of men (from whom he shrank unless they were as fastidious as himself). He could pity men and animals, and wish to better their lot; but for men *as* animals he had an aversion. When he could turn his eyes back, away from conflict, as he did when he wrote of old and dying people, he could still see the world as a lovely viceless thing for the eye to rest upon. He could still believe in peace, leisure, and acceptance. (p. 198)

Frank Swinnerton, in his The Georgian Scene: A Literary Panorama *(copyright 1934 © 1962 by Frank Swinnerton; reprinted by permission of Holt, Rinehart and Winston, Publishers), Farrar & Rinehart, 1934.*

The disease from which [Galsworthy] suffered was pity . . . or not so much pity as an insupportable anger at the sufferings of the weak or the impoverished in a harsh world. It was as if some portion of his mind had been flayed and bled at every touch. . . . And, for me at least, it robbed his later work of interest, since the novelist must be pitiless at least when he is at work.

And it filled me with disappointment. I think I must have been the first person really to take Galsworthy seriously as a writer. For most other people who knew him then—except of course for the lady who subsequently became Mrs. Galsworthy—he was still an amiable, rather purposeless man-about-town. . . . But I had already recognized in him a certain queerness, a certain pixylike perversity . . . and a certain, slight, authentic gift. So that I had expected him, if he persevered, to provide for us another—a possibly sunnier kind, of Trollope, and I very much did not want him to become overserious or emotional.

And suddenly there was Turgenev—the most dangerous of all writers for his disciples—Turgenev and emotionalism appearing in the mentality of that sunny being with the touch of genius. . . . (pp. 125-26)

It might have been true to say that he was not a born novelist and, from my particular angle, it might be true to say that he never was a novelist at all. But writing is not all novel-writing, and there were departments of the art of projecting things on paper in which he really excelled and was conscious that he excelled. It is true that a writer must be born a writer. But it is true, too, that a born writer can be made over . . . to his detriment; and I do not think that any real writer can have ever been so made over as the unfortunate young Galsworthy. (p. 135)

To me it became apparent gradually that Galsworthy was probably never meant to be a novelist. Or it would be more just to say that thoughts of the world of injustice pressed too strongly on him to let him continue to be a novelist. . . . I can assure you that I felt a genuine pleasure and impatience at the thought of coming across a person with the aspects for me of an authentic genius . . . and if I perceived a threat to the prospect of the fruits of that genius growing eventually ripe beneath the sun, I was proportionately dismayed. And I thought I perceived that threat. I foresaw for a moment his preoccupation with the unhappinesses of lovers and the helpless poor . . . and that preoccupation leading him to become not a dispassionate artist but an impassioned, an aching, reformer.

The premonition was too true. *Villa Rubein* was a novel of a sunlit quality. But its successor, *The Island Pharisees*, was already a satire, and *The Man of Property*, which came next, was an attempt to cast discredit on the marriage laws of the day. And after that, in his novels, he was the reformer almost to the end.

And unfortunately his temporal success as novelist obscured his much greater artistic achievement with the drama. His novels suffered from his dogged determination to find ironic antitheses. His one 'effect' as a novelist was to present a group of conventionally virtuous, kindly people sitting about and saying the nicest things about all sorts of persons. . . . A divorced woman is thrown over their garden hedge and breaks her collar bone, and all the kindly people run away and do not so much as offer her a cup of tea. And that goes on forever, the situation being always forced to bring in that or some similar effect. (pp. 138-39)

But the same dogged determination to present antitheses which produced an effect of monotony in the later novels was exactly suited to the theatre. There effects are of necessity more fugitive and need to be harsher—more cruel. And the keen pleasure that, at the play, the mind feels at appreciating how, unerringly, Galsworthy picks up every crumb of interest and squeezes the last drop of drama out of a situation . . . that pleasure is the greatest humanity can get from a work of art. It is the greatest because pleasures, shared as they are in the playhouse, are contagious and can be unbounded. And it is one of the most legitimate of man's pleasures.

When you came away from the first performance of *The Silver Box* you knew that something new had come into the world . . . a new temperament, a new point of view, a new and extraordinarily dramatic technique. And the conviction was strengthened by each new play. For myself I preferred *Joy* to all the others because it was more a matter of dramatic discussion than of situations and because it had some of the lightness that had distinguished the *Villa Rubein* of our youths. But the characteristic of building up antitheses which, monotonous as it becomes in the novel, is always legitimate and exciting in the swifter moving play, that characteristic distinguished as much his handling of situation as of staged controversy. . . . No other modern dramatist had anything approaching Galsworthy's loftiness of mind, his compassion, his poetry, his occasional sunlight or the instinctive knowledge of what you can do on the stage. And by himself he lifted the modern stage to a plane to which until his time it had seemed impossible that it could attain. (pp. 139-40)

> *Ford Madox Ford, "Galsworthy," in his* Portraits from Life *(copyright © 1936 and 1937 by Ford Madox Ford; 1965 by Janice Alaine; reprinted by permission of Houghton Mifflin Company), Houghton, 1937 (and reprinted by Greenwood Press, 1974), pp. 124-42.*

[Galsworthy] created human beings who are free because they are completely passionate, and he created others who are real because they live their lives in ignorance or disregard of philosophical problems. The best examples of the first are women, and the best examples of the second are men—particularly old men.

The women are Mrs. Bellew in "The Country House," Mrs. Noel in "The Patrician," Anne Stormer, Olive Cramier, and Nell Dromore in "The Dark Flower," Noel Pierson in "Saint's Progress," and Irene Forsyte in "The Forsyte Saga." With two exceptions these are mature women, and with one exception they are married. Their passion is by no means a plaything; it is not in the superficial sense of the word romantic. It is, Galsworthy seems to say, the fundamental thing in their lives as it is the fundamental thing in all human existence. It is the thing which redeems society from too much comfort, from too much money, from all its crueler or dingier aspects. It is the divine fire in an otherwise earthy world. With this in mind, one cannot perhaps object that the women who possess it are considerably alike. They are invariably quiet with a hunted quietness; they are soft and mysterious and beautiful; they suffer without end from the grosser qualities of husbands, fathers, relatives, and friends who set respectability above private integrity, who honor law before love.

One cannot object, that is, on the score of poetry or philosophy; but one can object on the score of fiction. This very sameness which makes a half-dozen women impressive as documents robs them of validity as characters. They are almost completely lay-figures which their creator has employed to preach a sermon on the necessity of passion. Take their passion away and little remains except a colorless, stereotyped beauty. It is not they who feel the passion in the first place; it is Galsworthy. So even they do not redeem him altogether from the charge that his fiction is more himself than mankind, more propaganda than truth. It is as if he had decided in the calm of his study that passion is important and had invented some people to put it in; not as if he had found the people first and presented them initially as people, with passion as only one, if an important one, of their qualities.

The old men of Galsworthy, however, are indisputably a triumph. They are obviously the fruit of observation, and one suspects that they are the persons whom Galsworthy has most relished living among. He understands them perfectly; he remembers even the most trivial thing that they do; they are marvels of objective and interesting reality. He has arrived at them through a prolonged study of the institution of the family. Although upon occasion he has seemed to be discussing the family as a sociological problem, he has at all times given an accurate, living picture of it; it has lived for him as people live for any first-rate creative writer —with flesh-and-blood reality. (pp. 222-23)

[Neither] the plot nor the theme is the crowning virtue of "The Forsyte Saga." That virtue inheres in its complete and permanent picture of a certain kind of life. The family which it describes is almost bewilderingly large, and it has a sufficient variety. Only Soames and Irene are uniquely one thing or another—types around which a war of forces could be supposed to wage. The rest either stand for different stages of social growth or are in themselves mixtures of many qualities. The essential fact is that they are real. They exist as acquaintances of the reader, being born, working, loving, marrying, growing old, and dying in the various houses which the reader visits so often that they become as familiar as his own. . . . The death of Old Jolyon is . . . one of the most magnificent deaths recorded anywhere in fiction. The old man was a ripe, confessed pagan, enjoying his money, his wine, his food, and his children to the utmost limit, and incidentally, as with all true pagans, feeling if only fitfully the urge of beauty in a wider and freer world than the one into which he had been born. (pp. 224-25)

[On the other hand] Galsworthy has little respect for the desires his young people are moved by [in "A Modern Comedy"]—so little, indeed, that his [later] trilogy is not finally effective either as tragedy or as comedy. (pp. 225-26)

> *Carl Van Doren and Mark Van Doren, in their* American and British Literature since 1890 *(copyright, 1939, by Prentice-Hall, Inc.; reprinted by permission of Prentice-Hall, Inc., Englewood Cliffs, New Jersey), revised edition, Appleton-Century, 1939.*

Of Galsworthy's liberal and traditional crusading, one may ask by what right it enters the novel, and secondly, what is the relationship between the informing idea and the *form* of the novel? The answer to the first question is in Galsworthy's justification of his choice of material and method. Believing that a feeling for the great problems of humanity and of society was the first requirement for a novelist, he insisted on freedom to throw himself in his own way into the battle of ideas. After writing *The Man of Property,* he came to feel that his strength lay in writing to a polemical strain through character. . . . [Faith] in independence and in the untrammelled exercise of creative power was the cornerstone of Galsworthy's work.

Along with this freedom to choose his own material went his belief in the value of objectivity in presentation. . . . (p. 41)

He thought the duty of the realist was to be faithful to the seething multiple life around him and to reach out and grasp the fullest expression of the individual rather than keep forever under critical shelter. This belief explains much of his naturalistic method of analysis, his careful documentation, and his lawyer's skill in the sifting of evidence. (p. 42)

Galsworthy built his novels, like his plays, to present a clash of ideas. . . . In *The Man of Property,* the clash is between Bosinney's devotion to art and beauty, which draws him to Irene, and the principle of self-preservation represented by Soames's property. . . . [Galsworthy] felt that the only way to defeat Forsyteism was to leave them masters of the field, property *an empty shell.* So he made the end tragic, remorseless. This novel probably best illustrates the relationship between the informing idea and the form of his novels. His modern sense of drama afforded him considerable scope and frequent opportunities for that tinge of irony or unexpectedness in expression which he believed necessary in any author who is to survive the rust of Time. (pp. 44-5)

The polemical dramatist or novelist almost inevitably pays the price of not having a strong sense of character. Galsworthy said that he created characters who have feelings which they cannot express. This may be due to Galsworthy's typical English repression, which he found in his Forsytes. . . . How painstakingly Galsworthy worked with his characters is shown by the trouble that he had with Bosinney. Originally, he did Bosinney subjectively and felt with him mentally while exerting his artifice to keep people from seeing that he had done so. Then he found Bosinney repulsive and changed him to an objective being, swinging the focus entirely into the Forsyte eye. . . . It may be that Galsworthy's characters are spun too exclusively out of his own temperament and therefore lack variety.

If so, Galsworthy's people at least reflect a creator of dignity and gentility. (pp. 46-7)

> *J. Gordon Eaker, "Galsworthy and the Modern Mind," in* Philological Quarterly, *January, 1950, pp. 31-48.*

I think that in "Justice," as in "Strife," it is because Mr. Galsworthy so carefully eschews any show of sympathy with one character, or of antipathy against another, that the charge of cinematography is preferred against him. . . . Mr. Galsworthy never takes an unfair advantage. He dispenses with many quite fair advantages. Is this because he is merely a detached and dispassionate observer of life? The reason is the very contrary. It is because he is fulfilled with pity for the victims of a thing he vehemently hates, and because he is consumed with an anxiety to infect his fellowmen with this hatred and this pity, that he strives so unre-

mittingly to be quite impartial. He knows that a suspicion of special pleading would jeopardise his case. He is determined to give us no chance of soothing our nerves by saying to him "Oh yes, no doubt there is a lot in what you say, but you have let your feelings—which do you great credit—run away with you." He doesn't mind losing the credit for having fine feelings and being regarded as merely a cold-hearted person who just wants to frighten and depress us, so long as he does succeed in his object of frightening and depressing us. (pp. 566-67)

In some of his works he does certainly lay himself open to a (very superficial) charge of inhumanity. In "Strife" he showed us a conflict, and in "Fraternity" a contrast, between the poor and the rich; and the implicit moral of the play was that this conflict would be for ever. If things are irremediable, why, it might be asked, harrow us about them? . . . Mr. Galsworthy's answer would be that to recognise the sadness of things is a duty we owe to honesty, and is good for our souls. In "Justice," however, there is no fundamental pessimism. Mr. Galsworthy sees that our criminal law and our penal system are clumsy, mechanical, mischievous. But he sees them as things not beyond redemption. A little spurring of the scientific intelligence in us and of our common humanity is all that is needed to induce reform. Perfect justice there can never be, of course; but the folly and barbarism of our present method—which is far less barbarous and foolish now than it used to be—can be amended. (pp. 567-68)

> *Max Beerbohm, in his* Around Theatres *(reprinted with permission of Mrs. Eva Reichmann), revised edition, Rupert Hart-Davis, 1953.*

Galsworthy's novels were to become outstanding examples of 'middle-brow' literature, one of the most interesting literary phenomena of our time.

'Middle-brow' literature—not to beat about the bush—is inferior literature adapted to the special tastes and needs of the middle class and of those who consciously or not adopt the values of that class. It may be inferior for any number of reasons—every bad book has its own particular quality of badness—but to come within the category of 'middle-brow' it must maintain, whatever its particular brand of inferiority, certain proprieties sacred to the bulk of readers of the more superior lending-libraries. Though permitted to titillate with the mention and even the occasional vision of the unmentionable, it must never fundamentally shake, never stretch beyond breaking-point, certain secure complacencies. It is worth making this point because it would be quite wrong to see 'middle-brow' literature as merely qualitatively mediocre, better than bad literature but worse than good. Its distinctive feature is not its quality but its function.

It would not be fair to discuss *The Man of Property* simply as 'middle-brow.' As opposed to Galsworthy's later books, this novel has its core of seriousness, its spark of genuine insight which is not merely incidental but central to its very conception.

This spark is the theme of property and its effect upon the personal relationship of the Forsytes. *The Man of Property* begins as satire and it is, without reaching to any marked degree of subtlety, effective satire. What is particularly well conveyed is the significant contradiction in the relationships of the Forsyte clan between their dislike and suspicion of each other and their colossal sense of solidarity before any outside threat. The close, oppressive family ties based on no affection or even friendliness; the obligatory 'good living' in which no one shows the slightest talent or even much pleasure; the unceasing pressure and pre-occupation of acquisitiveness; the underlying assumption that human relationships are merely an extention of property relationships (a wife as a man's proudest possession): all this comes across effectively in the early chapters of the book. Robert Liddell has criticized Galsworthy's upholstery on the grounds that his method of presentation makes for merely crude differentiation between characters:

> Each Forsyte, or group of Forsytes, is built up from the background; we learn to know them apart by their furniture or their food. Old Jolyon had a study 'full of green velvet and heavily carved mahogany,' and when he gives a family dinner the saddle of mutton, the Forsyte *pièce de résistance,* is from Dartmoor. Swithin has an 'elaborate group of statuary in Italian marble,' which placed upon a lofty stand (also of marble), diffused an atmosphere of culture throughout the room! His mutton is Southdown. . . .

> This is not at all a clear way of distinguishing character. . . . If you collected and multiplied traits of the kind Galsworthy has here given, you might in the end arrive at some slight discrimination of character. But it is obvious that this is an extremely laborious way of doing things. One ought rather to deduce from the character of any Forsyte, if he had been well drawn, what sort of furniture he would be likely to have, and what he would be likely to offer one if one dined with him—if it is really a matter of interest to know.

But surely this is to miss the whole point of Galsworthy's method. What *is* the character of any Forsyte abstracted from his furniture and his saddle of mutton? . . . It is nonsense to assume that behind Timothy or Swithin Forsyte there is some mysterious, disembodied 'character' waiting to be expressed by some sensitive artist like Virginia Woolf or Ivy Compton-Burnett.

Unfortunately the satire of *The Man of Property* is not sustained. It could not be, for there is insufficient sincerity, insufficient indignation behind it. The Forsyte characters, though credible enough, are too politely treated. Like all pusillanimous writers Galsworthy is afraid to let his characters develop to their own logical extremes. He is for ever drawing back, blurring, sentimentalizing. Of the 'pure' Forsytes only Soames is given anything of a free hand.

As it goes on *The Man of Property* becomes less and less satisfactory and this is because Galsworthy completely blurs the central conflict of the book—the conflict between humanity and property. The representatives of humanity—Irene, Bosinney, young Jolyon—turn out to be a poor lot; they are not more humane than the Forsytes, only more romantic. . . . Soames's actions are, compared with Bosinney's, eminently justifiable. Bosinney's overspending in the

face of numerous perfectly reasonable undertakings betrays not fine feelings but sheer incompetence; yet so hazy and wishy-washy and romantic are Galsworthy's positive values that we are invited to identify Bosinney and Irene with Art and Beauty, struggling against the tyranny of Property. In fact throughout *The Forsyte Saga* nobody really struggles against the tyranny of the Forsyte view of property. Young Jolyon, the humane rebel, is quite prepared (there isn't even a moment's conflict) to accept money from his father whose values and property-principles he affects to despise. Galsworthy's own positive is betrayed not as opposition to the Forsytes but as the sentimentalizing of them. Old Jolyon is his ideal. That is why his satire which, as D. H. Lawrence remarked, had at the beginning "a certain noble touch," soon fizzles out. (pp. 96-8)

> *Arnold Kettle, "John Galsworthy: The Man of Property," in his* An Introduction to the English Novel, Vol. II, *edited by Basil Willey, Hutchinson's University Library, 1953, pp. 95-9.*

The Man of Property is not an entirely convincing novel; Galsworthy is a good deal better at social satire than at depicting scenes of passion—some of these are distinctly melodramatic. But the satire is sufficiently prevalent and incisive to make it a fairly memorable novel—certainly one of the best to come out of Edwardian England. Galsworthy draws the Forsytes as purely social beings: rather more than mere caricatures, but something less than deeply conceived fictional characters. Hence, perhaps, their air of existing on the same plane of reality as their furniture and hangings, stuffed and gilded objects rather than authentic persons. It is impossible to imagine them outside the inevitable setting of their tall, overfurnished houses in Kensington or Bayswater. . . .

Turning from *The Man of Property* to the succeeding volumes that make up *The Forsyte Saga,* and still more to the following trilogy, *A Modern Comedy,* which follows Soames's fortunes through to the mid twenties, one is struck and disconcerted by the way in which Galsworthy sentimentalises the Forsytes, and transforms Soames from something very like a villain into the admired and endorsed central intelligence of the sequence. (p. 135)

Defiance of convention had, perhaps, made [Galsworthy] a novelist, but once he was established he was entirely repossessed by all the fundamental assumptions of his class and upbringing. . . . For all his admirable personal qualities—he was a tireless supporter of good causes and gave away a large part of his earnings—it is difficult to be fair to the later Galsworthy as a writer. He continued, of course, to be an excellent story-teller, with a lively feeling for intrigue. But once he ceased to be a satirist his work lost all emotional coherence. His view of reality was hopelessly soft-centred. The sludge of sentimentality, presented in a prose shrieking with exclamation marks, is perhaps the most intolerable feature of the later sections of *The Forsyte Saga.* Even in his pre-war work a degree of sentimental evasiveness is apparent. In that wildly successful play *Strife* . . . , Galsworthy appears to be dealing seriously with a social issue—the effects of a prolonged strike in a tin-plate works. But the piece remains a nullity: insight is sacrificed to slick contrivance.

In his final years Galsworthy was wholly given over to flattering the Forsytes of the world, as though to placate them for his initial unkind treatment. To the end he retained inviolate those instinctive assumptions of the British ruling class that outsiders find so obnoxious; an effortless sense of unquestioned superiority and a corresponding condescension. . . . (p. 137)

Bernard Bergonzi, "Man as Property" (originally published in Spectator, February 15, 1963), in The Turn of a Century: Essays on Victorian and Modern English Literature (© Bernard Bergonzi 1973; reprinted in the U.S. by permission of Harper & Row, Publishers, Inc., Barnes & Noble Import Division, and in Canada by permission of A. D. Peters & Co.), Barnes & Noble, 1973, pp. 134-38.

Fifty years ago naturalism was the great new movement in the English theater, and John Galsworthy was its dignified prophet. But yesterday's masterpieces have become today's museum-pieces, and Galsworthy's voice is stilled. If he had been a bad dramatist, there would be no critical problem, but his plays have the virtues—serious content, clear structure, interesting characters, brilliant individual scenes—that usually guarantee long life in the theater; some of his scenes, such as that of Falder's isolation in *Justice,* are as good now as they ever were. As a whole, however, his work has not worn well, and what astonished its first audiences now often seems pallid or melodramatic or naive. My purpose is to suggest that this lack of durability is the fault not of Galsworthy's incompetence but of his strict adherence to naturalist theory.

Unlike many of his contemporaries, Galsworthy was not so adept in literary techniques that he could choose whichever he felt best. Where the careers of most dramatists of the period show a gradual move away from realism, Galsworthy was from the beginning to the end true to his original ideas, and his sole attempt at another mode (*The Little Dream . . .*) is a self-confessed failure. By temperament, by instinct, he was a realist. . . . The public acclaimed *Strife* in 1909, and in 1910 *Justice* had such a sensational closeness to real life and to problems of immediate interest to its audience that it produced changes in the regulations governing the solitary confinement of prisoners.

In the next decade, Galsworthy, with Shaw and Granville-Barker, led the Renaissance of the New Drama. (pp. 65-6)

The heavily plotted play had triumphed in the nineteenth century. Audiences apparently demanded that all the non-spectacular forms of theater be based on an elaborate sequence of events designed to arouse emotion and directed to moral ends, so that even the lowliest of melodramas share a tendency which in the higher forms, such as the well-made play, becomes an end in itself. Galsworthy's plays belong to the same tradition, and their taut, clear structure produces exactly similar experiences of suspense, irony, and catharsis. *The Silver Box* is typical of his favorite method, wherein both plot and meaning depend on the fortuitous parallelism between the actions of the two leading characters.

Usually Galsworthy will couple a contrast in concept between the privileged and the underprivileged with a chance conjunction of events in the plot—pregnancy, for example, in *The Eldest Son,* or theft in *The Silver Box*—to create an artificial parallelism out of which the meaning and the events of his play arise. In *Strife* the structure is very clear both in the simultaneous overthrow of Anthony and Roberts and in the use of the classic device of the well-timed death (of Annie Roberts) to bring about the dénouement. Ironic contrast, again usually fortuitous, is a favorite trick, sometimes made crudely obvious. . . . [The] gradual revelation of a secret, one of the hoariest techniques of the old drama, forms the basic plot of *The Skin Game, A Bit o' Love,* and *Loyalties.* On occasion the machinery emits loud creaking noises; Galsworthy did not altogether subdue his liking for "strong" curtains, for instance, or for using the chance entrance of a character as the mainspring of the action. . . . While the endings of his plays are not often so neatly arranged as those of the well-made plays, they all nevertheless bring a series of events to a definite close beyond which life does not in any sense continue. The dénouement of *The Mob,* in which Stephen More is accidentally knifed, is the most blatant example of a manipulated ending based on poetic, rather than blindfold, justice. This evidence does not suggest that his plots depend wholly on character.

Technique controls idea, and the way Galsworthy arranged the events of his plots amalgamated with the way he saw life—as a battle between the individual and society—to produce many of the characteristics of the melodramatic formula typical of the nineteenth century theater, that is, the conflict between Good and Bad. Galsworthy, to be sure, abandoned the noble heroes and dark-browned villains of the popular theater; Falder is no more a hero than his judge or his employers are villains. But in their place we have a dehumanized villain, Society (sometimes with such human embodiments as the police), against which all humans battle with varying degrees of skill, knowledge, and success. In the five plays which end with the death of the leading figure (*Justice, The Fugitive, The Mob, Loyalties, Old English*) we can see the closeness to melodrama. Each of the central characters is a basically good person who, because of events outside his control, is brought into jeopardy. Unable to defend himself, unable to speak forth and proclaim his position with any strength, he grows increasingly isolated as his enemies turn on him and his friends prove powerless. As a result of this carefully arranged isolation of characters who remain basically good throughout, their deaths result not from simple accident perhaps, but certainly from accidental and untypical behavior.

The same inarticulate isolation, the inability even to decry one's fate or welcome it, means that the final conflict is between neither ideas nor characters but emotional attitudes; instead of coming to focus in the death scenes, the previous suggestions about character and idea are simply abandoned. (In Ibsen's plays, for example, the final scenes are the most complex; in Galsworthy's the most stark.) These are all characteristics familiar both in the reputable plays of Augier or Dumas *fils* and also in melodrama. . . . The emotionality of Galsworthy's final scenes was deliberate. Like his predecessors, he arranged his plots to produce any of a range of emotions from shock or horror to humor and whimsical irony. We have his own testimony as to his intentions. (pp. 67-9)

A similar problem arises with Galsworthy's characters, who owe a great deal more to his predecessors and to his audience than to his desire to reflect reality. When his plays first appeared, he was praised for bringing back to the stage a wide range of social classes—one of the standard measurements of realism. . . . Unfortunately, Galsworthy's common men have a higher proportion of titles and country homes than we might today think fit. . . . His low-life characters . . . have . . . many fewer lines than his socially acceptable people, usually because they are in the position of servants or others who speak only when spoken to. He rarely allows them to occupy the stage alone, and when he does the effect is often unfortunate. . . . We can see that he is attempting to create dramatic interest from such people, but when he succeeds it is usually by means of a traditional type, such as the low-life philosopher, Mr. Bly, in *Windows*. One perceptive critic of the time [Edward Storer] pointed out that many of his characters go back to old stage types and that even his great hero of the common man, Falder, "is haunted by that ghost of English melodrama, the desire to do the right thing, which in this connection is nearly always the sentimental, stupid and wrong thing." Galsworthy's characters are, in fact, part of the long process of the humanization of basic stage types which Shaw noted as typical of the theater of the eighteen-sixties and described as "a discovery of . . . sympathetic qualities in personages hitherto deemed beyond redemption."

There is no doubt that Galsworthy's restriction of real understanding to what Masefield called his "gallery of country-house people" strongly lessens the realistic effect of his plays today. Try as he might, it was impossible for him to escape entirely from the class and kind of character that his audiences accepted as legitimate for dramatic study. He took the characters given to him by Jones, Pinero, and Grundy and stretched them as far as he could. (pp. 69-70)

The point to be emphasized about Galsworthy's characters, and about his plots, is not that his method is necessarily wrong or inferior to another method. Quite obviously his practice is different from that of his immediate predecessors and usually has a more worthy, or more serious, aim. It may well be good drama, but—we must not call it realism. The desire to mirror real life on the stage is a perilous ambition, for the conventions of the theater die hard; but they do die, and the more dead they become, the more recognizable they are. In Galsworthy's case, the conventions of the older theater remove the sense of actuality, so that "theater-land" triumphs again.

Let us assume for the moment that Galsworthy could have escaped the influence of the theater and successfully captured his own view of real life. A second force—his temperament—acts with equal subtlety and greater inevitability to bring about his present neglect. As is apparent from both his life and his work, Galsworthy was that rare being, a consistent moralist. It is therefore doubly unfortunate that he chose the techniques of realism in which to express himself, because the dictates of moralism and the dogma of realism are in direct conflict, and in his work they so successfully undermined each other that his morality was cheapened and his scientific impartiality destroyed. . . . It is extraordinarily difficult to provide both an accurate reflection of contemporary life and a play that is meaningful and bearable. The individual point of view always distorts, and unedited transcripts are only spasmodically appealing. It is certainly true that Galsworthy's temperament was so strongly and naturally moral that by itself it undermined the actuality of his plays. (pp. 71-2)

Galsworthy's work rarely contains either the fervor or the particularity of the platform-speaker, and rarely sacrifices dramatic integrity for the sake of proving a point or arguing an issue. Galsworthy only incidentally deals with problems which he believes to be soluble. He is interested not so much in their removal as in recognition of their sources in human nature, and any minor problem in his work is at once related to a concept, to something which is not "soluble" but "comprehensible.". . . Like Shaw, Galsworthy had the potential for a greater permanence than the problem playwrights because his moralism ran so deep that he could not see the world in other than moralistic terms and had a totally consistent view of the events of real life.

Why then did this permanence remain potential? He himself gives us the clue in his formulation of the basic concept of his realist theory. The dramatist's best course was, he wrote, "To set before the public no cut-and-dried codes, but the phenomena of life and character, selected and combined, *but not distorted,* by the dramatist's outlook, set down without fear, favour, or prejudice, leaving the public to draw such poor moral as nature may afford.". . . But if drama wishes to rise above the merely entertaining and to reveal meaning in any way, it must immediately become moralistic in that it expresses an organized and consistent point of view. In this sense, Shaw and Strindberg, Chekov and Ibsen, are all moralistic (though they differ widely in their use of realistic techniques). The realism of their plays is only a means to an end. A doctrinaire realist, on the other hand, if he wishes to go beyond the "slice-of-life" and have any point at all, has twice as much trouble as the non-realist. Like the non-realist, he must select his material, but unlike the non-realist he must order it *with the pretense* that he is not selecting or ordering at all. He is simply presenting the naked truth. Unfortunately, as soon as the pretense is discovered, the logical structure of his plays collapses—disprovable by the very particularity in which he sought his strength. But this is not the truth, we say, nor anything like the truth!

There is no doubt that the pretense in Galsworthy's work is apparent. His ordering is obvious in the fact that every natural act or real person in his plays stands in a clear relationship to his moral theme—there is nothing here, as in life, of the random or the irrelevant. . . . [The] world of his plays is not just controlled but created by a particular set of principles. It is such tightness of structure that has doubtless led to the charges of propagandism, since in failing to provide an atmosphere in which either characters or actions are in any way independent of his moral argument, Galsworthy destroyed the vitality, the complexity, and hence the realism of his plays. (pp. 72-3)

> *Gary J. Scrimgeour, "Naturalist Drama and Galsworthy," in* Modern Drama *(copyright 1964, A. C. Edwards; with the permission of* Modern Drama*), May, 1964, pp. 65-78.*

Galsworthy tried to escape from the clubman's image by impersonating, in his picaresque satirical novel *The Island Pharisees,* a young Belgian beatnik he had met, an embittered wanderer never at a loss for a gibe at the established. It was no good; he kept the offbeat character but made the central figure a young man like himself. The latter was a mouthpiece, certainly, for an all-out attack on the ugliness of the big cities, the horror of the slums from which his own family drew much of its money, the willful blindness, the sexual hypocrisy, he found everywhere; but he was also irredeemably locked in the comfortable world of . . . upper-middle-class society. . . . (p. 109)

He himself was always perfectly well aware of what later came as an unpleasant surprise to many of his radical admirers—that though he wished to make the world a better place, he did not wish to make it a different one. He had acquired in some quarters, he noted, "the reputation of a revolutionary—a quaint conceit," adding that "the constant endeavor of his pen has merely been to show Society that it has had luck; and, if those who have had luck behave as if they knew it, the chances of revolution would sink to zero."

Besides, he wished to emphasize quite another aspect of himself as a writer:

> I've neither the method nor the qualities of a social critic. I've only detachment in so far as I can examine *myself* in contact with life . . . [my books are] simply the criticism of one half of myself by the other half . . . there's quite enough of the dried-caste authority element in me to be legitimate subjects for the attack of my other half . . . [my works are] not a piece of social criticism— they none of them are. If anything, a bit of spiritual examination.

As with the world at large, so with his own world, which was the world of Forsytes. . . .

[Time] is steadily making nonsense of Virginia Woolf's dismissal of him, along with H. G. Wells and Arnold Bennett, as one of those novelists who "write of unimportant things . . . spend immense skill and immense industry making the trivial and the transitory appear the true and the enduring," and from whose novels "life escapes."

From Galsworthy's best work life has patently not escaped. The Forsyte stock lives in his pages, with "gray unmoving eyes hiding their instinct with its hidden roots of violence, their instinct for possession. . .". Galsworthy knew it, felt it in his bones, filled it with the extraordinary pulse of sexual energy that drums through all his best work, recorded it from an ironic distance. . . .

There was something Roman about those bleak yet vital Victorians of Galsworthy's. If he needs a modest epitaph— well, he was the noblest Forsyte of them all. (p. 111)

> *J. W. Lambert, "The Galsworthy Saga," in* Horizon (© *1967 The Sunday Times), Autumn, 1968, pp. 106-11.*

John Galsworthy received in his lifetime every honor a British man of letters could decently dream of receiving— the offer of a knighthood, which he refused; the Order of Merit, which no Englishman has ever refused; the Nobel Prize, which showed that a country-gentleman writer could also be a figure of world literature. Even in 1929, a first edition of "The Man of Property" could fetch ̃ 138 (then about $670) in an auction at Hodgson's in London. For nearly 30 years he was king of the English novel, but only in a constitutional (perhaps even a Pickwickian) sense—a king and no king. He influenced giants like Thomas Mann, was read in France and taken seriously in Russia, but in his native England he ruled chiefly in the hearts of the middle-brows. The intellectuals spurned him. He was never on the shelves of the public libraries because borrowers were always taking him out; he was never on the shelves of the serious students of the novel because they thought him not worth studying.

Compare him with Joyce, Lawrence and Conrad, and Galsworthy hardly exists as a novelist. He belongs to that narrow, conservative, somewhat slipshod range of late-Edwardian, quinto-Georgian British writers who cared less about words than what lay behind the words—the bourgeois men who couldn't understand Flaubert's solitary agony in the service of art and who were even faintly embarrassed by Henry James. They were men who liked society at least as well as they liked literature, and they even had energy left over from their near-art to create societies . . . [Galsworthy founded the P.E.N. Club].

If devotion to literature had entailed becoming lousy, bearded and Bohemian, Galsworthy would have rejected literature. (p. 57)

"Justice," "The Skin Game," "Strife" still have the power to move, since the author himself was so evidently moved by his persistent theme of the wrongs done in the name of his own class to the underdog. . . . This profound yet simple humanitarianism of Galsworthy is wholly admirable; that it does not make admirable art is another matter, and it is perhaps ungentlemanly to raise it.

The themes of the plays, the particularizations of social injustice, presuppose the bigger theme of "The Forsyte Chronicles". . . . As with C. P. Snow's "Brothers and Strangers" sequence, the whole structure rides on the very period it chronicles; the novelist had his whole subject more or less mapped out, but he had to wait for successive slices of time to reveal the nature of the *mise en scene*. (p. 59)

[Galsworthy] starts by castigating a family and its way of life, often with shafts of superb irony, but by the end he has identified himself with the change-hating Forsytes. He is ultimately on the side of the ruling class, whichever form it takes. The rights of the underdog must be promoted, but this is not a duty of the radicals; it is a paternal responsibility of a class we had thought to be dying.

There is no point in denouncing Galsworthy for his change of direction. "The Forsyte Saga" was life's work, and to sustain a consistency of attitude throughout a long life is beyond any man. And, ultimately, the whole chronicle must stand or fall as a work of art—a moving tapestry of flesh-and-blood creations, set against a history that is realized as tangible, sensible actuality. There can be no doubt that "Forsyte's" characters are alive. (p. 60)

The whole work is an astonishing creation. Why, then, is it not great literature?

In the first place, the writing is not distinguished. It is content with old rhythms, clichés, the easy way out—the modes, in fact, which most appeal to lending-library readers and are so transparent that we feel little is lost when transference of the book is made to the small screen. (p. 62)

[There] is more concern in "The Forsyte Saga" with contrivance, with the neat arrangement of patterns, with the mechanical devices of "plot" in the old 19th-century manner than with the direct observation of life. . . .

The Forsytes are *limited* creatures. They are creatures of society, not of their own inner demons. They do not exemplify Ophelia's "We know what we are but know not what we may be"; they are all too predictable. If you like, they are not quite mad enough. . . .

"The Forsyte Saga" is a great television triumph, since the Galsworthian conception has the near-coarseness, the near-melodramatic simplicity of superior soap opera; it has been waiting all these years to slide into its true medium—the leisurely, middlebrow television serial. (p. 64)

> *Anthony Burgess, "Seen Any Good Galsworthy Lately?," in* The New York Times Magazine *(© 1969 by The New York Times Company; reprinted by permission), November 16, 1969, pp. 57-64.*

Federico García Lorca

1899-1936

Spanish poet and dramatist born in rural Andalusia near the city of Granada. García Lorca was an exceptionally attractive man of intense vitality and personal charm. He combined a knowledge of Spanish literature with folk and gypsy poetry to create an idiom at once traditional, modern, and personal. Moving to Madrid in 1919, he lived for several years at the "Residencia de Estudiantes," a flourishing center for writers, critics, and scholars of cultural liberalism. García Lorca devoted himself almost entirely to poetry from 1920-30. During this time his growing reputation as a gypsy poet or modern troubadour disturbed him and he considered turning to teaching. In 1929 he spent a year in New York, producing *The Poet in New York,* which illustrated his horror at a mechanized civilization. Returning to Spain, García Lorca devoted himself to drama, founding and codirecting "La Barraca," a traveling experimental theater under federal sponsorship. In both poetry and drama, García Lorca's themes were Andalusian in their fantasy and folk elements, yet universal in their conflicts of life and death, fantasy and reality, fulfillment and sterility, vital female and inadequate male. His most important lyrical work, *Lament for the Death of a Bullfighter,* shows his genius in masterly construction and dramatic impact. García Lorca had never been a political poet but his treatment of the conflicts inside Spanish society made his work abhorrent to Franco's supporters. Shortly after the outbreak of the Spanish Civil War, when he was at the height of his powers, he was assassinated, apparently by nationalists.

PRINCIPAL WORKS

Romancero gitano (poetry) 1928
 [*Gypsy Ballads,* 1953]
Bodas de sangre (drama) 1933
 [*Blood Wedding,* 1939]
Yerma (drama) 1934
 [*Yerma,* 1941]
Llanto por Ignacio Sánchez Majías (poetry) 1935
 [*Lament for the Death of a Bullfighter,* 1937]
Poeta en Nueva York (poetry) 1940
 [*Poet in New York,* 1940]
La Casa de Bernarda Alba (drama) 1945
 [*The House of Bernarda Alba,* 1941]

Garcia Lorca's poems use the art of words to exalt the arts of deeds. "Manly" prosody, made suspect in the English tongue by the practices of such philistines as Kipling, is now retrieved by this aesthetic performance in [A. L. Lloyd's] English translation. . . . Writers in English can learn from the work of this Spanish gypsy who learned from our Whitman and wrote an ode to him. Our poetry at its full would reconcile passion recollected in tranquillity (the style of Wordsworth) with action induced through agitation (the style of Whitman).

The external of Garcia Lorca's art is his handling of free assonantal verse. (pp. 167-68)

It is not surprising that Garcia Lorca's verses rang through the breadth of his land from the lips of illiterate persons long before his aesthetic populism led him to its political expression. The internals of his art, its surrealist extensions of symbolist association are of an inherently popular nature. . . . (pp. 168-69)

Above all, this work is important as propaganda. It does not come straight out; everything is held in suspense, implicit. . . . As is essential also to poetic propaganda which does come straight out, this propaganda is moved by magic —seemingly unpredictable; compact of mystery, vitally fatal. As with all men of genius, Lorca's life, his work, his death were one—consummated in the classic destiny that his last poem should have been a bullfighter's elegy. . . . The actuality of his anti-Fascism makes his poetic philosophy unutterably touching in its indication of the mystic meaning of the bullfighter's conquest of the beast and the scientific meaning of the art of revolution's conquest of the mill. (pp. 169-70)

> *John Wheelwright, "The Poetry of Lorca," in* Poetry (© *1937 by the Modern Poetry Association; reprinted by permission of the Editor of* Poetry), *December, 1937, pp. 166-70.*

[Garcia Lorca's] poetry is a curious blend of folk song and sophisticated speech. There is in it the quality that one finds in the Scots ballad and the Elizabethan lyric and the Greek Anthology. What is said is said definitively, authentically, stamped and sealed in a tradition of speech that easily outlasts the dictatorial orator of the moment, even while the poet dies for it. Much of this came from his Andalusian childhood: the landscape, animals, children, sailors that he had known, the annual pleasures of the countryside, the regular excitements of the religious processions; and also there was the preoccupation with the gypsies there, as settled in their own way, but fleeting and mysterious. Andalusian ballads and gypsy songs make up a large part of his poetry; through them he made his appeal to the people. . . .

These ballads and songs [in *Poems*] are peculiarly local and native, with undertones that only an Andalusian would fully grasp. . . . And the specific recurrent imagery of olives, jasmine, fig trees, salt pits, the smell of the Sierra, the little squares of the towns, the ponies in the mountain—all this will be for most of us a dream landscape. What makes it *seem* so real to us is that Lorca, without being a storyteller, constantly gives the sense of life to his pictures: men riding, women on the balustrade, gypsy girls dancing. In effect it is what Burns does so easily and simply in his Scots poems. . . . So Lorca . . . savors and sweetens a people and landscape that he loved deeply and intimately.

But though like Burns in his realism and his nature-sense and like him also in his musical knowledge (he composed, sang his own songs, had the respect of de Falla), Lorca is far beyond in linguistic sophistication. He uses every effect of symbolism, fantasy, super-realism, and he has the astringent difficulty and corresponding pleasure of solution that most modern verse has, and that Blake, rather than Burns, had. Particularly in the *"Casidas"* there is an imaginative reach for the reality beyond mere description: "The roses search in the forehead . . . for a hard landscape of bone"— "I want to live with that obscure child . . . who wanted to cut his heart on the high seas"—the rose, the landscape, the child, the sea are becoming symbols of Lorca's own world out of the popular world that he knew, and this would have been developed, undoubtedly, as Rilke, Yeats and Eliot have developed theirs, had he not been so stupidly put to death.

> *Peter Monro Jack, "The Poetry of Garcia Lorca," in* The New York Times Book Review *(© 1939 by The New York Times Company; reprinted by permission), September 3, 1939, p. 2.*

The difficulties confronting any translator of Lorca are formidable. His manner is the manner of the Andalusian *romance,* which has no equivalent in English, and which, transposed into English, divorced from the movement and cadence of the folk-music that is its very soul, becomes merely floppy, meaningless doggerel. It is possible to preserve much of Lorca's wild imagery; but in Spanish the justifying context of this imagery is the singing or speaking voice, and translation destroys the context and accordingly falsifies the imagery. The translatable element in "Bodas de Sangre" is slight enough: a negligible plot, no analysis of character, with here and there a bit of dialogue that would come through in any language. What gives the tragedy its passionate life is the music that cannot be translated. (p. 21)

> Saturday Review *(copyright © 1940 by Saturday Review, Inc.; reprinted with permission), January 13, 1940.*

With each fresh addition to our knowledge of Federico Garcia Lorca, the poet's genius becomes more impressive. That extraordinary brillance which struck one at once, in the first few of his poems to be translated, has turned out

by no means to be an intermittent or accidental thing—it was sustained. Brilliance came as naturally to him . . . as dullness or preciosity to others; it was simply his speech. Nothing could be more remarkable, [in] . . . *The Poet in New York,* than the apparently inexhaustible fertility of Lorca's imagination. It was everywhere at once, it was prodigal, it was fantastic—the subjective and objective worlds rolled up and ignited in a single ball—the quotidian married singularly to the classic, the folksong crossed with the baroque. To call him a surrealist is a mistake, for to be a surrealist is to be something else than a poet, something less than a poet: surrealism is perhaps one of many names, merely, for the substratum out of which poetry is made. Lorca devoured all the properties of surrealism, stuffed his cheeks with them, like a conjuror, blew them out of his mouth again as poems—but so he did with everything else that he fed on. The papery guitars, the ingeniously misplaced eyes, the little traplike mouths cropping out of the sides of heads, and all the rest of that slightly sinister and somehow iodine-tinctured phantasmagoria of the followers of Loplop and synesthesia, these are certainly here, in the New York poems, but they have been made into poetry.

On the whole! There are times, let us admit, when the prodigality of image does seem to be indulged in for its own sake, and when the virtuosity and rapidity become blinding: the Gongoresque multiplication of idea carries one too far, and on too wide a front: too many things are required to be embraced at once, as if one tried to organize a single wave from end to end of the Atlantic. But even so, the fault is more often ours than Lorca's—*he* knows perfectly well what he is doing, and the tiniest or queerest item of the sargasso which his wave lifts will presently yield its meaning, like something heard afterward, like an echo. Back will come the main theme, the recurring preoccupation, of this book—pain, pain and suffering, fear of death and injury, the agony of the conscious mind in the presence of universal pain. . . . (pp. 276-77)

If there is nothing in the present collection quite as good as the *Lament for the Death of a Bullfighter,* which was perhaps the finest of all Lorca's poems, there is nevertheless much that is magnificent. The "Ode to Walt Whitman"— bitter, comic, wry-mouthed, double-faced—is devastating: and so are the New York poems, "Unsleeping City," "Blind Panorama" and others. There has been no more terribly acute critic of America than this steel-conscious and death-conscious Spaniard, with his curious passion for the modernities of nickel and tinfoil and nitre, and for the eternities of the desert and the moon. He hated us, and rightly, for the right reasons. Intensely Spanish, he is best of course in Spanish, which, next to English, is the best of all poetic languages. . . . (p. 278)

> *Conrad Aiken, "After All, I Am a Poet," in* The New Republic *(reprinted by permission of* The New Republic; *© 1940 by The New Republic, Inc.), September 2, 1940 (and reprinted as "Lorca, Federico Garcia" in his* Collected Criticism, *Oxford University Press, 1968, pp. 276-78).*

Lorca had a right to Surrealism as non-Spanish poets have not; his native literary tradition stems from Gongora. And the modern Spaniard has cut loose from the idea of a religious hell so recently that the private hell of the subconscious floats closer to the surface in both Dali and Lorca than, nowadays, in artists of other nationalities. These facts must be borne in mind by the reader who, like myself, distrusts Surrealism's worth and pretensions and the worth of any poet who adheres too rigorously to its tenets. In the case of Lorca, we have proof of his poetic worth in his non-Surrealist work. The brilliant and popularly inspired *Gypsy Ballads* were published in 1928. . . . His Surrealist period in America and Cuba followed. Later, Lorca published his "Lament for Ignacio Sanchez Mejias" (already translated into English by A. L. Lloyd as "Lament for the Death of a Bullfighter"), and in that late and superb poem we can see what the poet finally did with Surrealism. He used it as Baudelaire used "Gothic": he made it humane and the vehicle of emotion.

His ballads get at the nerve centers directly. Their oral tradition comes through at all points; we understand why this poetry is sung by illiterate people all over Spain. Objects in them move, glitter, give off heat, cold, and odor; expand and contract, glow and resound, and the heart of the reader goes through corresponding processes; is made to feel. They are grown out of the heart as wheat or grapes are grown out of the ground. (pp. 283-84)

> *Louise Bogan, "Federico Garcia Lorca" (1937, 1940), in* A Poet's Alphabet, *edited by Robert Phelps and Ruth Limmer (copyright © 1970 by Ruth Limmer as Trustee), McGraw-Hill, 1971, pp. 283-84.*

Lorca would have enjoyed the hard Irish, I think, and admired both their folksiness and their preciosity. He was not lachrymose; he knew better than to break up his lines to weep; unlike many writers who identify themselves with the emotional states of women, he never invested himself with melancholy. He knew, as perhaps Unamuno did not, that for the tragic sense of life gaiety was no accident but essential. He knew that if the play was tragic it was play still—"gaiety transforming all that dread." It is good to have, in this first collection of his dramas [*From Lorca's Theatre: Five Plays*], these specimens of his friendly invention, his rashness, his fun, and always his brilliance, a kind of light vanished from our literature, if it ever shone there. Even the formal silk hat, in which he comes on to address the audience in the author's prologue to "The Prodigious Shoemaker's Wife," reminding them that the poet does not demand benevolence but attention—even this tall silk hat is a symbol of his profusion: when he takes it off, it becomes illuminated with a green light from within. He tips it over and a gush of water falls from it. He seems embarrassed and retires; but he did not really need to beg our pardon.

> *Rolfe Humphries, "So Bright an Andalusian," in* The Nation *(copyright 1941 by the Nation Associates, Inc.), November 1, 1941, p. 430.*

[The] world première of Federico Garcia Lorca's play [*If Five Years Pass*], offered by the Jane Street Group at the Provincetown Playhouse, is here briefly mentioned in the interest of theater as well as news. . . . I should like to say at once that this vehicle of dream (no dreamer) constituted for me the most intense experience in modern theater I have received outside the books. Frankly an experiment—it is one of two surrealist plays projected by its author, Spain's greatest poet-dramatist—the piece necessarily employs a system of private and received symbols precisely

figured by actors although in no way to be naturalistically interpreted by them. The theme can be identified with one of the White Queen's in "Through the Looking Glass": *remembering forwards;* and its working depends upon an ambiguity which is as exciting as it is pure. And here it is tragic. I think the effect can only be defined as the physical acting out of metaphor: as trope summons trope in the lines, the figures recall, accept, or impel other figures, subjects, things. It is of course no more astonishing that Garcia Lorca has been only twice before played in this country than that Brecht is completely unplayed. In the work of both these men the stage is returned to the poet and poetry is made. (pp. 17-18)

> *Kappo Phelan, in* Commonweal *(copyright © 1945 Commonweal Publishing Co., Inc.; reprinted by permission of Commonweal Publishing Co., Inc.), April 20, 1945.*

[Lorca's] songs have a peculiarly diaphanous and evanescent quality. His sensitiveness enabled him to catch those fleeting moments to which coarser temperaments are blind, and his skill translated these into airy melodious verse, in which all that exists is the impression of a single moment. Lorca, intent on conveying the pure essence of poetry, gives only the central thrill. When his sensibility found unexpected relations between things and was able to illuminate what others had only half noticed, with deft brevity he touched on the vital relation, the point of identity or resemblance between one impression and another and produced the image which secured this. What counts is the choice of an image, or of a scene which does the work of an image in suggesting wider associations of thought. Lorca uses his sensibility to evoke something beyond the event which provides his material. These poems are not in any limited sense descriptive, nor are they abstract. They move through varied and vivid stages, through exact and loving observation, to the evocation of an experience in its imaginative unity. Lorca seems to possess by nature the new way of transforming inchoate states of consciousness into concrete pictures. His mind was stored with memories and what his eyes or ears noted passed into his poetry. (p. 193)

He was the first European poet to use modern methods of imagery and suggestion to create a poetry of simple people [in *Poema del Canto Hondo*]. . . . Every detail tells. Every touch is not only perfectly conceived imaginatively but is entirely true to the human subject. Though Lorca throws himself into the lives of his Gipsies and sees everything through their eyes, at the same time he keeps his own delicate, special touch in the speed with which he shows just what a situation or a sensation means, what imaginative significance it has, what its decisive impression on him is. Lorca absorbed some of the discoveries of modernism so easily that he seems to have been born into them. His art shows no traces either of effort or of conscious modernity. In him the modernistic ways of looking at experience seem to be perfectly natural not only in himself but in the characters whom he presents.

Lorca's interest in this grim and primitive Gipsy life led him to publish in 1928 *Romancero Gitano (Gipsy Ballads)*, and to win with it a success unparalleled for poetry in his time. It was his masterpiece. Even he, who was usually diffident and dilatory about publication, felt no hesitation about this book. . . .

His dramatic instinct needed something wider than song could give him, and he found it in the Spanish *romance,* the ballad which dates back to the fourteenth century and has been perfected by many great poets both known and unknown. It has none of the slackness and immaturity of the English ballad: it has a regular line based on a fixed number of syllables, and a whole poem is held together by a single assonance which runs through it instead of rhyme. The traditional *romances* have a wonderful economy and concentration, and Lorca could follow their manner without surrendering any of his own special effects. He might even claim that in applying this ancient form to a modern sensibility he had a precedent in Luis de Góngora who in the seventeenth century used the *romance* to blend popular themes with the advanced manner of his epoch. (pp. 194-95)

In the *Romancero* Lorca carried to perfection that harmony of primitive and cultivated elements which can be seen in his earlier poetry. Though his subjects are drawn from a small part of life and his characters act on elementary motives, he never fails to set the imprint of his own sensibility on them. There is no artificial simplicity in these ballads. There is no moment which is not pure poetry or in which Lorca does not give an experience in its exciting fullness. The poems are not, even at a first reading, easy. Yet they have won a great popular success and are loved and quoted by many almost illiterate Spaniards. The reason is not only that they reflect some dominant qualities in the Spanish soul but that Lorca's sensibility is so fine and so sincere that simple men, whose minds are not touched by science or its substitutes, can see directly what he means and recognise its affinity to their own experience. (p. 196)

The poems have a deeper unity than [the necessary symbols]. Though Lorca tells his stories for their own sake with an almost dramatic impartiality, he creates his own self-consistent world of the imagination. He reduces human life to a few essential elements, to the unrationalised emotions and desires of simple men and women. The humanity which Lorca portrays has a natural directness and candour. The characters, sketched in a few deft strokes, stand in their own strength with all their primitive forces at work.... These characters are not facets of the poet's inner life or symbols of his thought; they are figures of drama who engage our interest by their personalities and their destinies. Even when Lorca shifts his point of vision from the present to history or legend, his characters are equally alive.... Lorca's dramatic and plastic genius created a homogeneous world in which some simple and essential kinds of human life are vividly presented in his dramatic persons. He makes his own little universe which so imposes itself on us that we accept its laws without question.

The *Romancero* is much more than dramatic: it is almost pure poetry. To every phase of his Gipsy lives Lorca gives the abundant riches of his sympathy and sensibility, and weaves his visual fancies in the frame of their dreams and deaths. His unexpected juxtapositions of images, the brilliance of his details and of his symbols, his complete avoidance of anything trite or false or exaggerated, all help to secure an astonishing level of imaginative achievement. He sees not only the physical setting of his characters but its meaning for the imagination. When he first mentions the Gipsies, he not only shows what they look like but more subtly what they are.... (p. 215)

The *Romancero* is a book of astonishing brilliance, of un-

failing poetry, in which a modern technique is adapted to traditional means and primitive subjects. In it Lorca has absorbed the most important lessons of modernism and avoided it excesses. His tone is marvellously sustained. We never cease to feel that we are seeing things as the Gipsies see them or would see them if they had the power to make their feelings definite. By a remarkable stroke of insight Lorca uses his modern manner for a primitive outlook, and the fit is perfect. His sense of mystery, of irrational actions, of magical powers in the universe, of the way in which passion dominates the mind and imposes illusions on it, is not only true to his Gipsies but perfectly adapted to his impressionistic method. People so unsophisticated as these see things in this vivid, unrelated way and do not wait to arrange their thoughts in logical categories. The ease of Lorca's purely poetical appeal owes much to his subject. Through it he can take great risks of expression but be sure that they will succeed, because after all his Gipsies are human beings whose approach to life has the instinctive immediacy which is also that of a poet. Nor is it fair to complain that in taking such a subject Lorca shirks the urgent issues of his time. His Gipsies are the humble people of Southern Spain and differ in few essentials from true Spaniards of the same district and class. These were the people whom Lorca knew, and he was right to make them his subject because he felt for them that special affection which awoke his curiosity and his imagination and set his powers to work. The result is a book which has a special place in our time because it shows not only that the outlook of a highly civilised poet is in many ways that of the simplest men and women, but that the new devices which have been invented to express a modern sensibility are not restricted to urban and sophisticated subjects but may be applied with great success to the dark passions and obscure fancies of an almost primitive consciousness. (pp. 218-19)

> *C. M. Bowra, "Federico García Lorca, 'Romancero Gitano'," in his* The Creative Experiment *(copyright © 1949 by Macmillan & Co., Ltd; reprinted by permission of Macmillan, London and Basingstoke), Macmillan, 1949 (and reprinted by Grove Press, 1958), pp. 189-219.*

[*The House of Bernarda Alba*] is about the attempt to preserve honor in the face of the sexual instinct. What is honor? Encountering the idea in a Spanish author, one is sent back to the classic Spanish playwrights of the seventeenth century. Isn't there a play of that period in which a husband must save his honor by killing the wife he knows to be innocent—because everyone else thinks her guilty? A student of Spanish tradition supplied me with quotations like these: "Dishonor is death, honor is life.... Honor being comparable to life, one can kill to defend it." "This dependence of honor on other people's opinion argues precisely its not being egotistical, but eminently social. Every man of dignity has to preserve intact his patrimony of social honor, of which each is a depository." All of which is to go but a step farther than Shakespeare's Fortinbras, who could find quarrel in a straw when honor was at stake....

[This] kind of honor was once the very center of a civilization's scheme of values and, second, that even in Lorca an echo of its old dignity and meaning is heard. Bernarda, in short, is not a villain of melodrama but the representative of a philosophy and a tradition.... On the other hand, it would be absurd to forget the centuries between Lope and Lorca. The latter comes forward to show how hideous and destructive the old ideal can be in the family life of some modern Andalusians of the middle class. (pp. 217-18)

[It] is Ibsen and not Sophocles we think of when Lorca gives a social grounding to his dramatic inevitability. "Each class does what it has to," says one of the sisters in another of the little formulas that sum up the play. Napoleon said that in modern times politics is fate; Lorca seems to be saying that economics is. Walled in by their economic situation, by their class, his people do what their fathers did before them. On her husband's death Bernarda orders the shutters closed for eight years of mourning. "That's what happened in my father's house, and in my grandfather's." Martirio [says that] . . . "things repeat themselves. I can see that everything is a terrible repetition." (p. 219)

What the "terrible repetition" is for Bernarda's family is sensed by all. Their grandmother is mad. Although Lorca gives her few lines, he contrives—and there is no higher tribute one could pay to his dramatic genius—to give her maximum weight. Her two little intrusions on the stage action are not only breathtaking theater; they sum the whole play up. "This is where you will all end" is the idea that follows both from the action and from constant harping on "terrible repetitions." . . . Yet the grandmother—being used dialectically—has also the opposite function of suggesting the earlier, healthier stage in a tradition now debilitated and sterile. She can dream her way back to romance and fertility. She forms a connecting link with the "unlikely landscapes full of nymphs or legendary kings" which Lorca says are pictured on the walls of the set. Because Bernarda is not linked to the ancient wisdom, she rushes stupidly into disaster. Adela asks her why people used to invoke Saint Barbara against evil omens, and Bernarda replies: "The old people knew many things that we've forgotten."

The way in which this remark is given broader reference by its context is Ibsenite, like the idea of society as fate. An Ibsenite symbolism pervades the text. . . . (pp. 219-20)

More interesting is Lorca's use of the Ibsenite device of a single, central metaphor that spreads itself, horizontally as it were, over the whole story and vertically onto different levels of meaning. Like Ibsen, Lorca puts his central image in his title. The house is the main character of the play. *Indoors* and *outdoors* are the chief spatial entities. *Doors* themselves are crucial as being at once barrier and bridge between *in* and *out*. *Windows* are equally significant, for in Spain a lady is courted at her window and it is through the window that the villagers look out upon life. The neighbors are always at their windows and are always curious to learn if you are at yours—and you are, though you hope they don't know it. In other words, all the houses are supposed to be closed; each inmate is fighting for his own privacy, his own identity. But all the houses are really open, for each inmate is fighting against the privacy of others, against letting them live their own lives. (pp. 220-21)

The play—especially Poncia's speeches—has made us aware that the neighbors are listening, that many of them "can read thoughts at a distance," that the shutting of doors and windows, physical or spiritual, is unavailing. . . . With every repetition of the word *silence* we are more aware of its futility. Lorca is writing the epitaph of old Spain, not a tribute to it. The Franco government is quite

right to find the recent *première* a threat to all the regime stands for.

The constant implied reference to society recalls the Ibsen of the "modern" plays. So does the ironical symbolism by which the reference is made. So, finally, does the over-all structure and dramaturgic method. Lorca follows Ibsen as Ibsen followed some of the ancients, in adhering pretty closely to the unities of time, place, and action. (pp. 221-22)

Lorca uses Ibsen's famous analytic method: you find out what has been going on from *obiter dicta* and innuendoes. (pp. 222-23)

"Silence" is the first word Bernarda speaks and the last. She speaks it many other times. She and others use synonyms like *hush* and *sh!* and *quiet!* . . . The repeated mention of silence is reinforced by actual silences. The pauses are as eloquent as anything in the dialogue. (p. 223)

Ireland and Spain are two of the remaining vestiges of Catholic-peasant civilization. Lorca's play springs from this civilization, gives it amazingly full expression, and is a bitter rejection of it. If the Franco government is not prepared to permit such public rejections, one can hardly be surprised. If Ireland *is* prepared to permit them, so much the better for her—and her future. (p. 231)

> *Eric Bentley, "The Poet in Dublin" (1950), in his* In Search of Theater *(copyright © 1948, 1949, 1950, 1951, 1952, 1953 by Eric Bentley; reprinted by permission of Atheneum Publishers, New York), Atheneum, 1953, pp. 215-32.*

Though not by any means the greatest Spanish poet of his time, Lorca is the most intensely and nationally Spanish. This, however, he does not express in patriotism, as an Englishman would do were he so extremely English as Lorca is Spanish. He is also one of the most narrowly regional of Spanish poets; and at the same time, paradoxically enough, he is the most popular and universal in his appeal both inside and outside Spain. His appeal is never more universal than when he is writing, at home, about his native Andalusia. It is never more parochial and provincial than when he is self-consciously trying to be 'cosmopolitan', under the influence of Whitman, in the poems written in, and about, New York and the Caribbean. Andalusia is Lorca's *querencia*. The *querencia* is the exact spot which every Spanish fighting bull chooses to return to, between his charges, in the arena. It is his invisible fortress or camp. It is not marked by anything but the bull's preference for it, and may be near the centre, near the barricade, or between the two, as the bull chooses. The nearer the bull is to his *querencia* or stamping-station, the more formidable he is, the more full of confidence, and the more difficult to lure abroad into the territory of the bullfighters, for their territory is wherever the bull is most vulnerable, and least sure of himself.

During Lorca's sojourns abroad, or in Madrid, he always returned for poetical strength to his native province; even when he did not return to it in person, he returned in imagination, memory, and dreams: and it never failed him as a source of strength and inspiration. It was from there that he was most difficult to lure abroad into the intellectual territory of the enemy, the territory of bad verse and of adverse criticism, where the critics can take advantage of the vulnerability of the poet, just as the 'toreros' do of the weakness of the bull when he stays outside of the magic and magnetic radius of his *querencia*. A poet can only get into that enemy territory by writing poorly about things he cannot feel instinctively. That is what happens to Lorca when he leaves Andalusia. He is like his ancient fellow-countryman, the giant Antaeus, who rose with strength redoubled each time he touched his mother-earth.

The cities of Granada, Córdoba and Sevilla, the three capital cities of Andalusia, always recur in that order in the poems of Lorca. After Granada the ancient Roman Córdoba comes second in his heart. He is attracted by something shadowy, nostalgic, and melancholy in both these towns which have outlived their greatest splendour. Sevilla, the gay, beautiful, and ever young giantess with the huge carnation between her teeth is too powerful and raucous to engage the same tender and intimate love that he feels for Granada or Córdoba.

That Lorca, one of the most narrowly regional poets of modern times, should be at the same time one of the most universally appreciated among his contemporaries, is just one more of those delightful little paradoxes which make bearable the present stereotyping dehumanisation, unification, and bureaucratic centralisation of human life. (pp. 8-9)

A body without reaction is a corpse: so is any social body without tradition. 'Reactionary' Spain has, during this century, produced better poetry than any other country; and this is chiefly due to her preoccupation with spiritual necessities rather than immediate physical conveniences.

At first sight some of the great poetical plays of Lorca will seem far-fetched because his characters prefer broken pockets, broken bank balances, and even broken hearts, to broken spirits. But those characters are true to life in Spain: and if they were true to life here, there would be more poetry here. There are no substitutes for morality, honour, and loyalty, either in themselves (as we are so painfully learning) or as the substance of poetry and drama. (p. 12)

There is one poet in contemporary English literature who is deeply conscious, as Lorca was, of the *sound* of words; that is Dylan Thomas: he extracts the maximum of meaning from words through their sound. So does Lorca. They are both musicians: more than any poets of our times, they have studied the evocative force of sound in words. Thomas is a dealer in thunder and lightning, Lorca deals rather in the sound of rivers and leaves, and the irridescences of lights and waters. Strength is Dylan Thomas's salient quality, though he is by no means without subtlety. Subtlety is Lorca's chief quality though he is by no means without strength. They both derive from countries where there is a very strong musical and vocal tradition, and where singing is a natural function of the people. (The success of the Welsh miners' choirs in Spain was only equalled by that of the Spanish singers and dancers in Wales.) (p. 13)

[The] popular tradition is one of the main influences in Lorca's work; but it has been vastly exaggerated by some critics, excusably perhaps, since it is so rare in the modern world that it immediately distinguishes a living modern poet who is lucky enough to have undergone that influence. But Lorca grafted on to the tree of popular tradition his own gorgeous ramification of the sophisticated and highly *literary* Gongorine tradition, which is the very opposite of the simple popular folk-lore with which he blended it so harmo-

niously. Thus he performed the miraculous operation of combining the most cultivated artifice of baroque poetry with the ingenuous art of the people, and of reconciling the treasures of the library to those of the earth and sky of his native sierra. He was influenced in turn by many of the other great poets of the Golden Age ... who formed a galaxy only equalled in literary history by that of our own Elizabethans and Jacobeans. (pp. 13-14)

Nearly all Lorca's most flowery work is vertebrated with a sinewy spinal-cord. However much he luxuriates externally into such sparkling froth ..., it is the froth of good strong champagne—with a body to it. There is always a central design to his work. The two principles, that of luxuriation and that of economy, wrestle harmoniously in nearly all the best Andalusian art, as if a sort of tropical oriental luxuriance were being pruned and ordered by the cold hard axe of Romanity. (p. 21)

Lorca's achievement, throughout his career, is reflected, as by an infallible index, by the effectiveness of his images. His poems stand or fall by them. They are the pulses by which we measure his health, beating strongly and normally in his *First Poems,* his best plays, the *Lament for the Bullfighter,* the *Canciones,* the *Cante Jondo,* but by fits and starts, irregularly, in his *New York Poems* and his *Diván de Tamarit.* Whereas a Castilian poet like Gabriel y Galán can write a superb poem without a single metaphor, simile or image, they form both the glory and (sometimes) the weakness of Lorca's work. He has periods when they are consistently successful, other periods when they are not, and it is very rare that he ever mixes good and bad images in the same poem. (p. 24)

Latin 'nature poets' differ entirely from the German and English Romantics. When I read Wordsworth, I feel that all his rocks, trees, and mountains are more intelligent than human beings, whereas his human characters, wherever they can be unearthed, are almost without exception imbeciles and nit-wits. I feel that there is something deeply perverse, intellectually suicidal and misanthropic about this transposition of values. In fact I think the whole Romantic principle (in its bad sense) can be defined as something perverse, a sort of centrifugal panic in which the poet escapes from himself: a principle that subordinates the immediate to the remote, the evident to the occult, the normal to the abnormal, the lucid to the obscure, the moral to the immoral, and the present to some Utopianised future or romanticised past. ... The difference in the Latin-Mediterranean type of 'nature poetry', seen at its best in the *Georgics* of Virgil, is that there is no brown study, no Buddhistified blurring and blending with 'the Whole', to the detriment of all outlines and sane values. Where a Latin poet creates a darkness, as in Saint John of the Cross's *Dark Night of the Soul,* it is not for the sake of merging with that darkness alone, nor the losing of all contours in a brown study; it is simply to rid the mind of a less intense form of reality, so as to give it all the more power to seize the more intense reality of God. The proof is in the fact that this kind of mystical poetry makes you wide awake, and the other soothes you almost to sleep; and this is the difference between the mystic and the mistagogue. The nature poets of the Latin races tend to differentiate, to particularise, and even to anthropomorphise the objects about which they write, as Virgil did with his bees, bringing them out clearly from their background. The tendency of the northern poets is to let nature envelop them around with moss, clouds, weeds, and flowers, until we and they disappear in a dream of mental vegetation and vapour.

Lorca, who had known intense suffering in childhood and throughout the rest of his life, since he was never to know the normal command of his muscles and limbs, grew up amongst those countrymen who, different from the poetical excursionists, know the particular in nature, and not a single entity with a capital N. The things that attract his attention most as a poet are always in his immediate surroundings, with their peasants and their animal population of bees, butterflies, nightingales, cicadas, frogs, and lizards. . . . In dealing with the smaller creatures of the earth, he affects a sort of Lilliputian minuteness, almost Franciscan in its intimacy, which in its detail reminds one of the exquisite treatment of bees by Virgil and Góngora, or the even more perfect treatment of the fable of the Town and Country Mouse by Horace in his satires. We are reminded of the pre-Romantic poets in our own literature, the exquisite Drayton of the *Nymphidia,* the speech of Mercutio about Queen Mab, and certain passages of *A Midsummer Night's Dream.* The very important difference is that we are torn by Lorca between a comic grotesqueness and a heartrending pathos with which he invests these slightly humanised, tiny creatures of the fields. He notices on the lizards their 'litle white aprons', calls them 'drops of crocodile', and 'dragons of the frogs', seeing their 'green frock-coat of a devil's abbot'. But Lorca's small animal and insect world, though conceived with a childish directness of vision, is no dream world of Titanias and fairies, but the real old world we inhabit ourselves, seen in miniature, with startling clearness, as through the wrong end of a telescope. Its fierceness remains undiminished by microscopic proportions, and becomes all the more startling because of them and because of a sort of Goyaesque and Bosch-like mixture of the human with the Lilliputian.

The description of the voices of the frogs 'freckling the silence with little green dots' is another uncanny but perfect image to those who have heard the frogs of the southern marshes, at sundown, start up their chorus with the twinkling of the stars. When I say Lorca partly humanises his creatures, I do not mean that he detracts from their peculiar frogginess, lizardliness, or whatever it may be. The touch of humanity seems to enhance and emphasize their innate quality as frogs, snails or ants, by the sheer force of contrast. [At the age of five] Lorca used to love harrowing and terrifying the peasants by imitating the priest's 'hell-fire sermons'. Some of his poems, of a seemingly trivial nature, are so poignant that one sometimes indignantly and resentfully accuses the poet of going out of his way to make one suffer. (pp. 26-8)

[The] disconsolate mood recurs with insistence and power in Lorca's early work: and it returns even more powerfully in his later plays in which he invariably deals with what we call 'unpleasant subjects'. But in these later plays, the cruelty which he flings in one's face almost aggressively, as if to relieve his own sufferings, is tempered and balanced by the Euripidean stature of the protagonists, their innate strength, their willingness to accept suffering (since there is always a way out of cowardice or compromise) and their capacity for resignation. We accept his plays as we would accept them from scarcely anyone else dealing with the same subjects. It is his sheer artistic mastery which makes us accept them, and the realisation that his compassion is, after all, one of the main motives for burning both himself and us with such anguish. (p. 30)

In the end it is clear that Lorca is not deliberately inflicting pain on the reader, in order to shock or annoy him; but that he feels so poignantly that he has to share this feeling with others. This is the motive underlying his insistence on themes of cruelty. We know that in his life he was cheerful, full of fun, a radiant and kindly personality, and that considering the extent and nature of what he had to suffer, there was not much perversity in his make-up, as modern poets go.

Together with this sense of pain one feels almost everywhere in Lorca's poetry, even at its gayest (and it can be very gay) there goes also the sense of a lurking, imminent and violent death. (p. 31)

His eternal wrestling with the theme of death had its justification, just as Keats's preoccupation with the same theme. It came out of strength rather than weakness. The event proved that it was no illusion. His own violent death, and that of nearly three million Spanish men, women, and children, could already be sensed in the air, like a coming thunderstorm, for many years before the Terror was unleashed. It was publicly threatened on all the walls. One could not escape from being confronted with skulls and crossbones with bloodthirsty inscriptions chalked up everywhere. . . . In the repeated wrestling with the idea of death, Lorca generally increases the stature of life, and intensifies it. All those people who repeatedly seek out death to risk their lives do so chiefly because they are overflowing with a surplus of life. They get a stimulus from the presence of death as a healthy body does from a cold bath. (pp. 37-8)

In Lorca's greatest sustained lyrical poem, the *Lament for the Death of the Matador (Llanto por Ignacio Sánchez Mejías),* we see a duel between Life and Death, enacted almost as a ritual dance between the superb, overflowing vitality of the matador and the cold shadow of Absence, while each augments and enhances the stature and the mystery of the other. In all his early poems in which he treats the subject of death we feel that the dual process is at work, which he carries to such a supreme triumph in the *Llanto.* Many of the earlier poems are rehearsals of this towering spiral in which the two forces contend in a sort of ecstasy; but there are also heights of serene lyrical contemplation which are exceptional in such a young poet. . . . (pp. 38-9)

'Romancero' means a collection of 'Romances'. This is by far the most famous and popular of all Lorca's collections of verse. . . . The romance is the Spanish equivalent of our ancient popular ballad-form; and the latter is the only means by which we can possibly translate it, since the Spanish 'romance', instead of rhyming, requires an assonance in every second line, which continues right through the whole poem, and, in the long run, produces a stronger effect than our rhyme. . . . Lorca, who while we are reading him appears to be a very spontaneous and facile writer, must have expended prodigious study and pains on the Romance form; his assonance is very much more pronounced than that of other Spanish poets. On analysing his use of vowel sounds, one finds that the extra emphasis which his own vowel assonance sounds acquire is usually due to their having been entirely suppressed from the rest of the line in which they occur. This is a true feat of profound technical engineering. (pp. 40-1)

[The] two books of his songs, or *Canciones,* ... were written mostly between 1921 and 1924, but not revised or published till many years later. In some of these he sets out to capture half-meanings and impressions that are difficult, vague, and remote, and literally to give to 'airy nothing' a name and address. 'Rien que la nuance', Verlaine's motto, 'nothing but the mere shade', flickers like a will-o'-the-wisp over some of these pages. (p. 62)

In Lorca's work, as in that of his two friends Falla and Salvador Dali, the tradition finally balances perfectly with their revolutionary innovations, though there is a violent struggle at first to dominate the irruption of the new forces in their work. Of the four Spaniards who loom so great in the world of modern art, Picasso is the only one who remains an iconoclast, in a state of perpetual fission. (p. 66)

Lorca's chief public activity was concerned with the stage, in reviving the masterpieces of the Golden Age under his own direction, and in travelling round with puppet shows and companies of his own. He was responsible for a national revival of poetic drama. He wrote many plays which he produced himself. Some like *Así que pasan los Cinco Años* were experimental.

The best verse dramas of Lorca fill several volumes and are generally remarkable alike for their stage-craft and the quality of the verse that sustains them. (p. 67)

[While in the United States, Lorca] was unable to establish a real contact with the Americans or their way of life. The result on his poetry was entirely negative. He underwent while there the intellectual influence, if not domination, of Salvador Dali, his friend, who is also a great artist of international repute, but a far more complicated personality than Lorca, more resilient and aggressive, with a far wider range of sympathies and interests, and at home anywhere from the U.S.A. to Catalonia. Lorca attempted to follow the Catalonian into the complex world of surrealism, and lost his depth. In Lorca's New York poems, the *Poeta en Nueva York,* his metaphors and images fall out of focus; his verse becomes loose, plaintive, and slightly mephitic. It took him quite a long time to recover his poetical eyesight and insight after he returned to Spain. In his long *Ode to Salvador Dali* he applauds the clear vision of the Catalan painter, but seems to lose a grasp on his own; yet the poem nevertheless contains some fine lines. We are reminded, in Lorca's American venture, of Burns when he went into high society at Edinburgh and started to write like a courtier and gentleman of the world. It was a fiasco. Lorca's talent is not cosmopolitan, and it did not flourish far from the scent of the orange groves of the South. Even in his two *Odes to the Sacrament,* which were written under the intense stimulus of religion, Lorca fails to organise the chaos in his imagery and the impact on his mind of Dali's work.

Lorca reached the height of his achievement in his *Llanto por Ignacio Sánchez Mejías;* here he remained true to his native Andalusia, to the earth and the landscape from which his verse derived its strength, flavour and perfume; yet he was not under the restriction he imposed upon himself in the *Romancero,* that of the coldly impartial and ironic spectator. On the contrary, he was expressing his grief for a beloved friend, one of the greatest bullfighters of all time, who was also a cultured literary man, a good farmer, a great horseman, and a popular figure who was equally beloved by all for his goodness of heart, as well as

for his prowess and valour. The death of Ignacio Sanchez Mejías was a public calamity in Andalusia. (pp. 71-2)

The fourth part of the *Llanto* in which he takes final leave of his friend, ends with a verse which might serve as an epitaph for the poet himself:

> It will be long before there is born, if ever,
> An Andalusian so frank, so rich in adventure;
> I sing your elegance with words that moan
> And remember a sad wind among the olive trees.
>
> (p. 77)

> *Roy Campbell, in his* Lorca: An Appreciation of His Poetry *(copyright, 1952, by Yale University Press), Yale University Press, 1952.*

[Although Lorca has been compared with Synge], Lorca entirely lacks Synge's grotesque humour. This may partly be because he is more part of the world he describes. With Synge we feel that he is an observer, sometimes completely fascinated, at others ironically detached. He has buried himself in the world of Irish folk-lore with extraordinary intensity, but in himself he still remains to some extent the lyrical poet, the symbolist who has re-discovered the strange people and nature of his own country. Lorca had also learned much from the French symbolists, and while writing his peasant plays, and even before, he was also writing stylized and symbolistic drama. The finest play in this vein is *Rosita La Soltera,* which combines a rather static plot with some extraordinarily beautiful lyric writing. His peasant plays also contain elements of symbolism, but he never quite seems to escape from the magic circle which his native Andalusia made for him. That is why with their lyrical beauty and their strangeness they are so enchanting.

When the three plays, *A Fatal Wedding* [also published in America as *Blood Wedding*], *Yerma* and *La Casa de Bernarda Alba (The House of Bernarda)* [published in America as *The House of Bernarda Alba*], are grouped together as a trilogy, this is not merely because they all have a peasant setting. Though the characters and atmosphere in each are distinct, they treat the same fundamental theme; as Hjalmar Gullberg has said, they deal with the tragedy of motherhood. ... Lorca seems to disapprove of Catholic bigotry, as O'Neill did of Puritanism, but to regard it as inseparable from the Spanish temperament. (pp. 345-46)

The idea that marriage was instituted for the procreation of children, and not for sexual satisfaction, is inherent in all Christian morality. But in *Yerma* it is given such a tense expression that a Scandinavian reader is immediately reminded of Ibsen's highly idealistic conception of the relations between the sexes. There is, however, no doubt that Lorca himself held the opposite view. In the symbolic scene between the Male and the Female especially, the subjects of married love and child-bearing are treated with fearless enthusiasm. The greatest heights of poetry reached in the play are found in the description of Yerma's disappointed mother-love, and her dreams of the child that she wanted. For her importunate husband her feelings are cool, while her love for Victor is suppressed by her Spanish notions of honour. We already notice here the same hostile attitude to conventional religion which is to be found in Lorca's last play. (p. 349)

In the person of Bernarda, unconcerned about human life, but determined to preserve an appearance of decency in the grim house where she reigns, Lorca has created his most complete female character, a counterpart to old Cabot in O'Neill's *Desire under the Elms*. No more than O'Neill has Lorca succeeded in explaining the psychological reasons for the triumph of ruthlessness and bigotry over ordinary human instincts. Both Cabot and Bernarda are terrifying personifications of this bigoted attitude. O'Neill's play is bolder and more generous in conception, but in spite of all the attention to realism, *The House of Bernarda* has an inner lyrical quality which O'Neill lacks. Both these peasant plays show how Ibsen's basic problem, the conflict between individual and social morality, is expressed in the terms of peasant life. It is significant that O'Neill, in order to make his play convincing, had to move it back to the more primitive conditions of last century. Lorca has been able without undue difficulty to set his play in contemporary Spain, and gains thereby in genuineness, both of setting and plot. (pp. 350-51)

> *Martin Lamm, in his* Modern Drama, *translated by Karin Elliott, Basil Blackwell, 1952.*

Poetic drama in English remains unsure of itself, highbrow and cultish—unless *Elizabeth the Queen, Venus Observed,* and *The Cocktail Party,* which are fairly well accepted in the show-shops, are to be called poetic drama.

Federico García Lorca also wrote poetic drama, very much as Yeats and Eliot have taught us to understand it, yet his plays are neither cultish nor middlebrow-Ersatz: they are theatre-poetry which lives naturally on the modern stage. Lorca did very little theorizing, but he found, at a very early age, in pre-Franco Spain, singularly direct ways to use the stage for the purposes of poetry. It is true that he is not a creature of the commercial theatre. Madrid in his time had a theatre corresponding to Broadway, but Lorca was always in more or less hidden opposition to it. He was the director of "La Barraca," a group of University players which was subsidized by the government and toured the provincial towns and cities of Spain with a repertory of classics. It is evident that his own plays owe a great deal to this experience. La Barraca found an "off-Broadway" audience in Spain, and since then Lorca's plays have found audiences in France, Switzerland, Germany, Mexico, South America, and college towns all over this country. No one has succeeded in producing him successfully on Broadway, but in being rejected by the timid snobbery of Times Square he is in excellent company. And there is no doubt that he can by-pass the taboos of the market, and reach a wide contemporary audience in free Europe and the Americas.

Lorca's theatre-poetry fulfills many of the prescriptions of Yeats and Eliot, but it is strongly marked by his unique genius, his rare combination of talents. And it is nourished by the Spanish tradition, which was showing new vitality just before Franco put out the light. These matters are already clear in his early play, "The Love of Don Perlimplin for Belisa, in His Garden." *Don Perlimplin* is a romantic farce, slighter and lighter than his most famous pieces, *Blood Wedding* and *The House of Bernarda Alba,* but it is a small masterpiece. When he wrote it he was already in control of his difficult art.

The story is old, lewd and rather savage: that of the old man married to a lusty young wife, one of the standard situations of neoclassic farce. But Lorca, without losing sight of the farce, lifts it to poetry also, and poetry of power and freshness. (pp. 337-38)

[The] basic situation of the old man and the young wife, . . . in Baroque continental comedy, or on the Restoration stage in England, is usually treated in the hearty, simple-minded mode of broad farce. Cervantes wrote a brilliant interlude of this kind called *The Jealous Old Man,* in which the fun is based on the disharmonies of human physiology, and the audience is expected to sympathize solely with the triumphant wife. Lorca expects us to remember that worldly old theme, and he emphasizes both its theatricality and its ancient, classic quality in the characters, their language, and their costumes. . . . [The] cast of characters is made to seem as old as nightmare, almost eternal.

But just because the farce and its people seem so ancient, it strikes us as not only farcical but also sinister. Lorca, while keeping the cynical old tale, with its neoclassic stagey glitter, also views it in the perspective of a later, gloomier and more romantic age; he transposes it to bring out also the love-death theme. That theme also is traditional in European literature. . . . Lorca certainly seems to echo the theme here with a full sense of its deep roots, especially in Don Perlimplin's lyric on the mortal wound of love, and in the final scene in the garden, which has the ceremoniousness of the dark old erotic rite.

It is an extravagant notion to combine farce and *Liebestodt,* but Lorca knew that it was extravagant. It is by means of the *style* of the piece that he makes an acceptable fusion of such disparate elements; for a knowing style implies the limitations of mood and viewpoint which the author has accepted in advance, and thus makes them acceptable and comprehensible to the audience. Lorca indicates the style of his play in its subtitle: "An Erotic Alleluya." An *Alleluya* is something like a valentine: a love-poem decorated with pictures, gilt cut-outs, lace paper and the like; something heroic, overdone, absurd: an *extravagant* offering to the beloved. All the elements of the production, music, sets, costumes, acting, should obey the requirements of this style. And one must remember that it is a Spanish style, akin perhaps to those drawings and paintings of Goya's— wounded cavaliers, frightening moustachioed old women, greedy young women in discreet mantillas—in which the remains of 18th Century elegance are seen in a sombre light.

Though this play is so unlike anything in English, it is a species of poetic drama. And it achieves much that Yeats and Eliot sought with only partial success. They were both lyric poets first and dramatists second; and both tended in their early efforts to approach poetic drama as though it were an overgrown type of lyric. (pp. 341-42)

Lorca also was a lyric poet before he succeeded on the stage, and his lyric verse shows (like that of Yeats and Eliot) the all-pervasive *symboliste* influence. He is an authentic poet, even by the exigent standards of our masters. But from the first he drew also upon the resources of the old and popular Spanish tradition of balladry: his first collection is entitled *Romancero Gitano,* "Gypsy Balladier." And the ballad is a far more promising clue to drama than the "pure" *symboliste* lyric, precisely because it typically suggests a story: a situation, contrasted characters, a significant event. The *symboliste* lyric, on the other hand, owes its purity to its source in the single feeling of the isolated poet. It is very difficult to derive from it the sense of separate but interacting lives; the movement of real change; the significance of a deed or an event: in short, the objectivity of drama, which is founded (however indirectly) upon sympathy and perception. We must simply recognize, I think, that the inspiration, the poetic point, of the *symboliste* lyric is not dramatic, while that of the ballad is.

It is clear that the whole conception of *Don Perlimplin*—the gentle, absurd, heroic old man; the animal-beauty and her mother; the weepy servant, the struggle with love's cruelty —struck Lorca as poetic. The narrative sequence is itself poetic, like that of the ballads we know. One can conceive a ballad version of *Don Perlimplin,* but not a *symboliste* lyric which would really capture the theme. Thus in trying to get the poetry of the play one must consider not only the passages in verse, beautiful though they are, but the movement of the play as a whole. The poetry is in the characters and their relationships, in the conception of each of the four scenes, and especially in the sharp but quickly-resolved contrasts between them. Cocteau's formula applies exactly to *Don Perlimplin:* "The action of my play is in images, while the text is not: I attempt to substitute a 'poetry of the theatre' for 'poetry in the theatre.'" . . . And as soon as we feel the poetry in the whole sequence, Lorca's prose has its poetic effect as well as his music and his visual scheme. Lorca is such a virtuoso of the theatre that he can use and control all of its resources to present his poetic vision. (pp. 343-44)

[If] the story is not strictly a myth, it has the qualities our poets seek in myth: it seems much older and much more generally significant than any history which is literally true; yet Lorca does not seem to have thought it up, but rather to have perceived it, or heard it, in the most intimate chamber of his sensibility. In embodying it on the stage he is careful to preserve this oft-told feeling, like song, or a tale by a grandmother. (pp. 344-45)

The deeply Spanish nature of Lorca's art does not prevent it from speaking to us. His sense of history—"the masquerades which time resumes"—is very modern; in his ability to mingle the most contradictory perspectives in one composition, and to shift with sureness from the pathetic to the farcical-frightening, he is in the class of our favorite poets. And he writes poetry of the theatre as our poets would like to do. We cannot use his Spanish language, or the symbolic language of the moral and aesthetic forms of his tradition. But we can learn to read it, and to discover thereby an authentic modern poetic drama. (p. 348)

> *Francis Fergusson, "Don Perlimplin: Lorca's Theatre-Poetry," in* The Kenyon Review *(copyright 1955 by Kenyon College), Summer, 1955, pp. 337-48.*

Lorca rediscovered for the drama the tragic image, that long lost mechanism that could trace out the journeys of the human psyche as it went down to hell or ascended to heaven, or both. His lament, sustained through three plays and woven through with the "deep song" of Spain, his cry over the breakdown in the Spanish provinces of the primal relationships generated by human nature, take us back to the Agamemnon trilogy of Aeschylus and the Theban plays of Sophocles.

Before discussing the plays, however, there is something which must be said: to enter into the tortured Spain depicted by Lorca is bound to be a humiliating experience for a Catholic, whether through fear of the truth or through rage at the public exposure of it or through a genuine perplexity that what we as Catholics "looked for is not fulfilled: the gods bring unlooked for things to pass." But the "gods" spoken of by Euripides are ourselves; it is we who shape the moralities that bring about calamity and the strangulation of life. In "Ecclesiastes" it is written: "Only this I have found, that God made man right, and he hath entangled himself with an infinity of questions." (pp. 472-73)

The language spoken [in "Blood Wedding" by the] peasants, both rich and poor, is dry like the hot climate that sears them, direct and to the point like the caste system that separates them, and austerely beautiful like the land they talk of having or not having. Only one character in this play bears a personal name: Leonardo Felix; he is the poor man become conscious of his desires to the point of fighting for them against others. The "others" are designated by their status in life: Mother, Bridegroom, Father, Bride, Wife, Mother-in-law. By these names the fatality of tradition is quietly yet unmistakably emphasized. It is a tradition which carries these people from generation to generation into marriages which in turn help to bring other marriages about, that is, blood weddings. (p. 473)

Yerma, the name of the young woman who is the central character of ["Yerma"], is an invented name and means "barren" in Spanish. The forces that work ruin in "Blood Wedding" are also in the background of this play, at times breaking out in a plain statement which highlights the intensely personal dilemma of Yerma: she wants children very much but is married to a man who is for some reason unable to give them to her. She symbolizes a type of young provincial woman in whom the depths of love, asleep in human nature, have never been fully awakened, yet who has allowed herself to be married off to someone picked out for her, content with the promise of children and a home for them.

Yerma's desire for children is really pure; like the Bride in "Blood Wedding," she is [a] "mirror of the earth." Her longing for a child is metaphysical: she wants only what God has made. (p. 474)

[In] the third tragedy "The House of Bernarda Alba," finished by Lorca just before the outbreak of the Civil War in 1936, the stifling morality of the other two plays has reduced a house containing ten women, and only women, to a hell of absurd, stupid suffering and maniacal hypocrisy. This is the play which Lorca has specifically labelled "A Drama About Women in the Villages of Spain" and which he said is a "photographic document." This can only mean that the House of Bernarda Alba is Spain itself, Spain become a matriarchy in which men are distrusted and hated, whose essential manhood is unloved, and who in turn make their bodies into a thing to be sold to women they do not love but who have money and property.

Stephen Spender claims that this play is a failure because the subject which the women are always talking about, man, does not appear in the play. He has badly misread the play, for it opens with the tolling of bells which are being rung for the funeral Mass of the Father of the house who has just died—man, the author is saying, is dead in this house! . . .

Lorca's plays are not propaganda. In their complex images he has exposed the terrible fault that walks on four feet right out of the Garden of Eden: the most fundamental human relationship possible, that of man with woman, had foundered: the gears of life had slipped in the heart of Spain.

In these plays the feminine principle of conservation takes over the family, the State and, for all practical purposes, the Church; or it could be put the other way: the necessary bias in the Church to conserve, to guard the integrity of faith, extends itself ever so easily to the bias of the State. The State is anxious to preserve an authority rooted in families which have ruled for centuries, and these families conserve themselves so that they may more easily conserve the State. It is a closed, a dead system of morality, says Lorca, and it is evil: it prevents human relationships and destroys the very thing everyone wants to preserve: the family. And it crucifies the poor, closing them off from opportunity and denying their right to a portion of the earth.

Lorca never specifically implicates the Church, though, for the Catholic as he reads, the Church is there in the background, for he knows that, finally, she is the custodian of all morality. Her fault is perhaps a temporary condition of inertia, of "the weightier things of the law left undone." Nevertheless she must share in the blame for what happened. (p. 475)

> *Anthony Aratari, "The Tragedies of Garcia Lorca: The Dramatist as Prophet," in* Commonweal *(copyright © 1955 Commonweal Publishing Co., Inc.; reprinted by permission of Commonweal Publishing Co., Inc.), August 12, 1955, pp. 472-75.*

Federico Garcia Lorca suffered a grave mishap on arriving in New York in 1929. He found himself in a friendly, plain, cordial, expressive, and at the same time inaccessible city. . . . He did not speak a word of English. It was a hard experience for one of his sensibility.

New York is not popular with poets. Someone has said that New York killed Dylan Thomas. Another Spanish poet termed New York "the dragon's head." . . . In "Poet in New York" Garcia Lorca gives us the ineffable measure of his confusion.

Like other Spanish and Mediterranean poets, Lorca is a poet of synthesis. The synthesis of New York was very difficult. Baffled by Manhattan, Lorca tried the opposite: disintegration, with the help of vanguardist irreverence and the patronage of the saint of Long Island, Walt Whitman. . . . He saw a thousand other things normally seen only by small children who can neither speak nor understand. The result is stimulating, with hectic images and a harsh crystallization of semi-conscious impressions.

"Poet in New York," in spite of the theme and the supposed cosmopolitan tonalities, is a book of less resonance than others by the same poet. It is not the cosmopolitan that leads to the universal, as the author of the introduction seems to think, but the particular and local. Nothing better for Lorca than to be, and seem, Spanish. Or better still, to be from Granada. And in Granada, from the Generalife or Albaicin.

If the surrealists cultivate the world of the subconscious, we are undoubtedly merged and equal in that world, since the writers of this school, despite their surface mannerisms, are all disconcertingly alike. . . . Nevertheless a notable amount of originality is to be found in Lorca's "The King of Harlem," "Fable and Round of the Three Friends," and "Jewish Cemetery." In all of them the image of the true Lorca appears, despite the abracadabra (horses' skulls, speculative cows, pheasants' eyes in which stupendous things are happening, singing spiders, colts celebrating mass and prophetic drops of water). But Garcia Lorca could play at schools of poetry, if he liked, as he could play at religion and metaphysics. He had his own accent and his own repertory of forms. (p. 7)

> *Ramon Sender, "Alone in a Friendly Yet Inaccessible City," in* The New York Times Book Review *(© 1955 by The New York Times Company; reprinted by permission), October 9, 1955, pp. 7, 30.*

I often met García Lorca during the years 1924-1928 in Madrid at the Residencia de Estudiantes with its sun-bathed terraces overlooking the city. There he radiated magic, and great and humble did obeisance to his twin demons [drama and poetry]. At one moment he would hold us all in suspense as he recited one of his romances or ballads on the death of Antoñito Camborio, the gypsy, "dark as the green moon," whose life was taken away by the Guadalquivir. Then he would sit down at the piano, and he would sing to his own accompaniment his setting of the fifteenth-century *Mudejar* song "Tres Morrillas" ("Three Moorish Maidens"). Soon after that I used to go to hear him play his *cantares* for the celebrated Sevillian dancer and singer La Argentinita in the Teatro Eslava, which in those days was directed by Spain's foremost man of the theatre, Gregorio Martínez Sierra.

In the "Romancero gitano" . . . he stresses the heroic struggle of the cave-dwelling gypsies of Granada against society, personified in the Civil Guards, transforming by his own intuitive sense of folk rhythms, and his knowledge of ancient ballads, the Romanichal into a mythological dream-hero vanquished by his everlasting enemy, the world of reality.

In the more mature "Poema del cante jondo" . . ., however, he stylizes the essentials of Andalusian gypsy song with glimpses of the great *cantaores* of a past age, such as Juan Breva, Silverio and La Parrala, when *Cante jondo* was the exclusive possession of the *aficionados*, and the patrimony of the Romanichals, who sang for themselves, or as they said, *entre cabales*. We then realize as we listen to the poet that tragedy was implicit in Lorca's genius from the beginning. At times the theme of death becomes an obsession of his, as though he continually discovered signs pointing to his own early death. . . .

The poems of death culminate in the "Lament" on the death of his friend, the bull fighter Sánchez Mejías, in the bull ring, the finest elegy in all modern Spanish poetry. . . . [The] first part of the elegy is an expressionistic monodrama with phantom voices repeating again and again the fatal phrase *"A las cinco de la tarde"* (at five o'clock in the afternoon). The rhythm of the fatal phrase clangs incessantly in the brain of the mourning poet as each grim detail of the tragedy reaches his consciousness, the five strokes of knell booming from innumerable clocks. He sees the dead bullfighter slowly mount the tiers carrying his death on his shoulders toward the dawn. At last, when the soul has departed, the poet-minstrel sings of one who possessed the longing for death and of the sadness of his once-valiant gaiety.

Walter Starkie, "The Demons of Garcia Lorca," in Saturday Review (*copyright © 1960 by Saturday Review, Inc.; reprinted with permission*), November 26, 1960, p. 49.

Lorca was neither a "political" nor a "surrealist" poet—in whatever sense these terms are used nowadays. He was, however, a *popular* poet in that special sense reserved to Spain: a poet whose work is loved and acclaimed by the illiterate and the sophisticated alike for those immediately discernible characteristics through which the Spanish people identify themselves. And he was a *difficult* poet, in the modern phrase, because he attempted to create a personal idiom by relating his understanding of a folk world with the values of an industrial world. In this attempt, he adapted materials and techniques from sources as remote as the medieval Arabic poets and as recent as Breton and Dalí. Yet to recognize his poetry alone is to omit his important dramatic work, for which poetry was, in one sense, a preparation. Poetic and dramatic both, his genius grew not out of advance-guard literary or political movements, but out of a richly functioning Spanish tradition barely surveyed by most present-day criticism. To approach him as an artist at all, one must realize the extent of his integration with that tradition, and understand the kind of sensibility able to thrive so well within it. (pp. iii-iv)

Unlike Yeats, Lorca had no set poetic system; unlike Eliot, his poetry and plays show no line of religious or ideological development. And if a good deal of his early work (in *Libro de Poemas, Canciones* and *El Maleficio de la Mariposa*) is nurtured by Jiménez' exquisitism, Lorca never perfected the older poet's glittering style of expression, perhaps because he could not be contained by the kind of arduously cultivated objective perceptivity it required. Lorca was more like Unamuno and Dylan Thomas: a self-dramatist possessed by the effort to describe the conflict of natural forms seeking escape from death and thereby lighting up the intensest of living moments. And so behind the mask of the gypsy in *Romancero Gitano* and of the Negro in *Poeta en Nueva York,* Lorca succeeded in being more personal than in the subjective lyricism of *Canciones.* In the same way, his *Lament* for the bullfighter is perhaps more intensely Spanish than his strongly honor-ridden plays about women. We should expect of a poet whose temperament is dramatic an acutely personal way of speaking that is not at the same time merely confessional. And similarly, of someone possessed by the idea of capturing reality in the conflicting flashes of the moment, we should expect a gradual discarding of ornament, poetic ritual and symbolism for the barest, most essential kind of prose, such as we find in *The House of Bernarda Alba.* (p. x)

Somewhere in a letter to Jorge Guillén, Lorca wrote that poetry is made out of love, force, and renunciation. The statement tells us something about the springs of his personality; it also says much about his literary procedures, his themes, and his problematical forcing of the door of the constant enemy, death. For what are these three paradoxical elements but a synthetic figure for human pride—a figure which attempts to assert the meaning of life against death? This is what Mariana Pineda stands for: in the end

her triumphant love, her struggle to make it pervade her action, her self-sacrifice, and through this, her powerless fight against martyrdom and its dehumanizing consequence of being turned into an abstraction. The triple complex of love-force-renunciation appears in the "erotic aleluya" *Don Perlimplín,* in *Yerma,* in *Blood Wedding,* in a more diffuse form in *Bernarda Alba,* as a fight against sterility, false honor (the tyranny of "whiteness") which is both chastity and death. Human pride is the ability to declare through a course of self-sacrifice what human love, however misunderstood, must affirm in the teeth of death and its own destruction. The figure of human pride is present in the gypsy's contention against the weapons of the law, in his erotic code, and in his last disdainful encounter with death. It is also present in the ever-new, ever-repeated encounter between the bullfighter and the bull, which must end in death, and, if fought well, in glory.

Reality, Lorca said, is prose, what lives now, the present tense: *it is.* The beauty of truth is poetry, timeless, always existent, all tenses. To be made conceivable, reality requires the poet's strategy, and poetry needs for its truth what Lorca called "the opening of the veins"—the expression of human pride in love, force, and renunciation. Understood in this way, Lorca at the end of his life was writing for very high stakes—and the only ones by which he could sustain his vision of human pride. (pp. xii-xiii)

Before seeking to estimate the distinctively modern qualities of his poetry, we must understand his art as primarily an expression of national genius. The main aspects of the Spanish lyric tradition which find a new culmination in Lorca's poetry are: the medieval Arabic-Andalusian art of amorous poetry together with the early popular ballad; the Renaissance synthesis in Spain of the Greco-Latin poetic art, accomplished by the sophisticated "conceptist" poetry of Luis de Góngora; and the broad body of Andalusian gypsy art known as *cante jondo,* "deep song." (p. 20)

Romancero Gitano (Book of Gypsy Ballads) . . . is the realization of poetic sensibility which has achieved technical mastery over its materials. Here the poet's restless imagination has at last found a form in which to cast his personal cosmology. Less slavish to the letter of folkloric devices, Lorca has begun to create a respectable folklore of his own. The characteristic concentration upon a theme in single monotone, which occurs in the conventional Andalusian song, is replaced in *Romancero Gitano* by a solid variety of thematic materials. These are elaborated in subtle musical patterns with a personal emphasis which marks the matured poetic spirit. Written in the traditional octosyllabic meter, these ballads become a series of re-invented *cantares de gesta.* They partake of the anonymous folk character upholding a tradition distinctive for its magical re-creation of language and its exaltation of natural phenomena and pagan feeling. Spanish poets beginning with Jiménez sought to eschew the anecdotal qualities of the old *romance* and to reshape the form according to new inventive techniques. And this is Lorca's first accomplishment in *Romancero Gitano.* He has re-created the classical style of the old ballad and given it a new tonal quality which is distinctly modern. (pp. 65-6)

The constant struggle of the gypsies is against a universal repression whose edict is death. They themselves, however, own the moon's proud body which they hammer on a forge in the intimacy of the surrounding night. (p. 67)

Lorca's use of the traditional ballad gradually merges with his whole esthetic procedure. This use is not the mere exploitation of a theme for the discursiveness of some folkloric poetaster; it is a marriage between the language of personal perception and the language of popular feeling. Lorca's esthetic demands continually enhance a subjective element of gypsy atmosphere in Andalusian life which others have overworked as an exotic attraction without particular spiritual significance. . . . But *Romancero Gitano* was in no sense a consummation of artistic purpose. Lorca's spirit was still hungry, as is the spirit of every poet who feels the burden of "the song I shall never sing." For Lorca was not interested in the popular elements of Andalusian culture alone. In his restless seeking of a bond between the habits of an older cultural perception and the values of the modern world, he felt compelled to experiment ceaselessly with different forms. (p. 77)

Just as Lorca discovered in Dalí's art a courageous instinct to deal with phenomena of pure form, so in the body and spirit of Christ he found committed the "love and discipline" by which he also sought to implement his poetry.

For Lorca, the Holy Eucharist was the religious counterpart of his own esthetic; in the unity of the godhead was the same concretization of form symbolized. Through this unity one might aspire to find "love and discipline" outside the characterless flux of the world. (p. 83)

Lorca speaks of his Odes as spiritual exercises, as attempts to overcome a sense of artistic irresolution and personal despair. (p. 84)

Lorca's short stay in New York resulted in the volume *Poeta en Nueva York*. It is the work of a new spiritual insight and of a largely incoherent prophetic vision. Tormented and mutilated, but still sensually realistic, the poems included in this volume carry a peculiarly important message to the modern age. It is easy to think of them as the fabrications of a mind which has lost its balance, as the outpourings of a surrealist gruesomely constructing an anti-human nightmare world. Certainly they are Lorca's most difficult poems. Musically discordant, disrupted in meter, poured into an arbitrary autonomous form, cascading with the fragments of exploded metaphor, they seem to contradict the whole of his previous procedure. But their secret is that a new world of imagery has been created to embody the fervid spiritual effort which informs them. The intricate imagistic and metaphoric terminology of *Poeta en Nueva York* proceeds from a vision of the world which, finding no expressive instrument in the traditions of any communicative medium, demands of the poet a new imaginative invention. (p. 85)

For Lorca, New York is a symbol of spiritual myopia, where man is unable to cope with the disease of body and soul because he cannot see the nature of his dislocation, because he has lost sight of those elemental natural forces which a people living close to the soil understand instinctively. (p. 87)

Lorca discovered a solid base for his poetic drama precisely in Lope and Calderón. Like Lope, he is essentially a lyric poet whose dramatic instinct grew out of a sense of communication he felt himself able to establish with the people. He too was possessed with the need to create spectacle, a visual and musical supplement to the art of the spoken word. Lorca's work also has a close moral affinity with Calderón's drama. Like Calderón, he seems to reduce life to a symbolic formula, holds that traditional Spanish respect for honor, and sees on life's flashing mosaic face the essential mask of death. But if on these terms Lorca's drama lacks the old unity, it is because he could not find grace, as Calderón did, in heaven, or absolution from the sins of human perversity on earth, the Catholic Church notwithstanding. He had no answer to the questions which most obsessed him. But he was fired with the fine musical imagination of a minstrel, and the sharp sense of death magnified—magnified as a garden in the clear morning light, to the least inconsiderable weed. With the first he wove out his dramatic idea; with the second he set his scene; and with both he opened the eyes of an audience which had not been stirred by such display for over two centuries.

Growing out of his consistent innovations in the lyric medium, Lorca's development as a dramatist fulfilled the imaginative pattern of his whole art. (pp. 108-09)

The positive dramatic thing which Synge was seeking and trying himself to do in the theatre was also the business of García Lorca. For, like Synge and Yeats and Lady Gregory when they set out to create a national literature for the Irish theatre, Lorca was rebelling against the realistic middle-class drama, which in Spain had succeeded in shutting off from the stage the rich atmosphere of folk speech and imagination. Lorca tried to break through the commercialized theatre with its vulgar parades of life twisted into the neat cynical gesture, the always triumphant negative morality. What he, like those leaders of the Irish movement, proposed to put in its place was the sense of the magic of language to which only a people still attached to the rituals of the land could respond with authentic pleasure. (p. 110)

The strength of Lorca's folk drama lies precisely in his use of woman as bearer of all passion and earthly reality: the wild superb nature of which Synge had spoken. With Lorca it is not simply an accidental choice. The Spain which let its blood for Christ secretly admired the Virgin more. The Virgin prevailing over all early Spanish church art was the symbol of earthly fecundity as well as the mother of divine mercy. The Spaniard often seems to mistrust his male saints for not suffering enough or convincingly. Spanish women saints, however, were always known to suffer magnificent and terrible martyrdom. The character of the *dueña,* the woman chaperon, very early became a convention in the Spanish theatre. And she, as the repository of good earthy frankness, knew the world's tricks and provided the audience with the protective motherly domination which it sought in woman. The Don Juan legend has been a popular and recurrent theme in Spanish literature because it re-affirms the generously fertile nature of woman as distinct from the abstract and essentially barren male lover who finds no permanence except in the arms of death. The Spaniard has been somewhat contemptuous of his philandering Don Juan, who instead of conquering women should have been conquering the New World, or even his own small plot of ground.

Lorca's heroines are modern versions of the warm matriarchal type found in all Spanish literature. They are magnetic fields inevitably drawing tragedy to themselves from a too ardent faith in the right of their natural instincts. Again, they are islands which the world cannot touch with its soiled and makeshift logic. Because their humanity is such an extremely procreative answer to life, they threaten to disrupt the mere man-made machinery of social law, which is, finally, a substitution for life. They are the affirmation to the question of the ultimate which man, with the beam of social exigency in his eye, is always begging. When they lose the sense of integration in life which is necessary to them, the world trembles and comes apart. Thus it is as martyrs of frustrated love, from the heroine of *Mariana Pineda,* who dies on the gallows, to the suicide of the youngest daughter in *La Casa de Bernarda Alba,* that Lorca's women uphold the insistent theme of his tragedies. (pp. 151-53)

The personal dilemma of the poet reflected in his plays, which to some extent are the enactment of that dilemma, is precisely that of his heroines in the folk dramas: frustrated love. In personal terms lack of fulfillment suggests a conflict of sexuality through its insistence on unresolved impasse in the plays, and through it increasingly an uncontainable eroticism which *wills* the impasse. . . .

Lorca's dramatic experiments like *Mariana Pineda, Don Perlimplín, Así Que Pasen Cinco Años,* etc., all treat the problem of romantic love ironically. (p. 195)

In the folk dramas which culminate with *La Casa de Bernarda Alba,* romance no longer exists even as an ironic statement. The poet, identified with all his heroines, perpetuates desire endlessly in an eroticism which, like Yerma's, ends in a metaphysical suicide, or like Doña Rosita's, spreads itself through the fields and wells and walls of Granada's circumambience. The refuges into which all his protagonists escape are in a sense fatally predetermined by the enormity of their excessive and unfulfillable need which they realize cannot be ratified by the society and situation in which they find themselves. And they correspond, in this way, to the poet in the jail of his richly surging world of sexuality which can neither be contained without a sympathy as gigantic as his own or broken through without catastrophe. But just as the first is never encountered, so the second gradually seems, as the dénouement of play after play, more a result of the same paralyzed circumstance than a revealing resolution of a many leveled tragic insight. It is the personal dilemma which prevents Lorca's folk dramas as well as his other plays from rising so often out of pathos to real tragedy. At the same time, however, it makes for Lorca's unique sincerity as an artist and shows why a tragedy of personal validity must fail in the modern world, where it remains unresolved finally in terms of social criticism, in terms of a society which inevitably degrades as it makes meaningless personal integrity. (p. 196)

The secret of Lorca's whole art is that as a poet he had an overwhelming impulsion to supplement the written word by a union of various artistic media; and that despite the consequences to which this led him, he succeeded in remaining primarily a poet. . . .

Few serious modern poets dealing with the heterodox world of the present are content to face it with so few original ideas. And most of the ideas in Lorca's work can be found embodied in the themes and conventions he adapted from Spanish literature. Notable in his folk plays are the insistence on themes of honor, the defeat of innocence when seeking justification in anarchic instinct, and the unconsummated love or marraige whose outcome is spilt blood and death. These appear in his poetry as the quest for spiritual permanence through sensual reality—a search peculiar to the Spanish temper with its mystical investment in what Unamuno has called "the tragic sense of life." (pp. 197-98)

In passing from the lyric-dramatic form of *Romancero Gitano* to the poetic form of his folk tragedies, he was repeating the process of dramatic adaptation as it occurred in the Golden Age. This was the transformation of the original epic into the popular ballad, and then directly into the drama, where both theme and character were continually preserved, though the literary forms had been changed. When Lorca made his gypsy the *modus vivendi* of *Romancero Gitano,* he proved that he could dramatize within a supple ballad form a well-recognized aspect of Spanish life; and in universalizing the gypsy so that the reader was able to identify himself, Lorca had found the hidden door which leads from poetry into the theatre. The same precise use of invention accompanies his entrance into the drama. For he was again transposing his subject into a recognizable traditional frame when he substituted for the silent, bronzed gypsy, agonized in his dream, the frustrated woman, agonized in her love. (pp. 199-200)

Lorca's use of musical motifs as dramatic support was another aspect of his poetry which emerged through imagery to assume a considerable part in his drama. (p. 201)

As still another esthetic complement, the ballet weaves its way into the plays. This is especially notable in sections of his "surrealist" attempts where certain characters exist only to mimic the main action of the play, as the Girl seeking her lover, who encounters the buffoons in the last act of *Así Que Pasen Cinco Años.* (p. 202)

Finally, there is in Lorca's art the imaginative dramatization of conflict between abstract and concrete forces, developing directly from his concerns as a poet into his inventions as a dramatist. There are at least three characteristic ways in which this dramatization occurs in Lorca's imagery.

The first is as a sudden awakening of animate or inanimate things to an awareness of heightened power which is not ordinarily prescribed in their nature. All Lorca's poetry is full of such imagery; but in his later work, through continual condensation, it becomes almost a stylistic habit, which is his particular signature in contemporary poetry. (p. 204)

A second way in which Lorca dramatizes the conflict between abstract and concrete forces is by revealing the compulsion of one element or quality of nature to become another and throw off its own inevitable form to live vicariously in one of its own choosing. Seeking such a change of identity, for instance, are glow-worms who want to be eagles. (p. 206)

The third facet of Lorca's imagistic inventions in this representation of conflict between abstract and concrete forces can be described as the achievement of a sense of halt in the rush of things forever in motion; the need of all life to find fixity, permanence, and its own endurability in rest. This is closely allied to the second process which deals with the complement of the same problem: the everlasting hunger for motion, change and illusion. Relevant here are Lorca's symbols of the mirror, the profile, the stone, and the backwater of a stream. (p. 208)

Edwin Honig in his Garcia Lorca *(© 1944, 1963 by New Directions; reprinted by permission of New Directions Publishing Corporation), New Directions, revised edition, 1963.*

To Lorca the gypsy was the embodiment of the free spirit of man, the closest person to that mystic existence he longed for and sought after all of his life. (p. 5)

Thematically, Garcia Lorca's theatre revolves on a single axis: *the preservation of Honor leads to the frustration of love, hence, of life itself; this frustration, in turn, becomes a despair which leads to Death.* This is always the major theme, the premise which serves as a point of departure for many variations. Starting there, he develops richly colored situations and populates them with strong central characters, personages who live passionate lives whether their emotions find expression or are repressed. However they react, they are primarily pawns of Fate, for it is this dark force which governs the entire premise. The theme, with Fate as its primary cause, represents the nucleus of Lorca's drama.

The first definable element of the theme is Honor. As Lorca sees it, it is a traditional code based on law, superstition and religion which orders a strict interpretation of Spanish life. Though originally the code served the desires of society for betterment, its gradual twisting by taboos and pharasaical dominance has made it an instrument of oppression. Because Fate so decrees, however, it is an instrument of self-torture rather than a weapon in another's hand. Thus, Lorca's characters are their own enemies. Prevented by this gnarled idea of the preservation of Honor, his creations fail to live "normally." . . . [The] instigating force behind every one of Lorca's plays is Honor. His central characters all live, react and die in the shadow of the burdensome code. (pp. 291-92)

Lorca connects the preservation of Honor with the frustration of love by making the latter result entirely from the former. Hence, Honor represses love. And this process is activated primarily through another important element in the dramas—Time. It is only through the lapse of time that the code of Honor becomes more and more excruciating. Time always has an undeniable role, one that serves to point out and emphasize the torment of frustration within the characters of respective plays. It, therefore, fits into the pattern of plot development as a catalytic agent. (pp. 292-93)

With the aid of Time, the element of frustration appears in some aspect in all of Lorca's drama. . . . It is Lorca's consistency in the treatment of frustration that serves to unite his theatre in spite of the diversification of situation. (p. 293)

The last phase of the primary theme is the topic of Death. This frustration of love, of life itself, leads unequivocally to Death. The path is inevitable in the context of life as Lorca sees it. Death, through its infallible presence, adds the intrigue that permeates the plots. . . .

The thematic content of Lorca's theatre, therefore, resolves itself into a pattern. Fate supersedes all action. Honor is a tool, the means through which Fate controls Man. Time provides the stimulus to plot, dissolving illusions that usually maintain human actions on a predictable level. Once Hope is eliminated by Time, the mind becomes frenzied with despair. The subsequent frustration leads directly to the separation of soul and body, by violence or through the spiritual death of the soul by seclusion from life. (p. 294)

The burden of carrying this thematic hierarchy falls mainly on the female characters. Lorca sees woman as the more tragic figure because of her role as bearer of children, prisoner of tradition, and servant of man. As he views her, Lorca observes the great sorrows which Fate has bestowed upon her existence. Man, however, appears as a passionate creature whose selfishness oppresses woman. He is free to act beyond the rules, ironically the same precepts which strictly govern her life. While she must remain at home obeying his commands, he experiences the freedom of the fields or expresses his natural instincts with another woman or may even choose not to satisfy his wife. These actions or inactions, depicting the unevenness of life under artificial rules, prompted the playwright to adopt the woman's cause and to portray her as the tragic figure reality had made her. (p. 295)

The final values of Garcia Lorca's theatre are found in the concept of totality of expression. As Lorca's life clearly shows, the playwright had an intensive background in many of the major art forms—music, painting, poetry, recitation. (p. 299)

The joint adventure, for Lorca's theatre is always that, of music, dance, art and poetry, contributes to a unified theatre of extensive range under the single purpose of his theme. His is a drama of dedication to humanity in which he longs for the freedom of the spirit from the artificial encumbrances of society. Lorca may laugh at the foibles and traditions of such a society, or he may show the human spirit naked at the whipping post of Fate, but his purpose is always the same. His theatre is a vivid interpretation of a codified existence and the evils it has engendered, and it remains as the undying hope his characters could never possess. (p. 300)

Robert Lima, in his The Theatre of Garcia Lorca *(copyright © 1963 by Robert Lima), Las Americas, 1963.*

Poem of the Deep Song (Poema del cante jondo) [was] written from 1921 to 1922 but not published until nearly ten years later. A wail *(grito)* like a sheet of sound envelops the book. It begins in the huts or olive groves, spreads to the valleys and plains, enfolds the mountains, becomes identified with the horizon: the *grito* is the poem. . . .

The presence of violence creates, in Gustavo Correa's terms, a tremendous tension that is released by the cry, linguistically taking the form of a metaphor. The entire book embodies a desperate urge to communicate and thus to ward off silence. It is a syndrome of communication symbols, including road, crossroads (cross), arrows, bows, archers, weather vanes, wind, and river. Within this set of symbols, the idea of arrival is equated with communication, and the concept of not arriving *(no llegar)* stands for death. Lorca's poems are populated by horsemen who never reach the end of their journey. Among other death symbols are the stillness of the air, the dryness of the land, the cisterns, the candle and lanterns (always present at a wake), and the ubiquitous knife.

These symbols hover over the crossroads and threaten with

extinction the various possibilities of communication implied in the coming together of roads.... (pp. 157-58)

The real *cante jondo,* said Lorca, belongs to nobody; it floats like thistledown in the winds of time, beyond the reach of literature. Despite this assertion, the *cante jondo* became very much Lorca's property in the twentieth century. Not only did it supply him with the inspiration lacking in his first book, it also responded to his masterful touch, and he was able to turn it into literature without in any way altering its basic feeling. (p. 159)

Faced with the elemental brutality of life, the human being raises a cry to the four corners of the earth. This is the nature of the "deep song," an exercise in communication considerably older than European poetry. From this primitive base Lorca developed a modern-day gypsy mythology....

The songs *(Canciones),* written simultaneously with the poems of the *cante jondo,* represent a playful and airy interlude in Lorca's career. The reader is very much reminded of the early poems composed at Granada, except that in the present case impish sensibility expresses itself with more subtlety and sophistication. Snatches from folk lyrics, useless songs for children (the adjective is Lorca's), an occasional tone poem in the provocative *cante jondo* manner, lullabies—these various ingredients are handled with a pristine touch that never appears again in Lorca's work. The poet is taking one last romp in that mountain meadow of his boyhood before violence, tension, and frustration—the chief marks of his adult writing—place their seal on his art forever. (p. 160)

Brevity and pithiness characterize much of Spanish literature. The *romance* tradition constantly offers Spanish poets an example of simple, direct expression. To this influence must be added that of the *coplas.* These brief poems of folk origin, usually not more than three or four lines in length, center around the work and play of the people, and are more thoroughly popular than the *romances,* which developed from epic poetry. Unlike the *cante jondo,* which otherwise is quite similar, the *coplas* display less grief, and were sometimes designed for dancing.... Lorca, whose art is rooted in popular traditions, could scarcely fail to succumb to their charms.

Many of his *canciones* obviously depart from the example of the *coplas,* but as usual his deft imagination imparts a subtle suggestiveness that is the mark of sophisticated art. Sometimes the suggestion is prompted by the title; on other occasions, there will be a single phrase charged with overtones that greatly increase the connotations of the entire poem. (pp. 161-62)

More than anything, the songs in [*Canciones*] preserve the wonder of being alive, the surprise necessary to poetry. Reading them, one recaptures the pure mystery of objects, the sense of delight that made one shiver as a child and welcome with warm arms life's flow and variety.... (p. 163)

The brilliant sensual metaphors of the gypsy ballads are justly famous. A poet must be a professor of the five senses, said Lorca, sight first and then touch. In a country where official prudishness is nearly always hypocrisy, Lorca cut through social standards with shocking ease. His work fastens upon the human body, so often absent or sub-

limated in Spanish poetry, and celebrates the flesh as a source of song. (p. 179)

The change provided by New York proved to be cataclysmal. No sharper contrast can be imagined than that between rural, agrarian, and tradition-bound Spain and the roaring twenties of New York.

More than any other happening in the long evolution of mankind (even more than the development of rationalism), industrial society is responsible for destroying the close, vital relationship between man and the cosmos that Lorca had evoked in his gypsy ballads. The advent of the machine age and the metropolis effectively established the here and now of man, underlining his responsibility and his aloneness. In terms of the magical style of Lorca's poetry, there could be no bond between New York and the cosmos. The moon, wind, sun, and stars would not deign to mingle with the prosaic-minded inhabitants of this immense city which had competently displayed its independence from nature and was attempting to control it. Reversing the rôle of the American innocent abroad in a sophisticated cultured, and cynical Europe, Lorca became the vulnerable European from a "backward" country, peculiarly unprepared by temperament as well as nationality for New York's modernity. The magic, delicate, primitive house of his poetry came tumbling down.

Poet in New York is a description of this collapse and of the painful process of picking up the pieces. The personal intervention of natural and mythical elements provided the gypsy with a sense of design and inspired his life with awe. In New York this sense of order crumbles, and chaos prevails. Mythical figures are systematically assassinated by negative symbols. The prevalent concepts are "hollow" *(hueco)* and "vacuum" *(vacío).* Everywhere the exuberant warmth of the gypsy ballads is replaced by the impersonal coldness of the New York herds; impending catastrophe is suggested by the symbols of shipwreck *(naufragio),* dance of death, and destruction of planets. The sea and snow, pulled out of their natural context, are prime tokens of that fearful silence against which the *cante jondo* had intuitively risen.

Although a baneful influence in the gypsy ballads, the moon, nevertheless, was filled with mythic grandeur. She was still the goddess with whom, according to Pliny, all things wax or wane. In *Poet in New York,* we watch her systematic decline, first into symbols of stagnation and horror—sharp bone splinters, a horse's skull; and finally into the degradation of the fat woman, a pathetic Preciosa passing through a sick multitude. The moon has lost its mythical force.... (pp. 181-82)

[It] is not until halfway through the book that he gains a firm grasp on his technique and channels the violent flood of surrealistic imagery into a meaningful direction.

Amidst this welter of facelessness and repressed emotions, Lorca's first act was to find a substitute for his gypsies. The Negro, too, was a primitive soul, persecuted by an entire class, and kept from being a child of nature by the artificial canyons towering above him. Lorca responded immediately, but he could not create a Negro myth. It was primitivism outside a tradition, and this made all the difference. The olive-colored gypsies belonged in their caves and on the beaches of Andalusia; the black man did not belong in apartments or subways.... At all events, the Negro became the first sympathetic element in Lorca's New York poetry. Perhaps the doorman at John Jay Hall, Columbia University, inspired "Ode to the King of Harlem." In the ludicrous actions of the first stanza, there is a reflection of the now-debased myth-maker and also of the ridiculous position of an African native tending doors for New York students. . . . (pp. 183-84)

Across the amputated symbols of natural life, the warm, vital murmur of the Negroes reached Lorca's heart. . . . But mostly New York was anguish. In the face of it, he could only proclaim the perpetual wakefulness of live flesh, still surrounded by such negative symbols as snow and dead dahlias. . . . (pp. 185-86)

Lorca's Manhattan is inhabited by broken objects, hapless creatures, demons, and jungle animals. This bizarre conglomeration has interfered with a true appreciation of the value of *Poet in New York,* a value heightened by the book's inspired compassion and the fact that it contains some of the best surrealistic poetry ever written. . . . But Lorca's passionate dismay and aroused tone of indignation is far removed from the intellectual calculation of the surrealist movement, and he avoids the exhibitionistic element so enjoyed by the Parisian poets. (p. 190)

Arabic-Andalusian poetry is of limited intellectual content, mainly descriptive, and bound by rigorous form. One of its chief attractions for Western readers has been its predominant sensuality, called by the scholar García Gómez a "frenzied adoration of physical beauty." Lorca was drawn by both the sensuality and the extravagance of metaphor, for these poets of the African deserts and Andalusian sierras spent their genius in creating elaborate, mannered imagery that makes extended reading of their verse similar to passing through a labyrinth wrought by a tortured imagination. The rashness of their similes must have enthralled Lorca, who had already learned the art of exaggeration from Andalusian folklore; when he saw a threaded needle compared to a comet, oars to eyelashes, and eyebrows to a half-moon, he knew he was among his equals in relating the seemingly unrelated. The bathos of Arabic poetry, its exalted feelings about trivial things, would also have appealed to Lorca. (p. 199)

If *Divan at the Tamarit* is a reliable indication, Lorca's conscious efforts to cultivate the Arabic vein came to naught. The projected book, in the form it has reached us, adds nothing new, and some of the imagery seems especially forced, proving, in a poet like Lorca, that his inspiration was actively engaged elsewhere [in writing plays]. (p. 200)

Death cut short the development of a series of poems provisionally entitled "Sonnets of Dark Love." The four examples we have in the collected works give a tantalizing glimpse of Lorca approaching middle age, possessed by the usual strange stirrings, and preoccupied by a need for form and measurement.

As he mused, free from the violent repulsion of previous works, on the nature of death, he saw himself gathered into the silence of the earth, symbolized by moss, stiffened doves, and the inert branch. The "pulse of his style," his need to communicate, will be checked forever in an unreflecting "chaste mirror." The mythical images are latent but not vital in these final poems. Instead, he seems to have been working towards a new manifestation of the synthesis between man and his natural environment. (p. 203)

The tremendous emotional impact of the *cante jondo,* [Lorca] said, could only be attributed to "dark sounds" (*sonidos negros*) which are inspired not by the gentle classical muse but by the *duende,* the spirit of the earth. The *duende* wells up from the deepest quarters of the blood and takes hold of the artist as he is creating. It responds most readily to music, dance, and spoken poetry, because a warm and living body is needed for it to make its presence felt. (p. 206)

Lorca . . . seems to have adumbrated the Jungian idea of the archetype—that hidden form or image sleeping in the blood that is quickly released by certain objects, sounds, or works of art. Lorca, of course, knew nothing of Jung, but he was well aware . . . that there are terrors which date beyond body, and that there are subjectively known forms which art, since its origins, has communicated by intuition, or, as he put it more poetically, by means of the "mirrors of the stars." . . . In his poetry he tried to evoke such images as much as possible. His lecture on the *duende* lists a series of objects that to him ultimately suggested death, and whether or not each one connotes a similar feeling for every reader, the implication is, as Jung declared, that these forms call forth from the unconscious a reaction that is shared by mankind. . . . (p. 207)

Among the many instances in Lorca's poetry that reveal the presence of the *duende,* we may recall, from "Lament for Ignacio Sánchez Mejías," these four suggestive lines . . . :

> His eyes did not close
> when he saw the horns near,
> but the terrible mothers
> raised their heads.

Upon first reading the phrase "las madres terribles," an uncanny feeling overcame me, and subsequent readings have always produced a shudder similar to the effect upon Housman of those stray lines of poetry that made the stubble of his chin bristle. The Terrible Mother has left numerous traces in mythology. . . . Lorca probably knew nothing about these mythological details, but the *duende* was present, and the phrase provokes from the reader a response that is explained at least in part by Jung's theories.

If we recognize Lorca's lecture on the *duende* as a statement concerning his own art, we can view his work in a new perspective that will explain much that has been dismissed as sheer whimsy, playfulness, or even perversion. Playfulness it is, but at the level of mythological creation. Studies have shown that Lorca's most common metaphor is one in which everything intermingles, in which the most antagonistic elements are related to each other, and it has been concluded that he had an eye for synthesis and analogy. But primitive myth demonstrates that early man did not view the world with an analytical eye, separating things into cause and effect; rather, the impulse behind myth seems to have been to underscore, in Cassirer's phrase, "the consanguinity of all things." (pp. 207-09)

Lorca's [visions are] . . . "strange," therefore, only to our non-mythic orientation, our rational atomization of reality. Lorca's violent reaction to New York may have been due to an awareness that industrial civilization had made the world a duller place in terms of the imagination. . . . [He] believed there was a language of primitive relationships forgotten by modern man. . . . (p. 209)

Howard T. Young, "The Magic of Reality," in his The Victorious Expression: A Study of Four Contemporary Spanish Poets *(copyright © 1964 by the Regents of the University of Wisconsin), University of Wisconsin Press, 1964, pp. 139-216.*

In all his later plays Lorca used metaphors taken from nature, varying rhythms of language and musical sound, brightly contrasting colors, and many songs and dances to transform the experiences of Andalusian life into a poetry of the theatre.

The theme in all of Lorca's work is frustration, and the center of the dramatic conflict in his mature plays is to be found in the frustrations of women, who he believed were the bearers of all passion and the source of every form of earthly creativity. On the surface this frustration emerges primarily in sexual terms, but finally the world of Lorca's theatre is ruled by the power of death. In his tragedies he ties up and twists the strands of people's passions so tightly that only the "tiny knife, the tiny golden knife" of death can probe the center of the conflict. Like all Spaniards, Lorca understood and felt life only through death. Death is man's mentor, his companion, and his greatest achievement.

Robert W. Corrigan, in his preface to "The Authority of the Theatre," by Federico Garcia Lorca, in Masterpieces of the Modern Spanish Theatre, *edited by Robert W. Corrigan (reprinted with permission of Macmillan Publishing Co., Inc.; copyright © 1967 by Macmillan Publishing Co., Inc.; © 1967 by William I. Oliver), Collier Books, 1967, p. 352.*

Lorca's passion is rooted in an established social context. The tragedy in his plays comes from the tension between passion, which is necessarily always entirely individual and personal and whimsical, and the society in which the individuals move, which defines them and also gives a particular value and shading to passion and its manifestations. In Lorca, the conflict is between passion and honor, where passion is the mark of the personal (willful and private and powerful in its needs) and honor that of the social (rigid and public and equally powerful in its rules and taboos, the denial of needs). (pp. 89-90)

Bernarda Alba is an extreme distillation of social honor; she exemplifies a passion that has gone too far in excluding the mortally impulsive, irrational, emotional, self-indulgent. It has become in its extremity antipassion....In effect, Bernarda is a Satanic spirit, living in an atmosphere of death, perversion, and denial. [The House of Bernarda Alba] starts with a funeral and ends with a suicide; between we have sadism, insanity, onanism. There are black curtains on the windows. Sexual passions are outside this territory: the stallion drumming in his stall; the village escapades. No men appear on stage. The setting is on the edge of action. The only action that occasionally can burst out in Bernarda Alba's house is the poultrylike squabbling of the sisters, a parody of life.

In *The House of Bernarda Alba* . . . we get an extended examination of the pathology of social passion, of an honor that is contemptuous of the individually human, that is, finally, self-defeating. (p. 95)

Bernarda Alba climaxes [Lorca's] trilogy of the tragedy of passion by seeming to assert that it is "honor," passion perverted by a sense of the social that excludes the human, which somehow survives and even triumphs, however abominably, over the personal passion. We may thus read these tragedies as concluding on a pessimistic note: the world of Bernarda Alba is one in which human impulses may not range freely, must be constrained, even expunged, even at the risk of the ugliest consequences, of perversions of passion and of life, including madness, self-stimulation, torture, suicide. . . . But the victims, whatever the intimidation, unless they conspire in their own long day's dying, hold on to life, one way or another. Even as Bernarda Alba is hysterically improvising her sterile stagecraft for the future, managing the appearance of Adela's suicide ("Take her to another room and dress her as though she were a virgin"), arranging to face death daily, another daughter, Martirio, mutters: "A thousand times happy she, who had him." . . . The personal, physical passion continues to assert its independent power. Honor may finally turn to antipassion, as in Bernarda Alba, certainly with its own power, but the primal force is personal passion.

Lorca's tragedy, then, resides in the domain of passion: passion destroys itself and its possessors, the personal can ultimately only come in conflict with the social, the social enlarges itself into vengeance or into death-serving sterility. . . .

But to celebrate passion is to celebrate life, living, feeling, reaching, erring: vitality, vivacity, whimsicality, impulsiveness, energy of every sort. There is a final rightness about Lorca's characters who strive toward goals that define them as they live, as there is about Oedipus, and to fail is simply—and greatly—to be human. (pp. 97-8)

Morris Freedman, "The Morality of Passion: Lorca's Three Tragedies," in his The Moral Impulse: Modern Drama from Ibsen to the Present *(copyright © 1967, Southern Illinois University Press; reprinted by permission of Southern Illinois University Press), Southern Illinois University Press, 1967, pp. 89-98.*

Kahlil Gibran

1883-1931

Lebanese poet, mystic, and painter. Author of the immensely popular *The Prophet,* Gibran is one of the best-selling poets to write in the English language. His small books, Biblical in style and often illustrated with his own allegorical drawings, have been translated into more than twenty languages. Gibran's poetry and prose is distinguished by its metrical beauty, an ecstatic spiritualism, and a vision of a mystical, serene love. This latter quality makes his work, particularly *The Prophet,* a popular choice for marriage ceremonies. A moderately successful Arabic poet, Gibran came to the United States in 1904, where he met Mary Haskell, a Bostonian headmistress who was to become both his inspiration and adviser. According to their love letters, published in 1972, this relationship was never physically consummated. Nevertheless, it proved artistically and personally rewarding for Gibran. His best works were written in English during his years in the United States.

PRINCIPAL WORKS

The Madman, His Parables and Poems (poetry and prose) 1918
The Forerunner, His Parables and Poems (poetry and prose) 1920
The Prophet (poetry) 1923
Sand and Foam, A Book of Aphorisms (prose) 1926
Jesus the Son of Man, His Words and His Deeds as Told by Those Who Knew Him (prose) 1928
The Earth Gods (poetry) 1931
The Wanderer, His Parables and His Sayings (prose) 1932
The Garden of the Prophet (poetry) 1933
Prose Poems (poetry) 1934
Tears and Laughter (poetry and verse) 1946*
The Secrets of the Heart (poetry and prose) 1947*
Nymphs of the Valley (prose) 1948*
A Tear and a Smile (poetry and prose) 1950*

*year of first English-language publication of works previously published in Arabic

---

[In] those parables and poems which Gibran has given us in English he curiously seems to express what Rodin did with marble and clay. Both sculptor and poet show an imagination which goes to the mountains and the elements for strength, a desire to give human things a universal quality, a mellow irony, and a love of truth which is not afraid of platitudes. Rodin compared Gibran to William Blake. But the parables collected in *The Madman* are more reminiscent of Zarathustra's maskings and unmaskings, of the long rising rhythms of Tagore. The English language never seems a fit medium for work of this nature. It is too angular, too resisting to hold the meanings which Oriental literature crowds as thickly and dazzlingly as jewels on an encrusted sword-hilt. (p. 510)

> *The Dial (copyright, 1918, by The Dial Publishing Company, Inc.; reprinted by permission of J. S. Watson, Jr. and Scofield Thayer), November 30, 1918.*

On the wrapper of ["The Prophet"] it is written that Rodin called Kahlil Gibran the Blake of the twentieth century. May rest and glory be an everlasting ecstasy to the soul of Rodin, who was a good sculptor! But Blake, if he could have understood "The Prophet," could no more have written it than he could have written "Endymion." . . .

To the Occidental Kahlil Gibran seems to have a genius for parable and an extraordinary talent for scrambling metaphors together beautifully. Here in this resting place we can repose indefinitely and reassure ourselves, and if need be we can go on indefinitely in the same vein, . . . imagining that with every period we are getting nearer to the Oriental's poetry. But presently we will begin to [see] . . . that Kahlil Gibran does something which our critical phrases are not at all designed to cover. Behold he comes to us with a book he has written, a thin black book, curiously illustrated, and he puts it upon the table and, standing behind us with a long white beard, says sepulchrally in a beautifully modulated voice: "Open and read, ye seeker after truth." Straightway the wind sighs in the empty book shelves, whence the beloved volumes we know have vanished, and the lights of our familiar chandelier grow peculiarly dim; and we open and read strange words, marvelling. We, poor Occidentals, who have known so many fakirs, find ourselves in the mood for a spiritual séance. It is not Blake we are reading, or Shelley, or Dowson, or Peacock, or any of the other names we know and love so well; dimly we feel that it is no friend of ours we read, that never in this book will we see the humble thoughts we have held so long in our own poor voiceless hearts spring to our eyes alive and deified, free and glorious at last. Here before us are strange metaphors. Here is not what we love in poetry; here is not the splendid echo of our own unlovely voices. Then as we close the book and lay it thoughtfully and a little contemptuously aside, there come back to us like spirits certain shining phrases that we know cannot be else but English poetry. "A dawn unto his own day, With sails full set awaits the wind." And then we tear our hair desperately, for we know that some one is going to ask us how we like the poetry of Kahlil Gibran and is not going to be put off with spiritualism.

Say then, desperately, if something must be said, that the beauty of Kahlil Gibran, of Tagore, of the stories Bain has published, and of all kindred things from FitzGerald to the Talmud lies not in the strange language in which all of them are couched, but in the interstices of this strange language; that through these interstices comes seeping liquid drops of something we feel instinctively is lovely; say on, either that it is something Oriental, and let the capitalization of the adjective cover up our ignorance as best it may, or else, with more courage, say that it is Absolute Futility. One will be as right as one is wrong. At least here in Absolute Futility is a definition towards which the mind can yearn and which can justify, even if it remains incomprehensible, the pleasure we derive from reading Eastern poetry.

Curiously enough, by such a standard "The Prophet" shrinks to a rather inconsiderable book. It has in it, it is true, traces here and there of the precious Oriental liquid we described. But now that the lights of our chandelier are once more brilliant we can return with more confidence to the ancient phrases we more nearly understand and observe clearly that Kahlil Gibran's struggles with a Northern language and familiarity with a Northern literature have done him harm, not good. Unfortunately, he has not aped the best we have. He is didactic, he is incompact, he is careless; the English in his writing is not excellent. The exotic, fascinating liquid of Kahlil Gibran is not so freely flowing as Tagore's. Again we tear our hair.

And thus, again, a senseless joining of two names completes a circle. "The Prophet" is not a book for the lovers of Blake. It is a book for those who love the Oriental mind and who find that Kahlil Gibran has not been altogether spoiled by Occidentalism.

> *Fillmore Hyde, "Oriental Liquid," in* The Literary Review, *December 8, 1923, p. 334.*

Kahlil Gibran has expressed [in "Sand and Foam"] in a series of unrelated apophthegms the mystical intuitions of life which he organized systematically under various headings in "The Prophet." Although fragmentary, they all, of course, derive from the same ecstatic sense of a reality of which our conscious, actual life is at best a poor parody. And in much of his writing the conscious is explicitly opposed to the unconscious. He writes, for example: "If I were to choose between the power of writing a poem and the ecstasy of a poem unwritten, I would choose the ecstasy. It is better poetry." It is in . . . preference for the inarticulate to the articulate that the weakness of his doctrine, however typical it may be of Oriental wisdom, consists. It may be impossible to embody ecstasy in words without loss to its ideal essence, but only by attempting to embody it can it become real. And Gibran not only in his

doctrine, but also in his expression is too apt to seek an infinite satisfaction to the neglect of finite concentration. Nevertheless this book justifies his claim that "life in rhythmic fragments moves within me." It is full of the simplicity of spiritual illumination, of an awareness of the timeless in a world of time, and this is combined with a natural shrewdness characteristic of the truest mysticism. (p. 253)

> *Times Literary Supplement (© Times Newspapers Ltd., 1927; reproduced from* The Times Literary Supplement *by permission), April 7, 1927.*

[*Sand and Foam*] contains sentences which possess the predominantly intellectual tang of the aphorism: "A disagreement may be the shortest cut between two minds"; but for the greater part it offers us expressions of feeling that are not always inevitable. One cannot but feel a certain gratitude, however, to the poet or sage, whichever he may be, for the honesty of his idealism. (p. 265)

> *The Dial (copyright, 1927, by The Dial Publishing Company, Inc.; reprinted by permission of J. S. Watson, Jr. and Scofield Thayer), September, 1927 (and reprinted by Kraus Reprint Corporation, 1966).*

[Gibran's] earlier works were written in Arabic—prose poems: *The Broken Wings, Spirits Rebellious,* and a number of plays. These were published in the United States, Egypt and Syria, and soon made him known to the entire Arabic world, which extends—ethnically and linguistically—from China to Spain. The character and depth of his influence upon that world may be inferred from the fact that it gave rise to a new word: *Gibranism.* Just what this word means Gibran's English readers will have no difficulty in divining: mystical vision, metrical beauty, a simple and fresh approach to the so-called problems of life.

About ten years ago, in this, the land of his adoption, he began to write exclusively in English, and those ten years have been sufficient for him to create a corresponding impression upon the Anglo-Saxon world as well. The books he is known by to this world are *The Madman, The Forerunner, The Prophet, Sand and Foam,* to which must be added *Jesus, the Son of Man,* and a collection of twenty drawings without text.

These books are sparks from one fiery trail, parts of one coherent structure, the successive presentment of a simultaneity—a presentment which has by no means come to an end. For Gibran's most widely known poem, *The Prophet,* which deals with man's relation to his fellow-man, is the first of a trilogy, to be followed by *The Garden of the Prophet,* having for its theme the relationship between man and nature, and *The Death of the Prophet,* the relationship between man and God. It is not possible to "get" Gibran without some sense of these organic relations, any more than it is possible to sense the vast sweep of Michelangelo's genius by looking at the Sistine ceiling, panel by panel, through an opera glass. (pp. 141-42)

Gibran's works, it is true, form a sequence; they represent the "pilgrim's progress," each is a "station of the cross"; but each one contains and is the whole, in the same sense that each branch of a tree is itself a tree, and each leaf a tree in miniature. To achieve these unities is the problem of the artist, who labors to conceal all evidence of labor, and this being so, he prefers to keep such matters to himself.

The theme of Gibran's books is one with his major interest, and his major interest is in *life*. He aims to discover some workable way of feeling, thinking, living, which shall lead toward *mastery*—how to serve the forces which enslave us until they are by us enslaved. Such, I take it, is his purpose, his "message," but having said so much I should be remiss not to call attention to the extraordinary dramatic power, deep erudition, lightning-like intuition, lyrical lift and metrical mastery with which that message is presented, and the beauty, beauty, beauty, which permeates the entire pattern, with which everything he touches seems fairly to drip, as it were. (pp. 142-43)

> *Claude Bragdon, "A Modern Prophet from Lebanon," in his* Merely Players *(copyright 1929 by Claude Bragdon; 1957 by Henry Bragdon; reprinted by permission of Alfred A. Knopf, Inc.), Knopf, 1929, pp. 139-47.*

Although the late author of "The Earth Gods" [Gibran] was a resident of this country, it is the thought and the mysticism of the land of his birth, Asia Minor, which dictate his utterance. And the literature of the East has shaped the utterance. There is in his lines something of the sensuous surge of the Song of Solomon. His three gods, earth-born and master Titans of life, that appear on the mountains are no mere intellectual concepts. They are corporeal beings, capable of high thought, but also are of their native earth. They are gorgeous gods, as were those of Babylon. . . .

This is not verse penned by an Occidental, toying with worn philosophies, wearied with striving to pour the new wine of an industrial civilization into the old bottles of polite literature. . . .

It would be our guess that "The Earth Gods" is something in the nature of a translation out of one of the author's Arabian works. It is something new, not grandiose but very nearly grand, sweeping and invigorating. In it the voice of older civilizations speaks to the upstarts of the West, albeit with something of sadness, yet with a large tolerance, like elders giving of their matured profundity to children concerned with small and perishable things. (p. 23)

> The New York Times Book Review (© *1931 by The New York Times Company; reprinted by permission), May 17, 1931.*

I do not think the East has spoken with so beautiful a voice since the *Gitanjali* of Rabindranath Tagore as in *The Prophet* of Kahlil Gibran, who is artist as well as poet. . . . Two of the drawings are specially moving, one a lovely drooping figure of a girl, the arms outstretched as in crucifixion with the hands nailed to the hearts of two other figures.

I have not seen for years a book more beautiful in its thought, and when reading it I understand better than ever before what Socrates meant in the *Banquet* when he spoke of the beauty of thought, which exercises a deeper enchantment than the beauty of form. . . . Our own words to each other bring us no surprise. It is only when a voice comes from India or China or Arabia that we get the thrill of strangeness from the beauty, and we feel that it might inspire another of the great cultural passions of humanity. (pp. 168-69)

> *George William Russell [A.E.], "Kahlil Gibran," in* The Living Torch, *edited by*

> *Monk Gibbon (reprinted with permission of Macmillan Publishing Co., Inc.;* © *1938 by The Macmillan Company), Macmillan, 1938, pp. 168-69.*

[In the preface to *Secrets of the Heart* Gibran is called] tremendous, electrifying, [dynamic], amazing, momentous, catapulting, powerful, frightening, funereal, and again tremendous. Gibran is, of course, none of these things. He is a sensitive poet, with the insight and compassion of the visionary who longs to heal the eyes of the blind. There is passion in some of these tales, along with a nostalgia for that Golden City of which he dreams—what Blake calls Eden and F.S.C. Northrop "the undifferentiated aesthetic continuum." Gibran calls it Iram, the City of Lofty Pillars, in a play of that name, in which he discloses so much of his own beliefs.

"The Madness of John" and "The Ambitious Violet" are two of the best sketches in this collection, demonstrating two diverse moods, one compassionate irony and the other the thrust of the rebel. Great poets are rebels and there are paragraphs in this book that could be quoted effectively by the crusading politician. John asks: "Tyranny and submission . . . which of these gave birth to the other?" Again Gibran writes: "In the mouth of society are many ailing teeth. . . . The decayed teeth of Syria are found in her schools wherein today's youth is taught tomorrow's sorrow." Gibran was an exile from his country and an excommunicate from his church. The revolutionary insights of a writer such as Gibran in forms that appeal to the heart and to the imagination, will be read by hosts of people who never read a political tract or listen to an ideological address. (p. 286)

> *B.D., in* Canadian Forum, *March, 1948.*

[The three stories in "Nymphs of the Valley"] are pale, sentimental and trite. They might be of service as balm to an overtired guest wishing at his bedside a not unpleasant book for sedative perusal. The style is overornamented. Even familiarity with the decorated phrasing of the East does not lead us to condone paragraphs wherein three or four unrelated similes crowd one another. And though there is much sweetness, it recalls pachouli, not attar.

Gibran's proverbs and shorter parables in previous volumes remain his best work. They have an easy grace similar to good conversation. . . . But this present book, whatever may be its value and popularity in Arabic, has no savor even in the smooth translation.

> *Robert Hillyer, "Three Ornamental Parables," in* The New York Times Book Review (© *1948 by The New York Times Company; reprinted by permission), April 18, 1948, p. 27.*

Though an Oriental . . . [Kahlil Gibran] preached no exotic religion. Though virtually venerated as a saint, he lived among the Greenwich Village artists and painted beautiful figures and remarkable portraits. Yet to hosts of his friends and thousands of readers in many lands he was known primarily as a poet and prophet. Clearly this was no ordinary man. An endowment such as his, rare at any time, seemed almost unbelievable in our own lurid Twenties. Perhaps that is why he received no more attention than he did from the mass of the public. But to his own followers and admirers Kahlil Gibran loomed very large.

A succession of little black books came from his pen . . ., a dozen or so, and they were like no other books of the time. Poetry, parables, dramatic dialogues, aphorisms, all touched with a strange beauty. . . .

The two dozen pieces making up ["Secrets of the Heart"] are like a sampling of the variety of Kahlil Gibran's work. They include prose tales and fables, poems of varying length and even a dramatic piece that somehow reminds one of the No plays of Japan. Most are mystical, all are rich in beauty. In a poem entitled "My Countrymen," he cries out:

> Hypocrisy is your religion, and
> Falsehood is your life, and
> Nothingness is your ending;
>   why
> Then, are you living? . . .

For writing things like this he was excommunicated from his church and exiled from his country. Yet today he is a classic there and one of the great heroes of the little Syrian nation living among the cedars of Lebanon.

> *Henry James Forman, "Work Is Love Made Visible," in* The New York Times Book Review *(© 1948 by The New York Times Company; reprinted by permission), July 25, 1948, p. 19.*

Gibran's principal success, "The Prophet," is like all his work Biblical in style, this-worldly in outlook, sentimental in tone. Its success, "nicking the minute with a happy tact," is certainly comprehensible. The large reading public which had given up going to church but still liked chants, and whose parents when socially enthusiastic read Carpenter's "Toward Democracy" and when personally romantic the FitzGerald "Rubáiyát," now could find both mild marching music and seemly serenade in the Kahlil canon.

Gibran had made himself an English which, like the Synge-Yeats "Kiltartan" dialect, was a tongue which no one had ever spoken but which was an effective literary invention for creating a dramatic atmosphere. When to this is added that Gibran, who began as something of a rebel, ended as a cheerful acceptor of the universe, yes, and of today and the West, no wonder that he has a stanch public that has put him above criticism by reading him devoutly at christenings, marriages and funerals.

"A Tear and a Smile" is a collection of early work translated by a fellow Syrian. But apart from a certain asperity toward the clergy and the rich—a natural resentment that success naturally abated—it clearly belongs to the canon.

The author is certainly not a poet's poet, nor will his work contribute to poetry's progress. But he helps many people if not to translate and construe at least to transpose their experience. This message has in it neither the opium of supernaturalism nor the alcohol of the revolutionary faith. Its potion-equivalent may be found in those beverages which imitate the color, claim the flavor and repudiate the stimulant of coffee.

> *Gerald Heard, "Kahlil Gibran: Comforter and Friend," in* The New York Times Book Review *(© 1950 by The New York Times Company; reprinted by permission), February 19, 1950, p. 5.*

At the time I knew [Kahlil Gibran,] he had perfected an art which is traditional in the East, the art of the relater of the apologue or parable. At a dinner table or in a lecture hall he would relate such stories with grace and point, and listeners would realize how well fitted the apologue or fable or parable is for conveying wisdom. They were Kahlil Gibran's finest expression; they are published in "The Prophet."

The collection published under the rather trying title "A Tear and a Smile" is earlier work. It is in prose and verse. The pieces were written in Arabic; as we have them here they are translation; we cannot know that distinctiveness they had in the original. In this translation they are too Biblical in their language and in their rhythm.

> *Padraic Colum, "Commonplaces from the Arabic," in* Saturday Review *(copyright © 1950 by Saturday Review, Inc.; reprinted with permission), May 20, 1950, p. 21.*

A lot of romantics are going to hate this, but they might as well know the truth: Kahlil Gibran is buried in a gift shop.

He lies in state, the coffin covered with plastic flowers, counters on either side selling souvenirs, in the old Mar-Sarkees monastery at Bsherri in the highlands of Lebanon. Meanwhile, his 20,000-word essay *The Prophet* has become Alfred A. Knopf's best seller of all time. This year the four millionth copy will pass over the counter.

Fewer than 2,000 copies were sold in 1923, the year Knopf brought out the first edition by the young Lebanese immigrant, whom he had met in a New York coffeehouse. The book began a heavy run after World War II. By the early Sixties it was starting to appear on best-seller lists at campus bookstores across the United States. Now words of *The Prophet* are replacing traditional biblical wisdom at hip public events, especially weddings:

> Ay, you shall be together even in the
>   silent memory of God.
> But let there be spaces in your
>   togetherness.
> And let the winds of the heavens dance
>   between you.   (p. 54)

In Lebanon, his work went unnoticed until the people of Bsherri [his birthplace] learned that Gibran had left them all future royalties from his books to be used for "civic betterment." . . .

Representatives from leading Bsherri families administered the Gibran fund without much conflict until royalties started to swell. With increased money came greater power and people began to push and shove to get on the committee. . . .

[Now] Bsherri has two committees and two lawyers. Knopf is holding a hefty sum in a New York bank until . . . they can figure out who gets it. The Lebanese Minister of the Interior has been called in to set up peace talks. And an estimated half-million has been frittered away in fees for lawyers and executors. (p. 55)

> *Sheila Turner, "Tales of a Levantine Guru," in* Saturday Review *(copyright © 1971 by Saturday Review, Inc.; reprinted with permission), March 13, 1971, pp. 54-5, 70.*

By my account, Gibran has outsold all American poets from Auden to Whitman. Moreover, his success lies outside the traditional minarets of merchandising and promotion. His publisher, Alfred Knopf, advertised "The Prophet" only once—and found that the campaign's net effect was to reduce sales. Since then Knopf has relied entirely on word of sophomore. He once theorized in audible wonder: "It must be a cult. But I have never met any of its members. I haven't met five people who have read Gibran."

For those benighted few in Alfred Knopf's tight orbit, an encapsulation of "The Prophet" is in order. If you are in spiritual distress, if you wish to read a work in which life takes on the bittersweetness of a Chopin Ballade, in which the opalescent beauty of philosophy is miraculously pinned to the page, glistening like a Morpho butterfly—then by all means buy the collected works of Vladimir Nabokov. Of all the limp, mucid hooey now being sold without a prescription, "The Prophet" is the most blatant and outrageous. At its best, it is precisely what Huckleberry Finn called the King's speeches, "full of tears and flapdoodle." At its leakiest it is *"Also Sprach Zarathustra"* written in mauve icing on a cake of halvah. (p. 9)

Many of [Gibran's] pen and ink sketches still survive. They show a technical competence and a sedulous, sexless imitation of the great: Masaccio without profundity, Blake without revelation. As a young writer he was equally vaporous and even less original; he had not yet found a writer to imitate. (p. 24)

Gibran is manifestly a late instance, very familiar to biographers of Ruskin and Carlyle, of the impotent *ubermensch* oscillating between terminals. Celebrity and withdrawal, ecstasy and celibacy, shyness and pontification—these are the classic polarities that produced so many of the 19th century's geniuses and charlatans.

Which was Gibran? I suspect that he was neither. His letters reveal a naif too complete to permit guile. His beliefs, like his writings, were infantile but authentic. The extravagant claims on his behalf were not, after all, made by the author but by his hysteroid disciples. (pp. 24, 26)

In the beginning, Gibran's small estate was worth some $50,000, benison enough for a village of ten thousand souls. But in the following decades, Kahlil was to be regarded as a real-life version of The Man Who Corrupted Hadleyburg. Bsherri was eaten by royalties. For with the campus revival, the coin that came to the little village totaled over $1-million. (p. 26)

I despise the work, not the man. . . . Gibran, of course, cannot be blamed for [acts by anyone else]. What he *can* be blamed for is his own softheadedness, for the unfocused, uncritical, tragically contagious view of man and God. In this he was not alone; he merely crystallized a tendency that has always been present in American letters. In Gibran's era you could find it in the high writings of, say, Thomas Wolfe ("O lost, and by the wind-grieved ghost, come back again") or in Hesse's "Demian," about which critic George Steiner once fumed, "That is not literature, it is incense." Today it has surfaced in the writing of Rod McKuen and Richard Brautigan. And, like everything else, it has been politicized. You can find it on the right in Ayn Rand's paeans to selfishness, and on the left in the cyclamatic "Greening of America," in which Charles Reich genuflects to the youth who adore their boots more than life itself.

Yet if only one of these authors survives to lecture posterity I am certain of his identity. It will be Kahlil Gibran speaking through "The Prophet." Why? First, because of Gibran's Law: the more complex the epoch, the simpler must be its solutions. The harder the time, the softer its lit.

Add to that, Kanfer's Law. Nutritionists tell us that if the body is deprived of cholesterol it will manufacture its own. Similarly, as the public is deprived of oleaginous philosophy, it makes its bards from hacks or journeymen. The ostrichlike assurances that once burbled from women's magazines are gone. "The Ladies' Home Journal" and "Seventeen" now discuss abortion and busing. Nick Kenny and Edgar Guest are no longer syndicated by newspapers. "Collier's," "The Saturday Evening Post," "The Woman's Home Companion," all, all are vanished, like Almustafa, in the mist. The public seeks its comfort in pop lyrics, or in remembrance of things past. (In Gibran the sources are combined: "Half of what I say is meaningless; but I say it so that the other half may reach you" is a snippet from the author's slim volume, "Sand And Foam" —quoted almost verbatim and without acknowledgment in the Beatles' song, "Julia.") (pp. 26, 28)

As organized religion loses its authority, disorganized religion fills its place. . . . Gibran's prose is pseudotestamental and his portrait of the prophet resembles those chromos of Jesus that are supposed to have materialized on old linen. (p. 28)

Perhaps the most quoted non-Prophet line Gibran ever wrote was, "We shall never understand each other until we reduce the language to seven words." This fatuous yearning for inarticulateness has become part of the new illiteracy. Indeed, talk show guests *have* reduced the language to seven words: Like; I mean; ya know; oh Wow!

Personally, I prefer the "Oxford English Dictionary," writers with large working vocabularies and readers who can challenge assumptions and question shibboleths. As for the celibate who knew all about marriage, the expert on life who shrank from the dirt of sexuality, the palsied surgeon of men's souls, he was, in fact, a social, psychological and biological ignoramus. (pp. 28, 30)

No, Gibran will not do; not even as entertainment. . . . Gibran's dictates are, ultimately, too simple, too sweet and too transparently bogus. Those who follow him end helpless before true tribulations and dumb before logical argument. . . .

For those who have not read "The Prophet" then, I offer my envy and a parting word: Don't. For those who have not only read but also loved the Gibran *oeuvre,* I can but quote the thought of the Chosen and the Beloved about his own notions:

> If these be vague words,
>   then seek not to clear them.
> Vague and nebulous is the
>   beginning of all things
> But not their end.

No indeed. The time for eagles and falcons is upon us; the era of the ostrich is over. Adolescents, Campus Cordials, middle-aged delinquents, it is time to put away childish things, to investigate and alter the world, not to cower under its surface, covered by sand and foam. (p. 30)

Stefan Kanfer, "But Is It Not Strange that Even Elephants Will Yield—and that 'The Prophet' Is Still Popular?" in The New York Times Magazine *(© 1972 by The New York Times Company; reprinted by permission), June 25, 1972, pp. 8-9, 24, 26, 28, 30.*

Lady (Isabella Augusta Persse) Gregory

1852-1932

Irish playwright, producer, poet, folklorist, and historian. Lady Gregory is best known for her influence on Yeats, although she was herself a competent playwright. Her best works are those in which she displays her rich knowledge of Irish legend and her keen ear for rural Irish dialogue. During her marriage to Sir William Gregory, an Irish member of Parliament, Lady Gregory led an extremely active social and political life. Upon his death the 40-year-old widow withdrew from her full life for a short time, then emerged to take on a vigorous role in the Irish literary revival. A latecomer to the theater, her importance is such that she is called by some the Mother of the Irish Drama. She provided inspiration and financial backing for many young Irish writers, and with Yeats and J. M. Synge founded the Abbey Theater in Dublin which she managed for many years. She was also one of the founders of the Irish National Theater Society. An aristocrat, Lady Gregory immersed herself in the common people, and from them she learned many riches of Irish living and legend, recorded in her several books on Irish folklore.

PRINCIPAL WORKS

Autobiography of Sir William Gregory (editor) 1894
Mr Gregory's Letter Box (editor) 1898
Ideals in Ireland (editor) 1901
Cuchulain of Muirthemne (translator) 1902
Poets and Dreamers (translator) 1903
Gods and Fighting Men (translator) 1904
Spreading the News (drama) 1904?
Kincora (drama) 1905
The White Cockade and *The Travelling Man* (drama) 1905
A Book of Saints and Wonders (folklore and history) 1906
Hyacinth Halvey (drama) 1906
The Rising of the Moon (drama) 1906
The Kiltartan History Book (folklore and history) 1909
Seven Short Plays: Spreading the News, Hyacinth Halvey, The Rising of the Moon, The Jackdaw, The Workhouse Ward, The Travelling Man, The Gaol Gate (drama) 1909
The Image (drama) 1910
The Kiltartan Moliere (translator) 1910
The Kiltartan Wonder Book (folklore and history) 1910
The Full Moon (drama) 1911
Irish Folk-History Plays, first series: *Kincora, Grania,*
Dervorgilla (drama) 1912
Irish Folk-History Plays, second series: *The Canavans, The White Cockade, The Deliverer* (drama) 1912
New Comedies: The Bogie Men, The Full Moon, Coats, Damer's Gold, MacDonough's Wife (drama) 1913
Our Irish Theatre (autobiography) 1913
The Golden Apple (drama) 1916
The Kiltartan Poetry Book (translator) 1918
The Dragon (drama) 1920
Visions and Beliefs in the West of Ireland (compiler) 1920
Hugh Lane's Life and Achievement, with Some Account of the Dublin Galleries (nonfiction) 1921
The Image, and Other Plays: The Image, Hanrahan's Oath, Shanwalla, The Wrens (drama) 1922
Three Wonder Plays: The Dragon, Aristotle's Bellows, The Jester (drama) 1923
Mirandolina (translator) 1924
The Story Brought by Brigit (drama) 1924
On the Racecourse (drama) 1926
Three Last Plays: Sancho's Master, Dave, The Doctor in Spite of Himself (drama) 1928
My First Play: Colman and Guaire (drama) 1930
Coole (essays) 1931
Lady Gregory's Journals (edited by Lennox Robinson) 1946

When I asked the little boy who had shown me the pathway up the Hill of Allen if he knew stories of Finn and Oisin, he said he did not, but that he had often heard his grandfather telling them to his mother in Irish. He did not know Irish, but he was learning it at school, and all the little boys he knew were learning it. In a little while he will know enough stories of Finn and Oisin to tell them to his children some day. It is the owners of the land whose children might never have known what would give them so much happiness. But now they can read Lady Gregory's book to their children, and it will make Slieve-na-man, Allen, and Ben-bulben, the great mountain that showed itself before me every day through all my childhood and was yet unpeopled, and half the country-sides of south and west, as populous with memories as her Cuchulain of Muirthemne will have made Dundealgan and Emain Macha and Muirthemne; and after a while somebody may even take them to some famous place and say, 'This land where your fathers lived proudly and finely should be dear and dear and again dear;' and perhaps when many names have grown musical to their ears, a more imaginative love will have taught them a better service.

I praise but in brief words the noble writing of these books, for words that praise a book, wherein something is done supremely well, remain, to sound in the ears of a later generation, like the foolish sound of church bells from the tower of a church when every pew is full. (pp. 34-5)

> *William Butler Yeats, "Thoughts on Lady Gregory's Translations" (1903), in his* The Cutting of an Agate *(reprinted with permission of Macmillan Publishing Co., Inc.; copyright 1912 by Macmillan Publishing Company; 1940 by Bertha Georgie Yeats; and in Canada reprinted by permission of Miss Anne Yeats, M. B. Yeats and the Macmillan Co. of London and Basingstoke),* Macmillan, 1912, pp. 1-35.

Lady Gregory has such an unquestionable genius for the theatre, so deep an intimacy with Irish folk-lore, and so fine a patriotism, that one opens her "Irish Folk-history Plays" with a sense of the highest expectation. Nor, if one bears in mind all that is implied of the title of these volumes, will that expectation be disappointed. The plays are folk stories, and the author has been careful throughout not to cram them into the Greek or French mould, and so sacrifice to artistic symmetry their essential flavour. Of the two volumes, one is devoted to Tragedy and one to Comedy, and in each case the subject is approached from the point of view of the peasant mind, and in that refinement of the peasant dialect which Lady Gregory has made peculiarly her own, and which she seems to write every year with increasing richness and variety. Indeed, the language alone is enough to make these plays interesting. . . . The rhythm and richness of [the] speech animates every page, and more than compensates for the absence of certain qualities which the modern mind insensibly demands in imaginative play-writing. In the first and strongest of the tragedies, "Grania," Lady Gregory has been bold enough to make a three-act play with only three characters. . . . This is by far the most successful of the tragedies. The story is a fine and simple one. It brings great qualities into action, and the character of Grania is boldly and yet subtly drawn. If the two Kings had been as solidly conceived, the play might have been a really great one, and, even as it is, it remains throughout a fine and moving thing.

In the Comedies one finds Lady Gregory in a more familiar mood. Yet the three plays in the volume strike each of them a very different note, the first of them alone approaching that vein of ingenuous farce with which its author's name is most usually associated. In this play ("The Canavans") the story is of Elizabethan Ireland, and the quality of the plot can be judged from the nature of the chief incident, when, in the Second Act, the time-serving miller's vagabond brother, in order to liberate himself and his brother from prison, dresses up as Queen Elizabeth (in the guard-room) and imposes on the vain young officer who is set to watch them. The remainder of the play is on the same plane, a plane which seems too grossly farcical till one reads the examples which Lady Gregory gives in the Appendix of current folk-stories about Queen Elizabeth.

One realises, then, that in the folk-story imagination knows no boundaries. None the less the play remains the least interesting of the volume. Its extravagance (in spite of some good character drawing and admirable dialogue) is too much for the English palate. "The White Cockade," which follows it, is far more disciplined. It is a good story, well told. Sarsfield, the principal character, is strongly and romantically drawn, and there is real feeling in the contrasts between the futility of James Stuart and the bravery and high hopes of the Irish whom his cowardice betrays. The last play ("The Deliverer") is a political allegory, the actual story of which is that of Moses and the Egyptian. The Israelites in this case are undeniable inhabitants of county Galway. What strange mischance has transported them to the banks of the Nile we are not told, but the change of sky has in no way diminished their raciness of speech and character. . . . There is a lesson for Ireland in every line, and the lesson is driven home with all Lady Gregory's unfailing humour and certainty of touch. The two volumes may be thoroughly recommended to all who are interested in the Irish theatre, and, if they do not always show their author in the vein in which we know and appreciate her best, they none the less contain much work which must rank with the best she has given us. (pp. 602-04)

> *C. T., "Lady Gregory's Irish Plays," in* Contemporary Review, *October, 1912, pp. 602-04.*

Of the five plays in [*New Irish Comedies*], only two have any real dramatic quality; but all have positive value, though not in equal degree, as intimate studies of Irish life and character. In dialogue they are frequently, sometimes extraordinarily, felicitous, racy in expression, rich in quaint and characteristic metaphor, and strokes of spontaneous humor and simple pathos. Occasionally they exhibit flashes of imaginative eloquence and passion. But, on the other hand, they are often sorely in need of revision and compression in long passages where the author, with a fatal fluency, weakens a serviceable motive, whether comic or serious, by merciless reiteration. As this fault is chiefly observable in her more farcical interludes, there is a presumption that it is due to haste rather than to lack of ingenuity or invention. In her best moments she can be vigorous, concise, and dramatic, but, throughout her writings, a tendency to diffusiveness and over-elaboration is strongly marked. On the printed page, where the flavor of the speech exerts a peculiar appeal, this is a matter of comparatively minor importance; but on the stage, where action is all important, the effect is mischievous and frequently disastrous.

There is much capital reading in "The Bogie Man," "The Full Moon," and "Coats," but these pieces are the merest sketches, devoid alike of dramatic substance and reasonability. At the bottom of each of them is an essentially comic idea which might easily have been more skillfully handled. The personages are alive, and the talk humorous and quaintly characteristic, but perpetually revolving about the same point, which soon becomes blunted by repetition. . . .

[It] is in the brief episode of "McDonough's Wife" that Lady Gregory exhibits her best dramatic and imaginative powers. It is a blend of sordid domestic tragedy and legendary fantasy. . . . Though written in prose, it is essentially poetic in its ideas, and is especially notable for the picturesque vigor, conciseness, and mingled realism and fancy of its literary form. . . . It seems to be a pity that Lady Gregory should have devoted so much time to the development of her comic vein, which, though productive, is seldom precious, instead of the tragic, in which her "McDonough's Wife" suggests infinite possibilities. But even in her comedies her complete mastery of all the external national characteristics has been of incalculable value to the Irish Theatre. (p. 555)

The Nation *(copyright 1913 by The Nation Associates, Inc.), May 29, 1913.*

Lady Gregory is the only playwright of to-day who writes comedies that have poetry in them. Her people talk lyrics and ballads. Most of her plays have a weakness—they are not firmly articulated, and too often they give the impression that a subject has been talked out rather than that an action has been brought to an end. Of the plays in [*The Image and Other Plays*] this might be said of three out of the four—*The Image, Hanrahan's Oath, The Wrens.* The fourth play, *Shanwalla,* is different; it is compact, and there is something hushed about it.

Shanwalla is a three-act play about a horse and a ghost, and the Connacht woman in Lady Gregory can rise with power in what has to do with these entities. The atmosphere is different from the usual Kiltartan play—it is not of the crossroads nor the marketplace, but of a gentleman's house in Ireland at the Stable-side. In *Shanwalla* there is nothing loquacious, nothing rhetorically tragical; everything is compact and hushed; the characters are all simple and all well-marked, and there is dramatic tension and power in it. It is one of Lady Gregory's best plays.

The others are typically Kiltartan; they are comedies of language, and they put us into contact with a rich and warm and quaintly cultivated humanity. There is a theme in each of the plays, a theme, rather than a plot, along which the people talk, and what we remember of them is the picturesque talk of the people who have had leisure enough to acquire a vocabulary and a wonderful stock of metaphor, not to speak of a rhythm that constantly rises into hexameters. Lady Gregory has kept note-books of this countryside talk, and her comedies make an anthology of phrases, partly traditional, partly improvised, of the Irish countryside. But no phrase is left sticking out. All are used as if they had never been on a collector's pages. The speeches are delightfully entertaining, but the Irish voice is needed to give the proper flow, intonation, and rhythm. (p. 572)

Padraic Colum, "Lady Gregory's Plays," in The Dial *(copyright, 1922, by The Dial Publishing Company, Inc.; reprinted by permission of J. S. Watson, Jr. and Scofield Thayer), November, 1922 (and reprinted by Kraus Reprint Corporation, 1966), pp. 572-73.*

[If *Three Last Plays*] are not the best of [Lady Gregory's] abundant dramatic output, they hold well to her high level; there is the same deft craftsmanship, and the fine sense that in reading or seeing her work you are in the presence of literature, and the unfailing sheer delight. . . .

Ever since she began writing plays, Lady Gregory tells us, she "had a desire to write one on Cervantes's great theme." The result is all the better, doubtless, for the long brooding. Something, surely, of the tolerance, the mellow understanding, the philosophical acceptance of the world's buffets, which the author has had to cultivate during her often stormy career, have gone into the shaping of her Knight of the Sorrowful Countenance, a figure who moves through scenes of sheer farce not only vestured in unsullied dignity, but touched by a fine compassion, in the three-act play obliquely entitled "Sancho's Master." . . . Lady Gregory's gently deflating art brings everything to the level of lovable humanity. Sparingly, but effectively, she uses those twists of Irish idiom with which she has made us familiar. They are like a check-rein, so that no matter how far the steed may prance into ancient times and Spanish scenes, he is ever and again brought deftly back into a universal focus. (p. 500)

As a reading play, "Sancho's Master" has the fault that the playwright's devices by which Lady Gregory crowds into the second and third acts so many of the noble and pathetic Don's adventures, make for a disjointed effect and a bit of a strain upon credulity.

The second play, "Dave," is typically Gregorian. The absurd intoxication of family pride is held up to laughter and riddled with an irony which the noble author has never surpassed. . . . But the major theme is again compassion—a cry against that kind of cruelty which tells the friendless waifs of the world that they are bad and despicable until in fact they become so.

Without the text of Molière's "Le Bourgeois Gentilhomme" before us, it is nevertheless evident that "The Would-be Gentleman" is a rendering so literal that it leaves little to say in praise of the self-effacing translator, but makes it possible to say that this particular masterpiece of the great Frenchman is still as actable and delightful and as true in its farcical irony as it was in the days when the elegant court of France laughed at it. (p. 501)

Shaemas O'Sheel, in Saturday Review *(copyright © 1928 by Saturday Review, Inc.; reprinted with permission), December 8, 1928.*

Where lies [Lady Gregory's] dramatic genius? First, in her use of Irish country dialect, that speech rich in imagery and imagination, an English to which Gaelic has given a strange twist. Yeats had set her gathering folklore, and she visited much among the country people around her home and had an impeccable memory for their speech, and in that speech most of her plays are written. . . . Lady Gregory's speech has not the wild poetry of [Synge's], but perhaps it is more authentic. She, Synge, and Padraic Colum were the first to discover that you could write quite seriously and beautifully about "poor" people, quite seriously and beautifully about people who spoke with a country accent, who spoke in dialect. Shakespeare and other writers had used such people in their plays but they had always used them for cheap, comic relief, to make the gallery laugh. It was for Synge to take a poor old woman living in a little cottage in the west of Ireland, and her son and her daughters, and shape out of those humble materials the most tragic and moving short play in the English language. It was for Lady Gregory to take a policeman, a butcher, a postmistress, and a telegraph-boy in a country village and out of these apparently farcical materials to build a high, delicate comedy. She learnt much from Molière, his quick patter of dialogue culminating in some long, eloquent speech. Perhaps she learned to love words too much and in her later plays might bury her situation under a load of beautiful fantastic phrases, an imagination run riot, a rich, curious dialogue, in detail of great beauty and subtle wit but undramatic in its essence. There are moments in drama when the only thing that matters is speed; like some ship flying to port before a tempest, all must be thrown overboard to lighten the ship, it must rush under bare poles; but Lady Gregory, stern at the helm, refused to sacrifice a single bale of merchandise or shorten a yard of sail, and in the end her craft is waterlogged, ready to sink under the weight of its own wealth.

This is an exaggerated statement; no play of hers has utterly foundered, yet some of them would have been greater successes if, at their most dramatic moments, the dialogue had been thinner. (pp. 59-60)

So varied was her output that it is best to consider it under certain easily defined heads. First, her short comedies, mostly early work and almost faultless. The more one studies these plays the better one appreciates her genius for construction. She realised, as every dramatist should, that construction is the bones of a play; once get them right and clothing them with flesh—with dialogue—is an easy matter. So she took great pains over her construction, and the result is seen, for instance, in *The Jackdaw* or *Hyacinth Halvey.* How superb are the situations, how they grow every moment in richness, piling themselves up like a great wedding-cake, tier above tier, crowned at last by some triumphant absurdity. Of the longer comedies I think *The Image* the finest; thin the dialogue a little here and there, and it is a beautiful character-piece, profound and entertaining. (She was aware of her over-rich dialogue and once allowed me to prune *Damer's Gold.* Few authors would be modest enough to submit to such a thing.)

The pieces in the two volumes of *Folk-History Plays* never had a great popular success. Yet *Kincora, The White Cockade,* and *The Canavans* deserve to be more often played. The first two are very early work and lack just that quality which was to mar some of her late work—the quality of thickness. *The White Cockade* qualities are of the most delicate, the play trembles between comedy and tragedy; *Kincora* has stouter qualities and is a fine heroic play; *The Canavans,* delicious farce. But greater than all these plays is *Grania,* a play that can easily stand beside *Deirdre of the Sorrows.* Here is a tragic legend treated with all the richness of folklore, here are situations simplified to the last degree—there are but four characters and the play is a long one. I do not know how it succeeds on the stage, for Lady Gregory could never get a cast in Ireland to her liking and therefore would not let it be performed.

She loved the noble tragic failures of history, the dreamer, the man with an impossible, unrealisable ideal. And so we have old Malachi Naughton in *The Image,* Patrick Sarsfield in *The White Cockade,* Parnell in *The Deliverer,* Don Quixote in *Sancho's Master,* Christ in *The Story brought by Brigit.* Feeling as deeply and as passionately on political affairs as any modern Irish dramatist in our years of acute national distress, no breath of contemporary politics blows across her plays. (pp. 61-2)

[She] wrote three plays unique in Irish drama—*The Golden Apple, The Dragon,* and *Aristotle's Bellows.* The first is not quite successful, there are too many scenes, the plot is confused; but the other two plays are entirely successful. These plays are realistic fantasy; it is only by such a contradiction of terms that they can be described. There are kings and queens and witches and magic charms and dragons and cooks mixed up with all the homely things of everyday Irish life in a most delightful way. The plays could take place nowhere but in the imagination of a genius; they brought beauty and extravagance into our Theatre when it had grown tragic and grimly realistic. (pp. 62-3)

> *Lennox Robinson, "Lady Gregory," in* The Irish Theatre, *edited by Lennox Robinson (reprinted by permission of Macmillan, London and Basingstoke), Macmillan, 1939, pp. 53-64.*

Lady Gregory created, in the main, slender but delightful farces. . . . From [the] contrived little farces, so shrewd and vivid and yet so superficial, Lady Gregory, however, moved to the high estate of comedy with one short masterpiece. In *The Workhouse Ward* . . . her preoccupation with common folk produced two remarkably vivid and charming characters. (p. 551)

In satire Lady Gregory revealed an incisive talent and in her three-act comedy *The Image* . . . she achieved a critique of Irish character that goes far beyond the scope of genre painting. . . .

Lady Gregory also gave expression to the national struggle of the people from whom she was separated by religion and English affiliations. Many of her patriotic pieces were melodramatic or pedestrian, and even the well-known *Rising of the Moon,* in which a police sergeant connives in the escape of a revolutionist who has moved his spirit, is a very modest accomplishment; the sergeant's conversion is an affair of sentiment rather than a result of characterization, although the effect is tense and poetic. But for once, when her patriotism found roots in peasant life, Lady Gregory created a second short masterpiece, *The Gaol Gate.* . . .

Irish peasant realism found its first effective realization in the work of Lady Gregory, and her best plays, however slight, are exquisite. . . .

Her example assured the triumph of peasant drama and was followed by a number of younger writers. (p. 552)

> *John Gassner, in his* Masters of the Drama *(copyright 1940 by Random House, Inc.; reprinted by permission of Random House, Inc.), Random House, 1940.*

In the pages of [*Lady Gregory's Journals*] will be found mention of all those people (nearly all; not Joyce) whom we would rather read about than anybody else—Shaw, Yeats, Synge, O'Casey, "AE," Gogarty, Stephens, and the rest, all those people whose writing in the English language was the brightest and liveliest we have known in our time. Yet these journals, it is sad to have to report, are not particularly exciting, are, even, rather dull; they begin in 1919, except for one or two earlier entries, and by that time the devotion and energy were employed in keeping or recovering; the bold wit that started things were worn down, and Lady Gregory sounds like a tired old lady, trudging faithfully where she may once, however sedately, have danced.

> *Rolfe Humphries, "Aftermath of Excite-*

ment," *in* The Nation *(copyright 1947 by the Nation Associates, Inc.), May 17, 1947, p. 577.*

Lady Augusta Gregory . . . expressed the drama of Ireland even better in her living than in her plays. She cannot rank nearly so high as Synge; her plays lack the lyricism of Yeats; but what is most important, she did have a strong feeling for the everyday personal problems of the Irish people. These are best reflected in her one-act pieces. She was, however, a propagandist so that if the character of the persons who existed in her plays would not fit the twist of the plot which would carry her point, she did not hesitate to distort the character to suit her ends. It is for this reason that she failed to reach as high a rank as her other many talents would have given her. Her poetic feeling for the Western Isles and the hidden places of her native land is strong and almost always moving. Her faerie quality is easy to accept because the audience knows from experience that the seeming naïveté is chosen, not inflicted by an inadequate command of dramatic technique. (pp. 218-19)

In *The Rising of the Moon* . . ., to give the proper happy ending to her play, and, at the same time perhaps, to work for better understanding between the nations, she perverts the character of the British policeman so as to allow for the escape of the Irishman. It is good theatre if not sure drama. In contrast, *The Workhouse Ward* . . . is a carefully constructed and well integrated piece which develops naturally out of the characters of the two protagonists. . . . *The Image* . . . is an example of the weakness of Lady Gregory's work when she tries to expand her subjects and methods into the three-act form. She is excellent in her chosen field and was most effective when she remained in it. Many persons feel that she reached her highwater mark as a playwright with *Grania* . . ., which is a folk tragedy but little understood except in Ireland where it is admired extravagantly. She is remembered as a warm-hearted woman with a flair for the one-act play form as well as being a born organizer. . . . (p. 219)

George Freedley, in A History of Modern Drama, *edited by Barrett H. Clark and George Freedley (copyright, 1947, by Prentice-Hall, Inc.; reprinted by permission of Prentice-Hall, Inc., Englewood Cliffs, New Jersey), Appleton-Century, 1947.*

Certainly there is no trace in [Lady Gregory] or in her work of that ruinous Irish envy, the backbiting and biting back, that exasperates, and only sometimes amuses, the student of Anglo-Irish literature. She was without envy because she had—more than any of her contemporaries—a sense of place, an aristocratic virtue little honored in the Ireland of yesterday or today. It was easy, then, for those who held such virtues suspect, as smacking perhaps too much of the prerogatives and pretensions of an obsolescent Ascendancy, to dismiss Lady Gregory's endeavors for what she herself, and after her Yeats, called "the dignity of Ireland" as the work of a literary drudge, a maidservant of letters among masters of the word. Whatever the reasons, ironic or absurd, the sorry fact remains that Lady Gregory *has* been neglected by literary historians and by the critics. . . .

[Her] "popularisation" was of so high an order that Yeats could afterward weigh it with Malory's *Morte d'Arthur* "and feel no discontent at the tally." That is because Lady Gregory's work is "created"; it rings true to the spirit of the old Irish tales, if not always faithful to the letter of the manuscripts. (p. 253)

Kevin Sullivan, "Portrait of Lady Gregory," in The Nation *(copyright 1961 by the Nation Associates, Inc.), October 14, 1961, pp. 253-54.*

Spreading the News was . . . intended to be another wistful piece like *Twenty-Five;* the Russian-scandal theme was to be used to rob a girl at a fair of her good name. (p. 80)

For sheer high spirits perhaps it stands at the top of [Lady Gregory's] list. . . . It is true that she was to do better technically, but the thing is the work of a mature dramatic personality, showing us in miniature the kind of playwright she is, and how she differs from her great contemporaries, Yeats and Synge.

They differ widely from each other, but each in his way is a romantic; she is classic. She has gone for her lessons, not to Maeterlinck or to the minor Elizabethans, but to Molière and Congreve. . . . She who had been living for the last three years in the cloudy world of the ancient epics shows no trace of their influence when she comes to choose the form in which she will express herself. It is neat, taut, finished; a conundrum has been set and successfully solved. The classic approach was not fashionable in 1904, and neatness was bound to seem anecdotal. What matters, however, is not the form in which you express yourself, but the quality of what you have to express.

And the little play is not a mere farce, firstly because Bartley is a real human being, even if the scandal-mongers weaving their web round him are two-dimensional, and secondly because its underlying intention is serious. She is laughing at her characters, as every writer of comedy does, but she is laughing at what is universal in them, not at what is accidental or ephemeral; certainly not at what is 'peasant'. She is not even merely satirising 'the incorrigible Irish genius for myth-making'; the Irish may bring an extra bravura to the art, but we all practise it. We all relish a scandal, and take care to pass it on in better shape than we receive it. The credulous market-folk of *Spreading the News* have their counterparts in the drawing-room.

And so it was to be in all her comedies. *Hyacinth Halvey* was inspired by 'a well-dressed, well-brushed man' in the Abbey stalls. The counterparts of the paupers of *The Workhouse Ward,* kept alive by their joy in a quarrel, could be found in a St James's clubroom. And her cleverest technical feat, *The Bogie Men,* in which the protagonists are two chimney-sweeps, was the favourite with the elegant and worldly Hugh Lane, because, he said, it exactly paralleled his experience with his cousins.

Hyacinth Halvey was written about the same time as she made the first of her direct translations of Molière into 'Kiltartan', and it has strong echoes of Molière, being almost entirely a series of ding-dong duets. One of them develops into that typical Molière device, the dialogue that is really two separate monologues, neither party really listening to the other. . . . The contrast is in itself piquant between the elegance of the rhythm and the artlessness of what the characters actually say.

As characters, they have more to them than those of *Spreading the News;* they are fewer in number and the play is a little longer. (pp. 80-2)

Lady Gregory's characters are commonly lumped under the heading 'peasant', but in fact many of them are peasant only in the sense of not being Ascendancy; they have a much wider social range than the characters of Synge. (p. 82)

She . . . called *The Image* 'my chief play', it was the only one she insisted on having revived, and Dr Lennox Robinson likewise 'gives it the branch'. Yeats on the other hand said it was too slow in action and had an act too many, and reluctantly I find myself in agreement with him; indeed, I would say it has two acts too many. (p. 85)

[*The Image*] became involved with her theory of the 'heart-secret', the cherished dream that keeps each one of us alive, and ought never to have its impracticability revealed by being told aloud. To carry the weight of this symbolic meaning, she expanded the little story, and as so often happens, the meaning has escaped her and gone into a programme-note instead of into the play itself. Its only explicit statement is in the last-act speech of old Peggy, who is not a sufficiently impressive character to pervade, as she needs to do, the whole play. To say that is not to deny that the actual workmanship of *The Image*, the dialogue, the characters of the pushing wife and the three elderly men with their alternate vauntings and self-doubtings, are among her very best. (pp. 85-6)

[In] effect the two women [of *The Gaol Gate*] are archetypal figures of tragedy, the wife and the mother of the man who is to die. She might therefore well have left them without character, relying simply on the pathos of their situation to move us. Whatever she may think herself, she has done nothing of the kind. The two women, within the brief frame of a one-act play, are not only individualised but contrasted, in their quite different reactions to calamity. The dour courage of the one, the pathetic gropings after comfort of the other, make them complete human beings, far removed from the single-quality poetic abstractions of Yeats. (p. 135)

They typify eternally contrasted attitudes, these two; they bear a distant relationship to Volumnia and Virgilia; but they are not the less bewildered countrywomen from Derrykeel, real figures in time and space, and in the history of a country where solidarity against the oppressor has been the first duty for seven centuries. They are among her most complete creations and best acting parts. . . . (p. 137)

Not since *Twenty-Five* had she shown any signs of abating her view that love was not a ruling passion in Ireland. Now, in *Grania,* she has an apparent change of heart, and writes a three-act play with only three characters, who have nothing to talk about but love. To Yeats, who expressed scepticism over the subject, she explained that 'the talk of lovers is inexhaustible, being of themselves and one another'.

The paring-down of the cast list, by which *The Poorhouse* gained so much when it was transformed into *The Workhouse Ward,* continued to exert her mind; she speaks wistfully of writing a play for one actor and a scarecrow. . . . *Grania* has only three characters because it is in a special sense a triangle drama, with which no outsider has anything to do. (pp. 141-42)

As I see it, *Grania* is not in the strict sense a love-story at all. It is a play in which a woman is ousted from an emotional relationship between two men. The 'love' is that of man for man, of brother for brother; it is loyalty to the warrior band, and a corresponding resentment of the woman who takes away the warrior's freedom, makes trouble with his comrades, distracts him from his purpose in life. It is an attitude which filters through the play as light filters through crystal; which runs through the heroic Irish sagas as it runs through the Greek. Its continuing validity was borne out by all Lady Gregory had observed in the world around her, the world of the 'loveless Irishman', the peasant society which relegated women to serfdom, the middle-class intellectual society which left them only the donkey-work. (p. 145)

Only in one of her plays do I find the authentic note of physical passion between man and woman, and that is in the one-act tragedy of *MacDonough's Wife,* where the woman who inspires it is dead. . . .

Someone did her the honour of comparing this play with Synge's *Riders to the Sea,* but MacDonough is not a figure Synge would have drawn; he is altogether too heroic. (p. 147)

Elizabeth Coxhead, in her Lady Gregory: A Literary Portrait (© *1961 by Elizabeth Coxhead 1961; reprinted by permission of Harcourt Brace Jovanovich, Inc.),* Harcourt, *1961.*

[There] is nothing whatever mysterious about Lady Gregory. If there is one word that sums her up it is complacency —Victorian complacency, at that. To please Yeats she rewrote the early sagas and romances that had been edited by famous scholars in English, French, and German, but when she came to a line like "Will we ask her to sleep with you?" in *The Voyage of Mael Dúin,* Lady Gregory, remembering what the Dear Queen would have felt, turned it into "Will we ask her would she maybe be your wife?"

Yet I think the critic in the *Times Literary Supplement* who not so long ago told us that there would be no Lady Gregory revival was probably wrong. I expect more revivals of *Spreading the News, The Rising of the Moon, The Traveling Man* and *The Gaol Gate* than of *Riders to the Sea* or *On Baile's Strand.* We have to *learn* to appreciate the work of Yeats and Synge, and in doing so lose something of its original freshness, but anyone can appreciate a Lady Gregory play just as anyone can enjoy watching a children's game. Under the Victorian complacency is the Victorian innocence, and this is a quality that does not easily date.

I do not mean that she is unsophisticated. If Yeats had his Corneille for master and Synge his Racine, she has her Molière, and anyone who knows Molière will notice his little tricks in her comedies. . . .

But in spite of the Victorian complacency she had a genuine tragic sense. Naturally, it was a very limited one. . . . But within that Victorian framework she achieves remarkable results, as she does, for instance, in *The Gaol Gate.* (p. 32)

Frank O'Connor, in Saturday Review (*copyright* © *1966 by Saturday Review, Inc.; reprinted with permission), December 10, 1966.*

[Lady Gregory's] use of language can in many of these aspects be compared with that of her fellow director Synge. Although Lady Gregory and Synge applied their observations to entirely different purposes, both were scrupulously accurate in their transcriptions and sincere in their use of the language they adopted. However, besides using different dialects (Synge generally used the dialect of Wicklow), the two writers approached their characters and dramatic form from opposite directions: Synge elaborated, enriched, personalized his people until their speech spiralled into romantic poetry; Lady Gregory on the other hand was more concerned with outline and neatness, controlling the dialogue with balance and almost classical precision. (pp. 18-19)

Lady Gregory's use of 'Kiltartan' extended beyond the accurate recording of picturesque phrases and turns of speech picked up in the 'thatched houses' where she gathered her folklore and poetry. A comparison of the difficult iambic pentameter quatrains of *Colman and Guaire* with the rich and flowing imagery of her later plays indicates the natural and characteristic language of the peasant whose thoughts flow easily into hyperbole and similes drawn from the life about him. (p. 19)

Nearly always the language of the plays fits the characters like a glove: the direct, incisive language of the policeman in *The Rising of the Moon;* the more relaxed, 'visionary' speech of the character-building community of *Hyacinth Halvey* and *The Full Moon.* . . . (p. 21)

One might safely say . . . that the foundation of all Lady Gregory's work, whether in its final form comedy or tragedy, fiction or history, is that delight in 'our incorrigible genius for mythmaking, the faculty that makes our traditional history a perpetual joy, because it is, like the Sidhe, an eternal Shape-changer'. (p. 25)

Perhaps Yeats is correct in his distinction between Lady Gregory's comic vision and Synge's ["Lady Gregory alone writes out of a spirit of pure comedy, and laughs without bitterness and with no thought but to laugh."]; there is little harshness in her work, and even in *The Deliverer,* the nearest she comes to satire, the attack is too direct and explicit to be considered a comic guise. Preferring to 'sport with human follies, not with crimes', she moves one step further than Jonson by removing the sting altogether from her 'image of the times'. When her comic vision does extend beyond the borders of what Yeats terms 'pure comedy', it moves not towards judgment of society but into the realm of human tragedy, or backwards into farcical situation. (pp. 31-2)

It might be said that she approached her peasant characters in the opposite direction from Synge: she recognized the universality of the themes which appealed to her and then wrote of them through the framework of Kiltartan; Synge on the other hand, like Yeats, felt first, observed particular qualities and characteristics which appealed to him, and then expressed them in terms of the universal. She worked from without in; Synge and Yeats from within out. . . . In other terms, it might be said that Lady Gregory was more of the story-teller in her approach to drama, whereas her two colleagues were more the [poets]. (pp. 33-4)

Perhaps because of her high regard for the poetic dramas of Yeats and Synge, Lady Gregory tended to underrate her comedies. She self-deprecatingly explained, 'I had been forced to write comedy because it was wanted for our theatre, to put on at the end of the verse plays,' and frequently reiterated that tragedy was easier to write than comedy, implying her own preference for the latter. . . . But if we observe the notes she wrote concerning the genesis and structure of her plays, it is apparent that even when the idea appeared first as a tragedy, it willingly adopted the comic form. . . . (pp. 35-6)

[Through] restricted dialect and characterization she managed to express her universal comic vision. Closer examination reveals two basic themes which are both universal and persistent: the idealist and his shattered dream. As all who knew her attest, and as can readily be observed from her writings, Lady Gregory had a deep sympathy with the 'image-maker', the rebel who must stand alone, apart from his community and yet bound to it by his dream. (p. 63)

It is perhaps inevitable that the celebration of the rebellious individual should appear under the mantle of tragedy, for in Lady Gregory's universe, as in Yeats's, such is the fate of those who take destiny into their own hands. But as one observes in Yeats's heroic fool, clearly the struggle is worth it, for only in controversy against inevitable Fate or overwhelming odds does he realize his full strength. This is the message of Grania, Gormleith, the penitent Dervorgilla; it is the message of Ireland's history. And when we turn from the tragic 'tragi-comedies' to the 'pure' tragedies, *MacDonough's Wife* and *The Gaol Gate,* we find the same stirring call to inner strength and the independent spirit.

The world in which Lady Gregory's plays have reality is very much a peopled world, inhabited by characters who are all gifted with loquacity and infinite capacity to believe, their individuality a result of fertile imagination. Consequently she rarely scales the heights of heroic tragedy, for as Yeats pointed out, the spirit of laughter is a great deflater, and once Lady Gregory allows her little people to take on their wayward personalities, she is no longer in control. . . . (p. 72)

Lady Gregory's nationalism not only led her to the theatre, but dictated the themes of her plays. Constantly we are reminded that these are plays not only for Ireland, but of Ireland. (p. 87)

Lady Gregory's approach to her material was in fact classical despite the romantic motivating forces of nationalism and idealism. Just as she watches with delighted interest the creation of her characters, so too she applies the same penetrating observation to the development of structure. Because of this ability to stand back and observe the dramatic form with a critical almost impersonal eye, her plays tend on the whole to be clearcut in form, classical in simplicity. (p. 91)

Throughout her plays, in structure, dialogue, and characterization, there is ample evidence of . . . emphasis on balance. Mathematical precision is most obvious in those plays which depend on inter-action between two groups of characters, such as *Coats, The Bogie Men, The Jester, The Workhouse Ward,* where the characters are really only half of the whole or 'mirror-images', and where the theme is a variation on comradeship. It is apparent again in plays containing the more complicated concept of the mask, such as *The Rising of the Moon,* where the ballad-singer represents the policeman's antithetical self, and *Damer's Gold,* where young Simon symbolizes Damer's own youth. . . . (pp. 93-4)

Her comic world was very close to the world of musical comedy, for both require that spirit which makes action more important than reading and which comes out of the dialogue as well as the situation. *Spreading the News* has been made into a comic opera; in over half of her plays music and song are made an integral part of the plot and she exploits this even more in *On the Racecourse,* where the songs further the action and reflect the inner conflict and emotions of the characters. Occasionally, as in *The Rising of the Moon* and *Dervorgilla,* the music-maker himself comes on; usually the characters burst into song to mark a shift in emphasis or break in tension. On the whole she adapted ballads to this use, and it is not surprising to learn that her favourite brother Frank's hobby was collecting Dublin street ballads. (p. 99)

Besides music and song, Lady Gregory was fond of introducing costume and disguise into her plays. . . . Mechanical devices abound in the wonder plays, which is to be expected. . . . Although she introduced the dance in only one play other than the translations (*The Full Moon*), choreographic effects are introduced frequently. . . . Like Yeats, Lady Gregory 'saw' her plays as she wrote them. (p. 100)

[It] was nearly always with Lady Gregory that the company [Abbey Theatre] broke new ground; it was she who popularized the one-act play with its economy and concentration and fine theatrical effect, created a new form of history-play that gave characters and incidents immediacy and life, and introduced a new universe, the 'Gregorian' fantasy world of her wonder plays. (p. 101)

[Never] did she let the theatre of her nation infringe upon the essential dignity of the spirit, and if the bulk of her work does not represent 'the apex of the flame, the point of the diamond', it is worthy of the base. And in that strange mingling of the ironic and the pathetic, the tragic and the comic, the clarity of vision which penetrated the dusk of Cloon and the moon-drenched Galway quays, Lady Gregory deserves her place in the constellation so clearly marked by her friends and fellow image-makers who worked together for art and for Ireland. (p. 102)

> *Ann Saddlemyer, in her* In Defence of Lady Gregory, Playwright *(© 1966 Ann Saddlemyer), Dolmen Press, 1966.*

[Interest] in that strange and sudden flowering of talent which is called the Irish Literary Revival, and in Lady Gregory's vital and many-sided part in it, though somewhat stagnant during the generation that followed her death, is evidently on the increase. . . . No doubt the best of her theatrical productions are the one-act comedies and dramas which for long remained the most popular features of the Abbey Theatre repertory, and of which the obituarist of the London *Times* wrote, "It is not too much to say that her one-act plays—so humorous, so wise, so moving, so poetical even when most homely—are among the best in the language." Although the fashion for curtain-raisers and after-plays is in abeyance, these little pieces are capable of holding their own, whenever given, by their quick sense of character, their neat, Molière-like construction, and the charming lilt of their partly observed, partly stylized Anglo-Irish dialogue. As [Elizabeth] Coxhead has suggested, they might almost have been designed for television. (p. 95)

> *Desmond Shaw Taylor, in* Saturday Review *(copyright © 1976 by Saturday Review, Inc; reprinted with permission), July 19, 1976.*

(Francis) Bret(t) Harte

1836?-1902

American short story writer and journalist. Although Harte was born in New York and lived on the East Coast and in Europe most of his life, his most important literary years were the seventeen he spent in California. Going there as a youth, he worked as an itinerant gold-miner, schoolmaster, Wells Fargo expressman, journalist, and printer. His varied experiences provided him with the material for the sketches and stories by which he gained his reputation. He is best remembered for his short stories of local color, notably "The Luck of Roaring Camp" and "The Outcasts of Poker Flat." He helped to establish the *Overland Monthly*, a journal for western writing (including the work of Mark Twain), and edited it for two years. He was an effective sharp reviewer and his talents as a critic were evident in some of his satirical parodies. Harte captured the imagination of his Victorian reading audience by his style of presenting morality in contrasts of black and white. His move to the East Coast to write for the *Atlantic Monthly* began his decline in popularity. He sought desperately to maintain his talents but was never able to sustain or recapture them. After serving as U.S. Consul in Germany and Scotland for several years he retired to England, never returning to the United States.

PRINCIPAL WORKS

Condensed Novels (parodies) 1867
The Lost Galleon and Other Tales (poetry) 1867
The Luck of Roaring Camp, and Other Sketches (short stories) 1869
East and West Poems (poetry) 1871
Poems (poetry) 1871
Stories of the Sierras (short stories) 1872
Mrs. Skaggs's Husbands, and Other Sketches (short stories) 1873
Tales of the Argonauts (short stories) 1875
Gabriel Conroy (novel) 1876
Two Men of Sandy Bar (drama) 1876
Thankful Blossom; a Romance of the Jerseys, 1779 (short stories) 1877
The Twins of Table Mountain, and Other Stories (short stories) 1879
Flip, and Other Stories (short stories) 1882
In the Carquinez Woods (short stories) 1883
The Argonauts of North Liberty (short stories) 1888
Cressy (short stories) 1889
A Sappho of Green Springs, and Other Stories (short stories) 1891

Colonel Starbottle's Client, and Some Other People (short stories) 1892
The Bell-Ringer of Angel's, and Other Stories (short stories) 1894
A Protégée of Jack Hamlin's, and Other Stories (short stories) 1894
Barker's Luck, and Other Stories (short stories) 1896
Poetical Works of Bret Harte (poetry) 1896
Tales of Trail and Town (short stories) 1898
Mr. Jack Hamlin's Meditation, and Other Stories (short stories) 1899
From Sand Hill to Pine (short stories) 1900
Condensed Novels. Second Series. New Burlesques (parodies) 1902
Trent's Trust, and Other Stories (short stories) 1903

American humour, neither unfathomably absurd like the Irish, nor transfiguringly lucid and appropriate like the French, nor sharp and sensible and full of realities of life like the Scotch, is simply the humour of imagination. It consists in piling towers on towers and mountains on mountains; of heaping a joke up to the stars and extending it to the end of the world.

With this distinctively American humour Bret Harte had little or nothing in common. The wild, sky-breaking humour of America has its fine qualities, but it must in the nature of things be deficient in two qualities, not only of supreme importance to life and letters, but of supreme importance to humour—reverence and sympathy. And these two qualities were knit into the closest texture of Bret Harte's humour. . . . America is under a kind of despotism of humour. Everyone is afraid of humour: the meanest of human nightmares. Bret Harte had, to express the matter briefly but more or less essentially, the power of laughing not only at things, but also with them. America has laughed at things magnificently, with Gargantuan reverberations of laughter. But she has not even begun to learn the richer lesson of laughing with them.

The supreme proof of the fact that Bret Harte had the instinct of reverence may be found in the fact that he was a really great parodist. . . . Mere derision, mere contempt, never produced or could produce parody. A man who simply despises Paderewski for having long hair is not necessarily fitted to give an admirable imitation of his particular touch on the piano. If a man wishes to parody Paderewski's style of execution, he must emphatically go through one process first: he must admire it, and even reverence it. Bret Harte had a real power of imitating great authors, as in his parodies on Dumas, on Victor Hugo, on Charlotte Brontë. This means, and can only mean, that he had perceived the real beauty, the real ambition of Dumas and Victor Hugo and Charlotte Brontë. (pp. 181-84)

[His] kind of parody is for ever removed from the purview of ordinary American humour. Can anyone imagine Mark Twain, that admirable author, writing even a tolerable imitation of authors so intellectually individual as Hugo or Charlotte Brontë? Mark Twain would yield to the spirit of contempt which destroys parody. All those who hate authors fail to satirise them, for they always accuse them of the wrong faults. . . . And it is this vulgar misunderstanding which we find in most parody—which we find in all American parody—but which we never find in the parodies of Bret Harte. (pp. 185-86)

The same general characteristic of sympathy amounting to reverence marks Bret Harte's humour in his better-known class of works, the short stories. He does not make his characters absurd in order to make them contemptible: it might almost be said that he makes them absurd in order to make them dignified. (pp. 186-87)

[Yuba Bill] is one of those who achieve the noblest and most difficult of all the triumphs of a fictitious character—the triumph of giving us the impression of having a great deal more in him than appears between the two boards of the story. Smaller characters give us the impression that the author has told the whole truth about them, greater characters give the impression that the author has given of them, not the truth, but merely a few hints and samples. In some mysterious way we seem to feel that even if Shakespeare was wrong about Falstaff, Falstaff existed and was real; that even if Dickens was wrong about Micawber, Micawber existed and was real. So we feel that there is in the great salt-sea of Yuba Bill's humour as good fish as ever came out of it. The fleeting jests which Yuba Bill throws to the coach passengers only give us the opportunity of fancying and deducing the vast mass of jests which Yuba Bill shares with his creator.

Bret Harte had to deal with countries and communities of an almost unexampled laxity, a laxity passing the laxity of savages, the laxity of civilised men grown savage. He dealt with a life which we in a venerable and historic society may find it somewhat difficult to realise. It was the life of an entirely new people, a people who, having no certain past, could have no certain future. (pp. 190-92)

Most of us have come across the practical problem of London landladies, the problem of the doubtful foreign gentleman in a street of respectable English people. Those who have done so can form some idea of what it would be to live in a street full of doubtful foreign gentlemen, in a parish, in a city, in a nation composed entirely of doubtful foreign gentlemen. Old California, at the time of the first rush after gold, was actually this paradox of the nation of foreigners. It was a republic of incognitos: no one knew who anyone else was, and only the more ill-mannered and uneasy even desired to know. In such a country as this, gentlemen took

more trouble to conceal their gentility than thieves living in South Kensington would take to conceal their blackguardism. In such a country everyone is an equal, because everyone is a stranger. In such a country it is not strange if men in moral matters feel something of the irresponsibility of a dream. To plan plans which are continually miscarrying against men who are continually disappearing by the assistance of you know not whom, to crush you know not whom, this must be a demoralising life for any man; it must be beyond description demoralising for those who have been trained in no lofty or orderly scheme of right. Small blame to them indeed if they become callous and supercilious and cynical. And the great glory and achievement of Bret Harte consists in this, that he realised that they do not become callous, supercilious, and cynical, but that they do become sentimental and romantic, and profoundly affectionate. He discovered the intense sensibility of the primitive man. To him we owe the realisation of the fact that while modern barbarians of genius like Mr. Henley, and in his weaker moments Mr. Rudyard Kipling, delight in describing the coarseness and crude cynicism and fierce humour of the unlettered classes, the unlettered classes are in reality highly sentimental and religious, and not in the least like the creations of Mr. Henley and Mr. Kipling. Bret Harte tells the truth about the wildest, the grossest, the most rapacious of all the districts of the earth—the truth that, while it is very rare indeed in the world to find a thoroughly good man, it is rarer still, rare to the point of monstrosity, to find a man who does not either desire to be one, or imagine that he is one already. (pp. 193-95)

> G. K. Chesterton, "Bret Harte," in his Varied Types (reprinted by permission of Miss Dorothy Collins), Dodd, Mead, 1921, pp. 179-95.

Harte did perhaps six distinctive things for the short-story form. First, he threw over his stories, especially over his early masterpieces, a peculiar atmosphere of locality, one that to the readers of his day was startlingly new. He did for California what Dickens had done for London: he romanticized it; he gave it a mythology with a background perfectly in keeping. His methods of securing his localizing effect were unusual. Seemingly he made little of his setting: one may glance through one of his tales and be surprised to find only here and there a sentence touching upon landscape or surroundings, and yet one carries away from it local coloring as the dominating impression. Never does Harte, in notable contrast with many of his disciples, describe the landscape setting simply because it is unusual or unique. Always it is introduced as background, as scenery for his little theater, and, like all scenery, it is painted splashingly with swift impressionistic strokes. The tragedy of "The Outcasts of Poker Flat" is played before this drop curtain:

> The spot was singularly wild and impressive. A wooded amphitheatre surrounded on three sides by precipitous cliffs of naked granite, sloped gently toward the crest of another precipice that overlooked the valley. . . .

It is like directions to a scene painter. (p. 234)

The second element emphasized by Harte was a saving dash of the new Western humor. In "Tennessee's Partner" he has recorded that in the gulches and the bar-rooms of early California "all sentiment was modified by a strong sense of humor." The statement is illuminating: without this peculiar quality in his work, which often is an atmosphere rather than a quotable entity, Harte would have been as sentimentally extreme as Dickens, his master. The funeral scene in "Tennessee's Partner" would have been mere gush. (p. 235)

The third characteristic was his startling use of paradox and antithesis. The world he presents is topsy-turvy. Of the dwellers in Roaring Camp he notes that

> The greatest scamp had a Raphael face, with a profusion of blonde hair; Oakhurst, a gambler, had the melancholy air and intellectual abstraction of a Hamlet; the coolest and most courageous man was scarcely over five feet in height, with a soft voice and an embarrassed, timid manner. . . . The strongest man had but three fingers on his right hand; the best shot had but one eye.

This became a mannerism with Harte. His heroes are men whom the world usually brands as villains. "A Passage in the Life of Mr. John Oakhurst" illustrates his method perfectly. (p. 236)

His fourth characteristic concerns his methods of characterization. He peopled his stories with highly individualized types, with picturesque extremes in an abnormal social régime. They are not photographs, they are not actual individuals, they are composites made up by fusing the unique qualities of many actual men or women into a single personality. Yuba Bill is the dream of a romancer who has known or has read about many California stage drivers. Colonel Starbottle is redolent of the make-up box: he changes from story to story. He is a gargoyle, and yet for all that he is alive, for Harte had learned from his master, Dickens, that art of creating what in reality is a realm of Munchausen, and then, miracle of miracles, of actually breathing into it the breath of life.

The fifth distinctive element in his work is a splashy type of impressionism. His treatment of background we have noted: he painted with broad strokes and strong colors, and he applied the method to his characters. Usually he works with extremes, with incarnated peculiarities, sharply emphasized. From him it was that Kipling learned the secret of the colorful impressionistic epithet, of the telling comparison, the single adjective that flashes a vivid picture. Harte describes a certain squaw as "a berry-eyed old woman with the complexion of dried salmon." Her daughter he describes as having also "berry eyes, and a face that seemed made of a moist laugh." Another character he pictures as "a stout, middle-aged woman of ungirt waist and beshawled head and shoulders."

Finally, like James and Aldrich, who were contemporaneous workers, he emphasized the technique of his art. He, too, had found Poe by way of France, he, too, was a conscious workman who knew the rules. Like Poe, too, he brought to the short story the training of the experienced magazine editor, and it was a training that kept him so long upon short, single-issue effects that he grew powerless to work effectively with the longer units. . . . He was brilliant in short dashes, but he had not the patience to hold himself to a long and leisurely plot and to slow character development. There were other reasons for his failure: Harte

lacked moral basis; he was superficial; he was theatric. He was temperamental, too, like Irving, and worked by impulse. Moreover, he dealt with materials impossible to be prolonged to novel length. If one is to make John Oakhurst or Mother Shipton heroic, one must deal with episodes: must make impressionistic sketches of vivid moments: to go farther would be to relate mere picaresque miscellany. It was only within narrow limits with single situations and highly colored materials that he could work at all effectively or artistically. (pp. 238-39)

Unquestionably the influence of Harte upon the American short story has been greater than that exerted by any other American author, always excepting Irving. His influence was far greater than the quality of his work entitled him to exert. He was peculiarly fortunate: everything for a time conspired to give him the center of the stage. The imagination of the whole world had been fired by the California gold era and the field had been untouched by romancers: his material was timely to the moment. Dickens had just visited America and the fame of him and his work had penetrated every household; then had come the news of his death, and enormous space had been given to him in all the journals of the world and new editions had crowded upon one another, until everyone had his Dickens:—the reading public had been educated to appreciate the type of work that Harte was to give them. Moreover, he came at the moment when better art was demanded, when the feminized fiction of the mid-century was no longer satisfying the majority of the readers, and he gave them his work in a form that seemed to them to be peculiarly adequate. In him may be found all the elements that had characterized the popular fiction of the earlier period, and yet his fresh, wild materials, his new Western humor, and his peculiarly effective technique made him appear like the inspired creator of a new *genre*.

Great as has been his influence, however, he can never be a permanently commanding figure in American fiction. He lacked sincerity. (pp. 239-40)

In all of his work there is no experience, no genuine feeling, no sympathy of comprehension; it is the theater and not life. Moreover, the moral perspective of it is wrong. Men do not at will put on a new suit of morals as they put on a new suit of clothes. Ruled by emotion and not by principle, by the desire to create wonder and sensation in his reader rather than to interpret for him life, he tells not the truth, and the ultimate basis of all great fiction, be it long or be it short, is the Truth. (p. 241)

> *Fred Lewis Pattee, "Bret Harte," in his* The Development of the American Short Story: An Historical Survey *(copyright © 1923 by Harper & Row, Publishers, Inc.; reprinted by permission of Harper & Row, Publishers, Inc.), Harper, 1923, pp. 220-41.*

Harte's superiority as a parodist lies, first, in the sound literary instinct that led him to choose great subjects for his parodies. I am speaking, and shall speak throughout, only of his first series [*Condensed Novels*]. His second series failed because he ran out of great subjects, and tried to make shift with subjects that were really too slight for effective parody. Fifteen out of his seventeen subjects in the first series were the most eminent popular writers of his period. . . . Two of his subjects were not great literary figures by any means, but they were conspicuously associated with great social and political circumstances, and thus became themselves conspicuous. . . . (p. 247)

With all his keen discernment of weaknesses and absurdity, he never fails to communicate the sense that he is dealing with a great subject. In fact if I were trying to interest a modern student in these distinguished Victorians, I am not sure but that I would approach the task by way of Harte's parodies. One who reads *Miss Mix,* Harte's parody on *Jane Eyre,* will find Miss Brontë's preposterous ineptitudes and absurdities faithfully reflected, but yet he will get the impression that somehow, nevertheless, *Jane Eyre* manages to be a highly considerable piece of work. In *The Dweller of the Threshold* one confronts all the pinchbeck writing, all the baroque transcendentalism; in *Lothaw* one confronts the tireless climber and insatiable toadeater; but one cannot quite get away from the conviction that as literary men, Disraeli and Lord Lytton were extremely respectable figures, notwithstanding. (pp. 248-49)

Harte . . . is concerned exclusively with the author and does not engage the reader's mind upon any idea, story or style of his own; he deals in pure parody. (p. 250)

> *Albert J. Nock, "Bret Harte as a Parodist," in* The Bookman *(copyright, 1929, by George H. Doran Company), May, 1929, pp. 244-50.*

Harte's letters reveal how earnestly he desired to write successful plays and how he turned aside from more secure engagements to dramatize *Jeff Briggs' Love Story, Thankful Blossom, The Luck of Roaring Camp, Clarence,* and *A Blue Grass Penelope,* none of which saw the stage. (p. 112)

It is true that his works teem with dramatic situations, but the limitations which, while allowing him to become one of the great writers of short stories, prevented him from becoming a successful novelist, also prevented him from becoming a practical playwright. If the one-act play had been at that time a profitable branch of theatrical art, Bret Harte might have succeeded in it. But his sense of construction was lacking for a broader structure, as the failure of *Gabriel Conroy,* his one full-length novel, proved. It was partly the very wealth of his material, as it was with Dickens, which stood in his way. . . . More than that, Bret Harte's characters had become almost like historical personages, and even he could not take liberties with them. . . . It must be remembered, too, that Bret Harte, even at his best, is constantly skirting the edge of danger in his treatment of the sentimental, and the touch that heightened his characters for the footlights was in some cases fatal. But if he could have worked harmoniously in collaboration with a trained playwright, he might have produced significant plays, for his great contribution to modern literature, the portrayal of moral contrasts in human beings from an objective, unmoral point of view, is in itself essentially dramatic. (pp. 113-14)

> *Arthur Hobson Quinn, in his* A History of the American Drama from the Civil War to the Present Day, *Vol. 1 (copyright, 1927, 1936, by Prentice-Hall, Inc.; reprinted by permission of Prentice-Hall, Inc., Englewood Cliffs, New Jersey), F. S. Crofts, 1936.*

Dickens was the decisive influence one saw at once in Bret Harte's tales, in their play of humour and sentiment, their mannerisms, their style. The mood of Dickens's Christmas stories reappeared in some of them,—with their odour of cedar boxes, evergreens, toys, glue and varnish,—and his way of repeating a stock phrase to identify a character, along with his selection of taverns and bar-rooms as settings. Bret Harte even followed the master's theatricality and drops into bathos. Dickens himself had recognized the younger writer's indebtedness to him, moved as he was by Bret Harte's bold new gift.

Many of the American story-tellers of the new generation were influenced by Dickens, a power as despotic as Carlyle's in the previous age, and it may well have been he who crystallized Bret Harte's feeling for the miners and gave him a pattern to follow in presenting their lives. . . . Bret Harte soon outgrew this influence. He became the sort of writer whom others follow,—if not the master of a school, at least the inventor of a kind of tale that numbers of others developed in America and in England. As he matured, he left behind the more obvious traits of the school of Dickens, his melodramatic tendencies and abuse of the pathetic, for he had a keen eye and a mind of his own, with a fine-grained instinct of workmanship and a style that was natural, resilient, clear, light and quick. For the rest, the miners were only one of a dozen aspects of the Western life of which he was a capital observer,—politics, ranching, newspapers, schools, religion, business, lawyers and the law and the glittering and varied scene of San Francisco. (pp. 269-71)

Bret Harte's notorious abuse of coincidence, one of the weaknesses of his art, might . . . have been due [in part] to the character of the world he pictured, a chaos that crystallized in the brilliant Bret Harte heroines who expressed as they reflected this atmosphere of excitement and risk. These were the frank direct young women who were always ready to "lead the way" in the "trackless, uncharted *terra incognita* of the passions" and whom Henry Adams had in mind when he said that, alone among the Americans, Bret Harte, after Whitman, had insisted on the power of sex. (p. 276)

Practically all of Bret Harte's stories were drawn from events that really happened, as most of his characters were based upon actual persons, and he was nowhere truer to life than when he revealed the deep civilization that so often underlay the rough crust of the hardened frontiersman. (p. 280)

Bret Harte's stories were the prototypes of all the "Westerns," with all the stock characters that appeared in the later tales,—characters, fresh with him, that were "stock" in time,—the pretty New England schoolmistress, the sheriff and his posse, the bad man, the gambler, the heroic stage-driver, the harlot with the heart of gold. His holdups, lynchings, bar-room brawls and romantic idylls on mountain ranches were the models that hundreds of writers followed in the future, few of whom ever compared with him in workmanship, style or refinement, for Bret Harte was not only original, he was an artist. His people appeared in flashes only, he could not develop a character and consequently failed when he attempted novels and plays, and sometimes he was melodramatic and often sentimental, though as often masterly in manner, subtle and firm. He ignored the demand for happy endings and in many of his tales there were none of the young heroes and heroines of conventional fiction, and this, with his clarity and lightness of touch, his abrupt beginnings and informal air, defined a new kind of story of which he was the inventor. (pp. 281-82)

> *Van Wyck Brooks, "San Francisco: Bret Harte," in his* The Times of Melville and Whitman *(copyright, 1947, by Van Wyck Brooks; reprinted by permission of the publishers, E. P. Dutton), Dutton, 1947, pp. 258-82.*

Chronicler of the "forty-niners" in short fiction, theatrical creator of Western gullies and arroyos, Bret Harte has been acclaimed the first of a line of Western storytellers who entertained two generations of American readers. He brought a world of contrast, uncouthness, and primitivism, a world of gamblers, reckless adventurers, and outlaws to his startled readers; and these materials for a western Iliad led them to clamor for more and more. He did not, as has been asserted, originate the local-color story. Augustus Longstreet, James Hall, Harriet Beecher Stowe, Rose Terry Cooke, Rebecca Harding Davis, Caroline Kirkland, and others had all preceded him. But his stories of the late 1860's and early 1870's did capture the public fancy, spread immensely the popularity of the regional tale, and solidify it as a literary form. Thus his influence upon later American writers was extensive. He was followed by Joaquin Miller, Jim Gally, Josephine Clifford, Edward Eggleston, George Washington Cable, Constance Fenimore Woolson, and others; regional literary activity had swelled into a movement. Hence, though no claim of priority can be made for him, his impact upon the readers of his generation and upon other literary men makes his place in the history of the short story an important one. Fusing the Irvingesque sketch with the gargoyled characters and sentiment of Dickens, he succeeded in drawing indelible pictures of the California of the gold-rush era. (p. 217)

> *The Heritage of American Literature, Vol. 2, edited by Lyon N. Richardson, George H. Orians, and Herbert R. Brown (copyright, 1951, by Ginn and Company; 1962, by Lyon N. Richardson, George H. Orians, and Herbert R. Brown), Ginn, 1951.*

The consensus on Harte [at the time of this essay] is approximately what it was at the time of his death: that he was a skillful but not profound writer who made a lucky strike in subject matter and for a few heady months enjoyed a fabulous popularity; that once the artifice, narrowness, and shallowness of his work began to be perceived, he fell out of public favor; and that through the last twenty-four years of his life, while he lived abroad, he went on tiredly repeating himself in potboiler after potboiler, turning over his own tailings in a pathetic attempt to recapture what had first made him.

That estimate is not true in all its details or in all its implications, but it is broadly true. Harte *was* lucky, he *was* limited, he *did* swiftly lose his popularity in America, he *did* go on repeating himself. Of the scores of stories that he wrote during his years in Germany, Scotland, and England, all but a small handful return to the picturesque gulches of the Sierra foothills from which, in one blazing strike, he had extracted the nugget of his reputation. Now, no critic takes

him very seriously; he is read principally by children and students. And yet he cannot be dismissed. More than a hundred years after his first sketches and poems began to appear in *The Golden Era* in the late 1850's, he remains embedded in the American literary tradition, and it looks as if he will stay. It is worth trying to discover what is keeping him there.

Whatever virtues he had, they were not the virtues of realism. His observation of Gold Rush country, character, and society was neither very accurate nor very penetrating; neither was much of it firsthand. (pp. 223-24)

His geography sounds authentic, but when one attempts to pin it down to locality it swims and fades into the outlines of Never-Never Land. Harte had no such personal familiarity with the Sierra as his contemporaries Clarence King and John Muir had, and no such scientific accuracy of observation. (p. 225)

He did not have, as the great fiction writers have, the faculty of realizing real characters on the page in terms more vivid than reality. His practice was to select occupations and turn them into types; and though individual models were sometimes present, as in the case of the gambler-duelist prototype of Jack Hamlin, the gamblers, schoolmarms, stage drivers, and miners of the stories are usually predictable. (pp. 225-26)

Unlike Mark Twain's human swarm, Harte's characters do not strike us with their lifelikeness. They are self-consistent, they have clear outlines and logical coherence, and they speak a lingo that sounds suitably rough and crude. Yet they look *made,* and they are.

These are, in fact, early forms of some of our most venerable literary stereotypes. Since Harte it has been next to impossible for a writer to present a western gambler who has not some of the self-contained poise, readiness, and chivalry of Jack Hamlin and John Oakhurst. Even Stephen Crane, in his superb short story "The Blue Hotel," succumbed to the pattern that Harte had laid down. Since Harte showed the world how, every horse-opera stage driver has driven with the picturesque recklessness and profanity of Yuba Bill. The schoolmarms of our movie and television westerns owe about as much to Harte's Miss Mary, in "The Idyl of Red Gulch," as to Molly Wood in Owen Wister's *The Virginian*—and it should be noted, in Harte's favor, that "The Idyl of Red Gulch" came thirty-two years before *The Virginian.*

Harte's geography seems vague because he did not know the real geography of the Sierra well, and didn't feel that he needed to. His characters seem made because they *were* made, according to a formula learned from Dickens: the trick of bundling together apparently incompatible qualities to produce a striking paradox. (pp. 226-27)

Harte's popularity . . . was always greatest in direct proportion to the reader's distance from and ignorance of the mines. By a happy chance of lagging factual reports, his stories reached Eastern readers when they were still titillated by rumor but unsatisfied in detail. As in the Currier and Ives prints about the buffalo plains, art passed for fact until fact overtook it, whereupon it began to lose its currency even as art. Then, after his popularity had dwindled on the Eastern seaboard, Harte found still another audience, even more remote from the Mother Lode, in England, and that audience stuck loyally with him until his death and after. In a way, it was the worst thing that could have happened to him, for it helped keep him from becoming anything more than the writer he already was. (p. 228)

Bret Harte represented two very common American literary phenomena. For one thing he was victimized, as many of our writers have been, by the boom-and-bust freakishness of public favor. For another, he was that American type, the local writer whom fame has drawn away from the local, and who now has a choice between developing new themes and a literary manner more suitable for a sophisticated audience, or repeating from exile, with increasing thinness and unreality, the localism he has left behind.

The very perfection of Harte's little world of the local picturesque made it all but impossible for him to break out of it. Mark Twain, who had never been so typed or so limited, was freed by the variety of his own life and by the vitality with which he welcomed new experience; he escaped into travel literature, into history, into causes, into his rich nostalgia for boyhood and the river. But Harte was imprisoned in his own creation. Pressed for money as he always was, he dared not vary locale or tone. (p. 230)

And so, from necessity, timidity, incapacity, or whatever, Harte made hardly a gesture toward discovering new sources of stories. He did now and then turn to poetry, but "only as a change to my monotonous romances. Perhaps it is very *little change,* for my poetry, I fear, is coming from the same spring as my prose, only the tap is nearer the fountain—and filtered." (p. 231)

[In] the *Letters* there is a more personal Bret Harte, one who makes us realize almost with a shock how little Harte's personality shows in the stories. There he is as scrupulously aloof and "indifferent," as "refined out of existence," as the most rigorous dramatic ideal could ask. His characters, whatever else they are, are never made in Harte's image, but are themselves, creations, clean of any taint of their creator. Like the perfect little world of picturesque localism and romantic paradox that they inhabit, they eventually controlled their creator as much as he controlled them; they were a thing he hid behind.

Reading the *Letters,* one wishes that Harte had let himself be revealed more: he is himself more interesting than his gallery of types. For one thing, the letters give evidence that if he had chosen to, he might have become a lively, biased, and outrageous travel reporter in the jingoist tradition of Mark Twain. (p. 232)

Admitting that there is in them little honest observation of people or of nature, no real character, no accurate picture of a society however fleeting, no true ear for the lingo, no symbolic depth, no valid commentary upon the human condition, no inadvertent self-revelation, and no real weight of

mind, there is still something. There is humor—pervasive, unprudish, often still fresh and natural. There is good prose, and this is nearly unfailing. He was master of a flexible instrument, and if his language was rather more literary than native, if he leaned toward the King's English and never made of his dialect much more than a sort of decoration, he can hardly be blamed. Of all his contemporaries, only Mark Twain managed to make the vernacular do everything a true literary language has to do. Harte's prose was sometimes inflated and self-conscious, but more often it was markedly clean and direct. He was capable of a notable economy, passages and sometimes whole stories of a striking nervous compactness in which character, situation, and realized place come off the page instantly visual. Try the opening of "A Protégée of Jack Hamlin's," a story written as late as 1893.

Economy and a formal precision were part of both his temperament and his training. In *Condensed Novels,* a series of parodies written during the sixties, he had learned to boil whole novelists down to a few pages of essence. But it was his adaptation of the short story to Californian materials that created something like a revolution. His example emancipated writers in every region, confirming them in their subject matter and confirming them in their preference for the short story form. So great was Harte's influence upon the whole local color school that in 1894 he modestly felt compelled to deny, in an article for *Cornhill,* that he had invented the short story itself. Invent it he did not, but no historian of the short story can overlook his shaping influence upon it or his enormous influence in popularizing it through the expanding magazines. (pp. 234-35)

> *Wallace Stegner, in his* The Sound of Mountain Water *(copyright © 1969 by Wallace Stegner; reprinted by permission of Doubleday & Co., Inc.), Doubleday, 1969.*

Although Harte frequently asserted that he could vouch for the realism of his characters and situations, he romanticized his materials to a greater degree than many other local colorists, especially those who identified themselves more closely with the regions they portrayed and who wrote less to exploit the eccentric and picturesque for its own sake than for some other purpose. From Harte's example, however, many of them learned that their stories must have a tone and form if they were to be more than sketches or loosely developed tales, and only a few of them were able to match the technical skill which makes "The Luck of Roaring Camp" and "The Outcasts of Poker Flat," whatever they may lack in verisimilitude, important landmarks in the development of the American short story. (p. 77)

> *Arthur Voss, in his* The American Short Story: A Critical Survey *(copyright 1973 by the University of Oklahoma Press), University of Oklahoma Press, 1973 (and reprinted by the University of Oklahoma Press, 1975).*

O. Henry

1862-1909?

(Pseudonym of William Sydney Porter) Short story writer, humorist, and journalist. O. Henry was among the first to perfect the technique of the unexpected ending; this as well as a vivid imagination coupled with keen observation are characteristic of his style. In 1894 O. Henry bought a weekly newspaper, *The Iconoclast*, (later called *Rolling Stone*), and turned it into a vehicle for humor, satire, and burlesques. The venture soon failed and he became a columnist on the *Houston Post*. He fled to Honduras in 1896 to escape prosecution on charges of embezzlement from an Austin bank where he had been a teller from 1891-94. Returning a year later to Texas where his wife was dying, he was convicted and served for three years. Whether he was guilty or innocent is not known. O. Henry's stories were first published while he was in jail. It is believed that his pen name was the abbreviated name of a well-known French pharmacist, Étienne-Ossian Henry, which O. Henry found in the *U.S. Dispensatory* while serving as prison drug clerk. After his release he settled in New York City to make his living as a writer. His more than 250 stories may be divided into tales of the Southwest, Latin America, and New York City. Along with his wide range of locality goes his use of authentic dialect. He was a devoted and accurate observer of the common life about him and loved to write about ordinary people. As a weekly contributor to the *New York World*, O. Henry became a popular success. Many of his stories have been widely translated and writers continue to imitate his style. The fatalism and irony of his fiction penetrated his life as well, and he died of alcoholism. The O. Henry Memorial Award has been presented since 1918 for the best story published each year in an American magazine.

PRINCIPAL WORKS

Cabbages and Kings (short stories) 1904
The Four Million (short stories) 1906
Heart of the West (short stories) 1907
The Trimmed Lamp (short stories) 1907
The Gentle Grafter (short stories) 1908
The Voice of the City (short stories) 1908
Options (short stories) 1909
Roads of Destiny (short stories) 1909
Let Me Feel Your Pulse (short stories) 1910
Strictly Business (short stories) 1910
The Two Women (short stories) 1910
Whirligigs (short stories) 1910
Sixes and Sevens (short stories) 1911

Rolling Stones (short stories) 1912
Waifs and Strays (short stories) 1917

O. Henry seems to possess the happy gift of picking up gold pieces from the asphalt pavement. If occasionally his finds turn out to be tobacco-tags instead, you easily forgive him, it's so clearly a part of the jubilant and irresponsible game he is playing. It is the unpremeditated element that lends half the characteristic charm to O. Henry's writing. His faculty of vernacular observation rarely fails him. . . . O. Henry's stories are as disorderly as the streets of the city he loves so well. This newer collection [*The Trimmed Lamp*] shows not the least growth in the quality of his perceptions (always shrewd, but never deep), nor any hoped-for attention to good workmanship. Having learned a trick or two of construction,—the three-line surprise ending, for example,—he seems quite satisfied to go no further. Yet there is something irresistible about the stories, with all their crimes upon them; they are so buoyant and careless, so genial in their commentary, and so pleasantly colored by a sentiment which, if as sophisticated as Broadway itself, is still perfectly spontaneous and sincere. (p. 134)

> *Henry James Smith, in* The Atlantic Monthly (*copyright © 1907 by The Atlantic Monthly Company, Boston, Mass.; reprinted with permission*), July, 1907.

Already a legend has grown up about O. Henry. There is a prodigious curiosity about the man behind those quick flashes that light up so many corners of American life. For whether the corners the light has shone upon have been in this homeless city of strangers, whether on the borderland where the shadow of the conquistadores of Spain and the plains Indian lie mingled athwart the life and language of the Anglo-Saxon, whether in the somnolent Southern town . . ., [no] matter where the corners have been, the vision has been that of the American such as he was before Germany and Eastern and Southern Europe flooded through the gates where the immigration authorities stand guard.

William Sidney Porter . . . traveled in the very track which most confirms the true American in his birthright. . . . [There] exists in what he has written a record of that American's attitude—an attitude mixed of shrewd humor, of sentiment, of a certain daredevil mockery, (noted by Mr. Kipling,) and underlain by a seriousness which no matching with destiny for beers, or better or worse, can rob of a certain consecration and solemnity. Holder of a trust from on high, he feels himself somehow, and he may speak as from a pulpit at any moment—as O. Henry has done in that wonderful "Unfinished Story" of his and elsewhere.

The way the man . . . [makes] us see what he saw, in spite of the sordid fact that he wrote most of it to redeem his soul and body from the publishers in whose debt he perpetually stood, reveals to an enormous number of Americans their own inmost attitude toward all sorts of things that surround them . . .—the vast machinery of their own civilization which has become their master instead of their servant through sheer excess of their industry and energy; the enormous loneliness of the life it thrusts upon the millions who tend it. . . .

We all know that we have our private and secret, and, as some might think, cynical thoughts [which are], as nearly as may be, reflected in O. Henry's attitude. . . .

[O. Henry] is the man who—as many think—holds next to Kipling first rank among modern short story tellers in English—stories of the spontaneous, not the artificial type, mind you.

> *"Some Ohenryana," in* The New York Times Book Review *(© 1913 by The New York Times Company; reprinted by permission), January 12, 1913, p. 10.*

O. Henry's finest work was done [in New York]—inimitable, unsurpassable stories that make up the volumes entitled "The Four Million," "The Trimmed Lamp," and "The Voice of the City."

Marvellous indeed they are. Written offhand with the bold carelessness of the pen that only genius dare use, but revealing behind them such a glow of the imagination and such a depth of understanding of the human heart as only genius can make manifest.

What O. Henry did for Central America he does again for New York. It is transformed by the magic of his imagination. He waves a wand over it and it becomes a city of mystery and romance. It is no longer the roaring, surging metropolis that we thought we knew, with its clattering elevated, its unending crowds, and on every side the repellent selfishness of the rich, the grim struggle of the poor, and the listless despair of the outcast. It has become, as O. Henry loves to call it, Bagdad upon the Subway. The glare has gone. There is a soft light suffusing the city. Its corner drugstores turn to enchanted bazaars. From the open doors of its restaurants and palm rooms there issues such a melody of softened music that we feel we have but to cross the threshold and there is Bagdad waiting for us beyond. A transformed waiter hands us to a chair at a little table—Arabian, I will swear it—beside an enchanted rubber tree. There is red wine such as Omar Khayyam drank, here on Sixth Avenue. At the tables about us are a strange and interesting crew—dervishes in the disguise of American business men, caliphs masquerading as tourists, bedouins from Syria, and fierce fantassins from the desert turned into western visitors from Texas, and among them—can we believe our eyes—houris from the inner harems of Ispahan and Candahar, whom we mistook but yesterday for the la-

dies of a Shubert chorus! As we pass out we pay our money to an enchanted cashier with golden hair—sitting behind glass—under the spell of some magician without a doubt, and then taking O. Henry's hand we wander forth among the everchanging scenes of night adventure, the mingled tragedy and humour of The Four Million that his pen alone can depict. Nor did ever Haroun-al-Rashid and his viziers, wandering at will in the narrow streets of their Arabian city, meet such varied adventure as lies before us, strolling hand in hand with O. Henry in the new Bagdad that he reveals. (pp. 246-48)

It is hard . . . to illustrate O. Henry's genius by the quotation of single phrases and sentences. The humour that is in his work lies too deep for that. His is not the comic wit that explodes the reader into a huge guffaw of laughter and vanishes. His humour is of that deep quality that smiles at life itself and mingles our amusement with our tears.

Still harder is it to try to shew the amazing genius of O. Henry as a "plot maker," as a designer of incident. No one better than he can hold the reader in suspense. Nay, more than that, the reader scarcely knows that he is "suspended," until at the very close of the story O. Henry, so to speak, turns on the lights and the whole tale is revealed as an entirety. But to do justice to a plot in a few paragraphs is almost impossible. (p. 249)

[Let the reader read one of O. Henry's best stories.] After he has read it he will either pronounce O. Henry one of the greatest masters of modern fiction or else,—well, or else he is a jackass. Let us put it that way. (p. 264)

> *Stephen Leacock, "The Amazing Genius of O. Henry," in his* Essays and Literary Studies *(copyright, 1916, by Dodd, Mead & Company, Inc.; reprinted in Canada by permission of The Canadian Publishers, McClelland and Stewart Limited, Toronto), Dodd, Mead, 1916, pp. 231-66.*

[O. Henry's] worst defect was a fear and hatred of conventionality; he had such mortal terror of stock phrases that, as some one has said, he wrote no English at all—he wrote the dot, dash, telegraphic style. Yet leaving aside all his perversities and his whimsicalities, and the poorer part of his work where the desire to be original is more manifest than any valuable result of it, there remain a sufficient number of transcripts from life and interpretations of it to give him abiding fame. There is a humorous tenderness in "The Whirligig of Life," and profound ethical passion in "A Blackjack Bargainer." (p. 231)

No writer of distinction has, I think, been more closely identified with the short story in English than O. Henry. Irving, Poe, Hawthorne, Bret Harte, Stevenson, Kipling attained fame in other fields; but although Porter had his mind fully made up to launch what he hoped would be the great American novel, the veto of death intervened, and the many volumes of his "complete works" are made up of brevities. The essential truthfulness of his art is what gave his work immediate recognition, and accounts for his rise from journalism to literature. There is poignancy in his pathos; desolation in his tragedy; and his extraordinary humour is full of those sudden surprises that give us delight. Uncritical readers have never been so deeply impressed with O. Henry as have the professional, jaded critics, weary of the old trick a thousand times repeated, who found in his writings a freshness and originality amounting to genius. (p. 232)

> *William Lyon Phelps, "O. Henry," in his* The Advance of the English Novel *(copyright © 1916 by Dodd, Mead & Co.), Dodd, Mead, 1916 (and reprinted in* Waifs and Strays: Twelve Stories, *by O. Henry, Doubleday, Page & Company, 1917, pp. 231-32).*

Thousands of us are reading [O. Henry's] stories at present and realizing with astonishment that he was a great literary artist—with astonishment because, though we are only just arriving at this knowledge of him, we learn that he commenced to write before the end of last century, and has been five years dead. Even in America, where he belonged, recognition came to him slowly. . . . (pp. 196-97)

O. Henry can move you to tears as well as to laughter—you have not finished with him when you have called him a humourist. He has all the gifts of the supreme teller of tales, is master of tragedy as well as of burlesque, of comedy and of romance, of the domestic and the mystery-tale of common life, and has a delicate skill in stories of the supernatural. Through every change of his theme runs a broad, genial understanding of all sorts of humanity, and his familiar, sometimes casually conversational style conceals a finished narrative art that amply justifies Professor [Stephen] Leacock [see excerpt above] in naming him "one of the great masters of modern literature." . . .

For the scenes, incidents, and characters of his tales he had not need to travel far outside the range of his own experiences, and it is probably this that helps to give them the carelessly intimate air of reality that is part of their strength. He touches in his descriptions lightly and swiftly, yet . . ., his stories are steeped in colour and atmosphere. You come to think of his men and women less as characters he has drawn than as people he has known, he writes of them with such familiar acquaintance, and makes them so vividly actual to you. . . . You scarcely realize them as creations, they seem to walk into his pages without effort. His women are, at least, as varied in type and as intensely human as his men. . . . (pp. 200-01)

There were moods in which he saw New York in all its solid, material, commonplace realism, and moods in which it became to him "Bagdad-on-the-Subway," and was full of romance, as Soho is in Stevenson's "New Arabian Nights." His Wild West stories are a subtle blend of humour, pathos, and picturesqueness; some of his town and country stories delight you by their homely naturalness, others are alive with sensation and excitement, others again are pure fantasy or things for nothing but laughter. Then there are such as "Roads of Destiny," which, with a strange dream-like quality, a haunting, imaginative suggestiveness, unfolds three stories of the same man—as one might see them in prevision—showing that whichever way of life he had chosen he would have been brought to the same appointed end. The eerie touch of other-world influences is upon you in this. . . . (pp. 201-02)

It is in sheer art of narration, and in the breadth and depth of his knowledge of humanity and his sympathy with it that he chiefly excels. He was too big a man to be nothing but an artist, and the bigger artist for that reason. He has none of the conscious stylist's elaborate little tricks with words, for he is a master of language and not its slave. He is as happily colloquial as Kipling was in his early tales, but his style is as individual, as naturally his own, as a man's voice may be. He seems to go as he pleases, writing apparently just whatever words happen to be in the ink, yet all the while he is getting hold of his reader's interest; subtly shaping his narrative with the storyteller's unerring instinct, generally allowing you no glimpse of its culminating point until you are right on it. "The art of narrative," said Keogh, in "Cabbages and Kings," "consists in concealing from your audience everything it wants to know until after you expose your favourite opinions on topics foreign to the subject. A good story is like a bitter pill with the sugar coating inside of it"; and this art O. Henry practises with a skill that is invariably admirable and at times startling. (pp. 202-03)

"Cabbages and Kings," a series of stories held together by a central thread of interest, is the nearest O. Henry came to writing a novel. Toward the end of his career his publishers urged him to write one and among his papers after his death was found an unfinished reply to them setting out something of his idea of the novel he would like to attempt. It was to be the story of an individual, not of a type—"the *true* record of a man's thoughts, his descriptions of his mischances and adventures, his *true* opinions of life as he has seen it, and his *absolutely honest* deductions, comments, and views upon the different phases of life he passes through." It was not to be autobiography: "most autobiographies are insincere from beginning to end. About the only chance for the truth to be told is in fiction."

But his novel remains without a title in the list of unwritten books. Whether, if it had been written, it would have proved him as great an artist on the larger canvas as he is on the smaller, is a vain speculation and a matter of no moment. What matters is that in these twelve volumes of his he has done enough to add much and permanently to the world's sources of pleasure, and enough to give him an assured place among the masters of modern fiction. (pp. 203-04)

> *A. St. John Adcock, "O. Henry: An English View," in* Waifs and Strays: Twelve Stories, *by O. Henry (copyright © 1917 by Doubleday, Page & Company; reprinted by permission of Doubleday & Co., Inc.), Doubleday, Page, 1917, pp. 196-204.*

O. Henry has breathed new life into the short story. Gifted as he is with a flashing wit, abundant humour, and quick observation, no subject has terrors for him. If it be too much to say, in the old phrase, that nothing human is alien to him, at least the larger part of humanity is his domain. The very title of one of his books, "The Four Million," is a protest against those who believe that New York contains only four hundred people worth while. O. Henry backs the census-taker against the social arbiter. The rich and the fashionable are, in his tales, conceived much in the spirit of similar characters in melodrama, except that the ingredient of humour is put in to mitigate them. Indeed, they figure but seldom. But the poor and the lowly, . . . the whole "ruck and rabble" of life, so meaningless to the comfortable, unobservant bourgeois, are set forth always with keen knowledge, with a laughing humour, and not infrequently with a tender, smiling pathos. As this panorama of the undenoted faces of the great city passes before the reader, he becomes his own Caliph Haroun-al-Raschid, and New York a teeming Bagdad, full of romance and mystery.

The facility, the light touch of O. Henry, his mastery of the vernacular, his insight into the life of the disinherited, make it needless for him to resort to such inventions as Stevenson's learned Arabian, imaginary author of the "New Arabian Nights." The piquant and picturesque phrasing, the dash of slang, the genial and winning fancy seem to carry off the most fantastic situations. The Touchstone, the jester, the merry-maker has always enjoyed a certain license if he had but the wit not to abuse it. O. Henry's fun is never of the slapstick variety and his pathos never bathos. (pp. 277-78)

"The Trimmed Lamp" is of a piece with "The Four Million," filled with the tragi-comedy of life much as it appeared to Dickens and to François Villon. In "Heart of the West" the author exploits a vein many have attempted in a short story as well as in the novel—the so-called "wild West." But no one, it is safe to say, has brought so much fun and humour to the Western story. Cattle-king, cowboy, miner, the plains and the chaparral—material of the "dime novel," but all treated with the skill of a Maupassant, and a humour Maupassant never dreamed of. The merest sketch of them has a certain substance to it. Yet it is idle to compare O. Henry with anybody. No talent could be more original or more delightful. The combination of technical excellence with whimsical, sparkling wit, abundant humour, and a fertile invention is so rare that the reader is content without comparisons. (p. 280)

> *Henry James Forman, "O. Henry's Short Stories," in* Waifs and Strays: Twelve Stories, *by O. Henry (copyright © 1917 by Doubleday, Page & Company; reprinted by permission of Doubleday & Co., Inc.), Doubleday, Page, 1917, pp. 277-80.*

[O. Henry's] first story, "Whistling Dick's Christmas Stocking," had attracted the attention of *McClure's* because of its materials: it was the story of the Southern tramp migration at the end of the Northern summer and it was told evidently by one who himself had been a tramp. All that was known of him was rumor: he had been a cowboy, a tramp, perhaps a yeggman, certainly a soldier of fortune in Honduras and South America, and he was writing with strangely graphic pen of his own experiences. The demand for his work came almost exclusively from the new popular magazines of the journalistic type. . . . (p. 359)

The period of his apprenticeship may be said to have ended in December, 1903, when the New York *World* added him to its staff as short-story writer for its Sunday edition. The result was one hundred and thirteen stories in some thirty months—the heart of O. Henry. Never was writer seemingly so irresponsible, so whimsical, so chattily heterogeneous. He had been given perfect freedom, and his stories had shaken off all traces of models and conformity to standards and were pure O. Henry. Maupassant he read constantly, but it was only to stimulate his own sense of form, for behind his seeming lawlessness were art requirements the most rigid. His chattiness, his familiarity with the reader, his seeming digressions, his monstrous exaggerations, all held rigidly to one end: he would win his reader—completely, put him utterly off his guard, and then bring him up rigid at the last sentence, and the newspaper re-

quirements were that he should do it in the compass of a page. His stories of this period average 2,500 words. Entertainment was his only thought—entertainment of the vaudeville variety, won at any cost, even the sacrifice of truth and reality. He was a reporter sent out each week for a "story" from the Babylon of New York and he was to tell this story so that the jaded and *blasé* and sensation-surfeited readers of Sunday papers would be attracted to it, would be held on and on to the end of it, and would even be thrilled and rendered exclamatory by the totally unexpected climax of it, so much so that they would turn to the same page on the following Sunday. It was superlatively good journalism. No longer was it strange background and Jack-Londonlike adventure from first hand experience that won his readers: he was working now with New York City stuff concerning which until a few months before he had had absolutely no first-hand knowledge. His vogue now came not from his materials, but from his manner.

The elements of his art were not many. One notes first of all that his stories are generally trivial as stories—mere anecdotes. Any one of his *World* pieces may be reduced to the compass of a commercial traveler's "good one." And not even this figment of plot is the vital thing about the story: it is the style of the telling—O. Henry stands first of all for manner, and the chief ingredient of this manner is humor. He should be rated first of all as a humorist, as much so as even Artemus Ward or Mark Twain. He was a born humorist: his biography is larded with Eugene Field-like practical jokes, with cartoons and caricatures and outrageous drolleries. (pp. 359-60)

The second element of his art came from his journalistic sense. He knew the public for which he was writing—Mr. Everybody—and catered to his whims. . . . He knew precisely how much of the sugar of sentimentality the great average reading public must have, and how much of the pepper of sensation, and the salt of facts, and the salad dressing of romance. He had, moreover, the newspaper man's horror of heaviness, of surplusage, of the commonplace. The story must have "snap," "go," up-to-dateness to the moment; a "punch" in every sentence.

The third conspicuous element in his art is closely allied to the second—form, technique. He studied Maupassant, but Maupassant in turn might have added a certain glow to the cold finish of his own tales, could he have studied O. Henry. The American certainly was the more original of the two. Not enough has been made of the ingrained Americanism of the man. No one, not even Mark Twain, was more a product of our own soil. He was a finished oral story-teller of the Western hotel-foyer type before he had ever written a word of fiction. . . . The "nub" of the narrative is held to the last moment and then greeted with a roar of laughter. The embroidery of the tale, the skill in concealing the final crux, and the color and the momentum of it all depend upon the narrator. O. Henry is the crowned chief of the ancient American order of *That Reminds Me of Another*. To read him is at times almost to feel his physical presence. He slaps you on the shoulder, asks your advice on points of grammar and the wording of quotations, and you can almost hear his laugh when he springs his final ending. His art is the art of Poe: he has no thought beyond the immediate effect of his tale upon his reader. Poe often left his audience quivering with horror; O. Henry leaves them chuckling with laughter.

The last distinctive element in his art is the strangest of all the strange paradoxes connected with O. Henry. In this unschooled druggist, this cowboy and Main Street clerk, this Texas funny man, one would hardly expect to find verbal precision and wide range of vocabulary. Modern slang he used with outrageous abandon, but everywhere amid the slang are felicities of expression and strange verbal flavors that amaze one. Not even Henry James could choose words more fastidiously or use them more accurately. And yet should one attempt to illustrate this quality of his style one could find only sentences or at most paragraphs. Not one of his stories as a whole can be singled out for its distinction of phrase and its uniformity of beautiful style. . . . A paragraph of beauty ends in a caper; one reads a whole page at the height of Emerson, only to find its author grinning through a horse collar at the end; one may discover what seems at last a completely serious story of real life—yet beware! . . . What he might have done had he dropped his harlequin pen and done serious work at the height of his powers we may not say. We know, however, that he had, whenever he deigned to use it with seriousness, a vocabulary like a backwoodsman's rifle: every word striking the red with a precision that gives to the reader a continual thrill.

But brilliant as were the possibility of his powers, and distinctive as was his technique, his final place can never be high even among the writers of short stories. He did not take literature seriously: he was a victim of Momus and the swift ephemeral press. His undoubted powers were completely debauched by it. He became exclusively an entertainer, with no thought but of the moment, and no art save that which brought instant effect upon his reader. To accomplish that he would sacrifice everything, even the truth. One never reads his tales for their material—incident for its own sake—as one does Jack London's or Kipling's; nor do we read them because of the characters as one does Mary E. Wilkins's or Alice Brown's; nor for seeing life exactly as life is as one reads Garland or Norris: one reads them for the narcotic effects they produce. These tales of South America, of picaresque adventurers and New York shop girls—two hundred and forty-five of them in all—are not necessarily the truth: they are *opera bouffe*. (pp. 361-63)

He worked without truth, without moral consciousness, and without a philosophy of life. He created no characters: he worked with puppets, lay figures without souls—we see them moving before us, but we know them not at all; they are x, y, and z in his rambles in absurdity. He was a harlequin Poe with modern laughter in place of gloom: much that we have charged up against him we have also charged up against the creator of the "Gold Bug" and "The Black Cat," but he was utterly without Poe's reverence for the literature of power, he was without his simplicity, without his universality, without his ability to stand with the great serious literary creators of the world. (p. 364)

Fred Lewis Pattee, "O. Henry and the Handbooks," in his The Development of the American Short Story: An Historical Survey *(copyright © 1923 by Harper & Row, Publishers, Inc.; reprinted by permission of Harper & Row, Publishers, Inc.), Harper, 1923, pp. 357-76.*

Like Maupassant and Chekhov, [O. Henry] set out to capture the readers, not of books, but of newspapers. He was,

indeed, a newspaper man. And while he never told his story in the first paragraph but invariably began with patter and palaver, like a conjurer at a fair, it was the art of the anecdote that hooked his public. He planned, first of all, to make his theme straight and clear, as a preacher does who gives the text. Then he established his people with bold, brilliant strokes, like a great cartoonist. But the barb was always a surprise, adroitly prepared, craftily planted, and to catch him at it is an exercise for a detective.

This method is now old-fashioned. . . . When O. Henry overworked his method, . . . he could lack taste and inspiration. [When he had no feeling for the people in a story], he depended on his formula. But when he built back from a surprise that had gallantry and pathos in it—and he could have done it by musing on the fact that a Sarah Bernhardt went on tour after she had a wooden leg—then the formula was a help because of his peculiar endowment.

That endowment he had derived from an imagination grimly educated. O. Henry was at the other pole from the restless analyst Henry James. Only when he held forth, half waggish, half sentimental, did he write atrociously. He could call an unknown destination "the undesignated bourne," and he could call feet "walking arrangements." His was the era in which storytellers were often mock heroic, out of a jaunty, facetious self-consciousness. It was the other side of his glamour, his extraordinary power to go ahead at any risk into the most dangerous and most precious experiments. (pp. 264-65)

It was the Southerner in him who saw the charm of New York working girls, and saw the awful boardinghouse carpet that "grew in patches on the staircase." It was the Southerner who was so entirely at home outside that prudent vice, the instinct of self-preservation.

New York gave this wayfarer his chance. His life had been shattered into a kaleidoscope, and each bit seems to have been, not so much himself as one of the persons he had musingly, bitingly, lovingly, made part of himself. He was aware of multitudes, many in ironic plights and shabby circumstances. With the fashionable he was gauche. His tenderness, like Ernie Pyle's, dwelt on simpler people, the vulnerable who had a flame in them. He knew the worst, "the hideous veracity of life." He thought that "nearly everybody knows too much—oh, so much too much, of real life." But there was a mysterious elixir in "The Lost Blend." It was just water with a sparkle in it. O. Henry's blend had this simple magic in it: without it the eye cannot weep or even see. (pp. 265-66)

Francis Hackett, "O. Henry," in his On Judging Books: In General and in Particular *(copyright 1947 by Francis Hackett; 1975 by Signe Toksvig Hackett; reprinted by permission of Thomas Y. Crowell Company, Inc.), The John Day Company, 1947, pp. 264-66.*

In a sense, O. Henry was the creator of a new and acceptable American myth. He turned away from the prosperous levels of society, so popular at the time as a subject for fiction. He ignored the Four Hundred to deal with the four million. This choice was more the result of his previous misfortunes than of any interest in social reform, but its net effect was to produce an optimistic social myth. His stories mainly turned on the fortunes of humble folk . . .; a group that, on the whole, had been anonymous and inarticulate in

American life, and absent from American fiction.... In the rapid urbanization and industrialization of American life, their numbers were constantly increasing. They were the vast, hard-pressed, hard-working, lower middle class of the great cities, to whom the present was usually precarious and the future equivocal.

It was O. Henry's special gift to portray them as they saw themselves. They did not consider themselves proletarians, victims of an exploiting social order, tragic subjects for rescue or salvage. (pp. 112-13)

The workers of his stories were seldom defeated by their environment. They had confidence in their future, and he appeared to share it. He gave the old dogmas a new sanction in terms of the commonplace. His myth was the one which most Americans lived by, and wanted to believe. In an age of wealth for the few and poverty for the many, it asserted that all things were still possible to the common man, and that most of them would turn out to be good.

Thus, his stories pleased every type of reader. Social reformers counted him sympathetic to their aims. Apologists for an expanding capitalism found their complacency reinforced by his optimism; and, because he seemed to be a conservative, they were quite willing to praise him for being a democrat. The class about whom he wrote liked him for shedding on their existence a light of romance. (pp. 113-14)

O. Henry was neither a social reformer nor a social theorist. He was a middle-class American to whom respectability was precious. He thought he had forfeited it and accounted the loss a personal tragedy. The values which his stories celebrated were those from which he felt himself to be forever excluded. The decent respectability, the honorable ambition, the instinctive self-respect and sense of equality which he extolled as characteristic of common American life—these were the things about which he cared most. Sophisticated critics of a later generation, to whom his secret became known after his death, were inclined to consider him a sentimentalist, whistling in the dark to keep up his courage. Reformers of a radical cast, contemptuous of his social optimism, were to declare him a reactionary. But, nearly forty years after his death, the "common man" about whom he wrote, having survived two great wars and a decade of extreme economic misery, showed little indication of being persuaded that O. Henry's view of American life was false. (pp. 114-15)

> *Lloyd Morris, in his* Postscript to Yesterday: America: The Last Fifty Years *(copyright 1947 by Lloyd Morris; reprinted by permission of Random House, Inc.), Random House, 1947.*

[O. Henry was] the prose laureate of Manhattan Island. Today the "four million" of his "Bagdad on the Subway" have become nine million, the slang that highlights his dialogue has been superseded by other passing catch-phrases, and restaurants and hotels that served as his locale were razed a generation ago, but his tales of New York remain the standard by which all other literature on the subject is judged. Only a few months ago the editor of a great metropolitan newspaper wrote a book about Manhattan. The review he cherished the most, and carried in his wallet, was one that referred to him as a "latterday O. Henry." (pp. 6-7)

> *Bennett Cerf, in* Saturday Review *(copyright © 1948 by Saturday Review, Inc.; reprinted with permission), July 31, 1948.*

The imitators of the O. Henry "twist" flourished in the popular magazines for a long time and, although the demand for this kind of ending has considerably abated, one can still see the vestigial remains of it in the "short-shorts" featured by an occasional magazine. Aristotle called this particular virtue—or defect—of the tale, *Peripeteia*, and his translators coined from it the phrase "reversal of the situation."...

[Since] the quality of irony seems to have always permeated the short story, reversal of the situation will probably remain as a time-honored device with which to achieve it....

O. Henry preferred to think of his endings as the inevitable ironic working out of his stories.... He did not regard the method as a trick, but his imitators saw it so, and many writers after him mastered the trick and gained easy popular success, to the sad detriment of other qualities in their work. (p. 26)

> *Hollis Alpert, "Master of Narrative," in* Saturday Review *(copyright © 1949 by Saturday Review, Inc.; reprinted with permission), August 13, 1949, pp. 26-7.*

With his neatness and brightness, his rapid effects, mechanical often, sometimes crude, with his settings in all-night restaurants and furnished rooms, with his characters, shopgirls, policemen, clerks, chorus girls and men from "home," [O. Henry] seemed perfectly suited for readers of the "all-fiction" press. Describing himself as a "fictionist," addicted to the "writing game," as worried as a "retail butcher" about his bills, he worked like a night-copy writer, in shirt sleeves, at his desk, turning out stories on contract once a week. (p. 273)

New York was really O. Henry's own,—it seemed to belong to him by right,—although it was the field of so many story-tellers. This was because of his attitude towards it, the fresh curiosity with which he approached it, his feeling of wonder about it, on certain levels, all of which made for a literary virtue transcending his occasional cheapness and coarseness, his sometimes unbearable jocularity and meretricious effects. (p. 276)

O. Henry himself was one of those men who cannot pick up a bill of fare without seeing a story somewhere between the lines, a story that he has guessed or heard or composed from some casual clue while he listened perhaps to the man who was cleaning his hat. The settings were often boarding-houses, restaurants, hotels and sometimes the rush-hour in the streets when the department-stores were pouring out swarms of young creatures with the "shop-girl smile" that dazzled the recent arrivals from Iowa or Maine. Thousands of the shop-girls had come from far away themselves, and most of O. Henry's people were transients in the city, nomads in a roaming world and lodgers like himself,—it was natural that he saw New York as a quicksand shifting. (pp. 278-79)

O. Henry shared Dickens's vision of a happy domesticity, sharing as well his feeling for the city streets, for the crowds and the lights of the metropolis, the night-blooming cereus unfolding its dead-white heavy-odoured petals. With his brisk and often too obvious stories, too hard or too soft in the wrong way, O. Henry was occasionally an artist, nevertheless, who escaped from the mechanical formulas of the cheap magazines, the last to vindicate Howells's belief that the "more smiling aspects of life" were the most characteristic of America, as no doubt they had been. (p. 281)

> *Van Wyck Brooks, "New York: O. Henry,"* in his The Confident Years: 1885-1915 *(copyright, 1952, by Van Wyck Brooks; reprinted by permission of the publishers, E. P. Dutton), Dutton, 1952, pp. 271-82.*

O. Henry was a "popular" writer; the great majority of his stories were written in what he thought was the vernacular —in some kind of dialect, either of a rural region or of a district in a city. But unlike previous works in the tradition of colloquial writing, O. Henry's dialect turns out to be quite remote from speech; one is tempted to say that it is entirely artificial. What the reader witnesses in these stories is the corruption and attenuation of the relation between popular writing and the people it purports to describe. . . . Not only was he insensitive to speech rhythms, but he was quite unable to distinguish between the accents of the various regions of the country; his cowboys in the Panhandle talk in the same cadences and with a vocabulary indistinguishable from the cowboys on Broadway and the Bowery. O. Henry throws up a Chinese wall of verbiage between the reader and the object, and his writing is full of adjectives, "cute" solecisms, and badly mixed images. (pp. 72-3)

Scarcely any distinction can be made between the language of O. Henry's characters and the language of O. Henry himself. This is not the language of the folk-story, where either an identity of language exists between the teller and the subject, or where there is a ritualized separation of the formal language of the story from the vernacular; nor can it be mistaken for the technique of the sophisticated writer, who, utilizing the unique qualities of dialect, juxtaposes it to the traditional, complex, and discriminating language of literature. . . .

O. Henry was . . . a half-educated man, at ease neither with literature nor with semi-literateness; and one knows the direction in which he leads. He leads to Damon Runyon and the language of the modern "tough" detective story, to a contorted and abstract sense of the language, a nearly total absence of any sense of its genuine idiom and of the relation of speech to character and intelligence. O. Henry's language is awkward, silly, and inane, but it is not often ugly. In Runyon and his disciples, in the detective story, in Raymond Chandler and James M. Cain, the language has become horrid, a caricature of itself, too easy to imitate, incapable of color, flexibility, or precision. O. Henry is the midpoint of this decadence.

It is to O. Henry's credit, however, that, unlike later hacks, he is not pretentious about his writing. Because of this his tales retain some of the purity of the folk anecdote, the joke, or the simple reminiscence from which they arise; occasionally they display a bareness and directness of effect that is O. Henry at his best. The stories are about what folk stories usually are about—separated parents and children, separated lovers, lack of money, the gay highwayman, the encounter between city and country. The famous "trick ending" is employed in about 75 per cent of the stories. . . . The trick ending is used much more frequently in

the stories about New York than it is in those about the West. O. Henry believed in the therapeutic virtue of the West (one of his favorite tales concerns a city bum reformed by the strength, humanity, and clean living of the open range), which in itself worked the wonders that in the city only coincidence could accomplish.

In the stories about the city the coincidence surely was intended to offset the poverty, hunger, and loneliness that beset his lower-class New Yorkers. (p. 73)

Although O. Henry's ridiculous and inadequate changes of fortune are intended to divert the reader from the likely consequences of the stories, they actually reinforce the picture of the drab lives of his characters. The endings are a kind of half-hearted assurance that all is well, that Providence still watches—an assurance whose palpable improbability only suggests the reverse.

In an uninspired way, the trick ending is the counterpart of those ironic mechanisms for explaining American reality which Mark Twain and Henry Adams developed late in their careers. . . .

Adams and Twain responded to their perception of changing American realities with a sterile and mechanical pessimism that turned the New World into a dull and drab and hopeless thing. Here we find these two men at their weakest. O. Henry, who had neither their courage nor their intelligence, responded to these same realities with a simple obtuseness, and a precarious good humor that took the place of thinking. (p. 74)

> *Steven Marcus, "The Legacy of O. Henry: His Contribution to Popular Culture" (reprinted from* Commentary *by permission; copyright © 1954 by the American Jewish Committee), in* Commentary, *January, 1954, pp. 72-4.*

By the end of the nineteenth century the carefully made, ingeniously plotted story had become a well-established tradition, but it was during the first decade of the twentieth century that the type was carried to its ultimate lengths in the stories of O. Henry. None of his predecessors exploited the contrived story with quite such deliberate calculation or with more facility, and none achieved anything like the phenomenal popularity of O. Henry, who produced his stories for mass-circulation magazines and newspapers with the intent, as he put it, of pleasing "Mr. Everybody." (p. 121)

His manner is usually that of the garrulous taleteller, and his style is almost invariably breezy, flippant, and slangy, with puns, malapropisms, and big words being used for humorous effect. His stories are liberally sprinkled with asides in which he addresses the reader in a familiar and chatty tone. Literary allusions, often made facetiously, are common, and there are many references to other writers. (p. 122)

Although he usually used stock story formulas, O. Henry had an undoubted gift for devising ingenious variations on them. Coincidence figures largely in his stories, and they often have a surprise twist, or "snapper," as O. Henry called it. Unabashed sentiment and the broadest kind of comedy and burlesque are other conspicuous ingredients. In addition, O. Henry usually made his contrived stories illustrate some more or less serious theme. Most of his many stories of New York City . . . make the point that the humble, insignificant little people of New York are just as admirable and their lives as worthy of attention and interest as the members of the Four Hundred. (p. 123)

> *Arthur Voss, in his* The American Short Story: A Critical Survey *(copyright 1973 by the University of Oklahoma Press), University of Oklahoma Press, 1973 (and reprinted by the University of Oklahoma Press, 1975).*

[O Henry's stories are] about ordinary Americans in the late nineteenth and early twentieth centuries, human, funny, neatly related, always sure where they were going, accessible to a wide range of readers, and yet not at all ordinary in themselves, or in the language they at times employ, which is generally far more literate, far more conscious of what words can be made to do, far more *literary,* too, than their 'ordinary people' subject-matter, their lack of pretension, might at first suggest. . . . O. Henry is always making fun of himself, especially when he seems to be waxing literary, which seems natural to him but which may also have quite a bit to do with those two quarts of whisky a day.

It certainly has to do with his rejection of pretension in all its forms. 'Blinker,' he writes in [one] story, 'always remembered that he was a gentleman—a thing no gentleman should do.' (pp. 30-1)

A favourite story of mine *so far* . . . is 'Psyche and the Pskyscraper', which begins: If you are a philosopher you can do this thing: you can go to the top of a high building, look down upon your fellow men three hundred feet below, and despise them as insects.'

O Henry himself may have thought of his fellow human beings as insects, good for nothings or louts, but despise them he never does, philosopher though he is, from start to finish. . . .

Have the stories dated? Slightly, but very pleasantly. High buildings in New York are nowadays three times as high as three hundred feet. . . . In the world of O Henry, American society still has charm; and has not yet become vicious. But what dates these stories more than anything else is their splendid, clear, effective prose. William Sydney Porter was writing in an English not yet infected by the German dropsy. (p. 31)

> *James Brockway, "O Mr. Porter," in* Books and Bookmen *(© copyright James Brockway 1974; reprinted with permission), October, 1974, pp. 30-1.*

A(lfred) E(dward) Housman

1859-1936

English classical scholar and poet. Though not a native of Shropshire, Housman visited there as a youth and returned later in life to write his masterpiece, *A Shropshire Lad*. That particular piece of English countryside seemed to symbolize to Housman a pastoral mystery and enchantment, and the poem evokes these qualities. During his student days at Oxford, Housman excelled in classical scholarship, though his other studies fell short of his expectations (he did not receive a Pass degree in the Greats). It was also during these days that he formed his important relationship with Moses J. Jackson, which was to color the rest of his life and some of his somber poetry. Housman's homosexuality was in part responsible for his shy and retiring manner and his disappointment over his relationship with Jackson seems never to have healed. His contributions to classical journals while working in the Civil Service in London eventually earned him a professorship at London University, and later at Cambridge. Although more eminent as a classical scholar than as a poet, even his editions of Manilius, Juvenal, and Lucan show a facility with poetic diction. Confining himself to writing poetry only when inspired, which strangely enough was when he was most physically weakened, Housman's poetic output is meager. His themes are primarily ones of deprivation—loss of love, loss of fortune, loss of friendship, loss of life. Departing from the fashionable metaphysical poetry of his time, Housman in his famous Cambridge lecture, "The Name and Nature of Poetry," defined the function of poetry as the "transfusing of emotion, not the transmitting of thought." Because of his narrow range, Housman cannot be considered a major poet. He was, however, widely read in his time.

PRINCIPAL WORKS

A Shropshire Lad (poetry) 1896
Last Poems (poetry) 1922
The Name and Nature of Poetry (criticism) 1933
More Poems (poetry) 1936
Collected Poems (poetry) 1939

We should like to feel ourselves more excitedly in the midst of Mr Housman's work, but it will not go. A truth that we nearly hate whispers to us that there is no use pretending, that these lines [in *Last Poems*] lilt too doggedly and too sweetly to fall in quite with our more exigent, half-undiscovered harmonies, that many of the magic turns catch us cruelly absent-minded. And, most disappointing of all, for we are a little disappointed, and vexed at being so, we cannot seem to pool Mr Housman's pessimism with our own. (p. 190)

In the larger perspective his best work is seen to be a highly personal culmination point in a poetic tradition that is thoroughly alien to us of to-day, and nothing demonstrates this more forcibly than the apparent backwash in some of the *Last Poems*. There is no backwash in spirit or in style, there is simply the lessened intensity that allows general, underlying cultural traits to emerge. . . .

Such work as Mr Housman's, admirably simple and clear, classical, as it is, once more raises the doubt as to whether we can truly be said to be expressing ourselves until our moods become less frenetic, our ideas less palpable and self-conscious, and, above all, our forms less hesitant. Our eccentricities have much interest and diagnostic value to ourselves, but should it not be possible to cabin their power in forms that are at once more gracious and less discussible? (p. 191)

> Edward Sapir, "Mr. Housman's Last Poems," in The Dial (copyright, 1923, by The Dial Publishing Company, Inc.; reprinted by permission of J. S. Watson, Jr. and Scofield Thayer), August, 1923 (and reprinted by Kraus Reprint Corporation, 1966), pp. 188-91.

If there were some who thought that any successor to the "Shropshire Lad" must be an anti-climax, they may change their minds. At first shock the reader who has cherished "A Shropshire Lad" may think, as he comes upon the familiar rhythms and thoughts, that the second book ["Last Poems"] is an overflow from the first, a weaker repetition. But it will not take him long to discover that it is, in fact, a continuation, and a continuation at the old level. He will discover "The West," then "The Epithalamium," and one by one these new poems will creep into his heart and become part of him, as did the old ones. In a day he will not know from which of the two books many of these poems came. (p. 153)

It may be that, when these poems are arranged in chronological order, those who study them will be able to trace some slight development in Mr. Housman's style; but they will record no change in his themes, none in his attitude towards the world. All that could be said of the poet of "A Shropshire Lad" can be said of the author of "Last Poems": nothing less and nothing more. He has an unquenchable desire and no hope. He is acutely sensitive both to the cruelty and the beauty of life, but even when most intensely aware of them he sees both under the shadow of obliterating death and against the background of a blind featureless eternity about which he has no theories and with which he feels not even the slightest and most occasional mystical contact. It is a consolation that the cruelty will pass, and a torture that all human love and all natural loveliness must go with the blossoms into nothingness; he must endure the one when he can and enjoy the other while he may. Endurance is difficult and calls for perpetual self-reminders, and enjoyment when keenest brings the strongest return of the knowledge that it is transient. He is never visited by any glimmering of comfort regarding the ultimate meaning and destiny of things; "somehow good" has no reflection in his vocabulary; on the whole, should he qualify his agnosticism in terms he would incline to the view that the universe is under an evil government, if any. All the old characteristic broodings recur in the new collection. His soldiers who go doomed to the fight are types of all mankind, battling briefly against an invulnerable fate; whether they are kicking against the pricks, or stoically resigned, their preoccupation is the same, and their end the same. He puts it now with an ironic humour, which half conceals pain, now simply and directly out of the bared heart. (pp. 154-55)

No English poet has been so ruthless with himself as an artist; that alone would make him unique. He is equally singular in manner and in attitude: a sort of blend of Baudelaire and Heine who is nevertheless as English as he could be. Posterity, which always amuses itself with this game, may "place" him. What is certain is that he is bound to be a considerable figure in our poetical history, and that his poems, unlike many great works, will continue to be widely read. It is a strange quality in him that his very pessimism attracts those who like pessimism nowhere else. He is honest and courageous; he incites in the end, to honesty and courage; he stimulates enjoyment even while he laments; and his music is so beautiful that whatever he says must delight. Young men and lovers will find all their secret thoughts in him, and finding them will be comforted; and to poets he will be a standard. Whatever his limitations may be, he has written scarcely a line which is not perfectly musical, scarcely a word which is not accurate and necessary. He has disciplined himself to such a point that there is at least one poem in his new volume which does not contain a single adjective; he is always lucid, always truthful, and when he uses an epithet he uses it to some purpose. This is a matter apart from philosophy. Even hymn-writers could study him to advantage. (pp. 158-59)

> *J. C. Squire, "Mr. A. E. Housman," in his* Essays on Poetry, *Hodder and Stoughton Limited, 1923, pp. 152-59.*

In form Housman attains a compression of thought and a classical perfection of finished expression which are extremely rare; his spirit is one of stoical acceptance of the facts of life. His favorite themes are the inconstancy of man and woman, the transience of human joys and sorrows, the inevitable and unending oblivion of death. Variations on these themes are composed with an almost invariable simplicity and directness of manner, but in tones ranging from ingenuous humor to ironical cynicism. (p. 303)

> *John W. Cunliffe, in his* Leaders of the Victorian Revolution *(copyright, 1934, by Prentice-Hall, Inc.; reprinted by permission of Prentice-Hall, Inc., Englewood Cliffs, New Jersey), Appleton-Century, 1934.*

It is the unanimous verdict of his admirers that Housman is essentially a classical poet. Master of the Latin language, he has introduced into English poetry the economy, the precision, the severity of that terse and lucid tongue. His verses are highly finished, deeply pagan; they stand outside the ordinary current of modern poetry, the inheritors, not of the romantic age, but of the poignancy and stateliness, the lapidary quality of the poems of Catullus, Horace, and Virgil, or of the flowers of the Greek Anthology. This impression is heightened by the smallness of Professor Housman's output and by the years he devoted to finishing and polishing it, and, not least, by the stern and cryptic hints in the prefaces, with their allusions to profound emotions rigidly controlled, to a creative impulse ruthlessly disciplined and checked. This theory seems to have hoodwinked all his admirers; their awe of Housman as a scholar has blinded them to his imperfections as a poet. . . . The truth is that many of Housman's poems are of a triteness of technique equalled only by the banality of the thought; others are slovenly, and a quantity are derivative—not from the classics, but from Heine, or from popular trends—imperialism, place-nostalgia, games, beer—common to the poetry of his time. *A Shropshire Lad* includes with some poems that are unworthy of Kipling others that are unworthy of Belloc, without the excuse of over-production through economic necessity which those writers might have urged. Horace produced, in the *Odes* and *Carmen Seculare,* a hundred and four poems; Housman, not I think without intention, confined his two volumes to the same number. Yet a moment's silent comparison should settle his position once and for all. (pp. 47-8)

There are two themes in Housman: man's mortality, which intensifies for him the beauty of Nature, and man's rebellion against his lot. On his treatment of these themes subsists his reputation for classicism. But his presentation of both is hopelessly romantic and sentimental, the sentiment of his poems, in fact, is that of Omar Khayyám, which perhaps accounts for their popularity; he takes over the pagan concept of death and oblivion as the natural end of life and even as a not inappropriate end of youth, and lards it with a purely Christian self-pity and a romantic indulgence in the pathetic fallacy. By the same treatment his hero becomes a picturesque outlaw, raising his pint-pot in defiance of the laws of God and man, running away to enlist with the tacit approval of his pawky Shropshire scoutmaster, and suitably lamented by him when he makes his final escape from society, on the gallows. In the last few poems it is his own mortality that he mourns, not that of his patrol, but here again his use of rhythm is peculiarly sentimental and artful. . . . It must be remembered, also, that classical poetry is essentially aristocratic; such writers as Gray or Horace address themselves to their own friends and would be incapable of using Maurice, Terence, and the other rustics as anything but the material for a few general images. (pp. 49-50)

There are about half a dozen important poems of Housman, of which I think only the astronomical one (*Last Poems, 36*) is a complete success. Two were given us at my school to turn into Latin verses.

> Into my heart an air that kills
> From yon far country blows

was one, which would suggest to a Roman only a miasma; one has to put it beside "There is a land of pure delight" to realize its imperfection in English, and the other was

> With rue my heart is laden
> For golden friends I had,
> For many a rose-lipt maiden
> And many a lightfoot lad.
>
> By brooks too broad for leaping
> The lightfoot boys are laid;
> The rose-lipt girls are sleeping
> In fields where roses fade.

This I have been told is the purest expression in English poetry of the spirit of the Greek Anthology—one of the few things that might actually have been written by a Greek. Yet the first line is Pre-Raphaelite; "golden friends" could not go straight into a classical language, "lightfoot lad" is arch and insipid. The antithesis in the last two lines is obscure. Once again it is a poem in which not a pagan is talking, but someone looking back at paganism from a Christian standpoint, just as the feelings of an animal are not the same as the feelings of an animal as imagined by a human being. The other important verses are in *Last Poems*. There is the bombastic epigram on the army of mercenaries, again with its adolescent anti-God gibe, and the poem which in texture seems most Horatian of all:

> The chestnut casts his flambeaux, and the flowers
>   Stream from the hawthorn on the wind away,
> The doors clap to, the pane is blind with showers.
>   Pass me the can, lad; there's an end of May.

The first verse, indeed, except for that plebeian "can," has an authentic Thaliarchus quality—but at once he is off again on his denunciations of the Master Potter—"Whatever brute and blackguard made the world." Even the famous last stanza,

> The troubles of our proud and angry dust
>   Are from eternity and shall not fail.
> Bear them we can, and if we can we must.
>   Shoulder the sky, my lad, and drink your ale

suffers from the two "pass the cans" that have preceded it, and from the insincerity of pretending that drinking ale is a stoical gesture identical with shouldering the sky instead of with escaping from it. The poem does, however, reveal Housman at his poetical best—as a first-rate rhetorician. The pity is that he should nearly always have sacrificed rhetoric in quest of simplicity. Unfortunately his criterion of poetry was, as he explained, a tremor in the solar plexus, an organ which is seldom the same in two people, which writes poetry at midnight and burns it at midday, which experiences the sudden chill, the hint of tears, as easily at a bad film as at a good verse. Rhetoric is safer.

The Waste Land appeared at the same time as *Last Poems*,

and the Phlebas episode may be compared, as something genuinely classical, with them. The fate which Housman's poems deserve, of course, is to be set to music by English composers and sung by English singers, and it has already overtaken them. He will live as long as the B.B.C. (pp. 50-1)

Cyril Connolly, "A. E. Housman: A Controversy" (originally published in Chelsea, *May-June, 1936), in his* The Condemned Playground: Essays: 1927-1944 *(reprinted by permission of Deborah Rogers Limited, London; copyright © 1946, 1974 by Cyril Connolly), Macmillan, 1946, pp. 47-62.*

Like Hardy, Housman is unhappy, pessimistic, and the reason, though perhaps neither knew it, is that each saw the Victorian base crumbling or as having crumbled. Housman projects his pessimistic emotion into the melodramatic figure of the Shropshire lad, who passes from inexperience to sorrow, from illusion to bitter disillusion, from content to regret. . . . There is nothing to do but bear it out stoically and wait for death—which, if it comes by hanging, or shooting in battle, is all the more grimly appropriate.

Housman's plea for the functionlessness of art and of scholarship (for that is what his lecture on poetry and many of his scholarly papers amount to) is the cry of a man for whom civilization has lost its value-patterns. The echoing plangency of *A Shropshire Lad* and *Last Poems* comes from the heart of a man who can find nothing in the life and thought of his time that can, on a long view, give life a meaning. . . . Housman denied himself so much—turning from Propertius, the Latin poet whose work he loved, to devote his life's energies to editing instead the trivial Manilius, repressing his enthusiasms, shrinking from the light—because he could find no valid reason why what he liked was worth doing, because he could find no real basis on which to ground his life and work; and, being sensitive, afraid to do what he could not justify, he took the stoic view and saw himself living to endure rather than to enjoy. . . . The only real belief he held was that in his own integrity: his basic emotion was pride. All other values had dissolved save this, the last. It is no coincidence that James Joyce, as much unlike Housman in his life and work as one artist could be unlike another, also threw overboard all values except the pride and integrity of the artist. Both writers were idealists without ideals, which meant that their only ideal was integrity. And in both cases it was the receding tide of traditional values that left them in that plight. (pp. 19-21)

David Daiches, in his Poetry and the Modern World: A Study of Poetry in England Between 1900 and 1939 *(© 1940 by The University of Chicago), University of Chicago Press, 1940.*

It is tempting to regard A. E. Housman's poetry as classical—in its lucidity, its symmetry, its formal patterning, its laconic bite and edged intensity. Our disposition to do so is encouraged by the fact that Housman was a professor of Latin at Cambridge University and an eminent scholar of the classics. But, as has been frequently observed, Housman is actually the most romantic of poets, and he himself pointed to thoroughly "romantic" sources for his own poetry in naming "Shakespeare's songs, the

Scottish border ballads, and Heine''. The essentially romantic nature of his conception of poetry was confirmed in Housman's famous lecture, *The Name and Nature of Poetry*. To a Cambridge that had largely shifted its allegiance and worshipped new gods, Housman proclaimed the old gospel: his summary of the history of English poetry still saw the Romantic revolt as the one far-off divine event to which, from its first beginnings, the whole creation of English poetry had moved. (p. 291)

Two of Housman's constant themes are courage and stoic endurance, and these are themes which are almost obsessive for several of our best contemporary writers. To name only two, there are William Faulkner and Ernest Hemingway. The gap between Housman's Shropshire lads and Hemingway's bullfighters or boxers or big-game hunters may seem shockingly wide, but it is actually less wide than we think. The gap narrows when we place beside Housman's doomed young soldiers the typical Hemingway hero as man-at-arms during the First World War. The idioms used, I grant you, are sharply dissimilar. Hemingway's brilliantly realistic, acrid Midwestern American speech is a whole world away from the faintly archaic, wholly British idiom which is the staple of Housman's lyrics. (pp. 291-92)

The Hemingway hero, like Housman's, faces the insoluble "troubles of our proud and angry dust", and in his own way subscribes to the sentiment that

> Bear them we can, and if we can we must.
> Shoulder the sky, my lad, and drink your ale.

Of course, it must be added that the drink of the Hemingway hero is more likely to be *grappa* or brandy or seven-to-one martinis. (p. 294)

I do not mean to press unduly the Hemingway-Housman analogy. I shall be principally concerned with those qualities that make the finest of Housman's poetry perdurable. But I think that the comparison with Hemingway's can be extremely useful in opening up to a contemporary audience the problems which Housman faced and the characteristic failures and characteristic successes which he achieves. In both authors, so dissimilar in so many ways, there is a fairly narrow ambit of interests. The same theme and the same kind of character occur over and over. There is the danger of monotony, the danger of repetition. It seems sometimes to a reader that Housman has only one poem to write, which he writes and rewrites tirelessly, though oftentimes with very brilliant and beautiful variations. With the general narrowness of the ambit there is, as we have seen, the possibility of sentimentality. In general there is a serious problem of tone. The poem must not seem arch or cute. It must achieve its intensity while making use of understatement or laconicism. The close-lipped courage and the stoic endurance must elicit an intense sympathetic response and yet the hero, from the very terms of the situation, is forbidden to cry out or make any direct appeal for our sympathy.

This is the general problem that besets the presentation of the Hemingway hero: he is the tough guy who because of his very toughmindedness sees into the nature of reality and indeed is more sensitive to the tears of things than are those soft and blurred sensibilities whose very fuzziness of response insulates them against the tragic aspects of reality. Yet Housman is a poet who elects to work within a tiny lyric form, barred from the factuality and massively de-

tailed sense of the world which a writer of fiction like Hemingway rightfully has at his disposal. (p. 295)

Sentimentality is a failure of tone. The emotion becomes mawkish and self-regarding. We feel that the poet himself has been taken in by his own sentiment, responds excessively, and expects us to respond with him in excess of what the situation calls for. And so the writer who, like Housman, insists so uniformly upon the pathos of loss, upon the imminence of death, and upon the grim and loveless blackness to come, must be adept at handling the matter of tone.

Housman's great successes (as well as his disastrous failures) are to be accounted for in terms of tone. It does not matter that Housman never himself employs the term. *We* need it, nevertheless, in order to deal with Housman's poetry: for control of tone is the difference between the shrill and falsetto and the quiet but resonant utterance; it is the difference between the merely arch and self-consciously cute and the full-timbered irony; it is the difference between the sentimental and the responsibly mature utterance. Housman's characteristic fault is a slipping off into sentimentality. (One may observe in passing that this is also Hemingway's characteristic fault.) Conversely, Housman's triumphs nearly always involve a brilliant handling of tone —often a startling shift in tone—in which the matter of the poem is suddenly seen in a new perspective. (pp. 298-99)

I called Housman a romantic poet, a late romantic. If I have emphasized Housman the ironist, it is because I think his irony is important and that its presence does not make him the less a romanticist. But a more obvious aspect of his romanticism may be his treatment of nature.

Many of the poems—and not only those of *A Shropshire Lad*—are given a pastoral setting. The English countryside is everywhere in Housman's poetry. (p. 307)

Housman's view of nature looks forward to our time rather than back to that of Wordsworth. If nature is lovely and offers man delight, she does not offer him solace or sustain him as Wordsworth was solaced and sustained. For between Wordsworth and Housman there interpose themselves Darwin and Huxley and Tyndall—the whole achievement of Victorian science. The effect of this impact of science is not, of course, to make Housman love nature less: one could argue that it has rendered nature for him more poignantly beautiful. But his attitude toward nature is not that of the early Romantics and we must take into account this altered attitude if we are to understand his poems. (p. 308)

Housman expressed his characteristic attitude toward nature in the beautiful poem numbered XL in *Last Poems* his farewell to nature. The matter of the poem is the speaker's resignation of his mistress Nature to another. The resignation is forced; he does not willingly relinquish her. He has possessed her too completely to feel that she is less than a part of himself and his appetite for her is not cloyed. At this moment of conscious relinquishment, nature has never been more compellingly the enchantress. (p. 310)

Nature, for all her attractiveness to man, is supremely indifferent to him. This is the bedrock fact upon which the poem comes to rest, but if the fact constitutes a primal irony, it is accepted in this poem without rancor or any fierce bitterness. The very charm of nature is the way in which she can give herself freely to all of us who will strenuously try to claim her. And moreover, if nature, in this last stanza, is heartless and witless, she is still as freshly beautiful as the morning. Notice how concretely Housman says this in the closing lines. Nature spreads her dewy meadow as virginly fresh for the imprint of the feet of the trespasser as for those of the old lover who would like to believe that he alone possessed her. (p. 312)

[The] nature that Housman depicts seems to answer at every point the sensitive and melancholy mind that perceives it, and in its turn implies in its aloof and beautifully closed order the loneliness and austerity of the mind of its observer. . . .

The poem matches the immortality of nature with its own kind of immortality—the immortality of art. For, if nature, changeless through all the vicissitudes of change, is unweariedly the same, so also the experience that Housman has dramatized for us here may be endlessly repeated and is eternally recapturable. *Ars longa, vita brevis.* (p. 313)

> *Cleanth Brooks, "A. E. Housman" (1959), in his* A Shaping Joy: Studies in the Writer's Craft *(© 1971 by Cleanth Brooks; reprinted by permission of Harcourt Brace Jovanovich, Inc.), Harcourt, 1971, pp. 291-313.*

What is surprising . . . is not that Housman should have his devoted admirers but that he should have been taken seriously by so many to whom modern poetry seemed a cause. For in the history of twentieth-century poetry Housman quite unmistakably represents the cause of reaction. . . . It is sometimes hard to remember how very close the lifespans of Yeats and Housman were, for if Yeats outgrew the period into which he was born, Housman never did. (p. 46)

The surface glitters, no doubt of that; and it is Housman's special and rather odd diction which constitutes a major part of the attraction. . . . Even in *To an Athlete Dying Young,* where Housman's language is working as well as it ever did, and to as large an end, the diction seems everywhere the product of the will, of a fastidious choosing which can reproduce the effects of great poetry without becoming great itself. What it lacks is that sense of unspoken depth, suddenly discovered, which can come through a variety of means, but on occasion comes apparently through the diction itself. . . . (p. 47)

> *Donald Justice, "A Housman Centennial," in* Poetry *(© 1960 by The Modern Poetry Association; reprinted by permission of the Editor of* Poetry*), April, 1960, pp. 44-7.*

[Housman's poems] are nearly all about youth and love and youthful sorrow; some about soldiering; some about crime and death and suicide—all treated in a manner which breathes youthfulness, which is filled with images of youth (spring flowers, folk music and country dancing, sport and hill-climbing) and empathy with nature; they are not about men and women, but about lads and girls; and their very rhythms are the rhythms of the ballad and the folk song, unsophisticated and uncomplex. They are charming. But is it not a paradox that the man who wrote them was, to the world, a cold, bitter, touchy, taciturn professor, who seemed to have been born elderly, whose best friends were afraid of him, whose brother was accustomed to receiving

woundingly cruel letters from him, and who kept a personal notebook full of savage epigrams (with the names of the victims left blank) to be introduced into reviews or conversations whenever he found a suitable opportunity for giving pain? (p. 115)

We can understand one poem by itself; then a second; and then a third. But when we try to understand them as a whole, we fail. Yet Housman published them in carefully arranged groups. The poems were intended to be understood, but they cannot be. They are both explicit and obscure. They are frank, but limited, utterances. They represent both the betrayal and the concealment of a secret. This ambivalence becomes still clearer when we read some of the poems which Housman's brother discovered and published after his death: for these are much more candid than the earlier poems, as though he had grown tired of keeping his secret. (pp. 116-17)

One further paradox appears in his poetry. The lyrics in these three volumes are usually melancholy, and sometimes painfully sad. Personally Housman appeared to be a glum and disagreeable man, who seldom smiled. But he also wrote very funny poems, parodies, and squibs. His 'Fragment of a Greek Tragedy' is one of the most brilliant and penetrating poetic parodies ever written. (p. 118)

It might appear that his debacle in Oxford was the disaster which created most of his poetry—the wish for death, the hatred of the world, the incurable loneliness, all these are the accompaniment of failure.

But no. It was not that kind of failure. As one reads his poems one sees that the failure had something to do, not with ambition, but with love. Again and again he speaks of lost love, love misunderstood, love ending in bitter separation, love ending in death or the wish for death. And so one wonders whether he had been in love with some girl who mistreated him: especially when one hears that he usually spoke of women with hatred, and detested meeting them. But then one rereads his three volumes of poetry. The love in them is sometimes, but not always, love for a girl. It is more often love for a friend, who did not understand or who would not listen, and who went far away—enlisting in the army, or dying abruptly, or vanishing in the illimitable distance. (p. 119)

And when we look more closely into Housman's biography, we see that he had one special friend, from whom he later parted, and of whom he could never speak without emotion. This was a young scientist called Moses Jackson. . . . Housman never forgot [him]. His greatest work, the edition of Manilius, was dedicated 'To M. J. Jackson, who despises these studies,' with an exquisite elegiac poem in Latin by Housman; and among his papers after his death, his brother found Jackson's last letter, written to him when he was about sixty, with every faintly penciled word gone over in ink, to make it last a little longer.

Somewhere in those early years lies the secret which Housman wished both to reveal and to conceal. All that was left to him . . . was a cold heart, filled with bitterness increasing year by year. . . . (p. 120)

Housman once said that poetry was intended to harmonize our sufferings. Without his poetry . . . his sufferings . . . would be more difficult to understand, and far less easy to endure, or to forgive. (p. 121)

Gilbert Highet, "Professor Paradox," in his The Powers of Poetry *(copyright © 1954, 1960, by Gilbert Highet; reprinted by permission of Oxford University Press, Inc.), Oxford University Press, 1960, pp. 114-21.*

Out of his memories of the West Country, [Housman] constructed a curious dreamworld (well described by R. M. Hewitt as an "inverted Arcadia") in which Shropshire Lads drink beer, play football, commit murders, enlist in red-coated Victorian Regiments, and either die in outposts of the empire or are hanged in Ludlow Gaol. This pseudo-pastoral fantasy seems partly to conceal and partly to symbolize a profound emotional disturbance in the poet's life of which nothing is known. As C. M. Bowra has written, it is "unable to carry the weight of the fearful events which are assumed to take place". Housman certainly made the Voyage Within but he was too prim and fastidious to give more than some cryptic hints of what he found there. His Voyage Without was rather in the nature of a scholar's daydream of rustic virility and violence than a genuine exploration. Nevertheless, in a few poems he gave powerful expression to the division in the modern consciousness caused by the contrast between the development of the moral sense . . . and the dehumanized world-picture provided by the discoveries of the scientists. (p. 56)

Vivian De Sola Pinto, in her Crisis in English Poetry: 1880-1940 *(© V. de S. Pinto 1958 and 1961), revised edition, Hutchinson University Library, 1961.*

To Housman himself, his scholarship came first, his poetry second: he believed he had been put on earth not to write "A Shropshire Lad" (I never knew before [reading "The Letters of A. E. Housman," edited by Henry Maas] that this title was proposed by A. W. Pollard; Housman's own title had been "Poems by Terence Hearsay") but to produce a definitive edition of Manilius. His choice of this particular Latin poet may have been influenced by his own interest in astronomy, which is Manilius's subject, but the decisive factor was probably that the text presented an exceptional challenge to an editor. He was certainly under no illusions as to Manilius's literary merits. (p. 326)

Incidentally, I had occasion not so long ago to compare three translations of the last stanza of the Horace Ode,

Book IV, 7—one by Dr. Johnson, one by James Michie, and one by Housman. To my surprise, the one which departed most widely from the Latin was Housman's. Indeed, had I not known the source, I would have thought that it was a verse from a Housman poem. (pp. 326-27)

"Vanity, not avarice," Housman once wrote, "is my ruling passion," but I don't think he ever realized just how vain he was. A man who refuses honors like honorary degrees from universities or the O.M. from the State declines them not because he feels unworthy but because he feels that no honor can possibly do justice to his merits, and a poet who refuses to be included in anthologies of contemporary verse reveals that he considers himself superior to all of his colleagues. But vanity did not distort Housman's judgment. He was always aware of what he could and could not do. . . .

He was also a good judge of his own work. Most of the posthumously published poems are inferior. (p. 328)

Naturally, one cannot read Housman's letters without thinking again about his status and achievement as a poet. A minor poet, certainly, which, of course, does not mean that his poems are inferior in artistic merit to those of a major poet, only that the range of theme and emotion is narrow, and that the poems show no development over the years. On the evidence of the text alone, it would be very difficult to say whether a poem appeared in "A Shropshire Lad," published when he was thirty-seven, or in "Last Poems," published when he was sixty-three. I don't know how it is with the young today, but to my generation no other English poet seemed so perfectly to express the sensibility of a male adolescent. If I do not now turn to him very often, I am eternally grateful to him for the joy he gave me in my youth. (pp. 331-32)

W. H. Auden, "A Worcestershire Lad" (originally published in The New Yorker, *February 19, 1972), in his* Forewords and Afterwords, *edited by Edward Mendelson (copyright © 1973 by W. H. Auden; reprinted by permission of Random House, Inc.) Random House, 1973, pp. 325-32.*

Sarah Orne Jewett

1849-1909

American novelist, poet, essayist, and short story writer. Sarah Orne Jewett, a native of Maine, was one of the first and most skilled members of the local color movement in literature. A country doctor's daughter, Jewett's experiences in accompanying her father on his calls had an important formative effect on the sensibility that later led her to write evocative stories of New England character and experience. In her fiction subject matter and technique were intimately wedded, for her prose is as spare and austere as the rugged section of coastal Maine that was her home. As friend and companion of Annie Fields, the Boston hostess, she made many literary acquaintances and admirers. These connections together with her travels to Europe and her wide reading broadened her horizons beyond the borders of Maine. *The Country of the Pointed Firs* is considered her best book. Her influences were Flaubert, Zola, Tolstoy, and Henry James; she in turn influenced Willa Cather, who was later to edit a collection of Jewett's stories.

PRINCIPAL WORKS

Deephaven (short stories) 1877
Old Friends and New (short stories) 1879
Country By-Ways (short stories) 1881
A Country Doctor (novel) 1884
The Mate of the Daylight, and Friends Ashore (short stories) 1884
A Marsh Island (novel) 1885
A White Heron, and Other Stories (short stories) 1886
The King of Folly Island, and Other People (short stories) 1888
Strangers and Wayfarers (short stories) 1890
A Native of Winby, and Other Tales (short stories) 1893
The Life of Nancy (stories) 1895
The Country of the Pointed Firs (sketches) 1896
The Queen's Twin (short stories) 1899
The Tory Lover (novel) 1901
Verses 1916

Miss Jewett's talent at its best is so quietly delicate, its spiritual aroma so subtle, that to come to it is like coming to one of the quiet sea beaches or woody hill-sides of Maine she so tenderly describes for us. . . . [In] some of Miss Jewett's early writings, as "Old Friends and New," "A Country Doctor," "A Marsh Island," we feel that a certain faint charm is struggling unavailingly with an artistic method too monotonous; and in some of her later stories she has also her uninspired hours, where her subjects of common daily life have their uninteresting reaches and stretches which defy the delicacy of her touch. Moreover, in her historical novel, "A Tory Lover," she has clearly stepped outside her own art, and her art has refused definitely to accompany her on this hasty excursion. It is therefore the less surprising that the English public should have failed to discover and acclaim the exquisite portion of her work—let me sum it up here as thirty little masterpieces in the short story, and one book, "The Country of the Pointed Firs,"—by which I believe her position is permanently assured in American literature. (pp. 190-91)

[Her] work exhales a spirituality which is inseparable from her unerring perception of her country-people's native outlook and instinctive attitude to life. It is by this exquisite spiritual gravity interpenetrating with the finest sense of humour, intensely, even maliciously discriminating, that Miss Jewett seems to speak for the feminine soul of the New England race. (p. 191)

A clearness of phrase almost French is allied indeed to her innate precision of language. Her gift for characterization is exceedingly subtle, but neither rich nor profound. Her people are sketched rather in their essential outlines than in their exact lineaments. It is puzzling to say by what hidden artistic spell she manages so craftily to indicate human character . . . , but after a few subtle hints are dropped here and there, her people are felt to be living an intensely individual life, one all their own, beyond their creator's control or volition. This gift of indicating character by a few short simple strokes is the gift of the masters. Perhaps we shall touch near to the secret of Miss Jewett's power and the secret of her limitations if we say that her art is exceedingly feminine in the sense that she has that characteristically feminine patience with human nature which is intimately enrooted in a mother's feeling. . . . Miss Jewett's artistic attitude shows a completely sympathetic patience with the human nature she has watched and carefully scrutinized. Her gift is therefore the gift of drawing direct from nature, with an exquisite fidelity to what appeals to her feminine imagination—such as the infinite variety of women's perceptions in their personal relations; but the feminine insight only moves along the plane of her sympathetic appreciation, and she can invent nothing outside it, neither has she a depth of creative feeling apart from her actual observation of human life. She is receptive but not constructive in her talent. It is for this reason that her historical novel, "A Tory Lover," is almost a complete failure. All the men in the book are masculine ciphers, and its real hero, Paul Jones, never begins to live. On the other hand, when she is content to interpret for us the characteristic attitude to life of grimly hard-working New England spinsters, such as Miss Peck, in "Miss Peck's Promotion," or broad matronly natures such as the village wife, the herb-gatherer, in "The Country of the Pointed Firs," we get a delicious revelation of how men by nature play the second fiddle in women's eyes. Man as a boy, a lover, a husband, brother, father or friend, with his somewhat obtrusive personality as an honest, well-meaning, forceful creature, is shown us as filling up woman's mental background in Miss Jewett's stories; but woman herself it is that decides, arranges and criticizes her own life, and the life of her friends, enemies and relations, and of the whole parish—and the reader has a sense in her pages that should the curtain be dropped on the feminine understanding, the most interesting side of life would become a mere darkened chaos to the isolated, masculine understanding.

I have spoken of Miss Jewett's art as coming second only to Hawthorne's in its spiritual interpretation of the New England character. In originality of vision, and in intense and passionate creative force she is, of course, not to be compared with him. The range of her insight is undeniably restricted. Nevertheless, it makes the cosmopolitan appeal, that all art of high quality makes, and her work at its best, no less than Hawthorne's conveys to us a mysterious sense of her country people's mental and moral life, seen as a whole in relation to their environment and to their past, and reveals it as the natural growth of the very definite history of the many Puritan generations that have gone before them. (pp. 192-95)

To discover intimately the subtle laws by which individual character works, to catch the shifting shades of tone by which a man reveals to the onlooker how life is affecting him, is not a common gift; but to reproduce by written words a perfect illusion, a perfect mirage of life, with each character seen in its proper perspective in a just relation to the exterior world around it, with everybody breathing his natural atmosphere and a general sense of life's inevitable flux and flow diffused through the whole—this is such an artistic feat that we need not wonder that Miss Jewett has succeeded only when she is writing as a close and humble student of nature. . . . So delicate is the artistic lesson of this little masterpiece ["The Country of the Pointed Firs"] that it will probably be left for generations of readers less hurried than ours to assimilate. (pp. 197-98)

> *Edward Garnett, "Sarah Orne Jewett's Tales" (1903), in his* Friday Nights: Literary Criticisms and Appreciations *(copyright 1922, 1950 by David Garnett; reprinted by permission of Alfred A. Knopf, Inc.), Knopf, 1922, pp. 189-98.*

[From] description-at-a-distance, mental, moral, or physical, Miss Jewett was beautifully free. She was of New England ancestry, birth, and training. Her home was in a New England village and she always kept it there. The "at-

mosphere" of her books was the atmosphere she breathed. Her "types" were not so much the result of study and abstraction from observed subjects as the transcription of direct appeals which the life of her neighbors made to her own heart. Born thus through contact of life with life, they not only embody various human qualities, but they really possess souls. The reader can rarely speak of them as "quaint" or "bleak" or anything else that merely accords with literary convention. They are too personal to submit themselves to easy definition; so human, indeed, as generally to be humane. (pp. 160-61)

Miss Jewett is sometimes charged with taking too sentimental a view of New England life and character. In her recently published letters there appears a tendency to overwork the adjective "dear," and it is said that love for the land of her birth reacting upon a thoroughly feminine nature, left her with a keener vision for the pathetic than for the really tragic elements in the world about her. It may be admitted that she loved best the peaceful pastures and quiet weather of humdrum and half-humorous prosperity; yet the fact remains that she could not only picture the rigor of January and the languor of August as relentlessly as Mr. Hardy, but she could quite as readily introduce Humanity hand in hand with Trouble—and poignant trouble too. (pp. 162-63)

Weather plays so large a part in New England life; there is so much of it to the square mile that a genuine love of weather for its own sake is needful to any sympathetic acquaintance with the face of the country. This Miss Jewett felt in high degree. Then too, this weather, largely interpreted, has played no inconsiderable part in the development of New England character. It has represented an ever present condition—generally a hard condition—which must needs be patiently endured or ingeniously turned to account. This also she has realized and made much of; indeed she has gone so far as to develop an almost mystic sense for the symbolic nature of the seasons. Her characters may come upon the scene, hand in hand with trouble, like Mr. Hardy's, or humorously rejoicing in modest success. But whether pinched by the cold of winter and poverty like the two gently bred sisters in "The Town Poor," or lying dead in the lonely April night like Miss Tempy, these creatures of her brain seem to rule their fate and to retain the mastery of their souls. So in general the occasional tragedy and the frequent comedy of these New England tales are normal and wholesome, because, whatever the philosophers may say, men live and act in them as though their wills were free. (p. 166)

In her later books, notably "The Country of the Pointed Firs," she pictures the Maine coast, the Maine summer, and the people of the islands and harbor towns. . . .

It is in this book too that she brings us into closest intimacy with two people who exactly correspond to such a setting—Mrs. Blackett of the Island, and her middle-aged son, William. They are mother and brother to Mrs. Todd, who serves Miss Jewett in the Dunnett Landing stories as the chorus did the Greek dramatists, with her comment upon life's passing show and her ready philosophy. William and his mother are among the great figures of New England fiction in their delicacy and fidelity. They are unskilled in the ways of the world and their simplicity follows the pleasant path between the fields of humor and pathos with frequent though rarely forced excursions into both. It is, however, a simplicity that enhances rather than compromises their native dignity and purity of soul. Every true country minister or doctor in New England knows their type and counts the knowledge a chief reward of his profession. (p. 167)

Like Jane Austen, Sarah Orne Jewett was at her best when . . . painting her "two inches square of ivory." She exercised, too, an artist's privilege in choosing subjects that seemed to her worth painting. There is no realistic setting forth of rustic squalor, though degeneracy exists in New England hamlets as in most rural communities. (p. 172)

> *Edward M. Chapman, "The New England of Sarah Orne Jewett," in* The Yale Review *(© 1913 by Yale University; reprinted by permission of the editors), Fall, 1913, pp. 157-72.*

In reading over a package of letters from Sarah Orne Jewett, I find this observation: "*The thing that teases the mind over and over for years, and at last gets itself put down rightly on paper—whether little or great, it belongs to Literature.*" Miss Jewett was very conscious of the fact that when a writer makes anything that belongs to Literature (limiting the term here to imaginative literature, which she of course meant), his material goes through a process very different from that by which he makes merely a good story or a good novel. No one can exactly define this process; but certainly persistence, survival, recurrence in the writer's mind, are highly characteristic of it. The shapes and scenes that have "teased" the mind for years, when they do at last get themselves rightly put down, make a very much higher order of writing, and a much more costly, than the most vivid and vigorous transfer of immediate impressions.

In some of Miss Jewett's earlier books, "Deephaven," "Country Byways," "Old Friends and New," one can find first sketches, first impressions, which later crystallized into the almost flawless examples of literary art that make up these two volumes. One can, as it were, watch in process the two kinds of making: the first, which is full of perception and feeling but rather fluid and formless, the second, which is so tightly built and significant in design. The design is, indeed, so happy, so right, that it seems inevitable; the design is the story and the story is the design. The "Pointed Fir" sketches are living things caught in the open, with light and freedom and air-spaces about them. They melt into the land and the life of the land until they are not stories at all, but life itself. (pp. ix-x)

I have tried to gather into these two volumes ["The Best Stories of Sarah Orne Jewett"] the very best of Miss Jewett's beautiful work; the stories which, read by an eager student fifty years from now, will give him the characteristic flavor, the spirit, the cadence, of an American writer of the first order—and of a New England which will then be a thing of the past.

Even in the stories that fall a little short of being Miss Jewett's finest, there are many delightful characters and there is much beautiful writing. (p. xiii)

The stories chosen for these two volumes vary little in quality, though one may have one's favorites among them. Personally, I like "The Flight of Betsey Lane" better than "The Hiltons' Holiday," though the latter story was especially dear to Miss Jewett herself. I think I know why; that

story simply *is the look*—shy, kind, a little wistful—that shines out at one from good country faces on remote farms; it is the look *itself*—and therefore is a little miracle. To have got it down upon the printed page is like bringing the tenderest of early spring flowers from the deep wood into the hot light of summer noon without bruising its petals. (p. xiv)

There are many kinds of people in the State of Maine, and its neighboring States, who are not in Miss Jewett's books. There may be Othellos and Iagos and Don Juans, but they are not highly characteristic of the country, they do not come up spontaneously in the juniper pastures as the everlasting does. Miss Jewett wrote of the people who grew out of the soil and the life of the country near her heart, not about exceptional individuals at war with their environment. This was not a creed with her, but an instinctive preference. She once laughingly told me that her head was full of dear old houses and dear old women, and that when an old house and an old woman came together in her brain with a click, she knew that a story was under way.

Born within the scent of the sea but not within sight of it, in a beautiful old house full of strange and lovely things brought home from all over the globe by seafaring ancestors, she spent much of her girlhood driving about the country with her doctor father on his professional rounds among the farms. She early learned to love her country for what it was. What is quite as important, she saw it as it was. She happened to have the right nature, the right temperament, to see it so—and to understand by intuition the deeper meaning of all she saw.

She had not only the eye, she had the ear. From childhood she must have treasured up those pithy bits of local speech, of native idiom, which enrich and enliven her pages. The language her people speak to each other is a native tongue. No writer can invent it. (pp. xv-xvi)

Much of Miss Jewett's delightful humor comes from her delicate and tactful handling of this native language of the waterside and countryside, never overdone, never pushed a shade too far; from this, and from her own fine attitude toward her subject-matter. This attitude in itself, though unspoken, is everywhere felt, and constitutes one of the most potent elements of grace and charm in her stories. She had with her own stories and her own characters a very charming relation; spirited, gay, tactful, noble in its essence and a little arch in its expression. In this particular relationship many of our most gifted writers are unfortunate. (p. xvii)

If I were asked to name three American books which have the possibility of a long, long life, I would say at once, "The Scarlet Letter," "Huckleberry Finn," and "The Country of the Pointed Firs." I can think of no others that confront time and change so serenely. (p. xviii) [Willa Cather revised this sketch of Sarah Orne Jewett for publication in her "Not Under Forty" (1936, Alfred A. Knopf). While much of the text is the same, the last paragraph excerpted here was omitted in the revision.]

> *Willa Cather, in the preface to* The Best Stories of Sarah Orne Jewett *(copyright 1910, 1924 by Mary R. Jewett; 1927 by The Riverside Press; reprinted by permission of Houghton Mifflin Company), Riverside, 1927 (and reprinted by Peter Smith, 1949), pp. ix-xix.*

If you read [Sarah Jewett's] letters as we have read Aldrich's and Lowell's, you are bothered by the too frequent use of the adjectives 'little' and 'dear.' A faint odor of rose leaves emerges. You are reminded of her inability to portray passion in her books. She always paints the gentler emotions: blinding hates and jealousies, the fever of lust and the thirst of avarice never throb there. Even her few lovers are almost invariably wooden and silly. And yet [recall Willa Cather's high praise of "The Country of the Pointed Firs" (see excerpt above)]. . . .

Serene [as Willa Cather wrote] is the very adjective to use. It suggests the unhurried sureness of her pictures of Maine life, the radiant simplicity of her spirit which bathed her scenes and characters in its own delicate, but uncompromising light. She has withstood the onslaught of time, and is secure within her limits, because she achieved a style. . . . Without style Sarah Jewett's material would be too slight to attract a second glance. With it she has created—not a world, but a township in the State of Maine. (pp. 144-46)

Her words are sometimes crude and fumbling. It demanded the fullness of Miss Jewett's vision to keep her from lifeless photography on the one hand, and strained exaggeration on the other. (pp. 147-48)

There is a stark New England Sarah Jewett does not show, sordid, bleak, and mean of spirit. She looked at nature in its milder moods, and at mankind in its more subdued states of tenderness and resignation. But she did not live in an unreal paradise. She was aware of all these aspects, she simply did not emphasize them. . . .

Miss Jewett does not generally deal with the central facts of existence. You do not remember her characters as you do the atmosphere that seems to detach from their rusty corduroys and the folds of their gingham dresses. Her township was on the decline, and to her eyes it was a place where emotion was recollected in tranquillity. (p. 149)

'Ethan Frome' was written only fifteen years after 'The Country of the Pointed Firs,' but it reveals in every respect the mark of another generation. Mrs. Wharton's is a violent story depending for its effect on the tightness of its plot. It is breathless, sinister, its three characters are seared in the furnace of love and hate until all that is left are shells of human impotence. Yet if you read it directly after 'The Pointed Firs,' strong and intense as the newer book is, it seems like a *tour de force*. It is a brilliant novel, but Starkfield might be anywhere: it is penetrated with little of the distinctive flavor of New England. The vitality is more on the surface than it is in Miss Jewett's book.

The distinction and refinement of Sarah Jewett's prose came out of an America which, with its Tweed rings and grabbing Trusts, its blatantly moneyed New York and squalid frontier towns, seemed most lacking in just these qualities. They are essentially a feminine contribution, and the fact that they now appear more valuable than anything the men of her generation could produce is a symptom of what had happened to New England since the Civil War. The vigorous genius of the earlier golden day had left no sons. Emily Dickinson is the heir of Emerson's spirit, and Sarah Jewett the daughter of Hawthorne's style. In the whole group of proud Brahmins whom Miss Jewett knew, and revered as far wiser and stronger than herself, there is not one with her severity of form and subtle elimination. Their words are heavy and diffuse, lacking balance, lacking

concentration. And so they are sinking slowly, while hers go lightly forward, and she takes her place next [to] Emily Dickinson—the two principal women writers America has had.

It is easy to object to Miss Cather's list of lasting American books. 'Leaves of Grass' and 'Moby Dick' throb with a deeper potency than any of them. But 'The Country of the Pointed Firs' is impressive in its quietness, and it has gained the end suggested to its author by Flaubert—it has made us dream. (pp. 150-52)

> *Francis Otto Matthiessen, in his* Sarah Orne Jewett *(copyright © 1929 by Francis Otto Matthiessen; 1957 by Mrs. H. G. Neubrand; reprinted by permission of Houghton Mifflin Company), Houghton, 1929.*

If [Sarah Orne Jewett] had a problem, it was, at first, that of putting a certain distance between herself and her material, in order to acquire literary poise. But that problem . . . was easily solved. There were no financial barriers to keep her from knowing the world outside of South Berwick. Boston was open to her, and, with Annie Fields as companion, she could soon count Longfellow, Lowell, Aldrich, and Howells among her friends. There was travel also: England, with visits to Arnold and Tennyson, Paris, Italy, Greece, the West Indies. And there were books, not merely the classics of her own country and England, not merely her beloved Thackeray, the Brontë sisters, Donne and Herbert, but the French and Russians also, Tolstoy and Turgenev, Zola, Daudet, Maupassant, Bourget, and Flaubert. If she knew South Berwick, that was not all she knew, and if she was provincial, she was provincial by choice.

With this equipment—the close, sensitive knowledge of the people she wrote about, and the awareness of a larger world of culture and refinement—she went tranquilly about her work, carefully selecting whatever served her personal needs and her literary purposes. "Écrire la vie ordinaire comme on écrit l'histoire," she copied out of Flaubert and pinned on her secretary. That is what she tried to do. But to write about ordinary lives as if one were describing the great pageant of history one must see in ordinary lives something of the grandeur and significance of historical events. That gift, so far as a certain limited kind of ordinary life was concerned, Miss Jewett had. (pp. 102-03)

But one is always conscious of Miss Jewett's limitations. She was lost the moment she stepped outside her Maine villages, whether she wrote of Boston, or Irish immigrants, or the American Revolution. More important, she was safe, even in Maine, only within her chosen emotional range. The stronger feelings, the more violent passions, the more harrowing griefs, she could not portray. Her methods, however suitable for the portrayal of pathetic situations, failed when she was confronted with tragedy. (p. 103)

There is, in short, nothing that we can admire her for except those delicate powers of perception that, under favorable circumstances, she could exercise so fruitfully. In other respects she was merely a New England old maid, who had a private income, traveled abroad, read the *Atlantic Monthly*, and believed in piety, progress, and propriety. She may have read Turgenev and Flaubert, Voltaire and Donne, but she praised Thomas Bailey Aldrich for his "great gift and genius of verse," called Tennyson the greatest man she had ever met, and thought *Pendennis* superior to *Anna Karenina* because more Christian. (p. 104)

We may grant that she is only a minor writer, that the kind of pleasure her work offers only remotely resembles the effect of great literature, that the insight she gives us into men and women is only fragmentary. We may grant that her attitude is essentially elegiac, and that she writes of a dying world of old men and old women. We may even grant that her aims were virtually those of the other regionalists. But there is a difference. For a moment her people live and breathe. For a moment, as we yield to her art, we feel that here is a master, though a master of a tiny realm. (p. 105)

> *Granville Hicks, in his* The Great Tradition: An Interpretation of American Literature *since the Civil War (reprinted with permission of Macmillan Publishing Co., Inc.; © 1933, 1935 by Macmillan Publishing Co., Inc.; 1950 by Granville Hicks), revised edition, Macmillan, 1935.*

To the regional story Sarah Orne Jewett brought understanding, knowledge, humor, and a thoroughly disciplined talent. At the time she wrote, the former way of life in Maine was coming to an end. . . . She described this world realistically but leisurely, with sympathy and poetic mood. Although her stories are mainly sketches, and contain little of the romantic element, they are composed daintily, with restrained refinement, and give evidence of gracefulness in structure and composition. Her style is tender and essay-like and free from gargoylish characters and the dialectal excesses that marked much of the regional fiction at the time she began writing. (p. 286)

Sarah Orne Jewett accomplished what few local colorists ever did—she portrayed the universal in the local. (p. 287)

> The Heritage of American Literature, *Vol. 2, edited by Lyon N. Richardson, George H. Orians, and Herbert R. Brown (copyright, 1951, by Ginn and Company; 1962, by Lyon N. Richardson, George H. Orians, and Herbert R. Brown), Ginn and Company, 1951.*

"Little" was the adjective that even Miss Jewett's closest friends came to apply by masculine instinct to her work. When T. B. Aldrich was editor of the *Atlantic,* he wrote to tell her, "Whenever you give me one of your perfect little stories the whole number seems to bloom." Rudyard Kipling, feeling quite sincere, told her of his satisfaction with *The Country of the Pointed Firs* as a perfect little tale, and Miss Jewett was unendingly happy with the compliment. Howells, having been sent a copy of her newest book, *Strangers and Wayfarers,* spoke of writing about it in a forthcoming study and apparently forgot to implement the promise; but he did state that everybody felt a love for her work. "Your voice is like a thrush's in the din of all the literary noises that stun us so," he added, and it was in the direction of the noises, and not of the little bird's song, that his own work was turning. (p. 10)

[Edward Garnett, the English critic and essayist,] could not, like the New England friends, approve of her sketches merely because they were realistic pictures of Maine scenery, so he looked for and found in them a higher art than realism where the scene presented invokes "immense reaches of life around it." Taking her own phrase from *Deephaven* that nothing in particular happened, he found in the "nothing" of one of her tales, "The Hiltons' Holiday," an epitome of universal family life. Here, for the first time, Miss Jewett begins to become free as an artist. (p. 15)

What neither her intimates nor her scornful critics of the Marxian enlightenment cared to see was that Sarah Orne Jewett, lady of South Berwick, hostess on Charles Street, faithful worshipper at the shrines of Victorian literary greatness, was, at her best, an artist with a theory of her craft and a skill in it that were independent of a fashionable new realism or a familiar landscape. . . . [The] exquisite telling, the fading away, the bringing out of all the possibilities, waited on the arrival of an artist who had already lived with the little everyday things and knew that any one of them could be made the portent of a meaning as deep as the mystery of life itself. The sprigs of late-blooming linnaea that William Todd picked for his mother's guest and gave her without speaking, the sweetbrier roses that Martha, the maid, brought in from the garden when her lady came home —these any visitor to New England can see and recognize. To discover in such a wildflower an image of the bloom on the rocky ledges of New England character is the quality of distinction in Miss Jewett's art. (pp. 17-18)

The process of composition . . . is at the heart of the problem of what she set out to do and what she achieved. Over a period of time she noticed things and received suggestions of character, laying them aside quietly in her memory. The design for a story came quickly and it was rapidly put down in words—words for which she herself hardly seemed responsible. It was a mystery, this gift of literary creation, a wind blowing where it listed and she not knowing whence it came nor whither it went. (pp. 28-9)

Perhaps her favorite word to which she turns for music in many a paragraph is the word "remembrance," with its overtone of old and far-off things and people. In the story of the individual, the incident of the moment has value only as a revelation of the long, unbroken record of the past. The farm and the spume-beaten house by the shore have interest now because there appear on them the marks of yesterday, such as "the heavy piece of old wreck timber . . . full of treenails" that lay by the path to Elijah Tilley's house. Where people come together, as at the Bowden family reunion, Miss Jewett's memory reaches far back to groups of simple country folk celebrating the immemorial rites of festival and friendship. . . . (p. 37)

[Memory]—and this, it seems, counts for a great deal of what she meant by the heart of any of her stories—is never a dead process. Only the things that have a past are really alive, and old people who have lived much are more interesting than the excitable and passionate young. (p. 38)

[Little] things . . . , seen through the eyes of remembrance, become the clues to that distinctive quality of a personality or a place. They are among the familiar objects of experience which, as Van Wyck Brooks points out about Emily Dickinson, become portents and symbols to the creative artist. . . . With Miss Jewett the symbols never stretched as far or suggested as much as for her poetic contemporary in New England. She placed each of hers in a human rather than a divine setting. They were, except for their background of sea and land, pieces of human property—a house, a boat, a thick cotton-striped shirt, a sewing machine; and they interested her because they bore the mark of hands. Into her sketches, as into an old-fashioned whatnot, she placed a collection of Maine souvenirs, each with its story of a person and an enduring human loyalty.

How to make such trivial things interesting was, of course, her great problem, as it was Wordsworth's. (p. 39)

It is quite apparent that fiction which depends on experiences so inward and so prompted by memory rather than observation is a highly specific form of prose art. It sets up as the standard of excellence a rarefied, intimate, and subjective human event or an impression of character as elusive as friendship itself.... What can be defined and discussed of the deliberate structure of a novel—its architectonics, the variety and interlocking of its characters, its pictures of place and society, and above all, its subject matter of social comedy and high drama—these are mostly repudiated as being incidental to the heart of achievement.

As a criterion of fiction, then, any one of the principles of this creed may be used to illuminate a novelist's work, but it does so only in part and sometimes mistakenly. Every artist gives himself to his work, but what he gives is still a matter of debate and analysis for his commentators. (pp. 40-1)

A corner of Maine was the field of her imagination, and within that corner a small group of men and women left behind in the processes of social change. Young love, the favorite theme of the novelist, interested her only when seen in retrospect over the years, and when she brought young people in love into *A Country Doctor* and *The Tory Lover* something other than the love-making caught her fancy. Her thought was absorbed only by people who were young when she was a child. That the incidents of their lives were commonplace disturbed her no more than it did Wordsworth so long as she could identify herself with them and create a like identification for the readers of her stories.

Within the limits set by these principles both Miss Jewett and Miss Cather were happy to see the goals of their writing. They sacrificed the broad range of incident, comment, and character for the sake of an intense effect. So as to have tranquillity in which creation could occur undisturbed, they were willing to forego the clash of exciting events in their own lives and to record little of it in the lives of their characters. Only items of experience that passed the test of being remembered, of returning unforced to the mind, were worthy of being dealt with, for they only, and not a catalogue of things seen, could be worked into their kind of picture and their kind of mood. They shied away from the grand passions of love, war, and adventure, preferring the quiet, enduring loyalties of family and property inside a restricted area, the village or the tight-knit group of neighbors. By withdrawing toward the center of the human situation rather than becoming immersed in its many and constantly changing outward manifestations, they believed that the small and private thing they saw and felt and recorded would be conveyed unchanged in its poignancy to their readers. In such a process of birth and bearing, the children of their mind would be theirs, living images of creation. (pp. 42-3)

> A. M. Buchan, in his "Our Dear Sarah": An Essay on Sarah Orne Jewett (copyright 1953 by the Committee on Publications, Washington University), Washington University Studies, 1953.

Sarah Orne Jewett was a writer of deep pure feeling and a limited capacity for emotional expression: there is always, one senses, more behind the language than actually comes through it. In her best work she employed—it was an instinctive and inevitable choice—a tone of muted nostalgia. She knew that the Maine country she loved so well was slowly being pushed into a social impasse: it could not compete in the jungle warfare that was American life in the late nineteenth century. But even as this knowledge formed and limited her vision of things, she did not let it become the dominant content of her work, for she understood, or felt, that the obsolete also has its claim upon us. She was honest and tactful enough not to inflate her sense of passing and nostalgia with the urgencies of a heroism that could only have been willed; in her bare, linear stories about country people struggling to keep their farms alive, she made no false claims, for she saw that even when one or another figure in her Maine country might be heroic there was nothing distinctively heroic in the spectacle of a community in decline, a way of life gradually dying. But she knew—it was an enviable knowledge—that admiration and love can be extended to those who have neither the vocation nor the possibility for heroism. She paid a price, of course. In a country where literature has so often been given over to roaring and proclaiming and "promulging" it was nearly impossible for so exquisite an artist—exquisite precisely because she was, and knew she was, a minor figure—to be properly valued....

The people in *The Country of the Pointed Firs* are eccentrics, a little gnarled by the American weather and twisted by American loneliness; but it is not for a display of these deformities that Miss Jewett presents them. She is interested in reaching some human core beneath the crusted surface and like so many other American writers, like Anderson and Frost and Robinson, she knows the value and pathos of the buried life. That is why it is harmful, despite the fact that her stories are set in the same locale, to speak of her as a regional writer; for regional literature, by its very premise, implies a certain slackening of the human measure, a complacent readiness to accept the merely accidental and unusual. (p. 24)

Like other books dealing with a relatively simple society, *The Country of the Pointed Firs* gains organic structure from its relaxed loyalty to the rhythms of natural life. The world it memorializes is small and shrinking, and the dominant images of the book serve only to bound this world more stringently: images of the ranked firs and the water, which together suggest the enclosing force of everything beyond the social perimeter. But meanwhile a community survives, endowed with rare powers of implicit communication: to say in this world that someone has "real feelins" is to say everything.

Finally the book is a triumph of style, a precise and delicate style such as we seldom find in nineteenth century American prose. The breakdown of distinctions between prose and verse which occurs under the sponsorship of romanticism and for a variety of reasons is particularly extreme in America, where it produces two such ambiguous figures of genius as Melville and Whitman—this breakdown hardly affected Miss Jewett. Very probably this is one reason she remained a minor figure while Melville and Whitman were, occasionally, major ones. But at the moment there is much to be gained from a study of her finely modulated prose, which never strains for effects beyond its reach and always achieves a secure pattern of rhythm. (pp. 24-5)

The Country of the Pointed Firs is not a "great" book; it isn't *Moby Dick* or *Sister Carrie* or even *The Great Gatsby*. It cannot sustain profound exegesis or symbol hunting. In fact, all it needs is appreciation. But living as we do in a country where the grand too easily becomes synonymous with virtue and where minor works are underrated because major ones are overrated, it is good to remember that we have writers like Miss Jewett, calmly waiting for us to remember them. (p. 25)

> *Irving Howe, "Cameos from the North Country," in* The New Republic *(reprinted by permission of The New Republic;* © *1954 by The New Republic, Inc.), May 17, 1954, pp. 24-5.*

The Berwick in which [Sarah Orne Jewett] grew up was unusually conscious of its past, probably because its inhabitants realized that its history did not accord well with the national pattern of development. Though the town had at one time seemed a potential rival of Portsmouth or possibly even of Boston, by the time of Sarah Jewett's childhood it had lost practically all of its important ocean traffic. However unimportant to the nation as a whole, this local decline seemed disastrous to some of the proud citizens of Berwick. Young Sarah must have observed this attitude in her grandfather, Theodore Furber Jewett (1787-1860). He could easily remember the time of Berwick's prosperity, and like many other good Federalists he seems to have blamed Jefferson's Embargo for his section's economic decline. (pp. 135-36)

However much credence Miss Jewett herself gave to this interpretation of the New England decline, her use of this theory enabled her to direct her readers' attention to the question of historical development. (p. 137)

Upon the entire performance of Miss Jewett's masterpiece, *The Country of the Pointed Firs . . . ,* lay an awareness of the past. Although she put much less of the explicit history of the region into this book than she had done with *Deephaven,* she assimilated better the spiritual essence of the past. It is true that Dunnet Landing was, like Deephaven, a New England seaport in decline and that it looked backward to mourn the passing of a better day. (p. 140)

Thus, when Miss Jewett turned at the end of her career to the historical novel, it was not a suddenly acquired interest in the past that provoked her to write. And however much she may have been motivated by the popularity of the historical novel at that particular time, she prepared herself carefully and wrote enthusiastically. If her story of the American Revolution did not succeed, it was much more her inability to live imaginatively in the masculine world of action than it was her lack of sympathy for the period of which she was writing. (p. 141)

It would, of course, be far too much to attribute to Sarah Jewett the critical power implied by the historical mind in its ripest development. But that she valued it so highly argues well for the clarity of her perceptions. (p. 142)

> *Ferman Bishop, "The Sense of the Past in Sarah Orne Jewett" (originally published in* University of Wichita Bulletin, *February, 1959), in* Appreciations of Sarah Orne

Jewett: 29 Interpretive Essays, *edited by Richard Cary (copyright 1973 by Colby College Press), Colby College Press, 1973, pp. 135-43.*

Although Miss Jewett's expressed purpose was to inform the world about her home district and its inhabitants, she is not a local colorist pure and simple. She portrays indigenous scenes, characters, and customs, with native perspicuity and understanding; she only occasionally casts a romantic sheen over her materials. She does not merely describe, she works into the texture of her descriptions reserves of knowledge and experience drawn from long and sensitive intimacy with her milieu. She construes environment as a pictorial backdrop, but also as a powerful determining influence. She does not resort to blatant misspellings in idiom and dialect. Some of her people are unquestionably quaint or queer, but they also have a strong streak of the universal—George Quint, for instance, or William Blackett. Instead of yielding to the richness of these elements, she handles them with wise authority. Fidelity to vision and tranquility of tone earmark her method. It has brought her accolades from many quarters. (p. 18)

Miss Jewett, with an art perhaps too serene to appeal to the uninformed city audiences she had in mind, superimposes upon each other two worlds—one lost and one misunderstood. The most frequent criticism of her rendition is that she screens out of it all the coarse and contemptible actualities of life in favor of a too pervasive charm and refinement. She is accused of feminine fastidiousness, aristocratic bias, esthetic myopia, and downright ignorance. Her depictions of locale are condemned as idyllic and many of her characters cited as paragons of purity. She is very generously excused on the score that, while aware of the starker sides of existence, she deliberately evades them out of fidelity to her purpose of bringing out only the best.

A close examination of Sarah Jewett's world will reveal that none of these criticisms is entirely justified. She does not uniformly dulcify her scenes, nor do her people invariably demonstrate redeemable virtues. She knows the ugly underside of nature as minutely as its happier facets, and she seldom shrinks from presenting the despicable in human motives or behavior. (pp. 30-1)

High among Miss Jewett's articles of faith are belief in the fabled tranquility of the past, in the genteel acceptance of one's lot—good or grim, and in the ineradicable benevolence of humankind. It is not deficiency of art or vision that impels her to stress the buoyant over the dire experience. It is a matter of maidenly decision. Her training and status lend substance to the view that life is on the whole a sequence of pleasantly muted interchanges, only occasionally obstructed by enmity or irreparable tragedy. She sees life in its variegated shades but, secure in her conviction that happiness is the highest moral purpose, she selects her tints to suit herself. (pp. 32-3)

Can Sarah Jewett meet the test of reality with so decided an inclination? Does the social distance between herself and her subjects militate against genuine comprehension of their secret and subtle responses? The answer lies in the unshakeable authenticity of her collective portrayal.

She allows no barriers to stand between herself and her basic materials. She takes every advantage of the democratic fluency between classes in the area to absorb intimate reactions at the farther end of the scale. Forty years of transit through the wider world of culture failed to take the country out of her. She moves with the discretion of a more fortunate sister or daughter among the citizens of her region, protectively colored by her native knowledge of formalities and language. Beginning in childhood, she acquired a fathomless understanding of the works and ways of her neighbors through close and impulsive intercourse. And she has the gift of empathy. Sharing their monolithic religious faith and uncomplicated graph of values, their naïve pleasures and antipathies, she can slip without discomposure into their very identities.

Quite frequently Miss Jewett assumes the role of detached spectator in her sketches and stories, but this is a tactic to secure the benefits of an added point of view. This device of course contributes texturally to her success in imbuing her reconstructed world with a sense of verity. But the qualities which pre-eminently mould her art into a likeness of life are her elemental knowledge of and sympathy with "the country out of which I grew, and where every bush and tree seem like my cousins!" (pp. 33-4)

[A] dogged surge of spirit which gradually succumbs to the limitations of flesh is in fact the outstanding attribute of the men and women who inhabit Sarah Jewett's little world. The exhilaration of ocean conquest has given way to almost stoic resignation. Meager subsistence from fishing, farming, and the patronage of summer visitors is the best that they can hope for. This dwindling downward from competence to poverty has put a stamp of repressive hardness on the souls of natives who go about their daily rounds with a curious quietude, as though knowingly guilty of a huge defection yet unwilling to accept the blame for themselves. They have pride, a quirky sense of humor, and relish for their slow-paced, self-possessed lives. They seem to be waiting, perhaps for renascence, calmly imbibing wisdom from the boundless vitality of the sea and the unbroken rotation of the seasons.

Old people predominate. Because Miss Jewett revered the aged as trustees of a past she loved, and because the youth of Maine migrated to greener pastures, young adults seldom play large roles in the small communal dramas. . . . Love is never passionate and courtships are most often duels of wits won by crafty, mature women. When marriages occur, they almost always come in the winter of time. . . . (p. 38)

Men are distinctly secondary in Miss Jewett's overwhelmingly female world. Not many have the sagacity of country-doctor Leslie, the solidity of marsh-islander Israel Owen, or the unadulterated goodness of David Berry. Omitting some of the resourceful fishermen, personalities run to weakness, deception, and shiftlessness. . . .

By one means or another—marriage, inheritance, subtlety, utter helplessness, or force of character—women determine the shape and color of life in this subdued domain. Widows and spinsters are in the majority. Their families long dead, they have become accustomed to living alone, are frightfully neat, and follow undeviating schedules of daily activity. They show inordinate curiosity about the slightest occurrence in the parish, ready to lay praise or blame upon friend or foe. They treasure their last rusty black satin "going-out" dresses and other sentimental remnants from the splendid shipping days.

A recurring type is the versatile, self-reliant female who

will not be deterred by circumstance. . . . From copious reserves of courage or tenacity they draw the spiritual energy needed to carry them through their comfortless situations. Many are women who turn out to be better "men" than their menfolk.

Miss Jewett usually equips her more feminine or inept elderly ladies with compatible and complementary sisters. They have lived so long together in self-contained seclusion that there is little to distinguish between one and the other. (p. 39)

With the uninsistent firmness of an assured artist, Sarah Jewett draws a small but vital portrait of a special place and people, more profoundly authentic than any in her own time and one excelled by few in any time.

From earliest maturity Miss Jewett was convinced that "the real drama of life" was to be found in "a dull little country village." In the city, . . . "[the] delicate cadences are lost in the blare of heavy tones." With this limiting principle as guide, she treats such themes as are best illustrated by her typical dull village. The themes themselves are broad and fairly simple; it is her implementation of them that is subtle. (p. 41)

The fabric of her work is shot through with [the decline of New England], which amounts to a mood as well as a theme. In the sketches Miss Jewett speaks directly from primary observation of persons and scenes that corroborate her point. She also resorts to expository statement in her narratives, but in these she is apt to utilize symbols of nature, situation, character, or action to fortify her intent. . . . The reign of poverty and apathy in a region once virile and self-reliant is the main spur to Miss Jewett's creative impulse. It drives her into an almost tragic revelation of the effects of defeat, defeat necessary to a people for proper recognition of their essential selves.

Miss Jewett's ingrained preference for the older generation and her distrust of the emerging technological culture lead her into numerous contrasts between the genteel values imbedded in her memory and the more raucous current ones. (p. 42)

Physical nature, whether beneficent or ill-favored, serves as more than backdrop in Miss Jewett's stories and sketches. She engages it actively in symbol and analogy . . . , and she also employs it thematically to grasp its psychic impress upon man.

In its salutary aspect nature imparts to country people a sense of the strength and purpose of the world about them. They listen to the words of sea and field and forest, absorb the meanings of the universal creative power, and accept instincts as truth. . . . On the reverse side of the shield, nature lies in wait for man with persistent hostility as he ineffectually tries to subdue its vigor. Worsting him in the lonely places, nature irresistibly covers up the traces of his fatal struggle. (pp. 42-3)

Contrasts between [country and city] . . . infiltrate all of Miss Jewett's important work. In her mind this polarity is allied with her theme of the decline of New England and her antithetical view of past and present. The wane of rural areas is a direct consequence of economic innovations in the cities. The country represents a treasury of all that is good in the past; the city, all that is dreadful in the present. (p. 44)

Miss Jewett's outstanding virtues of expression are simplicity, clarity, and economy. Her prose flows effortlessly, uncluttered by studied phrases or tortured figures, and gives off a subdued radiance. . . . (p. 51)

The felicity of her style is most manifest in her management of native idiom. She extracts the peculiarities of speech from the earth of their origin, turns up their roots with some of the soil still clinging, yet preserves unharmed their vibrant connection with life. (p. 52)

Her first stories, formal exercises imitative of current magazine standards, are overplotted, savorless, and disposed to gratuitous homily. Characters and conversation are unbelievably stilted. Locale is generalized, exerting no appreciable effect upon people or situation. (p. 88)

The later stories, which reflect her victory over mere technique, are practically devoid of plot. A sequence of events is readily evident, but it does not necessarily move toward a revelatory climax. The single incident which betrays in a flash an aspect of character, or a man's knowledge of himself, or a man's relation to his universe is not part of Miss Jewett's repertory. She favors, instead, ordinary instances in the lives of ordinary people: a lonely holiday, a trip to town, a father's doubts, a family leave-taking, a train ride.

Her principal concern is not action but character—more precisely, the interpenetration of character and environment; moreover, the long, slow, internal relevancies develop without galvanic stimuli. (p. 89)

In her 1893 Preface to *Deephaven*, Miss Jewett reviews the reasons that impelled her to write about her own region. The Civil War, railroads, immigration, summer visitors, and the exodus of young natives effected extraordinary changes in rustic life. She felt obliged to honor Plato's dictum that "the best thing that can be done for the people of a state is to make them acquainted with one another." The diminution of respect for old customs and culture, the frivolous alteration of traditional architecture, and the loss of individuality made it urgent to reanimate the values of the hallowed past for the heedless present. To help city and country folk understand each other, and to expose the current age to the finest ideals of expired or expiring generations—in one or the other of these respects, this is what all her novels are about. (p. 132)

Sarah Orne Jewett's work is a considerable contribution to American literature. Of her novels, *Deephaven* and *The Country of the Pointed Firs* will always extend a vital personal record of the people, conditions, and values of nineteenth-century rural New England to generations desiring intimate knowledge of the national past. (p. 157)

It has been shown that Miss Jewett's finished art is deficient in some of the significant phases of a mature culture. She was neither philosopher nor sociologist, but she was an observer and interpreter who did the type of observing that precedes speculation and the kind of interpreting that resists collectivization. She has this in common with many American writers who have been more concerned with substance than with subtlety, and she fits, therefore, into a middle place in several lines of development in American literature. In style and content she relates to Washington Irving; in mystical advocacy of nature to the transcendentalists Emerson, Thoreau, and Whitman; in gentility of realism to Howells and Henry James; in choice of locale

and characters to Harriet Beecher Stowe; in themes, if not treatment, to Hawthorne. Without ascribing definite influence, it may safely be said that her grace of expression has been perpetuated in similar fields by Willa Cather and John Steinbeck; that her characters have reappeared with appropriate mutations in the poetry of E. A. Robinson and Robert Frost; that her situations, if not moods, are to be found in Edith Wharton's New England aspect; and that her concept of a fruitful, renewable *York*-napatawpha county is not unlike Faulkner's mythos. (pp. 157-58)

It is not too much to claim that Sarah Orne Jewett is without peer among her contemporaries in the reliable depiction of her chosen time, place, and personalities. (p. 159)

> *Richard Cary, in his* Sarah Orne Jewett *(copyright 1962 by Twayne Publishers, Inc.; reprinted with the permission of Twayne Publishers, A Division of G. K. Hall & Co., Boston), Twayne, 1962.*

It is curious that Miss Jewett's literary career should have opened and closed with the same literary form: the looseleaf novel in which a female narrator gives the reader sketches of persons and places in a small Maine village. She must have had a sense from the beginning of the perfect medium for her talent and laid it aside, consciously or not, for the two decades that elapsed between *Deephaven* and *The Country of the Pointed Firs*. It was to take her all of that time to perfect her character sketches of village and farm people, for the difference between success and failure in this delicate art was always a hairline. The danger that stalked her was sentimentality.

There is little to be said about *Deephaven* or about the three small collections of stories and essays that followed it: *Old Friends and New* . . . , *Country By-Ways* . . . , and *The Mate of the Daylight, and Friends Ashore*. . . . They have charm, but it is a pale, wistful charm. (p. 7)

She now turned to the conventional novel form with *A Country Doctor*. . . . It is only in parts successful. It fails to hang together, and although this was a common fault in the Victorian novel, it is more noticeable in a book as short as *A Country Doctor*. . . .

The development of the relationship between the doctor and his ward, as she accompanies him on his calls and learns all he can teach her, inspired by Miss Jewett's own experiences with her father, is the finest part of the book. (p. 8)

The disjointedness of *A Country Doctor* is corrected in *A Marsh Island* . . . , a charming, concentrated, well-balanced little novel of rustic love in the haying season. (p. 9)

The decade from 1886 to 1896 Miss Jewett devoted to the short story, producing five collections. . . . These include all of her memorable fiction except *The Country of the Pointed Firs*. The stories, almost without exception, succeed in direct proportion to their proximity to Miss Jewett's home base. . . . Miss Jewett is at her most triumphant with the proud, dutiful, aristocratic old maid in reduced circumstances. (pp. 11-12)

Miss Jewett told Willa Cather once that "when an old house and an old woman came together in her brain with a click, she knew that a story was under way." The old women are her particular trademark, with their shrewdness and humor and plain common sense and dutifulness and, above all, their ability to look the world straight in the eye without being in the least impressed. (p. 13)

With *The Country of the Pointed Firs* . . . , Miss Jewett returned to the fine straight highway of her first book but now with all the experience of twenty rich years of observing and recording. The novel of the Maine village, the string of loosely connected tales of characters in the same locale, was what she did best; indeed, it is her claim to enduring fame. . . . Dunnet [the village in *The Country of the Pointed Firs*] may be seen too idyllically, if realism is what one wants, but . . . they have been selected to substantiate the author's thesis that Dunnet is a lovely place, full of integrity, good neighborliness, thrift, and industry, as neat as it is honest, as tactful as it is unaffected, as simple as it is profound. No doubt she could have chosen types to illustrate the contrary; Miss Jewett was too much a doctor's daughter not to have heard about degeneracy in small, isolated New England communities. But what she chose to depict was the charm of the coastal village, and that such charm exists every visitor can testify. No other author has begun to catch it as she did, and it is unlikely now, with Maine drawn more and more into chain-store and television civilization, that there will be much of it left to catch in the future. (pp. 15-16)

> *Louis Auchincloss, "Sarah Orne Jewett," in his* Pioneers & Caretakers: A Study of 9 American Women Novelists *(© 1965, University of Minnesota), University of Minnesota Press, Minneapolis, 1965, pp. 6-19.*

The Country of the Pointed Firs is the most sustained of the works which mark the high point of Sarah Jewett's art. Although it lacks something of the breadth contained in [other pieces] . . . , its confident movement is deep. (p. 290)

The great strength of *The Country of the Pointed Firs* is its sane estimate of the limited value of the fact that Dunnet Landing is out of the way and different. No attempt is made to relate it to a wider world. The values maintained there— loyalty, courage, honesty—are right for it. If they are not more widely applicable, this does not reflect the provinciality of Dunnet Landing but rather the loss the world has sustained by changing. A rooted age is indispensable to the life portrayed. . . . The world of Emerson and Thoreau is still intact in the hands of the elderly ladies who are its keepers, and Miss Jewett can move unselfconsciously from the flora to the residents because time has matched their movements to one another. The narrator, coming from the world of the city, sheds her anxieties in her commitment to Mrs. Todd's back-country interests, but she does not do so to escape life. Rather, in Thoreauvian fashion, she has exchanged anxious living for life, for an acute consciousness of the succession of the minutes and the myriad of things brought to the senses in each hour of the day. Daily life in Dunnet Landing follows a well-established pattern, but, as the narrator appreciates, this commitment to routine frees the inhabitants from care about the future and enables them to get the most from the natural pleasures of the present. (pp. 290-91)

> *Larzer Ziff, in his* The American 1890's: Life and Times of a Lost Generation *(copyright © 1966 by Larzer Ziff; reprinted by permission of The Viking Press, Inc.), Viking, 1966.*

The passage of time in [Miss Jewet's] stories is governed by concern for the survival of her community: characteristically, she celebrates the stability of social order in affirmative moments of return and continuation, or she records its decline in the definitive moment of departure and farewell. The persistence of her quest for permanence in her scenes of country life is suggested by the markedly static, highly pictorial manner in which they are rendered. (p. 204)

The action of the stories, when there is any, is usually set in motion by an event which threatens the stability of a character's place in his community: there is an economic failure or a domestic loss; sometimes an unexpected arrival or a sudden departure, more often a death. Her characters are given what may be called a primary situation that takes its meaning from a social context: they are unmarried or widowed, old or poor. Next, they are endowed with certain secondary personal qualities that are (or sometimes are *not*) of use to them in their efforts to make the best of things. The action concludes when economic independence or domestic security has been achieved, and the individual's position in his community has been restored. In such a world action is thought of chiefly in defensive terms, and rarely acquires any positive value of its own.

Miss Jewett's optimistic belief in the permanent values of country life remained unshaken by her sensitive observation of the large, inexorable forces of social change which were gradually undermining them. (p. 206)

In her best work Miss Jewett refrained from an excessively sentimental or didactic treatment, but she was never able to free herself completely from these weaknesses. The problem was perennial, for her writing was ultimately devoted to portraits of characters who embody ideal moral qualities. (p. 207)

The province of Miss Jewett's greatest literary achievement lies somewhere between a simple recording of personal experience and an imaginative manipulation of it into more elaborate artistic patterns. As she moved away from the purely personal, she gained formal qualities of proportion and perspective. When she left the personal too far behind, the tone suffered, and sentimentality and melodrama increased. She found her most favorable medium of expression in a form which is not exactly a sketch or a story, but which may be described by such phrases as genre scene, dialogue piece, and character portrait. (p. 208)

Miss Jewett's gifts were not those of the novelist. If her capacity for the invention of incident and the construction of plot was limited, her ability to handle the problem of character development was equally restricted. At the outset of her career she was painfully aware of the lack of drama in her stories. (p. 210)

Sarah Jewett never really mastered the dramatic art of character development. Most often she bypassed this problem altogether, perfecting instead the precision of her description of dialect, gesture, and landscape, and filling out the character of the sensitive observer of these external realities by a discreet and effective use of her own personal response to them. In her best work she made as complete and economical a use of her own experience as possible, inventing relatively little. The result is a subtle blend of observation and autobiography. . . .

[Out] of the rhythm of her life there emerged the pattern of a larger order which became a primary fable for the revelation of her country world in its totality, a fable in its essence of the impact of experience upon the receiving mind, relating the individual to the community in which he lived, the village to the world beyond. This narrative design was that of the outsider who makes a visit to a village or country locale and has a series of brief experiences. This visit pattern, present in many of the stories and in all of the longer fiction except *The Tory Lover,* made its earlier important appearance in *Deephaven* . . .; evolving slowly for many years, it received its most commanding, definitive statement in *The Country of the Pointed Firs.* . . . The time limitations imposed by the visit fitted the modest dimensions of her personal experiences, and the presence of an outside observer provided additional justification for the practice of defining character in terms of external circumstances. (p. 211)

In *The Country of the Pointed Firs* the author has broken away from the static treatment of the visit pattern as a head-on confrontation between different environments; she has turned it into an interesting developmental situation in which her outside observer ceases to be merely a summer visitor and is accepted temporarily as an inside member of the village community. In the relationship of the two women there is ample opportunity for the expression of her own mixed feelings about provincial life without bringing them into open conflict as she had in "A White Heron," *A Country Doctor,* and *A Marsh Island.* As she told Willa Cather, an artist needed the detachment of an outsider and the experience of a native. Miss Jewett found that the presence of the visitor would provide the occasion for the revelation of the knowledge available only to the native, and the sympathy and appreciation of the native could be acquired by the visitor, who might—and often did—lack these indispensable qualities. The villager could, in fact, remake the stranger in his own image. Miss Jewett had learned to create perspective and drama through a projection of herself. (p. 218)

> *Paul John Eakin, "Sarah Orne Jewett and the Meaning of Country Life," in* American Literature *(reprinted by permission of the Publisher; copyright 1967 by Duke University Press, Durham, North Carolina), January, 1967 (and reprinted in* Appreciation of Sarah Orne Jewett: 29 Interpretive Essays, *edited by Richard Cary, Colby College Press, 1973, pp. 203-22).*

Ever since Willa Cather, in the preface to the 1925 edition of *The Country of the Pointed Firs,* judged it to be one of three American books which had "the possibility of a long, long life" [see excerpt above], criticism has been attempting to define more accurately the qualities which make this work a classic of its kind, and which suggested to Miss Cather that it should rank with *The Scarlet Letter* and *Huckleberry Finn* in importance. In the light of the present corpus of American fiction her judgment must appear somewhat arbitrary, although it is obvious that she wished, in part, simply to praise a book in which she took particular

interest by comparing it with two novels which were then its best-known predecessors. Unfortunately her statement has not always been understood in this context, and Miss Jewett's book has either suffered badly from the comparison, or has profited from it in an equally misleading fashion. Miss Cather's judgment may, however, lead to more profitable approaches in understanding *The Country of the Pointed Firs;* she may have recognized in all three books the treatment of a mode with which she herself was much concerned, namely the pastoral. Since Miss Jewett's work clearly belongs to this mode, while the other two books use it as a motif, the problem is to discover what distinguishes *The Country of the Pointed Firs* from other pastorals.

As a literary mode the pastoral describes a retreat both in time and place to an enclosed green world. This retreat expresses man's dream of an ideally ordered and independent existence, and his desire to escape from the complex realities of social ills and natural process (change, decay and death). In his essay "The Oaten Flute" [in *Harvard Library Bulletin,* May 1957], Renato Poggioli suggests a useful distinction between two kinds of pastoral: that of innocence and that of happiness. In the pastoral of happiness the bucolic landscape represents a place of erotic fulfillment, while the pastoral of innocence is essentially a domestic idyll presented in terms of old age rather than youth. . . . Miss Jewett's pastoral clearly belongs to the latter type, for as has often been remarked, the world of Dunnet Landing is curiously a world of old people in which sexuality plays no part. The exclusion of this element of natural process points to another concern of pastoral: its constant preoccupation with the arresting of time and change. But if pastoral seeks to present a vision of life held in stasis, it nevertheless ultimately recognizes the inevitable truth of mutability: *Et in Arcadia ego.* It is the extent to which the narrator or central character is consciously aware of this truth which determines the extent to which a reconciliation with time is finally achieved. (pp. 249-50)

Unlike the river scenes in *Huckleberry Finn,* or the Salem to which Hawthorne's narrator returns in the introduction to *The Scarlet Letter,* the landscape of Dunnet Landing in *The Country of the Pointed Firs* represents the totality of the narrator's desired experience. The lasting achievement of the book stems, in fact, from the emotional ambiguity evoked in the reader towards this experience. Constantly aware of the impossibility of regaining such innocence, we are drawn in spite of ourselves into the charmed circle of Dunnet Landing and its inhabitants; unlike the narrator, we can never quite evade the poignant realization that we have already passed beyond it. (p. 254)

> *David Stouck, "The Country of the Pointed Firs: A Pastoral of Innocence" (originally published in* Colby Library Quarterly, *December, 1970), in* Appreciation of Sarah Orne Jewett: 29 Interpretive Essays, *edited by Richard Cary (copyright 1973 by Colby College Press), Colby College Press, 1973, pp. 249-54.*

Amy Lowell

1874-1925

American poet, essayist, and biographer. The leading proponent of the Imagist School in American poetry, Amy Lowell is remembered for her strong-minded theorizing on poetics, her support of other poets, and her massive biography of John Keats. Born of a distinguished New England family, Amy Lowell became a literary legend in her lifetime. Her eccentric personality, outspoken ways, and enormous girth, however, were better known by the public than her poems. Her Cuban cigars, she confided to friends, were her doctor's advice to aid her mild but chronic indigestion. Having been slender as a girl, her obesity caused by a glandular condition was difficult for her to accept. After publishing a volume of undistinguished verse *(A Dome of Many-Coloured Glass),* Lowell met Ezra Pound in Paris on one of her European tours and became a fervent convert to imagism. (Pound was later to rename the movement Amygism.) Her own poetry, while acknowledged for its vitality and exoticism, has been criticized as being pretentious and superficial, and she is generally categorized as a minor, but interesting, poet. *What's O'Clock,* containing the best of her later work, was published posthumously and awarded the Pulitzer Prize in Poetry in 1926.

PRINCIPAL WORKS

Dream Drops; or Stories from Fairy Land, by a Dreamer
   (poetry) 1887
A Dome of Many-Coloured Glass (poetry) 1912
Sword Blades and Poppy Seed (poetry) 1914
Six French Poets: Studies in Contemporary Literature
   (essays) 1915
Men, Women and Ghosts (poetry) 1916
Tendencies in Modern American Poetry (essays) 1917
Can Grande's Castle (poetry) 1918
Pictures of the Floating World (poetry) 1919
Fir-Flower Tablets (poetry) 1921
Legends (poetry) 1921
A Critical Fable (poetry) 1922
John Keats (biography) 1925
What's O'Clock (poetry) 1925
East Wind (poetry) 1926
Ballads for Sale (poetry) 1927
Fool o' the Moon (poetry) 1927
Poetry and Poets: Essays (essays) 1930

During the past year something has happened in the sphere of the arts quite as important, in my opinion, as the European war in the sphere of politics and international relationships, or the discovery of radium in that of science. A new poetic form, equal if not superior in value to *vers libre,* has made its appearance in English. The discoverer is a woman. Had it been a man, we should probably all have heard by now of the richness of the find. Since there seems to be some danger that only a few will appreciate its significance, I venture to draw the public attention to it.

I do this the more willingly, because in her preface to *Sword-blades and Poppy Seed* Miss Amy Lowell, who is the true discoverer of this form, has modestly and mistakenly stated that it is not altogether her own invention, but was first employed by a French poet, Paul Fort. Now, for the uninitiated, I may say that M. Fort is a poet who possesses great facility in writing the alexandrine, the French classic metre. Unsatisfied with the chill regularity of this measure, he has attempted to fit it to his temperament, which is that of an improvisatore or ballad-singer, by interspersing his poems with bits of prose, whenever his rhyme-invention flags. (pp. 32-3)

Upon this purely typographical device in M. Fort, Miss Lowell's imagination fastened itself. She is almost unique among present-day poets in possessing the ability of writing equally well in rhymed metre and in *vers libre.* She has practiced her art long enough to understand that the really great poetry which will survive, depends upon its sound quality and its substance quality, upon its appeal to the ear as well as to the eye. It seemed to her that there must be some way of fusing together unrhymed *vers libre* and rhymed metrical patterns, giving the rich decorative quality of the one and the powerful conciseness of statement of the other. In short, she was seeking some means whereby she might free herself, and other poets after her, from a constant and dogmatic adherence to a single metre throughout a single poem. (p. 33)

Miss Lowell had scarcely begun her attempt to follow Paul Fort before she realized that what she was doing consisted not so much in adapting a French form as in creating a new English one. For one thing, she was faced at the outset by the fact that the English language, since the break-up of blank verse, has no form which is standard, like the French alexandrine. She found it possible to vary the rhythm and metre of these strange new poems of hers almost at will, following the inner emotion of the thing she had to say. Swift-flowing metrical passages might be succeeded by *vers libre* recitatives; connecting links of prose could be used as a relief to the ear, and to lead up to some new metrical passage, and so on. In short, here was the opportunity, long sought, of displaying, within the limits of a single poem, all the resources of her art.

In my opinion, Miss Lowell has, in her latest examples of this peculiar form, resolved in a great measure the difficulties which confront all English poets who attempt to say something new today. (p. 34)

> *John Gould Fletcher, "Miss Lowell's Discovery: Polyphonic Prose," in* Poetry (© *1915 by The Modern Poetry Association; reprinted by permission of the Editor of* Poetry), *April, 1915, pp. 32-6.*

As usual with her, Miss Lowell's title is exact. *Legends* is a volume consisting of eleven narrative poems, most of them on themes selected from folk-lore. Their sources are various. A few she has created herself. "A Legend of Porcelain" is obviously from the Chinese; "Dried Marjoram" is English. "Witch-Woman" comes from Yucatan; "Memorandum Confided by a Yucca to a Passion-Vine" comes from Peru; "Many Swans" from North America, or, more specifically, from a Kathlemet myth. The other legends are European, Amerindian, or Down-Eastern. Evidently the volume is a Mythology of All Peoples in brief. It is at least Miss Lowell's reaction to universal mythology. . . .

Her private library is one of the best in New England, and it is not idle. The result of her reading and observation is that she can pack her legends with a mass of brilliant detail, which distinguishes them sharply from the stark narratives of the original. At her worst this detail almost suffocates the theme; usually it gives life to the bare bones of the story. Her own character, moreover, justifies this handling; she is a pluralist, not a monist. And she is telling myths that belong to her personally as well as to the races that originated them. (p. 222)

She shows . . . in the volume, remarkable ability to handle large forms. At this point in the discussion, a deficiency in critical vocabulary troubles me. If Miss Lowell were a painter, one would certainly speak of her excellent composition, but composition in painting and composition in writing are two different things. One is safer in saying that her poems possess balance and movement. The movement is diversified by certain common devices, such as interludes (like the choruses in "Many Swans") and tangents (like the end of "Memorandum"). The number of these devices, whether for unification or diversification, is limited, and yet they can be built into more combinations than a bridge hand. The comparison is unfortunate, perhaps, for there is nothing mechanical about poetical form; one can't just shuffle and expect it to come out right. It is complex and organic like the human body. All this is primer talk, but it is a quotation from an unwritten primer. The point is that Miss Lowell builds—or composes—her poems as well as a painter of the first rank, instead of as badly as a British novelist.

Poetical form has, of course, another and smaller aspect. It is the handling of the individual lines and stanzas, corresponding somewhat to the brushwork in painting. Here, too, *Legends* shows up excellently; her verse becomes increasingly supple. In former volumes she was apt to use a single mode of verse. Thus, *A Dome of Many-Coloured Glass* was written in rhymed stanzas; *Sword Blades and Poppy Seeds* in unrhymed cadences; *Can Grande's Castle* in polyphonic prose. She now uses all her former modes in a single poem, and uses them all with greater freedom than before. She varies from one to another in accordance with the swiftness of the movement and the intensity of the mood (and lyric poets will be shocked to discover that the most intense mood does not usually call for rhyme and metre). This technique is admirably suited to programme music.

In her brushwork, however, a serious weakness appears. It is to her misfortune as a writer that she reads so well. Before an audience she can make her worst lines sound convincing; for this reason she is sometimes not so careful as a poet would be who recited wretchedly. Only Miss Lowell's best oral manner can carry over the line in "The Ring and the Castle" where Benjamin Bailey says:

> He died, they say, at the sight of my present.
> I laughed when I heard it—'Hee! Hee! Hee!'

"Hee" rhymes with "three." Another bad line which she mends in the reading occurs in "Memorandum"—"Blue dims rose." In print the line is almost without meaning.

It is healthy that a poet should get the big things right and fail only in the little; the trouble with poetry in the decade before us was just the opposite. It is healthy also that a poet should go on developing from year to year, instead of dying above the shoulders at the age fixed by Mr. Mencken. I cannot say pompously that this latest volume contains Miss Lowell's best work, but it contains her work that I like best. (pp. 224-25)

I have come to believe that one's estimate of Miss Lowell is bound up with one's estimate of American poetry in general. The new and excellent qualities of our literature are abundantly represented in her work, as is also our national tendency to be ragged. We must wait till the indefinite time when American literature has been judged before judging her. She is, at any rate, one of the three graces or nine muses upon whom our poetry stands or falls. (p. 226)

> *Malcolm Cowley, "Programme Music," in* The Dial (*copyright, 1921, by The Dial Publishing Company, Inc.; reprinted by permission of J. S. Watson, Jr. and Scofield Thayer), August, 1921, pp. 222-26.*

No one has fought, in theory and in practice, the battles for the experimental artist, for a wider aesthetic appreciation with more determination than Amy Lowell. And no one has shown such ability to learn from her own experiments. Preëminently the poet of the external world, her later work pierces the shining surfaces of her technic. Poet, propagandist (she was one of the first members of the Imagists and three collections of their work were published in America under her supervision), lecturer, translator, biographer, critic . . . her verve is almost as remarkable as her verse. (p. 135)

Through all her work runs an eager inquisitiveness; it accounts for her preoccupation with technic, color, form and the surfaces of art. It explains why so definitely American a poet could write so sympathetic and authoritative a volume on foreign tendencies as her *Six French Poets*. . . . It is her catholicity of taste, her subjugation of prejudices that make such a book not only a notable interpretation but a contribution to criticism. (p. 136)

No poet living in America has been more fought for, fought against and generally fought about than Amy Lowell. The thing which has stirred so many admirations and antagonisms is her implied and often direct challenge to the lazily sentimental reader as well as to the placid manufacturers of predigested verse. It is this positive quality that has caused so much opposition, especially among negative people. . . . Nor has she been an advocate merely for her school, a special pleader. It is true that in her critical work and general discussions she has taken up the sword for *vers libre* and the Imagists most frequently; but she has also wielded a lusty cudgel for all of the radicals in poetry and for all the new tendencies in the other arts as well. Nothing could be more descriptive of her dual rôle—the combination of poet and propagandist—than the title of her second volume, *Sword Blades and Poppy Seed*. . . . (p. 137)

In *A Dome of Many-Colored Glass* . . . it is difficult to discover even the proverbial "promise" of most first books. It is hard to believe that our most consistent innovator could have written such wholly trite verses as the ones entitled "Apples of Hesperides," "Suggested by the Cover of a Volume of Keats's Poems," "The Road to Avignon," "The Boston Athenaeum." And it is equally inconceivable that Miss Lowell, who would cut off her right hand rather than let it commit a *cliché*, could ever have written such gems of banality as:

> Life is a stream
> On which we strew
> Petal by petal the flower of our heart.

(pp. 137-38)

Sword Blades and Poppy Seed . . . reveals an entirely different Amy Lowell. The book brims not only with another kind of poetry but with an unexpected belligerence. The author fights for her poems with almost superfluous zeal in a preface which argues that "the poet must learn his trade in the same manner and with the same painstaking care as the cabinet-maker," that "poetry should exist simply because it is a created beauty," that "the trees do not teach us moral lessons" and that "the poet must be constantly seeking new pictures to make his readers feel the vitality of thought." (p. 138)

When one turns from the writer of doctrinaire prefaces to Amy Lowell the writer of poetry, an entirely different personality is encountered. Many of the traits are the same—the vigor, the pugnacity, the power of the sharply cut line—but they are transmuted into something that is more delicate and yet more forceful. What is most striking in this volume is the uncommon sense of hearing a sensitive, aesthetic femininity unbosom itself in a decidedly masculine utterance. Throughout the volume one observes this queer mixture. Miss Lowell's objectivity is so great that she finds one sex insufficient to express herself. Not that she assumes the male attitude too anxiously or too often; the intellectual form of her work is hermaphroditic rather than sapphic. It assumes both sexes with equal dexterity. Contrast, for instance, so purely feminine a concept as "A Gift" with so lusty and virile a love-song as "Anticipation." Or turn from the point-lace and lavender archness of

"Apology" to the brusque speech of "The Cyclists" with its speed and incision. (p. 140)

But it is an experimenter that she is most arresting. Her interest in form is something like a passion with her. Yet even the most tenuous of her imagist verses have more than the form as their impetus. So with the experiments in long *vers libre* and "polyphonic prose," which Miss Lowell with eager catholicity has adopted from the French. The latter form, as she uses it, becomes a flexible medium with its prose structure, its irregular meter, its sudden incidental and almost accidental rhymes. (p. 142)

With her next book, *Men, Women and Ghosts* . . . , Miss Lowell fulfilled the hopes of her friends. Her antagonists found little comfort in the new volume, for its author escaped from their dark pigeonholes, shook off the neat labels with which they had ticketed her, and proceeded to do all the things which they had proved she was incapable of doing. They said she could not tell a direct, readable story; and *Men, Women and Ghosts* is a bookful of them. They said she could write only in irregular rhythms and bizarre images; so she gives them a 627-line eighteenth century love-poem, with all the conservative modelling and precision of Pope. They said she was at home only in the limbo of foreign futurism; and here (in "The Overgrown Pasture") are four straightforward, almost over-dramatic poems of everyday New England.

One of the most remarkable things about this volume is its extraordinary range of subjects, treatment and forms. Chaucerian stanzas, "unrelated" *vers libre,* strict ballad measures, polyphonic prose, conservative couplets, free-rhymed verse, monologues in dialect, stiff little tercets—in her handling of these Miss Lowell reveals her skill as the most versatile woman that has ever written poetry in America. Perhaps, after all, the most amazing thing is neither the amount of topics nor the variety of forms that interest her, but the astonishing success with which they are employed. Restless, penetrative, alert, Miss Lowell's reactions are a fresh surprise to the reader and an impetus to the artist. (pp. 144-45)

[In] *Can Grande's Castle* . . . the teller of stories, the artist and the experimenter are fused. Possibly the strangest thing about this energetic book is that it is actually taken from other books. Even the title is borrowed. And yet the use of another poet's phrase explains not only itself, but the volume it prefaces. (pp. 147-48)

By using [Richard] Aldington's phrase as her title, Miss Lowell lets us understand that the contents of the new volume are the result of what she has read. But in the writing, her reading becomes real; her creative excitement makes what she has got from pages of history-books far livelier than her life. It is obvious that she could not possibly have experienced these things. Their vividness is due to the fact that, thrown back into the past, either by the war (as Miss Lowell claims), or, as is more probable, by a subconscious search for fresh material, an artist has taken a list of dates, battles, proper names together with Rand McNally's Geography and vitalized them. It is this objective and dramatic sense that makes her audience feel the reality of her historical revaluations. . . . (p. 148)

The volume is composed of four long semi-declamatory, semi-narrative poems, all of them in "polyphonic prose," with which John Gould Fletcher has experimented so often. Concerning this form, Miss Lowell has an extremely interesting digression in her preface. A glance at her poems in this manner shows not only how far she has gone from the original innovation of Paul Fort (which consisted, for the greater part, of regular prose passages alternating with regular rhymed ones) but how greatly she has progressed beyond her own previous efforts in this mode. With its many changes of rhythm and subtleties of rhyme, it is practically a new form; dignified, orchestral, fluid. It is a form of almost infinite possibilities; it can run the gamut of *tempi* and dynamics on one page; it can combine the thunder of great oratory with the roll of blank verse and the low flutes of a lyric. If Miss Lowell has done nothing else, she has enriched English as well as American literature with a new and variable medium of expression. (pp. 148-49)

Pictures of the Floating World . . . may well come to be Miss Lowell's most popular book. It retains her vigor with an increase in delicacy. (p. 151)

It is obvious that Miss Lowell agitates whatever she touches; under her provocative observation not even the most static thing can remain quiescent. Whether she writes about a fruit shop, a bather, a violin sonata, dolphins in blue water, a broken fountain or a Japanese print, everything flashes, leaps, spins and burns with an almost savage intensity. And, though motion frequently usurps the place of emotion, the speed is not without its graces and changes in tempo.

Although *Pictures of the Floating World* contains some of Miss Lowell's most aggressively brilliant examples, it also includes many of her quieter successes. "Madonna of the Evening Flowers" is one of the poems that combine magic of verbal and color sensitivity. (pp. 152-53)

Legends . . . is closely related to *Can Grande's Castle*. . . . And here, in these varied pages, are eleven stories from seven different backgrounds. Lacking the sweep of the four earlier canvases, the new narratives are chiefly interesting as stories. The first poem, however, "Memorandum Confided by a Yucca to a Passion-Vine," must be rated among the poet's finest moments; it is a startling *tour de force,* shining with colors strange even for Miss Lowell, exotic and metallic as the scene it describes. As in her previous books, this poet makes even the most casual descriptions an adventure in excitement.

It would be doing scant justice to Miss Lowell to conclude this chapter without an appreciative line regarding her recent work in the formal measures. Her touch has grown lighter and surer without sacrificing the accent which is definitely hers. (pp. 154-55)

A consideration of her volumes must make it plain that Miss Lowell's range is the most obvious of her gifts. But it is not the greatest. She strikes single notes as sharply as she sounds experimental chords. When her completed works are some day appraised in a detailed study of American poetry, it will be found that her versatile energies have expressed a poet who is half-singer, half-scientist, and the groping, experimental period she helped represent. (p. 156)

Louis Untermeyer, "Amy Lowell," in his American Poetry Since 1900 *(copyright ©️ 1923 by Henry Holt and Company; reprinted by permission of Holt, Rinehart and Winston, Publishers), Holt, 1923, pp. 135-56.*

Miss Lowell is one of the great personalities of our time and one of the great aristocrats of literature. No one who has heard her talk will ever forget it. . . . Miss Lowell's great achievement as a poet lies precisely in the fact that her poems are the most important things about her. She has succeeded in creating poems which owe her nothing but their creation, poems which are not the publications of her heart nor the revelations of her philosophy, but finalities, entities, existences. Her distinction is that she has practised poetry as an art. And it is the recognition of that fact which should keep her work in a living perspective, and in all times and seasons safe from mummifying fame. (p. 510)

[The] poetry of Miss Lowell will be glass, colored glass but glass nevertheless, to those who merely read it, who are incapable of seeing it, touching it, sensing it. While to those who are capable of experience it will give the intense experience of great art. It is throughout, in its failures as well as in its successes, the work of a conscious and controlled intelligence. (p. 513)

This quality of artistic intention, this passion to make, to perfect, is evidenced as much in Miss Lowell's experiments with rhythm as anywhere else. In so far as these experiments raise questions of technique they do not concern us here. It is neither in spite of nor because of *vers libre* that Miss Lowell is a poet. But as illustrative of her attitude toward her medium they are of the first importance. They indicate in a way nothing else can her sense of words and combinations of words as material out of which an imagined form may be created. In her failures, as in the failures of artists in other media, this sense takes the shape of a desire for "effects". So in *A Waltz by Bartok* she reproduces a waltz rhythm at the expense of writing a poem. In her successes she subdues herself to what she works in, maintaining from the inside as it were an artistic purpose and a perfect control over her material which gives her patterns, old or new, conviction and firmness and a kind of necessary rightness for which there is no adequate term. There is nothing labored, nothing calculated, nothing interlineated or overwritten. One would say, as undoubtedly Miss Lowell would say herself, that the impulse had brought its own form. And yet there is an intensity and a perfection which only the refining and controlling intelligence of the artist can give. (pp. 513-14)

I find it almost impossible to write of [*Legends*] without dissolving into mere exclamation. "Memorandum Confided by a Yucca to a Passion Vine" is simply superb. It is complete utterance. There is nothing more that can be said. The rising of the moon at Cuzco is one of the unforgettable experiences of a life time. In a world of metal, of thin gold and clashing silver, of clear metallic sound, of suns rising "with one deep bell-note of a copper crashed gong", the figure of a dance unfolds. And the dance is beautiful and terrible as the *Sacre du Printemps* is beautiful and terrible, more colorful perhaps, perhaps less centripetal, but equally intent. Nothing else in the book seems to me as fine and yet almost all is fine. "A Legend Or Porcelain" has moments of greatness, "Many Swans" is deeply and inexplicably moving, "Witch-Woman" in its action equals the "Memorandum" but only in its action. And all these poems with the possible exceptions of "The Ring And The Castle" and "The Statue In The Garden" have the movement, the rhythm appealing to eye as well as to ear, of the ballet. And the best of them, the "Memorandum", is the expression toward which Miss Lowell's poetry has moved. . . .

There is no poet in America or England who can equal her at her best in her own field. But there are poets in both countries whose lyrics must be preferred to hers. (p. 518)

[*Pictures of the Floating World*] is of the first importance for its bearing upon a problem of poetic theory with which Miss Lowell's name has been associated, the problem of Imagism. The manifesto of the original Imagists is well known and contains, as has been often remarked, nothing new nor unfamiliar. It was a shifting of emphasis based upon the recognition of the simple fact that a poem is a work of art and not an edited epigram. But some of the original Imagists and practically all their thousands of disciples have taken the name by which they distinguish themselves seriously and devoted themselves to picture making. With the result that they do not write poetry. Coleridge long ago observed "that images, however beautiful, though faithfully copied from nature, and as accurately represented in words, do not of themselves characterize the poet." The relation of words to objects in the external world is not mathematical, not necessary, not logical. It is emotional. . . . In the sense of the word in which these people are Imagists Miss Lowell is not an Imagist and never was. Her power to transfer objects into words is merely a function of her power as a poet. She achieves the poetic statement. She never permits her verse the gesture of the exclamatory forefinger indicating nothing. And if the imitation of her technique has strewn the museum cases of minds incapable of poetry with the glass flowers of fraud, she is not to blame. (pp. 519-20)

Any attempt at this time to "place" Miss Lowell, either in relation to the poetry of her own day or in relation to the tradition of English poetry, would be fantastic. The fertility and energy of her own creative faculty no less than the profound changes now taking place in the body of English poetry would very shortly demonstrate the inadequacy of the conclusion. But it is neither too early nor too late to point out the fundamental quality of her work and to insist upon it in the teeth of the devouring and omnivorous fame which, in a world of literary reviews, lies in wait for even the best of poets. It is a quality which appeared first in her first book, which is mature in her last, and which will leave her greatest work (work which we may or may not yet have seen) secure in that kernel of poetry which, because it is neither concerned with the communication of the symptoms of emotion nor with the revelation of contemporary truth, escapes for its handful of generations the familiarities of time. It is the quality of art. (p. 521)

> Archibald MacLeish, *"Amy Lowell and the Art of Poetry,"* in The North American Review (*reprinted by permission from* The North American Review; *copyright* © *1925 by the University of Northern Iowa*), *Spring, 1925, pp. 508-21.*

[Lowell's] life was essentially the triumph of the spirit over the tragedy of the body. She was a sick person from her early girlhood, yet her energy exceeded that of a dozen minor poets. Every obstacle except poverty blocked her path. . . . [In only] thirteen years of public literary life, broken though they were by illnesses and eyestrain and a series of operations, she rose, through bored indifference, through ridicule and controversy and hatred, to complete victory, dying 'at the zenith of her fame'. . . .

Those thirteen years, in which she proved herself poet, critic, biographer, scholar, and controversialist, coincided with a great revival of poetry in the United States. America had reached a point in civilization where the arts were bound to flourish; and so vigorously did they do so that a World War with its subsequent inflation and depression was unable to stunt them. It was the time-spirit alone that caused Amy Lowell to publish her first book in that surprising year 1912; but her championing and development of the Imagist tenets in 1914 speedily made her the center of a storm which ventilated and refreshed all American literature, experimental or conservative, verse or prose; and her own literary achievements soon conquered a continent and left her one of the two or three leading influences in the poetry of a nation. (p. xii)

[The title of *A Dome of Many-Coloured Glass*] is from a well-known line in Shelley's 'Adonais': the 'dome' is there used to symbolize life itself, in all its brilliant variety and fragility, a construction in the empty light of eternity. Yet the life recorded in the book is not that of humanity, but of one shut out from humanity. This exclusion itself becomes the theme of the book: it is the veiled record of frustration; a dedication of an otherwise useless life to poetry; a blind, almost hopeless, determination to succeed.

On the surface there is little promise of success. The book is sincere but restrained, dignified but conventional. There are poems about the seasons, about one's longings, about things. There are sonnets, building up to the predestinate last line; there is syllabic blank verse, with every urge of cadence ironed out; there are unrhymed hexameters and some rhymed stanza-patterns, original yet not seeming so. The book might tell the story and the tastes of a thousand women; yet only one woman could have written it, as we now can see in light touches there and there. As with the Italian primitives, the attitudes are the stock ones, but the landscape behind is fresh—the flowers are real flowers and the weather real weather.

It is this honesty which constitutes the greatest promise of the book. It was built of what she knew. There are memories of childhood—of her grandfather's house at Roxbury, of the fruit-garden at Brookline, of the field of blue gentians at Medford, of climbing in trees or watching brook-trout. The most personal poem in the book is 'The Fairy Tale,' which records the curse upon her earliest years. (p. 187)

The influence of Keats, of course, is strong in the book, yet not after the customary manner. There are no imitations of his poems or mannerisms, no borrowings, no seeing things through his eyes or describing them with his pen. But the format of the book is his; the title comes from Shelley's elegy written to him; two poems offer him direct homage; and the first, and best, poem in the book, 'Before the Altar,' uses the basic symbol of his 'Endymion.'

This altar is pagan; the deity is the moon. A man stands worshipping; he has nothing to offer, except his life, his heart, to a moon which gives no sign of answer. No Indian Maid offers a perplexed comfort, no choruses celebrate a coming marriage in the skies; there is nothing but a despairing, unassuageable desire.

Although this poem is iambic and rhymed, the irregular line-lengths and rhyme-pattern show the influence of French *vers libre*. Miss Lowell later was to claim it as her first experiment in free verse. (p. 188)

A Dome of Many-Coloured Glass contains few hints of the real Amy Lowell, with her gustoes and wit and daring and drama and ideas and colors and sounds: it represents rather Miss Lowell as she then underestimated herself, blighted by properties, and almost paralyzed by despair. Furthermore, although her material was genuine as far as it went, the conventionality of the expression made it unconvincing. (p. 190)

A Dome of Many-Coloured Glass was, briefly, the traditional 'first book' in which the author had gone as far as she could by herself, and had succeeded in saying a few things of her own, though not in her own way. It is to be respected for the persistence, almost the heroism, of working ten years without any instruction or aid from outsiders; and for the boldness in supposing that alone and unaided one could produce great poetry. But in those days, few people knew that there was anything to *learn* about writing poetry: one read, one wrote, and that was all. (pp. 191-92)

Amy Lowell's career really began with *Sword Blades and Poppy Seed*. She was forty years old. Her ten years of writing virtually unaided had brought her as far as she could go without expert aid; her first volume *A Dome of Many-Coloured Glass*, had as it were cleared her brain; her association with Pound and the Imagists had opened her eyes and sharpened her technique; and finally we might suggest that even the schism [between Pound and Lowell] had done its bit by making her completely independent. (p. 253)

[Lowell] believed that poetry was a spoken art—was communicative and not merely self-expressive—that no poem was complete until it had functioned in the mind of its audience. This belief not only saved her from the vitiating preciosity of 'Art for Art's sake,' but caused her to build her poems of genuine human material in an emotional, or dramatic, structure. Thus the Imagist monotone became varied and alive. (pp. 254-55)

The very title of *Sword Blades and Poppy Seed* proclaims a reaching out beyond Imagistic ends. 'Sword blades' are fighting truths; 'poppy seed,' lulling dreams. The title-poem is a fantastic tale explaining that these two, truth and beauty, are the twin functions of literature. This idea is presented in narrative form: the poet buys his swords and seeds of a strange old man ('Ephraim Bard, dealer in words'), pays as price his whole existence, and the sun rises. (p. 255)

[Polyphonic prose] is the most various and supple poetic form ever devised in English. It runs without let or hindrance from one rhythm into another, according to the mood of the moment; it allows the use of any and every device known to versification, the only restriction being that 'the sound should be an echo to the sense.' Nothing quite like it had ever been known in English before. . . . Miss Lowell, in her search for a form capable of the greatest versatility and expressiveness, invented polyphonic prose, and later used it for some of her most magnificent work. It is a difficult form, however; not many others have been able to manage it.

The three pieces of polyphonic prose in [*Sword Blades and Poppy Seed*] ('The Basket,' 'In a Castle,' and 'The Forsaken') are three tragedies of love, with contrasted heroines, one cold, one adulterous, and one faithfully loving. 'The Basket' is a symbolic puzzle which Miss Lowell always refused to explain. But again we find a man consumed by a passion which is inadequately returned; art and religion are elements in the affair; the conflagration is the familiar disaster; and the moon with geranium eyes at the end is again the sterile, unresponsive, maddening symbol. 'In a Castle' is a tale of Gothic crime ending in murder and suicide. 'The Forsaken' is the prayer of a girl who has been callously abandoned.

As with the narratives, most of the lyrics in the book are conventional in form—indeed, just about three-quarters of the book, counting by pages, is metrical. The best lyrics, however, are those in free verse. 'A Lady' and 'The Taxi' proved by all odds the most popular of the volume. 'The Captured Goddess,' which opened the first section of the book, gives the first evidence of that fresh delight in pure color which later was to blind so many critics to the solider qualities of her work. (pp. 257-58)

The surface of [the] poems [in *Can Grande's Castle*] is a brilliant series of magic-lantern dissolving views of the past. They depict various civilizations at those critical points when one is hurled against another, to the subjugation and even the destruction of the physically weaker. But the real subject is not historical: it is rather the survival of civilization in the eternal struggle against war. The superficial pictures are splendid with the colors of life; they represent the arts and amusements which constitute a civilization; but behind these pictures are at work the acquisitive and destructive forces which give meaning to the poems—a meaning anything but splendid. The surface is life, the depths are death; combined, the result is history.

In reading *Can Grande's Castle,* then, one must watch the flow of seemingly unrelated pictures of carnivals and triumphs and love-affairs and horse-races with an eye to what they signify in human society, for they were selected to illustrate and explain the civilization under discussion. The flow is life itself; war is the death-force that destroys them. The splendor of the surface sheds no glamour upon the meaning; Amy Lowell was not glorifying war. (pp. 469-70)

Amy Lowell, after the historical studies which produced *Can Grande's Castle,* delved yet deeper for *Legends,* going into folklore, which is the very tap-root of literature. Her new book contained seven symbolic tales, three tales of superstition, and one dramatic lyric. (p. 557)

The first poem, 'Memorandum Confided by a Yucca to a Passion-Vine,' (or 'From a Yucca to a Passion Vine,' as the running-title put it—which in her letters she sometimes reduced briefly to 'The Yucca'), is a Peruvian legend. . . . It is another poem of that moon-worship which had been the theme of the first poem in her first book. . . . The Inca texture of the poem is a triumph, from the opening torrid sunrise and the chattering animals, to that extraordinary reascent of the defiled moon at the end; and of course Amy Lowell would never miss the gold temple of the Sun, the silver temple of the Moon, and the garden of precious metals. The versification swings from rhymed meter to unrhymed free verse and back with such deftness that it is quite unobtrusive. The action is so dramatic and the poem so musical that it is almost a ballet. . . . (p. 558)

Amy Lowell was predestinate to write a biography of John Keats. The history of her book might be traced back to the day when the girl of fifteen, devouring Leigh Hunt's *Imagination and Fancy,* discovered that a poet called Keats had once lived, and was actually in her father's library. But it really begins when the woman of thirty-one bought all the Keats material in the Locker-Lampson sale, including the manuscript of the 'Eve of St. Agnes'; this became the nucleus of her own collection, which grew steadily until it was, as she believed, the largest in the world. (p. 672)

When she began this collection, she had already been writing poetry for a few years, but she always claimed that she learned more about poetic composition from the manuscript of the 'Eve of St. Agnes' than from any book or human being. . . . [It] was Keats, of all poets, who was nearest to the Imagist ideals: none other had ever attempted so thoroughly to describe things as they appear to the senses illumined by the imagination, without the intrusion of morals or personalities. It was Keats who had opened Amy Lowell's five senses, and had taught her the meaning of love, physical and spiritual. It is significant, I think, that they both had a cult of the moon. (pp. 673-74)

It is not surprising, then, that the format of her own first book was copied from the format of Keats's 1820 *Lamia;* the first and best poem in it utilized the moon-symbol of *Endymion,* and two other poems were frankly inspired by Keats. (p. 675)

The biography which she proposed to write was to be simultaneously a psychological novel, a book of poetic criticism, and a contribution to scholarship. (p. 677)

John Keats she saw, not as a Poet, a Being Apart, with dishevelled locks, wild eyes, and a halo, but rather as the kind of pleasant young man who might live next door, with a remarkable gift for writing. (p. 679)

[The] chief genius of her book [lies in her] sympathetic, unsentimentalized narrative of a thoroughly human young man, as he lived, worked, and died. One does not feel him as belonging essentially to another century and civilization: the differences of costume and custom, which would figure so largely in the picturesque type of biography, are here relegated to their proper unimportance. It is a psychological novel indeed, though without dabbling in the superficialities of the 'stream of consciousness' or the profundities of psychoanalysis—a psychological novel in which the chief strands of the narrative are Keats's brain, his heart, his nerves, also his vocation, his money, and his disease. Particularly, it is a study of the development of his genius. . . . (pp. 679-80)

But her best work was done in straightening out Keats's relations with Fanny Brawne. The mawkish and false interpretations of that affair had worked to the great discredit both of the young girl and her lover; and it was Amy Lowell who first applied a sympathetic common sense to the tragic situation. (p. 680)

The biography as a whole showed remarkable insight into poetic psychology, such as was possible only for one poet writing on another. Amy Lowell traced the emergence and heading up of Keats's inspiration; quoted the best lines and told why they were good. . . .

As a work of scholarship, the book is such a contribution to knowledge that no one henceforth can write on Keats without taking Amy Lowell's book into account. (p. 682)

But though she kept the proper subordination of scholarship to criticism, and criticism to biography, the scholarship

sometimes obtruded, chiefly because she enjoyed it so much. Full of the ardor of the chase after facts, she was sure that the excitement would be communicated; but the unscholarly reader, interested only in the results, was confused when she made up her mind in print. (p. 683)

There can be no question but that death cut Amy Lowell's career short. She showed not a sign of having been written out; her work was advancing steadily, interrupted though it had been by the biography of Keats. She should have had at least a decade more. (p. 723)

And though ten years have passed since her death, the time has not come yet to pronounce upon her place in the poetic firmament. Such a judgement cannot be passed until the poet has sunk into obscurity and then re-emerged. The poetry of Amy Lowell has not been forgotten. Her books sell; the anthologies find it essential to include specimens of her work; the historians of American poetry discuss her achievements lengthily. She remains a living force.

But it is possible to indicate some of her achievements.

First of all, unquestionably she wrote poems—and how many expert versifiers achieve reputations without ever quite achieving a single poem! The test is simple but severe. Look over the anthologies issued in her lifetime, and observe how irretrievably the bulk of verse then thought worth preserving has faded and disintegrated, until scarcely a single adjective is left. What experiments that failed! what promises never fulfilled! But Amy Lowell's poems are as fresh and vital as when they were first written. Their gusto and brilliance and tenderness are untouched. Indeed, if anything, they seem to have matured: future generations will never conceive how perverse and puzzling many of these poems appeared at first printing, which now are so straightforward, unaffected, and inevitable.

In her work, she extended the strait limitations of the poetry of her day, in both method and substance.

Her sense of larger rhythms led her to transcend the metrical foot as the basis of her *vers libre;* she used the line, or cadence, as the fundamental unit, emphasizing also the paragraph or strophe as a larger unit. Her structures were built both according to the thought and the feeling; and her polyphonic prose established the ultimate of the principle of rhythmical (or dramatic) variation.

In substance, she got away completely from her predecessors' doleful egotism, effeminacy, and conventional moralizings, by recording life as one knows it, not as former poets had written of it. Her flowers came from the gardens of Sevenels or the fields of Dublin, not from the limited *hortus siccus* of the literary past. Her five senses ranged freely in her search for sharper and more inclusive perceptions of reality. In 'Lilacs' alone one may study out how she saw shapes and colors, heard sounds, smelled perfumes, touched things, appreciated spatial relationships, then brought her culture to bear upon her subject, invoking its aesthetic significance and its historical past, until the depths of her experience were stirred, to release a variety of seemingly unrelated things; yet at the end, her completed poem was a human unity.

Amy Lowell was the first of our poets to take full advantage of the civilizations across both the Atlantic and Pacific, and yet remain thoroughly American.

She brought back to life the limited and over-conventionalized emotions deemed appropriate to verse, and added others, until the whole range of human feeling was laid open. Her poems express gusto, wit, anger, fun, sensuousness, fear, tenderness, contempt, despair, bitterness, and delight of all kinds. Thus she broke completely with the traditional poetic monotone, which in some quarters had reverted to actual intoning. This suppleness of voice informs all her poems, long and short, and accounts in part for their effectiveness when read in public. But besides being dramatic, her poems are also musical; they inspired hundreds of composers to write for permission to set her lyrics.

Her variety of subject-matter was endless. She told stories of all kinds, realistic, romantic, symbolic, about times past and present; she also wrote lyrics, satires, monodramas, and epics after her own formula. As a result of this profusion, she was the despair of the contemporary pigeon-holers, who were at a loss to place her, in spite of the fact that her personality came out clearly in all she wrote. That she wrote objectively as well as autobiographically added to the difficulty.

But the sensorial and emotional aspects of her writings were usually the expression of her thought. She experienced life intelligently as well as passionately; her convictions about it were the true substance of her poetry. She had various things to say, and she had to say them. Whether studying the course of human history or delving into the dim foundations of the individual soul, she wrote honestly, courageously, and brilliantly. Her poetry thus expresses the complete human being: it includes brain as well as the heart and senses. But the public, used to verse that was intellectually negligible, and even believing that intelligence and poetry were incompatible, usually overlooked her message—which was as well, for that message was often dangerously liberal.

Thinking as well as feeling, she naturally became a critic as well as poet. Criticism in America has so often been confused with book-notices that her importance in this field has been underestimated; but there can be no doubt that she won her place among the few critics of importance whom America has produced.

Her attitude towards the arts was actually a contribution to aesthetic philosophy. Taking for granted that happiness was the test of a successful life or civilization, she placed the higher pleasures—the arts—as the purpose and climax of our existence. This conviction of hers was so complete that she hardly bothered to labor so obvious a point; but it is the implication and trend that lay behind all her aesthetic dicta. These dicta, scattered through her prefaces and other critical writings, could easily be arranged into a complete system. Had she lived longer, she might well have done so herself.

She was far more explicit about her conceptions of poetry. It was the expression of experience, to which nothing human was alien; and to express experience more effectively, she extended the bounds of rhythm and form. She did not seek for originality in her theory, but for fundamentals, which she was content to clarify and reaffirm. Her indebtedness to the Imagists and such other theorists as Hunt and Hulme was obvious and frank; perhaps only her theory of symbolism was wholly her own.

The development of her theory of criticism is demonstrated in her three critical books. *Six French Poets* introduced the chief post-*Symboliste* writers to America, and opened their new realms of experience to her readers. *Tendencies in Modern American Poetry* detected and defined the deep trend of the 'New Poetry' and made its chief personalities vivid in the public mind. Amy Lowell's treatment of their poems as springing on the one hand from their lives and on the other from the time-spirit was precise and convincing. Her *John Keats* went still further. It was scholarly in its accumulation of facts, critical in her explanation of his work, and creative in the telling of his life.

But had Amy Lowell written nothing at all, she still would have earned an important place in American literary history by her crusading for the New Poetry. She, more than any other single person, challenged and defeated the forces of public ignorance, indifference, and contempt, and of aesthetic egotism, snobbery, and envy. Her rousing of the public was something of a miracle. In 1912, it believed firmly that Beauty was Prettiness plus a Moral, that all poetry was effeminate, and that all the great poets were dead forever. It had no taste, no knowledge; it was disturbed at vitality, fluttered at originality, indignant at significance, and completely baffled by the unfamiliar. But never once compromising with the public lack of taste, she made it listen to the works of our leading poets and buy their books, coerced the dictators of literary fashions to support them, and in spite of parodies and violent personal attacks, broke the belief that America could produce no poetry, and built up a national audience. When a nation supports a great art, a renaissance is in progress.

Of course she did not do this single-handed; she was merely the chief spokesman for a national art. Advertising breaks down after a while, if the goods do not come up to specifications. Her championing of Imagism succeeded, where a hundred imitative movements since have failed, because the principles of Imagism were the results of the lengthy observations and arguments of many persons. The poets were already writing, the poetry magazines were beginning to appear, and the New Poetry was already well rooted when Amy Lowell took charge. But it was the moment for somebody who combined creative ability, critical integrity, and a powerful personality to take the leadership. Amy Lowell was the person who assumed that leadership.

The result was a general rejuvenation of American literature. Even those who despised Free Verse and Imagism found themselves writing with greater clarity and conciseness and intensity and truthfulness.

These were the public accomplishments of Amy Lowell; of the private ones, the full tale will never be told. She constantly was seeking out good poets in the making, talking over their manuscripts, recommending them to editors, even selling their poems for them at times. Literary merit was her sole test here: she discounted personal friendships and enmities as far as possible. Any private charities were chalked up as service to the art, never as personal obligations.

Hampered by constant illness, by a late beginning, by all the forces of bitter egotisms and literary enmities, and an early death, none the less she fought her way to the top. Elsie Sergeant spoke truly when she said: 'Amy Lowell was a dynasty in herself.' (pp. 723-28)

S. Foster Damon, in his Amy Lowell: A Chronicle, *first edition, 1935 (copyright 1935, 1963 by S. Foster Damon; reprinted by permission of Archon Books, Hamden, Connecticut), Archon Books, 1966.*

One day when Amy Lowell was sixteen, a Boston schoolgirl—"ugly, fat, conspicuous, and dull," she told her diary—

"Oh Lord please let it be all right, & let Paul love me, & don't let me be a fool"—

One day in her father's library she found *Imagination and Fancy*

(A book by Leigh Hunt, subtitled *Selections from the English Poets, illustrative of those first requisites of their art; with markings of the best passages, critical notices of the writers, and an essay in answer to the question "What Is Poetry?"*).

She read it, she devoured it, she seized upon the poets quoted: Shelley, Coleridge, Beaumont and Fletcher, Keats;

Keats most of all.

Then in her busy school days and again in her young womanhood, jilted, ill, despondent, she forgot herself in Keats.

All her life she was in love with John Keats, she was the sweetheart, the disciple, the wife, the adoring aunt, the invalid mother of John Keats. . . . (p. 278)

For his dear sake she befriended and scolded dozens of young poets, most of them neither grateful nor talented;

For his dear sake she assembled manuscripts and letters, the world's largest collection of Keatsiana;

For his dear sake she wrote a memorial biography, working night after night to decipher the almost illegible notes he left on the margins of his books, and rupturing the blood vessels in her eyes from too much study.

Three months after publishing her two-volume life of Keats she had a fatal stroke.

She died from overwork, she died for the love of John Keats. (p. 279)

Malcolm Cowley, "Poem for Amy Lowell," in The New Republic *(reprinted by permission of* The New Republic; © *1936 by The New Republic, Inc.), January 8, 1936 (and reprinted in* Think Back on Us . . . : A Contemporary Chronicle of the 1930's by Malcolm Cowley, *edited by Henry Dan Piper, Southern Illinois University Press, 1967, pp. 278-82).*

In one of the early issues of *Poetry,* founded in Chicago by Harriet Monroe in 1912, Miss Lowell saw pieces by Ezra Pound, listed as a young Philadelphia poet, and some unusual verses signed "H.D., Imagiste.". . . The summer of 1913 she went to England to see what it was all about. She visited Henry James, who, old and disappointed, told her that if she wanted to write she should stay in America. She met all of the Imagistes. She found out all there was to know about Imagisme—how a young Englishman, T. E. Hulme, had conceived the idea, how Ezra Pound had become the sponsor for the movement, and how H.D. and

John Gould Fletcher, also Americans, were enthusiastic over it. Her future course was determined by the time she left England. She was not *an* Imagiste; she was *the* Imagiste. (p. 81)

To Miss Lowell Imagism was never more than a stimulation. The celebrated Imagist credo published in *Some Imagist Poets: an Anthology* (1915)—calling for the *mot juste,* free choice of subject, organic rhythm, exact imagery, definiteness, and concentration—is only a part of the Amy Lowell credo. Imagism merely gave her the clue for developing a style as distinct as her own individuality. (p. 82)

And writing was by no means all that filled Miss Lowell's career. She was employing a new idiom, and she felt dutybound to acquaint America with its effectiveness. The verse she wrote was for the ear, and no one could recite it as well as she. (pp. 82-3)

Miss Lowell's genius did not lie in her talent; it lay in her energy. She was not a born poet. She made herself a poet through strength of will and determination. Perhaps she will remain (as she is regarded now) more important for her personality and her influence than for her writing. Yet there seems to be a lasting ring in her often repeated cry for man to emancipate himself from those conventions which bar him from enjoyment of the world's beauty. . . . More than half of her poems are narrative—legends, ballads, historical tales. In her emphasis on sense impression she usually lost the story. When she did not lose it, she created an effective tale—as in "The Book of Hours of Sister Clotilde" and "Sky Blue and Blood Red". . . . Amy Lowell was not a Keats. But she was one of the most successful of the many Keats imitators. (pp. 83-4)

Vernon Loggins, in his I Hear America . . . : Literature in the United States Since 1900 *(copyright 1937 by Thomas Y. Crowell Company; reprinted by permission of Thomas Y. Crowell Co., Inc.), Crowell, 1937.*

Was she a great poet? Was Amy Lowell a poet at all? . . .

She was reputed to have said that the Lord had made her a businessman, but that she, herself, had made herself a poet; and Harriet Monroe, who had many traits in common with her, always insisted that Amy Lowell had everything but genius. (p. 183)

When *A Dome of Many-coloured Glass* appeared. . . , it was exactly the sort of book to be expected of a New England Lowell. Examining it now, more than three decades after its publication, one can agree with almost everything that had been said of it by the critics of its own time. The poems it contained were delicate, feminine, yet flat and honest; they were innocent of verbal distinction, and yet had less clumsiness and more polish than the later work written in the flush tide of her notoriety. S. Foster Damon [see excerpt above] has summed up the entire book in a single sentence: "As with the Italian primitives, the attitudes are the stock ones, but the landscape behind is fresh—the flowers are real flowers and the weather real weather."

Meanwhile, the first book opened the excitements and the fervors of the literary world to her. She was no longer Miss Amy Lowell of Sevenells, but Amy Lowell, the poet, who had published a book, and if her quick, intelligent mind (for her critical abilities always ran far beyond the reaches of her creative powers) knew that her first book was not all it should have been, she resolved to learn, to experiment, to spread her range of feeling over wider areas, to make a real test of whatever talents and abilities she felt that she possessed. (p. 187)

The impressionistic freedom, the flowing, fluctuating rhythms of vers libre seemed to open new possibilities for the art of poetry and Amy Lowell studied them carefully.... [When she met Ezra Pound in London, it] was a case of the irresistible force meeting the immovable object, of Mahomet and the mountain coming together; great things were bound to happen and, of course, they did. The "poetic renaissance" now swung out into a full stream of achievement—and publicity.

After Amy Lowell's battle for vers libre was over (and it was over in 1922), after the corpses had been counted and the survivors decorated (they were very few in number), one felt that something had been achieved. The public had actually caught something of the general excitement felt by the poets; the dead weight of dull and academic verse (in its worst sense) had been lifted and cleared away, and an atmosphere was created in which every good poet of the period felt himself at liberty to work. (pp. 187-88)

With each new book of poems, Amy Lowell's reputation increased, and if some of the better critics were silent, the furore she caused on lecture platforms, the vigor, the valor, and good sense with which she fought for the poetry of others as well as her own brought sustained applause from her large audiences.... Everything around her seemed to be prospering, her work seemed to be gaining the widest possible recognition, her house seemed always to be filled with admiring friends. But from time to time, through the words or hints of friends who admired her as a person, she received a few doubts—worded delicately, of course—the intimation of something that was not overwhelming praise. (p. 189)

Amy Lowell's imagination was vivid, often exact and always clear, and she could describe a flower, the effect of beech and of pine trees as they appeared to her sight through a heavy sunlight or an object of art with memorable vividness. Like many writers of the 1920's, ... Amy Lowell was, among other things, a poet of virtu, celebrating her favorite bric-a-brac, her memories of brightly costumed periods in history, and of fine furniture. Of the school to which this style of writing belongs, Amy Lowell's "Patterns" will remain as good an example as any. The poem still retains its traces of color and movement, yet one feels always that it is a portrait of an eighteenth-century scene re-created by a writer whose feet are too firmly planted in the nineteenth or twentieth century. Despite, or perhaps because of, the theatrical note which enters it, "Patterns" will remain the most representative of all Amy Lowell's more ambitious poems.

"The Sisters," a study of Elizabeth Browning and Emily Dickinson, also contains Amy Lowell's characteristic conversational manner and lively interest in her subject. But a lesser-known poem, "On Looking at a Copy of Alice Meynell's Poems Given to Me Years Ago by a Friend," has a distinction and a delicacy she rarely attained.... [We] find ourselves praising her for the remarkable something that speaks best *between* rather than *in* the lines of this poem and all her poetry. (pp. 190-91)

Horace Gregory and Marya Zaturenska, "Amy Lowell, Literary Statesman," in their A History of American Poetry: 1900-1940 *(© 1942, 1944, 1946 by Harcourt, Brace and Company, Inc.; reprinted by permission of Horace Gregory), Harcourt, 1946 (and reprinted by Gordian Press, 1969), pp. 182-91.*

Sword Blades and Poppy Seed . . . disclosed the fact that in the two years [since the publication of *A Dome of Many-Coloured Glass*] Miss Lowell had learned more than she had in the previous ten [years of studying poetry]. Although about three-fourths of the book consisted of poems in meter, the best poems were those in vers libre, a mode of writing verse on which she commented in a preface. To the French term "vers libre," which had already won acceptance in English, she preferred the term "unrhymed cadence" for several reasons. It connotes the fact that the basis of this species of writing is, as she termed it, "organic," varying with the rhythms of breathing. And it connotes the intermediate patterning of such writing: less regular than metrical verse, but exhibiting, more pronouncedly than prose, the occurrence of stresses and of what she called a "curve," by which she seemed to mean a greater premonition of an appropriate ending in any beginning. Yet in spite of the flexibility and "subtlety" of cadenced verse, she insisted that "it is constructed upon mathematical and absolute laws of balance and time."

Moreover, for three poems dealing with thwarted love Miss Lowell chose "polyphonic prose," which she described more fully in the preface to a later volume, *Can Grande's Castle*. (pp. 18-19)

Vers libre or free verse is of course in no degree synonymous with Imagism. The latter is a species of doctrine and practice connected with the referential content of verse; the former is a species of doctrine and practice connected with the phonetic structure of verse. But the two were often concomitant. Amy Lowell believed herself to be a practitioner of Imagism; she certainly *was* a practitioner of free verse. It was this auditory aspect of her evangel that evoked the most passionate controversy. And, as her discussions of her technical innovations exemplify, an auditory concern was conspicuous in Miss Lowell's own consciousness.... Miss Lowell's emphasis on poet as minstrel, however much by chance it augured a future of radio and television, was in its literary result a reaffirmation of a tradition of the past, and tended to exclude from her verse, save only occasionally, the more or less clearly indicated overtones of meaning and undertones of preconception characteristic of poetry of first importance today.

From Miss Lowell's prose in her explanatory prefaces, and of course elsewhere, several others of her traits can be adduced. For one thing, her innovations are not indicative of a salient originality. Though she acquired a considerable skill in verse technique, her novelties were, as she acknowledges in her account of "polyphonic prose," developments of what she had found in other writers. For another thing, allied to her enthusiasm for new poets and poetries was a decided tendency to overstate. She declares that the laws governing free-verse cadences are "absolute" and "mathematical." Yet nowhere does she provide any definitions of these laws, any criteria with respect to which absoluteness might be established. (pp. 20-1)

[Although] Amy Lowell was accounted leader of the Imagist movement after Pound withdrew . . . , it is questionable whether she is best described as an Imagist poet. Ezra Pound certainly thought not; he derisively termed her views and verse "Amygism." A distinguishing feature of Imagism as originally propounded was brevity. The genesis of an Imagist poem was to be the presentation of an image—usually, though not necessarily, visual—not depicted with all the details appropriate to it, nor even with all the constituents ordinarily thought of as essential to it. Rather, it was to be identified through some one of its features or aspects. This single focus would oftenest be conveyed, however, through a comparison or allusion to something else. By virtue of this comparison, a new insight into the nature of the originating image would be communicated. Furthermore, the comparison might confer upon the image a status in some wider realm of reference—nature, life, love, time, eternity—but, again, often by implication from a compact mention, though the derivative image might be somewhat more discursive. (Ezra Pound has spoken of this mode of generating a poem as "a form of superposition.") (pp. 22-3)

[While] Imagism was congenial to her penchant for noticing her surroundings, the Imagist stress on conciseness was quite antipathetic to her temperament. Whatever Miss Lowell's virtues, succinctness, except sometimes in repartee, was not among them. Her energy and enthusiasm impelled her to write on, often beyond the limit that a more careful artist would set for himself. She was lavish in her use of repetition as a means of coherence and emphasis. (Perhaps this repetitiveness was in part the meaning of her term "return.") (p. 25)

Imagism typically begins with the thing seen, and finds for it a significance. Symbolism begins with a significance, and finds for it an embodiment in an image. This "significance" may be a conviction or attitude or mood definite enough to be expressed as an assertion; but more characteristically, it is so subtle or elusive as to seem inexpressible with any exactness apart from the particular embodiment given to it in the poem. Miss Lowell was by no means a Symbolist in the more narrowly technical sense; yet a half-dozen or so of her poems can be found in the whole range of her work that similarly elude dogmatic analysis. The frequently anthologized "Meeting-House Hill" is one such poem. Another is the narrative "The Book of Hours of Sister Clotilde" in her second book. (pp. 25-6)

Miss Lowell's command of cadence and color, and her ability to sustain animation, are amazing. But to be amazed so prolongedly results at last in exhausted stupefaction. The experience is akin to traversing interminable corridors adorned with tapestries whose patterns are intricate, insistent, and, finally, incapacitating. (pp. 30-1)

When Miss Lowell's biography, *John Keats,* was published . . . , she had achieved the book into which she had put her most intense and prolonged efforts, her deepest interests, and probably what became her chief ambition. She might well have been satisfied with a posthumous fame as the outstanding Keats scholar of the twentieth century. (p. 42)

F. Cudworth Flint, in his Amy Lowell *(American Writers Pamphlet No. 82;* © *1969, University of Minnesota), University of Minnesota Press, Minneapolis, 1969.*

Eugene O'Neill

1888-1953

American playwright and recipient of the Nobel Prize for Literature in 1936, the first of his countrymen to be so honored. The son of a professional actor, O'Neill was brought up on the road. Motivated by his father's wish that his sons attend college, O'Neill enrolled in Princeton in 1906. With the pressure of his mother's recurring mental illness, his own failure to pass college examinations, and a short and unsuccessful marriage, O'Neill attempted suicide and then ran away to sea. His years as a seaman yielded much material for his later writing. It was during a period of convalescence in a tuberculosis sanatorium that he assiduously applied himself to playwriting. O'Neill studied for a year at Harvard (1914), joining George Pierce Baker's drama workshop. Shortly thereafter, the Provincetown Players performed his *Bound East for Cardiff*, marking the beginning of both his career and of serious American theater. His work falls into three periods. The early plays, written 1913-18, are primarily one-act dramas of the sea. The seven plays written between 1921 and 1925 are much larger in ambition and earned O'Neill the acclaim of his contemporaries. With the exception of *Desire under the Elms*, most of these plays have not stood the test of time. The mid-1920s through 1934 are a continuation of the second period and mark the midpoint of O'Neill's career. During this time he experimented with many stylistic devices including the interior monologue, stream-of-consciousness dialogue, the aside, symbolic masks, the chorus, thematic repetition, and mythological motifs. *Mourning Becomes Electra* is the masterpiece of this period. O'Neill retreated from public life abruptly in 1934 and for twelve years worked on a cycle of one-act plays (of which *Hughie* is a small masterpiece) and a cycle of full-length plays. His work was frustrated by disease and repeated suffering from alcoholism and family neuroses. The last and finest stage of his career began with the triumph of *The Iceman Cometh*, and O'Neill re-emerged to resume the throne that he had relinquished. In this period he reaches the universal through the personal; there is no better example of this than the torturous working out of his past in *Long Day's Journey into Night*. Critics have often found fault with O'Neill's literary abilities, disparaging his use of language and philosophical pretensions. His best work, however, transcends his technical limitations with the power of its passion and its masterful sense of theater.

PRINCIPAL WORKS

Before Breakfast (drama) 1916

Bound East for Cardiff (drama) 1919
The Dreamy Kid (drama) 1919
Ile (drama) 1919
In the Zone (drama) 1919
The Long Voyage Home (drama) 1919
The Moon of the Caribbees (drama) 1919
The Rope (drama) 1919
Where the Cross Is Made (drama) 1919
Beyond the Horizon (drama) 1920
Diff'rent (drama) 1920
Gold (drama) 1920
The Straw (drama) 1920
The Emperor Jones (drama) 1921
Anna Christie (drama) 1922
The First Man (drama) 1922
The Hairy Ape (drama) 1922
All God's Chillun Got Wings (drama) 1924
Welded (drama) 1924
Desire under the Elms (drama) 1925
The Fountain (drama) 1925
The Great God Brown (drama) 1925
Lazarus Laughed (drama) 1927
Marco Millions (drama) 1927
Strange Interlude (drama) 1928
Dynamo (drama) 1929
Mourning Becomes Electra (drama) 1931
Ah, Wilderness! (drama) 1933
Days without End (drama) 1934
The Iceman Cometh (drama) 1946
A Moon for the Misbegotten (drama) 1952
Long Day's Journey into Night (drama) 1956
A Touch of the Poet (drama) 1957
Hughie (drama) 1959

We have in O'Neill evidence a-plenty of a predisposition for the dramatic that is as pronounced as the Barrymore inheritance. But we have one who has lived so remote from the theatre that he has been uncorrupted by the merely theatrical and has carried over into his own workshop not one of the worn stencils and battered properties which are the dust-covered accumulations of years.

This same remoteness, which so freshens the air of [*Beyond the Horizon*], is probably responsible, also, for its considerable impracticability. He was an impractical playwright, for instance, who wrote into his play the character of a two-year-old girl and gave her two long scenes with business to do and lines to speak. He might have known that the part would have to be given to a child disturbingly, almost comically older than the baby called for by the context.

Certainly it was a quite impractical playwright who split each of his three acts into two scenes, one outside and one inside the Mayo farmhouse. (pp. 136-37)

Some of a novelist's luxuries must be forgone by a writer when he goes into the theatre, and one of the lessons he must learn is that the ever illusion-dispelling process of dropping a curtain, releasing an audience and shifting a scene is accepted twice and sometimes three times by a modern audience without even an unconscious resistance. But any further interruption works havoc with the spell. It may be reported here that, at the second performance, the third act was telescoped into a single scene, and it may be guessed that the play would not only be a better knit but a much more popular piece if the same violence were done the other acts as soon as possible. (p. 137)

> *Alexander Woollcott, "'Beyond the Horizon',' in* The New York Times *(© 1920 by The New York Times Company; reprinted by permission), February 8, 1920 (and reprinted in* O'Neill and His Plays: Four Decades of Criticism, *edited by Oscar Cargill, N. Bryllion Fagin, and William J. Fisher, New York University Press, 1961, pp. 135-39).*

As a rule, the plays of O'Neill are singularly uninviting on the printed page. The dialogue is raw and prosaic, in texture quite undistinguished, and the author has made no attempt to appeal to the imagination by way of the stage directions, which are not lifted above the baldness of the prompt-book. These plays appear too often, in short, as rather second-rate naturalistic pieces that owe their eminence, not to their intrinsic greatness, but, as Marx said of John Stuart Mill, "to the flatness of the surrounding country." (p. 99)

But Eugene O'Neill has another vein in which he is a literary artist of genius. When he is writing the more or less grammatical dialogue of the middle-class characters of his plays, his prose is heavy and indigestible even beyond the needs of naturalism. People say the same things to one another over and over again and never succeed in saying them any more effectively than the first time; long speeches shuffle dragging feet, marking time without progressing, for pages. But as soon as Mr. O'Neill gets a character who can only talk some kind of vernacular, he begins to write like a poet. (p. 100)

Two of Mr. O'Neill's chief assets are, first, a nervous driving force that carries the audience inescapably along; and, second, a gift for the eloquent use of the various forms of the American vernacular. (p. 103)

Mr. O'Neill has another qualification which sets him completely apart from the other American dramatists, who have so far done very little more than modify the conventional American comedy in the direction of Shaw or Sinclair Lewis: he nearly always, with whatever crudeness, is expressing some real experience, some impact directly from life. The characters and the scene in O'Neill are sometimes forbiddingly bleak . . . but they are likely at any moment, by taking on the power and the awfulness of naked natural forces, to establish a violent contact between themselves and us. . . . Mr. O'Neill, with this sort of subject from ordinary middle-class life [in *Welded,* a monotonous drama of marriage,] does not pay enough attention to style. A play, like anything else that is built of words, is primarily a work of literature, and even the most vigorous dramatic idea cannot be trusted to make its effect without the right words to convey it. All but the greatest of actors are liable to betray a careless text, but an accurate and brilliant text will manage to speak for itself in spite of the very worst. The expressiveness of Mr. O'Neill seems to diminish in direct proportion to his distance from the language of the people. At one pole, you have *The Hairy Ape,* certainly his best-written play; at the other *Welded,* perhaps his worst. In *All God's Chillun Got Wings,* you see his quality rising and falling—between the stale language of stock-company melodrama and the vivid, the racy, the real. (p. 104)

> *Edmund Wilson, "Eugene O'Neill as Prose Writer" (1922) and "'All God's Chillun' and Others" (1924), in his* The Shores of Light: A Literary Chronicle of the Twenties and Thirties *(reprinted with the permission of Farrar, Straus & Giroux, Inc.; copyright 1952 by Edmund Wilson), Farrar, Straus and Young, 1952, pp. 99-104.*

[O'Neill's] spirit was made up of almost equal parts of deeply articulate proletarian and surface poet, with both blended to an undistinguishable whole. In using the noun "proletarian," I do not mean to indicate that he was in any way a social-radical. The underdog in one of his plays is a trapped, snarling, futile being, with recalcitrant feelings that lead only to fears, and profanities, and heavy toil, and the swishing of fists against his companions, and with barely enough mind to realize—in his most depressed moments— his own insignificant and enslaved condition. In his first plays, O'Neill wrenched human beings from the heaving mud of life but did not give them sermons, and voluble "aspirations" toward "freedom." Their dialogues were more restrained and cogent under his direction than they would have been in actual saloons, dives, ships, and jungles, but they were usually, in faithful and innate detail, expressions of the characters themselves, as far as any creator could make them so and still retain the unobtrusive aversions and dislikes that formed his individuality. . . .

Of course, ten years can turn topsy-turvy the surfaces and even the purposes of a man, and the present Eugene O'Neill has become the hero of a more polished and restricted environment . . . and the former boisterous renegade-creator has altered to a reserved and polite-mannered gentleman, with a distant look in his eyes. Practically the same alterations can be observed in his latter plays, *All God's Chillun Got Wings, Desire Under the Elms,* and *The Fountain,* where the old O'Neill is abdicating to a more "aesthetic," refined, and redundant creator, who does not seem to care for his former oaths, and gasping cries from the darker bottoms of life, and sledge hammer dénouements, and probings of vicious realities. Yet, in spite of these changes, I do not believe that his basic spirit has died but merely that he has been surfacely hypnotized.

I think that he will eventually return to the deeper "fountains" of his genius and that now, at thirty-eight, he has been only temporarily led astray from his fundamental purposes and attainments. (p. 18)

> *Maxwell Bodenheim, "Roughneck and Romancer," in* The New Yorker (© 1926 by The New Yorker Magazine, Inc.), February 6, 1926, pp. 17-18.

Strange Interlude is a play of exceptional merits almost entirely spoiled by technical infelicities. Mr O'Neill has developed the aside and the soliloquy to a point where they correspond to the interior monologue, the stream of consciousness, as it is used by contemporary novelists; and it happens that he is so good a dramatist that possibly he alone, of all our playwrights, does not need the method. Frequently the soliloquizing of the characters told us something we might not otherwise have known; it was not always important, but it was informative. The complex asides (to use the old name) almost invariably repeated something which the excellent dialogue . . . had already made plain. . . . The moment these asides become unnecessary, they become impertinent and one recognizes the absurdity of the technical device, for in all the time of the aside, the other character stands waiting. One compares these unnecessary interruptions to the course of the drama with the scenes where O'Neill has done his most dramatic writing, where the tremendous swing of his drama simply compelled him to drop his method, and where, if the method were legitimate, it would most suitably be employed.

One of these scenes is the conversation between Nina Evans and her husband's mother. . . . Here is one of the richest complications of motives our stage has given us; all through it the minds of the two women must be racing with thousands of half-formed thoughts, with overpowering emotions. And O'Neill has given them to us with hardly a break in the continuous statement and question and reply between the two; everything needful is directly spoken, although these two characters have less reason to be frank with each other than others in the play. They are driven to dramatic utterance by the intensity of emotion; where the others are intense, they fumble with O'Neill's tricks.

I do not wish to suggest that O'Neill has deliberately tried a stunt; there is nothing meretricious in him and he sincerely believed, I am sure, that he could not, in any other way, give the dimension of depth to his characters. He underestimated his own power. (pp. 348-49)

[In] his glum, humourless brooding over his characters O'Neill has endowed them with passions, and that isn't a common thing in the theatre. As they are now projected they are shadows on a wall, gigantic, but still shadows. In proper perspective they would have a vehemence of life, a tremendous energy. Even in the dreary reaches of the present production they maintain a certain hold on you; in the end, by dint of talking about themselves, they make themselves known. They are enmeshed in a philosophy which is almost meaningless to me, although I have met it in almost all of O'Neill's later plays. "Life IS," even if the IS recognizes no WHYS, does not seem to me particularly meaningful or exceptional thematic material. The play, of course, runs away from the author's invocations to mystic forces; the characters in it engage in heroic battles with each other, with time, with themselves, with fate. They

don't give a hang whether life is and the fact that God is a woman does not console them; they struggle to make life, create it, protect it, to give it meaning and nobility and beauty. If Mr O'Neill had only let them! (pp. 349-50)

> *Gilbert Seldes, in* The Dial (*copyright, 1928, by The Dial Publishing Company, Inc.; reprinted by permission of J. S. Watson, Jr. and Scofield Thayer), April, 1928 (and reprinted by Kraus Reprint Corporation, 1966).*

More than any other contemporary American dramatist, [O'Neill] has made his career one long series of experiments with stagecraft; he has never for long remained contentedly in one position; he has moved restlessly from out-and-out realism (as he saw realism to be—which, it must be confessed, is a thing peculiar to Mr. O'Neill) to poetic melodrama, from poetic melodrama to poetic monologue, from monologue to something very like opera (*Lazarus Laughed*), and, finally, in the latest and finest of his experiments, which has been awarded the Pulitzer prize, to something very like a stream-of-consciousness novel for the stage. (p. 315)

Mr. O'Neill has always been much preoccupied, as indeed any dramatist worth his salt ought to be, with the secret dynamics of the mind or psyche. One has always thought of him as a kind of desperate, even despairing, epistemologist of the soul. One sees him perpetually as in pursuit of this elusive and complex ephemerid, stalking it with a net, lying in wait for it with a microscope, trying, as it were, to conjure it with verbal incantations; even, at times, when his subtlety has seemed to fail him, assaulting it with a sort of intellectual hammer. The pursuit has been earnest, passionate, gloomy, relentless. There have been moments when his intensity has become so humorless and—let us admit it—obtuse as to seem grotesque, even comic. And, nevertheless, one has always, despite these occasional miscarriages of effect, enormously respected his honesty and zeal. (pp. 315-16)

In *Strange Interlude* he is still wearing the robes of the prophet; he appears to be suggesting to us that he is getting at something very secret and esoteric; we are going to be told something extremely important about life, and miraculously new. And precisely what this message is we never find out.

But, fortunately, there is much more than this. The play is really a novel for the stage—a novel (thanks largely to the use of the asides) pitched in the key of the interior monologue. . . . One has always felt, a little, that Mr. O'Neill's sense of character was oddly deficient. He sees a shape, a guise, a color, an emotional tone, a *direction* (if one may apply such vague terms to the sense of character), but somehow or other he very nearly always just misses the last quintessence of what one calls individuality. . . .

[His characters] think, in their asides, the things which the *situation* would naturally and inevitably demand of them, but they do not think the things exactly, or richly, which their own inner *identities* would demand of them: they have not, in other words, that ultimate surplusage of sheer *being*, in their own rights, which a Shakespeare would have given us. One feels, rather, that Mr. O'Neill has come to them from outside, has made for us a set of admirably lifelike puppets and has urged them into a series of admirably plausible actions, but that there are very few moments when any of these people become subtly or powerfully or aromatically *themselves* and, *ipso facto,* run away with the scene as a first-rate character creation ought to do.

And it is precisely in the asides that Mr. O'Neill had, of course, his golden opportunity to bring this about. (p. 317)

One still feels a kind of hollow and melodramatic unreality in Mr. O'Neill's realism: an operatic largeness which is not quite life itself. And, nevertheless, it would be ungracious and dishonest not to admit that this play seemed to the present reviewer the finest play by an American which he ever saw on the stage—and the most moving. (p. 318)

> *Conrad Aiken, "O'Neill, Eugene" (originally published under a different title in* New York Post, *July 21, 1928), in his* Collected Criticism *(copyright © 1935, 1939, 1940, 1942, 1951, 1958 by Conrad Aiken; reprinted by permission of Brandt & Brandt),* Oxford University Press, 1968, pp. 315-18.

No other American writing to-day has so many ardent well-wishers as Eugene O'Neill. . . . We have watched his progress from days of his first one-act plays with their promising strength, through the realism of *Beyond the Horizon, Diff'rent,* and *Anna Christie,* and the failure of *The Straw, The First Man,* and *Welded,* and the experiments and expressionism of *The Emperor Jones, The Hairy Ape, All God's Chillun,* and *Desire under the Elms,* to the mystery of *The Fountain* and *The Great God Brown.* And while *The Great God Brown* is by all odds his finest work, and finer work in many respects than the other plays would have led one to expect of O'Neill, it still leaves one with the tantalizing feeling that the dramatist is capable of doing still better, that his definitive masterpiece is just around the corner. (pp. 230-31)

Not only, like most moderns, does he see man as a subordinate part of nature, the sport of incomprehensible and meaningless natural forces within and without himself, a passive and helpless victim who can only suffer and vainly struggle in the grip of powers which he cannot understand, let alone cope with; not only, that is, is O'Neill a naturalist and a determinist: he is also a pessimist, who sees everything as predetermined for the worst. In all tragedy we expect the protagonist to lose his battle outwardly, and in modern tragedy we expect him to succumb to nature; but O'Neill goes farther. He shows us man as undergoing an inner defeat. For the defeat his protagonists suffer is spiritual; they end in a spiritual frustration, a spiritual failure. His is an extreme development of what we have found to be the special theme of contemporary American tragedy. His favorite topic is the degradation and disintegration of character. His heroes lose both the world and also their own souls. Irony is fundamental in O'Neill's view, for the disparity between human wishes and the brute facts is inevitable, and it is a bitter irony. Indeed, since not only all man's hopes but the very self of man is doomed to betrayal, and since all aspiration and all effort are futile, ironic is not so good a word for such a world as sardonic. Not that all O'Neill's plays are utter gloom, for at least he is not a misanthrope. But the most that can be said is that he treats his poor creatures with pity, not with contempt. The dramatist at any rate is sympathetic, though life is inane and inscrutable, derisively and ingeniously malignant.

The agencies of destruction in O'Neill's world are varied and complex. . . . [In] a few of his earliest pieces, [O'Neill] made considerable use of chance and circumstance. In the later plays it is not an intangible evil fate that pursues man. Sometimes he is broken by the might of nature. . . . [He] has never forgotten the part played by the primal facts of existence. They are the foundation of all he writes. Sometimes society takes the rôle of hostile victor. . . . [Ordinarily] the destructive force itself is an inner one: the mind goes to pieces because of its own inner conflict. (pp. 232-34)

All things work together for the ruin of men, with a sort of mocking grimness.

O'Neill's dramatic world, then, has obvious limits: not only is it tragic, but it is confined to the tragedy of frustration. . . . The point about O'Neill's folk is less that they have been denied the good things of the world than that they have been denied life itself. (pp. 235-36)

If O'Neill's world has an effect of narrowness and scantness, this effect is in part due to the materials with which he works, for a dramatic world of human abundance cannot be created out of dehumanized human beings. There is, however, another reason why his world lacks body and fullness. His particular mode of characterization does not leave an impression of solidity, and in general his concern is not to project a fully imagined and created world, an independent, self-sufficient, opaque, three-dimensional affair in which solid, fully existing men and women move about. (p. 236)

Because O'Neill's whole interest is centered on the essential springs of action, his people are likely to appear elementary—I think the truer word is elemental. They are manifestations of such primal forces as hate and fear and cupidity and sexual desire. (p. 237)

One of his dramas might be described as the automatic working-out of a complicated system of forces which at the start are in a state of unstable equilibrium. Possibly that description sounds unduly mechanical; yet it is significant that one is tempted in discussing O'Neill to use physical rather than human terms, to speak of forces rather than of human individuals. (p. 239)

One reason why he was the first American playwright to join the anti-realistic reaction called expressionism may be that the newer technique offered him a line of less resistance than the old, in that it freed him from the necessity of trying to transform his forces into concrete individuals, and gave him a chance to solve many of his problems, as in *All God's Chillun,* by means of devices which are facilely mechanical. His plays have tended more and more to work themselves out like the equations of physics. (pp. 241-42)

I hesitate to call O'Neill a thinker, for in his plays there is little sign of logical processes; but by means of intuition guided by his feeling he has arrived at understanding. If he has reasoned little about life, he has contemplated it long and hard. (pp. 242-43)

The Great God Brown [is] a piece of work so astounding, so uncanny, so unlike everything else of O'Neill's, that it requires separate consideration. (p. 245)

Some of O'Neill's traits are still obvious in *The Great God Brown*—his tendency to symbolize, for instance, and his preference for the elemental and abstract have been given free rein. His passion and his insight are the same, but raised to a higher degree than one would have thought possible for him. But the differences are more striking. First of all, he has been able to control and to sustain his effort throughout; here not only is there no going to pieces, but there is even no such unevenness as in *The Emperor Jones* and *The Hairy Ape*. But most astonishing is his ability to write, his power of expression especially on the highest emotional levels. The play is full of passages of breathtaking poetry. By frankly abandoning all effort at realism, he seems to have freed himself for soaring flights unlike anything in his previous work. The poet in him whom one had begun to fear was tongue-tied has found his proper utterance at last. The tragedy is no longer unrelieved, for it is not stark but clothed in the beauty of poetry. (pp. 246-47)

> *T. K. Whipple, "Eugene O'Neill," in his* Spokesman: Modern Writers and American Life *(copyright © 1928 by Prentice-Hall, Inc.; reprinted by permission of Prentice-Hall, Inc., Englewood Cliffs, New Jersey), Appleton, 1928, pp. 230-53.*

The title [of *Mourning Becomes Electra*] . . . intends to dispose at the start of [its] relation . . . to the Greek drama. (p. 522)

It will be obvious that the American dramatist, as the Greek did, used a well-known outline which he could fill into his purpose. . . . But to dismiss the matter by saying that Mr. O'Neill has merely repeated the classic story in modern terms is off the track. Let it go at that and you will miss even the really classic elements in the play and get only the Greek side of it that is self-evident and that would be easy for any dramatist. (p. 524)

The magnificent theme that there is something in the dead that we cannot placate falsely is in the Greek plays and in the O'Neill play. The end of the play is by imaginative insight Greek in spirit: Lavinia goes into the house, the blinds are closed forever, the stage is silent, the door shut, the exaltation is there, the completion, the tragic certainty. Finally, the peculiar kind of suspense employed in the play is Greek. The playwright has learned the adult suspense of the classics as compared with the adolescent sense of it, hit off happily enough at times, that reigns in the romantic drama of the North. Classic suspense does not depend on a mere crude strain, wondering how things will turn out, however entertaining and often dramatic that effect may be. . . . In the classic form where the outcome is already known, lies the highest order of suspense. Knowing how things will end, you are left free to watch what qualities and what light will appear in their progression toward their due and necessary finish. You hang on what development, what procession exactly of logic, ecstasy or fate, will ensue with them, what threads of beautiful or dark will come into their human fabric. . . .

Along with these more accessible and manifest likes and dislikes, there are numerous points about Mr. O'Neill's play that so far at least as the Greek original goes, are variations or additions. The most brilliant of these is the incest motive, coming toward the last of the play. (p. 525)

The two gifts that Eugene O'Neill up to now has displayed are for feeling and for dramatic image. His plays have often conveyed a poignancy that is unique in the modern drama, you felt that whatever was put down was at the dramatist's own expense, he paid out of himself as he went. His great theatre gift has been in the creation of images that speak for themselves, such for instance as the tittering of the Great Khan's ladies-in-waiting at the western Marco Polo, the dynamo in the play by the same name, and another, images so vivid that their mere repetition in people's talk makes the play sound better and more complete than it ever was. Sometimes this dramatic image spreads to the scope of a dramatic pattern that is the whole sum of the play. This happened not in more recent and elaborate plays, such as *Strange Interlude*, but in at least two of the earlier, *The Emperor Jones* and *The Hairy Ape*, where the whole plot was like an expanded sentence. In *Mourning Becomes Electra* Mr. O'Neill comes now into the full stretch of clear narrative design. He discovers that in expressive pattern lies the possibility of all that parallels life, a form on which fall infinite shadings and details, as the light with its inexhaustible nuances and elements appears on a wall. He has come to what is so rare in Northern art, an understanding of repetition and variation on the same design, as contrasted with matter that is less deep or subtle, though expressed with lively surprise, variety or novelty. It is a new and definite state in his development.

None of the old tagging appears in this play, no scientific terms that can be mistaken for psychological finalities. The feeling of Orin toward his father, for example, or of the daughter toward him, is not labeled. They are motives contrived to speak for themselves, and no specious explanation appears to be offered. The lapses in taste, as regards the writing itself, the trite jargon or the pushing of a situation to an obvious extreme, have vanished. The interest in shocking the bourgeois, not always lacking hitherto, has matured into the desire only to put in the truth. On the other hand the feeling remains. If not always as lyric as before, it has spread out into a more impersonal and distributed but no less passionate element in the play. The novelties and causes, masks, labor, sex, and asides, devices, are not in evidence, or rather have moved inward whatever there was in them beyond sheer theatrical effectiveness. (pp. 527-28)

In *Mourning Becomes Electra* the end is fulfilled; Lavinia follows her direction, the completion of herself and her own inevitable satisfaction are seen. It may be that here life, as the Greek proverb said, wails as to a tomb. . . . When the play ended, and the last Mannon was gone into the house, the door shut, I felt in a full, lovely sense that the Erinyes were appeased, and that the Eumenides, the Gentle Ones, passed over the stage. (pp. 528-29)

> *Stark Young, "'Mourning Becomes Electra'," in* The New Republic *(reprinted by permission of* The New Republic; *© 1931 by The New Republic, Inc.), November 11, 1931 (and reprinted in* Literary Opinion in America, *Vol. II, edited by Morton Dauwen Zabel, revised edition, Harper & Row, Publishers, 1962, pp. 522-29).*

[O'Neill] has made the most exhaustive studies of frustration in its various manifestations. Beginning with studies of simple defeat in *Beyond the Horizon* . . . , and *The Straw*, he went on to examine the disintegrating effect of the lust for wealth in *Gold* and *Marco Millions*, of maladjustment to environment in *The Hairy Ape* and *All God's Chillun Got Wings*, of sexual passion in *Diff'rent*, *Welded*, and

Strange Interlude, of metaphysical bewilderment in *Dynamo.* In dramatizing these themes he has shown the utmost ingenuity, employing all his knowledge of theatrical resources to contrive forms suited to the expression of the subtleties that engage his attention. The seriousness of his purpose, coupled with his mastery of the theater and his sympathetic comprehension of all the stages of disintegration, have made him our principal dramatist.

In O'Neill, as in the novelists and poets, some vague hope struggles against the prevailing gloom, and he is not content to leave that hope inarticulate. Side by side with his study of disintegrating forces he carries on a quest for some principle of redemption. (pp. 253-54)

In *Lazarus Laughed* other persons share the hero's courage so long as they are with him; when they can no longer draw on this source of confidence, their old cowardice triumphs. So with the play itself: we feel its power as we read it, but later contemplation can discover little significance in its emphatic affirmations. What does the affirmation of life mean? We cannot affirm the value of life in the abstract; we can only affirm the value of those forces in life that work for ideal ends. His inability to discover those forces, and show them to us, robs O'Neill's affirmations of all vitality. Indiscriminate hope is as pointless as indiscriminate despair, as his manner of turning from one to the other shows. (pp. 254-55)

O'Neill's restless preoccupation with one type of frustration after another suggests that he is not satisfied with his own analyses and has no assurance that he has found the poison responsible for the destruction he sees. Nor has his search for an antidote been more successful: though the right mood can inspire vigorous and momentarily effective affirmations, despair promptly follows hope. Few writers are less predictable than O'Neill, but it is significant for the future that in *Mourning Becomes Electra* he seems to be concerned with suffering for its own sake. The theme that in the hands of the Greeks touched the most fundamental problems of human destiny offers O'Neill only an opportunity to portray futile lives and to ask himself questions that he cannot answer.

It cannot be denied that most of O'Neill's plays affect the emotions of the spectator, in whom they arouse a distress like that by which the author is agitated. But one has a curious sense, as one watches these plays unfold, that they are somehow beside the point. One is even a little irritated because one feels that some profound truth has just eluded one. (p. 255)

> *Granville Hicks, in his* The Great Tradition: An Interpretation of American Literature since the Civil War *(reprinted with permission of Macmillan Publishing Co., Inc.; © 1933, 1935 by Macmillan Publishing Co., Inc.; 1950 by Granville Hicks), Macmillan, revised edition, 1935.*

Since my early critical interest, many years ago, in [O'Neill's] work, there has persisted a legend that my close friendship with and personal affection for him have induced in me a critical astigmatism as to his defects as a dramatist. (p. 112)

We are, I suppose, friends for better or worse, till the water-wagon or continued bad work in the case of either doth us part, and that—disturbing as it may be to some—is that.

When I started to confect this chapter on him, I had an inclination to give it the title, "The New O'Neill." I refrained for the reason that, though the O'Neill of today is a considerably changed man from the O'Neill I have known in past years, no man ever really changes so greatly as to warrant any such absurd politico-journalistic caption. Yet that there has been a change in the old O'Neill is unmistakable.

When I first knew him, back in the earlier Nineteen Hundreds, he exuded all the gay warmth of an Arctic winter. To say that he was a melancholy, even a morbid, fellow is to put it mildly. Life to him in those days—and not only life but his stock-taking of his own soul—was indistinguishable from a serial story consisting entirely of bites from mad dogs, fatal cancers and undertakers disappointed in love. (pp. 114-15)

One of the greatest recent changes that has come over him, however, is a recapture of the humor that was in him in those distant days before even he began to write, in the days that I have described in the volume called "The Intimate Notebooks of George Jean Nathan," when, at the dives known as Jimmy the Priest's and the Hell Hole, where he made his residence, he was part and parcel of such low buffoonery as has seldom been chronicled in the biography of *homo literarum Americanus.* There was a long period when humor and the O'Neill drama were strangers —the period when he himself was in the spiritual, mental and physical dumps—although even then, despite the seeming skepticism of his critics, there were occasional fleeting symptoms of that grim humor which was in him in the old, previous days and which was struggling pathetically and often baffled to come again to the surface. But the new O'Neill humor is not a grim humor; it is a kindly and gentle and often very tender humor, wholly unlike any that has fitfully edged its way into even those of his plays that have not been abruptly catalogued by his critics as "morbid," "gloomy," "lugubrious," or what not. Much of his prospective work must surely testify to the fact.

As one of his critics, I have never been one, incidentally, to be persuaded that O'Neill's drama is exactly what the majority of his commentators have professed to regard it, to wit, a drama almost uniformly bereft of any and all traces of humor. . . . To argue that O'Neill has not had humor because a lot of it has been of the grim variety is to argue, on the same ground, that neither had Chekhov any.

Another change in O'Neill is a mood of optimism and faith that has supplanted his old, indurated pessimism and disillusion. Where formerly his outlook on life and on himself was generally glum and bitter, there is in him now evidence of a measure of philosophical rosiness and trust. . . . Life and the world and the agonies of humanity are still, of course, a source of much brow-wrinkling for him, and not a little meditative pain, but back of it all one can vaguely hear a tune singing in his heart. (pp. 116-18)

It has come as a surprise to many that O'Neill had it in him to write such an amusing comedy [as "Ah, Wilderness!"]; one containing as many legitimate loud theatre laughs as any first-rate comedy by a professional comedy writer seen hereabouts in some time. (In order to fit the play into the usual theatre time, indeed, it was necessary for O'Neill to cut out twenty-four minutes of laughs which unduly invaded his main story.) Why it should be a surprise, I don't know. It is beside the point to repeat that in certain of O'Neill's antecedent work we have had evidence of his humor. But it is less beside the point to call attention again to the silly idea that, because a dramatist writes gravely on grave topics, he must arbitrarily be devoid of the comic gift. (p. 122)

In this play O'Neill has abandoned temporarily his avid experimenting with complex new dramatic forms and has worked in the simplest and most forthright. I am glad to observe the happy and eminently satisfactory result, for it seems to me that there is sometimes a dogmatic and faintly strained effort on his part to evolve a new and strange dramatic form where the more conventional and established form would not only serve his immediate purpose just as well but even, perhaps, a little better. (p. 123)

We now turn to less pleasant news. . . . "Days Without End" [his most recent play] is not only, along with "Welded" and "Dynamo," one of the poorest things he has written but which, in addition, is one of the dullest that has come to the more ambitious stage in some time. [It] . . . is one of the most unbroiled plays that has been composed upon its general theme. And to make matters worse for those of us who believe in O'Neill's very considerable talent and better for those who don't, the fellow actually considers it the best play he has ever written!

From beginning to end, save for two brief flashes, this "Days Without End" is a tournament in collegiate theorizing artlessly bamboozled into a superficial aspect of grave experimental drama by a recourse to masks and to the technical device . . . of co-ordinating the narration of a hypothetical fiction story with the actual lives of the immediate characters. It comes to the old tale: when O'Neill goes in for pure emotion, he is a sound and enormously effective dramatist; but when he ventures into theorizing and philosophizing, he is—to be very gallant about it—far from palatable. In the present play, he had a play of pure emotion, exalted emotion even. But every time it pops up its head he gives it a mortal clout with a pseudo-ratiocinative bladder. The result is chaos—and tedium. (pp. 123-24)

"Days Without End" may be a testimonial to O'Neill's newly found optimism, but it is hardly one to his older gift for sound dramatic writing. (p. 126)

> George Jean Nathan, "O'Neill," in his Passing Judgments (copyright © 1933, 1934, 1935 by George Jean Nathan; reprinted by permission of Julie Haydon Nathan), Knopf, 1935, pp. 112-26.

Primitivism scored its first great popular victory with the early plays of Eugene O'Neill. The dramatist owes little to Gertrude Stein or Sherwood Anderson, although it is said that he was an early and appreciative reader of *Three Lives*. O'Neill goes back for his origins to Kipling, Jack London, and Joseph Conrad, to an early and innocent primitivism. Yet he did not need to rely upon these gentlemen for materials, for few of our authors—even Jack London himself—have knocked around more than has Eugene O'Neill. (p. 332)

All God's Chillun Got Wings is the finest drama of O'Neill's first period. Despite the threatening toughs of the early scenes, despite the grinning African mask which Jim's sister has given him as a wedding gift, despite the raw joke at the end of the play on poor, faithful, religious Jim, the play is too poetic . . . to be thoroughly primitivistic. For the first time the psychology of his characters is not obvious, but subtle. One of the finest touches in the play is the portrayal of the hostile attitude of Jim's sister, Hattie, who is an educated negress, a school teacher. Hattie fancies that she is detached, objective, yet her reactions are innate, defensive. Then, too, O'Neill has made as good a use of symbolism in this play as in any that he has written. Not alone the African mask, nor the wedge of buildings in the opening scene which separates a street of blacks from a street of whites, nor Jim in black and Ella in white deserted on the sidewalk after their marriage, suggests the universal oppressiveness of race distinction; the play is filled with details capable of sudden importance and significance. The audience before it leaves the theatre reads meanings into all things, as Ella does, setting them without exception into the categories, black and white. . . .

With the two-act play *Diff'rent* . . . , Eugene O'Neill turned to Freud for themes for his dramas. More and more psychoanalysis interested him and his later work was to be done largely in this field. . . . O'Neill abandoned primitivism because he plainly saw its limitations. It takes only a certain amount of skill to prepare raw food, and primitivism did not extend his powers. The psychoanalytical play— even granting that its characters are made by formula—is more challenging. Fully aware of the larger demands—and also of the larger rewards—Eugene O'Neill turned to the analytical study of frustrated and abnormal lives. (pp. 339-40)

O'Neill [in *Desire Under the Elms*] has shown clearly the will to mastery which made New England what she was in her hey-day, the time of this play. Whether this will expressed itself in lust for property or lust for the flesh, its most characteristic expressions, it was seemingly a pure thing, cauterized by its own burning. The penetration of the dramatist to this essential understanding of vice, with the consequent elevation of his play so that it is no merely ribald attack upon Puritanism, makes *Desire Under the Elms* great. It is a tremendous revelation of the mainspring of Yankee character, and there is none other like it. No ordinary stage career, however, will prepare actors properly to play its parts. (p. 695)

His fierce hatred of the Yankee impelled O'Neill to write one of the great plays of his career in *Mourning Becomes Electra*. . . . Provided that he has the technical skill, a repressed and directed fury in a dramatist, if allowed to surge through violently opposed characters, as in this play, is likely to produce something of consequence; and if *Mourning Becomes Electra* is not of the first consequence, there is no modern drama at all, and our faith in the contemporary theatre is mere delusion. (p. 711)

The Hunted moves with a tragic swiftness and certainty which outpaces the tempo of *The Homecoming*. The action throughout is tremendously elevated by the struggle for dominance between Christine and Lavinia. Christine, who, in *The Homecoming*, attains to something of the dignity of Lady Macbeth, shrinks in this play pitifully before the relentless attack of her daughter upon her security, upon her dream of bliss, even upon her hope of flight. There is something of the remorselessness of Strindberg's women in these two—the frenetic fury of the sex turned upon itself—as they lash out at each other, and there is achieved suspense of the highest tension as Christine and Lavinia play for control of the hapless Orin, who, however weak and indecisive, may become, with the proper stimulation, as dangerous as Orestes armed with an axe. (p. 715)

Although O'Neill achieves a wholly adequate climax for his trilogy at the end of *The Haunted,* his third play, when Lavinia, having renounced her lover and accepted the fate of the Mannons, turns on her heel and marches into her ghost-filled home, O'Neill's action breaks badly before it sets towards its goal. This is because he has taken too easy a path with Lavinia, whom, despite the admirable drawing of *The Homecoming* and *The Hunted,* he does not wholly understand. Her characterization, furthermore, is enfeebled by a dramatic necessity which O'Neill does comprehend. He realizes that his sea will break with a more terrific roar if it can draw back before the final, devastating lunge. Lavinia must herself catch some vision of rapture before she surrenders to her doom. The weakness of the vision supplied mars the drama. . . . [When Lavinia returns from her trip to the Orient], we are startled at the transformation in her—the grimness, the statuesqueness which reminded us of her military father, are gone, and in their place are a youthfulness and a sensuousness reminiscent of her mother, a reminiscence enforced by the dramatist's insistence on a physical resemblance of Lavinia to the Christine of Act I of *The Homecoming.* If this were mere psychoanalytical nonsense, we could endure it; but whatever the Freudian overtones, this new Lavinia's resemblance to the old Christine has moral and aesthetic indications we cannot ignore. We are told that Lavinia, during a sojourn with her brother on a coral isle, has become infatuated with the conception of pagan love, stimulated by the attentions of an adoring native chief. That is, she has virtually accepted her mother's philosophy that sensuous passion is the one categorical imperative of life. It is easy for O'Neill, with his conviction of Yankee hypocrisy, to accept this change in Lavinia as natural, but it is not easy for anyone who really knows New England to accept it. (p. 716)

Lavinia realizes her way is marked with death and, allowing Peter [her fiancé] to believe the worst of her, she sends him from her. Thus in the end she reachieves that tragic greatness the dramatist momentarily robs her of. Like Ephraim Cabot, she transcends defeat, accepting life as her punishment for being born. . . . Thus in the end, almost in spite of himself, but with an aesthetic conscience which transcends private considerations and makes all motives pure, O'Neill does final justice to the race of Mannons and the detested Yankees. (pp. 717-18)

[The] writing of his trilogy apparently did as much to cleanse the emotions of the dramatist as the performance did for those of his audience. (p. 718)

Autobiographical or not, *Days Without End* marks the most complete retreat of O'Neill's creative career. It may be eminently satisfying to those who, like Arthur Hobson Quinn and Richard Dana Skinner, see that career wholly in terms of a poet's quest for spirituality; but it is a renunciation of the hedonism of *Lazarus Laughed* and of the pagan "natural right" to love by which O'Neill has tried and condemned New England morals in *Dynamo* and *Mourning Becomes Electra.* It is not easy, either, to reconcile its tardy endorsement of the Church with Ponce de León's

recognition of the "enemy" in the Churchman, whatever his guise. No, *Days Without End* is hardly a logical capstone to the work of O'Neill: it is, however, a symbol that he has rejected the philosophy of his creative work (as proceeding too much from his ingenious Loving devil?) and is ready to reaffirm his faith in traditional things. . . . There is, it would seem, reason for both delight and anxiety in *Days Without End:* joy because O'Neill has rejected a palpably false philosophy of life, and fear that the acceptance of tradition may ruin the dramatist. Is Eugene O'Neill such that only a Promethean position is possible for him, if he is to do creative work? Is he one of those who need to feel themselves in opposition to the gods, to do work beneficial to man? Let us recognize that, however wrong-headed his plays have been, they have been provocative of thought on matters few of his contemporaries have consistently touched. Can we spare this Promethean fire for candlelight? . . . [Our] concern is wholly for the artist; we agree that the man has found himself. (pp. 719-20)

> *Oscar Cargill, in his* Intellectual America: Ideas on the March *(reprinted with permission of Macmillan Publishing Co., Inc.; copyright 1941 by Macmillan Publishing Co., Inc.; 1969 by Oscar Cargill), Macmillan, 1941.*

'Nobility of spirit'—to be able again to believe in one's self, to have a firm purpose in life, 'a will and power to live,' all this is the recurrent theme in nearly all the plays of Eugene O'Neill. But at the same time he has also found its recipe to be as elusive as all the vagaries and new purposes of the generation after the war. . . . To say that he has at last found a final recipe for living is to speak against the evidence. For each new play has broken new ground, and revealed a new purpose. What will be the end of the story?

Perhaps, and probably, this almost amateur readiness to undertake a new doctrine is the most American trait in Eugene O'Neill, that and a certain courage—even rashness —to proclaim it. As an American, O'Neill knows there is something wrong with the world; but it is rather more of the intellectual knowledge of the observer than the deeply felt personal experience of the participator. (pp. 125-26)

In spite of the changes that have come in O'Neill's ideas on life and its problems, all of his plays can be said to have one central theme. It is the persistent question that he has put to life, and as persistent has been the variety of the answers: the why and the how of failure, and of the disintegration of personality that is the sign of failure. His characters are ever discovering the always imminent possibility of losing the way, of missing the motive that might give life a meaning and keep personality intact. In a word, how can one find, not success perhaps, but the compensation of peace and happiness? Nearly all of his plays, and all of the more significant, have never lost sight of this central problem. He may have toyed with atheism and socialism— and he has—but it has always been for its bearing on the life of the single individual. O'Neill never thinks in masses. His earlier plays dealt more specifically with the failure to find the way; his later, speaking more generally, have found some sort of answer that will bring some variety of peace. (p. 130)

> *Philo M. Buck, Jr., "The New Tragedy," in his* Directions in Contemporary Literature

(copyright © 1942 by Oxford University Press, Inc.; reprinted by permission), Oxford University Press, 1942, pp. 125-48.

O'Neill, like every significant writer ... was not the product of merely theatrical developments or impulses. He was, above all, a unique personality; and despite the complacencies of those who see a playwright merely as an accessory to the fact of theatre or the fact of economics, a real dramatist is a real personality. He was, at the same time, a veritable seismograph of the ideas, viewpoints, and promptings of the new age. He reflected a general discontent with a materialistic America on the part of the younger creative sons of the age, a sense of frustration, a general straining for enriched experience, and an assimilation of European thought and dramatic art. He responded to these underground stirrings and rumblings with crude but impressive intensity. His impressiveness resides, in fact, not in the discovery of unique ideas but in his absorption of these ideas and even more importantly in the raw personal passionateness with which he employed them on the stage. (p. 640)

The nature of this greatness cannot, however, be summarized coldly. It is a matter of his generally somber and sardonic tone, of his demoniac possession and writhings, and of reality honestly caught, intensely hated and passionately defied by him. His realism has indeed neglected reality as a phenomenon that might be clarified or ameliorated by social analysis and action. O'Neill has been extravagantly acclaimed as a mystic by the Catholic critic Richard Dana Skinner, when as a matter of fact many of his perceptions have caught and appraised reality realistically and psychologically while his visions have merely possessed that sense of eternity or kinship with nature which is any poet's prerogative. On the other hand, O'Neill has been severely criticized for treating the social realities of his time only tangentially or without awareness of their existence as a social problem. The fact is that he has rarely regarded them as worth treating artistically except as manifestations of the struggle between man's will and fate, between passion and circumstance, and between forces of the inner self. This has resulted in much ambiguity, exaggerated ineffective emotionalism, and chafing against imponderables on his part.... Even in his metaphysical flight, O'Neill has caught the reality of common people living on sea or land; he has presented humanity struggling against inherited or acquired limitations and facing racial prejudice, proverty, the hardness of a stony soil, the frustrations of puritanism, and the effects of a materialistic world which thwarts or perverts the spirit. (p. 641)

The one possibly serious difference between his effects and those of the greatest tragedians (including Chekhov) is that O'Neill's characters are too often only pseudotragic, since they lack greatness of spirit and stamina. Their quest is too intangible, their discontent is too febrile, and their desire too introverted. They coddle their frustrations and submit too supinely to their disease or their defeat. O'Neill, in short, has performed too many symphonies on the sensory system. This creates greater "theatre" than "drama." It can be added, however, that since there is in effect no Mason and Dixon's line between the two, his "drama" benefits from his "theatre," just as his theatre sometimes suffers from his drama. Perhaps, too, our concept of tragedy needs modification. (p. 644)

O'Neill indeed practically created American naturalistic drama without actually confining himself to it in these plays, and such work as *Tobacco Road* and *Of Mice and Men* would possibly have remained unaccepted but for his potent example. Nevertheless, he was an eclectic theatrician and a poet who could not accept even the semblance of a straitjacket in naturalism. (pp. 651-52)

The so-called aside [which allowed his characters to express their unconscious thoughts verbally] in *Strange Interlude* is not so much related to the older conventions of the drama as to the stream-of-consciousness technique of Strindberg's expressionist plays and James Joyce's *Ulysses*. And this, too, was a notable innovation in the theatre....

O'Neill, it is true, paid a heavy price for so ambitious an undertaking. The aside is sometimes overworked or obvious, and it becomes somewhat tiresome even when it is entirely appropriate. (p. 656)

John Gassner, "Eugene O'Neill and the American Scene," in Masters of the Drama *(copyright © 1940 by Random House, Inc.; reprinted by permission of Random House, Inc.), Dover, 1945, pp. 629-61.*

The Iceman Cometh is ... made of ice or iron; it is full of will and fanatic determination; it appears to have hardened at some extreme temperature of the mind. In the theatre today, it is attractive positively because of its defects. To audiences accustomed to the oily virtuosity of George Kaufman, George Abbott, Lillian Hellman, Odets, Saroyan, the return of a playwright who—to be frank—cannot write is a solemn and sentimental occasion. O'Neill belongs to that group of American authors, which includes Farrell and Dreiser, whose choice of vocation was a kind of triumphant catastrophe; none of these men possessed the slightest ear for the word, the sentence, the speech, the paragraph; all of them, however, have, so to speak, enforced the career they decreed for themselves by a relentless policing of their beat. What they produce is hard to praise or to condemn; how is one to judge the great, logical symphony of a tone-deaf musician? Pulpy in detail, their work has nevertheless a fine solidity of structure; they drive an idea or a theme step by step to its brutal conclusion with the same terrible force they have brought to bear on their profession. (pp. 81-2)

O'Neill has neither the phenomenal memory which serves Farrell as a substitute for observation, nor the documentary habits which, for Dreiser, performed the same service. In *The Iceman Cometh,* the scene is a cheap bar somewhere in downtown New York in the year 1912; the characters are the derelict habitués of the back room—a realist's paradise, one would think. But it needs only a short walk along Third Avenue today (or the armchair method of inquiry) to solidify the suspicion that, unless drinking *moeurs* have changed in the last thirty-five years, O'Neill is an incompetent reporter. In the day and a half that elapses on the stage of the Martin Beck, none of the characters is visibly drunk, nobody has a hangover, and, with a single brief exception, nobody has the shakes; there are none of those rancorous, semi-schizoid silences, no obscurity of thought, no dark innuendoes, no flashes of hatred, there is, in short, none of the terror of drink, which, after all, in the stage that Harry Hope's customers have presumably reached, is a form of insanity. What is missing is precisely the thing that is most immediately striking and most horrifying in any human drunkard, the sense of the destruction of personality. Each of O'Neill's people is in perfect possession of the little bit of character the author has given him. (pp. 82-3)

What shreds of naturalism cling to this work are attached to and encumber the dialogue; the language has the wooden verisimilitude, the flat, dead, echoless sound of stale slang that makes Farrell's novels and the later works of Sinclair Lewis so stilted. O'Neill here has not even the justification of sociological pedantry, which these other writers might bring forward. His intention is symbolic and philosophical, but unfortunately you cannot write a Platonic dialogue in the style of *Casey At the Bat*. O'Neill might have studied the nature of illusion through the separate relations to illusion of a group of characters *(The Three Sisters)*, but his people are given but a single trait each, and they act and react, in the loss and recapture of illusion, not individually but in a body. Bare and plain, this play has the structure of an argument; its linguistic deficiencies make it maudlin. How is your wife getting along with the iceman, the characters roar, over and over again, and though death is the iceman, the joke is not appreciably refined by this symbolic treatment; rather, it is death that is coarsened.

Yet it must be said for O'Neill that he is probably the only man in the world who is still laughing at the iceman joke or pondering its implications. He is certainly the only writer who would have the courage or the lack of judgment to build a well-made play around it. This sense of one man's isolation is what, above all, gives *The Iceman Cometh* its salient look. . . . Its solitariness inside its rigid structure suggests the prison or the asylum or the sound of a man laughing in a square, empty room. (pp. 84-5)

> *Mary McCarthy, "Dry Ice," in* Partisan Review *(copyright © 1946 by Partisan Review, Inc.), November/December, 1946 (and reprinted as "Eugene O'Neill—Dry Ice," in her* Sights and Spectacles: 1937-1959, *Farrar, Straus, 1956, pp. 81-5).*

O'Neill has hardly ever given up his opposition against the conventional theatre, against the play that is "satisfactory" in the sense of Bronson Howard. Like many lesser men of the Little Theatre Movement he absolutely refused to show a picture of life on the stage that was distorted by conventions dear to the paying majority. It is true, once, in a mood of relaxation, he . . . followed the beaten path. This happened when he composed the charming comedy *Ah, Wilderness!* . . ., the only one of his plays in which we find humour. Nevertheless, it is his outstanding characteristic that he carefully avoided the conventions cherished by the customers of the commercial theatres, and tried to introduce old and new conventions from other countries or even to invent new ones. Moreover, he was quite ready to face life in its American form. Not because he thought it perfect. He felt no desire to glorify the United States in his art, nor did he wish to escape from them. The American form of life was the one he knew best; therefore he made it his main subject. Like Sinclair Lewis, H. L. Mencken and other intellectual leaders of his generation he looked at his countrymen and their problems in a detached and critical way. And the young people who were going through the experience of the war and the post-war era shared this attitude; they read and admired Lewis and Mencken, and they proclaimed O'Neill the first dramatist of America. O'Neill's freedom from any escapist love of Europe and its tradition by no means prevented him from a close study of European literature, especially of the modern dramatists. Signs of his knowledge of Ibsen, Strindberg, Shaw and Synge are frequently met with in his plays.

The strongest impression we get in surveying O'Neill's plots and figures is the deterministic mood that pervades them. If one of his human beings appears to be a free agent this is the result of an abbreviation necessitated by dramatic economy. It is manifestly impossible to unfold in a play all the influences and conditions that have made the behaviour of a person what it is according to the deterministic creed. As a dramatist O'Neill can only relate characteristic actions to the most decisive of their causes. In many of his plays the milieu in the widest sense of the term appears as a force shaping character and destiny. In the early one-act plays the sea and its atmosphere function in this way. . . . Another shaping power that dominates the will is race. In O'Neill's negro plays *The Emperor Jones* . . . and *All God's Chillun Got Wings* . . . the racial characteristics of the main figures have a decisive effect on their behaviour and fate. A further determining factor is heredity. (pp. 5-6)

[O'Neill] was more and more fascinated by the drama going on within a single soul, if this old-fashioned word can still be used in connection with his modernistic psychological studies. He accepted the view according to which the mind is a complicated mechanism whose nature, not discernible as long as it is functioning normally, is disclosed if a crisis comes on or if a mal-formation has taken place. (p. 11)

It is not astonishing that O'Neill's psychological interest led him on to the phenomenon of the split personality. He has evolved methods of making split personalities capable of dramatic representation. . . . The personification of the good and the evil propensities of the soul remind us of the allegorical methods of the mediaeval and the Puritan moralists. O'Neill has used this primitive method to reveal the struggle in a modern soul in a striking manner. (pp. 13-14)

O'Neill remains for us the restless seeker, the man of many creeds and many forms. His great dramatic power appears in the skill with which he develops drama out of themes that are hardly promising in themselves. His intense interest in psycho-analysis is not an asset in a dramatist. Some of his plays remain interesting case studies. The more completely he analyses his figures for us the less is there of the mystery of life in them. But O'Neill undertook the task of interpreting his figures in the terms in which many of his contemporaries interpreted their own reactions and conflicts. It cannot be said that this interpretation always sprang from his immediate experience. Often he was fascinated by a theory. This, I think, is the reason why his plays —except perhaps *The Emperor Jones* and *Desire under the Elms*—remain admirable experiments. We respond to them intellectually and with part of our emotions, but there is not that complete and unreserved response exacted by the masterpieces of dramatic art. Even so, he has drawn unforgettable pictures of modern man, haunted by many clashing beliefs, superstitions and longings, often his own worst enemy, entirely unable to save himself. (pp. 14-15)

> *Rudolf Stamm, "The Dramatic Experiments of Eugene O'Neill," in* English Studies: A Journal of English Letters and Philology, *Vol. 28, 1947, pp. 1-15.*

For O'Neill, the "sickness of today" which he conceived as the only possible big subject, resulted from the death of the old God and the failure of science and materialism to give any satisfactory new one for the surviving primitive religious instinct to find a meaning for life in, and to comfort its fear of death with. Was not this the primary source of all man's blundering unhappiness? This sickness—the disorientation of the individual—became O'Neill's major theme. The unhappiness, in an extraordinary variety of illustrations, furnished him with the stories of his plays. In general, O'Neill's characters were of two kinds: those who regarded themselves as "belonging," as identified with something that transcended their personal lives; and those who, having lost any conviction of such relationship, were desperately seeking an equivalent for it. For both kinds of character, O'Neill's plays showed that life was apt to be tragically frustrating. (p. 179)

O'Neill was to acknowledge, ultimately, that he was not interested in the relation of men to men but only in the relation of men to God. Like the characters of his plays, he lived in a society less godless than deprived of God—was this why he achieved, in his finest plays, a poignancy and power unique in the modern theater? . . .

Writing for those deeply aware of the absence of God, O'Neill repeatedly stated their pathetic need of an assurance that man's fleeting life in time and space can be noble; of a new ideal to measure the value of our days by—only to suggest that all merely mortal dedications must, in the end, prove inadequate. If men were to have an intensified feeling of the significant worth of man's being and becoming, it would be achieved only through identification with something larger than and superior to themselves. (p. 180)

Never directly concerned with social criticism, O'Neill nevertheless furnished an oblique commentary on the America of his day. In studying the various substitutes for a relation to God through which men seek satisfaction, he frequently dealt with two which, in effect, were the normal, prevalent ones in the United States: material success, and personal achievement, or "self-expression." In his plays, these appear as the most fruitless of dedications. (p. 181)

O'Neill's two finest plays—*Desire Under the Elms* and *Mourning Becomes Electra*—dealt with the relation of men to God at a time when this relation, as he conceived it, still retained a genuine reality. Both plays were placed in the American past, in the New England of the mid-nineteenth century, when the Yankee conscience, beginning to lose its authority over the external world, was likewise beginning to turn inward, to become repressed, sinister, poisoned by doubt and suspicion, morally sick. The old Puritan God was sinking into twilight; and no longer permitted to be divine, was becoming diabolic. The warped, perverse life which O'Neill portrayed in *Desire,* and in the trilogy of *Electra,* could have obtained only when a sick conscience confronted a dying god. Both were doomed, but both still lived, so a vital relationship existed. And—since, in it, men, however sinister, identified themselves with a transcendent moral force, however malign—this relationship was also potent; though potent only for evil, for destruction, for catastrophe. Thus, O'Neill was able to make both plays true tragedies; and the *Electra* trilogy a tragedy in the Greek sense, in modern psychological terms with Fate and the Furies working from within the individual soul.

This was why, in these plays, O'Neill achieved a moral elevation lacking to any of his plays about contemporary life. . . .

The effect of these plays, in the theater, was eloquent proof that O'Neill's thesis, seemingly so remote from contemporary American life, remained a living issue to many more people than might have been anticipated. (p. 183)

> *Lloyd Morris, in his* Postscript to Yesterday: America: The Last Fifty Years *(copyright 1947 by Lloyd Morris; reprinted by permission of Random House, Inc.), Random House, 1947.*

If we put aside Bernard Shaw as an author who, while producing some of his finest work during the twenties and thirties of this century, established himself on the stage before the outbreak of the First World War, we must all recognize that the only between-war playwright endowed with those virtues which are the mark of true genius was a scion of the American stage. Eugene O'Neill is not only a symbol of the dramatic movement that flourished so rapidly and with such resultant fruitfulness during the century's third and fourth decades; he also stands, a powerful and vibrant figure, over all his playwriting colleagues throughout the world.

He has genuine dramatic stature, yet the colossus does not by any means plant itself firmly upon the soil, nor is it lacking in cracks and fissures. Richly endowed with genius, O'Neill presents himself as a man who, whatever his strength, is wanting in that one final element of power and balance out of which greatness is born. He has strength of passion; he is not content to serve the stage merely with trivial themes of domestic interest; he ponders deeply upon man in relation to the universe in which he lives; more nearly than any author writing in English he approaches the great entrance-hall to tragedy's temple.

Two things only are lacking. First, we sense in O'Neill's career a strangely uneasy relationship between the man and the theatre of his time. When we confront such dramatists as Sophocles, Shakespeare, Molière, Racine, we feel that there is a perfect adjustment between their desires and the stage for which they write. At times they may endeavour to seize from the theatre effects almost beyond its reach, but in general they restrain themselves, with apparent content and harmony, within limits set by the very nature of the theatrical art of their ages. Not so does O'Neill impress us. All too often he suggests that he is impatient of the restrictions and that he is attempting to shatter them or to wrest from within them something the theatre is incapable of yielding. Frantically, almost hysterically, he turns from style to style, from device to device. (p. 880)

This constant and restless movement in his career, this phrenetic seizing upon new devices, maybe ultimately depends upon his unconscious recognition of the essential lack in him of what is the essential instrument of the great playwright. With the deepest regret we must confess that O'Neill is not a finished literary artist. No words of rich import and beauty wing themselves from his pages; we remember his scenes but not the language in which they are couched; again and again as we reach an emotional climax in one or another of his dramas a wave of disappointment comes flooding in upon us. Where we had confidently expected to find lines instinct with loveliness and majesty all we have heard are sharp cries, broken phrases, the clichés rather than the originalities of expressive language. (p. 881)

A young dramatist is always blessed by the stars when he finds easy access to a theatre, and in this respect it was lucky that, in the years of the First World War, O'Neill found, in the Provincetown Players, an acting group ready to present his earliest efforts. At the same time we must remember that this was a collection of amateurs, and the fact that O'Neill began with them is likely to have intensified his own inherent aloofness (despite his having been born 'in the profession') from the commercial theatre. Instead of being forced to adapt his visions to the requirements of the ordinary playhouse, O'Neill began by finding a group of enthusiastic but technically inexperienced amateurs of the stage anxious to present his pieces as they were written and eager to idolize this young genius of their very own finding. (p. 882)

Immediately following the appearance of *Days without End* O'Neill let it be known that he was engaged in penning a great cycle of dramas depicting a section of American life. What this will be like we cannot, of course, even guess at: all we may say is that his first contribution to this his latest work, *The Iceman Cometh* . . . , is a vastly disappointing play. The characters talk too much; we become wearied with the constant repetition of the phrase "pipe-dreams"; the philosophy of the scenes is confused. Set in a wretched saloon where the flotsam and jetsam of society gather, it concentrates attention upon a certain travelling salesman, Hickey, who is accustomed to come there at periodic intervals for a drinking-bout. . . . What this farrago of despairing scenes implies no one can tell: O'Neill's latest play is perhaps his poorest.

In a sense the dramatic career of this strange author is representative of the American theatre as a whole. From about 1918 to the present time the New York stage has been one of the most vital in the world, and when we consider its contributions collectively we may readily admit that it has exhibited a vitality and a strength which cannot be matched anywhere else within these years. On the other hand, those last refinements which alone can bring greatness are lacking. It is as though we were constantly approaching and never arriving at our destination. (pp. 892-93)

> *Allardyce Nicoll, "Eugene O'Neill," in* World Drama: From Aeschylus to Anouilh *(reprinted by permission of Harcourt Brace Jovanovich, Inc.), Harcourt, Brace & World, Inc., 1950?, pp. 880-93.*

It would be nice to like O'Neill. He is the leading American playwright; damn him, damn all; and damning all is a big responsibility. It is tempting to damn the rest and make of O'Neill an exception. He *is* an exception in so many ways. He has cared less for temporary publicity than for lasting and deserved fame. When he was successful on Broadway he was not sucked in by Broadway. The others have vanity; O'Neill has self-respect. . . . O'Neill has always had the grown-up writer's concern for that continuity and development which must take place quietly and from within. In a theater that chiefly attracts idiots and crooks he was a model of good sense and honor. (p. 233)

But his gifts are mutually frustrating. His sense of theatrical form is frustrated by an eloquence that decays into mere repetitious garrulousness. His eloquence is frustrated by the extreme rigidity of the theatrical mold into which it is poured—jelly in an iron jar. Iron. Study, for example, the

stage directions of [*The Iceman Cometh*], and you will see how carefully O'Neill has drawn his ground plan. There everyone sits—a row of a dozen and a half men. And as they sit, the plot progresses; as each new stage is reached, the bell rings, and the curtain comes down. Jelly. Within the tyrannically, mechanically rigid scenes, there is an excessive amount of freedom. The order of speeches can be juggled without loss, and almost any speech can be cut in half.

The eloquence might of course be regarded as clothing that is necessary to cover a much too mechanical man. Certainly, though we gained more by abridging the play than we lost, the abridgment did call attention rather cruelly to the excessively schematic character of the play. Everything is contrived, *voulu,* drawn on the blackboard, thought out beforehand, imposed on the material by the dead hand of calculation. We had started out from the realization that the most lifeless schemata in this overschematic play are the expressionistic ones, but we had been too sanguine in hoping to conceal or cancel them. They are foreshadowed already in the table groupings of Act I (as specified in O'Neill's stage directions). They hold the last act in a death grip. . . .

It would perhaps be churlish to press the point, were O'Neill's ambition in this last act not symptomatic both of his whole endeavor as a playwright and of the endeavor of many other serious playwrights in our time. It is the ambition to transcend realism. (pp. 239-40)

At one time he performed a historic function, that of helping the American theater to grow up. In all his plays an earnest attempt is made to interpret life; this fact in itself places O'Neill above his predecessors in American drama and beside his colleagues in the novel and poetry. He was a good playwright in so far as he kept within the somewhat narrow range of his own sensibility. When he stays close to a fairly simple reality and when, by way of technique, he uses fairly simple forms of realism or fairly simple patterns of melodrama, he can render the bite and tang of reality or, alternatively, he can startle and stir us with his effects. If he is never quite a poet, he is occasionally able—as we have seen in *The Iceman*—to create the striking theatric image.

But the more he attempts, the less he achieves. . . . A hundred novelists have dealt more subtly with hidden motives than O'Neill did in his famous essay in psychological subtlety, *Strange Interlude,* a play that is equally inferior as a study of upper-class Americans. Then there is his desire to re-create ancient tragedy. Although no one is more conscious than he that America is not an Athens, the "Greek dream"—the desire to be an Aeschylus—has been his nightmare.

The classic and notorious problem about tragedy in modern dress has been that the characters, not being over life-size but rather below it, excite pity without admiration and therefore without terror. Though O'Neill has talked of an "ennobling identification" with protagonists, he has only once tried to do anything about it: only in *Mourning Becomes Electra* are the characters over life-size. Unhappily this is not because of the size of their bones but, as it were, by inflation with gas, cultural and psychological.

The cultural gas is the classic story. The use of classic stories has been customary for so long, and has recently come into such vogue again, that writers have forgotten their obligation to make the stories their own. (pp. 244-45)

We are told that myth is useful because the audience knows the plot already and can turn its attention to the how and why. To this I would not protest that all adapters, including O'Neill, change the mythic plots, though this is true; what I have in mind is, rather, that they do not always change them enough. Events in their works have often no organic place there, they are fossilized vestiges of the older version. We ask: why does this character do that? And the answer is: because his Greek prototype did it. In *Mourning Becomes Electra* the myth makes it hard for O'Neill to let his people have their own identity at all, yet to the extent that they do have one, it is, naturally, a modern and American identity, and this in turn makes their ancient and Greek actions seem wildly improbable. Heaven knows that murders take place today as in ancient times; but the murders in O'Neill are not given today's reality.

Instead, the characters are blown up with psychological gas. O'Neill has boasted his ignorance of Freud, but such ignorance is not enough. He should be ignorant also of the watered-down Freudianism of Sardi's and the Algonquin, the Freudianism of all those who are ignorant of Freud, the Freudianism of the subintelligentsia. It is through this Freudianism, and through it alone, that O'Neill has made the effort, though a vain one, to assimilate the myth to modern life. Now, what is it that your subintellectual knows about Freud? That he "put everything down to sex." Precisely; and that is what O'Neill does with the myth. Instead of reverent family feeling to unite an Orestes and an Electra we have incest. *Mourning Becomes Electra* is all sex talk. Sex *talk*—not sex lived and embodied, but sex talked of and fingered. (pp. 245-46)

O'Neill is an acute case of what D. H. Lawrence called "sex in the head." Sex is almost the only idea he has—has insistently—and it is for him only an idea. Looking back on what I wrote about him a few years ago, I still maintain that O'Neill is no thinker. He is so little a thinker, it is dangerous for him to think. To prove this you have only to look at the fruits of his thinking; his comparatively thoughtless plays are better. For a non-thinker he thinks too much. Almost as bad as sex in the head is tragedy in the head, for tragedy too can decline into a doctrine and dwindle into an idea. . . . Tragedy is hard, but the idea of tragedy ("the tragic view of life," "the tragic sense of life," and so forth) is seldom evoked without nostalgic longing. (p. 246)

Aristotle's view of tragedy is humane; [that popularized by Robinson Jeffers] is barbaric without the innocence of barbarism; it is neo-barbaric, decadent. O'Neill is too simple and earnest to go all the way with Jeffers. Puritanism and a rough-hewn honesty keep him within the realm of the human. But *Mourning Becomes Electra* does belong . . . [to] a world that titillates itself with tragedy in the head. Your would-be tragedian despises realism, the problem play, liberalism, politics in general, optimism, and what not. Hence *Mourning Becomes Electra* is unrealistic, unsocial, illiberal, unpolitical, and pessimistic. What of the *Oresteia*? It celebrates the victory of law over arbitrary violence, of the community over the individual. It is optimistic, political, social, and with permissible license might be called liberal and realistic as well. *O tempora, o mores!* If one does not like O'Neill, it is not really he that one dislikes: it is our age—of which like the rest of us he is more the victim than the master. (p. 247)

Eric Bentley, "Trying to Like O'Neill" (1951), in his In Search of Theater *(copyright © 1948, 1949, 1950, 1951, 1953 by Eric Bentley; reprinted by permission of Atheneum Publishers, New York) Atheneum, 1953, pp. 233-47.*

O'Neill seems to visualize the process of living as a stream of consciousness in which the lifeline is always becoming fouled. He writes generally of normal life perverted, twisted, and rotted by some excess, mania, whim, or crank. As early as *Diff'rent* . . . , a major character announces that "Folks be all crazy and rotten to the core, and I'm done with the whole kit and caboodle of them." The playwright was not discouraged by his vision; rather he has continued to probe, to attempt to discover the motives of human conduct. His frequent choice of the sea or the farm as his background may be due to their symbolic value; life on shipboard as the world in miniature, the farm juxtaposing the order of nature and the disorder of man.

But in his mystical as well as in his realistic plays, O'Neill demonstrates the acute sense of form which was to make him an early leader of American expressionism. The structure of the play, the pattern of the action, even the shaping of the dialogue always follows a strict design, usually one devised for that particular play. (pp. 65-6)

In characterization, too, O'Neill prefers to follow a pattern. His characters are not necessarily stereotypes, but he is at some pains from early in his career to make sure that the relation of each character to his central theme or action shall be apparent. Later he was openly to employ real masks. In his early works he is willing to suggest the "humour" or manner of any one character by using the mask less literally. (p. 67)

This use of the matériel of the theater, settings and make-up and action, on several levels achieves an effect similar to the effect of poetic language, and accounts for the impact of much of O'Neill's work in spite of the lack of poetic language in his dialogue. (p. 68)

Alan S. Downer, in his Fifty Years of American Drama, 1900-1950 *(copyright © 1951 by Gateway Editions, Ltd.), Regnery, 1951.*

A Moon for the Misbegotten is *Desire Under the Elms* grown old and hoarse and randy. There is the familiar puritan triad of greed, land and sexual repression. There are a demonic old man, a stony unrewarding farm, a vital Demeter of a woman. The finale is lit by an apocalyptic dawn, and the whole play is reddened by whisky, like a bloodshot eye. There is an opening which is really a prologue, with the cunning son (two in *Desire Under the Elms*) deserting the farm with a sum of money stolen from the miser father. This opening imparts to both plays a curious, desolate aspect, as if normal self-interest, in the person of the departing sons, had stealthily forsaken the vicinity; those who are left are survivors in a waste.

A Moon for the Misbegotten, however, is not laid in the period-past of the gold rush but in the golden bootleg twenties, on a Connecticut tenant farm, an old box of a house raised up on blocks of timber. The characters are not New Englanders of the original stock but Irish supplanters. The heroine is a gigantic young woman, one hundred and eighty pounds broad and tall, who carries a club to defend herself;

as the daughter of a bootlegger and shifty, shiftless farmer, she is known throughout the neighborhood for her herculean sexual prowess. A sort of Olympian knockdown comedy is enacted between the trickster father and the virago daughter, but this comedy is at bottom sad, for the daughter is in actuality a virgin with a strong maternal heart and the father a grimy cupid with benevolent matrimonial plans for her.

These plans center on a middle-aged alcoholic of educated pretensions, the son of a well-known Thespian who owned farm property. Here the theme of puritanism suddenly appears, like an elemental blight. Behind the pagan façade of Irish boasting, drinking and ribaldry is revealed a wheyey sentimentality and retching hatred of sex. With the nuptial couch all readied in the tar-papered lean-to, James Tyrone Jr., man of the world and Broadway rakehell, makes his true confession: he is a man who, like Stephen Dedalus, has wronged his dying mother, and wronged her again, a thousand times over, when, escorting her body home on the train, he entertained a prostitute in his drawing-room while Mama was in the baggage car ahead. In his moment of opportunity, he sobs himself chastely to sleep, a guilt-sickened altar-boy.

This moment, in which the bootlegger's daughter discovers that this middle-aged man is really "dead," emotionally speaking—an exhausted mummified child—is a moment of considerable poignancy. The defeat of all human plans and contrivances is suddenly shaped in the picture of the titaness sitting staring at a stage moon with a shriveled male infant drunkenly asleep at her side. The image of the survivors takes on a certain grotesque epic form; the woman, stage center, like a gentle beached whale, appears for an instant as the last survivor of the world.

What disturbs one here, however, as in so many of O'Neill's plays, is the question of how far the author himself is a victim of the same sentimentality and self-pity that is exhibited clinically in the characters; how far, specifically, O'Neill himself is taken in by the "tragic" figure of James Tyrone Jr., who is merely a pitiable wreck. My impression is that O'Neill himself does not know, that he puts the character forward like a question, which he hopes may be answered favorably. The crudity of the technique makes it hard to descry intention. Nevertheless, despite this, despite the tone of barbershop harmony that enters into all O'Neill's work, this play exacts homage for its mythic powers, for the element of transcendence jutting up woodenly in it like a great home-made Trojan horse. (pp. 86-8)

Mary McCarthy, in The New York Times *(© 1952 by The New York Times Company; reprinted by permission), August 31, 1952 (and reprinted in her* Sights and Spectacles: 1937-1959, *Farrar, Straus, 1956, pp. 86-8).*

[Mr. O'Neill] alone among our dramatists looks beyond his people to the agents that control them. His men and women are torn by worries which they do not—cannot—give each other, even as they are scarred by bruises which their strong arms are not strong enough to have inflicted on one another. They stray into no Utopia which is above the moral law. Nor do they lead those guarded, vicarious lives that make for the pleasant artifice from which high comedy is spun. They are not prattling shadows, strutting for the sake of recreation in a playroom of their own fashioning,

but unprotected men and women, set down sternly in a world that is not man-made, who face its rawest issues with an awesome directness. Their curiosity extends beyond their neighbors' well-being, just as their woes are greater than their rent-day worries, because, instead of assuming their place among men, they search for their place in the scheme of things. Like Yank in *The Hairy Ape* they want to "belong," to be a part of the life force and an expression of it, to feel the solace of an unavoidable submission to powers which are beyond their control, or the affirmation that comes from identifying themselves with the larger agencies that engulf them. They are the visible cogs in the invisible machinery of the universe, violent with its violence even as they are broken by it. They grapple with these mysteries as Jacob wrestled with his God. (pp. 41-2)

The forces with which Mr. O'Neill's people contend may be cruel but they are never indifferent. Unwilling to brood over his characters from afar, they enter in their daily lives as the silent, mocking witnesses of their doom, or the grimly active participants in their undoing. They are personal, finite gods whose interference is so immediate and undeviating that they lose no time in trusting oracles or priests to relay their intentions. They do not hide in the shadows of the heath but palpably abide in the great hall of Dunsinane. It is because they speak directly, and because Mr. O'Neill seeks to have his audiences feel the impact of these greater forces as personally as both he and his characters feel them, that he has no other choice than to work as a symbolist. It is his only possible way of expressing inexpressible things. As a symbolist who is both a mystic and a romantic, his plays abound in tangible manifestations of divine concern, of the interest of the larger forces of the world in the small affairs of men, and of the close relationship that he believes to exist between man and nature.

His men and women belong to a fierce but a caring world. The eye of God may be angry but it is never closed. (pp. 42-3)

The connection that exists between . . . larger agencies and the men and women of Mr. O'Neill's plays is more frequently ironic than tragic. Indeed, in many respects it is the acuteness of his sensing of the life force as ironic that has stood in the way of his development as a tragic dramatist. His irony is bitter, melancholy, and unflinching. But as irony it does not rise above pain or exult in the manner of tragedy. It asks us to smile in a sad way at the savage joke that the gods can play on men far more often than it invites us to share the divinity that suffering can bring to man. Too often he leads his people downward rather than letting them rise again from hell, because his preoccupation is so frequently the trick—the dirty trick—that fate has up its sleeve, rather than the ennobling protest that the tragic dramatists have put into the hearts of men.

The undoing of many of his people is so certain that the interest shifts—as it does not in true tragedy—from the men and women who are tested and broken to the destructive agents that test and break them. The inevitability of their outward doom becomes of more importance than the inevitability of their inward undoing. Because instead of tearing the heart by the picture that he paints of the martyr's anguish in the arena, he permits the attention to fasten itself with a grim fascination upon the prowess of the lion that is bound to devour him. It is Mr. O'Neill's awareness of the sad humor in events that causes him in *The Emperor Jones* to send his terror-stricken emperor circling through the protecting forest until he stumbles out of it and into the hands of his pursuers at the very point at which he entered. (p. 46)

The tragic and ironic forces with which Mr. O'Neill deals he handles with a power that is uniquely his own. It is a power born of the grim forces which are his subject matter. Like them his writing surges onward because it must; because it shares with them their quality of inevitability. It has no time for the subduings of a blue pencil skillfully wielded or for the niceties that are so dear to the lesser men and that would do so much to conserve its strength, because it is as wasteful of itself as nature is and seems to be equally casual in its editing. Its force is most resilient when Mr. O'Neill's concern is not the sciences that man must master with his mind but the crude elements of nature that he must battle with his arms, because it is as an emotionalist, and not a thinker, that Mr. O'Neill excels. His strength is of that great, raw, shaggy kind that Whitman's was. It is soberer, starker, and infinitely more grim. But it is no less torrential, savage as it is, with the same energy, heavy with the same profusion and cumulative in the same headlong way.

Mr. O'Neill's are vigorous words unloosed in vigorous cadences. (p. 48)

Of recent years, as Mr. O'Neill has grown as an artist and grown away from immediate contact with his early material, and as his field of exploration has ceased to be the world of fact and become the world of modern psychology and mysticism, an increasing self-consciousness has manifested itself in his work. His thought has often been impeded in its statement because of the "mystical patterns" and "overtones" that, as he himself has described it, lie "dimly behind and beyond the words and actions of the characters." An acute illustration of that confusion and of the involutions of his own mind which he expects an audience to follow in the terms of an elaborate symbolism, is *The Great God Brown*. . . . (p. 50)

If in spite of his exceptional courage and his no less exceptional power, Mr. O'Neill seems an unsatisfactory genius, it is because he comes so frequently within the range of greatness without achieving it completely. His plays are peaked with greatness rather than sustained by it. (p. 52)

[*Mourning Becomes Electra*] is one of the most distinguished achievements of Mr. O'Neill's career. It is—as the dull word has it—uneven, but so—as the no less dull retort phrases it—are the Himalayas. It has blemishes which are obvious, especially as it reaches its third section. But it remains to the end a *magnum opus* beside which *Strange Interlude* and most of the earlier, simpler plays sink into unimportance. For it is an experiment in sheer, shuddering, straightforward storytelling which widens the theatre's limited horizons at the same time it is exalting and horrifying its patrons. (pp. 53-4)

As Mr. O'Neill rehandles this venerable story it preserves its awesome fascination. It emerges, as it has always emerged, as one of the most gripping melodramatic plots in the world. It also comes through its present restatement as a tragic melodrama of heroic proportions. The poetic beauty the Greeks gave it is lacking in Mr. O'Neill's prose modernization. But the dilemma remains, and so does much of the agony and exaltation that belong to it. Mr. O'Neill's treatment of it is vigorous with the kind of vigor our theatre

rarely sees. It is stark, unadorned and strong. It has dignity and majesty. Nearly the whole of it is possessed of such an all-commanding interest that one is totally unconscious of the hours its performance freely consumes.

That it is longer than it need be seems fairly obvious, as does the fact that, like so many of O'Neill's plays, it stands in need of editing. . . . Deprived of plotting which sweeps forward to a climax, and dealing with the conscience-stricken course of its avengers, it goes a tamer, more uncertain way. Nor is it helped by the incest motive Mr. O'Neill has added. It rises in the last act, however, to a final curtain that is Greek in its whole feeling and flavor. (pp. 56-7)

If Mr. O'Neill remains "news"—definitely "news"—the reasons are almost intrusive. Whatever his shortcomings may be (and they have been fairly manifest), he occupies a position as proud as it is solitary. . . .

What has set him most squarely apart, and granted him a fine loneliness among the dramatic talents of our time, has been the subject which he has made his most constant concern. Whether he has stated this in terms of cheap and juvenile irony (as he most certainly did in the melodramatic excesses of those earliest "My-Gawd-what-a-chanct-I-got" one-acts), or expressed it with the white heat of tragedy (as in the first two parts of *Mourning Becomes Electra*, before the play became mired in Freud), his characters have almost always dared to look beyond their relations with their neighbors and sought to find their place in the universe. (p. 59)

John Mason Brown, "O'Neill and God's Angry Eye" (1930), "'Mourning Becomes Electra'" (1931), "Moaning at the Bar" (1946), and "O'Neill in Retrospect" (1953), in his Dramatis Personae: A Retrospective Show *(copyright © 1929, 1930, 1934, 1938, 1940, 1944, 1946, 1948-1955, 1957, 1958, 1962, 1963 by John Mason Brown; reprinted by permission of The Viking Press, Inc.),* Viking, 1963, pp. 39-66.

It is indisputable that O'Neill's plays are nearly always more impressive on the stage than on the printed page. I should very much like to see [*Long Day's Journey into Night*] done on or off Broadway. If such a play is "impractical" for our theatre, so much the worse for our theatre. The play is the testament of the most serious playwright our country has produced.

To say this is not to set oneself down as an unqualified O'Neill admirer. O'Neill was a faulty craftsman; he was not a sound thinker. Though he probably read more extensively and profoundly than most of our playwrights, O'Neill could not by any "universal" standard be considered a cultivated man. His view of life is circumscribed, he is often raw, naive, sentimental and pessimistic in a somewhat adolescent manner.

Yet to dwell on these shortcomings as if they negate the value of the man to our stage and to our culture is to confess one's own inadequate and bloodless response to the world we live in. For in a time and place where life is experienced either as a series of mechanistic jerks or sipped in polite doses of borrowed sophistication (when it is not dully recorded in a sort of statistical spiritual bookkeeping) O'Neill not only lived intensely but attempted with perilous honesty to contemplate, absorb and digest the meaning of his life and ours. He possessed an uncompromising devotion to the task he set himself: to present and interpret in stage terms what he had lived through and thought about—a devotion unique in our theatre. (pp. 214-15)

From [a] sense of guilt—all his characters suffer it in one form or another—and a corresponding sense that the guilt feeling is in itself a sin or at least a fatal blemish comes a constant alternation of mood. Every character speaks in two voices, two moods—one of rage, the other of apology. This produces a kind of moral schizophrenia which in some of O'Neill's other plays has necessitated an interior monologue and a speech for social use (*Strange Interlude*) or as in *The Great God Brown* and *Days Without End,* two sets of masks. In this everlasting duality with its equal pressures in several directions lies the brooding power, the emotional grip of O'Neill's work. (pp. 215-16)

O'Neill's work is more than realism. And if it is stammering—it is still the most eloquent and significant stammer of the American theatre. We have not yet developed a cultivated speech that is either superior to it or as good. (p. 216)

> *Harold Clurman, "'Long Day's Journey into Night,"* in The Nation *(copyright 1956 by the Nation Associates, Inc.), March 3, 1956 (and reprinted in* O'Neill and His Plays: Four Decades of Criticism, *edited by Oscar Cargill, N. Bryllion Fagin, and William J. Fisher, New York University Press, 1961, pp. 214-16).*

With the possible exception of one or two, even [O'Neill's] best works nearly always suggest that they intend more than they succeed in embodying and that—possibly because the aim is so high—they are, in certain respects, less adequate to their purpose than the plays of lesser men. For all that he is so prolific, he has no facility; there is a continual, seldom wholly successful struggle, not only with the central conception but even with the language itself, so that one often gets the impression of positive clumsiness, as though neither the imagination nor the tongue was quite articulate enough to achieve full or clear expression.

His themes have, at the same time, been extraordinarily varied. But neither the variety of themes nor the restless, sometimes extravagant experimentation with forms and unusual technical devices is the result of the exuberance of a skillful craftsman trying everything because he has discovered in himself a kind of universal competence. Neither do the varied subject matters suggest that vivacious type of mind which, having no center of its own, exhibits an eager concern with everything suggested to it. On the contrary, an intense, almost pathologically introverted personality obsessed with what is really a single idea, seems to be seizing, one after another, upon themes or forms of expression and then dropping them after more or less prolonged experimentation because each is discovered to be less closely related to a central concern than it seemed at first sight to be. (pp. 77-9)

[A] brooding temperament is even more fundamental in him than any specific predilection for the drama, and the history of his development as a writer begins as significantly with his discovery of that temperament as it does with his early familiarity with dressing rooms. (p. 81)

Bound East for Cardiff and . . . other short plays of the sea . . . reveal not only O'Neill's penchant for "strong" incidents and his preference for primitive, not wholly articulate characters, but also his persistent sense that pure rationality cannot exhaust the meaning of any really important situation. It is significant that the dying hero of his first produced play should be chiefly concerned with what God will think and significant also that the hero of *Ile* . . . should be a fanatical whaling captain whose wife goes mad when a sudden opening of the ice makes him break his promise to head south. Many of O'Neill's characters were to be obsessed by something stronger than themselves and it is that obsession, that relation to something good or evil bigger than their conscious minds, which makes them interesting to their creator. (p. 82)

Before the end of 1918 he had written a number of one-act plays, and the five dealing with the sea are characterized by a compactness and clarity not to be discovered in many of his later works. The very fact that they are short prevents over-complication or confusions and it is noticeable that as O'Neill turned to longer plays he showed a tendency, not only to lose himself in the uncertainty of his own emotions, but also to allow the intrusion of themes which did not concern him as deeply as he perhaps at the moment supposed. (p. 83)

O'Neill seems to waver somewhat in the judgment which he passes upon the imperatives outside themselves which men obey. Sometimes—most often perhaps—they enslave. But he never loses the sense that those who recognize them gain some sort of stature, attain some sort of eminence—either good or evil. As he came later to attempt more clearly defined tragedies, he realized that what the catastrophes of the mere unhappy play most obviously lacked was magnitude, and that the first step in the creation of a tragic effect must consist in giving that magnitude to catastrophe by relating it to something real or illusory outside of man's mere rationality as well as outside his mere animal desires. (pp. 86-7)

To George Jean Nathan, O'Neill once wrote: "The playwright of today must dig at the roots of the sickness of today as he feels it—the death of the old God and the failure of science and materialism to give any satisfactory new one for the surviving primitive religious instinct to find a meaning for life in, and to comfort its fears of death with. It seems to me that anyone trying to do big work nowadays must have this big subject behind all the little subjects of his plays or novels, or he is scribbling around the surface of things." This is surely not only explicit enough but stated in terms so familiar as to be commonplace, and O'Neill's distinction can hardly consist in the fact that he has arrived at such a conclusion. It does, however, consist in part in the fact that he has found original symbols through which to present the conviction and told exciting stories which take on meaning in the light of it. . . . The crude and obvious fact that life is vivid and restless, exciting and terrible must be turned by tragedy into some peace-giving beauty. O'Neill is not concerned simply with saying that it is. As a writer of tragedy he is attempting to get beyond the mere fact. (pp. 92-3)

It is impossible to say just how conscious O'Neill may have gradually become of all he had learned of his own aims, powers, and limitations in the course of writing more than a score of plays. Unconsciously, at least, much clarification had taken place by the time he came to compose *Mourning Becomes Electra*. Some time before he had come to realize clearly that he was concerned with "the relation of man to God"—with, that is to say, the relation of man to something, whether that something is the universe itself or merely the enduring laws of his own being, which is independent of local or temporary conditions. Now he realized also that tragedy is essentially a story of some calamity growing out of that relationship and that it differs from the story of any failure, however calamitous, involving merely human relationships by virtue of two facts: On the one hand it involves a great deal more; on the other, the protagonists take on a dignity they cannot otherwise have. But the would-be writer of tragedy today labors under an almost insuperable difficulty. He lives in a society most of whose members are either confused and uncertain or explicitly deny that any such relationship between man and God exists; that there are any problems to solve except problems to be faced by men so entirely the product of temporary conditions, that even their past is no more than a ghost which it is their business to lay as promptly as possible. (pp. 104-05)

No radical solution of the difficulty seems possible and perhaps none is. To ask for a tragedy "modern" in every sense is to ask for a play whose characters must have toward the universe as a whole an attitude which would render them no longer typically modern. Hence the choice seems to be inevitably a choice between genuine tragedies about people more or less remote from us and mere demi-tragedies like *Strange Interlude* about ourselves. Nor can it be said that O'Neill has ever completely solved the perhaps insoluble difficulty though he has, I think, come nearer to doing so in *Mourning Becomes Electra* than in any of his other plays. (p. 106)

Obviously O'Neill is moved by the conviction that . . . debasement of a story of passion and crime to the police court level is not inevitable; that there remain to us depths and dignities which could lift it into a different realm if they were properly exploited. And *Mourning Becomes Electra* is precisely an effort to exploit them. . . . [The play attempts] by means of the sheer intensity with which it presents strength of character and high passion, to make these things seem sufficient in themselves and to demonstrate that the possibility of emotional greatness has not departed from us. It is, in effect, the tragic poet's answer to a charge which he himself had previously seemed to make, to the charge that both the sense of sin and the sense of greatness have disappeared from the human consciousness along with the religious sanctions which supported them.

Perhaps the difference between Aeschylus and O'Neill is to some degree a measure of the extent to which the weakening of the sanctions has weakened the emotions which they supported, if they did not create. But the difference between what the Greeks could feel and what we can feel is not as immeasurably great as it may sometimes have seemed when we were in the presence of tale-tellers who accepted too readily the police-court view of human nature. And in that fact lies a measure of the importance of the play. In no other of O'Neill's major works do the characters make with equal success the attempt to lift themselves by their own bootstraps, to gain stature, less by relating themselves to something outside, than merely by virtue of the strength that is in them. It is far less mystical than even

Strange Interlude; it accepts without protest the validity upon its own level of a purely rational psychology. But it also manages somehow to reassert human dignity and to prove by the emotional elevation it manages to maintain that to explain human conduct even in Freudian terms is not necessarily the same thing as to explain it away. (pp. 110-11)

[O'Neill] is a mystic and . . . to him the essential fact about human life is not that manners and creeds vary from place to place and from time to time but that two phenomena— the conflict between good and evil and man's desire to feel himself in harmony with something outside himself—eternally re-appear. It is likewise true that the persistence of these phenomena is also a chief concern of the Catholic Church, and if one assumes as correct and final the Church's attitude toward them, then it is natural that its standards of truth should be regarded as highly relevant to the judgment of any man's work. But if, on the contrary, one assumes that Catholic teaching represents only one of the attempts to formulate and solve problems more universal than even Catholic theology itself, then one may assume, not only that its terms are not necessarily the most appropriate to O'Neill, but also that his most significant treatment of his themes may have been those in which he seemed to be either solving or failing to solve problems in a highly original way rather than in that single play where he seemed to bring himself at last to the acceptance of a ready-made solution which he had rejected many times before.

To whatever extent it may finally appear that the best of O'Neill's work falls short of absolute greatness, it is not likely that his failure will be found to consist in a failure to accept soon enough or fully enough any intellectual formula. Both as an intellectual and as an emotional conception *Mourning Becomes Electra* at least is in the true grand manner. To find in it any lack one must compare it with the very greatest works of dramatic literature, and to do that is to realize that the one thing conspicuously missing is language—words as thrilling as the action which accompanies them. . . . If the language came, we should be swept aloft as no Anglo-Saxon audience since Shakespeare's time has had an opportunity to be. But no such language does come and *Mourning Becomes Electra* remains, therefore, only the best tragedy in English which the present century has produced. That is the penalty we pay for living in an age whose most powerful dramatist cannot rise above prose. (pp. 118-20)

> *Joseph Wood Krutch, "Tragedy: Eugene O'Neill," in his* The American Drama Since 1918: An Informal History *(reprinted by permission of George Braziller, Inc., Publishers; copyright © 1957 by Joseph Wood Krutch), Braziller, 1957, pp. 73-133.*

Although O'Neill broods over death, it adds nothing but confusion to call him a tragic dramatist. . . . O'Neill's question, which in the late plays became sharper and more accurately perceived, was simply how man, bereft of faith in God, might confront the inevitability of death. That was hardly a new question, far too commonplace to please those who put a premium on originality. Moreover, O'Neill's answer to the question was an ancient one, although it has a modern appeal. The mood of the late O'Neill combines Romanticism and Stoicism. (pp. 111-12)

It would be interesting to discover whether Eugene O'Neill knew that in his treatment of time he was closer than in any other respect to the Greek drama. He was not successful in finding a modern equivalent for the Greek Fates or for Nemesis. The attempt to make the Oedipus complex perform this service in *Mourning Becomes Electra* succeeded only in reducing the Greek story to the level of rationalistic psychology. Where O'Neill did succeed, however, and for his purposes it was probably the only place necessary for him to succeed, was in his representation of a world in which, as in most Greek tragedy, there is no future. (p. 112)

We must suppose that the notion of an effective action taken in the present was not consistent with the view of the world that O'Neill had adopted, or was coming to adopt. Other efforts in that direction (*Lazarus Laughed, Dynamo*) also fail. The idea of decisive action seems to have been associated in O'Neill's mind with fantasy. In *The Iceman Cometh, A Touch of the Poet,* and *A Moon for the Misbegotten* all thought of taking action to change things is set forth as the product of illusion. The one function of the present is to reveal the past. Only the past is real. (p. 114)

O'Neill, whose affinities with Strindberg are well known, may be said to represent the secularized man of Christendom living at a time when the built-in optimism of Western society is being exhausted. He is unable with the old latent assumptions to cope with the disruptions of an age of violence; and he is even less able to return to religious life, out of which a belief in the future had originally sprung. It was but natural, therefore, to turn to the kind of skeptical reassurance-in-chaos which had sustained the late Classical age, in other words to a new Stoicism. (pp. 114-15)

The skepticism of O'Neill is nowhere more in evidence than in his handling of the theme of illusion. This is not so much because he sets about to destroy illusion in the name of reality as because the question of illusions is linked to his time-pessimism, with its essentially foreclosed future. Illusion therefore not only includes self-deception or "pipe-dream" but also every kind of hope, excluding only the hope of death. The attitude here is unflinching. We remember Ibsen's greater flexibility, able at one time to oppose illusory "ideals" for the sake of truth itself, but also able, in *The Wild Duck,* to understand the wisdom of the life-illusion when it is a necessary defense against destruction. O'Neill shows no hint of such practical compromise. There is no value according to which illusion (art, self-fulfillment, hope, religious faith—anything future-oriented) might be tolerated. And there is no alternative to illusion but death. (p. 118)

O'Neill [insists] upon stripping man of every role, every pattern of order, every formation of his mental powers through which he builds those "lies" upon which life and culture depend: that is, those indirections by which we find directions out. All figurative knowledge is . . . dismissed, so that O'Neill is not only anti-religious . . . but also anti-aesthetic.

O'Neill was anti-religious only in so far as the object of the quest is concerned: he was always extremely religious in terms of the quest itself. The letter to George Jean Nathan in which he spoke of finding a substitute for the old, dead God is famous, as is also his remark to Joseph Wood Krutch that he was interested only in the relation of man to God. Henry Hewes is right to speak of the "constant recognition," in *Long Day's Journey into Night,* of "man's quest for religious ecstasy." Where the quest seems ready to discover its object, however, O'Neill was either ill at ease or emphatically negative.

Similarly, O'Neill was dedicated to art in so far as art can be understood as a quest. Writing was his vocation, and few men have labored at it so consistently against such odds. If part of the odds came from ill health, another part came from the fact that, as Joseph Wood Krutch said, he had no aptitude for writing, no concern with the *mot juste.* I think it safe to say that he had no *confidence* in art as form. His vocation of writing plays was not followed for the purpose of achieving the right forms incarnating the right conceptions but rather to use writing to wrestle with life. This accounts for the strength and weakness of his work. It is weak at almost every point where we care to ask an aesthetic question, and therefore, by implication, where we care to ask the question of what is being affirmed outside of man. It is strong wherever we care to look at man coming to terms with himself in a world of total darkness.

O'Neill thus affords us a clear example of the close, if usually unacknowledged, connection between art and religious or philosophical assertion. To be concerned about the creation of a work of art is to be able to back off far enough from the existential battles to adopt a standing place, on the basis of which the form of the work of art may be established. Those who say, therefore, that O'Neill lacked only the ability to write well miss the point. To be concerned about writing well would have been to deny the very obsession which impelled him to write in the first place. It would have assumed a stasis, a sense of completion or wholeness which his radical pessimism had completely overthrown. In a situation in which the only reality is death and the only question how to meet it, necessarily a tormented question, there are no values, proportions, relationships, traditions, or ultimates according to which the artistic work might be fashioned and judged. The particular existential power of O'Neill's work and its aesthetic ruggedness go hand in hand. (pp. 119-20)

There may indeed be many things in [the late plays] which are to be explained on the basis of the playwright's idiosyncrasies, but the struggle between life and death is not one of them, nor is the purgation of the fear of death. In these respects, O'Neill is but one of a much larger company today for whom the ancient life-death battle is the paramount reality. For these the major problem of man is how he is to find himself in a world in which the ultimate reality is a return to nothingness. Here the Stoic virtues of resignation, courage, and purgation of passion become relevant. The Stoic element in all the nonreligious versions of existentialism is very strong. Courage and resignation are the only virtues which apply to Heidegger's situation of being on the edge of the abyss. They are the first virtues which apply to the world Sartre has described. They are the starting point for the assertion of manhood proclaimed by Camus. If it was Kierkegaard who first convinced modern man that his situation is desperate, O'Neill is but one among many who have answered neo-Stoically that despair is only to be overcome by having the courage to acknowledge it as the inescapable fact of our existence.

If Paul Tillich is right that the basic anxiety of our age comes from the threat of meaninglessness, it is not difficult to see that O'Neill offers a remedy for that anxiety. His plays declare that the meaning of life is its inevitable progression toward death. This is not, of course, an assertion which gives meaning to any of the particularities of life. In fact, it drains them of meaning. But it is a way of redeeming existence from meaningless anarchy by showing that its pattern is basically simple and imperturbable. The bleakest philosophy is preferable to chaos. (p. 122)

I believe O'Neill's stance is wrong. It is responsible for his failure to come to terms with the particularities and contingencies of living which many of us are not ready to declare of no importance. Be that as it may, no other playwright of the American stage has shown us as much of the grandeur of the dramatic imagination. He makes the rest of our theater seem petite, and very timid. (p. 123)

> *Tom F. Driver, "On the Late Plays of Eugene O'Neill," in* The Drama Review *(copyright © 1958 by* The Drama Review*), December, 1958 (and reprinted in* O'Neill: A Collection of Critical Essays, *edited by John Gassner, Prentice-Hall, Inc., 1964, pp. 110-23).*

By American standards [O'Neill's] reputation was surely justified. No other native playwright had been at once so skillful, original, exciting, prolific. None had been so bold, uncompromising, influential. Now, after some thirty years, one is further impressed by discerning a pattern in the earlier plays, a tendency obscured perhaps by infusions of psychology and sex, by theatrical gimmicks. I mean the religious element. Beginning about 1922 O'Neill wrote play after play of personal suffering, passionate intensity, religious aspiration—allegorical works, dramas of conversion, apocalyptic plays. The serious playwright "must dig at the roots of the sickness of today," O'Neill announced, a sickness which he traced to "the death of the old God and the failure of science and materialism to give any satisfying new One for the surviving religious instinct to find a meaning for life in and to comfort its fears of death with." Digging at his own roots, describing his own symptoms, he pursued strange gods. One, the contrary of his own temperament, was the embodiment of those affirmative qualities which O'Neill so desperately lacked. This was, of course, Nietzsche's Dionysus. O'Neill had become a disciple of Nietzsche and from him learned not only to substitute Dionysus for Christ but also the satyr for the ape. In this way he temporarily answered his objections to modern Christianity and to scientific Darwinism. From Nietzsche he learned, further, to urge struggle in place of resignation, ecstasy in place of apathy, affirmation of life in place of denial. Moreover, he now found it possible to transfigure into mystic vision and rapture his old formula for survival: dope-dream and drunkenness. (p. 219)

Prior to *The Iceman Cometh* O'Neill had always felt that love was the prime component of faith. He had his characters plead for love, profess it, pursue it, but seldom experience it in any but the most elemental or immature way. His heroes, at odds with the world, sought the remoteness of the cosmos, the protection of the womb, the anonymity of the grave. In their self-obsession they were actually indifferent to the suffering of other men, although they avowed their love for Man. The triumph of *Long Day's Journey Into Night* was the consequence of O'Neill's emergence from the fog, of his ascent from the bottom of the sea, long

enough to give love an ascendancy over peace and to find it in his heart to absolve his misbegotten family. The play is one of self-discovery and of spiritual victory. It is at once O'Neill's most religious play and his most genuine tragedy. (p. 223)

> *Edwin A. Engel, "O'Neill, 1960," in* Modern Drama *(copyright 1960, A. C. Edwards; with the permission of* Modern Drama*), December, 1960, pp. 219-23.*

I would nominate *Strange Interlude* for [these] refulgent honors: as the most atrociously ill-written and ill-conceived play of our time, as the falsest "masterpiece" in the theatre, as very likely the worst play that has ever been written by a dramatist with a reputation. And what makes its current revival such an occasion for outrage is precisely the reverent atmosphere surrounding the event, the fact that as the first offering of the Actors Studio, that *soi-disant* savior of the arts of the theatre in America, it is being presented as Revelation, crammed as full of stars as the Milky Way and made to blot out by its sheer pretentious gaseous bulk, its surrogate presence, any glimpse we might have had of an area of hope for maturity on our native stages and among our audiences.

I beg my readers' indulgence. I can't decide which is greater, my anger or my despair, and I can't be temperate. . . . Bathed in the piety and idiot enthusiasm of that audience for whom O'Neill is holy writ, assaulted in our intelligence, aesthetic faculties and simple hope of physical survival, we came as close to conceiving an irreparable hatred for the theatre as only such a misuse of it as this can bring you to. (pp. 68-9)

It is a commonplace to speak of O'Neill's verbal deficiencies, but in *Strange Interlude* they are at their most flagrant because the play is literally nothing but talk—grotesquely artificial dialogue and those intolerable asides which have been seen as a profound theatrical innovation but which instead constitute one of the most colossal dramaturgical evasions on record.

The asides either tell the audience what it already knows or serve to choke the action of the play; the one thing they never do is contribute to any understanding of the characters that could not have been gained through direct speech, if O'Neill had been capable of that. It is just the playwright's task to make dialogue illuminate inner states, to fuse expression with the not-to-be-expressed. And indeed the fantastic ineptitude of *Strange Interlude* can be seen by measuring it against any work by Strindberg, the master whom O'Neill plundered and so badly misunderstood, and who in seven minutes on the same themes of sexuality, repression and the ravages of passion could convey precisely through dialogue unfathomably more than O'Neill in his four-and-a-half-hours of mutterings.

Quarter-baked Strindberg, tenth-rate Freud—the play is a vast mine of reductive psychologizing, spurious philosophy, adolescent mysticism, unrealized emotion and sentimentality on an epic scale. (pp. 69-70)

If you are a masochist, there is nothing I can say, I have in fact helped you. But if you merely wish to subject yourself to O'Neill, out of unresolved confusion or lingering respect, I suggest you choose instead the film of *Long Day's Journey Into Night*. In that play, as in a few others of his last years, O'Neill broke through, became an artist and found the form for his vague floating passion for the "big things." In *Strange Interlude* the big things have no form, no language and, finally, no existence whatsoever. (p. 71)

If there is one point around which hard critical opinion, as distinguished from chauvinistic rhetoric or inarticulate zealotry, has coalesced it is that O'Neill's last plays constitute his strongest claim to permanent stature. It is a thin claim when measured against the accomplishments of his European contemporaries such as Shaw, Brecht or Pirandello, or his immediate predecessors like Ibsen, Strindberg and Chekhov. But at least *The Iceman Cometh* and *Long Day's Journey Into Night* do not have to be ashamed in that company, whereas we have been made increasingly aware of how inexorably the plays of O'Neill's middle period, upon which his aggrandizement has chiefly been built, are slipping out of consciousness, literature and indeed any reality except an antiquarian one. (p. 72)

O'Neill's desires outrun his capacities [in *More Stately Mansions*], as they do almost everywhere in his work until the last phase, when through a reduction of scope and what we might call a localization of language he was able to fuse his moral and aesthetic intentions, to find a rhetoric which did not escape like a balloon from his feeling and a structure in which his thought did not appear dwarfed.

But here the fusion is not achieved; the moral and metaphysical critique and vision exist mostly as a series of statements and isolated confrontations which lack an organic base and a coherent impulse. As elsewhere in O'Neill there is a strenuous attempt to compensate for this condition through an atmosphere of portentousness, a heavy air of "high" poetry, apocalypse, fervid declamations and mysterious psychological irruptions. (p. 74)

O'Neill, if we needed any more proof, was the victim of his ill-defined encounter with "Tragedy" and the "Soul," forever trying to embody them in works which . . . could not be compelled into clarity or convincing life; when the coercion stopped and he gave form to what his imagination had truly known and not merely aspired to, art at last became possible. (p. 75)

> *Richard Gilman, "Between Anger and Despair" (1963), and "Mr. O'Neill's Very Last Curtain Call" (1964), in his* Common and Uncommon Masks: Writings on Theatre, 1961-1970 *(copyright © 1971 by Richard Gilman; reprinted by permission of Random House, Inc.), Random House, 1971, pp. 68-75.*

As some of the dust begins to settle over the controversial reputation of Eugene O'Neill, and our interest shifts from the man to art, it becomes increasingly clear that O'Neill will be primarily remembered for his last plays. The earlier ones are not all without value, though none is thoroughly satisfying. Some contain powerful scenes; some have interesting themes; and some are sustained by the sheer force of the author's will. Still, the bulk of O'Neill dramatic writings before *Ah Wilderness!* are like the groping preparatory sketches of one who had to write badly in order to write well; and in comparison with the late O'Neill even intermittently effective dramas like *The Hairy Ape, All God's Chillun Got Wings,* and *Desire Under the Elms* are riddled with fakery, incoherence, and clumsy experimental de-

vices. No major dramatist, with the possible exception of Shaw, has written so many second-rate plays. (p. 321)

O'Neill came to prominence in the second and third decades of the century, when America was just beginning to relinquish its philistinism in order to genuflect before the shrine of Culture. The American culture craze was largely directed towards the outsides of the literature, which is to say towards the personality of the artist rather than the content of his art; and the novelists and poets inducted into this hollow ritual found themselves engaged in an activity more priestly than creative. O'Neill's role was especially hieratic, however, since he had the misfortune to be the first dramatist with serious aspirations to appear on the national scene. . . . But to a large body of hungry critics and cultural consumers, who were indifferent to the quality of the product so long as it was Big, O'Neill was a homegrown dramatic champion to be enlisted not only against Ibsen, Strindberg, and Shaw, but against Aeschylus, Euripides, and Shakespeare as well. (pp. 321-22)

Afflicted with the American disease of gigantism, O'Neill developed ambitions which were not only large, they were monstrous; he was determined to be nothing if not a world-historical figure of fantastic proportion. Trying to compress within his own career the whole development of dramatic literature since the Greeks, he set himself to imitate the most ambitious writers who ever lived—and the more epic their scope, the more they stimulated his competitive instinct. The scope of his own intentions is suggested by the growing length of his plays and the presumptuousness of his public utterances. *Mourning Becomes Electra,* which took three days to perform, he called "an idea and a dramatic conception that has the possibilities of being the biggest thing modern drama has attempted—by far the biggest!" And his unfinished eleven-play "Big Grand Opus," as he called it, was designed to have "greater scope than any novel I know of . . . something in the style of *War and Peace.*" At this point in his career, O'Neill, like his public, is attracted to the outsides of literature, and he wrestles with the reputation of another writer in order to boost his own. But to O'Neill's public, ambitions were almost indistinguishable from achievements; and the playwright was ranked with the world's greatest dramatists before he had had an opportunity to master his craft or sophisticate his art. (pp. 322-23)

Subjected to closer scrutiny, the very qualities which had inspired so much enthusiasm in O'Neill's partisans now seemed the marks of a pretentious writer and a second-rate mind. Pushed about by this critical storm, the winds of literary fashion shifted, and O'Neill's reputation was blown out to sea. Although the playwright was awarded the Nobel prize in 1936, obscurity had already settled in upon him, and it deepened more and more until his death in 1953. During these dark years, ironically, O'Neill's real development began. Before, he had prided himself on having "the guts to shoot at something big and risk failure"; now, he had the guts not to bother himself about questions of success and failure at all. Maturing in silence, stimulated only by an obsessive urge to write and a profound artistic honesty, he commenced to create plays which were genuine masterpieces of the modern theatre. Most of these were not published or produced until after his death, some by the playwright's order. In proscribing *A Long Day's Journey into Night,* O'Neill was trying to hide his family's secrets from the public eye; but O'Neill's desire to keep his works off the stage was undoubtedly influenced, too, by the hostile reception accorded to *The Iceman Cometh* and *A Moon for the Misbegotten,* the first of which failed on Broadway, the second, before even reaching New York. The public and the reviewers, having found new idols to worship (the Critic's prize the year of *The Iceman Cometh* went to a conventional social protest play by Arthur Miller called *All My Sons*), began to treat O'Neill with condescension—when they thought of him at all. And he was not to be seriously reconsidered until 1956, when a successful revival of *The Iceman Cometh* and the first Broadway production of *A Long Day's Journey* brought him so much posthumous recognition that his inferior work was soon dragged out of storage for some more unthinking praise. (pp. 323-24)

Aside from the one-act sea plays, which are modest in scope and relatively conventional in form, O'Neill's early drama tends to be Expressionist in its symbolic structure and messianic in its artistic stance. Both O'Neill's Expressionism and messianism, I hasten to add, are borrowed, ill-fitting robes. By the time O'Neill begins to write, the theatre of revolt is an established movement in every country except America, where the theatre has produced nothing more exhilarating than the fabricated fantasies of Fitch, Boucicault, and Belasco. Thus, the drama of the continent constitutes an untapped mine of material, and O'Neill, recognizing its potentialities, becomes the first dramatist to exploit it; with the aid of the Provincetown Players, he does for the American awareness of European drama what Shaw and the Independent Theatre did for the English.

Although O'Neill is originally considered a wild, untutored genius, therefore, his early work is clearly the offshoot of a very intellectualistic mind, attuned more to literature than to life. Aligning himself with the more radical of the rebel dramatists, he is soon impersonating their postures, imitating their doctrines, and copying their techniques. One can detect the influence of Ibsen, Toller, Shaw, Gorky, Pirandello, Wedekind, Synge, Andreyev, and others in the early plays of O'Neill, but chief among his dramatic models in this period is August Strindberg, whom O'Neill, in his Nobel prize acceptance speech, called "the greatest of all modern dramatists." . . . O'Neill's relation to his plays . . . is very Strindbergian: he is almost always the hero of his work, trying to work out his personal difficulties through the medium of his art. (pp. 324-26)

As an experimental dramatist, O'Neill would naturally be attracted to the greatest innovator in the modern theatre; and O'Neill's Expressionism is certainly indebted to Strindberg's dream techniques. The difference is that Strindberg's formal experiments grow out of his material, while O'Neill's seem grafted onto his, and thus give the impression of being gratuitous and excessive. . . . Thus, O'Neill uses Expressionistic devices to communicate ideas which he is either too inarticulate or too undisciplined to express through speech and action. And his masks, asides, soliloquies, choruses, split characters and the like are really substitutes for dramatic writing (most of these conventions are borrowed from the novel), provoked not by a new vision but rather by a need to disguise the banality of the original material. Thus, instead of opening up uncharted territory, O'Neill's devices invariably fog up already familiar ground,

as for example the interminable soliloquizing of *Strange Interlude* which, instead of going deeper into the unconscious mind, merely compounds the verbalized trivialities of the characters with their trivial unspoken thoughts. Moving from mono-dramas to miracle plays to historical dramas to mob plays to Greek tragedies, O'Neill appears to experiment largely for the sake of novelty without ever staying with a form long enough to perfect it. (pp. 327-28)

O'Neill exposes the philosophical incertitude of the Strindbergian rebel—the pain, the doubts, the confusion. But although there are undoubtedly genuine feelings beneath all this, O'Neill's spiritual crises seem very literary, and his expression of them comes to him secondhand. Furthermore, one is never convinced that O'Neill has read very deeply in those philosophies that he affirms and rejects; his works display the intellectual attitudinizing of the self-conscious autodidact. It is this aspect of the early O'Neill, in fact, which most arouses the spleen of the second generation of his critics. "Mr. O'Neill is not a thinker," asserts Francis Fergusson, while Eric Bentley [see excerpt above] adds, "He is so little a thinker, it is dangerous for him to think." Both critics go on to demonstrate how O'Neill's superficial treatment of fashionable ideas was his main appeal to a superficial and fashionable audience; and both have shown how emotion and thought fail to cohere in his drama. . . . O'Neill's failure, I would suggest, is not a failure of mind so much as a failure of feeling. It is not that he is incapable of thought but rather that he is incapable of *thinking like a dramatist,* communicating his ideas through significant action. And this may be because all of his ideas, in this period, are borrowed rather than experienced. Thus, we find notions of Tragedy out of Nietzsche, of the Puritan Booboisie out of Mencken and Nathan, of the Racial Unconscious out of Jung, of the Oedipus Complex out of Freud, and of Hereditary Guilt out of Aeschylus and Ibsen —all grafted onto plots which are largely unconvincing, irrelevant, or inconsequential.

In fact, the major components of his plots, in this particular phase, are romantic love and swashbuckling adventure, both treated in a manner more appropriate to the melodramatic stage of his father, James O'Neill, than to the theatre of revolt. Ironically, O'Neill always thinks he is defining himself *against* this kind of theatre. . . . (p. 333)

O'Neill's attempt to introduce large themes into his work is a sign of his rebellion against the mindless nineteenth-century stage, but he has assimilated more of "the old, ranting, artificial romantic stuff" than he knows. . . . In O'Neill, everything seems to render down to romance or sex, despite the fact that the author has an extremely naive conception of sexuality. One has only to note his puerile sentimentalization of whores, his Romantic idealization of chaste women—or still worse, his laughable ideas about extramarital affairs, exposed in that fantastic *Strange Interlude* scene where Darrell and Nine cold-bloodedly decide to mate only to produce a child, and discuss the liaison in the third person for the sake of scientific impartiality.

Allied to O'Neill's treatment of sex is his treatment of incest, which is also romanticized in the pulsing accents of *True Confessions* magazine. In *Mourning Becomes Electra,* for example incest becomes as common as weeds, and equally inevitable. . . . "Fierce, bruising kisses" are called for in almost every one of O'Neill's earlier plays—the more fierce and bruising when they are incestuously motivated—

accompanied by bathetic odes to Beauty and jerky apostrophes to Nature. But sex in O'Neill remains without complexity, darkness, or genuine passion, the mentalized fantasy of an adolescent temperament, and totally incompatible with the portentous philosophical attitudes it is meant to support. (pp. 334-36)

[*The Iceman Cometh*] is a chronicle of O'Neill's own spiritual metamorphosis from a messianic into an existential rebel, the shallow yea-saying salvationist of the earlier plays having been transformed into a penetrating analyst of human motive rejecting even the pose of disillusionment. O'Neill's "denial of any other experience of faith in my plays" has left him alone, at last, with existence itself; and he has looked at it with a courage which only the greatest tragic dramatists have been able to muster. *The Iceman Cometh,* despite its prosaic language, recreates that existential groan which is heard in Shakespeare's tragedies and in the third choral poem of Sophocles's *Oedipus at Colonus,* as O'Neill makes reality bearable through the metaphysical consolations of art. O'Neill has rejected Hickey's brand of salvation as a way to human happiness, but truth has, nevertheless, become the cornerstone of his drama, truth combined with . . . compassionate understanding. . . . Expunging everything false and literary from his work, O'Neill has finally reconciled himself to being the man he really is.

This kind of reconciliation could only have come about through penetrating self-analysis; and it is inevitable, therefore, that the process of self-analysis itself should form the material of one of his plays: *A Long Day's Journey into Night.* . . . Here, combining the retrospective techniques of Ibsen with the exorcistic attack of Strindberg, O'Neill compresses the psychological history of his family into the events of a single day, and the economy of the work, for all its length, is magnificent. Within this Classical structure, where O'Neill even observes the unities, the play begins to approach a kind of formal perfection. Like most Classical works, *A Long Day's Journey into Night* is set in the past. . . . And like most Classical works, its impact derives less from physical action (the play has hardly any plot, and only the first act has any suspense) than from psychological revelation, as the characters dredge up their painful memories and half-considered thoughts. (pp. 348-49)

O'Neill . . . is not only the author of the play but also a character in it; like Strindberg, he has written "a poem of desperation," composed in rhythms of pain. . . . The play, written as he tells us "in tears and blood," was composed in a cold sweat, sometimes fifteen hours at a stretch: O'Neill, like all his characters, is confronting his most harrowing memories, and putting his ghosts to rest in a memorial reenactment of their mutual suffering and responsibility.

Because his purpose is partially therapeutic, O'Neill has hardly fictionalized this autobiography at all. (p. 349)

In view of this fidelity to fact, it is a wonder that O'Neill was able to write the play at all, but he is in astonishing control of his material—the work is a masterpiece. While *The Iceman Cometh* has fewer arid stretches and deeper implications, *A Long Day's Journey* contains the finest writing O'Neill ever did—and the fourth act is among the most powerful scenes in all dramatic literature. O'Neill has created a personal play which bears on the condition of all

mankind; a bourgeois family drama with universal implications. *A Long Day's Journey* is a study of hereditary guilt which does not even make recourse to arbitrary metaphors, like Ibsen's use of disease in *Ghosts*. (p. 350)

In the plays that follow, O'Neill continues to work the vein he had mined in *The Iceman Cometh* and *A Long Day's Journey:* examining, through the medium of a faithful realism, the people of the fog and their illusionary lives. And in writing these plays, he stammers no more. In the lilting speech of predominantly Irish-Catholic characters, O'Neill finally discovers a language congenial to him, and he even begins to create a music very much like Synge's, while his humor bubbles more and more to the surface. Despite effective comic passages, however, O'Neill's plays remain dark. (p. 358)

[*A Touch of the Poet* and *A Moon for the Misbegotten*] are minor masterpieces; *The Iceman Cometh* and *A Long Day's Journey* major ones. And in all four plays, O'Neill concentrates a fierce, bullish power into fables of illusion and reality, shot through with flashes of humor, but pervaded by a sense of melancholy over the condition of being human. Like Strindberg, therefore, O'Neill develops from messianic rebellion into existential rebellion, thus demonstrating that beneath his Nietzschean yea-saying and affirmation of life was a profound discontent with the very nature of existence. O'Neill's experiments with form, his flirtations with various philosophies and religions, his attitudinizing and fake poeticizing represent the means by which he tried to smother this perception; but it would not be smothered, and when he finally found the courage to face it through realistic probes of his own past experience, he discovered the only artistic role that really fit him. In power and insight, O'Neill remains unsurpassed among American dramatists, and, of course, it is doubtful if, without him, there would have been an American drama at all. But it is for his last plays that he will be remembered—those extraordinary dramas of revolt which he pulled out of himself in pain and suffering, a sick and tired man in a shuttered room unable to bear much light. (p. 359)

> Robert Brustein, "Eugene O'Neill," in his The Theatre of Revolt: An Approach to the Modern Drama (© 1964 by Robert Brustein; reprinted by permission of Little, Brown and Co. in association with the Atlantic Monthly Press), Atlantic-Little, Brown, 1964, pp. 329-59.

We do not read Sophocles or Aeschylus for the right answer; we read them for the force with which they represent life and attack its moral complexity. In O'Neill, despite the many failures of his art and thought, this force is inescapable. (p. 103)

Not only has O'Neill tried to encompass more of life than most American writers of his time but, almost alone among them, he has persistently tried to *solve* it. When we understand this we understand that his stage devices are no fortuitous technique; his masks and abstractions, his double personalities, his drum beats and engine rhythms are the integral and necessary expression of his temper of mind and the task it set itself. Realism is uncongenial to that mind and that task, and it is not in realistic plays like *Anna Christie* and *The Straw,* but rather in such plays as *The Hairy Ape, Lazarus Laughed* and *The Great God Brown,* where he is explaining the world in parable, symbol and myth, that O'Neill is most creative. His interest is not the minutiae of life, not its feel and color and smell, not its nuance and humor, but its "great inscrutable forces." Hence the bathos and redundancy of his language, for a temperamental insensitivity to the accurate word and the exact rhythm is encouraged by the requirements of his enterprise; the search for finality tempts him toward the big and inexact words. (p. 104)

To O'Neill the acquisitive man, kindly and insensitive, practical and immature, became a danger to life and one that he never left off attacking.

But it developed, strangely, that the American middle class had no strong objection to being attacked and torpedoed; it seemed willing to be sunk for the insurance that was paid in a new strange coin. The middle class found that it consisted of two halves, bourgeoisie and booboisie. . . .

Boobish and sophisticated: these were the two categories of art; spiritual freedom could be bought at the price of finding *Jurgen* profound. (pp. 106-07)

O'Neill did not win his worldly success by the slightest compromise of sincerity. Indeed, his charm consisted in his very integrity and hieratic earnestness. His position changed, not absolutely, but relatively to his audience, which was now the literate middle class caught up with the intellectual middle class. O'Neill . . . had become a physician of souls. Beneath his iconoclasm his audience sensed reassurance.

The middle class is now in such literary disrepute that a writer's ability to please it is taken as the visible mark of an internal rottenness. But the middle class is people; prick them and they bleed, and whoever speaks sincerely to and for flesh and blood deserves respect. O'Neill's force derives in large part from the force of the moral and psychical upheaval of the middle class; it wanted certain of its taboos broken and O'Neill broke them. (p. 107)

Whoever writes sincerely about the middle class must consider the nature and the danger of the morality of "ideals," those phosphorescent remnants of a dead religion with which the middle class meets the world. This had been Ibsen's great theme, and now O'Neill undertook to investigate for America the destructive power of the ideal—not merely the sordid ideal of the Business Man but even the "idealistic" ideal of the Poet. (pp. 107-08)

To affirm that life exists and is somehow good—this, then, became O'Neill's quasi-religious poetic function, nor is it difficult to see why the middle class welcomed it. . . . [O'Neill] solves the problem of evil by making explicit what men have always found to be the essence of tragedy—the courageous affirmation of life in the face of individual defeat. . . .

O'Neill, unable . . . merely to accept the tragic universe and unable to support it with man's whole strength—his intellect and emotion—prepares to support it with man's weakness: his blind faith. (pp. 109-10)

For the non-Catholic reader O'Neill's explicitly religious solution is likely to be not only insupportable but incomprehensible. . . . [He] feels that life is empty—having emptied it—and can fill it only by faith in a loving God. The existence of such a God, Pascal knew, cannot be proved save

by the heart's need, but this seemed sufficient and he stood ready to stupefy his reason to maintain his faith. O'Neill will do no less. It is perhaps the inevitable way of modern Catholicism in a hostile world. (p. 110)

O'Neill has crept into the dark womb of Mother Church and pulled the universe in with him. Perhaps the very violence of the gesture with which he has taken the position of passivity should remind us of his force and of what such force may yet do even in that static and simple dark. (p. 113)

> *Lionel Trilling, "Eugene O'Neill," in* After the Genteel Tradition: American Writers, 1910-1930, *edited by Malcolm Cowley (copyright © 1964 by Malcolm Cowley; reprinted by permission of Southern Illinois University Press), revised edition, Southern Illinois University Press, 1964, pp. 103-13.*

[O'Neill's] work suffered more than any other dramatist's from the general desire for 'significance'. His dramatic talent amounted to genius, but only within a very narrow framework—that of naturalistic drama; and only a fraction of O'Neill's output was naturalistic. The majority of his plays are top-heavy experiments, unable to support dramatically the load of meaning borrowed piecemeal from Nietzsche, Freud, Jung and Adler. . . . (p. 109)

With *Desire under the Elms* . . . O'Neill made a sudden but, unfortunately, temporary break with his intellectual and stylistic experiments. Using a simple naturalistic form he achieved in this play the highest imaginative peak of his career. His other plays of a comparable stature were all direct and painful distillations of his own experience, and they are at their best when they come nearest in every detail to that experience. *Desire under the Elms* is pure imaginative creation, no nearer to the everyday realities of O'Neill's life than *Phèdre* was to Racine's, yet also no less real than *Phèdre*. The psychological patterns are present in this play for critics to dig out, but they are deep down, an integral part of the dramatic situation, as in *Hamlet* or *Oedipus Rex*. (pp. 112-13)

[In *Mourning becomes Electra*,] O'Neill tried to write a version of the Orestes story which would be as relevant to the twentieth century as Aeschylus's *Oresteia* was to Athens. His method was to transplant the story to New England at the time of the Civil War, and to give sexual motivation to every twist of the plot. His result was merely to belittle his archetypes. . . . Once again O'Neill is signposting, using a modern shorthand, writing from outside. In several scenes the authentic O'Neill style, the dramatic muscularity of the first scene of *The Emperor Jones*, begins to reappear; but it is soon swamped again by the ideas. A character in *Strange Interlude* said that 'Herr Freud' had 'a lot to account for'—not the least of which is this period of Eugene O'Neill's work. Looking back over the plays, with all the men putting their heads in their mistresses' laps and calling them mother, one can validly wish that the characters would stop behaving, within their given framework, with such predictable conventionality. (pp. 115-16)

In [*Long Day's Journey into Night*] O'Neill achieved all that he had been moving towards in his others. The constant see-sawing of the relationship between characters dates from as far back as the first scene of *The Emperor Jones*. The multiple aspects of personality, which in the masks of *The Great God Brown* had been mere idea-mongering, are here presented naturalistically and movingly. (p. 118)

The general attitude to O'Neill is strangely ambivalent—he is approached with a peculiar mixture of veneration and distaste. . . . O'Neill always demanded serious attention because he so constantly threatened the stage with high astounding terms—which then often turned out to be mere bombast. With such extremes of quality in his work it is essential to separate ruthlessly the successful from the merely ambitious. For O'Neill was like the proverbial child —when he was good, he was very very good. (p. 120)

> *Bamber Gascoigne, "Eugene O'Neill, 1888-1953," in his* Twentieth Century Drama (© *Bamber Gascoigne 1962), Hutchinson University Library, 1967, pp. 109-20.*

[O'Neill's] material seemed indeed infinite, as infinite as the mystery of human personality, which was his true subject. (p. 43)

[He] was not Shaw, not a thinker; hiiiiiiiiiiis overwhelming gift as a dramatist was a consciousness of the ineradicable stain of human sin perpetuating itself through the generations—a vision of Old Testament man as American. The drive to power he saw as an infectious madness of the race, but he abstains from moral judgment as if in deference to predetermined fact. It is the configuration of power that absorbs him, working and changing at intimate quarters, in the family nest, in the sexual divide. In this tragic game whole personalities are caught up, nourished, destroyed, and it is from this sense of the single human personality before whose private pestilences and appetites any conviction of the objective world must falter that O'Neill's drama derives its strength and meaning for us. (p. 44)

> *Arlene Croce, "Old Testament Man as American," in* National Review (© *National Review, Inc., 1968; 150 East 35th St., New York, N.Y. 10016), January 16, 1968, pp. 43-4.*

This is how O'Neill's theatre-poetry works; it is a matter of structure, rhythm, cadence, coming from life and flowing back into life again. It is not, in the first instance, a verbal matter. The easy thing to say of O'Neill is that he cannot write. He said it himself. . . . But *Long Day's Journey* is a poetic play because of the coherence of its elements and the depth at which the coherence is achieved. The elements are not, in the first instance, verbal; they are movements of feeling, gestures, relationships, the things that Yeats called Life when he invoked two rival 'ways', the other being Words. It is the urgency and coherence of these elements that makes the play poetic. What we demand of the words is that they will not shame the feelings placed in their charge: everything else is a bonus. If Shakespeare writes like an angel and O'Neill stammers like poor Poll, this is a fair measure of the difference between them; but it should not blind us to the fact that O'Neill has something of that poetic and theatrical sense which prompted Shakespeare, in *Macbeth,* to bring in the Porter's scene immediately after the murder scene. If we put the two men irrevocably apart, it is only after putting them, in this respect, together. The impact of *Long Day's Journey* comes from finesse certainly not verbal but, to a high degree, formal, a finesse of structure; so that the excitement of waiting to see whether the

ingredients are combined in an innocent or a catastrophic way goes along with a formal excitement. . . . (pp. 157-58)

Before the arrival of *Long Day's Journey* there was little enough to be said about O'Neill except what Mary McCarthy said [see excerpt above], that the poor man had a writing problem as other people have a money problem or a job problem. Even Eric Bentley [see excerpt above], who spent many years trying to like O'Neill, found his patience exhausted by the effort of producing *The Iceman Cometh.* And yet, after all, we have a masterpiece of the Old Drama, proof that the thing can be done. (p. 160)

> *Denis Donoghue, in his* The Ordinary Universe: Soundings in Modern Literature *(reprinted with permission of Macmillan Publishing Co., Inc.;* © *1968 by Denis Donoghue), Macmillan, 1968.*

In order to destroy one tradition, the playwright must create another. When O'Neill rejected the conventional [melodramatic] formula, he had to forge his own form. So his dramatic career is a series of experimental efforts to find a satisfactory vehicle for "life." The autographical bias of his plays, which has been extensively documented by biographers and critics, is not so much an instance of narcissistic preoccupation as it is evidence of dissatisfaction with a dramatic tradition. O'Neill wanted to write about contemporary life. The life he knew best was his own. His experimental method consisted in casting about for ways to embody his experience, in trying various approaches that range from stern "realism" in *Desire Under the Elms* and *Beyond the Horizon,* to expressionism in *The Hairy Ape* and *The Emperor Jones,* to adaptations of Greek and Renaissance stage conventions like the mask and chorus or the aside. He was never satisfied; he would not settle for forms that did not encompass the whole of life. Drama, he said, had to deal with life; "fate, God, our biological past creating our present, Mystery, certainly"; this was the only subject worth writing about.

One of his most interesting and, for our purposes, most informative experiments is his adaptation of the *Oresteia* of Aeschylus to an American situation. In the light of his search for form, it is understandable that O'Neill should be attracted to Greek tragedy. After a century of puritanism, sentimentality and scientific attack, the Christian tradition that had served Renaissance drama so well was—at least for the time—defunct. Greek tragedy dealt with "the Mystery" within a conventional structure; it came out of a relatively homogeneous culture and was well supplied with legendary themes. In short, the Greek playwrights had a form at hand; they needed only to shape their material to it. O'Neill set out to borrow both form and content from Aeschylus. (pp. 27-8)

Mourning Becomes Electra follows the general outlines of the Aeschylean trilogy very closely. The playwright borrows the three-play division, the sequence of events and the climatic order. (p. 31)

O'Neill is striving to revitalize the legend, to render its values in modern terms. He must, therefore, find a complex of cultural attitudes, which the audience will recognize and (hopefully) accept, to provide the dimension which an Olympian Providence supplies in the *Oresteia.* O'Neill tried to find this complex of attitudes in a theory of behavior that was "in the air" when he wrote the play—the psychology of Sigmund Freud. (p. 40)

When O'Neill chose Freudian psychology to motivate the action, he extended the dimensions of his play-world into areas as broad (if not as transcendent) as the Olympus of Aeschylus. The Freudian view of behavior invokes a region as mysterious as the dwelling-place of the gods and sees human motivation as guided by impulses as imperative as divine commands. As the social dimension of O'Neill's action extends into the Puritan past, so the broader dimension extends into the unconscious where drives are determined by infantile experience.

Like the Puritanism, the Freudianism of the play is popular and unscientific. *Mourning* is not a carefully documented case study nor was it intended to be. The fact that the doctrines of Freud were widely misunderstood and vastly oversimplified by the public and the popularizers, did not prevent the playwright or the novelist—who often did not understand them either—from using the attitudes toward human behavior that the theories suggested. However imprecisely, the public knew that Freud insisted on the relevance of the sex drive to life-adjustment, on the dangers of repression, on the importance of dreams as a key to self-knowledge in these areas. The "Unconscious" or subconscious was a deep, dark, cellar-like place from which proceeded equally dark impulses like the urge to marry your mother; "repression" was a dangerous damming-up of such urges and led to abnormal inversions. The biological determinism of nineteenth-century Naturalism also had prepared the ground for the psychological determinism of these theories. Whether or not the public approved, Freudianism, as it was understood or misunderstood, represented in the 1920s a definite complex of attitudes about the importance of the psychic as a key to human behavior.

O'Neill himself insisted that his knowledge of the psychoanalysts was unscientific and fragmentary, and that he was guided more by intuition than by any theory. (pp. 40-1)

The plot of *Mourning Becomes Electra* is remarkably faithful to the *Oresteia*. Its characterization, symbolism and tone, however, are determined by O'Neill's interpretation of the Puritan heritage, by Freudian psychology, and by the corollary motif of salvation by spatial remove. The effect of these non-Hellenic elements is a shift of focus so radical as to produce a complete inversion of the play's meaning. (p. 49)

Death is the goal of O'Neill's Puritan; he meditates on it, he walks in its shadow, he lives for it. Since this Puritanism does not include a theological dimension, Death is an end in itself, not a passage to another world.

Thus Death is not merely a thematic image in the play or simply a way of dispatching the personae and cleaning up the stage. It is the epiphany that concludes the action, the vision to which the plot progresses. If Greek tragedy included the death of the hero, it also provided a means of encompassing the idea of death in a framework of death-and-rebirth. O'Neill's modifications, however, result in a hopeless reiteration that death is final, absolutely conclusive, the end. (p. 51)

> *Thomas E. Porter, "Puritan Ego and Freudian Unconscious: 'Mourning Becomes Electra'," in his* Myth and Modern American Drama *(reprinted by permission of the Wayne State University Press; copyright © 1969 by Wayne State University Press),*

Wayne State University Press, 1969, pp. 26-52.

The Chinese influence in O'Neill's last plays has been almost ignored by the critics. Many writers have pointed out the central theme in the late plays, the contrast between reality and fantasy, the idea that man through his "pipe-dreams" of fantasy creates an imaginary world that enables him to endure the tragedies of existence.

The view, of most O'Neill criticism, is that although the late plays are his best work, they represent a philosophical nihilism that rejects the Christian sources of Western civilization. Many critics add their belief that the slow failure of O'Neill's health was the major cause of the nihilism in these final plays. The truth is more complex. . . .

The advent of World War II and his increasingly poor health shattered his struggle to unify his sympathy towards Taoism with the conflicts of the American society. Yet in this impossible struggle for a synthesis of eastern and western thought, O'Neill achieved a new dimension in his plays. This new dimension is the sense of learning to balance good and evil, to endure the raging polarities of existence, to reconcile pipe dream and reality. If the surface theme in these plays always seems to be the gap between pipe dream and reality, the deeper theme is always the necessity of reconciling them. (p. 192)

Behind the uneasy, western conscience of the characters who still cry for individual salvation, lies a world where the conflict between reality and fantasy can be resolved only if selfishness and worldly power are suppressed in favor of a simpler, more objective, Taoist way of life. It is no accident that most of the characters in the late plays live in a relatively timeless world of desire and imagination. They are cut off from the world of time by their inability or their unwillingness to fit into the practical materialistic nature of American society. One of the stages of Taoism is to find the source of power which reconciles a man with the Tao, the universal energy which unites the opposites and permits one to escape the earthly limitations of time and environment.

Consequently, the major characters in the late plays turn away from the practical demands of time, but they are unable to fit into the timeless world of spiritual values because they are still part of a dissolving western society rooted in the search for material possessions and a self-centered salvation. I do not mean to imply that the Chinese Taoist influence is dominant in the last plays, merely that it is strongly there. It is mixed particularly with the sense of "fate," which O'Neill derived from Greek tragedy, and with the sense of "pity," which came from his Catholic background. The striking interest of O'Neill's final plays is their widening out beyond national barriers into an area where various religions and philosophies flow together. (p. 193)

Some day it would be revealing for an American theatre to produce five of the last plays in the following sequence: *A Touch of the Poet, More Stately Mansions, The Iceman Cometh, Long Day's Journey Into Night,* and *A Moon for the Misbegotten.* . . . Such a sequence progresses from a more objective, historical view of the nature of the American family to a subjective, contemporary view of family ties and illusions. In *A Touch of the Poet* and *More Stately Mansions,* the European tradition of class differences creates an agonizing conflict in early Nineteenth Century America between the public dream of democratic equality and the private desire of materialistic wealth and power. The other three reveal the contemporary collapse of the family, its retreat into the pipe dreams of security that make the members of a family cling together despite their increasing separation from any essential connections with society. Together all of these plays are a powerful indictment of American family life presented with mature insight and a rare compassion. (p. 195)

[Every] American playwright today must still measure himself against the depth and ambition of O'Neill. All of the recent, familiar critical warnings about O'Neill's limitations are of little consequence. Ponderous, sentimental at times, an awkward prose writer who tended to bathos rather than the incisive metaphorical insight that marks the great writer —these faults cannot disguise the achievement. (p. 196)

James Schevill, "Eugene O'Neill: The Isolation and Endurance of an American Playwright," in his Break Out in Search of New Theatrical Environments, *edited by James Schevill (© 1973 by James Schevill; reprinted with permission of The Swallow Press, Inc.), Swallow, 1973, pp. 190-97.*

[In *Long Day's Journey into Night,* having] overcome the need to prove himself a thinker and poet, a fuzzy combination of Shaw and O'Casey spiced with a bit of Nietzschean suffering, O'Neill was free to be what he superbly was: a dramatist of courage and force who understood very well how to construct the tensions and rhythms of a play so that it becomes infused with crude theatrical life and capable of sustaining the needs of the singular vision that gave it birth. (pp. 52-3)

What O'Neill presents us with in his last plays is the result of an almost complete rupture of his artistic manner; what has gone before in no way prepares one for what will follow. . . . When O'Neill found his world and his words, he had made no place for himself to come from; he was simply suddenly where he wanted to be, suddenly a master of his art.

What took him so long, one wonders? And what finally caused the transformation to take place? (p. 53)

O'Neill, like so many American writers of the period, suffered from the ugly-truth fixation, a peculiar form of literary reaction that sets in generally after a long period of stylized convention and artificial sentiment. When O'Neill came into the American theater, it had never known anything except such a period, and he therefore found it easy to gain attention from those who wanted to see our drama have something to do with life again. Unfortunately, what O'Neill considered life in those days had about as much reality to it as did the melodramas in which his actor-father, in a bitter quest for financial security, had toured the country. In all the rough, tormented examples of humanity he created in his early work, there shines the simplistic faith of the writer who created them, a faith that believes that a serious work of art perforce must thrust upon its public something that public would rather not know about or consider.

Such a faith, had it been unadorned, would possibly have made O'Neill no more dangerous than any other naive

realist. However, O'Neill had other ambitions for his talent. He had, after all, wanted to be a poet and had gotten his notions of literary lowlife from Baudelaire, a poet who had had the good sense to realize that if one must write about whores, it is best to use them as symbols for reflection rather than object lessons about life. A dramatist cannot, of course, be reflective about his characters, at least so that it shows in the finished work. If he is to get poetry into them he must find dramatic forms that allow one to realize that an ugly truth has its rights also to verbal glory. Thus we have those strange dramatic limbos in which *The Hairy Ape, The Emperor Jones,* and *The Great God Brown* are played, twilight worlds that are every bit as artificial and "theatrical" as the melodrama O'Neill believed he was waging war upon. Again and again in these plays, ugly truths are prodded into a wobbly transcendence of their humble origins, while human speech is tortured into something the playwright thinks is the proper manner of address in heroic surroundings.

Such a notion might produce, at best, a few odd moments of good verse if the playwright were truly a poet. O'Neill was not, and these attempts to get dramatic prose to do poetry's work almost ruined him as a dramatist as well.

Another affliction of O'Neill's was his obsession with the idea of restoring antique forms of tragedy for modern use. It follows that if an ugly truth is ready for the world as its stage and poetry as its language, it is ready also for the dignity of participation in a tragic myth. No matter if the myth can't be abstracted from the society that created it without losing much of its meaning and all of its terror. If one knows that the characters involved are meant to be the descendants of Electra, Agamemnon, Orestes, *et al.,* then, though their behavior appears peevishly lunatic in a modern world that has its own sense of tragic necessity, one will be forced to accept them as representative of the dark and consistent destiny of our species.

All this would be enough for hours of tedious drama. Yet O'Neill had still another weakness to overcome. He was from time to time addicted to the idea that he was meant to transmit to us the philosophic and scientific fashions of his time in a manner that would make them dramatically compelling. How he fared in this form of drama can be seen, if one has the curiosity necessary to endure its nine acts, in *Strange Interlude,* a mixture of Shavian morality, Freudian psychology, and novelistic technique that only a theatrical press agent would call Joycean. This is a play . . . in which O'Neill, aiming for a drama of infinite size, achieved one of interminable length. (pp. 53-4)

O'Neill demonstrated for all who followed him every pitfall a modern dramatist, especially an American, has in his path.

But how is one to understand the transformation? How is one to explain the simple force of *Long Day's Journey into Night* or *Moon for the Misbegotten,* or the culminative power of *The Iceman Cometh*—a play whose faults are truly easily forgotten and whose vision of failure in America is, Miss McCarthy, no pipe-dream?

I would only guess at the cause. Perhaps as he withdrew more and more from the social life of the theater he found less need to dazzle it with innovation. Perhaps he saw life more clearly as it receded from him. Perhaps the ghosts he called upon demanded that he take no liberties in perpetuating their memory. But it is no matter why O'Neill became the great dramatist he always wanted to be. That he did is a judgment as indisputable as any judgment about the nature of art can be. Reading his life, one discovers that he thought himself, in his romantic way, damned. One honors him because, returning his romanticism, one sees in him a rare symbol of redemption. (p. 54)

> *Jack Richardson, "O'Neill Reconsidered" (reprinted from* Commentary *by permission; copyright © 1974 by the American Jewish Committee), in* Commentary, *January, 1974, pp. 52-4.*

It has been said of the soil of Bordeaux that if it were not, thanks to the grape, the most valuable in the world, it would be the least valuable; in something like the same fashion, if Eugene O'Neill had not written a couple of our finest plays, he would be among the least regarded of our playwrights. What a graceless writer he is, groping after thoughts of no great novelty or merit! (p. 47)

> *Brendan Gill, in* The New Yorker *(© 1975 by The New Yorker Magazine, Inc.), March 31, 1975.*

"Long Day's Journey Into Night" is a most unlikely masterpiece: (a) it is boring; (b) one knows all there is to know by the end of Act 1; (c) nothing happens, or rather, no matter what happens, nothing changes; (d) its creed is hopelessness.

The mystery is why, having spent the long day watching the four Tyrones disintegrate and slip into their separate stupors, we feel so exhilarated. Have we enjoyed the day? Has the drunken misery at any moment been (even a la Baudelaire) joyful? Is there any cause for hope? No, no, no. What buoys us, what redeems us, is simply the fact of their survival. Despite their guilts, the total responsibility of each for the wreck of the whole, their failures, their bitterness, their fights, their fates, they endure—and more, they continue to love and need. Granted, it would have been better for them not to have been born, but having been born, it is encouraging that none of them, even those who would have liked to, have died. If these, our frontiersmen in the wilderness of despair, persist, how much more have we, with less miseries, to live for.

In a winking mood, O'Neill ends his play with a dope-saturated Mary Tyrone remembering her marriage to James Tyrone. "We were so happy for a time," she says, Curtain. Is the notion of happiness merely a mockery of the present? —that is the easy reading. But the fact of happiness having existed once, even briefly, makes it impossible to preclude the possibility of happiness, as long as there is life. Is hope reasonable for the Tyrones? Not very. And it is just such unreasonableness that makes humans grand.

> *Carll Tucker, "O'Neill Explores the Wilderness of Despair," in* The Village Voice *(reprinted by permission of* The Village Voice; *copyright © by The Village Voice Inc., 1976), February 9, 1976, p. 99.*

Rainer Maria Rilke

1875-1926

Greatest of the twentieth-century German lyric poets. Rilke sought all his life to find, as his translator J. B. Leishman wrote, "symbolic, or 'external' equivalents for experiences that were becoming ever more 'inward' and incommunicable, and which, when he tried to communicate them, were continually bringing him up against the limitations of language." Delicate and frequently ill, Rilke nevertheless traveled throughout his life, living and writing at various times in Paris, Russia, Scandinavia, Italy, Austria, Egypt, and Spain. Chameleon-like, he picked up bits and snatches of identity in his travels, having decided at the age of twenty-five that his actual lineage did not accurately define him. It is questionable which experiences were lasting, although most critics agree that his association with the sculptor Auguste Rodin had a significant influence on his aesthetics. His experimental novel, *The Notebook of Malte Laurids Brigge,* may be viewed as a restatement of the essential connection of love and death which recurs throughout his poetry. Rilke's greatest poems are the magnificent *Duino Elegies,* in which the poet ultimately celebrates the ecstasy of existence through the acceptance of death and pain.

PRINCIPAL WORKS

Vom lieben Gott und Anderes (short stories) 1900
  [*Stories of God,* 1932]
Auguste Rodin (biography) 1903
  [*Auguste Rodin,* 1919]
Das Studenbuch (poetry) 1905
  [*Poems from the Book of Hours,* 1941]
Die Weise von Liebe und Tod des Cornets Christoph Rilke (prose poem) 1906
  [*The Story of the Love and Death of Cornet Christopher Rilke,* 1927]
Neue Gedichte (poetry) 1907-8
  [*New Poems,* 1964]
Requiem (poetry) 1909
  [*Requiem, and Other Poems,* 1935]
Die Aufzeichnungen des Malte Laurids Brigge (novel) 1910
  [*The Notebook of Malte Laurids Brigge,* 1930]
Die Sonette an Orpheus (poetry) 1922
  [*Sonnets to Orpheus,* 1936]
Duineser Elegien (poetry) 1923
  [*Duino Elegies,* 1931]
Briefe an einen jungen Dichter (letters) 1929
  [*Letters to a Young Poet,* 1934]

[Rilke's] vision was full and perfect long before the World War was dreamed of. But it is since the war that that vision has seemed most pertinent and persuasive to minds wearied and bewildered by the destructive thunder of the wheels of a mechanical civilization. They turn to Rilke; they seek to stand with him at that point of the inner life at which the self and the universe are no longer divided, at that point in which the soul *consents* to its continuity with an order unmiraculously perceived as divine and receives all phenomena into itself. A great vigilance and a great stillness of spirit have lead Rilke to an attitude unique in the history of either letters or thought. It is in vain that critics speak of Dostoevsky, of the undoubtedly decisive effect upon Rilke of his visit to Russia. It would be equally in vain to speak, as I am tempted to do, of Wordsworth and of "wise passiveness." Experience rather than learning will open that door. But most people, hot of heart, violent of will, are excluded from the moods that are the material of Rilke's poetry. Unlike Wordsworth, he does not need the grander aspects of nature; he avoids the complications of the human scene. A face, a street, a remembered legend, a caged animal, an heroic gesture suffice to induce in him that mood of contemplation in which he sees "into the life of things" by being no longer divided from them. In this habitual mood of his the common contradiction between mind and nature, subject and object, is abolished. (pp. 148-49)

Significant for Rilke's development are, I suspect, the poems in which he remembers his childhood and adolescence. He retained, long beyond the wont of men, the child's ability to let day and dream be a continuous country. Later day and dream became appearance and reality, became the self and the universe, became the thing and God. . . . From the periphery where one *observes,* his temperament carried him effortlessly to the center where one *experiences.* Truth comes to him who keeps the vigil of eternity. . . . From these interpretative statements it is easy to derive Rilke's silent opposition to the naturalistic movement in literature; it is equally easy to see why all the expressionistic poets consider him their master. . . . (pp. 151-52)

He is so little known among us—more like a legendary name than a living poet—that what is needed is first of all to make him and his work accessible to the lover of poetry. . . . Rilke uses the entire vocabulary of the language. There are no prosaic words. . . . It is in harmony with this principle that Rilke has abandoned all licenses and verse devices. His syntax is always the syntax of prose. (It is in this respect that the translator is forced to betray the poet most grossly.) Hence his verse has an initial naturalness and fluidity. On the other hand, it will be observed that Rilke constantly uses alliteration and internal rhyme and is an incomparable master of the contrasts and harmonies of vowel music. But the use of these methods is never facile. Language is to Rilke more than a means of expression; it is a material like marble or gold or alabaster which has its own laws and possibilities and methods of treatment. It must be wrought into a beauty proper to it as substance. But the poet never forgets the emotional and conceptual aspects of speech. Hence words must be significantly beautiful; alliteration becomes symbol of meaning and orchestration of thought. (pp. 157-58)

> *Ludwig Lewisohn, "Rilke," in his* Cities and Men *(copyright 1927 by Harper & Brothers), Harper & Brothers, 1927, pp. 146-57.*

Often Rilke seemed to change for those who read him over a long period, often he seemed to shed his skin, at times to wear a mask. Now the collected works show an amazingly unified picture. The faithfulness of the poet to his own essential being is far greater, that essential being is far stronger, than what we once called his versatility or even his changeableness.

We pick up volume after volume, turn the pages, humming to ourselves the opening words of beloved poems, first from one and then from another, begin to search out special favorites and lose ourselves again in the wide bright forest of these poems. And in each volume we find imperishable poems that have stood the test of time, among the very earliest, hesitant works no less than among the latest. In the first volume we rediscover those lovely tones that so gently and deeply entranced us thirty years ago, those quiet simple verses full of astonishment and tremulousness of soul. . . . In the second volume the *Book of Pictures* reminds us of the powerful impression of correctitude and formal power it once made on us, and we linger for a long time over the *Book of Hours,* which once was our favorite and that of the girls we knew. In the third volume, the last of the volumes of poetry, is unfurled the classical piety of the *New Poems,* and in the *Duino Elegies* the summit of his work is attained. Remarkable, this journey from the youthful music of Bohemian folk poetry to this point and to *Orpheus,* remarkable how this poet so consistently begins with what is simplest and as his language grows, as his mastery of form increases, penetrates deeper and deeper into his problems! And at each stage now and again the miracle occurs, his delicate, hesitant, anxiety-prone person withdraws, and through him resounds the music of the universe; like the basin of a fountain he becomes at once instrument and ear.

The two following volumes contain the prose writings, among them that favorite, unforgettable *Malte Laurids Brigge.* . . . The translations occupy the final volume of the works, and here once more all the poet's great virtues are displayed: his mastery of form, his certain instinct in selection, and his persistence in the pursuit of complete understanding. Gems like the translation of Guérin's *Centaur* are there, André Gide's *Return of the Prodigal Son* and Paul Valéry's poems. (pp. 337-38)

When the poet Rilke died a few months ago one could tell clearly enough from the attitude of the intellectual world—partly from its silence but even more from what was said—how in our time the poet as the purest type of the inspired human being, caught between the mechanical world and the world of intellectual industriousness, is forced as it were into an airless room and condemned to suffocate. (p. 339)

It is no accident and it is not, although at times it might appear so, by any means a simply literary matter that the figure of the poet Rilke has become of such importance for our time. . . . The phenomenon of Rilke . . . can be described in this way: in the midst of a period of violence and the brutal worship of strength, a poet becomes a favorite, indeed becomes a prophet and model, for a spiritual elite, a poet whose essence seems to be weakness, delicacy, devotion, and humility, who, however, turned his weakness into an impulse to greatness, turned his delicacy into strength, turned his psychic vulnerability and fear of life into a heroic asceticism. And this is the reason that Rilke's letters and his personal life and his legend belong so very much to his work, because in his nature he is so very typical of what is unprotected, homeless, uprooted, threatened, yes, suicidal in the spiritual man of our time. He prevails not because he was stronger but because he was weaker than the average; it is the sick and threatened quality of his nature that so powerfully summoned up and strengthened the healing, incantative, magical forces in him. And so he has become a beloved and comforting image and model for the spiritual man and artist who does not withdraw from suffering, who does not flee from and renounce his own time and its fears, nor his own weaknesses and dangers, but through them, a sufferer, achieves his faith, his ability to live, his victory. This road led him as poet to a new form, suffered for and battled for, that often resonates through and through with strain. As a human being his fate made him humble and kindly. And it is with full right that his followers reckon the many splendid letters he wrote as an essential and valid part of his work. (pp. 340-41)

> *Hermann Hesse, "Rainer Maria Rilke" (1928), in his* My Belief: Essays on Life and Art, *translated by Denver Lindley (reprinted with the permission of Farrar, Straus & Giroux, Inc.; copyright © 1974 by Farrar, Straus & Giroux, Inc.), Farrar, Straus, 1974, pp. 337-43.*

Rilke seems never to have found a potent inspiration in the life and literature of Germany. The two countries which made the strongest appeal to him and had the greatest influence on his art were Russia and France. It was his visit to Russia which inspired *Das Stunden-Buch;* it was the years he spent with Rodin in Paris which helped him to write his *Neue Gedichte.* The difference between these works shows how much his circumstances affected Rilke and how intensely he appreciated two widely different civilisations. What he admired in Russia was the old Holy Russia, the country of saints and pilgrims, of simple faith and longing for some degree of absorption in the divine being. In the *Stunden-Buch* he dramatised himself in a rôle that enabled him to express half-hidden thoughts and desires which might seem alien and inappropriate to a cultivated citizen of Central Europe, but were entirely right for a lonely, contemplative Russian monk. The *Stunden-Buch* marked for him the end of an epoch. When he had written it, he seems to have felt that for the time being he had written enough in lyric form about himself and his own feelings. He was indeed to return years afterwards to the poetry of the self and to revive in a new form some of the ideas which may be seen in the *Stunden-Buch,* but in the interval he turned to a different kind of poetry, to something more objective, less personal, and in some senses less intimate.

The causes and character of the change are somewhat complex. Rilke seems to have felt that he had said all that could be said about his feelings, that to continue writing as he had hitherto written must mean the repetition of what he had already done, and from this his artistic conscience revolted. He needed a new outlet for his energies, and he found it in France. The precise direction which his art now took was to some extent determined by his admiration for Rodin. He was deeply interested in sculpture, and in Rodin he saw a great creative genius who towered above contemporary artists by the strength and independence of his work. For some months he lived in Rodin's house, and the close contact which he found there with another art than his own affected him in a remarkable way. He saw that Rodin's sculpture was largely the result of a great tradition, and to the masterpieces of this tradition, whether Greek or Medieval, he brought the full powers of his studious, perceptive and devoted mind. Instead of living among dreams he lived among works of visual art until, by a natural process, he wished to make his own poems like them—self-sufficient, perfectly wrought and rich in content. He had indeed attempted something of the same kind in *Das Buch der Bilder,* where in a number of descriptive poems he achieved a degree of objectivity which seems a foreshadowing of what was to come. But the peculiar character of the *Neue Gedichte* does not lie simply in their being more objective than Rilke's earlier poetry. These poems were written with a different conception of the nature of poetry, and in consequence they are fuller and finer than anything he had yet written. They move to a different rhythm; they are more concentrated, more vivid, more visual. And, what is more remarkable, they were largely written in accordance with a theory of poetry. (pp. 87-9)

To describe this process he found a figure which fitted his ideas—the medieval stonemason who turned his feelings into the permanent shape of the stone cathedral. In other words, the poet's many experiences must be transmuted into something independent and complete, something which stands in its own right and needs for its understanding no reference to the poet's life and thought and feelings. (p. 91)

However independent he wanted his poetry to be, its independence would not be of the impersonal, pictorial, Parnassian kind. He started with an act of faith that every experience would ultimately become part of himself and that out of this enriched and complex self his poetry would emerge. But he also felt that when his poetry came, it would not be personal and subjective like his own earlier work but self-sufficient and complete in itself like a masterpiece of the visual arts.

Rilke's theory, then, might be regarded as an attempt to harmonise and combine two different views of poetry. On the one hand it demanded the fullness which comes from living in the imagination, from yielding to every impression, and in this it recalls the Romantics with their eager quest of sensations and their belief in the unique nature of the poet's calling. On the other hand it recalls Mallarmé's conception

of the ideal poem as something absolute in itself and free from anything that might be called the private tastes of its maker. The two views are not easily reconciled; for the one asserts the importance of everything that the poet feels, the other demands that the poet's individuality must be omitted from the actual poem, which exists in its own world of pure art. But Rilke's attempt to combine the two views is intelligible in the light both of his time and of his own development. He saw, as others saw, that the Romantic personality was in many ways destructive to poetry, while the impersonal art of the Parnassians omitted too much. And in his own experience he had both known the ardours of an intense inner life and felt the majesty of works of art which were somehow complete in themselves. In his last years he turned again to the poetry of self-revelation, but before that he went through a time when he deliberately tried to lose himself in impressions, hoping that out of them he would create an objective and self-sufficient art.

In this task Rilke was helped by his temperament. . . . He knew, as few have known, the state of pure receptivity, the true aesthetic condition, and when something was given to him on these terms, it stayed with him until it became a part of himself. From such moments he made his poetry, and naturally he sought them of his own choice. . . . In his search for them he looked all about him, in the life of large towns such as Paris, in the monuments of the past, in the unfamiliar sights of foreign places, in sculpture and painting and architecture. He passed much of his life in solitude that his impressions might not be sullied or shaken by the impacts of personal relations or the stress of living. He regarded his aesthetic task as all-important, and faced it with unrelaxed determination and self-denial. In his search for beauty he was extremely hard on himself. For it and through it he lived and worked. (pp. 92-4)

Where others have found a unifying principle for themselves in religion or morality or the search for truth, Rilke found his in the search for impressions and the hope that these could be turned into poetry. To this task he gave his religious fervour, his moral earnestness, his intellectual integrity. For him Art was what mattered most in life. . . . His concern with the arts was so serious and so single-minded that he tried to recapture through aesthetic appreciation the power and the vision which had gone to the making of masterpieces. The extraordinary thing is that he succeeded and found sources of original poetry in the works of other men.

Many of the poems in the *Neue Gedichte* are concerned with works of art. They vary greatly both in manner and in quality, and, on the whole, it seems true to say that the more Rilke liberates himself from a purely appreciative state, the more original and striking his work is. So long as his poetry is dominated simply by the impression which a masterpiece has made on him, he is more of a critic than a poet. . . . It is still the inspiring masterpiece that matters. This is true even of poems like *Früher Apollo* and *Die Fensterrose,* which are far from being merely descriptive. . . . (pp. 95-6)

In other poems of the *Neue Gedichte* he develops . . . his ideas about death. With these he was much occupied and, though he never combined them into a doctrine, they form a coherent whole whose parts appear in different poems. The result is that when Rilke writes about death, his work is curiously exciting and mysterious. (p. 107)

In his aesthetic life, . . . Rilke not merely found subjects for poetry but was able to find himself through these subjects and to create new and intensely personal poems in which an old idea was transmuted through his vision of it. Thus he succeeded in both parts of the task which he set himself. His poems were certainly not 'emotions' but 'experiences,' and they had that independence and completeness which he saw symbolised in the stone cathedral. No one else could have written them, and on them all is the unmistakable imprint of his workmanship. (p. 110)

[He] was able to make his poetry intensely suggestive and full of associations. This richness may be seen to great advantage in his similes, in which no modern poet has equalled him. Small and trivial things, which he had noticed and which are in themselves insufficient to make a poem, become vitally important when attached to some larger theme. . . . By his similes Rilke makes his poems far fuller and truer. They bring out the associations which his subjects have for him, and suggest hidden depths of meaning.

The similes would hardly be as successful as they are if Rilke had not set them in contexts where everything seems to be said in plain unassuming words. Unlike some other poets of his generation, such as Stefan George and Gabriele d'Annunzio, Rilke uses a very simple vocabulary. He avoids recondite 'poetical' words, and some of his finest effects are made through an apparent simplicity. There is a complete lack not only of decoration, but even of any attempts at an elevated style. . . . (pp. 114-16)

In the *Neue Gedichte* Rilke not only opened up new subjects for poetry, but he found a secret beauty in many unrecognised subjects. He was not a modern poet in the sense that he found charm in the discords and paradoxes of modern life. But he kept a singularly open mind and explored the possibilities of many subjects which had not before been introduced into poetry. Because of his love of artistic objects he found much to admire and understand in subjects so different as the Cathedral at Chartres, San Marco at Venice, small Flemish towns and islands in the North Sea, statues of the Buddha and of Artemis, of Adam and of Apollo. Through works of art he found his way into the study of the past. . . . But his study of these was always primarily that of one who looked to see what strangeness of charm or interest they might have for him. He savoured the relics of the past as if they were works of art, and when he placed them in his poetry, it was always for some permanent element which he found in them. Sometimes this might seem unimportant. At other times, as in his poems on the Buddha or on the figures of the Christian saga, he found something that in spite of its apparent remoteness was singularly intimate and modern.

Rilke in fact tried to widen the range of poetry, to find undiscovered subjects which would show how much closer poetry lay to the life of every day than many of its practitioners assumed. In this main task he was triumphantly successful. In the *Neue Gedichte* he showed that in common sights and in threadbare stories there lurked vast possibilities for the poet who had the courage and the insight to find them. He was always original, even in his failures, and his particular combination of gifts is without parallel in our times. No other poet has been so careful, so touching, so sensitive, so widely appreciative. He had a wonderful way of investing apparently unimportant things with a magic light, and to what he saw through his receptive imagination he brought all the resources of a richly stocked memory and a consummate sense of the associative value of words. He lacked Stefan George's moral splendour, but he had something which George never had, a tenderness and a sensibility which made his verses throb with emotion or seem to pierce with clairvoyant vision to the heart of life. By his achievement he showed that the cult of the Beautiful need not mean the destruction of personality nor the creation of a colourless, shapeless type of mind. By his earnest and hard-won appreciation of masterpieces he widened and strengthened his nature, and by finding material which illumined some of his most intimate ideas he emerged from his aesthetic discipline a far richer personality, ready for the great tasks of his last years. (pp. 119-21)

> *C. M. Bowra, "The Neue Gedichte," in* Rainer Maria Rilke: Aspects of His Mind and Poetry, *edited by William Rose and G. Craig Houston, Sidgwick & Jackson, Ltd., 1938 (and reprinted in America by Gordian Press, 1970), pp. 85-121.*

When Rilke had completed his *Duineser Elegien* in 1922, he announced the event to his friends in words that may seem to us strangely ostentatious for so unassuming a man. We must, however, realise that he considered them as a task entrusted to him and to be performed with obedient self-effacement. Rarely has a poet waited so patiently for the moment of utterance and schooled himself so zealously in the smallest details of life, in order adequately to comply with his 'Diktat.' Yet he did so with no pride and no desire to be remarked and honoured. It was an unselfish cult of the self, an impersonal self-dedication.

Although, therefore, the personal element abounds in the Elegies and Rilke's individual associations and reminiscences constantly obtrude themselves, the purpose which he pursued was an objective one. (p. 125)

He realised that he was as far removed from his goal as at the time when he had completed the *Stunden-Buch,* and he felt that his purpose could be achieved only when subjective utterance and objective statement intimately coalesced in a work that directly purported to treat of human life and destiny. *The Duino Elegies* are this work.

It would be wrong to conclude that Rilke was pursuing a didactic purpose in his poetry. He did not wish, nor did he think that it was possible, to bring a message that might help and comfort others. It is the poet's task, he maintained, to justify, not to relieve, suffering. . . . (p. 128)

This conception of the poet's duty explains the texture and the movement of the Elegies. They begin with lament, but end with praise. Rilke felt that accusation and lament, however deeply concerned with the most universal human distress, express a purely negative attitude and signify immaturity if they are not finally, without being annulled, elevated to praise. The poet must proceed from the expression of distress to eulogy of the world which has caused his distress. . . . But this was no easy assertion of faith. With his extreme sensibility he fully experienced both the inadequacies and the perfections of life, and for many years it was his constant endeavour to recognise that the distresses and the felicities of life, even death and life themselves, could not be separated from one another. It was his final conviction that they belong together, necessarily and intimately, and that they form what he variously called 'a Unity,' 'one Being' and 'the Whole.' The many delays to which the writing and the completion of the Elegies were subjected were due to Rilke's search for this supreme truth and to his inability for a long time to express it adequately, though he had found it. Without it he was unable to pass beyond the limits of lament, for it was his sense of the unity of all things which allowed him to proclaim that which had hitherto caused him distress. (pp. 128-30)

Viewed in the light of this 'effort,' the Elegies are the crowning achievement of Rilke's work; and in particular they appear as the completion of his task when they are compared with *Die Aufzeichnungen des Malte Laurids Brigge.* In *Malte* he had written an elegiac novel, the history, subjectively told, of one who was doomed to destruction because he was incapable of doing more than recognising that life was distressing and man inadequate. (pp. 130-31)

In both works life, death and love are the predominant themes, but the accents are differently placed. At the time when Rilke was preoccupied with the continuation and completion of the Elegies, he would recommend *Malte* to those only who could read it 'against the grain.' The reason for such repeated warnings is to be found in Rilke's later attitude of eschewing lament purely as lament. His work on the Elegies was painfully retarded by his experiences in the War. More deeply than ever he was immersed in distress, personal, spiritual and cultural. He had almost approached the stage when he felt sufficiently mature to affirm and praise. But the War drove him back on himself and in the almost only notable poem which he wrote during that period, in *Fünf Gesänge August 1914,* we find him retracing his steps and moving from praise to lament. (pp. 131-32)

Rilke's experiences in the War had diverted him from the path of his true enquiry, which was the search for the answer to the question: "How can we exist in the face of our inadequacies in life, death and love?" . . .

[He] was able to regain that clearness of vision and to acquire that measure of human self-esteem which allowed him to sound the theme of praise in the Elegies. He was [then] able to define the true relation between life and death, and to recognise that despite our many inadequacies we are intended to perform a high and immortal task. . . . By accepting human sorrow and distress and, while not ceasing to lament the nature of man, vindicating his existence, he was able to carry out his resolve.

Rilke does not ask: "How shall we act, knowing ourselves to be inadequate in life, love and death?" His question is not an ethical one, even as his poetry is not meant to be didactic. Rather he considers the ultimate and metaphysical reasons for human existence: "How can we exist?" (pp. 134-35)

These two conceptions, that life and death form a unity and that death is the consummation of life, explain Rilke's terse and recondite thoughts concerning the youthful dead in the *First Elegy.* They are immature when they die, since their death had had no opportunity to ripen within them. For them therefore death is strange and their first experience in death is slow regain. But as life and death are one, we, the living, can be of use to them until finally they outgrow our aid and then it is we who have need of them. . . . (p. 138)

[Though] the *First Elegy* foreshadows the scope of the whole work, and though an answer has been found for the question of human usefulness, there can be no doubt that as yet the theme of lament vastly predominates. No adequate justification of human existence has been given, and indeed the Elegies that follow pursue the examination of life and continue the theme of lament. (p. 139)

[The] *Second Elegy* instances two reasons for lament, which must be distinguished, for upon this twofold result depend the further development of the Elegies and the final answer to Rilke's question. First, the nature of man generally is at all times transient and evanescent. Secondly, the life of man in the modern world suffers from the absence of valid external symbols for the inward actions of his soul. (pp. 140-41)

The *Second Elegy* for the first time voices this complaint, but it is left to the *Seventh Elegy* to develop it more fully. The *Second Elegy,* also for the first time, hints that the lovers share our human imperfection. The woman who loves is, nevertheless, a figure approaching perfection. Compared with her, man is untutored and inadequate when he loves. He falls immeasurably short of the achievements of woman in love. . . . When a man loves, he does so with his selfish instinct and his blood, and he is the instrument of dark biological forces. The *Third Elegy* laments this male inadequacy in love. Neither mother nor maiden elicits the tumults of blood, nor are they able to soothe and fully restrain it. (pp. 142-43)

In the *Fourth Elegy* the lament becomes more extended and profound. In language and imagery of unusual suggestiveness, but replete with esoteric meaning, Rilke passes judgment on human nature. No simpler words could convey his thought which, concerned with the limitations of human consciousness, must itself transgress the sphere of ordinary consciousness. Dealing with the inexpressible, it is intuitive rather than rational. (p. 143)

Our consciousness is never pure, never without an 'opposite.' For our every feeling, desire and intention there exists, inevitably, something contrary. We are at home in enmity. Backgrounds of contrast are our essentials. We cannot pursue our feelings to their pure end; from outside they are restricted and corrupted until they become matter-of-fact, like the life of a dancer which, in reality, is a bourgeois affair. . . . Nothing in our lives is truly genuine, except some hours in our childhood, during which we are in contact with more than the mere past and not concerned about the future. Lacking adult consciousness, there is for us in childhood no 'opposite' to disconcert us and we are happily occupied with that which lasts and are fit to take part in a pure event. The Elegy therefore ends in praise of the child, whose death, Rilke says, has none of the beauty of maturing, but is as ugly as bread that grows hard or as the core of an apple, and yet does not make the child malicious while depriving it of so much.

This Elegy is one of the most representative of the series, expressing Rilke's profoundest aims and desires. More than anything else he wished that love, thought, feeling and action should be 'pure,' that is, complete in themselves, unalloyed by any consciousness of an 'opposite.' (pp. 144-45)

The *Fifth Elegy,* the last to be written, indirectly continues this train of thought. Rilke's praise had hitherto been elicited by two human figures only: the lover and the one who dies young. . . . Later his interest was aroused by two additional human figures, and for no very dissimilar reasons: the acrobat and the hero. The former is the subject of the Fifth, the latter of the *Sixth Elegy.*

Stimulated by one of Picasso's pictures, Rilke in the *Fifth Elegy* describes the life of the acrobats as more than ordinarily human, more transient even than that of other men. . . . The fugacity of their existence has this particular quality, that it is nearly a 'pure event.' They are playthings in the hands of grief, which continually turns and twists them into the same postures. There is no joy in this spectacle, and the interest of the onlookers who surround them like the petals of a blowing rose can only be due to the fact that it awakens in them displeasure at their own fate. But that the actors themselves feel the pain of their vocation and are yet able to smile—this makes them worthy of praise even to the angel, so that their activity can become a model for us. In this world we may be material in the hands of death which, like a milliner, works us up into manifold ornaments for the cheap hats of fate. But beyond, there may be a place where lovers succeed in pure love. They would then be like the acrobats and we should be happy spectators. (pp. 146-48)

The *Sixth Elegy* is devoted to the hero. . . .

[The] *Seventh Elegy* immediately proceeds to the glorification of existence. At the point when the value of human life in this world seems to have been completely denied, Rilke proclaims its virtues. (p. 149)

For happiness, Rilke continues, is greatest when it is not visible, when it is an inward possession. Our real world is inward and invisible. We are, he continues, experiencing in our age the decline of that which is concrete and visible. Mental images are substituted for the permanent houses of other times. The creations of our age are stores of energy (triumphs of mechanical science) which are as shapeless as the wearing speed that we extract from everything. Our age knows temples no longer. But though our hearts thus go to waste, we are nevertheless inwardly building greater statues and pillars. At every turn the world has taken there have been such disinherited men as we now are, to whom neither the past nor the future belonged. This should not confuse us, but should urge us to preserve those shapes which we still appreciate. For there they have stood, secure amid uncertainty and fate. And Rilke, addressing the angel whom he now will not solicit, proclaims to him the beauty of human creations and achievements, of cathedrals, music and love.

For the first time in the body of the Elegies praise outweighs lament. In some of the preceding poems there had been eulogy. But it had concerned isolated members and individual representatives of humanity (the lovers, the prematurely dead, the acrobats, the hero), never the race as a whole. Now we are all entitled to share the praise which Rilke has to bestow. Such regret as exists is mainly occasioned not by inadequacy on our part, but by the inevitable trend of history. In this *Seventh Elegy,* therefore, one of the two laments voiced in the *Second Elegy* has been answered. Man in the modern world has no meaner mission than his ancestors. It is in truth a greater task: to build invisibly that for which they were able to find outward and visible images.

The path now seems clear for final praise, the answer to the

wider question concerning man generally: "Why, being inadequate, should we exist at all?" Rilke does not proceed to give this answer immediately. In the *Eighth Elegy* he returns to lament. This shows that lament is not removed by praise, that even in the most affirmative estimate of our human value the realisation of our inadequacy subsists; for in the *Eighth Elegy* the theme of lament is sounded with no abatement of poignancy.

Human nature is compared with that of the animal. The animal, says Rilke, lives an 'open' life; it is not burdened with our consciousness of an 'opposite.' Death is not its opponent. Death lies behind it and it moves steadily towards God, into pure space. . . . It is different with us. Rilke believed that we, by the very nature of our existence, move 'behind' God, though we are at one with Him. (pp. 151-53)

The greatest pain of life is departure from the womb into the world, so that even birds and bats are dismayed when they must leave their nests and venture to fly. Serenity of joy is known only by those minute creatures which are bred not in a womb, but on earth. (p. 155)

The idealistic conception of human destiny is foreign to Rilke. He believed that our existence is not more dignified, but a little darker, than that of other beings, and more evanescent, like the smile of a wind. Why then, he asks in the *Ninth Elegy,* knowing the sadness of our lot, should we not wish to depart from it? . . . The reply to this question is at last the answer to Rilke's enquiry in the Elegies, the solution of his problem. The query at the beginning of the *Ninth Elegy* must be read in conjunction with that of the First concerning the usefulness of human existence. The purpose of our existence, he says, is not happiness or knowledge or experience. We exist because existence is in itself of value and because everything which exists apparently appeals to us and depends on us for its future existence, though in this world we are the most fleeting creatures of all. But we pass on into another world, and it is our task to ensure for other beings a form of continued existence. We accomplish this task by expressing their hidden and inner meaning and by taking this possession 'across' with us. The purpose of our existence is to praise and extol the simple things of existence. (pp. 156-57)

The existence of man is justified. He has a purpose in life which is not invalidated by his many inadequacies; he has an immortalising mission, and he can, after all, enter death and meet the approving angels. With this affirmation of life achieved, Rilke is now entitled to say, in the *Tenth Elegy,* that pain and sorrow are not a passing season of our life, to be sped and curtailed, but our permanent abode in life and death. We do not enter a land of happiness in death, and we should not spend our life, as we do, in a perpetual effort to appease and mitigate our distress. The principle of the whole of our life, in this world and the next, is sorrow.

To convey these concluding thoughts, Rilke employs an allegory of suffering which fills the *Tenth Elegy.* He contrasts life and death as the City and the Land of Pain. In life we do all we can to remove and conceal sorrow. We have arranged our life like a noisy fair to distract us from death and to reward those who are a little more skilful than others. It is only the children, the lovers and the animals who have no share in this shallow gaiety. (pp. 159-60)

In this concluding Elegy, which follows immediately upon

the vindication of human existence, Rilke fulfils one of his purposes, "das Leben gegen den Tod hin offen zu halten." It was not his purpose to give any complete account of human existence in death. He merely intended to demonstrate the unity of life and death by exhibiting their common principle—suffering—in an allegorical action, in which, moreover, only those are concerned who die young. (p. 161)

What is true of this Elegy applies to the work as a whole: the composition depends as much on the poet's reminiscences (which remain unexplained) as on the play of imagination and the elaboration of thought. From such varied poetic impulses there has nevertheless resulted an entirely homogeneous creation.

To many, however, it will seem that Rilke has left the last word unsaid. References to the Deity are singularly infrequent and guarded in a work that so pre-eminently treats the most fundamental issues. (pp. 161-62)

The Elegies reflect [his] tendency to speak of man and the world without approaching God directly. He is now the ineffable and unapproachable Divine Being of the Old Testament. In many respects Rilke's religion approximates more to the creed of the Old Testament than to that of the New, and frequently he can accept neither. He is averse to the belief in the need of a divine intermediary and in the dogma of original sin. His desire for an 'open' life, unhampered by the presence of any 'opposites,' is finally explained only by the necessity for him to move freely towards God, and he could not believe that our life in this world made the path to Him any the more circuitous. (pp. 163-64)

This conception of man's relation to God explains, too, the figure of the angel as presented in the Elegies. . . . The angels, both according to Rilke's conception and in Christian thought, are the perfect and glorious first-created of God. But Rilke's definition of their perfection does not agree with that of the theologians. They are, on a higher plane of existence, what the animals are on a lower—a foil to man, stable and decided beings, re-creative even in their intensest abandonment of feeling. They are an example to man of his ultimate purpose, for his task is accomplished in them; and because this is so they are a source of terror to man, for man, while occupied with making the world invisible, is yet attached to it. . . . For this conception it is hardly possible to find a rational explanation. It is a matter of Rilke's personal belief. (pp. 165-66)

The *Duino Elegies* are written on the transcendental plane of the angel. (p. 167)

He projects the world into the angel, where it becomes invisible. At the same time, however, he looks upon it with human eyes, attached to its concrete substantiality. The Elegies are therefore also written on a human plane at a guarded distance from the angel.

These distinct yet intimately connected attitudes on the part of the poet largely determine the texture and the style of the Elegies, for his speech seems to come from a region that lies midway between two worlds, one of which is accessible to us, while the other transcends us by far. (pp. 168-69)

In each of their aspects the *Duino Elegies* reveal a man who has dwelt in another world and on his return must say what he has learned of human life and destiny. This was the task which Rilke had to accomplish after he had completed *Malte Laurids Brigge*. (p. 170)

> *E. L. Stahl, "The Duineser Elegien," in* Rainer Maria Rilke: Aspects of his Mind and Poetry, *edited by William Rose and G. Craig Houston, Sidgwick & Jackson, Ltd., 1938 (and reprinted in America by Gordian Press, 1970), pp. 123-71.*

To Rilke everything was to be accepted, nothing denied. All things were to be seen, loved, filtered into the unconscious, there to be turned magically into names: and then the poetry *is* the naming. And the naming must in a sense be beyond love, even, lest it carry with it an implied partiality or judgment. (p. 332)

It is no wonder that Rilke is the most difficult of contemporary poets, and no surprise that he is ultimately the most rewarding. Is he perhaps the first great poet of the unconscious? Freely and dangerously, with immense courage, but also with miraculous judgment, he dared to accept the dark, fluid, "private world"—the private world with all its idiosyncratic secrets; and, with a kind of instantaneous ordering of the chaos, turned the inside out, projected the dream back again into the world as a new object. No poet before him had been brave enough to accept the *whole* of that private world, as if it were unquestionably valid and potentially universal. There is no compromise in Rilke. . . . Rilke's power was his ability to carry that perishable, affective gleam so swiftly across the border of consciousness and into so strong a constellation of design, where mysticism and a genius for prosody meet, that the gleam survives and the nonsense is summarily translated.

Sometimes, it is true, we hardly know into what—his process is too quick for us, the references too blind altogether. When this occurs no amount of explanation serves much purpose. But even here there is a "poetic" meaning which is sufficient: the tone, the implication, the music, is enough. . . . There is a sense in which we can say that poets are ultimately ranked in accordance with what might be termed their intellectual *play-content*: not, that is, according to *what* they think, but for the range, richness, ease and delight with which they manage a maximum amount of reference to thought, and thought of the best order. No other poetry of this century vibrates with so much of this *reference*. To think of Yeats or Eliot is to think of neater and smaller worlds altogether, worlds that give themselves more readily, and perhaps even more vividly, but that nevertheless are sooner traveled. Rilke's is a world which to some extent remains permanently unexplored.

The *Sonnets to Orpheus* . . . is, with the *Elegies*, Rilke's finest work—the two books really belong together, shine the better for each other's presence, and should some day be published in one volume. (pp. 332-33)

> *Conrad Aiken, "Rilke's Greatness," in* The New Republic *(reprinted by permission of* The New Republic; ©1942 *by* The New Republic, Inc.), *October 19, 1942 (and reprinted as "Rilke, Rainer Maria" in his* Collected Criticism, *Oxford University Press, 1968, pp. 331-33).*

Rilke regarded the Elegies as the crown of his achievement. We can understand why. (p. 73)

In the Elegies Rilke used a new form. With the exception of the Fourth and the Eighth, which are written in the German equivalent of English blank verse, they are written in *vers libre*. The rhythm is predominantly, though by no means invariably, dactylic, and this gives a more regular tone than is usual in *vers libre*. The staccato effect which seems almost inevitable to the form is avoided by the construction of large paragraphs, the use of *enjambement,* the way in which images are sometimes sustained through a long passage, the prevailing sombreness of tone. The absence of rhyme, of stanzas, of regular rhythm, contributes to the effect in a remarkable way. The element of song is entirely lacking. Its place is taken not by quiet meditation but by nervous, excited, discursive thought in which sensibility plays a large part. It is hard to find a label for this kind of poetry. It is undeniably full of thought, even of argument, but it does not prove a thesis or move to a regular plan or appeal directly to the understanding. It appeals to the nerves and the emotions. Rilke almost anticipates the psychological sequence which T. S. Eliot used in *The Waste Land,* but he does not change with such leaps and jerks from one subject to another and he still keeps a poem, more or less, to a single theme. He even makes his intricate movements a little clearer by a certain amount of unpoetical matter. There are moments when he seems near to prose. Yet even then it is not argument that appears but thought that has not quite been raised to an imaginative level. The Elegies may be regarded as poems of nervous brooding. Their mood is that of a man who has withdrawn into himself and lived for long with his sensations and thoughts, until they have passed into himself. Such poetry would be inconceivable in anyone not deeply absorbed in himself. Everything passes into him, registers its impression on his sensibility, and becomes part of a metaphysical scheme which he creates to cover what is given to him. What before were exterior objects are now symbols of great issues. They are even more. They exist only in the poet and get their importance from what he feels about them. He seems to have abandoned his belief in an external world and to have replaced it by a system in which there is nothing but sensations existing in the mind. It is obvious that for such a system a special kind of verse is needed. The *vers libre* of the Elegies is well fitted to express the subtle and sinuous movements of a soul communing with itself. (p. 74)

It is hard to say what the main subject of the Elegies is. It might be said to be man's place in the world, and this is to some extent true. But the Elegies may be read at two levels, almost in two different ways. They are in the first place the record of the poet's own hard struggles to be a poet, of his efforts to come to terms with his inspiration, to find an answer to his own private problems. And in the second place they are the poetry of all men who struggle and are beset by doubt and despondency. The poet moves from his own struggles and his solution for them to the assumption that others are like him and that what is true of him is true also of them. As a poet he speaks for humanity. Their lot is his, though he sees it more clearly and feels it more acutely. (pp. 75-6)

Rilke knew that his own life passed between extremes. On the one side were the rare, rapturous, perilous, appalling moments when poetry came to him. These, following Mallarmé's precedent, he symbolised by Angels. There were other moments which he had known in his childhood when life seemed complete and rounded. The first moments were

rare, the second had passed beyond recall. Rilke spent much of his time waiting for the one and regretting the other. This intermediate condition was largely one of "Angst", of acute and unsolved apprehension. It was from this that he strove to deliver himself; it is this which permeates the Elegies and sets so much of their tone. Rilke longed for an Absolute, for sustained rapture in creation. He found instead that he was at the mercy of his instincts, his doubts, his uncertainties, his inability to feel at home anywhere for long. To sustain himself he clung to those hours which remained brightest in his memory and in which he seemed nearest to his ideal. (p. 76)

The evil of life lies in its incompleteness. That is the problem as Rilke sees it. But it is not all that he has to say. As the Elegies advance, they become more hopeful and consoling. . . . In the Tenth a final solution of the problems and paradoxes is offered. From irony, defeat, despair he turns to joyful trust. His method must not be misunderstood. The later Elegies do not contradict the earlier in the sense that one argument contradicts another. They are later stages in a voyage of discovery, riper knowledge which succeeds incomplete acquaintance with the mysteries of living. What is said in the earlier Elegies is true so far as it goes, but it is not the whole truth. Man is indeed a creature of extremes, torn between opposing destinies, and from this arises much of his futility. But behind this there is a reason. In the universe all is right, and those who think enough will see this clearly. The solution which Rilke propounds appeals to the heart as well as to the intellect. It comforts as well as satisfies. But to give it its full force he has first to state all the difficulties in all their drabness and darkness. The solution is only satisfactory if we have really felt what it is meant to solve.

Rilke's solution turns on two fundamental ideas, related in his scheme of life, but ultimately distinct and distinguishable. They are Transformation and Death. The first is the theme of the *Seventh Elegy,* where Rilke proclaims that life is glorious because it provides the material for something more permanent and more important. (pp. 84-5)

The *Tenth Elegy,* in all its allegorical complexity and subtlety, picks up many previous hints and gives a Gospel of Death. It is a kind of Pilgrim's Progress, a parable of man's state between the ordinary town with its noisy and aimless activities and the real life outside. This real life is shown by a Lament ("Klage") to one of the youthfully dead, and it contains all that matters. Rilke develops an idea familiar from *Neue Gedichte* that the dead have a fuller, more real existence than the living. (p. 88)

Rilke saw death not as annihilation but as self-transcendence. He wished to get back to the roots of life, to be like his Eurydice mingled in the earth, to be absorbed in the springs of creation. Like all poets, he imagined a sphere in which he could create in untrammelled ease, and he identified this with the state of the dead. He felt that when he lost himself in intercourse with the Angel, he was to that degree sharing in death. Death was for him a fuller existence not only because his creative moments involved a self-surrender like it but because through death he had known the vivid, stirring power of grief. (p. 89)

While the Elegies moved from the thought of the poet's inspiration to a cult of death, the Sonnets were inspired by a single death to a cult of song. They were written as a memorial for a young girl whom Rilke greatly admired, and from the thought of her death they move to an appreciation of life, of all that she showed when alive and to much else that this suggests. In Orpheus, the singer who tries in vain to call up his beloved from the dead, Rilke found a symbol for himself. But what concerns him is not the attempt to regain Eurydice but the cosmic function of the great poet in whom Nature herself seems to speak. In his kinship with the brute creation, his power to move natural objects by song and so to transform them, in teaching that the body is a tomb from which the soul must escape, Orpheus presents points of resemblance which Rilke could well use. The symbol was good and released many hidden powers in him.

The concept of Orpheus dominates the first part of the Sonnets, and here Rilke implicitly corrects the more rigorous view of death which he put forward in the Elegies. The Spirit of Song, which is in Orpheus and himself, has roots both in life and in death. . . . (pp. 90-1)

In the Sonnets Rilke shows what poetry meant to him, what he got from it and what he hoped for it. The dominating mood is joy. It is a complement to the distress and anxiety of the Elegies, and in Rilke's whole performance the two books must be taken together. While the Elegies reveal his pangs and struggles when he was not creating poetry, the Sonnets tell of his joy when he was. His life passed between extremes of frustrated waiting and rapturous creation, and he assumed that the common human state was like his own, that it knew the misery of aimless emptiness and the concentrated activity of inspiration. His theory of Transformation bridged this division to his own satisfaction. The Sonnets are the songs of his victory. (p. 96)

> C. M. Bowra, "Rainer Maria Rilke," in his The Heritage of Symbolism (© copyright 1943 by Macmillan & Co. Ltd.; reprinted by permission of Macmillan, London and Basingstoke), Macmillan, 1943, pp. 56-97.

Of modern poets Rilke is the great solitary, the preeminent individualist. All his major ideas have the common object of leading a man back into himself. The idea of transformation of the external into an inner reality, of a man dying his 'personal death' and thereby achieving self expression in the last act of his life, of unrequited love being nobler than love which finds its natural satisfaction: all these major Rilkean ideas contribute to the establishment of an ideal for man which consists in his remaining always concentrated within himself and rejecting any kind of experience which would diminish the intensity of his effort to apprehend the infinite. . . . Rilke's world was bounded on the one hand by the material form of the art-object (das Ding), and on the other by the immaterial realm of Platonic Ideas (such as the sublime concept of the Angel in the *Duino Elegies*). Between these two extremes there was little room for the human, and indeed in few of Rilke's poems are the emotions expressed ordinary human ones. It is chiefly by reason of the distinctive nature of his emotional experiences that Rilke impresses us as being a religious poet. (pp. 167-68)

Rilke was one of the very few great myth-makers of modern times. If he started as a symbolist he succeeded more than did any other poet of that school in creating universally valid images for those processes of the human spirit which urge man to be continually aspiring beyond himself.

It took many years for Rilke's powers to develop fully. He was not a dogmatic poet, and he never assumed the promethean mask that Yeats and Rimbaud so proudly wore. The power of his mature verse is the power born out of weakness being painfully overcome. . . . He always regarded himself as a servant rather than a master; as the servant of powers before which man must humble himself. (p. 168)

The influence upon him of his first experience of Russia is evident in his first important poetical work, *Das Stundenbuch*. Here Rilke reveals himself as a God-intoxicated man. The poems celebrate the greatness of God . . ., His omnipresence and identity with all life, and seek to express the poet's mystical states in which he felt himself to be intimate with the deity. (p. 170)

Rilke was constitutionally averse to the essence of Christianity, for he saw it as a world- and life-negating religion which pirated to a Beyond the benefits which man should enjoy in the present. . . . Rilke conceived it as his task to "exalt the present and the real," and a religion which required man to stake his hopes on a future life and abjure the things of the earth and the experiences of the senses was anathema to him. (p. 172)

[It] was his will to be changed, to progress, step by step, towards complete self-realisation, that made Rilke, after a not very promising start in the Romantic vein, a major religious poet. (p. 174)

In *Neue Gedichte* the Rilkean world becomes clearly defined; the peculiar climate of sensibility in which one finds oneself on reading the *Duino Elegies* and the *Orpheus Sonnets* has been evolved. In this volume Rilke first expressed some of the ideas he was to develop in his maturer work, and, what is equally important, he made great progress in building up his means of expression "so as to say everything." (p. 175)

Rilke's visions were not dynamic apocalypses of the Blakean type but rather subtle, but no less vivid, apprehensions of existence as pure being and of the correspondences subsisting between his inner states and the external, natural world. His mysticism consisted in the expression of marginal conditions of human feeling, intuitions of the essential relatedness of the human and natural worlds and the cosmos as a whole. It would be inaccurate, though, to speak of him as a nature mystic. "I do not think," he wrote in a letter, "anybody has ever experienced more vividly to what an extent art goes against Nature; it is the most passionate inversion of the world, the return journey from infinity on which you encounter all the honest earthly things." Art could not proceed from nature, he said elsewhere, without despair, without a Fall. . . . Rilke had no Rousseauesque sentiments about nature. He saw in it . . . the primal, unconscious chaos (witness the third *Duino Elegy*); but yet, trustingly, he submitted himself to its direction. His mystical experiences were not of the kind that are attained by means of asceticism or rigorous disciplines. They were 'given' to him, and were independent of his volition. (p. 176)

[The] poetry which Rilke wrote to express and extend his experience . . . is one of the most successful attempts a modern man has made to orientate himself within his chaotic world. (p. 178)

The philosopher Martin Heidegger has said that his work has been an attempt to express in philosophical terms the truths which Rilke expressed symbolically in his poetry. It was Heidegger, remember, who defined the human situation as "being exposed to nothingness." Rilke confronted that nothingness. He experienced both the metaphysical despair of Pascal and the despair at the spiritual desolation of modern life that drove Nietzsche insane, and he came out of that experience with a characteristic phrase on his lips: "dennoch preisen" (praise nevertheless, praise in spite of). It was a phrase that Neitzsche's Zarathustra would have approved. Praise and celebration in the face of and in full consciousness of the facts that had caused other minds to assume an attitude of negativity, was the declared object of both Rilke and Nietzsche. . . . Nietzsche and Rilke, believing respectively that they had extended the frontiers of thought and feeling, took upon themselves the task of affirming *the whole,* of accepting and transfiguring pain, suffering and evil.

Rilke's poetry moves between the poles of praise (*Rühmung*) and lament (*Klage*). The two themes, he emphasised, were complementary. . . . The predominant note in the *Duino Elegies* is one of lament, whereas in the *Sonnets to Orpheus* praise predominates. Suffering and pain were experiences which had to be endured, had to be regarded as merely "*one* of the seasons of our interior year", for only when it grew out of such experiences could praise be valid. (pp. 180-81)

It was Rilke's desire in his poetry to open up again the way to the infinite, to extend the contingent and material into the realm of the eternal and spiritual. . . . (pp. 187-88)

> Stuart Holroyd, "Rilke: The Visionary Individualist," in his Emergence from Chaos (copyright © 1957 by Stuart Holroyd; reprinted by permission of Houghton Mifflin Company), Houghton, 1957, pp. 166-90.

The first sensation one is likely to have on reading Rilke is that he was far too sensitive; there was none of that tough-mindedness about him that one finds in Eliot or Hemingway. He is the sort of person that W. S. Gilbert might have satirised. What is one to feel about a description [of Rilke] like this?:

> Through the crowd on the Graben [Prague's main street] a young man slowly makes his way, clad in an old-fashioned black frock coat, wearing a black cravat round his outmoded collar and a broad-brimmed black hat. This strange apparition holds a brightly coloured flower in his hand, a long-stemmed iris. He bears it along solemnly, as though he were carrying a blessed candle in a procession. . . . He seems to be looking for somebody that nobody has yet seen in these streets. . . .

This is an account of Rilke at twenty, by Steiner-Prag, a contemporary observer. In the same way, when one reads Rilke's letters—so many of them passionate effusions to older women—one cannot help feeling that he was a mother's boy, and never grew out of it. When one learns that his mother brought him up as a girl, dressing him completely in girl's clothes until he went to school, and even then playing games with him in which he would be 'little Sophie' (her

'sweet little daughter') one can only recoil, and turn hastily to Hemingway's stories of *his* early childhood in the Michigan backwoods.

But in spite of this, Rilke has a kind of toughness that is quite peculiar to him: a Baudelaire-like capacity to accept his own pain and transmute it; to hammer it into creation. (p. 49)

The remarkable thing about the young Rilke is not the excellence of his poetry; if he had died at the age of twenty-five, no one would have remembered him. It is the fact *that he so thoroughly dramatised himself in the role of poet.* The life of Rilke is an astounding case of *self-creation.* (p. 50)

Rilke might almost be said to have made himself a poet by an act of will. . . . He *envisaged* his ideal of the poet, and then quite deliberately *acted* the poet until he became one. He widened his receptive powers; and when the great experience of Russia came, he was ready for it. The broad rivers, the forests, the vast cathedrals and churches, the general feeling of a people untouched by Western materialism, produced a sudden heightening of his sensibilities, an ecstatic receptiveness. After the Russian experience, his work became 'saturated with religion.' . . . J. B. Leishman has said that everything Rilke saw or felt in Russia was a revelation of God. It is quite clear that for the young poet, for whom the world up till then had been a gloomy, hostile, difficult place, Russia seemed like a spiritual Utopia. No doubt the Russia of 1900 was not quite the Russia that Rilke wanted to imagine; what matters is that the image of 'holy Russia' changed him from a mere poet to a visionary, and in doing so, made him into a far greater poet. (p. 56)

Malte is a great book because it is such an extraordinary evocation of a man on his own in a foreign city: the conflict between his certainty of his own power as an Outsider, and his feeling of being negated by the immense number of people who live their lives as if he did not exist. There are moments in it when Malte seems to achieve the power of insight that reconciled Hesse's Steppenwolf to his unfulfilment; the moment, for instance, when he passes the shop with the two masks hung outside the door: one of the drowned girl who was taken from the Seine, and smiles with such tranquillity; the other of Beethoven, symbol of the will to conquer. . . .

If *Malte* is a less perfect book than *Niels Lyhne,* it is because Rilke lacked the staying power and detachment to shape the book as a novel. (p. 57)

Since the *Elegies* might well be called the greatest set of poems of modern times, it would not be fair to try to give an impression of them here. They have had as much influence in German-speaking countries as *The Waste Land* has in England and America; although it would perhaps be more accurate to compare them to Eliot's *Four Quartets.* Their central theme is that of the angel: Rilke's certainty of the need for a higher order of existence. (It is significant that the *Elegies* were finally published at about the same time as *Back to Methuselah.*) (p. 58)

The idea that dominates the *Elegies* is the concept of human suffering, and the concept of a vision that makes human suffering seem unimportant. . . . But most important is the fact that Rilke's 'religion' in the *Elegies* is the Nietzschean religion. (p. 59)

Rilke's *Elegies* are a plea for an effort of will to assimilate more; a plea for less indifference. . . . Rilke felt, as Hesse did, that human life is spent in continual perplexity, continual boredom or misery or doubt. The moments of supreme detachment, when we stand above our own experience and somehow see a meaning in it, come too rarely. . . .

[The] men who have the greatest sensibility often wish they could get rid of it (like Whitman wishing he was a cow, or T. E. Lawrence envying a soldier caressing a dog). They are half afraid of it. They are afraid of insanity. But the strain occurs only in the halfway stage. Rilke recognised that what is needed is an *effort of affirmation*. Of course there is strain for a man standing between two stools. He must make up his mind which one he wants to sit on. If he decides for the lower one (as Lawrence did) he should sit on it. If he decides for the higher one, he should make the effort of will to achieve the new state of consciousness, and make an attempt to bully his experience, instead of allowing it to bully him. This may be an unpoetic way of expressing the philosophy underlying the *Elegies* (and an oversimplification, of course), but it is the language that precedes action, and Rilke's failure lies in the fact that he never tried to bridge the gap between words and action. Perhaps he loved words too much; and although this is fortunate for us; it made his life a tragedy. (p. 61)

The essence of his philosophy is contained in the phrase '*dennoch preisen*,' to praise in spite of. These two words contain the essence of Rilke's greatness. . . . When Rilke first used that phrase 'to praise in spite of,' James Joyce's *Ulysses* had not been published, and Hemingway had not even begun to write. Yet the phrase defines the greatness of *Ulysses* and *A Farewell to Arms*. (p. 63)

Rilke, too, was capable of envisaging . . . an act of complete affirmation; his 'Orpheus' of the *Sonnets to Orpheus* makes it all the time:

> Praising, that's it! As a praiser and presser
> he came like the ore from the taciturn mine
> Came with his heart, oh, transient presser,
> for men, of a never-exhaustible wine.
> Voice never fails him for things lacking lustre. . . .

But Rilke could never make this boast of himself. Voice *often* failed him for 'things lacking lustre.' Like the early Yeats, he had all his life hated ugliness and misery and turned away from it. That effeminate, Jamesian prose was not the instrument for taking the worst reality by the throat; and could one honestly expect lyrical poetry to do all that Joyce did in *Ulysses*?

No, the truth is that, great as Rilke was, he reached his deepest insights in theory rather than in practice. Towards the end he *saw* quite clearly that the really great poet should be an Orpheus, living with such intensity that 'voice *never* fails him'—not for anything. But he did not put this into practice throughout his life. In the *Sonnets*, he strives to be Nietzschean in his refusal to shudder and turn away. . . . This, of course, is pure Zarathustra—the man who has so far transcended his 'human-all-too-human' limitations that nothing horrifies him. But Rilke himself never achieved such greatness. He wandered from castle to castle, mansion to mansion, reading the bad poetry of rich women, and engaging in 'serious conversations' with all kinds of imbecilic members of the nobility. In between

times he was a chronic hypochondriac, and something of a figure of fun in the Bunthorne manner. In short, after reading too many of the Letters, or one of the many biographies of him, one cannot help turning with relief to someone like Hemingway, who errs on the side of being thickskinned rather than oversensitive.

This is not intended as a literary criticism. [It] is not about literature, but about existentialism. Rilke's contribution lies in the fact that he did, actually, learn a great deal from his own life, and reached certain conclusions which, even if he didn't live up to them himself, are of inestimable importance in the search of the Outsider. It is important to realise that one cannot speak of Rilke the man and Rilke the poet as if they were one and the same. The poet was triumphant; the man was miserable. (pp. 63-4)

> *Colin Wilson, in his* Religion and the Rebel *(copyright © 1957 by Colin Wilson; reprinted by permission of Victor Gollancz, Ltd.), Houghton, 1957.*

[Rilke's] growth was astoundingly rapid. The "late" Rilke is the Rilke of the *Sonnets to Orpheus* and the *Duino Elegies,* both published in 1923; but the first of the elegies was written in 1912, at the age of only thirty-seven. At that time Rilke was already popular, beloved, and famous (the critics, though, "discovered" him much later). There is sometimes a cloying, almost embarrassingly naked sentiment in the works that first established him, in the *Book of Hours,* the *Stories of God, The Song of the Love and Death of Cornet Christopher Rilke* (a bittersweet virtuoso piece that has sold over a million copies). But his curve rose fast. *The Notebooks of Malte Laurids Brigge,* drenched with the fear of dying, mark the end of a period. The great *New Poems* mark the climax of another. Under the impact of Rodin's art and attitude towards art, Rilke had become the language-sculptor who fashions "the things" in all their truth; nothing must be applied or brought to them: it is all *in* them, in their detail, their hidden dimensions. This is the Rilke who taught us to "see" essences: The Dog, The Leprose King, Blue Hydrangea, Lady Before the Mirror, The Beggar, Unicorn, Buddha. In the essences he "saw," there was always Death, not the personal death that horrifies Malte, but Death at the root, behind, and in the very constitution of "the things." The "late" Rilke rose to his ultimate insight into the condition of true poetry: the poet is Orpheus, descended to the dead, eating with them of their food, to return transformed and "knowing" so that he may "render the unending praise." This is what the *Sonnets to Orpheus* say. The Mirror Sonnet begins: "Mirrors: no one yet has *knowingly* described your *essence*"; it is an "Orphic" song of knowledge and praise. (p. 149)

The *Duino Elegies,* Rilke's greatest work, are exceedingly difficult for anyone who comes upon them for the first time. Even the German reader must struggle with their uncommon use of common words, with their sentences that tear open to let displaced parts of speech press into the gap, with their obscure allusions and mystifying or wildly farfetched metaphors (when fully understood, they will appear wonderfully apt and illuminating). But the deepest difficulty, and the source of all others, lies in the strangeness of the experience into which they lead us. Out of them rises a unique image of life, death, and love, a world of heart-felt correspondences.

The way to the "Elegies," Rilke suggested, is not through elucidation. One must try and reach out to those "farthest feelings" . . . that are almost beyond the sayable. Their language of "lyrical totals," of "condensation and abbreviation" (Rilke's terms), is the language of new experience, and has to be learned.

The "First Elegy," simpler in design than others, asks: Where can we, alone and insecure in our fleeting existence, find support? And how can we become more than ourselves? For what we are is not enough, by far.

We cannot turn to the Angels. Who are they, those "almost deadly birds of the soul," "dawn-red ridges of all creation," "spaces of being, shields of bliss, tumults of tempestuously rapt feeling, and suddenly, singly, *Mirrors*," as the "Second Elegy" calls them? They are the triumphant accomplishment of creation in whom "the Visible," the transient, "the things," are gloriously transformed into the greater reality and surpassing strength of "the Invisible"; while "we, where we feel, evaporate." Were the Angel to take but one step towards us, our heart would leap up to him in one lethal upbeat ("Second Elegy"). There is no refuge in the Angel. . . .

Nor can we turn to fellow-man, for there is no such thing as fellowship. Even in the embrace of love are we utterly alone. And the animals, secure in their instinctive knowledge of the world, refuse to make common cause with us groping ones. There is pitifully little left we can turn to—perhaps some insignificant but remembered, revisited thing, some small, capricious habit, comforting because it stays and does not choose to desert us. Even the night we long for disappoints us, whether we face it alone or with the beloved one. For love does not make the lovers one; it merely covers up their separateness. . . .

But are not we ourselves, perhaps, needed? Have we not at times been called upon in a vague, allusive, easily missed yet unmistakable way? For ". . . our task is to stamp this provisional transient earth into ourselves so deeply, so hurtfully and passionately, that its essence may be 'invisibly' resurrected in us" (Rilke—in a letter to his Polish translator). This is what those questioning calls of spring, of a melody, of a star, meant to say. But we did not listen. We were still waiting for the wrong thing, for the impossible, for a beloved one to come and end our loneliness. And so we mistook these urgings for signs heralding her advent. Yet we could not have kept her if she had come, for whenever the "great, strange thoughts" enter and stay, our heart is full, since these "great thoughts," and not love, are the task of our lives. . . . Our yearning for love should rather make us praise *die Liebenden* ("the loving ones"), a term by which Rilke means those exceedingly rare women who so loved and who were so cruelly deserted that in their very ruin they found strength to create a memorial to their grief. . . . (p. 153)

"Voices, voices"—our heart, no longer distracted, hears them if it listens with the superhuman concentration of those kneeling saints whom "God's gigantic call" bodily lifted from the ground (the mystical levitation), and who kneeled in the air and did not know it. What *we* hear is *not* God's voice—how could we endure it when even the Angel is terrible beyond our enduring? What we may hear is silence endlessly forming into "the uninterrupted message" now wafting towards us, breath-like, from the dead. It

comes from those who died in childhood or youth and left us in grief. They want us to understand that there was no injustice in their dying so young. They are still not "weaned from earth," and any bitterness that galls our grief will slightly hamper "their spirits' pure motion" towards eternity. . . .

To those young ones, being dead is "arduous and full of catching up" so that they may in time "feel a bit of eternity." But do not we, the living, make too strong a distinction between life and death? Angels, it is said, often do not know whether they walk among the living or the dead. The eternal current unceasingly roars through both these realms, unceasingly rushing human beings of all ages from one to the other, its voice outsounding the voice of life and the voice of death.

The last, brief section . . . takes us back to the "Elegy's" main theme, in a bold, inevitable curve. The early-departed may need us now, but soon they will grow away from their earthly origins. It is *we* who need *them*: we need the deep sorrow of their passing. For our "blessed progress" often springs from deepest lament. . . . (p. 154)

Rilke said that the "Elegies" and the "Sonnets to Orpheus" were "dictated" to him. The "First Elegy" was written . . . at Duino Castle, near Trieste (hence the name); a voice, out of a raging storm, had given him the opening line. The "Elegies" are the work of a consciousness which passionately rejects the distinction between life and death, between a here and a beyond, between sorrow and joy. Man is transient, perishable, fleeting, like all the "visible" and earthly. But man's consciousness stands "vertically" upon this fleeting, beloved earth, capable of grasping the "visible" with such deep, hurtful passion that its essence will be "invisibly" resurrected in him. (pp. 154-55)

> *Stanley Burnshaw, in* The Poem Itself, *edited by Stanley Burnshaw (copyright © 1960 by Stanley Burnshaw; reprinted by permission of Holt, Rinehart and Winston, Publishers), Holt, 1960 (and reprinted by Schocken Books, 1967).*

"Am *I* the man to interpret the Elegies correctly?" wrote Rilke to his Polish translator who had asked him for help in his difficult task. . . . Rilke claimed the right to be as perplexed by them as the translator was. "They are infinitely beyond me," Rilke said. And having thus assumed, once again, the attitude of solemn innocence and genteel mysticism which had become the Orphic letter writer's second nature, Rilke proceeded amply to supply the translator's demand. (p. 148)

[Rilke] was *extremely* "Classical" in the period of *Neue Gedichte* and *Der Neuen Gedichte Anderer Teil* . . ., when he wrote his *"Ding-Gedichte,"* the poems of concrete things, and was "Classical" with such extremeness that his work acquired a quality not dreamed of by any previous classic; and it is precisely the very "unclassical" sense of the disturbed relations between within and without that lurks behind his extreme intensity. For the "thingness" of these poems reflects not the harmony in which an inner self lives with its "objects"; it reflects a troubled inner self determined to transcend its troubles by immersing itself in "the things," indeed by invading them with a greed of appropriation which Rilke thought was inspired by his intimate knowledge of Rodin's work but which was in truth more like Van Gogh's. Rilke's captive Panther, for instance, the first thing-conquest of *Neue Gedichte*, is surely a zoological relation of Van Gogh's Sunflowers, those rapacious "things" that draw the whole world into their dark centers.... As early as 1910 he denounced his dwelling upon "things" as inhuman, obstinate, and greedy, and in 1914 marked his conversion with the poem *"Wendung,"* "Turning Point," which proclaimed the new beginning.... The work of sight is done; now the work of heart is to begin, the work of liberation, freeing the imprisoned images of things which he had overpowered, as if in an act of war, and which, in their strained captivity within his imagination, he no longer recognizes as true. (pp. 154-55)

In *The Duino Elegies* saviour and saved have, in a most drastic maneuver of reversal, changed parts: no longer is it the visible things that save the unquiet inner spirit by granting it a refuge in their unshakable "objectivity"; on the contrary, it is the invisible inner spirit that redeems the visible world threatened with destruction. The poor soul which once called out for redemption has acquired the power to save "the things."... For salvation lies in infinite subjectivity. This is why in the *Ninth Elegy* the question asked by the First and, still more insistently, by the Fifth, *Wer aber sind sie ...?* (meaning "Who are we?"), appears to be resolved in at least one respect. For whatever our ultimate human destiny may be (*"wer wir am Ende auch seien"*), it is clear now that we are the owners of subjectivity, the artisans of the heart, the householders of infinite inwardness; and being all this, we are called upon to gather into ourselves the visible world which has been abandoned by the Spirit. For *"immer geringer schwindet das Aussen"* —the "reality" contained in the outer world is fated to lose ever more of its substance (*Seventh Elegy*). Fragments of the real, it is true, still fly across the eyes of the soul, opening it to glimmers of sense; yet, like meteors, they expire in darkness. (pp. 156-57)

Thus the meaning of the persistent sadness of the *Elegies* is at last revealed. Its cause was a formidable misunderstanding between the soul and the world. The soul still hankered after that measured harmony between within and without, between the true feeling and the true gesture, the sublime peace and Hegelian Classical accord which Rilke, at the end of the *Second Elegy*, so beautifully evokes in remembering the Greek stele of Orpheus, Eurydice, and Hermes. For the soul was not yet initiated either into the secret of its unhappiness or the mystery of its grand task. Desirous of taking roots in the *"Fruchtland,"* the orchard of reality, the soul was saddened by its being helplessly forced to pass through and surpass everything that in the external world seemed, but only seemed, to bid it enter and be at home. It sought love and found only the love which widowed itself as well as the lovers in the very act of the embrace: because the consummation did not keep the promise given to the heart on that first walk through the garden (*Second Elegy*), or the love that committed adultery in the very wedding night as the beloved features merged with the infinite in which she was no more (*Fourth Elegy*). Or the soul labored in the servitude of art only to be dismayed by the emptily dazzling "too much" of acrobatic virtuosity unaccountably emerging from the pure "too little" of its natural endowment (*Fifth Elegy*). And all the while it did not know that its search had to be in vain because the world that it desired as its home was under notice

from the Spirit; and far from being ready to receive the soul, the world itself was asking to be taken into the soul's invisible house. (pp. 157-58)

There are two difficulties with which *The Duino Elegies* are likely to disturb the mind of even a very accomplished reader; and now at least one of them resolves itself. This is the question: Is the condition of man described in this most "ontological" of all modern works of poetry meant to be *the* condition of man, or only the state of our humanity at this particular moment of its history? Is it Rilke's meaning that the human being, ever since the Fall, has been the displaced person of the universe, unemployable in his soul by angels, men, or beasts alike, as the *First Elegy* laments? Or *was* there a time, the days of Tobias, brought back in the *Second Elegy*, when on occasion he might have traveled hand in hand (*"Jüngling dem Jüngling,"* a youth to another youth) with even the most radiantly mighty of angels? . . . [Because] man and Spirit are what they are, there *was*, among the Spirit's seasons, the time of Tobias; there *is* the time of the *First Elegy*, the time of the agony suffered by the soul of man in its "alienation" from himself and Nature and angels alike; and there *will be* the time of the *Ninth Elegy*, the time of the transformation of the world into the invisibility of the Spirit's very own substance. (pp. 159-60)

The voice, which at Duino [Rilke] had heard in the wind, spoke again at Muzot. His breathlessly ecstatic letters announcing, in February 1922, the completion of the *Elegies* show that he had experienced that mighty onrush of inspiration almost as St. John, in that drafted poem of 1915, received his Revelation. . . . Now that the Lord has decided wholly to reveal himself, St. John must write without even looking at what it is he writes. For this too is necessary: that it should be written and recorded. And what Rilke recorded at Muzot was the yearning of all things to be transformed into the invisible substance of human subjectivity, and the poet's resolve to fulfill their desire.

Would all things come to nothing in that consuming inwardness? No. Or be reduced to those riverbed "abstractions" which were repugnant to Rilke when he met them in the art of his contemporaries? No. Or, maintaining their "still recognizable form," simply be "transformed" into poetic images? No. Rilke's meaning lies in a different category of thought; and it is only the theological prudishness of the age that can prevent the reader from thinking about the "Apocalypse" of *The Duino Elegies* in theological or—which perhaps amounts to the same—Hegelian terms. For words like "resurrection" or "transubstantiation" fit the cataclysmic event, in which the *Elegies* culminate, better than the idiom that literary criticism or any amount of "empathy" puts at our disposal. . . . It is in this Hegelian manner that *The Duino Elegies*, concerned as they are with the seemingly contradictory task of rescuing the *visible* world in the *invisibility* of inwardness, touch upon the mystery within which the perishable bread, remaining bread, is invisibly transubstantiated, and the perished body, restored to its bodiliness, is invisibly resurrected. If Hegel has tried to convert this mystery into dialectic philosophy, Rilke has turned it into the apocalyptic poetry of a human inwardness that takes over the divine agency of salvation: "Nowhere will be world but within." (pp. 168-70)

Erich Heller, in his The Artist's Journey into the Interior and Other Essays *(copyright © 1965 by Erich Heller; reprinted by permission of Harcourt Brace Jovanovich, Inc.), Random House, 1965.*

A work of art, says Rilke, is the product of having been in danger, of having gone to the very end of an experience, beyond which no man can go further. It should spring from necessity, and be judged by its origins, that is, by the dangers that had to be overcome. For the danger is as necessary as the suffering it brings. (p. 61)

The Notebooks of Malte Laurids Brigge (Die Aufzeichnungen des Malte Laurids Brigge) is a record of the terrible before it meets the tender, and Rilke warns that it must be read against its current, for it is not directed against life but against human weakness and error. The power that feeds Malte's suffering could also nourish his joy. Rilke calls the book a negative mold of which the grooves are suffering, though the casting would be bliss.

Two of the greatest contradictions that Malte faces are God and death. Rilke blames Christianity for nearly extinguishing God in human experience. A God held by belief or the forcing of the heart to hold something as true leads to a distinction between the saved and the damned that has no basis in human experience. "The view that one is sinful and needs ransom as premise for God is more and more repugnant to a heart that has comprehended the earth." Such a view leads you to condemn suffering, and to suppress impulses in yourself which, although sometimes called evil, may hold your real strength.

Confronted by the suffering of a whole city, Malte in Paris feels himself annihilated. The sick and the dying evoke his sympathy so strongly that he is left dissolved, without will, desire, or defence, like a vacant spot. He walks behind an epileptic on the street, and he feels his own strength pass into the body of the sick man. Rilke is Malte here. "I was torn out of myself . . . through all their burdened lives," he writes from Paris to Lou Andreas-Salomé. "I often had to say aloud to myself that I was not one of them, that I would go away again from that horrible city in which they will die." Malte prays that God will grant him the grace to write beautiful verses and thus prove to himself "that I am not inferior to those I scorn." He pities them but he cannot accept their suffering. (pp. 62-3)

Through the deaths that occur in *The Notebooks of Malte Laurids Brigge* and Malte's attitude toward them, Rilke tries to show that people no longer understand what death means. It remains the great contradiction, the opponent of life, the frail glass of our happiness, out of which we may be spilled at any moment.

Rilke rejects a Beyond because it denies this world for the sake of one unknown to us. As a result, the dead and our whole past are inaccessible to us. Malte clings to the absolute power of time, which his experience constantly denies. This power orders most people's experience; things happen within their appointed boundaries, and events are fairly predictable. When he loses faith in this order, he loses the sense of both his past and his future. The character of Count Brahe suggests another way of looking at time. In his consciousness, all awareness of change has disappeared. Chronological sequence means nothing and neither does death, since for him everyone he has ever taken into his memory continues to exist. But Malte, denying his past and thereby losing his future, is left with no more room to

stand on than a tin soldier. Having eliminated what he cannot understand, he becomes one of the disinherited children of the seventh *Duino Elegy (Die siebente Elegie)*, "to whom no longer what's been, and not yet what's coming, belongs."

If you reject what you cannot understand, you will find that life is indeed simpler for you, but, at the same time, more uncertain. You cannot be sure of your progress, because you cannot distinguish between problems actually solved and problems only postponed. So your life unfolds like a desert, for nothing can take root there. When a tree grows, death grows there as well as life, says Rilke; because it is full of death, it sends out a rich expression of life. So the man who is learning how to live must bring back God and death as a necessary part of human experience.

Rilke believes that you see things as they are only when you can affirm the unity of all existence, a unity in which suffering, death, and the unreality of the past are no longer a threat. Only then can you see that terror and bliss are two faces of a single head that looks in one direction or another, depending on how you meet it. Malte himself knows this, without being able to act on it. He says, "If my fear were not so great, I should console myself with the fact that it is not impossible to see everything differently and yet to live." Although he is afraid to change, he admits that he feels himself standing before something magnificent. One more step and he could understand and approve of his suffering; his misery would be bliss. But he cannot take that step and he feels that he is broken.

To keep from being broken you must be as strong as water; beat it and it yields, yet it is still water. So a man, too, can choose to be changed instead of broken by suffering. "These states of rigidity may easily be transformations, inner alterations, to be followed by renewed existence and awareness of ourselves when the alteration has taken place." Malte prays that he might not be inferior to those he despises. But grace can come to him only when he includes them in his prayer, when he does not see what is repulsive, but what is. (pp. 63-5)

In *The Notebooks of Malte Laurids Brigge . . .*, Rilke suggests the breadth of knowledge that a poet must have. For the sake of one verse he must have known the sick, the dying, the beloved, the movements of animals, the gestures of flowers, the screams of women in childbed, and many roads in many countries. He should wait and gather experience before sitting down to write. But, more important, he should not write of these things too soon. He must forget them and have the patience to wait until they come again. Not till then can the poem happen. (p. 67)

Of his life in Paris, from which Malte's story grew, Rilke remarked that he would have been spared much suffering if he had been able to objectify his fears, to shape things from them, and so set himself free by the very act of creation. . . . Whatever the artist's stated intention may be, his real purpose is to reach what Rilke calls a more intact state in the center of his own being.

The artists who do this most easily are those who have a tangible medium of presentation for all things, regardless of subject matter. Rodin could see the particular world as a system of surfaces; his medium shaped what he saw. Rilke, too, wished to be a craftsman. He was not interested in a sculptural reshaping of his work, however, but in the inward shaping of artistic processes. He knew that what he needed most was clay rather than an instrument of feeling, a medium through which he could shape the whole of his life.

But for a poet, where does this medium lie? In a more thorough knowledge of his own language and its past development? In a particular study or cultural background? Rilke's attempts at study programs always broke down, due to the strange feeling that he was returning by a roundabout way to some inborn knowledge, and he soon admitted that the poet's medium is not any intellectual pursuit. Lou Andreas-Salomé had warned him that words do not build like stones. Because they are symbols for indirectly transmitted suggestions, they are far less substantial than stones. To create, the poet must learn how to live. (pp. 68-9)

In the *New Poems (Neue Gedichte)*, Rilke achieved his "Werk des Gesichts," learning from Rodin and Cézanne the patient observation of physical things. Visiting the museums and parks in Paris, listing subjects for poems, and systematically crossing out those that he completed, he sustained for a little while the ability to write without waiting for inspiration, to transform his observations—indeed his whole life—into art. He soon realized that this kind of transformation made dazzling poems but did not really open the secret lives of things: "I sit here and gaze and gaze until my eyes hurt, and . . . recite it to myself, as though I were supposed to learn it by heart, and still haven't got it."

The turning in the poem, then, is from a superficial mastery of things to a real one, which comes only when he loves what his sight has gathered. (pp. 79-80)

The *Sonnets to Orpheus (Die Sonette an Orpheus)* are hymns to this change that keeps things rather than kills them. Now, when Rilke writes of a rose, he no longer encumbers it with elaborate metaphors; he speaks directly to the flower of the inner world. . . . (p. 80)

Now, when he writes about the woman who loves without being loved in return, he does not take the viewpoint of an individual. Whatever singled her out has fallen away and left the core of her feeling standing free. She is not described; there is no one to describe, just as the man who rejected her has also lost his identity. All you can know for certain is that his coldness closes behind her love as heedlessly as water.

The poet asks of the woman in the sonnet only what he asks of himself: to live so openly that she can affirm all that happens to her, even this loss. Only then will the direction of her feeling be endless. Then she is both the bow and the target, self-containing and complete. The images in the poem are simple; they describe nothing, they are the language of feeling itself. (pp. 81-2)

The salvation of things, then, lies in the poet, but the salvation of the poet lies in the poem. Only he can turn loss into joy when he steps into the darkness of his own mind and recognizes there all that he has ever seen or felt. Rilke learns how to live from his angel, who is blind and gazes into himself at the whole world. In order to see things as they are, the poet too has become divinely blind. (p. 82)

> *Nancy Willard, "How to Live: Rainer Maria Rilke," in her* Testimony of the Invisible Man *(reprinted by permission of The University of Missouri Press;* © *1970 by The Curators of the University of Missouri), University of Missouri Press, 1970, pp. 61-82.*

In the first of his *Duino Elegies,* when he is talking about the living and the dead and the relationship between them, Rilke says that we who are living all make the mistake that we differentiate too sharply. In this case, that we make a distinction between life and death which is not there. All Rilke's work is about integration. The integration of life and death is only one aspect, but the most important; it shows clearly his belief that there is a continuity of consciousness which makes a total event. It is the simple message that incoherence is in us, not in the world. . . .

The reader new to Rilke is likely to find the *Sonnets to Orpheus* almost incomprehensible. But Rilke himself did not understand them . . . at least, not at the beginning. There could hardly be a better example of what T. S. Eliot had in mind when he said "the poet does many things upon instinct, for which he can give no better account than anybody else". Just over a year after he had written these poems Rilke tells a correspondent: "I myself have only now, through reading these poems aloud, gradually begun to understand them." He is careful not to say that he does understand them, and two months later we find him saying, "sometimes I myself have to struggle for the meaning which has made use of me to break through into the human sphere, and even I understand certain passages only in isolated moments of grace". . . .

[Rilke's] first great cycle of poems was written around the turn of the century, a collection in three parts called *The Book of Hours*. Much of it is a song of praise to darkness, and this darkness is the inexplicable region where truth is concealed. It lies outside our consciousness, so it is dark. This is where the poet wants to penetrate; his aim is simply truth. And this is where the monk, the fictitious writer of these "prayers" which are *The Book of Hours,* places his God. But not only here. Light and dark are complementary, differentiated only by our senses. The realm is total, and this total realm is God, so he exists in the light (that experience which is visible to us) as well as in the dark (what is, as yet, inexplicable). . . .

Rilke gives the impression that he is talking about the infinite, but his poetry is based on natural fact, which is always an amalgam of finite change. This is nature, the tangible in movement, but always tangible. The drops of water in the ocean *can* be counted, if not by us. The God of *The Book of Hours* is visible and can only be visible to the poet in the manifestations of life perceptible to human senses. . . .

This God is the same Poet who is later called Orpheus. At the end of *The Book of Hours* Rilke presents an image of this immanence and change which is even closer to his later use of Orpheus, because here we do see the human contour. . . .

Rilke told some friends that the sonnets he had written in February 1922 grouped themselves in a flash round the figure of Orpheus seen in an old engraving. He could not have invented a better story. It matched exactly his attitude, by which I mean his conception of truth. Something magical happens when a poet, or any kind of artist, finds the right material. Or the material finds him. He looks out from it as if through a mask, different but recognizable, as we recognize a familiar person in a dream, though the figure may be changed utterly by the mysterious workings of our unconscious. Once he had emerged from his inspiration, this dredging of the unconscious, Rilke did not (for a time) know himself in these words, knowing only that he had made something which fulfilled him completely. Indeed, his whole effort was to remove the differentiation of self and world. . . .

"Paris", says Rilke, "became the basis of my will to form." And Rodin, he says, "made me work like a painter or sculptor *before nature,* inexorably comprehending and reproducing the features of the model". His ambition now was to make the poem as objectively representative, as independent in space, as the visibly isolated work of the sculptor, disconnected from its maker. The poet's vision, too, had to be transformed into a tangible thing. Rodin's words, "You must work and have patience", remained Rilke's guiding principle to the end. . . . Patience is the open and receptive attitude, untouched by human necessity. Rilke found it in Rodin, he found it in nature, and he found it in Orpheus, so different now from the impulsive human figure of that earlier poem.

Rilke was no classical scholar. He knew only what most people know about the Orpheus legend. First, that the music of Orpheus was magical, giving him power over animate and inanimate nature. Second, that he visited the realms of the dead in a vain attempt to bring Eurydice back to the world of the living. Third, that in his death he was torn to pieces by savage women, followers of Dionysus, and scattered over the earth. And finally, that after his death he was regarded as a high priest of religion and even a god.

These are the features which form the substance of Orpheus in Rilke's *Sonnets.* He is the universal poet with magical powers of transformation, working like nature itself: for him there is no distinction between life and death—he is equally familiar with both realms; by being scattered over the earth he becomes part of the earth and so exists in everything. . . . He is form and movement, existence and continuity. (p. 1494)

The *Sonnets* are about fusion, the fusion of the many into one. Orpheus stands for this complete integration. In an essay which he wrote in 1919 and called *Primal Sound,* Rilke talks about what he calls our "five-fingered hand" of the senses. Each sense covers a separate sector, like a finger. What guarantee have we that these five sectors do cover the whole of possible experience? Between the sectors, the fingers, there are gaps. To extend these sectors and combine them to cover all perception is, says Rilke, not unnatural but supernatural. The supernatural, in this case, means of course more than *we* can perceive of the natural world. It is not beyond nature, it is beyond us. And the supernatural, says Rilke, is the province of the poem.

In his essay Rilke implies that, if we had this supernatural ability to perceive with one all-embracing sense, we should then experience—see, smell, taste, touch, hear—all the senses rolled into one, indistinguishable from each other—what he calls primal sound. . . . So, although the *Sonnets* are grouped round the figure of a musician and are therefore drawn towards the terminology of sound, there is an effort to make the different terms of sense-perception interchangeable. This is confusing but logical. . . .

"Praise, that's it!" says the poet in one of these sonnets. This is the function of Orpheus's song, and this is the function of the poet, who identifies himself ideally with Orpheus. By "praise" Rilke means more than the process of giving affirmative utterance. He means also the attitude of complete and patient acceptance. "Praise" is a celebration of *all* existence, even the apparently vile and immoral aspects—these are a limited human classification. "There is no choosing and no rejection", he says in *The Notebook of Malte Laurids Brigge.* Truth comes from all the evidence, not from selection on grounds of moral judgment. Now the material of life is allowed to choose the writer, not the writer his material. We are spared nothing. . . .

Orpheus represents primal sound. He comes and goes, says Rilke. The movement is cyclic and complete. The magical power attributed to Orpheus in legend is simply, as I suggested earlier, the working of nature itself. Magic is only the establishment of connexions we haven't seen before and can't quite see now. Establish every cause, or connexion, and you explain every event. In the total realm which Orpheus represents, all forms are connected, every form is in movement and becoming something else, so every transformation is not only possible but inevitable. Orpheus could have changed straw into gold, but this was left to a later Germanic imagination—perhaps the first German economic miracle. Orpheus himself as not only a transformer but as an object undergoing transformation is presented by Rilke in a sonnet which describes his death, in a peculiarly Rilkean way. Everything in life is both an agent of change and a subject which is being changed.

In the legend Orpheus is said to be a follower of Apollo (some versions say he was Apollo's son). His actions clearly associate him with the god who is a symbol of order. When he tames wild nature he establishes form by revealing, magically, that connexions do exist between the particles we call chaos. Nothing is absolute in his realm. Life is drawn from death, creation from destruction. But the legend describes a single process—creation. What we call destruction is a stage in creation and is therefore creative. And so it is in Rilke's sonnet. He follows the legend in telling how Orpheus is torn to pieces by the Maenads, wild women, followers of Dionysus, the god of licence and disorder. . . .

Nature is the universal poet; and in the *Sonnets* Rilke shows how well he has learnt the lesson from Rodin: to work "*before nature,* inexorably comprehending and reproducing the features of the model". Comprehending and reproducing—this is what is meant by being both a listener and a mouth of nature. He is characterizing his own effort as a poet. His theme is transformation, and his work is transformation. At the centre of transformation is Orpheus, the smallest particle, a material divinity, more credible than the gods some religions have made into distant giants.

"Speak and proclaim", says Rilke in the ninth Duino elegy. He is conducting a dialogue with himself, like Orpheus. In this elegy he implies that it is no use talking about the infinite or the intangible or the metaphysical. The things of this earth are the only material for human vision. And again he coalesces time and space when he says: "*Here* is the time of what can be uttered, *here* its home." And by "here" he means this world, what we have, what we can perceive. It is a mistake to think of him as an otherworldly poet: his supernature, his poetry, is based on nature—in its widest as well as smallest sense, meaning everything within the range of human perception.

The only purpose he ever attributed to his poetry was the preservation of tradition. In the *Sonnets to Orpheus* he felt he had made a contribution in this respect. These poems are material objects. He hoped they were as true and as representative as those works of handcraftsmen which were his own inheritance and which he once described as "secret equivalents of life". Everything is movement and continuity. (p. 1495)

> *Idris Parry, "Rilke and Orpheus," in* The Times Literary Supplement (© *Times Newspapers Ltd., 1975; reproduced by permission), December 12, 1975, pp. 1494-95.*

[Rilke's] moods and decisions and changes of place are largely governed by the progress of his poetry.... Four places, or images of places, stand out. First, Russia, which he visited ... at the turn of the century.... It is this orthodox Russia, with its spirituality and remoteness from the technological civilisation of the West, which gave him what he called 'the foundation of my experiencing and receiving'. The Paris of Rodin and of the Picasso of the Blue Period provides the other pole of his poetry, 'the basis of my desire to create form'. Duino, the castle near Trieste, is the place in which the *Elegies,* the greatest venture of his life, are begun in 1912; and Muzot, a little mediaeval manor house in the Swiss Valois is where, ten years later, in the memorable month of February 1922, the *Elegies* and several other collections are concluded.

There are a few men among Rilke's friends—among them André Gide and Paul Valéry, both of whose work he translated into German—but, above all, his friends were women. [It] seems as though [almost] all these countless, highly-charged erotic relationships were merely there to provide figures in the pattern of his work, examples of feeling in its different intensities. (pp. 835-36)

The history that needs to be written and never has been written, Rilke once said, is the history of feeling. Men differ from each other from one era to another in respect of their capacity for feeling and experience, and certain images in Rilke's poetry—'the grey horse in Russia', 'the rope-maker in Rome', 'the potter on the Nile', a window of Chartres Cathedral—are presented as significant emblems of their respective historical eras precisely because they are seen as expressions of the human potential for feeling in any one era of history. And when T. S. Eliot writes that, in this age of ours, 'human kind cannot bear very much reality', he provides the experiential ground on which the poetic argument of the *Duino Elegies* is based

For there is, indeed, an argument: the ten elegies with their powerful, heavily-stressed lines, whose beat derives from the classical elegiac distich, consist of a carefully organised series of images in which the story of our strengths and weaknesses, of our realities and of the possibilities that are in our grasp, is told. In calling Rilke the poet of feeling, I do not wish to suggest that he is lacking in thought. This vision or, as we might almost say, ideology of feeling is a complex thing, richly elaborated and deeply considered. To me, the most astonishing aspect of his poetry is that, in it, feeling, thought and image are united, and that it is his achievement as a lyrical poet which forces us to revise such doubtful antitheses as 'thought' and 'feeling', which causes us to think again about our arid separations. . . .

The *Elegies* are an attempt to describe our condition, not in terms of static abstractions, but as the flowing re-enactment of a major change in man's history which Rilke understands as a history of feeling.... Poetry, then, is the activity which keeps 'the still recognisable form' alive, and thus makes human sense of the world. And in the profusion of poetry written during those last 20 years of his life, Rilke returns to this theme of the poetic validation in countless different ways: now through the celebration of flowers, beasts and birds, now through the exploration of the myths of Orpheus and Eurydice and of the ancient gods, now through the poetic re-creating of man-made *things*. Yet the moods are by no means always solemn. In the poem, 'The Unicorn', for instance, that fabulous animal is presented with an Alice-in-Wonderland-like gaiety. It is a creature of the children's longing and imaginative surmises, a beast so powerfully imagined by them that it simply could not resist their desire for it to *be,* and so, Rilke says, it *was,* fed on a strange, fairy-world variety of corn, fed on the merest possibility of being.

A remarkable thing, so it seems to me, has occurred in this poem and many others like it: that intensity of experience and feeling which I mentioned is no longer a part of the explicit poetic argument. Instead, it *shows,* gently and joyfully, the achieved images that issue from the process. The voice of the age has not been silenced but transcended. Like the fly in the amber, the historical is preserved in the aesthetic.

It is time, though, to consider some of the obvious objections to Rilke's vision. Is this validation of the world through poetry not a highly esoteric affair? If, in the end, the temptation of exclusiveness and esotericism is overcome, this is because what Rilke is invoking is, not an isolated poetic faculty, but all our creative faculties as symbolised and represented by the poetic. The value and meaning given to the world in the act of poetic re-creation are not some aestheticist ornaments, they represent our attempts to make sense of the situation in which we have been placed; our strenuous attempts, blessed, at times, with the uncovenanted grace of ease and felicitous resolution. And the 'immanent' divinity implied in Rilke's later poems is born of a protest against the theologians' conception of a god unsullied by contact with the earth and the world of men, a god whose transcendence is absolute and inaccessible. Invoking the divine in the language of the earth, Rilke is calling it back to the earth, which is God's creation, after all. And the words which are meant to describe him are offered up as a kind of living proof that we have only one language for God and men and their world; that we have to use words when we talk to each other; and that the language-and-experience of poetry, like the language-and-experience of religion, are inseparable from our common humanity. (p. 836)

> *J. P. Stern, "Rilke: Words for God and Men," in* The Listener (© *British Broadcasting Corp. 1975; reprinted by permission of J. P. Stern), December 18, 1975, pp. 835-36.*

Gertrude Stein

1874-1956

American novelist, poet, critic, and playwright. Not a great writer but a bold experimenter, Gertrude Stein is important for the ways in which she defined new attitudes and perspectives in twentieth-century literature and art. As a student at Harvard's Radcliffe College from 1893 to 1897, she studied psychology under William James. She did advanced work in brain anatomy at Johns Hopkins University from 1897 to 1902 but did not take a degree in medicine. Being of independent means, Stein moved to France in 1903 with her lifelong friend, companion, and secretary, Alice B. Toklas. For more than a generation her home in Paris at 27 rue de Fleurus was a center for artists, writers, philosophers, and critics. At the height of the American literary expatriation in the 1920s, many members of the younger generation of American writers came to her for advice and encouragement, among them Hemingway, Sherwood Anderson, and Fitzgerald. Picasso, Braque, Matisse, and other avant-garde artists greatly impressed Stein and she began collecting their work and championing them in her writings. With the help of her brother, Leo, an art critic, she greatly encouraged Picasso at the beginning of his career. Stein attempted to do, in prose, something of what her friend Picasso had done in art, cultivating a style akin to abstractionism. A verbal technician, her special emphasis was on the tools of writing: words and structure. Her most consistent genres for communicating her ideas were criticism and autobiography. Her two popular autobiographies, *The Autobiography of Alice B. Toklas* and *Everybody's Autobiography*, show her gifts and her considerable wit. The first of these is not itself experimental and gained for her a wider readership. Stein came into public prominence by the combination of her autobiography, her lecture tour of America in 1934, and her "mothering" of American G.I.s in the Second World War. In spite of her long battle to be published, she never ceased to regard herself as a genius and the center of modern literature. In *The Autobiography of Alice B. Toklas*, Stein has Alice recounting that she personally knew three geniuses in her lifetime: Picasso, Alfred North Whitehead, and Gertrude Stein. Her name was prominent in the literary reviews of her time and she is remembered as an author whose style reached the ultimate in abstraction, a literary "cubist."

PRINCIPAL WORKS

Three Lives (short novels) 1909
Tender Buttons (prose poems) 1914
The Making of Americans (novel) 1925
Composition as Explanation (essay) 1926
Lucy Church, Amiably (novel) 1930
The Autobiography of Alice B. Toklas (autobiography) 1933
Four Saints in Three Acts (play) 1934
Lectures in America (essay) 1935
Narration (essay) 1935
Everybody's Autobiography (autobiography) 1937
Ida (novel) 1941
Wars I Have Seen (essays) 1945
Brewsie and Willie (essays) 1946
Things As They Are (novel) 1950

"Lie on this, show sup the boon that nick the basting thread thinly and night night gown and pit wet kit. Loom down the thorough narrow."

Surely one does not have to be persuaded into liking the happy chunks of verbalism Miss Stein has given us here, the sharp ticking off of the words, with a plunge at the end like a boat grounding on thick mud. . . . Here, after all the varnish, is the return to the primitive. (pp. 408-09)

In Miss Stein's case the satisfaction stops with the form itself. Even the nursery rhyme, by its semblance of a "message," goes farther in this particular than the [quotation] from Miss Stein.

We find, then, that Miss Stein's method is one of subtraction. She has deliberately limited her equipment. . . . I should say that she had ignored the inherent property of words: that quality in the literary man's medium which makes him start out with a definiteness that the other arts do not possess. That is, if the musician plays G-sharp he has prescribed no definitions; but if the literary man writes "boy" he has already laid down certain demarcations. Now, obviously, any literary artist who sets out to begin his work in a primary search for music or rhythm, and attempts to get this at the expense of this "inherent property of words" . . . obviously this artist is not going to exploit the full potentialities of his medium. He is getting an art by subtraction; he is violating his *genre*. One might, in a pious moment, name this the "fallacy of subtraction." The formula would apply to a great deal of modern art.

Miss Stein continually utilizes this violation of the *genre*. Theoretically at least, the result has its studio value. If the academies were at all alive, they would teach the arts in precisely this manner. By approaching the art-work from these exorbitant angles one is suddenly able to rediscover organically those eternal principles of art which are, painful as it may be to admit it, preserved in all the standard textbooks. (pp. 409-10)

Perhaps it has been noted with resentment that up to this point I have avoided discussing Miss Stein's use of associated ideas. I have done so because associated ideas *per se* are of no more value than are the Ozark mountains *per se*. Their encroachment into art is justified only when some sound aesthetic value is acquired thereby. And their value, it seems to me, lies precisely in the opportunity they offer for throwing into relief the *functions* of the art-work. . . . A logical sequence (the perfectly lubricated novel, for instance) moves with a minimum of relief; the purpose is to conceal the form beneath the matter; the form is used to "sell" the matter. But if I wanted to emphasize, say, a transition; not try to sneak across a transition, but to throw it into relief so that the reader knew that at this moment he was going through a transition; I could get this by a chain of associated ideas, used like steps going in one direction. I should move from point to point by a *psychological* sequence rather than a *logical* sequence. To illustrate rather bluntly; let us suppose a series of nouns, running from ideas of complete stability, into ideas of inceptive motion, then gentle motion, then accelerated motion, speed, precipitancy, and finally ending in some violent cataclysm or explosion.

But this, obviously, would bring in the need of the taboo. To produce this art-form, I should have to rule out ideas of precipitancy at the beginning, and ideas of stability towards the end. The work of art, then, implies the erection of a temporary set of values, true at least for the particular problem at hand. But in the first flush of our "freedom," certain artists like Miss Stein refuse to recognize even these temporary taboos. Here is the absurdity of romanticism, or individualism; here we see carried to the extreme the tendency to take the personality of the individual as a virtue in itself; for the only unity of these associations is the unity of their having been written by one person—which is the absurdity of Dadaism. (pp. 410-11)

At any rate, Miss Stein does get this aesthetic value at times into her sentences. And at such times they have a *raison d'être* not merely as fever charts, but also as bits of art. But here again the choppiness of her subject matter limits her achievements enormously. (p. 411)

Miss Stein, by her short sparrow-pecks, can get a certain analytic form, the form of her sentences. But the synthetic form of paragraph or stanza, or beyond, of the art-work *in toto,* is denied her. While even her analytic form is seldom brilliant, and shows beyond a doubt that the focus of her attention is elsewhere. This, of course, results in her being diffuse. And her method leaves us with too little to feed on. One might almost say that it argues for the insignificance of significant form. Further, her book is a continual rebeginning. No sentence advances us beyond the sentence preceding. For such advances involve this synthetic form, and this synthetic form can be brought out only by a greater stability of subject matter. (pp. 411-12)

Kenneth Burke, "Engineering with Words," in The Dial *(copyright, 1923, by The Dial Publishing Company, Inc.; reprinted by permission of J. S. Watson, Jr. and Scofield Thayer), April, 1923 (and reprinted by Kraus Reprint Corporation, 1966), pp. 408-12.*

In a style which appears to owe nothing to that of any other novelist, [Gertrude Stein] seems to have caught the very rhythms and accents of the minds of her heroines [in *Three Lives*]: we find ourselves sharing the lives of the Good Anna and Gentle Lena so intimately that we forget about their position and see the world limited to their range, just as in Melanctha's case—and this is what makes her story one of the best as well as one of the earliest attempts of a white American novelist to understand the mind of the modern Americanized negro—we become so immersed in Melanctha's world that we quite forget its inhabitants are black. And we discover that these histories have a significance different from that of ordinary realistic fiction: Miss Stein is interested in her subjects, not from the point of view of the social conditions of which they might be taken as representative, but as three fundamental types of women: the self-sacrificing Anna, who combines devotion with domination; the dreamy and passive Lena, for whom it is natural to allow herself to be used and effaced from life by other lives; and the passionate and complex Melanctha, who "was always losing what she had in wanting all the things she saw." Behind the limpid and slightly monotonous simplicity of Gertrude Stein's sentences, one becomes aware of her masterly grasp of the organisms, contradictory and indissoluble, which human personalities are. (pp. 237-38)

Sometimes [the] writings of Gertrude Stein make us laugh: her humor is perhaps the one of her qualities which comes through in her recent books most clearly; and I should describe them as amusing nonsense, if "nonsense" were not a word which had so often been used in derogation. . . . If I should say that Miss Stein wrote nonsense, I might be thought to be implying that she was not serious or that she was not artistically successful. As a matter of fact, one should not talk about "nonsense" until one has decided what "sense" consists of. . . . (p. 244)

Widely ridiculed and seldom enjoyed, she has yet played an important rôle in connection with other writers who have become popular. . . . Most of us balk at her soporific rigmaroles, her echolaliac incantations, her half-witted-sounding catalogues of numbers; most of us read her less and less. Yet, remembering especially her early work, we are still always aware of her presence in the background of contemporary literature—and we picture her as the great pyramidal Buddha of Jo Davidson's statue of her, eternally and placidly ruminating the gradual developments of the processes of being, registering the vibrations of a psychological country like some august human seismograph whose charts we haven't the training to read. And whenever we pick up her writings, however unintelligible we may find them, we are aware of a literary personality of unmistakable originality and distinction. (pp. 252-53)

Edmund Wilson, "Gertrude Stein," in his Axel's Castle: A Study in the Imaginative Literature of 1870-1930 *(reprinted by permission of Charles Scribner's Sons; © 1931 by*

Charles Scribner's Sons), Scribner's, 1931, pp. 237-56.

Miss Stein has been called the mother of modern literature. Her revolutionary theories about the use of words undoubtedly influenced James Joyce's *Ulysses*, which has in turn influenced almost all serious fiction produced since its appearance. (p. 323)

She is realistic, and therefore unbookish and unimaginative. The words which dart about in her poems without regard for the ordinary laws of language sequence or of musical cadence are commonplace words, frequently monosyllables. They repeat themselves endlessly, and frequently get into juxtapositions which suggest humor, but rarely beauty. They symbolize nothing. But they do follow the most common of all language patterns—the pattern of dreams, of reverie. . . .

Yet in working out these charts, Miss Stein has rendered a valuable service to herself and to all writers. She has shown how inadequate conventional prose and verse are for recording actual mental processes. She has shown how demoded our language laws have become. She has tried to get the individual word where it belongs—attached always to the concept it represents. (p. 326)

The Making of Americans is very Henry-Jamesian. But Miss Stein's investigative mind is decidedly her own. She digs into moral institutions, and shows that they are largely follies. The book is a treatise on ethics, a psychological analysis of the most thoughtful workmanship. Throughout, Miss Stein as the recorder of the history is thinking out loud. She is not in a state of reverie; on the contrary, she is employing all of her intellectual faculties. Her language is thought in the nude—not thought dressed up in the clothes of time-worn rhetoric. (p. 327)

If a great new English prose is in the making, and if Ernest Hemingway, as James Stephens thinks, is its prime mover, then Gertrude Stein is its creator. For there is not a stylistic device employed by Hemingway and his numerous followers which had not been first worked out and used by Gertrude Stein. According to existing standards, she is not a poet nor a story-teller, but she is a creative thinker. She has discovered new functions for words. (pp. 327-28)

Vernon Loggins, in his I Hear America . . . : *Literature in the United States Since 1900 (copyright 1937 by Thomas Y. Crowell Company; reprinted by permission of Thomas Y. Crowell Co., Inc.), Crowell, 1937.*

Gertrude Stein's importance, so far as literature was concerned, lay less in her actual writings than in her reforming influence on the tones and cadences of prose. From her practice as well as from her singular discourses *How to Write* . . . and *Narration* . . . it appears that words for her had qualities—color and sound—besides their meaning, and sentences had—or ought to have—something like what in music would be called a tune. When she herself wrote obscurely it was because she undertook to do with mere color and sound more than words can do, as if she were humming lovely or witty tunes without pronouncing the words. She did not fall into any ornate or precious classicism. Instead, she evolved her linked, symmetrical, diversified cadences from familiar American speech, much as Mark Twain had done in his tall tales and in *Huckleberry Finn*. (p. 339)

Carl Van Doren, in his The American Novel: 1789-1939 *(reprinted with permission of Macmillan Publishing Co., Inc.; copyright 1921, 1940 by Macmillan Publishing Co., Inc.; 1949 by Carl Van Doren; 1968 by Anne Van Doren Ross, Barbara Van Doren Klaw, and Margaret Van Doren Bevans), revised edition, Macmillan, 1940.*

In all the world, in 1903, there was but one literary person who had anything approximating a scientific or realistic (for they are essentially the same thing) interest in primitive mentality. And that one person was Gertrude Stein. (p. 312)

Yet the current literary vogue of 1903 and her psychological studies, while they may be used in explanation of Gertrude Stein's work, have less to do with its actual inception than had certain events in the world of art, events which Miss Stein witnessed as a sympathetic and intelligent observer after her arrival in France, for shortly, under her brother's expert tutelage, she became a discriminating critic and patron of the new art, and helped to "discover" Cézanne, Matisse, Derain, Picasso, and Juan Gris. Just at that time art, which had seemingly exhausted the possibilities of impressionism, received a new stimulus in the discovery of the high merit of negro sculpture, introduced from Northern Africa. Though Vlaminck is believed to be the first to apprehend the worth of the simplified emotional form of this sculpture, and Modigliani to make the most effective early use of it in painting, Pablo Picasso (who had contracted to paint Gertrude Stein's portrait) lived with the Spanish sculptor, Agero, designer of bas-reliefs on African models, and must have done some very acute thinking about this time on the subject. It was while she was sitting for her portrait for Picasso that Miss Stein began work on the "Melanctha" story in *Three Lives*. . . . To the prevalent enthusiasm in Paris among the artists whom Gertrude Stein knew well must be assigned the immediate origin of this first, and all-important, tale of Gertrude Stein. (p. 314)

["Melanctha"] is the first genuinely primitivistic study in American literature. The author, with extraordinary penetration, has seen that it is not always the jarring of wills, the conflict of violent natures, which makes the course of love uncertain; she has discovered, with the help of her medical science, that the element of "timing" is an important one in passion. Doubtless there are earlier uses of this theme in world literature, but it is exceedingly difficult to recall them. Miss Stein, to enforce the theme and to show how easy love is when both natures are ripe for it, throws Jem Richards and Melanctha Herbert together at the end of the tale. Yet there is to be no happiness for the girl who had learned to be "safe" in love. Her faith shaken in herself since her affair with Jeff Campbell, she insists on marriage with Jem only to drive him from her by her very insistence. Consumption is a final irony, for Melanctha had burned herself out before disease destroyed her. "Melanctha Herbert always loved too hard and much too often." Thus the tale is a consistent study of a type, the analysis of an ardent, self-consuming nature. (pp. 315-16)

Both for historical reasons and for intrinsic merit, "Melanctha" must be ranked as one of the three or four thoroughly original short stories which have been produced in this century.

The other two stories in *Three Lives* are of less consequence than "Melanctha." Like it, they are portraits aiming to set forth the generic or essential things in the characters studied. Like it, they owe a great deal to the new painting. Indeed, Gertrude Stein tells us that she did the actual writing of these stories facing Cézanne's *Portrait of a Lady* which she had recently acquired. How much her use of adjectives reminds us of the laying of heavy brush strokes of primary color on canvas! (p. 317)

Now, just as Pablo Picasso arrived at "pure" art, by reducing painting from representation to solid geometry, to fragmentary solid geometry, and finally to plane geometry, so Gertrude Stein may be said to have tried to produce "pure" literature and to have progressed by comparable stages to this end. The first stage in this progress may be said to be an effort to formulate abstract conceptions of people. This effort is seen in *The Making of Americans,* Miss Stein's 900-page novel. . . . (p. 318)

The Making of Americans is without dialogue and without action; Miss Stein calls it "a description"—which is accurate. "Events," asserts Miss Stein, ". . . should not be the materials of poetry or prose." Characters, however, are delineated in the book and are recognizable. In fact, in her account of the dressmakers and governesses employed by the Herslands, in her brief record of the relations of Mary Maxworthing and Mabel Linker, . . . Miss Stein is still very close to the method which she employed in *Three Lives.*

The next stage in Gertrude Stein's progress towards pure abstraction in type drawing may be said to be represented by "Ada" in *Geography and Plays.* . . . It was in order to do "portraits" of this sort that Gertrude Stein gave up the composition of *The Long Gay Book* and *Many Many Women.* She had discovered that it was impossible to eliminate the narrative interest from fiction (as *The Making of Americans* reveals) and have much of anything of value left. The word-portrait is much nearer the brush-portrait than is the novel; consequently in its favor Miss Stein abandoned fiction writing. "Ada," her first portrait, we now know to be a study of Alice B. Toklas, the companion for twenty-five years of Gertrude Stein. In form, "Ada" may be said to correspond to the "fragmentary solid geometry" stage of Picasso's painting. It is not the story of "Ada" precisely; yet by reading the fragmentary material about her brother's love affairs, about her letters to her father, and about her grandmother's way of smelling flowers and eating dates and sugar,—in a word, by *moving about* the character —we certainly gain some sort of notion of her.

The third and final stage of Miss Stein's progress towards the abstract, which means *the complete elimination of narrative,* might be represented by any number of "portraits" selected from Miss Stein's work. . . . Not only narrative is eliminated, but the fragments of the portrait are related to each other only through an association suggested by the sounds of the words. Miss Stein has filled her picture as would Picasso by letting the form of one object suggest another. (pp. 319-20)

After achieving pure "abstraction" in portraiture, it was only natural that Gertrude Stein should try "still lifes" (her phrase) and "landscapes." Most of the material in *Tender Buttons* belongs to the "still life" category, while the things called "plays" are really "landscapes." . . . A purely scenic thing with words and music, but without representa-tion or narration, might produce on the stage something of the effect of a cubist landscape in painting. And that is precisely what *Four Saints in Three Acts . . .* did.

Although she has succeeded in writing something which may "revolutionize opera," the course which Gertrude Stein has followed since creating *Three Lives* cannot be said to have been a profitable one. It is true that the present has no comparative standards save in painting for the judgment of her later work, and the future must decide whether portrait painting, still life painting, and landscape painting of the sort that she has done with words have any usefulness. She herself has passed judgment on her fiction writing by abandoning it, yet the present, moved by her early studies and cold towards her painting, may fairly question whether she has not been unduly and unwisely influenced by Picasso, and whether, in transferring some of his ideas to literary composition, she has properly defined her medium. (pp. 320-21)

> *Oscar Cargill, in his* Intellectual America: Ideas on the March *(reprinted with permission of Macmillan Publishing Co., Inc.; copyright 1941 by Macmillan Publishing Co. Inc.; 1969 by Oscar Cargill), Macmillan, 1941.*

One of the many interesting things about *The Making of Americans* is its date. It was written . . . (1906-1908), when Gertrude Stein was young. It precedes the war and cubism; it precedes *Ulysses* and *Remembrance of Things Past.* I doubt if all the people who should read it will read it for a great while yet, for it is in such a limited edition, and reading it is anyhow a sort of permanent occupation. Yet to shorten it would be to mutilate its vitals, and it is a very necessary book. (p. 251)

This is a deeply American book, and without "movies" or automobiles or radio or prohibition or any of the mechanical properties for making local color, it is a very up-to-date book. We feel in it the vitality and hope of the first generation, the hearty materialism of the second, the vagueness of the third. . . . In beginning this book you walk into what seems to be a great spiral, a slow, ever-widening, unmeasured spiral unrolling itself horizontally. The people in this world appear to be motionless at every stage of their progress, each one is simultaneously being born, arriving at all ages and dying. You perceive that it is a world without mobility, everything takes place, has taken place, will take place; therefore nothing takes place, all at once. Yet the illusion of movement persists, the spiral unrolls, you follow; a closed spinning circle is even more hopeless than a universe that will not move. Then you discover it is not a circle, not machinelike repetition, the spiral does open and widen, it is repetition only in the sense that one wave follows upon another. The emotion progresses with the effort of a giant parturition. Gertrude Stein describes her function in terms of digestion, of childbirth: all these people, these fragments of digested knowledge, are in her, they must come out.

The progress of her family, then, this making of Americans, she has labored to record in a catalogue of human attributes, acts and emotions. Episodes are nothing, narrative is by the way, her interest lies in what she calls the bottom natures of men and women, all men, all women. (p. 252)

In [the] intensity of preoccupation there is the microscopic observation of the near-sighted who must get so close to their object they depend not alone on vision but on touch and smell and the very warmth of bodies to give them the knowledge they seek. This nearness, this immediacy, she communicates also, there is no escaping into the future nor into the past. All time is in the present, these people are "being living," she makes you no gift of comfortable ripened events past and gone. "I am writing everything as I am learning everything," and so we have lists of qualities and defects, portraits of persons in scraps, with bits and pieces added again and again in every round of the spiral: they repeat and repeat themselves to you endlessly as living persons do, and always you feel you know them, and always they present a new bit of themselves.

Gertrude Stein reminds me of Jacob Boehme in the way she sees essentials in human beings. He knew them as salt, as mercury; as moist, as dry, as burning; as bitter, sweet or sour. She perceives them as attacking, as resisting, as dependent independent, as having a core of wood, of mud, as murky, engulfing; Boehme's chemical formulas are too abstract, she knows the substances of man are mixed with clay. Materials interest her, the moral content of man can often be nicely compared to homely workable stuff. Sometimes her examination is almost housewifely, she rolls a fabric under her fingers, tests it. It is thus and so. I find this very good, very interesting. "It will repay good using."

"In writing a word must be for me really an existing thing." Her efforts to get at the roots of existing life, to create fresh life from them, give her words a dark liquid flowingness, like the murmur of the blood. She does not strain words or invent them. Many words have retained their original meaning for her, she uses them simply. Good means good and bad means bad. . . . (p. 253)

An odd thing happens somewhere in the middle of this book. You will come upon it suddenly and it will surprise you. All along you have had a feeling of submergence in the hidden lives of a great many people, and unaccountably you will find yourself rolling up to the surface, on the outer edge of the curve. A disconcerting break into narrative full of phrases that might have come out of any careless sentimental novel, alternates with scraps of the natural style. It is astounding, you read on out of chagrin. Again without warning you submerge, and later Miss Stein explains she was copying an old piece of writing of which she is now ashamed, the words mean nothing: "I commence again with words that have meaning," she says, and we leave this limp, dead spot in the middle of the book.

Gertrude Stein wrote once of Juan Gris that he was, somehow, saved. She is saved, too; she is free of pride and humility, she confesses to superhuman aspirations simply, she was badly frightened once and has recovered, she is honest in her uncertainties. There are only a few bits of absolute knowledge in the world, people can learn only one or two fundamental facts about each other, the rest is decoration and prejudice: She is very free from decoration and prejudice. (pp. 253-54)

[In] that slow swarm of words, out of the long drone and mutter and stammer of her lifetime monologue, often there emerged a phrase of ancient native independent wisdom, for she had a shrewd deep knowledge of the commoner human motives. Her judgments were neither moral nor intellectual, and least of all aesthetic, indeed they were not even judgments, but simply her description from observation of acts, words, appearances giving her view; limited, personal in the extreme, prejudiced without qualification, based on assumptions founded in the void of pure unreason. . . .

It was not that she was opposed to ideas, but that she was not interested in anybody's ideas but her own, except as material to put down on her endless flood of pages. Like writing, opinion also belonged to Miss Stein, and nothing annoyed her more—she was easily angered about all sorts of things—than for anyone not a genius or who had no reputation that she respected, to appear to be thinking in her presence. (p. 259)

> *Katherine Anne Porter, selections from two essays (originally written in 1927 and 1947), in her* The Collected Essays and Occasional Writings of Katherine Anne Porter *(copyright © 1970 by Katherine Anne Porter; reprinted by permission of Delacorte Press/Seymour Lawrence), Delacorte Press, 1970.*

As readable as it is singable, [*Four Saints in Three Acts*] is to me an esthetic experience. Like a fine wine, a sunset or a wedding night, it is to be enjoyed, not defined; like a Picasso, Gris or Braque, it might be interpreted but refuses to be explained. Program notes add nothing to it, as they add nothing to a symphony.

While it was intense and dramatic, it had little to do with cognition. . . . *Four Saints in Three Acts* makes no literal sense, as indeed the title foretells, for two of the five words are inaccurate; there are more than four saints and more than three acts, and no one I'm sure doubts Miss Stein's ability to count. It was intended to do something to us, not to tell us something. Of the average book it can be said that you can't take it with you, but of *Four Saints* it is on the contrary true that you can. It is not informative, like *The Making of Americans,* but it is invigorating and vastly inspiriting. Precisely like a piece of music, though in a different medium, it boils something inside you to the exploding point, serves as an intensifier, acts like sunspots on the unsteady psyche. People who resent it, and of course many were infuriated, expect too little of it; they want something they can put their finger on, and its quality is far too subtle and intangible for that. (pp. 51-2)

Miss Stein, believing there was more in [words], and less, than the dictionaries taught, said in *Everybody's* that she liked "anything a word can do." She showed it excitingly in *Four Saints.*

She understood words in Webster's sense, too, as we devote them to practical use, for she was expert in the traditional employment of language, as no phrase proves better than the famous, acutely stylized "A bell within me rang," to announce Miss Toklas' trio of geniuses. Starting with the familiar "that rings a bell in me," she turned it around and thus seized the advantage of association with the idiom and avoided the disadvantage of a literal copy. But in addition she had to decide on one of several possible words and orders: "A bell rang in me, a bell in me rang, a bell rang within me, within me a bell rang, in me a bell rang." One choice of words and one order alone carry the greatest emphasis and significance and best catch and hold a reader's attention, and Miss Stein hit on them unerringly. A recent misquotation of it as the "little bell which rang in my head'' shows how it could be muffed. It wasn't enough for her to boast that she was a genius; she must phrase her claim in such a memorable and distinguished manner that we would not miss it nor forget its impact. The masterly form of her statement, it seems to me, verifies its content. (p. 53)

Tender Buttons is to writing . . ., exactly, what cubism is to art. Both book and picture appeared in, belong to, can't be removed from, our time. That particular quality in them which is usually ridiculed, the disparate, the dispersed, the getting onto a horse and riding off in all directions, the atomization of their respective materials, the distorted vision, all that was not imagined but rather drawn out of their unique age. If the twentieth century makes sense, so do Stein and Picasso. (p. 67)

Miss Stein's sentences should be read as one "reads" a painting composed of real and unreal elements, or of displaced fragments. The impressionists, whose poet was Mallarmé, separated colors into their parts, but they would unite again. The cubists separated objects into pieces which all the king's horses and all the king's men couldn't put together again. Miss Stein was equally destructive. (p. 69)

The poems and novels were not meant as puzzles.

Miss Stein's works can of course be taken literally, in somewhat the same manner in which one investigates a passage in Joyce, with dictionaries and encyclopedias at one's elbow. You dissect them, or rather vivisect them, though you're the one to be hurt and you derive little benefit from it; at the same time the magic vanishes. Either you try it on a fine example of Stein and the essence of it evades you, or you try it on an example so obvious that the effort is superfluous. (p. 70)

Miss Stein did not write in fragments, but instead gave us the fragmentation, the ultimate dissolution of the traditional literary form. It was atomic dissolution in the world of letters; she turned down the lamp for the sake of the big explosion.

Dissolution, destruction, atom and fission suggest contemporary manifestations infinitely more momentous than Miss Stein's writing had ever pretended to be, or ever seemed to be either to her friends or foes. It would be as erroneous to read into her work the ultimate meaning of the modern world as to read into it nothing. (pp. 72-3)

If she resembled most authors in being an unreliable judge of her own works, she resembled all authors in the unevenness of her production. Some books are worth more than the others. Some of them should have been edited, or even cut remorselessly. . . .

In directing the posthumous publication of her remaining manuscripts, she acted on the conviction that, since the passage of time had disclosed the indubitable importance of her early work, so would her late work, if given a chance, win eventual recognition. For some writers, like Flaubert, as for some painters, like Cézanne or Ryder, a work is never finished; to the day of their death they could keep on improving it. For others, like Miss Stein, a work is finished as soon as it is inscribed. (p. 238)

[Some] books abound in discouraging pages, and other volumes, it seems to me, are more notebook than finished work, even though to her they were complete; they are the

inception, not the development, of ideas, more interesting after you know Gertrude Stein than when you are trying to make her acquaintance. For making her acquaintance, nothing is better than *The Autobiography of Alice B. Toklas.* As for the less traditional works, *Three Lives* should properly come first. *The Making of Americans* deserves try after try, and preferably in the abridged American edition; taken slowly, and not too much at a time, it will prove rewarding. After that, *Tender Buttons* is essential, for here is the kind of Stein that launched a thousand jibes; this represents the big break with the sort of books to which we had been accustomed, and once you have succumbed to it, you can take anything, you have become a Stein reader. *Lucy Church Amiably, Operas and Plays, Four Saints* and *Four in America* are to be recommended. But *Brewsie and Willie, Wars I Have Seen* and *Yes Is for a Very Young Man,* among the better known works, are less stimulating despite some excellent passages. Some of the later writing has gone slack, it is diffused, and we hunt in vain for the verve of the *Autobiography* and the evocative power of *Four Saints* and the incomparable charm of "Rose is a rose is a rose is a rose." (pp. 238-39)

W. G. Rogers, in his When This You See Remember Me: Gertrude Stein in Person *(copyright © 1948 by W. G. Rogers; reprinted by permission of Holt, Rinehart and Winston, Publishers), Rinehart & Company, Inc., 1948.*

[Gertrude Stein] had conceived it as part of her mission to "kill" the nineteenth century "dead,"—"quite like a gangster with a mitraillette"; and, concerned with a continuous present alone, she had begun to convince herself that her work was "really the beginning of modern writing." Her story *Melanctha* in *Three Lives* . . . was the "first definite step," as she wrote later, "away from the nineteenth century and into the twentieth," and there was a grain of truth in this, though the same claim could have been made for several other compositions by contemporary writers. At that moment the movement of "modern art," so called for many years, was also beginning in Paris with Matisse and Picasso, and Gertrude Stein and her brother Leo were friends of the protagonists and even brought Picasso and Matisse together. . . . Gertrude, sharing their point of view, wrote as it were in conjunction with them, endeavouring to parallel in words their effects in paint. . . . Gertrude was certainly the first to follow them in writing. (pp. 435-36)

No one could ever have denied the power or the note of originality that characterized Gertrude Stein's first three stories about the "good" Anna, the "gentle" Lena and the graceful intelligent Negro girl. . . . The main characters were intensely real and alive. . . . That Gertrude Stein was a true creator, one of the rare minds who originate styles, could never have been questioned by a reader of these three stories, entirely new as they were in the vision as well as in the manner that was to mark her work for forty years. (pp. 437-38)

With the rhythms that characterized her style, these writings were marked by a certain lucidity because they had all been composed in a state of excitement, for she was possessed in each case by a subject that stirred her emotionally first of all and brought her faculties clearly into focus. She had "something to say," in other words, when she wrote about Lena, Melanctha and Anna, and when she told the story of the modern art-movement,—the real theme of the *Autobiography of Alice B. Toklas;* and who had more to say than she when she told, at the end of *Wars I Have Seen,* the story of the "coming of the Americans" in 1944?. . . [When] she began to "write cubistically," as her brother Leo called it, she dispensed with the subject that had stirred her and focussed her mind. So her writing became a chaos of words and rhythms. At the moment when Picasso was painting her portrait, he was entering his own cubistic phase, . . . and Gertrude Stein followed him again in *The Making of Americans, Tender Buttons* and the portraits that seemed to parallel his work in paint. She also, in her literary still-lifes, disintegrated objects, apparently aiming at an incoherence that was later supposed to express the distortions and disruptions and discords of a world in collapse, and various young writers were influenced by her powerful individuality, her original simplifications and the movement of her style. (pp. 438-39)

> *Van Wyck Brooks, in his* The Confident Years: 1885-1915 *(copyright, 1952, by Van Wyck Brooks; reprinted by permission of the publishers, E. P. Dutton), Dutton, 1952.*

If Gertrude Stein had never lived, sooner or later works very much like those she produced would have been written by someone else. Once a particular set of conditions was present, her arrival was inevitable—like an event in chemistry.

She told the story of her life and work more completely and more obsessively than any other writer of her time. But her purview was subjective to the point of myopia and she was as self-satisfied and as full of contented whimsies as a cat on a hob. (pp. xiii-xiv)

Gertrude Stein belongs in the last phase of the governance of reason; she is one of the last daughters of the Enlightenment. While she spent a lifetime trying to escape the nineteenth century, her career belongs to its sunset phase—to the era of William James and John Dewey, George Bernard Shaw and the science of economic reform, of the "Boston marriage" and votes for women, of the incandescent lamp and the Michelson-Morley experiment.

She believed exclusively in the power and efficacy of the rational mind when all of her major contemporaries in art and literature were examining with fascination the power of the non-rational as a source of aesthetic communication. She believed in consciousness as a positive glory when the temper of her time ran toward intimations that an understanding of the unconscious might be a major source of wisdom.

In her lifetime a general public would not take her seriously at all, while an intellectual public took her all too seriously. Americans obsessively driven somehow to understand what they could not anyhow experience made her the Sacred Cow of modern letters and all but succeeded in separating the figure from her work. Yet behind the romance of her reputation she was simply a writer who produced something confoundingly new, something based in the lively vision of a knowledgeable personality and an erudite mind. She may not endure, as James Joyce or Picasso may not endure. But our history would be poorer and narrower without her, and generations to follow may not knowingly deny themselves the pleasure of her company. (pp. xiv-xv)

If it is difficult to be passionate about her work, it is equally difficult to be passionate about a Brancusi bird or a Mondrian canvas. But it is easy and perhaps necessary to be passionate about her devoted practice of the art of language without reference to utility. . . . [A] passion for Gertrude Stein's valiant explorations has been the history of her admirers who tend, almost unanimously, to praise her methods at the expense of the writings that document them, and to regard her less as a subject to be examined than as an object to be accounted for, or simply acclaimed.

Her influence—in the verifiable sense that Whitman and Henry James, Flaubert or Proust, Rilke and Hopkins have been influences—has been all but nil. Her small, easily recognized effect on the careers of Ernest Hemingway and Sherwood Anderson has been vastly overemphasized and subsequently accepted as something significant mainly by critics who deal most congenially in the secondhand. (p. xv)

The way in which she maintained integrity of life—the artist's life—was her real and resonant influence. . . .

In a writing career that lasted more than forty years, Gertrude Stein separated literature from history, from sociology, from psychology and anthropology, even from knowledge itself. As a poet, she destroyed the connecting tissues that hold observed realities together and, as a writer of novels, she attempted to remove from the body of literature the very sinew and bone of narrative. She preached that literature was an art not necessarily dependent upon any of these, and she practiced what she preached. While she believed that most writers failed to allow writing to express all that it could, in her own practice she scrupulously saw to it that writing expressed less than it would.

Among writers driven in one way or another to find the limits of language, she had forebears in the poets of Alexandria, in the translators of the King James Bible, in John Lyly, in Góngora, in Marivaux; and on the continent of Europe she had active contemporaries in the figures of Max Jacob and Pierre Reverdy in France, Carl Einstein in Germany, for a time Pär Lagerkvist in Sweden, and Ramón Gomez de la Serna in Spain. (p. xvi)

> *John Malcolm Brinnin, in his introductory note to* The Third Rose: Gertrude Stein and Her World *(copyright ©, 1959, by John Malcolm Brinnin; reprinted by permission of Little, Brown and Co.), Little, Brown, 1959 (and reprinted by Peter Smith, 1968).*

Whatever the sterilities and the self-infatuations in her work, [Gertrude Stein] was a woman of extraordinary insight. She understood men who were writers, she understood fellow minds. Her influence was enormous because writers could pick up extraordinary suggestions from her thinking. She studied the world, from her mind as its center, with an intensity that literally made her a stream of consciousness, and writers could find particles of thought anywhere in this stream. Because of her quickness and her social sense, she was able to size up people quickly, and many of her verbal judgments on people—carefully repeated in her more popular books—are unforgettable. She said of a well-known novelist who has been "promising" all his life—"He has a certain syrup, but does not pour."

But if Gertrude Stein herself has become finally unreadable, it is because she did not think in terms of books at all but in orphic sayings, sentences, rhythmic paragraphs that brought home the sound of herself thinking to herself. She was fascinated by ideas, the outlines of things, the possibilities inherent in all subjects, the hidden voice of the individual beneath his social personality. Unlike so many writers today, who see their opportunity only in the generally accepted, she was utterly fearless and tried everything; there was nothing she ever found in her own mind that seemed alien to literature. If courage were the same as creativity, Gertrude Stein would have been Homer. But creativity is a matter of achieving whole works, not of ideas for books or brilliant passages in books. Gertrude Stein could make a Hemingway or Anderson or Fitzgerald—at times even a Picasso—glow with ideas. But when she sat down to write, she let the stream of all her thoughts flow as if a book were only a receptacle for her mind. One came to suspect that her widsom was more in the realm of theory than of actuality. . . .

Gertrude Stein dreamed of finding the formula that would put all other modern writers behind her. She thought she had found it, and she went on writing with the imperturbable smile on the face of a Buddha; she trusted in her thoughts as if she were Moses tuned into the Almighty. But the trouble with these pure thinkers in art, criticism, and psychology is that the mind is always an instrument, not its own clear-cut subject matter. No one, not even a Freud, has ever been really sure just what pure mind is; Freud had too much respect for the truth to think that he had found a realm absolutely detachable from everything else. Gertrude Stein's error was not that she thought of herself as a "genius"—who can say what that is?—but that she identified this genius with pure intellect. She even defined a genius as a representative of the human mind, partly because he understands, without submitting to, the force of human nature. Artists, she thought, are slaves to human nature, are bound by resemblances, subject to sorrow, disappointment, and tears. But "the human mind writes what it is . . . the human mind . . . consists only in writing down what is written and therefore it has no relation to human nature." There is the root of her delusion and of the intolerable conceit that unheedingly drove her work into a corner. Gertrude Stein had a very good mind. But it was not as good as she thought it was, or else she would not have assumed that literature can be written about nothing but the mind itself. (p. 52)

Alfred Kazin, "The Mystery of Gertrude Stein," in The Reporter (© *1960 by The Reporter Magazine Co.), February 18, 1960, pp. 48, 51-2.*

[While] the impetus of [Gertrude Stein's] literary practice was nineteenth century, she was right in maintaining that its result was wholly consonant with the twentieth-century scene and that she provided a remarkably acute sense of its intellectual decorum and habitude. She was if anything more "modern" than Eliot and Pound. What attracted such younger artists as Hemingway to her was her conviction not only that "the past did not matter" but that the present was overweeningly demanding and that its "spirit" and rhythms had to be continuously sustained in literature. Her primary contribution to twentieth-century literature was methodological. Except when she wrote reminiscences (and she did these superbly and with great popular success), her work was only indifferently related to context. Its major

objective was to illustrate and to refine the manner of fusing the "seeing" and the re-creation of an importunate present moment. (p. 10)

Miss Stein is concerned [in her style] to preserve the essential experience from the accidents of flow. (p. 14)

The danger is that words, so scrupulously separated from familiar or suggestive contexts, come to have an abstract role and meaning, which they do not vividly and recognizably describe. But this is not only a risk Miss Stein is willing to take; it it substantially what she wants to do. For objects, she says, do not present themselves manageably to the consciousness in a riot of colorful detail; they are (as is experience) eligible to gradual change, in each successive detail preserving what they have had before altering it slightly and in minute degree. No more eloquent testimony of the shrewdness of her energy of attention is available than the famous play upon "pigeons" in *Four Saints in Three Acts*. (p. 15)

When Miss Stein defined the process of writing, she thought of it as a delicate balance of motion and form, the form providing the present context, the motion formally (and gracefully) described in terms of it. For Miss Stein was always striving for such balances, a balance such as is achieved in a ballet, where the dancer combines motion with the illusion of a fixed point within a formally described space. . . .

To perfect the balance of movement and form, there must be many repetitions, as there are for example in the play on "pigeons" and "grass" of *Four Saints in Three Acts*. Miss Stein set down as the second of her three "rules of composition" that to maintain a "continuous present" one must "begin again and again" (*Composition as Explanation*). Repetition is an essential strategy in composition; it guarantees similarity and forces the consciousness upon the nature of the thing seen while at the same time it provides the avenue along which movement and change may occur. Hence Miss Stein's writing is often accused of being monotonous and wearisomely repetitious; but it is deliberately so, to preserve it from being superficial. Deliberate simplicities ("a rose is a rose is a rose") are an important characteristic of modern prose style. They are as effectively a rendering of experience and a scenic reflectiveness in the writing of Hemingway, for example, as the syntactic effusions of Faulkner are a means of recording his sensibility in relation to his material. (p. 20)

Her "novels" have a static quality; sometimes they are empty of overtly significant movement, even of conventional content. Her characters endure experience more often than they initiate it. And the major signs of development within her fiction are an increasing complexity of attitude and a change of relational terms. The fiction "develops" by accretion in much the same way as sentences move into paragraphs—neither situation calls for much movement in either space or time. (p. 21)

[Miss Stein] limited herself deliberately in the matter of subject, having a distaste for "subjects" as such, and worked often within a "scientifically pure," an isolated, situation. The result was a method repeated and refined, almost obsessively practiced, but above all immune from the worst gaucheries of naive naturalism. . . .

In many respects Miss Stein's concern over the limits of

complication in writing seems overly anxious and fastidious. . . . She deliberately wrenched words not only from familiar context but from almost any context at all. Yet the effects are intermittently extraordinary, though even the most dedicated follower at times admits to weariness. (pp. 24-5)

The effect [of Miss Stein's observations] upon her literary practice was to reduce its scope and to introduce one after another kind of abstraction and attenuation. She set about deliberately eliminating time from human consideration, moving from the idea of "history as generations" of *The Making of Americans* to the pure stasis of her late plays. Having been left with space, she tried to purify it, holding it in the syntactic balance of the carefully limited sentence and protecting it from the threat of superficial and destructive motion. She worked hard at the task of reducing connotation to the bare minimum necessary to suggest a context of any kind. In consequence, she was left with a very much reduced field of deliberation: not surrealistic or impressionistic, not at all realistic, a world of concepts all but deprived of percepts, providing an intellectual music of successions and echolalic improvisations. (p. 27)

The progress [in "Melanctha," from *Three Lives*] from vague desires to initial experiments in satisfaction, to major crisis and failure, is brilliantly intricate. The burden of movement is assumed by words and phrases. Miss Stein "begins again and again," she "uses everything," she maintains a "continuous present." The pattern is that of a spiral moving within and beyond several levels and stages of passion and knowledge. The language changes and remains the same; slight additions and qualifications indicate advances and retreats, and Melanctha's progress in "wisdom" is shown in a successively sharpened emphasis in the language. Perhaps the key word is "trouble"; it suggests a commitment to experience without a full understanding of it. Trouble occurs when passion is forced beyond the comprehension of those involved in its expression. Jeff Campbell, for example, "had never yet in his life had real trouble." Melanctha always "could only find new ways to be in trouble." Because neither is able to redeem "wisdom" from the menace of "trouble," the relationship fails. (p. 32)

The personal tensions are communicated naturally and easily, while in Miss Stein's first writing (*Things as They Are*), the language clumsily interferes and the conflicts are handled in an interplay of artificial and unreal poses. "Melanctha" strikes one as a peculiarly effective piece, whose place in modern literature is important in a wide variety of ways. It is, for one thing, a triumph of analysis of the kind that Henry James (who at the time of its writing was producing his most complex works) could never have achieved. This is in itself a fact of more than ordinary importance, since it suggests a broadening of perspective in the functions and uses of analysis. Its application to the minds of relatively "unlettered" persons pointed away from the clumsy assumptions of contemporary naturalists who seemed to think that subconsciously a person's emotional status was as complex as his background and social level dictated. It is infinitely superior, in analytic correctness and appropriateness at least, to Dreiser's fumbling attempts to define Sister Carrie's "vague yearnings for the ideal." Sherwood Anderson's sketches of lonely, inarticulate souls come closer both in type and in merit; but An-

derson lacked Miss Stein's intensity, and his analyses often settled into formula characterizations. . . .

"Melanctha" succeeds in part because it assumes an equality that underlies social discrimination, an equality of feeling and emotion.

[It] has done much—much more than the early naturalists were able to do—by way of breaking down artificial barriers of class, manner, "culture." The "simple soul," the "peasant complex," the "servant's mind" are all ruled out. Miss Stein may be said here to have initiated or shown the possibilities of an entirely new type of "novel of manners." (p. 33)

Four Saints in Three Acts is a play upon the will toward saintliness, and upon the quality of saintliness as a human disposition and temperament, as "Melanctha" was an analysis of passion in its move toward social complication. It is, therefore, as a whole, an aesthetic object without context except what the concept of abstract disposition of saintliness can give it. It makes an elaborate design out of a possible and a probable form or type of human disposition. Since this disposition is saintliness and neither passion nor convention, the effect is ceremonial and gay and colorful and—within Miss Stein's own scope of apprehension—beatific. These are all available to emotional response, but the play lacks what she always regarded as an "audience trap," the building of suspense through plot, the directing of the audience's sense of time and event, stimulating the need for audience to reconstruct themselves in terms of the drama that was unfolding.

One way of appraising Gertrude Stein's value in modern literature is to say that she was pre-eminently a theorist (a "scientist" of sorts), who offered some illustrations of what she thought literature should be. It is true that we are always busy examining her creative work as demonstration, to "see if composition comes out as she says it should." There is no question of her value as a critic whose primary function was to define language and to examine its place in the work of art. Perhaps it is, after all, her main claim to eminence. It would be a false reading of her work, however, to say that it served only to validate her theory. The work often stands by and for itself. It does not stand by itself in the manner of other contemporary masterpieces, however. Its merits are essentially those of a work designed to break new experimental ground. It is tendentious in the most useful and illuminating sense that word might have. Its limitations are a result of her virtues; one may truthfully say that the limitations are necessary to the virtues. (pp. 42-3)

Three Lives is a minor masterpiece of great significance to modern writing because it is intrinsically good and impressive as literature and was received as such by many of her sensitive contemporaries; *The Making of Americans* cannot be so regarded, but must be thought of as the most elaborate of all demonstrations, intrinsically great but valuable because its merits come from its elaborate illustration of a theory of time and history; *Four Saints in Three Acts* is similarly beautifully successful but never truly separable from the variety of theoretical convictions from which it emerged. There are other pieces that move somewhere between the level of demonstration and the status of *sui generis* masterpiece. Some of these, like the novel *Ida,* the little books *Paris France . . .* and *Picasso,* and *The Geo-*

graphical History of America, have frequently a strong and persuasive identity as books of unaffected wisdom; they are original and characteristic of their author, but they are also, in the sense in which she was capable of being so, profound. (p. 43)

[Gertrude Stein's position,] as critic or theorist or both, is distinctive and yet an important part of modern criticism. Despite Miss Stein's overwhelming "presence" on the modern literary scene, she actually asks for and even demands an impersonal literature. It is true that many of her works are gratuitously personal, and that often she coyly peeps out at the reader from behind whatever large object conceals her. But unless we wish to assume that most or all of her critical discourses are merely self-ingratiating, the appeal in them is to a literature divested not only of specific autobiographical meaning but of the traditional structural implications of literature. These virtues are considerable because the limitations are so enthusiastically admitted and so significantly assumed. There is nothing specious about Gertrude Stein; to call her a supreme egotist does not convict her of simply posing before her Picassos for personal gain. She has had much to say, and she has often said it with a stubborn (perhaps a naively truculent) persistence. When her manner of saying it is penetrable, and it often is, the ideas are worth the value that she has been able to give them. She will, at any rate, merit a position in literary criticism as the person who carried as far as it might go William James's analysis of consciousness. Beyond that, she has stared hard at the prospect of an art objectively hard and autonomously real, using its instruments in strangely new but often startlingly effective ways. Much of what she has done to prove her theoretic convictions falls far short of enabling her to do so. She has had many failures, and in any case the perspective of an old maid eccentric can scarcely be expected to yield large truths consistently. There is a wide margin between her profound insights and her more obvious and banal observations.

These conditions limit her usefulness, but they do not destroy it. She has the undoubted strength of the creative person who is able to call upon her powers of imagination to prove what literature might be. (pp. 44-5)

> *Frederick J. Hoffman, in his* Gertrude Stein *(American Writers Pamphlet No. 10; © 1961, University of Minnesota), University of Minnesota Press, Minneapolis, 1961.*

[The] *Autobiography* is an inspired gossip column which stands up to any amount of re-reading. It may be inaccurate, it certainly is unfair, but it is a model of its kind.

Besides being the best-seller which it deserved to become, the *Autobiography* (written in six weeks) triumphantly demonstrated the disciplines to which Miss Stein in her arcaner studies had for so long submitted. Every parody of her has failed because one cannot parody the monotonous boredom of her writing unless one has an equal amount of learning and intelligence to suppress; a smaller mind will lack the courage to be so dull. (pp. 283-84)

> *Cyril Connolly, "Gertrude Stein," in his* Previous Convictions, *Hamish Hamilton Ltd., 1963, pp. 282-85.*

Gertrude Stein's development as a writer of fiction was wholly technical. All that she had to say as a story-teller

and moralist is clearly set out in her first and least unconventional book, *Three Lives.* . . . But however we measure her subsequent work—and not a great deal of it charms us into sitting up all night to read it through—the intelligence of her concern for style and form, and the general usefulness, are undeniable. From the first she put herself in the main line of innovation and experiment in modern letters. . . . In content *Three Lives* is not very different from the genre realism of the '90s or of Dreiser's earlier work. In form, however, dramatic movement has already half dissolved into abstract patterns of notation rhythmically repeated. The results endorse the experiment; Melanctha Herbert in particular, subtle, intelligent, attractive, dependent, self-abasing, is surely one of the few wholly believable women in American fiction. In *The Making of Americans,* even more in the arrangements of "Objects Food Rooms" in *Tender Buttons* . . . , these rhythmic patterns of resemblance and repetition—which now begin to appear as verbal patterns first of all—are increasingly dominant. The different stages of "living" dissolve into phases of timeless being. Change, causal sequence, action of any sort tend to disappear altogether. (pp. 248-49)

The best use to make of her work she herself pleasantly suggests at the end of the section, "Food," in *Tender Buttons:*

> Next to me next to a folder, next to a folder some waiter, next to a foldersome waiter and re letter and read her. *Read her with her for less.* [Emphasis added]

Just so: in such matters the modest principle of *with-though-for-less* can become a whole interior way of life—if not transforming in itself, then the cause that transformations are in others. Beyond question the forms and the language of contemporary literature are healthier because Gertrude Stein played her honest and reasonable games with them. If her example also had the effect, historically, of endorsing a certain imaginative complacency in the younger writers who put themselves to school with her—Hemingway for one—their failure to grow out of that complacency is not, strictly, her fault. (pp. 252-53)

> *Warner Berthoff, in his* Ferment of Realism: American Literature, 1884-1919 *(reprinted with permission of Macmillan Publishing Co., Inc.; copyright © 1965 by The Free Press, a Division of The Macmillan Company), Free Press, 1965.*

Whether we think of Gertrude Stein as a sage, a mountebank, or an authentic poet, one fact has to be admitted: she has been a formidable phenomenon, influencing other writers more than one likes, perhaps, to realize. Nor can it be denied that the impact of her personality and "unintelligible" linguistic compositions tended to encourage a spirit of anti-intellectualism among her contemporaries. But this fact is paradoxical. Gertrude Stein was herself a keen student of philosophy; and although the voice that speaks in her work is often playful and sometimes, in spite of her wit, uncompromisingly ordinary, the structure of her underlying ideas reveals that she had thought deeply about man's essential humanity and about the nature of the cosmos in which this humanity is possible. (p. 4)

[To] the reader who takes pains to decipher the recurrent ideograms in *The Geographical History of America,* or who has focused upon such "difficult" compositions as *An Acquaintance with Description* and *How To Write,* it seems clear that she was exploring some of the problems of meaning brought to the fore by such different linguistic philosophers as I. A. Richards and Ludwig Wittgenstein.

It is also abundantly clear that not only was she familiar with the great philosophical systems of the past, but that her explicit repudiation of systematic philosophy (and dogmatic religion as well) stemmed not from any distaste for metaphysics but from a deep dissatisfaction with systems that did not adequately recognize, or account for, her own primary philosophical intuition. (p. 5)

[It] is quite possible to associate her ideas with Hegel's theories of language and culture in *The Phenomenology of Mind.*

A close reading of Stein has persuaded me that she was very likely familiar with this work. In any case, the movement of thought in much of her writing seems to parallel the dialectical movement of the Hegelian world spirit in a moment of transition and transformation, namely, the twentieth century. . . . *Tender Buttons* embodies the appearance of the new as bare abstraction in an isolated mind. *The Geographical History of America, or The Relation of Human Nature to the Human Mind* is a meditation on the general spiritual impoverishment and abstractness of American consciousness. *Doctor Faustus Lights the Lights* dramatizes the psychic process of alienation from nature and the salutary transformation of the archetypal images of the Western Mind into the concrete actuality of experience. According to my view, Gertrude Stein was always recording, not experiences, but the "experiencings," of the Hegelian world spirit as an internal drama on the simultaneous stage of her own consciousness and of Western man's—a drama in which the actors are words, those relatively stable objects of the human mind in a changing world. (pp. 24-5)

The first thing that strikes the reader of her work as a whole is that the emotion contained in it is a genuine cosmic emotion (almost religious, according to James's definition of religion), but focused less upon first and last things than upon the potentialities and latencies of experience. Her metaphysical thinking is thus naturally concerned with the mystery of creativity—with the primal source of emergent novelty in the world and of creative insight in man. For although she was a thoroughgoing temporalist and pluralist, in the best Jamesian tradition, Stein recognized, like James himself, the miraculous element in the advent of the *new;* and in her life and work it was always the new that she cared about most. Her theory of the possible discontinuity between being and existence is an effort to describe this miracle. (p. 29)

Although Gertrude Stein always welcomes the advent of novelty and the challenge of the unexpected, her deepest emphasis is actually on possibility and on creativeness. In her life, moreover, she conveyed her vision in a way which seems to have liberated people, making them feel that the "new" was able to come to birth in them, and through them. (No doubt few people ever worked out the subtlety of her thought on this subject. It was probably communicated by the direct impact of her personality and her witty conversation.) (p. 45)

It would be easy, I suppose, to criticize her philosophy for a certain inconsistency or irrationality at its core. Yet it might be very difficult to prove that the real universe is any more rational or consistent than the picture one gets from studying *The Geographical History of America.* (p. 64)

Gertrude Stein's real concern, however, is not to explain the world, but to describe or inspire the *act of presence* by means of which the human mind and cosmic beauty are simultaneously realized. . . .

[The] significant point is that even in her philosophic writing she does demand and evoke from her readers an active creative effort. Thus her deepest ideas are merely suggested—condensed in gnomic phrases or flashed out in a pregnant juxtaposition of ideas—but never rigorously elaborated with any view to helping the reader. In all this she seems oddly akin to those Eastern sages who refuse to explain the disaster of existence and yet make the severest demands on those disciples who would obtain salvation. (pp. 64-5)

No doubt the total volume of Stein's work belongs to the phenomenology of mind rather than to literature: in her effort to grasp and set down her moments of concentrated vision she failed again and again, and she published her failures along with her successes. But her method of discipline was contemplation—involving creative dissociation; her conscious goal was the new word to express a new and purified perception of common reality. Given these clues, one may expect to find extraordinary riches (both psychological and linguistic) in many hitherto baffling passages. (pp. 66-7)

Gertrude Stein's conscious purpose was verbal, not mystical in any religious sense. It need not surprise us, therefore, that her unconscious daemon often aided her with all that subtle and witty grasp of linguistic relationships and depth of verbal meaning which is perhaps the prize gift of every man's unconscious mind. The strange vitality with which some of her most interesting passages vibrate, however, seems especially due to the phenomenon of "overdetermination" of meaning—the susceptibility of a given word or phrase to multiple interpretation. This is one of the chief hallmarks of unconscious activity, whether neurotic or creative. And the reader often finds one strange conjunction in particular: a seemingly trivial perception, or a pointed but unimportant flash of wit, linked verbally with a murmured suggestion of ritual, prayer, purgation, and renewal. Is it fanciful to point out that Gertrude Stein was rather more of a genuine sage, if not a frustrated mystic, than she cared to admit? (p. 67)

[Riddles] anciently were more than rhetorical complications. Along with runes and charms, they were "dark sayings" which bore testimony to the magic of the word. . . . This double connotation is singularly appropriate to the strange yet vital writing—when considered as an organic whole—which makes up *Tender Buttons.* For the little book does bear witness to a kind of magic power inherent in words; and beneath its verbal surface the reader can find extraordinary patterns of linguistic relationship. At the same time, I believe, by way of these very relationships, he will discover that the force at work here is psychic in its origin and spiritual in its goal. The pressure that holds the words in place and gives them all their latent power is the mysterious force of a total personality in the process of self-exploration and self-organization. Throughout the whole, indeed, one feels this pressure as a kind of steady effort—exerted against the resistances inherent in the very nature of language—to arrive at, rather than merely to express, some insight of paramount importance.

I believe, in other words, that *Tender Buttons* should be regarded as a mandala, a "magic circle" or enclosure for the unconscious mind, originating in its maker's unconscious but elaborated, with more or less conscious purpose, as an act of self-creation. In this case the mandala is worked out in words. In speaking of the "unconscious" I do not of course intend to revive the hoary accusation that Gertrude Stein produced her work by means of automatic writing. An authentic mandala is not merely an arrangement of symbols from the unconscious—symbols especially vital to the personality that produces them; it is also a highly organized form, presented by means of the dance, painting, or words. It points toward unity, toward the spirit and spiritual perception, for it is designed to unite the conscious intellectual perceptions of its creator (or the one who uses it for meditation) with his unconscious psychic drives and intuitions. Thus it functions both as a chart, so to speak, of the total self and as an instrument in that self's awakening. In the hands of a disciplined artist, an original mandala may become a creative form, aesthetically significant as well as pleasing, because it incorporates new materials and revealing insights. (pp. 71-3)

I think that Stein made a deliberate effort to revive the root meanings of English words—to recover the pictorial element in them and so attach them again to sensory perception. For primitive root meanings are essentially pictorial, though changes in the forms of the words that carry them have almost completely obscured this fact in English. At any rate, I believe it was in the sense of root meanings as picturing reality that Gertrude Stein described the writing of her middle period as painting. (p. 78)

There is a good deal of dross in [her] total product: some apparently aimless punning, much trivial playfulness, and a great deal of seemingly frivolous humor. But there are also many passages in her books which reveal a musical structure and the development of meditated themes—beautiful passages, with a strange quality of depth and suggestion. It is reasonable to conclude that, though she also published her failures, her successes gave her such a sense of revelation that she went on trying, in spite of the failures. (p. 96)

Like an invocation, [the poems in *Tender Buttons*] serve to summon repeatedly the lightning flash of subliminal intuition—the creative point. But because the poet was consciously aiming at fresh names for simple objects and experiences, her intuitions seem to concern themselves only with the objectivity and transpersonal power of language. Thus for all their elusive gaiety and droll personal flavor, these poems tell us little enough about the personality and experience of Gertrude Stein, and almost nothing about their ostensible subject matter. Read at the appropriate depth, however, they tell us much (as we have seen) about the interior energies of words. And when we take them seriously as a mandala, we find that they also reflect the psychic process or ritual that Jung calls "individuation." (pp. 112-13)

There is something poignant in the disparity between the depth of insight and the surface flatness not only of *Tender Buttons* but of nearly all of Gertrude Stein's work. This very quality may also serve to illuminate much that is flat and trivial in contemporary art and life. Gertrude Stein saw

beneath this flatness. And like [Robert Frost,] another poet of the New England tradition (in which Gertrude Stein must stand), she had to overcome her fears of both depth and height by confronting her own soul. (p. 139)

As I understand *Doctor Faustus Lights the Lights,* the play contains no dogmatic postulates concerning theology, but affirms a "highest value" and identifies it with what the developed personality treasures. We need not be deceived by the coy banality of the "pretty pretty dear" phrases with which the man from over the seas addresses Marguerite Ida and Helena Annabel. In this *Faustus* of hers Gertrude Stein is addressing our intelligence and intuition, not our conditioned, conventional feelings; and she makes this appeal, in part, by a tone deliberately light and almost satirical, with touches of farcical humor. In context, it is plain that she is speaking of the "pearl without price," the "treasure hid in a field," the one thing needful for which a man might well lose the whole world—that is, in Biblical terms, the soul. In more modern language one can speak of that contact with the riches of racial wisdom and intuitive vision which possession of the key, the anima, confers upon the individual Self. This is, of course, a deeply religious idea. (pp. 182-83)

There is a sense in which her very preoccupations, including her almost casual assumption of the naturalistic viewpoint, attest to that estrangement of man from nature and the past which so well characterizes our time. But though in *Doctor Faustus Lights the Lights* she projects the image of alienation very vividly, she clearly suggests . . . a possible resolution of the difficulty. In an age of anxiety she affirms the fact that wholeness of experience is possible. Equally important, however, is the fact that in an era of propaganda, corrupted language, and the breakdown of communication she works for a language that has been purged of its unclean service to Mammon.

Nevertheless, just as Gertrude Stein's impressive though baffling personality can hardly be understood in terms of sanctity—or even in terms of Oriental "liberation"—so her expressions of harmony and presence must not be understood as revealing any traditional religious attitude, either Eastern or Western. Self-discipline and spiritual exercises may have made her a creative force. But it cannot be said too plainly that in cosmic vision, as well as in personal relationships, she was a singularly tough-minded realist. She was noted for her wit and gaiety and a deliberately prosaic quality of thought and perception; there was very little that was exalted in her language or in the feeling she expressed. (pp. 192-93)

[To] people who find yoga and kindred subjects interesting, the odd thing about Stein's long habit of spiritual exercises is that they were focused—by her own account, at least—on trivial or evanescent objects. Her cosmic vision is one of temporal flux and vanishing: there is no sense here of eternal meaning or purpose, no goal beyond the present moment. Her present moment, in fact, is not obviously identifiable with the "eternal now" of the mystics. Thus, in a lifetime of effort and disciplined attention, what she sought to realize was succession, on the one hand, and a kind of abstract universality on the other. What she tried to express was the shifting scenes and objects arbitrarily selected for attention, or to construct out of the chance concatenation of objects in any moment, a "composition." She wanted to convey the essential nature of living creatures or of objects moving in space, and by the intensity of her own mental activity to project motion into still lifes. . . . Most of the spiritual masters of East and West alike have realized the self in a spirit of religious dedication to the divine—or at the very least, as in Hinayana Buddhism, in a spirit of universal compassion and a desire to lead suffers out of nature and the cosmos and into the Clear Void. But Gertrude Stein traveled light, rejecting all such aims as well as all religious formulations. (pp. 200-01)

There is audible in much of her work a note of singing—as if she were aware of a divine chorus and her own inevitable part in it. Perhaps this concept of the "chorus" was one of her semantic discoveries while writing *Tender Buttons*. But no matter what her subject matter was—and as she became more playful in tone, she wrote more and more frequently about "saints and singing"—she was never solemn or conventionally religious. She had wit and a love of the comic; since her object was only to be present both to her writing and to her reader, she gives the impression of childlike intentness, as if she were concentrating upon each movement in an absorbing game. Her work is filled with a feeling of delight and freedom from care, even when she is describing the wars she has seen. (pp. 207-08)

For Gertrude Stein there is a harmony between man and the universe, but it is not a heavenly harmony—not the music of the spheres. It is not a process in time or a result of progress or an event in history. It is perhaps "the choir invisible of those immortal dead who live again" in masterpieces, who are present to the world and to themselves, participating in experience, contemplating it, loving it, dreaming about it, and expressing it in the forms of art. She rejected all forms of mysticism, theology, or systematic philosophy which would place the harmony of things beyond experience. The chorus as she conceived it is a harmony of separate and distinct voices—not a transcendent or an immanent paean in which the many are resolved into the One.

So there is little exalted rhetoric in her writing. But there is a great deal of joy—in the pleasures of perception, of imagination, of play and song. When one lives consciously in the actual present, one is "doing nothing" in exactly the way saints are "doing nothing" when they pray or sing or perform their ritual tasks. The song is intent and serious only in the attention devoted to it. It asks for nothing, but finds everything. (pp. 208-09)

The Geographical History of America is . . . in some ways her crowning achievement. A triumph of lost ground regained, it is as full of wit, song, and gaiety as anything she ever wrote; but it is also, despite the minor difficulties involved in reading it, a coherent expression of her special metaphysical vision.

The experience of self-division and crisis was evidently also the basis for *Doctor Faustus Lights the Lights*. As we have seen, this curious work may be understood as a symbol of the failure of science and the purely intellectual outlook to confer meaning and joy upon experience. It is also a paradigm of that widespread ailment of our time—the collapse or partial disintegration of the successful and apparently well-integrated personality on the threshold of its autumnal years. It dramatizes a common cause of this ailment—the rebellion of the buried psychic functions against the overdeveloped but ultimately sterile intellect, which has domi-

nated life too long. Gertrude Stein understood very well, I think, the experience of self-alienation presented here. Again, as in *Tender Buttons,* the "villain" is the ego. There she had written, "Act so that there is no use in a centre." In *Doctor Faustus,* it is Faust's ego that is sent to hell. Thus, in both compositions, reconciliation is achieved through ego transcendence. The power of the Jungian symbols to express dynamically the truth of modern man's predicament and its solution must have led her at last, after thirty years of nonsymbolic writing, to acknowledge the occasional value of symbolism in art, as Picasso had already done in his *Minotauromachy* (1935) and *Guernica* (1937). (pp. 210-11)

Most important of all, perhaps, is the fact that she felt so keenly the need for sacred experience in a world that is secular in more than one way—temporal and evanescent as all its values and creations seem to be. Committed to her time's rejection of tradition, yet disgusted with its slick and meaningless clichés, she found in the deepest levels of her own being a passion for communion, "presence," and the sacred word. But because of her commitment to the current world view of natural science, she found it impossible to believe in any all-embracing divine order, either personal or impersonal. This too is a dilemma that has frustrated and sometimes tortured a great many of the most sensitive and intelligent men and women of this century.

Apparently she resolved the dilemma for herself by means of a kind of vatic art, suggesting a personal experience of harmony that in our time seems incommunicable. But the very unintelligibility and dislocations of such writing provide a magnifying glass for language itself—a glass that forces the reader to look again, and much more carefully and honestly than he has looked before, at every ordinary word. She always seems to be saying, therefore, often almost inadvertently but sometimes quite deliberately, that until we have cleansed the doors of perception and common speech, we have not earned the right to speak to one another of anything very profound. (pp. 211-12)

It might be noted here how much Gertrude Stein resembles the teachers of Zen Buddhism—in her predilection for jokes and riddles, in her matter-of-fact language and fondness for non sequiturs and sudden absurdities, in the playfulness that got her a reputation, in certain quarters, for being a mountebank, and in her pursuit of the creative act that would be both technically "without any technique" (because beyond it) and spiritual at the same time. She and such painters as Paul Klee were intuitively close in this regard to those Zen masters of swordsmanship, archery, and painting who found the experience of ultimate reality in concentrating on their craft with increasing devotion. But nowhere is she so much in the true spirit of Zen as in her method of suggesting, but never actually stating, the true nature of the goal she reached throughout her long period of concentration. (pp. 213-14)

Allegra Stewart, in her Gertrude Stein and the Present (*copyright © 1967 by the President and Fellows of Harvard College; excerpted by permission of the author and publishers*), *Cambridge, Mass.: Harvard University Press, 1967.*

["Melanctha"] is probably Gertrude Stein's most important literary achievement, ... Not of least importance is the fact that, as Carl Van Vechten long ago pointed out, it is "perhaps the first American story in which the Negro is regarded as a human being and not as an object for condescending compassion or derision." . . . [The story] attempts to trace the curve of a passion, its rise, its climax, its collapse, with all the shifts and modulations between dissension and reconciliation along the way. This is the center of the story and its *raison d'être*—the passion and its death between two persons of opposite type. . . . (pp. 302-03)

In her next book [*The Making of Americans*], Gertrude Stein was to base much on her declaration that all human beings can be reduced to two types, what she called the "attacking" type and the "resisting" type. (p. 303)

If formerly her model was Cézanne and her ambition was a literary distortion of reality analogous to his painterly distortion, her model now is Picasso in his cubist phase and her ambition a literary plasticity divorced from narrative sequence and consequence and hence from literary meaning. She was trying to transform literature from a temporal into a purely spatial art, to use words for their own sake alone. (p. 304)

> *Mark Schorer, in his* The World We Imagine: Selected Essays *(reprinted with the permission of Farrar, Straus & Giroux, Inc.; copyright © 1948, 1949, 1953, 1956, 1957, 1959, 1962, 1963, 1968 by Mark Schorer), Farrar, Straus, 1968.*

[Gertrude Stein's] stories, poems, and plays lie beside the mass of modern literature like a straight line by a maze and give no hold to the critic bent on explication. Art to be successful at nearly any time dare not be pure. It must be able to invite the dogs. It must furnish bones for the understanding. Interest then has sought the substitutes that she provided for it. (p. 80)

Gertrude Stein has mostly been . . . an anecdote and a theory and a bundle of quotations. . . . Once admired by a few without judgment, she is now censured by many without reason, and that perplexity her work and person have created, as Coleridge noted the connection, has contained sufficient fear to predispose some minds to anger. (pp. 80-1)

The writings of Gertrude Stein became a challenge to criticism the moment they were composed and they have remained a challenge. This challenge is of the purest and most direct kind. It is wholehearted and complete. It asks for nothing less than a study of the entire basis of our criticism, and it will not be put off. It requires us to consider again the esthetic significance of style; to examine again the ontological status of the artist's vision, his medium, and his effect. None of the literary innovators who were her contemporaries attempted anything like the revolution she proposed, and because her methods were so uncompromising, her work cannot really be met except on the finest and most fundamental grounds. *Finnegans Wake,* for instance, is a work of learning. It can be penetrated by stages. It can be elucidated by degrees. It is a complex, but familiar, compound. One can hear at any distance the teeth of the dogs as they feed on its limbs. With Miss Stein, however, one is never able to wet one's wrists before cautiously trusting to the water, nor can one wade slowly in. There the deep clear bottom is at once. (p. 87)

One way in writing of not coming near an object is to interpose a kind of neutralizing middle tongue, one that is neither abstractly and impersonally scientific nor directly confronting and dramatic, but one that lies in that gray limbo in between, composed of the commonest words because its objects are the objects of every day, and therefore a language that is simple and unspecialized, yet one whose effect is flat and sterilizing because its words are held to the simplest naming nouns and verbs, connectives, prepositions, articles, and pronouns, the tritest adjectives of value, a few adverbs of quantity and degree, and the automatic flourishes of social speech—good day, how do you do, so pleased. This desire to gain by artifice a safety from the world—to find a way of thinking without the risks of feeling —is the source of the impulse to abstractness and simplicity in Gertrude Stein as it is in much of modern painting, where she felt immediately the similarity of aim.

Protective language names, it never renders. It replaces events with speech. It says two people are in love, it does not show them loving. Jeff and Melanctha talk their passion. Protective language, then, must be precise, for in a world of dangerous objects which by craft of language have been circumvented, there remains a quantity of unfastened feeling that, in lighting elsewhere, will turn a harmless trifle into symbol. Name a rose and you suggest romance, love, civil war, the maidenhead. The English language is so rich in its associations that its literature tends to be complex and carry its meanings on at many levels. . . . Protective speech must cut off meanings, not take them on. It must find contexts that will limit the functions of its words to that of naming. Gertrude Stein set about discovering such contexts. (pp. 89-90)

The transfer of emotion must be made by means of every physical resource (rhythm, pattern, shape, and sound). How interminably her lovers talk, and how abstractly, yet her rhythms and repeating patterns make an auditory image of her lovers' passion. (p. 90)

In her effort to escape a purely protective language and make a vital thing of words, Gertrude Stein unsettled the whole of prose. Her abstractness enlarged the vocabulary of exciting words and made for some of the dullest, flattest, and longest literature perhaps in history. Her experiments in disassociation enlivened many dead terms and made her a master of juxtaposition. They also created bewildering and unpleasant scatterings of sound. Her success in uniting thought and feeling in the meaning and movement of speech showed that rhythm is half of prose, and gave it the power of poetry without the indecency of imitation. It also nearly made her a mystic and sent her wildly after essences and types. She studied grammar creatively, as few writers have, though little concrete seemed to come of it, and she was sometimes made to sound an utter idiot by present tense and Time. She rid her works of anecdote and scene and character and drama and description and narration one by one and in both a theoretical and applied way raised the serious question of their need and function. None of her contemporaries had her intellectual reach, few her persistence and devotion, though many had more industry and insistence on perfection. (pp. 95-6)

She reads easily when an impatient mind does not hasten the eye. We habitually seek some meaning and we hurry. But each word is an object to Gertrude Stein, something in a list, like the roll call of the ships, and lists are delightful simply for the words that are on them. . . .

I think that sometimes she brings prose by its own good methods to the condition of the lyric. And everyone knows some perfectly beautiful lyrics that mean hardly anything. (p. 96)

> *William H. Gass, "Gertrude Stein: Her Escape from Protective Language," in his* Fiction and the Figures of Life *(copyright © 1958, 1962, 1966, 1967, 1968, 1969, 1970, 1971 by William H. Gass; reprinted by permission of Alfred A. Knopf, Inc.), Knopf, 1970, pp. 79-96.*

Edmund Wilson [in *Axel's Castle*] supplies us with Paul Valéry's view of the symbolist revolution:

> Literature, according to Valéry, has become "an art which is based on the abuse of language—that is, it is based on *language as a creator of illusions, and not on language as a means of transmitting realities* [my italics]. Everything which makes a language more precise, everything which emphasizes its practical character, all the changes which it undergoes in the interests of a more rapid transmission and an easier diffusion, are contrary to its function as a poetic instrument."

Valéry's statement raises several issues crucial to our discussion. First of all, Valéry had the foresight to distinguish between language used in a one-to-one correspondence with objective reality and language with little or no correspondence with reality. To the symbolists, the only true poetic language is one with no corresponding ties to reality. The justification for such a theory was grounded in the belief that a poem should create an alternative reality in opposition to, or at the very least in a creative dialogue with, social reality. (pp. 3-4)

Valéry's statement appears only a decade prior to the first stories of Gertrude Stein. I entitled this book *Gertrude Stein and the Literature of the Modern Consciousness* because I concur with Valéry's feeling that modern literature has become the showplace for a revolutionary use of language. (p. 4)

In an 1881 lecture entitled "Reflex Action and Theism," William James (one of Gertrude Stein's most significant instructors) said:

> We have no organ or faculty to appreciate the simply given order. The real world as it is given objectively at this moment is the sum total of all its being and events now. But can we think of such a sum. . . . Does the contemporaneity of [a million disjointed events] . . . form a rational bond between them, and unite them into anything that resembles for us a world?

Our syntax, our ways of combining words, is grounded in Aristotelian logic—a logic that made considerable sense at the time of its inception and makes less sense every century since. A linguistic logic based upon laws of direct causality and linear time cannot authentically correspond to a universe of possibilities such as James describes. And James's model of the world is our modern inheritance. (p. 5)

It is not surprising to hear that Gertrude Stein began her academic career as a psychologist concerned with manipulating attention through unorthodox linguistic structures. . . . Miss Stein's syntax, like that of the symbolists before her, seeks to disturb the reader's conventional consciousness of words and their so-called corresponding realities and compels the reader to enter a realm of aesthetic possibilities and values foreign to his experience in his practical reality. To differentiate literary work such as Miss Stein's from what we earlier called the didactic or informational, I would use the term "consciousness altering." The meaning of my term is twofold.

First I refer to the ability of such literature to alter the quality, the phenomenology, of the reader's consciousness. By qualities, I refer to density (the diversity of phenomena that can exist simultaneously in the mind), continuity or discontinuity (the breaks, if any, that occur in the flow of consciousness), and speed (the duration of mental time taken for the phenomenon to pass through the reader's consciousness). (p. 7)

In addition to altering the quality of consciousness such writing alters the quantity—the size—of the field of consciousness. I use the phrase "consciousness expansion" with caution, since it is presently linked in the public mind with drug experimentation. However, this is exactly what such literature proposes to do. It is more than a coincidence that William S. Burroughs, the leading American novelist of the drug experience, studied Gertrude Stein's method as a student at Harvard. . . .

Although I feel the main thrust of her work centers on this issue of language and consciousness, I am in no way neglecting the purely literary and, most importantly, purely human concerns of her work.

One reason I am drawn to Gertrude Stein's work is the skill with which she wears the masks of both poet and psychologist. I see her works as demonstrations, perhaps the most developed demonstrations of our age, of the consciousness and language problem. But what gives her art the human interest it holds is the fact that her psychological laboratory is the world of human personality. (p. 8)

One factor we must keep in mind is that for Gertrude Stein psychology meant the psychology of William James and his followers. In the first decade of this century the work of Freud and Jung was virtually unheard of. The problems that psychology examined—What is consciousness? How does consciousness relate to the whole personality? Is consciousness continuous or discontinuous? What is the meaning of automatic functioning? How does unconscious knowledge pass into consciousness?—grew out of James's massive *Principles of Psychology*. . . .

Foremost among [Gertrude Stein's assumptions] is the Jamesian assumption of the universe as pluralistic. The world was seen as teeming with possibilities, any of which could be actualized if man chose to do so. (p. 12)

The radical individualism of Thoreau and Whitman carries this premise to its logical conclusion. If a man is the total of what he lives, a man may choose to radically alter his personality by radically altering his life style. This belief assumes an extreme plasticity of character, a belief many of us take for granted. . . . In Europe one's life is one's life: a struggle within the boundaries of personality.

I am insisting on this distinction because it is a crucial idea in Gertrude Stein's personality theory. She is one of the very few American writers of our time who reject the Lockean model of a limitless plasticity of character. She follows James in seeing the personality in terms of a fixed nature, a central "core," subject to alteration by experience, but only subject to change within the limitation imposed by the entire character structure. (pp. 13-14)

The broken time flow in *Ulysses* is justified by the fact that any character's stream-of-consciousness statements have roots somewhere in past experience. By contrast all the action in "Melanctha" takes place in what Gertrude Stein calls the "continuous present." The illusion of eternal presentness is supported by a number of stylistic devices—the most obvious being Miss Stein's use of present participles. (p. 19)

The discontinuous narrative is preferred over the linear narrative because Melanctha is the same person throughout. The incidents at the beginning of her life are no more significant in molding her character than the incidents at any other point in her life. The character is always in the present because for Gertrude Stein the present is "the twentieth-century moment of composition." For a character to live for the reader, the character must always be who she is, must always be *being*. And being implies the continual reassertion of what is through all its slight permutations, a process that Miss Stein links with motion pictures. . . . (pp. 20-1)

The analogy to motion pictures leads us to Gertrude Stein's second device to reveal the differences in consciousness flow—*graduated degrees of syntactic displacement*. . . . Sentences are repeated with the slightest alterations. . . . The sentence structure is changed ever so slightly by commas. Commas are inserted not for syntactic correctness but for rhythmic, tonal emphasis. The same words are put into a different sequence in order to emphasize the recurring sameness and the recurring difference of the thought. These changes are graduated. By graduated I imply that the changes increase in number and complexity in direct relation to the emotion to be conveyed. . . .

It is because of these graduated, minute syntactic changes that Gertrude Stein's prose can be called "cubistic." (p. 21)

Beginning with "Melanctha" and continuing throughout her entire writing career, Gertrude Stein explores the possibility of decelerating mental time. "Melanctha" represents the first step in a lifelong series of experiments to discover the relationship between decelerated time consciousness and its correlative in language, particularly in syntactic patterns.

The third quality of the conscious flow revealed in the Melanctha speech patterns is density. By density I imply the number of mental events that can be simultaneously held in the consciousness. (p. 23)

When Gertrude Stein spoke of listening to the *movement* of words rather than merely what the words said, it might be because she was concerned with the *quality* of character consciousness as opposed to the contents of character consciousness. (p. 24)

The Making of Americans can be considered a "history of everyone who ever lived, is living and will live" because for Gertrude Stein all persons can be fitted into her characterology. The roots for her characterology are found in *Three Lives*. . . . The title "making of Americans" is meant to be taken literally. From the immigration of grandparents to the youngest American in the book, . . . the aim is to show how the *American* consciousness is forged through the passage of generations. Such an encyclopedic task would be absurd from the start unless we grant some common pool of personality characteristics that exist as a constant from generation to generation. (pp. 32-3)

Miss Stein wrote that her favorite novel was Richardson's *Clarissa Harlowe,* and it is perhaps from Richardson that Gertrude Stein learned the technique of occasionally decelerating time to emphasize select action. . . . The decelerated time flow stretches the boundaries of the character's quintessential act, and makes it appear more important than it might appear in sequential, ontological time.

A second reason for decelerated time is related to Gertrude Stein's theory of human personality. . . . For Gertrude Stein the "bottom nature" of every character is revealed in the nature of their repetitions. There is a direct correspondence between the rhythm of personality and the sentence rhythm. Every violation of conventional syntax, every word inversion, unqualified dangling clause, every repeated phrase or word is an indicant of consciousness. The changes in the field of consciousness from generation to generation are revealed both linguistically and syntactically. (pp. 38-40)

If you grant Miss Stein's assumptions about personality and consciousness, her stylistic experimentation can be seen as an outgrowth of a writer's attempt to capture life by language, to capture the process of living by recreating English to make it a language more process-oriented.

I think that it is in the paintings of Cézanne that the closest analogy to what Gertrude Stein was attempting in literature can be found. (p. 45)

The possibility that unconventional language might lead to new areas of consciousness intrigued Gertrude Stein. . . . She was simply an American woman in France sensitive to the modernist revolution in the arts, and capable, through intuition and bumbling as well as through intellectual intention, of coming upon certain truths concerning the relations between language and consciousness.

Gertrude Stein lived in a literary period bubbling with linguistic experimentation. . . . There was a widespread interest bordering on faddism in mysticism, the East, hypnosis, magic, mythology, Freud, Jung, child perception, drug experimentation. To suppose that Gertrude Stein's work can all be traced back to such intellectual currents is foolish. . . . With a single-mindedness bordering on preposterous megalomania she stubbornly kept writing according to her most singular program. (pp. 56-7)

The distinction between Miss Stein's compositions and methods of automatic writing is difficult to establish but valuable to indicate. Automatic writing is the release of the contents of the writer's unconscious mind at the moment of composition without conscious author intervention. As the phrase "automatism" suggests, the conscious attentive stream is frozen, blocked off, so that the locus of attention is directed inward. In Gertrude Stein, the attention, the conscious perceptual apparatus, is heightened in intensity, so much so that synesthesia occurs—she speaks of *Tender Buttons* as the first composition to totally mix sight with hearing with sense. In this moment of heightened perception, words emerge in the mind which are *not* words of conventional semantic correspondence.... (p. 62)

Miss Stein makes a great, conscious effort to avoid familiar word combinations in *Tender Buttons*. Such avoidance of semantic correspondences must imply a conscious processing of linguistic data. No subject recorded under hypnotic trance, no author of automatic writing, has yet produced a composition with the particular nuances of *Tender Buttons*. (p. 64)

Tender Buttons is a mirror for our nonsense, a dictionary for our daily distraction, a child's first guide to the twentieth century. A symphony for meaning-laden ears. A master score of phenomenology and psychology, naïveté and wisdom, nonsense and sense. (p. 67)

What is drama for Gertrude Stein, and how does her definition mark a break from the definitions provided by our literary tradition? (p. 70)

She reminds us that all plays take place in a highly particularized space. A play is, first of all, that which takes place behind a curtain, on a stage frontally located apart from the audience. The play is something presented for the consideration of an audience. But considerably more may be presented for an audience's consideration than dialogue. Take for example the fact of the actors' presence, the setting, the lighting, the curtain. These elements are usually considered secondary and subordinate to the message. But must they be?

For Gertrude Stein the stage area is analogous to a circus ring.... The circus is an area of magical possibilities sealed off from objective reality. It is a particularized area with "a great deal of glitter in the light and a great deal of height in the air." (p. 71)

Her theater turns away from naturalism to enter a realm of high fantasy or romance. Rather than attempting to simulate social reality on stage, she uses her talents to create an alternative, imaginative reality. This alternative reality is created entirely through verbal magic and setting. (p. 72)

In the early 1930s Gertrude Stein began work on a long philosophical poem that was to mark the pinnacle of her experiments with the language/consciousness problem.... This poem, *Stanzas in Meditation,* is at the present time the most neglected of Gertrude Stein's major compositions. (p. 82)

The most specific aid we can bring to an examination of *Stanzas* is the corpus of Gertrude Stein's philosophical assumptions that rest behind her compositional methods. It has been my contention ... that Gertrude Stein's literary work represents an attempt to capture James's pluralistic universe through the development of an experimental syntax. Conventional English syntax compels its user to accept the model of a sequential, linear time/space realm that is not true to the modern, post-Heisenburgian world view. One of the most curious of psychological phenomena that conventional syntax tends to screen out from everyday, individual consciousness is the phenomenon of *simultaneity*. (pp. 82-3)

In *Tender Buttons* the Jamesian universe of flux and proc-

ess is dramatized by the processual syntax; the description, the verbal embodiment of the object, is as plastic, as multidimensional and as protological as objective reality itself.

In *Stanzas* a different approach prevails, both toward objective reality and the linguistic embodiment of it. Instead of scrambling sentence elements to eliminate the possibility of intelligible recombination the very opposite technique is employed: the central device of the poem is the conscious maximizing of semantic possibility. Each line of each stanza contains multiple options of readings. Each stanza, therefore, also contains multiple readings and so on through each part. (p. 84)

Each line contains all the syntactic variants previously contained in separate poetic lines. The reader of the lines creates, or, rather, reenacts the poem by focusing his attention on the multiplicity of word connections both within and beyond the individual line. (p. 85)

By placing an equal perceptual stress on the perception of each word the conventional ideational hierarchy behind conventional syntax is rejected. When each word of an utterance is subjected to its own, individual moment of magnification no noun conventionally labeled as sentence subject is any more important than any article or conjunction. Each word in an utterance emits a glow, a force field equal to that of any other word. So the possibilities of multiple linkages between words is intensified. Such words in a poetic line establish "territories" or "zones" of semantic intelligibility. But since the words chosen to fit into the lines of *Stanzas* are the simplest of pronouns, articles, and conjunctions—words intentionally chosen for their limited field of semantic reference—the multiple readings generate a multiplicity of apparently trivial and commonplace utterances, often to the determined reader's chagrin. (pp. 85-6)

What does all this insight into the poem's structure mean? One of the enormous paradoxes evident in the reading of *Stanzas* is that the discovery of technique does little to open the poem to exposition. Once the key to this possible reading is explored the reader is left with several most central questions: what is this poem about and what justification does it have for its existence other than as a magnificent tour de force of ornate syntax? As a philosophical poem what does it reveal of Gertrude Stein's philosophy and its relation to that of James, Whitehead, and Santayana? (p. 88)

As a psychology student she was concerned with automatism (the total shutting out of the perception of external reality so that the internal constituents of consciousness might be examined). From Melanctha of *Three Lives* to the still lifes of *Tender Buttons,* her literary career centered upon the effort to utilize a syntax most evocative of the true nature of things as she endlessly pondered them in her isolated consciousness.

The key question, repeated endlessly throughout her *Lectures in America, How to Write,* and *Geographical History* is: How do I, as a writer, come to know of the world what I know? (pp. 91-2)

This extreme sensitivity to the most minute changes of reality in process could only come about, paradoxically enough, through a determined isolation from direct perceptual activity.... It is only when speech can be focused upon as an isolated object for introspection that one's awareness of the gradualness of syntactic change can be intensified dramatically.

I am suggesting that this is exactly what Gertrude Stein accomplished in *Stanzas*. She forced herself to focus upon bits of commonplace conversation and put them through all their conceivable syntactic combinations until they emitted a glow and, like the still lifes of *Tender Buttons*, became tranformed from dully perceived commonplace to objects for aesthetic contemplation. The vibratory syntax in *Stanzas* represents nothing more than a revelation into how the human mind meditates upon reality—through the endless coming to terms with its changes. (pp. 92-3)

Poets who have followed in the wake of both Stevens and Gertrude Stein—George Oppen, Robert Duncan, John Ashbery—are engaged in the same struggle Miss Stein articulated in *Stanzas*: They are meditating upon the word and word structures that would dare to contain and encompass pluralistic reality. . . . [Her] exploration of the various consciousness states and their correlatives in language has become our modern literary legacy, our locus for aesthetic success or failure: our meditative foundation. (pp. 98-9)

In *Art by Subtraction: A Dissenting Opinion of Gertrude Stein*, B. L. Reid boldly declares that Gertrude Stein's contribution to twentieth-century literature is nil, that she had impact on no other artists save a few cranks, and that she will be forgotten entirely in a decade or so. . . . But regardless of my or Mr. Reid's opinions the fact remains that Miss Stein followed a program essential to modern literature. John Malcolm Brinnin suggests that if Gertrude Stein had not lived and written in the manner in which she did, someone else would have had to. (p. 128)

> *Norman Weinstein, in his* Gertrude Stein and the Literature of the Modern Consciousness *(copyright © 1970 by Frederick Ungar Publishing Co., Inc.), Ungar, 1970.*

Gertrude Stein's method of composition is to make statements which cannot be disproved even when they may be ignored. Who could argue with this statement from *Tender Buttons*: "Light curls very light curls have no more curliness than soup. This is not a subject." Even in her "normal" writing like *The Autobiography of Alice B. Toklas* her way is to proceed from one unshakable (though not necessarily correct) affirmation to the next. She begins her book *Paris France* by informing us: "There are two things that french animals do not do, cats do not fight much and do not howl much and chickens do not get flustered running across the road, if they start to cross the road they keep on going which is what french people do too." It is impossible to refute a statement made in a poem; poetry is by nature true and affords blanket protection to anything one wishes to

say in it. Gertrude Stein is a poet in this sense. Like Picasso, she is *building*. Her structures may be demolished; what remains is a sense of someone's having built. (p. 74)

> *John Ashbery, "G.M.P.," in* ARTnews *(© 1971 by* ARTnews*), February, 1971, pp. 45-7, 73-4.*

[Though Stein's] *The Making of Americans* and *Tender Buttons* tend toward the opposite poles of metonymy and metaphor, they are both recognizably 'modernist' and both pursue the same general artistic aim—to render that elusive quality, 'existence'. Her use of repetition with slight variation in her earlier, metonymic prose has the effect of converting the dynamic into the static, the temporal into the spatial, for the pace of the narrative is heavily retarded and we are scarcely conscious of progressing at all. This is consistent with the aim of metaphor-oriented symbolist and imagist verse, or Pound's definition of the 'image', which 'presents an intellectual and emotional complex in an instant of time.' The instantaneousness is an illusion inasmuch as language is necessarily extended in time, but it is an illusion easier to achieve in the metaphorical mode of poetry than in the metonymic mode of prose. Gertrude Stein showed that by an artful use of repetition-with-slight-variation both lexical and grammatical, prose might achieve a similar effect; and since repetition of this kind is natural to casual vernacular speech, the method lent itself to a writer like Hemingway who wanted to be both a realist and a modernist. (p. 85)

> *David Lodge, in* Critical Quarterly, *Spring, 1975.*

It has been Gertrude Stein's fate to be known more as a "personality" than as a writer, a fate she would have strenuously condemned. Stubborn and implacable about the virtues of her work, she was for a time virtually its only enthusiast, and even her biographers have tended to slight it. . . .

Gertrude Stein made the English language "an artist's medium," a sort of prose imitation of the Cubist practice of portraying an object on all sides at once. Having abandoned direct narrative early on, her work became increasingly dense and repetitive once she had discovered the stylistic principle that could be described as a gradual incrementation of detail. In her later books, this principle was put to relentless use, sometimes with great effect but more often to the point of tedium. (p. 30)

> *James Atlas, in* The New York Times Book Review *(© 1976 by The New York Times Company; reprinted by permission), April 11, 1976.*

(Johan) August Strindberg

1849-1912

Swedish dramatist, novelist, short story writer, poet, and essayist. The father of expressionistic drama and the most versatile of modern playwrights, Strindberg was called by Eugene O'Neill "the most modern of moderns, the greatest interpreter in the theatre of the characteristic spiritual conflicts which constitute the drama—the blood—of our lives today." A man tormented by frequent bouts with mental illness, three disastrous marriages and three bitter divorces, and permanent scars from a troubled childhood, for a time Strindberg was more notorious for his scandals than famous for his literary genius. His father, an impoverished shipping agent and his mother, a servant, were married just before his birth. The scars that family life left on the sensitive Strindberg were described in the autobiographical novel, *The Son of a Servant*. His work can be roughly divided into three periods: 1870-80, an apprentice decade spent writing historical romances; 1885-90, a productive period of pessimistic naturalistic dramas; and 1898-1912, his expressionist period. Strindberg's technically superb naturalistic plays are characterized by a disturbing misogyny. The war of the sexes is a familiar theme of the work of this period. Following a severe struggle with insanity which he chronicled in *Inferno*, Strindberg entered his expressionist period, which is generally considered to be his most difficult and most excellent. He ended a self-imposed exile from Sweden in 1907; his return did not bring peace but rather culminated in the "Strindberg Feud of 1910-12," a showdown between radicals and the literary establishment. In spite of all the conflict, he is Sweden's greatest dramatist. Thanks to Bernard Shaw, who gave his Nobel Prize money to the project, Strindberg's works are slowly being translated.

PRINCIPAL WORKS

Mäster Olaf (drama) 1872
  [*Master Olaf*, 1915]
Röda Rummet (novel) 1879
  [*The Red Room*, 1913]
Tjänstekvinnans son (autobiographical novel) 1886-87
  [*The Son of a Servant*, 1913]
Fadren (drama) 1887
  [*The Father*, 1907]
Le Plaidoyer d'un fou (autobiographical novel) 1887-88
  [*The Confession of a Fool*, 1912]
Fröken Julie (drama) 1888
  [*Miss Julie*, 1913]

Kamraterna (drama) 1888
  [*Comrades*, 1919]
Till Damascus (drama) 1898-1904
  [*To Damascus*, 1933-35]
Advent (drama) 1899
  [*Advent*, 1912]
Dödsdansen (drama) 1901
  [*The Dance of Death*, 1912]
Påsk (drama) 1901
  [*Easter*, 1912]
Ett drömspel (drama) 1902
  [*The Dream Play*, 1912]
Brända tomten (drama) 1907
  [*After the Fire*, 1913]
Spöksonaten (drama) 1907
  [*The Spook Sonata*, 1916]

[Strindberg's] campaign against feminism, which otherwise could have served a good purpose by curbing wild militancy, was defeated by its own exaggerations. . . . [He] was utterly incapable of objective thinking, and under the sting of his miseries in love and marriage, dislike of woman turned into hatred and hatred into frenzy. Henceforth, the entire spectacle of life presented itself to his distorted vision as a perpetual state of war between the sexes: on the one side he saw the male, strong of mind and heart, but in the generosity of strength guileless and over-trustful; on the other side, the female, weak of body and intellect, but shrewd enough to exploit her frailness by linking iniquity to impotence and contriving by her treacherous cunning to enslave her natural superior:—it is the story of Samson and Delilah made universal in its application. Love is shown up as the trap in which man is caught to be shorn of his power. The case against woman is classically drawn up in "The Father," one of the strangest and at the same time most powerful tragedies of Strindberg. The principals of the plot stand for the typical character difference between the sexes as Strindberg sees it. . . . (pp. 87-8)

Unfortunately, Strindberg's abnormal vision falsifies the things he looks at, and, being steeped in his insuperable prejudice, his pictures of life, in spite of the partial veracity they possess, never rise above the level of caricatures. (p. 89)

Extending the significance of his own personal experience to everything within his horizon, and erecting a dogmatic system upon this tenuous generalization, Strindberg reached the conviction that the purpose of living is to suffer, a conviction that threw his philosophy well into line with the religious and ethical ideas of the middle age. Yet even at this juncture his cynicism did not desert him, as witness this comment of his: "Religion must be a punishment, because nobody gets religion who does not have a bad conscience." This avowal preceded his saltatory approach to Roman Catholicism. (pp. 97-8)

The keynote to his literary productions is the cry of the agony of being. Every line of his works is written in the shadow of the sorrow of living. In them, all that is most dismal and terrifying and therefore most tragical, becomes articulate. They are propelled by an abysmal pessimism, and because of this fact, since pessimism is one of the mightiest inspiring forces in literature, August Strindberg, its foremost spokesman, deserves to be read and understood. (p. 105)

> *Otto Heller, "The Eccentricity of August Strindberg," in his* Prophets of Dissent: Essays on Maeterlinck, Strindberg, Nietzsche and Tolstoy *(copyright © 1918 by Alfred A. Knopf Inc.; reprinted by permission of Alfred A. Knopf, Inc.), Knopf, 1918, pp. 71-105.*

There are both magnificent poetic fantasy and implacable naturalistic causality in the final scene of *Miss Julie,* and, unlike some of Strindberg's other play endings, it makes no concessions to sentimentality. It is obviously because of Strindberg's close allegiance to the naturalistic program that *Miss Julie,* unlike his previous play, *The Father,* and his next, *Creditors,* lacks a moral thesis. "The naturalist has abolished God with guilt" are Strindberg's own words in the Preface, and the play has few traces of his usual misogyny. . . . He says in the Preface that love in any higher sense is impossible between two persons so different. But he also wanted his play to be an example of the adaptation to social conditions of Darwin's doctrine concerning the survival of the fittest and the destruction of the weak in the struggle for existence. Miss Julie, the descendant of a decadent noble family, goes under, while Jean, with healthy proletarian blood in his veins and a robust appetite for life, is a "race-builder," the progenitor of a new social species. (p. 114)

If our response to the ending of the play is rather less joyous than [he intended] it is because Strindberg, his professed objectivity notwithstanding, has conceived of Miss Julie's destiny tragically. She is the refined aristocrat who succumbs in the struggle with the coarse proletarian Jean. For the fact of the matter was that Strindberg's Darwinism had already for some time clashed with his growing antidemocratic sentiments and his cult of the superman. (pp. 114-15)

The last step in this development is marked by *By the Open Sea* . . . , where Strindberg creates a superman in his own image. The hero of the novel, the fishing inspector Borg, is a genius, but he is a superman only by virtue of his gigantic intellect; physically he is small and frail, and psychologically he is a tense and excitable decadent with some of Strindberg's own susceptibility to changing emotions. His

tragedy is his failure to maintain his superiority over the rabble without having the exquisite machinery of his mind picked to pieces by the crude population of fishermen among whom he lives. His fate is a little like Miss Julie's, and when in the last scene of the novel he sets sail for the open sea in a full storm he is sailing toward death just as surely as Miss Julie's walk from the kitchen to the barn with the razor in her hand is a walk toward death. Strindberg's otherwise often brutal superman cult is here softened by his conviction that the superman is a dying species and that the pygmies will inherit the earth. (p. 116)

> *Martin Lamm, "'Miss Julie'," in his* Strindbergs dramer *(copyright © 1924 by Martin Lamm), Albert Bonniers Förlag, 1924 (translated and abridged by Otto Reinert, and reprinted in* Strindberg: A Collection of Critical Essays, *edited by Otto Reinert, Prentice-Hall, Inc., 1971, pp. 105-16).*

Like another Dante, [Strindberg] haunted the shades of a modern Inferno; but, unlike Dante, in searching for God he found the devil. In his sympathetic contemplation of the tragedy of human destiny, is felt the strange, sweet pathos of one who is somehow strong and good; yet evil, the knowledge of evil, so obsessed his consciousness that he stands forth today as that artist of modern times whose power of painting the evil genius of humanity, of turning up the seamy side of the garment of life for our horrified yet fascinated contemplation, is unique and incomparable. In his lifetime, he sought to annex the entire domain of the human spirit; and yet this search for cosmopolitan culture, for the highest, deepest reaches of the artistic consciousness, left him as it found him, a plebeian of the soul. (p. 6)

Little heed has been paid to Strindberg's early dreams for social betterment, as embodied in his *Swiss Tales.* They form a cardinally suggestive link in the chain of his spiritual evolution; for after this one flight into the blue of social idealism, Strindberg reverts to the passionate individualism which signalizes his greatest work throughout his career. Yet, it is something added to our conception of Strindberg, this knowledge that Strindberg fiercely protested against the human servitude imposed by the material conditions of modern life. Civilization has been paid for too dearly—thus early Strindberg speaks in resonant tones. As a social reformer, Strindberg showed himself to be pure communist. Abolish private ownership, and require of every man all that in reason and in conscience he can bring himself to contribute. The European dynasties must go, in the interest of the future of the average man; militancy must yield to the visionary ideal of world-peace. This strange anomaly of the Berserker-like Strindberg previsaging the tranquil communist state of the far future has a certain piquant charm—the charm of naïve inconsistency. The optimistic spirit of the utopist expires in the bosom of the temperamental pessimist. The later Strindberg sinks to the mean level of crass actuality and of individual strife, bafflement and trial. (pp. 20-1)

It was the fatal weakness of his temperament, as well as of his esthetic creed, to generalize from personal data, to identify the individual with the universe. It is the fundamental weakness of all thesis-literature: to put the part for the whole. Like a camera held too close to the object, Strindberg throws into ghastly disproportion that which is nearest to him. No artist of modern times has been so pre-eminently successful in the shattering of perspective. (p. 31)

There is no error so crass as that of presuming, with hasty generalization, that Strindberg was essentially eccentric—dementedly swinging off from the central realities of life. This inner meaning of Strindberg's temperament lies at the very heart of his nature, which pulsed violently in the midst of the most fantastic realities. Never did artist so persistently cleave to the centre of his own being in his effort to project for the world's inspection the inner significance of contemporary existence. Strindberg is the most ego-centric dramatist who has ever lived. If Shakspere was actually, as Mr. Frank Harris vehemently implies, the Strindberg of the Elizabethan era, by the same token is Strindberg the Shakspere of the Nietzschean age—a supremely daemonic bohemian of the soul. (pp. 37-8)

Strindberg has been called the only dramatist of genuinely Shaksperean order in modern times—assuredly true in the dramatic sense that in the consciousness of no other contemporary dramatist do conflicts, antitheses, crises, emanate such trenchant, virile reality. The secret of his marvellous appeal is his headlong participation in the destinies of his dramatic characters. It is because he threw himself so vehemently into the arena of dramatic struggle and dramatized his own tremendous struggle that his art works seethe with such vital force and energy. (pp. 38-9)

Strindberg pays woman the high honor of holding her to be a foeman worthy of the sharpest steel of man. He holds woman fully worthy of man as an antagonist in the duel of sex. In his plays, woman fights for her own hand with unlimited will-power and intellectual skill.

Strindberg can only be properly understood if we realize that the duel of sex is not always a contest for sex supremacy. It is a contest, as Strindberg so diabolically shows in *Creditors,* of the woman for the right to illicit gratification of her own instincts—regardless of honor, fidelity, or modesty. Or it may be, as in *The Link,* a mortal struggle for the possession of the child. (p. 53)

> *Archibald Henderson, "August Strindberg," in his* European Dramatists *(copyright © 1926, by Prentice-Hall, Inc.; reprinted by permission of Prentice-Hall, Inc., Englewood Cliffs, New Jersey), Appleton, 1926, pp. 3-72.*

Thrice shipwrecked in marriage, [Strindberg] could still render an account of the relations of man and wife which the world, no matter how much it disapproved of him personally, must gravely ponder before it could proceed in its old brutal, nonchalant way. For here was more than the account of petty bickering or noisy brawls with which some authors chose to adorn their tales; here was the assertion that sex is a fatal magnet drawing together two venomous antagonists armed with secret knives—that in this duel the spiritually inferior, the woman, is the stronger because more realistic and unscrupulous. Held by varying degrees of conviction and horror, readers and playgoers, Americans as much as the rest, deliberated Strindberg's thesis long enough to have their own thoughts, their own constructions of life, affected by it, as we shall see.

Strindberg arrived at his conception of the "war of the sexes" by slow stages. . . . The fact that the author was wed always to what are euphemistically termed "superior women" may have had something to do with convincing him that the woman has every advantage in an encounter with the male, particularly the nineteenth century male with his chivalrous notions of womanhood (learnt from his mother, who is the first to betray him); but the conquests which Strindberg himself made of these superior women can just as certainly be cited as the source of his idea that the person of low birth, who hasn't the handicap of chivalrous associations, easily dominates women of the upper class—an idea he developed in *Miss Julie.* (pp. 575-76)

Aside from *Marriage,* the work of Strindberg which has been influential in America is confined definitely to five or six plays. . . . *The Father* pictures a cavalry captain, who has continued to live with his wife for twenty years merely for the sake of his daughter, now goaded to madness when he opposes his wife's wishes in regard to the child's education. The play is extraordinarily effective, granted that a character could be as diabolically possessed as the wife. On the stage this wife is convincing as Svengali is convincing—a fascinating study of a sadist, yet few would be willing to generalize about the whole sex from her, as Strindberg does.

Miss Julie (known only as a one-act play in America) is undeniably one of the best pieces of theatre of modern times; it is a triumph of dramatic art to get an hour of breathless entertainment out of one setting and only three characters—two of them servants. Who had accomplished this before Strindberg? The play expounds one of his favorite ideas: that in the encounters of aristocrat and plebeian, where the former is reduced to equality by sentimentality, the latter always triumphs. Neurotic Countess Julie (Strindberg, too, had had his Countess) dares to flirt with the man-servant, John, and after being taken by him, can think of no satisfactory way of escape . . . , until John at the end of the play puts a razor in her hand and directs her to the door. No work of Strindberg shows better than this how women (as he contends) survive in the sex duel only because the chivalric code protects them; once Julie has sacrificed this protection she has no will to oppose the brutal implicit command of her servant-master.

Again, in *Creditors,* Strindberg tries to demonstrate that woman, though inferior to man in intellect, is his superior in the inevitable struggle between them because she regards the code as a mere convenience and is completely lacking in moral sense. Tekla, the fantastic vampire who dominates this play, is the epitome of evil, a compound of all the horrendous traits that Strindberg imagined could ever occupy the tenement of woman. *The Stronger,* shortest of all Strindberg's dramas, is a monologue . . . during which the wife, with growing sureness as she senses her victory, asserts her superiority over the other woman, who does not get a chance to reply before her antagonist sweeps out and the curtain falls. This one-act play is a milestone in the evolution of the experimental drama and deserves full praise from the standpoint of the theatre, even if the meaning of the play wholly changes with different actresses in the rôles—so indefinite is the characterization. *The Link* sets the stage with a divorce court—a sensational case in which a local baron and his wife are to be separated is on the calendar. Even in the face of the dissolution of their legal bond the couple are bound together by their common anxiety to spare their child, for whose future they have already made arrangements. The clumsy conscientiousness of the young judge leads the woman to vilify her husband, and the baron to retort, so that before they can check themselves, they are wrangling in the open court—with the result that the judge takes from them their child and places him under a stupid guardian, offensive to both. Inferior as theatre to *Miss Julie* and *The Stronger, The Link* is much more convincing than either. Even the railing at Heaven, so apt to be melodramatic, coming at the end of a tragedy, seems consistent with the overwrought condition of the principals as the curtain falls on this play.

The Dance of Death—a tedious, two-part play covering long years of bickering and mutual loathing—gets its title from the fact that both husband and wife, unwilling to appeal to the divorce court in this instance, wait for the release of death which the husband's failing health seems to promise. Yet perhaps the supremely ironical passage in Strindberg is found at the end of *The Dance of Death*— when the wife, who has exulted over the fallen and dying man, admits he was good and noble, and with her hatred no longer to sustain her, feels her own dissolution near. It is the Unconscious, so it would appear, who is the true enemy of both. As soon as these puppets fall from the strings, new figures will be attached, and the dance will begin all over.

It is one of the extraordinary things in modern literature—a thing for which Freud has an explanation—that every writer who has been peculiarly absorbed by sex has also been much concerned about God. Strindberg is no exception to this generalization and his *Dream Play,* a fantasy governed by chance association in which even the characters split or multiply, blur or vanish, is his thesis in divinity. Brahma, the World Soul, has been prevailed upon by the World-Mother, Maya, to propagate himself—and as a result of this heavenly sin, the mating of Spirit with Matter, and of Idea with Sense the world is born, filled with creatures who vainly aspire to free themselves from matter. Every joy is checked by pain. Strindberg, to be brief, has elevated woman into a force responsible for all the evil in the universe. This is a pretty myth, and as plausible as any, yet if it were absolutely true, not to be given human credence, since it frees the male sex altogether of any responsibility.

It would seem impossible to thrust the critical scalpel between the man and his work in judging Strindberg. Unfortunate in love and indubitably chiefly at fault in this, he judged all womanhood from the women whose lives he helped to warp; hypersensitive, he recorded more accurately than anyone else the vindictive responses of the woman to whom love was still a subtle whip: and the accuracy of his reporting is responsible for the great power of his plays. His tortured Baronesses, his Alices, and his Julias convince only the prejudiced that they are representative of their sex; their obvious sickness moves Strindberg's audiences to compassion, which lends force to his plays. As a dramatist he is to be condemned for the capriciousness of his action, which is plausible only with warped characters, and for the generalization implicit in the action. No man ever labored harder than he (Was he trying to convince himself?) to make the exception seem the rule. And few men, surely, have brought more art to the business. (pp. 579-82)

> *Oscar Cargill, in his* Intellectual America:
> Ideas on the March *(reprinted with permis-*

sion of Macmillan Publishing Co., Inc.; copyright 1941 by Macmillan Publishing Co., Inc.; 1969 by Oscar Cargill), Macmillan, 1941.

Strindberg looks back to the Romanticists. When he was not a conscious disciple of Rousseau, he was an unconscious disciple. He is Romantic in the vulgar sense of expressing passion quite openly, quite toweringly, and of pushing it to an extreme or to an eccentricity. He is Romantic also in the deeper sense of trying not only to recognize the magnitude of the passions but also to discover their proper status. He is both an intense lover and a precise analyst of his love. In himself he recognizes two kinds of love, the two kinds which Western tradition has called *eros* and *agape,* human and divine, sexual and sacred. Contrary to current assumption, the Romantic idea has not been an unambiguous endorsement of either. The Romanticists rediscovered *eros* and *agape* precisely by rediscovering their ambivalence. . . . What we call the Freudian approach, the stress on ambivalence, the sense of the subterranean, and the intellectual analysis of these, is pure Romanticism, and if Freud has given us the most systematic documentation of this approach, Strindberg has given us not only the most circumstantial case history but the ultimate Romantic self-analysis along Freudian lines. . . . Almost alone among autobiographers Strindberg told everything without telling more than everything. He was a great descriptive artist, and if he alternately loved himself to the point of narcissism and despised himself to the point of indignity, he somehow contrived to make these tendencies his servants. Though in the plays and novels self-dramatization plays an inordinate role, the autobiography is suprisingly literal. It should be taken as, among other things, the historical foundation upon which the fiction and the drama are an imaginative superstructure. Art was a sort of sublime self-indulgence for Strindberg, autobiography and history a self-discipline. The discipline consisted in a compulsion to get rid of his past by exactly recording it. (pp. 198-99)

Modernism is a development from Romanticism, a development partly by revulsion but just as much by continuation. Freud is a Romanticist; he is also correctly regarded as a Modernist. He gave a new concrete embodiment to Romantic principles, thus fulfilling one of the deepest urges of Modernism. This is the sense in which Ibsen and Shaw are Modernists. This is the sense in which Strindberg is a Modernist.

"Modern" is the word which would occur to any reader of those parts of Strindberg's autobiography which, before Freud, though after Stendhal, describe very fully the author's mother fixation. Strindberg's account of his childhood is already so analytic that the work of the psychoanalyst is supererogatory. (p. 199)

Strindberg's love of theater is his narcissism. He insisted on *seeing* his destiny lamented. Is not this very Romantic? Is it not also very Modern? (p. 200)

The life work of Strindberg may be arranged in three concentric circles. Tangential to the outermost circle are his occasional works, translations, essays, and treatises; within it are the autobiographies which are the raw material for Strindberg's art works; within the second circle are the novels, a rough attempt to impose form upon the chaos of his experience; within the inmost circle as Strindberg's central achievement are his plays. . . . Taking the whole body of plays together we find two extreme types, both Swedish in inspiration: at one end the chronicle history play, at the other the fairy play. Strindberg modified both these forms. After Büchner, and at the same time as Shaw, he helped to shape an informal and intimate type of chronicle play. After the German Romanticists, and at the same time as Maeterlinck and W. B. Yeats, he made out of fairy tales a delicate and sophisticated theater. More important than these extreme forms are Strindberg's deviations from the rival simplicities, namely his own quasi-tragic naturalism and his own kind of fantasy, deviations which were both intensely personal and intensely European. (pp. 201-02)

We often find that the inventors of "new" forms in modern literature carry a formula as far as it can go. Having reached the North Pole they can go north no longer. That is true of Strindberg. Having invented his new naturalistic form Strindberg did not proceed to use it. He abandoned it, and in his next great period of dramatic productivity—the last dozen years or so of his life—he writes on another pattern. If the earlier formula had been the duet in a naturalistic setting, the later formula was the solo in an Expressionistic setting. If the earlier pattern had been Strindberg's conflict with Siri von Essen, the later was that of a solitary old man looking back over his buried hopes and past opportunities. If the form of the earlier plays was Antoine's Naturalism, the form of the later plays is a new sort of intimate theater which Strindberg himself requires us to associate with Max Reinhardt, who opened his Chamber Playhouse in Berlin in 1906. In a memoir written for the actors in his little Stockholm theater, Strindberg wrote: "Reinhardt brings the idea of chamber music into drama: intimate nature of spectacle, emphatic statement of the theme, care given to the execution." The theory of Chamber Drama, as further expounded in the memoir, is not of course a retraction of the theory of theater expounded in Strindberg's naturalistic days (in the preface of *Miss Julia* for instance). At both times Strindberg stresses the prime need of a single powerful motif, at both times he outlines a scheme for an intimate theater with a small auditorium and its attendant effects upon dramatic style. The Memoir goes on to deplore calculated effects, passages written for applause, brilliant acting roles, tirades and display: in fact the whole bag of professional tricks, most of which the earlier Strindberg had resorted to and some of which the most austere later Strindberg did not actually eliminate.

Perhaps the most challenging thing in the Memoir is what Strindberg says about dramatic form. Dramatic criticism had been a battle of centuries as to the correct or the best form of drama—whether Greek, Shakespearean, neo-classic, or "well-made." Strindberg's declaration that form must be left fluid so that a theme may be allowed to find whatever form suits it best is perhaps the obvious retort to all this sort of squabbling. But it is the kind of obviousness which apparently only a genius is equipped to discover at the right moment. Fluid form! Certainly Strindberg lived up to his own injunction—always feeling his way, always trying to discover organic and expressive shapes for chaotic experience. Nowhere is this clearer than in the plays of the last period. (pp. 203-05)

Strindberg's self-dramatization, like Rousseau's, like Nietzsche's, is a fact but not in itself a refutation of all his views or a condemnation of all his achievements. Strind-

berg, moreover, differs from these men not, it is true, in being a neurotic or in being a genius, but in being a man whose genius itself is neurotic. In most neurotic geniuses the genius, I should think, is the healthy part of them. In Strindberg this is probably not always so. His visions are themselves mad. If they are of value—and I think they are —it is because morbid symptoms are but exaggerations of "normal" symptoms. The gigantic pictures of insanity and nightmare are but enlargements of the images and dreams of the sane. They too are human and universal. (p. 208)

No more than many other plays which appear under such rubrics is *The Ghost Sonata* one of the "world's greatest plays." But it is a brilliant and complex piece such as none but Strindberg would have dreamed of attempting. Perhaps its best qualities are its superficial qualities: color, rhythm, shifting tempi, *élan,* cleverness, atmosphere, and theatricality. Nevertheless it has a core. The ending does indeed indicate Strindberg's failure to find a meaning in life which he could confirm from inner experience. His religion is always pasted on. But this very fact is what makes the religious plays—except for their forced conclusions—much richer than the religious drama of most other moderns. The latter tend to write self-conscious religious propaganda. Strindberg represents the modern would-be religionist much more explicitly when he so patently fails in simple, positive faith. And it is his undignified maneuvering, his vacillation, his passionate insincerity, his wriggling to and fro, that make his spiritual escapades interesting and almost amusing. Most of our more recent neo-religious poets are solemn and sour, and exact from us an almost funereal deference. They are consequently tiresome and unconvincing. Strindberg we begin by taking with a pinch of salt. But the salt does not lose its savor, and we end by taking him seriously if not *au pied de la lettre.*

Perhaps the Strindberg we come to respect is neither the dazzling lunatic of the naturalistic "tragedies" nor the melodramatic mystic of the dream plays. It is the less unequivocal, more ironic Strindberg of what he calls his "comedies." *Comrades* contains the essential teaching of Strindberg on women. It is also sane—which means that in it Strindberg evinces some appreciation of the thick, ambiguous texture of life itself, and of the consequent need for some sort of moral as well as dramatic irony, of the need for not taking tragedy too tragically. The point is perhaps more deliberately advanced in another "comedy"—*There Are Crimes and Crimes*—as the title best implies. (pp. 209-10)

While Ibsen is known as a negative skeptic but was really a positive believer, Strindberg, known as a dogmatist, was above all a skeptic. That is clear from *There Are Crimes and Crimes.* Perhaps all the Chamber Plays, intentionally or not, bear witness to it. In them we see his inability to believe not only the materialism of his youth, which he now openly abhorred, but also the religion which he pretended to have discovered later and which he was to go on parading till the day when he asked that the bible should solemnly be laid upon his corpse. (p. 212)

What is Strindberg's place in the history of drama? . . . Strindberg was a man of the nineteenth century—indeed almost a synopsis of the century's beliefs, illusions, and attitudes. His dramaturgy is of the epoch in that he remains in the peep-show theater of illusion, suspense, individual psychology, and domestic tragedy. What he tried to do was to intensify, not destroy, all these. The intimate theater is a device to that end. And too many imitators of Strindberg have drawn upon this "bourgeois" Strindberg—upon the wild sexual emotion of the naturalistic "tragedies," upon the unconvincing religiosity of the dream plays, upon the shrill egoism, the false horticultural denouements, and the like. I am thinking again of the Expressionists. In Strindberg and in all these there is a great deal of the world weariness of "decadence" and much less, perhaps, of the promise of a future. (pp. 213-14)

A living seismograph, Strindberg can feel the twentieth century coming, can feel a gathering in the air of all the hate and ferocity of renewed barbarism. (p. 214)

> *Eric Bentley, "August Strindberg," in his* The Playwright as Thinker: A Study of Drama in Modern Times *(copyright 1946, 1974 by Eric Bentley), Reynal & Hitchcock, 1946, pp. 193-215.*

[*Comrades*] came in its final form to include elements of bitterness and brutality at least somewhat suggestive of the naturalistic tone and manner. *The Father,* in marked contrast to *Comrades,* is pure tragedy. A slight touch of the comic in its opening scene is soon buried forever in the rapidly developing, intensely tragic central action of the play. Here for the first time Strindberg develops a motif which is to become central in his later plays: the head-on, savage collision of two wills, usually those of a man and a woman, each seeking absolute mastery over the other, neither willing to yield, and with the weaker though finer will being finally crushed by the stronger, less scrupulous will. . . . Strindberg had been immersing himself at the time he wrote *The Father* in that group of pseudo-scientific psychologists of the day (Liébeault, Bernheim, and others) who had been investigating such phenomena as hypnotism, mesmerism, and some of the more inclusive aspects of mental suggestion; and his play from one point of view is but a brilliant dramatic exposition of some of the psychological theories that he had come upon in this reading. *The Father* gains its terrifying tragic reality, its intense actuality, however, from the fact that Strindberg is here telling the story of his own marital life. Strindberg himself is the Captain, breaking inexorably bit by bit under the insistently horrible pressure of a stronger will. The best commentary on *The Father* is, in consequence, the autobiographical volume *The Confession of a Fool,* written shortly after *The Father* and containing all of the psychological motifs employed by Strindberg in the drama. . . .

[It] should be apparent that in certain technical elements in this play Strindberg has felt the impact of earlier traditions in the drama. One finds echoes of both Shakespeare and the Greek theatre in Strindberg's otherwise so-modern play. . . . That Strindberg had the Greek drama in mind seems apparent from his use of sharply concentrated action, his employment of a very small number of dramatis personae, and his observation of the unities of time and place. The Omphale motif is an even more striking illustration of the influence of a Greek tradition on Strindberg in this play. It should be stressed, however, that these traces of an earlier dramatic tradition are on the whole incidental rather than basic in *The Father.* They have been so thoroughly assimilated by Strindberg that they seem in no way artificial adjuncts to a play otherwise so undeniably Strindbergian in every essential respect. . . . Strindberg managed

. . . to break through the heavy superstructure of quite static outward detail which had made the usual type of naturalistic play so essentially undramatic. He uses, indeed, what the naturalists called "a slice of life" as the basis of his drama; but he does not follow orthodox dramatic naturalism in permitting the action to flow entirely haphazard. Strindberg is too much the born dramatist to become a merely doctrinaire naturalist, much as he was impressed at this stage in his development by the possibilities of the naturalistic view of human life as applied particularly to the conception of dramatic character. (pp. 28-9)

True to the doctrinaire naturalist's conception of character as a product of heredity and environment, Strindberg has his central characters [in *Miss Julia*] reveal bit by bit in the course of the dialogue the particular elements in their heredity and in their environmental backgrounds which determine their every action. . . . In none of Strindberg's other plays dealing with the conflict between man and woman has he been more objective, less inclined to side with one party or the other in the course of the dramatic conflict. In this respect also *Miss Julia* satisfies the naturalistic concept of the drama. Instead of showing, as Strindberg almost invariably does, a marked sympathy for the man in such a struggle, the dramatist through most of this play reveals no perceptible tendency toward taking sides, and in the closing scene one feels that Strindberg's sympathies lean a bit toward Miss Julia. (pp. 30-1)

In the highly charged dramatic scenes of *The Creditors* hatred lurks everywhere, ready to spring into devastating explosive action; the dialogue is handled with uncanny virtuosity; never has a play been written with a more concentrated, tightly knit construction. Though all of this gives to the play something of an artificial, schematic quality not at all characteristic of *The Father* and only at times present in *Miss Julia, The Creditors* was the first play by Strindberg successfully performed on the Continent (Berlin in 1893), and it has remained to our day among the most frequently played of Strindberg's dramas both in Europe and America.

The fascination which abnormal psychological phenomena held for Strindberg in his full-length naturalistic plays from just after the middle of the 1880's carried over into a number of less important plays—the three one-act plays, *Pariah, The Stronger,* and *Simoon*—which he wrote in order to provide a repertoire for the experimental theatre which he attempted unsuccessfully to establish in Copenhagen in the late 1880's. . . . It was at this time that Strindberg first came to read Edgar Allan Poe, whose horror themes and intricate detective pattern intrigues fascinated him and left their mark clearly upon both *Pariah* and *Simoon.* (p. 31)

The opening scene of . . . *The Keys of the Kingdom* reveals Strindberg at his best in the poetry of deep personal pathos; but after this promising beginning the play rapidly deteriorates into a succession of rather pointless, and only slightly coördinated, satiric episodes. *The Link,* on the other hand, is among Strindberg's more important naturalistic dramas. It is a case of "court reporting," a re-telling in dramatic form of Strindberg's own divorce case; and as such it fulfils most of the thematic and technical demands of the naturalistic theatre. (p. 32)

[The] haunting power of [*To Damascus*] emanates substantially more from the form in which the play is written than from the story in itself. This form is revolutionary in every respect. Turning away entirely from the severe, concentrated construction of his naturalistic dramas, Strindberg here composes simply a series of tableaux, related to each other by what may be called poetic moods rather than by any sharply defined outward action. The play differs from Strindberg's earlier naturalistic dramas also in that the fundamental dramatic struggle involves a conflict between man and God rather than a struggle between two human wills; and God (The Unseen One) never appears in the play, though he directs and controls the action. Strindberg's most daring technical departure in this play lies, however, in his curious blending of reality and fantasy, a blending as in the materials and the processes of a dream. This is what gives the drama its remarkable, purely Strindbergian quality; for Strindberg himself during the Inferno period, and not infrequently thereafter, found it at times difficult to distinguish between reality and fantasy, life and the dream. It was this that gave to *To Damascus* that "terrifying half-reality" to which Geijerstam referred. This weird, only half earthly manner is to stalk again and again in Strindberg's plays, most successfully, as we shall see, in *Easter* . . . and *The Dream Play* . . . and finally in the series of Chamber Plays. . . . (p. 35)

Were it possible for non-Scandinavian students of the drama to identify themselves intimately enough with Scandinavian history to be in position to respond adequately to [his] historical dramas, Strindberg would certainly be recognized everywhere among those very few dramatists who rank close to Shakespeare in the historical drama. As it is, Strindberg's eminence in the naturalistic and expressionistic drama is universally recognized while his historical plays remain the precious possession of Strindberg's own nation alone. (p. 37)

Strindberg's primary concern in these plays is with character rather than with episode or mere complications of plot. In the matter of dramatic structure these plays (with the striking exception of *Gustaf Vasa*) depart almost as completely from the firm, tight construction of Strindberg's naturalistic plays as did *To Damascus*. . . . [The] structural pattern of Strindberg's . . . historical plays is on the whole curiously fluid, suggestive of moods in a tragic vein rather than of clear-cut dramatic conflicts; and the dramatist does not hesitate to employ in the course of the solemn progress of action in these plays a variety of subtly meaningful lyric adjuncts to give greater richness, body, and direction to the plays. (pp. 37-8)

Gustaf Vasa, looked upon by many as the greatest of Strindberg's historical dramas, is less musical in manner than are *The Saga of the Folkungs* and *Erik XIV*. In general structure it is sharp and clear, almost architectural in its lines; its central character, King Gustaf Vasa, is drawn in bold, striking outline; and the dramatic conflict is presented in clearly perceived ethical terms. But even this play does not lack its poetry, particularly in the first two acts, where the King does not himself appear and yet his person dominates everything, casting its giant shadow over action and dialogue and determining with a strong master hand the destinies of his subjects. It is by a series of massive indirections that we first become aware of the King's presence and his power. Not until the third act does he actually appear on the stage. Seldom has Strindberg been so imaginative in handling the element of dramatic suspense. (p. 39)

[In form *The Dream Play*] somewhat resembles *Easter* and *The Bridal Crown*, for these plays had experimented liberally with what might be called the poetry of symbolism. But *The Dream Play* carries these techniques much farther, adopting techniques that are more closely related to the revolutionary dramatic form of *To Damascus*. . . . Strange as is the weird procession of eerie tableaux in *To Damascus*, the drama is held together by an at least vaguely outlined "story" as well as by its subtly integrated play of moods and ideas. In *The Dream Play*, on the other hand, Strindberg has eliminated entirely any succession of episodes forming a pattern or a story. The "action" of the play is wholly phantasmagoric, entirely irrational, ignoring both time and space relationships, and following the lawless vagaries of the pure dream world. Never had a dramatist indulged in a more capricious play of fantasy. The only thing that holds the play together at all is its mood, which finds periodic expression down through the drama in the daughter's plaintive lamentation: "Life is evil! Men are to be pitied!"

As Strindberg approached old age, isolated, living almost completely within himself, his imagination never ceased working in the most original of manners on the material of life that drifted into his ken. Each of the four Chamber Plays illustrates this, but none more startlingly than *The Spook Sonata*. Never has Strindberg been more bizarre: the stage is not only peopled with ghost-like living human beings, mummies appear in the action, dead men suddenly come to life and walk, living persons turn suddenly into mummies. The characters are caricatured, distorted, twisted into horribly grotesque forms. Though the point of departure for his play is a real-enough situation, Strindberg develops a world of wraiths and monsters in order to give adequate expression to the monomaniac view of human life that possessed him at the time. (p. 43)

Though the view of life expressed in *The Spook Sonata* is substantially the same as that of *The Dream Play*, the former drama is borne by no note of pity, no infinitely sad compassion toward mankind. In *The Spook Sonata* life is not only sad, it is evil to the very core, worthy only of annihilation. Given this view of human life and Strindberg's fantastic imaginative capacities, it is little wonder that *The Spook Sonata* attains the ultimate in bizarre stage effects. One type of expressionistic drama could be carried no farther. . . .

[His] last play, *The Great Highway*, [is] a magnificently conceived, but only in part well executed, autobiographical drama in the manner of *To Damascus*. The play is Strindbergian to the core, reflecting his faults as well as his virtues, giving expression to the petty as well as to the noble strain in his restless, always-searching spirit. In certain of its central monologues *The Great Highway* reaches poetic heights never surpassed, and seldom equalled, in Strindberg's earlier plays; but the drama as a whole reveals a Strindberg in decline, tired and resigned to the dissolution which was creeping in upon him. (p. 44)

Arik Gustafson, in A History of Modern Drama, *edited by Barrett H. Clark and George Freedley (copyright, 1947, by Prentice-Hall, Inc.; reprinted by permission of Prentice-Hall, Englewood Cliffs, New Jersey), Appleton-Century, 1947.*

Among the qualities held in common by the early Strindberg and the late, chief in significance is the intense 'subjectivity' in his art. It was as though he saw the whole of life focused upon himself, as though nothing existed save for the purpose of impinging on his personality. Oppressed by this concept, he continually interpreted events, not in relation to other events, but in relation to things that had happened to him: in his play *After the Fire* the Stranger speaks in the author's name when he declares that

> however life shaped itself, I always became
> aware of connexions and repetitions. I saw
> in one situation the result of another earlier
> one. Or meeting *this* person I was reminded
> of *that* one whom I had met in the past.

The result is that every one of his plays is a kind of reflection of himself: of the purely objective style in dramatic art he is entirely innocent.

Along with this must be noted a peculiar attitude towards reality which, although appearing in an intensified form only among his later plays, is early adumbrated in diverse scenes. For Strindberg material reality does not possess the same significance it did for Ibsen, and this expresses itself both by a greater selectivity and by a tendency to allow appearances, phenomena, to dominate in his plays. Not only is the spiritual of greater consequence to him than the physical, the physical at times almost seems to cease to exist, to prove itself merely a figment of the mind.

A third characteristic is the fact that, while his genius was a forceful one, hardly any other author of equivalent stature has shown himself so strongly and yet fitfully influenced by others as he has. In philosophy he passes under the spell of Buckle, Kierkegaard, and Swedenborg; in art he is swayed by a variety of writers from Byron to Maeterlinck. The consequence of this is twofold: that often two diametrically opposed styles are apparent at one single period of his career, and that that career exhibits a variety far greater than what is usually to be found in the work of a great dramatic author. (pp. 550-51)

Three things in especial Strindberg did. First, in the supreme concentration of the dramas of his middle period, he showed how much even the closely packed realistic plays of Ibsen lacked of essential dramatic economy. Secondly, he came as near as any man towards creating a modern socialtragedy. And, thirdly, in his latest works he achieved what might have seemed the impossible—producing theatrical compositions that in effect are wholly subjective. In the long range of his writings his hands touch now the early romantics, now the realists and naturalists, now the expressionists, now the surrealists, and now the existentialists. There is no author whose range is wider or more provocative. In him the entire history of the stage from 1800 to the present day is epitomized. (p. 562)

> *Allardyce Nicoll, "Strindberg and the Play of the Subconscious," in his* World Drama: From Aeschylus to Anouilh *(reprinted by permission of Harcourt Brace Jovanovich, Inc.), Harcourt, Brace & World, Inc., 1950?, pp. 547-63.*

[What] is radically novel in Strindberg's attitude [is] his conviction that the woman problem is completely unsolvable. Men and women are different, and this means both

that they want different things and that each is determined to dominate. If one could conquer the other, then some sort of peace based on subjugation might be achieved. If either could be as consistently ruthless as he sometimes is willing to be, then he might achieve such a peace. But irrational love, the desire and need of one for the other, makes this impossible. Men and women can neither consistently love nor consistently hate. Each is condemned to a hell of conflict and frustration until one or the other is destroyed. Man is too irrational a creature ever to achieve a rational order even in his personal life.

I must confess that I do not know who first used the phrase "the battle of the sexes." In any event Strindberg is as much responsible as anyone for the popularization of the conception behind the phrase. . . . (p. 30)

The significant fact about Strindberg, however, is not simply that he popularized the assumption that some sort of sex rivalry is inevitable. Not only did he make irreconcilable conflict the central fact in the relation between men and women but also, by analogy, he made it the central fact in the whole problem of the good life. No good life in the classical sense is possible because a good life would demand the resolution of conflicts which can never be resolved. The woman problem is not only basic; it is also typical of the whole human dilemma. (p. 32)

Like Ibsen, Strindberg influenced the form as well as the tone and mood of the drama. . . . [He] at one time thought of himself as a practitioner of Zola's naturalism, and both *Countess Julia* and *The Father* are in a more or less naturalistic form. But as he grew more frantic and apocalyptic he threw off the pseudoscientific, pseudo objectivity of naturalism and developed a visionary subjectivism most typically represented by *The Dream Play,* in which the logic and the mechanisms of the dream state are used to make comments upon human life, with special stress upon its irrationality.

This particular play is generally and probably properly credited with being the precursor of the whole nonrepresentational modern drama, including Italian futurism, post-World War I "expressionism" in Germany, and the experimental theater of the Russian twenties and thirties. Certain of O'Neill's plays, notably *The Hairy Ape,* show its influence and so do many other American experimental plays including Elmer Rice's once famous *The Adding Machine.*

No sort of consistency, however, either of thought or of method is to be expected of Strindberg, who is always violent and extreme. At one period he turns Christian and writes of resignation and Christian piety. But the center, or rather the vortex, to which he tends to return always involves irrational and unresolvable conflict. (pp. 32-3)

His temperament is the believing temperament, not the skeptical one. He changes his mind and goes wholeheartedly from one extreme position to the other. Hence he can write nihilistic plays or he can write Catholic plays. But there is little place for a "nevertheless" in either. The thing that is most original and powerful is what you get when the pendulum swings all the way, as it does in *The Father, The Dream Play,* or, to mention another of the "expressionistic" works, *The Ghost Sonata.*

The last two probably represent most completely the desperation to which he is led by the conviction that man is torn between irreconcilable impulses and that the universe itself puts him on the horns of a dilemma. It is not merely that in both the central characters are frustrated and destroyed, that their hopes and plans are defeated. All the hopes and plans of man must be frustrated because they involve impossible reconciliations, of which the need to reconcile the hatred of man for woman with the desire of one for the other is an example. The only conclusion to be reached is that enunciated by the goddess in *The Dream Play* which is simply, "Men are pitiable creatures." (pp. 33-4)

> *Joseph Wood Krutch, "Strindberg and the Irreconcilable Conflict," in his* "Modernism" in Modern Drama: A Definition and an Estimate *(copyright © 1953 by Joseph Wood Krutch; 1977 by the Trustees of Columbia University in the City of New York), Cornell University Press, 1953, pp. 23-42.*

Unlike Ibsen, Strindberg, who was astonishingly copious, did not confine himself to the Theatre but poured out novels, volumes of autobiography, essays and treatises; and in Sweden he is regarded as a great all-round man of letters, as important outside the drama as he is inside it. . . . [In] the Theatre he is recognised to be one of the rare masters. (pp. 289-90)

He may not have been the solid master builder that Ibsen was, but it could be argued that he possessed, or was possessed by, a more natural genius for the drama. . . . [He] responds at once to the discipline of the Theatre, and is able to appear successfully and severely realistic or creatively experimental in his method, just as he pleases. The strange elements are still there, often casting sinister shadows, but the dramatist himself is masterly, fully in control of whatever the stage demands. . . . What seems a limitation to many writers in the Theatre, the fact that the dramatist cannot speak directly for himself but must devise an action and characters to represent him, steadied and strengthened this writer, who may have been saved from the madhouse by the playhouse. (p. 290)

[That] mysterious borderland between consciousness and the unconscious which Ibsen discovered in his later plays was where Strindberg mainly lived, never entirely leaving it throughout all his angry journeyings. He was an Ibsen with the door off the unconscious, and out of its darkness came the muttering rumours of vast conspiracies against him, the figures of strange persecutors, the sweet-smiling, infinitely seductive, yet terrible image of Woman. . . . Strindberg's idea of women [was] not persons belonging to the opposite sex but angels turning into devils. . . . And in those plays in which he shows us a wife destroying a husband, Strindberg, using a naturalistic method, displays the same almost diabolical ingenuity. (p. 291)

To us outside Sweden, Strindberg seems strongest in the Theatre when he is not in the middle region of his historical and national plays but at one end or the other of his dramatic territory, in the naturalistic technique and apparent realism . . . of *The Father* and *Miss Julie* (that powerful and most subtle little play, in which the class war is superimposed upon the sex war, as it was later at times by D. H. Lawrence), or, at the other extreme, in his final experiments, designed for his own theatre, *The Dream Play* and *The Spook Sonata*. Here . . . we have completely realistic

scenes blended with highly subjective drama, taking place in the inner world of vague associations, premonitions, hopes out of time and fears beyond space, archetypal joys and griefs, and those fateful coincidences that Jung has called 'synchronicity'. . . . In his frantic search for God, down all manner of crazy by-ways, in his angel-demon attitude towards Woman, in his bewildering and unattractive oscillations between monstrous arrogance and self-pity, . . . Strindberg may seem merely a grotesque figure; but in the Theatre, where so many conscientious and respected writers display nothing but minor talent and industry, he has genius: he was—and still is, for we must not imagine we are ahead of him yet—a master. (p. 292)

> *J. B. Priestley, in his* Literature and Western Man *(copyright © 1960 by J. B. Priestley; reprinted by permission of A. D. Peters and Company), Harper & Row, Publishers, Inc., 1960.*

To all appearances, August Strindberg would seem to be the most revolutionary spirit in the theatre of revolt. Actually, that distinction must go to Ibsen, but Strindberg is certainly the most restless and experimental. Perpetually dissatisfied, perpetually reaching after shifting truths, he seems like a latter-day Faust with the unconscious as his laboratory—seeking the miracle of transmutation in the crucible of his tormented intellect. The metaphor is precise, for transmutation—the conversion of existing material into something higher—is the goal of all his activity, whether he works in science, turning base metals into gold, or religious philosophy, turning matter into spirit, or in drama, turning literature into music. His entire career, in fact, is a search for the philosophers' stone of ultimate truth through the testing of varied commitments. In his theatre, where almost every new work is a new departure, he experiments with Byronic poetic plays, Naturalistic tragedies, Boulevard comedies, Maeterlinckian fairy plays, Shakespearean chronicles, Expressionistic dream plays, and Chamber works in sonata form. In his religious and political attitudes, he covers the entire spectrum of belief and unbelief, skirting positivism, atheism, Socialism, Pietism, Catholicism, Hinduism, Buddhism, and Swedenborgian mysticism. In his scientific studies, he ranges from Darwin to the occult, from Naturalism to Supernaturalism, from physics to metaphysics, from chemistry to alchemy. His literary work is one long autobiography. . . . More than any other dramatist who ever lived, Strindberg writes *himself,* and the self he continually exposes is that of alienated modern man, crawling between heaven and earth, desperately trying to pluck some absolutes from a forsaken universe.

Because of his restless Romanticism, and particularly because he initiated an alternative "anti-realistic" theatre in opposition to Ibsenist "realism," Strindberg has generally been regarded as Ibsen's antimask, the nonconformist Bohemian in contrast with the stolid, practical bourgeois. . . . [The] contrast between the two playwrights, while unquestionably strong, has been somewhat overemphasized at the expense of their similarities. As a matter of fact, both are part of the same dramatic movement, sharing certain general traits which have rarely been explored.

Undoubtedly, Strindberg himself is largely to blame for this unfair emphasis, since he had a tendency to define himself *against* Ibsen, and spent most of his career directly or indirectly attacking what he thought to be the older man's themes and forms. (pp. 87-8)

Where do Ibsen and Strindberg join hands in the theatre of revolt? Quite clearly, in their basic artistic attack. Both are essentially autobiographical writers, exorcising their furies by dramatizing their spiritual conflicts; both are subject to a powerful dualism which determines the changing direction of their themes and forms; and both are attracted to the more elemental aspects of human nature. But above all, both are Romantic rebels whose art is the unrelieved expression of their revolt. (p. 90)

Strindberg's early plays—works like *The Freethinker, The Outlaw,* and *Master Olof*—are often strongly reminiscent of Ibsen's *Brand* and *Emperor and Galilean* in their rebellion against God, sometimes even embodying open attacks on God as the author of madness and the father of evil. In the epilogue to *Master Olof,* for example, it is God who maliciously introduces misery into the world ("The creatures who live [on Earth]," He declares, "will believe themselves gods like ourselves, and it will be our pleasure to watch their struggles and vanities"), while it is Lucifer, the rebellious son who, Prometheus-like, tries to bring good to man, and is outlawed for his pains.

Strindberg's identification with Lucifer, rebelling against a mad, merciless, mechanical Will, is quite clear throughout the first phase of his career. In his opposition to established authority, Strindberg also identifies with related figures like Cain, Prometheus, and Ishmael—all rebels against God—willingly, and sometimes rather theatrically, embracing their pain and torment as well. . . . Strindberg's admiration for religious rebels presses him well beyond the usual revolutionary postures to an embrace of Satanism, under the spell of which he practices black arts, worships the occult, and studies the transmigration of souls, pursuits which he considers dangerous and diabolical. (pp. 91-2)

[While] Ibsen's messianism remains consistent, Strindberg's is gradually tempered by his fears of divine revenge from an omnipotent power. Even when he considers himself a freethinking atheist, these fears are never far from the surface. He became an unbeliever, as he declares in *Inferno,* when "the unknown powers let slip their hold on the world, and gave no more sign of life." But when these "unknown powers" do begin to appear to him in the 'nineties, his messianism becomes less and less defiant, until he finally becomes convinced that the powers are personally guiding his destiny, and revealing themselves to him in every material object. (pp. 92-3)

Ibsen continues to reject God; Strindberg wavers between affirmation and negation, finally giving way to a melancholy fatalism which one never finds in Ibsen. For while Ibsen works through to a Greek tragic *form,* his rebellion remains strong and constant. Strindberg finally works through to a Greek tragic *mood,* his rebellion partially dissipated by his effort to accept and understand.

On the other hand, while Ibsen is the more faithful rebel, Strindberg is the more faithful Romantic, for he will make fewer concessions to the world beyond his imagination. It is here, in the comparative degree of their involvement in the world of others, that the essential difference between the two playwrights is exposed, for Ibsen offers a superficial deference to external reality which Strindberg totally refuses. (p. 94)

Classicism is a mode totally alien to Strindberg, even when he seems to be exploiting it. For even the techniques of "Naturalism" are, for him, a springboard for his unabashed Romanticism. Unlike Ibsen, he is unable to test his subjective responses on the objective world because, also unlike Ibsen, he doesn't much believe in the objective world. Anticipating Pirandello, Strindberg works on the assumption that the world beyond his imagination has no fixed form or truth. It becomes "real" only when observed through the subjective eyes of the beholder, and (here he differs somewhat from Pirandello) especially "real" when the beholder has poetic, clairvoyant, or visionary powers. Strindberg's subjective relativism explains why his art always turns inexorably in on himself and his own responses; in a world of elusive truth, only the self has any real validity. Thus, if Ibsen is primarily concerned with self-realization—or blasting avenues of personal freedom through the cramped quarters of modern society—Strindberg is primarily concerned with *self-expression*—or justifying the superiority of the poet's vision in a world without meaning or coherence. Both are Romantic goals and closely allied. But since Strindberg lacks even Ibsen's grudging respect for external reality, he is by far the more self-involved Romantic, one who worships the "cult of the self" (as he puts it in *Inferno*) as "the supreme and ultimate end of existence." In his personal life, this ego-worship often takes the form of severe psychotic delusions in which Strindberg loses his grip on reality altogether; and it robs his art of such Ibsenist virtues as self-discipline, detachment, and dialectical power. But it provides Strindberg with a Dionysian vitality which carries us along in spurts of ecstasy, lyricism, irrationality, cruelty, and despair—and a dramatic technique which, in his early plays, is almost totally free from the need for balance or moderation, and, in his later ones, has almost totally burst the bonds of restraining rules.

Because of his commitment to a subjective art, it is impossible to analyze Strindberg's work without some reference to his life, especially to that dualism which, like Ibsen's, plagued him throughout his career. In Strindberg's case, this dualism was psychological rather than philosophical, and began at the moment of his birth. The child of a tailor's daughter who had seen domestic service, and a *déclassé* shipping agent who claimed to have noble blood, Strindberg was inclined to regard these circumstances as the source of all his later troubles, interpreting them in a manner which is always psychologically revealing, if not always psychologically accurate. In *The Son of a Servant,* for example, Strindberg expressed his conviction that—since he was conceived against his parents' will (i.e., illegitimately)—he was born without a will (i.e., essentially passive and feminine). And since he identified his father and mother with the highest and lowest classes of society, he concluded that this inheritance accounted for his vacillation between peasant servility and aristocratic arrogance. (pp. 94-6)

The consequences of Strindberg's ambivalence towards his father were later to be realized in his ambivalence towards all male authority, notably in his alternating rebellion against and submission to the higher powers. His ambivalence towards his mother had a different effect, determining the shape of his love life and his general attitudes towards women. Like those Romantics described by Mario Praz in *The Romantic Agony,* Strindberg had split his mother in two—the chaste Madonna and the erotic Belle Dame Sans Merci—and, unconsciously recapitulating his early feelings later in life, he vacillated between an intense worship of the female and an even more intense misogyny. Strindberg was himself aware, in more lucid moments, that his misogyny was "only the reverse side of my fearful attraction towards the other sex" (in his early years he had even been a partisan of free love, companionate marriages, and feminism!). Yet, caught in a tight neurotic web, he was never able to transcend his ambivalence, and alternated between regarding women as evil vampires, sucking out his manhood, and virtuous maternal types who gave him the comfort he so sorely craved.

Sometimes he revealed this ambivalence by dividing women into two distinct classes: (1) the "third sex"—composed of emancipated females—whom he detested for their masculinity, infidelity, competitiveness, and unmaternal attitudes, and (2) older, more motherly women (generally sexless). (pp. 96-7)

As for his obsession with female domination, Strindberg's desire for a mother reduced him to a weak and passive dependent, while his intellect rebelled against his childlike state. In short, Strindberg wished to have the purity and passivity of the child and the masculine aggressiveness of the adult. Desiring to dominate and be dominated, seeking *eros* and *agape* in the same woman, he was the victim of contradictory needs which left him in perpetual turmoil and confusion.

I must apologize for this bare Freudian treatment of Strindberg's dualism; but so much of it has been established, or at least suggested, by Strindberg himself that the analysis is essential, especially since the roots of Strindberg's art are so clearly sexual and pathological. In Strindberg's dualism, moreover, we will be able to see the nucleus not only of his sexual problems, but of his various artistic, scientific, religious, and philosophical attitudes as well. For the struggle in Strindberg's mind between the male and the female, the father and the mother, the aristocrat and the servant, spirit and matter, aggressiveness and passivity, is the conflict which determines the direction of his career. If we project Strindberg's dualism onto the whole of his drama, we shall be able to understand his development from Naturalism to Expressionism, from scientific materialism to religion and the supernatural, from a convinced misogynist to a resigned Stoic with compassion for all living things. We shall also understand the changing nature of Strindberg's revolt, for his conversion from messianic prophet to an existential visionary is directly connected with the resolution of Strindberg's conflicts after years of horrible suffering.

The mature writings of Strindberg fall into two well-defined periods, separated by the *Inferno* crisis—a dark night of the soul lasting five or six years, during which Strindberg wrote no dramatic works at all. To his first period (1884-1892) belong works like *The Father, Miss Julie, Creditors, Comrades,* and about nine one-act plays, in which the recurring subject—treated further in the essays, stories, and autobiographical novels written during this period—is the battle between men and women. Almost all of these works are conceived in a Naturalistic style, which is contradicted in execution by a number of non-Naturalistic elements—especially the author's undisguised partisanship of the male character and the masculine position. Strindberg's control of the Naturalistic method is further weakened by his tendency to strip away all extraneous surface details, and sometimes even to sacrifice character consistency and log-

ical action, for the sake of his concentration on the sex war. (pp. 99-100)

Strindberg's readings in Nietzsche must also have confirmed him in his sexual attitudes, for the philosopher shared many of Strindberg's prejudices. . . . (p. 101)

Under this influence (which lasted until the philosopher went mad, and sent Strindberg a letter signed *Nietzche Caesar!*), Strindberg continues to develop a rigorously masculine program, which consists in despising weakness, worshiping the superhuman, and regarding life as a war to the death between master and slave, strong and weak, possessed and dispossessed. Strindberg also shares with Nietzsche an overwheming contempt for Christianity, a religion he declares is fit only for "women, eunuchs, children, and savages." And since he finds Christianity to be a weak and female religion, he begins to reject the softer Christian virtues—like compassion, sympathy, pity, and tenderness—as also suitable only for women.

In their place, Strindberg exalts the hard masculine virtues. The most admirable quality for Strindberg, at this time, is strength—strength of will, strength of intellect, strength of body. Thus, his male characters are often conceived as Nietzschean Supermen, endowed with the courage to live beyond the pale of commonplace bourgeois morality. For Strindberg professes to find a grim pleasure in the tragic quality of human existence and the tough, predatory character of human nature. (pp. 101-02)

As for the Strindberg hero, he may look like a Nietzschean strong man, but he is quite often in danger of being symbolically castrated. For while the author, in his paranoiac fantasies, will identify with the robust heroes of antiquity, his artistic honesty makes him put these fantasies in perspective: his Hercules is often robbed of his club and set to do women's tasks at the distaff. (pp. 102-03)

In all these plays [*The Father, Creditors,* and *Miss Julie*], the antagonist is a woman—more accurately, an emancipated woman—an Omphale who will not rest until she has reversed roles with her Hercules, and assumed his position of authority. The conflict of these plays, therefore, is provided by the opposition of male and female, and the issue is not resolved until one of them has conquered. As a member of the "third sex," the typical Strindberg heroine (Laura, Miss Julie, Berta, Tekla) has a strong masculine streak in her nature too—sometimes even stronger than the man's, for while he occasionally expresses a childlike desire for tenderness, she remains adamant until she feels herself invulnerable. The paradox of this struggle, therefore, is that while the male is physically, and often intellectually, superior to the woman, he frequently falls victim to her "treacherous weakness"; for, in all plays but *Miss Julie,* the heroine lacks honor and decency, pursuing her ends by subtle, invidious, and generally "unconscious" means. Yet, even when Strindberg permits the woman her victory, he feels compelled to demonstrate her basic inferiority. When she competes with the man in a worldly career, as in *Comrades* and *Creditors,* it is only through his help that she succeeds at all; and the man must be brought to realize, as Strindberg was brought to realize, that the sexes cannot coexist on equal terms. (pp. 103-04)

Miss Julie is undoubtedly the closest thing to a Naturalist drama that Strindberg is ever to write. The hero and heroine—as "characterless" as real people—have been provided with an elaborate social-psychological history, and are controlled by their heredity and environment; the action is loose, natural, and compact without being plotty; the dialogue has the aimlessness of real speech; and the acting style, makeup, costumes, settings, and lights have all been designed for a minimum of artificiality.

Yet, despite all these unusual concessions to the "real," *Miss Julie* is not, strictly speaking, a Naturalistic work—partly because of the ballet, mime, and musical interlude Strindberg introduces into the work in the middle, but mostly because the author is constitutionally incapable of Naturalist impartiality. (pp. 113-14)

The Father and *Miss Julie,* twin prayers in Strindberg's worship of the masculine and the finest works of his first phase, are followed within a few years by a profound spiritual crisis, during which Strindberg's last resistance to the feminine and religious aspects of his nature is broken, and after which his art undergoes an emphatic change. Strindberg's harrowing diary of this crisis, *Inferno*—along with *The Road to Damascus,* an autobiographical trilogy written after the crisis was over—documents the history of his artistic, sexual, and religious "conversion." (p. 119)

Of all the works that Strindberg wrote during [his next] period, *A Dream Play* is probably the most typical and the most powerful. To judge from the parallel dreams of Jean and Julie, Strindberg always believed in the significance of the dream life; but here he has converted this conviction into a stunning dramatic technique. Though the "dream play," as a genre, is probably not Strindberg's invention—Calderón, and possibly even Shakespeare in *The Tempest,* anticipated his notion that "life is a dream," while Maeterlinck certainly stimulated his interest in the vague, spiritual forces "behind" life—the form is certainly his own, in which time and space dissolve at the author's bidding and plot is almost totally subordinate to theme. The Dreamer, whose "single consciousness holds away" over the split, doubled, and multiplied characters is, of course, Strindberg himself, who is also present as the Officer, the Lawyer, and the Poet, and, possibly, as Indra's Daughter. As he describes the Dreamer in his preface, "For him there are no secrets, no incongruities, no scruples and no law. He neither condemns nor acquits, but only relates, and since on the whole, there is more pain than pleasure in the dream, a tone of melancholy, and of compassion for all living things, runs through the swaying narrative."

Because of the absence of "secrets," *A Dream Play* is even more self-exploratory than *The Father;* but although a direct revelation of Strindberg's unconscious mind, it is almost entirely free from any personal grievance. For Strindberg, the drama is no longer an act of revenge, but rather a medium for expressing "compassion for all living things." In *A Dream Play* the world is a pestilent congregation of vapors; the miseries of mankind far exceed its pleasures; but, for these very reasons, humans must be pitied and forgiven. The prevailing mood of woe in the work stems from the author's sense of the contradictions of life, some of which are suggested by the Poet in the Fingal's Cave section. (p. 126)

Always ashamed of being human, Strindberg rejected the external world so completely that he often bordered on insanity. But except for his most disordered years, he was usually able to convert pathology into a penetrating, power-ful, and profound drama. This transformation was perhaps his most impressive achievement, for his art was in a constant state of flux, always yielding to the pressures from his unconscious. When he learned to control his misogyny in later years, and soften his resistance to the female principle, he faced life with the quietism of a Buddhist saint, sacrificing his defiant masculinity to the need for waiting, patience, ordeals, and expiation. But though his mood had changed and his spirit was chastened, his quarrel with God was never far from the surface. His rebellious discontent, expressed through a drama of perpetual opposition, had simply found its way into a dissatisfaction with the essence of life itself. (p. 133)

> *Robert Brustein, "August Strindberg," in his* The Theatre of Revolt: An Approach to the Modern Drama *(copyright © 1962, 1963, 1964 by Robert Brustein; reprinted by permission of Little, Brown and Co.), Little, Brown, 1964, pp. 87-134.*

Strindberg's work is, in a sense, overunified and suffers from so urgent a need for coherence that he must incessantly trace and guarantee connections in a way characteristic of the obsessed and fearful mind. (p. 57)

The initial critical difficulty is a product of the very thing we are seeking to demonstrate. It can be stated thus: Strindberg's mind is intricately coherent but it is not balanced. His mental and artistic economy depends on his power to accommodate a phobic fertility of terrifying proportions. He and his characters are constantly threatened. (p. 58)

Strindberg ... sensitively anticipated much of Freud's more systematic explanation of *dream-work,* through condensation, displacement, and secondary elaboration. Strindberg understood these processes and his critics must "read" this same idiom of multiple awareness and be content to trace and retrace inner connections not always in simple logical order. Furthermore, ... the kind of unity that Strindberg seeks is gained at the expense of detachment—his characters are not free to choose, they cannot release their obsessive grip long enough to change, to choose or learn, they lack the illuminating irony and self-humor which is the emotional expression of this missing freedom. His art as a result is often cramped and rhythmically broken. (pp. 58-9)

Strindberg's seemingly most indirect plays are quite direct guilt-fantasies about the rape of innocence necessitated by all forms of masculine assertion. Strindberg could neither avoid these betrayals of innocence nor escape their psychic consequences. . . .

[The] hopeless desire to escape was, characteristically, evident to him, for he knew of his "exile's longing for a lost sunny existence". . . . Strindberg writes a puritan-cum-romantic drama as intense as tragedy and as it were expanding its authentic area of being. His is a tragedy of formal but unavailing redemption. The romantic is literal-minded; he wishes to possess anything he can imagine—hence ideals are not limits or measures, nor are they guides to action for the romantic as they are to non-romantics who see ideals as things to be aspired after but by definition never achieved. Instead, they are literally demanded and sought as possessions. The romantic is a person who believes that any change is degradation—that is, any change of the things he already admires and loves. At the same time, he wants the rest of the world to be brought up to conformity with those rare islands of truth and beauty which he already "possesses" and which in his austere epistemology alone are known and alone exist. There is a radical tension here, and where there is radical tension drama can be made. The romantic vision had to explore itself, for it obviously is shaped by its own dialectical oppositions. Thus, one can commit the genetic fallacy in the study of romantic literature and confuse the first imaginative phase of romanticism with its whole historical development. For the romantic, Strindberg, change *is* degradation, it is a falling away from the Truth, from Privilege, a loss of essential access to the primal place and source. (pp. 59-60)

Furthermore, as a romantic, Strindberg was necessarily opposed to the impositions of the reigning social order, not so much for what these things were in themselves (he is essentially apolitical), but because becoming a citizen of one's historical moment involves surrender of the valid selfhood of the child. Political institutions are the manifest instruments of the changing processes of history as surely as they are its products. They are the agencies of change on the psychological level just as definitely as they are the inhibitors of change on the social and political level. Under this pressure, there is in a man like Strindberg a constant tension between the fierce wish that the past must and shall be ineradicable, so that the "valid" and beautiful first experiences of childhood may be forever preserved untarnished, and the need for forgetfulness, so that the evidence of the active process of self-corruption shall not overwhelm the mind and make for sick remorse and moral failure. Unhappily, of course, the tenacity of memory necessary to hold the "true" moments of past innocence before the mind reinforces fruitless recollection of "sin," "error," and all such deviations from the perfection of technical innocence. Fearing the substitutions of invalid for valid that sublimation requires, Strindberg thus enfeebled his powers of repression and left himself both as a man and as a dramatist incapable of dividing time's unified flow.

This porous relationship to the action of past time has a direct effect on what Strindberg writes about, the way he shapes it, the very style he works in. He never enjoys serenity. Everything important has already happened before his plays begin; the marriage has been consummated; the child has been born; the hatred matured. Original sin is not a concept but a fact for him, as it would be for anyone who restores time to an undivided state. (p. 61)

Most of Strindberg's dramas are petrified *situations,* not *problems* admitting of solution. People find themselves stalled in relationships they can neither control nor abandon. In the primitive sense, they are *fascinated* with each other as Julie and Jean are in *Miss Julie.* Men and women confront each other on an island, literally or figuratively beleaguered, in a state of siege with no extra increment of energy to help them to imagine alternatives. If irony did nothing else it should afford the image of viable alternatives. Yet, these paralyzed situations, unlike the plays of Beckett and Pinter which descend from them, are full of fierce, useless energy. The characters are witty and quick, they think fast, they yoke together images of exotic and domestic things in a ready, plausible fashion. . . .

The precise juncture in human experience which Strindberg repeatedly dramatizes is the point at which passion passes over into despair and spiritual death. And his protagonists have just this kind of desperate alertness until, at last, they can no longer supply the counter-energy to maintain the equilibrium of relationship with another or within their own soul. (p. 62)

Thus, like many obsessed artists, Strindberg is prescribing through his characters not only to the maladies of the species but to himself. There is little evidence, however, that he absorbed anything very useful to himself from his art. The wisdom of his novels and his plays is clearly bought at the most preposterous prices and is the reward of weariness, not self-knowledge. . . . Strindberg's characters see almost everything, but they learn little. More crucially, they suffer terribly, they react to that suffering, and yet they organize no denser view of reality. The Aeschylean maxim, so central to tragic experience, that "we learn by suffering," clearly has little efficiency in Strindberg's world.

This failure to compile an organic body of convinced experience made Strindberg's private existence a manifold and incessant agony. It also throws light on his development of a seminal dramatic art. It is an art rooted on the "mania for sincerity". . . . This mania is complexly rooted and it seems insatiable. The compulsively sincere man wants to avoid being misunderstood, which is to say he wants no strong opinion registered about him or about his actions which contradicts his own. On the other hand, he wants to be understood. This is quite another matter. To be understood demands strong, searching opinions of him and his actions and work or he feels isolated and ignored. Hence, Strindberg and his masculine protagonists constantly force consequences they require but cannot tolerate; they are yearning but defensive, implore truth but resist the honest response. They demand high intelligence in others but are allergic to its expressions. They feel the moment they learn better through criticism, that the criticism is applicable only to a prior, now-corrected self which they disown. Thus, the criticism is no longer relevant, and if it is not relevant to them it is not truly just. This protective mechanism can be detected in Strindberg and his repertoire of hypersensitive victims again and again. (pp. 62-3)

Strindberg takes the objects of experience and sets them forth in a direct manner as if we were first seeing what they are. This suggests a deficiency in mystery and interest, yet these depictions of experience are intensely interesting and even mysterious in the impeccable exactitude of their emotional astigmatism. (p. 65)

Strindberg is the least philosophical of dramatists. There is no real thought going on in his plays. True, he busily collects ideas in the rain forests of late nineteenth-century theosophizing, but they are preserved in his plays only as dead, period decorations, pressed flowers in the already crowded Victorian interiors of his scene. (p. 67)

Strindberg's plays rest on a devastated vision of an absurd, divinely abandoned world. Strindberg seriously believed that we, here, are the dead caught in the illusion of life, and he actively mourned a sense of a *deus absconditus,* felt Nietzschean deprivation in the God who is dead. This feeling makes for a mocking sense of the littleness, impermanence and, above all, the staginess of left-over human action which is the proper imaginative matrix of the Absurd. (pp. 68-9)

[His] dramatic art is one of anticlimax just as his life view, tied as it is to certain romantic axioms about time and value, is one of necessary and constant anticlimax. Things and people *originally have* value and are separated by the process of life from this value. So life is a despoiler of that innocence which is alone valuable. A normal spectrum of values which would counterbalance technical innocence with experience as, say, in Goethe, is not maintained in Strindberg's world, which is a strange, uneasy mixture of the primitive and the sophisticated. Not only was the content of Strindberg's unconscious mind more readily accessible to him than it is to most men, but he was often absorbed into its hectic activity and lived with startling immediacy in a world of contagion, arbitrary collocations of events and meanings, roiling images, and ruinous superstition. It is hard to say with Strindberg where event leaves off and metaphor begins. One feels meanings being gestated and born in his plays, it is almost biologically intimate. It is also why some of his plays are confusing and hard to explain. They mix categories, and Strindberg, normally, lacks any power to create a raisonneur who can subordinate confusion or regulate relationships and readings himself through parable and structure.

Strindberg's plays lack almost wholly the choral, summarizing and reorienting element which from Greek drama onward has been the other half of the turbulent descent into the agon of suffering and risk which we call tragedy. It is not too much to say that Strindberg as a brilliant victim of superstitious reflexes, had no power to coordinate alternate meanings and hence could not create artistic conflict in what we think of as a dramatic fashion. He could depict persecution and advertise consequent suffering, and there is an unmatched monochrome consistency to his representation of fear, decomposition, stalemate, torment, and struggle without outlet. (p. 69)

Tragedy is radically of life. Its roots are there, and tragic is one way life can seem when one is in it.

Strindberg, for all his powers, remarkable and preternaturally acute as they are, lacked above all the power to be in life, to rest there, and to believe in its decorum. Hence he wrote gripping but incomplete plays. They are at once more penetrating and more superficial than other great plays. (p. 70)

> *R. J. Kaufmann, "Strindberg: The Absence of Irony," in* Drama Survey 3 *(copyright © 1964 by the Bolingbroke Society, Inc.), 1964 (and reprinted in* Strindberg: A Collection of Critical Essays, *edited by Otto Reinert, Prentice-Hall, Inc., 1971, pp. 57-70).*

[Strindberg] has meant the renewal of the modern drama, and thereby also, the gradual renewal of the theatre. It is from him and through him that naturalism received the critical blow even though it is also Strindberg who gave naturalism its most intense dramatic works. If one wishes to understand the direction in which the modern theatre is actually striving and the line of development it will probably follow, it is certainly wise to turn to him first of all. (p. 24)

Strindberg's distinctly new creative work in the drama, where he is, more than in any other area, an *imaginative writer,* begins first after he had gone through the religious

crisis out of which he emerges, on the whole, freer of alien influences, entirely absorbed in himself, enclosed in his own suffering and his own shattered, agonizing world. It is as if, confronted by the need of finding expression for these new, complex conditions of the soul where nothing is at rest, where all is unquiet, anguish, a never ceasing vacillation, where feeling is replaced by feeling, faith by doubt, when existence itself and the external world seemed to him to crumble, to dissolve; as if he then no longer found the old form sufficient, but had to press forward, seeking a new one in which all this could be reflected, one which was as restlessly changing and complex as the conditions of the soul which it should make intelligible. (pp. 24-5)

Hereafter, the drama—and the direct, intimate confession —is his true expression. And it is conceivable that it was to be the drama because it is in all respects, his most personal form, his finest tool.

Strindberg himself characterizes *Advent* as "a mysterium." And not only here but also in *To Damascus* there is a mood of the Middle Ages, of Catholicism, and of severe and naïve religiosity which afterward always remains. I do not know if Strindberg specifically had the medieval drama in mind when he created this motif of the passion play to which he returns time and time again. But in the freedom with which the dramatic theme is handled, in the seeming looseness and the apparently fortuitous juxtaposition of the scenes which one feels in reading but which on the stage is not noticed, and in the immediacy anchness of the narration there is much of the medieval drama. But still, quite naturally, everything is entirely new. (pp. 25-6)

In regard to form, he succeeded completely for the first time in making a reality of all that he was profoundly seeking, in the chamber plays, in these extraordinary dramas which open a whole new world to our eyes, as rich in human experience as they are in poetry. (p. 26)

In the presence of these dramas no one can fail to see how insufficient the naturalistic form is and how narrow its limits. For no one can doubt that Strindberg, if he had been forced to develop the themes in *The Spook Sonata, The Pelican,* and *The Black Glove* in one fixed realistic plane, never could have wrung from them that fullness of moving humanity which has made them stand as the most profound and remarkable imaginative writing that he produced. Nor, can anyone doubt that it was just through the new mode of expression which he created that Strindberg was able to speak so directly and openly to us, to touch hidden strings in our consciousness which we perhaps had sensed but whose sound we had never before heard.

One may add that Strindberg is not a great dramatic writer because he found this new form.

But that this form allowed him to show the full magnitude of his greatness.

Strindberg's drama such as it gradually became signifies in all respects revolt and renewal. And one cannot imagine that it will have anything else but a revolutionary effect on modern drama because it so completely destroys the old foundations, creates new ones instead, and so clearly shows a way which leads forward.

Ibsen, who was long the modern writer *par préférence* because he exhaustively plodded through all of the social, sexual, and mental-hygienic ideas and ideals which happened to come up for discussion, merely weighs us down with his perfectly consummated and fixed form, impossible of further development; and besides, only fills, in an admirable way, an unoccupied place which otherwise would have been empty. Strindberg, on the other hand, opens a perspective forward which is stimulating and exciting and allows us a premonition of what lies deepest within us, not because he informs us about what we think or ought to think—for how often do we really share Strindberg's opinions?—but just because in him we find the very disquiet, uncertainty, and faltering pulse of our own day.

A new form has never been created more beautifully or more completely as a result of inner personal compulsion.

And yet, as the form finally appears to us, it is never purely and simply the fruit of personality; innumerable other factors have also had their influence: everything which lives and moves about the writer, all he has seen and experienced, all of the life and time which was granted to him. The *form* never becomes entirely his personal property, but that of his time and perhaps posterity's well. (pp. 27-8)

[It] has been Strindberg's fate—and probably will continue to be for a long time yet—that he is valued first and foremost for his bad qualities, both as a writer and a man. All of his repellent and morbid features were seized upon; these have been regarded as the most interesting. For this best suited modern literature.

Perhaps, however, Strindberg can be viewed more reasonably without therefore losing any of his magnificence or interest. Perhaps one may love the beauty and the value in his work, and understand, but not love, its inferior qualities.

It would then be easier to see entirely without prejudice where he is greatest as an imaginative writer and where he falls short.

The sweeping renewal of the modern drama which Strindberg represents in his later development cannot be explained away. It is a revolt against the old, not a development from it. And it is this, his last achievement, that makes it impossible to circumvent him even if one has entirely different purposes and goals.

Ibsen can be circumvented like a milepost with a Roman numeral on it. But Strindberg is in the middle of the road and one is allowed to pass, only after one first understands him and what he actually signifies. (p. 29)

If the struggle for a new form does not also mean the struggle for a deeper personal view, then for heaven's sake it should be avoided. And if one does not need to understand Strindberg's importance one ought to leave him alone.

All I want to affirm is that Strindberg's newly created dramatic form, despite all its subjectivity, nonetheless corresponds to an artistic instinct in our age. (p. 30)

Foremost may be mentioned the intimate theatre which arose from the drama of Strindberg and whose founding Strindberg himself brought about through his remarkable preface to *Miss Julie.*

"First and last a small stage and a small auditorium" is the demand he makes. And afterward he always holds fast to it, throughout his entire development. His own theatre comes

into existence chiefly to put this idea into practical effect. And here it acquires its most interesting form through the introduction of the so-called "drapery stage." This is the most extreme consequence, and it is better and more sensible than stopping halfway.

But whether this way is, on the whole, the right one is another question. Many of his plays—like much of naturalistic drama in general—could be played to advantage on such a stage. But many, and among them the most important ones, could only lose by it.

The fact cannot be avoided that a small stage implies, first and foremost, reduced possibilities. Such a stage is confined within a small space from beginning to end. When an effect built upon contrasts is necessary it is helpless and can do nothing. It has no possibility of expression through proportions, distance, and antitheses. (pp. 30-1)

The merit surely lies in the fact that in a time of confusion in such matters this theatre really implies a definite style. But in this there lurks a danger for the actor which weighs even heavier and which has already been felt—the danger that instead of enriching his acting skill and liberating his imagination, he is led to *stylize* his presentation, killing his individuality. Stylization is the antithesis of all art, and in our day it is the spectre which threatens everywhere. One need only think of a "stylized" landscape painting hung as a background to give "atmosphere"—as happened in Strindberg's theatre, and which he insisted upon in, to choose an example, the last scene of *The Spook Sonata*—in order to understand what the end would be.

On this point, and for that matter, in his whole attitude toward the theater, in his suspicion of it and his wish to see it changed quite simply into an awe-inspiring pulpit for the playwright, Strindberg is no more than the exponent of his own generation's taste and ought not to be regarded as anything else. It would be unfortunate if his instructions were taken *ad notam.* Unfortunate both for the effect of his own dramas and for later development. (pp. 31-2)

> *Pär Lagerkvist, in his* Modern Theatre: Seven Plays and an Essay, *translated by Thomas R. Buckman (reprinted by permission of the University of Nebraska Press; © 1966 by the University of Nebraska Press), University of Nebraska Press, 1966.*

There is a kind of tragedy which ends with man bare and unaccommodated, exposed to the storm he has himself raised. . . . All primary energy is centred in this isolated creature, who desires and eats and fights alone. . . . And when these isolated persons meet, in what are called relationships, their exchanges are forms of struggle, inevitably.

Tragedy, in this view, is inherent. It is not only that man is frustrated, by others and by society, in his deepest and primary desires. It is also that these desires include destruction and self-destruction. What is called the death-wish is given the status of a general instinct, and its derivatives, in destructiveness and aggression, are seen as essentially normal. The process of living is then a continual struggle and adjustment of the powerful energies making for satisfaction or death. . . .

The work of August Strindberg is the most challenging single example, within this range of tragedy. (p. 106)

For Strindberg, naturalism was primarily an attitude to experience, which determined the substance of his art. Dramatic method followed from the nature of this experience. The principle of selection was quite fairly called 'naturalism', in line with the philosophical rather than the critical uses of this term. Strindberg wrote, for example:

> The naturalist has abolished guilt by abolishing God.
>
> (pp. 109-10)

Strindberg's power as a dramatist is his emphasis on process:

> The psychological process is what chiefly interests the newer generation; our inquisitive souls are not content with seeing a thing happen; they must also know how it happens.

In this sense Strindberg is pre-eminently the dramatist of a dynamic psychology. He is extraordinarily creative in a purely technical way: in the capacity to find new and dynamic forms through which psychological process can be enacted. The merit of this kind of commitment is in any case its particularity: the convincing detail of an actually destructive relationship. Yet it is true of Strindberg, as of so much psychology in our century, that behind the particularity of detail there is a very firm and even rigid body of generalisation and assumption. To show that a particular relationship is destructive can be empirical and dynamic, but the effect is lessened, in any final analysis, when we realise that the relationship follows from an assumed general condition. Nothing whatever has been shown about relationship, and the particularity of detail can be mere embellishment, if the finally governing assumption is a personal isolation in a meaningless world. Relationship is then by definition destructive: not only because isolated beings cannot combine, can only collide and damage each other; but also because the brief experiences of physical union, whether in sexual love or in infancy, are inevitably destructive, breaking or threatening the isolation which is all that is known of individuality. . . . (pp. 111-12)

[In Strindberg's drama the] Lord is the Lord of Heaven, not the Lord of Earth. All created things have been separated from his mercy; only in the lapse back into death can the possibility of mercy reappear. Humanism has quite disappeared, as tragedy has entered the bloodstream. For such a vision of God is the late-mediaeval view that humanism had challenged: of a God separate from His creatures, who while they live are beyond his reach, and who in the act of living create hurt and evil, their energy turning to fever and the flow of desire turning to self-destruction, until death comes to release them.

It would be difficult to overemphasise the persistence of this pattern in twentieth-century literature. It is a characteristic half-world from which God is absent, or is present only in absence, but in which evil and guilt are close and common, not only in particular relationships but as a kind of life-force; an element that is finally recognised below and beyond individual aspirations and beliefs. While this pattern holds, every actually destructive relationship can be brought, as experience, to its support, and we often fail to notice how interpretation and selection are being consciously and unconsciously guided by the conviction of a general truth. Superficially, this literature is empirical, and it is significantly often autobiographical or founded on reported cases. But the kind of warrant this gives has to be set against the presence in such works of the characteristic absolutes, which are held to be empirical or even scientific in character, and which support a determining general pattern. This is normal in any structure of feeling which is powerfully supported by a particular culture. What is called dogma is the dead tissue, of used and separated beliefs. But the real dogma is in the assimilated pressures, the habitual ways of perceiving and acting, which create an experience and then offer reflection as truth.

The line from Strindberg can be traced in a number of ways. In the drama, the significant line is American, through Eugene O'Neill to Tennessee Williams. In England, the clearest example is the work of John Osborne, though here it is joined or entangled with a particular kind of social feeling, which can be superficially related to the liberal tradition. (pp. 114-15)

> *Raymond Williams, in his* Modern Tragedy *(copyright © 1966 by Raymond Williams; with the permission of the publishers, Stanford University Press), Stanford University Press, 1966.*

Strindberg is the artist as neurotic, and criticism must begin by coming to terms with the life and the personality that were both source and subject of one of the most remarkable imaginative achievements in modern literature. We think of him as that other brooding Scandinavian genius, more original than Ibsen, perhaps, but also less accessible—paradoxically so, since of the two Strindberg seems to have had much the shorter "distance between the blood and the ink." It rarely occurs to us to search the reticent Ibsen's conventional public life for the originals of his dramatic fictions, but between us and a clear perception of Strindberg's work stand the thrice-married misogynist, the suspicious and ungrateful friend, the paranoid hater of dogs and lesbians, the frustrated gold-maker, and the receiver of messages from the occult in cloud formations, names of hotels, and crossed twigs in the road. Because Strindberg's real and projected selves are so indistinct, we have until recently had more about Strindberg "the possessed" than about Strindberg "the maker."

Today, the new orthodoxy in Strindberg criticism is that everything that matters about him is present in his writings and that their faithfulness to the outer facts of his life is an issue that can be left for biographers to settle. (pp. 1-2)

But the critic's problem of what to do with Strindberg's biography is not quite so easily disposed of. . . . [A] critic who chooses *not* to disregard the stresses in Strindberg's literary and marital career from which his works erupted is not necessarily failing to mind his proper business. The old conundrum about writers—"Does the life explain the work or the work the life?"—usually poses a false choice. The alternatives are particularly crude in the case of someone like Strindberg, who wrote his life and lived his imagination more fully than just about any other major author we can think of. Among moderns, perhaps only Kafka is an expressionist in the same radical sense. And both, significantly, are writers whose bizarre inscapes have become familiar landscapes of the modern consciousness and whose private nightmares have become common myths.

After Shakespeare's, no playwright's world is so inclusive

as Strindberg's. But while Shakespeare's world is so densely and variously populated and so omnivocal that the playwright himself eludes discovery, over much of Strindberg's there hovers, like some unaccommodated residue of private psychic matter, a monotone of petulance with life. Strindberg lacks Shakespeare's generosity of spirit and his intelligence of imagination. (pp. 2-3)

Since poverty was not the least of Strindberg's many difficulties, he sometimes wrote just for a living. It is striking how often money is a major plot motif in his works. There were, happily, other times when he delighted in the sheer exercise of his creative powers and artistic skills. But there was hardly a single extended period in his productive life when writing was not also a therapeutic effort to sublimate psychic pain. Words for Strindberg could punish and vindicate, conjure and exorcise. No wonder his creativity did not always keep up with his industry. (p. 3)

But next to Leonardo's or Goethe's, Strindberg's achievement over a wide range of intellectual and artistic activity appears less universal than simply versatile—shallow and sometimes silly, and frenetic rather than grand. As a belated polyhistorian he may have been doomed to be an anachronistic failure; already the fragmentation of human knowledge had gone too far. But that does not keep the versatility from being something that Strindberg partisans are more inclined to apologize for than to glory in. He expended his extraordinary gifts indiscriminately on ephemera, esoterica, and personal vendettas and on sublime visionary parables, brutal transcripts of actuality, and lovely childlike legends. One understands why critics have felt both tempted and obliged to turn to the life in order to bring light and shape to the huge, heterogeneous canon—to discover its core and continuity not in the works but in their creator.

But Strindberg was as "characterless" a character as any he ever created—a "soul complex" multiply motivated, a dark chaos past finding out. (p. 4)

He desired nothing more ardently than the bliss of quiet domesticity with wife and children (though his own were not to cry at night and their diapers had to be kept out of his sight), but he could never resolve the traditional dilemma of seeing woman both as madonna and as corrupting temptress and latent prostitute. His wife had to be both sensuous and virginal, motherly and submissive, a housekeeper and a soul companion. That a man and a woman who want nothing more than to live together in love invariably end up torturing one another seemed to him another move in the cruel game "the powers" play with the poor human pawn.

His intellectual development was as volatile as his emotional life, as if ideologies after a while turned as menacing as women and friends. At one time or another, Strindberg occupied just about every political, philosophical, and religious position available to a late-nineteenth century intellectual, sometimes returning to positions he had violently abandoned earlier. (pp. 4-5)

After the stern and joyless pietism of his childhood, he moved in the late 1860s and the 1870s through Unitarianism and Darwinistic agnosticism, arriving at atheism in the late 1880s. The paradoxes of Kierkegaard's pseudonymous personas took him to a moral impasse (he discovered Kierkegaard's religious stage only later). Kant's moral imperatives

left him wondering whether it was he who was stupid or Kant who was muddled. (p. 5)

During the Inferno crisis in the mid-1890s—a nervous breakdown which in Strindberg, characteristically, took the form partly of near-suicidal terror and partly of ecstatic, semimystical epiphanies—he once again changed his ideological furniture, abandoning atheism when the powers began to persecute him. Roman Catholicism attracted him, but he never converted, and he tried theosophy only until he discovered that the leader of the cult was a woman, Mme. Blavatsky. (pp. 5-6)

Strindberg's personal tragedy was that he was forever reaching out for what it is not in the power of life to grant. All he wanted was professional fulfillment, the world's love and respect, sexual passion forever renewable, family happiness, peace of mind, and supernatural reassurance that human existence has meaning. It would never have occurred to him that this way of describing his desires is in any sense funny. There are humor and wit in Strindberg, although mostly of the sardonic sort, but even his self-ironies have a Promethean ring. A lifetime of suffering taught him that his demands on the ultimate were preposterous, but he never learned to reduce them. And yet, for an author who so single-mindedly sought catharsis of his existential discontent, it is remarkable how seldom erring artistic tact betrayed him into whining self-pity.

Strindberg's embarrassing versatility is therefore neither lunatic hubris nor meretricius fickleness responding to literary fashions. As no religious creed and no philosophical system for long could still his metaphysical hunger or mediate between his sense of personal guilt and whatever agent was responsible for burdening him with it, so no single literary form sufficed for the expression of his riven self. Without the mystic's temperament, he had a mystic's impulse toward some single, comprehensive experience of reality, an "*Anschluss mit Jenseits*" ("union with the beyond"), and with all his insecurities, conflicts, and phobias —his whole impossible personality—he still possessed some reservoir of resilience that allowed him to adapt his creativity to his turning quest. (p. 7)

Strindberg's lyrical and satirical nondramatic verse does not translate easily, and its largely occasional nature reduces its interest for non-Swedish readers. For all Strindberg's skill in music and despite the fugue-like form of the chamber plays, the symphonic orchestration of some of his historical and expressionistic plays, and his dramatic use of musical leitmotifs (Beethoven and Mendelssohn in *To Damascus*, Haydn in *Easter*, Bach in *A Dream Play* and *Charles XII*), his verse, including his dramatic verse, is not particularly musical, and only a few of his plays and novels have anything resembling a musical structure.

But even outside of Sweden there is growing recognition of Strindberg's achievement in prose fiction. His range here is hardly less than in drama, and even the most summary comment must do more than recognize the Dickensian quality of Strindberg's eccentrics (he never attempted Dicken's mystifying intrigues) and the influence of Balzac, "the great vizard," whose comprehensive and tolerant objectivity Strindberg himself—rather surprisingly—acknowledged had taught him how to "look at life with both eyes" and to submit to fate's ministrations of bitter medicine. (p. 12)

Strindberg's fiction includes the acid vignettes on the vanity of human wishes for wedded happiness in *Married* and the fevered monologues of a modern Job in the Inferno books, the episodic social and topographical panorama of *The Red Room* and the claustrophobic hallucinations in *The Roofing Feast*. But the variety is not incoherence. Both the robust and sunny peasant realism in *The Natives of Hemsö* and the vicious attacks on thinly disguised real-life models from the contemporary Stockholm intelligentsia in *Black Banners* rise at times to a mode of grotesquerie, hilarious in the former and demonic in the latter. Both *The Natives of Hemsö* and *By the Open Sea* are naturalistic demonstrations of the destruction of exceptional individuals by the ethnic and physical forces of the alien environments they enter and seek to control. (p. 13)

The culminating phase in Strindberg's drama is the period of four years from the spring of 1898 till the spring of 1902 when he wrote eighteen plays, of which all but four or five are major items in his canon and which represent all his four major dramatic genres: realism, history play, expressionism, and lyrical allegory. From the viewpoint of literary history, the Inferno years may be considered a fortunate interlude in Strindberg's life, an apparently sterile but actually highly germinal period that was followed by his astonishing psychological recovery and an equally astonishing burst of dramatic creativity. Criticism can only despair of encompassing in a single descriptive definition an achievement that includes all the great history plays, *To Damascus* and *A Dream Play*, *The Dance of Death*, *Easter*, and *The Bridal Crown*. But even in the apparently most realistic of these plays, *Crime and Crime* and *The Dance of Death*, there is a core action of religious symbolism akin to that in the two modern mystery plays *Advent* and *Easter* and in *The Saga of the Folkungs*, Strindberg's most Shakespearean history. Strindberg's naturalistic world view did not survive the Inferno experience.

The final phase is marked by the four chamber plays he wrote in 1907 (he added a fifth and rather different one in 1909) in order to provide his Intimate Theater in Stockholm with a repertory suitable to its small stage and its limited technical and financial resources. (pp. 15-16)

Strindberg's recurrent dramatic motifs define rather than explain the human situation: the ambiguities of childhood guilt, the uncertainty of identity, sex as the fatal mutual attraction of two hostile species whose struggles serve some mindless life force, vampire figures that drain others of their vitality, endless household drudgery, disgust with physicality, the eternal return of the same sorrows and frustrations, myths of expiation of personal and collective sin. He discovered archetypes in the kitchen and in his own family squabbles and overdrawn bank accounts. He dispensed with traditional patterns of action, because such patterns presupposed stable laws of causality and character continuum. He writes about souls that break under pressures from somewhere out of a dark chaos. Not plot suspense but the thrust of dialogues in which people catechize one another in words resonant with metaphysics accounts for the palpable dramatic intensity of his best plays. (pp. 16-17)

As a theorist of drama, Strindberg is important mainly as the author of the manifesto of naturalistic playmaking and staging with which he prefaced *Miss Julie* and for his advice on theatrical production in his *Open Letters*. Nowhere

does he even begin to formulate a systematic theory of expressionism, and he never uses that term for the kind of drama he is credited with inventing: symbolical, dreamlike in its free and open form, of fluid space and fractured time, and with generic rather than individualized characters. But then he didn't need to; he wrote the plays. (p. 18)

> *Otto Reinert, in his introduction to* Strindberg: A Collection of Critical Essays, *edited by Otto Reinert* (© *1971 by Prentice-Hall, Inc.; reprinted by permission of Prentice-Hall, Inc., Englewood Cliffs, New Jersey), Prentice-Hall, 1971, pp. 1-25.*

For Strindberg a novel dramatic style, a certain fluidity of scenes, combined paradoxically with much condensation of reality, and situations and characters abstracted by symbolization and intensified by distortion became an inner necessity. It became necessary for him to represent states of mind which precluded Aristotelian logic and that both undermined and went beyond realism.

It became imperative for Strindberg to discard realistic drama in order to come closer than realism could to reality —the reality of his tensions and insights; and to leave naturalistic drama behind in order to be natural on the non-Euclidean plane, as it were—the plane of depth psychology, on the one hand, and the plane of spiritual experience, on the other. Romanticism would not satisfy his need for the expression of tensions too exacting for a mere romantic flight into the blue or an easy escape into some medieval landscape of elves, magicians, and knight-errants. Mere symbolism would not do either, except as a secondary decorative detail or shorthand for mystic imaginings. Symbolist moods were bound to be too indistinct and mild for his intense temperament; although the attractiveness of Maeterlinck's poetic artistry brought Strindberg to the verge of imitation in some minor pieces, Strindberg would not content his irascible spirit with "Maeterlinckéd sweetness," as one punster, recalling Milton's "linked sweetness long drawn out," called Maeterlinck's mesmeric mood-poetry.

Allegory was not an alien mode of drama for Strindberg; it influenced his early play *Lucky Per's Journey*. But allegory was too impersonal a form for the expression of "inwardness" and the maneuvering of symbols was too artificial. *Spontaneity,* the constant overflow of powerful emotions, is the essence of Strindberg's latter-day art, which is *compelled,* rather than calculated, art. What we call the expressionist phase of his writing is the form of expression that brought him closest to the source of his feelings in an underground of fears and fancies and ambivalences of love and hate. Strindberg plunged into this underground, which some will call his "unconscious" and others his "preconscious"; and by whatever name it is called, it was a fascinating as well as frightening world that he reached. He emerged from it with enough bizarre material to bewilder and entrance a modern public which could match his personal discoveries with those of modern "metapsychology" and could outstrip his grotesque vision of the world with its own experience of the twentieth century since World War I. (pp. 2-3)

Already in *Lucky Per's Journey*, his first important play, ... Strindberg had reached for an imaginative and comprehensive, rather than a "closed" and narrowly realistic, action. The rapidly moving scenes of this play, which has been described as "a Swedish *Peer Gynt*," afford a kaleidoscopic view of the world, modified by disenchantment. The play, outwardly playful and rather facetious, has the external trappings of romantic fairy-tale comedy, and Strindberg once declared that he had intended it for children only. But the abundance of sardonic imagination in the work contradicts the author's protestation of innocence and shows him to have been striving for the same scattering grapeshot style of dramaturgy that culminates in the fragmented world of *A Dream Play*. By comparison, the naturalistic plays of domestic relations with which he first impressed the world, especially *The Father, Miss Julie,* and *Creditors* . . . , contract the dramatic action in order to intensify it. Yet even in these works we find a comprehensive imagination at work, for the private conflicts become a universal duel of the sexes. In *Miss Julie,* in addition, the war of the sexes is paralleled by a conflict of the classes (the frigid Miss Julie's antagonist is not merely a *man* but her father's *valet*), and this parallel between private and social conflict continues to exercise Strindberg's imagination in the expressionistic plays, even as late as *The Ghost Sonata* . . . , in which the Cook takes all the nourishment out of the food of the masters of the household.

Even in Strindberg's deadly parlor games of domesticity will be found that striving for largeness of reference that made him distinguish in one of his critical pieces between the "little" naturalism he scorned in hack writings and the "big" naturalism to which he aspired. Moreover, he treated these conflicts early and late as conditions of *being* or existence rather than as individual peccadilloes or perversities. They exemplified the ambiguousness of human relationships and the ambivalent nature of the affections. Ultimately, it was human nature itself that caused the rifts between man and woman, while the misery of mankind implicated the nature of the world rather than merely the perversity of an individual. There was no help for being alive in the world, as his latter-day Buddhist leanings taught him half a century before the vogue of the new avant-garde of Beckett and Ionesco in the 1950's. "Use your head, can't you, use your head, you're on earth, there's no cure for that!" says the protagonist Hamm in Samuel Beckett's *Endgame*. Ultimately, it is the "human condition" that Strindberg found burdensome, and it is the World, Existence or the "illusion" of existence, that he rejected out of hand in *A Dream Play*.

There is just one difference, but an extremely significant one, between Strindberg's despairing view of life and the despair of the mid-twentieth-century dramatists: he did not seek "morbid gain" from his negations; he sought *healing* instead. He was not at all willing to accept defeat for the human spirit. The latter-day plays, with the strong exception of his powerful and monstrous sex-duel drama *The Dance of Death,* represent a search for salvation rather than a wallowing in damnation. Strindberg's heart is full, not frozen. And whatever we may think of the ultimate note of faith in his work, the penultimate one of *longing* for faith is a positive quality in the plays and is based on a premise of hopefulness. It is plainly stated in *The Ghost Sonata* when the Student declares his belief that the Liberator is approaching and he prays that the dying Young Lady will awake into a world in which the sun doesn't burn, where friends are pure, and where love is unflawed.

In this one respect Strindberg remained a nineteenth-century man: he treasured a beam of optimism in the Cimmerian night of his world picture; and this is reflected in his poetry, in verbal embellishments that do not altogether escape a certain degree of Victorian sentimentality and decorativeness. This tendency goes counter to the rationalist temper of our day and the bland detachment or matter-of-fact coolness of expression favored by it. (pp. 9-10)

John Gassner, "Strindberg the Expressionist," in Eight Expressionist Plays, *by August Strindberg, translated by Arvid Paulson (reprinted by permission of New York University Press; copyright © 1945, 1957, 1960, 1961, 1963, 1972 by Arvid Paulson), New York University Press, 1972, pp. 1-12.*

Although he was not to "solve" anything, least of all the enigma of his nature, August Strindberg fiercely proposed himself as dilemma and laboratory, making his life a succession of attempts—blind or lucid, apocalyptic or sly—to get hold of his own truth, which he regarded as extreme but still humanly representative, the way all writers in some fashion must. What he succeeded in doing—no writer has ever done it more violently—was to place his nature on exhibition, objectifying its contradictions, confusions, and ambivalences in the most amazingly varied forms. Yet we have to remember that Strindberg was an artist, a being for whom "nature," his own or any other, is as much an invention as a given fact.

Having multiple souls of his own, Strindberg sought alternately to give reign to one of them at the expense of the others, to fix them all in equilibrium, and to escape from all of them at the same time. Like most imaginative writers, he no doubt did this last thing best in his plays and fiction. (pp. 83-4)

He was immensely complex, and trickier than we think, a site of warring faculties and impulses but no simple victim of them; he was tragedian and clown, insurrectionary and quietist, obscurantist and seer. No playwright ever contained in his private and public experience so much of the raw material we think of as "dramatic" and none was ever so histrionic outside the work.

Few can have spread their intellectual and creative energies as widely. . . . But along with his plays (more than sixty of them) Strindberg wrote novels and short stories; poetry; sociological and literary essays; art criticism; historical works; seven books of autobiography; scientific, quasi-scientific, and alchemical studies; and even treatises in such far-flung areas as Scandinavian folklore and Sinology, besides all this being a brilliant, innovative painter. (pp. 84-5)

He considered *A Doll's House* a "scandalous" work and seems seriously to have believed that Ibsen was the ringleader of a feminist conspiracy, one of whose objectives was his own downfall. There is scarcely a significant play of Strindberg's, to say nothing of most of his other writings, that doesn't bristle at some point with sexual hostility or reveal a strange, mystical bitterness toward women.

Yet there is a whole other side to the matter. We know, for one thing, that Strindberg's anti-feminism was in no sense political, that it was accompanied by a conviction, for which he publicly fought, that women had been the victims of legal injustice; in that sense he was at least as much a believer in women's rights as Ibsen. (p. 86)

The connection of sex and writing, and the derogation of the latter as damaging fantasy, are recurrent motifs in Strindberg, indications, if we don't put too much on them, of how difficult he found it to keep separate what we ordinarily do so matter-of-factly; the carnal and the contemplative, daydreaming and formal imagination. In any case, *A Madman's Defense* had been written in a spirit of what he had convinced himself was scientific objectivity, though it was in fact as "literary" as anything he ever wrote. *The Father* appears to have emerged out of the same state of self-deception, although by now very much less complete.

The Father is enshrined now as Strindberg's first "naturalistic" play and, along with *Miss Julie,* the one he wrote soon after it, as one of the masterpieces of the genre. The vicissitudes of that genre come to our attention at this point. It is greatly significant that almost as soon as Strindberg had been identified as one of the leaders of naturalism he hastened to call himself a *nyanaturalist,* a "new" one. It was true that in their contemporary subjects and colloquial manner, their dealing with problematic immediate life, Strindberg's plays (and novels) of this period resembled those of the movement's acknowledged leaders, Zola and Hauptmann chiefly; but the differences were more important.

While the "old" naturalists were drawing upon sociological data and organizing their works according to principles of fidelity to social reality and repudiation of gross theatrical artifice, Strindberg, with a much more naturally histrionic sensibility and a greater access to unconscious and irrational sources, created plays of psychic and spiritual warfare which went far deeper dramatically, at the same time as they were more truly modern. For these reasons "naturalistic" is an inadequate and misleading term to describe his plays of contemporary life.

Above all, what distinguishes Strindberg's effort and achievement in *The Father*—and in *Miss Julie* even more—from those of the naturalists is the presence in them of self, personal existence. As different as their methods were from one another's, Strindberg and Ibsen share the honor of having brought drama back to individual being, to subjectivity and human specificity, after nearly two centuries during which the stage's uses had been almost wholly for the exhibition of archetypes. In these plays of Strindberg's experience is no longer codified, made into a system of emblematic gestures within a universe of accepted, unexamined meanings, but is allowed to issue forth in singular, unruly unexpectedness.

The Father can be said to be a domestic drama, but only in the sense that it takes place within a home and concerns family relationships. The first of Strindberg's plays of marital and sexual torment (its specific characters and setting will be used fifteen years later for his definitive work of this kind, *The Dance of Death*), it exhibits a ferocious struggle for power between a husband and wife, with their daughter as the prize. (pp. 90-1)

Yet the chasm isn't so neatly identified as being between husbands and wives, or even men and women. The wife's chief tactic is to plant doubt in the husband's mind as to whether or not he is actually the child's father. A theme rising directly from Strindberg's obsession with his own legitimacy, its presence in the play moves past that particularity to become a question—as it must have been for

Strindberg all along—of what we might call the legitimacy of existence itself. For *The Father* gives off a sense of terror emanating from something wider and more mysterious than the details of the marital combat, from a region where the absence of any validation of our beings makes itself felt. . . . [The] Captain says of the struggle that "it's like fighting with air, a mock battle with blank cartridges. A real betrayal would have acted as a challenge. But now my thoughts dissolve, my brain grinds emptiness."

The speech reveals Strindberg's deepest anxiety, the metaphysical anguish that lay beneath the clinical facts of his psyche and was the true source of his creative power. For, as is true of the protagonist in this play, it was the opacity of the world, its infliction of a mysterious suffering having to do with the uncertainty of our identities, the divisions in our nature, that so affected him, alternately plunging him into acute depression, inspiring him to demented alchemical raids on existence's secrets, and rousing him to furious megalomanic rebellion. (p. 92)

This is not to say that *The Father* isn't "about" sexual and marital strife; Strindberg is not writing allegory. But it is about these things in much the same way *Hamlet* is about a familial and dynastic situation: these matters constitute the drama's occasion, its means of bodying forth something that will be palpable, actable, capable of being *seen.* Behind the details of event exists the play's true story, which is larger, less explicit, and more permanent than the physical life chosen for its exhibition. The invisible has always to be made known through the visible but is never conterminous with it, and the resulting gap between idea and incarnation is the theater's perennial problem. (pp. 93-4)

Strindberg wrote *Miss Julie* at great speed a year or so after finishing *The Father.* We cannot know the sources of what he had learned about dramaturgy in the interim, or what acts of criticism he might have performed on his previous work, but a leap had taken place. For all its "violent power" and original perception, *The Father* had been structurally and procedurally a rather conventional play, one that adhered fairly closely to theatrical traditions of orderly, accumulating plot and straightforward dialogue. With *Miss Julie* Strindberg's technical means expand, the body of the work becomes more supple and elusive, the dialogue gains a capacity for dangerous surprises, not in terms of its "content" but in the sense of being unpredictably organized, of not following the established theatrical grammar of progressive exchange and interchange. (p. 95)

[Strindberg] embraces the dilemma—the social and sexual antinomies—in a clasp of reconciliation, not factual or "real" but aesthetic. This is to say that while the sexes and the classes may war blindly in actuality and may do so forever, within the work of dramatic art they exist in interpenetration, necessary to each other, illuminating each other, arising as they do from the imagination, whose truths are indivisible.

Therefore, the first thing to see about *Miss Julie* is that the conventional description of it as a duel to the death between "objectively" irreconcilable opponents is false; the play's movement is instead that of a continual confrontation between aspects of the self. . . .

[For] all its accuracy as socio-sexual portraiture, its firm grasp of the observable phenomena of the life of the period, *Miss Julie* is not finally a psychological or sociological document, not a tragedy of contemporary misalliance or inequality. It is not a tale of the wreck of passions and aspirations but an anatomy of them. For all Strindberg's interest in his characters as representatives of determinable social and sexual realms, he is more interested in them as figures in an internal landscape of doubt, ambivalence, insurrection, and submission; his characters confront one another with a despairing sense of otherness, as agents of his own self-division. Such a concern is of a more durable order than that of the clinical gaze upon what is not the self. (pp. 100-01)

Whether they were farces, melodramas, or naturalistic and sober tales, plays for a long time had been images of wholeness, continuity, and coherence, stable little models for the reinforcement of the audience's illusory sense of their own world's fixity. *Miss Julie* establishes a counterworld of discontinuity, fragmentation, and contradiction, not simply as its theme but as its manner. This is the true purpose of the breaking up of the logical patterns of stage dialogue and the introduction into plot of a multiplicity of motives that Strindberg talked about. (p. 101)

Miss Julie was followed over the next three or four years by a number of plays more or less in its vein of *nyanaturalism,* among which perhaps the most durable are *Creditors* and *Playing with Fire*. But then in the early 1890's Strindberg entered on what he called his "inferno" period, a time when he suffered his nearest approach to actual madness. During these three or four years, most of which were spent in Paris, he engaged in attempts to make gold and in other alchemical research, underwent profound if rather cloudy religious and mystical experiences, and wrote only one work of permanent interest—a far-seeing essay in aesthetics called "On the New Arts, or The Risk in Artistic Production"—and nothing whatsoever for the theater. Then in 1897 he emerged with his creative faculties seemingly intact, the first product of this restoration being a new play, *To Damascus,* which was as radical in its relation to the body of existing drama as *Miss Julie* had been ten years before. (pp. 103-04)

On the most immediate level *To Damascus* is a product of the religious experiences Strindberg had had during the inferno period, two chief elements of which had been his excited discovery of his countryman Swedenborg and his intense interest in the Catholic Church. The title refers of course to the journey Saul was making when he underwent the mystical visitation that turned him into Paul. (p. 104)

How then can we account for its importance to modern drama? To begin with, the influence it exerted was actually part of a broader one emanating from an entire genre of Strindberg's late writing for the theater. *To Damascus* is the first of his "dream plays," of which the drama with that title, written in the same year as *To Damascus, Part III,* is the best known. From the works of this genre, which include, for all their special intentions, most of the later "chamber plays" and his last work for the stage, *The Great Highway,* arose a model of a new kind of dramatic procedure. It was not entirely without precedent, but it went beyond into a previously unoccupied imaginative zone. (pp. 105-06)

What was Strindberg actually proposing, or rather telling us he had in hand? The dream plays have sometimes been interpreted as plays written *as though they were dreams,* as

though they had been authored by the unconscious storytelling mind. Yet what Strindberg says is that his play attempts to "reproduce the disconnected but apparently logical *form* of a dream," a very different matter. It is the logic of disconnection, a logic operating outside wakefulness, beyond ordinary processes of intellection, that is decisive here.

It was an internal principle of dramatic construction that had almost no direct antecedents in the theater, although models for it existed in recent poetry and certain types of new fiction. (p. 107)

The structures of the dream plays, while reasonable—logical—in themselves, were therefore not so by the criteria of accepted dramaturgy. Nothing was brought down with a louder crash than the Aristotelian unities of time and place, which had been broken before but not in such a thoroughgoing way. For time and space have disappeared as stable entities. (p. 108)

Along with this dreamlike procedure of having one place give way to another without narrative preparation, Strindberg goes immeasurably further in breaking up the unity and stability of characters than he had done in *Miss Julie.* There his characters had been internally divided, but now they separate out into other characters: the Lady has several guises, none of them adopted as a matter of narrative tactics—she is not impersonating someone else—but in the manner of that dream mechanism whereby a single being is afforded diverse shapes. (pp. 108-09)

Strindberg demonstrated how to borrow the methods of dreaming while keeping authority over their uses. The effect was to release new parts of the self into availability for artistic acts. In one of those apparent cultural coincidences that are really signs of a change in the universal air, Strindberg was finishing *To Damascus* and writing *A Dream Play* at the same time that Sigmund Freud was working on *The Interpretation of Dreams.* Freud always considered that book the keystone of psychoanalytic theory, since, as he said, to possess the secrets of dreaming was to be on "the royal road to the unconscious." And in the unconscious Freud first explored through the investigation of his own dreams he discovered the same things Strindberg had: that there are no "secrets" there, no "incongruities," "no scruples," and no negatives-everything is possible.

The access Strindberg's dramaturgy gave to the unconscious meant that irrational material could now be presented throughout a play, as part of its very texture, instead of being confined as it had been in the past to *irrational characters*-madmen, say, or persons temporarily crazed by passion. Above all, it could be presented without comment or apology; it would not have to undergo a later "correction" into rationality through denouements, happy or not, which emphasized conscious, normative values. It isn't hard to see how from this accession rose the possibility of the surreal and the absurd in the drama of our era. (p. 110)

Many years later, after there was no one left who could testify to what his presence had meant and he had been frozen into one of the narrow legends of modern literature, a countryman, the novelist Pär Lagerkvist, spoke of what had been done to him [see excerpt above]: "It has been Strindberg's fate, and probably will continue to be for a long time yet, that he is valued first and foremost for his bad qualities, both as a writer and a man. All of his repellent and morbid features were seized upon.'' Perhaps so; but there is a counterpressure to that fact, which comes from the continuing presence in living imaginations of the example he gave of creative unrestraint, visionary daring. (p. 115)

> *Richard Gilman, ''Strindberg,'' in his* The Making of Modern Drama: A Study of Büchner, Ibsen, Strindberg, Chekhov, Pirandello, Brecht, Beckett, Handke *(reprinted with the permission of Farrar, Straus & Giroux, Inc.; copyright © 1972, 1973, 1974 by Richard Gilman), Farrar, Straus, 1974, pp. 83-115.*

Dylan Thomas

1914-1953

Anglo-Welsh poet and prose writer. Dylan Thomas, painstakingly careful of his craft and hopelessly careless of his own physical well-being, is probably the greatest lyric poet of his generation. Born in Swansea, Wales, he was educated at the local grammar school where his father was senior English master. Success and its resultant acclaim came early to Thomas; his first volume, *18 Poems,* published when he was only nineteen, was widely noticed and enthusiastically reviewed by several important critics. Subsequent volumes excited greater attention and Thomas was catapulted into the position of public figure, a role that led to his self-destruction. Thomas is essentially a poet whose images are drawn from nature, a poet of celebration, an intensely visual poet. His major poetic themes are limited but elemental—birth, childhood, sex, death. In the last few years of his life he found it difficult to write poetry and turned to prose. *Under Milk Wood,* a play for radio, is generally considered the most distinguished piece of this period. He died of acute alcoholism at the age of thirty-nine while on one of his speaking tours of the United States.

PRINCIPAL WORKS

18 Poems (poetry) 1934
Twenty-five Poems (poetry) 1936
The Map of Love (poetry) 1939
The World I Breathe (prose and poetry) 1939
Portrait of the Artist as a Young Dog (autobiographical
  short stories) 1940
New Poems (poetry) 1943
Deaths and Entrances (poetry) 1946
Twenty-six Poems (poetry) 1950
Collected Poems, 1934-1952 (poetry) 1952
In Country Sleep (poetry) 1952
The Doctor and the Devils (drama) 1953
Quite Early One Morning (prose) 1954
Under Milk Wood (drama) 1954
Adventures in the Skin Trade, and Other Stories (short
  stories) 1955
The Death of the King's Canary [with John Davenport]
  (novel) 1977

[Thomas's] basic device (which Joyce later systematized) is

the invention of words. . . . Dylan Thomas, in writing poetry, is not expressing so much as discovering his feelings. . . . The poet conventionally offers what he knows he has found, but Thomas offers the process of discovery itself. This unfinishedness is regarded by some as an insult to the reader, but in reality it is characteristic, honest, and one of the most attractive aspects of his work.

The invention of words, then, is inevitable in the expression of the half-perceived, incoherent sensations and ideas. (p. 22)

At his best, Thomas reminds us of the Old Testament, James Joyce and Hopkins all at once. It matters little whether he reads them: his language partakes of all three.

In his later poems (since 1936) Thomas has diluted [his] verbal surprises. That his poems still startle our complacency is a proof that his first appeal was not due to mere bogus verbalism. It is well that he is losing some of these habits, which lead to preciousness of the most pompous kind. Not that it is to be despised, for preciousness itself can reveal a wealth of unsuspected fact. All poetry is precious.

I do not agree with a critic who said that there were two types of poems in the 1936 volume, 'sense' and 'nonsense' poems. The poems scarcely differ in method, and are made sensible by the pervading presence of the Bible and sexual symbolism. . . . The fervency of [the Biblical] references is due to the fact that the Bible appears as a cruel and crazy legend, as seen through childish memories of hot-gospelling and the diabolical grimace of the Welsh Bethel. The Biblical element is further confused by a primitive metaphysics, related in the last analysis to a sexual interpretation of the universe. . . . (pp. 23-4)

The philosophy is simple: the universe is sexually dynamic; bird, beast and stone share the same (sexual) life with man (an advance on the pretty pantheism of Wordsworth), but, for-ever conscious of sin, Thomas conveys this as something terrible. . . . Death is present from beginning to end.

The 'horreur de la vie et l'extase de la vie' of Baudelaire are evenly balanced in Dylan Thomas. His universe is dynamic, frighteningly active and alive. . . . Death, not life, is the measure of time. . . . So it is that the life-death problem in Dylan Thomas is as unresolved as the sex-sin problem. (pp. 24-5)

His poems are admittedly subjective, and their structure is remarkably simple. Not only is the 'main moving column' of words present; there is in consequence a strong core of subject round which the imagery is grouped. For this reason, although many people are dismayed by the accumulation of imagery and pseudo-imagery in the poems (for he is a spendthrift poet), the poems are far from being chaotic. Thomas's fundamental simplicity is shown in two of his finest poems, 'The hand that signed the paper felled a city' and 'The force that through the green fuse drives the flower.' These two poems reveal a classical ability to develop fully a simple subject. They alone would prove him a considerable poet. (After painting his complex portrait of Gertrude Stein, Picasso needed all his genius to draw like a child.) (p. 31)

Dylan Thomas's poems are somewhat coarse-grained because of the profusion of imagery, most of it in overtones, grouped round the centre. But in the best poems, as in 'In Memory of Ann Jones', the magnifying habit scores heavily. In more recent poems there is less over-laying, and in 'There was a Saviour' there is evidence of a more refining process of selection. Technically, Dylan Thomas has achieved nothing new. His alliterative and inventive tricks are as old as poetry. His personal rhythms are not unusual when compared with those of Hopkins. He writes with equal ease in fixed and loose forms. His outstanding merit, when compared with the other young poets, is his rich vocabulary, his sensual appreciation of words, his intense persuasive idiom which reveals him as one who is reaching towards all that is most living in our language. (p. 32)

The characteristic tone of his poems is grave and depressing. There is sorrow in his wit, which is grim. This grimness is to be found also in his stories, such as 'The Burning Baby' and 'The School of Witches', where it reaches cruelty.

Dylan Thomas is fundamentally a poet of the feelings, and is not a visual poet. He does not see clearly, and consequently is a cuckoo in the nest of the 'New Verse' observation poets. His main object is to feel clearly, which he has not yet achieved. . . . He seeks the world in himself, and consequently his work is entirely autobiographical.

His future depends on an enlarging of his simple vision of the sexual basis of life, and it is to be hoped that he will not abandon his essential subject. That problem itself, and his evident conflict as to its solution, should provide him with an inexhaustible and vital theme. He is potentially the most modern of the young poets now writing, because of his assimilation of Joyce, Freud and the Bible, and because so far he has rejected the influence of the generation immediately preceding his own. . . . Technically he has little to do save to give his verbal inventions a better grounding in reality and in philology, to concentrate even more on that 'main moving column', and to concede less to that delight in a grimace by which every poet is tempted. (p. 33)

Francis Scarfe, "Dylan Thomas: A Pioneer," in his Auden and After *(reprinted by permission of Routledge & Kegan Paul, Ltd.), George Routledge & Sons, Ltd., 1942 (and reprinted in* A Casebook on Dylan Thomas, *edited by John Malcolm Brinnin, Thomas Y. Crowell Co., Inc., 1960, pp. 21-33).*

One of the most interesting things to watch, in the perpetual backwards-and-forwards evolution of poetry, is the emergence and development, during any given period, of a new fashion—and by fashion one doesn't mean fashion in form so much as fashion in tone. . . . We remember how distinct and strange was Mr. Eliot's voice, in 1911. . . . [It] remains the most *characteristic* voice of the period from 1916 to 1930.

If it was the individual problem which fed and concerned Mr. Eliot . . . Mr. Auden changed the tune and tone in the early thirties by the simple device of social multiplication. Like the sociologists and politicians of the time, Mr. Auden thought in numbers, in plurals; and by objectifying in his verse this preoccupation with classes, groups, units, currents of economic and social change and currents of idea, Mr. Auden found a "voice" which was almost as influential and as readily *received* as Mr. Eliot's. Valedictory, valetudinarian, statistical, latinate, neatly abstract and generalized, its abandoned workings and rusty tramlines began to turn up everywhere, together with the ruined boys, the unnecessary workshops, guides in shorts pursuing flowers, and the short-haired, mad executives. Yes, it was something we all knew about, all right, and Mr. Auden did it brilliantly; but although the influence was useful, in that it expanded the objective of poetry, as against Mr. Eliot's increasing contraction of it (unless we except here *The Waste Land*), the method, as imitated by others and even by himself, became at last somewhat dehydrating. . . . [The] corrective turned out to be, what surely no one had expected, a kind of up-to-date euphuism.

Mr. Dylan Thomas started it: with a natural and strong love of language and of words for their own sake, and of English roots as against Latin, he reacted violently, perhaps too violently, from the fashionable desiccation of diction; and the consequence has been a spate of poetic purple, on all sides, which still shows no signs of abatement. Mr. Thomas's style and speech, nevertheless, like those of his two predecessors, was very much his own, *sui generis:* a fast-moving tide of images, nouns and noun-clusters, free-associational in its direction, but the association that of an imagination with enormous relish and gusto, and sense of color and, kinesthetically, of thrust and texture as well. The question was, however, and remains, whether a method so wholly devoted to the voice and the word, so deliberately given up to sound and fury, or good Elizabethan ranting (for which there is a great deal to be said), can ultimately be directable to more than one kind of poetic effect. Word-magic as a *quality* of poetry is one thing, but poetry as *nothing* but magic—one sees the limitations. . . . The euphuism was already showing signs of self-destruction, both in Mr. Thomas's hands and in those of his many imitators; and his own new book [*New Poems*] is certainly in this regard disappointing. There are good things in it, but they aren't better, as they might be, despite the slackening of the fever and a discernible tendency to more conscious control. (pp. 371-73)

Conrad Aiken, "The New Euphuism," in The New Republic *(reprinted by permission of* The New Republic; © *1944 by The New Republic, Inc.), January 3, 1944 (and reprinted as "Thomas, Dylan," in his* Collected Criticism, *Oxford University Press, 1968, pp. 371-73).*

Mr. Thomas's most recent book, *Deaths and Entrances,* shows, not a theme, not meditation, but simply obsession; —obsession with birth, death, and love, and obsession mainly in a muddle of images with only the frailest ineptitude of structure. Rhyme schemes begin and break. Rhythms start off and falter, into incoherent prose. Image repeats image, in a tautology of meaning. If a poet rhymes, he must twist his rhymes to the exigencies of impulse, or illumination; not, as Mr. Thomas very often does, twist, and so falsify, his illumination to the exigencies of rhyme. And when he determines to keep his purpose, being too unskilful in words, he nearly-rhymes. Near rhymes have their virtue, but only if they come as deliberately as true rhyme, and have, against each other, the proper weight, accent, and length.... Syntactically Mr. Thomas makes wonders of awkwardness; not, one feels, from theory, but because his words are nearly automatic, his words come up bubbling in an automatic muddle.... And like a child, learning to talk, or a journalist, Mr. Thomas deals in the striking, but rootless image, and in the cliché turned—*once below a time, all the sun long, happy as the heart was long —a bad coin in your socket:* word-tumbling without either gravity or point, or point of fun (as when Lewis Carroll writes "Either you or your head must be off, and that in about half no time").

Mr. Thomas does indeed work, as a child works, towards form and coherence.... [His] poetry as near as may be is the poetry of a child, volcanic, and unreasoning, who has seldom read, and little cared for, the poets of his own language, and allowed them little power over his own manipulation—or rather automatism.... The power which these poems appear to exercise over readers does not reside in sense, demonstrably; it does not reside in music, it does not reside in an ordered, musical non-sense. The unit, one realizes, in Mr. Thomas's poetry, is neither poem, nor stanza; it is phrase or line, which by accident suggests the next phrase, or the next line, the solipsist image which suggests the next solipsism; power resides in the novel suggestion, in these massive solipsisms, of the strange, the magical, the profound; and in fact their strangeness is little else than the strangeness of Mr. Thomas, their profundity little beyond the Indian-ink deepness of an individual, their magic little else than what appears to be a black magic. (pp. 119-22)

Mr. Thomas, as I say, cannot help what bubbles into him and bubbles out; but to invest these black magical bubblings, as critics feel them to be, with greatness,—in spite of here and there a fancy, even a "sublime" fancy (though often it is "the sublime dashed in pieces cutting too close with the fiery four-in-hand round the corner of nonsense"), here and there even a poem—to do that deserves many descriptions, of which I will mention only one, that it seems a little out of date. The "new romanticism", of which Mr. Dylan Thomas's poetry is the exemplar, became articulate and "new" some twenty years ago in the hey-day of *Transition;* and as Mr. Wyndham Lewis made plain in attacking *Transition* in *The Diabolical Principle,* it was not new even then. (p. 122)

> Geoffrey Grigson, "How Much Me Now Your Acrobatics Amaze," in his The Harp of Aeolus and Other Essays on Art, Literature and Nature *(reprinted by permission of Geoffrey Grigson), George Routledge & Sons,*

> *Ltd., 1947 (and reprinted in* A Casebook on Dylan Thomas, *edited by John Malcolm Brinnan, Thomas Y. Crowell Co., Inc., 1960, pp. 115-24).*

[Dylan Thomas's] moods of literary mischievousness alternated with phases of a poetic grandeur, as in *The hand that signed the paper,* so that one became temporarily reassured, and hopefully waited for further manifestations of this magnificent clarity.

And that, in any satisfying and final degree, we are still waiting for. (p. xii)

[Because] of his complexity, his unusually startling and fertile flow of images, and his conceptions of other realities, Dylan Thomas has been connected, in the minds of some readers, with the Surrealists whose ideas and work have gained a publicity ... simultaneously with the appearance of his poetry. (p. 31)

Thomas's rhythmic monotony was the result of his early fixation on the iambic pentameter, the most suitable metre for the young writer who wishes to make a grand and dramatic gesture. One of his technical battles has been, throughout the whole of his poetic development, the discovery of a substitute for the pentameter. (p. 45)

[It] is apparent that the poet's theory of creating an image, of letting that image war with another image to produce a third image, and so on, is little more (or less) than a rationalisation of a process which may only be guessed at by the creator of the poem. In actual fact, Thomas's poems seem to proceed by a simple associative mechanism, controlled by his rhythmic scheme and fed by his cultural and verbal habits. Again and again this mechanism takes the same turn, though in different circumstances, leading one to suppose that the poet has a certain almost inflexible stock of verbal habits or responses, which occur unceasingly and with only the slightest variation as he grows older, to whatever initial stimuli his original poetic impulse produces.... To my mind, a more serious fault of Dylan Thomas's early poems is their *diffuseness.* (pp. 46-7)

In all the poetry of Dylan Thomas one may similarly find two ... elements: inquiry, and a terror of fearful expectation.... If there is little joy in the poems of Dylan Thomas, it is because his inquiring, clinical intellect has prohibited it. His probings have laid bare the tumour: his labours "towards some measure of light" have unearthed those things which are antithetical to a joyous lyricism. (p. 65)

The main body of work so far produced by Dylan Thomas is admittedly difficult: its rhetorical violence, individual and personal imagery, and its paradoxes among other things help to make it so.

The writer seems to have grown into his poems, or the poems to have grown round the writer, so that he is unable or unwilling, for the most part, to abnegate his personality, to divorce himself from his work, and, stepping back to explain as impersonally as possible, and having regard to the opinions and experiences of his readers, what he is writing about. (p. 85)

Dylan Thomas, thrown back upon himself, produced a poetry of his own, the startling elements of which had never before been combined in the unity of one man's work.

What was his theme? Not the limited countryside, not post-war depression, not Communism, not the beauty of the mechanical world. It was *Man*. (p. 97)

My own final impression . . . is that Dylan has realised . . . the need for technical development, and the existence of other tones of mind than that of clinical enquiry. But by this recognition does not come the necessary physicking of the poet's over-indulgence in words, a sharpening of his sense of humour (though, as another critic has observed, as a person, Dylan is very humorous), care in his use of old or invented epithets or, what is most important in a writer who intends to write about the grandeur and pathos of living, the ability to be humble without being self-pitying, and strong without being self-righteous. (p. 105)

The period beginning with 1945 seems to indicate a new consciousness of the need for technical progression, for religion and humility, and an unambiguous statement of compassion. But over all it marks Thomas's recognition that man must grow older, must become inevitably separated from young things, and must eventually die.

The adolescent reader might assert that Dylan was never uncertain of that last fact. (p. 110)

It is in [his] seemingly artless reminiscences that Dylan can score so highly over his contemporaries; and it is when he decorates such essentially simple and moving memories with a festoon of verbal turgidity that his admirers become most despondent about him. (p. 115)

Throughout the book . . . [*Deaths and Entrances*] the poet is forcing himself to take a stand . . . even though he is uncertain of the necessity or value of that stand. He is striving with the shapes bred from his own wilderness. And, of course, he is suffering. No man may write well unless he has suffered, and there is that in *Deaths and Entrances* which leads me to believe that the poet has suffered. (pp. 122-23)

It is a poetry of loneliness and fear rather than one of unconquerable endeavour. And there, to my mind, is Thomas's weakness. Another fundamental point of weakness in this latest work lies in the fact that detail and imagery are inadequate to the framework which they are required to occupy. (p. 123)

Is [Dylan Thomas] swindling his readers, asking their tolerance and appreciation of work which is counterfeit and sham? It is true that his nature is such that he wishes to make an impression on his audience, to parade before them a striking personality. But, if he does this legitimately, that is, by *being* such a personality, and by producing such poems as will elucidate this personality, where then is the swindle? The audience knows the sort of thing it is going to be shown: if they like it, well and good; if they don't, then they should go to another playhouse. There can be no question of swindle, though.

Nor do I see anything in Thomas's work which, judged relatively to his own personality, could be called "sham" or "counterfeit". If there is a deficiency in his work, this deficiency grows from a similar deficiency in the poet's personality, I believe. But that work seems to be the sincere expression of his personality, good or ill, and therefore no sham. (p. 130)

He is fond of the *dramatic gesture,* . . . which he habitually produces by a mouthful of fine words. . . . The ability to roll . . . words on his tongue may be an elemental childlike ability . . .; but the gravest charge one may bring is that it is empty rhetoric; a primitive Celtic mechanism, and in no way a deception. Only a court set up in these times of rationing, utility and austerity could condemn a Romantic poet for indulging in the extravagant taste of fine words! (p. 131)

[Dylan irritates] when [he] chooses for himself a difficult way of saying something which is essentially simple, or when, by his music and rhetoric, he magnifies a triviality. He seems naturally apt to make a tremendous pronouncement of something that is essentially commonplace. Just as an intoxicated man might. . . . (p. 133)

Take away Thomas's right to state a simple, fundamental theme, in his own way, and you take away his whole method of working; for this method is based on the statement of an elemental truth in his first stanza, and the restatement of this truth, with appropriate varieties, in each subsequent stanza. That is to say, he states a thesis, and repeats that thesis without development. (pp. 133-34)

I feel that Dylan Thomas is extremely (and unconsciously) ill-balanced; yet, in that unbalance, lies much of his 'charm', and most of his function as a 'Dog among the Fairies'; that is, a cataclysmic force among those poets deadened by traditionalism, or made ineffectual by hypersensitivity. His choking verbalisms, his fixations on certain threadbare or obscure epithets, his inability to resist inorganic alliterations, his wilful obscurity, his deafness to certain obviously poor rhymes, his preponderating rhythmic monotony, his careless use of words, the overstress or understress created by his rhetorical mechanisms, the overemphasised pathos and arrogance, the self-pity, the lack of humour, the poverty of historic background (reflected in his self-sufficiency), all these are evidence, and to spare, of a lack of *maturity*. But, unless such unbalance is known to the poet, it is less than just that he should be called a forger, and his works fakes. (p. 135)

> *Henry Treece, in his* Dylan Thomas: 'Dog Among the Fairies', *Lindsay Drummond Ltd., 1949.*

For all his apparent debt to Donne and Herbert and the English metaphysicals, Thomas is only in the most distorted sense a metaphysical poet himself. He is in fact our most consistently and extravagantly primitive poet, and I mean no dispraise by this just yet. He came to poetry with a natural Eleusinian sense of life, and he has done his best to deepen that sense as the matrix of his poetry. His own poetry is all explicitly in praise of a life-process which bears less relation to Bergson than to Heraclitus or to Empedocles. It is overtly prelogical; in Thomas' process, logical opposites like Being and Not-Being fold naturally into one another; death and life are directly interchangeable terms by virtue of the process which throws them up as merely different specifications of itself. To insist that Thomas *thinks* as, say MacNiece thinks, is to ignore the fact that the language in which Thomas' "thought" is carried on belongs to those fine days before Plato's *Parmenides* when Not-Being still Was. I am not, of course, saying that Thomas "babbles"; he doesn't. But he has anachronized the world back into his process with little concern for the cost. Christ, for instance, is in Thomas no Christian Christ, but amoral and pre-Christian: all Adonis. Moreover, his process is not only prelogical (which doesn't matter in a poet of Thomas' skills) but also premoral (which, I think, does matter).

Put it this way. Thomas' poetry is in praise of Process ("the force that through the green fuse drives the flower"); his typical problem has been the reconciliation of the individual with the process: how can a man have a history or destiny apart from the process, especially when his relation to it is one of making second-order statements about it, like the artist? Up to now, the artist-participant whose vision gives form to the process itself has been Thomas' answer. (pp. 99-100)

It is, for obvious reasons, not altogether easy to come to terms with this Eleusinian apocalypse and its passionate prophet. It has, after all, generated poetry of extraordinary vitality in the hands of a poet who lives it as a matter of faith. And for all its rigorous prelogicality, it is not therefore philosophically invalid. But there are, I think, two major objections, one concerned with the method of its carrying out, and the other concerned with its human cost. To celebrate life means to celebrate its particularities as much as the universal behind them; and given the apparent strength-in-particularity of Thomas' poetry, it is perhaps imprudent to suggest that Thomas is more in love with Process than the small creatures who have to live it. But for all the flurry of creatures, mice, foxes, badgers, etc., who clamber on to Dylan's ark, it seems clear to me that if Thomas is a Franciscan, he is the Francis of symbols, without tenderness. These animals are heraldic; they are not foxes *qua* foxes, but Process-foxes, and what Thomas loves in them is not their individual lives but the smell of the processed fox. (pp. 100-01)

What makes him a magnificent poet, that thudding vitalism in which winds whack and hills bounce, cuts him off from the completion of his poetic and human skills. Thomas is a primitive poet, and the cost of that primitive celebration is the loss of the civilized virtues and the problems of civilized men. The cost is, I think, already taking its toll; at least I find in these late poems [in *Collected Poems*] a renewed belligerency about Life which shows itself in increasing rage and self-disgust, the rage of a man who feels that Morality or a Christian Christ is on the point, despite all his efforts, of getting a foothold in the Process via the back door. A lover's quarrel with Process should be worth watching; not until then will these mysteries be either moralized or civilized. (p. 101)

> *William Arrowsmith, in* The Hudson Review *(copyright © 1953 by The Hudson Review, Inc., 1976 by William Arrowsmith; reprinted by permission), Vol. VI, No. 4, Winter, 1953-54 (and reprinted as "From 'The Wisdom of Poetry'," in* A Casebook on Dylan Thomas, *edited by John Malcolm Brinnin, Thomas Y. Crowell Company, 1960, pp. 99-101).*

[Thomas's prologue to the collected edition of his poems] is a great hail to the natural world, and man as a part of it, and might be taken by the careless reader as an impressionist outpouring of celebratory exclamations:

Huloo, my prowed dove with a flute!
Ahoy, old, sea-legged fox,
Tom tit and Dai mouse!
My ark sings in the sun
At God speeded summer's end
And the flood flowers now.

Yet in fact this spontaneous-seeming poem is a cunningly contrived work in two movements of fifty-one lines each, with the second section rhyming backwards with the first—the first line rhyming with the last, the second with the second last, and so on, the only pair of adjacent lines which rhyme being the fifty-first and the fifty-second. Whether the ear catches this complicated cross rhyming or not, it is part of a cunning pattern of ebb and flow, of movement and counter-movement, which runs through the poem. This single piece of evidence is perhaps enough to prove that, for all the appearance of spontaneity and sometimes of free association that his poems present to some readers, Thomas was a remarkably conscientious craftsman for whom meaning was bound up with pattern and order. No modern poet in English has had a keener sense of form or has handled stanzas and verse paragraphs—whether traditional or original—with more deliberate cunning. It is worth stressing this . . . because there are still some people who talk of Thomas as though he were a writer of an inspired mad rhetoric, of glorious, tumbling, swirling language which fell from his pen in magnificent disorder. He has been held up by some as the antithesis of Eliot and his school, renouncing the cerebral orderliness of the 1920s and the 1930s in favour of a new romanticism, an engaging irresponsibility. On the other hand there are those who discuss his poems as though they are merely texts for exposition, ignoring the rhyme scheme and the complicated verbal and visual patterning to concentrate solely on the intellectual implications of the images. The truth is that Thomas is neither a whirling romantic nor a metaphysical imagist, but a poet who uses pattern and metaphor in a complex craftsmanship in order to create a ritual of celebration. He sees life as a continuous process, sees the workings of biology as a magical transformation producing unity out of identity, identity out of unity, the generations linked with one another and man linked with nature. Again and again in his early poems he seeks to find a poetic ritual for the celebration of this identity. . . . (pp. 51-2)

He had no desire to be difficult or esoteric. He drew on the Bible and on universal folk themes rather than on obscure late classical writers or Jessie Weston's *From Ritual to Romance*. In *Under Milk Wood* he puts into simple yet powerful and cunning words a day in the life of a Welsh village, with each character rendered in terms of some particular human weakness or folly. Unlike Eliot, Thomas accepted man as he was: he had a relish for humanity. By the end of his life he had learned to be both poetically honest and poetically simple—a difficult combination, especially in our time. . . .

Was he a great poet? Against him it can be argued that his range was severely limited, that (in his earlier poems) he overdid a handful of images and phrases to the point almost of parodying himself, that many of his poems are clotted with an excess of parallel-seeking metaphors. I doubt if he wrote a dozen really first-rate poems; these would include, among those not hitherto mentioned here, 'In the White Giant's Thigh' and 'In Country Sleep'. In his favour it can be claimed that at his best he is magnificent, as well as original in tone and technique, and that he was growing in poetic stature to the last. Perhaps the question is, in the most literal sense, academic. It is enough that he wrote some poems that the world will not willingly let die. (pp. 60-1)

> David Daiches, "The Poetry of Dylan Thomas" (originally published in The English Journal, October, 1954), in his Literary Essays (© 1956 by David Daiches), Oliver & Boyd, 1967, pp. 50-61.

Call him what you will, tragic poet, bard, poet of sublimity; the point is that [Thomas's] proper character is a lofty, a heroic one. You will look in vain in his poetry for wit, elegance, polish, and all the graces which makes us preserve many a lesser poet—graces which, indeed, can be found in his own prose. You will find anger, but it will be no common anger, but the wrath of Achilles. You will find despair, but it is the despair of Philoctetes. So with everything he feels. Compare "A Refusal to Mourn" or "Ceremony After a Fire Raid" or "After the Funeral" with John Crowe Ransom's "Bells for John Whiteside's Daughter" or Walter de la Mare's "Sunk Lyonesse," and it will be manifest to you that Thomas never achieves, indeed never attempts, certain ranges of emotion.

Although he comes through love to his faith, we never see him, in the poems, really thinking how others think or feel; they exist simply as objects of his own emotion. In his poetry he is capable of immense emotion for another; but he cannot stand in another's skin. As we read him, we are shaken by what he feels for another, not by the sufferings and the feelings of that other. . . . I have remarked, indeed argued, that Thomas' imagination could transport him anywhere, through all space and all time; but it is also true that, wherever it takes him, he sees nothing but himself. He can enter into worm and animal, but he will look out through his own eyes. He can create worlds; but he creates his worlds in his own image, and remains the center of his own thought and feeling. He is not a Dante, a Chaucer, a Shakespeare, or a Browning, who stood inside the men they made; he is a Keats, a Byron, a Yeats, or an Eliot.

These two limitations—his restriction to certain ranges of emotion and his restriction to one character—must not be taken too seriously, for they amount to this: that he was a lyric poet of the lofty kind. But also they cannot be disregarded; a poet so restricted must either aim at and achieve the sublime, or he fails. When the conception underlying his poem is a powerful and lofty one, and controls all the devices of his poem, Thomas is magnificent; when the conception is trivial, or when his treatment of it does not sufficiently manifest it, he is utterly disappointing. . . . [When] the high conception is wanting, energy becomes violence and noise, the tragic passions become the melodramatic or the morbid, ecstasy becomes hysteria, and the high style becomes obscure bombast. (pp. 74-5)

> Elder Olson, "The Nature of Poetry," in The Poetry of Dylan Thomas (© 1954 by The University of Chicago), University of Chicago Press, 1954 (and reprinted in A Casebook on Dylan Thomas, edited by John Malcolm Brinnin, Thomas Y. Crowell Company, 1960, pp. 72-9).

When he was not catching queer fish in the stream of the unconscious, Thomas was singing the praises of the instinctive life. His finest poems are those in which he conveys a feeling of man's co-existence with nature. His radio play *Under Milk Wood* describes the life of a Welsh fishing village from sunrise to nightfall, and his characters, brilliant and authentic though they are, never come out of the dream state of unconscious existence. Life proceeds guided by the rhythm of the rising and setting of the sun, and not one of the inhabitants of the village is able, by an act of will, to assert man's autonomous existence, his independence of nature. Nature, the mother of all, broods over all the poems Thomas wrote, and shelters man with her dark wing. In a note to his *Collected Poems* Thomas said that they were written "for the love of Man". No doubt they were, but Man is as variously interpreted a word as God. Man, in fact, is not present in Dylan Thomas's poetry. The lusting blood, the dreaming unconscious mind are present; but man the creator, the being fully conscious of his high destiny, is an alien figure. (pp. 77-8)

The legend of "fierce, fine and foolish Thomas, poet, roisterer and lover of mankind," as one popular journalist described him, is a falsification of the facts for it ignores an important aspect of the man's character—his weakness. . . . Dylan Thomas's finest poems are a triumph over his native weakness of character. He himself has told how he had to labour over them to give them such permanence as they may possess. In such a way he created some half-dozen perfect and immortal poems—an achievement sufficient to absolve any man. . . . He was a poet of faith, and it is in those simple but subtly-wrought poems in which he affirms his faith that he is at his best. Faith came easily to him, but it did not come often; at least the passionate faith that gave birth to *Poem in October, A Winter's Tale, Fern Hill*, and *A Refusal to Mourn the Death, by Fire, of a Child in London*, was the exception rather than the rule with him. It was a transfigured Dylan Thomas who wrote these poems, quite a different man from the legendary figure, who, though he would not be dictated to by men or the institutions of men, was nevertheless a slave to his instincts and suffered from that indetermination which is characteristic of his brilliant race. (p. 80)

Dylan Thomas's god had little in common with the God of the Christians. He demanded no sacrifice of man. No particular effort of will was required in order to attain to the condition of unity with him. Only a complete absorption in the life of the senses. . . . (p. 81)

If we say that Dylan Thomas was wholly preoccupied with sex we are in danger of giving the wrong impression that he was an erotic poet. He was in fact far less erotic than D. H. Lawrence. His attitude to sex, in his poetry at any rate, was almost clinical. Sex was for him the overwhelming mystery. Without it no living thing could overcome its separateness; by it all things were made as one. Whereas the pantheist normally sees God in all things, Thomas saw sex in all things. In fact sex, together with the processes analogous to it in the natural world, was Dylan Thomas's god. The sexual act between man and woman was therefore invested with a grave significance. The act that created life was symbolical of the moment of death; for death was the entry into the womb of the universe, and as man and woman surrender their separate identities at the moment of union, so does man give up his identity when submerged by death. (p. 83)

The implication in his poetry seems to be that man fulfils his function in this life at those moments when he absorbs himself in nature and thus returns to the state of pristine unconsciousness.

Death is one of the major themes in Dylan Thomas's poetry. (p. 84)

Equally important as, and in a way complementary to, the theme of death, there runs through Dylan Thomas's poetry another theme: that of pre-natal life. Coupled with the genesis theme it was predominant in *18 Poems*. It is perhaps expressed most clearly in the poem *Before I knocked and flesh let enter*, where the condition of pre-natal life is described in terms similar to those used when he speaks of life after death. (p. 86)

When he was not probing into the unconscious he became what he really was: a bard in the old sense of the word, a descendant of Chaucer or Villon or of his own great mediaeval compatriot Dafydd Ap Gwilyn. His lack of interest in metaphysical issues was responsible at once for his limitations and for his greatness. His simple vision invested his poems with a certain grandeur and enabled him to divine what Hopkins called "the freshness deep down things." (p. 87)

Throughout his first two books of poems the themes of time's irrevocable passage and death's inexorable approach constantly recur. It was this fear of death which kept him bound to Christianity, even though he longed to move away from it.... [His] attitude to death gradually changed, and as it did so he moved further away from the Christian attitude to life, which he could never find congenial, and became more confirmed in his pantheism. (p. 89)

Thomas wrote always out of a sense of delight. Sometimes it was only delight in the sound of words, as in much of his obscurer poetry where we often feel that he has sacrificed sense to sound; in his best poems it was delight in nature and in his own feeling of identity with it that inspired him; in his dramatic writings it was delight in human character and in his own irrepressible sense of humour. Delight abounds in his writings and humbles the critic who might approach him too academically.... And whatever criticism may be levelled against him there will always remain something quite beyond criticism: the perfection of *Fern Hill* and *Poem in October* and the assured mastery of poetic craftsmanship which he revealed in writing *A Winter's Tale* and *In Country Sleep.* (pp. 91-2)

Stuart Holroyd, "Dylan Thomas and the Religion of the Instinctive Life," in his Emergence from Chaos *(copyright © 1957 by Stuart Holroyd; reprinted by permission of Houghton Mifflin Company), Houghton, 1957, pp. 77-94.*

[Thomas] is a fine, bold, original and strong poet whose work is marred by two great drawbacks. First, a disastrously limited subject-matter. There are really only three subjects treated: (i) childhood, and the associated topic of what it is like to remember one's childhood; (ii) the viscera; (iii) religion. The first is very well handled, but really nobody could improve on the *Portrait of the Artist as a Young Dog* as saying all that can be said about growing up, and if you add the related group of verse pieces, chiefly the quasi-Wordsworthian *Poem in October*, you really find that there

is nothing left to do. The second, the viscera, is of course an important subject, and the early poems with their obsessive concern with anatomy and crude physical sensation are fine and valuable poems, but here again you can say the last word, and say it pretty quickly. Thomas has added almost no good love poetry to the language, because he always seems to treat sexual love as an affair of glandular secretions and the mingling of fluids, which is only true as far as it goes. The third subject, religion, seems to me Thomas's worst pitch; he never succeeds in making me feel that he is doing more than thumbing a lift from it. Indeed it is only a helpful subject to him in those poems which are content to leave every important matter to be settled by the reader. (p. 69)

[The] second great flaw which keeps Thomas's poetry at a remove from greatness [is] the suspicion (which has, goodness knows, been voiced often enough) that his writing, in the more 'difficult' poems, is quasi-automatic. It is perfectly possible to furnish even his wildest pieces with a 'meaning' (i.e. a paraphrasable content or set of alternative paraphrasable contents), but the gnawing doubt remains as to whether the writer really *cared* whether it meant anything precise or not. (pp. 69-70)

This, by the way, would be the place for a few remarks in contradiction of one of the most obstinate absurdities that bedevil discussion of this poet: the idea, brought up on occasion by his supporters and opponents alike, that he is a divinely inspired simpleton.... [It] is obvious to anyone who reads the poems carefully that Thomas put into them a good deal of ordinary common-or-garden cleverness and capability of the breadwinning, examination-passing type, not a fanciful fourth-dimensional 'poetic' afflatus. This is clear from the very great skill with which he has assimilated his literary influences, the chief of which are, of course, Hopkins and Yeats, though there is a noticeable streak of William Empson.... Thomas is also a brilliant parodist, another sure test of acuteness of the ordinary day-to-day type (no fool ever wrote a successful parody even if, which I doubt, a fool ever wrote a successful poem).

To turn definitely to the credit side, there is, of course, all the obvious—magnificently and overwhelmingly obvious—grandeur, generosity and harmony of these poems. (pp. 70-1)

John Wain, "Dylan Thomas: A Review of His Collected Poems," in his Preliminary Essays *(reprinted by permission of Macmillan & Company, Ltd.), Macmillan, 1957 (and reprinted in* A Casebook on Dylan Thomas, *edited by John Malcolm Brinnin, Thomas Y. Crowell Co., Inc., 1960, pp. 68-71).*

Obsessed and possessed, working in a complicated rapture of language whose stormy play with contraries and opposites made for a texture and tension sensational and immediate on the surface and ambiguous at the center so that despite the great heat one labored for the light—this *sui generis* poetry presaged, it was soon being said, a return to the individual, a new romanticism, in short, all that which the poetry of the early thirties with its brilliant investigations of the diseased body politic had moved away from. But never was poetry less romantic in the usual sense of the word.

Whereas the romantic poet subscribed to a religion and a heroic religion of the self in all its phases, forms, as culture bearer, as sensitive medium, as interpreter of the many modes of feeling and being, as grand brooding figure summing up the many shapes of men, Thomas broke with all that, especially in his first poems, turning to the anatomy not of the self but of its animal other, the body, an animal without soul, nor the possibilities of it entertained save in some ghosted mythic "mothers-eyed" racial-recapitulation seed-of-Adam sense. As D. H. Lawrence said in one of his letters that he was less interested in his characters as members of a class and culture, of given occupations and specific heritages than as psychological constellations, knots of force, hate, love, and chemic impulsions, so Thomas, not writing love poems but sex poems, to coin a phrase, discarded all traditional attitudes, including those of the personal. Lover and beloving are not selves but exchanging forces on a dark field. As parts of this geography of the under-skin tissue and muscle world they are stripped down to their first meaning of meeting.... As other poets wrote of gods, he wrote of God, God's Mary in her grief, and Jack Christ. Treated very freely in the beginning, almost as mere parts of an imaginative order, it is only later that they become symbols and signs for the precarious life of the spirit in a world not found but lost.

One has the feeling that, wild on his own chimeras, Thomas just kept at bay the dreadful gorgons, the frightful adversaries of spirit, reason, and flesh. "What's never known is best." And this by energy combating despair. In any case, his early work, which has been described as baroque, with its proliferation of metaphor from metaphor, partakes always of whirling unrest, wild struggle of material against form in a tension so coiled that motifs seem ever about to break away from the center, to fly out into the chaos of space. That they do not testifies to the organizing powers of concept, wonderfully beleaguered but unifying. All his snails, fish, birds, quayside rails, endowed with dramatizing vitality, go at breakneck speed round the mysterious eye and center of the poem. (pp. 111-12)

In his later poems he foregoes his more gordian complexities; another kind of equilibrium has been found. The less accessible, more arbitrary, more interior world where the conceit, the paradox, the pun, the double play on words, the clashings and forcings waged their action has been exchanged for a more open, exterior world. He abandons some of his masked impersonality, he is less private and more direct.... As in certain poems—I am thinking especially of *Ceremony After a Fire Raid* and *A Refusal to Mourn*—feeling is caught up in so formal a devotion that the language seems to become the language of rite and liturgy, and the poems ceremonial structures, invocations to the tragedy of birth and existence. The power of absolute poetry is that it always sounds like absolute truth.

Thomas has been called a poet of faith and whatever that may precisely mean it remains that he put man back on one of his grandest stages, in the theatre of heaven and damnation, that he saw him as well in his most universal aspects, *not* as dense commuter, tool, and cypher. It also remains that in our urban age of relativity, pessimism and scepticism he wrote of the exuberant powers of the natural world and its capacities to nourish and sustain, and the powers of the human spirit to withstand, in moments at least, its natural adversaries—of the god-like in man by which he may

leap the wall of days, mazes, death, to find transcendence in the vision that, despite time, is timeless. One may call Thomas's faith of praise for essential being his energy before the "tossed blood" of despair that knows "the terrible world my brother". (p. 113)

[*The Collected Poems*] is a voice of marked consistency and identity. A few dominant themes, present from first to last; the words in single poems all working to become one word, such is the drive for unity and compression; because the range of meanings is long, cross-cutting, far-flung, combating, the sense of great pull, from circumference to center. To compare this voice to a nightingale's will not do. It is too original, too complicated. One wants a *rara avis* for comparison, of extraordinary cross-breeding, many-tongued and heaven-diving. But Bird, yes, descanting on its themes as if they had been learned before the Flood.

In a cold dry age Dylan Thomas's poetry spoke and speaks for the holy unholy waters of blessed rage and exultance. This heir to Rimbaud, Blake, Hopkins, the Bible, with his "cinder-nesting columns", his "priest, water", that bring to mind the "temple-haunting martlets" of Shakespeare and "the moving waters at their priestlike task" of Keats, has created the new language of a vision. It is enough to alter the subtle currents of that stream that comes from we know not where, far before, no doubt, the Pierian springs were made known by the Muses. (p. 114)

> *Jean Garrigue, "Dark Is a Way and Light Is a Place," in* Poetry (© *1959 by The Modern Poetry Association; reprinted by permission of the Editor of* Poetry), *May, 1959, pp. 111-14.*

[Thomas] did not dramatize his personal life in his poetry, or build himself up as a 'character.' He did these things in conversation, and in the sketches and short stories, brilliant improvisations, which were fundamentally an extension of his genius for conversation. His poems are exceedingly individual, but they are also impersonal; when he writes about his childhood he is not so much recalling particular experiences as transforming them into a vision of innocence before the Fall. Yet at the same time, he is a concrete rather than a generalizing poet; he does not, like Mr. Auden, take a more or less abstract theme and proceed to relate it, in a detached way, to particularized observations about man and society. Both the appeal and the difficulty of his poetry come from the fact that it is a poetry of unitary response.... [Urgent] contemporary themes of stress, doubt, division in the self, tragic irony and tragic choice, do not enter into Dylan Thomas's poetic world. It is a world quite at one with itself. At the heart of his poetic response to experience there is a baffling simplicity. (pp. 35-6)

[*The Map of Love*] had a great and in many ways unfortunate influence on some of the younger English writers of that time, in particular on the movement called at first the New Apocalypse, and later, when it became a wider and even more shapeless stream of tendency, the New Romanticism. The prose pieces in *The Map of Love* were not at all like the straightforwardly descriptive and narrative, funny and pathetic pieces of *Portrait of the Artist as a Young Dog,* which came out in the following year, 1940. They were much influenced by the belated English interest in the French Surrealist and Dadaist movements.... The prose pieces in *The Map of Love* are not strictly Surrealist—they are too carefully worked over, as to their prose rhythms, and so on—but they have a semi-Surrealist flavour in their superficial incoherence, their reliance on shock tactics, and the cruelty or obscenity, or both, of much of their imagery. They are failures on the whole, artistically, but they have a real interest in relation to the total pattern of Thomas's work. They are his *pièces noires,* the pieces in which he accepts evil: they are one side of a medal of which the other side is Thomas's later celebration of innocence, and the benignity of the Reverend Eli Jenkins [in *Under Milk Wood*]. In writing these pieces, Thomas was grappling with, and apparently succeeded in absorbing and overcoming, what Jungians call the Shadow.

Perhaps because of the comparative failure of these prose pieces, *The Map of Love* was the least popular of Thomas's volumes. . . . Yet it contains some of Thomas's most memorable poems. (pp. 44-5)

[In] tone, in style, in subject-matter Thomas is a much more various, a much less narrowly consistent poet, than people make him out to be. In *Eighteen Poems,* for instance, there is, in the ordinary senses of these words, no human or religious interest; the sonnets, at least, in *Twenty-five Poems* have a remarkable religious interest; and 'After the Funeral' and some other poems in *The Map of Love* have a human interest that is new. . . .

I have been told that some work he did on a documentary film on the bombing raids, which in the end was found too grim for public release, had a profound effect on his imagination; an effect that may partly explain the retreat, in many of his later poems, to the themes of childhood innocence and country peace. Certainly, in these years, Thomas did more and more tend to turn, for the central themes of his poetry, to his Welsh childhood. The same episodes which, in *Portrait of the Artist as a Young Dog,* had provided material for comedy, now, more deeply explored, brought forth a transformation of memory into vision; a vision of a lost paradise regained. (p. 47)

[Seven late poems in *Deaths and Entrances*] have a larger and looser, a more immediately apprehensible rhythmical movement than most of Thomas's earlier work. They do not aim at dark, packed, and concentrated, but at bright, expansive effects. Their landscapes are always partly magical landscapes. (p. 48)

The seven poems ['Poem in October,' 'A Winter's Tale,' 'Fern Hill,' 'In Country Sleep,' 'Over Sir John's Mill,' 'Poem on His Birthday,' 'In the White Giant's Thigh'] . . . are likely to remain Thomas's most popular pieces. But for the special effect he is aiming at in them he has eliminated that quality of cloudy pregnancy which, rightly or wrongly, was for many readers one of the main fascinations of his earlier poems. It is not that these eloquent, sincere, and moving long poems are in any sense shallow; they make us gloriously free of a visionary world; yet there does remain a sense, if the Irishism is permissible, in which the depths are all on the surface. The poems give what they have to give, grandly, at once. One does not go back to them to probe and question. A passion for probing and questioning can, of course, vitiate taste. Yet there will always remain critics . . . to whom these lucid late successes are less 'interesting' than other late poems, more dense and obscure, much less certainly successful but carrying the suggestion that, if they *were* successful, their success might be something higher still.

The quality that Thomas jettisoned in these late, long poems, rightly for his purposes, was a quality of dramatic compression. The title poem of *Deaths and Entrances* is, for instance, almost certainly on the whole a failure: if only for the reason that Thomas does not provide us with clues enough to make us bother about what is happening. (p. 50)

[Although] Thomas's attitude to life was, as he grew older, an increasingly religious, and in a broad sense an increasingly Christian one, he was certainly not a poet, like Mr. Eliot for instance, to whom dry theological and metaphysical speculations were, in themselves, poetically exciting. His world was not a conceptual world and his coherency is not a conceptual coherency. (p. 53)

> *G. S. Fraser, "Dylan Thomas," in his* Vision and Rhetoric, *Faber and Faber Ltd., 1959 (and reprinted in* A Casebook on Dylan Thomas, *edited by John Malcolm Brinnin, Thomas Y. Crowell Company, 1960, pp. 34-58).*

[Dylan Thomas] was exciting because his language was brilliantly rich, gaudy, reverberant and lavishly spent, and he was exciting because, with less apology and more force than any of his contemporaries, he turned the power of his imagination upon the great primary issues of birth, death, sex, and eternity. (p. xi)

As a man, Dylan Thomas was available to anyone on earth. He loved people and gathered them about him with a warmth which, as many of them testify, they do not expect to meet again. As a poet, Dylan Thomas was and is available only to those who regard language and the imagination as divine rights to be continually possessed and repossessed and who regard the art of poetry as a profound source of knowledge. He wanted readers, and though in his lifetime he too often gained merely companions and "ardents," as he termed his star-struck followers, his poems are still an open invitation to all men to share the world he made. (pp. xii-xiii)

Dylan Thomas is an experience. Submission to that experience may result in puzzlement, wonder, love, a widening of horizons, a quicker sense of life as it is lived, or any of a dozen other forms of participation and understanding. (p. xiii)

> *John Malcolm Brinnin, in his introduction to* A Casebook on Dylan Thomas, *edited by John Malcolm Brinnin (copyright © 1960 by Thomas Y. Crowell Company; reprinted by permission of Thomas Y. Crowell Co., Inc.), Crowell, 1960, pp. xi-xiii.*

Touch Thomas' poems wherever one will, there is the madness and the splendor of man. He sought out the truth of sense and imagination and found that "when logics die,/ The secret of the soil grows through the eye." The secrets he revealed through unborn embryos and sacerdotal herons are finally the secrets of mankind itself: "Four elements and five Senses, and man a spirit of love." (p. 193)

> *Leon Edel, "Boily Boy and Bard," in* Opinions and Perspectives from The New York Times Book Review, *edited by Francis Brown (copyright © 1964 by The New York Times Company; reprinted by permission of Houghton Mifflin Company), Houghton, 1964, pp. 189-93.*

[No] major English poet has ever been as Welsh as was Dylan. His instincts were those of a countryman, as is most of his imagery, yet he was happy only by the sea. (p. 63)

One early theme, or set of themes, of which he quite quickly wearied was madness, witchcraft and diabolism in general; he soon recognized this type of morbidity as adolescent and essentially derivative.... His preoccupation with death, however, grew stronger and more profound with the passing years. The subjective basis for this preoccupation—his belief that he had not long to live—was in some ways transcended by his own sort of pantheism, by the identification of himself and his mortal body with all nature:

> The force that through the green fuse drives the flower
> Drives my green age: that blasts the roots of trees
> Is my destroyer.

This famous poem was first written in the summer of 1933, but the concept remains central throughout his work....

Finally, there is what might be loosely called a Freudian synthesis in his poems between the death wish and the urge to procreate, expressed now through one set of images, now another, often through several sets simultaneously, physiological, biblical, even astronomical: death and life cease to be antitheses, but are the yin and the yang of one great, mysterious process that the poet shares through his own body with all nature. Such, in crude oversimplification, was Dylan Thomas' principal contribution to English poetry. (p. 66)

> Constantine Fitzgibbon, "Young Dylan Thomas: The Escape to London" (copyright © 1965, by Constantine Fitzgibbon), in The Atlantic Monthly (copyright © 1965 by The Atlantic Monthly Company, Boston, Mass.; reprinted with permission), October, 1965, pp. 63-70.

From the very first moment of its existence, even in the womb, even when the "seed [is] at-zero," the self, for Dylan Thomas, includes all the cosmos, lives its life and is lived by its life. There is no need to achieve by expansive stratagems of sensation or imagination an identification with all things. That identification is given with existence itself and can never be withdrawn. There is no initial separation between subject and object. The self is not set apart from things or people which are other than itself.... Thomas from the beginning contains in himself the farthest star. He is the center of an adventure which is the total cosmic adventure, and, after the first experience of a birth which is a coming into existence of everything, there is no possibility of adding more to the self. What exists for Thomas as soon as anything exists at all is a single continuous realm which is at once consciousness, body, cosmos, and the words which express all three at once. (pp. 191-92)

The entire expanse of the cosmos, both spatial and temporal, is as close to him and as intimately known as his own body, or as the body of a woman he loves. He is always "in the safe centre of his own identity, the familiar world about him like another flesh".... Thomas' use of the traditional relation of microcosm and macrocosm is more than the manipulation of a metaphor. It is a way of expressing a literal fact in the universe of his poems. To understand and accept this literalness is the key by which his most difficult poems may be unlocked. The contradictory images of his poems are not metaphors or symbols. They describe something as exactly as the poet knows how. . . . Throughout his poetry what might in another poet be asserted as a metaphor or simile is affirmed as literally true. (pp. 192-93)

This overlapping of mind, body, and world means that language which in conventional speech would apply to only one of these realms can be used by Thomas to describe all three simultaneously. (p. 194)

Thomas tries to create structures of words which cannot be understood piece by piece, but only by a single leap which carries the reader into the meaning. . . .

Thomas' language calls attention to itself as language. It is not an instrument which dissolves in its own use, but is its own world. It is not a transparent medium through which the reader sees undistorted an object which remains detached from consciousness. (p. 195)

[The] possession of the world through its spontaneous transformation into images is not dry, cerebral, or abstract. It coincides with the passionate apprehension of things through the senses. The poet penetrates the world, identifies himself with its processes, lives its secret life. (p. 196)

Certain culminating passages in his late poetry are magnificent expressions of a world which is a single activity in the present moment of a thousand separate forms of life, each asserting its distinct violence of existence to make a total "sermon of blood". . . .

The fact that the act of love is the best symbol of the interpenetration of all things in the "linked night" shows the transiency of any instant of the cosmic life. If things can only continue to exist as a process, this means that they can only continue to exist by changing. To live is to burn like a fiery torch through time, but it is possible that the torch may burn out, and it is certainly necessary that new fuel continually be added to the fire. In Thomas' world nothing remains itself for long. (p. 199)

Nothing can endure as itself for more than an instant, and what replaces it is not a modulated form of what filled the previous moment. It is something entirely different, depending not on continuity with what preceded but on its complete annihilation. In order for one instant to come into being there must be a destruction of what existed the moment before, and out of this void the solidity of the new moment comes. (p. 200)

In the end this discontinuity becomes a law of continuity. It is certain that the next instant will have nothing to do with the present one. This fact comes to be experienced as something constant. . . . Time in Thomas' world is an ever-experienced discontinuity. (pp. 201-02)

This elementary town is God. God is an anonymous totality of being. . . . To God distinctions of good and bad, innocent and guilty, are nothing, since he sees all created things in terms of their inevitable return into "the winding dark". (p. 203)

Time and all the things of time must constantly recommence. In describing a world of "endless beginning". . . , Thomas, like Descartes or Malebranche, affirms the old doctrine of continuous creation. The death that obsesses him and undermines his world is not the change of one form of existence into another. It is the perpetual return of all things into the neutrality of God. (p. 204)

Human beings can reach the darkness of the genetic sea in a way which is possible to no other creatures. A man may reach God through the intermediary of another human being. This possibility is explored in all Thomas' poems about love. It is the key to the meaning he gives to sexual experience. (p. 205)

Only a certain kind of poetry will be possible in such a world, so detached is each moment from all the others. . . . The center . . . is the poet's consciousness, but it is also the anonymous darkness, the "god of beginning" out of which all images come. The poet "lets" an image be made in him. It is not a matter of volition or reasoning. These operate only in the construction of the finished poem out of its raw material, or, rather, the poet's will operates in a negative way in the genesis of a poem. He permits the images to come into being within his consciousness. The center is "a host of images," that is, at once the possibility of a vast number of images and the negation of each one, since none is commensurate with its source. The host of images is beyond contradiction. It both contains and denies all the images which may come from it. . . . No image which does not come from the central seed will be the stuff of real poetry, and yet the central seed demands that any poem must be what Picasso once called his paintings: "a horde of destructions." (pp. 206-08)

> *J. Hillis Miller, "Dylan Thomas," in his* Poets of Reality: Six Twentieth-Century Writers *(copyright © 1965 by the President and Fellows of Harvard College; excerpted by permission of the author and publishers), Cambridge, Mass.: Harvard University Press, 1965, pp. 190-216.*

In some instances, Donald Davie declares [in *Articulate Energy*, Thomas] exploits a 'pseudo-syntax'. 'Formally correct, his syntax cannot mime, as it offers to do, a movement of the mind.' Within the context of his argument, which he illustrates with the seventh 'Altarwise by owl-light' sonnet, this is a telling criticism. But by considering the whole vision of the poet, it is possible to grasp the larger intelligibility of his syntactical manoeuvres. Syntax represents order and succession in the sentence, the spatio-temporal design. Since Thomas, in the early poems (basically those published before 1940) generally takes the position of a humanity wronged, 'double-crossed' by the natural order, it might be argued that an attack upon syntax constitutes the appropriate linguistic gesture. He does not, it should be noted, utterly discard syntax as extreme verslibrists have done, but manipulates an inexorable movement to his own ends. If the most pervasive trend in his poetry is to make 'a merry manshape of your walking circle,' to humanize an alien cosmos, then this verbal strategy is consistent, enacting the poet's equivocal relationship to the analogue in reality. In the later poetry, where Thomas has managed to 'Suffer the heaven's children through my heartbeat,' giving time and space a human shape, the problem of pseudo-syntax has, appropriately, evaporated. In 'Fern Hill,' time is the gentle warder, in whose chains the child is permitted to sing; in 'Poem on his birthday' he exultantly sails out to die with the sun blooming and the world spinning 'its morning of praise.'

Thomas may have discovered in the aural euphony of these late poems a kind of supra-syntax, reconciling the subjective flow of images with the inflexible facts of order and succession embodied by normal syntax. In terms of Thomas' vision, the later poetry expresses beatific harmony between man and the stern conditions governing his existence. Certainly their flow of sound and meaning is in sharp contrast to his earlier work, which generates energies that, as Thomas noted, often exceed the limits of single poems and lead in the direction of a corporate meaning. One must ask whether any of Thomas' poems do offer to mime 'a movement of the mind.' Radically romantic in attitude, he is, like Rimbaud, devoted to the mind as renovator rather than recorder of mental reality. Since syntax represents in language the mundane order, it is here that poetic alterations must be made, and new movements undertaken.

Thomas . . . is concerned to develop a mythology of mankind. This is like the myth of Prometheus in the sense that he is striving to acquire fresh powers for man, but the Promethean defiance expressed in such poems as 'I see the boys of summer' ('But seasons must be challenged or they totter/Into a chiming quarter') grows into the reconciliation noted in the later poems, a reconciliation reaching the intensity of epiphany in such poems as 'Vision and Prayer.' The energy of his poems is intrinsically more complex, too, than the simple gift of light and heat. Like fire in the myth of Meleager, it consumes the self that expresses it: 'The force that through the green fuse drives the flower . . . is my destroyer.' Thomas' allusion to Meleager in the second 'Altarwise by owl-light' sonnet affirms [the] paradoxical identity of creative and destructive powers within the context of the individual life. . . . In the sonnets, and indeed in Thomas's poetry as a whole, this relationship prevails: the child's rise entails the parents' decline as surely as one bicycle pedal requires a complement. (pp. 57-8)

The techniques generating energy in Thomas' poetry can all be traced back to the primal force, sometimes abstractly construed as time, as it is resisted, accepted or converted by man. (p. 61)

> *D. F. McKay, in* Critical Quarterly, *Spring, 1974.*

In Dylan Thomas' play for voices, *Under Milk Wood*, the radio-program format eliminates many standard dramatic devices. The effect depends on the evocative power of the language, which must replace scenery, costumes, and lighting in delineation of roles and definition of setting. . . . [The] patterns established by the different voices—individual themes and tones, and their contributions to central ideas—are of the utmost importance. (p. 74)

The language used by First Voice . . . is appropriate to his role as shaping artist. The syntax is that of a conscious, lucid speaker; for he, with the audience, regards the operations of the dreaming unconscious from a conscious perspective. Though he uses long complex sentences with accumulations of modifiers and metaphors, yet there is a sentence structure, with a subject-verb basis, which is lacking in some of the speeches of other voices. His metaphors also operate on the conscious level, often denoting qualities that are logically appropriate to the subject because of its appearance, situation, or use. (pp. 75-6)

Second Voice's language seems to spring from unconscious sources more than First Voice's, and the syntax of his speeches is one indication of this difference. Second Voice speaks in long phrases or sentences with little internal punctuation, and he repeatedly fails to supply the subject-verb basis, leaving that to artist First Voice. . . .

However, the real difference between the two narrators is not so much rhythmical or syntactical (since part of the appeal of shaped rhythm is to the unconscious) as logical. Their uses of language have different bases. Even First Voice's allusions to the sexual element in dreams ("organ-playing wood," "bucking ranches," "jollyrodgered sea") are essentially wordplay, homonyms and dual meanings depending on the shape and sound of words. In contrast, Second Voice employs words almost solely as indicators of meaning; and their referents are completely contained in the world of dreams. His language consists largely of archetypal images springing from the collective unconscious (the sea, the phallic trout); and these images appear through processes of transmutation and metamorphosis rather than through intellectual comparison. His words are representations of realities perceived directly by the unconscious mind, not substantive objects in themselves. (p. 78)

[The] voices of *Under Milk Wood* form a complex pattern of tones, attitudes, and levels of awareness. The dramatic record of the struggle for understanding works through many individual situations, and each character reveals his own struggle in a personalized vocabulary, made up of variations on a common colloquial pattern. Second Voice's mythic language speaks for the element common to all these visions. But First Voice works with both particular and universal aspects of the struggle, leading the audience through the "rhythmic, inevitably narrative" structure that he imposes to a whole view synthesizing specific and general, external and internal, elements. In his role as shaping artist, he works with description, statement, metaphor, and wordplay to present a unified vision of the human struggle to see, to understand, and to love. (p. 88)

> *Cynthia Davis, "The Voices of 'Under Milk Wood'," in* Criticism *(reprinted by permission of the Wayne State University Press; copyright 1975 by Wayne State University Press), Vol. XVII, No. 1 (Winter, 1975), pp. 74-89.*

Thomas was the first modern romantic you could put your finger on, the first whose journeys and itineraries became part of his own mythology, the first who offered himself up as a public, not a private, sacrifice. Hence the piercing sacrificial note in his poetry, the uncontainable voice, the drifting, almost ectoplasmic character of the man, the desperate clinging to a few drifting spars of literary convention. Hence, too, the universal acclaim for his lyricism, and the mistaken desire to make him an heir to Bohemia or to the high Symbolist tradition.

Writers said of Thomas that he was the greatest lyricist of our time. The saying became a platitude. It was unquestionably true, but what did the word mean? It meant that, in contrast to the epic pretensions of many of the leading modern poets, he was the only one who could be called a singer. To call him the best lyric poet of our time was to pay him the highest, the only compliment. Nearly everyone paid him this splendid compliment and everyone knew its implications. Few realized, however, that this compliment marked a turning point in poetry. (p. 141)

Thomas is in somewhat the relation to modern poetry that Hopkins was to the Victorians—a lone wolf. Thomas resisted the literary traditionalism of the Eliot school; he wanted no part of it. Poetry to him was not a civilizing

maneuver, a replanting of the gardens; it was a holocaust, a sowing of the wind. (p. 142)

Thomas' technique is deceptive. When you look at it casually you think it is nothing. The meter is banal. It is no better and no worse than that of dozens of other poets his age. There is no invention and a great deal of imitation. There is no theory. But despite his lack of originality, the impress of Thomas' idiom on present-day English poetry is incalculable. (p. 143)

It is hard to locate the distinctiveness of Thomas' idiom. There are a few tricks of word order, a way of using a sentence, a characteristic vocabulary, an obsessive repetition of phrase, and so on—things common to many lesser poets. Again, if we scrutinize his images and metaphors, which are much more impressive than the things I have mentioned, we frequently find overdevelopment, blowziness, and euphemism, on the one hand, and brilliant crystallization on the other. But no system, no poetic, no practice that adds up to anything you can hold on to. The more you examine him as a stylist the less you find.

What does this mean? It means that Thomas is a quite derivative, unoriginal, *unintellectual* poet, the entire force of whose personality and vitality is jammed into his few difficult half-intelligible poems. To talk about Thomas as a Symbolist is dishonest. Once in Hollywood Aldous Huxley introduced a Stravinsky composition based on a poem of Thomas'. Huxley quoted that line of Mallarmé's which says that poets purify the dialect of the tribe. This, said Huxley, was what Thomas did. Now anybody who has read Thomas knows that he did the exact opposite: Thomas did everything in his power to obscure the dialect of the tribe—whatever that high-and-mighty expression may mean. Thomas sometimes attempted to keep people from understanding his poems (which are frequently simple, once you know the dodges). He had a horror of simplicity—or what I consider to be a fear of it. He knew little except what a man knows who has lived about forty years, and there was little he wanted to know. There is a fatal pessimism in most of his poems, offset by a few bursts of joy and exuberance. The main symbol is masculine love, driven as hard as Freud drove it. In the background is God, hard to identify but always there, a kind of God who belongs to one's parents rather than to the children, who do not quite accept Him. (pp. 144-45)

Thomas, with no equipment for theorizing about the forms of nature, sought the "forms" that Hopkins did. The chief difference between the two poets in terms of their symbols is that Hopkins draws his symbology almost entirely from the God-symbol. God, in various attributes, is the chief process in Hopkins' view of the world. Sex is the chief process in Thomas' view of the world.

Thomas' idea of process is important. The term itself is rather mechanistic, as he uses it. He always takes the machine of energy rather than some abstraction, such as spirit or essence. Hence the concreteness of his words and images; obscurity occurs also because of the "process" of mixing the imagery of the subconscious with biological imagery, as in Hopkins. But there is also a deliberate attempt to involve the subconscious as the main process: Thomas' imagination, which is sometimes fantastic, works hard to dredge up the images of fantasy and dreams. Very often the process fails and we are left with heaps of grotesque images that add up to nothing. I would equate the process in Thomas' poetics with his rather startling views of the sexual process. Aside from those poems in which sex is simply sung, much as poets used to write what are called love poems, there are those poems in which sex is used as the instrument of belief and knowledge. Using the cliché of modern literature that everyone is sick and the whole world is a hospital, Thomas wants to imply that sex will make us (or usually just him) healthy and whole again. And there are suggestions of Druidism (perhaps) and primitive fertility rites, apparently still extant in Wales, all mixed up with Henry Miller, Freud, and American street slang. But sex kills also, as Thomas says a thousand times, and he is not sure of the patient's recovery. In place of love, about which Thomas is almost always profoundly bitter, there is sex, the instrument and the physical process of love. The activity of sex, Thomas hopes in his poems, will somehow lead to love in life and in the cosmos. As he grows older, love recedes and sex becomes a nightmare, a Black Mass.

Thomas moves between sexual revulsion and sexual ecstasy, between puritanism and mysticism, between formalistic ritual (this accounts for his lack of invention) and vagueness.... His dissatisfaction with his own lack of stability is reflected in his devices which tend to obscure even the simple poems; he leaves out all indications of explanation—quotation marks, punctuation, titles, connectives, whether logical or grammatical. In addition he uses every extreme device of ambiguity one can think of, from reversing the terms of a figure of speech to ellipsis to overelaboration of images. There is no poetic behind these practices—only catch-as-catch-can technique. One is always confused in Thomas by not knowing whether he is using the microscope or the telescope; he switches from one to the other with ease and without warning. It is significant that his joyous poems, which are few, though among his best, are nearly always his simplest. Where the dominant theme of despair obtrudes, the language dives down into the depths; some of these complex poems are among the most rewarding, the richest in feeling, and the most difficult to hold to. But, beyond question, there are two minds working in Thomas, the joyous, naturally religious mind, and the disturbed, almost pathological mind of the cultural fugitive or clown. On every level of Thomas' work one notices the lack of sophistication and the split in temperament. This is his strength as well as his weakness. But it is a grave weakness because it leaves him without defense, without a bridge between himself and the world.

Thomas begins in a blind alley with the obsessive statement that birth is the beginning of death, the basic poetic statement, but one which is meaningless unless the poet can build a world between. Thomas never really departs from this statement, and his obsession with sex is only the clinical restatement of the same theme. The idealization of love, the traditional solution with most poets, good and bad, is never arrived at in Thomas. He skips into the foreign land of love and skips out again. And he is too good a poet to fake love. He doesn't feel it; he distrusts it; he doesn't believe it. He falls back on the love-process, the assault, the defeat, the shame, the despair. Over and over again he repeats the ritualistic formulas for love, always doubting its success. The process is despised because it doesn't really work. The brief introduction to the *Collected Poems* sounds a note of bravado which asserts that his poems "are written for the love of Man and in praise of God." One wishes they were; one is grateful for, and slightly surprised by, the acknowledgment to God and Man, for in the poems we find neither faith nor humanism. What we find is something that fits Thomas into the age: the satanism, the vomitous horror, the self-elected crucifixion of the artist. (pp. 147-49)

Karl Shapiro, "Dylan Thomas," in his The Poetry Wreck: Selected Essays, 1950-1970 *(copyright © 1955 by Karl Shapiro; reprinted by permission of Random House, Inc.), Random House, 1975, pp. 139-49.*

Nathanael West

1903(?)-1940

American novelist, born Nathan Wallenstein Weinstein in New York City. West, the precursor of black humorists, is considered a master of the absurd and grotesque. His distinction lies in his utilization of a cool, spare prose style to produce a passionate invective against the barrennesss of modern society. An undistinguished student, West was admitted to Brown University through a mistake in identity. There he assumed his pen name along with rather foppish ways. In 1924 West went to Paris. The surrealist influences he was exposed to there are evident in his first novel, *The Dream Life of Balso Snell*. He moved in literary circles (S. J. Perelman married his sister) and was associate editor of *Contact* (with William Carlos Williams) in 1932 and associate editor of *Americana* (with George Grosz) in 1933. He married Eileen McKenney (the subject of the book and movie *My Sister Eileen*) in 1940 and seven months later they were killed in an automobile accident. An innovative and serious craftsman, West achieved little fame in his short life. However, the publication of his *Complete Works* in 1957 kindled interest in him and he is beginning to receive the critical acclaim denied him during his lifetime. *Miss Lonelyhearts* and *The Day of the Locust* are considered his masterpieces.

PRINCIPAL WORKS

The Dream Life of Balso Snell   (novel)   1931
Miss Lonelyhearts   (novel)   1933
A Cool Million: The Dismantling of Lemuel Pitkin   (novel) 1934
The Day of the Locust   (novel)   1939

"The Complete Works of Nathanael West" . . . contains some of the best writing that has been produced by an American in this century. . . .

West was one of the few novelists of the thirties who succeeded in generalizing the horrors of the depression into a universal image of human suffering. His "particular kind of joking" has profoundly unpolitical implications; it is a way of saying that the universe is *always* rigged against us and that our efforts to contend with it invariably lead to absurdity. This sort of laughter—which, paradoxically, has the most intimate connection with compassion—is rarely heard in American literature, for it is not only anti-"radi-cal" but almost un-American in its refusal to admit the possibility of improvement, amelioration, or cure. (pp. 66-7)

"The Day of the Locust" was West's first attempt to explore the implications of the compassionate view of life he had arrived at in "Miss Lonelyhearts." Gloomy as it seems, this view of life provided a sound basis for writing comedy. "Miss Lonelyhearts" and "The Day of the Locust" are comic novels, not simply because they contain funny passages but because they are about the inability of human beings to be more than human, the absurdity of the human pretense to greatness and nobility. The fact that West has enormous respect for the fury and the hunger behind these pretensions, the fact that he does not demand of people that they surrender their dreams, the fact that he responds to the pathos of their predicament—none of this compromises the comedy. "It is hard," West tells us in "The Day of the Locust," "to laugh at the need for beauty and romance, no matter how tasteless, even horrible, the results of that need are. But it is easy to sigh. Few things are sadder than the truly monstrous." This is one of the lessons that comedy teaches—neither to laugh at the need nor to be taken in by the results. It is also the animating principle of true sympathy, which is why West's "particular kind of joking" has so deep a kinship with the particular kind of compassion that is allied to intelligence and is therefore proof against the assaults of both sentimentality and cynicism. (pp. 74-5)

Norman Podhoretz, "Nathanael West: A Particular Kind of Joking" (originally published in The New Yorker, May 18, 1957), in his Doings and Undoings (reprinted with the permission of Farrar, Straus & Giroux, Inc.; copyright © 1957, 1964 by Norman Podhoretz), Farrar, Straus, 1964, pp. 66-75.

Perhaps the most remarkable things about West's career are its unevenness and its development. West's early writings are bitter, extremist, near surrealist and aggressive. The criticism underlying them is based on a disgust that is not far from hysteria: the language is obscure, extravagant, privately allusive and contemptuously scatalogical.

Yet after this unrelated little essay in intellectual gaucherie, West could suddenly strip his writing of all pretence, of all arrogant obscurantism, and produce a novel of the direct and economic intensity of *Miss Lonelyhearts,* in which every word is used exactly and functionally—and then again, in *A Cool Million,* forsake a personal style for mock-heroics and parody. Only several years later, when he had emerged from his incubatory period in Hollywood, and had written *The Day of the Locust,* was it apparent that West was somewhere on the way to integrating his gifts, to merging his bitterness and savagery into a wider, more organic pattern without losing his edge. *The Day of the Locust* marked his most important advance, the step from a political to a human view of drama. Basically, West was always a sociological writer, moved by the horrible emptiness of mass lives; and in this sense all his books are indictments, not so much of economic systems, but of life itself. *Life is terrible,* that was the despairing conclusion that led nowhere and which was the motive spring for his novels. For West there was no religious redemption to be found in human weakness, no transfiguring sense of good-and-evil, no compensation in the physical life. Seediness, apathy remained just seediness and apathy. The joke was on civilization, and West's own attitude was inexpressible through the perversion of great tides of compassion into relentless observation. So just as *Miss Lonelyhearts* is West's greatest book, because it is conceived most purely as a formal work of art, and is flawless within its structure, *The Day of the Locust* is his most mature because in it his criticism of life is not intruding between the characters, nor his pity confronting them. They exist simply in their relation to one another; the hidden reformer in West has contented himself with being an artist. (pp. x-xi)

Perhaps most important is West's view of character and his treatment of it. For none of his people are seen "in the round," as individuals created for their own distinctiveness; nor yet are they exactly "types" or vehicles for ideas in the Aldous Huxley manner. West uses subsidiary characters as an architect uses windows—to let in light on a central character and to show, but not offer him, escape. They exemplify modes of living that are never developed beyond the point where they become absurd; and at one point or another they all become absurd. These are West's primary characters: Beagle Darwin in *Balso Snell,* Shrike, Miss Lonelyhearts in *Miss Lonelyhearts,* Shagpoke Whipple in *A Cool Million,* Homer, Faye Greener and Tod in *The Day of the Locust.* But around them, and though they are main characters they never "come off" in the sense that West makes them succeed in their lives, there are a host of abnormal minor figures, whose abnormality and pathos act as a series of reservoirs, almost in the form of a Greek chorus, for West's savagery and inverted violence. (p. xvi)

In its awareness of political technique, its devastatingly true analysis of unrestricted Capitalist method, its foreshadowing of Americanism turned into a possible Fascism, *A Cool Million* is brilliantly successful. Unfortunately, having decided on a mock-melodramatic style ("when our hero regained consciousness,") . . . West sacrificed the stylistic hallmark that makes a writer's work compact and homogeneous. (p. xvii)

West's Hollywood is made up of degeneracy and brothels, of failure and sexual desire, of cock-fighting and third-rate boarding houses. But more than anything it is made up of significant boredom, of an etiolated ennui: the whole canvas on which the motiveless actions take place acquires a Breughel-like stillness, as if all the monstrous things going

on were part of a very ordinary pattern. And, indeed, the pattern of all West's books is ordinary; it is only the extraordinary stylized grotesques on the edge, the narrative logic that touches the rim of fantasy, that charge it with the nervous garishness, the disproportionate perspective that, like the beautiful hunchbacks in *Balso Snell,* mock normality with their own freakishness. (pp. xxi-xxii)

> *Alan Ross, "The Dead Center: An Intro-*
> *duction to Nathanael West," in his* The
> Complete Works of Nathanael West *(re-*
> *printed with the permission of Farrar,*
> *Straus & Giroux, Inc.; copyright © 1957 by*
> *Farrar, Straus & Giroux), Farrar, Straus,*
> *1957, pp. vii-xxii.*

Miss Lonelyhearts has too long been denied recognition as one of the great short novels in American Literature. West's masterful use of poetic imagery in the novel form is incisive, brilliant; his story is powerful, its emotional impact overwhelming, its significance profound. Technically, the novel is marred, to some extent, by a loss of artistic control in the final chapters, but despite this flaw, the book deserves a niche in the history of American Literature, not only on the basis of literary merit, but also because it is the answer of the 1930's to the great poem of the 1920's—T. S. Eliot's *The Waste Land.* I do not know whether West intended his novel as a reply to Eliot. The similarities in theme and imagery seem too obvious to be accidental. West's intentions, at any rate, are of little significance; his novel is an answer to the optimism implicit in Eliot's vision of man and society. Though Eliot's poem is a somber and depressing view of modern man and his culture, it is a view brightened by hope. Eliot's optimism is particularly obvious when his vision is contrasted with West's. (p. 91)

The inhabitants of West's waste land, as I shall presently show, are similar to the inhabitants of Eliot's. The major difference in the two visions is in the cause of the cultural and moral aridity. To West, the human being appears a misfit in an undirected universe. . . .

West's tragic vision of human life is the same vision Eugene O'Neill dramatized in *The Iceman Cometh,* probably the most despairing play of our time. Both writers see man's ideals and ideas as nothing but pipe dreams. These empty dreams, as man's only defense against the brutality of reality, are essential if he is to go on living.

I make much of West's despair because it is the fact that eluded me when I first read *Miss Lonelyhearts.* The columnist's plight is so pathetic, his desire to succor his fellow sufferers so attractive, his Christ dream so appealing that he remains a sympathetic character to the end of the novel. Miss Lonelyhearts in the final chapters, however, is a madman; he has severed all contact with reality. The theme of the novel demands that the reader experience pity, not sympathy, for Miss Lonelyhearts in his madness; but West, in his final chapters, does not exert sufficient artistic control over his story and his own feelings (I suspect) to withdraw his reader to an observer's position. (pp. 92-3)

Like Eliot's protagonist, the hero of *Miss Lonelyhearts* is given the opportunity to view the waste land in which he lives. What both protagonists see . . . is a world without values. There is one major difference: Miss Lonelyhearts' world has no values, not because man has thrown them over, substituting superficial values for good ones, but because the human being has reached a time in his history when he can no longer delude himself. None of his philosophies or dreams has ameliorated or accounted for the presence of evil, for the pain, the suffering, the misery of human existence. In the three letters that open the novel, the writers are victims, completely innocent victims, of forces beyond their control. They in no way deserve the suffering they are undergoing. . . . For these sufferers the flame of their agony is reality. Their protective illusions have burned away. But reality cannot be endured without dreams, and in desperation the anguished victims write to Miss Lonelyhearts. The unknown writer of the newspaper column becomes their only hope of salvation; in his column they seek "The Word."

Miss Lonelyhearts' waste land, therefore, is more than a reflection of man's personal and cultural degeneration; it is a land in which evil and human suffering stalk in their naked horror. No sensitive viewer of this land can observe the anguish and retain his sanity. The inhabitants of the waste land are, from necessity, breathing dead men. The death mask is their alternative to facing the horrors of life. The chief spokesman of these inhabitants is Shrike, named for the butcher bird that impales its prey on a thorn or twig while tearing it apart with its sharp hooked beak. . . . Shrike, like all human beings, must have some defense against reality. One of the nasty products of "this unbelieving age," he lives by impaling the dreams of others and ripping them apart: he makes a joke of everything. (pp. 93-4)

Miss Lonelyhearts, too, had been a joke machine until the column he had begun as a joke forced him "to examine the values by which he lives. This examination shows him that he is the victim of the joke and not its perpetrator." He is the victim because the people he had planned to laugh at reveal to him the horrors of life; their agonized pleas penetrate to his heart. He can no longer ignore the reality of human existence. Like Melville's Captain Ahab, West's Miss Lonelyhearts concludes that there is no such thing as justice in the universe; human evil is merely an eruption of universal evil. The two characters experience the same awful insight. Their subsequent madness takes different forms because they are a century apart in the history of man. There is no fight in the twentieth century columnist, no need for vengeance. Captain Ahab had something to hate, something to struggle against. He could defy the gods, hate the injustice of the universe, reject the cruelty of man. Miss Lonelyhearts has no opponent. . . . (pp. 94-5)

When he looks up to the sky for a target and can find none, Miss Lonelyhearts has reached that moment of complete despair that the French existentialist writers a few years later were to term *Nauseé*, or The Absurd. Miss Lonelyhearts' creator, however, was no existentialist. He could not move out of his despair; he could only joke about man's attempt to curtain reality, write a satire on the Christ dream —the salvation of Eliot's Waste Land. . . .

The Christ dream for Miss Lonelyhearts . . . is a form of madness; it can cut him off from reality, making the dead world seem alive. As a product of his age, however, Miss Lonelyhearts cannot rationally accept Christ, and religion is meaningless to him. (p. 95)

Miss Lonelyhearts knows, therefore, that if he gives himself over to the Christ dream he will be cutting himself off

from reality. But what else can he offer Sick-of-it-all and Broken Hearted, whose own dreams have evaporated in the hellish flames of reality? He is their last hope, and he cannot ignore them. He must help his fellow men, suffer for them, become the living Christ. Christ is his natural inevitable haven, though he realizes it is an empty dream. Christ, as Shrike declares, is the Miss Lonelyhearts of Miss Lonelyhearts—the ultimate, vacuous hope of the desperate. The columnist also knows that "Even if he were to have a genuine religious experience, it would be personal and so meaningless, except to a psychologist." The Christ dream, Nathanael West is saying, can perhaps provide personal escape, but it is not the salvation of the waste land; it is not, as in Eliot's poetry, the means of personal and thereby universal salvation. (p. 96)

At the end of the three days of symbolic entombment, Miss Lonelyhearts arises. His suffering is over; he has become the rock. West's use here of the symbol of despair, the rock, to symbolize his protagonist's withdrawal from reality makes clear his attitude toward the Christ dream. (The symbol may also be a satirical reference to the effectiveness of the Church in aiding suffering mankind.) (pp. 99-100)

Miss Lonelyhearts is a brilliant, profound expression of despair, able, a quarter century later, to evoke the feeling and mood of its period better than any other novel, including *The Sun Also Rises*. Reading the novel is a painful emotional experience, not unlike that produced by reading *The Waste Land*. But in Eliot's Waste Land regeneration is possible; in West's there is no hope of salvation. (p. 101)

> *Edmond L. Volpe, "The Waste Land of Nathanael West," in* Renascence 13 *(reprinted by permission of the author and the publisher), Winter, 1961 (and reprinted in* Nathanael West: A Collection of Critical Essays, *edited by Jay Martin, Prentice-Hall, 1971, pp. 91-101).*

Nathanael West is not, strictly speaking, a novelist; that is to say, he does not attempt an accurate description either of the social scene or of the subjective life of the mind. For his first book, he adopted the dream convention, but neither the incidents nor the language are credible as a transcription of a real dream. For his other three, he adopted the convention of a social narrative; his characters need real food, drink and money, and live in recognizable places like New York or Hollywood, but, taken as feigned history, they are absurd. (p. 238)

There are many admirable and extremely funny satirical passages in his books, but West is not a satirist. Satire presupposes conscience and reason as the judges between the true and the false, the moral and the immoral, to which it appeals, but for West these faculties are themselves the creators of unreality.

His books should, I think, be classified as Cautionary Tales, parables about a Kingdom of Hell whose ruler is not so much the Father of Lies as the Father of Wishes. Shakespeare gives a glimpse of this hell in *Hamlet*, and Dostoievsky has a lengthy description in *Notes from the Underground*, but they were interested in many hells and heavens. Compared with them, West has the advantages and disadvantages of the specialist who knows everything about one disease and nothing about any other. He was a sophisticated and highly skilled literary craftsman, but what gives all his books such a powerful and disturbing fascination, even *A Cool Million,* which must, I think, be judged a failure, owes nothing to calculation. West's descriptions of Inferno have the authenticity of firsthand experience: he has certainly been there, and the reader has the uncomfortable feeling that his was not a short visit.

All his main characters suffer from the same spiritual disease which, in honor of the man who devoted his life to studying it, we may call West's Disease. This is a disease of consciousness which renders it incapable of converting wishes into desires. (pp. 240-41)

A sufferer from West's Disease is not selfish but absolutely self-centered. A selfish man is one who satisfies his desires at other people's expense; for this reason, he tries to see what others are really like and often sees them extremely accurately in order that he may make use of them. But, to the self-centered man, other people only exist as images either of what he is or of what he is not, his feelings towards them are projections of the pity or the hatred he feels for himself and anything he does to them is really done to himself. Hence the inconsistent and unpredictable behavior of a sufferer from West's Disease: he may kiss your feet one moment and kick you in the jaw the next and, if you were to ask him why, he could not tell you.

In its final stages, the disease reduces itself to a craving for violent physical pain—this craving, unfortunately, can be projected onto others—for only violent pain can put an end to wishing *for* something and produce the real wish of necessity, the cry "Stop!" (pp. 242-43)

As used by West, the cripple is, I believe, a symbolic projection of the state of wishful self-despair, the state of those who will not accept themselves in order to change themselves into what they would or should become, and justify their refusal by thinking that being what they are is uniquely horrible and uncurable. To look at, Faye Greener is a pretty but not remarkable girl; in the eyes of Faye Greener, she is an exceptionally hideous spirit.

In saying that cripples have this significance in West's writing, I do not mean to say that he was necessarily aware of it. Indeed, I am inclined to think he was not. I suspect that, consciously, he thought pity and compassion were the same thing, but what the behavior of his "tender" characters shows is that all pity is self-pity and that he who pities others is incapable of compassion. Ruthlessly as he exposes his dreamers, he seems to believe that the only alternative to despair is to become a crook. (p. 243)

West comes very near to accepting the doctrine of the Marquis de Sade—there are many resemblances between *A Cool Million* and *Justine*—to believing, that is, that the creation is essentially evil and that goodness is contrary to its laws, but his moral sense revolted against Sade's logical conclusion that it was therefore a man's duty to be as evil as possible. All West's "worldly" characters are bad men, most of them grotesquely bad, but here again his artistic instinct seems at times to contradict his conscious intentions. I do not think, for example, that he meant to make Wu Fong, the brothel-keeper, more sympathetic and worthy of respect than, say, Miss Lonelyhearts or Homer Simpson, but that is what he does. . . . (p. 244)

> *W. H. Auden, "Interlude: West's Disease,"*
> *in his* The Dyer's Hand and Other Essays

West saw the seeds of disillusionment and contradiction sown in the American image, had the vision to recognize their relevance far beyond the tempests in political teapots to which many of his friends sacrificed their creative energy, and maintained a comic perspective which causes his anger and despair to emerge with a timeliness characteristic of that art which on the primary level manages to embrace the timeless. (p. 31)

In *Balso Snell,* West introduced his readers to the eccentric, the mystic, the pervert, the crippled, and the disillusioned who were to be credibly presented as major players in his later novels. The themes of cheating, distorted reality, and the Dostoevskian paradox of good and evil occur throughout the book, although they emerge in self-conscious references and images. In the absurdly tweedy figure of Miss McGeeney West first suggests the sterility of modern woman and the failure of sexual gratification. . . . Miss Farkis, the bookstore clerk in *Miss Lonelyhearts,* is [her] direct literary descendant. . . .

Employing [a] picaresque technique in his first novel, West satirizes the classic myth of "revelation" which the technique has traditionally illustrated. Balso, the itinerant hero, begins his journey by entering the anus of the Trojan Horse, but unlike Odysseus, Dante and Ishmael, there is no discovery of ultimate truth awaiting him at the end of his voyage. . . .

The Trojan Horse is Balso's world, and like its Homeric predecessor it represents evasion and deceit. For West the modern world is no more honest in the dreams it offers man than the Trojan Horse had been in the dreams of peace with which it tempted the besieged citizens of Troy. The horse as a symbol of sham reappears in *A Cool Million* in Sylvanus Snodgrasse's fatuous panegyrics and in the grotesque rubber figure at the bottom of Claude Estee's swimming pool in *The Day of the Locust.* . . .

Balso Snell journeys into the dream world of the self in a classic effort to assess his own personality. He approaches religious mysticism, sexual expression, and literary detachment in a manner that foreshadows the agonized gropings of Miss Lonelyhearts. (p. 33)

In Balso we see developing the bitter cynicism of Shrike. . . . (p. 35)

West was remorseless in exposing the dreams by which man strives to escape the violence and emptiness of life, and *Balso Snell* is a catalogue of the delusions which were to be the subjects of his later work—Christianity, the success dream, artistic detachment, the innocence of childhood, the return to nature, and political idealism. Miss Lonelyhearts, as Balso Snell's successor, runs the full gamut of these delusions. (p. 37)

Like Swift, West distrusted the very pattern of life, and he found the same impossibility of adjusting to the discrepancies between man's ideals and his accomplishments. West realized, with Swift, that the purpose of satire is to ridicule what one is to demolish, although he did not consistently recognize that the ingredient of humor is essential to effective satire. (pp. 38-9)

West believed that modern society, like Balso Snell in the horse's interior, moved without direction, and this concept is the essence of his vision of man's comic nature. In the rebellion against his own society, the satirist is often eyed with suspicion and disfavor. Thus, readers have made a ready identification of West with the "cultured fiend" in *Balso.* . . . West was, indeed, a great despiser, and he repeatedly satirized the things he despised; however, the objects of his satire were not men themselves, but the masks which men wore. . . .

Balso Snell . . . is an artist's sounding-board, and from it West obviously learned a great deal. He had hoped that his first novel could be more than a literary exercise, that it might make an effective attack on artiness and superficiality. But because he attacked these subjects with such vindictiveness, and because he threw out conventional plot structure and character development while substituting no alternative literary pattern, *Balso Snell* became one with the very qualities of pretentiousness which it satirized. (p. 39)

The distinctive prose style which West created [in *A Cool Million*] is inflated by mock-heroic language and flawed by limiting topical references. The social impulses which he attacks are still illusion, and the outcome of illusion is still physical or spiritual dismantling, but in concentrating his attack within the sphere of capitalist legend, West created a distinctively political novel. The book succeeded at all only because West, though politically angry, managed never to lose his temper. (p. 40)

Only the occasional emergence of West's peculiar humor and the absence of Utopian idealism distinguish *A Cool Million* from the other novels of class struggle and economic collapse which were characteristics of the 1930's. (p. 41)

In all West's work there is a fascination with violence that is related to Dostoevsky's concentration on the distorted and the painful, but that also has distinct counterparts in the American literary tradition. . . . Poe and West shared the ability to create a nightmarish atmosphere which has strong roots in the anguished fancies of Ann Radcliff and Horace Walpole. While Poe believed that the lyric poem was the most appropriate vehicle for demonstrating the nightmare of life, West felt that the short novel could better accomplish that purpose. (p. 43)

For West, Lemuel's role [in *A Cool Million*] is not a tragic one. The author suffers with many of his characters, even if he does so in a curiously indifferent manner, but he suffers less with Lemuel than with his other misguided "fools." It is the content of their dreams, however, which makes the sufferings of Balso Snell, Miss Lonelyhearts, and Tod Hackett ennobling. Even though *A Cool Million* makes a violent critique of the *milieu* in which Lemuel's dream is cultivated, West is so out of sympathy with the character of that dream that he has little sympathy for Lemuel. . . . From his tortuous experience with life, the mock-hero emerges with only physical alterations—the grotesque alterations of a circus clown. (pp. 45-6)

A Cool Million lacks the poetic description, the feeling of economy, and the complexity of expression of *Miss Lonelyhearts* and *The Day of the Locust,* but as an artist's opportunity to detour, practice, and sample, *A Cool Million* bore fruit in *The Day of the Locust* just as *Balso Snell* did in

Miss Lonelyhearts. Historically, *A Cool Million* is important as the first complete disavowal of the American dream of success and one of the first suggestions of Fascism, but what he had to say about a Fascist America, West said with far greater power in his very unpolitical last novel. (p. 47)

> *David D. Galloway, "A Picaresque Apprenticeship: Nathanael West's 'The Dream Life of Balso Snell' and 'A Cool Million'," in* Wisconsin Studies in Contemporary Literature *5 (© 1964 by the Regents of the University of Wisconsin; reprinted by permission of the publisher), Summer, 1964 (and reprinted in* Nathanael West: A Collection of Critical Essays, *edited by Jay Martin, Prentice-Hall, 1971, pp. 31-47).*

One could search West's novels with great care and never find a suggestion of introspective delicacy; one would not even find psychologically perceptive dialogue. That is not West's way. He is not interested in analyzing character; he is interested in correlatives of a psychological state. Intent on creating archetypal characters in an age of psychoanalysis, West probably felt that Freudian psychology was indispensable. But West is not interested in great subtlety; it is sufficient that the images convey the disorder.

The vague uneasiness we feel when reading West is often due to our subliminal perception of this Freudian dimension. It is not pleasant to be reminded as emphatically as West reminds us that our behavior is rooted in sexuality. It is particularly offensive when the proponent of such a view believes, not with Freud, in the potential beauty of sex and in the need to liberate its creative energy, but in the power and ugliness of sex, in sexuality as the opposite of spirituality. (p. 3)

Dark as West's world view was, it was probably the manner in which he translated that view into art that ultimately alienated his audience. West was both too European and too modern for an American audience bred on a national proletarian realism. Despite West's American idiom and topical setting, his influences were intensely European, as a casual glance reveals. In a list of major influences including Baudelaire and the French symbolists, the French surrealists, Kafka, Dostoevski, Joyce (and one suspects, Conrad), only T. S. Eliot can by any stretch of the imagination be considered American. Even Jung, Freud, mythology, mysticism, and the Bible had not been used in American literature quite the way West has used them.

Perhaps what puzzles us most about West is his distance from realism and naturalism. A keen observer, his effects are nightmarish rather than realistic. Always opposed to middle-class realism, West preferred a deeper level of reality, a preference probably derived from expressionists such as Kafka, and from surrealists such as Breton and Eluard, as well as their precursors Lautréamont and Apollinaire. Perhaps from them he learned that the most cruel but most efficient way to overcome conventionalized or dramatized feelings was to make fun of them. Probably from them he learned to shun the traditional forms of comedy and tragedy and to prefer a combination of the serious and the comic. To them he probably also owed his peculiar use of the grotesque. . . . Equally derivative were certain aspects of his pessimism, such as a theatric sense of futility. Perhaps even his use of prophecy had its origin in surrealism, but more than likely, in tone and symbolism, he is most indebted in this respect to the Old Testament prophets. Finally, in his violent rejection of the human condition, he is surrealist, for "the idea of warfare against the purely human condition of man occupies the dark center and focus of surrealism." (pp. 4-5)

West's created world, a blend of sordid realism and nightmarish fantasy, was probably influenced by Baudelaire's own created half-world. . . . Like Eliot, West believed that art was not self-expression, and like Eliot, West's art deals with intensely personal experience, with internal conflicts and emotional dramas which are in some degree common to all men. Perhaps more important, from Eliot West derived some of his symbolism—particularly that of the wasteland; and his vision of the contemporary scene seems to have differed little from Eliot's, except for a suggested solution: West had none. (p. 6)

The ability to create subtle and complex tensions is one of West's finest achievements. A study of his style is, to a large extent, a study in tension. West's device, in creating a state of tension between the reader as participant and as spectator, allows for, and often demands, a comparison between reader and fictional character. The comparison is a spontaneous and unconscious one, but one that nevertheless tends to destroy reader empathy at the same time that it creates it. This paradox occurs because the reader is a participant and spectator on two levels: on the simple vicarious level, and on the experiential level. In essence, the reader not only observes the characters, he observes himself; not only does he participate empathetically in the characters' ordeal, he participates in a new emotion, much as if the work were a "real" stimulus to which he would respond. (p. 27)

West's symbolic brilliance . . . proceeds not from the abundance of symbols—although they are abundant, nor from their coherence—although they are generally clear and well integrated, but from their application. Perhaps so little has been made of West as a symbolist because his symbolism, like Kafka's, has not one application but several unrelated and seemingly contradictory ones. The obscurity occurs because West, attempting to suggest or evoke as many meanings as possible, seems to have taken pains to avoid overloading one symbolic interpretation at the expense of another. Thus West was careful to maintain the precarious tension between the mythic, religious, and psychoanalytic symbolisms in *Miss Lonelyhearts* in order that all three might remain operative.

This attempt to embrace many meanings helps explain the disparate readings of *Miss Lonelyhearts*. The reader's interpretation will depend in large part upon his sensitivity to one set of symbols at the expense of the others. The sensitivity need not, of course, be a conscious one. It is necessary to realize that West, like Kafka, appeals to man's private instincts and deepest feelings, to that unconscious "nightmare world which is always just below the surface." (pp. 34-5)

Grotesque elements, perhaps Kafkaesque and surrealist in origin, are a conspicuous part of West's method. Often, . . . the grotesque consists of a combination of heterogeneous and incongruous details; but more often, it consists of distortion for artistic effect. Either way, the effect is disturbing. More than a stylistic device calculated to shock,

the grotesque is a method of characterization: it gives his characters their unique, energetic individuality. If one is unable to conceive of West's characters in any other way, it is because they are described in no other way.

Perhaps even more important is West's ability to make grotesqueness atmospheric. West spends little time creating atmosphere, and yet it is always there. He creates it briefly, casually, as if in passing; but it is passed over so often that it seems never to leave the stage, an effect achieved by re-triggering a previous impression. A part thus serves to evoke a much greater grotesque whole. (p. 36)

There is a tendency at first glance to dismiss West's jokes as pubescent humor in bad taste. Such a view tends to ignore not only their abundance, their existence in every novel, but the element of conscious artistry in West. . . . It was his precious ability to create miniature portraits of a society steeped in vulgarity. . . . A mark of his inherent good taste was his ability to transcend the manifestations of that pervasive and sickening vulgarity. Much of this ability to temper the unsavoriness of his subject resulted from his pose of amused "detached observer of the ironies in the human struggle," and from a vision conveyed in comic idioms such as clichés. (p. 45)

In [his] later major works, West has made of the cliché a thing of art. He has used it for reasons of subtlety; and by varying the language slightly, he has preserved all the echoes of the old while creating something new and original. (p. 48)

[A] theatric sense of absurdity . . . is the rock on which he built all his novels. It merely seems to loom larger in *Balso Snell* because of the novel's formlessness and because his method, in this work, is one of direct attack rather than indirect implication. Instead of placing his characters in situations which reveal futility and absurdity, as he does in *Miss Lonelyhearts* and *The Day of the Locust,* West in this work makes the characters and their very problems absurd. The problems raised in *Balso Snell* are treated in a fashion calculated to create this effect. One has, and is meant to have, the feeling that these are not problems that one can take seriously. This response is vastly different from one's feelings about the problems in *Miss Lonelyhearts*.

West is able to accomplish this effect in *Balso Snell* not by dealing with trivial problems as opposed to those dealt with in *Miss Lonelyhearts* and *The Day of the Locust,* but by choosing banal or unbelievable incidents to dramatize the problems. Add the element of melodrama to banality or incredulity and one creates a problem that is a farce not worthy of serious consideration. (p. 65)

Strident and garish as it is, *Miss Lonelyhearts* is a novel most delicately poised between agonizing pessimism and ironic amusement. It was a balance too fine for West to achieve in any other novel. Perhaps he achieved it in *Miss Lonelyhearts* because in it he first gives voice to violent despair and because, though it is his most personal, subtle, and important philosophic statement of life, it followed too soon after *Balso Snell* to escape that novel's broad comic irony. (p. 72)

In *Miss Lonelyhearts,* West has seized upon a myth, just as Joyce and Eliot had in *Ulysses* and *The Waste Land,* in an attempt to bring order to a disordered world, and to give the action a timeless truth. In the legend of the dead Fisher

King he found a myth which was rather perfectly suited to his heightened sensitivity to despair and decay.

Although dealing with legend or myth, West does not allow himself to be restricted by it. *Miss Lonelyhearts* is the symbolist masterpiece that it is precisely because West has merely incorporated the Grail and Oedipal legends into a larger conception. More than a modernization of a legend, *Miss Lonelyhearts* is a modern myth. (pp. 91-2)

Ultimately, what is so remarkable about [*Miss Lonelyhearts*] is the range and depth of its archetypal conception. Apparently casual responses are far from casual. The richness of the novel resides in symbolic or archetypal dimension residing in almost every detail. (p. 94)

Miss Lonelyhearts is the near perfect work it is because as a myth, it is not a dream—not even a grotesque nightmare. Its pattern, like that of myth, is consciously controlled. . . . That West consciously constructed his myth to give "certain spiritual principles" a bitter, ironic twist is not only characteristic, but revealing; it suggests that West, like many moderns, was prone to a psychological interpretation of myth. Since Freud's Oedipal studies and Jung's analysis of the collective unconscious, such psychological interpretation has become widespread. West's success in adding this psychoanalytic dimension to the classic archetypal drama of *Miss Lonelyhearts,* in psychoanalyzing Miss Lonelyhearts *imagistically,* is his most brilliant achievement. . . . (p. 95)

Miss Lonelyhearts may strike many, particularly religious readers, as an unpleasant, even ugly novel, and not without some justification. Nevertheless, despite its many unfortunate anti-religious overtones, one misunderstands West and does him a disservice if one fails to realize that the attack is against that kind of religiosity which seeks to escape involvement in human suffering by explaining and justifying its existence. . . . The subtle symbols, the allusive conception, and the bitter ironies are all part of West's attempt to disguise his emotional involvement in an agonizing perception, and are his way of preventing the novel from being sentimental. They make a simple reading impossible. *Miss Lonelyhearts* is an enormously compressed and complex novel; to pretend that it is simple is to pretend that West was neither a symbolist nor a highly allusive writer. (p. 101)

West, himself, was fully aware of the superficial unreality of his characters; they posture and are psychologically paper thin because "Psychology has nothing to do with reality nor should it be used as a motivation. The novelist is no longer a psychologist." The characters do not live and breathe, but they do disturb. They act upon the reader in this way because they strike a chord within him which makes him supply the nuances—nuances drawn from his own psychological makeup. (p. 160)

This incompleteness of presentation, along with the subsequent additions of the reader, results in the reader's peculiar ambivalence. The characters are unlovely but nonetheless pathetic; unpleasant and unsympathetic, and yet capable of arousing pity. One has the distinct impression that such a mixed response is due less to West's fusion of feeling and satire than to reader identification. The reader is experiencing an objectified self-pity or self-contempt.

Identification as an aspect of West's art is not an unquestionable hypothesis. However, if one rejects this theory,

one finds it hard to explain one's great involvement; it is difficult to remain indifferent to the characters. They are upsetting, and it seems that if they do not arouse the reader's pity, they arouse his anger. In either event, his response seems to be as much the result of his own self-concept as of the objective presentation of character. If one's world view is similar to West's, one's response is probably that of pity muddied by anger; if one's view differs, one may still feel pity, or one may feel anger. Either response is hard to justify textually. The characters are too ambiguous, and one may find passages to support either emotion.

The ambiguity is undoubtedly intentional; it is not only part of West's world view, it is a reflection of his secretive nature. Such ambiguity cannot be condemned as inartistic, because it is not the result of shoddy craftsmanship but rather of the nature of the portrait. It is one thing to condemn an author for an ambiguous portrait, but another to condemn him because one's own attitude toward the portrait is ambiguous. Both ambiguous portraits and responses are true to life, but the former, unlike the latter, may or may not be related to artistic problems. There is a peculiar power in the latter form of ambiguity: it is the power to arouse thought. This ability to engage the reader's intellect as well as his emotions is characteristically Westian; the reader feels as well as understands the implications of the problem presented. This kind of total involvement of the reader is demanded by most important writers.

It is this ability to breathe life into otherwise unlifelike, often grotesque, characters that makes West so remarkable and so modern. And it is his ability to communicate his own intensity that brings them to life. (pp. 160-61)

West probably selected [sex to dramatize his characters' ineffectualness] because of its universality and its symbolic value. The disorder of the individual mirrors the disorder of the society. Sexual inadequacy is ineffectualness at its most primitive biological level. Tied up in one vivid image are man's social, biological, psychological, and "metaphysical" inadequacies—man's inadequacy before the "laws of life." (p. 163)

Perhaps, ultimately, what makes West's work so unpleasant and upsetting is [his] ability to generalize an image of man as a diseased, endlessly suffering victim. For some, there is something vaguely indecent and terrifying about such an image, about exposing such suffering. William Carlos Williams, a close friend of West's, inadvertently summed it up as well as it probably ever will be: "Should such lives," he asked, "as these letters [in *Miss Lonelyhearts*] reveal never have been brought to light? Should such people, like the worst of our war wounded, best be kept in hiding?" For many readers the answer is "yes"; for them, the "private masochistic alchemy by which West tried to erase the vision of suffering humanity he saw around him" results in a work of art with, to paraphrase Wordsworth, a greater proportion of pain than may be endured. Most, however, feel differently, and therein lies a hint of the dimension of West's achievement; for only a very fine writer could have transcended such a vision of unrelieved, unbearable human suffering. (p. 166)

Victor Comerchero, in his Nathanael West: The Ironic Prophet *(copyright © 1964 by Syracuse University Press), Syracuse University Press, 1964.*

In the reappraisal of the literary 'thirties, West has caught up with and overtaken most of the triple-decked Naturalists whose solemn and often infelicitous documentations no longer are devoured with relish. (p. 307)

Being a radical in the 1930's (and West was a faithful subscriber to Party manifestoes) did not necessarily mean that one had to write ritualistic proletarian novels or Whitman-esque exhortations to revolt. There was another kind of writing, Edward Dahlberg called it "implication literature," tinged with "just as deep a radical dye." West belonged to that select company of socially committed writers in the Depression decade who drew revolutionary conclusions in highly idiosyncratic and undoctrinaire ways: in the eerie episodes of Dahlberg's *Bottom Dogs* and *From Flushing to Calvary,* in the nightmarish poems of Kenneth Fearing, and in the pointed buffoonery of S. J. Perelman. Like these writers, West supported the objectives of the Left while retaining the verbal exuberance, the unplayful irony, the nocturnal surrealist fancies associated with a certain school of expatriate writing in the 'twenties.

Had West (and the same might be said of Fearing), been merely an unaffiliated rebel, an inveterate non-joiner suspicious of causes and unburdened by any social philosophy, his satire and humor would hardly have been condoned by the Communists. (p. 308)

West could not be accused of divorcing dreams from reality, but the literary and artistic streams that fed his bizarre imagination—the French school of the *fin de siècle,* Dostoievsky, squalid pulp fiction, the comic strip, the cinema—set him apart from the Proletarians who saw no revolutionary significance in myths and dreams. For this reason, despite such discerning readers as Josephine Herbst, Edmund Wilson, Fitzgerald, William Carlos Williams, Angel Flores and others, the Movement never took West to its bosom. In misconstruing his humor and failing to explore his baleful Wasteland, it committed both a political and an aesthetic blunder. (pp. 309-10)

Plainly [West] is an exorcist of a kind, for all comedy is cathartic; and clearly he tried to become on occasion a "satiric propagandist." *A Cool Million* is an anti-capitalist satire, its well-defined targets obvious in 1934 to any Communist, Fellow-traveler or even liberal. It is hardly an example, however, of the socially conscious fiction the Left-Wing was calling for, and it displays the Westian idiosyncrasies that kept him from becoming an acceptable political marksman for the Party: pessimism, an impatience with codes, and an inability to accommodate revolutionary parables to his gothic imagination.

At his most authentic, West is the "universal satirist." His humor is savage and sad, in contrast to Perelman's brash spoofing, and it springs, I think, from his tragi-comic view of the world, from his wry awareness of the disparity between secular facts and his suppressed religious ideals. His slapstick ends in a scream; the self-hatred of his characters, their efforts—sometimes grotesque and always painful—to find answers or relief, only curdles his pity. In *A Cool Million,* as in his other novels, the real culprit is not capitalism but humanity. (p. 316)

> *Daniel Aaron, "Late Thoughts on Nathanael West," in* The Massachusetts Review *(reprinted from* The Massachusetts Review; © *1965 The Massachusetts Review, Inc.), Winter-Spring, 1965, pp. 307-16.*

If Nathanael West appears to us from our present vantage point the chief neglected talent of the age, this is largely because he was immune to the self-deceit which afflicted his contemporaries; he knew what he was doing. Despite his own left-wing political sympathies and the pressures of friends more committed than he, he refused to subscribe to the program for proletarian fiction laid down by the official theoreticians and critics of the Communist movement. And he turned unashamedly to the business of rendering the naked anguish he felt, rather than projecting the commitment to action and faith it was assumed he should feel. Even more importantly he rejected the concept of realism-naturalism, refused to play the game (variously connived at by Dos Passos and Steinbeck and Farrell) of pretending to create documents rather than poetry. He returned, despite the immediate example of three decades of falsely "scientific" writing, which sought to replace imagination with sociology, the symbol with the case report, to the instinctive realization of the classic American fictionists that literary truth is not synonymous with fact. West's novels are a deliberate assault on the common man's notion of reality; for violence is not only his subject matter, but also his technique.

His apprenticeship was served in Europe, in the world of the Left Bank, where from the Surrealists he learned (his finger-exercises are to be found in his first book, *The Dream Life of Balso Snell*) a kind of humor expressed almost entirely in terms of the grotesque, that is to say, on a perilous border-line between jest and horror. Yet his Surrealist-inspired techniques—the violent conjunctions; the discords at the sensitive places where squeamishness demands harmony; the atrocious belly-laughs that shade off into hysteria—are not very different, after all, from the devices of *Pudd'nhead Wilson* or *Gordon Pym.* West is, in a sense, then, only reclaiming our own; yet, in another, he is introducing into the main line of American fiction a kind of sophistication, a view of the nature of art, of which our literature was badly in need.

It is possible for an American, of course, to find in his native sources, his native scene and his American self cues for the special kind of horror-comedy which characterizes West's novels. The uneducated Twain once did precisely that, and the half-educated Faulkner has pretended at least to follow his example. Yet in Twain everywhere, and in Faulkner more and more as the years go by, there is evident a presumptuous, home-made quality, which mars their work whenever they pass from the realm of myth to that of ideas. Nothing is more bald and thin than the back-porch atheism of Twain's *The Mysterious Stranger,* except perhaps the red-neck Protestantism of Faulkner's *A Fable.* (pp. 485-86)

In one of his few published critical notes [West] declares: "In America violence is idiomatic, in America violence is daily." And it is possible to see him as just another of our professional tough guys, one of the "boys in the backroom" (the phrase is applied by Edmund Wilson, in a little study of our fiction, to West along with John O'Hara). This is not to deny, though West himself tried to, that West is, in some meaningful sense, a Jew. He is enough the child of a long tradition of nonviolence to be racked by guilt in the face of violence, shocked and tormented every day in a world where violence is, of course, daily and most men are not at all disturbed. In *Miss Lonelyhearts,* he creates the portrait of a character, all nerves and no skin, the fool of pity, whom the quite ordinary horror of ordinary life lacerates to the point of madness. His protagonist is given the job of answering "letters to the lovelorn" on a daily newspaper; and he finds in this job, a joke to others (he must pretend in his column to be a woman, for only women presumably suffer and sympathize), a revelation of human misery too acute for him to bear. It is the final modern turn of the gothic screw: the realization that not the supernatural, the extraordinary, but the ordinary, the everyday are the terrors that constrict the heart. (p. 487)

Miss Lonelyhearts is, finally, the comic butt who takes upon himself the sins of the world: the *schlemiel* as Everyman, the skeptical and unbelieved-in Christ of a faithless age. But such a role of absurd Christ is West's analogue for the function of the writer, whom he considers obliged unremittingly to regard a suffering he is too sensitive to abide; and in no writer is there so absolute a sense of the misery of being human, though he also believes that such misery is a more proper occasion for laughter than tears. He is child enough of his time to envision an apocalypse; but his apocalypse is a defeat for everyone. The protagonist of *Miss Lonelyhearts* is shot reaching out in love toward a man he has unwillingly offended; while the hero-*schlemiel* of the more deliberately farcical *A Cool Million: or The Dismantling of Lemuel Pitkin* (in theme and style a parody of Horatio Alger), staggers from one ridiculous, anti-heroic disaster to another, becoming after his death the idol of an American fascist movement. But the true horror-climax of his life and the book comes when, utterly maimed, he stands on the stage between two corny comedians, who wallop him with rolled-up newspapers in time to their jokes, until his wig comes off (he has been at one point scalped), his glass eye pops out, and his wooden leg falls away; after which, they provide him with new artificial aids and begin again.

It is not until *The Day of the Locust,* however, which is West's last book, and the only novel on Hollywood not somehow made trivial by its subject, that one gets the final version of the Apocalypse according to Nathanael West. At the end of the book, a painter, caught in a rioting mob of fans at a Hollywood première, dreams, as he is being crushed by the rioters, the phantasmagoric masterpiece he has never finished painting, "The Burning of Los Angeles." West does not seem finally a really achieved writer; certainly, no one of his books is thoroughly satisfactory, though there are astonishing local successes in all of them. His greatness lies like a promise just beyond his last novel, and is frustrated by his early death; but he is the inventor of a peculiar kind of book, in which the most fruitful strain of American fiction is joined to the European tradition of avant-garde, anti-bourgeois art, native symbolism to imported *symbolisme*. The Westian or neo-gothic novel has opened up possibilities, unavailable to both the naturalistic semidocumentary and the over-refined novel of sensibility, possibilities of capturing the quality of experience in a mass society—rather than retreating to the meaningless retailing of fact or the pointless elaboration of private responses to irrelevant sensations. Putting down a book by West, a reader is not sure whether he has been presented with a nightmare endowed with the conviction of actuality or with actuality distorted into the semblance of a nightmare; but in either case, he has the sense that he has been presented with a view of a world in which, incredibly, he lives.

Yet the importance of West's work was scarcely realized in his own day; and it would be misleading even now to speak of his general influence. Though his novels continued to move younger writers, and though the last few years have witnessed not only a growing critical acclaim, but attempts to extend his audience by stage adaptations and moving-picture versions, West is still more admired than directly emulated. (pp. 488-89)

The alienated *schlemiel*-heroes of Saul Bellow surely owe something to West's protagonists, whose anguish never quite overbalances their absurdity; and everywhere in the Jewish American novelists of the last two decades, West's influence is felt, if only as a temptation toward sheer terror rejected in favor of sentimentality or some abstract espousal of love. Though lonely in his own time, West was not really alone in his attempt to redeem French horror for the American soul, as Poe had once redeemed that of Germany. . . . (p. 490)

> *Leslie A. Fiedler, in his* Love and Death in the American Novel *(copyright © 1960, 1966 by Leslie A. Fiedler; reprinted with permission of Stein and Day/Publishers), revised edition, Stein and Day, 1966.*

Though veiled by vulgarity and a deliberate contempt for the weaknesses of readers, *Balso Snell* undoubtedly deals with one of the central themes of literature: the conflict between idealism and materialism. Balso is in part a realistic man, alive to the comfort that can be gained from the monistic and idealistic view of the universe, but too aware of the pragmatic foolishness of such a viewpoint to derive much solace from it. (p. 47)

The essential cause of Miss Lonelyhearts' despair is seen in *Balso,* for both heroes are questers, fruitlessly searching, one reverently, one cynically, for a central unity, an Over Soul, that will make the meaninglessness of multiplicity into the ultimate truth of some essential oneness. Balso searches through his song in praise of the circular. Miss Lonelyhearts' need for unity and order, so great as to border on insanity, forces him into trying constantly to balance and compose the multiplicity of the physical universe into static, ordered harmony. Like Balso, however, Miss Lonelyhearts must face the sad truth of man's dilemma: "Man has a tropism for order. . . . The physical world has a tropism for disorder." . . . This kind of antagonism is but one manifestation of constant competition in West's world. This conflict may be simple Darwinistic strife. It may be the spiritual Darwinism postulated in *Balso* and fully dramatized in *Miss Lonelyhearts,* so that Miss Lonelyhearts cannot accept the purely physical man but instead must compete with Christ, attempt to *be* a modern Christ. Between different political systems, neither good, the conflict may, as in *A Cool Million,* grind to destruction the simple bumpkins, the Lemuel Pitkins, of the world. Or the hostile camps may be divided into actors and audience, one cheating, the other hating, as in *The Day.* Wherever one looks in the world of West, there is some kind of conflict, irreconcilable, insoluble, horrible.

Like *This Side of Paradise,* however, *Balso,* as a work of art, is weakened by the fact that it is not so much the book of a grown man as the book of a precocious boy who in himself reflects many men. (pp. 57-8)

Surrealism and the writings of James Joyce, two related

sources, also illustrate how West reflects and yet satirizes his influences in *Balso*. The influence of the former is seen in the chaos of the dream life of Balso, for surrealism wished to capture man's disconnected dream life and preserve that mysterious world in art. However, to the surrealist's contention that the dream life may reveal an inner man who is higher than the purely animal creature, West directs his satiric attack. Even though a man may remove himself from everyday reality to the point of absurdity (as, for instance, when Balso reads a pair of letters within a dream within a dream), even then the simple truth is always the same: man is an animal.... West satirized what he felt was Joyce's artistic pretentiousness ..., [especially] the chaos and remarkable transformations of Joyce's famous *Walpurgisnacht* in *Ulysses*. (pp. 59-60)

Obviously, West is satirizing Joyce, but even more obviously West reflects the influence of that great artist. The form of *Ulysses,* a journey through chaos, makes the form of *Balso* what it is. Even more, the dominant ideas of *Ulysses,* the quest for truth (or the father) and the rejection of false gods, are the central concepts of *Balso;* and West accepts the idea, if not the prose, of Joyce's "yes" to the body. (p. 61)

Disgust, anti-intellectualism, and glorification of the physical man are important aspects of Dada, and all are central to *Balso Snell*.... West's later novels contain only partial echoes of this first Dadaistic cry. Where *Balso* blasts at the intellect, the foundation of man's misery, the other novels dramatize the horrors that stem from specific dreams, the products of the mind. *Miss Lonelyhearts* presents the results of an attempt to live by the Christ dream. *A Cool Million* depicts the deluded life of a boy who takes the American, Horatio Alger dream seriously. *The Day of the Locust* portrays the horror of Hollywood, the lesser dream factory (for, of course, the mind is always the major dream manufacturer). (pp. 63-4)

In its fusion of form and content, *Miss Lonelyhearts* is the best novel West was ever to write. To the novel nothing should be added and nothing could be taken away. Its stark simplicity of language and sentence structure, a bareness achieved by continual pruning and sharpening through six revisions of the novel, creates a peculiarly nightmarish etching of shadows and decay unlike the art of any other American novelist. In addition the book has a warmth, a compassion, which exceeds that of West's other novels. The warmth is especially apparent in the increased depth with which West treats the dilemma of humankind in its need for a dream. Earlier, in *Balso Snell,* West had implied that the wisest thing man can do is to accept himself as an animal and to avoid dreams completely, for in dreams there is only misery. Such an attitude was naïve: an oversimplified solution of a very young man. In *Miss Lonelyhearts,* West probes deeper. The horror of a life lived without any dream is illustrated by the joke-machine called Shrike. Terrible as it is, even a bad dream is better than no dream at all, and this idea, from *Miss Lonelyhearts* on, is constant in West.... The pathos of [man's] need to dream, while forced by his nature to choose dreams that will not soothe his pain, is explored with both horror and compassion in *Miss Lonelyhearts,* and in *Miss Lonelyhearts,* unlike *The Day,* the pity is greater than the horror. (pp. 96-7)

In ... imagistic terms the characters subordinate to Miss Lonelyhearts become merely simplified states of mind. Jux-

taposed pictorially against the growing alienation of Miss Lonelyhearts from the world of reality, the minor characters serve primarily as contrast and chiaroscuro. This static, pictorial quality is also true of the actions, which seem like candid snapshots of people caught in mid-air against a background of dull sky and decaying earth. Each action becomes a symbol of an abstract state of mind and heart, and leaves one remembering a series of almost independent pictures rather than with a memory of the developing actions.... The pictures are, in reality, sensory portrayals of the inner heart and mind of Miss Lonelyhearts.... This pictorialization, West felt, was the writer's fulfillment.... (pp. 104-05)

[The] images make the abstract concrete. They pictorialize the inner feelings. They partially explain the peculiar power of West's writing, with its nightmarish involvement in a world of hallucinations and shadows. In this approach to writing, West owes a good deal to surrealism. In the success with which he makes his distorted world of half-light come alive, perhaps more alive than the world of everyday toast and tea, he is indebted only to the intensity and power of his own imagination. (p. 106)

A Cool Million is more than a mock-melodramatic burlesque of the American success dream. It is a fearful cry against the dangers inherent in that dream. Used by opportunists, even those who believe the clichés they mouth, the American dream could be the stepping stone to a dictator. As the first significant novel satirizing the incipient fascism West saw in America, *A Cool Million* is worthy of study. (p. 132)

A Cool Million is a sad commentary upon the confident faith of the founding fathers: a sad decline from the lyric of Hail Columbia! happy land! or the concept of America, the land of the free and the home of the brave. But in the face of the American depression, it would have been surprising if West had not written such a book. What West does is to restate his constant theme in a contemporary context. The quest for something to believe in continues, and it again ends in despair. Where *Balso* indicts the folly of the quest of art, where *Miss Lonelyhearts* mocks man's dreams of Christ, *A Cool Million* attacks the American success dream. West had hoped to make *A Cool Million* an American *Candide,* but though it is not that, it does present an essential Candidean truth: the progress of the industrious and honest man is from shirtsleeves to shirtsleeves.

Like the previous novels, *A Cool Million* offers no real solutions. It mocks the American way, derides the "conspiracies" of the Bolsheviki and the International Jewish Bankers, and attacks bitterly the American Fascist movement. If the novel suggests anything affirmatively, it is that life was better in an earlier time. (pp. 136-37)

[If] there is any constant pattern in the novels of West, it is the pilgrimage around which each novel centers. In each the hero is in search of something in which he can believe and to which he can belong. The search may be made skeptically as in *Balso,* or with religious fervor as in *Miss Lonelyhearts,* or ironically as in *A Cool Million* and *The Day;* but the result is always the same: tragic disillusionment. The quest is similar to the dominant motif of *Ulysses,* and it is undoubtedly this concept in Joyce's work, as well as the pathos of the Jewish outsider Bloom, which impressed West so tremendously and made him read *Ulysses* again and again. Not to bend the knee to either church or Mother, to reject and then to seek: it was a theme worthy not only of an Irish Catholic but of an American Jew.

It is more than likely, therefore, that the reason West's novels are involved in the Quest is his rejection of a heritage, both familial and racial, that burdened West just as Joyce's heritage weighed on that great nay sayer. West's consciousness of his theme is evident from the beginning epigraph of *Balso,* "After all, my dear fellow, life, Anaxagoras has said, is a journey" . . . ; and it is as a journey, dominated by a quest which ends in disillusionment, that West's novels should be read.

But what is this promised land that is being sought in the novels of West? It is no land of milk and honey, nor is it one of perfume and spices. It is an interior land, and the search is for interior security and order, for the "beloved balance" that J. Raskolnikov Gilson seeks so desperately in *Balso.* (pp. 148-49)

Always, though obliquely and episodically, with a kind of Grecian inevitability, the action of [*The Day of the Locust*] is moving toward increasing violence, toward the mass destructive orgy in which the novel hysterically ends.

The characters that West uses in this nightmarish novel are grotesques, and they are similar in the cause of their grotesqueness: the need for an emotional life. Both comic in the tastelessness of its results and tragic in its yearning, this emotional need leads to architectural monstrosities built formlessly of plaster and paper; it leads to brothels and cockfights and pornographic movies and endless attendance at funerals, to vicarious lust and violence furnished by movies and newspapers, to violence even in the Hollywood premieres. For both rich and poor, however, there is an ever lessening sensibility to such shocks, and as the sensibility decreases there comes the emotional death which leaves each person with the vague feeling that he has been betrayed. (pp. 171-72)

The half-world [of *The Day of the Locust*] can be divided into spectators (the cheated whose emotional needs demand satisfaction) and performers (the cheaters who are attempting to satisfy the emotional needs of others). The roles, however, occasionally shift, for in the world of grotesquerie all men are both performers and spectators. . . . (p. 173)

The particular mythology that West was concerned with in *The Day*—pertinent to West's own time but timeless in its implications—is a drama about man's emotional needs, the frustration of those needs, and the need for a scapegoat to vent one's rage upon. This is, of course, good Jung, and it is completely pictorialized in the vision of the cheated pursuing those they have forced to do the cheating. (p. 183)

Part of the impact of *The Day* stems from the way in which West strives in prose for effects similar to those of certain painters. . . . [In] painting the gloom, pain, potential violence, and terrifying blankness of the human starers (or cheated), West worked in Goyesque style, painting in the darkest colors and with the most frightening of distortions. In treating the mob, West did not satirize or paint with pity. . . . West painted the mob with respect, for he knew "its awful anarchic power." . . . This mass, chaotic power is most effectively suggested by images of "wild, disordered minds" at work. . . . The influence of Daumier's car-

icatures is most apparent in the depiction of the Hollywood performer-cheaters. (pp. 184-86)

Goya darkness (the audience-starers) is, then, opposed in *The Day* by Daumier caricatures (the artist-performers). In addition *The Day* reflects the influence of certain Italian artists, among them Salvator Rosa, Francesco Guardi, and Monsu Desiderio, whom West calls "the painters of Decay and Mystery." . . . These painters are surrealistic in tendency: the work of Rosa is intimately involved with destruction and pain; the work of Guardi and Desiderio is full of images of falsity similar to those on a movie lot, where "there were bridges which bridged nothing, sculpture in trees, palaces that seemed of marble until a whole stone portico began to flap in the light breeze. . . . These images of pain and falsity exist on every page of the novel, and they are typically associated with the performer-cheaters. Often the images of falsity are highly colorful and lend a phosphorescent air and a carnival atmosphere to the novel. . . . It is the contrast between the carnival atmosphere and the horrible reality that makes for a good part of the impact of the novel, for what it obviously suggests is a Babylon doomed to destruction. The sharp contrast also creates a nightmare world made out of the grotesque world of dreams, evoked by the sights in carnival mirrors that distort the human form into weird and magical shapes, realized in the sounds of some eternal bedlam, where the cries of the sufferers in their pain and misery drift out eerily into some eternal, uncaring fog.

In *The Day* the grotesqueness of man's creation is horrible in its falsity, but *The Day* also creates the feeling of some elaborate artifice in God's creation. (pp. 188-89)

The Day is not as perfect a book as *Miss Lonelyhearts.* One reason is that *The Day* is more ambitious, as is apparent textually in its greater cast of characters, greater complexity of plot and idea, and more subtle distinctions of thought and imagery. This greater ambitiousness, however, does not excuse the fact that the middle of *The Day* seems at times to be rambling, without effective direction, especially in the extended treatment of Earle Shoop and his Mexican companion. Nor does it alter the fact that the novel's insistence upon falsity everywhere eventually seems a little overdone, rather monotonous, and a bit irritating. Even more significant, though, is that the greater formal perfection of *Miss Lonelyhearts* rests on a more effective handling of viewpoint. . . . Miss Lonelyhearts' ambivalent attraction toward and repulsion from the grotesques he pities and detests at the same time is realized dramatically through West's choice of viewpoint. On the other hand, Tod Hackett, as an artist, is merely curious about the grotesques he sees. . . . Ultimately this difference in viewpoint leads to a difference in the warmth of the novels. . . . (p. 192)

The only valid appraisal of [West's] nightmares is the test of their congruousness and their power. West's writing stands such tests. To use the word of Henry James, West's world is *done,* not *done* in any realistic or naturalistic sense, but still *done.* Most of all, it is realized in surrealistic conceits. These, more than any other single thing, make for the horrid, nightmare quality of West's universe. The conceits demonstrate man's role as a clown in a foolish dreamplay called life, and the poor art of the Creator and Director of the dream-play seems evident in the fact that the machinery creaks and the still-life background is just as phony as the death rattles of the actors. . . . Love becomes a vending machine, a place of deposit. Life becomes a fraud devised by some super Hollywood producer.

These conceits, pictorially, symbolically, and dramatically, help to create a world of irreconcilable conflict, where life is not to be taken seriously but is really a terrible prank played by some malevolent prankster. In a world where even the continued existence, to say nothing of the meaning and importance, of the human race is open to question, West's world of conflict and dreams has the ring of truth for even the most common of common men. (pp. 210-11)

> *James F. Light, in his* Nathanael West: An Interpretative Study *(copyright © 1971 by Northwestern University Press, Evanston, Ill.), second edition, Northwestern University Press, 1971.*

[*The Dream Life of Balso Snell*] does not deserve either neglect or disparagement. It is one of the most complex books this side of James Joyce, and its complexity is coherent, not chaotic. West was a widely read young man. In his first book, he reacted to his reading in three ways: he rejected the ultimate value of literature; he laid the foundation for his novel in allusions of an unusually destructive sort; and he put into practice a number of the lessons he had learned from his favorite authors, while succeeding in creating an unmistakably original work. (p. 24)

West has wasted no time in proclaiming his book a portrait of the artist turned inside-out. This technique of announcing the multiple motifs of a novel on the first one or two highly compressed pages is precisely that of James Joyce. The first two pages of *A Portrait of the Artist as a Young Man* foreshadow all the themes of the book. The epigraph to *Balso* introduces, ironically, the ignoble journey of the protagonist, the journey of the reader into the microcosm of humanity's dream life, and the life-long search of West for some escape hatch from his ironclad nihilism. The mention of Anaxagoras prepares us for the problem of the One and the Many, the metaphysical question which has occupied philosophers in one form or another since the pre-Socratics and which occurs in bizarre contexts in *Balso*. (pp. 25-6)

Balso Snell is, above all, a rejection not merely of Art, not merely of West, but rather a rejection of life itself. The implied syllogism is that life is worth living only if man can give life meaning through spiritual activity. But all spirituality is either a sham or reducible to physiological causes. Therefore, life is not worth living. Granted, the novel does constitute a revolt against art and a flagellation of the Self. But it is also an attack on Catholicism, Judaism, Christian Science, philosophy, history, music, poetry, scholarship, courtly love, the home, and patriotism. West launches his attack on the universal by means of attacks on particulars. (pp. 49-50)

West attacks the various manifestations of the spirit in two ways, by the facetious allusion and by the Westian dialectic. The first works on the principle of guilt by association; any name summoned up by one of the grotesques in *Balso* is certain to be diminished by the company it keeps. The dialectic pits thesis against antithesis and lets them destroy each other. The most important of these antitheses are Old World versus New World, Jews versus Christians, Monism versus Pluralism (in various contexts), realistic art versus abstract art, health versus mortification of the body, sanity versus insanity, mind versus body, delirium (or delusion) versus cynicism, optimism versus pessimism, art versus "animal acts," the consciousness against itself (reflection), the conventional pose versus the eccentric pose, ideal unity (system) versus material unity (disintegration), cynicism versus sentimentality, and man versus woman. This dialectic assures that no positive values will be inferred mistakenly from West's negativism. It rejects equally the two halves of human existence, mind and body, and in so doing rejects their sum—life. (p. 50)

To seize upon the uniqueness of West's nihilism it is helpful to compare his spirit with that of Dada. Dada was nihilistic, but directed its disgust at the past. . . . Dada was destruction, but it was destruction with a better future in mind. . . . West's nihilism encompassed not merely 3000 years of history, but all the possibilities of life itself. For West, the future offered no hope, because neither the body nor the spirit offered meaning or value. West's nihilism was, therefore, absolute, whereas that of the Dadaists, as vigorous as it was, was relative.

West differed from the Dadaists in technique also. Dada placed great importance on chance. . . . West gave his imagination free rein in conjuring up the unusual, but the final product was the result of reworking and creative integration. (pp. 53-4)

The Dream Life of Balso Snell is an exercise in total nihilism cast in an ingenious nihilistic form. By means of his nihilistic dialectic, the author systematically disposes of the various contestants in the world's intellectual arena. By means of facetious allusions and the satirizing of his own models, he wages battle against literature, nullifying what might have been interpreted as positive elements in his own work. By linking his characters and situations to literary tradition, he exposes "real life" for as great a fiction as the novel itself. His attack is comprehensive and it is at one with the method in which it is carried on. But the book is also a first novel, and, as such, it has a further interest as a proving ground for the talents which account for the eventual success of *Miss Lonelyhearts* and *The Day of the Locust*. West shows in *Balso* that penchant for caricature which he finally developed to a Dickensian fineness. Furthermore, all his later books employ a scenic or episodic technique similar to that of his first novel. His prose is, at the beginning as at the end, vulnerable to analysis only in terms of painting. And his comedy, though it varies somewhat from book to book, never compromises the cold eye of satire that so mercilessly exposes the human condition in *Balso Snell*. West need not have been ashamed of his first novel. It lacks the stature of *Miss Lonelyhearts* or *The Day of the Locust*, but it is an extraordinarily original work, and it is successful on its own terms. (pp. 54-5)

> *Gerald Locklin, "'The Dream Life of Balso Snell': Journey into the Microcosm," in* Nathanael West: The Cheaters and the Cheated, *edited by David Madden (© 1973 by David Madden), Everett/Edwards, 1973, pp. 23-55.*

The Cheated was the original title of West's last book, *The Day of the Locust*. All of West's characters have been cheated of self, whether they belong to the frenetic group of performers West calls masqueraders, or to the faceless, uneasy mob whose appetite for a vital identity is served by the masquerade. As Tod Hackett reflects, the anarchic audiences who throng Hollywood's cinema openings are the cream of America's madmen because they realize that they have been betrayed by the promise of life for the free individual.... West's characters are all poorly made, like Homer Simpson, because all that remains of real identity is a vestigial self felt as a restless desire for completion. The audience's demand that they be furnished with a full, authentic existence is insatiable, so that they are always ready to provoke and then to follow "the necessary promise" of a new con man into the violence that makes them feel alive. The growing recognition runs throughout West's work: the dissolution of self makes the existence of individual, artist, and nation three dependent coordinates of a con-game.

West described his first novel, *The Dream Life of Balso Snell,* as "a protest against writing books," and the reasons for the protest are perfectly clear in the artist's hatred of the audience who requires him to be a confidence man:

> Some day I shall obtain my revenge by writing a play for one of their art theatres. A theatre patronized by the discriminating few....
> In this play I shall take my beloved patrons into my confidence and flatter their difference from other theatregoers.... Then, suddenly, in the midst of some very witty dialogue, the entire cast will walk to the footlights and shout Chekov's advice:
> "It would be more profitable for the farmer to raise rats for the granary than for the bourgeois to nourish the artist...."
> In case the audience should misunderstand and align itself on the side of the artist, the ceiling of the theatre will be made to open and cover the occupants with tons of loose excrement.   (pp. 304-05)

Art is an excrement in that it seems to be a waste, a by-product, of the fundamentally selfish, yet symbiotic, relationship of artist and audience: the audience needing the stimulating illusions of the artist in order to feel that it exists and the artist needing someone to see his illusions for the same reason. More specifically, as the anecdote about dumping excrement suggests, art is a sadomasochistic shell game in which the artist's covert desires to demean are released to the delight of the victims, who have in effect "asked for it" by stimulating his desires.... The secondary, by-product nature of art is further indicated by the book's repeated explanation that creativity is a vehicle for sexual conquest and by the frequent suggestion that the content of art is inconsequential as long as it seems excitingly portentous; standing before his "cringing audience," another performer climaxes his act "by keeping in the air an Ivory Tower, a Still White Bird, the Holy Grail, the Nails, the Scourge, the Thorns, and a piece of the True Cross".... The thesis that art is a deceitful act of aggression fulfilling the ulterior needs of performer and viewer is chiefly borne out in the long literary leg-pull of the book. We begin by entering the anus of the deceitful Trojan horse, and after complicated stories-within-stories-and-dreams which explode in our faces after asking to be taken seriously, we finally come to a conclusion that defines the whole work as an excremental act, a wet-dream. (pp. 306-07)

In both *Miss Lonelyhearts* and *The Day of the Locust* West extends his inquisition of the art-game to an exhibition of the art by which everyone lives. Human life is exposed as a set of tricks and rituals by means of which one persons asks another for assurance, with the implied promise that confidence will be returned if the other cooperates in the game. People exist by inducing others to trust roles. (p. 307)

The supreme form of confidence, religious faith, is the dramatic center of *Miss Lonelyhearts.* ... Christ, the ultimate Miss Lonelyhearts, is the sovereign conferrer of belief; and West's protagonist, once he finds it impossible to betray his readers' trust anymore, is forced to search for a self that will give validity not only to his role but to Christ's. The design is basic West. A tormented, cheated mob forces a man to attempt to fashion an authentic self that will make his role effective in giving the mob authenticity in turn. Miss Lonelyhearts must play the part that the shadowy Dr. Pierce-All does in *The Day.* He must indicate the road to life. Such is the interdependence of all of West's huddled artifacts—people, animals, and things in a continuum of gaudy sterility—that one has the awesome sense that if anyone in this world came to genuine life, Miss Lonelyhearts' whole "world of doorknobs" would indeed follow suit miraculously. Christ is the answer, Miss Lonelyhearts knows, but he is also aware that for him Christ is another trick, a "hysteria" in whose "mirrors ... the dead world takes on a semblance of life".... However, tricks and mirrors are all that is available, so in a grimly comic parody of the existentialist hero's quest to create himself, West's hero willfully attempts to indulge the deception to the hilt. (p. 308)

Skeptical of his own roles and the illusions on which they are built, the West hero is vulnerable because of his inability to cloak himself completely with a façade. Wanting to find a believable role, yet despising the lies of which roles are made, he maintains an envious love-hate relationship with those who have apparently achieved invulnerability through manipulation of illusions—Shrike and Betty in *Miss Lonelyhearts* and Faye Greener in *The Day.* Betty and Faye share the "power to limit experience arbitrarily" ..., Betty to the order bounded by gingham apron and party dress, and Faye to the mental screen where she projects a bright confetti of fragmented film-strips. (p. 309)

In West's fiction the fool-role is crucial above all because it represents a way of dealing with a diminished self; in this sense, we may say, all of West's characters are fools.

Miss Lonelyhearts is thus more successful as the Holy Fool than as the magician-priest. In fact, in the transformation that takes place in the last pages of the novel he seems to achieve his desire to become a man of confidence. (p. 311)

One major attribute of West's self-doubt as an artist, his haste to laugh at himself before we do, gets the best of him in his next novel, *A Cool Million.* (p. 312)

Nevertheless, *A Cool Million* is not merely regressive; seen in the context of West's career, it represents his progressive generalization from the self-doubt of the artist to an understanding that this provides a key insight into a national as well as a personal malaise. Whenever West has a new or deepened perception his first instinct is to parody it. Thus *A Cool Million* bears much the same relationship to West's last novel that *Balso Snell* does to *Miss Lonelyhearts....*

A Cool Million allows us to see still more clearly that in dealing with the duplicity that he perceived at the center of existence, West could not create a potent master-manipulator of confidence as Melville could. Melville makes the existence of the self an enigma, but the figure he places before us has a full, probing power even if the source of the power be a mystery. In West, the dissatisfied boredom and sense of vague betrayal indicate that the self does in fact exist, but only as a minimal presence. (p. 314)

The suspicion that somehow, some unnameable agent has cheated them of something valuable sifts like the smell of smoke through the empty souls of *The Day of the Locust.* West's ability to capture this mood is perhaps the most remarkable quality of the novel, but the book also has a certain diffuseness everyone has noted. In *Miss Lonelyhearts* plot was coterminous with meaning; the flesh and bone of *The Day* never quite connect, in part because West makes his most ambitious attempt to deal with the individual, artistic, and national crises of confidence that he feels are interrelated. The three threads of plot weave in and out of each other in the sort of disquieted ballet performed by the masqueraders and the mob that watches. (p. 315)

The Day of the Locust elaborates the idea of radical exhaustion in image after image of somnolence, impotence, and sheer tiredness. The god of love lies face-down in a pile of old newspapers on a movie set, Homer Simpson sleeps as if after centuries of stone breaking that have left him a hulking, tired shell, the betrayed mob stands listlessly about with shabby clothes and worn personalities. The dissolution of core vitality which is the individual's existential condition is also his national heritage, a social-hereditary strain of spiritual debility. The energy that broke stones can now only construct fairy-tale edifices of lath and paper, a fantasy culture that in turn dupes and eviscerates its creators in an endless cycle. (pp. 316-17)

West is a confidence trickster not primarily because his style sometimes leers heavily at us but because his writing becomes a game of confidence that makes writing possible. His bitter self-doubt, activated by the role of magical guru the modern artist is asked to play, turns instinctively to the ludicrous strategies of make-believe. The game takes its strength from the confidence it seeks to win from us, the audience. Anticipating that confidence (this is the crucial initial "leap" of faith in the game), the artist first tricks himself, as it were, into commitment to his work. It is as if the writer by his tone must never fully admit to himself, at least while the pen is in his hand, that he is trying to tell the truth, for he hasn't sufficient confidence for that role, and the realization would make art impossible for him. Like Tod Hackett, he must remind himself ironically that he is a painter, not a prophet. He commits himself to art as a trick to win confidence in the face of doubt, beneath which is a need for belief. Having admitted that art is a trick, he can allow himself to have faith in it insofar as it is an enticing game, and his skill both expresses and preserves that precarious conviction. West's artistry thus becomes a mental judo that makes the force of doubt lend momentum to confident creation. Solid images change surreally from one thing to another, natural facts bend like rubber artifacts, metaphors are absurdly reified, pretense and reality blend into each other and dissolve. The fictional world is fantastic and full of ironies to remind one level of the writer's consciousness that a trick is being played; but the surreal world must be made vividly, exactly, with disciplined craft because it must also convince, win belief. If the writer is intelligent, perceptive, and lucky, then his bizarre lies will coincide with and betray the lies that exist in our lives. And this is the con-artist's truth. This is West's delight in meticulous tall tales that circle around the rooted doubt that feeds them.

It may be objected that every artist is in a sense a confidence man who tries to win our belief in his illusions of reality. And further, Schiller has told us that all art is a game. But not every artist has a radical self-doubt which is so close to the surface and which is so much "compensated" by a bravura of fantasy and trickery, both stylistic and thematic. The account of West's genius that I am attempting to give is the same account of the artist that his work dramatizes; it is one of his central subjects, and the bizarreness of his presentation is as acute as his intimate self-awareness. Neither is a reductive description. If we are all tricksters, then art can be one of those tricks that illumine instead of darken our knowledge. Literature is a fabrication, a tissue of words, lies told in the service of truth—that complacent cliché becomes fresh, the tired phrase becomes vivid insight again in West's four brief novels. (pp. 318-19)

> *Warwick Wadlington, "Nathanael West and the Confidence Game," in* Nathanael West: The Cheaters and the Cheated, *edited by David Madden (© 1973 by David Madden), Everett/Edwards, 1973, pp. 299-322.*

Nathanael West, I believe, was influenced by both naturalism and existentialism, although he is seldom mentioned with the naturalists. Strange. . . .

Nathanael West has moments when he is the beaten soldier on the battlefield of despair, as darkly pessimistic as the most pessimistic existentialists. At other times, West is hopeful. . . . West leans far in the pessimistic direction, but not as far as we probably think. We don't have to slash our throats after reading West. (p. 181)

West's naturalism needs to be emphasized as a balance to the remarks on surrealistic grotesqueness that have made him seem a non-American or even un-American writer, an unhealthy, little "alien." The small sales of all his books in his lifetime can be traced, in part, to a sense of strangeness in his presentation of the world. Even today West is not well known outside academic circles, if there. Nevertheless his bizarre distortion of persons and events does not bar him from the mainstream of the naturalistic movement, even though this is usually thought to be "realistic" rather than "surrealistic." It is not. (p. 184)

The chief difference [between West and other naturalists] is that West has more examples [of grotesqueries] than the other writers. . . . West is only carrying to their natural conclusions the impulses of the naturalists.

Moreover, . . . the grotesque is a typical American genre. . . . In other words, . . . Nathanael West did not have to go outside his native literature to find an influence on his writing.

Many critics have claimed that a characteristic of naturalism is the extensive documentation of details. West's novels are notable for their brevity. But naturalism is not intrinsically dependent on quantitative criteria. If it were, Sherwood Anderson and Stephen Crane would have to be cast aside, and few would exclude them from the tradition of the naturalists. The endless pages of dreary Dreiser and numbing Norris do not make the works deterministic, *determinism* being the one essential quality of this literary movement. . . . Nathanael West achieves much real power in a few pages of careful writing and judicious selection of devastating details because he knew it is not freight or bulk that is required for naturalism; the deterministic vision of life is. Dreiser, Dos Passos, and Farrell could have learned something about restraint from West. West's criticism of the naturalists has too often been read as a blanket condemnation. Actually his chief complaint is their length. . . .

However, something in the style of West definitely *is* like that of the literary naturalists—its detachment. Supposedly these writers were scientists who dispassionately recorded whatever unfolded, without comment. West never intrudes himself into his books, but tersely records the activities of the distorted and grotesque characters. I think Leslie Fiedler overstates his case about West's rejection of this detached style [in *Love and Death in the American Novel*, for] . . . West is not a writer of case reports. . . . (p. 185)

West's detachment is only a matter of indirection and not uninvolvement, in any case. Any writer, including a naturalist, selects the material he wants to convey; he arranges it in any pattern he wants; he can, for example, kill off or save his creatures; he can send them to the electric chair or into the arms of a loved one. If anything, naturalists are more involved in their characters' lives than are any other writers because they are always promoting theses. Never are they merely letting characters work out their own destinies; their destinies are set when the authors begin to write. (pp. 185-86)

A true point of difference between West's style and the naturalists' is his use of comedy. He makes the reader writhe and smile, grimace and chuckle simultaneously. Strict naturalists are rarely amusing—intentionally. They do not see the plight of their characters as anything but serious and pathetic. Who would ever laugh at Studs Lonigan? It is part of the war within West that he sees his characters' plight as silly and ludicrous as well as heartbreaking, calling for laughter as well as tears. It is here that West's naturalism blends into existentialism's sense of absurdity and makes for his unique gifts as a novelist. It is impossible to have a stock response to his work. . . .

West's grotesquerie has an element that is not the same as the grotesque in many other American writers. . . . [Others] writing in this vein are not noted for their smiles, however uncomfortable. Rather, they inspire terror. Their horror is oppressive, often frightening. West's is like theirs, but adds a European element that is oddly funny. It is this comic aspect of his writing more than anything that made him seem bizarre in his own day. Yet partly because of West, black humor has become common in modern American writing. . . . (p. 186)

This formerly "un-American" tendency in West is mingled, however, with a very American sense of optimism. Black laughter is one impulse toward a helpless and almost despairing acceptance of the problems that West depicts in his novels. . . . His war within his fiction is . . . between his desire to throw up his hands because of the absurdity of human behavior and all activity and his other desire to work to remedy social evils. Much of West's satire is inherently optimistic, for only someone who believes in the possibility of change can ridicule so angrily. . . . Like a good healthy-minded American, he thinks that something must be done to uplift the downtrodden. Like a good nihilistic European, he thinks something must be done to downtrod the uplifted. His optimism leads him to want a new tomorrow for his broken people, even something like "a better way of life"; his pessimism leads him to a tortured self-mockery. . . . Only recently, really, has it been possible for all but the avant-garde to understand West's tensions. (pp. 186-87)

Freudian psychology has played a conspicuously large part in West's emphasis upon sexual frustrations. The overwhelming feeling is of stagnation of the body, which is a swamp. From this muck, miasmic emotions seep out, only to smother themselves later. All the naturalists deal with similar psychological factors, though not always in such a concentration of deadness. (pp. 187-88)

Violence in West erupts because of inhibitions and frustrations of basic drives. There is a strange leaden quality to the violence in West's books, even though they are memorable for their cockfight and lamb slaughter, for a scalping and an assassination. He believed that an American writer uses it to capture the flavor of American life: "In America violence is idiomatic. Read our newspapers. To make the front page a murderer has to use his imagination, he also has to use a particularly hideous instrument." . . . West was at the beginning of the trend. Yet no one ever reads him for gratuitous violence; he is interested in the reasons behind it. (p. 189)

West makes his readers uncomfortably sensitive to one aspect of their physicality. As with Jonathan Swift, the accusation is often "neurosis" or "filthy-mindedness," either term meaning the same thing actually, but West is trying to puncture the scented, floral-designed toilet paper wall that man builds around himself. *Balso Snell* is not West's best book, but it is not flawed simply because it is scatological. Perhaps, like Swift's *A Tale of a Tub*, as years pass, justification will be found or excuses made for the inclusion of a degrading reality about men's bodies. Without a doubt there is a double standard of respectability that favors the safely established writer over the living one —especially in the academic world. There is nothing like being dead for two hundred years to make critics excuse a writer's "flaws," even turn them into virtues. (p. 192)

He clearly was not a propagandist; yet he was critical of conditions in America, especially proto-fascism in *A Cool Million* and materialistic American dreams in *The Day of the Locust*. As with the mainstream naturalists, the social criticism is more pronounced than the specific alternatives to bad conditions. . . . West, like the naturalists generally, may not always know what he wants for his creations, but he knows it is not *this* and not *that*. . . . *The Dream Life of Balso Snell* has little social protest, but the last three novels do. The difficulty arises because West's work comes so close to the most pessimistic strain in naturalism, just where it blends into the hopelessness of existentialism. But he was not a writer of total despair. (pp. 193-94)

West's sense of the absurd is best illustrated by the endings of all his books. Each one is a means of undercutting the dreams or potentialities of the protagonist. . . . These endings definitely militate against a reading of optimism in

West, but the reader must always consider the aesthetic force of a death or unhappy ending in a novel. West faced the problem of being thought a Pollyanna if he allowed his characters to win. In fact, without a stark ending, a novel may seem to be unimportant. The social realities presented seem not worth much consideration since the problems are solved in the book itself. Like the naturalists, West did not want his works to be tossed aside as escape literature; he wanted them to remove social problems where possible.

Unlike Sartre's existentialism, West's sees little freedom in the characters' choices. There is no defiance of conventional morality, as there is at the end of *The Flies,* or of anything else. West wrote at the time when senselessness was just becoming a felt fact. At the beginning of any shift in philosophy or feeling, fiction writers are probably uncertain about how to handle their beliefs. Especially with existentialism, it was hard to see beyond utter hopelessness. The Dadaists could only grunt and rip up things. What is amazing, actually, is how West could guide his writing to the extent he did, without choking on his own despair. Later writers, like Sartre, could approach the same *Weltanschauung* with more appreciation of its malleability. It was something with which *they* were to work. In West the existentialism almost works him.

Even in Hemingway, who was writing during the same years and experiencing the same philosophical pull, the mood is of greater control over a meaningless reality.... The best is made of a bad situation. In West, the mood is that the worst has been made of a terrible situation.... West cannot create even the temporary clean, well-lighted places, be they bull rings or fishing boats. His works are much closer to the philosophical abyss. The only stay against harsh reality is an uncoated recognition of the facts.

If there is one existentialist concept West deals with the most, it has to be *Angst.* His world is full of unnamed fears and terrors. I think this feeling is a further development of the many frustrations portrayed in naturalistic fiction. Lurking inside his truncated people are emotions that move around like psychic indigestion. They can point to the spot, but they cannot belch. Sometimes they cannot even point to the spot where it hurts. It might seem that the anxieties of the characters are sexual and nothing else. But modern interest in Freudianism can lead readers to oversimplifications. West uses the sexual blocks as metaphors for all human anxieties. He never envisions an orgiastic utopia. The trouble is not always isolable; it is a condition of being alive. (pp. 196-97)

The lack of identity of people in the modern world is an issue almost worn out with over-insistence. But surely it is a predominant theme in Nathanael West. It was not so commonplace in his day.... But interestingly enough, West cannot retreat, except fleetingly, to a pre-industrial, more satisfactory world, as can Steinbeck in *Tortilla Flat* or Sherwood Anderson can in *Poor White.* He does not romanticize the past, except in *A Cool Million* in a few scenes, primarily as a satiric contrast to the present. When he depicts a country "idyll" in *Miss Lonelyhearts,* it is to dismiss it as an evasion of the hard truths. It is almost as if West excludes history altogether. What concerns him is the stark, streaked reality of his own day.. This feeling of pain ties West to modern existentialist beliefs as well as to naturalism. (pp. 197-98)

[Just] below the surface of the comedy and the restrained writing is a river of tears that threatens to flood the page. Unlike many naturalists, he portrays no easy villains to blame.... The naturalists' sympathy has developed into the existentialists' *Weltschmerz.* It should be pointed out that much of the pity and sorrow that resulted is self-pity. There is no one to turn upon for relief. The weeping and gnashing of teeth are as much for the authors as for the creations. Without his black laughter, West might have been sentimental. (p. 198)

There is another paradox in West's attitude toward the suffering masses. The deformed, the retarded, and the weak are his victims; they whimper from their soiled, little corners. He pities them immensely. But he dislikes—elsewhere—the very people whose pains he empathizes with. The clash here is between naturalistic proletarian sympathies and existentialist elitist disdain for the ignorant majority. (p. 199)

West's answer to the metaphysical shriek beginning to fill the thought of his time is neither suicide nor acceptance. It is thin, ironic laughter. Readers must notice the grotesque comedy in the very center of the most sorrowful events. (p. 200)

The final major characteristic of existentialism I wish to discuss is the desire for what Heidegger called an *authentic* life. All of West's protagonists seek such a life; they want to live meaningfully and honestly.... The trouble, as West feels it, is that practically all lives are not authentic. He represents a logical outgrowth of naturalism in this respect, I think, since he is only saying in more extreme form what the naturalists had said earlier. That is, they documented the tediousness and limitations of characters living lives thrust upon them by biological and environmental and accidental circumstances. The naturalists implied that some of these discontents are remediable; West is not so sure. (p. 201)

West wrote at a period when the inherent optimism of most naturalists for improved conditions was souring, turning into a more pessimistic intellectual *milieu,* the one that has predominated in the nineteen-forties, -fifties, and -sixties. In a way he stands suspended—one might say crucified—between hope and hopelessness, between anger and *Angst,* bleeding from all his wounds. (p. 202)

Daniel R. Brown, "The War Within Nathanael West: Naturalism and Existentialism," in Modern Fiction Studies *(copyright © 1974, by Purdue Research Foundation, West Lafayette, Indiana, U.S.A.), Summer, 1974, pp. 181-202.*

Oscar (Fingal O'Flahertie Wills) Wilde
1855-1900

Irish-born dramatist, essayist, novelist, and poet. Oscar Wilde was undoubtedly better known in his lifetime for his scandalous lifestyle than for his literary theories and their execution in his dramas. However, subsequent generations have regularly revived his delightful comedies of manners, and it now seems likely that his work will survive his notoriety. He was born into a family to whom scandal was no stranger. His father, Sir William Wilde, was a prominent surgeon whose sexual dalliances led him into one of the most scandalous libel suits of the time. His mother was a writer of some fame as well as a champion of Irish nationalism. Wilde got off to a brilliant scholastic start at Trinity College, Dublin, and Magdalen College, Oxford. At the latter he came under the influences of John Ruskin and Walter Pater. Deciding to make writing his career, Wilde came to London and quickly became the leading proponent of the Art for Art's Sake Movement. His bizarre costumes and extravagant conversation put him at the center of literary London society. During the early 1880s he published his first book, *Poems* (a rather undistinguished collection), made a brilliantly successful lecture tour of the United States and England, and married Constance Lloyd, the daughter of a well-off Dublin family. According to most sources the marriage was successful for several years and there was no evidence of Wilde's later homosexuality. However, in 1891 he met and became infatuated with Lord Alfred Douglas, son of the Marquess of Queensberry. At the same time he entered into his period of greatest creativity, publishing *Intentions,* an important collection of critical essays outlining his aesthetic theories; and his witty comedies, of which *The Importance of Being Earnest* is his masterpiece. His relationship with Douglas, the Marquess's violent disapproval of this relationship, and Wilde's own ill-advised legal action against the Marquess set up a chain of events that led to Wilde's imprisonment on charges of homosexual practices. He continued to write during his two years in prison, most notably the poem *The Ballad of Reading Gaol.* After his release he retired to France, and his attempts to revive his literary career were unsuccessful.

PRINCIPAL WORKS

Poems (poetry) 1881
The Happy Prince, and Other Tales (short stories) 1888
Intentions (essays) 1891
Lord Arthur Savile's Crime, and Other Stories (short stories) 1891
The Picture of Dorian Gray (novel) 1891
Lady Windemere's Fan (drama) 1893
Salome (drama) 1893
A Woman of No Importance (drama) 1894
The Ballad of Reading Gaol, and Other Poems (poetry) 1898
An Ideal Husband (drama) 1899
The Importance of Being Earnest (drama) 1899
De Profundis (essay) 1905

What Dorian Gray's sin was no one says and no one knows. Anyone who recognizes it has committed it.

Here we touch the pulse of Wilde's art—sin. He deceived himself into believing that he was the bearer of good news of neo-paganism to an enslaved people. His own distinctive qualities, the qualities, perhaps, of his race—keenness, generosity, and a sexless intellect—he placed at the service of a theory of beauty which, according to him, was to bring back the Golden Age and the joy of the world's youth. But if some truth adheres to his subjective interpretations of Aristotle, to his restless thought that proceeds by sophisms rather than syllogisms, to his assimilations of natures as foreign to his as the delinquent is to the humble, at its very base is the truth inherent in the soul of Catholicism: that man cannot reach the divine heart except through that sense of separation and loss called sin. (pp. 204-05)

In his last book, *De Profundis,* he kneels before a gnostic Christ, resurrected from the apocryphal pages of *The House of Pomegranates,* and then his true soul, trembling, timid, and saddened, shines through the mantle of Heliogabalus. His fantastic legend, his opera [*Salomé*]—a polyphonic variation on the rapport of art and nature, but at the same time a revelation of his own psyche—his brilliant books sparkling with epigrams (which made him, in the view of some people, the most penetrating speaker of the past century), these are now divided booty. (p. 205)

James Joyce, "Oscar Wilde: The Poet of 'Salomé'" (originally published in Italian in Il Piccolo della Sera, *March 24, 1909), in* The Critical Writings of James Joyce, *edited by Ellsworth Mason and Richard Ellmann (copyright © 1959 by Harriet Weaver and*

F. Lionel Monro; reprinted by permission of The Viking Press, Inc.), Viking, 1959, pp. 201-05.

The difficulty about Wilde as a playwright was that he never quite got through the imitative phase. *The Importance of Being Earnest* is the nearest approach to absolute originality that he attained. In that play, for the first time, he seemed to be tearing himself away from tradition and to be evolving a dramatic form of his own. Unhappily it was the last play he was to write, and so the promise in it was never fulfilled. . . . For, paradoxical as it may sound in the case of so merry and light-hearted a play, *The Importance of Being Earnest* is artistically the most serious work that Wilde produced for the theatre. Not only is it by far the most brilliant of his plays considered as literature. It is also the most sincere. With all its absurdity, its psychology is truer, its criticism of life subtler and more profound than that of the other plays. And even in its technique it shows, in certain details, a breaking away from the conventional well-made play of the 'seventies and 'eighties in favour of the looser construction and more naturalistic methods of the newer school. (p. 61)

In *The Importance of Being Earnest,* in fact, Wilde really invented a new type of play, and that type was the only quite original thing he contributed to the English stage. In form it is farce, but in spirit and in treatment it is comedy. Yet it is not farcical comedy. Farcical comedy is a perfectly well recognised class of drama and a fundamentally different one. There are only two other plays which I can think of which belong to the same type—*Arms and the Man* and *The Philanderer.* (p. 63)

As far as plot and construction are concerned [Wilde's comedies] are frankly modelled on the "well-made play" of their period. Indeed, they were already old-fashioned in technique when they were written. The long soliloquy which opens the third act of *Lady Windermere's Fan* with such appalling staginess, and sends a cold shiver down one's back at each successive revival, was almost equally out of date on the first night. Ibsen had already sent that kind of thing to the right-about for all persons who aspired to serious consideration as dramatists. Luckily the fame of Wilde's comedies does not rest on his plots or his construction. It rests on his gifts of characterisation and of brilliant and effective dialogue. Both these gifts he possessed in a pre-eminent degree, but in both of them one has to recognise grave limitations. His minor characters are generally first-rate, but he never quite succeeded with his full-length figures. He is like an artist who can produce marvellously life-like studies or sketches, but fails when he attempts to elaborate a portrait. Windermere and Lady Windermere, Sir Robert and Lady Chiltern, none of them is really human, none of them quite alive. As for the principal people in *A Woman of No Importance,* Lord Illingworth himself, Mrs. Arbuthnot and her son, Hester Worsley, they are all dolls. The sawdust leaks out of them at every pore. That is the central weakness of the play, that and its preposterous plot. But when you turn to the minor characters, to Lady Hunstanton and Lady Caroline Pontefract and Sir John and the Archdeacon, how admirably they are drawn! Did anybody ever draw foolish or pompous or domineering old ladies better than Wilde? (pp. 66-7)

Lady Bracknell is an immortal creation. She is in some ways the greatest achievement of the Wilde theatre, the fine flower of his genius. It is impossible to read any of her scenes—indeed, it is impossible to read almost any scene whatever in *The Importance of Being Earnest*—without recognising that for brilliancy of wit this play may fairly be ranked with the very greatest of English comedies. But though Lady Bracknell is wonderfully drawn, she is not profoundly drawn. As a character in so very light a comedy, there is, of course, no reason why she should be. I merely mention the fact lest she should be claimed as an exception to the statement that Wilde's more elaborate portraits are all failures. Lady Bracknell is brilliantly done, but she is a brilliant surface only. She has no depth and no subtlety. Wilde has seen her with absolute clearness, but he has seen her, as it were, in two dimensions only, not in the round. That is the weak point of all Wilde's character drawing. It lacks solidity. No one can hit off people's external manifestations, their whims and mannerisms, their social insincerities, more vividly or more agreeably than he. But he never shows you their souls. And when it is necessary that he should do so, if you are really to understand and to sympathise with them, as it is in the case of Mrs. Arbuthnot, for example, or Lady Chiltern, he fails.

Why he failed I do not know. Possibly it was from mere indolence, because he was not sufficiently interested. Possibly he could not have succeeded if he had tried. To analyse character to the depths requires imaginative sympathy of a very special kind, and I am not sure whether Wilde possessed this, or at least possessed it in the requisite degree of intensity. He had a quick eye for the foibles of mankind and a rough working hypothesis as to their passions and weaknesses. Beyond that he does not seem to me to have gone, and I doubt whether it ever occurred to him to examine the springs of action of even his most important characters with any thoroughness. So long as what they did and the reasons assigned for their doing it would pass muster in the average English theatre with the average English audience, he was content. (pp. 69-70)

The only one of his plays which seems to me to be written with conviction, because he had something to express and because the dramatic form seemed to him the right one in which to express it, is *Salome*—and *Salome* was not written for the theatre. . . . [When] Wilde wrote it, it was not with a view to its ever being performed, and so his genius had free scope. He was writing to please himself, not to please a manager, and the result is that *Salome* is his best play. *The Importance of Being Earnest* is written with conviction, in a sense. That is to say, it is the expression of the author's own temperament and his attitude towards life, not an insincere re-statement of conventional theatrical ideas. But *The Importance of Being Earnest* is only a joke, though an amazingly brilliant one. . . . (pp. 70-1)

St. John Hankin, in his The Dramatic Works of St. John Hankin, *Vol. III, Martin Secker, Ltd., 1912 (and reprinted as "Wilde as a Dramatist" in* Oscar Wilde, *edited by Richard Ellmann, Prentice-Hall, Inc., 1969, pp. 61-72).*

A wholesome dislike of the common-place, rightly or wrongly identified by him with the *bourgeois,* with our middle-class—its habits and tastes—leads [Wilde] to protest emphatically against so-called "realism" in art; life, as he argues, with much plausibility, as a matter of fact, when it is really awake, following art—the fashion an effective artist sets; while art, on the other hand, influential and effective art, has never taken its cue from actual life. In *Dorian Gray* he is true certainly, on the whole, to the aesthetic philosophy of his *Intentions*; yet not infallibly, even on this point: there is a certain amount of the intrusion of real life and its sordid aspects—the low theatre, the pleasures and griefs, the faces of some very unrefined people, managed, of course, cleverly enough. The interlude of Jim Vane, his half-sullen but wholly faithful care for his sister's honour, is as good as perhaps anything of the kind, marked by a homely but real pathos, sufficiently proving a versatility in the writer's talent, which should make his books popular. Clever always, this book, however, seems to set forth anything but a homely philosophy of life for the middle-class—a kind of dainty Epicurean theory, rather— yet fails, to some degree, in this; and one can see why. A true Epicureanism aims at a complete though harmonious development of man's entire organism. To lose the moral sense therefore, for instance, the sense of sin and righteousness, as Mr. Wilde's heroes are bent on doing as speedily, as completely as they can, is to lose, or lower, organisation, to become less complex, to pass from a higher to a lower degree of development. As a story, however, a partly supernatural story, it is first-rate in artistic management; those Epicurean niceties only adding to the decorative colour of its central figure, like so many exotic flowers, like the charming scenery and the perpetual, epigrammatic, surprising, yet so natural, conversations, like an atmosphere all about it. All that pleasant accessory detail, taken straight from culture, the intellectual and social interests, the conventionalities, of the moment, have, in fact, after all, the effect of the better sort of realism, throwing into relief the adroitly-devised supernatural element after the manner of Poe, but with a grace he never reached, which supersedes that earlier didactic purpose, and makes the quite sufficing interest of an excellent story. (pp. 127-29)

Dorian himself, though certainly a quite unsuccessful experiment in Epicureanism, in life as a fine art, is (till his inward spoiling takes visible effect suddenly, and in a moment, at the end of his story) a beautiful creation. But his story is also a vivid, though carefully considered, exposure of the corruption of a soul, with a very plain moral, pushed home, to the effect that vice and crime make people coarse and ugly. General readers, nevertheless, will probably care less for this moral, less for the fine, varied, largely appreciative culture of the writer, in evidence from page to page, than for the story itself, with its adroitly managed supernatural incidents, its almost equally wonderful applications of natural science; impossible, surely, in fact, but plausible enough in fiction. Its interest turns on that very old theme, old because based on some inherent experience or fancy of the human brain, of a double life: of Döppelgänger—not of two *persons,* in this case, but of the man and his portrait. . . . (pp. 132-33)

> *Walter Pater, "A Novel by Mr. Oscar Wilde," in his* Sketches *and* Reviews *(copyright, 1919, 1947 by Boni & Liveright, Inc.), Boni & Liveright, 1919, pp. 126-33.*

No one would deny to Wilde the title of a Prince of Paradoxers. And yet this acolyte of the obverse, to whom perversity was a passion, never created so puzzling a paradox as the paradox of his own life. He to whom humanity was always a disquieting problem has bequeathed himself as a

far more disquieting problem to humanity. Irony incarnate, yet unconscious, lay in his reiterated injunction that it is not so much what we say, nor even what we do, but what we *are* that eternally matters. . . . He early confessed that he "wanted to eat of the fruit of all the trees in the garden of the world"; and he went forth into the world with that passion in his soul. But he ate only the bitter-sweet fruit of the trees of pleasure; and it turned to ashes upon his tongue. If he ate of the fruit of the tree of knowledge, it was knowledge of evil, not of good. This master of the half-truth is condemned in the very phrase; it was the fate of his character not simply to know, but to wish to know, only the half of the truth, of the meaning of life. (pp. 260-61)

If Wilde could be termed virtuous in any sense, it was in no other than the professional sense. In his life as artist, it was his sincerity to be insincere. The final verity about the man is that, through the refractory lens of his temperament, all truth appeared encased in a paradox. Far from being universal or fundamental, truth to Wilde was so individual, so personal a thing that the moment it became the property of more than one person, it became a falsehood. If his art ever ceased to live for its own sake, it was because it lived for Wilde's sake. Indeed Wilde was of his essence what the French call *personnel;* and a work of art, as he phrased it, is always the unique result of an unique temperament. To Ibsen, creation in art consisted in holding judgment-day over oneself. To Wilde, creation in art consisted in the celebration of a holiday of mentality. In the guise of interpreter of the modern spirit, he was always happening upon the discovery of a great, an unique truth; and this he flippantly and condescendingly consented to communicate to that boorish monster, the public. Art was an ivory tower in which dwelt the long-haired seraph of the sunflower. The drama was merely a platform for the *flair* of the *flaneur.* All the world was a stage for the wearer of the green carnation. (pp. 261-62)

If Wilde could be said to have any morals, it was a faith in the artistic validity of poetic justice. If he could be said to have any conscience, it was the professional conscience of the impeccable artist—of Poe, of Pater, of Sainte Beuve. If he could be said to have a sense of right, it was a sense of the right of the artist to live his own untrammelled life.

Nothing is easier than acquiescence in Wilde's dictum that the drama is the meeting place of art and life. And yet nowhere more clearly than in Wilde's own plays do we find the purposed divorce of art from life. It was his fundamental distinction, in the rôle of critic as artist, to trace with admirable clarity the line of demarcation between unimaginative realism and imaginative reality. The methods of Zola and the Naturalistic school always drew Wilde's keenest critical thrusts. The greatest heresy, in his opinion, was the doctrine that art consists in holding up the camera to nature. He was even so reactionary as to assert that the only real people are the people who never exist. . . . The function of the artist, in Wilde's view, is to invent, not to chronicle; and he even goes so far as to say that if a novelist is base enough to go to life for his personages, he should at least pretend that they are creations, and not boast of them as copies. (pp. 263-64)

The Duchess of Padua is noteworthy for its tender lyrism, the delicate beauty of its imagery, and its glow of youthful fire; and despite its mimetic stamp, displays real power in instrumentation of feeling and in the temperamental and passional shades of its mood. The play links itself to Hardy and to Whitman, rather than to Shakspere, in its intimation of purity of purpose as the sole criterion of deed. For here Wilde, concerned less with the primitive basis of individuality than with the fundamental impulses of instinctive temperament, reveals life as fluid and evolutional. (p. 287)

Salomé is a fevered dream, a poignant picture—it is like one of those excursions into the *macabre* with which Wilde succeeded in fascinating the Parisians. In it one discerns the revolting decadence of an age when vice was no prejudice and sensuality no shame; we hear the resonance of lawless passion, and the reverberations of obscure, half-divined emotions. The characters stand forth in chiselled completeness from the rich Galilean background like the embossed figures upon a Grecian urn. (p. 291)

In *Salomé*, Wilde depicts a crystallized embodiment of the age, rather than the age itself. To the naturalism of sensation is super-added stylistic symmetry and, in places, what Baudelaire termed supreme literary grace. The influence of Maeterlinck is inescapable in the simplicity of the dialogue in places, the iterations and reverberations of the leading motives, the evocation of the atmosphere and imminence of doom. Nature symbolically cooperates in intensifying the feeling of dread; and we dimly entertain the presentiment of vast and fateful figures lurking in the wings. (p. 293)

It was Wilde's characteristic contention that there never would be any real drama in England until it is recognized that a play is as personal and individual a form of self-expression as a poem or a picture. Here Wilde laid his finger upon his own fundamental error. By nature and by necessity, the drama is, of all the arts, the most impersonal: Victor Hugo said that dramatic art consists in being somebody else. So supreme an individual was Wilde that he lacked the dramatic faculty of intellectual self-detachment. (p. 305)

The comedies of Oscar Wilde stem not from the Ibsen of *Love's Comedy*, but from the Dumas *fils* of *Francillon*, the Sardou of *Divorçons*, and the Sheridan of *The School for Scandal*. Nor are they lacking in that *grain de folie* which was the sign manual of Meilhac and Halévy, of Gilbert and Sullivan. In verve, *esprit* and brilliance Wilde is close akin to his compatriot and fellow townsman, Bernard Shaw; in both we find a defiant individualism, a genius for epigrammatic formulation of the truth, and a vein of piquant and social satire. Inferior to Shaw in most respects, Wilde surpasses him in two features: the sensitiveness of his taste, and the remarkable social ease of his dialogue. As an artist Wilde was generously endowed with the discretion which Henry James aptly terms the "conscience of taste"; and, unlike Shaw, he was far more intent upon amusement than upon instruction. (p. 309)

There is no term which so perfectly expresses the tone of Wilde's comedies as *nonchalance*. The astounding thing is that, in his sincere effort to amuse the public, he best succeeded with the public by holding it up to scorn and ridicule with the lightest satire. (p. 311)

While the dialogue of Wilde's comedies . . . contains more verve and *esprit* than all the French, German, and Italian comedies of to-day put together, nevertheless our taste is outraged because Wilde lacks a developed sense for character, and employs a conventional and time-worn technique. Wilde's figures are lacking in vitality and humanity; it is impossible to believe in their existence. (p. 312)

As Bernard Shaw may be said to have invented the drama of dialectic, so Oscar Wilde may be said to have invented the drama of conversation. (p. 313)

[In] Wilde's comedies the accent and stress is thrown wholly upon the epigrammatic content of the dialogue. (p. 315)

> *Archibald Henderson, "Oscar Wilde," in his* European Dramatists *(copyright © 1913, 1926, by Prentice-Hall, Inc.; reprinted by permission of Prentice-Hall, Inc., Englewood Cliffs, New Jersey), Appleton, 1926, pp. 253-320.*

Wilde believed in the policy of shocking people, and it had been so successful that he seldom considered the damage to himself. Yet certain passages in "The Portrait of Mr. W. H." and *Dorian Gray* indicated either ignorance on his part or a complete faith in the ignorance of his contemporaries. The age was ignorant; he was right about that. Though it has been said on good evidence that homosexuality was common, it was not understood. . . . Much that would today seem evidence of homosexuality was then regarded as merely bizarre or effeminate. (p. 226)

If it had not been for this confusion, Wilde would not have been likely to write the passage in "The Portrait of Mr. W. H." in praise of the higher love between man and man, with its direct allusion to Plato's *Symposium*, nor would he have indicated quite so frankly the relationship between Dorian Gray and Basil Hallward and that between Gray and Lord Henry, who is so obviously Wilde himself. We cannot help assuming that Wilde did not want to flaunt his homosexuality as such, for he went to some pains to deny the charge even among friends. He had done much talking about secret and splendid sins, but it was not his intention to be too specific. . . . What he did not anticipate was that, though readers of *Dorian Gray* seldom knew exactly what was bothering them, they were troubled, and they did feel that Wilde had somehow betrayed himself. The critic in the *Saturday Review* failed, in the course of his long diatribe, to define his objections to the book, but the strength of his emotion was unmistakable and ominous. He seemed to feel, moreover, as did other critics, that Wilde was providing evidence that could eventually be used to destroy him.

In spite of the gathering opposition, Wilde was entering his period of triumph. It is worth noticing that three of his plays were problem-plays, and that in all three conventional morality is satisfied. *Lady Windermere's Fan* inquires whether, when lovely woman has stooped to folly, she should tell her daughter, and it reaches its climax in the redeeming self-sacrifice of the sinner. *An Ideal Husband* poses the problem of the early misdeeds of a successful man and the self-righteousness of his wife. *A Woman of No Importance* tells the old story of wronged innocence, and ends with the triumph of the victim over her betrayer. All three of them plead for tolerance for the sinner, but only within limits long established by literary convention.

What, it may be asked, was Oscar Wilde, the preacher of art for art's sake, doing with problem-plays? The best answer is probably that *A Doll's House* was produced in 1889 and *Ghosts* and *Hedda Gabler* in 1891. The British stage, after a drab century, was being brought to life by the problem-play, and, though it may be doubted whether

Wilde was interested in the problems he dealt with, he was astute enough to know that the play-going public was. . . . The dialogue, needless to say, pleased audiences that had suffered from the stodgiest kind of dramatic writing, but it was not enough in itself to have given the plays their success.

His other two plays, usually listed by his admirers among his chief claims to greatness, were more purely characteristic. *Salome* owes much to Flaubert and Maeterlinck, but it has its original quality, a quality not calculated to reassure those who had been disturbed by *Dorian Gray. The Importance of Being Earnest* is not in that sense alarming, though, as Shaw has pointed out, it is hard and almost cruelly impersonal. What makes it uniquely Wilde's is that it is wholly composed of the brittle dialogue that figures in only a few scenes of the other plays, and that its artificiality, as more than one critic has pointed out, is perfectly sustained. Everyone talks like Oscar Wilde, including the governess and the clergyman, and, though there is sometimes a frantic grasping for witticisms, the talk is good. (pp. 227-28)

Art for art's sake! Nothing, actually, was farther from Wilde's mind. All his life he was preaching some sort of doctrine—his own version of paganism, or Socialism, or Christianity—and all his doctrines had at their core his dissatisfaction with the society of the eighties and nineties. That he never looked at the age closely enough to understand it, never discovered what was wrong with it or made more than sporadic gestures to offer a remedy, is obvious. His attacks were of the highly personal and melodramatic kind that one would expect. But he did have something that he wanted to say, and, in spite of all his pretenses, he said it. Unwilling to engage in lengthy debate with the Philistines, he sought to undercut their tedious arguments by his smashing announcement that everything they said was irrelevant. They could not apply their standards to him because he demanded judgment by his own standard, the standard of art. He did not, however, succeed in deceiving them, nor should we be deceived.

In saying that the artist must not choose as subject anything that is necessary or useful, or affects him deeply, or has immediate bearing on his life, Wilde was true to his professed beliefs, but he was disregarding the whole history of art, and he was limiting his own practice to an extent that, if he had been logical, would have proved intolerable. It is possible, under certain conditions and for certain special purposes, to look, not at what the writer is saying but at how the thing is said. Otherwise there could be no point in talking about artistic techniques. But, however important technical considerations may be, neither the author nor the reader is in practice indifferent to what is being expressed, and form and content are so closely linked that either can be understood only in its relation to the other. Wilde knew this as well as anyone. He represented a certain way of life, perhaps not admirable in itself but significant as criticism of the way of life then commonly followed. His attempt to conceal the fact only added to his symbolic quality. (pp. 241-42)

> *Granville Hicks, "Oscar Wilde and the Cult of Art," in his* Figures of Transition: A Study of British Literature at the End of the Nineteenth Century *(reprinted with permission of Macmillan Publishing Co., Inc.;* © *1939 by Macmillan Publishing Co., Inc.;*

> *1952 by Granville Hicks), Macmillan, 1939, pp. 217-66.*

Farce effervesces very quickly when it is not mixed with the ingredients of poetic fantasy as in Aristophanes' work or with the cement of earthy characterization such as one finds in Shakespeare's clowning episodes. Wilde's farce being neither imaginative nor earthy was quickly recognized by the best critic of his day—who was Shaw, of course—as "stock mechanical fun." At most, the epigrams gave a new fillip to the older farces of H. J. Byron, with which Shaw identified *The Importance of Being Earnest.* Wilde, however, had other resources than insouciance, and he succeeded in writing two clever comedies of ideas in his earlier produced plays, *A Woman of No Importance . . .* and *An Ideal Husband.*

Anticipating Somerset Maugham's *Our Betters* in the first of these, Wilde centered part of the play around the experience of an American girl in sophisticated English society. Here he struck cleverly at the American habit of knocking at the portals of aristocracy with quips like Lord Illingworth's remark that "American women are wonderfully clever in concealing their parents." The cream of the jest, however, lies in the fact that highly touted British society is itself pinchbeck, a point that Wilde presses home not merely in so dazzling and Shavian an epigram as his definition of the British ideas of health, "The English country gentleman galloping after a fox—the unspeakable in full pursuit of the uneatable" but in his entire gallery of hollow characters. . . . Restoration comedy of manners is revived here to perfection. . . . (pp. 589-90)

Loosely related to this social satire is the assault on the double standard which makes Mrs. Arbuthnot a social outcast whereas Lord Illingworth who gave her an illegitimate son goes scot free. Wilde failed to realize the point that conventional morality has saddled Mrs. Arbuthnot with an insufferable, masochistic conscience; and that consequently she becomes a bore. (p. 590)

An Ideal Husband is, in truth, a mess, but it is headed in the direction of comedy of ideas.

Wilde's contribution to the airing of the British theatre cannot be underestimated. It was his misfortune only that he was incorrigibly lazy and that his was not a mind of the first order. (p. 591)

> *John Gassner, in his* Masters of the Drama *(copyright 1940 by Random House, Inc.; reprinted by permission of Random House, Inc.), Random House, 1940.*

Reading and rereading Wilde through the years, I notice something that his panegyrists do not seem to have even suspected: the provable and elementary fact that Wilde is almost always right. *The Soul of Man under Socialism* is not only eloquent; it is just. The miscellaneous notes that he lavished on the *Pall Mall Gazette* and the *Speaker* are filled with perspicuous observations that exceed the optimum possibilities of Leslie Stephen or Saintsbury. Wilde has been accused of practicing a kind of combinatorial art, in the manner of Raymond Lully; that is perhaps true of some of his jokes ("one of those British faces that, once seen, are always forgotten"), but not of the belief that music reveals to us an unknown and perhaps real past (*The Critic as Artist*), or that all men kill the thing they love (*The*

Ballad of Reading Gaol), or that to be repentant for an act is to modify the past *(De Profundis),* or that (and this is a belief not unworthy of Léon Bloy or Swedenborg) there is no man who is not, at each moment, what he has been and what he will be *(ibid.).* I do not say this to encourage my readers to venerate Wilde; but rather to indicate a mentality that is quite unlike the one generally attributed to Wilde. If I am not mistaken, he was much more than an Irish Moréas; he was a man of the eighteenth century who sometimes condescended to play the game of symbolism. Like Gibbon, like Johnson, like Voltaire, he was an ingenious man who was also right.... He gave the century what the century demanded—*comédies larmoyantes* for the many and verbal arabesques for the few—and he executed those dissimilar things with a kind of negligent glee. His perfection has been a disadvantage; his work is so harmonious that it may seem inevitable and even trite. It is hard for us to imagine the universe without Wilde's epigrams; but that difficulty does not make them less plausible.

An aside: Oscar Wilde's name is linked to the cities of the plain; his fame, to condemnation and jail. Nevertheless (this has been perceived very clearly by [his biographer] Hesketh Pearson) the fundamental spirit of his work is joy.... Wilde [is] a man who keeps an invulnerable innocence in spite of the habits of evil and misfortune.

Like Chesterton, like Lang, like Boswell, Wilde is among those fortunate writers who can do without the approval of the critics and even, at times, without the reader's approval, and the pleasure we derive from his company is irresistible and constant. (pp. 80-1)

> *Jorge Luis Borges, "About Oscar Wilde" (1946), in his* Other Inquisitions: 1937-1952, *translated by Ruth L. C. Simms (copyright © 1964 by the University of Texas Press; reprinted by permission of Emecé Editores, Buenos Aires, República Argentina), University of Texas Press, 1964, pp. 79-81.*

In spite of their obvious debts to Milton, Keats, Tennyson, Rossetti, and Arnold (not to mention others), [Wilde's] early poems have considerable vitality and charm. You can take every one of them disapprovingly to pieces, yet they are readable in a way which more approved specimens of the art are not. They seem to make the Romantic poetry of England accessible to young readers who are not yet competent to appreciate the great writers. They represent the moment when Romanticism became classical—corresponding to the Parnassians in France—but with a classicism of joyous reminiscence, not of plodding obedience to rule and precept. They should be taken in the spirit of the Latin poetry of the Renaissance, when the subtle flavors of innumerable older writers were enthusiastically enjoyed, when every line and phrase was drenched in older poetry, yet there was something new about it all, some final touch of the writer's own personality. (p. 47)

Wilde had two distinct styles of writing, though he sometimes mixed them (as in the dialogues) with the happiest results. One of these was the aesthetic or symbolist, gorgeous and poetic, full of allusion and reminiscence and jewelled words (the purple patch, as it is aptly called), and the other light, worldly, cynical, paradoxical, full of laughter. In his plays he nearly always kept them apart, and on the few occasions when he does attempt the purple patch in his comedy-dramas, the result is failure. (p. 64)

With three artistically immoral plays and one masterpiece Wilde had achieved the money he thought he needed to realize his "immeasurable ambition," for which he had worked perhaps harder than is usually supposed.... But when Wilde had at last got his opportunity, what did his "immeasurable ambition" lead him to achieve? The post of Prime Minister, like his unacknowledged master Disraeli? No, he merely footed the bill for the ridiculous extravagances of the younger son of a Scotch marquess, who repaid him by getting him sentenced to two years penal servitude. In allowing this to happen Wilde not only ruined himself and his family, but completely betrayed the "Art" he had so often and so ostentatiously proclaimed to be the dearest thing in the world to him. He gave the British Philistine his most resounding triumph and at a stroke undid the patient work of two generations. The hatred of art, which is one of the few genuine emotions of the English-speaking peoples, was immensely fortified. It may be said of him that he contributed to prolong the barbarity of nations. (pp. 69-70)

It is not correct to put Wilde among the great writers. Compare him with his masters in poetry, Keats, Arnold, and Gautier; with his masters in prose, Ruskin, Pater, and Flaubert—Wilde's inferiority is instantly recognizable. But it is impossible not to feel that so violent a reaction on the part of society and its legal representatives showed that there was something as wrong with that society as with its prisoner. (p. 70)

> *Richard Aldington, "Oscar Wilde" (originally published as his introduction to* The Portable Oscar Wilde, *The Viking Press, 1946), in his* Richard Aldington: Selected Critical Writings: 1928-1960, *edited by Alister Kershaw (copyright © 1970, Southern Illinois University Press; reprinted by permission of Southern Illinois University Press), Southern Illinois University Press, 1970, pp. 39-70.*

The Importance of Being Earnest ... is a variant, not of domestic drama like *Candida* or of melodrama like *Brassbound,* but of farce, a genre which, being the antithesis of serious, is not easily put to serious uses. In fact nothing is easier than to handle this play without noticing what it contains. It is so consistently farcical in tone, characterization, and plot that very few care to root out any more serious content. (p. 111)

As its title confesses, it is about *earnestness,* that is, Victorian solemnity, that kind of false seriousness which means priggishness, hypocrisy, and lack of irony. Wilde proclaims that earnestness is less praiseworthy than the ironic attitude to life which is regarded as superficial. His own art, and the comic spirit which Congreve embodied and which Meredith had described, were thereby vindicated.... Wilde is as much of a moralist as Bernard Shaw but ...., instead of presenting the problems of modern society directly, he flits around them, teasing them, declining to grapple with them. His wit is no searchlight into the darkness of modern life. It is a flickering, a coruscation, intermittently revealing the upper class of England in a harsh bizarre light. This upper class could feel about Shaw that at least he took them seriously, no one more so. But the outrageous Oscar (whom they took care to get rid of as they had got rid of Byron) refused to see the importance of being earnest. (pp. 111-12)

[Wilde] has no serious plot, no credible characters. His witticisms are, not comic, but serious relief. They are in ironic counterpoint with the absurdities of the action. This counterpoint is Wilde's method. It is what gives him his peculiar voice and his peculiar triumph. It is what makes him hard to catch: the fish's tail flicks, flashes, and disappears. Perhaps *The Importance* should be defined as "almost a satire." As the conversations in *Alice in Wonderland* hover on the frontier of sense without ever quite crossing it, so the dialogue in *The Importance* is forever on the frontier of satire, forever on the point of breaking into bitter criticism. It never breaks. The ridiculous action constantly steps in to prevent the break. That is its function. Before the enemy can denounce Wilde the agile outburst is over. . . . (pp. 114-15)

The counterpoint or irony of Wilde's play expresses itself theatrically in the contrast between the elegance and *savoir-faire* of the actors and the absurdity of what they actually do. This contrast too can be dismissed as mere Oscarism and frivolity. Actually it is integral to an uncommonly rich play. The contrast between smooth, assured appearances and inner emptiness is, moreover, nothing more nor less than a fact of sociology and history. Wilde knew his England. He knew her so well that he could scarcely be surprised when she laughed off his truisms as paradoxes and fastened a humorless and baleful eye on all his flights of fancy. (p. 115)

> *Eric Bentley, "'The Importance of Being Earnest'," in his* The Playwright as Thinker: A Study of Drama in Modern Times *(copyright 1946, 1947 by Eric Bentley; reprinted by permission of Harcourt, Brace & World, Inc.), Reynal & Hitchcock, 1946 (and reprinted in* Oscar Wilde, *edited by Richard Ellmann, Prentice-Hall, Inc., 1969, pp. 111-15).*

I wish that some appropriate person would investigate and report to me why the epigram is so generally viewed as the arch-criminal of literature. For a reason that I have never been able to make out, even the best and most intelligent epigram is looked down on as being frivolous, flippant, and all too easy. Though it may be quoted for years on end and be as wise as it is witty, it is still regarded as a black sheep, unworthy of the respect of any mentality duly appreciative of such more copious literary forms as the *Congressional Record* and the cerebral ensembles of Walter B. Pitkin. (p. 87)

Take at random a few Wilde samples:

"The truths of metaphysics are the truths of masks." It took Brieux a whole two and a half hour play (*La Foi*) to say much the same thing, and not half so sharply.

"The history of woman is the history of the worst form of tyranny the world has ever known: the tyranny of the weak over the strong. It is the only tyranny that lasts." The major part of the great Strindberg's dramatic canon is devoted to proving just that.

"Cynicism is merely the art of seeing things as they are instead of as they ought to be." Here, in little, is, among other things, a critical appraisal of much of the classic Russian drama.

"The tragedy of old age is not that one is old but that one is young." Bataille consumed almost three hours to say the same thing in his admired *L'Homme à la Rose*.

"Ideals are dangerous things. Realities are better. They wound, but they are better." Yet Ibsen's *Brand*, Echegaray's *Folly or Saintliness*, Hartleben's *Rose Monday*, and many other such dramas enunciating the idea at great length are highly esteemed.

Along with the epigram, Wilde's sincerity, or rather alleged lack of it, is another favorite disparagement on the part of his critics. When they speak of sincerity, they obviously speak of it according to their own personal standards, not Oscar's. Oscar, for all his occasional self-mockery, was perfectly sincere in following his own lights, peculiarly colored though they were. When at odd times he was guilty of what seemed to be insincerity, it was only obliquely to ridicule the dull sincerity of others. The man's whole life, save in one or two instances, was a testimonial to his sincerity, such as it was. But since wit is so often regarded by the witless as a mark of insincerity—as Shaw, whose sincerity has been raised to a point of obstreperousness, has also discovered to his amusement—Oscar has been tagged with the label. (pp. 88-9)

It was not plot that interested Wilde, or that should interest any critic not given to an admiration of detective fiction and other such juvenile diversions. It was style, and at style, as at decoration, he excelled. "In all the unimportant matters," he declared without paradox, "sincerity, not style, is the essential." And his style in his dramatic time was as unrivaled as it is in ours. His sense of word and phrase and sentence is almost perfect. (p. 90)

> *George Jean Nathan, "Oscar Wilde and the Epigram" (originally published in* The Theatre Book of the Year, 1946-47, *Alfred A. Knopf), in his* The World of George Jean Nathan, *edited by Charles Angoff (copyright © 1952 by George Jean Nathan; reprinted by permission of Julie Haydon Nathan),* Knopf, 1952, pp. 87-90.

As a macabre novel, in spite of [its] noble ancestry, *The Picture of Dorian Gray* is not entirely successful. The thread of its narrative is too frequently interrupted by Wilde's esthetic preaching, by useless displays of esthetic erudition, by unnecessary descriptions of works of art and by paradoxical table-talk which have little bearing on the plot, except where Lord Henry dazzles and convinces Dorian. The conversation, at times, even distorts the plot. It allows a vague number of duchesses and other characters, doomed to vanish almost immediately after their first appearance, to wander into Wilde's novel, straight from the pages of *Vivian Grey* or of *Pelham*, in a frenzy of brilliant repartee and shrill laughter like the extras who suddenly give life to a court-scene in an old-fashioned light-opera. Between these pauses, where the atmosphere has been slapped on so thick that it clogs the machinery of plot, Wilde's plot itself reveals several curious weaknesses; had not the book been so hastily written that it is almost unjust to analyze it as if it were a carefully devised work of art, these weaknesses would suggest an unexpected mixture, in the author, of amateurishness and prudish guilt-feelings.

Wilde's naïvely romantic descriptions of low life, for instance, are full of pathetic echoes of the melodrama of earlier decades, of De Quincey's years of misery in the London slums where he met Ann, of the drug-addict poet James Thomson's *The City of Dreadful Night* and even of Charles Dickens; and they contrast oddly with Wilde's infinitely more sophisticated and knowing descriptions of high society. (pp. 50-1)

As a masterpiece of the macabre, it is infinitely less diffuse or rhetorical, and told with more economy and fewer tangles and snappings of the thread of narrative, than *Melmoth the Wanderer*. Wilde had indeed profited by the art of Balzac [Roditi notes elsewhere in this essay that Byron and Balzac were Wilde's favorite writers] and Flaubert; and when he revived the obsolete genre of the "gothic" or sartorial novel, he avoided much of the formlessness of *Melmoth*, *The Monk* or *Vivian Grey*, so that Wilde's tale now reads better than most of its literary ancestors and conforms more exactly to our stricter and more sober standards of plot, of atmosphere and of probability for the improbable.

But the true greatness of *The Picture of Dorian Gray* resides in the philosophical doctrine which the novel is intended, as a myth, to illustrate: [the] *Erziehungsroman* of dandyism. . . . (pp. 53-4)

> *Edouard Roditi, "Fiction as Allegory: 'The Picture of Dorian Gray'," in his* Oscar Wilde *(© 1947 by New Directions Publishing Corp.; reprinted by permission of New Directions Publishing Corporation), New Directions, 1947 (and reprinted in* Oscar Wilde, *edited by Richard Ellmann, Prentice-Hall, Inc., 1969, pp. 47-55).*

The best of [Wilde's] writing is only a pale reflection of his brilliant conversation. Those who have heard him speak find it disappointing to read him. *Dorian Gray,* at the very beginning, was a splendid story, how superior to the *Peau de Chagrin*! how much more significant! Alas! written down, what a masterpiece *manqué.*—In his most charming tales there is too great an intrusion of literature. Graceful as they may be, one feels too greatly the affectation; preciosity and euphuism conceal the beauty of the first invention; one feels in them, one can never stop feeling, the three moments of their genesis; the first idea is quite beautiful, simple, profound and certainly sensational; a kind of latent necessity holds its parts firmly together; but from here on, the gift stops; the development of the parts is carried out factitiously; they are not well organized; and when, afterwards, Wilde works on his phrases, and goes about pointing them up, he does so by a prodigious overloading of concetti, of trivial inventions, which are pleasing and curious, in which emotion stops, with the result that the glittering of the surface makes our mind lose sight of the deep central emotion. (n., p. 34)

> *André Gide, "In Memoriam," in his* Oscar Wilde, *translated by Bernard Frechtman (copyright © 1949 by Philosophical Library), Philosophical Library, 1949 (and reprinted in* Oscar Wilde, *edited by Richard Ellmann, Prentice-Hall, 1969, pp. 25-34)*

[Wilde] was an undergraduate all his life. He never grew up. His poetry never got beyond a college "quad" or a drawing room, or the verse that Blackwell of Oxford publishes at the expense of budding bards. And yet his lines to

Theocritus and his ode to *The New Helen* are among the finest of their kind in the English language.

The Picture of Dorian Gray! It came like a comet and was the talk of the town. Its provocative preface set forth his attitude towards life, which was that of a patrician to the decadence of ancient Rome. He wore a fringe like that of the Emperor Nero; and indeed his wit and terseness in packing reams of criticism in a few words likened him to Nero's arbiter of the elegances, Petronius. Just as did Caesar Borgia, Wilde modeled himself on the greatest and most blasé decadent the world has known. But his ideas of the elegances were extravagant. In a land of understatement he was an exaggeration.

He dressed like a continental tenor or a successful dealer in antiques who has been exalted to the peerage. He was in a sense a dealer in antiques, for he sold a store of the ancient classics to an astonished public. In the age of Nero he would have been entirely probable; but in Victorian London he was an anachronism. (pp. 52-3)

William Butler Yeats (another Dublin man), himself a great conversationalist, said that Wilde was the greatest talker he ever met. He could disarm and charm even when surrounded by envious enemies who would invoke the massed might of all the righteous dullards to destroy him. He had outraged all London. His brilliance was bad form and his inversions of accepted opinions were insufferable! "An honest God's the noblest work of man." Was he to be permitted to undermine the morals of a country whose mortality depends on hiding, if not suppressing, immorality? He was publicly flaunting vice in their faces. The sky fell. (pp. 54-5)

Ill-advised or not, quips and smart answers will not defend a culprit from the deadly ritual of the law. And even had Wilde been exculpated, there was within him an heredity that would have arraigned him again. (p. 55)

Flippant, superficial, facetious, a spoilt schoolboy? Very well; but what other attributes are there for the Spirit of Wit, this Puck? Would you have him Victorian? Wilde could not have been as successful had he been graver or more sincere. England, that insists on her poets having a bad conscience, or on preaching, cannot make a laureate out of a lyricist: Francois Villon would have never left Reading Gaol.

It is to the subconscious nature one must go if there is to be an assessment of the greatness of Wilde. His superficiality was his way of expressing his art. He was, not without a deep significance, attracted to Nero, who died proclaiming himself an artifex, a playboy. His was an Ariel-like attitude to life. But his prophetic soul was capable of assessing himself and leaving on record his own testimony in his *The Picture of Dorian Gray*. He knew what was happening to him. He could not lift a hand to prevent it without slaying himself. Just as Shelley was able to prophesy his own stormy death in the end of Adonais, so Wilde wrote early in life an account of what his end would be. Only natures of supreme genius have this prophetic power. These with an eye to see can read it all in his esoteric testament and apologia, *The Picture of Dorian Gray*. (p. 56)

> *Oliver St. John Gogarty, "A Picture of Oscar Wilde," in his* Intimations *(copyright, 1950, by Oliver St. John Gogarty; reprinted*

by permission of Thomas Y. Crowell Company, Inc.), Abelard Press, 1950, pp. 44-57.

In the heyday of Wilde's success, from the writing of *The Picture of Dorian Gray* to his abrupt fall from popularity, he seemed rather to turn away from his social ideals. The success of his plays, with their fabulous earnings, turned his head. . . .

Yet even at this period his writings contain a powerful element of social criticism. The English upper-classes represented in his plays are caricatured with clear hostility, and Wilde does not hesitate to pillory their corruption, their shallowness, their snobbery, their lack of genuine moral scruples. (p. 155)

A Woman of No Importance has, indeed, a general atmosphere of social protest, not only in the satirical and bitter (as far as Wilde was capable of acrimony) attitude towards the upper-classes, but also in the main plot, which is clearly built around a social problem, already sketched in *Lady Windermere's Fan,* of the inequality of men and women in modern society and the ruthlessness of the conventional social code towards the individual who, deliberately or unwillingly, acts against its arbitrary laws. The theme is partly imbued with that sentimentality which in a character like Wilde's always underlies his more obvious cynicism, but this quality is made less obvious by the sparkling wit with which the dialogue flits lightly over the whole range of social life and the political scene. The theme is presented conventionally, in the differing lives of Lord Illingworth, the successful and ruthless public figure, into whose witty conversation Wilde put much of himself, and Mrs. Arbuthnot. . . . (pp. 155-56)

Undoubtedly, in his treatment of [the] plot, Wilde was largely motivated by a desire to give the Victorians a rather sentimental theme of the kind to which they were accustomed, as a means of transmitting the brilliant verbal wit which was always the most pleasant ingredient of his plays —to the author even more than to the audience. Nevertheless, the particular choice of a plot is always significant, and I have no doubt that Wilde, who edited an intellectual woman's paper for some years, and who often had a high opinion of the capacities of the women he encountered in literary society, deliberately intended to draw attention to sexual equality of rights. I think it is also reasonable to assume that, like most cynics, Wilde had a strongly humane aspect to his character, which appears often in his works; *The Ballad of Reading Gaol* is one example, while in parts of *De Profundis* this quality is shown, almost, at times, to the extent of sentimental atrocity.

Nevertheless, however conventionally conceived may have been the main feminist plot of *A Woman of No Importance,* it is presented with great wit and much reason. Wilde's conclusions can be best summarised in a sound remark he made elsewhere, that he was against the existence of one law for men and one for women, and would prefer to see no law for anybody. (pp. 156-57)

Wilde's protest against [the] social enormity [of hanging] formed the main theme of the last and greatest of his poems, *The Ballad of Reading Gaol,* into which he condensed all the bitterness and pity engendered by his own prison life, and all of his renewed sense of indignation at social injustice.

The Ballad of Reading Gaol, as well as being the best and most original of Wilde's own poems, is also one of the few permanently successful propaganda poems written in the English language, an ironical fact when one considers that Wilde has been regarded, and usually regarded himself, as the high-priest of Art for Art's sake. At times it sinks into a rather banal sentimentality, but often it has a bare strength which is quite unlike anything else in Wilde's works. (pp. 165-66)

With all its literary faults, it remains unique in the history of penological literature. If Wilde had produced nothing else, this poem alone would have justified him as a writer. (p. 168)

George Woodcock, "The Social Rebel," in his The Paradox of Oscar Wilde (© 1949 by George Woodcock; reprinted by permission of Curtis Brown, Ltd.), Macmillan, 1950 (and reprinted in Oscar Wilde, edited by Richard Ellmann, Prentice-Hall, Inc., 1969, pp. 150-68).

One evening in 1892, the first of Oscar Wilde's four successful comedies had in London its first performance. It is said that after the last curtain the audience rose to cheer— and it had good reason to do so. Not in several generations had a new play so sparkled with fresh and copious wit of a curiously original kind.

By now the play itself, *Lady Windermere's Fan,* seems thin and faded. To be successfully revived, as it was a few seasons ago in the United States, it has to be presented as "a period piece"—which means that the audience is invited to laugh at as well as with it. Paradoxically, the only thing about it which can be taken seriously today is its fun, intentional as well as, occasionally, unintended. Few remember long what the story is about. But a dozen such epigrams as "There is nothing like the love of a married woman; it is something no married man knows anything about" are in quotation books and still pass in current conversation. It would probably be not too much of an exaggeration to say that it was the first theatrically successful English play since Sheridan to win a place in English literature. (pp. 43-4)

Wilde had, of course, already made himself famous, or at least notorious, in other ways and had become the best-known specimen of the new, irritating kind of writer called an aesthete. He had been delightedly shocking the public by proclaiming that the chief end of man is not the pursuit of Truth or of Virtue but of Beauty—which often found itself the enemy of both Truth and Virtue and which sometimes degenerated into mere Pleasure, sometimes trivial and sometimes forbidden. Wilde had not, himself, invented or even significantly developed any part of the doctrine. He had borrowed it partly from Walter Pater, who had taught at Oxford when Wilde was a student there, and partly from France, where aestheticism, known also as decadence, had already run a long course from Gautier down to Wilde's own contemporary Huysmans. He had published poems which *Punch* accurately described as "Swinburne and water." With a somewhat greater success he had also published the sensational prose tale *The Picture of Dorian Gray,* which was obviously inspired by Huysmans and in which a great deal of wit was mingled with a good deal of nastiness. Besides all that, he had written as well the "aesthetic" tragedy *Salomé,* forbidden performance by the Lord Chamberlain. With a great talent for publicity, he was, however, better known as a personality than as a writer and as such was known to thousands who had never read him.

Inevitably, when Gilbert and Sullivan decided to write an opera on the subject of the aesthetic poet, they made the hero dress in the knee breeches and silk stockings which were part of Wilde's favorite costume, and they made various allusions to his supposed behavior. To all this Wilde delightedly gave his unofficial collaboration. There is even some reason to believe that he may have been aware of the fact that the American lecture tour arranged for him by Gilbert and Sullivan's own agents was partly a publicity stunt to advertise in the United States the subject of the opera. Wilde simply accepted the publicity and depended upon his wit to escape the possibility that he might become merely a butt. He denied, for example, that he had ever walked down Piccadilly stopping from time to time to gaze with aesthetic rapture at the lily which he carried in his hand. Anyone, he said, could have done that. He did something much more difficult. Without ever having "walked down Piccadilly with a tulip or a lily in his medieval hand," he had made people believe that he had. Asked what he thought of *Patience,* he replied that "Parody is the tribute which mediocrity pays to genius." He thought that that single remark left the victory on his side. And I am not sure that it did not.

Lady Windermere's Fan was followed by three other comedies of which the last, *The Importance of Being Earnest,* was the most consistent, the most sustained, and the best. They were the first genuinely popular successes to be achieved by a man who had previously been "well disliked" rather than "well liked." Moreover, they represent the successful exploitation of a discovery which Wilde had previously made, namely that aestheticism, which was merely pretty-pretty in some of his poems, rather horrible in *Salomé,* and rather nasty in *The Picture of Dorian Gray,* could be employed to supply the paradoxical element in an original brand of wit. (pp. 44-6)

[He] had always had a great, unexpected sense of sheer fun; in the comedies he gave it rein, using intellectual and moral perversity only to add a certain spice. (p. 46)

[An] epigram has been very profoundly as well as epigrammatically defined as "a half-truth so stated as to be especially irritating to those who believe the other half." Wit is largely a matter of half-truths, of usually rather disillusioning, rather tough-minded half-truths, irritating to the unrelievedly idealistic. And aestheticism, even perversity and decadence, often supply these corrective half-truths. There was enough acid in Wilde's epigrams to dissolve a good deal of what we call Victoriansim. . . . Wilde made, therefore, his small contribution to the development of "modernism." (p. 47)

> *Joseph Wood Krutch, in his* "Modernism" in Modern Drama: A Definition and an Estimate *(copyright © 1953 by Joseph Wood Krutch; 1977 by the Trustees of Columbia University in the City of New York), Cornell University Press, 1953.*

[There] is something almost sacrilegious about the juxtaposition of Nietzsche and Wilde, for the latter was a dandy,

the German philosopher a kind of saint of immoralism. And yet the more or less sought-after martyrdom at the end of Wilde's life—Reading Gaol—adds to his dandyism a touch of sanctity which would have aroused Nietzsche's full sympathy. (p. 170)

Not for nothing have I coupled the names of Nietzsche and Wilde—they belong together as rebels, rebels in the name of beauty, for all that the German iconoclast's rebellion went tremendously deeper and cost tremendously more in suffering, renunciation, and self-conquest. . . . (p. 171)

> *Thomas Mann, "Nietzsche's Philosophy in the Light of Recent History," in his* Last Essays, *translated by Richard and Clara Winston and Tania and James Stern (copyright © 1958 by Alfred A. Knopf, Inc.; reprinted by permission of Alfred A. Knopf, Inc.), Knopf, 1958 (and reprinted as "Wilde and Nietzsche," in* Oscar Wilde, *edited by Richard Ellmann, Prentice-Hall, Inc. 1969, pp. 169-71).*

[In his parables,] Wilde is trying to relate his central intuition of youthful beauty to love and good works. That a kind of love-wisdom rather than any normal love is his true centre can be seen indirectly from the contrast of a natural and flower-like love with the soul in *The Fisherman and his Soul.* Wilde senses a dangerous co-presence of selfishness and spirituality, an all-too-solid presence of a transcendency directly associated with the "soul," and yet seemingly as *infertile as rich gems;* and as dangerous. How, then, may the "soul" and its jewelled and seemingly infertile Eros be related to love and Christian values? Young royal figures help most, since their human beauty lives and acts within the temporal order under the Crown whose rich stones symbolize the eternal.

In *The Happy Prince* the aim is clearer: the parable expresses the potential sovereignty of youth-beauty or love-wisdom even though, in our era, it is constricted. . . . [The Happy Prince] is a royal Eros. A Swallow, symbolizing the human self, leaves his lady, a Reed, because of her feminine ways, and rests beneath the statue, which is weeping for human misery. . . . [The Prince] gets the Swallow to strip the gold-leaf from his body piece by piece to relieve the destitute within the city. The Happy Prince symbolizes *that within the erotic vision which is not being used;* recalling to our minds those stores of "hidden kindness and power" in man of which Nietzsche speaks. . . . Though set on high where he can *see* "all the ugliness" and "all the misery" of mankind, yet he himself "cannot move"; but though his heart is of "lead," his beauty has the needed wealth; and after he is melted down and only his leaden heart survives with the dead Swallow, God in his good time will welcome both to his "garden of Paradise" and "city of gold." Every phrase is loaded. It is a consummate and final statement, even to the heart of lead. Though the emotion may be, or seem, worthless, it survives the fires of mortality. (pp. 141-42)

In *The Picture of Dorian Gray* the young hero of amazing beauty becomes, like the Star-Child, cruel and vicious, and though he remains outwardly young and perfect his advancing age and crimes are horribly objectified in the ever-changing and damning portrait, which recalls the externalized evil of *The Fisherman and his Soul.* . . . *Dorian Gray* contains one of Wilde's finest passages on jewels . . .; and it is surely the subtlest critique of the Platonic Eros ever penned. Throughout Wilde's thought-adventures there is this analysis of the interrelationship of soul, beauty and Christian goodness. (p. 143)

Not only was Wilde's a quest of a high order, but it had strong Christ-like affinities. The New Testament wavelength and Biblical style of the Parables is obvious; and from his youth onwards Wilde was deeply attracted, and in his works again and again engaged, by the Christian religion. In *Salome* a decadent and bejewelled paganism in a sulphurous atmosphere of beauty and blood-lust asserts itself statically and repetitively against the equally repetitive denunciations of Jokanaan, or John the Baptist, whom Salome desires. Always in Wilde the two worlds want to meet. Here they coexist in unhealthy opposition: the atmosphere is like pressure before thunder. (pp. 143-44)

[Wilde] must be judged in relation to the difficulties inherent in his life's central, Blakean, aim: to make of the senses elements of a new spirituality, to cure the soul by the senses and the senses by the soul. . . . This aim he carried through with a daring consistency; it motivated alike his aestheticism, his anti-social acts and his perception of Christ. About his lowest engagements there was an element of the sacramental. Of cruelty he knew as little as he knew of caution; his instincts were of a childlike, positive and embracing kind. In these terms he lived and acted in allegiance to the royalty of the crowned and diamonded Eros. His sin was total self-expression acted out in spontaneity "not wisely but too well"; and he took tragedy uncomplainingly in his stride. (p. 149)

> *G. Wilson Knight, in his* The Christian Renaissance *(reprinted by permission of W. W. Norton & Co., Inc.; copyright © 1962 by G. Wilson Knight), Norton, 1962 (and reprinted as "Christ and Wilde," in* Oscar Wilde, *edited by Richard Ellmann, Prentice-Hall, Inc., 1969, pp. 138-49).*

It is impossible for us to be just to Wilde because, although his contemporaries all agreed that his improvised conversation was superior to his writings, they also thought the latter much better than we do. Of his poems not one has survived, for he was totally lacking in a poetic voice of his own; what he wrote was an imitation of poetry-in-general. His prose letters to the *Daily Chronicle* about prison life are authentic, *The Ballad of Reading Gaol* is not. . . . Of his nondramatic prose, we can still read *The Happy Prince and Other Tales* with great pleasure, and *The Soul of Man Under Socialism* and *Intentions,* for all their affectation, contain valuable criticism, but "The Portrait of Mr. W. H." is shy-making and *The Picture of Dorian Gray* a bore. (pp. 321-22)

The typical fashionable play of the period was a melodramatic libretto *manqué;* indeed, a number of plays, including *Salomé,* which have long since vanished from the theater, are flourishing to this day in the opera house. Shaw's conclusion, which was valid for himself, was that the future of drama without music lay in the drama of thought. Wilde could not have taken the Shavian path because he was not a thinker; he was, however, a verbal musician of the first order. While *Salomé* could become a successful libretto, *Lady Windermere's Fan, A Woman of No Importance,* and

An Ideal Husband could not, because their best and most original elements—the epigrams and comic nonsense—are not settable; at the same time, their melodramatic operatic plots spoil them as spoken drama. But in *The Importance of Being Earnest,* Wilde succeeded—almost, it would seem, by accident, for he never realized its infinite superiority to all his other plays—in writing what is perhaps the only pure verbal opera in English. The solution that, deliberately or accidentally, he found was to subordinate every other dramatic element to dialogue for its own sake and create a verbal universe in which the characters are determined by the kinds of things they say, and the plot is nothing but a succession of opportunities to say them. Like all works of art, it drew its sustenance from life. . . . (pp. 322-23)

> *W. H. Auden, "An Improbable Life" (originally published in* The New Yorker, March 9, 1963), *in his* Forewords and Afterwords, *edited by Edward Mendelson (copyright © 1973 by W. H. Auden; reprinted by permission of Random House, Inc.), Random House, 1973, pp. 302-24.*

'I live in terror,' wrote Wilde, 'of not being misunderstood.' As it turned out, he need not have worried. His contemporaries liked or disliked him largely for the wrong reasons, the earlier twentieth century reacted decisively against him. Even today, with two major films on their rounds in Britain and television programmes innumerable, he remains curiously hard to understand. As a humorist he set out to amuse, as a successful humorist he paid the price of being taken less than seriously. The normal English attitude to humour is notoriously odd. Most of us look on it as a national asset, in wartime it becomes almost a mystique. But there is a puritanism in the English tradition which prevents the more boisterous and flamboyant types of laughter from flourishing unchecked. . . . (p. 138)

Most 'comedy' as the term is now understood keeps entertainment firmly under the thumb of instruction. . . . Nor does 'wit', when the Metaphysical and Augustan types have been exempted, fare much better. The very term in *Scrutiny* circles is a tainted one, at best associated with Bloomsbury, at worst with the *fin de siècle* and with Wilde most of all. (pp. 138-39)

Yet Wilde himself was one of the kindest and sanest of men, in addition to being a prince of entertainers. . . . (p. 139)

Wilde's values, I shall suggest, were not dissimilar to Blake's, though his life, or what public hostility chose to make of it, was less edifying, and his talents were inferior. He is an example, maybe an extreme one, of a writer whose insight belonged by and large to the camp of moral health, but whose creative gifts were limited to fields where moral health is always liable to suspicion. When he tried for seriousness as an artist he failed; as an entertainer he was more morally clearsighted than is usually allowed. (pp. 139-40)

In a deep sense he thought that Art *is* what we should normally call 'moral': that it is to do, that is, with order and beauty in perception and conduct, and with the ambition to make life itself a shaped and satisfying whole. He chose, however, to call this 'aesthetic' rather than 'moral'. . . .

The strategy of Wilde's terminology is easier to grasp when one remembers two more of the main distinctions he sees between Art and Life. Art is more ordered than life, he believes, and more beautiful. The supreme secret of beauty is form; which in men manifests itself as conduct, in nature as harmony, in art as style. Now man and nature are always changing. The sunset no sooner appears than it starts to fade; the colours alter as we watch them. Only in art is the beauty which natural scenery and conduct no more than hint at given shape, significance, and the prospect of permanence; only the artist can give to the beauty he sees a form that moves it towards its own ideal and preserves it from erosions of change. His shaping intelligence heightens the meaning of beauty; the medium he works in is more enduring than both the occasion of his art, and himself.

Wilde's perception that art is more ordered than life is reinforced, then, by awareness that it is more permanent; it comes as near to the immortal and the immutable as anything in a turning world ever will. This insight came to him, we need hardly remind ourselves, from Keats's Odes, mediated through the Pre-Raphaelite sensibility and already decisively diverted towards Pater. (p. 141)

Why is the world of art 'more real than reality itself'? Because it has more form, and so more significance, than reality. And why has it true ethical import? Because its standards, even though they exist only in man's own achievements and nowhere else in any possible world, offer something concrete and valuable to live towards. A rose or an *objet d'art* is, for Wilde, the unique inspirer of conduct. (p. 143)

The differences between art and life turn out to be much what Wilde said they were. On the one hand art adds significant form to events; on the other it removes them from the flux of reality to an abstract world of its own devising. (p. 144)

His most characteristic habit is one of paradox. 'Work is the curse of the drinking classes,' he writes, and naturally we are delighted, but why? Partly, no doubt, because the mere intention to shock by way of reversing a respectable cliché always is amusing, not only to adolescents to whom it comes fairly naturally as a form of humour, but to the incurable iconoclast biding his time inside most of us. But the intention of shocking is only part of the story. The real joke is that the cliché Wilde reverses is itself hopelessly and perniciously stupid, so that there is irony at the expense of those who are actually shocked, as well as good-humoured laughter for those who are not. Do we really believe that drink is the curse of the working classes? Of course not. Do we say that we believe it? If we do, we deserve any fate a satirist might devise. Wilde's wit performs, therefore, the traditional task of irony, sorting its audience into sheep and goats by challenging to a response which is human and real instead of being conventional and dead. Though his pose is to shock for its own sake, the pose, in this instance, is his technique. Mistaking pose for real intention is precisely the trap Wilde sets for his readers, and the *raison d'être* of his irony.

If we examine more closely the clichés Wilde turns inside out, we shall see that almost always he has behind him either genuine insight (as in the theories of Art and Life I have already discussed), or genuine humanity (as in his great essay, *The Soul Of Man Under Socialism*), or genuine detestation of cant and humbug (as in his Comedies, and much of the recorded conversation). What looks like, and is intended to look like, a prolonged flirtation with cynicism is in fact a running battle against obtuseness, hypocrisy and cant. What seems at first sight an affront to responsibility is on second sight a jest at the expense of the pseudo-responsible. Stupidity and insincerity are confronted with formulae decked out to look more deplorable than themselves, yet actually pointing back towards the minimal respect for good sense and good nature which they violate. (pp. 145-46)

> *A. E. Dyson, "Oscar Wilde: Irony of a Socialist Aesthete," in his* The Crazy Fabric: Essays in Irony *(copyright © A. E. Dyson 1965; reprinted by permission of Macmillan, London and Basingstoke), Macmillan, 1965, pp. 138-50.*

From Wilde descends the whole comedy of entertainment in our century, Somerset Maugham, Noël Coward, Frederick Lonsdale, the lighter plays of Terence Rattigan, the Aldwych farces of Ben Travers, the comedies of William Douglas-Home. What all these successors of Wilde lack, however, is the perfect finish, the almost Mozartian gaiety, which having laid melodrama and the desire to shock aside, Wilde was able to achieve with such grace and charm in *The Importance of Being Earnest*. (p. 194)

> *G. S. Fraser, in his* The Modern Writer and His World: Continuity and Innovation in Twentieth-Century English Literature *(© 1964 by G. S. Fraser), revised edition, Frederick A. Praeger, 1965.*

It is possible to regard Wilde's four principal plays as a series of attempts to resolve a particular clash between manners and morals, between style and content, between the author and his characters. The problem which faced him, as a dramatist, was a very specific one—that of finding a world fit for the dandy to live in; fit, in the sense that such a world would help to make clear the meaning of being a dandy. Considered in general terms, the role of the dandy is defined largely by his alienation from the social world in which he lives. He is the visible emblem of nonattachment. His best audience is himself; his favourite view, that presented him by his mirror. (pp. 501-02)

For the dramatist the accommodation of such a figure presents special problems. In so far as his role is mythic and not individualized he requires for his embodiment a special form of play. Drama usually involves its characters in ethical judgments; the dandy elaborately abjures them. Drama is an exploration of character in action; the dandy is self-consciously static, and the art he requires of the dramatist is precisely that which sees the mind's construction in the face. The dramatic role of the dandy would seem to lead into a world where, of necessity, everything was amoral, inconsequential, and superficial. Was it possible to create such a figure and such a world, and yet produce a play which itself would be none of these things? This, basically, was Wilde's problem. He solved it only once with complete success, in his last play, *The Importance of Being Earnest*. In the varying achievement of the three plays which preceded it, however, we can see what were the conditions for such a "solution", and this enables us to understand more clearly the nature of Wilde's single dramatic masterpiece.

Lady Windermere's Fan . . . , Wilde's first play, illustrates very clearly the difficulties that beset a dramatist whose aesthetic ideology includes a belief that manners take precedence over morals and style over content. . . . The play, in common with *A Woman of No Importance* and *An Ideal Husband,* has as a central theme the hazards of precipitate and inflexible moral judgment—in this case a wife judging, or misjudging, the nature of her husband's liaison with another woman—and the way in which that judgment has to be modified. And it is in this modification that the dandy has his special role to play. The critical problem in all the plays arises from the nature of the wisdom the dandy dispenses and the relationship of this wisdom to the dilemmas which constitute the plot of the play. (pp. 502-03)

If the dandy as lover causes difficulty in *Lady Windermere's Fan,* the dandy as villain in *A Woman of No Importance* . . . causes considerably more. It would seem that Wilde had not yet grasped the fatal significance of making his dandy into a character, equipped, in however simple a way, with complexity of motive and a capacity for involvement in emotional affairs. By nature a bystander, the dandy is forced in these first two plays to become a participant, and confusion results. (p. 507)

In *Lady Windermere's Fan* [the dandy] had become a sympathetic lover and had been rendered null; in *A Woman of No Importance* he has been a faithless lover and is degraded into a melodramatic villain.

Involvement of one kind or another was the root defect of these plays, and in writing his third play, *An Ideal Husband* . . . , Wilde seems to have taken special care to keep his dandy free from commitment. . . .

Connected with Wilde's clearer insight into the dramatic requirements of the dandy was his decision to make the central plot of *An Ideal Husband* much wider, much more public in concern, than that of the earlier plays. Here, for the first and only time, a man's profession is central to the play. (p. 509)

However lightly it may be sketched in, the world of *An Ideal Husband* is a world where ambition and disgrace, love and suspicion, are possible. It is, uniquely in Wilde, a world of work. From his post of vantage the dandy may observe keenly and comment shrewdly, but he can never affect this world except through the arbitrary good fortune which the author has conferred on him. On his own, Goring is Wilde's most successful dandy; in the Chiltern-Cheveley world he is a wraith, lucky enough to be his author's Scarlet Pimpernel. His father's constant rebuke that he is wasting his time is not so easily dismissed as Wilde would like us to think. (p. 511)

And now Wilde begins to see that, if the dandy is to master the world, it can be only a world of his own making. Only in a *world* of dandies will his voice and actions become harmonious: a world where the categories of serious and frivolous will no longer apply, where every character can speak like the author and the author like every character, where everything that can be seen is harmonious and there is nothing that cannot be seen. The dandy can exist fully only in a world of idyll, of pure play. And at last, in *The Importance of Being Earnest* . . . , he finds himself in such a world. (p. 512)

Everything starts from language. The characteristic language of the dandy is the paradox, and the essence of paradox is contradiction. This draws attention to two things— the attitude or sentiment which the paradox is concerned to reverse, and the language itself in which the reversal is done. We should say of paradox that it is a form of expression which is at once critical and self-delighting. And the same definition would apply very well to *Earnest* as a whole. Wilde is able to achieve this extension and uniformity because in this play the language of the dandy is a language appropriate to everyone. In the earlier plays, where the dandy was a figure involved with others who were not dandies, his idiom belonged to him in a very personal way: we were driven to reflect on *his* criticism, *his* self-delight. But when all the characters can speak with the author's voice they are completely insulated against each other; the criticism is then cut free to apply to a world beyond the characters, to the world of the audience. And in their turn the audience cannot think of any of the characters critically, because the delighting, and self-delighting form of paradox creates a comic response which encloses these characters in a protective shell. (p. 514)

To think of Wilde's art as merely "escapist" is to oversimplify the position. What he gives us is a completely realized idyll, offering itself as something irrevocably *other* than life, not a wish-fulfilment of life as it might be lived. Consequently, to think of Wilde's idyll in terms of "aspiration" or "rejection" is as idle as the notion of "accepting" or "rejecting" Keats's *Ode on a Grecian Urn,* or the urn itself, or Mozart's *Marriage of Figaro.* "Truth in art is the unity of a thing with itself," and the truth in Wilde's dictum can be falsified by art too self-consciously pursued, as well as by life. *Salome,* Wilde's last produced play, is a monument to art, not art itself; it is as entangled with an aesthetic commentary on life as *A Woman of No Importance* is with a moral one. *Earnest* is the dramatic expression of a precise aesthetic ideology, where Art is seen as the supreme ordering and perfection of life. In such a play the plot can never be our sort of plot, and so, in Wilde, it is a farce; the characters can never be human, and so, in Wilde, they are pure and simple; the language has to be our language, but if it is the language of paradox it can continually contradict us. Such a play can contain oblique criticism of life, but it will never be a direct imitation of life, since that would imply an intrinsic value in life superior to that of art. Even at its most topical *The Importance of Being Earnest* avoids the didactic and the narrowly satirical, and remains resolutely faithful to its aesthetic aim. It was a success which Wilde achieved only once, and we can feel reasonably certain that the sudden ending of his dramatic career did not deprive us of any better play. (pp. 520-21)

> *Ian Gregor, "Comedy and Oscar Wilde,"*
> *in* Sewanee Review *(reprinted by permission*
> *of the editor; © 1966 by The University of*
> *the South), Spring, 1966, pp. 501-21.*

Up to a point Wilde patronizes life for its inferiority to art, but 'The Decay of Lying' has a second declension, which maintains that art inseminates life with its images. It brings color to what would otherwise be neutral gray. 'Think of what we owe to the imitation of Christ, of what we owe to the imitation of Caesar.' (p. 17)

The principal theme in 'The Decay of Lying' develops from overturning the conception of imitation. That art is an imitation of life, that life is an imperfect imitation of a supernal world of forms, were theories of famous men which Wilde was ready to revise. By his lights Plato had needlessly suggested that the forms were extraterrestrial, when in fact they were terrestrial, and could be found in the world of art. Art makes life imitate it. Whether the forms of art have any source or sanction beyond the human Wilde chose not to consider, sensing that metaphysical speculation would land him back in the romantics' camp. (p. 20)

> *Richard Ellmann, in his* Eminent Domain *(copyright © 1965, 1966, and 1967 by Richard Ellmann; reprinted by permission of Oxford University Press, Inc.), Oxford University Press, 1967.*

Wilde's own literary criticism was limited to short reviews, many of them unsigned. Like anyone else who has had a classical education (one should never forget that Wilde got a First in Mods and a First in Greats), as a critic he is primarily concerned with artistic form and mastery of language. His prose may sometimes be too lush—"Let me play you some mad scarlet thing by Dvorák"—and he sometimes makes statements which are meant to be provocative epigrams but, in fact, are sheer nonsense—"Nothing that actually occurs is of the smallest importance"—but his language is never ungrammatical nor his use of words sloppy. He knew Latin and Greek and French very well. When, as a reviewer, he is savage, which is not often, it is always over some misuse of words or some mistranslation. Though he never claimed to be a scholar, he was remarkably well-read. It is obvious from his review of two books on Sir Philip Sidney—one by J. A. Symonds, the other by Edmund Gosse—that he knew more about the literature of the period than either of them. (p. 208)

> *W. H. Auden, "In Defense of the Tall Story," in* The New Yorker *(© 1966 by The New Yorker Magazine, Inc.; reprinted by permission of Curtis Brown, Inc.), November 29, 1969, pp. 205-06, 208-10.*

[*The Ballad of Reading Gaol*] is a long sigh of repentance over the contradictions inherent in suffering and compassion—as "Helas!" sighs, more briefly and in French, over the conflict between passion and conscience. The weakness of both is the manner in which they call attention to themselves. Poetry may be, as Wilde insisted, the result of self-conscious effort, but his own poems too often show the strain of the effort. In his prose he used paradox to reconcile contradictions and, despite some excesses, the prose sparkles with life. But in the poetry contradictions are left unresolved and the effect is both stiff and languid. (pp. 9-10)

[*The Picture of Dorian Gray*] is a modern fairy-tale more than a novel. Like many a tale, it starts out with a wish: "If it were I," exclaims Dorian, "who were always to be young and that picture that was to grow old! . . . I would give my soul for that!" And it proceeds to relate how, in most unlikely fashion and with most unlikely consequences, that wish was fulfilled. The characters are cast accordingly: Dorian is the Beautiful Princess (gender is here irrelevant), Lord Henry a Wicked Witch, and Basil Hallward—whose art is a kind of magic—Fairy Godmother. The figures are placed in a setting, artificially lighted but casting real shadows, designed to please a childish taste for decadence while at the same time leaving room for a moral with which every good fairy-tale ends. (p. 14)

In a serious moment Wilde thought his story was possibly defective in being "far too paradoxical in style" and "far too crowded with sensational incidents." He was probably right, but neither fault is likely to trouble a reader who today is willing to accept the work as a fairy-tale rather than a novel. But then of course other defects begin to appear. A finely tempered artificiality is flawed by an occasional brush with realism—or what Wilde may have supposed was realism. When he steps out of the drawing room, for example, and descends to Sybil Vane's tenement, it is clear he has no knowledge of life below-stairs. He neither knew nor cared how people like the Vanes lived or might be expected to talk or act. They are borrowings from cheap popular romance (the same source provides the casual anti-Semitism of the "hideous Jew" who exploits Sybil) and have no place in anything so serious as a fairy-tale. The story falters over these characters not because it is artificial but because the characters are not of a sufficiently high order of artificiality. ("Realism," Wilde once remarked, "is always spoiling the subject matter of art.") Once back in the drawing room, however, among genuinely artificial articles Wilde is again at his best. So long, that is, as he keeps his characters talking. When they pause for a bit of stage business the effect is likely to be upsetting. None of them, for example, ever stands up or sits down: they "fling" themselves into armchairs, they "leap" from couches, they "saunter languidly" to doors and "pass listlessly" out of rooms. Their acrobatics, even or especially in slow motion, are exhausting. (p. 18)

[But] beneath the ostensible show of character and event, the glitter of conversation and sensational twist of incident, the story is an intensely imagined fantasy in which nothing really happens and there is only one character, a prescient author, who never appears. But everything is dominated by the Wilde personality and is a celebration of the essential hedonism of that personality which one might find boring or repulsive if it were not also essentially innocent and almost childlike in its gaiety. "Basil Hallward is what I think I am," Wilde wrote to an admirer, "Lord Henry what the world thinks me: Dorian what I would like to be—in other ages, perhaps." (p. 19)

The relation of the plays to *Dorian Gray* is that of a cannibal tribe to its sacrificial king. Bits and pieces of the novel's dialogue keep turning up in one or other of the plays—in all of them except *Salome*. (p. 21)

[It] is the failure of fantasy to fit into a tragic mold. As such it is a literary curiosity, little more. But there is a kind of fantasy that resists not only the tragic but also the comic mold. Like a tenth muse, fantasy of this kind is willful and elusive and far more rare in appearance than any of her nine sisters. But the lady did appear at least once to Oscar and, though he apparently did not recognize her and even at times thought little of her lunatic carrying-on, he was, despite himself, so possessed by her that he created an all but flawless piece of dramatic nonsense. The rational mind, uneasy except in the company of categories, can only call the result comedy, but it is in fact a unique form not only without antecedents but, until now at any rate, without certifiable descendants. When, in retrospect, Wilde claimed that he had given to dramatic form a mode of expression as personal as that of the lyric or the sonnet, he did not seem to have any particular play in mind, but in none of the plays is the claim so finely justified as in *The Importance of Being Earnest.* (p. 23)

The perfection of style in *Earnest* is the flawless encapsulation of the insignificant in a word or phrase and the significant arrangement of these into a finely artificial wholeness. One of the principles of this arrangement is, as Wilde pointed out, the use of the recurring phrase, simple or variant, to effect a unity in much the same way that the old ballads were bound together by simple or variant refrains. "Oh, that is nonsense," says Jack apropos of some excellent idiocy of Algernon's early in the play, and, as if the word were a leitmotif or running comment on the action itself, he keeps repeating at intervals in the sparkling confusion around him that this or that is nonsense. (p. 24)

The technique is simple, the effect on the whole quite splendid. Situation repeats situation, character reflects character, as refrain echoes refrain. The play is constructed like an elegant hall of mirrors in some highly sophisticated House of Fun where proper identities are less important in themselves than as occasions for the comic flash of image to image from glass to glass. Values of ordinary importance are happily distorted, inverted, or dissolved in the glitter of wit. (p. 26)

Earnest is a kind of comic heaven and, as in the heaven of scripture, there is no distinction between the sexes such as history affords—and seems to demand—nor is there, except in some comic mystical sense, marriage or giving in marriage. Sexual identity, like family and personal identity, dissolves in a glass brightly. Stripped of maleness or femality the person is flashed back at us in the hall of mirrors as absolutely and absurdly human in the beatific glow of its insignificance. (p. 28)

Jack and Algernon, though a world removed from metaphysics, are in their particular moment of boredom comic exemplars of the universal ennui hanging over man at every moment of his existence. The best, and perhaps the only safe, escape from this would seem to be through a hatch of laughter opened by gifted spirits in the dead center of ennui. Such at any rate was Wilde's route and after him the route of Samuel Beckett. For this exchange between Algy and Jack is, with scarcely a change of mode or mood, readily transferable from *Earnest* to *Godot*. The bored and funny bums of Beckett, waiting around with nothing to do, ramble on—apparently inconsequentially—in the authentic and exemplary manner of their elegant predecessors, Jack and Algernon. (p. 29)

A common form of insanity among many people is a predisposition to take themselves so seriously that they attach to the trivialities of their existence an importance all out of proportion to the reality of things. *The Importance of Being Earnest* corrects the imbalance and restores man to sanity for an hour or so (or about as long as he can take it) which is a bright and happy and joyous state of being. A trivial incident or attitude—a dropped handkerchief, an idle prophecy, a momentary sense of overweening self-importance—may, and frequently does, spark off tragedy. That is one of the reasons why the form of tragedy is inherently imperfect, out-of-joint, an incompletely developed negative of human existence. *Earnest* is the complete reversal of this ("it is only the superficial qualities that last," as dear Cecily Cardew says) and returns man in a flood of laughter to his scriptural state of insignificance. . . .

The other three comedies have little or none of this vitality. They are stylish but without style, fashionable but in the fashion of the day, and if we smile at them now it is the polite smile we reserve for the odd humors and curious antics of a grandparent. Character, plot, situation, and dialogue are all interchangeable from play to play. The moving figure in each is a female revenant with a touch of the blackmailer in her: Mrs. Erlynne's thing (*Lady Windermere's Fan*) is social blackmail; Mrs. Arbuthnot's (*A Woman of No Importance*) moral blackmail; Mrs. Cheveley's (*An Ideal Husband*) out and out blackmail. The moral is also the same: blackmail never succeeds, and true love—whether marital, maternal, or romantic—overcomes all the stratagems of the wicked and the wise. Even the accessories (a note, a fan, a letter) are the same. All this is stock. . . . (pp. 30-1)

What is original in these plays is, again, the Wilde personality in so far as it can express itself within the tiresome conventions of a fashionable stage. When the characters talk like Wilde, which is a good deal of the time, they sound brilliant; when they talk in character, they are prigs or bores or worse. . . .

To compare any of these plays with *The Importance of Being Earnest* is to recognize at once the difference between talent and genius, a distinction made much of by Wilde in a somewhat different connection. "I put my genius into my life," he told André Gide, "only my talent into my work." Despite a flippancy of tone, and always excepting *Earnest*, that is a just and accurate self-evaluation. Talent, however great, is limited to competence, and though competence may be of a high order, its limits are invariably fixed by prevailing literary tastes and standards. Talent matches itself against these, genius overcomes them. As an artist Wilde overcame them only once. (pp. 32-3)

> *Kevin Sullivan, in his* Oscar Wilde *(Columbia Essays on Modern Writers Pamphlet No. 64; copyright © 1972 Columbia University Press; reprinted by permission of the publisher),* Columbia University Press, 1972.

"Dorian Gray" was the first piece of work which proved that Oscar Wilde had at length found his true vein.

A little study of it discovers both his strength and his weakness as a writer. The initial idea of the book is excellent, finer because deeper than the commonplace idea that is the foundation of Balzac's "Peau de Chagrin," though it would probably never have been written if Balzac had not written his book first; but Balzac's sincerity and earnestness grapple with the theme and wring a blessing out of it, whereas the subtler idea in Oscar's hands dwindles gradually away till one wonders if the book would not have been more effective as a short story. Oscar did not know life well enough or care enough for character to write a profound psychological study: he was at his best in a short story or play. (p. 121)

I regard "Salome" as a student work, an outcome of Oscar's admiration for Flaubert and his "Herodias," on the one hand, and "Les Sept Princesses," of Maeterlinck on the other. He has borrowed the colour and Oriental cruelty with the banquet-scene from the Frenchman, and from the Fleming the simplicity of language and the haunting effect produced by the repetition of significant phrases. Yet "Salome" is original through the mingling of lust and hatred in the heroine, and by making this extraordinary virgin the chief and centre of the drama Oscar has heightened the interest of the story and bettered Flaubert's design. I feel sure he copied Maeterlinck's simplicity of style because it served to disguise his imperfect knowledge of French and yet this very artlessness adds to the weird effect of the drama. (pp. 130-31)

"The Ballad of Reading Gaol" is far and away the best poem Oscar Wilde ever wrote; we should try to appreciate it as the future will appreciate it. We need not be afraid to trace it to its source and note what is borrowed in it and what is original. After all necessary qualifications are made, it will stand as a great and splendid achievement. (p. 388)

It is said that "his actual model for 'The Ballad of Reading Gaol' was 'The Dream of Eugene Aram' with 'The Ancient Mariner' thrown in on technical grounds"; but I believe that Wilde owed most of his inspiration to "A Shropshire Lad." (p. 389)

"The Ballad of Reading Gaol" is beyond all comparison the greatest ballad in English: one of the noblest poems in the language. This is what prison did for Oscar Wilde. (p. 392)

Anyone who has read Oscar Wilde's plays at all carefully, especially "The Importance of Being Earnest," must, I think, see that in kindly, happy humour he is without a peer in literature. Who can ever forget the scene between the town and country girl in that delightful farce-comedy. As soon as the London girl realises that the country girl has hardly any opportunity of making new friends or meeting new men, she exclaims:

"Ah! now I know what they mean when they talk of agricultural depression."

This sunny humour is Wilde's especial contribution to literature: he calls forth a smile whereas others try to provoke laughter. Yet he was as witty as anyone of whom we have record, and some of the best epigrams in English are his. "The cynic knows the price of everything and the value of nothing" is better than the best of La Rochefoucauld, as good as the best of Vauvenargues or Joubert. He was as wittily urbane as Congreve. But all the witty things that one man can say may be numbered on one's fingers. It was through his humour that Wilde reigned supreme. (pp. 415-16)

[Wilde] will live with Congreve and with Sheridan as the wittiest and most humorous of all our playwrights. "The Importance of Being Earnest" has its own place among the best of English comedies. But Oscar Wilde has done better work than Congreve or Sheridan: he is a master not only of the smiles, but of the tears of men. "The Ballad of Reading Gaol" is the best ballad in English; it is more, it is the noblest utterance that has yet reached us from a modern prison, the only high utterance indeed that has ever come from that underworld of man's hatred and man's inhumanity. In it, and by the spirit of Jesus which breathes through it, Oscar Wilde has done much, not only to reform English prisons, but to abolish them altogether, for they are as degrading to the intelligence as they are harmful to the soul. (p. 546)

> *Frank Harris, in his* Oscar Wilde: His Life and Confessions *(© 1974; reprinted by permission of the publisher, Horizon Press, New York), Horizon, 1974.*

On its face the view that Wilde's art grew out of his initiation into homosexuality would seem somewhat exaggerated, if not dangerous, and it would . . . appear to contradict Wilde's own cherished belief that man's past is not deterministic of his future. . . . [If] there is any one overriding theme in Wilde's social comedies, it is that man must never become trapped into one perspective, but must remain ever flexible, continuing to develop his personality and preserving his potentiality of being, in order to be able to deal with the complex paradoxes of human existence. One of the virtues of an aestheticized life, after all, is that time can be abolished, and in "gathering the whole" and being able to live in all ages at once, one need never fear a past which can always be recreated. Art alone bestows on the world its meaning and value, serving for Wilde as the ultimate sanctifier of history. It can hardly be coincidence that so many of Wilde's protagonists are literally or figuratively orphaned heroes (and thus ontologically incomplete) whose mysterious pasts are "redeemed" at the end of their tales by being fictionalized—aesthetically "recreated," as it were—by a play of the mind; these purifying "reincarnations" stand, in some sense, as Wilde's effort not only to reverse one or another "flawed" history but to reconcile and harmonize the world of reality with the world of dreams. Interestingly, even Wilde's "fall" into homosexuality is explained in *De Profundis* as an attempt to aestheticize life. (p. 106)

[For] Wilde the "demonic universe" is not defined according to the conventional categories of good and evil, but reflects the metaphysical double-bind at the core of human existence; it is, in large part, a function of what Wilde saw as the fundamental alienation of aesthetic purity and ethical experience, of absolute beauty and human contingencies. The Decadents sought in their quest for purity to establish an absolute standard of value—Art—but it is the testimony of Wilde's works that absolutes, being by definition extrahuman, cannot be merged with life without destroying the integrity either of the absolute or of humanity. Ethics and human love may be the salvation of Life, but the co-mingling and compromise they demand can only mar the purity, perfect wholeness, and static perfection of Art; conversely, Art's beauty and perfection may stand at the pinnacle of sanctifying value, but the self-sufficient and isolated nature of that beauty denies in its very premises the need for human communion. However much he wished to fuse them, Wilde ultimately perceived the worlds of Life and Art to be two separate, tragically irreconcilable systems of value; to embrace the one, as his young fisherman learns, is to destroy the other. (pp. 107-08)

[He] discovered that balance was not unity and that one could not ultimately aestheticize life's ethical dimension—if anything, the very need to interlink aesthetics and ethics only confirmed once again the suspicion that Art was finally incapable of redeeming Life. We remember, after all, that Wilde's poet was both attracted and repelled by the Sphinx, and Wilde feared to the end of his life that behind its inscrutable mask there may indeed be no secret. . . .

The final message conveyed by Wilde's life and art, and by the Decadence in general, is that the attempt to heal the split between man's dreams of innocence and his fact of guilt is ultimately fatal, the quest for wholeness self-destructive. It is perhaps not a surprising fact of the *fin-de-siècle* that a group of writers so possessed of a "schizoid consciousness'' should take as one of their emblems that divided being, the androgyne—nor that they should eventually reverse the traditional iconography and come to see that figure as representative not so much of a ''completing'' union of opposites as of disease, sterility, and death. It was Wilde's unending dilemma that he could never bring himself to forsake either purity or humanity, and thus was forced into the ontological position of the androgyne, trapped between two worlds and unable to live comfortably in either. (p. 108)

Chris Snodgrass, in Criticism *(reprinted by permission of the Wayne State University Press; copyright 1975 by Wayne State University Press), Vol. XVII, No. 1 (Winter, 1975).*

Charles Williams

1886-1945

English novelist, poet, playwright, biographer, and essayist. Charles Williams is best known for his seven novels, supernatural thrillers which have as their theme the struggle between good and evil. Williams was a devout Anglican and religious themes recur in all the genres in which he wrote. London-born, Williams studied for two years at the University of London before lack of money forced him to drop out. In 1908 he joined the editorial staff of the Oxford University Press and there he spent most of his career. Just before his death, he was appointed lecturer at Oxford University and awarded an honorary M.A. A personable man with an active social life, Williams numbered among his friends Auden, Eliot, C. S. Lewis, Dorothy Sayers, and Barbara Ward. His poetry, less popular than his fiction, is remarkably original; he considered his Arthurian poems his most significant works and many critics agree with him. Although his novels were widely read in England during the 1930s, they were little known in the United States until the publication here of *All Hallows' Eve* in 1948. Serious critical interest in Williams has grown in the United States since that time.

PRINCIPAL WORKS

The Silver Stair (poetry) 1912
Poems of Conformity (poetry) 1917
Divorce (poetry) 1920
Poetry at Present (criticism) 1930
War in Heaven (novel) 1930
Many Dimensions (novel) 1931
The Place of the Lion (novel) 1931
The Greater Trumps (novel) 1932
Shadows of Ecstasy (novel) 1933
Thomas Crammer of Canterbury (drama) 1936
Descent into Hell (novel) 1937
Taliessin through Logres (poetry) 1938
The Descent of the Dove (religious essay) 1939
Judgement at Chelmsford (drama) 1939
The Figure of Beatrice: A Study in Dante (criticism) 1943
The Region of the Summer Stars (poetry) 1944
All Hallows' Eve (novel) 1945
Seed of Adam, and Other Plays (drama) 1948

For Williams, as for Plato, the phenomenal world—the world studied by the sciences—is primarily a reflection or copy or adaptation of something else. Nimue, the 'mother of making,' is that energy which reproduces on earth a pattern derived from 'the third heaven,' i.e. from the sphere of Venus, the sphere of Divine Love. But the poet does not use those words. What resides in the third heaven ('the pattern in heaven of Nimue, time's mother on earth') is called by him 'the feeling intellect' or *mens sensitiva*. The expression 'feeling intellect' is borrowed from Wordsworth's *Prelude*. . . . The important difference between the two poets is that where Wordsworth is thinking of a subjective state in human minds, Williams is thinking of an objective celestial fact. The Feeling Intellect may be attained for moments by human beings; but it exists as a permanent reality in the spiritual world and by response to that archtype Nimue brings the whole process of nature into being. Williams is here (perhaps unconsciously) reproducing the doctrine of the Renaissance Platonists that Venus—celestial love and beauty—was the pattern or model after which God created the material universe. (pp. 101-02)

The image of the Empire [in *The Vision of the Empire*] is the final form of something that had always haunted Williams and which he often referred to simply as 'the city.' The word is significant. Williams was a Londoner of the Londoners; Johnson or Chesterton never exulted more than he in their citizenship. On many of us the prevailing impression made by the London streets is one of chaos; but Williams, looking on the same spectacle, saw chiefly an image —an imperfect, pathetic, heroic, and majestic image—of Order. (pp. 104-05)

Such is Byzantium—Order, envisaged not as restraint nor even as a convenience but as a beauty and splendour. Perhaps no element in Williams's imagination separates him so widely as this from other writers. (p. 105)

Yet order, in the sense of discipline and civility, is not the whole of what Williams sees in Byzantium: if it were, the Roman empire might have been as apt an image as the Byzantine. He chooses the Byzantine because, whether rightly or wrongly, we think of it as something more rigid, more stylized, more scrupulously hierarchical, more stiffly patterned than the Roman. Its organization suggests something geometrical; and that was what Williams desired. His great saying 'Hell is inaccurate' implies his outlook on heaven. Deeply moved by even human order, he was also deeply aware of Divine Order as something of a flawless and mathematic precision imposing itself on the formless flux of natural moods and passions, imposing itself in the shape of virtue, courtesy, intelligence, ritual. (p. 106)

[*Song of the Unicorn* and *Bors to Elayne: the Fish of Broceliande*] introduce us to Williams's doctrine of Love. On this subject, as on so many others, he reaffirms the Romantic tradition but continues and elaborates it in modes that amount to a correction of earlier Romanticism. His most systematic statements in prose are to be found in the fifth chapter of *He Came Down from Heaven* and in *The Figure of Beatrice*. His master is Dante. Love means to him something that begins with what he calls a 'Beatrician experience'—the sort of experience that Dante records in the *Vita Nuova*. (p. 116)

The Beatrician experience may be defined as the recovery (in respect to one human being) of that vision of reality which would have been common to all men in respect to all things if Man had never fallen. The lover sees the Lady as the Adam saw all things before they foolishly chose to experience good as evil, to 'gaze upon the acts in contention.' Williams believes that this experience is what it professes to be. The 'light' in which the beloved appears to be clothed is true light; the intense significance which she appears to have is not illusion; in her (at that moment) Paradise is actually revealed, and in the lover Nature is renovated. The great danger is lest he should mistake the vision which is really a starting point for a goal; lest he should mistake the vision of Paradise for arrival there. . . . The Beatrician experience, like the Wordsworthian experience, is the summons to a discipline and a way of life—the long way recorded in the *Divine Comedy* or *The Prelude*.

The Beatrician experience does not usually last: nor, it will be remembered, did the Wordsworthian. Dante's Beatrice died—but even had she lived the story would have been much the same. The glory is temporary; in that sense Beatrice nearly always dies. But a transitory vision is not necessarily a vision of the transitory. That it passes does not prove it a hallucination. It has in fact been a glimpse of what is eternally real. (pp. 116-17)

In the first poem of all, *The Calling of Taliessin*, . . . Williams realizes, as perhaps only great poets do, that poetry is after all only poetry. It is not a substitute for philosophy or theology, much less for sanctification. Not even Virgil can be saved by poetry. That is the real meaning of the images in [*Taliessen in the School of the Poets*]. (p. 121)

What we . . . witness [in the Prelude to *Taliessen through Logres*] is a Beatrician experience going wrong. There is no mistake about its Beatrician quality; indeed nowhere, in my opinion, has the poet expressed so perfectly what he had to say about the human body. (p. 125)

Lamorack and the Queen Morgause of Orkney draws together into one vision all evils and all threats of evil that there are in Logres. In the first place it sets before us a fact about human passion which has not yet appeared in the poem. Not all loves—not even all life-long loves—begin with a Beatrician experience. (p. 128)

The whole poem marks strongly the difference between the technique of narrative or drama and that of the metaphysical ode. The obsessive love of Lamorack, which is what a dramatist would seize on, though vividly imagined, is used by Williams chiefly as the medium through which to show us the

> contingent knowledge of the Emperor floating into sight.

His concern is not with the psychological origins of evil but with its metaphysical 'procession,' its intrusion from nightmare into reality, the horrible stages whereby what ought not to be at all becomes an image, and what ought to be only an image becomes stone, and what ought to be only stone becomes a woman, and what ought to be only a woman becomes her son. For the whole tendency of Williams's myth of the Fall is to make us feel evil not as imperfection, nor even as revolt, but as miscreation—the bringing to be of what must not (and even in a sense cannot) be, yet now it is. . . . (pp. 131-32)

In [*The Star of Percivale* and *The Ascent of the Spear*] Taliessin has been shown principally as giving (though also, in some degree, receiving) a Beatrician experience. In the next, *The Sister of Percivale*, he receives more fully; he meets the Beatrice *par excellence* of his whole life. . . . The second and much more important thing about her is that she 'bled a dish full of blood' . . . to save a sick lady's life and died herself as a result. She is therefore the extreme instance in the poem of 'Exchange' or 'Substitution.'

This is perhaps the most difficult poem in the whole cycle and I am far from claiming that I have mastered it. All I can do is to begin with what is easiest and then go to what is next in hardness and so on till I find I can get no further. In its plainest sense the 'argument' is that Taliessin sees Blanchefleur newly brought to court with her two brothers and is, in a certain fashion, enamoured of her—I say, 'in a certain fashion' because this is a meeting of two unicorns, two celibates between whom nothing but 'intellectual nuptials' are at any stage in question. Let us now go up the second step in our stair of difficulties. Before Blanchefleur enters the courtyard Taliessin has been watching a slave girl (not the girl of the two previous poems) drawing water from the castle well. In her also he has seen the celestial light; of her also he has, if we must use the word, been enamoured. The Beatrician quality of the lady does not in the least 'kill' the Beatrician quality of the barbarian slave. Taliessin is living on that rung of the Platonic ladder whence the soul sees the beauty in all beautiful bodies to be one. Hence, as Williams says in one of the manuscript notes, he sees the slave and the lady as twins; 'Blanchefleur cannot be perfect to understanding without the slave.' This unity between the two is worked out by an extraordinary unity in diversity between two very different sensuous experiences which the poet establishes at the very moment of Blanchefleur's arrival. . . . The level continuity of the trumpet blast, made out of something so essentially warm and flexible as air from rounded lips and the rounded straightness of the arm, are both instances of that union between the geometrical and the vital which Williams so often expresses, both fit objects for 'Euclidean love.' Now a further step. The blazon of Percivale's house, and therefore of Blanchefleur's, is a star, as we have learned in earlier poems. And the slave's back is scarred—whether 'from whip or sword' we do not know. Taliessin has watched her at the well until that scar ('the mark flickered white in the light') has led him over 'the curved horizon' of her back into the contemplation of that same 'organic body' which he contemplated in Byzantium. . . . That is why, recognizing the unity between the slave and the lady, we can say 'The stress of the scar ran level with the star of Percivale.' The difference, to be sure, is quite as important as the unity. The scar symbolizes all the violence and suffering by which alone barbarian souls can be brought, against their will, into the confines of the City in order that, at a later stage they may, by their will, remain there. The star symbolizes the whole heraldic pattern which the City has for those who are native there, for whom law has been sublimated into honour, service into courtesy, discipline into dance. Blanchefleur and the slave are two as well as one. In the slave we see the back of something which in Blanchefleur reveals its face. Poetically this is driven home by the fact that we attend almost exclusively to the slave's back—the scarred shoulder, the 'smooth slopes,' the spine; but turning, Taliessin saw 'the rare *face* of Blanchefleur.' Perhaps that is what Blanchefleur is—the slave *turned around:* in older language, converted. And yet, by a further subtlety, Blanchefleur herself, Blanchefleur's face, is the back of something else. (pp. 137-40)

So far I think I understand. But all round this illuminated area there rolls and pulsates a mass of meanings that escape me. Williams himself wrote for me . . . this sentence: 'The perfect union of sensuality and substance is seen for a moment.' It is plain that the whole poem records the momentary vision of a unity which is more often invisible; but the terms sensuality and substance, borrowed from Lady Julian's *Revelations of Divine Love,* do not help me very much since I know neither what Lady Julian meant by them nor what Williams understood her to have meant. *Sensuality* in Middle English normally means 'the sensitive soul' which we share with animals, as distinct both from the 'vegetable soul' which we share with plants and the 'rational soul' which we share with angels: that is, it means the life of the senses. (What we call 'sensuality' is in Middle English called 'luxury' or 'gluttony.') Williams was not a Middle English scholar and we cannot assume at the outset that he fully understood Lady Julian's use of the word: but he certainly understood that *sensuality* in her language is not a term of disapproval. He found the key to her meaning (as another of his notes tells me) in the passage where she says that the City is built at the meeting place of Sensuality and Substance—at that very border line where the supersensible joins the sensible, where incarnation or embodiment occurs, where the Word (in some degree or on some level) becomes flesh. The poem we are considering is filled with imagery which suggests that we are between two worlds. The very first words in it are 'the horizon'—though I do not understand why this horizon should be located 'at the back of Gaul.' The image of an 'horizon' (a hard, straight line which at once unites and separates heaven and earth) is repeated in the level top of the wall on which Taliessin is lying. He is also, significantly, 'between' Arthur's hall and the horizon which are for a second united by a flash of lightning, just as the sensuous and substantial worlds are momentarily united in the Beatrician experience. The slave's back as she stoops makes 'a curved horizon' beyond which Taliessin sees her 'substantial' (supersensuous) nature, and 'the horizon in her eyes was breaking with distant Byzantium.' The shape of the hall is cut out against the western sky and thus makes a kind of horizon between Camelot and Broceliande. The bucket coming out of the well is visualized in the line, 'A round plane of water

rose shining in the sun.' The image is so 'mature with pure fact' that it can be enjoyed fully for its own sake: but the writer must have noticed and intended us to notice that 'a round plane' shining in the sky's light is an exact description of what every horizon contains. But there is still something more in the poem which I have not understood.

In these three pieces we have been shown instances of those acts of courtesy and exchange out of which the king's poet's 'household' or 'company' arose. In *The Founding of the Company* we get a fuller account of its character. The 'company' is an extension of the 'household'—an overflow, or reproduction, into Logres generally of the life lived in Taliessin's own house among his slaves, retainers, and squires. It is something subtly less than a religious order. It has not a rule, only 'a certain pointing': it has no name, no formal admission. It is also, I suspect, the most autobiographical element in the cycle. Something like the Company probably came into existence wherever Williams had lived and worked. In it the whole organic body is represented. . . . (pp. 140-41)

Dinadan, the knight of holy mockery, meeting Taliessin in the king's rose-garden on All Fools' Day, salutes him as the Master of the Company. . . . The absurdity lies in the fact that every one of God's lieutenants is, in the last resort, wholly superfluous. God needs none of them; 'of these stones' He can raise up prophets, doctors, priests, poets, philosophers, guides. Taliessin's cavalry charge turned the day at Mount Badon: but it was his men, not he, who did most of the killing. They needed him only as a figure-head; any other figure-head, had God so willed, would have done as well. And now Taliessin, with a superficial ruefulness in his smile and a delight far deeper than the ruefulness, recognizes this. He is unnecessary to Dindrane, to Logres, to the Company, even to poetry: nay, poetry itself is unnecessary.

Many writers have in a satiric spirit unmasked human grandeur, delighting to show us that the king, stripped of robes and ceremony, is but clay like other men and that (says Bacon) 'the masks, and mummeries and triumphs of the world' show more 'stately and daintily' by the candlelight of illusion than by the 'naked and open' light of truth. Any sixteenth-century writer—Shakespeare, Erasmus, Montaigne—can roll you out reams of such moralizing, almost in his sleep. Williams's view is different. He accepts all they say. He finds it so obvious as to be hardly worth saying. *Of course* the whole thing is a kind of make believe or fancy-dress ball. . . . [All] is, from a certain point of view, illusory. What then? What but to thank God for the 'excellent absurdity' which enables us, if it so happen, to play great parts without pride and little ones without dejection, rejecting nothing through that false modesty which is only another form of pride, and never, when we occupy for a moment the centre of the stage, forgetting that the play would have gone off just as well without us. . . . (pp. 144-45)

Two spiritual maxims were constantly present to the mind of Charles Williams: 'This also is Thou' and 'Neither is this Thou.' Holding the first we see that every created thing is, in its degree, an image of God, and the ordinate and faithful appreciation of that thing a clue which, truly followed, will lead back to Him. Holding the second we see that every created thing, the highest devotion to moral duty, the purest conjugal love, the saint and the seraph, is no more than an image, that every one of them, followed for its own sake and isolated from its source, becomes an idol whose service is damnation. The first maxim is the formula of the Romantic Way, the 'affirmation of images': the second is that of the Ascetic Way, the 'rejection of images.' Every soul must in some sense follow both. . . . But souls are none the less called to travel principally the one way or the other, and in the . . . poem (*The Departure of Dindrane*) this distinction of vocations is set before us. (p. 151)

In all the poems which deal with Taliessin's 'Household' we have seen various stages in the progress of his 'slaves' from barbarism to Christian ripeness. In *The Queen's Servant* we see the consummation of this process. This difficult and daring poem is best understood if we remember, firstly, St. Paul's longing to be rid of the mortal body not in order that he may be unclothed but that he may be clothed anew . . . and, secondly, that place in the *Purgatorio* where Virgil having brought Dante to the earthly Paradise sets him free from all tutelage and makes him henceforth emperor and pontiff over himself. We are shown, in fact, the moment at which a soul is redeemed into the glorious liberty of the children of God. Treating the poem allegorically you might say that Taliessin is here a type of Christ: but it is not an allegory and we had better say that Christ in Taliessin is operative—as in all our guides and teachers. (p. 155)

There is . . . throughout [*The Son of Lancelot*] an amazing counterpoint of ideas: the 'top tune' or . . . the focus which brings all into unity, is supplied by Merlin. His behaviour is, for me, a little obscured by technicalities of magic, a subject in which Williams was more learned than most of us. I am compelled to accept these as a mere romantic penumbra because of my ignorance; but I am quite sure that was not how they were written. Williams probably knew all about the 'anatomical body of light' and the 'illustration' of the 'grades.' Magic for him 'throws no truck with dreams': its instrument is 'the *implacable* hazel'—the straight, cut rod of discipline and measure. The conjuring of Merlin— the thrust of Time, Destiny, History—exhibits that mysterious onward pressure which brings events to pass: mysterious to us, because we are ignorant, but doubtless, in itself, as precise and articulate as a geometrical diagram. (p. 160)

[We] may point out that Merlin becomes wolf of his own will and Lancelot against his will and beyond his understanding. Lancelot is the beast 'that had lost the man's mind': Merlin is the man's mind using and controlling the beast's speed and strength. . . . Clearly, [Guinevere's 'unaesthetic'] state of evil is being contrasted with the aesthetic evil of the king. Arthur is an aesthete: imagination is the medium through which his egoism corrupts him. Guinevere is not at all an aesthete: she is an angry, mortally wounded woman whose thoughts go round and round the same circular groove. By the words 'unaesthetic womanhood' I think Williams means to direct our thoughts to something which is really characteristic of the feminine mind—that monopolistic concentration, for good or ill, on the dominant idea, which brings it about that in a woman good states of mind are unweakened and undissipated, or bad states of mind unrelieved, by fancy and speculation and mere drifting. Hence that tenacity both of good and evil, those chemically pure states of devotion or of egoism, which are hardly conceivable in my own sex. The lady in

Mr. Eliot's poem who said 'How you digress' was speaking for all women to all men.

A single poem is all we have to fill the gap of time between Galahad's birth and his arrival, as a young man, at Camelot. Perhaps if Williams had lived other poems would have come in here. Yet the arrangement as it stands is not an unhappy one, for the single poem *Palomides Before his Christening* is a poem of prolonged, monotonous stillness: it would be quite appropriate to imagine it filling fifteen or twenty years. Here, and here alone, Williams approaches the temper of Mr. Eliot's later poetry. The dry rock scenery, the artfully prosaic sentences, the sense of a vast pause, a vacuity, which may be the prelude either to conversion or despair, all remind us of the other poet. There is even an echo of Mr. Eliot's manner in the lines

The Chi-Ro is only a scratching like other scratchings;
But in the turn of the sky the only scratching.

The borrowing seems to me to be ill-judged. No two great poetic styles are less likely to mix fruitfully than those of Williams and Mr. Eliot. The passage about skeleton loves which comes a little earlier is also reminiscent: but the influence here might also be that of Miss Edith Sitwell's *Metamorphosis*—though I doubt whether Williams knew her poetry as well as he knew Mr. Eliot's. (pp. 162-63)

[Rushing] movement is the predominant quality of *The Last Voyage*. This does not mean that it has at all the kind of rushing movement we find in Shelley—much less the galloping movement of Swinburne. . . . The motion [here] is taut, vibrant: the sense of quivering compulsion is behind it. . . . The birds, which appear in the third paragraph are not here used as they would probably have been in an earlier poet to suggest speed; that has already been done, and will be kept going by the refrain 'The ship of Solomon (blessed be he) drove on.' They are land birds, doves, now 'sea travellers' because 'the land melts.' According to Williams's note 'For them (i.e. Galahad and his companions) all that was Logres and the Empire has become this flight of doves. Galahad as a symbol of Christ now has necessity of being in himself.' (p. 178)

[The] power of the symbol lies, I think, more in the simple idea that the solid land has become a flight of birds. It is this that makes us poetically believe that we are passing with all the speed of our 'arm-taut keel' beyond the phenomenal universe, through the 'everlasting spray of existence,' the 'sea of omnipotent fact'; that we are witnessing apotheosis. But, as in all poetry that attempts such themes with success, so here, the symbolical miracles are braced with flashes of acute recollection from the sensuous world. Thus the line 'down the curved road among the topless waters' brings before us exactly what we have seen from real ships—not 'waves' coming towards us, nor even 'waves' rising and falling, but (as if stationary in that split second of sight) a terrible road down into a shining valley. (p. 179)

I [consider] these *Arthuriana* as a book of wisdom—a book that makes consciousness. If I say that in this respect it seems to me unequalled in modern imaginative literature, I am not merely recording the fact that many of Williams's doctrines appear to me to be true. I mean rather that he has re-stated to my imagination the very questions to which the doctrines are answers. Whatever truths or errors I come to hold hereafter, they will never be quite so abstract and je-/

june, so ignorant of relevant data, as they would have been before I read him. (p. 191)

Consider, again, how in the matter of irony Williams begins where nearly every modern writer leaves off. No age has been more ironical than ours: irony has even been made by some critics into a necessary element of all poetry. To that extent Williams is a child of his age. But that kind of irony at which others arrive on their final goal is for him the starting-point. It is for him what you get over almost before beginning to write. The true goal is 'defeated irony': and it makes the lower irony (to me) look simply stupid—'swain-ish' as Milton would have said. The work of Lytton Strachey, read immediately after Williams's poetry, would, I suspect, sound pitiable. (p. 192)

Other modern myths depict a dialectical world. Keats's Titans and Wagner's Gods beget their opposites and are transcended by them. Williams paints a Co-inherent world: 'joy remembers joylessness.' If this is a truth at all it is certainly a more interesting and subtle truth, and a fresher, if not a newer, one. (p. 193)

Character is not there for its own sake, and what is there is stylized and limited for symbolic and lyric purposes. The wonder is that, despite this self-limitation, so much merely personal tragedy and even social comedy is interwoven with the myth. The persons are not abstractions. There is more merely human life in them than the poet, for his main purpose, needed to show. It gets out, it is irrepressible.

In 'Wisdom' then I believe the work abounds and even excels. Next for Deliciousness, and first for Deliciousness of rhythm and melody. This is the quality in which I consider the work most unequal—at least as posterity will read it. His own incantatory powers were very great and no line that he wrote did not sound musical when he recited it. But that is an advantage which, I suppose, many poets have had and which all must lose at death. We can judge the po-etry only as read without it. Metrically the individual poems fall into two classes: those in rhyming or unrhyming stanzas and those in continuous five-beat verse (with occasional internal rhyme). It is in the latter that the poet seems to me, at times, to falter. He is using Sprung Rhythm in which a single syllable may be a foot. This technique at its best can fling stressed monosyllables together so as to produce an unsurpassed weight and resonance. . . . On the other hand there are poems in which Williams has produced word music equalled by only two or three in this century and surpassed by none. *The Calling of Arthur* responds metrically to every movement of the emotion: startling and shrill in its opening stanza ('Black with hair, bleak with hunger, defiled'), dragging and fainting for King Cradlemas ('The high aged voice squeals with callous comfort'), rising into a rapid and more familiar rhythm as action begins ('The banner of Bors is abroad; where is the king') and then, at the end, using all its monosyllabic feet and clashing accents to convey an astonishing sense of violent and con-clusive action. . . . (pp. 193-95)

Less excited but even richer in pure sound is *The Crowning of Arthur*. Here a particularly fine effect is achieved by the long lines as they rise—one might almost say, as they *escape*—out of the mass of the shorter lines stiffened with heavy syllables and jewelled with internal rhymes. Thus in 'The King stood crowned; around in the gate' we ourselves stand rigid; in the last line of the same stanza ('Logres her-

aldically flaunted the King's state') that long waving word *heraldically* lifts us banner high above the crowd. (p. 195)

One might almost say that as Williams is the poet of 'de-feated irony' so he is the poet of the 'defeated senses,' or rather of the transmuted senses, of poetry which by an un-fulfilled invitation to the senses lures us beyond them; his poetical city 'is built at the meeting place of substance and sensuality.' He is in one way full of images: but where he is most himself each image is no sooner suggested than it fades—or, dare I say? *brightens*—into something invisible and intangible. (p. 197)

The world of the poem is a strong, strange, and consistent world. If the poem is rejected you will reject it because you find that world repellent. And that is a reaction which, though I do not share it, I can understand. It is certainly not a world I feel at home in, any more than I feel at home in the worlds of Dante and Milton. It strikes me as a per-ilous world full of ecstasies and terrors, full of things that gleam and dart, lacking in quiet, empty spaces. Amid the 'surge and thunder' of the *Odyssey* you can get a snug fire-side night in Eumaeus's hut. There is no snugness in Wil-liams's Arthuriad, just as there is none in the *Paradiso*. What quiet there is is only specious: the roses are always trembling, Broceliande astir, planets and emperors at work. Can we then condemn it, as Raleigh came near to con-demning *Paradise Lost* because it was insufficiently home-ly? Not, I think, unless we know that comfort and hearts-ease are characters so deeply rooted in the real universe that any poetic world which omits them is a distortion: an assurance which I, to my sorrow, lack. Perhaps the uni-verse of *Taliessin* and *The Region* is quite as like the real universe as what we find in *Pickwick* or *Tristram Shandy*. What provides relaxation in it, and thus, in a sense, takes the place of snugness, is gaiety—a stranger to poetry for some hundreds of years, but certainly no stranger to the universe. I am speaking of the gaiety of Dinadan, of Tal-iessin himself, of the stripped maids frolicking in Caucasia, and of the high courtesy and defeated irony which runs about the whole poem. There is a youthfulness in all Wil-liams's work which has nothing to do with immaturity. Nor is this the only respect in which his world offers the very qualities for which our age is starved. Another such quality is splendour: his world is one of pomp and ritual, of strong, roaring, and resonant music. The transparent water-colour effect of much *vers libre* is not found there. His colours are opaque: not like stained glass but like enamel. Hence his admirable hardness; by which I do not here mean difficulty, but hardness as of metals, jewels, logic, duty, vocation. Eroticism, in some form or other, is not a quality in which modern literature is deficient: but the pervasive eroticism— the glowing, pungent, aromatic quality—of these poems is different, and possible only to a poet who also appreciates austerity. Side by side with the splendour and the erotic perfume we meet celibacy, fasts, vigils, contrition, tragedy, and all but despair. This balance is true to the poet's origi-nals: and that truth also contributes to the strength of the incantation. It is an advantage which few refashioners of old myths have had. All through *The Ring* the original Ni-belungen story is pulling against the political and economic stuff with which Wagner wants to load it: all through Ten-nyson's *Idylls* the Arthurian story is pulling against nearly everything that Tennyson wants to say. There is no such tension in Williams's Arthuriad. It is in one way a wholly modern work, but it has grown spontaneously out of Malory and if the king and the Grail and the begetting of Galahad still serve, and serve perfectly, to carry the twentieth-century poet's meaning, that is because he has penetrated more deeply than the old writers themselves into what they also, half consciously, meant and found its significance unchangeable as long as there remains on earth any attempt to unite Christianity and civilization. (pp. 198-200)

> *C. S. Lewis, "Williams and the Arthuriad,"*
> *in* Arthurian Torso *(reprinted by permission*
> *of Oxford University Press, Inc.), Oxford*
> *University Press, 1948 (and reprinted by*
> *Oxford University Press, 1969), pp. 93-200.*

It is a pity, I think, that Charles Williams' best known works should be his fiction, for, extraordinary as the novels are, I find them the least satisfactory of his books. To begin with, he is interested, like Blake, in states of being rather than in individuals, and fiction is not an ideal medium for describing such. Second, it is virtually impossible, I believe, to describe the state of grace artistically, because to this state the capacity of the individual soul for expression is irrelevant; a commonplace person who can only utter banalities is just as capable of redemption as a genius; indeed, the chances of his redemption are probably greater. . . . If a writer pick a genius to represent the state of grace, he is almost bound to suggest that salvation is the consequence of genius, that the redeemed are a superior elite; but if, on the other hand, he chooses a commonplace person, banalities remain artistically, banalities, whatever glories they may conceal. The saved characters in Mr. Williams' novels, like Lester, are unsatisfactory from a literary point of view because of the unbridgeable gulf between their experiences and their power of describing them.

In describing the state of damnation this problem does not arise, and I know of no other writer, living or dead, who has given us so convincing and terrifying portraits of damned souls as Charles Williams. The popular notion of hell is morally revolting and intellectually incredible because it is conceived of in terms of human criminal law, as a torture imposed upon the sinner against his will by an all-powerful God. Charles Williams succeeds, where even Dante, I think, fails, in showing us that nobody is ever *sent* to hell; he, or she, insists on going there. If, as Christians believe, God is love, then in one sense he is not omnipotent, for he cannot compel his creatures to accept his love without ceasing to be himself. The wrath of God is not *his* wrath but the way in which those feel his love who refuse it, and the right of refusal is a privilege which not even their Creator can take from them. (pp. 552-53)

Judging by my own experience, I should advise readers to postpone reading Charles Williams' poetry until, through reading his prose works, they have become thoroughly familiar with his ideas and his sensibility. I must confess that, when I first tried to read his poetry, though as a fellow verse writer I could see its great technical interest, I could not make head or tail of it. Like the Blake of the Prophetic Books, Charles Williams has his own mythology which a reader must master, and previous geographical associations can make this difficult. To me, for example, the word "Caucasia" has certain geographical and ethnic associations which I had first to dismiss in order to accept it as the poet's term for the unfallen order of Nature. I can only say, however, that the more I read *Taliessin Through Logres*

and *The Region of the Summer Stars,* the more rewarding I find them. . . .

Perhaps the most remarkable thing about Charles Williams, . . . is what one might call the orthodoxy of his imagination, as distinct from his beliefs, for this is very rare in our technological culture. In describing the life of the body and its finite existence in time, most contemporary writers, whatever their beliefs, show a Manichaean bias, an emphasis on the drab and the sordid. If they are materialists they place the beautiful and the exciting in some temporal future; if they are professing Christians the only road to salvation they can imagine is the Negative Way of ascetic renunciation. Even the few who, like D. H. Lawrence, do not suffer from this bias, cannot find anything in the contemporary world to their relish and turn for sustenance to preindustrial societies.

Chesterton, a writer by whom, I think, Charles Williams was influenced, did try to keep his balance and his nerve, but in his praise of wonder and wine there is a shrillness of tone, an exaggerated heartiness which betrays an inner strain. In the work of Charles Williams I can detect no strain whatever; he can imagine Beatrice in the Finchley Road as easily as in 13th century Florence. (p. 553)

> *W. H. Auden, "Charles Williams," in* The
> Christian Century *(copyright 1956 by Christian Century Foundation; reprinted by permission from the May 2, 1956 issue of* The
> Christian Century*), May 2, 1956, pp. 552-54.*

[*Poems of Conformity*] is not a thrilling or satisfactory book. It is very much an early book where moments of insight flicker here and there, and one feels that the author did not distinguish them from the rest. . . . Until *Taliessin* he does not make a serious attempt upon the hiding-places of his power, and in *Conformity* he had hardly identified them. (p. 41)

[*Poems of Conformity*] is easy to criticize. There are echoes of other writers, Chesterton, Macaulay, Shelley (almost painfully in 'Ascension'), Francis Thompson; there are what he himself describes as 'jostled pieties' in the sprawling pantheism of 'Ode for Easter Morning' and 'The Repose of Our Lady: A Dirge'; there are good phrases which fail to come off in their poem, like 'the Riders of the Holy Ghost'; there are faults of literary taste and crudenesses of method. But over all there is poetic energy, the impact of real existence, authority in rhyme and metre and a grand alliance of intellect and imagination. (p. 47)

It was in meditation on war and his friends that he first began to approach the idea that his life was involved in the lives of all other people and not only of people he had chosen to love and live with. He recognized that he benefited from the effort and pains endured by others far from him and not at the time concerned with or for him. He saw that pains and effort could and would be inflicted within himself which would be part of the life of the effort and pains of those others.

This is the beginning of coinherence, the main concept of all his thought. Charles touched the idea without realizing how it was to develop in his mind, nor that from grief and remorse over the death of his friends it was to grow into a doctrine of life for friend and stranger. (p. 55)

He had from the first book of verse been poised between

the two ways of rejection of the world and its images as not valid vehicles of the spirit, or the acceptance and affirmation of them as capable of good. He had hovered about the idea that human life was unable to sustain a spiritual experience, that however gifted and devoted a nature attempted it, the mere living of courtship and marriage would maim and diminish love, if it did not kill it altogether—especially the beautiful and unheard-of kind of love. Throughout *The Silver Stair* there had seemed to him a lot to be said for giving up the girl, marriage and home, and preserving love always beautiful and untouched in his heart. It is the intense temptation of the 'aesthetic life' to Kierkegaard. . . . In *Poems of Conformity* and *Divorce* he still writes of love distinct from loving. In *Windows of Night* it is no longer so, unless 'Antichrist' is an instance. Love is now known under its human accidents, in relationship. . . . The beautiful and unknown kind of love is here at home, still beautiful, still at any moment unknown and unparalleled. There is no loss and no diminishing. The thing known is utterly different from the thing imagined, and in the knowing there is no loss or diminishing but gain and amazement. . . . The living of love has sustained the vision, it has illumined, explained and made the vision possible, and at every moment the living itself has been sustained by the vision. (pp. 63-4)

[C. W.'s novels] are hasty and leap from point to point in a style which deceives the reader into thinking that life could skim thus surely, but the drive behind them is the sense of a totally different kind of life within our apparent life, and of the choice of becoming that other at any moment, or not.

The novels are full of action with an element of violence. Their action moves beyond the material world, and develops from relations to, and beliefs in, a world of spirit and ideas. They all pass, sooner or later, through the material bounds of normal life, while maintaining normal life in the plot. People become animals, which variously represent their inclination of mind, cards make earth and wind, men live in undecayed life for hundreds of years, a house disappears. C. W.'s ideas were no sooner framed in mortal people and material surroundings then they bounded off into the eternal non-material world which he saw pressing through our lives, and were held by his genius and his style in a tension between the two which is 'existential', thrilling, sometimes unbearable, not always succeeding.

The first five novels are of one kind. *Descent into Hell* and *All Hallows' Eve* are darker and more complicated. They lack the feeling that they were written for the fun of the thing—or they gain by that, according to the point of view. But the interesting thing about the novels is that . . . [they] are power novels. They are all about that dream of necromancers and psychologists, the achieving of power. (p. 78)

Power, personality and sex fill his novels—but with what a difference! They are the starting point for him instead of the finishing post. His stories start at power and lead out to freedom and peace and love; they start at personalities and lead out to coinherence and unity; they start at sex and lead out to the full nature of matter and the body in glory. He was particularly liable to be influenced by the rage of sex and power, being a man of very strong sensibilities, great nervous tension, and intellectual ability which could throw up a thousand implications and shadows in any situation, and yet a man without the satisfaction of any position or power in the world. There is no doubt that he had a conviction of genius and an appetite for fame. He knew he ought

to be a literary power and he longed to be. But he did not altogether long, and he never consented to the longing. It is possible I think that he longed also to be a power in sexual love and to have great experiences in act and knowledge, and not only in the intellect and imagination. But this longing also he did not consent to. (p. 80)

Read the novels and see what exaltation there was in this man, what grappling with unresting opposites until he wrung strength and order from them, what joy and glory he found in daily life in an office, and, finding, was able to expose and make available for others. He had extraordinary intellectual powers and he could draw naturally on extraordinary subjects, but all was forced into the service of our common day, our concern with money, love, marriage, illness, unemployment, examinations, or bad temper. He also insisted with equal force that our common day should relate itself to extraordinary subjects and ends, to glory, to joy, to purity and power. (pp. 80-1)

[The] lovers in his novels are not bound to their smallest daily round. If they are truly lovers, however stunted like Damaris Tighe or misdirected like Henry Lee, they have contact with the full powers of love, those powers entirely beyond, but not different from, their own, and through their theology or discovered ideas they can achieve them. It is true too of vices and the bad characters. Irritation has contact with its full power of murder, willingness to cheat to pass an examination has contact with its full power of theft and sacrilege. But this development in evil is more common among our writers; the development in goodness is unique in C. W.'s novels.

In life, in his poetry and in his novels he was more interested in what people became than in what they were like before they felt the contact of mighty powers. Therefore he was no laborious portrayer of character. . . . [He] had no interest at all in mighty powers except as they concerned human life. But he did not revel in people as people, without relation to ideas. His characters then are not memorable. In fact, his women are poor. (pp. 81-2)

But the stories of the novels are so intensely interesting that they absorb the reader, and the characters do not trouble one as they might in a smaller plot. (p. 82)

It is easy to pick holes in the novels. They were written hastily, and they take enormous themes hastily for their own purpose with little knowledge and hardly any research, but the use made of them is never superficial. The quality of C. W.'s mind worked throughout all, and if the Grail, and the Crown of Solomon, and the Tarot cards, are used they are not brought in as trimmings or make-weights, but because C. W. grasped their own particular point and glory, and saw what a remarkable tale could arise from it. His ability to seize on a mystery and express it in his own experience and emotions has produced a handful of the most exciting novels one can read. They are not fantasies. Through considerable psychological complexities, their attitude to life is wholly positive and affirmative. (p. 86)

[His] plays had the strong point of being short, and in all their 'literariness' C. W.'s sense of crisis presented life in surprising situations, which made his plays 'good theatre'. . . . His development of style helped the later plays, *The House of the Octopus, Seed of Adam, Thomas Cranmer of Canterbury,* and the shorter ones, *The Death of Good Fortune, Grab and Grace, The House by the Sta-*

ble, *Judgement at Chelmsford,* but in *A Myth of Shake-speare, The Witch,* and *The Chaste Wanton* one really has very little idea of what is actually going on, and when people are killed one needs the stage directions to know who has killed whom. It matters extraordinarily little, for only in *The Chaste Wanton* does the action rank with the ideas, and in that it is only one action, the signing of the death warrant by the Duchess. . . . In C. W.'s plays the ideas and the language are the important things, and the action much less. He was at the opposite end of the dramatic pole from Ibsen and such a play as *Hedda Gabler,* which has acutely dramatic action and no ideas at all. (p. 104)

[*The Chaste Wanton*] was one of C. W.'s favourites in all his work, as his Duchess, the heroine, was his favourite woman. It is unwise to press biographical implications in a man's invention too far, but this play stands as an imagination of a profound alteration in the way of knowing love and therefore life. It is a picture of a life opening upon love and power, and then being broken, forced into an altered way of knowing all its good, and after the breaking finding a deeper reconciliation. *Divorce* had known the terror of crucifying love in oneself by ordinary living and thinking. *The Chaste Wanton* sees another terror, that of being crucified in love by the rejection of one's love. The verse of the play beats with an intensity and compression which gathers its meaning and flings it out in the pain of the breaking. (pp. 109-10)

Descent into Hell [was] a novel written from the deep place where his spirit was. It shows the states of love in action and love in loss without defining them; it knows the facts, not the names, as it says of the suicide on his return to the world. The result is a book which carries the reader into its own dream, further and further below the level of conscious patterns of thought and behaviour; love in action moves one way and love in loss moves another, and the separation becomes final; coinherence ceases when loss refuses to love and clings to knowing nothing but loss. The only reality presented in the book is love; all else is illusion— self, honours, possession, pleasure, hate, or sexual joy. Only poetry shares the reality of love, but in lower place. It is all worked out with the logic of a dream wherein there is no difference between a small cause and a large. But still there is a story—since the book is written by C. W. . . . It is a frightening book, and an almost wholly non-religious book, in spite of its reference to certain lines in the Bible. It is the life of a consciousness below the level of reasoning and thought, a journey through the roots of a forest which are deep under water, like the forest of Broceliande. Above are patterns and definitions and formulas, below are facts, huge, unproportioned, the bottom of the monstrous world. (pp. 134-35)

Coinherence, substitution, and exchange: the rest of C. W.'s life and work enlarged upon these as a way of life and a way of thought. All goes back to the Trinity and the Incarnation and the Crucifixion of Christ. . . . C. W.'s thought . . . conceives always a living responsible Nature, the three Persons reciprocally indwelling and coinhering. (pp. 136-37)

This coinherence works through all creation; love lives from our unloving natures or not at all; our darkened and unhappy natures live from light and love (however remotely and ignorantly) or we have no life. It is not a trick, or mere tantalizing, or a superficial synthesis of opposites, it is how life works. The means by which we can enter into this coinherence is by substitution and exchange. . . .

Nobody saw the difficulties more clearly than C. W., but nobody believed the possibility more strongly, or declared more vehemently that he saw it happening. In the first half of *He Came Down From Heaven* the pattern of it is worked out in Old Testament history and in the life of Christ. He follows it through the idea of forgiveness and reconciliation, and finally into the concept which he was to make peculiarly his own, the Incarnation which is love acting in and through the human body. From this arose not only his presentation of the glory of the body, but also his great conception of the City, which meant coinherence, substitution, and exchange in all the web of relationship that binds the body of humanity or the body of the Church together. (p. 137)

From now on, the word 'love' has always a double meaning in his thinking, as personal love, and as love in the City which may be felt in any of the concerns and relationships of people everywhere. . . .

Read *He Came Down From Heaven* to see the outline of C. W.'s thought, and then read *Taliessin Through Logres.* The poetry is the shape of that outline. The diagram of his thought rises line by line upon the mind as the diagram rose through the mosaic of Phoebus in the poem 'Taliessin In the School of The Poets'. . . . With the perception of a change of diagram comes a change of value, a change of life; every man has his own pattern, but the diagram it relates to is new.

> Infinite patterns opened
>   in the sovereign chair's mass;
>   but the crowned form of anatomized man,
>   bones, nerves, sinews,
>   the diagram of the style of the Logos,
>   rose in the crimson brass.

The style of the Logos might be roughly rendered the manner of loving. There is a new pattern of life, a new assessment of what is important and what we can work upon. The new diagram is not only a sacred sign of God, not an abstraction alone but an abstraction expressed in [the] very man, bones, nerves, and sinews, not lessened to the physical mortal specimen but crowning and transfiguring it. This is the centre of C. W.'s vision.

'Crowning' and 'transfiguring' are terms which need detailed filling out, and in the second half of *He Came Down From Heaven* C. W. goes on to do it. These three Chapters, V, VI, and VII, deal with exchange, substitution, and coinherence in the love we mean when we speak of falling in love, and its development in ordinary life between ordinary people everywhere. This is what C. W. called Romantic Theology. These chapters are a key to his new world. (p. 138)

There are two themes besides the main one of love-in-life. One is the necessity of change in the new life, and one the bearing of burdens by substitution. The good life is not just to be better, it is to be different. . . . Dedication, self-sacrifice, social service, all intellectual fortresses must be redeemed, must lose their own vindication of themselves and live a substituted life, vindicated and defended only by Love. (p. 139)

Taliessin Through Logres is a vision of the life of love. It concerns love between man and woman, in mind and body, and it concerns love in the City, in the linked organism of human society. It is a double kind of pattern, a diagram of the life and a map of how to live it. The whole nature of man is figured under the name of the Empire, and the different provinces suggest different parts of the body and their attributed activities. Britain or Logres is the head or place of thought and direction. . . . Within Logres, Camelot is the seat of ordinary life, of government, marriage, work and all affirmation. It is also, C. W. told me, the seat of all life without direct revelation of joy, therefore also of love in loss. Carbonek is the seat of dedication, of the Church, of the attempt to know goodness more directly than through work or home or art, the seat of the Hallows and direct communication. Byzantium, C. W. said, is meaning. ('Not life, nor death, but meaning,' he asked for in the Masque.) Sarras, the city of the soul, is everywhere by achievement, and so not marked, but implied for convenience to be an island city in the seas beyond the forest of Broceliande which covers all the coast of South Wales and Somerset and is rooted in the sea. The last book of poems, *The Region of the Summer Stars,* is concerned with a totally different geography from that of the struggling Empire, as its title shows. The poems should not be intermingled. The same characters move in the world of the summer stars, but to mix the poems up with the *Taliessin* poems is like mixing the chapters of two different travels by the same man. (pp. 146-47)

Taliessin Through Logres is the struggle of the poet to articulate his knowledge and in the articulation to know it further. After it, he moved securely in the world he had discovered. Although the poems do not encourage a particular kind of careful explanation they are not finally obscure, and their knotted language is less deceptive than the pure flow of *The Region of the Summer Stars,* where meditation is needed to penetrate the layers of life. (p. 154)

Taliessin Through Logres is wholly new. Its style is new, compressed and complex, with the drive of extreme simplicity. Its vision is a new discovery in the oldest themes of love and the body, just as his critical work is a new discovery in the oldest themes of English criticism, Shakespeare, Milton and Wordsworth. Not what it is, but that it is, and its existence so deeply experienced that some rumour of what it truly is penetrates to thought and speech. A natural and pure originality marked everything that C. W. wrote. Disagree with him if you will, but his communication is direct. There is nothing worn or common or dull in any of his work, no padding, no borrowed thought. His mind lived in Carbonek rather than Camelot, but it was the ordinary daily life of all of us that he lived there and enabled others to live. (pp. 154-55)

[Williams] stands to be judged as a man of original ideas, as poet and critic and man of religion, the man with direct spiritual insight who in the fashion of another age was called a prophet, not as a foreteller but as one who learnt of God directly and without overmuch human guidance. The histories and novels in his work are less. What remains are the Arthurian poems, the concept of reading and writing poetry as a way of knowing experience, and his religious vision.

As a poet, Bridges linked him once with Donne, and though the small quantity of his mature work must always lessen his standing, his work has the intellectual poetic quality of Donne, the union of human and religious love, and the transcendental vision which sees God break everywhere out of the forms and movements of humanity. Because his poetry is shaped by a faith it achieves a philosophic pattern which marks it out in twentieth-century verse, and though the pattern is different it brings the poetry into relationship with that of his great contemporary Yeats. (p. 192)

It is likely, and desirable, that he will not found a school in the sense that young poets will feel that the way to write is like he wrote, as has happened to Hopkins and to Eliot. C. W.'s inspiration is too personal, and his style too closely chiselled by his personal vision, for this to be anything but lamentable. His individuality of style came from compression of experience, and without the working of that inner life upon it the outer style would be mere spinning of patterns. But it is likely that he will have the subtle and far-reaching influence of a solitary. His unlikeness to others, his concern with his own vision of timeless things working in human experiences, sets him apart from his age, especially from the twentieth century, which is so deeply occupied in contemporary social, psychological, and political things, all particularly subject to time and time's changes. This makes it likely that C. W.'s work will powerfully affect certain kinds of minds, and minds looking for certain kinds of things—things original, things of faith and of understanding and of experience, things not of material values but of good and evil. (pp. 192-93)

[In *The Figure of Beatrice*] all his thought is gathered, with an orientation peculiarly his own. The flashes we saw in novels and biographies and verse and *He Came Down From Heaven* are here sustained and steady. Here is the eternal worth of the body, exchange and coinherence true and false, mystery, intellect, and psychology. . . . C. W. moves with unswerving speed and sureness among the stars and gulfs of heaven, tracking out the path.

The Figure of Beatrice is more than a recapitulation. It is a breakthrough into a further country. There is a frightening strangeness here and there in its phrases. A horrible pressure rises between the sentences in the chapter on the Inferno. Each sentence follows the last like a step onward in hell. (p. 194)

[In *The Figure of Beatrice*] the vision of evil is more homely than the vision of good. It is here that C. W. has gone furthest, as in his novels the examination of good was always outstanding in his generation of contemporary writing, which all had skill in examining evil. When he turned his attention on some common good, as duty, punctuality, accuracy, seeing through his eyes one saw it shine in a transfigured state, itself yet glorious, and part of the pattern that sustains our life. (pp. 194-95)

> *Alice Mary Hadfield, in her* An Introduction to Charles Williams *(© Alice Mary Hadfield 1959), Robert Hale Limited, 1959.*

Charles Williams' Arthurian poems constitute his own recasting of the Arthurian myth as he derived it from earlier sources, principally Malory. His unfinished prose essay, *The Figure of Arthur,* is, however, a retracing of the myth through all the principal early texts and, though undated, can, I think, be presumed to follow the poetry in Williams' career. (p. 38)

Williams wishes by means of this essay to ground his own myth in tradition by setting his Arthuriad within the framework of the historical legend. . . . [He] establishes immediately that the Grail is to him the thematic core of the Arthurian material and that the historical myth assumes meaning to him only when it focuses on the Grail. The fact that we today tend "to regard the Lancelot-Guinevere story as more important than that of the Grail," Williams takes to be a matter of historical accident. Thus, he sets out in *The Figure of Arthur* to restore what he considers to be the proper emphasis and equilibrium. (p. 41)

The union of Arthur and the Grail . . . becomes to Williams a gigantic and complex symbol of the union of civilization and Christianity. The attempt to unite the Grail and the Kingdom can almost be called a "type" (to use Williams' term) of the Second Coming. (p. 42)

Perhaps the greatest single image that Williams develops in remaking the Arthurian legend is that of organic unity and order. There would seem to be little doubt, moreover, that this is Williams' contribution; order and fact are so much a part of Williams' whole theology that he could hardly have helped seeing the Arthurian world as anything other than an ordered kingdom. The Arthurian world is, as we have noted before, marked by order at every phase of its existence. Yet this concept of order is not exploited in the cycle for its own sake; its presence in Williams nearly always denotes the sacred, the holy. (p. 67)

The logic of the Empire thus reflects the order of the universe; Arthurian Logres becomes a microcosm of the ideal cosmic civilization in which even the deviations from precision, as, for example, the curve of Iseult's arm, serve to redefine the straightness of the pattern that permits the curve. Order, in Williams' terms, is always the mode of God's existence and its manifestations in the world are His handiwork. (pp. 67-8)

To what purpose is Charles Williams using the Arthurian myth? First of all, it should be apparent that the cycle as a whole deals with the unifying of Christianity and civilization, of spirit and flesh, of form and matter. Thus it is that throughout the poem we find on every level themes and images dealing with order and Exchange. It should also be apparent that this order is constantly frustrated by man's desire for self-sufficiency and independence. The main theme of the cycle thus becomes the battle between order and chaos, charity and cupidity, love and pride, Exchange and possession. Such a theme is, of course, universal, and there can be little doubt that Williams saw these battles in terms as relevant to twentieth-century London as to Arthurian Britain. (pp. 83-4)

The first thing that strikes one reading Williams' novels for the first time is his use of the occult and the mythical. The first five novels make great use of frankly mythological properties (in the stage sense) and of frankly supernatural or subnatural personages and events . . . [which] furnish for Williams convenient and striking means of introducing the particular themes of good and evil, order and chaos, which he is attempting to express. In each case, we have almost the same technique. Williams forces an occurrence of tremendous cosmic significance into modern society and then settles back to watch its effects on ordinary human beings. Moreover, the intrusion of these cosmic phenomena generally results in an overthrowing of natural order that can only be restored by the actions of the hero. (p. 84)

The focus of interest in the novels is always on the earthly characters themselves and on their reactions to the sudden revelation of the supernatural forces that surround them. Thus Williams' novels are far from being simply supernatural adventure stories. They are in the first instance novels about morality and religion among men.

The heroes and heroines, moreover, of Williams' novels are generally passive in the midst of the universe-shaking events that reveal the latent good and evil tendencies of the lesser characters. (p. 85)

Goodness as well as evil is made universal by myth in *Descent into Hell*. It is clear that the substitution that is the center of the novel is a type of the Incarnation and Atonement. . . . Substitution is, as Williams says, the "heart of the Church" and, as such, becomes a matter of universal concern. . . . Thus, to Williams, the process that lies behind the Incarnation is repeated over and over again in the history of mankind. It need not even be spoken of; it is a matter of tacit consent, a problem of common courtesy. The apparently strange illustration of the doctrine in *Descent into Hell* is simply an extension of what is, in reality, an everyday occurrence, a "universal rule." So again, the mythological reference in the novel renders the particular universal and the mystifying ordinary. (pp. 92-3)

During the middle years of the 1930's, Williams' novels came more and more to deal with the problems of salvation and damnation in the contemporary world. The early thrillers, though important in showing the development of Williams' themes, generally treat good and evil as absolutes. Those who are condemned are condemned because they worship evil and despise good. Although the situations in these early novels reflect, as they are certainly intended to do, perfectly valid and meaningful theological and mystical states, they have not the general charity-cupidity theme that dominates the later novels and the poetry. The shift, I think, in Williams' writing during the 1930's is away from mystical vision and adventure and toward an attempt to picture salvation and damnation as they exist among the people of Williams' own time. What we find is an attempt to translate the kinds of mystical experience found in the early novels into less overtly fantastic literary situations. Thus, in *Descent into Hell* and *All Hallows' Eve*, there is a great deal less of the science fiction point of view that makes use of supernatural devices and props. But even in these novels, we still find an insistence on a mystical point of view that involves a frank intermingling of nature and supernature; the living and the dead associate, ordinary temporal bonds are broken, and the characters, under quite ordinary circumstances, indulge in mystical experiences without apology or pseudoscientific explanation. (pp. 93-4)

Taliessin through Logres . . . was published during this period. It is impossible to say how Williams happened to hit upon the Arthurian legends as an objective correlative to his major themes. Certainly his early Arthurian poems . . . contain only the merest "intimations of spirituality." It is possible to say, however, what Williams saw in the legend, and particularly in the Grail quest, since it provided him with a setting that was at once fairy and religious. If my assumptions concerning Williams' creative processes and development are correct, it must have become increasingly apparent to Williams that it was impossible for him to translate completely his major themes into ordinary contemporary circumstances since by their very nature many of these themes were semimystical. Consider, for example, the doctrine of Exchange, which in essence is an extension of the Incarnation and Atonement to all human intercourse. Although this theme is treated as matter-of-factly as possible in *Descent into Hell,* it is clear that its very presence gives the novel a semimystical atmosphere that, while not out of place, is considerably removed from the ordinary life with which the novel deals. It may well be, of course, that Williams' plan in *Descent into Hell* is to produce just this mixture of the miraculous and the ordinary, but, on the other hand, the mystical nature of the theme is better suited to a setting in which it can operate normally and upon its own terms. Thus, by adopting as objective correlative a myth that has as a part of its normal construction just these mystical and semimagical qualities—the Grail, Merlin, the prophets—Williams could very well let his own mystical concepts—the doctrines of Exchange, Beatrician love, Gomorrah—function on their own proper levels without having to force them into normal, everyday life situations to which they are by nature alien.

Second, in the Arthurian materials, Williams found a myth that could carry, without undue forcing, his primary theme of order and chaos. In Malory he found the story of the rise and fall of a would-be perfect civilization. Moreover, the key to a religious interpretation of that fall lay to his hand in the failure of the Grail quest. The theme of spiritual incest (Gomorrah) could be presented by Arthur's conceiving Mordred on Morgause. The practice of Exchange could be presented as the guiding law of the perfect civilization. The Fall of Man could be seen in the Dolorous Blow. On every level, the legend could carry Williams' themes. (pp. 95-6)

Williams uses myth referentially in the novels to render universal his specific and generally bizarre fictional situations. That is, in the novels Williams' method is to begin with the modern situation and then to extend his meaning through allusions to myth. In the poetry, on the other hand, we find Williams beginning and staying within the myth itself. . . . [Myth] is not used to generalize a specific situation but, conversely, is made to render specific a universal theme. We see the hope and failure of Logres as a whole; we see our contemporary Grail quest in fragments. To Williams' mythmaking mind, however, one thing is clear: both quests are failures. The hope in both cases exists in the company, the remnant, those to whom the doctrine of Exchange has operative validity. In the novels, this theme is often obscured by the fact that the chosen objective correlative cannot bear its weight. In the poetry, the theme takes on new meaning and new grandeur from the meaning and grandeur inherent in the myth itself. (pp. 100-01)

Charles Moorman, "Charles Williams," in his Arthurian Triptych: Mythic Materials in Charles Williams, C. S. Lewis, and T. S. Eliot *(copyright © 1960 by The Regents of the University of California; reprinted by permission of the University of California Press), University of California Press, 1960, pp. 38-101.*

Charles Williams is the most fascinating product of the English religious drama revival. . . . The unusual quality in Williams's work lies probably in his relationship to the material with which he deals. Where another writer might present the supernatural as a construct of belief and fan-

tasy, Williams always seems to be offering it as observed fact. (pp. 142-43)

Of all the modern religious playwrights, Williams is the least evangelical. Here, he says, is the way things are—things seen and unseen. The reader can accept or reject the vision as he wishes or as he must. It is Williams's achievement as a playwright that he can attract the unbelieving mind—in a willing suspension of disbelief—as well as the believing one; it is probably his weakness as a playwright that it is the mind, more surely than the emotions, that he attracts. (p. 147)

Whether or not Williams is actually attracted to the unusual for its own sake—and a book like *The Descent of the Dove* seems to indicate that he is not, that his style is the natural complement of his thought—theatrical production is likely to underline the difficulty of his work, to hint at the "exhibitionism" which seems to distress [some of Williams' critics]. His fondness for internal rhyme quite naturally turns up phrases in which he appears to be straining for effect, and such jarrings on the ear are likely to stay with the listener longer than the felicitous phrases. At their best, Williams's sentences are complicated, their rhythm unusual, his verse difficult to read; the demands that he makes on an actor are greater than those of any other modern writer of theatrical verse. (p. 163)

Gerald Weales, in his Religion in Modern English Drama *(copyright © 1961 by Gerald Weales), University of Pennsylvania Press, 1961.*

Many so-called heresies, Williams believed, are outraged, justifiably extravagant reassertions of some neglected aspect of orthodoxy. The central tenet of the poems [in *The Silver Stair, Poems of Conformity,* and *Divorce*] is that the Church, shrinking from the full meaning of the Incarnation, has severed the *Via Positiva* ("the Way of the Affirmation of Images") from the *Via Negativa* ("the Way of the Rejection of Images") and has glorified the latter at the expense of the former. (p. 261)

The love he celebrates is that which, precisely because it honors the body, enables a man and a woman to enter God's presence together. Above all other Christians, true lovers are entitled to affirm that they "believe in the Holy Ghost." As for the Incarnate Lord, how can we know Him more surely than by fiercely tender exploration of that flesh wherein He dwelt among us? (p. 262)

Perhaps the best way of being religious about sex is to keep it in its place with reverently joyful awareness of what it actually is. Due allowance must be made for the baroque concettism which sometimes characterizes Williams' style. (p. 264)

Strongly as the romantic impulse works in . . . Charles Williams, [his] Christianity restrains them from lapsing into pantheism, solipsism, or self-deification. . . . Yet between [him] and the non-Christian mystical poets the chasm, though wide, is narrower than one could wish. (p. 267)

Hoxie Neale Fairchild, in his Religious Trends in English Poetry, *Volume 5 (copyright © 1962 Columbia University Press; reprinted by permission of the publisher), Columbia University Press, 1962.*

If you can imagine grafting a Dorothy Sayers detective story onto the Apocalypse of St. John, the resulting fruit might be like a Charles Williams novel. His seven remarkable tales are transcendental thrillers, supernatural melodramas. In them, immeasurable powers are loosed, terrifying events follow, and the characters live, move and have their being in dimensions which sometimes appall, but through which Williams shows us the full implications of creeds too much taken for granted in repetition. (p. 197)

Human character is seen with intense penetration. Immemorial traits and attitudes of fallen man are vividly isolated, defined, and traced to their conclusions in works and fruits. The cold lust to exploit power at the cost of damnation is tracked along its course of self-destruction. The bodily and spiritual death that comes from total self-absorption is contrasted to the sometimes serene, but also sometimes life-consuming self-giving to both man and God. Fashionable attitudes of this century are shown to us as changes rung on the old sin of Pride. (p. 198)

A dearth of significant or consequential content is a plague of much modern fiction. A loss of the vision of the nature of man that has shaped Western Christendom is characteristic of much more. Williams's seven novels have a weight of content and a clarity of vision of the Christian image of man that lend them their special importance. (pp. 201-03)

In his novels, one of Williams's achievements is to restore the sense of the awesome, the other, the holy, in our religious life. (p. 204)

He was determined to remind us of the full implications of Christian creeds and worship. He would not allow them to be denatured and shrunken to a remote mythology and a distillation of ethics. Vast and terrible powers are seen operating in his stories—not somewhere else at some other time, but here and now. He brings all the drama of Heaven and Hell and the driving, operative energies of the universe into commonplace English country scenes or the streets of modern London. His pages present the full-dimensioned actuality of a Faith which, to many, remains only words, forms, or benevolent works. (p. 205)

One of Williams's favorite devices for the recapture of the immensity of the Christian vision of life and Creation is the use of apocalyptic events, by which he freshens our awareness that human life is lived at all times and in all places in a double dimension of the natural and the supernatural. He shows us that, in every act, we are in contact with more than the supernatural—the supra-natural—for it involves not only those aspects of nature that overreach human control or conception, but also Him Who is beyond nature because He created nature. (p. 206)

He sees the will of God and the will of Satan clashing in the world, but chiefly operating through the wills, decisions, actions and commitments of men. (p. 207)

A favorite theme with Williams, as it was with Dostoyevsky, who also sometimes used visionary images to express it, was that philosophies can get out of hand. (p. 208)

The lust for power is one of Williams's favorite themes. But since he is dealing in supernatural terms it is supernatural powers that are pursued rather than the ordinary economic, political, or emotional varieties. We see it as the impious attempt to usurp Heavenly powers, the primal sin of pride, the desire to be as God. This is the Faustian delusion: Seek ye first the kingdom of Hell and all the rest shall be added unto you. It involves sacrilege—the abuse of sacred things, the attempt to force the powers that derive from God into purposes that are not God's. (pp. 211-12)

The impious strivings for power are of several kinds, but in every case its disastrous element is that it willfully refuses to see or recognize the true nature of the forces mischievously invoked. There is in this something of the mythic or fairy-tale catastrophe of Pandora's box, the magical salt mill or porridge pot, and the water buckets of "The Sorcerer's Apprentice." (p. 212)

Williams is not sentimental about the powers of Creation, with that persistent and popular sentimentality which comes perilously close to being a heresy in Christianity. He is that subtle phenomenon, the Christian pessimist. His awareness of the dark possibilities of the immediate grows from knowledge of the nature of man and our fallen condition. Optimism, the counterbalance to despair, lies in the expectation of redemption, the making of all things new. Meanwhile, he knows that "The universe is always capable of a worse trick than we suppose." (p. 217)

Williams sees the dread forges of Creation much as Blake saw them in "The Tiger." There is a God of loving-kindness and mercy and bounteous redemption. But the objective powers of His universe are not supportable by human flesh, as witness the lethal radiations of outer space and the fearful tensions that bind the nuclei of atoms. God's forces exist—they *are*—and they will consume flesh that becomes caught in their fields, howsoever. (p. 218)

At the heart of the novels, increasing in clarification, intensifying in focus in the later ones, is a concept toward which all Williams's thought led him. This is his formulation of *substituted love,* which carries with it the related concepts of *coinherence* and *exchange.* I say his "formulation," for he did not invent the concepts. They are the facts of existence and are visible in the Creation, the Fall, the Incarnation, Crucifixion and Resurrection. It was Williams's gift to find dramatic images to heighten our awareness and strengthen our grasp of them. (p. 219)

At moments his dialogue is irritatingly brittle and mannered, almost a parody of Britishism. This is partly because, as in the detective story, the characterizations are flat. Yet it would be wrong to say simply that his characters are types, with the suggestion of cliché or superficiality. It is rather that he uses characters deliberately to typify the varied attitudes toward life demanded by his themes. His people have a life more of embodied idea than of flesh.

Although the plots are sensational and the pace swift, there is great intellectual demand upon the reader, increasing in the later novels. His narrative, as well as his dialogue, bristles with intellectual stimulation and is lit up by an epigrammatic sparkle. (pp. 230-31)

Even though several of the novels make no overt reference to Christ or the Church, his theological vision admits of no watering down into vague, comforting generalizations, soothing emotions, or canting spiritual inspirationalism. A crystal-hard mind is demonstrating the implications of a religion so demanding, as has been remarked of Christianity, that nobody would have made it up. He calls it "the intolerable gospel." (p. 232)

If you enter the world of Charles Williams and find yourself one of its citizens, you will retain that citizenship permanently, going often in and out of his borders, for it will take a long time to explore. You will find there a vast conception of both what you are, and where you are. (p. 234)

> *Edmund Fuller, "Many Dimensions: The Images of Charles Williams" (© 1949 Pellegrini & Cudahy), in his* Books with Men Behind Them *(copyright © 1959, 1961, 1962 by Edmund Fuller; reprinted by permission of McIntosh and Otis, Inc.),* Random House, *1962, pp. 197-234.*

[Williams'] material is always fantastic and esoteric, and it is always in some unorthodox way religious. The paradox of his fiction, and I believe the explanation of his hold upon his readers, is simply that for his fantasy he is not content with a willing suspension of disbelief. He demands the destruction of disbelief. (p. 113)

Each of Williams' novels is uncanny. In *The Greater Trumps* there is the same Tarot pack which fascinated Eliot when he wrote *The Waste Land,* the cards that reflect or direct the Great Dance of all that is. . . . The most impressive part is the evocation of the Dance that so fascinated the imagination of the Renaissance, as in the *Orchestra* of Sir John Davies. It is the mystery of order in chaos, the puzzle that so concerns our subtlest science today. . . . As we read, we feel that here is not a wildly inventive storyteller but a poet who sees into the heart of matter, side by side with the nuclear physicist. (pp. 113-14)

In general, the theme of Charles Williams is the Christian faith, seen from a rather special and individual point of view. . . . Williams confronts his readers with strange assertions and startling images. . . . (p. 119)

Here is an element of doctrine that Williams shared with [C. S.] Lewis: it is not the event provoking an emotion that is a spiritual danger, but the emotion itself. Williams maintains that emotions can not only be confided in others but exchanged with them.

This is co-inherence, Williams' most characteristic teaching. All men are brothers in more than a genetic or merely integrationist sense; he believes that when we are commanded to bear one another's burdens our Lord means us to support one another in the most intimate possible way. The type example, as the Lion is the type of all lions and of all strength, is the Substitution on the Cross. (p. 121)

It has been argued (with a "perhaps") that the passage of time is not an ultimate reality, that exchange between persons is possible, that materialism is not true. The "perhaps" is necessary: our scientific education presses upon us, as does the deceptive common sense of every day. We cannot "know" hell and heaven except by the testimony of our emotions. But that testimony can be denied or confirmed by the witness of other lives in literature; the expert authorities upon emotions are the poets.

So it is especially important to know whether such a witness as Charles Williams is truly a poet. It has been charged with sneers that he is not; in cross-examination it is charged that his credentials have been forged by fellow Christians and by personal friends. It is too bad if a man must be blamed for friendship, but indeed we who read him are few enough to be called a clique.

We cannot assert his authenticity by the evidence of his style. When he writes at his best, which is magnificently, it is in passages of such strange, uncanny action that when quoted in isolation they sound simply bad. More mundane pages are usually clear, but not always: astonishingly for a professional editor, Williams has some trouble with grammar. On the larger scale of structure he is better, although he learned slowly how to compose a novel. The later stories are admirably planned. The symmetry of paired characters in *The Greater Trumps* and *Descent into Hell* evinces a firm sense of design. Characterization is perhaps not important in stories of this particular type, but he has one rare excellence. It is recognized that good people are the most difficult to create in fiction and that Williams excels in presenting sanctity. But surely his greatest talent, and that upon which his authority as an honest witness must rest, is his ability to present to our imagination what is denied by our presuppositions, to make real what lies beyond reality. (pp. 123-24)

> *George P. Winship, Jr., "The Novels of Charles Williams," in* Shadows of Imagination: The Fantasies of C. S. Lewis, J.R.R. Tolkien, and Charles Williams, *edited by Mark R. Hillegas (copyright © 1969, Southern Illinois University Press; reprinted by permission of Southern Illinois University Press),* Southern Illinois University Press, *1969, pp. 111-24.*

[Williams'] human participants are usually of two kinds: those whose knowledge and endowments give them a special and understood objective, for good or evil, from the beginning; and those ordinary mortals who, at least early in their involvement, find themselves caught in an incomprehensible turmoil of events. Of the first kind, the figures are often mythical or legendary, or, if contemporary, have the qualities of such. . . . The second kind have no great names or accomplishments, but they are just as much agents of superhuman power. (pp. 143-44)

Just as characters in Williams' fiction are determined by allegiance, so is the progress of action. The basis is, of course, the warfare of good and evil, and the movement of warfare follows a standard pattern. Early in the action the aggressions or assertions of evil move rapidly, almost unchecked, whereas the proponents of good are slow and confused. Their own purposes are but gradually revealed to them; they lack the mobility, the devices, and the ruthlessness of their opponents. This is a classical relationship in romances. The rationale of evil, being self-aggrandizing or destructive or both, is easily formulated and put into execution; evil has many devices and enjoys early success, seemingly to the point of being invincible. Good lacks this advantage. Its proponents are required to discriminate between what actually is and what only appears to be of the enemy. Within themselves they have few of the resources, militant and diplomatic, which evil can command. Good must rely on itself, its own faith and durability. It must work within a restrictive frame of justice and mercy; it may not, like evil, injure wantonly and conquer simply in accordance with desire. Hence the forces of good often suffer early defeat and hold out in peril until fortunes begin to change. The change may have any of several causes or all. Sometimes evil weakens itself and deteriorates with prosperity. More important, the faith and fortitude of the good exert against trial an energy which is intrinsic though not at first called forth. And this strength, once mobilized, increases with onslaughts against it. This capability can scarcely be distinguished from such supernatural or divine assistance as cannot fail to triumph. (pp. 144-45)

[In] the romances of Williams there is no fundamental suspense. Rather there is what for many readers seems more gratifying—a temporary anxiety playing over a solid foundation of confidence. This anxiety may simulate genuine desperation when the forces of evil, in spectacular movement, seem invincible; conversely, when they are in rout, the punitive pleasures of confounding the enemy and the satisfaction in order re-established seem equal to those of a triumph which was really in doubt. Thus is generated an emotionalism which is like to be more facile *because* the possibility of irremediable disaster is never present. Some find in this a fraudulent appeal and exploitation, and liken the responses to those prompted by melodrama. . . . (p. 145)

Whatever the judgment on this objection, Williams makes his narratives exciting. Excitement resides in the external events, provided usually by disruptive and often exotic forces invading familiar places and commonplace lives; Williams seemingly cared little for exotic settings. Excitement also resides in the choices which his characters must make. They do not have psychic and emotional conflicts but rather debates with self over their allegiances. These spiritual crises so engage them that the deep feeling of meditation and inquiry are conveyed to the reader. With external and internal events, Williams regularly builds his romances to breathless, climactic scenes in which awesome powers vent themselves and stupendous, though familiar, truths are revealed in explosions of enlightenment. Excitement in these scenes often overpowers clarity, but an engaged reader will have little difficulty at the time in forfeiting the value which he places on intellectual tidiness. (pp. 145-46)

Much of the substance of Williams' fiction derives from his adoption of the material, both detailed and general, of inherited mythology. Most prevalent is the Christian, but echoes of Neoplatonic, gypsy, Islamic, Arthurian also abound; the last named is much more prominent in his poetry. . . . [He] made mythical material his own by subjecting its original disparities to his own syncretizing, by adapting it to contemporary persons and circumstances, and by fusing narrative which is mythical in origin with narrative of his own invention. (p. 148)

Into the associative framework of well-known myths Williams regularly fits pieces of recondite lore as well as incidents and symbols of his own making. Such is his skill in assembling and extending that he gains a double advantage: the unfamiliar material retains the charm of novelty while it is rendered intelligible and persuasive by its coalescence with the familiar.

For readers with a disposition to believe, the romances of Williams provide welcome assurances. Chief among these is a fortified confidence that right and order will prevail even against the gates of hell. Another is a vision of the ultimate unity of faiths and of stories which concern fundamental issues. Williams seems to have known that a desire to perceive unity, rather than fragmentation, is a strong motive in many minds and sensibilities, even in a time which has long been indoctrinated with the claims of analysis. (pp. 148-49)

W. R. Irwin, "Christian Doctrine and the Tactics of Romance: The Case of Charles Williams," in Shadows of Imagination: The Fantasies of C. S. Lewis, J.R.R. Tolkien, and Charles Williams, *edited by Mark R. Hillegas (copyright © 1969, Southern Illinois University Press; reprinted by permission of Southern Illinois University Press), Southern Illinois University Press, 1969, pp. 139-49.*

Williams' work seems full of false notes, unable to justify its pretensions, lacking in imaginative energy, dependent on theological notions rather than fictional insights. Why, then, do I take pleasure in it? What is the relation between my compulsive, embarrassed reading of these novels and the judgment which damns them? Are my enjoyment and my disapproval both valid responses? To what, exactly, do they respond?

On one level, the pleasure of reading a Williams novel is like that of indulging in high class detective fiction or ghost stories: pure escapism, made more appealing if it touches on important issues. But Williams demands to be taken more seriously than this. The ultimate source of his appeal, it seems to me, is the extraordinary ambition of the attempt he makes: not merely to write good fiction, not just to dramatize theological issues, but to create a new twentieth-century form, an equivalent for the great medieval allegories. The attempt fails, but it suggests important issues in the fiction of our time. (p. 150)

Many Christian intellectuals have been aware that the psychological and the theological might reveal equivalent truths; Williams' special contribution was to bring the supernatural into close relation with them. The supernatural, in his novels, is a bridge between psychology and theology. It provides objective correlatives for modes of feeling: a sense of the menace of the universe and the dangers of self-knowledge (the doppelgänger in *Descent into Hell*), malice and power-lust (the Snake and the Lion of *The Place of the Lion*), emotional conviction of the enduring force of art (the supernaturally long life of Nigel Considine in *Shadows of Ecstasy*). But the same images objectify theological truths. The doppelgänger means also the joy of accepted responsibility for one's freedom, the Lion and the Snake are emblems of divine energy, Considine's longevity signifies his sinful rejection of the human condition. Often—as in the examples given—the moral weight attached to the theological meaning contradicts that of the psychological meaning: Pauline's doppelgänger, a psychological evil, becomes a theological good. There are also simpler cases: Evelyn's rejection of others in *All Hallows' Eve* becomes rejection of God, Wentworth's psychological self-obsession in *Descent into Hell* turns diabolical. Such paradoxes of value help to establish the ambiguities of perception, the need to be capable of faith beyond perception.

Neither Tolkien nor Lewis is ambitious in this particular way. . . . Williams, in his effort to achieve significant fusion, invites comparison with the imaginative theological writers of the past: Milton, Dante. But any attempt at such comparison seems forced because Williams' work so conspicuously lacks grandeur and true cosmic scope. (pp. 151-52)

Williams reminds us of the cosmos within; he relies on

complexity instead of grandeur. The supernatural phenomena which abound in his novels hint the connections between the unfathomable depths of the personality and the mysteries of the larger universe, but there is no systematic cosmology. The City, emblem of man's community with God, recurs as a symbolic reference; its nature, however, is never specified.

To accept complexity as a substitute for cosmic range accords with the modern temper, yet Williams' novels have not generated wide enthusiasm: they remain the property of a cult. One reason may be that their complexity dissolves upon close examination because the fusion attempted seems finally inconceivable. The theological realizations of the novels subsume so much that they make psychological complexity (and consequently psychological realism) impossible. Theological insight is always in some sense complex; but in another, simple. Its special quality is finality: once achieved, it solves problems; no amount of verbal manipulation can convince one that the problems remain. Other problems emerge, but in a theological framework only salvation matters. (pp. 152-53)

Like the science fictionist and the classicist, [Williams] directs us toward important truths. His fiction seems more immediate than Johnson's, more broadly relevant than Isaac Asimov's, because psychological trimmings obscure its theoretical foundation. But since they are only trimmings they cannot fully engage us; they do not appear really to have engaged their creator. (pp. 153-54)

Williams' wise characters—Pauline's grandmother and Peter Stanhope in *Descent into Hell*, for example, or Sibyl in *The Greater Trumps*—all understand that the supernatural is only an aspect of the natural. It may violate normal expectation, but it would be dangerous to disbelieve for that reason, to make human comprehension the standard for judging omnipotence. Williams' attempt at literary fusion dramatizes his belief that the universe operates through equivalent fusions; human perception may be unable to grasp them, but faith maintains their reality. Modern skepticism, these novels hint, may reflect narrowmindedness rather than liberalism. (p. 155)

Williams' concern with man in his cosmic relations is central in his fiction; he faces the difficulty of turning abstract perceptions into recognizable experience. He takes none of the easy ways out; he does not retreat into the historic or mythic past, he does not create new worlds for his charac-

ters or in fact achieve true lyricism. Instead he tries to employ the conventions of the realistic novel, to convey the outlines of a social world inhabited by recognizable human beings and yet to serve more than realistic purposes. In his most compelling moments, he makes experience seem both plausible and reverberant with uncanny significance. . . . (pp. 157-58)

Charles Williams, reaching for more than [Graham Greene, Muriel Spark, and Iris Murdoch], achieves less. the attempt to fuse different levels of experience which dominates his novels is fundamentally allegorical, but he cannot commit himself to the limitations of allegory. His introduction of supernatural phenomena and events indicates also his impatience with realistic convention: he wishes to tell us that we must expand our conceptions of what realism is. Since what he wishes to say seems more important to him than how he says it, he sacrifices the imaginative life of his novels to purposes which are didactic rather than philosophic. The little sermons which keep intruding into his fiction suggest his greater concern with ends than with means; he is unable to confine himself to the structure of the realistic novel. (pp. 158-59)

[Uneasiness] remains after reading a Williams novel. The author cannot sustain the unification of experience and of sensibility that he attempts. At his best, near allegory, he attains great symbolic richness, but he cannot sustain that either; the temptation to didacticism overwhelms him. Williams' ideas are compelling and so is his fictional purpose, his attempt to unite what in experience seems disparate. In the early chapters of his novels, before one feels the full demands of realistic conventions, and at isolated moments later, he achieves his ambitious fusion. Finally, though, his aims exceed his literary ability. The fusion splits, one feels the novelist manipulating, hears the theologian exhorting, realizes how superior medieval methods are to this version of twentieth-century ones for conveying the subtleties of theology in imaginative form. (p. 159)

Patricia Meyer Spacks, "Charles Williams: The Fusions of Fiction," in Shadows of Imagination: The Fantasies of C. S. Lewis, J.R.R. Tolkien, and Charles Williams, *edited by Mark R. Hillegas (copyright © 1969, Southern Illinois University Press; reprinted by permission of Southern Illinois University Press), Southern Illinois University Press, 1969, pp. 150-59.*

(Adeline) Virginia Woolf

1882-1941

English novelist, critic, and essayist. Virginia Woolf was the daughter of Sir Leslie Stephen, the Victorian editor, scholar, and critic, and was related to some of the most prominent scholarly families in England, including the Darwins and the Stracheys. Woolf's fiction is usually compared with that of James Joyce, of whom she was an exact contemporary, and D. H. Lawrence. Her novels, according to William Rose Benét, "are noted for their poetic and symbolic quality . . . , their delicacy and sensitivity of style, their psychological penetration, their evocation of place and mood, and their background of historical and literary reference." During her lifetime, Woolf was perhaps best known as cohostess, with her sister Vanessa (wife of Clive Bell), of the Bloomsbury Group, which included Keynes, Forster, Spender, Strachey, and Fry; and as publisher, with her husband, Leonard Woolf, of early work by Forster, Eliot, Katherine Mansfield, and Freud, at their Hogarth Press. Virginia Woolf took her own life in 1941.

PRINCIPAL WORKS

The Voyage Out (novel) 1915
Kew Gardens (short stories) 1919
The Mark on the Wall (short stories) 1919
Night and Day (novel) 1919
Monday or Tuesday (short stories) 1921
Jacob's Room (novel) 1922
Mr. Bennett and Mrs. Brown (criticism) 1924
The Common Reader (criticism) 1925
Mrs. Dalloway (novel) 1925
To The Lighthouse (novel) 1927
Orlando: A Biography (novel) 1928
A Room of One's Own (essays) 1929
The Waves (novel) 1931
The Common Reader: Second Series (criticism) 1932
Flush: A Biography (biography) 1933
The Years (novel) 1937
Three Guineas (essays) 1938
Roger Fry: A Biography (biography) 1940
Between the Acts (novel) 1941
The Death of the Moth, and Other Essays (essays) 1942
The Haunted House, and Other Short Stories (short stories) 1943
The Moment, and Other Essays (essays) 1947
The Captain's Death Bed, and Other Essays (essays) 1950

A Writer's Diary (journal) 1953
Hours in a Library (essay) 1957
Granite and Rainbow: Essays (essays) 1958

Virginia Woolf seems to me the most interesting of the younger writers now living as well as the best of them, but her work is so individual that another writer can learn little from it, and I very much doubt if she will have a direct influence on her contemporaries. . . . [Her] art is perfect, but the gifts are personal and defy imitation. Mrs Woolf's writing is characterized by remarkable beauty of phrasing, and the merit of her work lies in the fact that the beauty of each line runs into the next one and forms part of the whole work. (p. 83)

To do this Mrs Woolf employs a particular method which she has employed before, but never so completely to the exclusion of other methods. . . . Here we learn everything as a fragment of memory passing through Virginia Woolf's mind. One thing calls up another, and we skip on to something very different, yet queerly linked with what went before. The story is tangled and inconsequent as are our digressions into the past. . . .

Things so recalled have a peculiar beauty, an added value, yes, and an odd reality, which the things we are passing have not got as we flash by in the 16-40 automobile of life. Every moment in life we are carried beyond the possibility of turning our heads to take a second look, and we are haunted by whatever it is—an old woman stooping to gather a dry stick, a child by the red currant bushes, the sun sweeping down between the clouds so that the valley is barred and chequered with light, like waking, years ago in the night nursery with the sun pouring in through the Venetian blinds. . . .

Our own memories are pale trodden-away things like the pattern of the linoleum in the parlour, her words fresh like childhood, or first love, and real—as poetry is. And we actually have to remind ourselves that Mrs Woolf is not drawing upon her memories, but her imagination, and that somehow she gilds everything she writes with the beauty of something remembered.

If she were not so individual she would almost certainly be a sentimentalist, as it is no doubt there are some people who would accuse her of being one. (pp. 84-5)

David Garnett, in The Dial *(copyright, 1923, by The Dial Publishing Company, Inc.; reprinted by permission of J. S. Watson, Jr. and Scofield Thayer), July, 1923 (and reprinted by Kraus Reprint Corporation, 1966).*

[Virginia Woolf] has, among other achievements, made a definite contribution to the novelist's art. But how is this contribution to be stated? And how does she handle the ingredients of fiction—human beings, time, and space? Let us glance at her novels in the order of their composition.

[*The Voyage Out*] is a strange, tragic, inspired book whose scene is a South America not found on any map and reached by a boat which would not float on any sea, an America whose spiritual boundaries touch Xanadu and Atlantis.... It is a noble book, so noble that a word of warning must be added: like all Virginia Woolf's work, it is not romantic, not mystic, not explanatory of the universe. (pp. 106-08)

[*Night and Day*] is the simplest novel she has written, and to my mind the least successful. Very long, very careful, it condescends to many of the devices she so gaily derides in her essay on *Mr. Bennett and Mrs. Brown*.... In view of what preceded it and of what is to follow, *Night and Day* seems to me a deliberate exercise in classicism. It contains all that has characterized English fiction for good or evil during the last hundred and fifty years—faith in personal relations, recourse to humorous side shows, insistence on petty social differences. Even the style has been normalized, and though the machinery is modern, the resultant form is as traditional as *Emma*. Surely the writer is using tools that don't belong to her. At all events she has never touched them again.

For, contemporary with this full length book, she made a very different experiment, published two little—stories, sketches, what is one to call them?—which show the direction in which her genius has since moved. At last her sensitiveness finds full play, and she is able to describe what she sees in her own words. In *The Mark on the Wall* she sees a mark on the wall, wonders what it is . . . and that is the entire story.... [She] reports her vision impartially; she strays forward, murmuring, wandering, falling asleep. Her style trails after her, catching up grass and dust in its folds, and instead of the precision of the earlier writing we have something more elusive than has yet been achieved in English. (pp. 108-09)

The objection (or apparent objection) to this sort of writing is that it cannot say much or be sure of saying anything. It is an inspired breathlessness, a beautiful droning or gasping which trusts to luck, and can never express human relationships or the structure of society. So at least one would suppose, and that is why the novel of *Jacob's Room* . . . comes as a tremendous surprise. The impossible has occurred.... The coherence of the book is even more amazing than its beauty. In the stream of glittering similes, unfinished sentences, hectic catalogues, unanchored proper names, we seem to be going nowhere. Yet the goal comes, the method and the matter prove to have been one, and looking back from the pathos of the closing scene we see for a moment the airy drifting atoms piled into a colonnade. The break with *Night and Day* and even with *The Voyage Out* is complete. A new type of fiction has swum into view, and it

is none the less new because it has had a few predecessors —laborious, well-meaning, still-born books by up-to-date authors, which worked the gasp and the drone for all they were worth, and are unreadable.

Three years after *Jacob's Room* comes another novel in the same style, or slight modification of the style: *Mrs. Dalloway*. It is perhaps her masterpiece, but difficult. . . . (pp. 109-10)

It is easy for a novelist to describe what a character thinks of. . . . But to convey the actual process of thinking is a creative feat, and I know of no one except Virginia Woolf who has accomplished it. Here at last thought, and the learning that is the result of thought, take their own high place upon the dais. . . . (p. 113)

But what of the subject that she regards as of the highest importance: human beings as a whole and as wholes? She tells us (in her essays) that human beings are the permanent material of fiction, that it is only the method of presenting them which changes and ought to change, that to capture their inner life presents a different problem to each generation of novelists; the great Victorians solved it in their way; the Edwardians shelved it by looking outwards at relatives and houses; the Georgians must solve it anew, and if they succeed a new age of fiction will begin. Has she herself succeeded? Do her own characters live?

I feel that they do live, but not continuously, whereas the characters of Tolstoy (let us say) live continuously. . . . And the problem before her—the problem that she has set herself, and that certainly would inaugurate a new literature if solved—is to retain her own wonderful new method and form, and yet allow her readers to inhabit each character with Victorian thoroughness. . . . There was continuous life in the little hotel people of *The Voyage Out* because there was no innovation in the method. But Jacob in *Jacob's Room* is discontinuous, demanding—and obtaining—separate approval for everything he feels or does. And *Mrs. Dalloway*? There seems a slight change here, an approach towards character-construction in the Tolstoyan sense; Sir William Bradshaw, for instance, is uninterruptedly and embracingly evil. Any approach is significant, for it suggests that in future books she may solve the problem as a whole. She herself believes it can be done, and, with the exception of Joyce, she is the only writer of genius who is trying. All the other so-called innovators are (if not pretentious bunglers), merely innovators in subject matter and the praise we give them is of the kind we should accord to scientists. . . . But they do not advance the novelist's art. Virginia Woolf has already done that a little, and if she succeeds in her problem of rendering character, she will advance it enormously. (pp. 113-14)

E. M. Forster, "The Early Novels of Virginia Woolf," (1925) in his Abinger Harvest *(© 1936, 1964, by E. M. Forster; reprinted by permission of Harcourt Brace Jovanovich, Inc.),* Harcourt, *1936, pp. 106-15.*

The historian writing fifty years hence of the literature of to-day will find in it a certain note of inhumanity. He will speak of our hostility to mankind, and he will remark how different Mr. James Joyce's attitude to his characters is from that of Scott, for example, or Jane Austen. A thorough dislike of their creations characterizes, indeed, the majority of modern novelists. Mr. Joyce hates and scorns his characters; Mr. Huxley's inspire him with disgust or with ill-natured laughter; Mr. Lawrence hews his down right and left in the name of his "dark god"; Mr. Stephen Hudson submits his, most severe test of all, to a scrupulous intellectual scrutiny. . . . The contemporary novelist does not walk through his crowds, on easy terms with them, good and bad, as Fielding and Thackeray walked through theirs. He is not among the works of his hands, but detached from them; he watches their movements as a scientist might watch the progress of an experiment. . . . They do not meet their characters on the same level as we should, if we were given the chance.

It may be said of Mrs. Woolf that she does meet her characters on this level. She accepts them as ends; she accepts them, that is to say, as people of the same status and existing in the same dimension as herself. She might walk into her novels and be at home in them. She stands in the same relation to her characters as almost all the chief English novelists have stood to theirs. Her attitude, like theirs, is eminently practical, tolerant, appreciative, intelligent; it has the good sense and sagacity of the English prose tradition.

The point is important, for an easy coming and going between the mind of the novelist and the world he creates has characterized the bulk of great fiction. It characterizes all the Russian fiction we know; it characterizes French fiction to the time of Flaubert; it has characterized English fiction up to Mr. Joyce and Mr. Lawrence. The advantage it gives to the novelist is clear. It endows his imaginary world with an everyday actuality, a toughness which will stand wear and tear. . . . For this practical, everyday, distinctively prose way of approaching the theme perhaps the best term is intelligence. It is not a purely intellectual quality; it consists rather in the use of the intellect and the imagination in a comprehensive but commonsense way, as if, exercised on imaginary situations, they were being exercised on the actual problems of life.

The quality of intelligence Mrs. Woolf has in a high degree. . . . All the notable English novelists of the past have possessed it; the only contemporary novelist, besides Mrs. Woolf, who has it in a striking degree is Mr. E. M. Forster. Mr. Joyce lacks it completely. . . . Mrs. Woolf's novels are an approximate image of the truth. The world she shows us is not of such vast dimensions as Mr. Joyce's, but it is on a perfect scale: there are all the elements in it that there are in any of the worlds we actually live in, and there is, moreover, a perpetual reference to the world itself, the modern world which looms behind and makes possible our smaller, personal worlds. (pp. 67-71)

Nothing was more striking in [*The Voyage Out* and *Night and Day*] than the undeviating sobriety of treatment, the absence of facility, the resolve to take all the factors into account and to be just to them all. The convention of the novel is accepted. The author, we feel, has resolved to take the novel as it is, and to make it do all that up to now it has done. In *The Voyage Out* she uses among other methods that of Chekhov. That book is still a little tentative, but *Night and Day*, which followed it, remains in some ways the finest of Mrs. Woolf's novels. In depth, in meaning behind meaning, some of the scenes in it are superior to anything else written in our time. . . . There are dull passages in [*Night and Day*]; the various threads of the story are not gathered up, do not become dramatic, until we are a

quarter of the way through, but once gathered up, they are never released until the end; the growth and development of the complex of situations is steady. One character after another is caught into the action; and it leaves none of them what they were before. The easy course, the short cut, is never taken; everything is worked out anew. For comprehensiveness of understanding the author has never surpassed *Night and Day*. Yet we feel, regarding Mrs. Woolf's later works, that there is something lacking in it: the satisfaction of the artist working within conditions shaped for herself. The given conditions, it is true, are scrupulously observed; but we feel them as a compulsion on the writer; they are too impersonal; they have not been resolved into a completely individual means of expression. *Night and Day* is a book which a writer might execute, submitting to the form rather than finding complete expression through it.

In the small volume of short stories, *Monday or Tuesday,* the experimentation with form began which later gave us *Jacob's Room* and *Mrs. Dalloway*. It is tentative, but lighter, more buoyant, than anything Mrs. Woolf had written before. *Jacob's Room* was a great advance; its plan was admirable; the recreation of a figure through memories and associations was a suggestive and perfectly valid device. The book contains several beautiful scenes, but it is not sure, like Mrs. Woolf's earlier and like her later work; it has a good deal of the sentimentality which so often comes out of the mind along with a first attempt to express something in it which has not been expressed before. When the artist tries to liberate his essential emotion towards experience, at first he is likely to liberate a great deal more along with it, until in this new kind of expression he learns to distinguish what is essential from what appears so. *Jacob's Room* has a more living quality than Mrs. Woolf's earlier work, but it is less critical. *Mrs. Dalloway* is the most characteristic work Mrs. Woolf has written. It is so unlike *Night and Day* that they can hardly be compared. It has not the earlier book's finely dramatic development or its intensity; but it is more organic and in a more living sense, it is infinitely more subtle in its means, and it has on all its pages, as *Night and Day* had not, the glow of an indisputable artistic triumph. As a piece of expressive writing there is nothing in contemporary English fiction to rival it. Shades of an evanescence which one might have thought uncapturable, visual effects so fine that the eye does not take them in, that only in the memory are guessed at from the vibration they leave in passing, exquisitely graded qualities of sound, of emotion, of reverie, are in Mrs. Woolf's prose not merely dissected, but imaginatively reconstructed. All that in the earlier novels was analysed is resolved in *Mrs. Dalloway* into evocative images. There is nothing left of the stubborn explanatory machinery of the analytical novel. The material upon which the author works is the same as before, but it has all been sublimated, and, although the psychology is subtle and exact, no trace remains of the psychologist. (pp. 72-6)

In a novel like *Mrs. Dalloway,* where the sensory impressions are so concretely evoked and are so much more immediate than they were before, a sort of rearrangement of the elements of experience insensibly takes place. In the traditional novel we have on the one hand the characters and on the other the background, each existing in a separate dimension, and the one generally more solid than the other. Sometimes the environment reacts strikingly on the characters, as for instance in *Wuthering Heights* and in Mr. Hardy's Wessex novels, but the reaction is not complex and continuous. It is indicated rather than treated, and the character and the background retain their peculiar values. But in *Mrs. Dalloway* they are more intimately connected; the one merges into the other; the character is suffused by the emanations of the things he sees, hears, feels; and almost inevitably what is presented is a complex of life, of which character and background are elements, both animate, rather than the living character stalking among inanimate things. The characters in *Mrs. Dalloway* are real; they have their drama; but the day and the properties of the day move with them, have their drama too; and we do not know which is the more real where all is real—whether the characters are bathed in the emanations of the day, or the day coloured by the minds of the characters. The result is less akin to anything else attempted in the novel than to certain kinds of poetry, to poetry such as Wordsworth's which records not so much a general judgment on life as a moment of serene illumination, a state of soul. . . . Mrs. Woolf is not concerned in *Mrs. Dalloway* with the character, which is shown in action, in crises (and novels are consequently full of crises), but with the state of being. To give it its value she catches it at a particularly fortunate moment, at a moment of realization; but the means are justified and are, indeed, the normal means of art. To reveal character the novelist concentrates on crises, comic or tragic, leaving untouched the vast, inert mass of experience: in concentrating on the daily existence when it is most significant Mrs. Woolf is in a different way obeying the same principle, the principle, indeed, of all imaginative art.

The Common Reader, in which Mrs. Woolf's mind deals with figures familiar to us all, shows it perhaps at its best. Her themes range from Chaucer to Conrad, from George Eliot to the Duchess of Newcastle, and in them all she shows the intelligence and practicality of temper of the critic. She has the informed enthusiasm which criticism should never lack but which is tending to disappear from it; her judgments have admirable breadth. The one important quality of the critic which she lacks is the power of wide and illuminating generalization. She holds the scales even, as she does between her characters in *Night and Day;* she uses her sensibility as she uses it in *Jacob's Room* and *Mrs. Dalloway.* It is the same mind, and we never doubt its competence to deal with anything which it fixes upon. (pp. 79-82)

> *Edwin Muir, "Virginia Woolf," in his* Transition: Essays on Contemporary Literature *(copyright © 1926 by The Viking Press, and renewed 1954 by Edwin Muir; reprinted by permission of The Viking Press, Inc.), Viking, 1926, pp. 67-82.*

Among contemporary writers of fiction, Mrs. Woolf is a curious and anomalous figure. In some respects, she is as "modern," as radical, as Mr. Joyce or Miss Richardson or M. Jules Romains; she is a highly self-conscious examiner of consciousness, a bold and original experimenter with the technique of novel-writing; but she is also, and just as strikingly, in other respects "old-fashioned." This anomaly does not defy analysis. The aroma of "old-fashionedness" that rises from these highly original and modern novels— from the pages of *Jacob's Room, Mrs. Dalloway,* and . . . from those of *To the Lighthouse*—is a quality of attitude; a

quality, to use a word which is itself nowadays old-fashioned, but none the less fragrant, of spirit. For in this regard, Mrs. Woolf is no more modern than Jane Austen: she breathes the same air of gentility, of sequestration, of tradition; of life and people and things all brought, by the slow polish of centuries of tradition and use, to a pervasive refinement in which discrimination, on every conceivable plane, has become as instinctive and easy as the beat of a wing. Her people are "gentle" people; her houses are the houses of gentlefolk; and the consciousness that informs both is a consciousness of well-being and culture, of the richness and luster and dignity of tradition. (p. 389)

But if, choosing such people and such a *mise en scène* for her material, Mrs. Woolf inevitably makes her readers think of *Pride and Prejudice* and *Mansfield Park,* she compels us just as sharply, by her method of evoking them, to think of *Pilgrimage* and *Ulysses* and *The Death of a Nobody.* Mrs. Woolf is an excellent critic, an extremely conscious and brilliant craftsman in prose; she is intensely interested in the technique of fiction; and one has at times wondered, so vividly from her prose has arisen a kind of *self-consciousness* of adroitness, whether she might not lose her way and give us a mere series of virtuosities or *tours de force.* (p. 390)

[In *To the Lighthouse*] one's irritation is soon lost in the growing sense that Mrs. Woolf has at last found a complexity and force of theme which is commensurate with the elaborateness and self-consciousness of her technical "pattern." By degrees, one forgets the manner in the matter. One resists the manner, petulantly objects to it, in vain: the moment comes when at last one ceases to be aware of something persistently artificial in this highly feminine style, and finds oneself simply immersed in the vividness and actuality of this world of Mrs. Woolf's—believing in it, in fact, with the utmost intensity, and feeling it with that completeness of surrender with which one feels the most moving of poetry. It is not easy to say whether this abdication of "distance" on the reader's part indicates that Mrs. Woolf has now achieved a depth of poetic understanding, a vitality, which was somehow just lacking in the earlier novels, or whether it merely indicates a final triumph of technique. . . . Certainly one feels everywhere in Mrs. Woolf's work this will to imagine, this canvassing of possibilities by a restless and searching and brilliant mind: one feels this mind at work, matching and selecting, rejecting this color and accepting that, saying, "It is this that the heroine would say, it is this that she would think"; and nevertheless Mrs. Woolf's step is so sure, her choice is so nearly invariably right, and her imagination, even if deliberately willed, is so imaginative, that in the end she makes a beautiful success of it. She makes her Mrs. Ramsay—by giving us her stream of consciousness—amazingly alive; and she supplements this just sufficiently, from *outside,* as it were, by giving us also, intermittently, the streams of consciousness of her husband, of her friend Lily Briscoe, of her children: so that we are documented, as to Mrs. Ramsey, from every quarter and arrive at a solid vision of her by a process of triangulation. The richness and copiousness and ease, with which this is done, are a delight. These people are astoundingly real: they belong to a special "class," as Mrs. Woolf's characters nearly always do, and exhale a Jane-Austenish aroma of smallness and lostness and incompleteness: but they are magnificently real. We live in that delicious house with them—we feel the minute textures of their lives with their own vivid senses—we imagine with their extraordinary imaginations, are self-conscious with their self-consciousness—and ultimately we know them as well, as terribly, as we know ourselves. (pp. 391-92)

The technical brilliance glows, melts, falls away; and there remains a poetic apprehension of life of extraordinary loveliness. Nothing happens, in this houseful of odd nice people, and yet all of life happens. The tragic futility, the absurdity, the pathetic beauty, of life—we experience all of this in our sharing of seven hours of Mrs. Ramsay's wasted or not wasted existence. We have seen, through her, the world. . . .

That Mrs. Woolf is a highly ingenious writer has been made glitteringly obvious for us in *Mrs. Dalloway* and *To the Lighthouse:* which is not in the least to minimize the fact that those two novels also contained a great deal of beauty. That she is, and has perhaps always been, in danger of carrying ingenuity too far, is suggested, among other things, by her new novel, or "biography," *Orlando.* Whatever else one thinks about this book, one is bound to admit that it is exceedingly, not to say disconcertingly, clever. In England as well as in America it has set the critics by the ears. They have not known quite how to take it—whether to regard it as a biography, or a satire on biography; as a history, or as a satire on history; as a novel, or as an allegory. And it is at once clear, when one reads *Orlando,* why this confusion should have arisen; for the tone of the book, from the very first pages, is a tone of mockery. (p. 392)

Mrs. Woolf apparently wants us to know that she does not herself take the thing with the least seriousness—that she is pulling legs, keeping her tongue in her cheek, and winking, now and then, a quite shameless and enormous wink. With all this, which she accomplishes with a skill positively equestrian, she is obliged, perforce, to fall into a style which one cannot help feeling is a little unfortunate. It is a style which makes fun of style: it is glibly rhetorical, glibly sententious, glibly poetic, glibly analytical, glibly austere, by turns—deliberately so; and, while this might be, and is, extraordinarily diverting for a chapter or two, or for something like the length of a short story, one finds it a little fatiguing in a full-length book. Of course, Mrs. Woolf's theme, with its smug annihilation of time, may be said to have demanded, if the whole question of credibility was to be begged, a tone quite frankly and elaborately artificial. Just the same, it is perhaps questionable whether she has not been *too* icily and wreathedly elaborate in this, and taken her *Orlando* in consequence a shade too far toward an arid and ingenuous convention. Granted that what she wanted to tell us was a fable, or allegory: that she wanted to trace the aesthetic evolution of a family (and by implication that of a country) over a period of three hundred years: and that she had hit upon the really first-rate idea of embodying this racial evolution in one undying person: need she quite so much have presumed on our incredulity? One suspects that in such a situation an ounce of ingenuousness might be worth ten times its weight in ingenuity; and that a little more of the direct and deep sincerity of the last few pages, which are really beautiful and really moving, might have made *Orlando* a minor masterpiece. (p. 393)

Conrad Aiken, "Woolf, Virginia" and "Woolf, Virginia" (originally published under different titles in Dial, *July, 1927 and February, 1929), in his* Collected Criticism *(copyright © 1935, 1939, 1940, 1942, 1951, 1958 by Conrad Aiken; reprinted by permission of Brandt & Brandt), Oxford University Press, 1968, pp. 389-94.*

[In] *A Room of One's Own* [Virginia Woolf] has, with extreme courage, defied a prevalent fashion among the intelligentsia, which is particularly marked in the case of her admirers. This book (it is really a long essay) is an uncompromising piece of feminist propaganda: I think the ablest yet written. Its main purpose is to defend women from the accusation of inferiority that is laid against them on the ground that they have failed to be geniuses. She proves her case in passages that in their perfect, rounded form, and in the warm yet restrained colour of their imagery, remind one of the great tawny chrysanthemums seen these days in the florists' windows. But make no mistake, she proves her case. (pp. 210-11)

It is all the more courageous because anti-feminism is so strikingly the correct fashion of the day among the intellectuals. (p. 212)

Now these intellectuals had always made an exception of Virginia Woolf, perhaps because she so obviously is the talent of this generation which is most certain of survival. She had therefore much to lose and nothing to gain by offending their prejudices. These considerations did not make her hold her peace, or blur a single argument. Her honesty is thus shown as remarkable as her sensibility; and that is not the only reason for respecting the author which emerges from this volume. Though she gives herself without stint to the material task of controversy, her temper remains serene. It is as if, advanced beyond the rest of us, she enjoys an extension of our human privilege of seeing a recovery to autumn, and knows that error, like winter, has an end. (p. 213)

Rebecca West, "Autumn and Virginia Woolf," in her Ending in Earnest: A Literary Log *(copyright 1931, © 1957 by Rebecca West; reprinted by permission of The Viking Press),* Doubleday, Doran, 1931, pp. 208-13.

Monotony can never be urged as a vice in Virginia Woolf. She has been able to carry a very sensitive mind into the dangerous purlieus of journalism, and is known even more widely as a publicist than as a novelist. She has brilliantly told us that the woman artist tends to suffer from her militancy. Wisely then she reserves her polemics for her articles, and so tempers anger with wit that she is able to make her most damaging points without the petulance that controversy so frequently engenders. The case for woman as creative artist has never been more effectively presented than in *A Room of One's Own* where she makes us partners in her thought process, and leads us on consentingly from step to step of her argument. We should concede to the woman as to the male novelist the privilege of communicating the imperfections of either sex. A savage emphasis in any direction we resent. Mrs. Woolf's singular fairness and impartiality are never in question, and the only hint of hostile bias is her portrait of Mr. Ramsay in *To the Lighthouse,* and in *Mrs. Dalloway* the portrait of Sir William Bradshaw. (pp. 328-29)

Mrs. Woolf in *The Common Reader, The Hogarth Essays,*

and in a series of articles, "Phases of Fiction," contributed to *The Bookman,* has made her views on fiction emphatically clear. She is dissatisfied with the work of the Edwardians, as she calls them, whose acclaimed leaders are Galsworthy, Wells, and Bennett.... Mrs. Woolf's contention is that the Edwardians think of character as something to be weighed and measured. They are complete materialists, and interpret human nature in terms of physical relations and external detail. Their books are imposing rubbish piles where poetry, subtlety, spirituality not only are indiscoverable but find no lodgment.... Mrs. Woolf's plea then is for poetry, and her regard for the writers of the past is proportioned to their poetic vision. Jane Austen alone she values on other grounds as a woman of genius who writes in a womanly way. (pp. 329-30)

Mrs. Woolf began her career with two novels in the traditional form. *The Voyage Out* is especially masterly, and the reader is not conscious that convention has hampered in any way the free expression of her mind.... With character-drawing and poetry in such effective combination we might think that a compromise had been reached which would realize Mrs. Woolf's idea for fiction. But she was evidently not content. She wrote another conventional book, *Night and Day,* and then in some of the short stories of *Monday and Tuesday* initiated her campaign of adventurous experiment. In her last book *The Waves* poetry has triumphed to the complete discomfiture of character. There are people with human names, tapestry figures that move only when some gust eddies along the wall, but no action unites them, and they bear a confused symbolic relation not with one another but with Life, Time, and Eternity.

The intervening books are more recognizably fiction,—a word whose definition we are willing to strain to the utmost limit provided that we retain even a shadowy action that binds a human group in a relation however shadowy. *Orlando* is fantastic biography, fiction if you will because invented, and entirely fascinating in idea and presentation. *Jacob's Room,* the first of her deviations failed to prove that her abandonment of tradition was justified. That she was more interested in writing this than *The Voyage Out* indicates that matter was in her mind that demanded its own peculiar medium of expression. (pp. 331-32)

Wordsworth's assertion is not to be disputed that every original author must create the taste by which he is appreciated. He was compelled to wait a few generations for full recognition, and Wordsworth is a major writer who cannot be considered very revolutionary in his assault upon tradition. Mrs. Woolf is definitely not a major, and her deviation from convention is much more drastic. Whatever posterity may do for her, the present penalty she pays for her courage and sincerity is a much more limited audience than her talent deserves. Her doom is the coterie, her reward a satisfied conscience. It would be folly to blame her open-eyed choice. In a large way the novel profits by intelligent experiment, and speaking in terms of her own activity it is probable that by her innovations she reached results that could not have been otherwise achieved.

Her main quest is for poetry and subtlety, and for a presentation of incident in closer consonance with reality than the exigencies of artificial plot-making permit....

Her gift of figurative speech would have suffered no impediment with the acceptance of the accustomed habit of fiction. But if we read her mind aright there were certain subtleties of poetry that could not so accommodate themselves. Poetry and prose considered from the aspect where they most diverge, and are therefore most characteristic, proceed from essentially different types of thinking. Prose thought is purposive, poetic thought is associational. There is much of the developed child in the poet. The darting inconsequence of the child's mind is a delight to its elders, though its operations need not have the profound significance that Wordsworth ascribed to them.... If we seek the real reason for Mrs. Woolf's rejection of consecutive fiction it was that she desired to record, as a poet might, the movement of the mind in revery. And the poetic results in her two best books are incontestable.

It would not be fair to her to suggest an uncontrolled disorder in their structure. *Mrs. Dalloway* and *To the Lighthouse,* despite their apparent dislocation are firmly fashioned. *Mrs. Dalloway* has the twofold unity of one day in London with Big Ben to chime off the hours. Comparison with Joyce's Dublin day is inevitable, but that has larger implications and deserves more nearly to be considered a day in the life of the race. In each book an effort is made to express simultaneity.... Older novelists used a slower clock, and there is something pauseful in the way they turn the wheels of time or stay their deliberate revolution to deal with events happening simultaneously. An electrical notation now copes with time's swift spinning. Transitions are sudden, and the return to progressive narrative is unprepared and sometimes non-existent.

But with all the stream-of-consciousness writers simultaneous time is less important than past time. They prefer to forget the temporal prison that confines us, and to assert the mind's contempt of the tenses. Past, present, and future are poetry's natural home. The less visionary poetic novelist does not by inclination inhabit the future, but memory is perpetually at her task of evocation. Remove the past from *Mrs. Dalloway* and the book would dwindle. Vagrant memories voyage backwards at the slightest hint, and though inconsecutiveness has been imputed to her as a fault she really errs in the direction of a too close articulation of experience past.... *To the Lighthouse* is a more satisfying book, for the past is in the story. We actually experience it, and then as the years pass we have the excitement and the pity of recapturing it. With what eerie tenderness do we not accompany the callous charwomen through the deserted rooms where once we lived! ... The book is a little masterpiece, for seldom have so much poetry, speculation, and character been compressed within so little space. (pp. 334-37)

Pelham Edgar, in his The Art of the Novel from 1700 to the Present Time, *The Macmillan Company, 1933 (and reprinted by Russell & Russell, 1966).*

Fundamentally dull people will not like Virginia Woolf, says Clive Bell, who admits that he likes her very much. Nor will people whose minds are neat and orderly and practical. Nor very emotional people who seek in fiction chiefly emotional release through identification. But many others, who find an initial difficulty, can overcome it simply by paying a little attention to their own undirected reveries— by exploring the stream of their own consciousness, and becoming aware of its movement.... It is our reveries, which psychologists have called the fundamental index of character, that fascinate [Mrs. Woolf] and that she chooses to record. (p. 221)

[We] have seen Mrs. Woolf as critic insisting upon success in characterization as the prime essential of the novelist's art. We have seen that she is dissatisfied with certain well-worn tools of the craft and disposed to experiment, and we have noted her peculiar aptitude in handling reverie. . . . Of her novels, *Mrs. Dalloway* has seemed to critics the outcome of deliberate experiment with a new method. (p. 226)

[*Mrs. Dalloway*] is a composition of reverie and dialogue, with brief snapshots of the outer aspect of people and things. We have the stream of consciousness and the stream of events. There are long reveries of Clarissa and of Peter, shifting as they notice things about them, or as a chance stimulus brings up a memory, or as they make some contact with people. When the characters are in groups, there is a symphony of reverie and dialogue—what they say aloud and what is drifting through their minds at the same moment. Sometimes Mrs. Woolf draws completely away from her characters, as in the passage inspired by the grey nurse who sits knitting beside the dozing Peter in Regent Park. While Peter sleeps, why shouldn't his creator play with her own mind?

What is the result? Has the character of Mrs. Dalloway been successfully projected? At the end Peter feels a curious stir at the sight of Clarissa coming towards him: "What is it that fills me with extraordinary excitement? It is Clarissa, he said. For there she was." Clarissa *is* emphatically. But there is nothing about which readers differ more than the so-called reality of characters, and perhaps for some readers she *isn't*. (p. 229)

The impression Mrs. Woolf gives of the trivial, tragic, confused, lovely, queer mix-up we call life is in one way disappointing, because it leaves us more at a loss than ever for a principle of order. And one of the satisfactions of art is that it simplifies confusion by selecting only certain forms and colors for its design. If by wearing blinkers and seeing only a few aspects of things, we have been able to persuade ourselves that we perceive an order and a meaning, Mrs. Woolf comes along and makes us face the infinite complications of the material. She exposes her reader to "constellations of stimuli," which form patterns of many motifs, the shape and color of each depending largely upon its relationship to each part of the whole design. The result—sometimes, at any rate—is that we become excited at the thought of living in so bewildering a world; and this too is pleasurable, though not quite so soothing as the illusion of simplicity and order. (pp. 230-31)

Realizing the nature of Mrs. Woolf's aim, we begin to understand certain effects of her books upon us. We feel ourselves becoming detached and contemplative, rather than involved and emotional. Her own detachment impresses all her critics, who account for it in various ways. . . . According to Clive Bell, she looks at her people through a cool sheet of glass; if she is watching a pair of lovers, she knows and puts down what they are feeling and saying. She herself feels the romance of the situation, but does not share the emotions of the actors. She is detached, and we too are detached. She can give the vision of someone feeling intensely; perhaps she shared the emotion when her imagination first projected the person and situation. But she has withdrawn from it and held it off for contemplation. (p. 244)

This effect of looking through glass at a picture may be one result of a constant quality of Mrs. Woolf's style—the concreteness of its visual imagery. . . .

[The] ease with which Mrs. Woolf slips in and out of people's minds keeps us from ever taking up a position permanently in any one character's mind. . . . There is a constant shift of focus—from one person to another, and from individuals to life in general. (p. 245)

It is because they bring these alterations in the movement of the mind that her books both keep one excited at the thought of living, and at the same time detached from living any special form of life that, if it comes to disaster, darkens the world. . . . It is . . . life in general with which Mrs. Woolf seeks a mode of communication. And this effort gives to her fiction the quality she finds very rare in English fiction—more often present in French fiction—intelligence. By intelligence she means neither brilliance nor intellectual power, but "the sense that the interest of life does not lie in what people do, nor even in their relations to each other, but largely in the power to communicate with a third party, antagonistic, enigmatic, yet perhaps persuadable, which one may call life in general." (p. 246)

Dorothy Brewster, "Virginia Woolf," in Modern Fiction, *by Dorothy Brewster and Angus Burrell (copyright 1934 by Columbia University Press; reprinted by permission of the publisher), Columbia University Press, 1934, pp. 218-47.*

[Both] *The Voyage Out* and *Night and Day* . . . were recognizably attempts to spin from the author's preoccupations coherent and continuous narratives. With *Jacob's Room* there was a change, and with two later books, *Mrs. Dalloway* and *To The Lighthouse,* narrative had given place to what must be considered Virginia Woolf's distinctive contributions to the modern English novel. These were curious weavings of impression and memory, the comings and goings of whimsical thoughts and fancies, sometimes from the moment, sometimes from yesterday, sometimes from long ago. Distastes for other individuals arose as if they were blown suddenly by a gust of wind; associations spread and narrowed, speculations jumped from nowhere, phrases came and went. A constant twitter of words and notions dominates these books. They specialize in disconnectedness. (p. 373)

Objective reality has little importance to Virginia Woolf; her interest is almost solely in the subjective. But not in what Aldous Huxley says is the only thing he cares about, the *Psyche;* rather in the flutterings of mood and fancy. She will take a person and show us the jumping of thought that goes on all the time in that person's consciousness. Having done that, she jumps to another person. And since she introduces us to several persons, who all jump in the same way, it is fair to assume that she has in her own mind some clear conception of these persons as separate individualities and believes herself to be successfully rendering those persons as individuals; but that is not my impression of them. Nor has the quiver and shake of their thoughts, for me, any deeper revelation than that of a kind of mental sickness, the sort of jumble that people have in their heads when they are going under or emerging from an anaesthetic. At such times, I agree, they are not very distinctly themselves. I should make this assertion of vagueness regarding *Mrs.*

Dalloway, To The Lighthouse, and *The Waves.* Of these books I should say, also, that they are extremely well-written, and full of ingenuities, the last-named full of beauty. *Orlando,* also, which is similarly very ingenious, is exceedingly interesting as narrative, and is easily comprehensible, but as far as I know does not pretend to be a novel. It is a calculatedly original work (but calculated originality is for me a contradiction in terms).

Some readers of Virginia Woolf apparently obtain a satisfaction from her work which they do not find elsewhere. For me, this work seems very clever, very ingenious, but on the whole creatively unimportant. It is all done with the wits; there is nothing in it for those who do not pride themselves upon intellectual superiority to the herd. There is nothing in it which is not offered to current middle class culture, the culture by which—post-Freud, post-Jung, and so on—all our younger minds are preoccupied by self-analysis. With the cleverness of young minds, they recognize in Virginia Woolf's characters leaps and states of mind familiar to themselves, and in that sense, making allowance for the difference of class, are doing no more than poor people do when they read novelettes. For if, recognizing a state of mind, or a whim, or a learned allusion, one acclaims in these books no more than recognizable phenomena, what is then left of Virginia Woolf's creative genius? She certainly does not purge by pity and terror.

What Arnold Bennett meant, I feel sure, in charging Georgian writers with ignoring the first essential of novel-writing, the creation of character, was that in the novels he had in mind (let us say that one of them was a book by Virginia Woolf, although I have no knowledge that he ever read a book she had written) there was no person seen and presented, as they say, in the round. In a book about Mrs. Brown, there was, for the reader, no Mrs. Brown. Virginia Woolf replied that there never was a Mrs. Brown, only a "Mrs. Brownness," the essential something which to Mrs. Brown is all that Mrs. Brown knows when she goes about her day's life. She claimed to be presenting not Mrs. Brown, but Mrs. Brownness. That sounds splendid. But in order to discover the Mrs. Brownness Virginia Woolf is forced to write solely of ruminative or introspective persons, and when she had carried her exploration to the four minds in *The Waves* she had reached as far as that particular method would take her. There were four poetic somethings; but they all thought alike. The reason for this, in my opinion, is that Virginia Woolf is essentially an impressionist, a catcher at memory of her own mental vagaries, and not a creator. She is aware, too, of many of the latest scientific facts and theories about human beings, but she is unable to imagine, to create, a human being who is not exactly like herself. Such a person as Arnold Bennett or Frank Swinnerton she could not—would not wish—to imagine. Nor Mrs. Brown either, I believe; for her Mrs. Brown is but a dream-jumble of odds and ends. She thinks she is pursuing the essential, but in fact she is too sensitive, highly-intelligent and playful in mind to have the emotional depth of an imaginative person. Psychologically she is as much at fault as the so-called realist, in thinking that if she chases every detail she will find truth. That is not the way to write great novels. Jane Austen was wiser and less anxiously exploratory; but Jane Austen had more creative imagination than cultivated brains. How odd that Virginia Woolf cannot see this. (pp. 374-76)

Frank Swinnerton, in his The Georgian Scene: A Literary Panorama *(reprinted with the permission of Farrar, Straus & Giroux, Inc.; copyright 1934 © 1962 by Frank Swinnerton; reprinted by permission of Holt, Rinehart and Winston, Publishers),* Farrar & Rinehart, *1934.*

It has often been pointed out that Mrs. Woolf's method has little to do with that of the ordinary novel. There is no conflict in her books, no sense of drama or dialectic; there is no progress through difficulties toward marriage or a deathbed. There is not even a story, in the usual sense of the word. Mrs. Woolf in her heart did not believe in stories; she thought of herself as living in a world where nothing ever happened; or at least nothing that mattered, nothing that was real. The reality was outside the world, in the human heart. Her literary method, based on this philosophy, was not to deal explicitly with a situation, but rather to present the shadows it cast in the individual consciousness. When the last shadows had moved across the screen and when the attentive reader had caught a glimpse of something motionless behind them—"this peace, this rest, this eternity"—Mrs. Woolf had nothing more to say. Her story had ended without having begun.

This method—as I think William Troy [see excerpt above] was the first to observe—is that of lyric poetry rather than fiction, and *Between the Acts* is the most lyrical of all her books, not only in feeling but also in style. The historical pageant is written chiefly in verse; the characters in their private meditations are always breaking into verse; and even the narrative passages have an emotional intensity and a disciplined freedom in the use of words that one does not associate with prose. Moreover, Mrs. Woolf uses almost as many symbols as Yeats does in his later work. (p. 383)

Malcolm Cowley, "Virginia Woolf: England under Glass," in The New Republic *(reprinted by permission of* The New Republic; © *1941 by The New Republic, Inc.), October 6, 1941 (and reprinted in* Think Back on Us ...: A Contemporary Chronicle of the 1930's by Malcolm Cowley, *edited by Henry Dan Piper, Southern Illinois University Press, 1967, pp. 382-84).*

[There] seem to be two sorts of life in fiction, life on the page and life eternal. Life on the page [Virginia Woolf] could give; her characters never seem unreal, however slight or fantastic their lineaments, and they can be trusted to behave appropriately. Life eternal she could seldom give; she could seldom so portray a character that it was remembered afterwards on its own account, as Emma is remembered, for instance, or Dorothea Casaubon, or Sophia and Constance in *The Old Wives' Tale.* What wraiths, apart from their context, are the wind-sextet from *The Waves,* or Jacob away from *Jacob's Room!* They speak no more to us or to one another as soon as the page is turned. And this is her great difficulty. Holding on with one hand to poetry, she stretches and stretches to grasp things which are best gained by letting go of poetry. She would not let go, and I think she was quite right, though critics who like a novel to be a novel will disagree. She was quite right to cling to her specific gift, even if this entailed sacrificing something else vital to her art. And she did not always have to sacrifice; Mr. and Mrs. Ramsay do remain with the reader afterwards, and so perhaps do Rachel from *The Voyage Out,* and Clarissa Dalloway. For the rest—it is impossible to maintain that here is an immortal portrait gallery. Socially she is limited to the upper-middle professional classes, and she does not even employ many types. There is the bleakly honest intellectual (St. John Hirst, Charles Tansley, Louis, William Dodge), the monumental majestic hero (Jacob, Percival), the pompous amorous pillar of society (Richard Dalloway as he appears in *The Voyage Out,* Hugh Whitbread), the scholar who cares only for young men (Bonamy, Neville), the pernickety independent (Mr. Pepper, Mr. Bankes); even the Ramsays are tried out first as the Ambroses. As soon as we understand the nature of her equipment, we shall see that as regards human beings she did as well as she could. Belonging to the world of poetry, but fascinated by another world, she is always stretching out from her enchanted tree and snatching bits from the flux of daily life as they float past, and out of these bits she builds novels. She would not plunge. And she should not have plunged. She might have stayed folded up in her tree singing little songs like *Blue-Green* in the *Monday or Tuesday* volume, but fortunately for English literature she did not do this either.

So that is her problem. She is a poet, who wants to write something as near to a novel as possible. (pp. 383-84)

It is always helpful, when reading her, to look out for the passages which describe eating. They are invariably good. They are a sharp reminder that here is a woman who is alert sensuously. She had an enlightened greediness which gentlemen themselves might envy, and which few masculine writers have expressed. (p. 384)

After the senses, the intellect. She respected knowledge, she believed in wisdom. Though she could not be called an optimist, she had, very profoundly, the conviction that mind is in action against matter, and is winning new footholds in the void. (p. 385)

The next of her interests which has to be considered is society. She was not confined to sensations and intellectualism. She was a social creature, with an outlook both warm and shrewd. But it was a peculiar outlook, and we can best get at it by looking at a very peculiar side of her: her Feminism.

Feminism inspired one of the most brilliant of her books—the charming and persuasive *A Room of One's Own.* . . . (pp. 386-87)

In my judgement there is something old-fashioned about [her] extreme Feminism; it dates back to her suffragette youth of the 1910's, when men kissed girls to distract them from wanting the vote, and very properly provoked her wrath. By the 1930's she had much less to complain of, and seems to keep on grumbling from habit. She complained, and rightly, that though women today have won admission into the professions and trades they usually encounter a male conspiracy when they try to get to the top. But she did not appreciate that the conspiracy is weakening yearly, and that before long women will be quite as powerful for good or evil as men. She was sensible about the past; about the present she was sometimes unreasonable. (p. 387)

> *E. M. Forster, in his* Virginia Woolf *(©
> 1942 by Harcourt Brace Jovanovich; © 1972
> by Cambridge University Press; reprinted by*

> *permission of Cambridge University Press),
> Harcourt, 1942 (and reprinted in* Modern
> British Fiction, *edited by Mark Schorer,
> Oxford University Press, 1961, pp. 376-90).*

Almost everything has been said, over and over, about Virginia Woolf's dazzling style, her brilliant humor, her extraordinary sensibility. She has been called neurotic, and hypersensitive. Her style has been compared to cobwebs with dew drops, rainbows, landscapes seen by moonlight, and other unsubstantial but showy stuff. She has been called a Phoenix, Muse, a Sybil, a Prophetess, in praise, or a Feminist, in dispraise. Her beauty and remarkable personality, her short way with fools and that glance of hers, which chilled many a young literary man with its expression of seeing casually through a millstone—all of this got in the way. It disturbed the judgment and drew the attention from the true point of interest.

Virginia Woolf was a great artist, one of the glories of our time, and she never published a line that was not worth reading. The least of her novels would have made the reputation of a lesser writer, the least of her critical writings compare more than favorably with the best criticism of the past half-century. In a long, sad period of fear, a world broken by wars, in which the artists have in the most lamentable way been the children of their time, knees knocking, teeth chattering, looking for personal salvation in the midst of world calamity, there appeared this artist, Virginia Woolf.

She was full of secular intelligence primed with the profane virtues, with her love not only of the world of all the arts created by the human imagination, but a love of itself and of daily living, a spirit at once gay and severe, exacting and generous, a born artist and a sober craftsman; and she had no plan whatever for her personal salvation; or the personal salvation even of someone else; brought no doctrine; no dogma. Life, the life of this world, here and now, was a great mystery, no one could fathom it; and death was the end. In short, she was what the true believers always have called a heretic.

What she did, then, in the way of breaking up one of the oldest beliefs of mankind, is more important than the changes she made in the form of the novel. She wasn't even a heretic—she simply lived outside of dogmatic belief. She lived in the naturalness of her vocation. The world of the arts was her native territory; she ranged freely under her own sky, speaking her mother tongue fearlessly. She was at home in that place as much as anyone ever was. (pp. 70-1)

> *Katherine Anne Porter, ''Virginia Woolf''
> (1950), in her* The Collected Essays and
> Occasional Writings of Katherine Anne
> Porter *(copyright © 1970 by Katherine Anne
> Porter; reprinted by permission of Delacorte
> Press/Seymour Lawrence), Delacorte Press,
> 1970, pp. 68-71.*

The evidence is clear enough in [Virginia Woolf's] work that the fundamental view of reality on which it is based derives from what was the most popular ideology of her generation. What is so often regarded as unique in her fiction is actually less the result of an individual attitude than of the dominant metaphysical bias of a whole generation.

For members of that generation concerned with fiction the

philosophy of flux and intuition offered a relief from the cumbersome technique and mechanical pattern of naturalism. . . . Like naturalism, it brought with it its own version of an esthetic; it supplied a medium which involved no values other than the primary one of self-expression. Of course one cannot wholly ignore the helpful co-operation of psychoanalysis. But to distinguish between the metaphysical and the psychological origins of the new techniques is not a profitable task. (pp. 65-6)

Possessing a mind schooled in abstract theory, especially alert to the intellectual novelties of her own time, Mrs. Woolf was naturally attracted by a method which in addition to being contemporary offered so much to the speculative mind. But the deeper causes of the attraction, it is now evident, were embedded in Mrs. Woolf's own temperament of sensibility. The subjective mode is the only mode especially designed for temperaments immersed in their own sensibility, obsessed with its movements and vacillations, fascinated by its instability. It was the only mode possible for someone like Proust; it was alone capable of projecting the sensibility which because it has remained so uniform throughout her work we may be permitted to call Mrs. Woolf's own. (p. 66)

From *The Voyage Out* to *The Waves* Mrs. Woolf has written almost exclusively about one class of people, almost one might say one type of individual, and that a class or type whose experience is largely vicarious, whose contacts with actuality have been for one or another reason incomplete, unsatisfactory, or inhibited. Made up of poets, metaphysicians, botanists, water-colorists, the world of Mrs. Woolf is a kind of superior Bohemia, as acutely refined and aristocratic in its way as the world of Henry James, except that its inhabitants concentrate on their sensations and impressions rather than on their problems of conduct. (Such problems, of course, do not even exist for them since they rarely allow themselves even the possibility of action.) Life for these people, therefore, is painful less for what it has done to them than for what their excessive sensitivity causes them to make of it. Almost every one of them is the victim of some vast and inarticulate fixation: Mrs. Dalloway on Peter Walsh, Lily Briscoe in *To the Lighthouse* on Mrs. Ramsay, everyone in *The Waves* on Percival. All of them, like Neville in the last-named book, are listening for "that wild hunting-song, Percival's music." For all of them what Percival represents is something lost or denied, something which must remain forever outside the intense circle of their own renunciation. No consolation is left them but solitude, a timeless solitude in which to descend to a kind of self-induced Nirvana. "Heaven be praised for solitude!" cries Bernard toward the close of *The Waves*. "Heaven be praised for solitude that has removed the pressure of the eye, the solicitation of the body, and all need of lies and phrases." Through solitude these people are able to relieve themselves with finality from the responsibilities of living, they are able to complete their divorce from reality even to the extent of escaping the burden of personality. Nothing in Mrs. Woolf's work serves as a better revelation of her characters as a whole than these ruminations of Mrs. Ramsay in *To the Lighthouse:*

> To be silent; to be alone. All the being and the doing, expansive, glittering, vocal, evaporated; and one shrunk, with a sense of solemnity, to being oneself, a wedge-shaped

core of darkness. . . . When life sank down for a moment, *the range of experience seemed limitless.* . . . Losing personality, one lost the fret, the hurry, the stir; and there rose to her lips always some exclamation of triumph over life when things came together in this peace, this rest, this eternity. . . .

What Mrs. Ramsay really means to say is that when life sinks down in this manner the range of *implicit* experience is limitless. Once one has abandoned the effort to act upon reality, either with the will or the intellect, the mind is permitted to wander in freedom through the stored treasures of its memories and impressions, following no course but that of fancy or simple association. . . . But experience in this sense is something quite different from experience in the sense in which it is ordinarily understood in referring to people in life or in books. It does not involve that active impact of character upon reality which provides the objective materials of experience in both literature and life. And if it leads to its own peculiar triumphs, it does so only through a dread of being and doing, an abdication of personality and a shrinking into the solitary darkness.

Because of this self-imposed limitation of their experience, therefore, the characters of Mrs. Woolf are unable to *function* anywhere but on the single plane of the sensibility. On this plane alone is enacted whatever movement, drama, or tragedy occurs in her works. The movement of course is centrifugal, the drama unrealized, the tragedy hushed. The only truly dramatic moments in these novels are significantly enough precisely those in which the characters seem now and again to catch a single brief glimpse of that imposing world of fact which they have forsworn. The scenes we remember best are those like the one in *Mrs. Dalloway* in which the heroine, bright, excited and happy among the guests at her party, is brought suddenly face to face with the fact of death. Or like the extremely moving one at the end of *To the Lighthouse* in which Lily Briscoe at last breaks into tears and cries aloud the hallowed name of Mrs. Ramsay. In such scenes Mrs. Woolf is excellent; no living novelist can translate these nuances of perception in quite the same way; and their effect in her work is of an occasional transitory rift in that diaphanous "envelope" with which she surrounds her characters from beginning to end.

For the novelist of sensibility the most embarrassing of all problems, of course, has been the problem of form. From Richardson to Mrs. Woolf it has been the problem of how to reconcile something that is immeasurable, which is what experience as *feeling* very soon becomes, with something that is measured and defined, which has remained perhaps our most elementary conception of art. . . . In Proust we see the attempt to achieve form on a large scale through the substitution of a purely metaphysical system for the various collapsing frameworks of values—religious, ethical, and scientific—on which the fiction of the nineteenth century had depended. In Joyce it is through a substitution of quite a different kind, that of a particular myth from the remote literary past, that the effort is made to endow the treasures of the sensibility with something like the *integritas* of the classical estheticians. And in the case of Mrs. Woolf, who is in this respect representative of most of the followers of these two great contemporary exemplars, the pursuit of an adequate form has been a strenuous one from first to last. (pp. 67-70)

[Already, in *The Voyage Out,*] one can observe a failure or reluctance to project character through a progressive representation of motives, which provides the structure in such a novelist as Jane Austen, for example, whom Mrs. Woolf happens to resemble most in this novel. For an ordered pattern of action unfolding in time Mrs. Woolf substitutes a kind of spatial unity . . . within which everything—characters, scenes and ideas—tends to remain fixed and self-contained. . . . [No] fulfillment is allowed; death is invoked; death supplies a termination which might not otherwise be reached since none is inherent in the plan. *Night and Day* is an effort to write a novel on a thoroughly conventional model, and the result is so uncertain that we can understand the rather sudden turning to a newer method. It is as if Mrs. Woolf had persuaded herself by these experiments (how consciously we may judge from her essay *Mr. Bennett and Mrs. Brown*) that her view of personality did not at all coincide with the formal requirements of the conventional novel. Of course she was not alone in this discovery for there already existed the rudiments of a new tradition, whose main tendency was to dispense with form for the sake of an intensive exploitation of method. . . .

Despite the number of artists in every field who assume that an innovation in method entails a corresponding achievement in form, method cannot be regarded as quite the same thing as form. For the novelist all that we can mean by method is embraced in the familiar phrase "the point of view.". . . "Method" in fiction narrows down to nothing more or less than the selection of a point of view from which character may be studied and presented. The drastic shift in the point of view for which Henry James prepared English fiction has undeniably resulted in many noticeable effects in its form or structure. But it is not yet possible to declare that it has resulted in any *new* form. . . . What Mrs. Woolf absorbed from [Dorothy] Richardson, from May Sinclair and from James Joyce, all of whom had advanced its use before 1918, was therefore only method, and not form. . . . Not until *Jacob's Room* does Mrs. Woolf attempt to use the method at any length, and in this book, with which her larger reputation began, we can first perceive the nature of the problem suggested by her work.

In one sense, the structure of *Jacob's Room* is that of the simplest form known to story-telling—the chronicle. From its intense pages one is able to detach a bare continuity of events: Jacob goes to the seashore, to Cambridge, to Greece, to the War. But what his creator is manifestly concerned with is not the relation of these events to his character, but their relation to his sensibility. The latter is projected through a poetic rendering of the dreams, desires, fantasies and enthusiasms which pass through his brain. The rendering is poetic because it is managed entirely by images, certain of which are recurrent throughout—the sheep's jaw with yellow teeth, "the moors and Byron," Greece. The theme also would seem to be a kind of poetic contrast between the outward passage of events and the permanence of a certain set of images in the mind. It happens that there is enough progression of outward events to give the book about as much movement as any other biographical (or autobiographical) chronicle. But one cannot point to any similar movement, any principle of progressive unity in the revelation of all that implicit life of the hero which makes up the substance of the book. As a sensibility Jacob remains the same throughout; he reacts in an identical fashion to the successive phenomena of his experi-

ence. Since he reacts only through his sensibility, since he does not act directly upon experience, he fails to "develop," in the sense in which characters in fiction usually develop. Instead of acting, he responds, and when death puts an end to his response, the book also comes to an end. "What am I to do with these?" his mother asks at the close, holding up an old pair of shoes, and this bit of romantic pathos is all the significance which his rich accumulation of dreams and suffering is made to assume in our minds.

In *Mrs. Dalloway* there is a much more deliberate use of recurrent images to identify the consciousness of each of the characters. The effort is not toward an integration of these images, for that would amount to something which is opposed to Mrs. Woolf's whole view of personality. It is toward no more than the emphasis of a certain rhythm in consciousness, which is obviously intended to supply a corresponding rhythm to the book as a whole. Moreover, in this work use is made for the first time of an enlarged image, a symbol that is fixed, constant and wholly outside the time-world of the characters. The symbol of Big Ben, since it sets the contrast between physical time and the measureless duration of the characters' inner life, serves as a sort of standard or center of reference. But neither of these devices, it should be realized, has anything directly to do with the organization of character: rhythm, the rhythm of images in the consciousness, is not the same thing as an order of the personality; the symbol of Big Ben is no real center because it exists outside the characters, is set up in contrast with them. By means of these devices carried over from lyric poetry, a kind of unity is achieved which is merely superficial or decorative, corresponding to no fundamental organization of the experience.

In her next book, however, Mrs. Woolf goes much further toward a fusion of character and design. *To the Lighthouse,* which is probably her finest performance in every respect, owes its success not least to the completeness with which the symbol chosen is identified with the will of every one of the characters. The lighthouse is the common point toward which all their desires are oriented; it is an object of attainment or fulfillment which gives direction to the movements of their thought and sensibility; and since it is thus associated with them it gives a valid unity to the whole work. Moreover, alone among Mrs. Woolf's works, *To the Lighthouse* has for its subject an action, a single definite action, "*going* to the lighthouse," which places it clearly in the realm of narrative. In fact, as narrative, it may be even more precisely classified as an *incident.* The sole objection that might be raised on esthetic grounds is whether Mrs. Woolf's method has not perhaps caused her to extend her development beyond the inherent potentialities of this form. The question is whether such a narrow structure can support the weight of the material and the stress of its treatment. More relevant to the present question, however, is the consideration that so much of the success of the book rests on the unusually happy choice of symbol, one that is very specially adapted to the theme, and not likely to be used soon again. Not many more such symbols occur to the imagination.

Certainly Mrs. Woolf does not make use of the same kind of symbol in her next novel; for in *The Waves* she returns to the devices of rhythm and symbolical contrast on which she depended in her earlier books. (*Orlando* is not a novel, but a "biography," and has only to follow a simple chronological order. Whatever hilarious variations its author plays on the traditional concept of time do not affect her adherence to this simple order.) (pp. 70-4)

What is unique [about *The Waves*] is Mrs. Woolf's effort to expand what is usually no more than an intuition, a single association, a lyrical utterance to the dimensions of a novel. In one sense this is accomplished by a kind of multiplication: we are given six lyric poets instead of the usual one. For what Mrs. Woolf offers is a rendering of the subjective response to reality of six different people at successive stages in their lives. We are presented to them in childhood, adolescence, youth, early and late middle-age. *"The waves broke on the shore"* is the last line in the book, and from this we are probably to assume that at the close they are all dead. Such a scheme has the order of a chronicle, of a group of parallel biographies, but Mrs. Woolf is much more ambitious. Each period in her characters' lives corresponds to a particular movement of the sea; the current of their lives at the end is likened to its "incessant rise and fall and rise and fall again." In addition, the different periods correspond to the changing position of the sun in the sky on a single day, suggesting a vision of human lives *sub specie aeternitatis*. (The ancillary images of birds, flowers and wind intensify the same effect.) . . . In conception and form, in method and style, this book is the most poetic which Mrs. Woolf has yet written. It represents the extreme culmination of the method to which she has applied herself exclusively since *Monday or Tuesday*. It is significant because it forces the question whether the form in which for her that method has resulted is not essentially opposed to the conditions of narrative art.

But this form is unmistakably that of the extended or elaborated lyric; and criticism of these novels gets down ultimately to the question with what impunity one can confuse the traditional means of one literary form with the traditional means of another. (pp. 74-5)

Because it is in an almost continuous state of moral and intellectual relaxation that Mrs. Woolf's characters draw out their existence, they can be projected only through a more or less direct transcription of their consciousness. . . . [The] method here is rarely if ever as direct as that of Joyce or his followers. Between the consciousness and the rendition of it there is nearly always interposed a highly artificial literary style. This style remains practically uniform for all the characters; it is at once individual and traditional. . . . For this reason the presentation of character by Mrs. Woolf gets down finally to a problem of style, to the most beautiful arrangement of beautiful words and phrases.

Here . . . Mrs. Woolf is pre-eminently the poet; for as an unwillingness to use motives and actions led to her substitution of poetic symbols in their stead so is she also compelled to use a metaphorical rather than a narrative style. In this practice of course she is not without precedent; other novelists have relied on metaphor to secure their finest effects of communication. But while such effects are ordinarily used to heighten the narrative, they are never extended to the point where they assume an independent interest. In Mrs. Woolf's books metaphorical writing is not occasional but predominate; from the beginning it has subordinated every other kind; and it was inevitable that it should one day be segmented into the purely descriptive prose-poems of *The Waves*. (pp. 77-8)

The images that pass through [Mrs. Woolf's] characters' minds are rarely seized from any *particular* background of concrete experience. There are few of them which we have not encountered somewhere before. They belong not so much to the particular character as to the general tradition of literature. The effect is of an insidious infiltration of tradition into the sensibility. And this effect is the same whether it is a straight description by the author, as in *To the Lighthouse*:

> The autumn trees, ravaged as they are, take on the flash of tattered flags kindling in the gloom of cool cathedral caves where gold letters on marble pages describe death in battle and how bones bleach and burn far away on Indian sands. The autumn trees gleam in the yellow moonlight, in the light of harvest moons, the light which mellows the energy of labour, and smooths the stubble, and brings the wave lapping blue to the shore.

or a presentation of mood, as in *Mrs. Dalloway*:

> Fear no more, says the heart. Fear no more, says the heart, committing its burden to some sea, which sighs collectively for all sorrows, and renews, begins, collects, lets fall. And the body alone listens to the passing bee; the wave breaking; the dog barking, far away barking and barking.

or a translation of ecstasy, as in *The Waves*:

> Now tonight, my body rises tier upon tier like some cool temple whose floor is strewn with carpets and murmurs rise and the altars stand smoking; but up above, here in my serene head, come only fine gusts of melody, waves of incense, while the lost dove wails, and the banners tremble above tombs, and the dark airs of midnight shake trees outside the open windows.

From such examples it should be apparent to what extent the sensibility here is haunted by the word-symbols of the past. . . . Some of [these passages] have the familiar charm of cherished heirlooms; only a few retain completely whatever power to stir the imagination they may once have had. Almost all of them depend for their effect on their associations to the cultivated mind rather than on their ability to evoke the fullness and immediacy of concrete experience. And the reason of course is that there is insufficient experience of this sort anywhere reflected in the course of Mrs. Woolf's work.

It is also clear in such passages how Mrs. Woolf has come more and more to cultivate language for its own sake, to seek in phrases some "independent existence" which will give them an absolute beauty in themselves. But detached from experience as they are they attain to no more substantial beauty than that of a charming virtuosity of style. It is not the beauty but the cleverness of Mrs. Woolf's writing which is responsible for the final effect on the reader. "No woman before Virginia Woolf has used our language with such easy authority," wrote the late Sara Teasdale. Indeed few writers of either sex have written English with the same mastery of traditional resources, the same calculated effec-

tiveness, the same facility. And when this facile traditionalism is allied with an appropriate subject, as in a frank burlesque like *Orlando,* the result is truly brilliant. It is only
when it is used as the vehicle for significant serious
thoughts and emotions, as in the larger portion of Mrs.
Woolf's work, that its charm seems false, its authority invalid, and its beauty sterile. (pp. 81-3)

• • • • •

Since her tragic death Mrs. Woolf's work has found its own
secure and appropriate place in the literature of our time.
That place has turned out to be neither so small nor so inconsequential as the prevailing tone here tends to predict,
nor is it so large as certain of her admirers and imitators in
the twenties hoped that it would become. Here again Time,
of which no one in her generation in England was more
painfully conscious, has altered or at least tempered literary
judgment along with everything else. Time has established
the balance.

For the pert severity of most of the objections to Mrs.
Woolf's novels the only excuse that can be made, apart
from the stock and always irrelevant one of youth, is that
they did at the time seem to represent a kind of facile emotionalism and moral attenuation that could spell no good for
the novel as a developing art form. But whatever threat
they may have offered has long since disappeared; and, as a
matter of fact, we are actually inclined to turn back with a
certain nostalgia to those very qualities of delicacy and elegance at which we took offense and which have now, alas,
almost universally departed from the novel. For example, it
now seems undoubtedly a mistake to have raised the hackneyed charge of sterility, to make the frequent confusion
between a writer's world and his treatment of it, to assume
that because a writer chooses to write about so-called
sterile people his own work is thereby necessarily sterile.
In rereading the best of Mrs. Woolf's novels, one is today
more likely to be impressed by the underlying vigor and
zest about the whole essential business of human experience, amounting at moments to ecstasy, as in the closing
lines of *To the Lighthouse* when Lily Briscoe turns to the
canvas upon which she has been working throughout the
book.

> There it was—her picture. Yes, with all its
> greens and blues, its lines running up and
> across, its attempt at something. It would be
> hung in the attics, she thought; it would be
> destroyed. But what did that matter? she
> asked herself, taking up her brush again. She
> looked at the steps; they were empty; she
> looked at her canvas; it was blurred. With a
> sudden intensity, as if she saw it clear for a
> second, she drew a line there, in the centre.
> It was done; it was finished. Yes, she
> thought, laying down her brush in extreme
> fatigue, I have had my vision.

Yes, we now can recognize that Mrs. Woolf too had her
vision, too narrow or special perhaps for most of us to
share with patience and sympathy, but her own and authentic. And all that matters is the high and exquisite art by
which she was able to render it. (pp. 87-8)

> *William Troy, "Virginia Woolf and the*
> *Novel of Sensibility" (originally published*
> *as three separate essays in 1932, 1937, and*

1952; reprinted by permission of the Estate
of William Troy), in his William Troy: Selected Essays, *edited by Stanley Edgar*
Hyman, Rutgers University Press, 1967, pp.
65-88.

[In her fiction, Virginia Woolf] attempted again and again
to find symbols for human existence; to construct scenes,
to weave patterns of imagery and feeling which would contain something of the vision that seemed always to be escaping before it had been fully apprehended; a dazzling vision which had changed the whole course of her art and
threatened to crack the walls of her being every time she
set out to recapture it. Again and again in these books she
introduces characters who are struggling to express the
inexpressible, whose intellect or imagination is taut with the
effort to reach beyond the frontiers of what has already
been discovered or created—images, in many guises, of the
artist herself. (pp. 242-43)

For these successive expeditions towards the inexpressible,
Virginia Woolf never chooses quite the same road, never
uses quite the same technique. Interior monologue is the
main instrument, appearing in all the novels, ranging from
the most mundane reflections to the pure poetry of Isa,
fluid and informal in all but *The Waves* where it becomes
static and formal, but used a little differently in each. In
Jacob's Room an extreme impressionism covers many
years and many different scenes by the slightest touches—a
paragraph of description, or a few thoughts, or a burst of
dialogue is often enough for each; with *Mrs. Dalloway* the
events and reflections of a single day fill a book of much the
same length; in *To the Lighthouse* two scenes of fairly
short duration in time are divided by a choral passage of
description, *Time Passes,* in which time moves infinitely
faster and actual events are only indicated here and there in
brief bracketed sentences. With *The Waves* the technique
is more radically altered, but is nevertheless a logical possible development from the earlier techniques; the new
form of the interior dialogue is only more deliberate and artificial, and an attempt is made to present it as if it were not
'interior' at all, but spoken, as it were, dramatically; the
choral interludes where the waves break on the shore and
the sun slowly crosses the heavens to mark the passage of
years are the development of devices already experimented
with in *Jacob's Room* and *To the Lighthouse.* The problem
in each of these books is the problem which lay concealed
all the time beneath the endeavour to leave out plot, and
concentrate on 'the soul': how shall one show the workings
of time on the lives of people? On each occasion she found
a new solution, but the curious structural uncertainty of her
next novel, *The Years,* makes one feel that she became increasingly dissatisfied with these solutions. *Between the
Acts* to some extent avoids the problem; one cannot tell
from it whether a new solution was emerging in her mind at
the time of her death.

It is perhaps impossible to analyse all that gives [Virginia
Woolf's] works their entirely unique and haunting quality,
that makes one feel that nowhere in the English novel have
such profound things been said about human existence, and
by the slightest means. One can only distinguish some of
the main elements in Virginia Woolf's art. Above all, her
astonishing sense of form and rhythmic pulse. *Jacob's
Room* seems to describe a perfect parabola, from the
opening when the cry of Archer is heard calling for Jacob

whom he cannot find on the beach, to the cry wrung out of Bonamy at the end for the Jacob he will never find again; and the end of *To the Lighthouse* seems to resolve all the themes of the book without one note wrong; it is as if one were listening to a flawlessly written piece of music and the emotional and intellectual satisfaction at the end is complete—though it must remain in the symbolism of the journey to the lighthouse and escapes any attempt at rational definition. There are themes which recur again and again, from novel to novel. The cry of 'Jacob! Jacob!' that rises from *Jacob's Room* is echoed by the cry of 'Mrs. Ramsay! Mrs. Ramsay!' from Lily Briscoe in *To the Lighthouse,* notes of an almost unendurable sadness that sounds softer or more poignant through all the books. It is round this sadness, this longing for something that cannot be reached or found again, that *The Waves* is constructed, where Percival who died in India repeats the theme of Jacob, the young man like a Greek statue come to life. The echoing sadness, and the continual questioning of life and death which accompanies it, are often deepened by the introduction and repetition of lines of poetry, 'O, western wind, when wilt thou blow', for instance, in *The Waves,* and 'Luriana Lurilee' in *To the Lighthouse.* The poets themselves are always present, Shakespeare, Shelley, Byron, the Greeks, their names appear again and again, and each time it is as if lamps were being lit; civilization, what man has created with art and learning—and with love—appears always as a light against darkness; Cambridge is imagined as emitting a radiance into the day as well as the night; in *To the Lighthouse* the *Boeuf en daube* dinner, with darkness creeping up the window panes becomes, as if by magic, no longer a dinner but an image of all this. Greece is one symbol among many she uses to create a sense of the past spreading illimitably round the lives of her characters; there are the strange skulls and bleached bones, the Phoenicians sleeping in the barrows, the old Barn like a Greek temple, the banners trembling above tombs. This sense of the past blends with the sea, the sound of waves breaking on the shore which is heard not only in *The Waves* but in *Jacob's Room* and *To the Lighthouse* as well; and when the pulse of time is not sounding from the sea it falls from clock-towers, in *Mrs. Dalloway* and *Between the Acts,* when the hour booms out over city or countryside. The past and its mystery; death and its mystery; love with its mystery, now transforming the whole of life with its glow, now savage as tigers; the dazzling surface radiance of the world and a terror and despair lurking always beneath; nowhere in modern writing have these things found symbols more audacious and memorable than in the novel-poems of Virginia Woolf, so that one can truly say that she enlarged the sensibility of her time, and *changed* English literature. (pp. 244-47)

> *John Lehmann, "Virginia Woolf," in English Critical Essays: Twentieth Century, Second Series, edited by Derek Hudson (copyright © 1958 by Oxford University Press; reprinted by permission), Oxford University Press, 1961, pp. 236-50.*

What . . . was Virginia Woolf's contribution to English literature? It was a very real, if in some sense a limited, one. She developed a type of fiction in which sensitive personal reactions to experience can be objectified and patterned in a manner that is both intellectually exciting and aestheti-cally satisfying. It is a delicate art. The robustness that makes itself felt in her criticism and in *Orlando* is not to be discovered in her characteristic novels, whose function is to distil a significance out of the data discovered by a personal sensibility and, by projecting that significance dramatically through the minds of others, to maintain an unstable equilibrium between lyrical and narrative art. She achieved that with greatest success in *Mrs. Dalloway* and *To the Lighthouse.* In the earlier novels the scales come down too heavily on the side of narrative, with the result that the lyrical elements are not properly fitted in; while in *Between the Acts* the scales are weighted on the lyrical side and the narrative is never wholly justified. *The Waves* introduces a not quite successful device for carrying on a narrative by means of lyrical monologues, while in *The Years* the reader senses a virtuosity in excess of the novel's requirements. Only in the two middle novels is the precarious balance maintained throughout: only in these is she able to refine life sufficiently to make it fully adaptable to her characteristic treatment.

The Victorian novelist tended on the whole to produce a narrative art whose patterns were determined by a public sense of values. Virginia Woolf, on the other hand, sensitive to the decay of public values in her time, preferred the more exacting task of patterning events in terms of her personal vision, which meant that she had on her hands the additional technical job of discovering devices for convincing the reader, at least during his period of reading, of the significance and reality of this vision. The English novel in the eighteenth and nineteenth centuries was essentially a public instrument; antithetical to lyric poetry. Its function was to utilize the preconceptions of readers in the presentation of a patterned series of events. (Lyrical poetry ignores, as a rule, public preconceptions and endeavours to communicate violently and directly a personal awareness of the poet's.) That the distinction between these two forms of art should be deliberately broken down in the post-Victorian period was only natural, for the distinction between public and private truth in every field was becoming blurred. There were many ways of responding to this situation: that of Virginia Woolf produced a type of art which, at its best, possesses a subtle and fragile beauty that will outlast the more rough-hewn works of many of her contemporaries.

Into the influences that affected her method we need not enter. The important thing is not that Proust or Joyce or any other writer influenced her writing, but that she developed a view of her art which made her susceptible to that kind of influence. Influences are not accepted passively by writers; they are actively embraced, and only when they coincide with the attitude the writer has already come to have: the important thing for the critic is to understand that attitude and its meaning for the writer's art.

It is doubtful whether the work of Virginia Woolf has permanently expanded the art of fiction. Her techniques are not easily isolated or imitated. But an author's greatness is not measured by the extent to which he can be imitated. Virginia Woolf can afford to rest her claims on her novels, which show her to be one of the half-dozen novelists of the present century whom the world will not easily let die. There can be little question that she was the greatest woman novelist of her time, though she herself would have objected to the separation of her sex implied in such a judgment. (pp. 153-55)

Virginia Woolf's novels, like James's, are characterized by an extraordinary blocking out of vast areas of life and a minute, vivid, at times nearly hallucinatory obsession with psychic experience. The intensity of her vision is so great that one feels the need to draw back from the particular, the subjective, to a detachment that will "explain" what is happening: a necessity Woolf admits in her use of techniques like the "Time Passes" episode in *To the Lighthouse* and the descriptions of sea and sky that introduce the various sections of *The Waves*. Her themes, unlike James's, usually have little to do with ethical problems. She dramatizes the mystery of life—the tensions between life and death, consciousness and unconsciousness, order and chaos, intimacy and isolation. (p. 24)

To the Lighthouse can be seen from a distance as a journey to a fixed point, the journey revealing to the sensitive child, James, the fact of there being two lighthouses, two "fixed points," two kinds of reality. Everything depends upon one's point of view and upon one's relationship, not only to the so-called objective world but to the minds of others. The desire to "be" is constant; the desire to *know* that one is, one exists, is superimposed on it; beyond this, there is the desire to establish one's "being" in terms of others. . . . (pp. 25-6)

The two impulses—toward identity and toward unity—are determined solely through relationships with others.

Yet the unity is always spiritual and, in spite of this, is always temporary. It should come as no surprise that Woolf does not concern herself with social questions in any but an incidental way, or that matters of a religious nature seem irrelevant. . . . [In Woolf's world there] is no distinction between the relationships of men and women and the relationships of women and women, men and men, adults and children. Where the Puritan mind establishes tension by its exclusion of the physical life deliberately and systematically, Woolf excludes it incidentally; it quite literally does not matter. (p. 27)

Having eliminated the vast complex areas of social, religious, and sexual concerns, Woolf is able to address herself to the primitive—or at least fundamental—question, "What is real?" If Woolf's characters appear to us creatures paralyzed in metaphysical wonderment, hence unable to live, it must be remembered that at the center of her work is life itself. . . . Only the sensitive can understand that nothing else matters except to live. . . . Yet the sensitive become by dint of their very sensitivity unable to simply "live," for they are committed to judgment and assessment and the establishment of order; and those who do no more than simply live cannot be conscious of the wonder of their experience.

To the Lighthouse . . . directly addresses the problem of knowledge and experience. The tension between Mr. and Mrs. Ramsay is partly accountable to their representing, not at all perfunctorily, the traditionally opposed talents for knowledge and for life. Mr. Ramsay is a professional phi-losopher who spends his time thinking. . . . Mrs. Ramsay, by contrast, is immersed constantly in time. One sees her always busy—knitting, mending, comforting a child, writing letters on the beach, opening windows and shutting doors, hiding the pig's skull on the nursery wall with her shawl. Lily thinks, after her death, of Mrs. Ramsay's instinct for humanity. . . . Moreover, Mrs. Ramsay is able by the magic of her being to make of the moment something permanent, to impose on the flux of life an order similar to the order of the artist. Her immortality, she thinks, consists in her kinship with others. . . . [Clearly] Woolf wants to make a distinction between reason and understanding in Kantian terms: reason being limited, for all its power, and understanding or intuition being freed from its dictates.

These evidently opposing forces, knowledge and experience, intellect and feeling, the masculine and the feminine tendencies, work to resolution. (pp. 28-30)

If the conclusion of *To the Lighthouse* seems to us dissatisfying, the complexity of life delivered over much too glibly to the demands of art, it is only because Woolf has taught us the ravages of an indifferent nature in the middle section, "Time Passes." . . . The achievement of order, then, is brutal and imposed upon from without when it is delivered apart from love. (p. 31)

The lighthouse as a final symbol remains an enigma because, like Melville's Moby Dick, it has been used to carry the burden of separate projections of meaning, the attempts of several individuals to come to terms with what is permanent within each of them in relationship to what is permanent "objectively"; the lighthouse carrying absolutely no connotations of good or evil, or a blend of both or neither, as Melville's whale does, but emerging instead as the fixed point of necessary order itself, ironic in that it can never be known except as a series of subjective experiences. It is the spiritualization of reality, once again the making immaterial of the "opaque," as Proust said. Arguments over the ultimate meaning of the lighthouse and the intention of the final pages are futile, since the novel is to be taken as a series of impressions in time, the final impression of unity being no more significant, perhaps, than Mrs. Ramsay's apparently basic feeling that there is no "reason, order, justice: but suffering, death, the poor." All depends upon point of view; Woolf shows the process of the mind in continual change, so that even those who are dead and ostensibly safe from further involvement are resurrected and given life again by their survivors. (p. 32)

Virginia Woolf was not one of the architects of the stream-of-consciousness novel. She read Joyce, Proust, and Dorothy Richardson and absorbed their lesson. Her peculiar contribution to the novel of subjectivity lay in her awareness almost from the first that she could obtain given effects of experience by a constant search for the condition of poetry. The influence of James Joyce upon her is much more profound than is generally believed. Indeed, she herself was prompt to seize upon *Ulysses* as a transcendent work long before it was published and only a few chapters had been serialized. (p. 63)

Light, tone, colour play through her cadenced works in a constant search for mood and with no attempt to impart an individual character to the style of thought. There is no attempt at portrait painting; rather does she try to evoke a state of feeling by a kind of mental poesy. The same vein of poetry runs through all the minds she creates for us. It is as if she had created a single device or convention, to be applied universally, in the knowledge that the delicacy of her perception, the waves of feeling, will wash over her readers as she washes them over her characters.

This is alike her achievement and its fatal flaw. The bright flame-like vividness of her books creates beautiful illuminated surfaces. There is no tragic depth in them, only the pathos of things lost and outlived, the past irretrievable or retrieved as an ache in the present. And in this she has fused the example of Proust as of Joyce. I think of *Mrs. Dalloway* as a Joycean novel, diluted, and washed and done in beautiful water-colour; and *To the Lighthouse* is Proustian in its time-sense, but again the medium is a kind of water-colour of the emotions.

Like Proust and Joyce, Virginia Woolf clearly expressed her aesthetic of fiction. Once she had grasped the lesson of her two great predecessors, she seems to have known exactly how she would apply it. But her definition of fiction is more impressionistic than the carefully evolved analysis Proust made of his *métier,* or the Aquinian aesthetic of Joyce. She adds little to what has been said, and once we divest her ideas of the eloquence in which they are clothed, we find them rather thin and unoriginal. (p. 64)

Virginia Woolf tried to catch the shower of innumerable atoms, the vision of life, the iridescence, the luminous halo. It was her way of circumventing the clumsiness of words. . . . However much Mrs. Woolf might assert the need to record the shower of atoms "in the order in which they fall," she neither accepted that order, nor believed in describing their frequent incoherence. Her method was that of the lyric poet. She was interested in the sharpened image, the moment, the condensed experience. She saw the world around her as if it were a sharp knife cutting its way into her being.

From James Joyce, Virginia Woolf seems to have obtained a certain sense of *oneness* and the isolation that resides within it: from him she learned how to give meaning to the simultaneity of experience. London is to Mrs. Dalloway what Dublin is to Leopold Bloom. But her London is a large canvas background with light cleverly playing over it and, unlike Joyce, her people are distillations of mind and flesh. Clarissa Dalloway's day in London, also a day in June, as in *Ulysses,* begins at nine in the morning and finishes early the next morning. (Indeed, in most of Mrs. Woolf's fiction, time is reduced to a few hours, so that even in *To the Lighthouse,* where a number of years are bridged in the middle passage, "Time Passes," it is but to link two single days at each end of that period.) (pp. 65-6)

[*Mrs. Dalloway's*] structure seems largely to be modelled on the multiple-scened chapter in *Ulysses* which is tied together by the progress of the vice-regal cavalcade through Dublin's streets. We are in many minds in the streets of London. But Mrs. Dalloway's mind, and that of Septimus Warren Smith, hold the centre of the book as did those of Bloom and Dedalus in *Ulysses.* The entire inwardness of the book, its limited time-scheme, the use of multiple views, so that we feel we have seen London through many eyes—and so are aware of it through many awarenesses—the glimpsing of certain characters and then the glimpse of them anew through the perceptions of the principal characters—all this becomes a subtle conversion to simpler ends of the Joycean complexities. But if Bloom and Dedalus are a father and son who meet for a brief moment at the end of a long day symbolically, as Odysseus met Telemachus after a lifetime of wanderings, Clarissa Dalloway and Septimus Smith seem to be two facets of the same personality—indeed, the projection by Virginia Woolf of two sides of herself. Mrs. Woolf's diary shows that she conceived this novel as an attempt to show "the world seen by the sane and the insane side by side." (p. 66)

The whole of the novel conveys poignantly Virginia Woolf's response to Joyce's success in reflecting how, in a big city, people's paths cross and dramas go on within range of dramas, and yet in spite of innumerable points of superficial contact and relation, each drama is isolated and each individual remains locked within walls of private experience. The book's brilliance, as writing and as poetry, lies in the skill with which Mrs. Woolf weaves from one mind into another. . . . This complex inner material could be rendered only by the use of brilliantly evocative prose-poetry. And this novel, like those which Virginia Woolf wrote after it, illustrates admirably the worth of the symbolist method in fiction. We have only to think of a Zola or a George Moore creating Clarissa after the manner of their naturalist doctrines to understand the difference. Clarissa would emerge as a commonplace woman, the façade described in detail, but no hint of the fascinating and troubled and mysterious personality behind her exterior. Mrs. Woolf extended with remarkable skill and literary virtuosity the creation of a novel that conveys inner experience. She was capable of finding the words that would show the world through her protagonists' minds: and she participated fully in the significant shift of emphasis, inaugurated by Henry James, from the outer social world—as explored by Balzac or the naturalists—to the sensibility with which that outer world is appreciated and felt.

If the general plan, the painting of the environment, is a scaling down of Joycean architectonics, the painting of the sensibility tends to be Proustian. And yet there is a significant difference. In Proust the odour of the lilacs is directly felt and explored with subtlety; his feelings well up out of the page and are carefully communicated. In Mrs. Woolf the odour bounces off the flowers and reaches the reader as a sharp, distinct but refracted sensation. One has indeed an effect of the bouncing-off of light and sound throughout the novel from people and objects and against the receiving mind. Proust touches experience directly. Mrs. Woolf's method is refraction, through a kind of high, tense awareness. The poetry is there on every page and always a synthesis—a pulling together of objects and impressions. (pp. 67-8)

Leon Edel, "The Novel as Poem" in his
The Modern Psychological Novel *(copyright*
© *1964 by Leon Edel), Grosset & Dunlap,*
Inc., 1964 (and reprinted in Virginia Woolf:

A Collection of Critical Essays, *edited by Claire Sprague, Prentice-Hall, Inc., 1971, pp. 63-9).*

In style, method, size, and shape, *Jacob's Room* would be the first distinctly Woolfian novel, but *The Voyage Out* asks right off her characteristic questions about the relation of the upper middle classes to life itself, their own lives as well as all others. Like *Mrs. Dalloway* and *Between the Acts,* it ponders the relationship of civilized consciousness to the prehistoric past that our consciousness sits trembling on. And it pleads with suffering and love to explain themselves.

Night and Day . . . comes from a craftsman looking before and after. It updates Jane Austen's heroines, gives them George Eliot's topics of conversation, and hurries them through London streets. . . .

[Nothing] . . . in *The Voyage Out,* called for so many fresh metaphors and surprising adjectives as the thoughts and dreams of the new young people occupied night and day in London. Katharine Hilbery ponders reality as an image-making Kant. Not systems—there is no Hegel in her—just reality. The creator who put her on paper was trying to find a way to show in fiction what life feels like. To show, not tell. From Dostoevski come illogical conduct and contradictions of personality, such as the mingling of love and hate that will deepen from *Mrs. Dalloway* on. Symbols to be central in later novels, the lighthouse and the breaking wave, enter surreptitiously. The novelist had yet to remove the large scaffolding of external fact erected by the earliest novelists and maintained by the Edwardians. Her second novel, like her first, was longer than any she would write in the next twenty years. The characters confess to each other as often as Dostoevski's. They spend more time than Galsworthy's riding omnibuses and looking for cabs. (p. 13)

The later novels tempt us to be flippant about the kind of novel *Night and Day* represents. The plot, moving to a happy ending through bumps of suspense and near melodrama, is a love-go-round. . . . There is some talk of cohabitation without marriage, but propriety wins. Such conventions of subject and technique do not prevent subtlety. . . . Sensitive, fumbling Katharine seems to be the heroine, and seems to engage a large part of the author, but it is possible to see all the people finally destined to happiness as indeed finally cleared away in order to let lonely Mary stay at her feminist post with us. (p. 14)

Jacob's Room . . . has interested literary historians because it makes new departures, particularly in the design of a rhythmic shorthand to expose streams of consciousness. Memories, thoughts, and sub-thoughts blend with impressions of external objects. With this novel the devices of narrative become at once more concentrated and more indirect. . . . A shuddering effect resulted when Mrs. Woolf submerged at once the narrator and the consciousness of the central character. Yet this device, germinal to the denser method of *The Waves,* leaves Jacob with a charm that would have worn off if he had meditated in our faces from childhood to grave. (p. 15)

Even [in *Jacob's Room*], where Mrs. Woolf begins to emulate the linguistic concentration of poetry, she resists the temptation to be timidly intense. She retains the Victorian virtue of scope. She enters the minds of most of the named characters, in this experimental novel as well as in those

before and after it. If she thinks she understands a character well enough to include him, she sympathizes enough to report his thoughts and feelings. Of the dozens of minds entered, whether or not their owners are made personally acquainted, most are sharing or exchanging impressions. In consequence, the mind entered is usually either a general mind or a representative local mind.

All the mental activity occurs within a firmly drawn external world. The method of drawing is impressionistic, sometimes expressionistic when the author sympathizes fully with her observers, but topography controls the impressions. . . . The past lives in the minds of the characters, but London lives too. (pp. 16-17)

[Experiment] introduced problems of its own. In the new economy, to take a small but nagging problem, alliteration sometimes makes sentences too rich. Overrichness will linger to burden *The Waves.* . . . The author does not pretend to nonexistence as the creating artist, but only to nonexistence as judge. . . . Symbols bind the characters in *Jacob's Room,* but the author does not trust them to remind the reader how hard life is to understand. She inserts essays that are readable enough, but are too many, and too many of them worry over life. The insertions both renovate the practice of Fielding and innovate in their own context, but they do not please those pleased by her later intensity of symbol. . . . She . . . had failed to achieve Ibsen's perfect fusion of actual and symbolic. (p. 18)

Suddenly in *Mrs. Dalloway* . . . the central character has no circumference. For the next four novels some of the characters perceived by the central consciousness are enclosed by a bounding line, but the author seems to look at some one character from the core inside. Beginners often produce a similar effect, but Mrs. Woolf was seeking a center for the thin-blown glass balloon of complete vision. She had a greater and greater hunger to convey her sense of life's essence, which could put any one mind at the center as well as the next. Even Proust, she believed, had not gone as far as a novelist might in awaking readers to the quality of life itself. Hoping to share with poets this power of awakening, she wished also to prove fiction generally capable of conveying essence along with appearance. . . .

Scenes in flashback would have been too rigid and too divisive. The past is sometimes mixed, sometimes fused, in the luminous halo of the present. We follow mental images from one person to another, either physically near at the moment or emotionally near in the past. Events of the past repeated as metaphors for the present can take the breath. . . . (p. 19)

[She] synthesizes the small dramas of perseverance and affection instead of analyzing stagy versions of passion. Mrs. Woolf made these novels realistic in the sense that they illuminate the lives of their readers. She did not escape with the naturalists, who describe events that happen to non-readers. *To the Lighthouse* incorporates plot, not by revealing that Miss Doyle and Mr. Bankes never married, but by showing, like *Mrs. Dalloway,* that the consciousness contains every day the greatest things that happen to the conscious: growth, friendship, quarrel, marriage, solitude, aging, death. . . .

[In *The Waves*] she drove her concrete images and phrase-making as near to abstraction as any novelist has risked driving them. She differentiates her six central characters by the allusions, attitudes, and metaphors of their brief soliloquies, which follow serially throughout the book, but she imposes a single undifferentiated style on the consciousness of all six. . . . [The] reader is unable to distinguish more than the six names before he is immersed in the central theme that we are all joined in a life of uniform flux. . . .

[The] story is itself "abstract." Their friendship differs only in chance detail from the loose bonds of others who might seem, both as individuals and as a group, to differ greatly from these. The story of growing up and aging is no more theirs than ours. . . .

In *Mrs. Dalloway* physical detail and reverie coexist; in *To the Lighthouse* they interweave; in *The Waves* they flow together through prose that has been too close to lullaby for all critics except those for whom the symbols suffice. (pp. 28-9)

On the novelistic side, the characters are individuals; on the poetic, where they fall into types, each positive has its negative. As they advance from childhood through youth and on to age, it gradually appears that it is not persons who are polar opposites, but only qualities abstracted from them. . . . Within the common style, speakers anticipate the discrimination of attitudes, symbols, and sensory debris in their minds by saying, I am Rhoda, I am Louis. Nothing so unnovelistic occurs anywhere else in the Woolf canon. Yet their effort of self-assertion wins an aesthetic response.

Of course the best training for the required discrimination is not the stringencies of, for example, Beckett—though Beckett is a good trainer—but Mrs. Woolf's earlier novels, beginning with the earliest. Old themes, images, and human relationships return here. The recurring motif of an earlier novel will anticipate a leitmotif in this one, if not specifically then in kind. (pp. 30-1)

In the other novels, including those after *The Waves,* separable elements can be admired. I would contend that scenes, devices for characterization, perceptions, evocations, and acquiescences should be valued for their own merits in all the novels but one. *The Waves,* unorthodox or inadequate in all the elements relied on by Scott and Balzac, either succeeds as a unified book (whether novel or not) or it fails. (p. 31)

The Years is of all the novels the most vulnerable to the charge of preciosity. Humor is kept on a tight leash. *The Waves,* like an encephalograph, discovered a style that reports at least one aspect of inner vibration. *The Years,* asking for comparison with other family novels about changing mores, seems to report snippets of trivia in conversation and thought. The methods of *Jacob's Room* are here mounted in a conventional frame. (p. 33)

Theory and doctrine never clog her fiction. Statements about experience in the novels, allotted to the minds of her characters, are fingers steadying the landscape of experience so that the new perspectives can work the easiest way. She transforms to a kind of postimpressionism what she learns of dreams, totems, and duration versus time. . . . She did not see Joyce's limitation as the choice of material that could not be made beautiful, but as a failure to make it beautiful. She could see some value in the raw blood offered by Joyce for readers as anemic as T. S. Eliot. For herself and other normal-blooded people, she prefers novels

of high finish. As long as language itself tells of life, she has no fear that pursuit of beauty will lead to excessive abstraction. *The Waves* may lead others to doubt her confidence. (p. 41)

Clearly she felt a tension between the responsibility to make fiction heighten life while portraying it and the responsibility to hold and assert social views courageously. The novels cover those views with layers of irony. None of her novels was unmistakably sympathetic with the proponents of woman's suffrage until *The Years,* when the fight she had personally supported was over. It would be hard to detect her alliance with the socialists in any novel before her last, although a Marxist could understand better than most the role of the economically deprived in the edges and crevices of her books. The psychological and fictional concerns in *To the Lighthouse* and the ontological concern in *The Waves* reduce the social interests of those novels to their narrowest in her work. More usually the spiritual lives of the characters unfold not only within the masonry and foliage of a physical setting . . . , but also against an appraised social fabric. We cannot speak of "Virginia Woolf's world" as we speak of "Dickens's world" or "Kafka's world" to mean peopled geographies that are persuasive but not representational. Her characters exist in two worlds: the subjective world she creates for them (and out of them), and the physical world that she holds too much in awe to alter for a merely fictional pattern. I think that this duality came from her unresolved impulses toward autonomous art and toward the shaping of evidence to support her conviction that the world she was creating was a world recognizable to all sensitive readers. Within the world that is "what life feels like," she put the stones of London.

None of the novels totally avoided the theme of resistance to Victorian damp and Victorian tyranny. With increasing insistence the books presented mystical experiences, and even basic doctrines, of escape from the senses into oneness with the all. Similar retreats from action have in recent years proved a representative ending, and possibly a fitting one, to the insistent individualism that accompanied Mrs. Woolf's early maturity. (pp. 42-3)

Carl Woodring, in his Virginia Woolf *(Columbia Essays on Modern Writers Pamphlet No. 18; copyright © 1966 Columbia University Press; reprinted by permission of the publisher),* Columbia University Press, 1966.

Virginia Woolf's feminism . . . was of a highly individualistic kind. . . . Far from believing that women should take on the characteristics of men, she believed it would be well, on the whole, for men to take on some of the characteristics of women. Her ideal was the blending of masculine intellect and logic with feminine intuition and imagination to produce what she called, borrowing a phrase from Coleridge, "the androgynous mind." She somewhat begs the question of whether these characteristics are naturally peculiar to the respective sexes, but seems to have considered them innate, subject to social conditioning. She believed that masculine one-sidedness—intellect and power without feeling and imagination—was the source of innumerable evils from bad art to bad politics and that unbridled masculinity led to the "arts of dominating . . . of ruling, of killing." Antigone was her heroine and Creon her archetypal tyrant. Shakespeare was the supreme example of "androgyny."

Virginia Woolf was, of course, sympathetic toward many of the aims of the suffragettes. In her books *Three Guineas* and *A Room of One's Own* she speaks at length of the injustices women had suffered from lack of legal rights, education, opportunity, and independence. . . . But the suffragettes erred, she thought, in using the methods of men—aggression and violence—and in accepting for themselves masculine values—power and physical strength. She not only believed in the traditional "nurturing" role of women, but emphasized it. Mrs. Ramsay in *To the Lighthouse* is a perfect example of the feminine mystique. (pp. 173-74)

[She contended] that *Moll Flanders* and *Roxana* are two of the very greatest English novels, that Charlotte Brontë would have been a better novelist if she could have "dined out." Her feminism underlies her famous criticism of Bennett and Wells: their work was made up of externals, they lacked intuition about the souls of their characters, they were one-sided. . . .

[However, one] knows from reading the novels and criticism that she has other themes, other insights, and that her concern for art and a true portrayal of life transcended her specialized concern for the role of women. The effect of the novels is certainly more of poetry than polemics, an effect, to use one of her own phrases, of "life itself." (p. 174)

> *Dorothy Zimmerman, "Woolf as Feminist,"* in Prairie Schooner (© 1971 by University of Nebraska Press; reprinted by permission from Prairie Schooner), Summer, 1971, pp. 173-74.

Between 1910 and 1930, many writers explicitly attacked the idea of compassion in literature. In revolting against what they thought of as the excessive piety, sentimentality, and complacency that characterized Victorian and Edwardian literature, writers often included compassion among the qualities that would distort the search for truth or muddy the clarity of the essential concept of human nature they tried to present. Poets like Ezra Pound and T. S. Eliot, as well as novelists like Virginia Woolf, D. H. Lawrence, and James Joyce, attempted, on the surface of their works at least, to veer away from an attitude of compassion, to penetrate the thickness of Edwardian literary fog and emotional dampness in order to reach a centrally significant truth about human experience. . . . [They] sought what was harder, firmer, what was humanly or metaphysically true no matter how bleak or difficult that truth might be. They were not, at least in their initial attempts, skeptical about the possibility of finding some metaphysical truth, some central essence of man. . . . (p. 179)

Virginia Woolf illustrates this consciously new and antiromantic point of view in *Orlando*. . . . More parable or essay than novel, *Orlando* is a comic survey course, complete with stylistic parodies, in English social and literary history from the Elizabethan age to the present. The central figure, Orlando, first as man and then as woman, lives through the more than three hundred years observing and experiencing the customs, attitudes, and atmospheres of the changing eras. Yet it is highly slanted social history. Mrs. Woolf seems to appreciate the adventurous energy of the Elizabethans, the macabre gloom of the Jacobeans, the gilded elegance of the restoration, and the witty eloquence of the eighteenth century. But nothing is attractive about her portrait of the nineteenth century. She sharply satirizes

the transcendant slush of Romanticism and expresses her greatest scorn for Victorian pretense and domesticity. . . . (p. 180)

Mrs. Woolf's most famous novel, *To the Lighthouse* . . . , comes closest to formulating a metaphysical truth, to dealing with that aspect of the human being which represents his eternal nature. The lighthouse itself, distant and ambiguous across the water, stands as the central symbol of meaning and achievement in the novel. Seeking the lighthouse, seeking the metaphysical truth about human nature, if successful, can provide focus for all human energy, and render subsidiary values, like compassion, trivial and irrelevant. As in many other versions of the searcher for the holy grail, for the object that would give meaning and direction to all human activity, Mrs. Woolf's symbolic searcher must suffer, must pass through the tumult of destruction and war, before he can reach the lighthouse. (p. 182)

The sense of personal victory in *To the Lighthouse* was, however, only momentary in Mrs. Woolf's fiction. Even the essay, "Mr. Bennett and Mrs. Brown" recognizes that truth or essence are, despite all human attempts, not permanent, that they are contingent upon the changes and relativities of history. (p. 186)

The emphasis on historical statement itself introduces compassion into the novel. Insofar as man is determined by history, conditioned by his time and place, he is unable to achieve or become all that he would wish, perhaps unable to realize the essential truths of human nature and experience. The author's statement that history limits the individual is also the author's statement that the individual may well not receive justice, may not find his truth no matter how dedicated his search or how wisely persistent his efforts. And the human creature who would be a self-consciously metaphysical entity but is necessarily compromised by social, psychological and historical accident receives compassion for conditions he cannot alter.

Mrs. Woolf's last two novels, *The Years* . . . and *Between the Acts* . . . , demonstrate the concern with social history more explicitly and directly than do any of the earlier works. (pp. 190-91)

The tension between the metaphysical and the historical, between man searching for a truth beyond himself and man bound to himself by time and history . . . , dominates only three of the novels, but they are Mrs. Woolf's three greatest: *To the Lighthouse, Mrs. Dalloway* . . . and *The Waves.* . . . In *To the Lighthouse,* the metaphysical search is completed, the truth, in symbolic terms, is achieved as Mr. Ramsay reaches the lighthouse and Lily Briscoe paints her picture. In the other two novels, truth is hidden, changed, or necessarily compromised, as man finds his essential truth, if at all, only at the price of his own destruction. In *Mrs. Dalloway* and *The Waves,* the tension between the metaphysical and the historical turns from a decision to a question of human survival, from a choice between two attitudes toward experience to a realization of the only terms on which experience is possible. With this realization comes the author's compassion for all her characters who wish to stand for something more permanent and more essential than they do. (pp. 192-93)

In terms of Virginia Woolf's career, *To the Lighthouse* alone is a moment, a point in time when experience gave the appearance of coherence and direction, whereas *The*

Waves depicts the general condition, the flux in which moments dissolve. Through history, through psychology, through the process of life itself, all the moments eventually dissolve, sometimes to the extent that mere survival, the possibility of keeping alive at all, becomes as much as the battered human being can manage. Compassion is a constant attitude, a point of view the author holds toward all those seeking the permanence of the moment, attempting to give life a direction and a meaning that can never be sustained. Man, looking for truth, is regarded with compassion because the truth either cannot be found or dissolves as soon as it is discovered.

Mrs. Woolf's revolt against the Edwardians, sufficiently evident in technique, was considerably less thorough than she thought it was. Trying to assert man's permanent essence, his eternal character, Mrs. Woolf often saw her crystallizations dissolved by time, by history, by the complexity and flux of human experience, by the very sort of environment and material intractability she so sharply criticized the Edwardians for relying upon. In addition, her attempts at hard truth frequently ended in soft compassion for the human being who could neither find nor face the hardness of truth. She was closer to Arnold Bennett than either she or her contemporary reading public would ever have acknowledged. "Yes, there it is," is, in Mrs. Woolf's novels, a summary and descriptive statement of man's condition, a resigned and limited conclusion, far more frequently than it is a moment of apprehension of eternal meaning or truth. (pp. 203-04)

> *James Gindin, "Virginia Woolf," in his* Harvest of a Quiet Eye: The Novel of Compassion *(copyright © 1971 by Indiana University Press; all rights reserved), Indiana University Press, 1971, pp. 179-204.*

"The things people don't say" were the things Virginia Woolf and her contemporaries, James Joyce and D. H. Lawrence, wanted to say. They shared an interest in making silence speak, in giving a tongue to the complex inner world of feeling and memory and in establishing the validity of that world's claim to the term "reality." That subjective reality came to be identified with the technique rather loosely called "stream of consciousness.".... Literary historians invariably make a trio of Joyce, Woolf and Lawrence, agreeing that they share this "metaphysical bias." We are, however, becoming as much aware of their singularities as of their shared attitudes and techniques. It is doubtful, for example, that Woolf and Lawrence used the famed stream of consciousness technique at all.

In a number of unexpected ways Woolf and Lawrence may be usefully compared. Each tended to attract disciples and antagonists in a way that made reasonably objective criticism during their lifetime almost impossible. Symbol and allegory hunters have come forth with extravagant interpretations of their work.... Both Woolf and Lawrence produced a highly personal vision of life in their works—at least by comparison with Joyce. Furthermore, Joyce was not a preacher; Lawrence was; Virginia Woolf was—as a feminist certainly if less certainly as a novelist. But such comparisons are less meaningful than Woolf's own perception that she and Lawrence had "too much in common—the same pressure to be ourselves." Joyce's more objective, encyclopedic, many-leveled prose never gave her the same shock of recognition.

Though so often mentioned together with Joyce and Lawrence, Woolf is neither so highly valued nor so well known as they are. She may partly be the victim of an obscuring personal legend created by her contemporaries. If so, she again recalls Lawrence; for Lawrence the writer was the victim of a far more obscuring personal legend, one arising out of both adulation and animosity and Lawrence's own strident prophetic stance. Happily, Lawrence has already survived his legend. Woolf has yet to survive hers. (pp. 1-2)

[Attitudes] toward her personality, her origins and her literary-political circle must have conditioned the onesidedness of the portrait that has come down to us and affected the reading of her fiction as "disengaged." Her novels may, however, justifiably claim to have represented a portion of "reality," even of social reality. (p. 4)

Virginia Woolf shared the restless experimentalism of her generation. The drive to begin anew may be seen as compulsion; it may also be seen as a kind of courage, an artistic strategy that is anything but soft. (p. 6)

But each of her completely new attempts did contain constants. One was her need to explore her double vision of reality.... When she divided novels into novels of fact and vision she was expressing a classification she thought inherent in life and in fiction. Contrary to what she seemed to be saying in her famous attack on Wells-Bennett-Galsworthy in her essay, "Mr. Bennett and Mrs. Brown," fact interested her as much as vision. If death was in the midst of life in all her novels, fact was always in the midst of vision.

The technique of writing about talk, a kind of fact, had been developed and perfected in the novel form. But how write about Silence? ... The paradox of talk about silence was one Woolf did not care to solve by authorial objectivity. She is one of the very few modernists who did not want objective (read dramatic) narration or a single center of consciousness. If she did write stream of consciousness, she wrote the simplest, the most lucid, probably the most superficial example of it. Her internal discourse is almost never discontinuous, never close to the pre-speech level and always carefully, almost too obviously guided by connectives which place it precisely. She did learn to internalize omniscient comment more skillfully. *Jacob's Room,* for all its departures from her first two novels, is painfully filled with unnecessary and obtrusive author comment. What she puts into her own mouth in that novel she learned to put into the mouths of others or to discard altogether. Although the musings of the London citizens who see the motor car pageant or the skywriting in *Mrs. Dalloway* may not connect various levels of life and reality for all readers, these musings are more skillfully interwoven into the texture of the novel than are the musings in *Jacob's Room.* Mrs. Woolf never wished to subordinate or to hide her omniscient powers. She wished to learn to use them in a new way.

Probably omniscience interested her because she wanted a method that would permit more than one person to speak in a way that dramatic narration would not permit. *Mrs. Dalloway* gave her one method and each of her subsequent novels gave her another. In no novel does one person speak. What she tried to develop may be called a kind of multipersonal method. It was one way for her to "keep form and speed, and enclose everything, everything." This paradoxical and inevitably frustrating aim was always before her.

How include everything when she was "as usual . . . bored by narrative" or obsessed by the inadequacy of the word novel? She called *To the Lighthouse* an elegy, *The Waves* a play-poem, *The Years* an essay-novel. She could say after *Orlando* was finished: "I feel more and more sure that I will never write a novel again," then, after her most daring departure from the novel form, *The Waves,* feel again attracted by traditional novel material and ask, as she was formulating *The Years:* "How give ordinary waking Arnold Bennett life the form of art?" If we were to decide her intentions as a novelist from her essay, "Mr. Bennett and Mrs. Brown," we should agree that she above all wanted to be faithful to Mrs. Brown. She insisted that the novelist never desert Mrs. Brown yet she deserted her frequently, if not always. In fact, a severe and common charge against her is that she did not create character. She may not even have wanted to. She wryly notes that a London *Times* review of *The Waves* praises "my characters when I meant to have none."

Thus she did in a sense constantly fight her medium, forcing it to do what it could not do and perhaps once or twice succeeding in the impossible—in making a work of fiction without character or narrative. (pp. 6-8)

In *Orlando* and *The Waves* Mrs. Woolf moves further and further away from the kind of modern novel she helped to define. Even in the Woolf canon *Orlando* is a sport, an "essay novel" on English literature, character and manners from Elizabethan times to the present, a fantasy with a main character who changes sex in 1683 and is over 300 years old when the novel closes in 1928. Though begun as a lark, *Orlando* may have served the more serious function of freeing its creator from dependence on the usual novelistic controls. It may have freed her for the creation of *The Waves,* if that novel is, as many critics believe, her best. *The Waves* can be called an anti-novel. The exciting artistic risk of that novel is the splitting up of personality into six voices only tenuously connected to external reality. Bernard, the talkiest of the six, wonders: "Am I all of them?" This novel, of voices without bodies or setting, may be an intellectualized tour-de-force that the common reader Mrs. Woolf prized would never return to, a kind of sport, like *Orlando.*

Her last two novels are re-combinations of familiar fictional strategies, as though the writer were enjoying a conventional holiday—one quite unlike the writer's holiday she said she was taking when she wrote *Orlando.* The principle of selection her mature works so suitably reflect deserts her in *The Years,* but reasserts itself in *Between the Acts* which more effectively evokes England than its predecessor. (p. 10)

We may come to see Virginia Woolf as less frail in her life and in her art than we have heretofore. Her productivity was, for example, striking. She did not match the torrential outpourings of her father, Sir Leslie Stephen, and other Victorians, but she did write 17 books in 21 years (too much perhaps by current standards). Her illness cannot make us ignore this fact. She appears to have been in life an example of the contrary states she explored in her novels: solid and shifting, male and female, a creature made up of fact and vision, subject to terror and ecstasy. (p. 12)

Claire Sprague, "Introduction" to Virginia Woolf: A Collection of Critical Essays *(copyright © 1971 by Prentice-Hall, Inc.; reprinted by permission of Prentice-Hall, Inc., Englewood Cliffs, New Jersey), Prentice-Hall, 1971, pp. 1-13.*

It was, I feel, a very happy idea to confine the selections from [Virginia Woolf's] diary to her reflections on her own career as a writer. Henry James in his notebooks, letters, and prefaces may have said more interesting things about literary technique, but I have never read any book that conveyed more truthfully what a writer's life is like, what are its worries, its rewards, its day-by-day routine. (p. 412)

Like every other writer, she was concerned about what particular kind of writer she was, and what her unique contribution could and should be. . . . What she felt and expressed with the most intense passion was a mystical, religious vision of life. . . . (p. 414)

What is unique about her work is the combination of this mystical vision with the sharpest possible sense for the concrete, even in its humblest form: "One can't," she observes, "write directly about the soul. Looked at, it vanishes; but look at the ceiling, at Grizzle, at the cheaper beasts in the Zoo which are exposed to walkers in Regent's Park, and the soul slips in." . . .

Though she took extraordinary pains over each book, she was a born spontaneous writer who never seems to have known periods when she was without a fresh idea; even while she was in the middle of writing one book, she got ideas for the next, and her output shows a greater variety than she is sometimes credited with. Each book set its particular problem and provoked in the author its particular psychosomatic reactions: "While I was forcing myself to do *Flush* my old headache came back—for the first time this autumn. Why should *The Pargiters* [*The Years*] make my heart jump; why should *Flush* stiffen the back of my neck?" (p. 415)

I do not know how Virginia Woolf is thought of by the younger literary generation; I do know that by my own, even in the palmiest days of social consciousness, she was admired and loved much more than she realized. I do not know if she is going to exert an influence on the future development of the novel—I rather suspect that her style and her vision were so unique that influence would only result in tame imitation—but I cannot imagine a time, however bleak, or a writer, whatever his school, when and for whom her devotion to her art, her industry, her severity with herself—above all, her passionate love, not only or chiefly for the big moments of life but also for its daily humdrum "sausage-and-haddock" details—will not remain an example that is at once an inspiration and a judge. (p. 417)

W. H. Auden, "A Consciousness of Reality," in his Forewords and Afterwords, *edited by Edward Mendelson (copyright © 1954 by W. H. Auden; reprinted by permission of Random House, Inc.), Random House, 1973, pp. 411-18.*

After James Joyce, whose *Ulysses*—with its plurality and parody of styles, its ironic juxtapositions of past and present, myth and realism, its use of stream-of-consciousness and other such 'spatial' modes—is the great classic in English of modernist perception, then Virginia Woolf's is probably the name we would next draw forth to show that English fiction after the First World War had a modernist phase. We have now come to take her as the imaginative contemporary of the great European and American modernists—Proust, Mann, Joyce, Faulkner—and as someone interested in the same kind of formal experiment, driven by the same kind of aesthetic aspiration. Her account of that aspiration, in her criticism and in the creative self-analysis of her *Writer's Diary,* has become a representative exploration of the modern artist's dilemmas and resources. We might name her thus with a certain caution, aware that Bloomsbury is not Montparnasse, that her sensibility can be private and shrill, that not all her books wear well, that her modern experience has a less extended social range than some of the other writers who embody modernism for us. Yet she is one of those writers who have disestablished something of the novel of the past and on those ruins built a new one, who visibly fought, on native grounds, the battle for new fictional modes arising from the challenges the novel had to face once James, Dostoevsky, Proust, and Joyce had written. (p. 121)

Once thing crucial to her importance is that she proposes a novel in which the devices of symbolist presentation become whole and entire, conditioning the total experience we read, and in which the characters live, the events occur. This is what Forster meant when he said she wrote by 'stretching out from her enchanted tree and snatching bits from the flux of daily life'. . . . But Virginia Woolf's novels, even the historical ones, dissipate, with varying degrees of success, the world of environment, the world of the socially conditioned, the notion of a life enacted through social forms and historical time; her books—at any rate her central ones, where she is best—substitute a prevailing state of consciousness, into and through which the world is filtered. (p. 122)

Like many of her successors in new fiction, [Virginia Woolf] was very much concerned in elaborating a new and commanding posture for the author; and, like them, she is a writer who not only patiently *embodies* a new aesthetic but is herself devotionally aesthetic, asserting the sovereignty of her own artistic sensibility and offering her art as a sequence of meanings and visions validated precisely *by* that sensibility. The sensibility itself was much shaped by a well-developed tribal body of assumptions about creative personal relationships and emotional states, and by the aesthetic upheaval that took place in Bloomsbury after the exhibition of Post-Impressionist paintings organized by Roger Fry in 1910 (a year Virginia Woolf regarded as the turning point into modern history). (p. 125)

To account for modernism's spirit in fiction, we must look not only to the novel's move towards a psychological-symbolist mode, but to the awareness, in those pursuing it, of the contingency of the universe from which a modern form must escape, in order to *be* a form. In this light, Virginia Woolf's mode is, for all the disturbance we know underlay it, an oddly joyous one. (p. 127)

Virginia Woolf moved, in her central fiction, into the realm of consciousness without being in a strict sense a psychological novelist, without concerning herself with psychic reasons, drives, archetypes, or 'unconscious' myths. Consciousness was a species of free action; and her new novel is nearer to being a reverie of the ego than an emanation of the id.

So, in short, for Virginia Woolf consciousness is intuitive and poetic rather than subterranean or mythopoeic; and hence it is the creative energy of the self which makes its own subjective time, its Bergsonian *durée,* out of the connective tissue linking the immediate moment with the past. . . . This is why Virginia Woolf's novels impress us not for their realism, not even their psychological realism, but for their sensibility. Only relatively is she interested in the psychological continuum, or the individual identity. The novel of consciousness affords the opportunity of a lyrical impressionism, a fiction of intensified sensitivity and fine sensations; and is rendered usually through a sensitive supraconciousness that works in association with the characters but which is the narrator's own, dominating and unifying the action. So, commonly in her novels, consciousness is permitted to shift not only temporally (backwards and forwards in time) and spatially (from this place to that) in the individual ego, but from character to character; while the characters often share a common focus in relation to an external symbol—like the lighthouse or the waves. Though the novelist remains in the same condition of immediate responsiveness as the characters, knowing little more than they, sharing their bewilderment and wonder, and though the events all remain essentially internal, the stream of consciousness is finally the emancipated associative flow of the novelist herself (who can function as an independent source of reflection in the absence of any character whatsoever, as in the 'Time Passes' interlude in *To the Lighthouse*). (pp. 128-29)

[Her] characters live between flux and pattern; and because the novels themselves are patterned and rhythmic she inevitably validates most of those characters who have an aesthetic and symbolist propensity of her own sort.

In so doing, she not only tends to poeticize modernism, but also to feminize and domesticate it. In *To the Lighthouse,* the male world is materialist, historicist, philosophical, public, a system of assessment and identity repudiated by the book, which celebrates the female world in which sensitivity, intuition, beauty, and domesticity unite. The men who 'negotiated treaties, ruled India, controlled finance' are excoriated and *protected* by sensibilities, notably Mrs. Ramsay's, attuned to higher matters, disdainful of the claims of history, abstract ideas, the materiality of things, all part of the 'fatal sterility' of the male. Because of this, the essential form of Virginia Woolf's novels, whatever the complexities of their pattern, is always finally that of the domestic novel of sensibility; and this limits the matter of consciousness with which she deals, too easily permits her states of 'rapture' and completeness. Her method, unlike that of Joyce or Forster, prescribes a large cutting away of much modern experience in the interests of keeping her fictional world intact.

To the Lighthouse is probably her best novel, but there is something unsolid and aloof about its achievement—as if its deliberated perfection of form cannot quite be substantiated through the materials of life with which the book must deal. Its two episodes, an evening and a morning ten years apart, split by an interlude which focuses those ten years of history into tiny parentheses, describe a world with Mrs. Ramsay in it and a world without her. Thematically, the book deals with a number of matters fundamental to Mrs.

Woolf's works: the relation of male to female, intellect to intuition, the difference between the isolation of pure thought and the social and humane quality of living, like Mrs. Ramsay, 'in beauty'. Mrs. Ramsay, a reconciling and invigorating force, is a unified sensibility.... With her beauty and her 'capacity to surround and protect', with her 'raptures of successful creation', Mrs. Ramsay is very much the book's centre; but that centre is removed midway. (pp. 130-31)

The world of the novel is scarcely penetrable from outside, by the real as opposed to the stylized contingencies of life. And as for the novel as a whole, that too is a total metaphor, shaped and fined, ending as it does with the last brush-stroke to Lily Briscoe's picture—in effect the signal for the total filling out of the composition. It ends *as* a composition, entire and of itself; while the flux may be the flux of consciousness, it moves inevitably towards a coherence, not of the human mind of the characters but of aesthetic composition. So pattern seems, finally, the pattern of art as artifice, and this limits the ultimate scale of Virginia Woolf's modernism. For all her registering of the evanescent, her work is on the one hand too crystalline and complete, on the other hand too dependent on her particular and personal sensibility, her self-conscious femininity, at times her quaintness and her whimsy, to be a guide for others. It is a peculiarly personal refinement of a tradition rather than the creation of a general style.

This, of course, does not limit her absorbing interest; but it does personalize it. Her sensitivity is infinitely rewarding; one re-reads her with pleasure. That should be enough—except that, precisely because of the rarity of the species, Virginia Woolf has not only become the great exemplar of the English experimental novel but, for a number of writers, an indicator of its limitations. Her own unease about her entire success in what she was doing, patent enough in *A Writer's Diary,* is evidence enough that in some ways this was a harsh sentence; while claiming to exemplify a new fiction, she had not thought to be the one and only proof of the pudding. But when writers of the thirties found the experimental novel bourgeois and private, and chose, as George Orwell had some sense of choosing, against it, it was largely Virginia Woolf they chose against, a fact that increased her guilt about what she was doing. And when in the 1950s, for different reasons, another generation of writers explicitly reacted against the experimental novel, it was not the novel of Proust they were reacting against (Snow and Cooper, for example, both greatly admired Proust) but the novel of Virginia Woolf and her few latter-day imitators. (pp. 132-33)

> *Malcolm Bradbury, in his* Possibilities: Essays on the State of the Novel *(copyright © Malcolm Bradbury 1973; reprinted by permission of Oxford University Press, Inc.),* Oxford University Press, 1973.

Like Joseph Conrad, Virginia Woolf values anything that art can salvage from a world that is "too dark altogether," yet like him too, she is careful not to make too large a claim: the darkness she depicts can never be dispelled. She is under no illusions that the resistance art can offer is tantamount to triumph, but even a stalemate is sufficient assurance for her of art's value in our lives. Here, I think, is where her chief importance lies for us today, both as an artist and as an aesthetician for modern practitioners of the

chaotic novel. In her, we may find hope for the future of a form currently in danger of being swallowed up by a vision that sees the futility of artistic control as the end rather than the beginning of a perpetual struggle.

In *To the Lighthouse,* Virginia Woolf handles chaos with such delicacy that the work seems almost too well-made to reflect her disturbing vision. Nevertheless, the balance between constructive and destructive forces is kept at such a teetering tension throughout, that the novel becomes an exciting, if subdued, contest between art and reality. If art's ultimate victory is tentative and precarious, it is still legitimate, for Virginia Woolf has not underestimated the power of her opponent. While her characterization of chaos lacks the terrifying aggressiveness accorded it by many contemporary writers, it is every bit as eerie, menacing, and devastating. Quietly seeping through the roots of our lives, it extirpates us quite as efficiently as much wilder forces, for it works from within *and* without. Like dusk descending slowly and silently, it settles over a scene until all forms become obliterated, and man himself is left a "wedge of darkness."

Because the darkness surrounding our lives originates in the pores of the human personality, we cannot say that it prevents us from knowing ourselves, but rather that this darkness is the deepest thing we *can* know about ourselves. (pp. 121-22)

By slipping in and out of her characters' minds, Virginia Woolf reveals all the subtle shifts in mood, idea, and response attesting to the fluidity of human consciousness; and her omniscient point of view enables her to define the remoteness of one mind from another with depressing clarity. (p. 122)

Though words are always inadequate conveyors of one's feelings, communication based on shared sympathies is always possible. When relationships are working well, silence will always transcend speech in eloquence of expression and exactness of thought.

The chaos emanating from within the human personality may, then, restrict self-knowledge and hamper relationships, but shared instinctive feelings can mitigate, if not overcome, the difficulty of having to live and love in such a world. Still, our lives are far more complicated than inner chaos alone would make them; to consider the other half of Virginia Woolf's vision, we must recognize the existence of outer chaos as well, which constantly undermines any order we may try to impose on the universe. This outer chaos is as quiet and invisible as the wedge of darkness at the core of our selves, but its presence is the most distressing fact of our existence because it denies everything we want to affirm, negates the value of our lives, and crushes out meaning with shocking swiftness. (p. 124)

Time is one important component of chaos because it gnaws away at our sense of stability, suggesting how little we can hope to know about life when the most that can be known in one lifetime is worth virtually nothing over the ages which will cover and forget us, bury our bodies and our knowledge as effectively as if we had never existed at all....

Another aspect of the outer chaos threatening us is the fluidity of the universe, which constantly undermines our sense of structure and security. For a human being to feel unanchored in the general drift of life is intolerable. (p. 125)

[In *To the Lighthouse,* the] tenuousness of man's significance is felt keenly as Mrs. Ramsay, her daughter, and her son die in parentheses—victims of time, chance, and the general entropic drive of the universe. As the darkness eats away at the products of a man's life in bigger and bigger gulps, both people and things sink into the chaos with remarkable impartiality. Man's values, dreams and creations are swept off into the chaotic flood which renders them inconsequential and meaningless, while his philosophical, moral, social, and spiritual systems are wiped out as so much presumption. Using Nature and Time as its primary instruments, the dark forces of chaos dominate, then demolish all the order man has brought to his uncertain life. . . . (p. 126)

It is obvious that for Virginia Woolf, art represents the ultimate resistance of the mind to the disordered life around us. . . . By facing squarely the aspects of chaos which threaten our security, art attempts to rescue for our benefit what the darkness is continually trying to remove. Thus, we see how the natural pull toward oblivion is met by the artist's struggle to pin down time and make it memorable; the tug toward fluidity is stayed by the permanence of the written word or painted line; the progress of decay is resisted by the vision which unifies and endures. The suction of natural things into a whirlpool of disarray is arrested by the imposition of aesthetic order which freezes reality; and the impulse of nature toward disintegration into unidentifiable atoms is thwarted by the unifying process of creativity.

The struggle of art against chaos is, then, a constant, agonizing, and intense one—infinitely exhausting, yet never futile. To shine a beam of light into the darkness and locate a truth which may be solidified into vision demands all of man's willpower and energy, but the war must be fought before man can ever satisfy his need for meaning. (p. 128)

The fact that chaos can be shaped to yield meaning does not imply, however, that the chaos itself is only an illusion; *its* inexplicability cannot be contested without gross falsification, and as a result, we must make sure that the process of formalizing never becomes too representational. That would constitute artifice rather than art, because as soon as chaos becomes defined, it disappears; and as soon as it disappears, we have a false sense of knowledge which leads us away from truth, rather than toward it. Chaos remains the reality behind appearances, *not* simply another appearance. Objectification is crucial, therefore, for *rendering* chaos only: it should not work to dispel it. This is probably the reasoning behind Lily's abstract method of painting [in *To the Lighthouse*], for a valid aesthetic principle must be an outgrowth of vision, and Lily's vision is one that acknowledges the reality of chaos, even while seeking to defeat it. (p. 130)

Virginia Woolf's concept of reality is introduced in the very title of the book, which emphasizes not the Lighthouse itself, but the movement toward it, producing an accumulation of multiple relative meanings as we watch it refracted through a succession of different perspectives and points of view. This mode of presentation characterizes every person, scene, and object that we encounter in the novel, and becomes ultimately the only way we can approach its reality. (pp. 133-34)

Action is unimportant in the writing of Virginia Woolf because the movement of our bodies cannot change our reali-

ties; these are created, changed, and carried exclusively in the mind. In a world of flux, every perception is relative to all the conditions converging at that instant to produce a particular impression in the imagination which alone constitutes its apprehension of reality at that moment. It is in our mental processes that we live out our lives. And there is no ultimate truth to be discovered, only a progression of perspectives to be held simultaneously in the mind. (p. 135)

Since chaos is a *mental* reality, it is the mind, too, which must struggle to provide relief through proper discipline of its own impulses toward order. Reality can be fixed only when the mind can concentrate on a focal point which gathers to it all the lines of diverse energies usually running rampant. Ordinary moments are characterized by parallel lines of thought which never converge, but move independently in separate spheres. (p. 136)

It is no coincidence that [Lily's] vision crystallizes immediately after she has been contemplating the Lighthouse, for it is only then that she deliberates on how to make the parts of her painting coalesce. . . . Like the jar that Wallace Stevens places in Tennessee, the Lighthouse becomes an organizing principle in a sea of chaos. Lily herself has not yet seen it this way, but she does make the decision to move the tree into the middle of her picture, thereby showing an as yet unconscious awareness of the principle: the particular object being placed in the center is an arbitrary choice, but once that object becomes the central focus, everything immediately gathers around it and becomes ordered. (pp. 138-39)

And Virginia Woolf works in exactly the same way: because she has rendered chaos so effectively as a major, ubiquitous element of reality, she must allow her reader, as she has her characters, an axis to keep the centrifugal forces from spinning out of control. This the reader finally finds in Lily herself, for her perception becomes the fundamental organizing principle to which the rest of the novel for us, and completes its experience as a meaningful investigation of reality. (pp. 139-40)

[But] artistic triumph is never anything more than temporary relief from the struggle which defines the sensitive life. There is no more touching testimonial to this depressing truth than Virginia Woolf's own death: walking into the sea, she finally found the only possible permanent relief by submerging herself in the chaos which closed over her at last, drowning out anguish, fatigue, and life itself. (p. 140)

> *Alvin J. Seltzer, "The Tension of Stalemate: Art and Chaos in Virginia Woolf's 'To the Lighthouse'," in his* Chaos in the Novel: The Novel in Chaos *(copyright © 1974 by Schocken Books Inc.), Schocken, 1974, pp. 120-40.*

The history of androgyny is one of eloquent but at times conflicting statements, and Woolf's place in that history is important because her work is the basis of many contemporary definitions. Critics of Virginia Woolf recognize androgyny's centrality to her theory and practice. . . . (p. 433)

Woolf . . . establishes the validity and uniqueness of women's literature. The woman writer has not written long sentimental phrases which in maturity she will throw away for the tough, analytic style and ideas of Gibbon and Johnson; rather, her uniqueness comes from the experience of living thousands of years in houses which have shaped her mind and her sentences. It is crucial that Woolf establishes this uniqueness, for it is the basis from which to develop a dialectical theory of androgyny. When she introduces androgyny . . . , she first visualizes the human soul balanced by male and female elements, both valid, both sustaining, both necessary. Like the literary styles, which have male and female sentences to express different experiences, and like literary traditions—which on one side may develop the epic and on the other the stream-of-consciousness novel— Woolf's two sides of the soul exist separately but in harmony and in close relationship. . . .

At first this definition is not an attempt to fuse the valid and independent natures into one asexual nature. Woolf initially seems to consider the androgynous mind bisexual, one that is basically male or female but in the process of freeing itself has experienced the other side of reality. The mind, thus, is not forced into a rigid stereotype but is allowed to roam the spectrum of experience and perception. The female side of the soul which has intercourse with the male side will not be boxed in by conventions which force it to respond in only one way; rather, by experiencing that which is opposite but complementary, the female side of the soul will be qualified by its complement.

But Woolf does not explore the potential of her initial statement on androgyny. Instead, she steps back and withdraws to adopt the more traditional version. (pp. 446-47)

If one looks carefully at her concern for objectivity, one can detect the influence of T. S. Eliot's theories of impersonality and unification of sensibility. Out of the fear which she exhibits in her diary [Farwell refers to an earlier quotation in her essay], Woolf feels that she is being too partisan in defending women, and instead of developing a theory of androgyny based on a belief in uniqueness of the individual parts of the whole, she succumbs to the pressure of her peers who are advocating a theory of objectivity in art. . . .

The obsession with unity was highly characteristic of the generation following World War I, an obsession which was both aesthetic and religious. Eliot insisted on the standard of a unification of sensibility that would bind together the thought and feeling which were separated under the influence of the Romantic theories. (p. 448)

This concept of unity is easily translatable into androgyny, and it is this version of unity which I believe Virginia Woolf adopts for her concept. Woolf, too, is obsessed with the idea of unity, and when she falls under these theories of art, androgyny is defined by fusion rather than balance. (p. 450)

With tongue in cheek [Woolf] argues that women should forget their grievances, their unique perceptions, and separate themselves from themselves and their works of art. Thus, while she consciously argues for androgyny in terms that will be accepted by her male peers, she, like Galileo, seems to whisper a rebuttal. While we are left with an ambivalent and limited concept of androgyny, we are also given the tools to go beyond that.

Like so many women writers wanting to write from their own experiences yet knowing well that men will be the final arbiters of their work, Virginia Woolf did not pursue some of her more radical insights into the writings of women. If she had, she would probably have outlined a much more comprehensive theory of androgyny, one which would have

acknowledged the individual differences of women and men but insisted on the validity and interdependence of each. As it is, Woolf withdrew from the implications of that move and spoke of androgyny in the traditional terms which equated the male with the universal. (p. 451)

Marilyn R. Farwell, "Virginia Woolf and Androgyny," in Contemporary Literature *(© 1975 by the Board of Regents of the University of Wisconsin System), Vol. 16, No. 4, Autumn, 1975, pp. 433-51.*

True humor is sanity itself, indeed a kind of exaggeration of sanity. One service which the publication of *Freshwater* does the reader is to show how art in Virginia Woolf can achieve this kind of humor, as in the transformation of her family in *To the Lighthouse*—and yet how inimical to her art was Bloomsburian gaiety—"we all talk at once and make such brilliant jokes as never was seen"—however much she may have thrown herself into it. *Orlando,* "the holiday escapade," was, she tells us, the result of "wanting fun, wanting fantasy." The result is a painful artificiality which reveals how different is the depth and naturalness in her masterpieces, even in her first and in some ways never surpassed novel *The Voyage Out,* when the striven-for settles out into the assured, the timeless, and the achieved. *Freshwater* is on a much less satisfactory level of send-up even than *Orlando,* and has the same coy breathlessness of time and place. . . .

The writing in both is almost deliberately arch, as if Virginia Woolf was both pleasuring herself with the sense of an in-joke, and sending it up, with the kind of malign detachment that lived somewhere at the back of her need to be made much of by the Group, and share in their self-approving gaiety.

Ske knew—none better—what form bad writing took, for herself as for others. . . . Escapades like *Orlando* and *Freshwater* draw . . . attention to the weakness of her own style, as though it was parodying itself. And she could not do this in a relaxed way, could not laugh at herself as those despised Victorians, Tennyson and Swinburne, could do: behind the gaiety is something like self-hatred, the frenzy of despair that was never far away. . . . [In these works] Virginia Woolf seeks in a self-damaging way to imitate and to identify with the self-congratulations of Bloomsbury; in her great novels she finds "a new and definite reality."

But one does not want to be too priggish about *Freshwater.* It has interest. Though the "fun" has evaporated, together with the family jokes, there remain some curiosities, even beauties. (p. 3)

When we first read *The Voyage Out, To the Lighthouse,* or *The Waves,* which should be before the age of twenty-five or so, we are not conscious of a complete personality at work in them or behind them, just as we are not when we read Shelley for the first time. They belong to the world of poetry rather than prose, and Rachel Vinrace, the heroine of *The Voyage Out,* has much of the purely visionary quality of Alastor, or of the heroine of Philip Larkin's extended prose-poem, *A Girl in Winter.* She does in fact have all the stuff of the novel about her, what Edith Wharton called the fringes we trail round with us through life, and yet she appears not to have: she inhabits an Elsewhere, the world where the waves are ceaselessly breaking like glass on the rocks below the lighthouse; where Mrs. Dalloway draws her needle through the green silk, and Rhoda rocks the petals in her basin.

Virginia Woolf herself did not of course live there, though the image of it and the struggle to realize the vision in her books was her greatest protection against madness. (p. 4)

John Bayley, "Cinderella in Reverse," in The New York Review of Books *(reprinted with permission from* The New York Review of Books; *copyright © 1976 NYREV, Inc.), July 15, 1976, pp. 3-4.*

William Butler Yeats

1865-1939

Irish poet, playwright, essayist, and autobiographer. Although he wrote distinguished work in other genres, it is as a poet that William Butler Yeats takes his place as a major figure in English literature. His is a rich and full poetry, a poetry replete with parodox, brimming with symbolic and mythologic allusions, and philosophical inquiry. Faced with a talent of such magnitude and variety, a brief summation is difficult if not unwise. Suffice it to say that Yeats is a poet whose later poetry was greater than his earlier; whose frequent subjects were love, politics, and philosophy; and who conceived of his poetry as part of a search for a philosophic and aesthetic system that would resolve the conflict between art and nature. He was born in Dublin, the eldest child of John Butler Yeats, a lawyer who gave up a moderately lucrative law practice to become an artist. Yeats spent his youth in Dublin, London, and Sligo, a port town, his mother's former home. The latter setting would be used in his earlier poetry. In 1887 he returned to London where he wrote for the *Yellow Book,* established important literary friendships, and became involved with Theosophy. His first volume of poetry was published in 1889. Yeats met and fell in love with Maud Gonne, a beautiful and fiery actress and Irish nationalist. She was the subject of most of his love poems and he pursued her, vainly, for two decades. In 1903 she abruptly married an Irish soldier; the marriage did not last and Yeats continued his pursuit. The nationalism that for Maud Gonne had a political outlet found a literary outlet in Yeats. He returned to Ireland in 1896 and became leader of the Irish renaissance in literature, establishing with Lady Gregory, Synge, AE, George Moore, and others the Irish Literary Theatre which became the Abbey Theatre of Dublin. Reacting against naturalism in drama and wanting to restore lyric drama to popularity, he wrote several plays for the Abbey. In 1917, after proposing to Maud Gonne and her daughter as well, and being rejected by both, he married Georgie Hyde-Lees, a spiritualist. From their joint experiment in spiritualism and automatic writing came *A Vision,* which set forth a cyclical theory of history. Yeats became a senator of the new Irish Free State in 1923, the same year that he was awarded the Nobel Prize in Literature.

PRINCIPAL WORKS

The Wanderings of Oisin, and Other Poems (poetry) 1889
The Countess Kathleen (drama) 1892

The Celtic Twilight (short stories) 1893
The Land of Heart's Desire (drama) 1894
Collected Poems (poetry) 1895
The Wind among the Reeds (poetry) 1899
The Shadowy Waters (drama) 1900
Cathleen ni Houlihan (drama) 1902
The Hour Glass (drama) 1903
Ideas of Good and Evil (essays) 1903
In the Seven Woods (poetry) 1903
The King's Threshold (drama) 1904
The Pot of Broth (drama) 1904
Stories of Red Hanrahan (short stories) 1904
Deirdre (drama) 1907
Discoveries (essays) 1907
Poetry and Ireland (essays) 1908
The Unicorn from the Stars, and Other Plays [with Lady Gregory] (drama) 1908
The Green Helmet, and Other Poems (poetry) 1910
Plays for an Irish Theatre (drama) 1911
Reveries over Childhood and Youth (memoir) 1915
Responsibilities, and Other Poems (poetry) 1916
The Wild Swans at Coole (poetry) 1917
Michael Robartes and the Dancer (poetry) 1920
Four Plays for Dancers (drama) 1921
Four Years (memoir) 1921
Later Poems (poetry) 1922
The Trembling of the Veil (memoir) 1922
The Cat and the Moon and Certain Poems (poetry) 1924
A Vision (essay) 1925
Autobiographies (memoir) 1926
Estrangement (memoir) 1926
The Tower (poetry) 1928
The Winding Stair (poetry) 1929
Words for Music Perhaps, and Other Poems (poetry) 1932
The King of the Great Clock Tower (poetry) 1934
Wheels and Butterflies (drama) 1934
Dramatis Personae (memoir) 1935
A Full Moon in March (poetry) 1935
The Herne's Egg (drama) 1938
New Poems (poetry) 1938
Last Poems and Plays (poetry and drama) 1940

In one of his books, [Mr. Yeats] writes that life seems to

him to be a preparation for something that never happens; and the quality of his voice suggests that thwarted desire which is expressed in so much of his work. He is, in poetry, what Mr. Galsworthy is, in fiction: he surrenders to life. I do not know of any one who can speak verse so beautifully and yet so depressingly as he can. The very great beauty that is in all his work does not stir you: it saddens you. There is no sunrise in his writing: there is only sunset. In his lyrics, there is the cadence of fatigue and of the lethargy that comes partly from disappointment, partly from loneliness, partly from doubt, and partly from inertia. "Innisfree," the beauty of which has not been diminished by familiarity, does not sound glad: it sounds tired. . . . One reads the beautiful poem in the sure and certain belief that Mr. Yeats will not "arise and go now, and go to Innisfree," but that he will remain where he is. There is no impulse or movement in the poem: there is only a passive wish and a plaintive resignation. (p. 272)

I am moved by the beauty of his work and distracted by its vagueness. I find in his writing and in his speech, great spiritual loveliness but curiously little humanity, and I have often wondered why it is that while Irishmen, even such as I am, are deeply moved by his little play, "Kathleen ni Houlihan," men of other countries—not only Englishmen—are left unmoved by it, unable, without a note in the program, to understand it. I have seen this play performed very many times. . . . It moved me as much when I last saw it as it did when I first saw it; and I do not doubt that if I live to be an old man, it will move me as much in my old age as it has moved me in my youth. But it does not move men of other races. That is a singular thing. It denotes, I suppose, that while there is much that is national in Mr. Yeats's work, there is less that is universal.

One rises from his work, as one comes from his company, with a feeling of chilled respect that may settle into disappointment. It is as if one had been taken into a richly-decorated drawingroom when one had hoped to be taken into a green field. . . . Mr. Yeats writes about things that he thinks; and thought changes and perishes, but feeling is permanent and unchangeable; thought separates and divides men, but feeling brings them together; and it may be that Mr. Yeats's aloofness from men is due to the fact that he thinks too much and feels too little. (pp. 297-99)

He is, so far as I am aware, the only English-speaking poet who did not write a poem about the War, a fact which is at once significant of the restraint he imposes upon himself and of his isolation from the common life of his time. I have never met any one who seems so unaware of temporary affairs as Mr. Yeats, and this unawareness is due, not to affectation, but to sheer lack of interest. He probably would not have known of the War at all had not the Germans dropped a bomb near his lodgings off the Euston Road. (p. 299)

The sense of age seems to have oppressed his mind for many years, perhaps for the whole of his creative life. He feels that he has outlived his generation and is lost in a period of time peculiarly alien to him. (p. 300)

Mr. Yeats is the greatest poet that Ireland has produced, but he has meant very little to the people of Ireland, for he has forgotten the ancient purpose of the bards, to urge men to a higher destiny by reminding them of their high origin, and has lived, aloof and disdainful, as far from human kind as he can conveniently get. (p. 305)

St. John G. Ervine, "W. B. Yeats" (originally published in a slightly different version in North American Review, *February, 1920 and March, 1920), in his* Some Impressions of My Elders *(reprinted by permission of The Society of Authors as the literary representatives of St. John Ervine; © 1922 by St. John G. Ervine), Macmillan, 1922, pp. 264-305.*

Mr. Yeats's "Later Poems" contains all the poems which Mr. Yeats wrote between his twenty-seventh year and 1921. The book, therefore, is a companion to the old volume of collected "Poems." (p. 160)

The book is anything but a duplicate of its predecessor, or even a twin. Mr. Yeats's poetry is other than it was. . . . The change has happened: still, in many essentials Mr. Yeats has not changed. His preoccupation with religion remains. His attitude towards civilisation is what it has always been. . . . [He] still, and in his poetry, stands for two cultures and two traditions, the aristocratic scholarly and the popular, both sustained by ceremony and fed by the free imagination; he has always cared about the world and Ireland and has not changed his opinions about their diseases.

Nor has the rigour of his artistic ideals altered. . . . He is the same man and the same artist; but he has developed. He has turned his attention from one thing to another; change has come from unchanging curiosity, certain faculties have matured and certain propensities diminished in consequence of a natural and normal passage from youth to middle age. Yet the integrity of the artist and the thinker remains unimpaired. In his writings all the important part of his spiritual and intellectual history is candidly and fascinatingly displayed and may be followed with—in both senses—admiration. (pp. 162-63)

The embroideries have gone, and, for the most part, even the allusions to old myths. And not only in this sense is there a new nakedness. Quite clearly Mr. Yeats, with labour as great as ever, has been aiming at bareness of statement, directness and economy of language and movement springing from the commoner rhythms of speech. He never could be called flowery; but he had certain poetical properties, less familiar when he began using them than when he finished, and his earlier music, as compared with his later, was obviously elaborate. Something has gone, but if one magic has been lost another has been gained; there is a deeper if less immediately enchanting music, the starkness of the language has a charm of its own, the thought is bolder and more clear cut, the pictures more definite and only requiring attention to become invested with a glamour not ready-made. (pp. 165-66)

He has deepened, and, in the best sense, hardened. Mr. Yeats will still be found often obscure by the running reader; but his obscurity now is never chargeable to what used to be called Celticism, to vague hinting or the auto-intoxication of a singer with a beautiful voice. Now he may be dark but is never dim. If he is hard at first sight to understand it is because he compresses overmuch, or because he gives us an allegory to which we fail to find the key, or because, with whatever exactitude, he is conducting an argument so subtle or recording a process so finely analysed that the reader who wishes to share it must make an intellectual effort on his own part. (p. 167)

Mr. Yeats is, of course, not always remote from the general reader; and a large proportion of those poems of his which he himself would consider his best are amongst his simplest and clearest, in conception and expression. Nevertheless, he is on the whole to be ranked with the learned and the intellectual poets, the cryptic and the hierophantic, the philosophers who explore strange regions of thought, the contemplatives who burrow into the recesses of the mind, the questioners who accept nothing which they have not closely examined, the scholars who make references of which the savour is reserved for those equal in knowledge, the experimentalists who are not satisfied with anything ready made in picture or rhythm, the craftsmen who labour for a perfection the nature of which few will comprehend. (p. 169)

J. C. Squire, "Mr. W. B. Yeats's Later Verse," in his Essays on Poetry, *Hodder and Stoughton Limited, 1923, pp. 160-70.*

If we do not ordinarily think of Yeats as primarily a Symbolist poet, it is because, in taking Symbolism to Ireland, he fed it with new resources and gave it a special accent which lead us to think of his poetry from the point of view of its national qualities rather than from the point of view of its relation to the rest of European literature. (p. 26)

Yeats found in Irish mythology, unfamiliar even to Irish readers, and in itself rather cloudy and vague, a treasury of symbols ready to his hand. He had thus perhaps a special advantage. The Danaan children, the Shadowy Horses and Fergus with his brazen cars—those mysterious and magical beings who play so large a part in Yeats's verse—have little more objective reality than the images of Mallarmé: they are the elements and the moods of Yeats's complex sensibility. But they have a more satisfactory character than such a French Symbolist mythology as Mallarmé's . . . because they constitute a world of which one can to some extent get the hang, where one can at least partly find one's way about. (p. 28)

Yeats's fairyland has become a symbol for the imagination itself. The world of the imagination is shown us in Yeats's early poetry as something infinitely delightful, infinitely seductive, as something to which one becomes addicted, with which one becomes delirious and drunken—and as something which is somehow imcompatible with, and fatal to, the good life of that actual world which is so full of weeping and from which it is so sweet to withdraw. (p. 30)

In Yeats, we find the aestheticism of Pater carried through to its consequences. What *is* the consequence of living for beauty, as beauty was then understood, of cultivating the imagination, the enjoyment of aesthetic sensations, as a supreme end in itself? We shall be thrown fatally out of key with reality—we shall incur penalties which are not to be taken lightly. There is a conflict here which cannot be evaded; and Yeats, even in his earliest period, is unceasingly aware of this conflict. But still he prefers to dwell most of the time in fairyland. . . . He would even transport his human love, his human desire, into the climate of that immortal world, where nothing that is ugly can jar and where nothing that is beautiful fades. . . . (p. 34)

With the development of [his] maturer style, it became impossible any longer to regard Yeats merely as one of the best of the English lyric poets of the nineties. The author of "The Lake of Innisfree," which had so delighted Robert

Louis Stevenson, had grown, in an interval of ten years during which nobody outside of Ireland had apparently paid much attention to him, to the unmistakable stature of a master. No other poet writing English in our time has been able to deal with supreme artistic success with such interesting and such varied experience. No other writer has been able to sustain the traditional grand manner of the poet with so little effect of self-consciousness. (p. 38)

Yeats, in his . . . dramatic works, has produced a theatre somewhat similar to Maeterlinck's. The productions of a greater poet, equipped with a richer and more solid mythology, these plays do, however, take place in the same sort of twilit world as Maeterlinck's—a world in which the characters are less often dramatic personalities than disembodied broodings and longings. Yeats's plays have little dramatic importance because Yeats himself has little sense of drama, and we think of them primarily as a department of his poetry, with the same sort of interest and beauty as the rest. (p. 42)

Yeat's prose, in its beginnings, when he is most under the influence of the Pre-Raphaelites and Pater, is a little self-consciously archaic—it has a Renaissance elaborateness and pomposity; and it is a little too close to the language of poetry—the meaning is often clotted by metaphor. But Yeats's prose, like his verse, has, with time, undergone a discipline and emerged with a clearer outline. Yeats is today a master of prose as well as a great poet. (p. 44)

Yeats has achieved [in *The Trembling of the Veil*] a combination of grandeur with a certain pungency and homeliness which recalls the more lightly and swiftly moving writers of the seventeenth century rather than the more heavily upholstered ones of the earlier Renaissance. The prose of Yeats, in our contemporary literature, is like the product of some dying loomcraft brought to perfection in the days before machinery. (p. 45)

Where the early Yeats had studied Irish folk-lore, collected and sorted Irish fairy tales, invented fairy tales for himself, the later Yeats worked out from the mediumistic communications of his wife the twenty-eight phases of the human personality and the transformations of the soul after death. Yeats's sense of reality to-day is inferior to that of no man alive—indeed, his greatness is partly due precisely to the vividness of that sense. In his poetry, in his criticism and in his memoirs, it is the world we all live in with which we are confronted—the world we know, with all its frustrations, its defeats, its antagonisms and its errors—the mind that sees is not naïve, as the heart that feels is not insensitive. (p. 58)

Edmund Wilson, "W. B. Yeats," in his Axel's Castle: A Study in the Imaginative Literature of 1870-1930 *(reprinted by permission of Charles Scribner's; © 1931 by Charles Scribner's Sons), Scribner's, 1931, pp. 26-63.*

[Yeats] is a striking example of a man whose poetic development has been from the one way of writing to the other, of a man who has tried to move from a partial to a complete way of looking at the experience he is putting into words. This change, and the success with which he has brought it about, is one of the reasons why his later poetry is so interesting, and is one of the facts which justify the assertion that Yeats is the greatest of living English poets. (p. 272)

The minor poets of the eighteenth century had a chilly poetic diction which hampered clarity, and the minor poets of the '90's had little clarity because they used a poetic diction which, one is tempted to say, was too warm. Closely connected with this, and in fact inseparable from it, they had a languorous and evasive habit of feeling, which is as dangerous to good writing as it is difficult to get rid of. What makes Yeats so worthy of admiration is that he did get rid of it. He tells us, in his *Autobiographies,* how, by sleeping upon a board (or at least by thinking of sleeping upon a board), by making his rhythms "faint and nervous," by contemplating the Dantesque image, by changing his subject matter and his vocabulary, he struggled to make his poems bare and clear, and expressive of the whole man. . . . His "quarrel with himself," to use his own phrase, has made Yeats a great poet. (pp. 272-73)

It is, of course, an over-simplification of the truth to say that Yeats has entirely turned from one way of writing to the other. He has not lost, he has enriched and perfected, the sensitive rhythms which were at the beginning the best thing about his style. What has happened is that Yeats has taught himself to give the exactly right, and hence unsentimentalized, emotional tone to what he wants to say. . . . Few poets have had more difficulties to escape from, more veils of unreality to break through—or, to change the metaphor, more intangible vapors to condense into solids—than Yeats. The late Romanticism of the '90's, Irish super-nationalism, the use of occult symbols, reliance upon a private metaphysical system; any one of these might have been the ruin of a lesser talent. But Yeats, in spite of what at times seemed unavoidable disaster, has triumphantly survived. Perhaps a life of action, and the anger it has sometimes generated—anger is an excellent emotion, if aimed at the right things, for a poet to cultivate—has helped to put iron into his style. (p. 273)

[There] is no better example of Yeats' genius than the way in which he chooses his refrains to give [a] double effect; it was essential to find the right words, and in nearly every poem, Yeats has found them. In his use of this device, as in everything else, we find the later Yeats making his poems a reflection of a complete experience, not of a discrete layer of experience only. (p. 277)

[What] is significant about [the] later poems is that the substitution, to use Yeats own description, of "sound for sense and ornament for thought," which was the fault of his early style, has given place to vigor and toughness, to a style where thought is substance and not accident, and which is able to communicate, in an entirely individual way, important emotions. (p. 279)

[Yeats' poetry] does not . . . abandon logic; it springs from a deeper well than mere logic ever swam in, and its coherence is far from "factitious." Even if we may sometimes feel that an individual poem is not entirely successful, the great majority of these poems do not grow commonplace with familiarity, nor are they easily forgotten. On the contrary they sing into the memory, and we feel, after contemplating them, that Yeats did himself no more than justice when he once wrote:

> There is not a fool can call me friend,
> And I may dine at journey's end
> With Landor and with Donne.

(pp. 280-81)

Theodore Spencer, "The Later Poetry of W. B. Yeats" (originally published in The Hound and Horn, *October-December, 1933), in* Literary Opinion in America, *Volume I, edited by Morton Dauwen Zabel (copyright © 1937, 1951, 1962 by Harper & Row, Publishers, Inc.; reprinted by permission of Harper & Row, Publishers, Inc.), revised edition, Harper, 1962, pp. 270-81.*

In this great poet's veins poetry grew like a rose, unfolding its dark secrets within his blood, colouring his veins with the beauty and richness of its nature.

With Mr. Yeats, poetry meant no escape from life; poetry *was* life—it was action as much as dream—and dream was a part of life, a refreshment, and a re-flowering. He believed in the unity of all lives. . . . (p. 75)

His genius is Belief that has found its natural form in a perfect proportion of beauty, unstained by Time, since Time has brought only its peacefulness, not its darkness, to this beauty. Here, indeed, we have one on whom the shadows of much earthly loveliness have fallen, and who has known the radiance of eternity and the wisdom that lies hidden in the heart of darkness. (p. 76)

Few artists can have given us so complete a record of the life of their soul—a record which is clothed in reticence and moves with a supreme dignity—as that given us by Mr. Yeats in his "Autobiographies" and the "Essays." . . .

The search for wisdom, the thirst for God—the dedication of his poetry, pure and impassioned, and flawless in its melodic line, to the ideal that ruled his life—we may find this record of the search for the Grail in "Autobiographies." (p. 82)

His poetry is a universal poetry, that speaks to all men, although his voice is that of the sea-cliffs of Ireland, of the sedge of the lakes of Ireland. . . . His voice is an Irish voice, but it speaks of a universal wisdom that existed in the beginning of things; and that wisdom was sought in many ways and on many paths. . . . (p. 83)

Edith Sitwell, "William Butler Yeats," in her Aspects of Modern Poetry, *Duckworth, 1934 (and reprinted by Books for Libraries Press, Inc., 1970), pp. 73-89.*

Yeats's attitude to what he calls the 'Tragic Generation,' the generation of *The Yellow Book* and the Rhymers' Club, was that of one who felt that their destiny was his own, and who yet felt dissatisfied with them and critical. The central point of his criticism was what involved him most deeply in his own work: the relation of their emotional, unbalanced lives to their accomplished, trance-like poetry. (p. 119)

He took his tradition, not so much from books (as he had at first imagined he should do), as from the lives of those people who created his cultural environment, and whose lives presented a picture of civilization to him in its most vivid form. Their lives, deeply rooted in the lives of their ancestors, saturate his later poetry; especially the poetry of *The Tower.* I only wish sometimes that he had allowed his interest to extend still further, outside the immediate circle of his friends, into the social life that surrounded him.

I believe that what distinguished Yeats from those other writers is not so much—as Dr. Leavis has said—his power of self-criticism, as his realism. He is far too rhetorical a writer to be self-critical. It is clear from the style of his prose that he must constantly be presenting himself to himself in a dramatic manner; and his conversation gives the same impression. He is capable, because he has the highest intelligence, and because his rhetoric is not the rhetoric of the politician, of passionate seriousness, of penitence, and of an almost excessive sense of responsibility. (p. 120)

Yeats was strengthened in his attitude to the life around him by certain of his intellectual experiences. The chief of these were the three influences of the Irish Literary Renaissance, Magic and Symbolism, and his interest in contemporary politics, which seem in the last years to have broadened into a prophetic concern (which resembles that of Stefan George, during and after the war) with the destiny of Europe. (p. 121)

Yeats is a poet who, finding himself in a desperate situation, has buttressed and shored up his work—as though it were, perhaps, his ancestral Tower—on every side. The reader is at every stage perplexed. First, he imagines that all is to be mystery and twilight and that he dare hardly listen, he must be so silent, for fear lest he disturb the fairies. To his disappointment he hears the fairy song grow fainter and fainter, until it disappears over the crest of the twilit hill. But Yeats has not disappeared. On the contrary, the reader now discovers that the fairies were only a part of a theory that by writing about them one could create a popular Irish ballad poetry. The fairies then merge into a theory of magic: but the magic, although much talked of, and although the poet never fails to produce a hush-hush solemn atmosphere, seems always to be something of a hoax. It has an element in it of spiritualist séances attended by a journalist, in order that he may broadcast his impressions of them.

In the first place, Yeats's attitude to magical events seems always to be that of a doctor instead of a witch doctor, and, in the second place, his poetry is only magical in the sense that he can produce a certain atmosphere. Yeats has written plenty of romantic poetry, plenty of obscure poetry, some nonsense, and much mystification, but nothing which one could say was magical. Nothing, for instance, which has the magical quality of Eliot's poem, *The Hollow Men*. (pp. 127-28)

What one admires in Yeats's poetry is, in fact, not its mystery, its magic or even its atmosphere: but its passion, its humanity, its occasional marvellous lucidity, its technical mastery, its integrity, its strength, its reality and its opportunism.

Why, then, is this romantic facade at all necessary? Or, since it exists, why does it not falsify the whole effect? The answer is that Yeats's poetry is devoid of any unifying moral subject, and it develops in a perpetual search for one. Although he has much wisdom, he offers no philosophy of life, but, as a substitute, a magical system, which, where it does not seem rhetorical, is psycho-analytic, but not socially constructive. Reverent as he is, he does not convey any religion; instead, we are offered, in such poems as *Prayer for my Daughter*, an aristocratic faith. (pp. 128-29)

Yeats has found, as yet, no subject of moral significance in the social life of his time. Instead of a subject, he offers us magnificent and lively *rapportage* about his friends. The only exception is in the poem called *The Second Coming*. (p. 131)

Stephen Spender, "Yeats as a Realist," in his The Destructive Element, *Jonathan Cape Ltd., 1935 (and reprinted by Jonathan Cape, 1938), pp. 115-31.*

[Yeats's] later poetry is . . . the *emotion* of the Poet as Poet (in the romantic sense) when faced with modern times, when forced to exist and to practice his art in the circumstances of the last forty years. If every generalization is bound to omit or to distort, and if this must be especially so of a generalization about the work of a poet, yet, in terms of this emphasis, the nature of the shift from the early to the later style becomes entirely plain. Yeats shifted from the effort to write the "poetic" poetry of the nineties to the concern, as poet, with what it was to be a poet amid the alien circumstances of his age. That is why he is so often, in his later poetry, writing about the artists, scholars, and beautiful women he has known, and their unfortunate lives. And that is perhaps why the unknown instructors or spirits who dictated a supernatural system to him through the mediumship of his wife, and prompted Yeats to offer to use the rest of his life explicating what had been dictated, rejected his offer, saying: "No, we have come to give you metaphors for poetry." Those spirits, it is certain, recognized their man. The poet intent upon Art so exhausted his intention and learned so much about that intention from others who were of like mind that his poetry became a revelation of the fate of Art and the emotion of the Artist in modern history. The will to seek one's opposite, the doctrine that one must seek one's anti-self, is at once the method by means of which Yeats found his genuine and peculiar theme, and one more example of the concern with acting a part which flows from the obsession with Art. The result has been a group of poems which will be known as long as the English language exists. (pp. 79-80)

Delmore Schwartz, "The Poet as Poet" (1939), in Selected Essays of Delmore Schwartz, *edited by Donald A. Dike and David H. Zucker (© 1970 by The University of Chicago), University of Chicago Press, 1970, pp. 72-80.*

[Yeats's] youthful plays, based upon folk-theme, enriched by a poetic imagination and an intellect of preciousness, were undoubtedly the finest plays in pure poetry produced during Yeats's years. In them the verse did not stay the action; their loveliness flowed naturally, with grace, ease, and power within the strict limits of the stage; and as such they were indeed an artistic indictment against the dramatic poetry or the rhetorical drama that passed for verse plays in the English theatre of their time. In them Yeats realised the fine instrument within his range. (pp. 73-4)

The story, the plot in Yeats's plays, is never very dramatic. All his themes are exceedingly simple, trivial in many cases; he shows little power of inventing a story, but he discovers in the trivial dramatic possibilities—for his intellect in many respects is ingenious rather than imaginative. You are rarely held by the intensity of the story; instead you are held spellbound by the intensity of thought and passion and by the consistent loveliness of apt speech, by the poetry. His plays have "poetry hid in thought or passion," as Coleridge says, "not thought or passion disguised in the dress of poetry". The outward sensuousness of his language is consumed by fiery thoughts or passions. Take away these and little is left to enrich the stage—it is, as I have said, bare of plot.

In this craft of play-writing, as in his lyric verse, beauty is taut and passion precise. The speech cadence is hesitant, yet full of verve and altogether impudently sweet. Yeats had no melodic ear; he could not measure words to musical stresses—he realised their significance, sought hard to employ them; but they were not at his command. In my opinion, that very lack of a musical ear offered remarkable compensation. It saved him, at worst, from an easy jingle of softly flowing sounds; from a monotony of regularity in well timed stresses. Indeed, his innocent offences against the laws of musical grammarians, his unconscious flaws in conventional melody, are responsible maybe for his curiously haunting harmonics in rhythm. These unexpected gaps staying his music, these hesitations in verbal sureness, altogether dramatise his cadence. His carefully poised verse is tuned, as it were, slightly off the note. Throughout one listens as to a folk-singer, in a constant fear that the thin run of melody will break on the perilous top note—altogether a tantalising music and a very personal music. Indeed, the very complex personality of this poet gives distinction to everything he writes. His most formal lines, the most.prosaic statement of his, stick in the mind, due possibly to some twist of syntax. Every quaint experience, passionate phrase, or queer thought becomes grist to his creative mill; while his own brooding on character gives an almost passionate importance to the commonplace. And through all appears the clear image of himself, impressionable—even gullible—in his momentary fierceness or foible. (pp. 79-81)

His . . . poetry never saw eye to eye with the middle classes. The bloodlessness, the loose sentiment of middle-minded verse was to him an abhorrence. There were, for him, only two commingling states of verse. One, simple, bucolic, or rabelaisian; the other, intellectual, exotic, or visionary. The middle minds lacked distinction, poise; their excursions into these states were the affectations of hikers —so he had little interest or patience with them. (p. 82)

The poetic plays of Yeats, those of his three phases, all spring from a lyrical impulse. That impulse never leaps beyond one act, and these one-act plays have all the attributes in content and in style of a lyric poem. They are sparse in substance and economical in speech, from his earlier wistfulness of loveliness to his later wispiness of power; for subject, there always appears the same conflict of spirit or intellect. In these plays majesty descends on threadbare speech; we gaze upon the sinewy thigh; through his invigoration, poetry on the stage again becomes sovereign. He had dreamed of a poetic stage, as I have said, with himself as main occupant; and that is what he has achieved. The influence of his distinguished work, particularly the influence of his earlier lyric plays, is seen in subsequent English and Scottish verse plays. . . . Yet, curiously, his influence on Irish poets produced no subsequent verse plays in the Abbey Theatre. (p. 85)

> *F. R. Higgins, "Yeats and Poetic Drama in Ireland," in* The Irish Theatre, *edited by Lennox Robinson (reprinted by permission of Macmillan, London and Basingstoke), Macmillan, 1939, pp. 65-88.*

There are two forms of impersonality: that which is natural to the mere skilful craftsman, and that which is more and more achieved by the maturing artist. The first is that of what I have called the 'anthology piece', of a lyric by Lovelace or Suckling, or of Campion, a finer poet than either. The second impersonality is that of the poet who, out of intense and personal experience is able to express a general truth; retaining all the particularity of his experience, to make of it a general symbol. And the strange thing is that Yeats, having been a great craftsman in the first kind, became a great poet in the second. . . . [He] had to wait for a later maturity to find expression of early experience; and this makes him, I think, a unique and especially interesting poet. (p. 299)

There was much also for Yeats to work out of himself, even in technique. To be a younger member of a group of poets, none of them certainly of anything like his stature, but further developed in their limited path, may arrest for a time a man's development of idiom. Then again, the weight of the pre-Raphaelite prestige must have been tremendous. The Yeats of the Celtic twilight—who seems to me to have been more the Yeats of the pre-Raphaelite twilight—uses Celtic folklore almost as William Morris uses Scandinavian folklore. His longer narrative poems bear the mark of Morris. Indeed, in the pre-Raphaelite phase, Yeats is by no means the least of the pre-Raphaelites. I may be mistaken, but the play, *The Shadowy Waters,* seems to me one of the most perfect expressions of the vague enchanted beauty of that school: yet it strikes me—this may be an impertinence on my part—as the western seas descried through the back window of a house in Kensington, an Irish myth for the Kelmscott Press; and when I try to visualize the speakers in the play, they have the great dim, dreamy eyes of the knights and ladies of Burne-Jones. I think the phase in which he treated Irish legend in the manner of Rossetti or Morris is a phase of confusion. He did not master this legend until he made it a vehicle for his own creation of character—not, really, until he began to write the *Plays for Dancers.* The point is, that in becoming more Irish, not in subject-matter but in expression, he became at the same time universal.

The points that I particularly wish to make about Yeats's development are two. The first, on which I have already touched, is that to have accomplished what Yeats did in the middle and later years is a great and permanent example— which poets-to-come should study with reverence—of what I have called Character of the Artist: a kind of moral, as well as intellectual, excellence. The second point, which follows naturally after what I have said in criticism of the lack of complete emotional expression in his early work, is that Yeats is pre-eminently the poet of middle age. . . . Most men either cling to the experiences of youth, so that their writing becomes an insincere mimicry of their earlier work, or they leave their passion behind, and write only from the head, with a hollow and wasted virtuosity. There is another and even worse temptation: that of becoming dignified, of becoming public figures with only a public existence—coat-racks hung with decorations and distinctions, doing, saying, and even thinking and feeling only what they believe the public expects of them. Yeats was not that kind of poet: and it is, perhaps, a reason why young men should find his later poetry more acceptable than older men easily can. For the young can see him as a poet who in his work remained in the best sense always young, who even in one sense became young as he aged.

But the old, unless they are stirred to something of the honesty with oneself expressed in the poetry, will be shocked by such a revelation of what a man really is and remains. They will refuse to believe that *they* are like that. (pp. 300-02)

T. S. Eliot, "Yeats" (originally delivered as
a lecture, 1940), in his On Poetry and Poets
(reprinted with the permission of Farrar,
Straus & Giroux, Inc.; copyright © 1943,
1945, 1951, 1954, 1956, 1957 by T. S. Eliot),
Farrar, Straus and Cudahy, 1957, pp. 295-
308.

Eliot's concern with tradition, his attempt to define his relation to the past, his attack on the romantic view of literature as the exploitation of personality, and his deliberate eclecticism in his choice of symbols from past cultures suggest some of the problems of the poet who lives in an age without a stable background. Self-consciousness about symbols and about tradition—and symbols depend upon tradition—is to be found increasingly among European poets from the last decade of the nineteenth century onward. Probably no poet was so aware of this problem and made such a gallant and sustained effort to solve it as W. B. Yeats. Yeats's poetic career . . . coincides with the development of that disintegration of belief which had so great an influence both on the technique and on the subject matter of literature. The phases of his poetic activity represent successive attempts to compensate for this disintegration by framing for himself symbolizations of experience in terms of which he could give meaning to his symbols, pattern to his thought, coherence to his interpretation of experience. (p. 128)

In his search for a compensating tradition Yeats went first to romantic literature, and then to mysticism of one kind and another, to folklore, theosophy, spiritualism, Neo-Platonism, and finally elaborated a symbolic system of his own, based on a variety of sources, and in terms of this was able to give pattern and coherence to the expression of his thought. It was a search for a system rather than a search for a set of beliefs; he sought a mode of expression rather than a set of dogmas to express. The problem for Yeats was not that of finding what he ought to say: his sensitive and restless mind provided him with a constant supply of subjects and attitudes. His problem was that of giving order and proportion to his insights. He did not even seek a point of view, for his mind, so much more elastic and all-embracing than Eliot's, would never be satisfied, as Eliot's was, with any single formulation of attitude. (p. 129)

It is a mistake to consider Yeats as a mystical poet. The true mystic is one who seeks to escape from an age of over-formulation by repudiating the orthodox categories and seeking identities and correspondences not recognized by more rational speculation. But far from seeking to escape from formulas Yeats is seeking to establish them. He does not wish to escape from orthodox religion but to find a substitute for it. He seeks to impose order, not, as the true mystic does, to break down a too neatly ordered system and get beyond it. . . . [While] Eliot was able to find [order] in orthodox Christianity, for Yeats, as for so many of his contemporaries, "Victorian science" destroyed the possibility of belief in orthodox Christianity, and he had to turn to less beaten tracks. That Victorian science had also, by implication at least, destroyed the possibility of belief in

these other systems did not matter, for Yeats had as a very young man believed in the scientific approach and allowed it to destroy his religious belief which could never after that be re-established, while he came to these other systems after he had repudiated Victorian science (which he soon grew to hate "with a monkish hate") which could thus have no further effect on his attitude. (pp. 131-32)

Yeats was attempting to solve two problems—the general problem of symbols in literature in an age lacking a common tradition and the particular problem presented by the confusions of the Irish situation. . . . It was, of course, a subjective order primarily, a pattern in his own mind which would enable him to utilize Irish material in his poetry. He was no politician and did not feel called upon to solve the practical problems of his time. But he was impelled to find a way of putting Ireland into some mental order, so that cultural symbols of dependable significance would be at the disposal of the artist. This double task— one posed by the cultural problem of his time, the other resulting from his relation to Ireland—was faced boldly by Yeats, and his development as a poet is the record of how he attempted to carry it out. (pp. 133-34)

It became increasingly clear to him that only in Ireland, only by defining his relation to Ireland and putting the symbols of Ireland in order in his mind, could he achieve the kind of poetic system he was groping after.

The Neo-Platonic ideas which he picked up at Ely Place and from Spenser and Shelley were used by Yeats at this time to give meaning and pattern to the Irish heroic themes which were coming more and more into his poetry. *The Rose* . . . is a collection of poems whose general theme is the symbolization of Platonic "ideas" by means of figures from Irish mythology and early history. (p. 142)

"The Rose of the World," perhaps the most perfect of his early poems, shows a careful discipline in language and control over form that are to be the outstanding features of Yeats's later poetry. The luxuriance and the romantic beating about the bush of his very first poems, when he sought his system in words merely ("Words alone are certain good") have given place to an artistic restraint which carries much greater power. . . . (p. 143)

Though Yeats's participation in Irish affairs at this time, his foundation of the literary societies, and his utilization of Irish material arose from his desire to satisfy his personal need as a poet, he nevertheless believed that in thus making use of Irish material he was contributing as much to Ireland as the politicians and the fighters. (pp. 146-47)

We see in the poems of *In the Seven Woods* the beginning of that epigrammatic manner which Yeats was to bring to perfection in *The Green Helmet*. A conscious and careful craftsmanship accompanies more realistic (i.e., personal and contemporary) themes.

Thus Yeats's verse becomes more severe and "classical" in manner while his themes become more personal and original. The older themes are not abandoned, but the newer ones keep intruding. (p. 158)

It is perhaps misleading to talk of the phases of Yeats's poetic career as though they succeeded and replaced each other: the truth is that, except for his very earliest period, Yeats never left anything behind, never repudiated an earlier position, but carried the past with him into the future in a way reminiscent of the "winding-stair" technique he uses in his later poems. He was constantly seeking a richer pattern, a more complex system, a more elaborate tradition, and he imposed his new patterns upon the old, integrating them into a richer unity, using myth and reminiscence as a means of carrying his youth into his old age. To live was, for Yeats, to "climb up the narrow winding stair to bed," and this image, so recurrent in his later poetry, is instructive. For the winding stair is both progressive and repetitious; at each landing one is above the same spot that one stood on at the lower landing, one is conscious of identity with one's lower self and yet of difference. The spiral staircase is a unity, with a definite pattern and a definite end—unlike the infinite straight line, and Yeats's progress is not in a straight line—the top of the spiral being a point which includes all the other positions in itself. The poetry of reminiscence that we find in *The Wild Swans at Coole, Michael Robartes and the Dancer, The Tower,* and *The Winding Stair* shows Yeats mentally ascending a winding stair, corkscrewing his way from the past to the present, from youth to age, advancing yet repeating, changing yet preserving, including earlier patterns in the present one. In an age without a tradition he has to build one out of his own life, making each phase of his life a chapter of a myth, and of the same myth. (pp. 167-68)

It is of course possible to explain the winding-stair symbolism in Yeats solely in terms of the esoteric system which he expounds in *A Vision;* this has been done by more than one critic, with great skill if with doubtful profit. For if this symbolism is to have any real significance in his poetry, it must be intelligible in more general terms, it must convey a meaning to the reader who studies with care the form and pattern of the later poems without continually glossing the text as he reads. If it is not thus intelligible, the poem is to some extent a failure. That some of Yeats's poetry does fail in this way—as a result of the confusion between mythology as framework and mythology as key to the meaning of the finished work . . .—can hardly be denied by the honest critic. (pp. 170-71)

But some of the dominant motives in Yeats's later symbolism can be interpreted without the aid of elaborate prose expositions—indeed, the winding-stair image can be given more significance if we do not attempt to narrow it down to the precise intellectual meaning demanded by the system expounded by Yeats in *A Vision.* One might make a useful distinction, in reading poetry, between interpretation by exclusion and interpretation by inclusion. The former restricts its concern to the conscious intellectual ideas held by the poet, and by doing so often sacrifices richness to precision and leaves the heart of the poem invisible, while the latter seeks to extend the implications of the images by seeing all their possible relations to each other and to the poet's work as a whole. In this way we can see the winding stair as at once the symbol of progress combined with repetition, a mark of the transition from youth to old age, an illumination of the place of memory, of reminiscence, in Yeats's endeavor to see his life as a unity, and even—to put it at its most grandiose—as a theory of epistemology. The truth is to be found by the patterning of opposites until they flow into each other in a single point. But the tower with its winding staircase is ruined at the top ("I climb to the towertop and lean upon broken stone") so that as a man grows old the past cannot be carried forward into a single point that includes both past and present, for by the time he has

reached that stage his faculties are decaying; the summit of the spiral is not a point but a ruin. One could play with this idea in a hundred different ways, and each would give some sort of insight into Yeats's mind. The balancing and unifying of opposites—truth being not a state of affairs but a mental activity—can be related to Yeats's view of life as a dance, as constant movement, both progress and repetition, in the midst of which the dancer is inseparable from the dance. . . . The situation in which we cannot tell the dancer from the dance is the top of the tower, the end of the spiral, where all opposites are fused. It is by this kind of symbolism that Yeats attempts to escape the dualism which meets us in all his earlier work; the pattern, the system, is not complete so long as the opposites remain opposites, eternally divided and opposed. Yeats's quest for order is concluded only when he finds a means of completing the pattern by fusing all life into a unity: though in ascending the winding stair we go continually in different directions and keep facing and opposing our former selves, when we reach the top we are at all points on the circle's radius at the same time. Further, in looking back we see our former selves, as it were, on the empty landings, and our progress is measured as much by our increased absence below as by our increased presence above. Here we have another symbol of the unification of opposites, presence and absence being interpreted in terms of each other. Thus the presence of these spiral images in Yeats's poetry can be related to the poet's advancing age and the problems which this brings, while the fact that poetry of reminiscence becomes so common in his work at this time bears out our interpretation very nicely. For as you carry the past with you into the future, the increase in the number of your absences, in the number of places where you no longer are, is a measure of·your progress; the more memories you have the older you are; and this leads us straight back to the winding stair again. (pp. 171-74)

The influence of Plotinus becomes increasingly noticeable in Yeats's later work. He seeks for a reality that lies outside time, and it is through this idea that he achieves the final resolution of his opposites. "Between extremities Man runs his course" and the problem is to destroy

> All those antinomies
> Of day and night.

If one could get outside time and outside memory, viewing all things simultaneously and at once, then one would have found the true pattern for reality—one could rest at the top of the spiral and see one's self on all parts of the winding stair at once. This search for an extra-temporal reality is reflected in numerous poems in *The Tower* and *The Winding Stair.* . . . One important aspect of Byzantium is that it is a city without time. (pp. 185-87)

Crazy Jane and Tom the Lunatic are characters whose function is to show the inadequacy of orthodox philosophy; only the inspired or the mad can rend the veil of time and see all life as a unity. (p. 187)

Yeats's search for a complete and systematic symbolization of experience—originating in his desire to compensate for a no longer tenable religious tradition—finally led him to a highly abstract and artificial philosophy from which ordinary human values had almost completely disappeared. If he could not obtain adequate pattern from life, he would do so from death. The poetry of his last years becomes increasingly bloodless, though always skilful and often impressive, and sometimes we begin to wonder whether he is a man like ourselves or

> Shade more than man, more image than a shade.
>
> (p. 188)

He was casting a very cold eye on life himself at this time. For over fifty years he sought for a philosophy to replace a lost tradition, that he might write better and with more confidence; and in the end his system conquered him. In his enthusiasm for the pattern that he was to impose upon experience he forgot about experience itself, so that while he retained his vigor he almost lost his humanity. In his last years his poetry was impressive but a little uncanny: he had cast too cold an eye on life. (p. 189)

> *David Daiches, "W. B. Yeats—I and II,"
> in his* Poetry and the Modern World: A Study of Poetry in England Between 1900 and 1939 *(© 1940 by The University of Chicago), University of Chicago Press, 1940, pp. 128-55, 155-89.*

Between the faint, vague, lovely wandering of [Yeats's] first romantic poems and the strong presentness, the urgent voice, of such a poem as *Byzantium,* is not only the distance between mediocrity and greatness but the distance also between a poet of private speech and the satin salons and a poet of public speech and the world. Yeats's later poetry is poetry of the world. It is the first English poetry in a century which has dared to re-enter the world. It is the first poetry in English in more than a century in which the poem is again an act upon the world. It is the first poetry in generations which can cast a shadow in the sun of actual things—men's lives, men's wills, men's future. With Yeats, poetry becomes an engine capable of employing all the mind, all the knowledge, all the strength. With Yeats, poetry ceases to be a closet avocation to the practice of which a man could bring only nostalgia, only melancholy, only fantasy, only arts and doubtings of escape. Writing as Yeats writes, a man need not pretend an ignorance of the world, need not affect a strangeness from his time, need not go mooning through an endless attic with the starlight clicking on the roof. The later poetry of Yeats is, then, the measure of the actual achievement of the poetic revolution associated with his name. (pp. 66-7)

[It] is . . . probable that this transition toward a poetry capable of accepting a political and revolutionary era upon its own terms is a transition capable, if effected, of reaching the greatest and most noble ends—the true ends of poetry—the ends of all the greatest poetry of the past. It is a transition capable of restoring a poetry of public speech.

It is a transition *capable* of that end. Whether or not it will actually achieve that end is another question. At the present moment, the transition is dangerously threatened from within by those who should be most responsible for its success. Certain of the young English poets, directly engaged in dealing with the revolution of their age, and consciously employing the methods of the revolution in their art, seem for some inexplicable reason to be doubling on their tracks. Or more exactly they seem to be engaged in pushing the use of idioms of living speech inherited from their predecessors on beyond the true limits of those idioms into the artificiality of a new closet poetry. Instead of the live phrases of passionate utterance to be found in Yeats—the human

rhythms, the beautiful simplicities of which the beauty is most apparent because it was always there but never till this moment seen—instead of all this, there is an inversion of naturalness which uses natural utterance for satiric and subjective ends. Auden and his imitators have chosen for their poetic language the living language of the time, but the living language in its most banal and deadened phrases. They have created from this stereotyped language a satiric, and sometimes a lyric, poetry of great power. But the meanings of this poetry are not outward toward the world but inward toward the private references of the poet.

The transition, therefore, may not ever be fulfilled. It may never move beyond its present tentative and incomplete position. (pp. 68-9)

> *Archibald MacLeish, in his* A Time to Speak *(copyright © 1940, 1968 by Archibald MacLeish; reprinted by permission of Houghton Mifflin Company), Houghton, 1941.*

Yeats does not regard poetry as complete in itself, with its own ritual and its own meaning. He sees it as part of a larger experience, as a means of communication with the spiritual world which lies behind the visible. For him the poet is almost a medium, an interpreter of the unseen, and his poetry is the record of the revelations given to him. (p. 185)

Yeats has his vision of what [the] new poetry will be. It will be marked by a return to imagination, to the state between waking and dreaming; it will cast out energetic rhythms and seek "wavering, meditative, organic, rhythms"; it will pay great attention to technique and employ, if they are necessary, even obscure and ungrammatical forms, but it must have "the perfection that escapes analysis, the subtleties that have a new meaning every day". Poetry is to be a record of a state of trance, and if it is to be a true record, it must take endless pains to secure its effect by the right rhythm and the right associations; for otherwise the state of trance is broken. This theory partly re-states some of the fundamental principles of lyric poetry, partly introduces the revolutionary notion that a poem is a charm or instrument of enchantment. Yeats finds the Symbolist doctrine to his taste not only because its high standards appeal to his artistic sense but because its mystical claims appeal to something mystical in him. But his mysticism is of a special kind. It is not aesthetic rapture, not pure vision, not creative ecstasy, but a belief in powers behind the visible world, powers that are evoked from dream and trance. For Yeats poetry is a communication with spirits, with an unseen order of things, and the poet is he who conducts the passage from one order to another and finds words for these mysterious messages. (pp. 187-88)

In its first stages Yeats' drama must be regarded as an extension of his lyrical poetry. Experiences too complex to be cast into lyrical verse may be put into plays without losing their essentially lyrical character. . . . In the symbolical expression of love *The Shadowy Waters* is Yeats' most sustained performance. . . . He calls the work a "story", and it is certainly more that than a drama. Its critical moments are not created by the events but by the emotions expressed. The beauty is of speech and sentiment; character and crisis have little importance. The tone of dreaming ecstasy, of withdrawal into an ideal world of dream, is marvellously sustained, but it is not dramatic. The beauty of *The Shadowy Waters* is really lyrical. Even the magical close relies for its effect on the emotions and ideas which it evokes, not on the situation of the characters. . . . (pp. 194-95)

The Shadowy Waters is the crown of the poetry which Yeats wrote under the example of Mallarmé as Symons explained it to him. In it the method of *Hérodiade* is carried to a highly personal conclusion, hardly in authentic drama but at least in dramatic lyric according to Symbolist rules. It is the poem of the poet's ideal love, of all such love as he understands it. His other plays of this period are not quite like this. They were meant to be acted and were acted. In them Yeats moved slowly to a more objective kind of drama and to a different manner of poetry. In each perhaps there are traces of Symbolist influence. . . . But what distinguishes these plays from *The Shadowy Waters* is that the language is less dream-laden and more suited to the action. . . . In these plays Yeats believed that he was following the tradition of English poetical drama and writing as Shelley wrote *The Cenci*. (pp. 195-96)

In his own way he still sought "pure poetry" and provided it in his plays. Poetical drama cannot be "pure poetry" if it is to be dramatic, and Yeats' plays are after all more poetry than drama. None the less in his development they mark an important stage. Just because he had to face a public with them and to make his meaning concise and clear, he was forced to trim and pare his language, to make it more forcible and effective, to be more objective in his presentation of people and events.

The fruits of this activity were remarkable. When in 1910 Yeats published the slim volume of *The Green Helmet,* his whole manner and outlook had changed. The elaboration, the mythology, the vagueness, the wavering rhythms, [had] disappeared, and in their place [were] simplicity, directness, plain vivid imagery, terse and concentrated rhythms. Yeats . . . remodelled his style and forged a powerful instrument which [seemed] to owe nothing to his earlier work. (p. 197)

The struggle between Soul and Self, between mind and heart, which had long occupied Yeats, was solved in his old age. The Self won. Yeats was still conscious of the mystical background to life, but what interested him most was life itself. He came nearer to it, was content to enjoy it. The result was a loosening in his style, an ever closer approximation to the language of every day, to old refrains and rhythms of ballads, to the simplest and most natural topics. In his *Last Poems* there is not even the stern majestic utterance of his mature work. He has flung the whole of himself into them and found at last a complete expression of his abundant complex nature. He is no longer torn by the conflict in himself between the man and the poet; he no longer wears what he calls a "Mask" to present himself to the world. The old age which he had dreaded as the end of poetry brought a greater power to create and a freedom from all hindrances. Yeats even came to glory in it, to wish to be "a foolish, passionate man". (p. 214)

Yeats' career is an instructive commentary on Symbolist doctrine. He was well fitted to welcome it, and through it he found his first real style. Even when he was brought down to reality and abandoned his earlier manner, he was still to a large extent a Symbolist; he still dealt with subtle and intangible matters behind the immediately visible world; he still saw the artist as a superior being who is almost necessarily out of tune with his times. But what marks him off from other poets of his training is that through Symbolism he found a way to create an extremely lively and concrete poetry about himself. He worked hard to rid his verse of all vagueness and looseness. What he lost in mystery he gained in power. To otherwise commonplace events he brought a wonder and significance, a vitality and enjoyment, which made them extraordinarily vivid and real. He attached great importance to the emotions, and since he was himself highly emotional and even passionate, he tried, with consummate success, to make poetry of them. Even in his most abstract themes there is a great intensity of feeling. He flung all of himself into his verse, till it contained the many qualities of his exuberant and abundant personality. (p. 218)

> *C. M. Bowra, "William Butler Yeats," in his* The Heritage of Symbolism *(© copyright 1943 by Macmillan & Co. Ltd.; reprinted by permission of Macmillan, London and Basingstoke), Macmillan, 1943, pp. 180-218.*

It is largely the discarding of the logical plan and characterization, the twin supports of conventional playwriting, that makes Yeats's dramas so elusive to traditional expectations of the form, and provokes the criticism that they are undramatic. Drama had always depended on an action that took a natural form as it is observed in life. . . . The logic of appearances; the close analytical plan with its explanation of relationships; the exposition of character and motive within a coherent moral order; the observance of time and space as they are accepted by common sense—all this is the foundation of Sophocles and Shakespeare, of Calderon and Corneille, of Molière and Congreve. And if a supernatural or dream world is presented, it is always a phenomenon having its place within the larger rational framework, as in *The Tempest*. Here, moreover, lies the common ground between drama in verse and drama in prose. *Deirdre* and *On Baile's Strand* are examples of it in Yeats.

The drama that was in vogue when Yeats was writing, the prose realism of Ibsen, Hauptmann and Galsworthy, reaches the extreme of dependence on natural logical appearances. Its critical purpose makes this inevitable, for it sets out to observe a "real" state of affairs and must achieve accuracy of diagnosis. To the extraversion of moralists and sociologists Yeats opposes in most of his plays a world inward and fanciful and spiritual; to their logic he opposes emotion; to their socially coherent plots his spiritually coherent visions. It is not only a question of "stylization," of beautiful verse and design, supported by formal elements of chorus and ballet, ennobling an action from life. . . . The mask, the patterned screen, the formal accompaniments of drum, gong, zither, and flute, the dance figures of the performers, design in the speaking of verse, are powerful independent means of evoking emotion; Yeats uses them in combination to give "musical" depth, a field of reverberation, to the action and to the language, which in itself employs rhythm, sound and image with the same intention. An early play like *The Shadowy Waters* relies entirely on the resources of language. The *Plays for Dancers* show the technique in its full development. And the poet's effect flows finally from an imagery of emotion that is intense in proportion to the complex use of different media towards a single end.

The result of such an assembling and ordering of symbols is to add a function to action itself. Instead of treating a plot that illumines human relations in their moral aspect, Yeats makes action into another signature of "emotion." It is not an end in itself, flowing from and dependent on what we call "character," but it evokes instead the intimacies, ecstasies and anguish of the soul-life. In these subtle plays relations between men matter less than the submission of a soul to the all-enveloping spiritual mystery. The coherent action-sequence that illustrates essentially the *moral* nature of life gives place to a complex pattern communicating a spiritual insight. In this pattern action is sometimes, it is true, an element of the seen life of human relations; more often it is an element of the unseen life of the soul and of spiritual powers, presented in poetry through anthropomorphic images.

In the mingling of these elements of seen and unseen, of natural and supra-natural, of human and divine, "action" comes to have the force of symbol, and conversely symbol assumes sometimes the character of action. (pp. 120-21)

In using action in this intricate and exceedingly free way Yeats has drawn on ordinary human life, on religious mystery, on folk-belief, on a mythical spirit-world, on a region of fairies and fantasies, on poetic legend, on occult spheres. The world he creates out of these various elements is not an "unreal" one, though it is very different from the world we are accustomed to find in drama. As a mental world that is relevant to our life it is real. The poet's means may often be those of fantasy, but his end is always to express something not at all fanciful or remote but exceedingly proximate: a mental, spiritual, emotional reality. *At the Hawk's Well*, for example, presents a feeling that is a substantial, gripping experience, it is "intense life"; only the object, the thing-to-be-attained is remote and elusive. Irrealities are symbols that evoke a reality.

The real fault in Yeats, I think, is not that his subject is unreal, uncorporeal, immaterial, but it lies in the *degree* to which he sometimes refines away the material world in too many directions at once. (pp. 122-23)

In Shakespeare and his contemporaries a world of spirit shapes itself upon a world of violent deeds because it was precisely this latter—the life of Renaissance man, a prince and adventurer, an amateur of love, ambition, power, intellectual and esthetic sensation—that raised the great moral and spiritual issues. The analysis of this life was the new subject for poetry prescribed by observation of the age. In this kind of work, therefore, spiritual experience flows from a real world of drama. In Yeats the new subject for observation is the life of the soul and spiritual powers, and so the progression is from inward to outward, unseen to seen, a sensuous world of drama shaping itself upon an ideal world of spirit. The novel can express mental experience directly. Drama is compelled to use symbolism, personification and myth. Yeats's use of a complex imagery of emotion was a vital method prescribed by the conditions of art and life in his time. The relative brevity of his plays depends on an acute judgement of what the method will stand. (p. 127)

Ronald Peacock, "Yeats," in his The Poet in the Theatre *(reprinted by permission of Routledge & Kegan Paul, Ltd.), Routledge & Kegan Paul, 1946 (and published simultaneously in the United States by Harcourt,*

Brace and Company, Inc., 1946, pp. 117-28.)

If we . . . decide to look into Yeats's plays for ourselves, we are apt to approach them by way of two very depressing literary movements—the "Irish Renaissance" and the Poetic Drama of the late-Victorian and post-Victorian era. The Irish Renaissance is depressing because it didn't exist, the Poetic Drama movement because it did. (p. 315)

It was Ezra Pound who introduced Yeats to the Noh plays, Japan's "unpopular" drama. They gave him a sort of dramatic equivalent for his new verse style: something terse, refined, solid, cryptic, beautiful. They also showed Yeats how to simplify his staging by radical conventions and how to combine music and dance with words without letting the words get swamped. Apart from such general principles, and the formal framework, Yeats's dance plays are as distinct from their Japanese prototypes as from Western drama. The Noh play can become anything you want to make it. (p. 322)

Yeats's most radical act was his rejection of the form common to Ibsen, Shakespeare, and Sophocles—the drama that was a moral analysis of character within a framework of more or less logical appearances. It is the absence of this form that the modern reader finds bewildering when he first encounters Yeats's plays. Is the play really there? asks the reader. What on earth am I supposed to do with these roles? asks the actor. And those of us who are more impressed ask: what does Yeats put in the place of the regular plot-and-character pattern? Our first inclination, especially if we have read his essays, is to say that he is following in the wake of Maeterlinck, and that what he is attempting is mood and atmosphere. One recalls that Yeats found in tragedy itself only emotion, and hence would not allow that Shakespeare is a tragedian. . . . Yeats's rejection of character was no mere whimsy. It is not the psychology of Cuchulain that concerns him, but the spiritual world to which Cuchulain can lead us. (pp. 322-23)

Eric Bentley, "Yeats's Plays" (1948), in his In Search of Theater *(copyright © 1948, 1949, 1950, 1951, 1953 by Eric Bentley; reprinted by permission of Atheneum Publishers, New York), Atheneum, 1953, pp. 315-26.*

[Any] poet today, even if he deny the importance of dogma to life, can see how useful myths are to poetry—how much, for instance, they helped Yeats to make his private experiences public and his vision of public events personal. He knows, too, that in poetry all dogmas become myths; that the aesthetic value of the poem is the same whether the poet and/or the reader actively believe what it says or not. He is apt then to look around for some myth—any myth, he thinks, will do—to serve the same purpose for himself. What he overlooks is that the only kind of myth which will do for him must have one thing in common with believed dogma, namely, that the relation of the former to the poet, as of the latter to the soul, must be a personal one. The Celtic legends Yeats used were woven into his childhood—he really went to seances, he seriously studied all those absurd books. You cannot use a Weltanschauung like Psychoanalysis or Marxism or Christianity as a poetic myth unless it involves your emotions profoundly, and, if you have not inherited it, your emotions will not become involved unless you take it more seriously than as a mere myth.

Yeats, like us, was faced with the modern problem, i.e., of living in a society in which men are no longer supported by tradition without being aware of it, and in which, therefore, every individual who wishes to bring order and coherence into the stream of sensations, emotions, and ideas entering his consciousness, from without and within, is forced to do deliberately for himself what in previous ages had been done for him by family, custom, church, and state, namely the choice of the principles and presuppositions in terms of which he can make sense of his experience. (p. 111)

[It] is one of the distinguishing marks of a major poet that he continues to develop, that the moment he has learnt how to write one kind of poem, he goes on to attempt something else, new subjects, new ways of treatment or both, an attempt in which he may quite possibly fail. He invariably feels, as Yeats puts it, "the fascination of what's difficult." (p. 112)

Further, the major poet not only attempts to solve new problems, but the problems he attacks are central to the tradition, and the lines along which he attacks them, while they are his own, are not idiosyncratic, but produce results which are available to his successors.... Yeats ... has effected changes which are of use to every poet. His contributions are not, I think, to new subject matter, nor to the ways in which poetic material can be organized—where Eliot for instance has made it possible for English poetry to deal with all the properties of modern city life, and to write poems in which the structure is musical rather than logical. Yeats sticks to the conventional romantic properties and the traditional step-by-step structure of stanzaic verse. His main legacies to us are two. First, he transformed a certain kind of poem, the occasional poem, from being either an official performance of impersonal virtuosity or a trivial *vers de société* into a serious reflective poem of at once personal and public interest. (pp. 112-13)

Secondly, Yeats released regular stanzaic poetry, whether reflective or lyrical, from iambic monotony; the Elizabethans did this originally for dramatic verse, but not for lyric or elegiac. (p. 113)

Which epitaph upon a poet's grave would please him more: "I wrote some of the most beautiful poetry of my time" or "I rescued English lyric from the dead hand of Campion and Tom Moore"? I suspect that more poets would prefer the second than their readers would ever guess, particularly when, like Yeats, they are comfortably aware that the first is also true. (p. 114)

> *W. H. Auden, "Yeats as an Example," in* The Kenyon Critics: Studies in Modern Literature from 'The Kenyon Review,' *edited by John Crowe Ransom (© 1951 by the Kenyon Review; reprinted by permission of Curtis Brown, Ltd.), World Publishing Co., 1951, pp. 107-14.*

The charm of much of Yeats's early poetry is ... slightly equivocal—dreamy and melancholy, passive and self-indulgent. ... (p. 13)

We should look, in the early poems, for [their] latent strength. Their weary, withdrawn note is a kind of protective colouring which Yeats has taken from his friends of the 1890's. (He was often, throughout his life, ready admiringly to imitate his minor, but never his major contemporaries. A natural leader, he liked to disguise himself as a follower, even of small men.) There is, of course, a paradox here. Yeats made himself a major poet, starting with the equipment and apparently the tastes of a good minor one—with a chaste but excessively 'poetic' diction, with exquisite but trite cadences, with a tendency to use symbols in a way that was decorative and even fussily so rather than deeply exploratory, with a narrow and rather wilfully sad range of moods, always just on the verge of the literary pose or the 'stock response'. He started, also, without much grasp of the outer world; his early poems rarely make us *see* anything; we can weave our own day-dreams round them, which is another matter. And though he acquired unique rank, among his contemporaries, as a visionary poet, it is probable that the merely *visible* world left him, to the last, rather cold. Usually he evokes it for us by a kind of trick, not describing the thing, but reminding us of our feelings about it.... We ourselves, most of the time, *make* Yeats's physical world for him. We believe in it, because we believe in Yeats, and rather as we believe in a painted Elsinore when Hamlet is talking. We can, in fact, think perhaps most fruitfully of Yeats's poems as speeches made by him at crucial moments in a long noble drama. No poet lends himself so little to the cold-blooded examination of his poems as isolated objects; no poet gains more from being read as a whole, with a full knowledge of his life. Yeats, as he grows older, acts, with growing assurance and spontaneity the difficult part of himself. The acting in the end, having gone through the stages of lyrical mime and heroic and satirical tirade, becomes almost naturalistic. (pp. 14-16)

Yeats's attitude towards the supernatural was a profoundly ambiguous one. He wanted, from a world beyond ours, in contrasting moods, two apparently quite contradictory kinds of assurance; one that we are, in fact, bound, as the Buddhists tell us we are, to the 'great wheel of existence' and shall reappear upon this stage, in various roles, again and again; the other that, as the Buddhists also tell us, we can escape ultimately from 'the great wheel'—but not to non-being, a concept which never attracted Yeats, but to some kind of finite timeless perfection. He was not sure (as perhaps no Western man who studies Eastern thought ever is) that he really wanted to escape from the wheel. Thus in the face of his 'symbolic phantasmagoria', he retains the freedom of inconsistency. His images of a Byzantine heaven in which he would be transformed into a golden bird (the artist becoming an eternal work of art) symbolized his desire to escape from the disorder, the irony, the failure of life; but so also other symbols—as when he says he would like to live again, even in a 'foul ditch', as a 'blind man battering blind men'—stand for a craving for life, at any level, the 'lust and rage' of which he speaks in his *Last Poems,* that grew stronger in him as he grew older. Often he hated life for not being perfection. Sometimes, also, he feared perfection for not being life. (p. 21)

Yeats felt that there was a tension between his life and his poetry. He thought sometimes of the poem as a kind of anti-personality which the poet builds up to compensate for or conceal personal weaknesses, of the poem as a 'mask'.... As Yeats's poetry matures, one of the things that happens is not so much that it becomes more 'personal', less of a 'mask', as that he gets more of his personality into it. He gets in things like irony, humour, arrogant irascibility, the coaxing manners of the professional Irish conversationalist, which in the 1890's he would probably have considered 'anti-poetic'; he gets in more of the prosaic detail of life, transformed by a poetic apprehension of it. (pp. 24-5)

Yeats was humble before the mystery of life. He never took either himself or his systems quite so seriously as some of his disciples have done. He was the last great poet in the English romantic tradition; and the only poet in that tradition, except Byron, with a genuine sense of humour and gift of wit. (p. 29)

> *G. S. Fraser, in his* W. B. Yeats, *Longmans, Green & Co. Ltd., 1954.*

[Yeats] was not content, as were most of the other Symbolist poets who were his contemporaries, to evolve a personal system of symbols which would adequately express his experience and would constitute a closed-in world, but wished his symbols to have the authority of an existence distinct from his own, to be projected upon some external, established and unchanging reality as were those of poets living in an age of faith.

It was typical of Yeats to require external authority for his symbolism at a time when other poets were content both to exist and to create within the confines of their own selves. He was always aware of the imperfection and transience of human life, and a recurring theme in his writings is the celebration of the transcendent, especially when it appears in the form of a work of art, for in making such a work man became superman, confounding time and change by embodying externally the inner processes of his intellect or imagination. . . . [It is a] Yeatsian principle that a thing becomes most completely itself when it has realised its opposite within itself. . . . Symbols gain in significance when they have some existence independent of the poet.

What saves Yeats from the intellectual flaccidity of most of the champions of occultism is his high ideal of the superhuman and his endeavour to attain to it himself by the discipline of his life and his art. (pp. 117-18)

[In] Yeats's poetry the external world is present only as a sort of foil to the inner subjective world, so that the latter may most fully realise and express itself through its struggle with its opposite. . . . Yeats was never a nature poet, and any natural imagery that appeared in his early work was an inheritance from the Romantic Movement rather than expression of the poet's true self. . . . Mind and heart, or spirit and flesh, are the twin springs which constitute the source of all that Yeats ever wrote. The whole man, and not merely the mind or the emotions, was involved in the writing of his poems, particularly the later ones, and it is to the whole man that they make their appeal. His is the poetry, not of nature, but of man, and his world is the world of the human spirit, both in its earthly and its transcendental manifestations. (pp. 121-22)

Yeats's [early] volumes . . . are full of artifice, and everywhere the influence of the Pre-Raphaelites, whom he so admired in his youth, is evident. But even while he was writing them he was, in his poetic theory, moving away from such work. . . . It was not until the twentieth century that he began to write out of his own experience of life. . . . (p. 122)

The exalted Image of Beatrice had enabled Dante, through

passion, to keep his buried self before his conscious mind, and thus to sustain the state of illuminative vision. Yeats never discovered an Image capable of doing this for him and consequently his poetry is a series of brilliant moments, moments of wilfully induced intensity, which marvellously mirror existence but do not resolve it. (p. 132)

> *Stuart Holroyd, "W. B. Yeats: The Divided Man," in his* Emergence from Chaos *(copyright © 1957 by Stuart Holroyd; reprinted by permission of Houghton Mifflin Company), Houghton, 1957, pp. 113-37.*

[Yeats's] strength lies in the magnificent way in which he accepts fallibility. This has nothing to do with his silliness, which is something less fortunate. It is a question of flexibility of tone. . . . (p. 32)

What is lasting in Yeats is traditional but not orthodox. Yet before that can be reached a great deal of Yeats's theoretical cant ought to be swept up. . . . Like Eliot, Yeats felt he had to have the support of beliefs. But he could find no acceptable dogma. So, aided by his wife and certain congenial spirits, he constructed for himself a system of beliefs out of astrology, neo-Platonism and spiritualism. . . . The hocus-pocus was necessary for Yeats as a person. It is not essential to the poetry. While Eliot's Christian orthodoxy is part of the order and allusiveness of his writing, Yeats merely needed the complication of his fairies and theosophy in order to write of the great common world of the passions. His delicacy is all in the poetry, not at all in the beliefs. . . . But at its best there is an extraordinary firmness about Yeats's poetic world: Helen and modern Ireland, Platonism, folk-lore and politics all have the same immediate conviction. For they are judged by the same values and presented with the same purity of language.

The values are traditional and when taken simply—which the poetry does not do—ideal. But there is a clear break between the tradition of Yeats's mature poetry and the tradition of his literary world. . . . Yeats [in his *Autobiographies*] defines his growth in terms of causes which he shows he knew well to be lost. In his public personality, as he chose to present it, the intelligence, which is everywhere, goes with a deliberate harking back.

Yet it is quite deliberate. Abstracted, the values which give strength to his mature poetry are not of our time. The *Autobiographies* show that they were still very much alive for him. (pp. 35-7)

Yeats's dogmas and orthodoxies encouraged in him a sort of triviality. In his maturity, his spiritualism was a game he played: he shuffled his symbols around, he quoted Plato and Plotinus as authorities, with a supreme disregard of the authoritativeness of his poetry itself. So, in his early verse: the aristocratic tradition became a dim mythology, nobility a rather dreary mountain-moving heroism and love a hopeless mist which enveloped everything. The Pre-Raphaelite mode in which he began and from which he fought free encouraged him in his taste for dreams. . . . But the dreams give only a shadowy hint, the waking gives the substance. And waking from a dream is, literally, a disillusionment. That is the theme of his later work. We know roughly what those disillusionments were: with his love affair with Maud Gonne, with Irish politics, with the Irish audience for whom he was writing plays, and finally, under the influence of Pound, with the mode of verse he had practised. . . . The disillusionment of his maturity comes from the conflict which he saw the traditions of the old world losing to the new world of Pound and Eliot. (pp. 37-8)

In Yeats's poetry the moving force is this clarity that comes too late: he knows his traditions and allegiances only when, for all practical purposes, they are finished. . . . (p. 38)

The theme of Yeats's youth was nostalgia for what had never been; that of his maturity, something between regret and remorse for a way of life he valued too late. . . .

In Yeats's poetry there is a continual tension between the bitterness of what he says and the strength and sweep with which he says it. Eliot has called him a poet of middle age. He seems to me to be the poet of old age in everything except his creative power. (p. 39)

Despite all the pride he took in his craftsmanship, Yeats's innovations are negligible; they have none of that dramatic importance of Eliot's. The most obviously "modern" apparatus he employs, his symbols, are effective almost in spite of the theory behind them. For he does not, in his real strength, use them as holdalls of meaning, private and a little inscrutable. They merely do their work along with the rest of the poem. . . . This is not symbolism at all; it is powerful use of the most telling imagery to hand. Because the imagery is used, and works, there is no need to be explicit. In the longer poems the metaphors have to do more, but that is because the poet is dealing with more complex and varying material. It is a difference in profundity, not in the nature of the imagery. Yeats's business, like any poet's, was always to say what he meant in the most effective and immediate way, not to define anything. (pp. 41-2)

Yeats's poetry then is modern with very little of the paraphernalia of modernism about it. It is modern because the tone of voice is that of the time. He may be magnificent, tender, ironical, or harsh, there is always a speaking voice that comes off the page. Nearly always, when he is most working himself up, that peculiarly unobstructed, intelligent honesty will break through. . . . With this honesty goes a willingness to face the disagreeable or shameful side of his feelings, and a pertinence in seeking out images and references which best suit his purposes, rather than, as in his earliest verse, those which soothe and flatter the reader. (p. 42)

The achievement is that these personal statements stand alone. They are not, at their best, idiosyncratic. The test is in the amount he had added to the common stock of poetry. . . . Yeats has the gift of all major poets that, though the large bulk of his writing may contain many indifferent poems, there is hardly one without something that sticks in your memory. His poetry bristles with lines which, once you have read them, seem completely inevitable; lines which, by their purity and economy, add a fresh dimension to the language. They give a new norm by which to judge poetic expression. (pp. 43-4)

What he did eventually derive from the Symbolists were mere surface tricks. . . . Yeats's poetry is the new flowering of a very old tree. (pp. 46-7)

A. Alvarez, "Eliot and Yeats: Orthodoxy and Tradition" (originally published in Twentieth Century), *in his* Stewards of Excellence: Studies in Modern English and American Poets *(reprinted by permission of Charles Scribner's Sons; and in Canada by Chatto & Windus, Ltd.* © *1958 by A. Alvarez), Scribner's, 1958 (and reprinted by Gordian Press, Inc., 1971), pp. 11-47.*

Yeats has . . . a consistent extraordinary grasp of the reality of emotion, character, and aspiration; . . . his chief resort and weapon for the grasping of that reality is magic; and . . . if we would make use of that reality for ourselves we must also make some use of the magic that inspirits it. What is important is that the nexus of reality and magic is not by paradox or sleight of hand, but is logical and represents, for Yeats in his poetry, a full use of intelligence. Magic performs for Yeats the same fructifying function that Christianity does for Eliot, or that ironic fatalism did for Thomas Hardy; it makes a connection between the poem and its subject matter and provides an adequate mechanics of meaning and value. (pp. 74-5)

[Yeats'] early poems are fleeting, some of them beautiful and some that sicken, as you read them, to their own extinction. But as he acquired for himself a discipline, however unacceptable to the bulk of his readers, his poetry obtained an access to reality. (p. 76)

When Yeats came of poetic age he found himself . . . in a society whose conventions extended neither intellectual nor moral authority to poetry; he found himself in a rational but deliberately incomplete, because progressive, society. The *emotion* of thought, for poetry, was gone, along with the emotion of religion and the emotion of race—the three sources and the three aims of the great poetry of the past. . . . The poets and society both, for opposite reasons, expected the poet to produce either exotic and ornamental mysteries or lyrics of mood; the real world and its significance were reserved mainly to the newer sciences, though the novelists and the playwrights might poach if they could. For a time Yeats succumbed, as may be seen in his early work, even while he attempted to escape; and of his poetic generation he was the only one to survive and grow in stature. He came under the influence of the French Symbolists, who gave him the clue and the hint of an external structure but nothing much to put in it. . . . He worked into his poetry the substance of Irish mythology and Irish politics and gave them a symbolism, and he developed his experiences with Theosophy and Rosicrucianism into a body of conventions adequate, for him, to animate the concrete poetry of the soul that he wished to write. He did not do these things separately; the mythology, the politics, and the magic are conceived, through the personalities that reflected them, with an increasing unity of apprehension. Thus more than any poet of our time he has restored to poetry the actual emotions of race and religion and what we call abstract thought. Whether we follow him in any particular or not, the general poetic energy which he liberated is ours to use if we can. If the edifice that he constructed seems personal, it is because he had largely to build it for himself, and that makes it difficult to understand in detail except in reference to the peculiar unity which comes from their mere association in his life and work. Some of the mythology and much of the politics, being dramatized and turned into emotion, are part of our common possessions. But where the emphasis has been magical, whether successfully or not, the poems have been misunderstood, ignored, and the actual emotion in them which is relevant to us all decried and underestimated, merely because the magical mode of thinking is foreign to our own and when known at all is largely associated with quackery and fraud. (pp. 94-5)

Yeats lacks, as we have said, the historical advantage and with it much else; and the conclusion cannot be avoided that this lack prevents his poetry from reaching the first magnitude. But there are two remedies we may apply, which will make up, not for the defect of magnitude, but for the defect of structure. We can read the magical philosophy in his verse *as if* it were converted into the contemporary psychology with which its doctrines have so much in common. We find little difficulty in seeing Freud's preconscious as a fertile myth and none at all in the general myth of extroverted and introverted personality; and these may be compared with, respectively, Yeats' myth of *Spiritus Mundi* and the Phases of the Moon: the intention and the scope of the meaning are identical. So much for a secular conversion. The other readily available remedy is this: to accept Yeats' magic literally as a machinery of meaning, to search out the prose parallels and reconstruct the symbols he uses on their own terms in order to come on the emotional reality, if it is there, actually in the poems—when the machinery may be dispensed with. This method has the prime advantage over secular conversion of keeping judgment in poetic terms, with the corresponding disadvantage that it requires more time and patience, more "willing suspension of disbelief," and a stiffer intellectual exercise all around. (p. 96)

> *R. P. Blackmur, "The Later Poetry of W. B. Yeats," in his* The Expense of Greatness *(copyright, 1940, by R. P. Blackmur), Peter Smith, 1958, pp. 74-105.*

"Among School Children" . . . is as centrifugal a major poem as exists in the language. Whoever encounters it out of the context Yeats carefully provided for it, for instance in an Anthology Appointed to be Taught in Colleges, will find himself after twenty minutes seeking out who Leda was and what Yeats made of her, and identifying the daughter of the swan with Maude Gonne (excursus on her biography, with anecdotes) and determining in what offical capacity, through what accidents of a destiny sought and ironically accepted, the poet found himself doubling as school inspector. So true is this of the majority of his major poems, that the anthologists generally restrict themselves to his minor ones, his critics practice mostly a bastard mode of biography, and his exegetists a Pécuchet's industry of copying parallel passages from *A Vision* (first and second versions), from letters and diaries, from unpublished drafts, and occasionally from other poems. Even Dr. Leavis calls his poetry "little more than a marginal comment on the main activities of his life." (pp. 12-13)

The place to look for light on any poem is in the adjacent poems, which Yeats placed adjacent to it because they belonged there. And the unit in which to inspect and discuss his development is not the poem or sequence of poems but the volume, at least from *Responsibilities* . . . to *A Full Moon in March*. . . . In the Age of Eliot, the poet is supposed to gather his interests and impulses and discharge them utterly in a supreme opus every so often, and evades this responsibility at the price of being not quite a major poet. Those weren't the terms in which Yeats was thinking; we misread him if we suppose either that the majority of the

poems are casual or that in each he was trying for a definitive statement of all that, at the time of composition, he was.

"Men Improve with the Years" looks like an attempt of this kind; it cuts off, of course, too neatly. The poet was once young, and a lover; now he is a monument, and no lady will love him. The quality of the rhetoric is impeccable, but the poem, on some acquaintance, appears to reduce itself to its mere theme, and that theme so simpleminded as to invite biographical eking out. The unspoken premise of Yeats criticism is that we have to supply from elsewhere—from his life or his doctrines—a great deal that didn't properly get into the poems: not so much to explain the poems as to make them rich enough to sustain the reputation. It happens, however, that "Men Improve with the Years" has for context not Yeats' biography but two poems about a man who did not undergo that dubious improvement: ["In Memory of Major Robert Gregory" and "An Irish Airman Foresees His Death"]. (pp. 14-15)

The Wild Swans at Coole is a book about death and the will. A component poem like "Men Improve with the Years" will no more pull loose from it than the "foolish fond old man" speech will pull loose from *King Lear*. It is a radical mistake to think of Yeats as a casual or fragmentary poet whose writings float on a current discoverable only in his biographable life. How much time does he not spend telling us that he has carefully rendered the mere events of his life irrelevant! . . . (p. 22)

Yeats' quarrel with nineteenth-century popular Romanticism encompassed more than its empty moons. He turned with increasing vehemence against a tradition that either laid streams of little poems like cod's eggs or secreted inchoate epics. Against the poet as force of nature he placed of course the poet as deliberate personality, and correspondingly against the usual "Collected Poems" (arranged in the order of composition) he placed the oeuvre, the deliberated artistic Testament, a division of that new Sacred Book of the Arts of which, Mr. Pound has recalled, he used to talk. It was as a process of fragmentation, into little people and little poems, that he viewed the history of European poetry, from the *Canterbury Tales* to the Collected Poems of, say, Lord Byron. (pp. 22-3)

He dreamed as a young man of creating some new *Prometheus Unbound*. One applauds his wisdom in not attempting that sort of *magnum opus*, but it was not likely that he should forget the idea of a work operating on a large scale. Each volume of his verse, in fact, *is* a large-scale work, like a book of the Bible. And as the Bible was once treated by exegetists as the self-sufficient divine book mirroring the other divine book, Nature, but possessing vitality independent of natural experience, so Yeats considered his Sacred Book as similar to "life" but radically separated from it, "mirror on mirror mirroring all the show." (p. 27)

"Day after day," Yeats wrote at the end of *A Vision*, "I have sat in my chair turning a symbol over in my mind, exploring all its details, defining and again defining its elements, testing my convictions and those of others by its unity. . . . It seems as if I should know all if I could but banish such memories and find everything in the symbol." On that occasion nothing came; the symbol was perhaps too limited. But the conviction remains with Yeats that a book, if not a symbol, can supplant the world; if not supplant it, perpetually interchange life with it. Nothing, finally, is more characteristic than his dryly wistful account of the perfected sage for whom the radiance attending the supernatural copulation of dead lovers serves but as a reading light:

> Though somewhat broken by the leaves, that light
> Lies in a circle on the grass; therein
> I turn the pages of my holy book.   (pp. 28-9)

> *Hugh Kenner, "The Sacred Book of Arts,"
> in his* Gnomon: Essays on Contemporary
> Literature *(copyright © 1958 by Hugh Kenner; reprinted by permission of Astor-Honor, Inc.), McDowell, Obolensky, 1958,
> pp. 9-29.*

[Yeats] was a symbolist poet—and never ceased to be one—who broke clean away from the French movement, with which he was only vaguely associated in his youth, to become not only a great poet but probably the greatest poet of this century. (p. 400)

If Yeats's dependence upon Irish characters and history gives him a superficial narrowness, a suggestion of provinciality (though behind every reference is something universal), then breadth, stature, greatness, are more than restored by his astounding ability to express, with passionate plain speech . . . wonderfully organised and most powerfully evocative, each succeeding decade. He is indeed the great poet of the second half of life, who by will and intellect, serving imagination, is able to see his own existence and that of his country raised to a kind of Homeric height. . . . Once he is past his youth, beyond the Aesthetic and Symbolist Movements, his poetry comes from a double act of creation: there are the poems, and behind them the heightened and heroic life out of which they come, itself a creation. (pp. 402-03)

[With] Yeats, from first to last, from theosophy, Rosicrucianism, magic, to automatic writing, spiritualism, the vast wheel in *A Vision,* ideas and beliefs are there to serve his poetry, the ideas to strengthen, the beliefs to light up, that poetic life, that specially created world of his own, out of which his verse comes. When he no longer needs them, as in so many of his last poems when he is playing the mischievous half-mad old man, speaking out about sex, then they are no longer there. (pp. 403-04)

Yeats is not a great poet by accident but by design, and the design, like the poetry, is entirely his own. He had some luck: his country was Ireland, where imaginative life still flourished; he lived in robust health to be old, unlike so many poets; but few men have done more with their luck; and the poetry he has left us, incomparable in this age in its combination of quantity, range and power, proves what poetic genius can accomplish with the aid, all too rare, of character, will, and a noble single-mindedness. (p. 404)

> *J. B. Priestley, in his* Literature and Western
> Man *(copyright © 1960 by J. B. Priestley;
> reprinted by permission of A. D. Peters and
> Company), Harper, 1960.*

Toward the end of his long career, William Butler Yeats wrote: 'I seek an image of the modern mind's discovery of itself.' He never described his own work more truly or more succinctly. Yeats spoke to the modern mind in every way. The rise of nationalism and the political problems that were to create two world wars, the shattering and challenging effects of new science on old beliefs, the reopening of every question of truth and value—all these elements entered his imagination and were there absorbed and transmuted into the symbolic structure of his poetry.

This alchemy illuminates the development of his poetry. Yet, curiously, Yeats is the least 'experimental,' in any obvious sense of that word, of the great modern poets. He does not throw whole poems into free-verse forms, does not violate significantly the ordinary rules of syntax or grammar, never gives a poem over wholly to colloquial idiom and its rhythms. He endeavored rather to invigorate the tradition within which he wrote. (p. 28)

Modern poetry as a whole tends to be tragic in its assumption that we are at a cultural dead end, in which myriad values [are] at cross-purposes. . . . The major poetic situation is the struggle of a heroic sensibility, or Self, to free itself from the condition of living death imposed by this murderous predicament. Clearly, the most elementary way to gain such freedom is to insist on the priority of instinct and emotion over all logical and systematic thought and over the demands of society. In many poems Yeats fastens on the sexual act and the mystery of sexuality as the ultimate sources of meaning. (p. 32)

Very early . . . Yeats begins to use the method of setting interpenetrating opposites against one another as a deliberate way of discovering the character of the human predicament and of exploring the challenge it offers. As one reads his *Autobiography* and other writings, one is recurrently struck by his almost professionally practical attitude toward the uses of supernatural symbolism. . . . His attraction to [various] cults and doctrines had many motivations, but one was overriding: a belief that they provided valuable clues to the unconscious life of mind and spirit and therefore to the sources of creative imagination. He sought a kind of anti-scientific science whose touchstones were the 'truths' of myth and art, a science that would therefore—from a poet's standpoint, at least—go beyond the materialistic thought systems prevailing in his youth and the vague bodiless religiosity that shuddered away from them. He wished, he wrote, to be able to 'hold in a single thought reality and justice'—the difficult 'reality' of experience and the 'justice' of pure vision.

'Pure vision' in Yeats is strangely related to ordinary experience. The world of symbols is not a humane or humanly ordered world, but men in their animal lives as well as in their aspirations are as it were its raw materials. As we have already [noted], it is charged with the sexual principle. (The interpenetrating cones or gyres by which Yeats diagramed the great cycles of thought and personality are a sexual abstraction in themselves.) (pp. 38-9)

[In] the famous 'Sailing to Byzantium' the speaker is an old man between two worlds. Or rather, he is deep within this world, which has all but rejected him and which he now wishes to repossess in a new way—by becoming part of a world of pure creativity in which the fleshly is transformed into the eternal. . . . Two worlds, two kinds of music, two sets of inhabitants, and the speaker between the two, seeking to make them one in his own person. It is man who has created the monuments of his soul's magnificence, but it is these monuments—his great works of art and thought, his spiritual creations, perhaps even God himself—which are needed now to carry him beyond the desperate moment in which he faces his own mortality.

A great deal can be 'learned' from 'Sailing to Byzantium' about attitudes toward death, sex, old age, and art. But whatever we thus learn is incidental to the terrible, blazing confrontation of the two spheres of being, each remote from the other yet inseparable from it. Yeats does not argue with or attempt to explain the human condition, nor does he subordinate to any specific doctrine his poem's anguished prayer for an ideal real enough to encompass and transform the speaker's experience and predicament. The poem comes close to pure symbolism, in the free play it allows thought and feeling over images of the widest possible relevance. (p. 40)

The relation of men to the great cycles of cultural history is another phase of this duality. In Yeats's later work especially the relationship assumes great importance. Do these cycles, in some measure, take their meaning from man himself, or is man merely the passive instrument of an indifferent deity or creative principle? Some of Yeats's finest plays deal with this theme, and in many works he uses as central symbols sacred events of myth and religion in order to present it as suggestively as possible. (p. 41)

Yeats [came] to see also his own personality and the relationships between science and religion as elements to be manipulated by art. In 'Sailing to Byzantium' the poet uses himself in his old age as such a symbolic and dramatic element. In his play *The Resurrection* he converts in a remarkable way the religious attitudes represented by his characters into aspects of the great oppositions defined in *A Vision*. Christ resurrected is but the fusion of pure physicality and pure spirituality mysteriously embodied. It is not the New Testament Jesus, but Dionysus reborn who ushers in a new phase of history. Greek disciple and Hebrew are confounded, while the Syrian, bearing within himself the memories of the 'fabulous formless darkness' before Greek civilization, recognizes the truth. The conception is similar to that of D. H. Lawrence's *The Man Who Died:* Christ paganized and 'revised' so that he now becomes one of those archetypal beings, 'created out of the instinct of man,' which, says Yeats in his *Autobiography,* may be 'the nearest I can go to truth.' (p. 46)

> *M. L. Rosenthal, "Yeats and the Modern Mind," in his* The Modern Poets: A Critical Introduction *(copyright © 1960 by M. L. Rosenthal; reprinted by permission of Oxford University Press, Inc.), Oxford University Press, 1960, pp. 28-48.*

It is very important to remember that with Pound, Yeats, and Eliot it is not the history of poetry or of literature that matters, but history itself. Poetry is actually secondary to anthropology and sociology in the writings of Eliot and Pound. Yeats alone tried to escape from this culture revolution with his head; but his own later poetry is much contaminated with cultural theorizing and historical prophecy. (pp. 90-1)

Yeats begins an essay on magic with these words: "I believe in the practice and philosophy of what we have agreed to call magic, in what I must call the evocation of spirits, though I do not know what they are; in the power of creating magical illusions, in the visions of truth in the depths of the mind when the eyes are closed. . . ." And in three

doctrines, he adds: that many minds can flow into one another and reveal a single mind; that our memories are part of the Great Memory of Nature herself; and that this great mind and great memory can be evoked by symbols.

This credo represents only one of the phases of Yeats' occultism, but it is one which he never rose above. Yeats' use of magic is closer to primitive science than it is to mysticism. There is in all spiritualist and theosophical activity an element of spite, based on the envy of modern science and its triumphs. Even Blake's cry that "Sir Francis Bacon is a Liar" partakes of this bitterness against rational science. Blake, however, appears to be more of a true mystic or gnostic than Yeats. Mysticism and magic are two different things, and it is on the latter inferior level that Yeats rested.

We should remember that in the great decade of Modernism, magic in such forms as spiritualism and theosophy reached its greatest popularity among artists and intellectuals; and that it was in fact an acceptable convention of the poet. Eliot's use of the fortuneteller in *The Waste Land* is a very *topical* allusion. Rilke himself indulged in spiritualism, even though he was aware that greater powers lay in himself than outside him. . . . Neither Blake nor Yeats made a distinction between mysticism proper and magic. We gather from this fact that both poets were exploring the possibilities of a cultural *mystique,* a *mystique* lying outside religion and outside modern rationalist science.

I take it that the failure to distinguish between mysticism and magic in Modern Poetry is deliberate and strategic. Religion is not a primary force in modern civilization and some substitute for religion must be found. So reasoned the Pounds and Eliots and Yeatses and Stevenses. Mysticism proper was therefore suspect; it lay at the very heart of religions. The mystical must therefore be intellectualized in some manner. (pp. 92-3)

Yeats' scrambling of mystics, alchemists, theosophists, neo-Platonists, and so forth, is his attempt to steer clear of both religion and philosophy. "Science" of course is his avowed enemy, but so are clericalism and orderly philosophical speculation. Occultism was to Yeats what anthropology was to Eliot—an instrument for fashioning the culture religion. It is commonly said about Yeats' interest in the magical that it helped him perceive his poetic images, or something equally silly. Yeats himself is responsible for that interpretation of *A Vision* and of most of his culture poetry. In reality, *A Vision,* like the notes to *The Waste Land,* the *Notes Toward a Definition of Culture,* or Pound's book on *Kulchur,* is a highly programmatic, even political work. The occultism suddenly jells into a practical psychology and ethics, providing not "metaphors for poetry" as the spirits whispered to Yeats, but a full-scale commentary on socialism, democracy, famous periods of history, and great men. The object of the book is to help create the cultural climate in which the poet can again take up the robes of authority, dethroning rationalism and clericalism. Everyone who loves poetry forgives Yeats this book, although it would be foolhardy to overlook its dangers. (pp. 93-4)

People generally agree that there are several Yeatses: the youthful romantic poet of love and the Celtic twilight, the Yeats of Ireland reborn, the Yeats of the Hermetic societies, and finally the Yeats of world culture. These appellations are grotesquely crude but in effect they give the well-known departments of Yeats' writings. And they are some-what related. The love poems are also folklore poems to a degree; the patriotic poems of the Irish revolution are also part of the folklore idealism and part of the esoteric explorations simultaneously; and the Culture poems are the final effort to project the subjective personal Yeats, the national Yeats, and the magus or alchemist Yeats into the figure of the seer of history. It is in this final phase that Yeats writes his occult book *A Vision*, in which he contends that he will adapt the symbolic and mythological techniques of Swedenborg and Blake to an interpretation of history, "historical movements and actual men and women." So here is Yeats acting precisely like Pound and Eliot. Yeats is a poet of true genius and not a mere opportunist, but he's off to make a sociological ass of himself all the same. (pp. 100-01)

Altogether, Yeats poses one of the central questions of the modern Classical poet, of which he is one of the gods. That question is also Eliot's question and Pound's question, namely, what is the position of the poet vis-à-vis history? From my point of view, I consider the question unreal and not worth the asking. If the self-consciousness of this attitude and the pompousness of it did not utterly defeat Yeats, that can only be because his genius never completely deserted him even throughout his intellectual soul-searchings. But it is my opinion that Yeats will always remain pretty much a poet of his time, because of his commitment to the historical role. The burlesque magus and spiritualist do not add to his stature; they detract from it; all the pronouncements about history and historical types are so much doodling in the margins of his mind. The poetry itself becomes affected; while the idiom steadily increases in subtlety and beauty, the feeling becomes more violent, turning against himself. Yeats could not make peace with age in any aspect; his central image becomes that of "this caricature," decrepit age tied to him "as to a dog's tail." Even that simple wisdom of reconciliation with age is denied him. That Byzantium symbol is a desperate remedy, no remedy at all. That vision of history is hardly a great vision after all but more of a travesty of the great cosmic systems of emanation which he had borrowed from the Hindus and the Neo-Platonists. The flaw in Yeats is his narrowly conceived idea of civilization; Yeats is quite eighteenth century in the long run. He loved Blake, but did he really learn anything from Blake? It appears not. There is no marriage of heaven and hell in William Butler Yeats—save in Byzantium. Think of the Byzantine mosaic and then try to set beside it the flowing angelography of Blake's pen. There is a complete divergence of imaginations.

The key with Yeats is the word "civilization," the alpha and omega of his culture philosophy. And civilization apparently is—Byzantium. Little wonder that Yeats, a scant generation after his death, is considered a master craftsman of the poem, and nothing else. (pp. 112-13)

> *Karl Shapiro, "W. B. Yeats: Trial by Culture," in his* In Defense of Ignorance *(copyright © 1960 by Karl Shapiro; reprinted by permission of Random House, Inc.), Random House, 1960, pp. 87-113.*

[In *The Rose*,] Yeats . . . touches the core of his inspiration. He is indeed a visionary poet, as he is claiming to be. But his vision is magical, not mystical. We shall make little of him if we are unable to believe that the elemental creatures did really go to and fro about his table. His evident

concern for masks and roles, and even for poses; a recurrent tone of scepticism, which is however less genuine than prudential; the unfashionableness of spiritualism; the general critical persuasion that he advances from ectoplasm to bronze; the comparatively small attention paid to his prose: all these have tended to encourage the view that his magic was little more than a picturesque embroidery on his cloak, which must vanish as soon as he went naked. In reality it is part of his mind. (pp. 306-07)

[Very] little, if anything, that came to him either in extrasensory perception or through occultist study [and recorded in *The Celtic Twilight*] appears to have any enduring importance, or much beauty, in itself. It is the mysteriousness of the intimations concerned rather than any real and meaningful coherence to be established among them that brings him to poetry. (pp. 308-09)

The greater part of *The Wind Among the Reeds* is given over to lyrics of frustrated love [written in his early symbolist manner]. It is in fact Maud Gonne's book. . . . In the 'slow moving elaborate poems' which Yeats directly associates with 'Rosa Alchemica' there are many . . . percurrent epithets, most of them to be fairly described as of the fainting sort. They knit perfectly with the long slow fainting rhythms to a total effect which is narrow, hypnoidal, and undeniably beautiful in the manner that the poet designs.

It is doubtful whether an attentive reader, uninstructed by biographers and literary historians, would divine that between this and the preceding collection of Yeats's poems there have arrived a grand passion and a new literary theory. Here first and foremost is the disciple of Rossetti and Morris still, doing what he has been doing before, but doing it very much better. Part of the increased effectiveness does certainly lie in the essentially symbolist technique of exploiting mythological material for the purpose of intimating mood and emotion. But although some of the poems are susceptible in a new degree to esoteric interpretation, the tensions between actual and ideal experience, between natural and supernatural upon which most are built, remain intelligible even when mysterious. . . . (pp. 319-20)

Yeats always composed aloud, and appears to have got very little assistance from the appearance of his verse on a page. To the end of his life he remained entirely ignorant of the notations of prosody, a subject in which poets commonly take, whether usefully or not, a certain amount of interest. (p. 322)

It is in the latter part of *The Wild Swans at Coole,* in poems composed shortly before the publication of the volume . . . , that we come upon a first cluster of poems enigmatic in a new way. They are contemporaneous with the beginnings of Mrs. Yeats's automatic writing, and are related—although the relation is sometimes in itself perplexing—to the 'explanation of life' which Yeats evolved from a study of the automatic writing, and to which he gave the title of *A Vision*. To what we can make of this work, whether in its first (1925) or drastically revised (1937) form, we are obliged henceforth frequently to appeal, since much that we immediately acknowledge as valuable in the later poetry contains a large admixture of matter that only some understanding of Yeats's elaborate 'system' seems to hold out any hope of rendering fully intelligible. (pp. 352-53)

A Vision . . . sees alike the spectacle of universal history and the disposition and progression of individual human beings as ruled by planetary influence. And indeed if we sufficiently juggle with the stars it is not difficult to make ourselves, being represented as their tennis-balls, seem to bounce on intelligible principles. *A Vision,* generated from an anxiety felt by a devotee of magic to find such principles, holds singularly little intellectual persuasiveness. What gives it a certain power—and its considerable utility for the development of Yeats's poetry—is its odd manner of telescoping a traditional astrological determinism with some irregular derivative of the Hegelian dialectic. The Heavens revolve, and a Golden or a Brazen Age returns. But as well as the Great Wheel there are the Gyres, interpreted in terms of which man shows as involved, to some artistically sufficient effect of drama and the dynamic, in a perpetual action of developing and resolving contradictions.

If we are to arrive at some understanding of *A Vision,* however, it is with the 'eighte and twenty mansiouns' of traditional astrology that we must begin. Or rather it is with these as Yeats qualifies them:

> Twenty-and-eight, and yet but six-and-twenty
> The cradles that a man must needs be rocked in.

Chaucer and his authorities are innocent of this mysterious retrenchment. It is at the heart of Yeats's system. (pp. 356-57)

[Although] the system excogitated in *A Vision* has a certain psychological validity, and is for this reason capable of enriching the poetry on many occasions, it seems to be the product of a somewhat depressive and even regressive phase in Yeats's life—one extending over a number of years, and coming to an end when he goes seriously to work on *The Tower.* (p. 362)

From now on much of Yeats's poetry is increasingly difficult. But he was well aware that Homer (although presently to be described as 'mad as the mist and snow') talks sense, and that the paralogical achievements of symbolism, with all that they have added to the resources of poetry, can be no more than adjuvant in any sustained and major utterance. This perception, which he shares with the other great and traditional poet of the age, Mr. T. S. Eliot, controls notably the deployment of his total powers in *The Tower.* (p. 369)

'Under Ben Bulben' was designed by Yeats as his last poem. It ends with his epitaph, and resumes in less than a hundred octosyllabic lines almost everything he has ever said. This inclusiveness neglects neither old prejudices (there are no such things, we want to tell him, as 'Base-born products of base beds') nor old hobby-horses: the persuasion, for example, so dear to the boy who could never manage sums, that 'Measurement began our might'. But there are few finer poetic testaments—and not least so in the manner in which the verses come home at the end and submit to the sobriety of actual historical process. . . . Yet in 'Cuchulain Comforted' there is a testament in a sense more nearly final still. It was written, we are told, out of a dream, and a prose draft 'dictated at 3 a.m. on 7 Jan. 1939'. Yeats never achieved a more mysterious poem. 'Thought hid in thought, dream hid in dream'—the phrase he had struck out more than forty years before for the sort of poetry he believed to be his—would be a fair description of it. And if explicators despair before 'Cuchulain Comforted', it may be only to an acknowledging of one truth about poetry in general which even a literary education ought not to drive wholly out of our heads.

Yet that is not a last word. Great poetry can never wholly disengage itself from religion and philosophy, or stand clear of what Matthew Arnold called 'the shadows and dreams and false shows of knowledge'. Yeats's system is as eccentric and obscure as Blake's. But, as with Blake, it is an integral part of some of his finest writing: a framework, rather than a scaffolding which may be stripped away. In the climate in which it matured there was much to encourage a hazardous luxuriance not in mystery but in mystification. It may be true, as one severe critic avers, that some of Yeats's most magical effects are no more than a sort of 'ad libbing' in an incantatory void. Still, his speculative efforts do represent an ordering, after a fashion, of such intuitions as lie at the roots of poetry, and it is necessary that they should be rigorously examined by scholars equipped for the task. From these roots come the magnificent exfoliations of his greatest lyrics. *The Chestnut-Tree* will be a good title for any finally adequate study of the poet:

> O chestnut-tree, great-rooted blossomer,
> Are you the leaf, the blossom or the bole?
>
> (pp. 420-21)

J. I. M. Stewart, "Yeats," in Eight Modern Writers, *edited by F. P. Wilson and Bonamy Dobrée (copyright © 1963 by Oxford University Press; reprinted by permission of The Clarendon Press, Oxford), Oxford University Press, 1963, pp. 294-421.*

Yeats's father once told him that poetry concerns itself with the creation of Paradises, and it is certain that the Otherworlds invented or adapted by a poet, whether demonic, purgatorial, or paradisal, are one index to the bias of his imagination. Yeats's multiple Otherworlds, critiques of "this world" both personal and social, are found throughout his prose and poetry. . . . The Otherworlds Yeats created he also, for the most part, inherited: there appear fitfully throughout his works almost all the notions of Paradise, Fairy Land, the Elysian Fields, and so on, that are common stock in folk tale, myth, and religion, and even the more eccentric Swedenborgian Otherworld is given houseroom. But as in all drawings from ample mythologies, the selection is determined by the characteristic impulse of the poet, and Yeats's Fairyland is neither Spenser's nor Shelley's, but his own, just as his Purgatory, whatever it owes to Dante or Swedenborg, is a mixture uniquely compounded.

In the early plays, the divorce between this world and the Otherworld is complete and tragic. . . . The tragedy [in *The Countess Cathleen*] is unequivocal: the Yeatsian Otherworld cannot intersect at all with the world of the poor, and though Cathleen is translated to heaven in a Pre-Raphaelite apotheosis, the poet is left wishing for death, his songs unsingable without their object. On the other hand, no attempt is made to deny the chilly brevity of the Otherworld. . . . (pp. 308-09)

The Otherworld, seen in the early plays chiefly in relation to sexual love (and peripherally in relation to poetry and song) takes on an ampler frame of reference in the middle and late plays, though Yeats never abandons his critique of human love through an Otherworld vision. (p. 311)

The Otherworld can be dramatized with a dry irony, too, as it is in that disillusioned play, *At the Hawk's Well . . . ,* where the forces for and against the Sidhe almost cancel each other out. (p. 313)

Where the Otherworld in *The Dreaming of the Bones* was a bittersweet night filled with clouds, winds, music, and the drifting pathos of separated lovers, the Purgatory of the play of that name is a mechanical time-interval, rather like the clocks with processions of grotesque figures that appear and disappear as the hour strikes. This is memory seen, not under its nostalgic aspect, but under its aspect of obsessive return. . . . No murder knife can stop the terrible repetition of the mechanical scene, and the image of the Old Man laying about him in futile expungings of his line while the Purgatory before him goes on undisturbed is Yeats's coldest statement on the irony of attempts to deal in peripheral ways with human fixation. . . . [Both] *Purgatory* and *The Dreaming of the Bones* may be said to embody the same reflection found in "A Dialogue of Self and Soul," but in one, the temptation against impassivity is nostalgia, in the other, obsessional sexuality (in the mother) and obsessional hatred-and-sympathy (in the Old Man): that is, we can regard the past with either love or hatred, and either makes our view less lucid than it ought to be. The metaphors for the inhabitants of the Otherworld change accordingly.

The final group of Otherworld plays refer to it under images of destruction and copulation, sometimes combined, sometimes separately: the copulation is usually with a magical beast or bird, a unicorn or a Great Herne, though it may be copulation with an icon as well. Sexual intercourse as a metaphor for the interaction of the Otherworld with this one appears in Yeats's earlier plays as seduction by a fairy mistress rather than by a divine animal; it was after his preoccupation with historical analogies (the swan, the dove) that he began to dwell more seriously on his metaphors for the same events (the Rough Beast, the Unicorn). (pp. 316-17)

Purgatory and *The Death of Cuchulain* are Yeats's last dramatic statements about the Otherworld: the first quails before the power of the impure images of memory to tyrannize over the mind, the other glories in the power of the memory to ransom the present by calling up a heroic past. The first deals with the unredeemed imagination, the second with the redeeming imagination.

In the relation of the Otherworld to this world, Yeats seems to suggest his view of the relation of art to life, though the terms are more equivocal, often, than that. It would be truer to say that the Otherworlds may represent the activity of the imagination on the events of experience. The imagination may paralyze, as in *Purgatory;* it may promise and not perform, as in *The Hawk's Well;* it may be a narcotic, as in *The Shadowy Waters;* it may be rejuvenating, as in *The Player Queen;* it may be frigid until "desecrated" by brute experience, as in *A Full Moon in March;* it may be temptation, as in *The Dreaming of the Bones:* or it may be the only source of value, as in *The Death of Cuchulain.* To know the whole canon of Yeatsian Otherworlds is to see Yeats "complete his partial mind" on the subject of his own genius. (p. 321)

> *Helen Hennessy Vendler, "Yeats's Changing Metaphors for the Otherworld," in* Modern Drama *(copyright 1964, A. C. Edwards; with the permission of* Modern Drama*), December, 1964, pp. 308-21.*

Yeats' account of the fortunes of the soul after death [in *A* *Vision*] owes much to Platonism and to Indian philosophy. Here, of course, are to be found the most fantastic aspects of Yeats' system. The system as a whole, he tells us, was dictated by the spirits through his wife's mediumship. And that account itself will be sufficient to disqualify it for most hard-bitten moderns. But extravagant as the book is, Yeats never really loses his hold on reality. And he does not lose his sense of humor. He says two things that make it easier for us to maintain our faith in him: in the first place, according to Yeats, the teaching spirits told him their object was not to instruct him in philosophy but to furnish him metaphors for his poetry. In the second place, Yeats closes his book with the declaration: "I would restore to the philosopher his mythology," and the term he chooses, "mythology," is significant. But Yeats goes on to raise the question of his own belief in his system. To that question he replies with a counterquestion: whether the word "belief," as the questioner will use it, properly belongs to our age. It is a fair question and a discerning question. To sum up, Yeats' fantastic system is frankly a fiction, a myth, but unless we are dogmatic positivists we shall at our peril utterly deny that it purveys truth. (p. 48)

I find in the later Yeats, by the way, a great deal of Nietzsche. The later Yeats rejoices in the celebration of man's sheer vitality and man's ability to do and to suffer. Nietzsche argued that in beauty "contrasts are overcome, the highest sign of power thus manifesting itself in the conquest of opposites." The artist, Nietzsche declared, creates out of joy and strength—not out of weakness—and the most convincing artists are precisely those "who make harmony ring out of every discord." The great artist is tested, Nietzsche felt, by the "extent to which he can acknowledge the terrible and questionable character of things," and still affirm the goodness of life.

These comments by Nietzsche apply beautifully to the magnificent poetry that Yeats wrote during the 'twenties and 'thirties. The Yeats of this period sees the typical tragic protagonist, a Hamlet or a Lear, as gay, "Gaiety transfiguring all that dread." (pp. 52-3)

The later poetry of Yeats does indeed "make harmony ring out of every discord"—in its rapt exaltation deliberately introducing the discord sometimes so that the poet may display his ability to resolve it. In one of his earlier poems Yeats wrote of Dante that he "set his chisel to the hardest stone." At the end of his own career it is always to the hardest stone that Yeats sets his chisel. (p. 53)

[The] restoration of the dimension of awe is the most significant thing about Yeats' treatment of Christianity. He pushes away all the timid Victorian pieties and the soft pre-Raphaelite distortions and appeals again to the Christian force that displays itself in Byzantine art or in the European middle ages. And, most important of all, in either case Yeats takes the Christian symbols seriously by bringing them into direct relation to man's perennial problems. (pp. 53-4)

As for Yeats' personal beliefs as distinct from the dramatization of beliefs which fill his poetry—this . . . is not easy to determine. The difficulty is in part that which dogs attempts to determine Shakespeare's personal beliefs. Like that great dramatist, Yeats throws himself into each new dramatic situation with sufficient ardor and conviction to give to each new poem his own personal energy, and thus to make it come alive. (p. 57)

But Yeats' ability to adopt varying stances—what Yeats could have called his power of negative capability—is the source of Yeats' great strength as a poet. (pp. 57-8)

Cleanth Brooks, "W. B. Yeats: Search for a New Myth," in his The Hidden God: Studies in Hemingway, Faulkner, Yeats, Eliot, and Warren (copyright, 1963, by Yale University), Yale University Press, 1964, pp. 44-67.

What is the mental atmosphere that makes Yeats's poems so individualistic? We might try to establish first the outer borders of his mind, with the initial admission that, as Yeats said, these are constantly shifting; and then its inner qualities. The intimation that seems to have been with him from his earliest days is that life as we generally experience it is incomplete, but that at moments it appears to transcend itself and yield moments of completeness or near-completeness.... In his early work Yeats conceives of the boundary line between the worlds of completeness and incompleteness as twilit, in his later work it is lit by lightning. Whether the light is blurred or stark there are strange crossings-over. (p. xvii)

And now we are led from a comparison of worlds to one of people. Man, according to Yeats's view, is a being who is always endeavouring to construct by fiction what he lacks in fact. Born incomplete, he conceives of completeness and to that extent attains it. We outfling ourselves upon the universe, people the desert with our fertile images. The hero does this unconsciously, the artist consciously, but all men do it in their degree. The dead bone upon the shore in 'Three Things' sings still of human love. Space and time are unreal, Yeats sometimes concedes to the philosophers, but he says they are marvellously unreal; they, and life and death, heaven and hell, day and night, are human images imposed like form upon the void. (pp. xviii-xix)

If we try to relate Yeats's poems more narrowly to the contrast between daimons and men on the one hand, and between man and his limitations on the other, I think we will see that each such contrast gains its force from a confrontation of passive acceptance with energetic defiance.... The pacific soul, which Yeats contrasts in his later verse with the military self, always offers a conventional way to heaven, and the self always rejects it, preferring the turmoil of this world, with its desperate search for words and images, to an easy and dumb-striking heaven. Every poem establishes alternatives to indicate only one choice is worth making, and that the agonized, unremunerative, heroic one.

These are not Yeats's ideas or beliefs; they are the mental atmosphere in which he lived, or if that term sounds too climatic, they are the seethings, the agitations of his mind which he learned to control and direct. His symbolism has to be understood not as a borrowing from Mallarmé, but as the only way in which he could express himself. 'I have no speech but symbol,' he wrote. His symbols are condensations of his theme that all struggle is futile except the struggle with futility, his recognition of the problem of the empty cornucopia, the crowded void. (pp. xx-xxi)

I sometimes think that we could try to codify the laws that govern the complexities of Yeats's poetry. Every poem offers alternative positions. While the choice between them may surprise us, we can be sure it will be based upon a preference for what is imprudent, reckless, contrary to fact,

but that in so choosing the poet does not act out of folly but out of understandable passion. The alternative is never completely overwhelmed, but remains like the other side of the moon, or, to use another of Yeats's images, like some imprisoned animal, ready to burst out again with its message of common sense or of renunciation of the world. The basic choice of the poem is reflected in the symbols, which either contain the same alternatives or at any rate imply them, as day implies night. The poem ends not in a considered conclusion, but in a kind of breathlessness, a breakthrough from the domain of caution and calculation to that of imprudence and imagination; the poem gathers its strength from putting down one view with another, from saying, against the utmost opposition, what must be said.

Usually the poems take one of two directions: either they are visionary, concerned with matters of prophecy, of the relations of the time-world and daimonic timelessness, or they are concerned with human enterprise, the relations of people with each other or with their own secret hopes and ambitions. In the visionary poems such as 'Leda and the Swan' or 'The Second Coming,' Yeats is concerned to intermesh the divine world with the animal, to show the world of time as centaurlike, beautiful and monstrous, aspiring and deformed. In the poems which deal with artists or with heroes or with other men, he wishes also to show how brute fact may be transmogrified, how we can sacrifice ourselves, in the only form of religious practice he sanctions, to our imagined selves which offer far higher standards than anything offered by social convention. If we must suffer, it is better to create the world in which we suffer, and this is what heroes do spontaneously, artists do consciously, and all men do in their degree. (pp. xxiii-xxiv)

The more one reads Yeats, the more his works appear to rotate in a few orbits. Again and again we are obliged to ask the same questions he asked. He was greatly concerned, for example, over the relations of his themes to his beliefs, especially because from the very beginning he adopted attitudes in different poems which seemingly conflicted with one another. This diversity, which he perhaps hit upon intuitively, he came to defend rationally in ways that most modern poets have left unexpressed. He displayed and interpreted the direction in which poetry was to go. (p. 1)

Themes and symbols in Yeats are questions of execution as well as of content, and style, with which he was so deeply concerned, was a question of content as well as of execution. Changes in rhythm, vocabulary, and syntax were substantive. Style, he considered, was the self-conquest of the writer who was not a man of action....

Beyond theme, symbol, and style is the general pattern or framework of Yeats's verse, in which each of these participates. Every poem embodies a schematization, conscious as well as unconscious, of his way of living and seeing; and all his poems form a larger scheme which we can watch in the process of evolving. The stature of his work, which seems to tower over that of his contemporaries, comes largely from this ultimate adhesion of part to part to form a whole....

Yeats's work, so strongly individualized, remains difficult to classify. It has been described as magical or occult poetry, but both terms must be rejected. (p. 2)

Yeats found in occultism, and in mysticism generally, a point of view which had the virtue of warring with accepted beliefs, and of warring enthusiastically and authoritatively. He wanted to secure proof that experimental science was limited in its results, in an age when science made extravagant claims; he wanted evidence that an ideal world existed, in an age which was fairly complacent about the benefits of actuality; he wanted to show that the current faith in reason and in logic ignored a far more important human faculty, the imagination. (p. 3)

Yeats is a romantic, but with compunctions. He admires imagination and individualism and excess and the golden future as much as Blake did, but he also at times evinces a strong strain of awareness that man's possibilities may not be limitless. He is unexpectedly interested in determinism; he insists on stateliness, courtliness, control, and orderliness as criteria for judging past, present, and future. His nature is not Wordsworthian, his heroes are not Byronic, his emotional expression is not Shelleyan. (p. 4)

It was as an Irish poet that he aspired to become known, and now that he is dead the category seems more fully established and distinguished from the state of being an English poet. Yeats's Irishism is of a special kind. Like Joyce's prose, his poetry makes use of national and local borders only to transcend them. He is Irish; he is also anti-Irish in an Irish way; and his interest in Irishmen is always subordinated to an interest in men. His method of treating his Irish background and subject-matter is therefore exceedingly complex. Ireland is his symbol for the world, and he is caught between estrangement and love for both.

His work finds its real centre in the imagination, which is both sensual and spiritual, with no other aim than the creation of images as lusty as itself. At its most extreme he asserts that the imagination creates its own world. There is also the reverse of this medal, an acknowledgment that the world should be the creation of the imagination but is not. These two conceptions underlie Yeats's early work as well as his late. . . . (pp. 4-5)

To voice these conceptions Yeats created three principal dramatic roles. The first, that of the seer, presents the power of the imagination and the comparative frailty of experience most strikingly. The seer has little or no personality of his own; he is often at pains to declare that his images are not remembered from experience but imaginatively inspired. He reports on moments of crisis when the tension between the ideal and the actual is greatest, as when the swan descends to Leda or the dreadful beast of the second coming slouches towards Bethlehem. Not many of the poems present so momentous a view, but those that do lend a prophetic firmness to the whole.

More often the protagonist of the poems takes the parts of victim and assessor. As the frustrated, unsuccessful lover of the early verse, as the hounded public figure of the middle period, as the time-struck, age-worn old man of the later work, he has always something of the scapegoat about him. The scapegoat's sacrifice is not, however, an empty one. To abandon himself to a hopeless passion and all its attendant suffering has the fruitful result of glorifying the beloved and, by implication, the perfect concord which his imagination conceives but cannot proffer. The lover's failure becomes symbolic of the defect of all life. To give up easy comfort and calm for the dangerous losing battle with vulgarity and prudery, as the protagonist and his friends do in Yeats's middle period, has the virtue of perpetuating those qualities which are imaginatively sacred, such as courage, freedom from abstract restraints, and creative force. To struggle against 'dull decrepitude' and death enables the speaker to defend life to its bitter end.

So, although at each stage he is victimized, the victimization is only half the story, the other half being the endowment of the situation with heroic consequence. (pp. 5-6)

His lifelong occupation with tragic drama is understandable . . . , for life is an endless competition between the imaginative hero and the raw material of his experience, the experience being necessary to bring out the heroic qualities to the full. The hero is one who sacrifices nothing of the ideal he has imagined for himself; death can do nothing but confirm his integrity.

Such are the lineaments that mark Yeats's work from first to last. They lend a strange excitement to it, as if it had all been written for an emergency, and to the search for what lie behind it, the choice among literary directions, the development of theme, symbol, style, and pattern. (pp. 10-11)

By becoming an Irish poet Yeats chose an art which would intensify the significance of a restricted area. For this intensification he needed rigorous discipline, and one means of securing it was to borrow for his poetry effects which had been achieved not by other poets but by practitioners of other arts. We cannot tell the precise degree of deliberateness in Yeats's borrowings, but they occur throughout the whole of his literary career and can hardly have been accidental. . . . Among his earliest poems was one which attempted to restate in words a painting by Nettleship; and among his latest was one, 'News for the Delphic Oracle', modelled in part from a cast at the Victoria and Albert Museum. He went to other arts more self-consciously: to the drama because it required lifelike passions at a time when he feared to be too ethereal; to the sung lyric because its strong rhythms and generalized sentiments precluded a private art; to the dance, which united an abstract, stylized, and symbolic pattern with visible action, because he needed an impersonal element in his work. (p. 20)

He apparently thought of tapestry as an art of great intricacy and rather limited means; looking for boundaries for his imagination, he may unconsciously have imitated the way that the artists he knew cut out excited rhythms, strong passions, and unexpected developments, in favour of a decorum and continuity of rhythm and feeling. He would devise an alternative to vulnerable intimacy, with the forms of life imbedded in pattern and beauty. It offered a texture suited to his intention of binding the world together. (p. 21)

The tapestry analogy manifests itself in various ways. Each of Yeats's early books is unified in tone, and each has the form of a series of related panels. He groups the details in each poem, as a rule, around a single image, such as an old woman, a lovely lady, or fairies on horseback. Grammatical devices enable him to secure an especially close texture. (p. 22)

The word 'phantasmagoria' was one which Yeats, following Rimbaud, Baudelaire, and Poe, grew fond of during the 'nineties. It designated for him that structure of related images through which he could express himself, and through which, as he later said, 'the dream and the reality' might 'face one another in visible array'. What was personal and transitory might be welded with what was impersonal and permanent through a group of images which had attracted men for hundreds of years. These images were phantasmagoric not in that they were illusory, but in that they represented, more than they participated in, the secret essences of things. (p. 62)

[Yeats] distinguished between two kinds of symbols, those 'that evoke emotions alone', and those 'that evoke ideas alone, or ideas mingled with emotions'. His clear preference was for the second sort. . . .

Among the intellectual symbols we can distinguish two sorts, or better, two functions: cooperative and emphatic. While any symbol could serve either function, the four elements of earth, air, fire, and water frequently are good examples of cooperative symbols. They set up eddies of association which are auxiliary to the main symbol of the poem. That main or emphatic symbol is a centre of attraction around which the mood gathers, and many of Yeats's poems, from 'The Rose of the World' to 'The Black Tower', are built around such centres. (p. 63)

Yeats's poetry is bound together by one unchanging conviction, the desirability of intense, unified, imaginative consciousness. But apart from this central pillar it reveals a series of points of view, sometimes parallel and sometimes divergent. What are we to make of his various attitudes towards reality, truth, life, death, and imagination? The question is of special moment because he kept increasingly as his career progressed to the ideal of writing poems of insight and knowledge which he had marked out for himself in youth. . . . The quality of the great writer, he maintained on one occasion, was '*Negative Capability,* that is, when a man is capable of being in uncertainties, mysteries, doubts, without any irritable reaching after fact and reason'. Yeats's conception of his art moved beyond this theory, because his verse depended, more than Keats's, on presenting a complete picture of the self, and to do so became full of reaching after fact and reason.

To explain and confirm his practice Yeats evolved a hypothesis which is closer to defining the situation in which the modern poet finds himself than negative capability. It might be described as *affirmative capability,* for it begins with the poet's difficulties but emphasizes his resolutions of them. . . . Yeats considered it the poet's duty to invade the province of the intellect as well as of the emotions. Neither the intellect nor the emotions can be satisfied to remain in 'uncertainties, mysteries, and doubts'; they demand the more solid fare of affirmations. (p. 238)

He is caught between the meaningless beliefs which the mob continually casts up before him, and the struggle to affirm on his own, individuality being a vital test of the affirmation's quality. The struggle is the more desperate because its sanction, his divinity—the sphere or world of completeness—is far-off and known only slightly. In this situation the poet receives help from tradition. . . . Old forms and situations give the poet dignity and reassurance. (p. 240)

His attitude towards scepticism is not entirely defined, but he was working towards some such generalization as this: in so far as scepticism prevents positive statement, it is a danger to art. Such scepticism feeds parasitically upon the beliefs of others, and cannot satisfy the mind. But in so far as scepticism is one of the obstacles which the poet masters in the course of his attempt to transcend the limits of his incompleteness, it may render his positiveness, wrung from him partly in spite of himself, more poignant, and more noble because marked with the scars of battle. It is the wind resistance which makes flight possible. In poems which scepticism has affected, the specific affirmation is often of less central consequence than the struggle with the incompleteness of the human situation; the poet labours to speak his whole mind, yet—such are his human limitations —even his most fervent utterances will reflect the incompleteness he cannot wholly overcome.

Yeats requires an art based upon affirmations, then, by representing it as the expression of the fundamental urge of living beings, to transcend themselves. It is necessary because, just as the artist finds in tradition an 'exposition of intellectual needs', so his art secures its value also by satisfying needs, his own and those of his readers, as fully as possible. . . . Art, then, to be genuine, must include those affirmations which will help to form 'a vision of reality which satisfies the whole being'.

Yet if such affirmations are only incomplete and limited expressions of the truth, how can they compose a vision of reality? Yeats answers, first, that the vision of reality which the poet gives us may be psychological; that is, it may be a vision of total human personality, and if so, the expression of divergent points of view and an awareness of the limits of each would contribute to the totality. . . . But Yeats, while he agrees with the therapeutic function of art, believes that it has also a revelatory function. He holds that the total expression of human personality must include our partial transcendence of our incompleteness, our intimations of a state which is not incomplete. To the extent that it furnishes these, the artist's vision of reality has an element of objective truth as well as of social and personal usefulness.

There are moments in Yeats's later life when he speaks of reality a little differently, when he has less confidence that our affirmations are even approximations of truth. At these moments he implies that reality is entirely distinct from human experience, that we cannot transcend our incompleteness. If it is so distinct, how can we establish any contact with it? Yeats suggests that we can express it through a series of contradictions. . . . Through focusing in themes and symbols the contradictory attitudes to which the world of appearance gives rise, attitudes which entrance his mind without securing its final allegiance, the poet presents reality as if by antithesis.

The conception of affirmative capability provides, in short, that poetry must centre on affirmations or the struggle for affirmations, that it must satisfy the whole being, not the moral, intellectual, or passionate nature alone, and that it must present a vision of reality. Our backs against the wall, we cannot decide whether reality is adequately described by our intimations of a state of completeness, or whether it is describable only as the opposite of all that we can see and imagine. In either case the artist must be its interpreter. Affirmative capability does not free him from the responsibility of intellectual search or understanding of experience, as negative capability might seem to; rather it forces him to live, as well as to write, in such a way that his consciousness will be inclusive. Any narrowness, any adherence to a given affirmation beyond the moment that it satisfies the whole being, any averting of the eye, destroys the vision.

The conception of affirmative capability is particularly suited to a time when there is no agreement over ultimate questions, when we are not even sure exactly what we think on matters that are so crucial and yet so obscure. It is suited to a time when man is not regarded as a fixed being with fixed habits, but as a being continually adapting and readapting himself to the changing conditions of his body and mind and of the outside world. We can keep silence altogether, but if we speak out we must do so in terms of some such hypothesis as affirmative capability. (pp. 243-44)

What emerges from a consideration of Yeats's whole poetic career is an impression of its seriousness and importance. All his work, in both poetry and prose, was an attempt to embody a way of seeing. That way is close to that of Blake and the romantics, but not identical with theirs. Like Blake, Yeats conceives of the imagination as the shaping power which transforms the world; but coming a century later, he has a tough-minded appreciation of the world's intransigence. He has little hope of building Jerusalem even in Ireland's green and pleasant land, and for him as for Keats, one function of art is to freeze life's inadequacies so as to render them harmless and beautiful. More than Keats or Coleridge, more perhaps even than Blake, he defends the imagination with the defiance of a man who sees himself as preventing the incursions of chaos. Yet his poetry is as much offensive as defensive. It fights its way beyond the frontiers of common apprehension, and brings previously untamed areas of thought and feeling under strong rule. (p. 245)

In modern poetry Yeats and T. S. Eliot stand at opposite poles. For while both see life as incomplete, Eliot puts his faith in spiritual perfection, the ultimate conversion of sense to spirit. Yeats, on the other hand, stands with Michelangelo for 'profane perfection of mankind', in which sense and spirit are fully and harmoniously exploited, and 'body is not bruised to pleasure soul'. So strongly does he hold this view that he projects sensuality into heaven to keep heaven from being ethereal and abstract. He presents this faith with such power and richness that Eliot's religion, in spite of its honesty and loftiness, is pale and infertile in comparison.

Yeats's richness, or better, his magnificence of tone, comes partly from the sumptuous images of his work, partly from the different levels of diction and the intricate rhythms at his command. His sense of decorum never fails him because he knows through long testing the value of everything; and this power to estimate things at their true worth contributes to his talent for general statement. . . .

In his endeavour to express these moments, he changed many elements of his verse, yet his identity is stamped upon them everywhere. His symbols keep altering, but the later symbols, in spite of their increased animation when compared to the earlier, are mature equivalents rather than new departures. His heroes also remain recognizable through many transformations; in his later writings they do not abdicate their thrones or take up island apiculture or go mad, but that is because they become aware of their essential isolation even when performing some communal role, and because their internal battle depends only slightly on external circumstance. They remain uncommon men, uncommon in their nobility, charismatic in the power with which they excite emulation and focus intellect and emotion. The heroes of the later verse are simply the heroes of the early verse who have, like their creator, matured.

The principles of growth and of stability keep constant watch on one another in Yeats's poetry. He was a many-sided man who by dint of much questioning and inner turmoil achieved the right to speak with many voices and to know completely the incompleteness of life. And if, as seems likely, his works will resist time, it is because in all his shape-changing he remains at the centre tenacious, solid, a 'marble triton among the streams'. (pp. 246-47)

> *Richard Ellmann, in his* The Identity of Yeats *(copyright © 1964 by Oxford University Press, Inc.; reprinted by permission of Oxford University Press, Inc.; and reprinted in Canada by permission of Macmillan London and Basingstoke), Oxford University Press, 1964.*

Yeats is the only poet of the twentieth century who has survived every change of my temperament and opinion. Often enough I turn from him in anger, even hatred, yet I always go back. . . . Yet all his belief and almost all his experience are as far from my own as if I had been born a Martian.

Something more than the verbal or even the figurative excellence of the poetry is needed to account for this, and I think the explanation lies in Yeats's irrelevance. More than any other modern poet in English he gathered and reshaped the entire cultural tradition of western man. The Americans, Pound and Eliot, were more brash, but Yeats in his slyer way was more piratical. From his broken tower on the edge of Europe he raided every storehouse, every kingdom. The evidence is his occultism. It is absurd to say, as some critics have, that his occultism was a personal aberration which the reader may safely disregard. Just the opposite is true: occultism is the entire fabric of his mind and work, his lifeblood from first to last. . . . This is hard for most of us to understand, even those who have studied the gnostic complexities and know something about the sources of Tristan and the Tarot pack. Occultism seems rather ridiculous. What have Theosophy and the Rosy Cross to do with anything? But behind them, in the long, long experience of *Tora* and *Rota*, lie the noblest and fiercest strivings of the Western spirit. Why there, why not in the public institutions of church and school? Simply because the whole is comprised by its parts: what lies hidden in the individual may be exposed in the mass only at great peril. Occultism is the one truly continuous history, the secret of the sanctuary at both Eleusis and Jerusalem, rising in every culture, claiming every prayer and every poem, in the concealed ecumenism of spiritual desire. Yeats fascinates us through the very longing and envy with which we observe his final celebration of that history, and perhaps even more through the hope that our own spirits, moving on such a different plane, may somehow still break through to that grand coherence. A forlorn hope; but forlorn hopes are sweetest. (pp. 192-93)

> *Hayden Carruth, in* Poetry *(© 1965 by The Modern Poetry Association; reprinted by permission of the Editor of* Poetry*), December, 1965.*

Yeats's starting place is the desire for a transfiguration of the present world and the present self. The everyday world must be transmuted into paradise, and the everyday self must be transformed into an heroic person, steeped in the supernatural. Yeats begins with a certain experience of the death of God: the scientific rationalism of Tyndall and Huxley. For them, as for so many men of the nineteenth century, God is either an exploded myth or is relegated to the realm of Herbert Spencer's "unknowable." In either case the self is defined as a dry collection of faculties, and the environment of the self is equally unliving. Man is left with a dead world of matter in mechanical motion. . . .

Against this world Yeats passionately rebels. He rebels in the name of a possible immanence of the divine spirit. The whole of human existence, every gesture, every incident, all the most commonplace utensils and acts must be irradiated with spiritual meaning. Only when the world is so transfigured can man be his proper heroic self. (p. 68)

The process by which society is made and unmade cannot be distinguished from the process of self-realization in the makers. At the center of Yeats's idea of selfhood is the notion of "unyielding personality, manner at once cold and passionate" . . . , a self full of "unpremeditated joyous energy". . . . Only such a self is worthy to be an avenue by which the supernatural enters society. . . .

Yeats started out in life with the project of transfiguring Ireland. (p. 73)

The human body is Yeats's favorite image of the concrete and real. . . . Incarnate man or woman holds the center of the stage because ultimate reality is not something vague and impalpable, the "One," or the "Idea of Ideas." It is a person or a congeries of persons. Yeats chooses for Plotinus, as he understands him, against Plato, and believes that behind all phenomena are not archetypal ideas but archetypal persons. The cosmos is made of the transformations of these eternal figures, "nothing exists but a stream of souls," and therefore "all knowledge is biography". (p. 74)

When Yeats tries to carry his project into practice, instead of a poetry "as cold / And passionate as the dawn" . . . , he can achieve only vagueness and wavering. An ominous vacillation is present in the essays from *Ideas of Good and Evil*. . . . In tension with the goal of an incarnation of the supernatural, there is the desire for a disembodiment of the world. Yeats dreams of an "autumn of the body" in which everything material will fade away and leave nothing tangible behind. He believes our scientific, critical age is about to pass and give way to "an age of imagination, of emotion, of moods, of revelation". (p. 75)

The world seems caught permanently in the moment when something is about to happen, and announces itself by premonitory flutterings, as of a wing in stone, or a child in the womb. But, instead of the birth of the new, there is only a hesitation, and then a further repetition of the signs which announce it.

These motifs are a precise representation of the present epoch of history. The world is now about to dissolve and become an essence, but so far this transition has not occurred, and Yeats's poems must describe, not the accomplished fact, but the crisis when the change is just going to take place. The phrase "almost disembodied ecstasy" wavers with characteristic hesitation. The ecstasy will be almost disembodied, but not quite, as "dove-grey" is not quite grey, and as the fluttering of leaves is a motion which is also stasis. . . .

Each personage in Yeats's early poems becomes aware of himself as "a whirling and a wandering fire" . . . , a sequence of many moods. Exhausted by this inner oscillation, he longs for fixity in the midst of whirling, but he finds only more moods, each replaced in a moment by another. The endless autumn of the mind will not give way to the immobility of winter. Since all inside is unstable, he turns to what is outside and beyond him. He goes to nature as the abiding place of an immanent spiritual force. Because he has had a glimpse of this beauty, he can find no peace in the everyday world. At the center of the "Rose of all Roses" . . . , though not at the petals' edge, it may be that there is peace.

When such a man seeks to reach peace at the center of the rose, his real adventure begins. (p. 77)

The situation of Yeats's personages is even worse than that of most men who seek eternal beauty. His early poems are based on a certain apprehension of the supernatural which he never betrays, even in his latest work. Instead of feeling that the divine world is a Platonic place of permanence and peace, Yeats experiences it as instability and turbulence. (p. 78)

In poem after poem the only rest he can find is an attenuated wandering. The most stable situation he can imagine still has a slight trembling, and even in the arms of his beloved or alone on an island he cannot escape from fluctuation. (p. 79)

Movement is everywhere, as the host of the air is everywhere. Once a man has had a vision of eternal beauty wandering on her way, he can never cease to be haunted by it. He is doomed to be unquiet forever. (pp. 79-80)

Such difficult knowledge accompanies the discovery that Unity of Being is possible only at rare moments of history. At all other times earth and heaven are incompatible, and to try to fuse them leads only to emptiness and unreality. This discovery leads Yeats to a crossroads, the "choice of choices."

The choice confronted when natural and supernatural are seen to be incompatible is both literary and personal. Yeats has sought in his writing to marry rock and hill to mythology. Now he finds that there are two forms of art. A writer may commit himself to one or the other, but not to both simultaneously. One kind of art takes delight "in essences, in states of mind, in pure imagination, in all that comes to us most easily in elaborate music". . . . The other delights in the whole man—blood, imagination, intellect, running together. One art leads upward to mystic ecstasy. The other leads to an art of "force," "personality," "the tumult of the blood". . . . Even the greatest artists of intellectual essences cannot carry the body to the summit of ecstasy, and even the greatest artists of personality cannot bring soul all the way to earth. A poet must choose either for personality or for the essences. (p. 81)

Now Yeats can see why his early art has led to vagueness and unreality, and why his search for self-fulfillment has turned into a chase after will-o'-the-wisps. His personal mistake has been to assume that he is destined to be a saint, just as his political mistake has been to assume that the Ireland of his day can achieve Unity of Being. He has believed that the life of the saint and the life of the poet can be reconciled and, through his attempt to combine them, has discovered their incompatibility. This discovery is a revelation about both art and selfhood. It shows him that there is no art of the way up. (p. 82)

Now that the situation is clear to him, he makes his choice resolutely. He rejects the "desire to get out of form, to get some kind of disembodied beauty," and chooses "to create form, to carry the realization of beauty as far as possible".... He makes his choice because he must. Reality, for him at least, lies only in the serpent's mouth. Though he remains true to this decision, the fact that two ways of life exist becomes an axis of his thought. (p. 83)

God does not want things to remain in static perfection, a hollow image of eternity. Once they have fulfilled the allotted circle of their existence, they have satisfied the need of the archetypes for material existence, and God then destroys them. He drives them to go beyond themselves into emptiness. There is only so much room in space at any one time, and the stage must be cleared for the next act of history. The plenitude of possible forms lives in the needle's eye of God, forcing the stream of time to flow forward into extinction in order to make room for new incarnations. To put it another way, all men are dancers, but they are not free to call the tune. (pp. 96-7)

Yeats's vision of history leads him ... to reaffirm the doctrine of "the Great Year of the ancients." There is an elaborate discussion of this tradition in *A Vision* . . . , and it is the basis of his cyclical theory of history. It means first the Indian or Platonic notion that after a certain long span of time, thirty-six thousand years or some multiple of that, all the archetypes will have incarnated themselves in time. There will have been one version of each possible form, and time will be fulfilled. The slow precession of the equinoxes will have completed a cycle, the movement of the zodiacal constellations will bring them back to their original position, and Aries will once more preside over the coming of spring. The creation will be returned to the beginning, and the impulse of eternity to actualize itself in time will be exhausted at last. . . .

Yeats escapes from the terror of history by affirming that everything is inevitable. (p. 97)

One of Yeats's strongest motivations is the desire for a systematic comprehension of the universe. (p. 98)

Reality is the irrational intensity of actual experience, and justice is the hidden law behind it. Yeats always seeks to hold these in a single thought. Respect for the tumult of the blood and a rage for order—these are the contraries in Yeats's own nature, dying each other's life, living each other's death. At times there is a wild oscillation from one extreme to the other, but his best work draws its strength from a tense copresence of these contraries. This is truest, perhaps, when it is least obviously the case. Yeats's most magically simple, sensuous, and passionate lyrics often hide his most esoteric thought. (pp. 98-9)

The final consequence of Yeats's sense of history is the worst of all. Not only is history determined and everywhere the same tale of violence, terror, and defeat, but each man is doomed, like each civilization, to suffer the same failure again and again. Yeats's vision of history culminates in a belief in the eternal return, for "a system symbolising the phenomenal world as irrational because a series of unresolved antinomies, must find its representation in a perpetual return to the starting-point". . . .

Everything in Yeats's thought leads him to reaffirm this doctrine. On the ring of history "everything comes round again." (p. 103)

Yeats has reduced everything to a comprehensive system, but it is a system which deprives human life of freedom and significance. No man's life is fortuitous. Each is patterned on eternal models. In spite of this, and even because of it, each life is meaningless suffering. . . . Man must suffer not only the eternal return of the same life but also the eternal return of all possible lives. It seems that he will be racked on the wheel of time forever. (p. 105)

It is not necessary to wait for the end of time or for the slow purgation of perhaps innumerable incarnations to reach liberation. After seeking it in vain through the world, Yeats has at last found what he wants at his own doorstep. He has discovered that every moment of life, in all its lowliness, can be the divine center itself. All direct approaches to God lead to further exile on the periphery. By renouncing them and choosing the circle in its poverty, Yeats finds himself miraculously at the center. This unexpected reversal is like the tangent curve in mathematics which disappears at infinity only to reappear again from the other direction. . . . As Yeats learned from Blake, contraries meet if carried far enough. . . .

Yeats's way of expressing the paradoxical nature of such a God revives an old definition of the deity. It is a definition which first appears in a twelfth-century pseudo-Hermetic treatise, the "Liber XXIV philosophorum": "God is an infinite circle, a circle whose center is everywhere and circumference nowhere.". . . In the center or outside the periphery—both places come in the end to the same thing, for the center is everywhere, and either extreme has escaped the whirling. God is no lofty source. He permeates the universe, from highest to lowest, equally present in all, and Crazy Jane's unholy body, possessed by all, is the place where all things remain in God. (pp. 123-24)

There are two kinds of knowledge: abstract, mediated, systematic knowledge, which reduces everything to common measure, making each man the exact copy of his neighbor, and immediate, irrational knowledge, the thought in a marrowbone. . . . Against the skeletonlike dryness of abstract thought must be set the living reality of bird, beast, fish, or man. These express ultimate truth, without knowing it, in every action. (pp. 124-25)

Ultimate truth cannot be known; it can only be incarnated in the action of some vital being. As soon as a man tries to know truth he cuts himself off from it, and falls into the realm of contradiction and abstraction. (p. 125)

Through his understanding of the richness of bodily life Yeats frees himself at last from the horror of the eternal return. His notion of repetition is significantly different from Nietzsche's. In Nietzsche it has a quasi-materialistic cause. Time is infinitely long; there is an infinite reservoir of energy; the amount of matter in the universe is finite; matter undergoes transformations according to unalterable laws; therefore in the course of time exactly the same arrangement of atoms will inevitably recur. The universe is a machine for repeating itself. In Yeats's thought, on the other hand, the eternal return is caused by the hunger of God for a perfect incarnation of the archetypes. God is an infinite potentiality, and therefore the supply of forms can never be exhausted. The Argo, the Trojan War, Leda, Helen, Hamlet, Ophelia, Lear's rage under the lightning—all these will return an infinite number of times, but each repetition will be slightly different from the others. (pp. 125-26)

Infinity, for Nietzsche, lies in the temporal dimension, in the way the motion of things continues forever, bringing the same objects and events back in innumerable repetitions. For Yeats, as for Blake, there is an infinite plenitude in every object, since each is unique. Each "bird, beast, fish or man" is a special representation of the totality and therefore of God himself. For a man to assert his limited situation with enough "heroic passion," forgetting all else, is to assert at the same time every other possibility and therefore to escape from limitation. Through narrowness he attains his ultimate particular freedom and his soul's disappearance in God.

Yeats has finally found what he sought in his youth, when he was deprived of his religion by Tyndall and Huxley. He has recovered an inherence of the supernatural in every corner of life.... If any parallel is needed for his fundamental thought it can be found in Zen Buddhism. (pp. 126-27)

God himself is irrational fury, the "there" where all opposites fuse. He can be most closely approached by man in experiences which carry the contraries to the point where they merge. So Yeats praises battle, drunkenness, rage, brutality, laughter, madness, revelry, wanton destruction or waste, the experience of great loss or failure, the moment of death. In these a man is most outside himself and can best receive the lightning bolt of revelation. They carry a man away from the rational world of distinctions and utility into the place where everything is present at once.... (pp. 127-28)

Battle, drunkenness, rage, and sex are among the best means of liberation, but one other way remains, and perhaps the most important: art. Like drunkenness and sex, dancing is a means of losing oneself to find oneself, and poetry is also a way of liberation. The culmination of Yeats's experience is a mode of poetry as well as a mode of life. His best poems begin with elements which are opposed or apparently unrelated, and bring them closer and closer in the dancelike rhythm of the poem until at the climax the opposites fuse in an explosion of intensity.

This explosion is the image. Yeats's use of an image, violent in its irrational particularity, as the resolution of a poem accords exactly with his praise of the intense moment of sense experience. Both are escape from the wheel of time. Both are a reconciliation of contraries. In Yeats's best poems the effect of the climactic image exactly parallels the experience it names. In the exclamatory image, wholly concrete, wholly resisting logical analysis, all the world and all the power of poetry are present at once, just as they are present in lightning flashing across the sky and obliterating past and future. In these final images Yeats reaches the summit of his art and at the same time the summit of his apprehension of life. (p. 129)

> *J. Hillis Miller, "W. B. Yeats," in his* Poets of Reality: Six Twentieth-Century Writers *(copyright © 1965 by the President and Fellows of Harvard College; excerpted by permission of the author and publishers), Cambridge, Mass.: Harvard University Press, 1965, pp. 68-130.*

Unity, escaping [Yeats] in life, was his in art. Yet his art is made of quarreling opposites—the grand and the commonplace, the personal and the impersonal, love and hate of Ireland—opposites that achieve oneness by a kind of conspiracy. Poems that show our time forth by whatever seems its opposite—by a noble response to ignobility—are nonetheless of our time, unmistakably. "The Second Coming," though lamenting ceremonies of innocence and recalling their air, has the air as well of a time without ceremony or innocence. Taking a look at time from the porch of timelessness, "Sailing to Byzantium," an artifact of our time, becomes an "artifice of eternity." (p. 4)

A symbol, for Yeats, was any thing of words or any concrete object that by correspondence with Anima Mundi, the Platonic memory up there, causes an influence to descend down here: "As above, so below," great Hermes said. The magical correspondence, working like a push button, causes a definite response; but response to the literary correspondence is at once certain and indefinite. As magus, Yeats employed the one to cure fevers; as poet, he was almost content with writing poems. (pp. 7-8)

His poems of the 1890s are filled with occult matters, "the Ineffable Name," for example, and Mme. Blavatsky's elementals. But references are not necessarily symbols. The best examples of symbolism are the poems Yeats wrote about the rose, emblem of the Rosicrucians and of the great work of alchemy. A natural shape that suggests unity, a rose brings many traditional blooms to mind: Dante's rose, the dark rose of Ireland, and the dozen roses one gives to a girl on occasion. "The Secret Rose," including these customary meanings and, apparently, uniting nation, love, and the occult, is secret nevertheless—not only remote but unknown and unknowable. Not multiple meanings but ultimate secrecy and the question mark that ends the poem guarantee symbol. (p. 8)

"Who Goes with Fergus?" the best poem of his prentice years, is one of the best of our time. Why else would Joyce's Buck Mulligan sing it to Stephen Dedalus on their tower, and why else would Stephen, brooding on mother, brood on it? Not only a poem of escape to "a woven world-forgotten isle," as Yeats puts it in "The Man Who Dreamed of Faeryland," this is a poem of retreat to infancy, the Land of Youth again, where, with mother and father in charge, love is no longer a bother.

William Empson found this poem an ambiguous thing—of ... perhaps, a type that, by saying nothing, allows the reader, projecting what he pleases, to say all. Is the opening line, for example, invitation or warning? And what about "now"? Empson asks, forgetting that now is a word that Irishmen like to end questions with. But much of the poem is plain enough: imagery of piercing, driving, and ruling seems paternal; the woods and "the white breast of the dim sea" are as clearly maternal. It is clear that Fergus, driving his brazen car, like a sun god, is still a man of affairs and that, ruling the shadows of the wood, the sea, and the comets, he has druid powers. Being with a man of this capacity, a benign papa who allows sporting on the green, makes one a child again. "Woven," the key word, implies a union here of disparate things unlikely in the world out there. Less ambiguous than it seems at first, the poem is an invitation to get away—especially from troubles with girls like Maud Gonne. But Empson is right in holding that what the reader is forced to project is the heart of the poem. Unlimited by the particulars of retreat, the poem becomes a form for a variety of feelings and their symbol: first a question, then a double chiasmus ("Young man . . . maid," "brood . . . brood"), then a triumph ("brazen cars"), and last a peaceful decline assured, yet slowed, by those excellent spondees. If "dishevelled" hints less than complete order and security, something unwoven, the hint is no more than a reminder of conditions off island; and, what is more, "dishevelled" implies hair, the material for tents. (pp. 10-11)

Yeats, having come to think himself sentimental, feared that self-expression would produce more soft and glimmering poems. But if he became his opposite, his verse would take on hardness and glitter. Through the mask of his opposite, he achieved the dramatic impersonality commended by Stephen Dedalus and, after him, by T. S. Eliot. No less personal than before he put the mask on, Yeats became to all appearances impersonal, at once involved with his affairs and so distant from them that he could display a courtier's nonchalance and the nonchalance of the artist. Balancing opposites, his mask brought unity—to the work. (p. 23)

[Yeats's] third period—much overlapping here and no clear edges—begins in 1918 perhaps. Poems of this period, improving the developments of the second, take another and a loftier character from new matter: the tower, the wheeling moon, and the trouble of growing old. Yeats and Wordsworth are alike in respect of this: both developed. As Wordsworth got worse and worse, so Yeats got better and better. By agreement among men of taste and judgment the later poems of Yeats—those in *The Tower* . . . , for example—are best. (p. 24)

As "The Lake Isle of Innisfree" is esteemed as a vision of escape, so "The Second Coming," as a vision of our world. Toward all of us—indifferent best and passionate worst alike—a monstrous threat comes slouching. But Castiglione's "ceremony of innocence" also stirs the bourgeois heart. However aristocratic, the falcon and his falconer make gyres public property; and the echo of Donne's "Anniversary" brings literary tradition to bear. Yet in their private capacities the beast and the sphinx, more than vaguely menacing, embody two cycles—the one before ours, the other, after. The first coming was that of Jesus, whose "rocking cradle" vexed the sphinx. Another Bethlehem will replace the Virgin's and another second-comer, her Son. Maybe this "rough beast" is also a second sphinx; but our knowledge of such matters is questioned at the end. (p. 31)

Occupying phase 15 of a temporal cycle, Yeats's Byzantium is at once in time and out of it, less an actual city, therefore, than a "holy city" or, at least, the half of one. His idea of this city was a long time growing. In 1907, when Lady Gregory showed Yeats the mosaics at Ravenna, Byzantium, encountered there, became for him a place of art: mosaics, domes, and goldsmith's work. He read books, in one of which he found Justinian and in another the mechanical golden bird of the Emperor Theophilus. When Yeats put his system together, his idea of Byzantium seemed a suitable climax (or fifteenth phase) for the Christian cycle. More or less out of time, the city became a refuge from time and, at once purgatory and paradise, a haunt of spirits. As for place: happily situated at the junction of East and West, uniting these opposites, the city would do as a

symbol of "unity of being." Going there became the process of unifying. . . . Of the two poems Yeats wrote about this compendious spot, "Sailing to Byzantium" . . . and "Byzantium" . . . , the second is more faithful to his ideas of the city, but the first is a better poem. (pp. 31-2)

"Once out of nature" or dead, the old man [in "Sailing to Byzantium"] will be gone into just the paradise for him—no love or nature around, but plenty of courtiers to sing to. This is one possible reading of the poem. Another is to find its theme the making of a work of art: bird, song, man, and the other things of nature, transfigured, become the unnatural golden bird, seated on Vergil's golden bough in Turner's picture. Like Keats's Grecian urn, the golden bird is beyond change—gold is the most stable of metals. But as the urn, out of time, brings news of a time, so the timeless bird sings of time, "Of what is past, or passing, or to come." The work of art, uniting timelessness with time, is an escape from time. Proust's novel makes this point and so, in a way, does Andrew Marvell's garden, a formal paradise with silver bird. Not garden, however, but voyage or journey provides the frame for Yeats's poem, an "archetypal" pattern that Joyce, Dante, and Homer had found useful. Nothing better and more customary for encounters with life, death, and, sometimes, art. (pp. 32-3)

Yeats, the student of interacting opposites, found [that] the terminal couplet of ottava rima, with its grandeur and finality, allows a triumph of sound and rhythm. Such triumphs bring "Sailing to Byzantium" from climax to climax until the final stanza, climax of all four. This structure of triumphs and conflicts is tightened by motifs—as of bird and song. Indeed, the parts consort well with one another. [This] work of art is the product of labor and great craft. . . . (p. 33)

Lacking the assurance of ottava rima, "Byzantium" . . . misses the monumental magnificence of its predecessor. . . . Rejected for "Sailing to Byzantium," the traditional image of the man-bearing dolphin demanded inclusion here—luckily; for it is the most memorable part of the poem. That the dolphins' port is not altogether ideal is suggested by the whores and drunks who throng it before closing time. The curfew from St. Sophia, announcing the purity of midnight, also torments the image-begetting sea. "All mere complexities" must endure the disdain of the purged and final image—pure, single, and eternal, whether soul or work of art. (pp. 33-4)

[Crazy Jane's] refrains . . . her derangement of matters, and her violations of the customary have the "irrational element" that Yeats, with "Sing a Song of Sixpence" in mind, thought poetry must have. (p. 38)

"Under Ben Bulben" (1938), grand and bare as the mountain itself, is the "gist" of what his sages, horsemen, and women "mean"—of all, in short, Yeats meant—of life, of death, of country and art. "Learn your trade," he tells Irish poets; sing the well-made song of "whatever is well made." Sing "the indomitable Irishry": the horsemen, peasants, saints, and drunks, the lord and ladies of "seven heroic centuries." What matter that no poet has taken his advice? His epitaph is example enough of what a poet can do:

> Cast a cold eye
> On life, on death.
> Horseman, pass by!   (p. 44)

There, cut in stone, is what Yeats stood for, put in a way to make the chills run down your spine: all that distance and nobility, all that craft. (p. 45)

William York Tindall, in his W. B. Yeats *(copyright © 1966 Columbia University Press; reprinted by permission of the publisher), Columbia University Press, 1966.*

[Each] of Yeats's books of poems is a strategic simplification, a trial account of his universe devoted not to the entire complex truth but to a particular bias which is dominant for the time being. Some are phoenix books; others, turtle books; what one longs for is the mutual flame. . . . (p. 110)

Yeats 'believed in' none of the public, institutional faiths. But he needed their authority, their momentum, or at least authority and momentum from similar sources. And he was a spectacular rhetorician. So he used each of the public faiths whenever he felt that one of its patterns of insight was specially relevant to the feeling of the poem. He may have been drawn to these local 'allegiances' by sensing a purely formal congruity between the pattern in the 'public' structure and the pattern implicit in the private feeling. This would account for the Way of the Cross in 'The Travail of Passion', to certify feeling akin to its own; or the figure of the Guardian Angel in 'A Prayer for My Son'. Similarly in the Crazy Jane poems the bodily imperative is a 'public' pattern of experience, with the force of public authority, complete with dogmas, rites, mysteries—and these by universal assent. The great advantage of the bodily imperative as a source of verbal communication is that it is prior to all conflicts of thought or belief; it under-cuts the contentious levels of experience. In lofty moments Yeats would invoke the Great Memory as the source and means of communication, and he would speak beautifully under its sign, but there would always be something problematic in its operation. The human body was more reliable; indeed, the body was the only universal Church to which Yeats would belong. (p. 114)

The Yeats of the *Last Poems* did not often laugh in the tragic joy of Lear and Hamlet; his laughter is too shrill for that. The apocalypse of these poems is a willed tumult, the poet goading himself into the role of a randy old man to repel the temptations of a laureate old age. (But there are great humane exceptions to this rule, such as 'The Circus Animals' Desertion', 'An Acre of Grass', and 'Beautiful Lofty Things'.) (p. 115)

Words for Music Perhaps . . . is a valuable book because it enables us to re-enact a movement of feeling downward into the limited, finite thing. The movement is touching in itself, in its compulsions and embarrassments; only the most sullen reader could fail to be moved and disturbed by this partial image of the human condition. The pathos of the book is that when Yeats had reached down into the finite Body there was little he could do with it; he saw no means of penetrating the finite without transcending it and thereby destroying it, as Roderick destroyed Madeline, in a rage for essence. The trouble was that he could not value the human body in itself; only when it agreed to wear a bright halo of animation.

It is painful dialectic. The poet for whom plenitude of being is everything finds himself kicking several of man's faculties out of the way in his rage for essence. The devotee of 'perfection' bows before fragments. In his most perceptive moments he knows that it is a desperate expedient, that even his Byzantine eternity is artifice. . . . If you reduce a human being to his consciousness, and then provide a diet of unknown thought, argument, and abstraction, you must face the risks involved; attrition, emaciation, a desert of mummies. Time and again in *The Tower* Yeats prays for a kinder unity. . . . But that book is a little too engrossed with its own exposure to allow much consideration for other people; apart from a few chosen friends, the rest are given as hot-faced bargainers and money-changers. (pp. 116-17)

'All Souls' Night' is almost a test case for the hazard of the human image. It is a thrilling poem; we are at once thrilled and shocked to find Yeats driving himself into such a terrifying corner. The position itself—we feel at once—is untenable. It is unnecessarily dissociative. . . . [The] intensity of 'All Souls' Night' amounts to this: a stern mind denying the most serviceable relations in a humane life, and holding this denial 'to the end of the line'. If intensity were enough, this poem, this action, would be one of the greatest achievements in modern literature, and we would assent to it without reservation and find in it none of the wilfulness which disturbs us now. But intensity is not enough, and may well serve no other purpose than to assure us that we exist.

Does this matter? Or is it the fury in the words that matters, and not the words?

The received opinion among readers of Yeats is that the classic poems are in *The Tower*. And yet by comparison with *The Wild Swans at Coole* the human image in that spectacular book is curiously incomplete; remarkably intense, but marginal; a little off-centre. Does this matter? Yes, it does; intensity is not enough. It matters greatly that *The Wild Swans at Coole* is at the very heart of the human predicament, groping for values through which man may define himself without frenzy or servility.

This book is concerned with the behaviour of men in the cold light of age and approaching death. The ideal stance involves passion, self-conquest, courtesy, and moral responsibility. Yeats pays the tribute of wild tears to many people and to the moral beauty which they embody; the entire book is rammed with moral life. Most of the poems were written between 1915 and 1919, and it is significant that those were the years in which Yeats was perfecting his dance-drama; because the dancer was the culmination of the efforts which Yeats made in *The Wild Swans at Coole* to represent the fullness of being as a dynamic action. (pp. 117-18)

The Wild Swans at Coole is committed to action; not to thought or concept or feeling, except that these are essential to the full definition of action. We are to register action as the most scrupulous notation of human existence, far more accurate, more 'creatural', than thought or concept—which are simplifications; far more comprehensive, too. Action is silent articulation of experience. Yeats's dancer has outdanced thought, summarized thought in a pattern of gestures. Her dance is an act of desire toward the God-state, or God-term; the dancer strives toward an 'essential' human image, an image of dynamic perfection freely formulated—fulfilled—at the end of the body-line. This is probably what Yeats meant in the well-known letter which he wrote a few weeks before his death, in which he said, 'It seems to me that I have found what I wanted. When I try to put all into a phrase, I say, "Man can embody truth but he cannot know it'." Truth is embodied in the figure of action, the dancer for whom meaning is embodied in gesture and gesture the only expression there is. Thought is not enough; even the 'thinking of the body': the most accurate annotation is that act which outdances thought and sums up human potentiality in gesture. (pp. 119-20)

[The] poems in *The Wild Swans at Coole* seem peculiarly 'central' to our experience. The burden of meaning has been placed firmly where it belongs, in people, and in the acts that embody their values. The book is an anthology of represented lives in which private vision becomes incarnate in public action. . . . The poems speak to us directly, to our sense of the human predicament; and in the last reckoning this is a more reliable mode of communication than the Great Memory or even the Body. The human image in this book is at once sweet and serviceable; it hides behind no platitudes that it can see; it does not feel called upon to take possession of the world or to set up as God. It acknowledges human limitation and tries to live as well as possible under that shadow. The image chimes with our own sense of the 'creatural' situation; it is continuous with our own unspectacular experience in its assent to common occasion. (p. 122)

[Unlike Eliot], to Yeats and [Robert] Lowell everything else in man is just as real as his mind. . . . The continuity of feeling between Yeats and Lowell implies that we live in the world as finite people, not merely zones of consciousness. Words alone are not, after all, certain good; as Yeats discovered. (p. 124)

Yeats found in Celtic folk-tales a great 'excess', a free range of the imagination, a flow of passionate experience, incorrigibly temporal, which he feared was lost in modern literature. We tend to smile, these days, at Yeats's traffic with legendary heroes, and yet our smile is idle and a little vulgar. When Yeats spoke of magical events he invoked and praised all those possibilities of the spirit for which there is no other explanation than the passion that incites them; and it was the passion he revered. By comparison, he thought his own time puny and timid, the work of the counting-house, except when it flowered beyond prediction in a great act, like the Easter Rising in 1916. (p. 132)

What Yeats missed in modern literature, besides 'excess', was 'emotion of multitude', a resonance of feeling which is primitive and fundamental. The modern well-made play or poem could have everything necessary for high art, he said, except emotion of multitude: unless it somehow touched and stirred that deep, primitive sense of life, it was bound to be meagre, superficial.

I am arguing that Yeats sought emotion of multitude and excess and found them in Celtic legends and never released himself from the human images they sponsored. If he revered the aristocratic hauteur it was because this was the nearest gesture he could find in history to the excess he found in legend. This partly explains one of the chief differences between the poems of Yeats and of Eliot. If we think of characteristic poems by Eliot, we can easily imagine them as paintings, or sculptures, or string quartets: this is what we mean, after all, when we say in some desperation that 'The Waste Land' has Cubist form. But Yeats's characteristic poems are cries, laments, prayers, stories, legends, rebukes; human sounds rather than objects. This

does not mean that he neglected to 'make' his poems. It means that the making of a poem, for him, largely consisted in making the sounds more and more responsive to a human occasion, real or imagined. (p. 133)

Yeats wanted a language capable of registering the full life of man; body and soul, matter and spirit. He might have wished for a better reality than the one proferred by his senses, but he laboured with the given, with 'the sigh of what is'. The human situation, to Yeats, is the place of long memory, where values are audible from generation to generation. This, indeed, is Tradition. (pp. 133-34)

Yeats thought of tradition . . . as a choir of voices in which the new voice is heard. The values of the past are not seen or inspected, they are heard, passed along through the generations in story, song, and rhyme. A race is unified because the passions of its people have gathered around a few images. The continuity of these passions is the emotion of multitude. This is what Tradition means, the concert of passions and the images that engage them. The individual talent is the 'excess', the flare of personality.

This explains why Yeats resorted to the drama. There is no more accomplished form for the representation of human life as a fully engaged experience, with all the faculties working at full stretch. . . . We often think that Yeats's plays are impossibly rarefied: we think this until we see them well played, and then we find that except for the very earliest plays they are much more resilient, much harder than their literary reputation has suggested. (p. 134)

Yeats's poems tend to present human life in the mode of drama, conflicts in place and time; value resides in the conflict, not merely in the victory. Hence, among other advantages, Yeats can free himself from the obsession with the transience of things which is one of the burdens of a visual culture. Eliot's poems concede that life may offer a few dazzling moments in which time stands still, but everything else is, as one of his poems says, 'a waste sad time stretching before and after'. (p. 136)

[This] is true of the vast majority of his poems from 'Adam's Curse' to the very last pages of the great book: these poems choose the living world for text, they are poems of place, time, memory, voice, conflict, personality. I do not find there a single poem in which Yeats releases himself from these obligations: he never composed a Supreme Fiction. That he occasionally wished to do so, I would not deny: the poems that spring to mind at once are, of course, the two Byzantine poems.

I have argued on another occasion that the best way to read Yeats's *Collected Poems* is to think of it as dramatizing a great dispute between Self and Soul; Self being all those motives which tie one to earth and time, Soul being the freedom of imagination transcending the finite. The dispute was never resolved. Yeats would lend himself to one side or the other, but always with misgivings, knowing the cost of severance. This is my chief quarrel with those who would read the Byzantine poems as if they were written by Wallace Stevens: these poems are not parables about the free imagination; they are poems about the dispute of Self and Soul at a time when old age and approaching death seem to vote resoundingly for Soul. (pp. 141-42)

'Byzantium' is a more spectacular poem than 'Sailing to Byzantium', but it is not as fine, as coherent or as just. This is not because the later poem is more dependent upon its handsome symbols but because it commits itself to its presumptive form at a stage somewhat short of moral understanding. It is as if 'Byzantium' were a very late draft for a poem never quite completed. Yeats is saying rather less than he seems to claim, making spectacular play with the heuristic possibilities of the symbols. The poem, in short, is weak in moral syntax. Perhaps this explains our hesitation, if we hesitate. The play is spectacular but heady, somewhat hysterical. A chosen tradition plays an important part in the poem, supplying most of the symbols and most of the feeling, but the function of the traditional lore is largely honorific and picturesque; most of it is present to make up a distinguished gathering. The tradition does not test, because there is not enough to test, not enough to criticize, not enough Fact to put to the measure of Value. The domes, bobbins, cocks, and dances reverberate imperiously, and Yeats draws wonderful music from these traditional instruments, but the tradition does not finally grapple with the individual talent. This is why 'Sailing to Byzantium' and—to choose another—'Vacillation' seem to me better poems, poems of reality and justice. (p. 144)

Yeats was a much more rooted poet than we have allowed, and he was much more rooted in the oral tradition of Ireland than we have been prepared to acknowledge. We often think that he was barred from the resources of Irish culture because he did not know the Irish language. And we think that the Irish tradition was itself severely damaged when Irish ceased to be the daily language of the majority of Irishmen. Admittedly, the Irish oral tradition was not a 'going concern' at the beginning of the twentieth century: Yeats was not Homer, with all the resources of a native tradition immediately available to him, ready for his hands. And of course the continuity of the Irish oral tradition was gravely undermined by the reduction of the Irish language to minority status. But the loss of the language, though tragic, did not mean that Irish culture was totally destroyed, that Irish memory was broken, or that the old Irish world was blocked off.... Yeats got from Irish sources what he needed for his poems; a sense of roots, a feeling of continuity, a sense of communal values issuing in speech and action, 'the dialect of the tribe'. (pp. 144-45)

> *Denis Donoghue, "The Human Image in Yeats" and "Yeats and the Living Voice,"* in his The Ordinary Universe: Soundings in Modern Literature *(reprinted with permission of Macmillan Publishing Co., Inc.;* © *1968 by Denis Donoghue), Macmillan, 1968, pp. 108-24, 125-45.*

Like Nietzsche, Yeats resists systematic definitions even when he attempts a conscious unity of thought; one senses in his work an unconscious repugnance to the formality of a completed gesture, an unambiguous vision. Even his most celebrated concept, the mysterious "Unity of Being," cannot be defined except as rhetorical tautology, the kind of abstraction Yeats despised. For he defines in 1937 his faith in his own Christ, "that Unity of Being Dante compared to a perfectly proportioned human body," yet goes on to say that this conception is an imminent one, differing from man to man and age to age. Beneath *A Vision* and its celebrated complexities is the phenomenal power of this mystical unity, which seems to have involved for Yeats extreme hatred as well as extreme love. Yet it is inexpli-

cable to the speculating Yeats himself: the "harsh geometry" of *A Vision* remains an incomplete interpretation.

Prophetic and apocalyptic, Yeats is yet intensely personal, his obsessions refining themselves until the cult of personality becomes a kind of mythologizing release. The romantic impulse toward the apotheosis of the ordinary, the immediate, the existential, is at constant odds with the classical, intellectual, harshly mathematical impulse in Yeats to turn everything to stone, to the clarity of gold and marble. (pp. 141-42)

In addition to the rich paradoxes of the poems and plays, the critic must contend with yet another voice—the patient, rational, and supposedly helpful voice of the essays. But the respectful intellect of the essays, with its elaborate accounting of the passage of the soul in Indian mysticism and asceticism, and its patient consideration of the philosophy of Berkeley and of others, is brutally undercut by the poems of the same years—the "Crazy Jane" sequence, for instance. (pp. 142-43)

[The] jagged tonalities of the last poems will not be reconciled by the theoretical claim for a dispassionate unity, just as certain poems, examined individually, will not support their apparent themes. Yeats's genius lies not in his ability to hammer his multiple thoughts into unity, but rather in his faithful accounting of the impossibility—which may lead one to the edge of madness—of bringing together aesthetic theory and emotional experience. His final work is characterized by irony, but more importantly by an incomplete blend of the "tragic" and the "mutable." What is tragic is intended to transcend or in some way justify the suffering Yeats or his legendary personae have experienced, and takes its most frequent immortality in the shape of a work of art; what is mutable is all that is left out, all that will not fit in—in short, life itself, the material of art itself. (p. 143)

The most general associations we have with Yeats's poetry are two—the golden bird on the Byzantine bough and the rape of Leda. It is significant that these two opposing images come to mind most readily, for they represent the obsessive claims of Yeats's art. Had he truly believed his early assertions in the 1901 essay, "Magic"—that our minds belong to a single mind, that our memories belong to the memory of nature itself, and that this great mind and great memory can be evoked by symbols—he would have remained a minor poet, content with the vague evocation of a mysterious and ineffable unity. Instead, his deepest instinct is to reject unity while he yearns for it; not only does he seem to reject it philosophically, like Nietzsche, but he seems to reject it emotionally as well. The epic and the dramatic impulses in Yeats far outweigh the lyric impulse, and that is why all his writings inform one another; the *Collected Works* constitute Yeats's being itself, the justification for his existence. But within the projected framework of a single book no single unity is possible, apart from the unity necessarily imposed upon the work by the passage of time, which the poet is anxious to record. The intellectual concept of unity is impossible for the artist to achieve, except at great cost to his art. It is not paradoxical to suggest that Yeats did not want unity, "Unity of Being," in any ultimate form. (pp. 157-58)

One of the outstanding features of Yeats's poetry and plays is the obsessive commitment to a transposing of daimonic knowledge into human language. Yeats has stated that he felt his plays are "not drama but the ritual of a lost faith." The human consciousness possesses something that is prior to itself and to individual existential experience; it is Yeats's sacred duty as a poet to translate the ineffable into a fable strong enough to bear the burden of this forbidden knowledge. (p. 165)

Yeats's tragic heroes are heroic because they are gifted with the audacity to undertake certain actions; though they fail, though they do not personally transcend their fates, they are heroic in their ritualistic enactment of the common human dilemma. We do battle, but battle with a shadow, a dream; we pit our human language against an inhuman language. Life may be an irrational bitterness, as Yeats says in *A Vision,* but the art that life makes possible must be both complex and simple, a presentation of timeless wisdom.

In the tragedies of Yeats one is struck by the ease with which characters assume their fates, and even by the playwright's offhand suggestion (usually introductory to the plays' actions) that the actors, the dancers, the "characters" onstage might be readily switched around. Obviously this is not realistic drama, yet it is surprising to see how totally Yeats has abandoned the most basic desire of the imagination—to be lied to in a realistic manner. Like contemporary dramatists of the absurd, Yeats refuses to sustain an illusion. (p. 167)

Yeats's compulsive desire to translate the lost faith into poetry necessitates his working with legendary and impersonal elements, his use of repetition and exaggeration and physical simplicity (especially his use of masks) having as its function the reinforcement of the archetypal structure of a myth that is previously known, or felt, by its audience. . . . He is quite obviously a man who has chosen to bypass the language of science for the language of myth, and *A Vision* is his apology for such a choice, a purely fictional objectification of ideas that were in his mind only slightly formed until the time, or times, at which he wrote the book. He has chosen deliberately the mystical belief of cyclical history over the more modern conception of progress, for, as he says in his notes to *The Words upon the Window-Pane* (the play is dated 1934, the notes, 1931), though man's knowledge is too limited to prove either concept of history correct, "the eternal circuit may best suit our preoccupation with the soul's salvation, our individualism, our solitude." His is a mythical organization of the world in which certain elements become gradually knowable. . . . (pp. 168-69)

The tragic fact of metamorphosis is at the heart of Yeats's poetry. Half consciously he seems to have chosen this primitive "logical thought" over the more commonplace and sanitary belief in the permanent isolation of human beings from one another and from the world of nature, whether animals, plants, or inanimate matter. The primitive imagination accepts totally the fact of miraculous change: what would be miraculous to them is our conception of a conclusion, an ending of spirit and energy. Such metamorphoses are not inexplicable, but are not subjected to explanations at all; indeed, the concept of an "explanation," the psychological demand for an explanation, is foreign to such thinking. The identification of hero with action, the fact of a heroic gesture *constituting* the entire history of a human being, is fundamental to the mythical world: not that one's life runs up to a certain moment in history, at which it is justified or redeemed or somehow explained, but that the

moment itself has always existed, as a kind of slot that will be filled by a certain person at a certain time. Thus action and passivity are perfectly mated. Violence and stillness are one. Yeats asks his famous question in "Among School Children"—

> O chestnut-tree, great-rooted blossomer,
> Are you the leaf, the blossom or the bole?
> O body swayed to music, O brightening glance,
> How can we know the dancer from the dance?

—and the answer is that we cannot know the dancer from the dance, man from his "dance," his shadowy struggle with the other-worldly antagonist. Yeats's tragedies are rituals of sacrifice in which the human element risks his humanity for supernatural knowledge (often through the flesh, through sexual intercourse with the other-worldly), is defeated or broken, and perishes into God—which is to say, into reality. Like man, God has no personal identity; God is the sum of all that is real, all that is consciousness, the historical necessity that man has resisted. Thus the plays are rites that set up the rejection of one kind of reality in favor of another, a reality that cannot be demonstrated or experienced but can only be suggested through holy images. (pp. 169-70)

> *Joyce Carol Oates, "Yeats: Violence, Tragedy, Mutability" and "Tragic Rites in Yeats's 'A Full Moon in March'" (originally published in* Bucknell Review, *Winter 1969-70 and* Antioch Review, *Winter, 1969-70, respectively), in her* The Edge of Impossibility: Tragic Forms in Literature *(copyright © 1972 by Joyce Carol Oates), Vanguard, 1972, pp. 139-62.*

For much of his long life Yeats used myth as both a defense against the power of his own insight and a means of releasing unconscious knowledge in poetry. There are signs of his awareness of this conflict in his early writings, but it took him a lifetime to come to terms with it; finally he employed the energy and pain of this struggle in constructing his greatest poetry. (p. 62)

[When] Yeats sees analogies in Gaelic legend, Greek Orphism, Christian myth, Rosicrucianism, and the vague mysticism of Theosophy, it is because, different as these are in origin and even in function, they are similar in one important respect: all of them express in symbolic form a human longing for regression and continuity, a simultaneous merging with past and future. Yeats used various myths and mystical doctrines to provide narrative and rite for his own mythical structure, which attempts to unite features of all yet is ultimately personal, since his quest for a unifying principle in myth expresses a demand for unity in his own soul and his own art.

In his prose, both autobiographical and critical, Yeats frequently refers explicitly to an awareness that his deepest "insight and knowledge" lie hidden within his unconscious self and can be brought to the surface only in poetry, through the agency of myth. (p. 63)

In Yeats's poetry, evocations of ritual are usually directly connected with his use of myth, primarily Celtic in his early poems and, in his later ones, the structure composed of Greek and other mythologies found in *A Vision.* (p. 185)

For Yeats dance is "a supreme ritual" which promotes

''unearthly ecstasy''; in *A Vision* and in his poetry he uses dance in a variety of ways but almost always with a ritualistic connotation. It is, moreover, a ritual of transcendence, for the movements of a dance, stylized and perfect, usually symbolize superhuman skill and knowledge. The dancer achieves control over nature; the silent, moving figure transcends the language in which he is described.

References to dance in *A Vision* suggest the writer's actual experience of illumination and synthesis as he approaches the mystery of existence.

In Yeats's poetry dance also symbolizes the fusion, balance, and harmony of extraordinary insight or knowledge. (p. 188)

Dance is the most widely known of the rituals that Yeats employs as poetic symbols. (p. 192)

The ritual to which Yeats was most drawn throughout his life was that of the dying and reborn god: Adonis, Attis, Osiris, and Dionysus. It was not only Frazer's *The Golden Bough* but other works, such as Thomas Taylor's *Dissertation* and Nietzsche's *The Birth of Tragedy,* which reinforced Yeats's inclination to consider ritual the ultimate act of control—over death itself. Yeats employs ritual rebirth as a motif most often in his drama; in his poetry, where it occurs less frequently, it is nonetheless important as theme and symbol. (pp. 194-95)

In Yeats's poetry ritual enacts an inner vision of permanent beauty, harmony, or courage, and in some of his poems the reader, like a participant in the transcendent experience of a rite, is involved in the creation of the miraculous—the dance or the work of art which unites opposing forces and defies time itself. In other poems, however, the contrast between the vision of immortality or perfection, which the rite enacts, and human mutability and failure creates a dramatic tension which is only partially resolved in the protagonist's or speaker's ''bitter'' acknowledgement of his own and man's limitations. (p. 200)

> *Lillian Feder, ''W. B. Yeats: Myth as Psychic Structure'' and ''W. B. Yeats: Prophecy and Control,'' in her* Ancient Myth in Modern Poetry *(copyright © 1971 by Princeton University Press; reprinted by permission of Princeton University Press), Princeton University Press, 1971, pp. 61-90, 185-200.*

Émile Zola

1840-1902

French novelist, essayist, and journalist. Émile Zola, naturalistic novelist and pioneer of the modern sociological novel, was an experimental writer who attempted to illustrate in his fiction the scientific theories of determinism. His twenty-volume "Les Rougon-Macquart," the saga of five generations of a family considered from the standpoint of the environmental and hereditary influences that determined their conduct, was his most ambitious effort in this direction. However, he is probably best known for his role in the notorious Dreyfus case. "J'accuse," his vehement open letter to the President of the Republic defending Captain Alfred Dreyfus, a Jewish army officer falsely accused of treason, is considered instrumental in the eventual pardon of Dreyfus. Born in Paris, Zola was raised in Aix-en-Provence where his father was an engineer. Zola returned to Paris at the age of eighteen and took a series of jobs, all the while reading voraciously and writing poetry. He eventually turned to writing novels and also began a career in journalism as a critic. In 1971 Zola published the first of the Rougon-Macquart novels, which were collectively to become the masterpiece of the French naturalist movement. Although these novels touched all classes of French society, those dealing with the working class are generally considered the best, among them *L'Assommoir* and *Germinal*. His intervention in the Dreyfus affair resulted in Zola being twice tried for libel. He fled to England, returning to Paris only after a general amnesty had been proclaimed. Although Zola's scientific conception of literature is today considered passé, he had a strong influence on such writers as Chekhov, Gorkii, Steinbeck, Dreiser, and Dos Passos.

PRINCIPAL WORKS

La Confession de Claude (novel) 1865
  [*Claude's Confession,* 1888]
Thérèse Raquin (novel) 1867
  [*The Devil's Compact,* 1892]
Madeleine Férat (novel) 1868
  [*Madeline Ferat,* 1880]
"Les Rougon-Macquart" (a twenty-novel series on the
    history of a family) 1871-93
  ["Rougon-Macquart novels," 1879-93]
Le Roman experimental (essays) 1880
  [*The Experimental Novel,* 1894]
"Les Trois Villes" (a three-novel series) 1894-98

["The Three Cities," 1894-98]
"Les Quatre Evangiles" (an unfinished four-novel series)
    1899-1903
["The Four Gospels," 1900-1903]

It is by his huge novels, and principally by those of the Rougon-Macquart series, that Zola is known to the public and to the critics. Nevertheless, he found time during the forty years of his busy literary career to publish about as many small stories, now comprised in four separate volumes. . . . [There] is very distinct interest in seeing how such a thunderer or bellower on the trumpet can breathe through silver; and, as a matter of fact, the short stories reveal a Zola considerably dissimilar to the author of *Nana* and of *La Terre*—a much more optimistic, romantic, and gentle writer. If, moreover, he had nowhere assailed the decencies more severely than he does in these thirty or forty short stories, he would never have been named among the enemies of Mrs. Grundy, and the gates of the Palais Mazarin would long ago have been opened to receive him. It is, indeed, to a lion with his mane *en papillotes* that I here desire to attract the attention of English readers; to a man-eating monster, indeed, but to one who is on his best behaviour and blinking in the warm sunshine of Provence.

In every [story in *Nouveaux Contes à Ninon*], without exception, is absent that tone of brutality which we associate with the notion of Zola's genius. All is gentle irony and pastoral sweetness, or else downright pathetic sentiment. (p. 135)

The consideration of the optimistic and sometimes even sentimental short stories of Zola helps to reveal to a candid reader the undercurrent of pity which exists even in the most "naturalistic" of his romances. It cannot be too often insisted upon that, although he tried to write books as scientific as anything by Pasteur or Claude Bernard, he simply could not do it. His innate romanticism would break through, and, for all his efforts, it made itself apparent even when he strove with the greatest violence to conceal it. In his *contes* he does not try to fight against his native idealism, and they are, in consequence, perhaps the most genuinely characteristic productions of his pen which exist. (p. 147)

*Edmund Gosse, "The Short Stories of
Zola" (1892), in his* The Collected Essays of
Edmund Gosse: French Profiles, *Vol. IV,
William Heinemann, 1913, pp. 125-47.*

[Zola's] office in the world has been like Ibsen's, to make
us look where we are standing, and see whether our feet are
solidly planted or not. What is our religion, what is our society, what is our country, what is our civilization? You
cannot read him without asking yourself these questions,
and the result is left with you.

There is the same mixture of weakness in his power that
qualifies the power of Ibsen, and makes his power the more
admirable. There are flaws enough in his reasoning; he is
not himself the best exponent of his own belief; there is no
finality in his precept or his practice. On the other hand, his
work has the same aesthetic perfection as Ibsen's, and as
an intellect dealing imaginatively with life, he is without a
rival. There is the like measure of weakness in Zola. . . .
Zola never was a realist in the right sense, and no one has
known this better, or has said it more frankly than Zola
himself. He is always showing, as he has often owned that
he came too early to be a realist; but it was he who imagined realism, in all its sublime, its impossible beauty, as
Ibsen imagined truth, as Tolstoi imagined justice. One has
to deal with words that hint rather than say what one
means, but the meaning will be clear enough to any one
capable of giving the matter thought. What Zola has done
has been to set before us an ideal of realism, to recall the
wandering mind of the world to that ideal, which was always in the world, and to make the reader feel it by what he
has tried to do, rather than by what he has done. He has
said, in effect, You must not aim in art to be less than perfectly faithful; and you must not lie about the fact any more
than you can help. Go to life; see what it is like, and then
tell it as honestly as possible. Above all he has shown us
what rotten foundations the most of fiction rested on, and
how full of malaria the whole region was. He did not escape
the infection himself; he was born in that region; the fever
of romanticism was in his blood; the taint is in his work.
But he has written great epics, and the time will come when
it will be seen that he was the greatest poet of his day, and
perhaps the greatest poet that France has produced. (pp.
162-63)

*W. D. Howells (from a review originally
published in* Harper's Review, *April 13,
1895), in his* Criticism and Fiction and Other
Essays, *edited by Clara Marburg Kirk and
Rudolph Kirk (reprinted by permission of
New York University Press; copyright ©
1959 by New York University), New York
University Press, 1959.*

[Thirty] years ago a young man of extraordinary brain and
indomitable purpose, wishing to give the measure of these
endowments in a piece of work supremely solid, conceived
and sat down to *Les Rougon-Macquart* rather than to an
equal task in physics, mathematics, politics or economics.
He saw his undertaking, thanks to his patience and courage, practically to a close. . . . It expresses fully and directly the whole man, and big as he may be it can still be
big enough for him without becoming false to its type. We
see this truth made strong, from beginning to end, in Zola's
work; we see the temperament, we see the whole man, with
his size and all his marks, stored and packed away in the

huge hold of *Les Rougon-Macquart* as a cargo is packed
away on a ship. His personality is the thing that finally pervades and prevails, just as so often on a vessel the presence
of the cargo makes itself felt for the assaulted senses. What
has most come home to me in reading him over is that a
scheme of fiction so conducted is in fact a capacious vessel.
It can carry anything—with art and force in the stowage;
nothing in this case will sink it. And it is the only form for
which such a claim can be made. All others have to confess
to a smaller scope—to selection, to exclusion, to the danger
of distortion, explosion, combustion. The novel has nothing
to fear but sailing too light. It will take aboard all we bring
in good faith to the dock. (pp. 156-57)

It was the fortune, it was in a manner the doom, of *Les
Rougon-Macquart* to deal with things almost always in gre-
garious form, to be a picture of *numbers,* of classes,
crowds, confusions, movements, industries. . . . The individual life is, if not wholly absent, reflected in coarse and
common, in generalized terms; whereby we arrive precisely
at the oddity [of] the circumstance that, looking out somewhere, and often woefully athirst, for the taste of fineness,
we find it not in the fruits of our author's fancy, but in a different matter altogether. We get it in the very history of his
effort, the image itself of his lifelong process, comparatively
so personal, so spiritual even, and, through all its patience
and pain, of a quality so much more distinguished than the
qualities he succeeds in attributing to his figures even when
he most aims at distinction. There can be no question in
these narrow limits of my taking the successive volumes
one by one—all the more that our sense of the exhibition is
as little as possible an impression of parts and books, of
particular 'plots' and persons. It produces the effect of a
mass of imagery in which shades are sacrificed, the effect
of character and passion in the lump or by the ton. The fullest, the most characteristic episodes affect us like a
sounding chorus or procession, as with a hubbub of voices
and a multitudinous tread of feet. The setter of the mass
into motion, he himself, in the crowd, figures best, with
whatever queer idiosyncrasies, excrescences and gaps, a
being of a substance akin to our own. Taking him as we
must, I repeat, for quite heroic, the interest of detail in him
is the interest of his struggle at every point with his
problem.

The sense for crowds and processions, for the gross and the
general, was largely the *result* of . . . the disproportion between his scheme and his material—though it was certainly
also in part an effect of his particular turn of mind. . . . We
feel that he *has* to improvise for his moral and social world,
the world as to which vision and opportunity must come, if
they are to come at all, unhurried and unhustled—must take
their own time, helped undoubtedly more or less by blue-
books, reports and interviews, by inquiries 'on the spot,'
but never wholly replaced by such substitutes without a
general disfigurement. Vision and opportunity reside in a
personal sense and a personal history, and no short cut to
them in the interest of plausible fiction has ever been discovered. The short cut, it is not too much to say, was with
Zola the subject of constant ingenious experiment, and it is
largely to this source, I surmise, that we owe the celebrated
element of his grossness. He was *obliged* to be gross, on
his system, or neglect to his cost an invaluable aid to representation, as well as one that apparently struck him as lying
close at hand; and I cannot withhold my frank admiration

from the courage and consistency with which he faced his need.

His general subject in the last analysis was the nature of man, in dealing with which he took up, obviously, the harp of most numerous strings. . . . [He] doubtless fell into extravagance—there was clearly so much to lead him on. The coarser side of his subject, based on the community of all the instincts, was for instance the more practicable side, a sphere the vision of which required but the general human, scarcely more than the plain physical, initiation, and dispensed thereby conveniently enough with special introductions or revelations. A free entry into this sphere was undoubtedly compatible with a youthful career as hampered right and left even as Zola's own. (pp. 160-62)

Taste as he knew it, taste as his own constitution supplied it, proved to have nothing to say to the matter. His own dose of the precious elixir had no perceptible regulating power. Paradoxical as the remark may sound, this accident was positively to operate as one of his greatest felicities. There are parts of his work, those dealing with romantic or poetic elements, in which the inactivity of the principle in question is sufficiently hurtful; but it surely should not be described as hurtful to such pictures as *Le Ventre de Paris*, as *L'Assommoir*, as *Germinal*. The conception on which each of these productions rests is that of a world with which taste has nothing to do, and though the act of representation may be justly held, as an artistic act, to involve its presence, the discrimination would probably have been in fact, given the particular illusion sought, more detrimental than the deficiency. There was a great outcry, as we all remember, over the rank materialism of *L'Assommoir*, but who cannot see to-day how much a milder infusion of it would have told against the close embrace of the subject aimed at? *L'Assommoir* is the nature of man—but not his finer, nobler, cleaner or more cultivated nature; it is the image of his free instincts, the better and the worse. . . . The whole handling makes for emphasis and scale, and it is not to be measured how, as a picture of conditions, the thing would have suffered from timidity. (pp. 162-63)

To make his characters swarm, and to make the great central thing they swarm about 'as large as life,' portentously, heroically big, that was the task he set himself very nearly from the first, that was the secret he triumphantly mastered. Add that the big central thing was always some highly representative institution or industry of the France of his time, some seated Moloch of custom, of commerce, of faith, lending itself to portrayal through its abuses and excesses, its idol-face and great devouring mouth, and we embrace the main lines of his attack. (pp. 165-66)

[The] singular doom of this genius . . . was to find, with life, at fifty, still rich in him, strength only to undermine all the 'authority' he had gathered. He had not grown old and he had not grown feeble; he had only grown all too wrongly insistent. . . . (p. 167)

There is simply no limit . . . to the misfortune of being tasteless; it does not merely disfigure the surface and the fringe of your performance—it eats back into the very heart and enfeebles the sources of life. When you have no taste you have no discretion, which is the conscience of taste, and when you have no discretion you perpetrate books like *Rome*, which are without intellectual modesty, books like *Fécondité*, which are without a sense of the ridiculous,

books like *Vérité*, which are without the finer vision of human experience. (p. 170)

Nana is truly a monument to Zola's patience; the subject being so ungrateful, so formidably special, that . . . the plunge into pestilent depths represents a kind of technical intrepidity.

There are other plunges, into different sorts of darkness; of which the esthetic, even the scientific, even the ironic motive fairly escapes us. . . . Our various senses, sight, smell, sound, touch, are, as with Zola always, more or less convinced; but . . . the mind still remains bewilderedly unconscious of any use for the total. I am not sure indeed that the case is in this respect better with [these] productions . . .— *La Faute de l'Abbé Mouret, Une Page d'amour, Le Rêve, Le Docteur Pascal*—in which the appeal is more directly, is in fact quite earnestly, to the moral vision; so much, on such ground, was to depend precisely on those discriminations in which the writer is least at home. The volumes whose names I have just quoted are his express tribute to the 'ideal,' to the select and the charming—fair fruits of invention intended to remove from the mouth so far as possible the bitterness of the ugly things in which so much of the rest of his work had been condemned to consist. The subjects in question then are 'idyllic' and the treatment poetic, concerned essentially to please on the largest lines and involving at every turn that salutary need. (pp. 171-72)

If you insist on the common you must submit to the common; if you discriminate, on the contrary, you must, however invidious your discriminations may be called, trust to them to see you through.

To the common then Zola, often with splendid results, inordinately sacrifices, and this fact of its overwhelming him is what I have called his paying for it. In *L'Assommoir*, in *Germinal*, in *La Débâcle*, productions in which he must most survive, the sacrifice is ordered and fruitful, for the subject and the treatment harmonize and work together. He describes what he best feels, and feels it more and more as it naturally comes to him—quite, if I may allow myself the image, as we zoologically see some mighty animal, a beast of a corrugated hide and a portentous snout, soaking with joy in the warm ooze of an African riverside. In these cases everything matches, and 'science,' we may be permitted to believe, has had little hand in the business. The author's perceptions go straight, and the subject, grateful and responsive, gives itself wholly up. It is no longer a case of an uncertain smoky torch, but of a personal vision, the vision of genius, springing from an inward source. Of this genius *L'Assommoir* is the most extraordinary record. (p. 173)

The mystery . . . is the wonder of the scale and energy of Zola's assimilations. . . . How, all sedentary and 'scientific,' did he get so *near*? (p. 175)

Grant—and the generalization may be emphatic—that the shallow and the simple are *all* the population of his richest and most crowded pictures, and that his 'psychology,' in a psychologic age, remains thereby comparatively coarse, grant this and we but get another view of the miracle. We see enough of the superficial among novelists at large, assuredly, without deriving from it, as we derive from Zola at his best, the concomitant impression of the solid. It is in general—I mean among the novelists at large—the impression of the *cheap*, which the author of *Les Rougon-Macquart*, honest man, never faithless for a moment to his own stiff standard, manages to spare us even in the prolonged sandstorm of *Vérité*. The Common is another matter; it is one of the forms of the superficial—pervading and consecrating all things in such a book as *Germinal*—and it only adds to the number of our critical questions. How in the world is it made, this deplorable democratic malodorous Common, so strange and so interesting? How is it taught to receive into its loins the stuff of the epic and still, in spite of that association with poetry, never depart from its nature? It is in the great lusty game he plays with the shallow and the simple that Zola's mastery resides, and we see of course that when values are small it takes innumerable items and combinations to make up the sum. In *L'Assommoir* and in *Germinal,* to some extent even in *La Débâcle,* the values are all, morally, personally, of the lowest—the highest is poor Gervaise herself, richly human in her generosities and follies—yet each is as distinct as a brass-headed nail. (pp. 175-76)

When we others of the Anglo-Saxon race are vulgar we are, handsomely and with the best conscience in the world, vulgar all through, too vulgar to be in any degree literary, and too much so therefore to be critically reckoned with at all. The French are different—they separate their sympathies, multiply their possibilities, observe their shades, remain more or less outside of their worst disasters. They mostly contrive to get the *idea,* in however dead a faint, down into the lifeboat. (p. 176)

> *Henry James, "Emile Zola" (1902), in his* Notes on Novelists, with Some Other Notes *(reprinted by permission of Charles Scribner's Sons; © 1914 by Charles Scribner's Sons, 1942 by Henry James), Scribner's, 1914 (and reprinted in* The Art of Fiction and Other Essays by Henry James, *Oxford University Press, 1948, pp. 154-80).*

The "social novel," which, fortunately, did not altogether succeed with Balzac, owing to his passionate temperament and the poetical impetus which he allowed to carry him away, was far more successful in the case of Émile Zola, who possessed a far calmer and more balanced disposition and was not betrayed by poetic inspiration.

This judgment is at variance with that generally accepted, because there hardly exists a history of modern French literature which does not take exception to Zola's attempt at "experimental fiction," directed towards the establishment or verification of "scientific laws," especially that of "heredity." But since other artists are pardoned for attempting an art which shall be, for instance, philosophy or morality, and Balzac himself is pardoned for laying down "social laws" in a cycle of novels, it does not seem fair to make Zola's theoretic illusion weigh upon him too heavily. It will be said that those other artists went wrong rather as critics than as artists, and that they applied morality, philosophy or social laws to their works from without; but Zola also went wrong in this respect as critic rather than as artist, and he too was only able to apply his "law of heredity" and the genealogical table of the Rougon Macquart to his work from without; because it was also not permitted to him to tear in pieces the nature of things and to make experiments where experiments were impossible. Perhaps the reason why people are severe with Zola and indulgent with others is that all are able to see at a glance the absurdity of experiments instituted upon facts that have been imagined, but all

have not sufficient acumen to discern the equal absurdity of poetry turned into morality or philosophy. But it is not only equity that demands an equal indulgence towards him as towards the others; for we must almost be grateful to him for having left to history a most significant document as to the extent to which heads were turned in the second half of the nineteenth century by the amorous intoxication and dizziness inspired by physiology, pathology, zoology and the other natural sciences. He formulated all this with the utmost simplicity of spirit in his experimental fiction. (pp. 312-13)

> *Benedetto Croce, in his* European Literature in the Nineteenth Century *(reprinted by permission of Alfred A. Knopf, Inc.),* Knopf, 1924.

[Zola's] "Lourdes" . . . is a study of a prodigious manifestation which he had witnessed within his own lifetime, the return of the supernatural to the modern world. This was a challenge to Zola's rationalism. (p. 103)

This study of Lourdes is made in all seriousness, and with great sympathy even for opinions which Zola regards as mistaken. And the novel is constructed with a high degree of formal skill. . . .

But . . . I do not regard "Lourdes" as one of the best of Zola's novels. In spite of the emotions aroused by both Marie and Pierre they somehow fail to register thoroughly as individuals. (p. 104)

Many of the individual novels of the [Rougon-Macquart] series have their themes, or subjects, like other novels, and develop them with art and imagination. "L'Assommoir" and "Nana" are certainly among the most skilful and moving pieces of fiction I have ever read. Only I do not regard them as philosophical novels. (p. 105)

Considered purely as novels, they are much better work than books like "Lourdes" and "Vérité". . . . And one reason for this may be that they are so much more purely works of the imagination, that they undertake to carry a much smaller load of social theory. The others make by comparison the impression of being doctrinaire, and fail to rise into the class of masterpieces. So that, on the whole, Zola serves to show us once again the difficulties of making fiction the vehicle of philosophy. (pp. 105-06)

> *Joseph Warren Beach, in his* The Twentieth Century Novel: Studies in Technique *(copyright, 1932, by Prentice-Hall, Inc.; copyright, 1960, by Mrs. Dagmar Doneghy Beach; reprinted by permission of Prentice-Hall, Inc., Englewood Cliffs, New Jersey),* Appleton-Century-Crofts, 1932.

Zola was a devotee of the Comtist doctrine of science, that "science alone would ensure the happiness and pacification of all the nations." And, as a corollary, it was added that literature in its effort to assist in this happiness and purification must become a hand-maid to science, utilizing all its powers to make the discoveries of science prevail, ever alert to the significance of new discoveries and ever ready to widen men's knowledge of its resources. (p. 283)

The form of the novel in particular, because of its convenient length, is a frame like a laboratory, biological and sociological, into which characters and situations are introduced and isolated, that their mutual dependence may be checked and ticketed, and general laws arrived at by induction in the orthodox manner. This can be done, Zola insists, if the artist becomes the sincere and dispassionate observer, and records with perfect objectivity the results of his observation. These will be the novel or drama. (p. 284)

Zola, who in his youth had been a journalist, armed himself with a notebook and went to the life of France to study it first hand, getting the facts that, when he had put them together, made his novels. In this sense it is true that naturalism is a species of extended and literary journalism.... And just as journalism of the higher variety has served excellently as a means for reform, so Zola and naturalism can be credited with the serious purpose of social reform. He painted with objective fidelity the ills of contemporary French society, roused the popular conscience, and when it was possible remedial legislation followed. (p. 286)

The Rougon-Macquart chronicles are a score of volumes dealing with the criss-cross of heredity in four and more generations, with each novel devoted to one specific member placed in a situation where his study will be edifying as a sociological "case." (p. 287)

That he adhered with remarkable consistency to this purpose in the larger number of the volumes of the series is a tribute to his self-effacement as a scientist; that as clearly in a few of the volumes near the end of the series he added something of his own is a tribute to Zola the artist. It is my sincere conviction that it is only on these last that Zola's claim for a large place in nineteenth century thought rests.

But Zola cannot be content with the impersonal and quite unobtrusive manner of the scientist working quietly in his laboratory and emerging quietly only after he has made his discovery. He must ballyhoo the performance and drag in the public to the exhibitions, and shock, even terrify them by the unexpectedness of his experiment. If his work has any social value he must startle his readers into thinking. (pp. 288-89)

Zola never ceased to call himself a naturalist. But he learned in his maturity to use his naturalism as a means to an end, and discovered, through it perhaps, a philosophy of life that has less connection with Zola the man of science. To be sure it was impossible for him to turn his back on science, or renounce his faith in his method. But more and more science became to him the means to great social ends, and literature more the handmaid of science than a department of experimental biology and physiology. And above all, because of his minute social studies, he acquired a faith in human nature, a belief in its essential soundness, that will make him a defender of the oppressed, but for a reason that has in it nothing of the sentimental love of the lowly or the liberal belief in democracy. (p. 293)

[Of] all his books I think it is *Germinal* that is from all points of view his best, and at the same time with a theme that touches our times most closely. Like all his others it is fully documented, so fully that it can almost serve as a text-book on coal miners and mining. (p. 295)

Here Zola has something more to maintain than the war between the classes, and the plea for a more adequate understanding between separated peoples. He is something more than the scientific sociologist painting the squalor of the oppressed, and the hatreds that oppression will always

engender. For the novel as it develops is more than an indictment of the capitalistic system, when one party must be wrong and the other right. What remains longest after reading is the humanity of the picture, and Zola's essential faith in the soundness at heart of the worker. He is not setting class against class, and passing judgment on a social evil; but examining the humanity of each of the warring classes, to see which fundamentally is the better fitted to survive. He asks for justice, not because of injustice done to the workers, but because they are better fitted to reorganize society. In this way, with this moral justification, *Germinal* is the first great proletarian novel, but with its faith based on no economic or sociological theory. (p. 296)

> *Philo M. Buck, Jr., "The Naturalist's Creed: Zola," in his* The World's Great Age: The Story of a Century's Search for a Philosophy of Life *(reprinted with permission of Macmillan Publishing Co., Inc.; copyright 1936 by Macmillan Publishing Co., Inc.; 1964 by Caroline Buck Reeves), Macmillan, 1936, pp. 282-305.*

Zola always makes a success of his first and final scenes, for he had what violinists call a "magnificent attack"....

Zola is famously at his best when he allows his imagination to brood over some one thing—the staircase in *Pot-Bouille*, the mineshaft in *Germinal*, the lonely house in the railway cutting in *La Bête Humaine*, the great sale of white millinery in *Au Bonheur des Dames*, the ruined garden of *La Faute de l'Abbé Mouret*—until it assumes the monstrous proportions of a nightmare or an hallucination. (pp. 201-02)

Uncommonly ill-read—especially for a Frenchman—in the literature, history and philosophy of the past, Zola was no thinker. You may search his novels in vain for a single interesting comment on life: everything is implicit. This, for a man whose stock of ideas was not only small but often fallacious, is unsatisfactory. Zola demands, in fact, too little of his reader. If he had been the exquisite type of artist, this might not matter; but he was slovenly and tasteless, he had more than a touch of Hall Caine (*Fécondité, La Faute de L'Abbé Mouret*), occasionally even of Marie Corelli (*Le Rêve, Rome, L'Oeuvre*). His illiterate, slapdash methods brought their own punishment: they robbed him of recognition by the best contemporary critics, who were so outraged by the vulgarity of his style and of his plots that they failed to perceive the rare epic quality of his imagination; and they firmly implanted in the public mind the image of a gloomy pornographer who thought the very worst of people in general and of his countrymen in particular. (p. 203)

Had he been born a contemporary either of Stendhal or of H. G. Wells, his generosity of mind, his vigorous and confident imagination, and that genius for broad depiction which triumphs over even the most commonplace and insistent detail, might have been expressed in a style better suited to vindicate his own dictum that a novel is "life seen through a temperament". (p. 204)

> *Edward Sackville-West, "Zola's 'La Débâcle'" (1941), in his* Inclinations, *Secker & Warburg, 1949, pp. 199-204.*

Zola aroused so much hostility in France in his lifetime that his thought, his Naturalism, has never been properly studied, nor has it received the consideration due it there. (p. 49)

At twenty-eight, with six books behind him, Zola seems to have done his first serious thinking about his profession. He saw that his talent was not for carefully wrought, psychological portraits like *Madame Bovary* and *Germinie Lacerteux*. He could never be *précieux*. Yet though long rhythms, broad panoramas, and great masses affected him most powerfully, he would not, like Balzac, indulge in mere portraiture or try to paint the whole of contemporary society. Balzac, like life itself, seemed to him to need an interpreter. Taine had taught him that, above everything else, the novelist must have a philosophy. (p. 50)

Zola utilized . . . most of the scientific "facts" of [Dr. Prosper Lucas' *Treatise on Natural Heredity*. The] greatest impression that it, and other similar volumes, made upon him was that one absolutely cannot escape his origins, but is completely the creature of heredity. Thus Naturalism, which we have defined as pessimistic determinism, was born. . . . (pp. 50-1)

It is remarkable in Zola's notes to discover that he did not wish to be "political, philosophical, or moral," but "purely naturalistic, purely physiological." In only one of his novels did he succeed in being "purely physiological." That is in *Le Ventre de Paris* . . . , an astonishing novel with its setting in Les Halles, the great public market of Paris. Here all men are classed as Thin or Fat, and the Fat live off the Thin, which, for the time being, Zola noisily insists is the law of life. In no other book of his is the *milieu* more important; yet the tale is not an ideal illustration of the influence of environment upon the human animal—it is too bizarre, Rabelaisian, fantastic. The observations are not those of a photographer, but those of a caricaturist. In this book, however, Zola exploited for the first time successfully the reportorial method of assembling all the minutiae of his background for a studied effect, a method which to many minds is Naturalism itself. Yet the one thing the Naturalists have in common is not this technique, as we shall see, but the philosophy of determinism. (pp. 52-3)

The effect of heredity or of environment may be studied in the case history of a single individual, as in *Nana,* or in the story of a whole society, as in *Germinal* . . . , Zola's next important novel. In the bulk of his books Zola is interested in biological determinism; in *Germinal* he is for once fairly absorbed by economic determinism. The book is a study of the revolt of the coal miners of Montsou, ground down by the operatives, brutalized by long hours, small pay, unsanitary and dangerous working and living conditions. (pp. 56-7)

[The] novel is not a "scientific" study, but rather a proletarian manifesto, and its popularity in the coal fields about Mons is readily understood. Zola has affected to believe that his naturalism has something in common with Marxism, and the general decadence of the upper classes is to be offset by the inherent strength of the proletariat. (p. 58)

La Terre is the most dismal of all Zola's dark books, perhaps because it is the most animalistic. The reader's sympathies are soon attached to the girl Françoise Mouche in her heroic efforts to resist the brutal physical attacks of her sister's husband, Butteau, which she is successful in doing, even though the sister's aid is invoked against her, until she is married to Jean Macquart, when, with child, she is at last overcome—only to realize, during the attack, that she is in love with Butteau. Him she protects after a fatal quarrel in which she is thrown upon a scythe, closing her lips to her devoted husband as she lies for hours dying. Françoise's extraordinary realization of her love seems intended to convey the theme of the book—the bestial quality of all affection—symbolized by the notorious and over-discussed fecundating of a cow at the beginning of the book. Yet Françoise's defection—and it may fairly be called that—is beyond the credulity of the reader. All the people in the novel live like swine save she; she seems, up to the last thousand words, to be the exception necessary for the proof of the rule and for artistic contrast in the story; when, therefore, she is shown to be like the others, the reader has had a surfeit of proof. His mind rebels. Zola has ridden the theme too hard. . . . Perhaps through hyperbole the book accomplished something in leading to franker discussions of the sexual basis of affection, though a good many other books had to be written before this was in any degree accomplished. (pp. 59-60)

Zola concluded the Rougon-Macquart cycle with one of his poorest novels, *Le Docteur Pascal* . . . , a book worthy of brief examination, however, since certain deductions may be made from it in regard to Zola. For narrative interest it has the aged Doctor Pascal's love for his niece Clotilde—a pretty piece of sentimentalism based, it is said, upon an illicit autumnal affair which the novelist himself had. To Pascal, however, is attached more than an amatory interest, for this elderly scientist has kept complete records of the whole Rougon-Macquart family and from these has formulated a science of heredity. The story develops into a contest between Pascal and Madame Félicité Rougon for the possession of these documents: he, to give them to the world; she, to destroy them for the sake of family pride. Clotilde shifts her allegiance from one to the other as the arguments of love and religion have force with her. In the end, however, the old lady triumphs and the documents are burned. Thus the novelist dodges the responsibility of summing up his "science" and his philosophy, which is plainly the task he should have set himself in the book that was to be the capstone of the series. While fatigue may be pled in his behalf—he had been occupied by the cycle for twenty-three years, it is not a valid excuse, since the novelist possessed sufficient energy to complete six more books and plan a seventh, which he doubtless would have finished, had not accidental death intervened.

The reason why *Le Docteur Pascal* is no summary of the Rougon-Macquart cycle, no statement of the laws of heredity, no final exposition of a philosophy, is that such a summary, statement, or exposition was for Zola impossible. (p. 61)

The question we are left with is, whether a Naturalist can be a moralist or, at least, the kind of moralist that Zola was? (p. 64)

> *Oscar Cargill, in his* Intellectual America: Ideas on the March *(reprinted with permission of Macmillan Publishing Co., Inc.; copyright 1941 by Macmillan Publishing Co., Inc.; 1969 by Oscar Cargill), Macmillan, 1941.*

On the morning of January 13, 1898, the conscience of mankind, which had been outraged at the injustice visited upon Captain Alfred Dreyfus of the French Army's General Staff, found a stentorian voice in Emile Zola. Zola, nearing sixty, the battle for literary naturalism won, was settling into the life of a worthy bourgeois when he was induced to interest himself in the Dreyfus Affair. He had become a Dreyfusard, but in this early January of 1898 Dreyfusard prospects were gloomy indeed. Then on the 13th on the front page of *L'Aurore,* the newspaper of Ernest Vaughan and Georges Clemenceau, appeared the headline-shout: "J'Accuse"; beneath was a long letter to Felix Faure, President of the French Republic, signed by Emile Zola. That day the circulation of *L'Aurore* leapt from a few score thousand to three hundred thousand, and the Dreyfus case was broken wide open again. (p. 141)

If I were to explain in three words the success, so far beyond Zola's hopes, of *J'Accuse,* the three would be: surprise, audacity, challenge. The timing of the letter's release proved to be perfect. Zola's name was famous enough to ensure that *J'Accuse* could not be greeted by the silence that kills without leaving a trace. And a daily newspaper was a prominent enough platform to reach a sufficient number of people to reopen the scandal. But the surprise lay in its form—a man-to-man appeal from one of France's literary giants, a leader in the profession of letters, to the political head of the nation. From his writer's eminence Zola spoke directly to the highest magistrate of the land. He spoke to President Faure with full mindfulness of official limitations placed upon that personage's actions but he detoured them by insisting upon the President's duty as a man.

Nothing at the time could have exceeded the breathtaking audacity of the letter's contents. Zola accused the War Ministry and the General Staff of the Army of a gross miscarriage of justice and of shocking efforts to conceal the miscarriage. He accused them collectively and singly by name. With the utmost courage he fired his accusations point-blank at high officials.

He then capitalized upon his surprising and audacious "break-through" of the anti-Dreyfusard defences by a ringing challenge. He dared the accused to bring him to trial for breaking the Libel Laws. This was the master-stroke. His taunting defiance stung the army into an unwise move —into putting Zola on trial in a civil court, exactly the step the Dreyfusards wanted to provoke.

Surprise, audacity, challenge—these were the tactics of the champion of truth. In executing them Zola employed a powerful rhetoric of indignation and a pulverizing ridicule. He marshalled facts and set them in a certain dramatic light so that their character of belonging in an "extravagant tragic serial romance" cannot be missed. His tone is adapted to his purpose—manly, open, frank, blunt, challenging, the tone of a man convinced of being right, of speaking by the dictates of conscience. Throughout there runs the strong current of his conviction that truth in the long run wins.

Most interesting of all, Zola spoke as an individual pure and simple and his letter was aimed at a single individual. He appealed to the pride and shame of Faure, to Faure's honor as a man, to Faure's qualities as an individual. Shall we not say, thinking of Paine, thinking of Paul, that the propagandist of truth is driven to speak from himself and that his appeal is to the individual heart and mind? (pp. 157-58)

Gorham Munson, "Zola's 'J'Accuse': The

Moment When Zola Was the Conscience of Mankind," in his 12 Decisive Battles of the Mind: The Story of Propaganda During the Christian Era *(copyright, 1942, by The Greystone Press, Inc.), Greystone Press, 1942, pp. 141-59.*

Zola has been declared not only obscene, but childishly so, and worse still, old-fashioned in his obscenity. To read his work seriously has been like facing the imputation of telling an old dirty joke. It is a charge which few have cared to incur. If we add to this the fact that the Rougon-Macquart has the misfortune to appear as a long family chronicle, although it is in fact a series of separate novels covered by the slenderest links, we can understand the oblivion to which it has been assigned. (p. 26)

Nothing perhaps can have seemed so serious a bar to achievement as his comparative lack of education. Education and taste were the two things he lacked to place him on a level with the classes he envied and despised. It is an ironic fact that it was ultimately to be in exactly these two spheres that the society he conquered was to be revenged upon him. (p. 27)

No nineteenth-century novelist, perhaps, succeeded so well in depicting the courage and honesty of the individual, aspiring workman of the century, and he does so with a lack of sentimentalism and a real understanding of the necessary limitations of such a life that is quite unique.

Such an exact class analysis if it had been rigidly adhered to, might well have produced novels that were text-books of political economy or social sermons rather than works of art. Zola, however, was too great an artist and too determinedly objective a writer to fall into this error more than occasionally. (pp. 35-6)

[Though] Zola needed the formal scheme of the [Rougon-Macquart] series to liberate his vast energies, and though he was often unaware himself of its secondary nature, most of the novels of the series, and, certainly, the best, were carefully planned as separate units, and if they interfered with the whole, the whole had to be remoulded. Frequently the members of the Rougon-Macquart are only formally the central characters, the real emphasis of the novels being placed upon other social groups, of whom the adventurers and outcasts from Plassans form useful observers. . . . He made little attempt, beyond an occasional explanatory reference which almost always appears forced, to connect the members of the family in one book with those in another. Such characters as do reappear have little consistency, except for Nana whose future had probably already been planned in detail when she appeared as the vicious little girl of *L'Assommoir.* . . . It was not the family heredity, nor even the theoretical class analysis that the family provided, with which Zola was concerned, however he may have wished to think so, but particular patterns of life which made immediate appeal to him. Nevertheless by establishing a broad general scheme and fulfilling it equally broadly, he insured that his artistic powers should be exercised over the widest possible field. (pp. 36-7)

Zola, like Dickens, mistrusted all the political parties. But whereas Dickens' political scepticism came from his view that all power was a corrupting influence on the will, Zola's contempt came largely from a general disbelief in the strength of the human will either for good or for evil. With his own abnormally developed will and energy, Zola was, perhaps, over-inclined to regard humanity as shifting, wind-swept sand whose apparent stability or direction was liable at any minute to be changed by some chance desire or momentary difficulty. (p. 40)

[For] Zola, as for Dickens, the picture of society which his analysis produced was too horrible to be passed over without some attempted solution. When the radical newspapers objected to his picture of the working classes in *L'-Assommoir,* Zola declared that as an artist he was concerned only with truth, not with opinions. This aesthetic creed of the naturalists was his constant sermon; but, nevertheless, it is possible to see a series of attempted solutions in the Rougon-Macquart novels which taken in conjunction with changes in his private life bridge the apparent gap between the objective novels of the family chronicle and the 'romans à thèse' and the propaganda novels of 1894 onwards. (p. 42)

Throughout his career Zola was attacked as a pornographic writer—a view which has since been increased in America by large numbers of illicit, hotted-up translations sold by book pedlars and in 'dirty' book shops. Nothing, in fact, could be less attractive than the squalor and disease which surround the sex life of his poor, the boredom and anxiety that beset his rich in their lovemaking. There are, however, certain romantic love episodes in Zola's work—though they are never cited by the smut salesman—about which an atmosphere of sensuality and excitement hangs that might be charged with the accusation of pornography. They are all of a very special kind: the innocent love of the very young, a sort of natural lovemaking of Adam and Eve before the fall. (pp. 47-8)

The answer to this sexual despair, the very core of his social pessimism, lies in Zola's own life. Nothing in Zola's early days in Paris had helped him to escape from his retrospective view of happiness, and his marriage seems to have proved to be no solution. Alexandrine was a good wife, ambitious, thoughtful for his needs, strong in character, emotionally profound. But she appears to have been only a supplement to his already deep mother-fixation. Had they been able to have children, all this might have been changed, but, unfortunately, this was not to be so. . . . [It] is only after his fruitful union with Jeanne Rozerat—a union which caused such misery to poor Alexandrine—that the picture changes. Already in *La Débâcle,* more openly in *Le Docteur Pascal,* and finally in *Paris,* the end of the long trilogy of Abbé Froment's road to a new faith, a note of hope appears—fecundity, work no longer as a drug but in happy knowledge that it will be carried on by posterity, a socialism gradual but sure because there is all the future in which to complete it—this was the faith which Jeanne Rozerat gave to Zola. It saved him from morbidity, and it ended his career as a great writer. (pp. 49-50)

The optimistic, cocksure bourgeois world of the 'forties and 'fifties was giving way to fin-de-siècle melancholy and ennui; all but the most obtuse felt the rotten boards creak beneath their feet, saw the scaffolding tremble above their heads. Zola, in his luxury and success, was seldom unconscious of these rumblings and groanings, and by his art, his force, his hatred, compassion and vulgarity, he drove the public to pile up his fortune as they queued to peer at the very hell they had spent most of their lives in avoiding. The peepshows were cleverly labelled—the Sanctity of the

Family, the Honour of the Army, the Virtues of the Poor, the Ideals of the Artist, the Traditions of the Peasantry, the Splendour of the Church, the Soundness of Finance—and in each there lay a putrescent corpse, far more terrible than the skeleton the poor reader had shut away so carefully in the cupboard of his own guarded conscience. Even now, the greatest of the novels—*L'Assommoir, La Terre, Germinal*—have the quality of nightmares; how much more appalling must they have been for the contemporary reader. (pp. 52-3)

He saw each novel as a separate picture, planned the whole shape in advance as would a painter. We have already said that the Rougon-Macquart series as a whole with its science, its heredity, even its social analysis, was always subordinate to the needs of the individual novels, equally the internal considerations of each novel—characters, events, time, place—were all subject to the demands of the logic of the total book.

From the earliest notes made for the series, it is clear that Zola realized his need to ensure this air-tight quality in his novels if they were to succeed. He affirms his decision to avoid Balzac's methods of presenting more than one group of society in any particular book. It is only in the later books like *Paris* that the very poor and the very rich are shown together, and it is clear from the unsuccessfully crude contrast, with its obvious moralising flavour, that his earlier decision was a wise one. His cuts into society were, in general, horizontal and not vertical. Within these horizontal sections, he planned each succeeding chapter as a separate step in the progressive logic of the whole. . . . Logical steps fused into a whole by passion, and by another quality which he does not mention, acute atmospheric sensitivity. A solidly established formal scheme given movement by emotional force and life by shimmering atmosphere—an Impressionist painting of the highest order. It is not 'Naturalism' but impressionistic technique which explains Zola's greatness. (pp. 54-5)

If the nervous undercurrent in Zola's life was made manifest spasmodically by mental obsessions and delusions, it was evidenced throughout his life by a physical hyperaesthesia which, like his obsession with numbers, is another great corner-stone of his creative powers. He saw, heard and, above all, smelt his surroundings more intensely than the normal person. To judge from his work we would suspect it was many years before this excess of physical sensitivity was integrated with the rest of his personality. It was responsible for the development within him of a poet—not the derivative, Romantic imitator of his youth, but a poet whose detailed powers of natural description allied him more to the Parnassian school, and who converted the natural phenomena he felt so intensely into images and shapes that finally give this side of his work a close link with the Symbolists. (p. 57)

The whole history of the Rougon-Macquart is the development of a detailed, realistic canvas into a statement of a mood, an atmosphere of a certain place and time within the same limited confines. (p. 62)

It has been said more than once that Zola's great novels are the forerunners of the epic cinema—of D. W. Griffiths, of Jean Duvivier or of Pabst—but excellent films though many of them would make, such a view ignores the fact that Zola's greatness lies in his use of words. He was a pictorial artist, but to say that his world would be better represented by the camera is the result of an age-old confusion of means and results in the arts. (p. 63)

If Zola's presentation of time and place supplies some key to the compulsion of his novels, his treatment of character gives the final answer. Zola was intensely interested in the physiological, medical approach to the human personality which the science of his youth propounded; one may well believe that the theories of Jeannet or Bergson would have attracted him as much as they did Proust, or that the views of Freud would have dominated him as they have later novelists. . . . As we have already noted, Zola began, like Dickens or Balzac, with characters that were largely humours. If he developed them, it was not by the enlargement of intellectual or emotional sympathy as George Eliot did, but by the unconscious infusion of his own personality into them. The Impressionist approach which he used could have led to a development of the interior monologue, as it did for Tolstoy, or to the tracking of memory as it did for Proust, but Zola's impressionism remained entirely fictional and external. Only one aspect of personal psychology really interested him deeply—the human will. It was probably this interest that attracted him to the works of Stendhal, at that time a neglected writer, and it is this interest that is predominant in his two 'psychological' horror stories, *Thérèse Raquin* and its later counterpart *La Bête Humaine*.

For the rest, character was for him merely a part of the general statement of his novels. Starting with a Balzacian realist approach, which was never entirely happy, he developed his humours in two directions; the central characters tended to be hardened into symbols, the others dissolved into 'humanity', crowds, groups. (pp. 66-7)

Central characters exist in all his novels, but they are a convention like the much advertised tenets of naturalism which he only supported one moment to deny the next. The approach to the scene is always external, and if that external viewpoint is sometimes for the sake of convenience labelled Gervaise or Étienne, the scenes in which they are present merge happily and easily into those in which they are not: the observer is always Zola's five senses. (p. 68)

With the publication of *L'Assommoir* in 1877, Zola leapt from extraordinary talent to a mastery of his medium that can, without distortion, be labelled genius. The theme had been maturing in his mind since 1869, and the most striking feature of the book is its deeply felt quality. The heroine, Gervaise, is perhaps the most completely conceived character, belonging to that great class of submerged, unindividual figures that make up the very poor, to be found in all nineteenth-century fiction. The tragedy of her limited fight —limited by education and circumstances—to win a pathetic little vision of individual happiness from an uncomprehended and uninterested world is treated with the greatest pity and the least false sentiment. In a note, Zola says, 'I must show all the world trying to bring about her ruin, consciously or unconsciously', and so we see it. . . . [In] incidental figures we have the whole world of strangers, of the educated, of the busybody and the official who beset and tyrannize and make small the submerged when they attempt to rise above the surface. The simple demands of Gervaise and Coupeau upon life, their capacity for gaiety, their childlike hopes and dreams are all attended by little incidents or remarks that foreshadow their futility. On

second reading, perhaps, the careful interlocking of the present hope with its future foundering seems a little careful, a little arranged, but, at first encounter, the effect of gradual, yet inevitable descent is overpowering. The tragedy and the horror would be unbearable—indeed a mere recapitulation of the events would make them ludicrous—if it was not for the concept of limited, pitiable, yet complete human dignity which marks Gervaise. It is perhaps almost unbearable, almost inartistic, when events finally reduce her human dignity to animal squalor—reality has outrun art. We may despise the bourgeois critics who shouted against the outrageous horror of *L'Assommoir,* but our special contempt must be reserved for those left-wing critics who did not find the picture of the submerged sufficiently noble. 'My characters', said Zola, 'are not bad, they are only ignorant and destroyed by the surroundings of crude need and misery in which they live.'

No account of *L'Assommoir* is complete, however, without mention of the humour of the scenes of prosperity and gaiety which intersperse the descent of Gervaise. Such humour is abundant in many of his books, but nowhere so successfully as in *L'Assommoir* and *La Terre*. . . . The humours of ignorance and superstition, of the oddities of the simple have been surpassed only by Dickens. . . . (pp. 111-13)

If *L'Assommoir* moves the reader's compassion for the submerged through the individual life of Gervaise, *Germinal* . . . uses the submerged community of the miners to compel his belief, if necessary, his hostile and frightened belief, in their right and their power to climb out of the hell to which indifference and greed have consigned them. If, in 1885, strike action was less rare than it had been when Dickens so sadly failed to grasp its necessity in *Hard Times,* it was still thought of by 'respectable' people as criminal violence. It was this aspect of bourgeois fear, this feeling that strikers were only collected criminals, violators of the sacred rights of property more vile than thieves because more dangerous, that Zola deliberately played upon. . . . *Germinal* is rightly regarded as one of the greatest novels of the masses. Nowhere perhaps have scenes of mass action been more deftly managed, nowhere the confused emotions and thoughts of simple people, treated like beasts and driven into self-defence that is often bestial, more directly made lucid without losing reality. Zola uses all his devices, and less obviously than in *L'-Assommoir*. The hero, Étienne Lantier, a stranger to the mining town, provides an observer for a community which has no self-consciousness. The building-up of that community through the lives of individuals makes a clear and detailed picture which later mass writers so often blurred by attempting to portray groups directly. Many left wing admirers, notably Barbusse, who have objected to the 'intrusion' of individuals, have failed to see that the force of compassion and anger which they praise rests exactly upon this method. Nowhere, too, is Zola's 'journalistic' approach—his visits to mines, his interviews with working men, his notes, his reading of reports—more truly vindicated than in the great imaginative scenes underground, the descents in the cages, the mining ponies, the flooded pits. (pp. 113-15)

L'Assommoir is Zola's most compassionate work, *Germinal* his most angry, but *La Terre* . . . is the most complete of all his novels. In it are brought together all the various strands of emotion which had competed for expression in the other Rougon-Macquart novels; in it Zola combines and blends more happily all the various methods of expression which had been individually perfected in its predecessors. It is a book of incidents and characters, that taken separately are the height of his exaggeration, his monstrous view of life, yet, united and fused, are the summit of his truth, his convincing projection of reality. (pp. 116-17)

But *La Terre* achieves greatness, that is denied to many of the other novels as rich in horror and irony, by the truth, the simple nobility of the hero and heroine, Jean and Françoise, whose greater feeling and finer aspirations are so skilfully woven into the same pattern of external coarseness and callousness as the sunken, brutalized mass around them, that they give a final conviction of mankind's possible redemption in the most vile swamps. This sense of nobility in the lower depths of life can only be compared to the greatest successes of Dostoevsky in *The House of the Dead* or *The Idiot*. (p. 118)

Zola's artistic genius was the expression of emotional and intellectual conflict. Peace came to his spirit with Jeanne Rozerat and his children; intellectual solution followed more slowly but was no less complete. Though a lifetime of writing made it natural that he should seek to express this final solution in books, its true expression lay in action. The courage, the generosity and the force which he showed in his defence of Dreyfus are the monument of these last years of positive conviction, they have their place in the history of France and in the history of human freedom, but they can only form a brief appendix to a study of Zola as a writer. (pp. 120-21)

> *Angus Wilson, in his* Emile Zola: An Introductory Study of His Novels *(copyright 1952 by Angus Wilson; reprinted by permission of William Morrow & Co., Inc.), William Morrow, 1952.*

For Zola the passion for art is sexual. Chaste in life we are potent in art. (p. 113)

Zola is the novelist of simplification, inflation, drama, the large, slack, crown-catching line. He seeks the pictorial. . . .

The Romantic dogma of death, failure and the hidden taint is responsible for the false twists in Zola's realism. (p. 115)

Like Balzac, Zola is the novelist of our appetites, especially of their excess in satisfaction or nausea, but he lacks Balzac's irony and subtlety. He is less civilised and less instinctively refined by the comic spirit. He excels until he exceeds, in atmosphere. . . . On the other hand, when he is not on his obsessive themes, he finely observes human nature.

[Meaning] and value in Zola lie in the rendering of life itself. It was necessary, one might say, to write novels of this kind because the 19th century saw the dehumanisation of man. Christianity had become meaningless. It was necessary to write about conditions simply because the dominant class were trying to live without knowing what their life was based on. The marvel is that Zola came so close to the skin of his people. He was able to do so perhaps because of his peculiar vice: the idealisation of the ugly. His obsessive taste for the revolting, the dreary, the bestial was an energy, and put him completely at one with the dreadful spirit

of the times; he was as ugly, disfiguring and, also, almost as ludicrous in his puffing and blowing as the early steam engines. But there is another reason for his success. Henry James gives us a clue to it when he reports, with a shock, Zola's decision to conduct research into popular speech, slang and foul language: Zola saw that this was not a barrier but the card of admission into the slum world. If he knew its language he would know its soul. . . . [In *The Dram-Shop*] Zola's following of bad words has led him, paradoxically, to the profoundest human feelings; and his own search for disgust and hatred is not proof against the surprising insinuations of the love that is mixed with the revolting—may even arise because of it. . . . Human beings have the right to their tragedy; they have the right to be incurable. Zola's sense of corruption was, no doubt, based on specious scientific theories; but it was a larger, more humane sense than the Puritan moralist's trite preaching of domestic virtue and the merits of the savings bank. (pp. 121-22)

> *V. S. Pritchett, "Zola," in his* Books in General *(© 1953 by V. S. Pritchett; reprinted in the U.S. by permission of Harold Matson Co., Inc., and in Canada by permission of A. D. Peters & Co.), Chatto and Windus, 1953, pp. 110-22.*

Zola and Flaubert have nothing in common except a few friends. Zola's naturalism arose out of a belief that the novelist could work, in a spirit of scientific determinism, alongside the biologist and doctor. His plan of the huge *Rougon-Macquart* series was conceived in that spirit; its twenty volumes would show what heredity and environment had made of the various branches of a family during the period of the Second Empire. And each novel would explore a certain territory or be concerned with a particular style of life, after Zola had made himself thoroughly acquainted with the facts. So, in order to write *Germinal,* one of the most ambitious and (if not widely popular) successful novels of the series, Zola spent six months taking notes in the coal-mining districts of North-Eastern France and Belgium. This preliminary documentation was an essential part of the naturalistic method. The novelist might imagine characters and situations, but the world in which they existed had to be an accurate copy of the real world. This 'documentary' fiction, something between literature and journalism, is not only still written but is on the increase, and there is a great deal of it both in Russia, where it is praised as 'socialist realism', and in America, where it is accepted as 'the low-down'; but Zola was its first and greatest practitioner, and made—or had made for him—the largest literary claims for it. But these claims, though never without serious advocates in Zola's lifetime and since, have not been approved by critics of weight inside or outside France; though the general tendency has been to ignore Zola rather than attempt any final judgment on him. (pp. 262-63)

[Zola] wrote a great deal that is immensely readable; most of his work has breadth and vigour, and the best of it has impressive power; he has an astonishing visual sense, combining an eye for detail with a panoramic style, like that of some painter of vast frescoes; he explores and describes his various selected territories and modes of life, many of them new to fiction, thoroughly and frankly and fearlessly. Next, he is much more than a narrow novelist with a thesis or purpose: his *L'Assommoir* (*The Drunkard*) is not simply a moral tale about the evil effects of drink in the Paris slums but is a genuine novel about a group of poor people. . . . His originality does not lie in his pseudo-scientific method, which need not be taken seriously, but in his genuine feeling for people in the mass and his sense of social justice, a natural sense that has nothing to do with political propaganda. Zola is far from being a Communist, but at his strongest—say, in *L'Assommoir, Germinal* especially, and *La Débâcle,* his picture of France's downfall in the war of 1870—he represents better than anybody the kind of novelist the Communists are always hoping to manufacture, chiefly through Party directives and resolutions of the Union of Writers. And his most impressive and memorable scenes, like tremendous moving pictures, are those in which he shows us not individuals but whole masses of people in motion, in a fashion that seems to belong to our age, mass-communicating through mass-media, rather than his. It is nonsense to say he is out-of-date—this comes from the criticism that has taken its tone from his arch-enemies, the Symbolists—because in what is central and original in him, his reportage, his concentration upon a particular way of life, an industry, a national crisis, his sense of people in the mass, he is more modern than most of the moderns, a novelist of our time. (pp. 263-64)

The trouble with Zola is that, beginning as he did with the idea that the new naturalistic fiction, if written on a grand scale, could be almost a scientific experiment, he forgot what literature is, and so it took its revenge on him. For literature does not put life under a microscope, remaining outside it to observe and to record what it is doing. Literature thinks and feels and imagines its way into life, expressing it from the inside. But with Zola we are always on the outside, and he is like one of those museum guides who tell us about everything and give us no opportunity of using our imagination. What he does is very difficult to do, and usually he does it very well, but it is not artistic creation. He is our special correspondent or guide to the markets and their workers, the financiers and cocottes, the dram shops and the slums, the big store and its assistants, the peasants sowing and reaping, and so on through the programme; but though he may instruct, entertain, horrify us, he weaves no spell about us, still leaves us outside the peculiar enchantment of literature. (pp. 264-65)

> *J. B. Priestley, in his* Literature and Western Man *(copyright © 1960 by J. B. Priestley; reprinted by permission of A. D. Peters and Company), Harper, 1960.*

As for Zola, there can hardly have been a modern writer so confused about the work he was doing. Consider the mechanical scientism to which he clung with the credulousness of a peasant in a cathedral; the ill-conceived effort to show forces of heredity determining the lives of his characters (so that a reader of *Germinal* unaware of the other volumes in the Rougon-Macquart series can only with difficulty understand why Etienne Lantier should suddenly, without preparation or consequence, be called "a final degenerate offshoot of a wretched race"); the willful absurdity of such declarations as "the same determinism should regulate paving-stones and human brains"; the turgid mimicry with which Zola transposed the physiological theories of Dr. Claude Bernard into his *Le Roman expérimental.* (p. 60)

Yet we ought not to be too hasty in dismissing Zola's intellectual claims. His physiological determinism may now seem crude, but his sense of the crushing weight which the

world can lower upon men remains only too faithful to modern experience, perhaps to all experience. If his theories about the naturalistic novel now seem mainly of historical interest, this does not mean that the naturalistic novel itself can simply be brushed aside. What remains vital in the naturalistic novel as Zola wrote it in France and Dreiser in America is not the theoretic groping toward an assured causality; what remains vital is the massed detail of the fictional worlds they establish, the patience—itself a form of artistic scruple—with which they record the suffering of their time. (pp. 60-1)

Insofar as a writer's ideas enter his literary work, they matter less for their rightness or wrongness than for their seriousness. And at least with some writers, it is their seriousness which determines whether the ideas will release or block the flow of creative energies. Zola shared with many late nineteenth- and early twentieth-century writers a lust for metaphysics. Christianity might be rejected, Christianity might be remembered, but its force remained. Among those who abandoned it there was still a hunger for doctrine, a need for the assuagements of system. They wished to settle, or continuously to worry, the problem of their relation to the cosmos. To us this may seem a curious need, since we are more likely to be troubled by our relation to ourselves; but in the last half of the nineteenth century the lust for metaphysics was experienced by people whose moral and intellectual seriousness cannot be questioned. (pp. 62-3)

Germinal releases one of the central myths of the modern era: the story of how the dumb acquire speech. All those at the bottom of history, for centuries objects of manipulation and control, begin to transform themselves into active subjects, determined to create their own history. (p. 64)

The myth of *Germinal* as I have been sketching it is close to the Marxist view of the dynamics of capitalism, but to yield ourselves to Zola's story is not necessarily to accept the Marxist system. Zola himself does not accept it. At crucial points he remains a skeptic about the myth that forms the soul of his action. His skepticism is not really about the recuperative powers of the miners, for it is his instinctive way of looking at things that he should see the generations crowding one another, pushing for life space, thrusting their clamor onto the world. His skepticism runs deeper. Zola sees the possibility that in the very emergence of solidarity—that great and terrible word for which so many have gone smiling to their death!—there would be formed, by a ghastly dialectic of history, new rulers and oppressors: the Rasseneurs, the Plucharts, and even the Lantiers of tomorrow, raised to the status of leaders and bureaucrats, who would impose their will on the proletariat. Zola does not insist that this must happen, for he is a novelist, not a political theoretician. What he does is to show in the experience of the Montsou workers the germ of such a possibility. As it celebrates the greatest event of modern history, the myth of emergence contains within itself the negation of that greatness. (p. 65)

A work of modern literature may employ a myth and perhaps even create one, as I think *Germinal* does, but it cannot satisfy its audience with a composed recapitulation of a known, archetypal story. With theme it must offer richness of variation, often of a radical kind, so as slyly to bring into question the theme itself. The hieratic does not seem a mode easily accessible to modern literature. We want, perversely, our myths to have a stamp of the individual, our eternal stories to bear a quiver of nervous temporality.

The picture Zola draws of Montsou as a whole, and of Montsou as a microcosm of industrial society, depends for its effectiveness mainly on the authority with which he depicts the position of the miners. Just as the novel is a genre that gains its most solid effects through accumulation and narrative development, so the action of Zola's book depends on his command of an arc of modern history. If he can persuade us that he sees this experience with coherence and depth, then we will not be excessively troubled by whatever intellectual disagreements we may have with him or by our judgment that in particular sections of the novel he fails through heavy exaggeration and lapses of taste. (pp. 68-9)

> *Irving Howe, "Zola: The Poetry of Natural-ism," in his* The Critical Point on Literature and Culture *(© 1973; reprinted by permission of the publisher, Horizon Press, New York), Horizon, 1973, pp. 59-76.*

There is every reason to suppose that Zola's political sympathies, at the outset of his career, were already oriented to the left. Yet, his concept of the creative artist as supreme among individuals threatened to make a shambles of whatever democratic principles he may have had. Next to the conservative pundits, whose fiats and taboos stifled the progress of art, *hoi polloi*—obtuse, sheeplike, fainthearted —were the target of his contempt.... But where do you draw the line between the people as common people and what is called "the public"? Zola—the young Zola—did not quite know and did not care: "Frankly," he averred, "I would sacrifice humanity to the artist."... He was henceforth reasonably satisfied that he could reconcile a fiercely personalized stance with the exigencies of humanitarian concern. He likewise saw himself as temperamentally suited to become a surveyor of temperaments. (pp. 9-10)

There was indeed abundant justification for Zola's claim that he presented French readers [in *L'Assommoir*] with the first piece of fiction ever devoted to the lower classes, the first that "smelled of the common people," the first that "did not lie." One may well wonder how in heaven some leftist critics found cause to reproach him for slandering the workingman. They missed the clear implication that society at large was responsible, not only for the prosperity of public malefactors such as *père* Colombe, but for the systematic degradation and subjection of the have-nots.

The proletarian "smell" came forth by means of an unheard-of stylistic device. Not content to record conversations in the vernacular, Zola so reported the *thoughts* of his characters. Thus, through a very extraordinary blend of direct and indirect discourse, *L'Assommoir* achieved a consistent "atmospheric" flavor. It did so at considerable risk, if only because slang forms are notoriously ephemeral. Beginning with the title-word itself, which no longer applies in that particular sense, examples of obsolescence have been garnered in an effort to discredit Zola's "philological experiment." The least this writer can say is that, on preparing, thirty-five years ago, a French-English glossary of one chapter of *L'Assommoir,* he found nine-tenths of its vocabulary to be miraculously fresh. Louis-Ferdinand Céline's *Voyage au bout de la nuit* was five years old at the time and already showing symptoms of linguistic arteriosclerosis. (pp. 21-2)

Nana was [a] "leaf" taken from the Book of Love—but the starkest imaginable, one which divested sexual desire or intercourse of the last shreds of idealization. *Nana* raised (or lowered) Woman to the status of a mythical force, at work to corrupt and disrupt society "between her snow-white thighs." A blind force, by the way, a mere instrument, wholly unconscious of its evil destination. But the instrument of whom—or what? On the one hand, Nana's story provided the true sequel of *L'Assommoir:* not only in the literal sense that the heroine was Gervaise's and Coupeau's daughter, but insofar as she, like her parents, had been preordained from birth to become chattel for the privileged few. Yet, on the other hand, any illustration of that old theme—the Devil and the Flesh—tends to establish man's lust, even the rich man's lust, as a law of nature; willy-nilly, it restricts to hypocrisy, to stuffy righteousness, the guilt of the upper classes. In short, the deterministic system to which Zola was beholden detracted somewhat from the value of *Nana* as a moral and social document. (pp. 23-4)

As a warning, . . . or as a prophecy, *Germinal* purported to be, and was, and remained ever after, Zola's most solemn utterance in the realm of "practical sociology." It presented the ruling classes with, according to him, an inescapable dilemma: either they would atone for their shameless exploitation of the downtrodden, of those they confined to the level of beasts, or they would sign their own death warrant. (p. 28)

Germinal surpasses *L'Assommoir* in that it is built on a heroic scale. The spotlight falls no longer on a handful of workingmen, but on the toiling, suffering masses presented as an entity; no longer on their ill-spent idle hours, but on a lifetime bereft of idle hours—unless you count as such the moments they devote to procreating, in mechanical abandon, the galley slaves (or avengers?) of the future. The devouring monster who faces them is no longer a mere alembic, a provider of oblivion, ensconced in a neighborhood tavern; it is the consortium known as the *Régie* (Governing Board), whose decrees, issued in Paris and carried out by local subordinates, resemble those of a remote and implacable deity. By no means does this aggrandizement result in a lack of individual characterization; yet, such is Zola's absolute mastery that personal lives appear to be—indeed are meant to be—submerged within the pulsating, swirling, random life of the whole. The mob scenes for which *Germinal* is justly famous serve to emphasize its emblematic quality. So does the invisibility of the *Régie*. So does the gnawing feeling, implanted on page after page, that both camps, however unevenly, are but the tools of a third force, call it Fate if you will, tortuously engaged in leading mankind, through blood, sweat, and tears, to an unknown destination. *Germinal* has all the features and—so does the author hope—the cleansing power of a Greek tragedy. (p. 29)

[It] must be admitted that his saga of the countryside [*La Terre*] breathed none of the warmth, and little of the urgency, which . . . pervaded the pages of *Germinal*. Despite the fact that the novelist went through his usual paces, revisiting his mother's native Beauce for on-the-spot documentation, the suspicion arises that the end product, qua novel, was primarily a rhetorical exercise based upon literary reminiscences. It was meant to relegate to their proper place the bucolic fantasies of George Sand—and in this it succeeded admirably. It also invited comparison with Balzac whose unfinished fresco, *Les Paysans,* bid fair to count among his greatest: perhaps a good enough reason why this direct challenge to an awesome predecessor lacked the imaginative power which Zola had brought or would bring to several others. As an observer of the rural scene he contributed little that was intrinsically new and seemed content to accentuate Balzacian traits. From Fourchon to Fouan, from Courtecuisse to Bécu or Lequeu, from Mouche to Mouche (pure coincidence?), family names retained their punlike, sometimes half-obscene quality. Greed and murderous hatred, not to mention uninhibited lust, supplied the main motivations as they had done in *Les Paysans*—only more so. Cunning remained the peasant's favorite weapon, but violence, already present in Balzac, was markedly on the increase. Comic relief turned to positive ribaldry. Where Balzac had made a wry jumble of human and animal life on the farm, Zola pointedly juxtaposed the insemination of cows and that of women, or again the birth of a calf and that of a child.

Harsh though it may sound, this estimate of *La Terre* does not purport to exonerate its original detractors. The work should have been recognized for what it was, for what the author intuitively felt it to be: "the living poem of the soil"; or, more accurately perhaps, the poem of man's incestuous attachment to the earth. The poem of Cybele as mother and mistress: equally demanding in both roles, yet strangely sparing at times, or at least capricious, in the dispensation of her bounties. A poem as removed from the paradisiacal climate of the Paradou garden as reality can be from a midsummer night's dream. The poem of fecundity, yes, but of fecundity through human fecundation. The earth's womb must be penetrated, the seed sown, the fruit reaped; men must sweat and men must die, so that "the bread of life may spring from the land." In this respect at any rate, *La Terre* far outdistanced Balzac's conceptions. Out of its manure-scented chapters there issued, willy-nilly, a paean to civilization: for, no matter how close to the brute man was depicted to be, he was also credited with a dim sense of direction and purposefulness. But for him the planet would forever remain a desert or a jungle. (pp. 33-4)

[In *L'Argent*] Zola presumed to open to his readers the *sanctum sanctorum* of modern capitalism—namely, the stock market. A rash venture on his part, since he knew nothing of its operations, never owned a share in his life, never even possessed a bank account. The true wonder, then, is not that *L'Argent* should fall far short of being a masterpiece but that it should be as competent a novel as it actually is. . . . *L'Argent* today remains unrivaled as a portrayal of the Stock Exchange and would need few transpositions to evoke for us, not the distant saga of speculation under the Second Empire, but that, closer to our times, of the Staviskys in France or the Insulls in America. . . . Zola does not issue a blanket indictment of his hero. Saccard's recklessness is taken to be but a malformation or misuse of the creative urge that makes the world go round. Not a little sophistry attaches to this judgment whose devious purpose it is to bring out an analogy with love. Money has no odor; money is what money manipulators make it. Likewise—and this is a note not heard in Zola's novels since *La Faute de l'abbé Mouret*—none of the filth that is being stirred in the name of love can defile love itself. (pp. 37-8)

By no means an impeccably constructed novel, *La Débâcle* stands nevertheless as one of Zola's most impressive achievements. It is a work of great scope and power, not unworthy of comparison with Tolstoy's *War and Peace.* Sweepingly majestic in its description of the battlefields, crystal-clear in its reconstruction of strategic or tactical maneuvers, masterly in its handling of enormous masses of men, it shows Zola at his narrative and epic best. Yet, the emphasis appears to be on individuals, combatants and noncombatants alike. There is merit in the author's later boast that he discarded, once and for all, the trappings, the flourishes, the heroics of the conventional war tale, substituting for them the naked truth: that of the smoke, the noise, the bloodshed, the stench, the pent-up brutality, the visceral fears, the cries of the wounded, the involvement of innocent bystanders—civilians, women, children. (pp. 39-40)

[Zola], not unlike Tolstoy, acquired the conviction that, by divesting the New Testament of its supernatural envelope, by breaking the Church's monopoly over it, one could extract from its teachings the charter of the future. And, again not unlike Tolstoy, he saw the artist as the apostle of the new faith. As if in anticipation of André Gide's famous axiom that good feelings make for bad literature, he, in the last decade of his life, endeavored to prove exactly the opposite.

Alas, he did not succeed. There are, to be sure, passages of great force and brilliance in Zola's triptych, *Les Trois villes* ([The Three Cities], . . . and in the unfinished "Four Gospels". . . .) This enormous production, however, while it bears witness to the author's unflagging stamina, is decidedly anticlimactic from a literary standpoint. It takes uncommon courage to follow abbé Pierre Froment's spiritual journey. . . . Of the three novels involved, the least unrewarding is probably *Paris,* if only because a certain grandeur attaches to the implicit contrast between the Paris of the Rougon-Macquart era and the new Paris of the coming century, hopefully reinstated in its former role as the capital of Thought. But then nothing less than heroism is required to withstand the heavy rhetoric, the utopian arbitrariness, the utter unreality of Zola's *Evangiles.* Even their symbolism descends at times to sheer puerility: the "Gospels" were to unfold the life story of Pierre Froment's four sons, pointedly christened Mathieu, Luc, Marc, and Jean after the four Evangelists; the patronymic itself, Froment (*wheat* in French), becomes an obvious emblem of fertility; Mathieu's wife, Marianne, borrows her given name from the girl in the Phrygian cap who traditionally personifies the French Republic; and that happy couple gives birth to twelve children who in turn present it, on its diamond wedding anniversary, with one hundred and thirty-four grandchildren and great-grandchildren. Were it not for lack of space, we might be tempted to probe more deeply into the whys and wherefores of Zola's messianic intemperance; we might even reach some instructive and not altogether damning conclusions; yet, one of them would have to be that, if *La Débâcle* came reasonably close to emulating Tolstoy's *War and Peace,* none of Zola's subsequent works even remotely offers itself as a counterpart to *Resurrection.* (pp. 42-3)

It is, I believe, extremely revealing that Zola should have sworn to Dreyfus's innocence "by my forty years of toil, by the authority that such labor may have given me." This is at once romantic nonsense and the reason why Zola's championship of Dreyfus is still remembered, whereas other participants in the drama, including Dreyfus himself, are readily forgotten. Let us face it: we went, we are still going, through experiences which dwarf the Dreyfus case; Zola's involvement in the specific issues thereof has, really, no greater relevance to our times than Voltaire's effort on behalf of Calas; but what matters in modern terms is that he entered the fray, not as a high-minded politician (assuming the breed exists), not as a man of action, not even as a writer systematically *engagé* in the Sartrean sense of the word, but as a *clerc* (Julien Benda's expression), *as a man of thought,* whose devotion to principles, and to principles only, prepared, nay, designated him for this extraordinary assumption of risk and responsibility. (pp. 46-7)

> *Jean-Albert Bédé, in his* Emile Zola *(Columbia Essays on Modern Writers Pamphlet No. 69; copyright © 1974 Columbia University Press; reprinted by permission of the publisher), Columbia University Press, 1974.*

Index to Critics

Ziff, Larzer
  Ambrose Bierce 1:94
  Sarah Orne Jewett 1:368
Zimmerman, Dorothy
  Virginia Woolf 1:543